REAL ESTATE INVESTMENT

Strategy, Analysis, Decisions

STEPHEN A. PYHRR is Associate Professor of Real Estate and Finance at the University of Texas at Austin, where he was instrumental in developing the undergraduate and graduate programs in real estate and urban land development. He earned his Ph.D. at the University of Illinois and is a graduate of the School of Mortgage Banking at Northwestern University.

Dr. Pyhrr is the author of numerous articles in the *Journal of the American Real Estate and Urban Economics Association, Appraisal Journal, The Real Estate Appraiser, Financial Management, Real Estate Review,* and *Mortgage Banking,* and speaks nationwide on real estate investment, finance, and taxation for professional organizations such as the Society of Real Estate Appraisers, the American Institute of Real Estate Appraisers, and numerous state associations of REALTORS®. He is also widely known for his pioneering work in the development of computer models for the financial analysis of income-producing real estate investment.

Dr. Pyhrr is associated with the real estate investment and property management firm of Davis and Associates, in Austin, Texas, and heads the firm's research and consulting division.

JAMES R. COOPER is Professor of Real Estate, Urban Affairs, and Legal Studies at Georgia State University. Previously, Dr. Cooper was a member of the faculty of the Wharton School of the University of Pennsylvania, the University of Pittsburgh, the University of Illinois at Champaign, and the University of Wisconsin at Madison. Dr. Cooper received his J.D. from The University of Pennsylvania.

Dr. Cooper holds an SRPA designation from the Society of Real Estate Appraisers, has taught national courses in appraising for both the SREA and the American Institute of Real Estate Appraisers, and is past director of the American Real Estate and Urban Economics Association.

In addition to numerous articles on housing and housing policy, investment analysis, valuation, and usury, Professor Cooper is the author of *Real Estate Investment Analysis,* an early book in computer simulation of real estate investment, co-author of *Real Estate and Urban Land Analysis,* and has produced real estate computer software such as the Illini-Cooper and REIG, USA™.

Dr. Cooper is a member of the bar of the District of Columbia and has been admitted to practice before the United States Supreme Court. He is currently a director of the Leedy Mortgage Company.

REAL ESTATE INVESTMENT
Strategy, Analysis, Decisions

Stephen A. Pyhrr, Ph.D./James R. Cooper, J.D.
University of Texas at Austin   Georgia State University

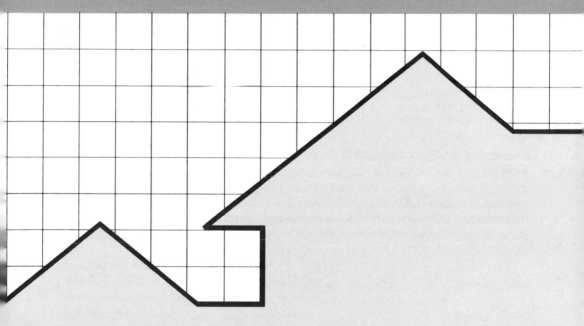

JOHN WILEY & SONS
New York • Chichester • Brisbane • Toronto • Singapore

Library of Congress Cataloging in Publication Data

Pyhrr, Stephen A.
  Real estate investment.

  Includes bibliographical references and index.
  1. Real estate investment. I. Cooper,
James R. II. Title.
HD1382.5.P93   332.63'24   81-24130
                         AACR2

ISBN 0-471-87752-2

Printed in the United States of America
  10

Preface

It has been said that the field of real estate investment is not crowded with high-quality advanced books. It has also been said that the real estate industry is not crowded with highly trained, educated business professionals who approach decision making in a rational and systematic manner. Traditionally, most real estate investors concentrated on a few key assumptions about a property and its economic future, examined a few rules of thumb, mulled over the situation, and then decided. Although some of the investment considerations were explicit, most of the mathematics of investment was left to the four horsemen of the implicit decision-making apparatus: judgment, hunch, instinct, and intuition (not to mention faith and gut feel). Even today, much real estate investment is dominated by market ignorance, irrational preferences and biases, and inability to cope with risk and uncertainty.

Because of the environment described above we were motivated to write this book. It has been ten years in the making, and there are few books to which it can be directly compared. What we have tried to do is to develop a normative framework for thinking about real estate investment problems. We see our effort as a pioneering and risky one—yet one that we hope will achieve high returns for our readers. We are anxious to see real estate decision making move ahead to new and greater plateaus of knowledge and skills, and we hope we can participate in that process through the writing of this book.

Readers of this book who apply what they learn will improve their chances of success in real estate investing. The imperfectly operating, disorganized, and highly stratified real estate markets afford investment opportunities that are not present in more organized and efficient marketplaces, such as those for bonds and stocks. One key to successful real estate investing and wealth accumulation is learning how to take advantage of these market imperfections through careful analysis and structuring of the financial and nonfinancial variables that affect investment returns and risks. In short, good strategic planning, market analysis, and financial analysis pay off in real estate investing!

Basic Objectives and Viewpoints

The basic objective of this book is to develop an analytical framework for real estate investment decisions by individuals and institutions. The framework considers the traditional methods of real estate investment analysis and the practical orientation of the majority of investors in the marketplace, as well as modern methodologies, techniques, and computer applications that are fast becoming preferred by sophisticated investors and analysts.

The cornerstones of the analytical framework developed are rate of return and risk concepts, which are related to the title of the text in the following manner:

• Strategy = return and risk *definition*
• Analysis = return and risk *measurement*
• Decisions = return and risk *evaluation*

The investment decision process is viewed as a return/risk trade-off process. However, it is not viewed simply as a financial and quantifiable phenomenon. Nonfinancial as well as financial considerations are integrated into the return/risk framework, with explicit considerations given to market, marketability, legal, political, social, and physical factors affecting investment decisions and performance.

Underlying our return/risk framework is the presumption that a decision maker can control, to a substantial degree, the returns and risks of a project through careful analysis and structuring of the financial and nonfinancial variables. Indeed, we can define real estate investment as the process of identifying and structuring projects in order to maximize returns relative to risks. (In financial management parlance, this process is called *maximizing financial wealth;* however little consideration is given to nonfinancial and nonquantifiable factors in financial management books.) Through greater expertise in the areas of market and marketability analysis, tax planning, and risk management, a decision maker can structure the purchase, operation, and termination of a property so as to increase investment returns relative to risks. We seek to improve the judgmental and structuring capabilities of both the student and the professional by way of the learning process resulting from the use of this book.

The primary viewpoint taken here is that of the *managing equity investor* — the key decision maker responsible for the location, acquisition, operation, and termination decisions of a real estate venture. To a lesser extent we will focus on the role of the *passive* equity investor. Due consideration is also given to the viewpoints of lenders, developers, architects and engineers, accountants, attorneys, promoters, government administrators, and consumers of urban space since their decisions and preferences influence, and often control, the ability of the managing equity investor to operate successfully within the investment environment.

Key Considerations Addressed

In designing this book we have placed considerable emphasis on the following factors:

1. *Increased demand for an advanced text.* There has been an extraordinary growth in the number of real estate principles courses offered in colleges and universities throughout the nation. This has produced a first generation of students ready for advanced real estate courses. Furthermore, career development and professional continuing education courses, as well as sophisticated investors, have all called for a book that is referenced and annotated, and this book takes a major step in that direction.

The book is designed to provide an advanced lesson plan for investment analysis at the advanced business undergraduate level and for graduate programs leading to the MBA and M.S. degrees. It is expected that some schools and colleges of architecture, planning, engineering, and accountancy may also choose the text for selected course offerings.

Throughout the creation of the book the authors also kept the professional real estate analyst and sophisticated investor in mind. Since the book starts with the rudiments of real estate investing and goes forward to the highest current state of the art, individual, corporate, and institutional investors in real estate may use the book to upgrade their analytical and decision-making skills. Reviewers have indicated that users of the book will want to retain it as a ready-reference desk book for solving particular problems as they arise.

2. *Theory/application versus problems/case studies.* Primary emphasis of the book is placed on theory, concept building, and practical application. While we use many short examples and one major case study (Aspen Wood Apartments) to illustrate the concepts and techniques in each chapter in Part III, cases and problems are atypical of the book's style and format. A casebook/problems manual, along with an instructor's manual of problem and case solution scenarios, will be published in the future.

3. *Analyzing real estate markets under changing conditions.* Although careful market and marketability studies are critical to the investment decision process, they are too often neglected or their importance is shortchanged by real estate investors. We place special emphasis on these subjects in Part II, and have devoted a chapter to the difficult topic of the complex impact of inflation, deflation, and real estate cycles on investment returns and risks. Both project and portfolio implications are addressed at length.

4. *Integration of management terminology and principles.* Normative methodologies for performing investment analysis, which consider the efficient allocation of human as well as financial capital resources, are developed. Most invest-

ment theories ignore the decision maker's time allocation problems associated with developing strategy, performing investment analysis, and making investment decisions. Most investment books implicitly and naively assume a one-shot investment analysis process that results in a go/no-go decision. In contrast, we advocate a stepwise investment analysis procedure which recognizes that investing is a discontinuous process during which knowledgeable investors develop drop/continue-on points (with the discontinuity of loops and feedback), and that investors have multiple investment objectives and constraints that are applied at different time stages in the process. One of the contributions we hope to make to the field is to demonstrate that different types of analysis (i.e., levels of sophistication) are appropriate for different kinds of property, different sizes of projects, and at different phases of the analytical process.

We have sought to adapt the terminology of management policy and strategy to the real estate investment process. In effect, the language of management by objective (MBO), resource audits, strategic profiles, monitoring and feedback, competitive threats, search for opportunity, etc. are used in order to break down the semantic barrier between academicians, business students, and real estate practitioners. This book is designed to bridge the gap and thus should be in tune with advanced undergraduate and MBA business school curricula.

5. *Application of modern capital budgeting techniques.* We place great emphasis on the importance of applying modern capital budgeting techniques and computer models to real estate investment analysis. After-tax cash flow analysis, discounted cash flow methods, and ratio and risk analysis techniques are explored in depth. Computer models developed by the authors are illustrated and will be made available at nominal cost to instructors and individuals (see Chapter 18). Numerous universities are using models developed by Pyhrr and Cooper, who are identified as pioneers in the field. Thus, we emphasize the development of technical competence in the measurement of returns and risks, after a subject property has been selected in earlier steps of the strategic framework. The process developed enables the investor to compare a project under analysis with the best available alternatives at the time.

6. *Tax planning and the Economic Recovery Tax Act of 1981.* Tax shelter analysis and tax planning concepts and strategies are given prominent status throughout the book, with a major chapter (Chapter 13) devoted to the subject. The many changes brought about by the Economic Recovery Tax Act of 1981 have widespread and significant impacts on the rates of return and risks of alternative investment media, and on investor preferences and perceptions. We explore in depth the various provisions of the 1981 tax act and their likely impact on investors and properties. At the time the act was passed (August 1981), the manuscript was in the final stages of completion. Although the tax planning chapter was rewritten and the 1981 tax act provisions noted throughout the text, many of the cash flow examples use tax assumptions that are not permitted under the new law, but are valid for the projects analyzed and purchased pre-1982. We compare and contrast throughout the text the provisions under the old and new law. For some time to come, most existing properties will remain under the provisions of the old law. The reader should understand both perspectives.

7. Emphasis on the assumptions that create the investor's rate of return. We emphasize that "the buyer should buy the assumptions that create the yield rather than the yield itself." Real estate investment analysis is thus a process of validating key assumptions such as income, expenses, financing, and resale. Those who can research a property and arrive at the most realistic set of assumptions will have the highest probability of success in real estate investing. As the old GIGO principle states, if you put garbage in your investment model, you get garbage out!

8. Realistic assumptions require an interdisciplinary, holistic approach. Because real estate is, by its very nature, an interdisciplinary subject, the interdisciplinary nature of real estate investment decisions is emphasized. The successful decision maker must possess a generalist's knowledge of architecture and design, engineering, construction, marketing, and management, in conjunction with a high level of expertise in urban economics and financial analysis. We believe that property returns and risks cannot be assessed intelligently and accurately without incorporating the above disciplines into a holistic approach to the investment process. Decision makers must learn to better understand the interrelationships and linkages between these areas and their probable impacts on investment returns and risks. A sound assumption base for a financial analysis cannot be developed without this knowledge.

Indeed, we believe that the conditions of uncertainty for business today are such that just as real estate must become more quantitative and statistically oriented, other business disciplines must become more holistic if their training is to be useful to future decision makers.

9. Distinction between existing and development projects. The nature and level of returns and risks, and the nature and extent of the analysis performed, are significantly different for development and existing project situations. Our focus is on existing, or ongoing, projects that are assumed to be completed and absorbed in the marketplace, or where a turnkey situation that promises completion is arranged with a developer. Thus, we will largely ignore direct involvement in a construction period and its attendant high risks. These subjects are, we feel, better reserved for a course and text on real estate development.

10. Background knowledge needed by readers. To take full advantage of this book, the reader should have some knowledge in the following subject areas: real estate principles and practices, accounting, finance, and mathematics. Our experience has indicated that a background course in real estate, although desirable, is *not* necessary for business students in graduate schools. However, at the undergraduate level we recommend at least one background course in real estate before undertaking advanced real estate investment analysis. Review of the following text (or a comparable one) will set forth the entry level for this book:

Alvin L. Arnold, Charles H. Wurtzebach, and Mike E. Miles. *Modern Real Estate* (Boston: Warren, Gorham & Lamont, 1980).

Although a background knowledge of computer software would be helpful, the illustrations used to explain computer simulation techniques will enable the novice to gain the skill to use the computer program studied without any prior training.

Organization and Content of the Book

In the various parts of the book the authors have sought, first, to present recent developments in the literature and the state of the art of analysis; second, to set forth a general normative methodology for analyzing investments in properties; third, to apply the analytical techniques to different types of property; and fourth, to present the state of the art in portfolio management both for individuals and institutions.

The book has five parts. *Part I* presents the current state of the art of real estate investment decision making. A statement of the nature and scope of real estate investments, an overview of the investment and feasibility process, and a comparison of traditional and modern decision making approaches serve as an introduction.

Part II introduces the difficult problem of analyzing real estate markets by evaluating how one might select a target SMSA given the process of growth and decline that characterizes metro areas. It then proceeds to present techniques of metro area market study and analysis of a given location within a real estate market. This part culminates with a significant chapter on the relationship between inflation, deflation, and real estate cycles. The reader is taught how to read the important economic indicators to evaluate the "timing" of investment purchases and sales, from both an individual project and a portfolio perspective.

Part III presents a strategy for the process of investment analysis and financial structuring of a particular investment project. The reader is taught how to use a basic financial feasibility model in the context of strategic planning. Selecting the ownership entity, discounted cash flow analysis, risk analysis, risk management, tax planning, financing and refinancing techniques, the art of negotiating, managing the property, and disposing of the property, are all intensively considered within the framework of a carefully developed 10-step process. A comprehensive case study—the 86-unit Aspen Wood Apartments presented at the end of each chapter—applies the concepts and techniques developed. While the case study can be treated as optional material, for most readers it will serve to integrate the material and make it seem more relevant.

Part IV applies the general methodology developed in Part III. It opens with a statement recognizing the importance of ethics in imperfect markets and provides a general scenario model for applying the techniques for selecting among alternative investments. The chapters within this part provide a wealth of source material to aid the reader in analyzing different types of investments: houses, small apartments, apartment projects, shopping centers, office buildings, industrial buildings and parks, special-use properties, and raw land investments. This applications section of the book provides a practicum for developing skill in using the 10-step model described in Part III. It also provides very valuable references and bibliographies for students who are doing case problems or developing input data for computer simulation. Institutional and corporate investors who are considering unfamiliar investments will, we have been advised, find the framework of analysis provided for each type of property a useful guide in reviewing investment proposals.

Part V has been sorely needed in advanced real estate curricula. Very little scholarly work has been presented in the field of managing investment portfolios that contain real estate assets as a major part of the portfolio. Indeed, most texts by specialists in finance act as though real estate assets do not exist as an investment alternative. Thus, Chapter 26 on institutional portfolio management, with real estate assets as a part of the portfolio, is a major first step in the direction of bridging the gap between securities analysts and real estate investors. Hopefully, the chapter's analysis and bibliography will produce research and writings that will merge the fields in the future. Chapter 27 is a first attempt in a book such as this to provide the individual investor with a method for managing a personal portfolio that contains real estate assets. We have sought to provide the reader with a systematic approach to wealth accumulation, using real estate, which could (ultimately) provide financial independence from the corporate institutions that seem to be the focus of interest of most of the finance literature.

The final chapter in Part V is the authors' attempt to forecast the future of real estate investing under the uncertain conditions of the next several years. Even if the reader disagrees with many of our forecasts and conclusions, the chapter should be a provocative exercise in the unsolvable problem of predicting future trends and in understanding the many economic, social, political, legal, and psychological forces that affect real estate investment.

Acknowledgments

While this book, which was ten years in the making, is a first of its kind, the authors are fully aware that they owe a heavy debt of gratitude to many real estate faculty members throughout the nation. We drew heavily upon the work of the scholars who have written for the *Journal of the American Real Estate and Urban Economics Association, Appraisal Journal, Real Estate Appraiser and Analyst, Real Estate Issues, Real Estate Review, The Journal of Real Estate Taxation,* and many Warren, Gorham & Lamont publications. The permissions granted by the National Association of REALTORS® organizations, such as the Institute of Property Management, Realtors National Marketing Institute, and others, were invaluable. We have sought, by way of cited permissions, footnotes, and acknowledgments, to indicate the names of the many professors, professional practitioners, students, and others without whose aid, wittingly or not, this book could not have been created. No doubt we have neglected to acknowledge some worthy person or source; for that unfortunate omission we extend our sincere apology.

We wish to express special thanks to our deans: Kenneth Black at Georgia State University and George Kozmetzky at the University of Texas. The patience and cooperation of our past and present department chairmen, Richard M. Forbes and Joseph Rabianski at GSU, and Lawrence Crum, Conrad Doenges, and Steve Magee at the University of Texas should not go unrecognized. Their aid and support were essential in this too long and difficult process.

Special thanks are due to Steven D. Kapplin, who was the primary author of

Chapter 25, "Institutional Portfolios" and to Larry E. Wofford who coauthored Chapter 26, "Developing a Personal Portfolio." Also we thank our good friends C. A. Davis and Edwin J. Bomer of the firm Davis and Associates in Austin, Texas who provided much of the information for the comprehensive case study that appears in Chapters 8–17.

The manuscript was typed, in its many versions, by Majorie Hudson, Leticia Vazquez, and Maria Lunday. Many useful suggestions were made by reviewers Kenneth L. Lusht, Larry E. Wofford, Donald M. Valachi, James F. Gaines, and Edwin J. Bomer. Ken Lusht took on a special burden as we worked to reduce a lengthy manuscript to publishable size. We do appreciate it. The work of Cynthia Hausdorff, our editor, in putting together the manuscript and in following through the production was patient, indefatigable, and deserving of great praise. Eugene Simonoff, of Warren, Gorham & Lamont did much to clear the path to completion. The authors also appreciate the comments and criticisms of the many students who reviewed parts of the book manuscript at various stages, including University of Texas students Scott Weaver, Richard Duncan, Jonathan Frank, John Ramzy, Mary Lanigan, and Michael Jacobs, who worked with Pyhrr, and the Georgia State students, too numerous to mention, who worked with Cooper.

We anticipate the embarrassment of the discovery of errors in the published text, by saying we are sorry, we have done the best we can, and we promise to do better next time. No one is to blame but us. Pyhrr/Cooper take complete responsibility. We wrestled with the problem of the male pronouns. We feel that women are equal, if not superior, and fully acknowledge it. In spite of our efforts an occassional "his" appears where it could be "hers." We hope that no individual will be offended.

Our fervent hope is that this new approach to real estate investment decision making will achieve its objective, which is to improve the quality of real estate education and knowledge. We are aware that there are many students and professionals in the field who are brighter and more knowledgeable than we are. We hope the book whets their intellectual curiosity and acts to challenge them to improve upon it. As in the past, in the future we will learn from them.

Both authors are aware of the tremendous burden writing places on their families. Cooper wishes to thank his wife, Dr. Nyda W. Brown, for being forthright with her anger resulting from the times he ignored her needs. Pyhrr thanks his wife, Daphne, for her love, understanding, and support during the writing of the book.

May we ask that those who discover errors or have comments to please contact the authors.

January 1982   Stephen A. Pyhrr/James R. Cooper

Contents

PART I   REAL ESTATE INVESTMENT: THE STATE OF THE ART   1

Chapter

1   The Nature and Scope of Real Estate Investments   3

What Is Real Estate?   The Many Dimensions of Real Estate Create
Opportunities   Investor Motivations   Participants in the Investment
Process   Investment Contrasted with Speculation   Summary

2   Overview of the Investment Decision Process   22

Framework for Real Estate Investment Studies   Investment Analysis vs.
Feasibility Analysis   Time Horizons for Investment Decisions: Life Cycles
Summary

3   Decision-Making Approaches to Real Estate Investment   44

Popular "How to" Approaches   Traditional Financial Decision
Approaches   Modern Capital Budgeting Approaches   Summary

**PART II   ANALYZING REAL ESTATE MARKETS UNDER CHANGING
            CONDITIONS   69**

**4   Searching for the Target Metro Area: Evaluating the Growth and Decline of
     Metropolitan Areas   71**

What Is a Metropolitan Area?   Patterns of Metropolitan Growth   The
Process of Urban Growth and Decline   Searching for a Target Metro
Area   The Growth Derby   Summary

5   **Market Studies   96**

Real Estate Markets   What Is a Market Study?   Economic Base
Analysis   Case Study: Using Economic Base Analysis to Forecast
Growth in Atlanta, Georgia   Market Studies—A Descriptive
Analysis   Summary   Appendix: Comment on Regional Planning
Models

6   **Marketability Analysis   120**

What Is Marketability Analysis?   Guidelines for a Marketability
Analysis   Summary

7   **Inflation, Deflation, and Real Estate Cycles   140**

Framework for Analyzing Inflation and Cycles   Impact of Inflation on
Investors and Properties   Inflation Cycles and Investment
Strategy   Other Real Estate Cycles   Summary

Appendix to Part II: Sources of Market Data for Real Estate Investors   179

**PART III   THE INVESTMENT ANALYSIS AND FINANCIAL
STRUCTURING PROCESS   185**

8   **Investment Strategy   187**

The Investment Analysis and Financial Structuring Process   Developing
an Investment Strategy   Summary   Aspen Wood Apartments

9   **Selecting the Ownership Entity   212**

Ownership Alternatives   Ownership Decision Model   Ownership
Selection Criteria   Noncorporate Forms of Ownership   Corporations
and Trusts   Real Estate Syndication   Summary   Aspen Wood
Apartments

10   **The Basic Financial Feasibility Model   246**

Important Concepts, Principles, and Techniques   The Basic Financial
Feasibility Model   Application of the Basic Financial Feasibility Model
Developing a Detailed One-Year Pro Forma   Summary   Aspen
Wood Apartments

11   **Discounted Cash Flow and Ratio Analysis   284**

Present Value and Internal Rate of Return   Discounted Cash Flow
After-Tax Analysis   Financial Ratio Analysis   Summary

12 **Risk Analysis and Risk Management   317**

Risk Analysis   Risk Management and Control   Summary   Aspen
Wood Apartments

13 **Tax Planning and Detailed Financial Analysis   341**

The Tax Law   Tax Planning Alternatives and Issues   Tax
Shelter Strategy   Summary   Aspen Wood Apartments

14 **Financing and Refinancing Techniques   385**

The Financing Decision Model   Debt Financing Alternatives   The
Refinancing Decision   Equity Financing Alternatives   Syndication
Offerings   Summary   Aspen Wood Apartments

15 **The Art of Real Estate Negotiations   425**

The Role of Negotiations   The Psychology of Negotiations   How to
Achieve the Objectives of the Negotiating Parties   Ending the
Negotiations—Final Settlement and Closing   Summary   Aspen
Wood Apartments

16 **Managing the Property   448**

What Is Property Management?   Who Needs Property
Management   The Property Management Process   Selecting the
Property Manager   Evaluating the Performance of the Property
Manager   Summary   Aspen Wood Apartments

17 **Termination of the Investment   478**

Disposal as Part of the Investment Cycle   Guidelines for
Disposition Strategy   Disposing of Property   Exchanges
Summary   Aspen Wood Apartments

PART IV PROPERTY SELECTION   515

18 **The Property Selection Process: A Plan for Earning a Good Track
Record   517**

Defining the Concept of a Modern Track Record   Sources of Computer
Software

19 **Apartments   523**

Track Record and Trends   Advantages and Disadvantages of Investing
in Apartments   Types of Investors and Investor Motivations   The
Nature of the Returns and Risks   Market and Marketability Analysis

Physical, Legal, Political, and Environmental Analysis
Analysis of Operations   Financing and Refinancing Techniques
Taxation and Tax Structure   Discounted Cash Flow Analysis
The Investment Decision   Selected References

20 Shopping Centers   540

Track Record and Trends   Advantages and Disadvantages of Investing
in Shopping Centers   Types of Investors and Investor Motivations
The Nature of the Returns and Risks   Market and
Marketability Analysis   Physical, Legal, Political, and Environmental
Analysis   Analysis of Operations   Financing and Refinancing
Techniques   Taxation and Tax Structure   Discounted Cash Flow
Analysis   The Investment Decision   Selected References

21 Office Buildings   564

Track Record and Trends   Advantages and Disadvantages of Investing
in Office Buildings   Types of Investors and Investor Motivations
The Nature of the Returns and Risks   Market and Marketability
Analysis   Physical, Legal, Political, and Environmental
Analysis   Analysis of Operations   Financing and Refinancing
Techniques   Taxation and Tax Structure   Discounted Cash Flow
Analysis   The Investment Decision   Selected References

22 Industrial Buildings and Parks   585

Recent Trends   Advantages and Disadvantages of Investing in Industrial
Buildings and Parks   Types of Investors and Investor Motivations
Market and Marketability Analysis   Physical Analysis of Site
and Improvements   Legal, Political, and Environmental Analysis
Property Management and Leasing   Risk Management and
Control Techniques   Financing and Refinancing Techniques
Taxation and Tax Structure   Discounted Cash Flow Analysis
The Investment Decision   Selected References

23 Other Income-Producing Properties   610

SINGLE-FAMILY HOMES, CONDOMINIUMS, AND SMALL APARTMENT
PROPERTIES   611

Recent Trends   Investment Advantages and Disadvantages   The
Nature of the Returns and Risks   Market and Marketability
Analysis   Physical and Structural Analysis   Legal, Political, and
Environmental Analysis   Property Management   Analysis of
Operating Income and Expenses   Analysis of Local Trends and
Uncertainties   Financing and Refinancing Techniques   Tax Problems
and Uncertainties   Rate-of-Return Analysis   Ratio and Risk
Analysis   The Investment Decision

Special-Use Properties

HOTELS AND MOTELS   625

Investment Advantages and Disadvantages   Types of Investors and Investor Motivations   Market and Marketability Analysis   Physical Analysis   Legal, Political, and Environmental Analysis   Property Management   Analysis of Current Operating Income and Expenses   Risk Management   Financing   Nature of the Tax Shelter   Cash Flow, Ratio, and Risk Analysis   The Investment Decision

NURSING HOMES   637

Investment Advantages and Disadvantages   Supply and Demand Analysis   Physical Analysis   Legal, Political, and Environmental Analysis   Property Management   Analysis of Operations   Tax Shelter Variables   The Investment Decision

Selected References

24 Land Investments   647

Track Records and Trends   Advantages and Disadvantages of Investing in Land   Types of Investors and Investor Motivations   Market and Marketability Analysis   Risk Management and Control Techniques   Physical, Legal, Political, and Environmental Analysis   Financing   Taxation and Tax Structure   Discounted Cash Flow Analysis   Selected References

PART V PORTFOLIO STRATEGY AND INVESTMENT OUTLOOK   663

25 Institutional Real Estate Portfolios   665

Introduction   Portfolio Choice   Real Estate Investing and Modern Portfolio Theory   An Extended Development of Portfolio Theory   The Impact of Portfolio Theory on Large Institutional Investors   Summary

26 Developing a Personal Portfolio with Real Estate   698

Adopting a Portfolio-Building Strategy   Basic Steps in Developing and Implementing a Personal Financial Plan   Summary

27 The Real Estate Investment Outlook   727

The Market Outlook for Different Types of Real Estate, 1982–1986   What Financing Will Be Available?   The Sprawling Costs of Urban Containment   Scenarios in Real Estate Investment Strategy and Planning   Conclusion

APPENDIXES   747

A   The Time Value of Money: Problems for the Student   **749**

B   Selected Compound Interest Tables   **751**

C   Present Value of $1   **775**
      Present Value of $1 Annuity   **776**

D   Mortgage Constant: Monthly Payment in Arrears   **777**

E   Accelerated Cost Recovery System Tables for Real Estate Assets   **779**

Table 1: All Personal Property
Table 2: All Real Property (Except Low-Income Housing)
Table 3: Low-Income Housing

INDEX   781

I

Real Estate Investment: The State of the Art

Our basic objective in this first part of the book is to develop an analytical framework for real estate equity investment decisions by individuals and institutions. We discuss the traditional methods of real estate investment analysis and the practical orientation of the majority of investors in the marketplace, as well as the modern methodologies and techniques that are increasingly preferred by sophisticated investors and analysts.

The cornerstone of the analytical framework presented is rate of return and risk analysis, often referred to as "wealth maximization." Investment decisions and the investment decision process are thus viewed as a return/risk trade-off process. However, the return/risk framework is not viewed simply as a financial and quantifiable phenomenon. Nonfinancial considerations are integrated into the framework, with explicit consideration given to market and location, legal, political, social, and physical factors affecting investment performance and investment decisions. Furthermore, it is argued that the decision maker can control to a substantial degree the returns and risks of a project through careful analysis and structuring of the financial and nonfinancial variables.

Chapter 1 examines the nature of real estate investment, its numerous advantages and disadvantages, and the various roles played by key participants in the investment process. Chapter 2 discusses our strategy/analysis/decision framework and the importance of the life cycles that affect the return/risk relationship upon which the investor's decision is based. In Chapter 3 we compare and contrast traditional "how to" approaches, traditional financial decision approaches, and modern capital budgeting approaches to investment decisions. Together these chapters synthesize the current "state of the art" in real estate investment.

1

The Nature and Scope of Real Estate Investments

A Neanderthal developer once rolled a rock to the entrance of his cave, and created Real Estate, providing the natural void with some additional attribute not found in nature, such as warmth, security, or exclusiveness. He had successfully interfaced land (a finite natural resource) with an artifact (the rock—the first solid core door) to serve an unmet need of a space consumer (a market). Eventually his possession of the cave over many moons became institutionalized as artifacts for the delineation of space became more sophisticated with survey monuments, county records, and equity courts. Real estate is therefore a manufactured product of artificially delineated cubage with an institutional time dimension (square foot per year, room per night, cave per moon), designed to interface society with the natural resource land.[1]

James A. Graaskamp

WHAT IS REAL ESTATE?

A real estate investment is often perceived as a physical product or entity. Since the dawn of history we have been possessed with the need to own and control physical things, and many of us believe that land and man-made improvements are the essence of real estate. To own or control a diversified portfolio of apartments,

---

[1] James A. Graaskamp, "A Rational Approach to Feasibility Analysis," *The Appraisal Journal* (Chicago: American Institute of Real Estate Appraisers), October 1972, p. 513.

shopping centers, office buildings, and industrial or other real estate is the goal of many individual and institutional investors. This bricks-and-mortar concept is probably the most common approach to the definition of real estate.

James Graaskamp has correctly pointed out, however, that the essence of a real estate investment is the space or the void, not the solids. The walls, floors, and ceilings are really worth very little. They are simply ways of delineating cubage. In fact, brick and mortar is a very clumsy way of delineating space. For example, at the beginning of this century high-rise office buildings were commonly built with walls five feet thick on the first floor and load-bearing walls and columns extended throughout the building. As technology changed from brick to steel construction and engineers discovered how to dispense with bulky exterior materials as well as space-consuming interior walls and columns, buildings became more efficient and far more flexible. In recent years developers have learned how to create more rentable square feet within the structure, reduce the bulk of the supporting structure, reduce the weight of the building, simplify the foundation design, and erect buildings on sites that formerly could not be used because of troublesome soil types. In short, developers have learned to create more artificially delineated space with less brick and mortar.

Real Estate as Space and Money over Time

The three-dimensional concept of real estate (i.e., as artificially delineated space) is important for understanding the nature of real estate. The concept is far more relevant to the investor, however, when a fourth dimension—time—is introduced. Investors are most interested in renting space over time. They are interested in renting an apartment unit per month, a motel room per night, or square feet of office space per year. Thus, real estate should be thought of as money flows over time.

Real estate investment analysis focuses on the conversion of space/time units into money/time units. While engineers and architects may prefer to think of real estate in a space/time context, land economists and real estate investors prefer to consider money flows over time. Investors are concerned with the amount of money needed to acquire the asset and with the cash flows they may expect over some future time period. Indeed, investors have recently devised sophisticated computer models that utilize internal rate of return and present value techniques to convert space/time concepts into money/time projections. Thus, the essence of real estate investment analysis is learning the techniques by which we can develop reliable methods of converting space/time into money/time.

The Investment Environment

Success in converting real estate space into money flows over time depends on how successfully the investor operates within the real estate environment. This environment can be depicted as the dynamic relationship between the real estate itself (site plus improvements) and three participant groups: (1) investor/developers who provide real estate space over time; (2) consumers, who use or consume the space provided; and (3) government, which provides the public infrastructure

EXHIBIT 1–1.   Conceptual Model of the Real Estate Investment Environment

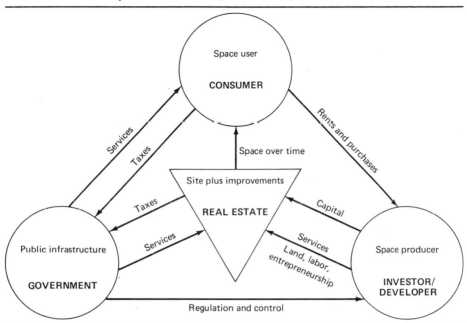

within which all real estate transactions take place. This relationship is illustrated in Exhibit 1–1.

The three cooperators must interact to find compromise solutions that permit them to operate successfully together over both the short and the long run. While the goals of the three parties are seemingly incongruent (consumers want lower rents; investors want higher rents; the government wants to tax away as much of the rent as possible), they all have a vested interest in achieving or maintaining financial solvency in order to survive. Neither the consumer, the investor/developer, nor government can require the others to make outlays which inevitably lead to insolvency. The power to force insolvency on others is the power to destroy an enterprise. While free enterprise depends on that war between private enterprises, it is not an acceptable relationship between public and private enterprises.[2]

Real Estate as a Stewardship

We have been living in an era of increasing government controls on every front. The use of *police powers* by local governments to regulate private property has increased substantially. The enforcement of master plans regulating land use, together with the development of more rigorous zoning ordinances, building

---

[2] James A. Graaskamp, *Two-Day Workshop: Real Estate Feasibility Analysis for the Appraiser,* prepared at the request of the American Institute of Real Estate Appraisers, Seminar Committee, 1976, p. 3.

codes, and subdivision regulations, attests to the growth of local government regulation. At the state and federal levels, growing concerns about how land use affects the living environment and the quality of life led to a barrage of legislation in the late 1960s and early 1970s, including the National Environmental Policy Act of 1969, the Clean Air Act Amendment of 1970, the Federal Water Pollution Control Act of 1972, the Coastal Zone Management Act of 1972, and the Housing and Community Development Act of 1974. Most states also enacted land use legislation and delegated the task of implementation to regional and county governmental bodies. In recent years very little new legislation has been enacted; greater emphasis has been placed on consolidation, modification, and in some cases retrenchment and simplification of the various existing land use programs at all levels of government.

Consumers have learned to act on their own behalf as well as through the governmental bodies that represent them. The power of consumerism is evident in every real estate transaction today—in the case of real estate leases, the law has increased the enforceable rights of tenants and provided them with expedient legal remedies if the landlord fails to perform the duties required by the lease agreement; in the case of residential loan closing statements, more effective advance disclosure of settlement costs to both buyers and sellers is required; and legislation on deceptive trade practices provides liberal legal remedies to consumers who feel that they have been deceived or cheated by real estate practitioners. Neighborhood groups have been organized in most metropolitan areas, and they are demanding their "sovereign" right to control land uses and regulate development efforts that affect their neighborhoods.

As a result of these trends, ownership rights in land have been shifted from the private to the public sector. Fee simple ownership no longer commands the same complete bundle of rights possessed in the past by the owner of record. Private sector businesses are being asked to assume broader social responsibilities than ever before, and to serve a wider range of human values.[3] Though it is obvious that the primary function of business continues to be the making of profits, there is no question that profit maximization must be tempered by another objective—serving the current needs of society and providing for the needs of generations to come. There is increasing support for the belief that a titleholder has no more than temporary possession of property during his or her lifetime and must act as a steward or trustee of the property for its future users. The successful real estate investor of the future must understand the words attributed to a Nigerian chieftan: "We have received this land from all those who have gone before and hold it for all those who are yet to come."

It is in such an environment that real estate investors must attempt to maximize investment returns relative to risks.

THE MANY DIMENSIONS OF REAL ESTATE CREATE OPPORTUNITIES

The advantages and disadvantages of real estate as an investment stem from the nature of the asset and the markets in which real estate is bought and sold. As a

---

[3] James R. Cooper and Karl L. Guntermann, *Real Estate and Urban Land Analysis* (Lexington, Mass.: Lexington Books, 1974), p. xxi.

first step the investor must thoroughly study the many dimensions of the asset and the marketplace.

It can be argued that real estate is a relatively weak product. The sales of an average manufacturing firm exceed its total assets each year, but the average real estate property generates sales (rents) equal to only 10–20 percent of the total cost of the property. The cash inflows are so weak that it takes 25 to 30 years for the mortgage to be fully amortized.

One might even argue that over the long run real estate is a poor investment. First, the investor buys a product whose location is fixed. If people choose not to drive to that location next year, the investor is in trouble. Second, the product is built to last, so the investor is committed to an investment that has a physical life of fifty years yet may become obsolete after only a few years. In contrast, automobile manufacturers build and sell new cars each year and hope that the planned obsolescence will occur on schedule. Third, the real estate product purchased reflects today's life style and standards. Fifteen years from now the investor may find that the investment is in the wrong place and represents the wrong life style.

The counterpoint to the argument just given is the recognition that these inherent characteristics of real estate present the entrepreneur with numerous opportunities to generate extraordinary profits. If the entrepreneur can learn to carefully analyze and assert some degree of control over the physical, legal, social, and financial aspects of real estate, then a strategy that will increase returns relative to risks can be developed. Clearly, if the investor can identify the best locations in town and a product that can be adapted to changing life styles, and then leverage the investment with mortgage funds, structure a tax shelter package that generates substantial tax savings, and manage the property professionally, he or she may very well be entitled to monopoly profits, or at least above-average returns.

The investor can also find many opportunities emanating from the imperfect market conditions that characterize real estate, including the following:

1. *Highly stratified, local markets.* This gives an advantage to experts who can correctly assess demand within the submarkets of a city.
2. *Heterogeneous products.* Investors who can perform market analyses to determine the product needs of consumers in local submarkets can design "a better mousetrap."
3. *Transactions are private, resulting in poor information flows.* Developing a good data base through local contacts and research will provide a competitive advantage.
4. *Poorly educated and unknowledgeable investors and industry participants.* A highly ethical, well-educated and trained professional has been the exception rather than the rule in real estate in the past, yet such a person can quickly gain a competitive edge.
5. *An unorganized market, with slow adjustments of supply and demand.* This causes relatively severe real estate cycles resulting in periods of overbuilding followed by periods of depression and underbuilding. Strategies can be developed to track these cycles and take advantage of their upsides and downsides. (See Chapter 7.)

6. *A high degree of government control of the market.* This gives rise to the need for more careful planning and analysis of political factors that affect development and ownership. Consultants prosper as government regulation increases and as the need for better feasibility and investment analysis increases.

Real estate is often described as the last bastion of entrepreneurship. Because of the imperfections of the marketplace, small investors are afforded opportunities that are not present in more organized, efficient marketplaces. While the average size of firms is increasing and financial giants like Bank of America and Prudential Insurance are playing more significant roles, most of the firms concerned with real property development and ownership are small. Even in today's complex and highly regulated economy there are still relatively few barriers to entry into real estate, and almost anyone can become an entrepreneur in this field.

INVESTOR MOTIVATIONS

Why do people invest? Some economists argue that individuals save a portion of current income to provide for future consumption and thus face investment decisions regularly. Rarely, however, is the consumption argument stated by real estate investors. Rather, most cite the financial and nonfinancial advantages and disadvantages of real property investments.

Investment Advantages and Returns

Investment incentives, motives, and returns are as diverse as the investors who acquire real estate. Individual motivations differ significantly from corporate or institutional objectives. The perceived advantages of certain real estate investments may vary over time and have to be reevaluated periodically in accordance with changing attitudes and strategies. These investment advantages and returns are generally a combination of the following:

Pride of Ownership   Many investors feel a need to own and control real estate for the sake of status and ego gratification. For many, real estate is a status symbol and a measure of greatness, importance, or success. While pride of ownership is most often associated with single-family dwellings, it is also prevalent, and sometimes overwhelming, with respect to commercial properties. The desire to create the most prestigious office building, corporate headquarters, or apartment complex, regardless of cost, has driven many an investor and developer into bankruptcy. In sum, real estate is a product that investors can feel and touch (the bricks-and-mortar concept). Owning real estate is an emotional experience for many people, and this is an important attribute to be recognized and dealt with.

Personal Control   Real estate, unlike other investment assets such as bonds and stocks, affords the investor an opportunity to exercise personal and direct control over the asset. If the real estate is owned directly, the investor can control decisions regarding purchase terms and price, leverage, form of ownership, operations, refinancing, and disposal of the property. For many investors, the desire to exercise direct control over a property, without interference from partners or other investors, is a significant reason for participation in real estate.

Self-Use and Occupancy   Many investors acquire real estate for their own use. The purchase of a single-family dwelling or condominium unit is a form of investment that provides both physical shelter and a tax shelter. In addition, the owner benefits from appreciation of property value and freedom from rent payments. An investor–occupant of a manufacturing plant benefits in a similar way. Medical doctors and dentists often prefer to own facilities designed to meet their particular needs.

Estate Building   Theodore Roosevelt argued that real estate was the surest and safest method of becoming independently wealthy. An investor can begin to build an estate by acquiring leveraged real estate, reinvesting the cash proceeds (which can be tax sheltered), and over the long run building up equity through loan amortization and appreciation of property value. Periodically, properties can be refinanced and the funds reinvested tax free in other properties, repeating the process. Tax-free exchange techniques are used to pyramid small properties into larger ones, or to convert high-risk properties into low-risk income properties that provide regular income during retirement. Real estate as a portfolio-building technique offers great flexibility for the investor.

Security of Capital   Safety of principal is a prime concern of many investors. Mortgage investors attempt to secure their investments by recording liens against properties and requiring personal guarantees and pledged collateral. Compared to other investment forms, real estate is generally believed to rank very high in terms of security of capital. It tends to be permanent, indestructible, and relatively scarce; demand usually exceeds supply; and price tends to be directly influenced by inflationary pressures. We will examine some of these claims and myths in detail in later chapters.

High Operating Yield   In the past some experts claimed that prime real estate would yield a before-tax return on total investment, including equity and debt, of 8–15 percent annually. Speculative real estate may show yields of 25 percent or more. Alternatively, through leases the investor is able to obtain a reasonably certain return with a minimum of risk. While such before-tax yields are attractive to pension funds, which are tax exempt and often prefer to buy debt-free properties, most investors prefer to evaluate properties on a leveraged basis and take tax shelter factors into consideration.

Leverage   One of the major attractions of real estate is the investor's ability to control a large asset with a small amount of equity capital. While most large manufacturing operations boast conservative debt ratios (debt/total assets) of less than 50–60 percent, most equity investors have debt ratios in excess of 70–80 percent. With a high degree of leverage, investors can use other people's money to parlay their equity yield to significantly higher levels. Leverage financing, thus, is a key factor in most real estate investments.

Tax Shelter Factors The real estate investor often seeks to shelter from income tax all cash flows earned by a property. In addition, the investor seeks to generate tax losses that can be used to shelter other earned income. Later, when the property is sold, the investor seeks favorable capital gains tax treatment on the (presumably) appreciated property value. In addition, taxable gains can be deferred through installment sales techniques or tax-free exchanges. In short, investors utilize tax-planning techniques to maximize after-tax cash flows over the long run.

Capital Appreciation and Protection Against Inflation In addition to receiving cash flow, tax shelter benefits, and equity buildup through loan amortization, the investor desires to receive a return from increases in property value. Appreciation can be caused by two factors. First, it can occur as a result of an increase in demand relative to supply in a noninflationary economy. An apartment property that is well located in an improving neighborhood, well designed, and professionally managed may substantially increase in value owing to the sheer pressure of demand. Similarly, price inflation may increase property prices dramatically. Historically, real estate has been a good inflation hedge, and diversified portfolios of real estate have outperformed stocks and other financial assets.[4] Without question, during the last decade the most significant amount of the investor's nominal return on leveraged real estate has come, on average, from the appreciation of property value due to inflationary pressure.

Investment Disadvantages and Risks

With the many apparent advantages and benefits emanating from real estate investments, why would any investor fail to commit a large portion of his or her savings to them? Perhaps because, after careful analysis, it becomes clear that many of the so-called advantages of real estate investment are really traps for the unwary. There are significant disadvantages, risks, and uncertainties associated with real estate investment (see also Exhibit 1–2).

Illiquidity Real estate is difficult to convert into cash quickly. The product is not standardized or traded on an exchange, and the time required for an investor to analyze the purchase is relatively long. Even after a purchase decision has been reached, time is required for negotiation of the sale, title search, preparing the necessary legal documentation, and arranging financing. At times financing is not available or interest rates make the purchase uneconomical. Also, the presence of illiquidity in situations of financial stress can easily lead to investor insolvency, bankruptcy, and personal ruin.

The Management Burden Most real estate investments require a significant amount of personal attention. Whether a tenant has agreed to manage a property

---

[4] For examples see Harris C. Friedman, "Real Estate Investment and Portfolio Theory," *Journal of Financial and Quantitative Analysis,* March 1971, pp. 861–874; Eugene Fama and G. William Schwert, "Asset Returns and Inflation," *Journal of Financial Economics,* November 1977, pp. 115–145; and Real Estate Review, *Analyzing a Real Estate Investment,* Portfolio 4 (Boston: Warren, Gorham & Lamont, 1974), p. 1.

EXHIBIT 1–2. Scenario of the Great Real Estate Depression of 1974

Descriptions and scenarios of the great real estate depression of 1974 are convincing evidence of the disadvantages and risks associated with real estate investments. In that year as a result of escalation of interest rates and construction and operating costs without corresponding increases in rents and sales prices, real estate values fell below costs and mortgage balances.[5] Gibbons and Rushmore vividly illustrate the perverse 1974 situation, which continued through 1976 in most areas of the country.

> Monetary policy was used in a meat ax fashion, dismembering the economy so thoroughly that the nation now has a splendid chance to achieve depression conditions rivaling the best the 1930's could produce. In real estate development, which is a highly levered field, sensitive to interest changes, the escalation of borrowing rates wrought extraordinary havoc, producing so many bankruptcies and mortgage foreclosures that the industry ground to a halt. . . .
>
> If one looks into the world of 1974, elicits interest rates being charged for various types of capital, and uses them to create overall capitalization rates, it will be apparent that application of such rates to property earnings will produce values far below costs to create the projects involved. So, feasibility died, and when it did, many incompleted realty projects failed financially and were abandoned. . . .
>
> . . . existing properties came under pressure from escalations of operating expenses, which cut deeply into net bottom-line earnings. If an owner found himself in the unenviable position of having a building with such a severely reduced net income, yet was under some compulsion to dispose of his property immediately, there was no way he possibly could avoid taking a huge financial bath. In fact, throughout the year, if a prospective purchaser who planned to bring new capital into an existing income property venture employed an appraiser for valuation guidance, the resulting appraised value probably would fail to equal even the mortgage position of the seller's investment.[6]

The gloomy picture outlined above illustrates some of the downside risks and disadvantages of real estate investments. Contrary to the beliefs of many optimists these downside situations tend to occur once or twice each decade.

---

on a net lease contract or the property is managed by the investor or through a management company, constant care must be given to the property to maintain its income and value. The property manager is responsible for achieving the cash flow projected by the investor, on which the investment decision was based. Many investors find property management an unpalatable aspect of real estate investment and one that can create severe mental and physical stress.

---

[5] James E. Gibbons and Stephen Rushmore, "Using Total Project Analysis to Compete for Investment Capital," *The Appraisal Journal* (Chicago: American Institute of Real Estate Appraisers), October 1975, pp. 491–516.
[6] Ibid., pp. 492, 495, 496.

Depreciation of Value   While inflation may be raising the monetary value of real estate properties, appraisers are quick to emphasize that *real* depreciation occurs from three sources: physical, functional, and locational. Periodically apartment owners eliminate curable physical depreciation by refurbishing units in order to raise rents and control expenses. Slumlords and owners of property on the wrong side of the tracks or in the wrong city can provide expert testimony on the adverse effects of location on value. The energy crisis has severely depreciated the value of many properties, especially those where the landlord pays for utilities.

Government Controls   Rent controls, controls on foreign investment and ownership, land use and density-of-development controls, flood plain and water runoff controls, antipollution and other environmental controls, monetary and fiscal policy, and full-disclosure requirements impose constraints on the development and use of property. These sociopolitical decisions have the combined effect of limiting development, restricting acquisition, reducing cash flow, and arresting growth. In housing, government controls and regulations have added thousands of dollars to the cost of purchasing and owning a home.

Inflation, Deflation, and Real Estate Cycles   Inflation made millionaires of many property owners who survived the 1974–1976 real estate depression. Since the values of existing properties tend to move with construction costs and the prices of new properties, investors who have enough carrying power to survive short-run down cycles will usually benefit over the long run in a growing economy in which price inflation is occurring. This is little consolation, however, to an owner of rent-controlled apartments in New York or Boston (or scores of other communities) when inflation raises operating costs by 9 percent a year and local authorities refuse or are slow to permit a pass-through of expenses to the tenants. Inflation is not very helpful to the owner of a free-standing warehouse or retail facility leased to a triple-A credit for twenty-five years without escalation-in-rent provisions to offset rising expenses.

Legal Complexity   The contracts between owners, lenders, and promoters are complex; they can make or break a transaction. The tax laws are also complex and change frequently and unpredictably. An investor who relies on tax shelter to provide a substantial portion of the returns can be adversely affected by tax law reforms.

Lack of Information and Education   The information essential to good decisions is imprecise, hard to find, and likely to be inaccurate.[7] Furthermore, investors often lack the interdisciplinary education needed for making sound investment decisions.

Weighing Advantages and Disadvantages

Every investor should be well motivated to carefully assess the risks, as well as the returns, that are expected from a property investment. Successful investors con-

[7] Sherman J. Maisel and Stephen E. Roulac, *Real Estate Investment and Finance* (New York: McGraw-Hill, 1976), p. 5.

sider many alternatives, then choose the best one and negotiate the best deal possible. This requires a careful analysis of the inherent advantages and disadvantages of each investment, followed by a translation of these parameters into a forecast of returns and risks. Plans should always be developed to minimize risks and the consequences of wrong judgment. Successful investors make the necessary contingency plans to control the bad effects of errors and events that cannot be forecasted with precision.

PARTICIPANTS IN THE INVESTMENT PROCESS

Successful investing also requires an appreciation of the roles, motives, and personalities of the key participants as well as the relationships among them. A thorough investigation of the participants involved in the real estate investment process was undertaken by a federal government task force.[8] Although the study focused on the housing process, the major participants and relationships are the same for any type of property, as can be seen in Exhibit 1–3. The participants are identified by their involvement in each of four phases of a project's investment cycle: (1) preparation or acquisition, (2) production or construction, (3) distribution or marketing, and (4) service or management. Most of the participants are risk-averse decision makers who are concerned first with their own survival. It is rare for any one individual or firm to assume all the responsibilities and risks of a complete project. Instead, during the development and ownership periods, the responsibilities are spread among many individuals, each of whom exercises some degree of control over the project and seeks to achieve a return level that will compensate for the risks perceived.

Real Estate Investor Roles

Investors can be divided into active and passive types.[9] If an investor packages, builds, or manages the property in addition to investing equity capital, he or she is classified as an active investor. On the other hand, if an investor invests equity capital only and does not take an active role in packaging, building, or managing the property, he or she is classified as a passive investor. Within the active investor category, three subtypes of investors are identified:

1. *Builder/developer.* The primary objective of a builder/developer is to realize a profit from the sale of real property, where the profit is measured as the difference between the sale price and the costs of producing the product sold.
2. *Packager/syndicator.* The primary objective of a packager/syndicator is to realize a profit from the sale of equity interests in properties to passive investors. This profit can be realized in the form of real estate commissions, packaging fees, and a share of investment returns.

[8] U.S. Department of Housing and Urban Development, *Study on Tax Considerations in Multi-Family Housing Investments* (Washington, D.C.: GPO, 1973), p. 257.
[9] Ibid., pp. 15, 21.

EXHIBIT 1–3.   The Housing Process—Major Participants and Influences

PREPARATION PHASE	PRODUCTION PHASE	DISTRIBUTION PHASE	SERVICE PHASE
Developer	Developer	Developer	Owner
Land Owner	Lending institutions (interim and permanent)	Real estate brokers	Maintenance firms and employees
Lawyers	FHA, VA, or private mortgage insurance company	Lawyers	Property mgt. firms
Real estate brokers	Contractors	Lending institutions	Insurance companies
Title companies	Subcontractors	Title companies	Utility companies
Architects and engineers	Craftsmen and their unions	FHA, VA or private mortgage insurance company	Tax assessors
Surveyor	Material manufacturers and distributors		Repairmen, craftsmen and their unions
Planners and Consultants	Building code officials		Lending institutions
Zoning and planning officials	Insurance companies		Architects and engineers
	Architects and engineers		Contractors
			Subcontractors
			Material manufrs. and distributors
			Local zoning officials
			Local bldg. officials

1 PREPARATION PHASE
A. Land Acquisitions
B. Planning
C. Zoning Amendments

2 PRODUCTION PHASE
A. Site Preparation
B. Construction
C. Financing

3 DISTRIBUTION PHASE
A. Sale (and subsequent resale or refinancing)

4 SERVICE PHASE
A. Maintenance and Management
B. Repairs
C. Improvements and additions

			Property taxes
			Income taxes
			Housing and health codes
			Insurance laws
			Utility regulations
	Banking laws		Banking laws
Real estate law	Building and mechanical codes		Union rules
Recording regulations and fees	Subdivision regulations	Recording regulations and fees	Rules of trade and professional association
Banking laws	Utility regulations	Real estate law	Zoning
Zoning	Union rules	Transfer taxes	Building and mechanical codes
Subdivision regulations	Rules of trade and professional associations	Banking laws	Laws controlling transportation of materials
Private deed restrictions	Insurance laws	Rules of professional association	
Public Master plans	Laws controlling transportation of materials		

SOURCE: *Report of the President's Committee on Urban Housing—A Decent Home* (Washington, D.C.: Government Printing Office, 1968) p. 115.

3. *Property manager.* The primary objective of a property manager is to realize a profit from managing real estate during the rental period. In the case of subdivision or condominium sales, the property manager may not play a significant role.

Key Decision Makers

Another approach to analyzing investor roles is to look at the decision makers who are responsible for the creation and ownership of the asset. Under this scheme the importance of a packager/syndicator is diminished, since this type of investor is seen as a middleman between buyers and sellers, who make the decisions. Likewise, a property manager is responsible for a property after acquisition and, consequently, is not responsible for the decision to buy, sell, or develop. While both parties may be influential in the development and investment decision, and indeed their roles are often critical, they are not the key decision makers.

The key decision makers are six: (1) the developer, (2) the joint venture partner, (3) the construction lender, (4) the permanent lender, (5) the managing equity investor, and (6) the passive equity investor. One common goal links all of these decision makers: Each is attempting to maximize returns relative to associated risks. Although our primary focus in this book will be on the managing equity investor and the passive equity investor, let us examine briefly the role played by each of the six. (See Exhibit 1–4.)

The Developer A developer wants the maximum possible return with the minimum financial and time commitment. The return generally consists of (1) a

EXHIBIT 1–4. Key Decision Makers

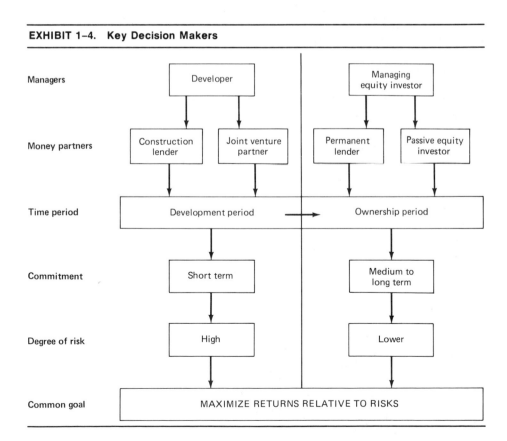

development fee, (2) profits on the sale to equity investors, and (3) a tax shelter and possible operating cash flows prior to the takeover of the property by equity investors. Developers may, and frequently do, take a long-term equity position in the property. To the extent that they do so, their goals are the same as those of equity investors and they should be considered as such.

The developer often does not carry out actual construction. Hence, the concept of builder should be distinguished from that of developer. Many successful nationwide developers of commercial properties, such as Trammell Crow, argue against the developer's taking on extensive building and contracting functions. They believe that developers should create new properties, minimize the size of their staff, and maintain maximum flexibility.

Typically, the developer has a short time horizon and wishes to minimize the duration of his or her involvement. The developer is selling time, in contrast to the passive equity investor, who is "selling money." The developer is anxious to push fledgling projects out of the nest and move on to new projects. Few of these entrepreneurs have a long-run interest in selecting tenants, supplying management and maintenance, and meeting mortgage payments.

The financial exposure of the developer comes in two distinct ways. First, the developer must expend time and money before being assured that the project will be built. Naturally, he or she seeks to minimize such expenditures. Second, the developer may miscalculate the total cost of completing the project and/or the value of the project once it has been completed. In many cases the developer will guarantee certain project occupancy and rental levels, and will be penalized by the lenders and equity investors if those levels are not achieved.

The Joint Venture Partner   A joint venture partner is an equity investor who provides a developer with equity funding during the development period in return for a share in the profits. The joint venture partner attempts to achieve the maximum portion of the development period returns based on the minimum possible financial commitment. The partner's return is based primarily on the difference between project value and project cost, and on the amount and terms of the debt financing. The partner's equity contribution often bridges a portion of the gap between project costs and available debt financing. No longer can the typical developer cover all project costs with interim financing funds. Most projects require substantial amounts of equity dollars to cover total project costs, thus creating the need for a joint venture partner.

The risk to the joint venture partner depends on the extent of the equity investment if no personal liability is assumed for debts. In cases in which the joint venture partner has personal liability on interim debt, the risk is much greater and relates to the amount of debt created as well as to the equity investment. In the event that the developer fails to properly perform his or her role, the joint venture partner may bear the entire loss and the difficult managerial task of completing the project that the developer has abandoned.

The Construction Lender   A construction lender provides short-term funds and is concerned with the total cost of completing the development according to plans and specifications, and with the commitment of a permanent lender to take over ("take out") the loan at the end of the construction period. Construction delays and cost overruns can easily push costs well above the developer's intended budget. The construction lender's risk is that these costs—or the portion financed by the lender—will exceed the amount of the permanent loan. When this occurs the interim lender must look to the developer or equity interests to cover the difference. If they are unable to do so, the construction lender is faced with a choice between foreclosing or converting the construction loan into a long-term loan or equity interest as a solution for the insolvency. The construction lender must weigh the risks of such undesirable consequences against the interest return (including origination fees and compensating balances) that may be earned by making the loan.

The Permanent Lender   A permanent lender, like a construction lender, is concerned with maintaining the safety of the loan while achieving the maximum possible return. While the construction lender has a short-term interest in the property and usually a take-out guarantee from a permanent lender, the permanent lender is prepared to fund a long-term interest with no take-out source. Therefore, he or she must be concerned with the long-term value of the project once it has been completed and is operating, and with the relationship of this value to the loan.

Permanent lenders, as well as construction lenders, are usually intermediaries acting as the fiduciaries of savers. As such, they are expected to comply with rigorous underwriting standards that are more conservative than those which most equity investors or developers would apply to their own position. Indeed, society depends on the lender to control the optimism of the developer and the equity investor.

In past years the underwriting record of lenders has been erratic. Throughout the nation many office buildings, combination-use buildings, apartment complexes, hotels, and industrial parks have been built without regard for the demand/supply trends that determine project feasibility. When money was available, lenders often lent it without serious regard for project feasibility. Lenders, as well as developers and equity investors, must assume more responsibility for the successful completion of projects. No commercial real estate project is complete or successful until it produces rental income sufficient to amortize the investment and provide a competitive return to the lenders and equity investors.

The Managing Equity Investor   A managing equity investor is responsible for *venture management*—structuring the investment package for the purchase of an existing or new property and managing the investment over the ownership period. He or she is also responsible for *property management*—hiring, firing, and overseeing the property management personnel. In the case of a new property, a managing equity investor often engages the services of a developer to build and deliver a completed project. This is often referred to as a turn-key job. While the project can be bought during the planning or construction phase, funding generally will not take place until the project is complete and operating. Thus, equity investors, like permanent lenders, will provide a take-out (purchase) commitment for the equity portion of a project. An equity investor who wishes to become a funding partner during the development period becomes, by definition, a joint venture partner.

Managing and passive equity investors do not (by definition) take development period risks, nor do they participate in development period returns. Their primary sources of returns are cash flow from operations, tax savings, equity buildup through loan amortization, and property appreciation. If the managing equity investor is also a syndicator/packager, he or she will also seek commissions and fees (or a proportionate amount of other benefits) as compensation for the amount of time spent analyzing and packaging an investment for sale to passive equity investors. Sometimes a syndicator takes an equity interest in the property in return for the services he or she performs, and becomes a managing equity investor in this manner. In any case, the managing equity investor should have substantial equity capital at risk.

The key distinction between managing and passive equity investors is the burden of management responsibility for the property and the venture over the ownership period. Even if the day-to-day responsibilities of accounting, marketing, conserving, and enhancing the value of the property are delegated to professional property managers, the overall burden of property and venture management falls on the managing equity investor. Indeed, he or she has the continuous duty of managing the property manager as well as the affairs of the venture that owns the property.

Both society in general and the mortgage lender in particular look to the managing equity investor for fulfillment of the responsibilities of ownership. Indeed, many individual and institutional investors prefer the active role of the managing equity investor. They believe that through the exercise of these rights that they can significantly enhance the performance of the project and, therefore, their own returns. On the other hand, there are institutions, business organizations, and individuals who would prefer to avoid such risks and responsibilities.

The Passive Equity Investor   A passive equity investor invests equity capital only, and does not take an active role in packaging, building, or managing the property. Like that of the securities investor, the passive equity investor's investment decision consists primarily of whether or not to buy, and if so, how much to buy. Like the managing equity investor, the passive equity investor makes a medium- to long-term commitment to a property. The primary sources of returns to such an investor are four: (1) cash flow from operations, (2) tax savings, (3) equity build-up through loan amortization, and (4) property appreciation. Since the risks of this form of investment are usually less than those of other forms, the passive equity investor is usually satisfied with less return than the managing equity investor would be willing to accept.

Passive equity investors obviously need managing equity investors to provide them with structured investment alternatives. They use many legal contrivances to create a passive role while shifting the management responsibilities to others. They can become stockholders of a corporation, shareholders of beneficial interest in a REIT, limited partners in a partnership, and so on. Many institutional investors, such as pension funds, foundations, and churches, must act as passive investors in order to obtain advantageous tax treatment and maintain their status as special legal entities.

The Interrelationship of Decision-Making Roles

The concepts of developer, construction lender or permanent lender, joint venture partner, managing equity investor, and passive equity investor presented here are simplified for our purposes; in reality these roles are complex and interrelated. The definitions are not perfect, and the separation of activities is not always clear-cut. Actors change roles and often play more than one role at a time. A developer, for example, may sell out only a fractional interest to equity investors, giving up all supervisory power and control but retaining the equity interest of a passive investor after the project has been completed. A construction lender may choose to take on the role of a joint venture partner in the development phase, fund the construction loan, and revert to the role of long-term lender upon completion of the project. An owner of land may decide not to *cash out* by selling the land to a developer; instead, the owner may seek to exchange his or her interest for that of a joint venture partner, or may seek to become a passive or managing equity investor and thereby avoid development risks. A wealthy individual seeking complete control over a project may choose to assume all the key investment roles—from developer through passive equity investor. The combinations are limitless.

As stated previously, our focus is on the roles of managing and passive equity investors. The real estate investment world is seen through their eyes, although it is necessary for each of these actors to be able to switch hats and understand the roles of all the other actors who influence their own decisions and investment activities.

INVESTMENT CONTRASTED WITH SPECULATION

Real estate strategies for maximizing an investor's returns relative to the risks are significantly different for different types of equity investors. In the United States the rules for responsible financial behavior derive from the puritan ethic embodied in Ben Franklin's *Poor Richard's Almanac:* Work hard; be thrifty; don't borrow. This puritan ethic led the average American to draw a distinction between speculation, which was considered bad, and investment, which was considered good.[10] One characteristic of Poor Richard's concept of an investment is that it is purchased and held for a substantial period. Buying and holding was considered ethically superior and more financially rewarding than in-and-out speculative trading.

Webster's dictionary defines speculation as an act of "engaging in business out of the ordinary, dealing with a view of making a profit from conjectural fluctuations in the price rather than from earnings of the ordinary profit or trade, or

---

[10] Roger Klein and William Wolman, *The Beat Inflation Strategy* (New York: Simon and Schuster, 1975), p. 46.

by entering into a business venture involving unusual risks for a chance of an unusually large profit."[11]

Speculative real estate might therefore be regarded as property that is purchased for the sole purpose of realizing a profit upon resale. Generally, no further capital is invested following acquisition; if any income is produced during the holding period, it is only incidental to the measurement of profits. For example, agricultural land normally remains under cultivation after acquisition by a speculator. However, property taxes, interest, and other carrying charges usually offset any revenues generated from the operation of the farm during the interim period.[12] In contrast to speculative real estate, investment real estate can be defined as a property that produces, or is capable of producing, periodic revenue as part of the total return from its operation and ownership.

In today's economy, in which inflation and competition have eroded the amount of current income from property and have resulted in increased reliance on future price appreciation for most of the investor's return, the traditional distinction between speculation and investment has become blurred. Poor Richard's way of investing is the wrong way to invest in a world characterized by high and volatile inflation and real estate cycles. If we seek to achieve high returns and control downside risks over the real estate cycle, we must be willing to make changes in the asset mix of our portfolio over time. In addition, we must devise investment strategies for predicting changes in property value more accurately, since this component of return and risk is most significant.

Investor motivation and the current market environment require us to rethink the concepts of investment and speculation and admit that price appreciation or depreciation, a variable that has historically been linked to speculation, should now be considered an integral aspect of investment and investment analysis. In addition, whether one is speculating or investing depends to a large degree on the nature of the analysis performed. If an investor attempts to *explicitly* measure the return and risk parameters of the project, even if the expected returns and risks are high, and bases his or her purchase decision on this analysis, then we can argue that this is an act of investment. On the other hand, if an investor is evaluating a project in which the returns are not estimated, and the method of analysis used is hunch, instinct, and intuition, then we are safe in arguing that the project would be a speculative venture.

SUMMARY

Real estate can be defined in terms of artificially delineated space, a physical product or entity, or a series of money flows over time. Real estate investment analysis focuses on techniques for converting physical space into projections of money flows over future periods and on the evaluation of those money flows relative to investor objectives. For the investor, success depends largely on the

---

[11] *Webster's Third New International Dictionary* (Springfield, Mass.: G. & C. Merriam, 1971).
[12] Lincoln W. North, *Real Estate Investment Analysis and Valuation* (Winnipeg, Canada: Saults & Pollard, 1976), p. 3.

ability to operate effectively in a complex environment. Ever-increasing government and consumer controls have reduced the ownership rights of investors and made it incumbent upon property owners to consider more carefully the needs of society, as well as their own profit motive, when engaging in investment activity.

Some people feel that real estate is too durable, becomes obsolete too quickly, and has too long a payback period relative to the total capital invested. However, the investor who makes good use of leverage and tax shelter provisions, chooses the "best" locations in town, and manages the assets professionally can consistently outperform the competition. The relatively inefficient real estate marketplace is often described as the last bastion of entrepreneurship, where anyone can become successful because there are few barriers to entry.

Real estate investments have both advantages and disadvantages for the investor. The advantages are many. They include pride of ownership, personal control, self-use and occupancy, estate building, security of capital, high operating yield, leverage, tax shelter factors, capital appreciation, and protection against inflation. Often overlooked, however, are the inherent disadvantages and risks: illiquidity, the burden of management, depreciation of value, government control, real estate cycles, legal complexity, and lack of information and education. These must be carefully assessed and minimized whenever possible.

Investors can change the nature of investment returns and risks by changing the nature of their involvement in a project. For developers and joint venture partners, the returns and risks tend to be high. For lenders, whose interest returns are fixed by contract, the risks are significantly reduced. In contrast, an equity investor assumes ownership risks and is responsible for meeting debt service payments and operating expenses, but does not assume development and building risks. Thus, the investor's specific role tends to define the nature of the returns and risks as well as the investor's management responsibilities. A passive equity investor has few or no project management responsibilities, whereas a managing equity investor assumes responsibility for structuring and managing the property and the venture that owns it. The key roles analyzed throughout this book are those of the managing equity investor and the passive equity investor.

2

Overview of the Investment Decision Process

Almost all real estate problems involve an investment decision—whether to buy and what to buy, whether to sell and at what price, whether to modernize or replace, whether to lend and how much to lend under what terms. . . . This transaction is the generating force in urban growth and change; it is the determinant of land use and thus builds our cities.[1]

—Richard Ratcliff

Real estate investment has been portrayed as a complex and dynamic enterprise. In essence, the investor is buying a new business each time he or she buys a property. Each investment has a distinct set of physical, market, legal, and financial characteristics. The better the investor understands this complex set of attributes and how they translate into investment returns and risks, the higher the probability that the investment decision will turn out to be successful. Also, the better the investor can manage the investment process, the greater the chances of success.

In this chapter we will develop the concept of investment analysis. Investment analysis deals with the return/risk relationships associated with existing projects, in contrast to feasibility analysis, which focuses on the return/risk relationships in the development of new projects. We will also examine the different life cycles that affect investment performance and perceptions—property, ownership, and investor life cycles.

[1] Richard N. Ratcliff, *Real Estate Analysis* (New York: McGraw-Hill, 1961), p. v.

FRAMEWORK FOR REAL ESTATE INVESTMENT STUDIES

Elements of the Investment Framework

Four key elements of a framework for the study of real estate investment are *strategy, analysis, decisions,* and *investment transactions,* as shown in Exhibit 2–1. Because we believe that a systematic approach should be developed for analyzing real estate investment problems and arriving at sound decisions, we focus primarily on the strategies, analyses, and decisions necessary to solve investment problems, and only secondarily on the transaction itself.

As a practical matter, a joint venture partner or managing equity investor must have considerable expertise in the mechanics of real estate transactions, while a passive equity investor can get by with only a general familiarity with those mechanics. There are lawyers to guide the investor through the legal maze, mortgage bankers to act as experts in financial details, and tax accountants to help structure the best possible tax shelter package. More critical is the need for trained counselors, advisers, and investors who can devise sound investment strategies, perform better investment and feasibility analyses, and render more profitable investment decisions. Thus, the critical need is for more professionally trained generalists who can manage the entire investment process, rather than for specialists who are experts in only one phase of that process.

Strategy   In making real estate investment decisions one begins by establishing an investment strategy—*defining* the acceptable return and risk parameters of a property. The investor's strategy should consist of four elements. First, the investor should *develop an overall investment philosophy,* a set of general principles that can be used as guidelines in making investment decisions. Second, the investor should *define objectives* and *establish decision criteria* that determine when objectives have been achieved. Next, the investor *develops plans and policies* to maximize the probability of success with the least time commitment. Finally, the investor *determines a strategy of analysis,* a plan that outlines how he or she will analyze properties and arrive at an investment decision. (In Chapter 8 we elaborate on each of these four elements of strategy.)

Analysis   The analysis of a property is fundamentally a task of *measuring* the return and risk parameters that form the basis of the investor's strategy. (See Chapters 10–13.) In measuring returns and risks the investor goes through various stages, which become more sophisticated as the analysis progresses and more data is collected. While the investor may begin with relatively simple nonfinancial tests involving location and "curb appeal" criteria, the final analysis may consist of internal rate of return, present value, and financial ratio and risk calculations and evaluation. At each stage of the analysis alternatives are compared and evaluated with respect to the investor's objectives.

Decisions   Investment decisions require a return and risk *evaluation* of all the alternatives relative to the investor's strategy. The investor is making decisions over a time horizon that includes both short- and long-run considerations. The investor must survive the short run in order to succeed over the long run. While

EXHIBIT 2-1. A Framework for the Study of Real Estate Investment

	STRATEGY (Return/Risk Definition)	Overall Investment Philosophy
Feedback		Objectives and Decision Criteria
		Plans and Policies
		Strategy of Analysis
	ANALYSIS (Return/Risk Measurement)	Stages of Analysis
Feedback		Analytical Techniques and Approaches
		Data Sources
		Comparison of Alternatives
	DECISIONS (Return/Risk Evaluation)	Project Decisions
Feedback		Portfolio Decisions
		Time Framework for Decisions
	INVESTMENT TRANSACTION	Buy
Feedback		Sell
		Exchange
		Finance

Feedback Mechanism

⌐ ⌐⌐ Attention is focused on these elements

the majority of decisions may be go/no-go project-type decisions, the investor may also be focusing on portfolio decisions and the goal of maximizing the value of the overall portfolio. For institutional investors like pension funds and life insurance companies, which are actively acquiring and selling projects throughout the country, portfolio decisions are becoming increasingly important. (These subjects are addressed in Chapters 25 and 26.)

Investment Transaction Often an investor decides to do nothing or to reject a project under consideration. These decisions do not result in investment transactions. In other cases an investment transaction will ensue and the investor will negotiate to buy, sell, exchange, or finance a property. Contracts and deeds will be drawn, closing arrangements made, and property management details arranged.

Feedback Throughout the investment process new information is constantly being acquired that may affect the investor's strategy, analysis, and decisions. The investor, operating in a dynamic cyclical environment, must constantly revise and update data and the decision-making system itself in order to outperform competitors. After all, the object of this rigorous study is to develop better decision-making skills. Better investment decisions are the surest way to achieve higher investment returns while managing investment risks.

INVESTMENT ANALYSIS VS. FEASIBILITY ANALYSIS

Investment and Investment Analysis

The *act* of investing involves the commitment of money (a capital outlay) in the hope of earning future income or a profit on that outlay. *Investment analysis* is the systematic evaluation of such capital outlays in relation to the expected income stream in order to render an investment decision. An overview of the investment analysis concept is shown in Exhibit 2–2.

Capital Assets Real estate investment analysis begins with the analysis of the proposed real property acquisition—that is, the capital asset. A *capital asset* represents various degrees of ownership and control of land and improvements. It can be a tangible asset, such as a rental house, a shopping center, or an industrial building, or it can be a financial or paper asset, such as a leasehold or mortgage note.

Equity Capital assets are purchased by an *equity investor,* the buyer, who is organized as one of a variety of legal entities—individual, joint venture, limited partnership, corporation, REIT, pension fund, and many others. The number of dollars that the equity investor spends to acquire the capital asset is defined as the *equity investment,* the *equity,* the *net worth,* the *owner's cash investment,* or simply the *total down payment.* Most of these terms are used interchangeably.

Debt The term *debt* has numerous synonyms, often being referred to as *liabilities, leverage, loans, lender,* and *other people's money.* The debt alternatives available to investors are numerous, including first mortgages, second

EXHIBIT 2–2.   Overview of the Investment Analysis Concept

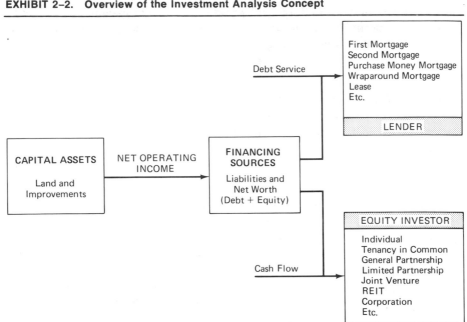

mortgages, purchase money mortgages, wraparound mortgages, and leases. In many cases the debt financing becomes a hybrid, taking on the characteristics of both debt and equity. For example, during the early 1970s mortgage loans with equity kickers or equity participations[2] were prevalent with large investment property transactions. They enabled lenders to take a "piece of the deal"—to obtain a cash flow return in excess of the contract interest rate specified in the mortgage note. In the early 1980s these hybrid arrangements again became popular.

Net Operating Income   The objective of owning or controlling a capital asset is to produce a stream of revenue or income. With the exception of non-income property, such as land, where appreciation of asset values is the primary source of income, *the net operating income (NOI) stream is the most important income stream* to both the lender and the equity investor.

The NOI is divided, by contractual arrangement, between lenders and equity investors after all operating expenses have been paid. The NOI portion that is received by the lender is called *debt service;* the residual, if any, is received by the equity investor and is called *cash flow*. Some often-used aliases for the term

---

[2] The right of a lender to a share of gross profit, net profit, or cash flow from a property on which the lender has made a loan; an additional payment or amount that may be paid to a lender over and above periodic fixed interest or fixed rent. (Source: Alvin L. Arnold and Jack Kusnet, *The Arnold Encyclopedia of Real Estate,* Boston: Warren, Gorham & Lamont, pp. 266, 444).

cash flow are *cash throwoff, equity dividend, net income after debt service, cash flow before tax,* and *cash flow from operations.*

Both lenders and equity investors look to the NOI stream from the property as the basis for their involvement. Their interests, however, are seemingly in conflict, since increasing the returns to one requires decreasing the returns to the other. An increase in debt service requires a dollar-for-dollar decrease in cash flow before tax. Since more is always preferred to less, each party negotiates so as to maximize its portion of the NOI. An acceptable financing or capital structure is achieved only when the property produces enough NOI to service the debt and provide an acceptable cash flow return to the equity investor. Consequently, the most difficult aspect of the investment process is locating a project that will produce a sufficiently high NOI to meet the minimum requirements of all the parties involved in the debt and equity financing process.

The Relationship of the Lender to the Equity Investor   The traditional economic relationship of the lender to the equity investor in real estate can be summarized as follows:

1. *Division of the net operating income.* The lender receives debt service while the equity investor receives cash flow.
2. *Debt-to-equity ratio.* The lender generally supplies the larger fraction (e.g., 75%) of the capital to finance the asset, while the equity investor traditionally has sought to acquire the asset with as little down as possible. The "golden rule" ("Whoever has the gold makes the rules!") suggests that the lender has traditionally controlled the financing rules and regulations in the investment property arena.
3. *Certainty of income.* The lender seeks a contractually guaranteed income. The lender expects such income to provide a return *of* the investment (loan amortization) and a return *on* the investment at market interest rates. In contrast, a rational equity investor is willing to accept higher risks but also expects a higher return. While this is not what happens in every case, these are the usual expectations.
4. *Priority of claim on income.* The lender has a senior or superior claim to the income from the project, while the equity investor has the residual claim on the income. The equity investor gets what's left over, if any.
5. *Priority of claim on assets.* The lender also has the first or senior claim on the assets in the event of a default in debt service payments. The equity investor often loses all his or her interest in the asset when foreclosure occurs. On the other hand, an inept lender may find the borrower still in control of the asset and may be forced to negotiate a settlement.
6. *A shorter investment time horizon.* In the past a lender generally made a commitment to a project for ten to forty years, the term of the loan, while the equity investor usually had a holding-period expectation of three to ten years with a typical investment property. Lenders thus had a relatively long-run viewpoint when analyzing a mortgage investment, while the equity investor

typically had a medium- to short-run viewpoint. Inflation and interest rate uncertainties, however, have increased the attention of both lender and equity investor to short-run solvency and profit considerations. With a high degree of inflation and interest rate uncertainties characterizing the marketplace, neither party is willing to make fixed long-term commitments.

Traditionally, equity investors have sought to maximize the use of leverage and often "mortgaged out" by obtaining long-term financing in excess of the cost incurred to develop or buy a property. More recently, however, because inflation has caused interest rates, operating expenses, and building costs to increase more rapidly than rents, and because of losses resulting from undercapitalized (overfinanced) projects, lenders have taken a more defensive position in real estate investment financing. Lenders are demanding more conservative capital structures—greater amounts of real equity dollars must be invested by borrowers. Lenders are also increasing their own interest in the equity investment by demanding equity participation in projects, either through joint venture positions or through 100-percent equity ownership positions. Also, lenders are hedging against inflation and interest rate uncertainties by using creative mortgage instruments such as variable-rate and renegotiable-rate mortgages (see Chapter 14). As a result, the traditional distinctions between debt and equity have become blurred. Hybrid financing devices are increasingly common, and the difference in realized returns between debt and equity investors is narrowing.[3] Institutions are accepting greater operating risks in return for greater yield expectations and protection against inflation.

Maximization of Wealth   Investment decisions are made with some objective in mind. Throughout this book we operate on the assumption that an investor's primary financial goal is to maximize wealth by making capital investments that offer some optimum combination of returns and risks that satisfies the investor's preferences.[4] Generally, investors want their rate of return to be relatively high; and they prefer more return to less. At the same time, other things being equal, they prefer their rate of return to be dependable and stable; that is, they prefer less risk to more risk. There is probably a group of people who ignore risk, who refuse to contemplate it, evidently hoping that it will go away if its presence is not admitted. We can label this group "unbounded optimists" or "risk ignorers," and might find its citizens in Boot Hill, San Quentin, Las Vegas, or working for land syndicators or development companies. We will tend to ignore the risk ignorers in this book.

The concept of wealth maximization through choosing the proper risk/return combinations is illustrated in Exhibits 2–3 and 2–4. The investor first *measures* the risk and return parameters for projects under consideration and then *evaluates* the projects by comparing them to each other and to his or her investment criteria,

---

[3] Stephen E. Roulac, *Modern Real Estate Investment* (San Francisco: Property Press, 1976), p. 18.
[4] Stephen A. Pyhrr, "A Computer Simulation Model to Measure the Risk in Real Estate Investment," *American Real Estate and Urban Economics Association Journal*, June 1973, p. 48. Reprinted in *The Real Estate Appraiser*, May–June 1973, p. 15.

EXHIBIT 2–3.   Return/Risk Measurement

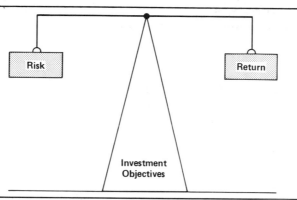

SOURCE: J. Thomas Montgomery, "Real Estate Investment Risk—Basic Concepts," *Appraisal Journal* (Chicago: American Institute of Real Estate Appraisers), January 1976, p. 12.

defined here as the investor's indifference curve or risk/return preference curve. In Exhibit 2–4 the investor's indifference curve is shown as line *ABC.* The investor is unwilling to accept any risk level in excess of "4" because the potential loss is too great to bear under any circumstances. Also, the investor is unwilling to invest in any projects that fall below line *AB* because these represent undesirable combinations of return and risk. The acceptable projects ("yes" possibilities) appear

EXHIBIT 2–4.   Return/Risk Evaluation

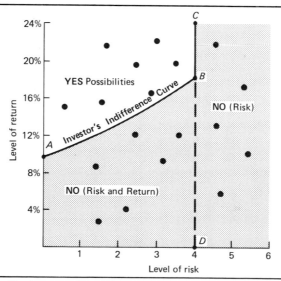

SOURCE: J. Thomas Montgomery, "Real Estate Investment Risk—Basic Concepts," *Appraisal Journal* (Chicago: American Institute of Real Estate Appraisers), January 1976, p. 20.

above the indifference curve, with the most desirable combinations of risk and return being the projects furthest above and to the left of line *ABC*. The most desirable projects are those which have the highest rate of return relative to the risks. For our purposes here, we can define risk as the probability of not achieving the expected rate of return.

In summary, investment analysis involves the measurement and evaluation of the returns and risks associated with proposed investments. Investment decisions and the investment decision-making process can be viewed as a return/risk trade-off in which the investor is seeking to identify, structure, and purchase projects that will maximize the return/risk ratio relative to his or her indifference curve. Later it will be shown that nonfinancial as well as financial considerations can be integrated into the return/risk framework, with explicit consideration given to market and location as well as other factors that affect investment performance and decisions.

Return and Risk Management   An integral part of investment and investment analysis is the management and control of risk. Many investors manage money, but "the really successful ones manage risk, the idea being not to avoid risk but to be skilled at identifying it, coping with it, and then living with it under acceptable circumstances."[5] Risks can be managed and controlled through application of the techniques of avoiding, transferring, and reducing. (The analysis and management of risk are discussed in Chapter 12.)

Underlying the return/risk wealth maximization framework developed in this book is the fundamental assumption that the decision maker can control, to a substantial degree, the returns and risks of a project through careful analysis and structuring of the financial and nonfinancial investment variables. Indeed, real estate investment analysis can be defined as the process of identifying and structuring projects in order to maximize the returns relative to the risks. Through greater expertise in the areas of market analysis, tax planning, financial analysis, and negotiation techniques (e.g., negotiation of lease escalations, exculpatory clauses in mortgages, etc.), a decision maker can structure the purchase, operation, and termination of a project so as to increase the returns *relative to* the risks.

Feasibility and Feasibility Analysis

While investment analysis has traditionally focused on the financial aspects of real estate investments, in which the primary goal of the investor is to *maximize financial wealth,* "feasibility analysis" has focused more on the nonfinancial aspects of the investment and the testing of the basic assumptions underlying the investor's financial analysis. Thus, feasibility analysis focuses on testing the marketing, legal, political, physical and social dimensions of a real estate project in addition to the financial dimensions. (We acknowledge, however, controversy in the use of these terms.)

A feasibility study is an analysis aimed at discovering whether a specific

---

[5] J. Thomas Montgomery, "Real Estate Investment Risk—Basic Concepts," *The Appraisal Journal,* January 1976, p. 14.

project or program can actually be carried out successfully.[6] In short, a feasibility study answers the fundamental question, "Will it work?" It explores every known alternative worthy of consideration in determining whether the economic and market climate is favorable for the effective implementation of a proposed real estate development. "In essence, a feasibility study is a forecast of things that will likely occur when the project is open for business . . . It tells the complete story of the why, when, and how of a project. Its conclusion will be critical to the investor, lender, and all others constructively involved in the project."[7]

James Graaskamp, in his book *A Guide to Feasibility Analysis,* states that a project is "feasible" when "the real estate analyst determines that there is a reasonable likelihood of satisfying explicit objectives when a selected course of action is tested for fit to a context of specific constraints and limited resources."[8] This definition is realistic, for it admits the presence in many situations of multiple investor objectives, both financial and nonfinancial. These objectives are usually peculiar to the individual investor and may be irrational in the narrow financial sense of maximizing financial wealth as defined in most investment textbooks. Certainly many headquarter buildings of major corporations are not designed to maximize financial return. Instead of maximizing anything, the investor is trying to find a "best fit." Relative to financial theory, this concept is similar to the goal of satisficing, in which investors are attempting to satisfy numerous goals and objectives, thereby exceeding minimum standards of performance and living within a given set of constraints and resource limitations.

The Distinction Between Existing and Development Projects

A useful distinction between investment and feasibility analysis is the one that can be drawn between existing projects and proposed projects. Feasibility analysis generally presumes a *development* situation in which the following conditions exist:

1. *A site or building is searching for a user.* The developer may be trying to determine the highest and best use for a tract of land that he or she owns or controls, or may be looking for a tenant for an empty office building that is nearing completion.
2. *A user is searching for a site and certain improvements.* This is the classic location decision. For example, a franchise hamburger operation may be looking for three new sites in a city, or a life insurance company may be seeking to locate a new regional office.

[6] Anthony Downs, "Characteristics of Various Economic Studies," *The Appraisal Journal,* July 1966, pp. 229–338. Reprinted in *Readings in Real Estate Investment Analysis* (Cambridge, Mass.: Ballinger, 1977), 1, 77–86.
[7] Lloyd D. Hanford, Sr., *Feasibility Study Guidelines* (Chicago: Institute of Real Estate Management, 1972), p. v. Also see Stephen D. Messner, Byrl Boyce, Harold G. Trimble, and Robert L. Ward, *Analyzing Real Estate Opportunities: Market and Feasibility Studies* (Chicago: Realtors National Marketing Institute of the National Association of Realtors, 1977), pp. 78–86.
[8] James A. Graaskamp, *A Guide to Feasibility Analysis* (Chicago: Society of Real Estate Appraisers, 1970), p. 4.

3. *An investor is looking for a means of participating in either of the situations just described.* The term *investor* here includes construction lenders, permanent lenders, developers, and equity investors.

In contrast, investment analysis generally focuses on existing or "ongoing" projects that are assumed to be complete and already absorbed in the marketplace. The development period and its risks are ignored. Rather, various assumptions regarding capital expenditures, rents, expenses, property value, and taxation are made for an assumed time horizon, and the investor tests the results of these assumptions against the investment objectives and criteria established at the beginning of the analysis. While the analysis of "likelihood" and risk may and should be an integral part of the investment analysis, the approach presumes a "going concern" rather than addressing the question, "How do we get the concern going."

An important distinction should therefore be drawn between existing properties, on the one hand, and development projects, on the other. The nature and level of returns and risks are significantly different for the two situations, as are the nature and extent of the analysis performed. Becoming involved in development activity (vs. existing projects) requires a critically different set of management skills and knowledge, risk-taking capacity, and analysis.

Types of Feasibility Analysis Reports

Various types of reports are often lumped together under the general term *feasibility study*. Actually, a "complete" feasibility study might include seven types of studies, any one of which could be the total assignment of the analyst in a particular situation:[9]

1. *Strategy study:* determination of investment/development objectives, policies, plans, and decision criteria.
2. *Legal study:* analysis of the various legal and political constraints and problems that may affect the project, including forms of organization, title, zoning, building codes, etc.
3. *Compatibility study:* the compatibility of the project to surrounding land uses, city or county master plans, public policies, and environmental standards.
4. *Market analysis:* macroeconomic studies, including regional analysis, economic base, and neighborhood or related aggregate-data reviews.
5. *Merchandising study:* consumer surveys, analysis of competitive property, sales and marketing evaluation and strategy, price and absorption rate studies, etc.
6. *Architectural and engineering study:* determination of alternative land use plans, structure and design alternatives, soil analysis, utility availability, etc.
7. *Financial/economic study:* cash flow forecasts, tax and tax shelter planning,

---

[9] Ibid., p. 7.

rate-of-return analysis, analysis of financing alternatives, holding-period analysis, *etc.*

As can readily be seen, the nature and extent of the feasibility study performed will be determined by the nature and extent of the problem that needs to be solved. It will also be determined by the sophistication of the decision maker who perceives the problem, the size of the project, and the budget available for such study. Too often the budgets for such studies are inadequate, and poor investment decisions are reached on the basis of inadequate information; the result may be financial disaster. Unfortunately, the approaches that have frequently been used to determine feasibility in the past are best likened to the science of decision making by consulting oracles, sticking one's head in the sand, calling in astrologers, or reading sheep's entrails.[10]

It should be obvious that the term *feasibility study* is no more useful or precise than is the generic term *theft,* which includes robbery, burglary, and embezzlement. Both terms cover a multitude of sins. Therefore, when the term *feasibility study* is used, it is necessary to define the concept of feasibility being used and the nature of the study being done. Seldom does an investor or analyst perform a complete feasibility study as defined here.

Appraisal vs. Investment and Feasibility Analysis

The appraisal process begins when an independent appraiser contracts to carry out field research, collect and analyze data, and estimate the value of a specific property as of a certain date. The appraiser typically uses the income, cost, and market approaches to value and reconciles the findings to arrive at a final value estimate; this becomes the conclusion of the appraisal report.

Clients have many reasons for engaging an appraiser, and the definition of "value" may vary, depending on the objectives of the assignment. The most common definitions of "value" are *market value* and *most probable selling price.* A less common definition is investment value. Appraisers are sometimes required to appraise value using other special definitions, such as insured value, liquidation value, assessed value, and book value.

Market Value As a result of much courtroom litigation, there are many definitions of market value. According to the American Institute of Real Estate Appraisers (AIREA), the most widely accepted definitions of market value include the following:

1. The highest price in terms of money that a property would bring in a competitive and open market under all conditions requisite to a fair sale, the buyer and seller each acting prudently and knowledgeably and assuming the price is not affected by undue stimulus.

---

[10] J. Thomas Montgomery, p. 11. For a discussion of problems with feasibility studies, see John R. White, "Non-Feasance with Feasibility = Failure: Improving the Quality of Feasibility Studies," *Urban Land,* October 1976, p. 6.

2. The price at which a willing seller would sell and a willing buyer would buy, neither being under abnormal pressure.

3. The price expected if a reasonable time is allowed to find a purchaser and if both seller and prospective buyer are fully informed.[11]

Certain conditions or assumptions that are implicit in the market definition are noted in *Real Estate Appraisal Terminology:*

1. Buyer and seller are typically motivated.

2. Both parties are well informed or well advised, and each is acting in what he considers his [or her] own best interest.

3. A reasonable time is allowed for exposure in the open market.

4. Payment is made in cash or its equivalent.

5. Financing, if any, is on terms generally available in the community at the specified date and typical for the property type in its locale.

6. The price represents a normal consideration for the property sold, unaffected by special financing amounts and/or terms, services, fees, costs, or credits incurred in the transaction.[12]

Unless the market is operating efficiently and producing equilibrium prices, it should be clear that market value is not market price. Such market conditions seldom exist these days.

Most Probable Selling Price The use of *most probable selling price* as the proper definition of value has been growing because it eliminates many normative assumptions about buyers and sellers, financing methods and costs, and current market conditions.[13] This definition appears to be a realistic reflection of current market conditions, as contrasted with the market value definition, which attempts to define normal medium-term equilibrium conditions. The most probable selling price is defined as "that price at which a property would most probably sell if exposed to the market for a reasonable time, under market conditions prevailing as of the date of the appraisal."[14]

Problems with Traditional Market Value Appraisals

Traditional market value appraisals have always played a key role in real estate financing and have been heavily relied upon to verify the legality and economic soundness of loans underwritten by lending institutions. Many investors and developers use appraisal data and conclusions in making investment decisions. It is argued, however, that traditional appraisals are inherently limited in their useful-

---

[11] American Institute of Real Estate Appraisers, Textbook Revision Subcommittee, *The Appraisal of Real Estate,* 7th ed. (Chicago, 1978), p. 23.

[12] American Institute of Real Estate Appraisers, *Real Estate Appraisal Terminology,* ed. Byrl N. Boyce (Cambridge, Mass.: Ballinger, 1975).

[13] Richard N. Ratcliff, *Valuation for Real Estate Decisions* (Santa Cruz, Calif.: Democrat Press, 1972), pp. 10–11.

[14] American Institute of Real Estate Appraisers, p. 52.

ness to decision makers who are faced with complex investment and feasibility problems.

The basic problem with most appraisals from a decision-making standpoint lies in the assumptions made on the first page of the appraisal report. The appraiser often assumes that the central issue is to determine market value. Then he or she assumes the viewpoint of "economic man," who is rational, intelligent, has good market information, and operates in an efficient market in the hope of maximizing the economic surplus of a single real estate property. In practice, market value is not usually the central issue. More often investors are concerned with "investment" value, or the expected rate of return or profit from an investment expenditure, and the final product of their study is some type of investment/feasibility decision. The investment/feasibility analyst sees a project from the viewpoint of a *particular* decision maker with a *particular* set of objectives and constraints. The decision maker may have noneconomic goals (including some that are irrational!), may work in a highly imperfect market in which accurate information is difficult to obtain, and may have considerable power to influence the final outcome. Indeed, the goal of an investor is to increase returns relative to risks through shrewd negotiation and investment structuring. Stated somewhat differently, the goal of an investor or entrepreneur is to create a monopoly (to whatever extent possible and for as long as possible) and thereby divert cash flows and other benefits to himself or herself—and the imperfections in the real estate marketplace often makes this possible.

In sum, a market value appraisal often does not solve many of the important problems of the decision maker. It is not usually decision or action oriented. In contrast, both feasibility and investment studies are structured to solve specific problems facing investors and developers. They are both action oriented, and the format of the study can be structured to answer the specific questions and problems facing the decision maker. Recently many appraisers have obtained the additional education and higher skill levels that will enable them to carry out feasibility and investment assignments rather than traditional market value appraisal assignments, in which many of the current problems are assumed away. Supporting this trend are lenders, investors, and developers, who are increasingly seeking market and merchandising studies and other economic studies to aid them in rendering more profitable decisions, rather than demanding appraisal reports that are file cabinet fillers for decisions already locked into contracts, promises, and concrete-and-steel structures.

TIME HORIZONS FOR INVESTMENT DECISIONS: LIFE CYCLES

In analyzing any real estate investment, the investor should recognize the life cycles that affect the return/risk relationships on which investment decisions are based. Decisions based on techniques and forecasts that do not consider these life cycles often have surprising, disappointing, and perhaps disastrous outcomes.

Three types of life cycles are of prime concern to investors. First is a *property life cycle,* which encompasses the entire development and holding periods from the idea stage through the demise of the project at the end of its useful economic life. Second is an *ownership life cycle,* which encompasses the holding period experienced by one ownership group from the day of purchase to the disposal of the property at the end of the period. Third is an *investor life cycle* that defines the type and amount of return and risk sought by the investor at different stages of his life.

Property Life Cycles

Every real estate investment has a property life cycle—it evolves through several distinct stages from its inception and development through its operation to the end of its productive life. This life cycle can be conceptualized as a pyramid and is explained by the acronym GLITAMAD, as shown in Exhibit 2–5.[15]

Investors can choose to invest in any stage of the pyramid. The upside of the pyramid (which generally spans one to five years) represents the development period, in which risks decrease as a project is developed and many of the uncertainties are eliminated. The developer is the dominant personality during this period. The top of the pyramid (end of tenancy stage) represents a completed and fully occupied project with established income, expenses, and cash flows. By this point the risks are minimal and the equity investor typically becomes the dominant personality. The equity investor dominates the downside of the property cycle. The downside spans a long period, typically forty to fifty years, and is characterized by increasing risks as the project ages. At the end of its useful life, the property is often ready for a new use and will enter a new property life cycle, beginning the GLITAMAD pyramid once again. If the property and location will support redevelopment, the developer again becomes the dominant personality. If not, the property will be abandoned or left vacant until new development is feasible.

Investors should choose carefully which stage of the life cycle they become involved in because each stage represents both a different return/risk situation and a different combination of returns—development profit, cash flow from operations, tax shelter, equity buildup through loan amortization, and appreciation (or depreciation) of property value. Consequently, each stage tends to appeal to a different type of investor. Furthermore, once the life cycle stage has been chosen, many of the basic return and risk parameters are established and may be difficult to change.

The Upside of the Property Life Cycle

The upside of the property life cycle corresponds to various stages of activity in real estate development. There are many uncertainties, and hence the risks are very high during the early stages. There is little (if any) cash flow, relatively limited tax shelter, and no equity buildup or property appreciation. The return is depen-

---

[15] Both the acronym and the concept were developed by Maury Seldin and Richard H. Swesnik, *Real Estate Investment Strategy* (New York: Wiley-Interscience, 1979), pp. 53–104. These authors were the first to clearly identify property life cycle stages in a return/risk decision-making framework.

EXHIBIT 2-5.   The Property Life Cycle Pyramid

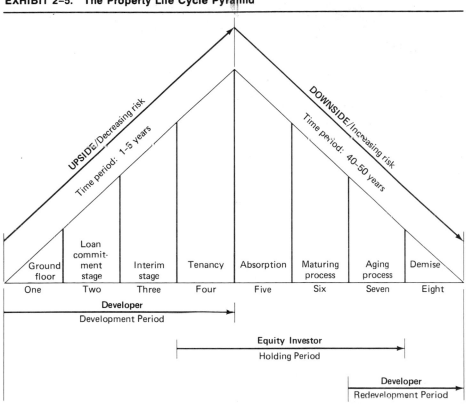

dent primarily on entrepreneurial profit—creating a property value that is greater than the costs of development. For example, a developer might hope to invest $800,000 in land and improvements that, when rented, will be worth $1 million, thereby earning a $200,000 development profit.

An investor who chooses to become involved in the early stages of development (e.g., the ground floor or loan commitment stages) usually demands a portion of the development profit to compensate for the high risks. By definition, the investor who becomes involved in this manner becomes a joint venture partner of the developer. The investor can fully share the development risks and returns with the developer; he or she can require the developer to guarantee a return; demand a preferential return from the developer; or do a combination of these things in order to avoid or shift many of the development period risks to others. In any case, to the extent that the investor takes development period risks, he or she should be compensated by receiving development period returns—a slice of the development profit.

As the development progresses, construction and permanent loan commitments are obtained (loan commitment stage), and the project is built (interim stage), the risks become less and more people are committed to the successful completion of the project. Equity investors often become involved at this point, often through syndications in which delivery of a completed and fully rented project is guaranteed by the developer and the equity funds raised are held in escrow until the project has been completed.

During the fourth stage (tenancy) the project is nearing the top of the pyramid. It is being leased to tenants and is producing income; the rents are at the top of the market because the project is new and desirable. In theory, the project is at the peak of its earning capacity at the end of the tenancy stage (top of the pyramid) and therefore can be sold at its highest price.[16] The rate of return required by equity investors in a competitive market should be at the minimum point because the risk should be at the minimum point. Clearly, the developer should be able to maximize expected profit by waiting until this point to sell the project, unless changing market conditions are expected to adversely affect the marketability of the project and discourage potential equity investors.

If the developer chooses to hold and own the project during the downside of the pyramid, he or she has by definition become a long-term equity investor. Today many developers choose to play dual roles, believing that they should not sell the valuable equities they create. Developers like the famed Dallas-based Trammell Crow seek to retain ownership of the properties they develop, except in cases in which financial partnerships are necessary to raise the cash needed to fund the difference between mortgage commitments and project costs.

The Downside of the Property Life Cycle

In a real economic sense, as a building and its neighborhood ages, the property value starts to decline and the risks become greater because the property is less desirable to increasing numbers of investors. Although the property's monetary value may be rising because of inflation, the improvements begin to wear out and eventually major replacements are needed.

The passive equity investor should be most comfortable in the first two stages of the downside (absorption, maturing process), which typically spans 15–25 years of economic life after completion of the project. Many institutional investors, such as pension funds and life insurance companies, prefer to invest in relatively new projects with an established track record. Other investors, often individuals or syndicates, prefer mature properties that may require some renovation but are in highly desirable locations where new competition is limited.

The stages through which every property must pass thus offer a variety of opportunities to investors with different objectives and preferences. Through subsequent purchases and sales of a given property, numerous investors or investment groups with differing investment postures can be satisfied.

Eventually every property deteriorates. Major repairs and renovations are necessary, and forecasts of income and expenses are increasingly uncertain. The

---

[16] This refers to the highest "real" price rather than the nominal dollar price, and implies that the project is fully leased at the end of the tenancy stage.

risks of investing become greater, and the investor is likely to gain the title of slumlord. Real estate advisers recommend that the inexperienced investor should be out and the professional investor in at this stage of the cycle. Also at this stage, a developer may enter the scene and undertake a major renovation of the property, seeking to bring the property back to a new absorption period and thus returning to the topside of the pyramid. This will prevent the property from going into the demise period, in which bulldozers are brought onto the site or the property is abandoned.

Attractive tax shelters can be created in the latter stages of the life cycle, since the useful lives of improvements are becoming very short and rehabilitation expenditures often qualify for favorable tax treatment. Nevertheless, the risks are high and the problems more difficult than at any other stage of the holding period.

Investment Strategy Implications

The stage of the pyramid at which the investor becomes involved is an important determinant of investment risks and returns. The life cycle pyramid concept suggests that there is a trade-off between risk and return such that it is impossible to simultaneously maximize returns while minimizing risks. Generally, the market in a free-enterprise system works in a manner that requires investors, on average, to take greater risks in order to achieve greater returns. However, while this is true in a general market sense, it is not true for an individual investor operating in a highly imperfect market. An equity investor or developer can exert influence on both the risk and return parameters of a project that is directly related to his or her skills, expertise, and negotiating ability. Thus, the investor can choose an overall return/risk profile by choosing the stage of the project life cycle at which he or she will become involved, and then alter that risk/return profile through entrepreneurship during the acquisition, operation, and termination stages of the project. These three stages make up what is called the *ownership* life cycle, to which we now turn.

The Ownership Life Cycle

An ownership life cycle is the period associated with one person or group's ownership of a real estate asset. While an ownership life cycle can conceivably cover the entire property life cycle—for example, when a developer builds and holds a property until it is razed forty years later—it generally encompasses a much shorter time span. For an aggressive young investor seeking to build wealth quickly, the ownership life cycle may consist of a one- or two-year holding period, while a conservative wealthy investor purchasing an existing shopping center may analyze a project on the basis of a ten-year ownership period.

The concept of an ownership life cycle has become popular in recent years as a result of the rapid acceptance of discounted cash flow methods in real estate investment analysis. The concept requires that all the anticipated costs and benefits of an investment be considered over the expected ownership period, and that the time value of money be used to equate future expectations with today's values.

The stages of the ownership life cycle may be defined as follows:[17]

1. *Acquisition:* Organization of the venture and development or purchase of property.
2. *Operation:* Property management and management of the venture that owns the real estate.
3. *Disposal or Termination:* Sale of the property and dissolution of the venture; or property exchange, foreclosure, gift, etc.

Each of these stages has unique cash flow and tax effects, and the investment analysis should consider the timing of these factors. Some analysts advocate the use of a discounted cash flow procedure, projecting after-tax cash flows each year over the expected ownership period, and calculating in the final step an internal rate of return on equity cash investment. Others advocate a discounted cash flow procedure for handling ownership life cycle considerations, but prefer a present value approach.

There is considerable debate about which discounting techniques and investment measures should be used to measure and compare the risks and returns from real estate investments. These will be reviewed in the next chapter. However, while brokers and investors often emphasize only one-year pro forma results, there is little disagreement among sophisticated investors that the entire ownership period should be evaluated when measuring project returns and risks.

The Investor Life Cycle[18]

It is commonly believed that investors experience a "life cycle" of their own, one that is related primarily to age, and that they seek different types of returns and risks at these different stages. Although the overall psychological and emotional makeup of an investor may remain relatively unchanged over his or her lifetime, definite cycles tend to characterize investment preferences and behavior as a person becomes older. For example, consider three key stages in a life cycle for an individual investor beginning a career after graduating from college: (1) the young investor, (2) the middle-aged investor, and (3) the older investor on the verge of retirement.

The Young Investor

According to Mark Twain, "The first half of life consists of the capacity to enjoy without the chance; the last half consists of the chance without the capacity." The young investor has relatively little equity capital and management experience but can look forward to thirty or forty years of increasing income and investable surplus funds, and has the energy and risk-taking capacity to build wealth rapidly.

---

[17] Also see Stephen E. Roulac, "Life Cycle of a Real Estate Investment," *Modern Real Estate Investment* (San Francisco: Property Press, 1976), pp. 297–306.
[18] Jerome B. Cohen, Edward D. Zinbarg, and Arthur Zeikel, *Investment Analysis and Portfolio Management* (Homewood, Ill.: Richard D. Irwin, 1977), pp. 602–9.

Having little to lose, the young investor usually seeks highly leveraged projects that require minimal management expertise. Often a single-family residence is the first investment, followed by a rental house, a duplex, a quadruplex, or a small apartment building. The young investor needs very little tax shelter, cash flow from operations, or equity buildup from loan amortization, but does seek to increase expertise quickly and to maximize property value appreciation.

Diversification is a difficult goal to achieve; the young investor usually builds a real estate portfolio one property at a time, and property types and locations will tend to be homogeneous owing to lack of expertise. In addition to mortgage debts, insurance premiums and monthly credit card payments are a considerable drain on the cash resources of the young investor. Debt also finances a car and furniture. It is difficult to build up a substantial cash reserve for anything but emergencies, and the net worth statement is but a gleam in the investor's eye at this stage.

The Middle-Aged Investor

At this stage the investor has probably reached the economic prime of life. Although earnings may not have peaked, the middle-aged investor has built up substantial liquid resources and equities in properties, and has greater financial mobility. Investment experience and expertise have been accumulated, and the investor is more sophisticated financially. Risk-taking capacity is at its maximum point—the investor can choose to become involved in development situations and commercial investments, such as shopping centers, office buildings, and motels, that require greater investment expertise.

Diversification will probably play a dominant role in the investor's strategy at this stage. Also, the need for tax shelter has increased as the investor's earned income has risen. Accumulation of wealth through property value appreciation continues to play a key role in the investor's strategy.

The Older Investor

As the investor grows older we expect more conservative behavior and greater aversion to risk. An investor whose prime earning years are over is less likely to pursue high returns, high risks, and capital accumulation alternatives. Rather, the investor will probably shift the portfolio into properties that create high current income, which can be used to augment retirement income. Selling real estate equities and taking back mortgage notes from purchasers is a common means of shifting income and risks in the manner desired while still maintaining an interest in real property.

A successful investor who has built a substantial portfolio of real estate assets over a lifetime may experience little or no decrease in tax bracket after retirement. The amount of ordinary income may in fact increase if the portfolio is shifted into investments that provide steady, but ordinary income for tax purposes. Thus, the desire for tax shelter may be sustained after retirement. In contrast, a relatively unsuccessful investor may need to supplement income from retirement investments by cannibalizing the accumulated investment fund. Periodically selling off assets to supplement income eroded by inflation may be a means of maintaining a given life style after retirement.

With age comes a certain weariness of investment and management responsibilities. Even for the successful managing equity investor, a shift of responsibility to younger and more aggressive individuals is usually warranted. The remaining portfolio can be restructured through an estate plan to accommodate the needs of family members, gifts to charities and foundations, and so on. The life cycle of the individual investor is over.

Institutional Investors

Little information is available that identifies the presence of distinct life cycles for institutional investors. Life insurance companies, pension funds, REITs and large-scale syndications are relative newcomers to real estate equity investment. They are constrained by their fiduciary responsibilities to their clients and by many legal and tax regulations that limit their investment flexibility. The goals and needs of institutions appear to change slowly in comparison to those of individuals; from a decision-making standpoint, therefore, investor life cycle may be a less relevant concept for the institutional investor. However, institutional investors do have personalities, and they do change their return and risk preferences as they become more experienced in the real estate investment game. For example, a number of life insurance companies, such as Prudential and Aetna, have evolved from residential lenders to commercial lenders and then to commercial developers. In searching for greater returns they have been required to participate in real estate activities that also produce greater risk of loss.

Integration of Life Cycle Concepts

Knowledge of life cycles should be used in formulating investment strategy. The interrelationship of the three life cycles discussed is pictured in Exhibit 2–6.

The investor first determines the amounts and types of returns and risks that are acceptable (investor life cycle). On the basis of this knowledge the investor can then choose the stages in the property life cycle (GLITAMAD) that represent acceptable return/risk situations. Properties are then located that meet the basic property and investor life cycle criteria; the investor analyzes each property using discounted cash flow methods that measure the return and risk dimensions over

EXHIBIT 2–6.   Interrelationship of Life Cycle Concepts

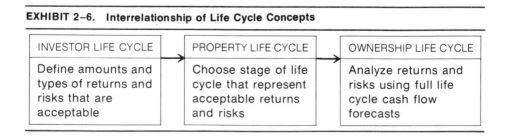

INVESTOR LIFE CYCLE	PROPERTY LIFE CYCLE	OWNERSHIP LIFE CYCLE
Define amounts and types of returns and risks that are acceptable	Choose stage of life cycle that represent acceptable returns and risks	Analyze returns and risks using full life cycle cash flow forecasts

the entire ownership period (ownership life cycle). When these steps have been completed, the investor has successfully integrated the three life cycle concepts into the decision-making process.

SUMMARY

This chapter presented an overview of the investment decision process. The four essential elements of our investment framework are strategy, analysis, decisions, and investment transactions, with least emphasis being placed on investment transactions. We begin by developing an investment strategy that *defines* the risks and returns acceptable to us and the methods we will use to achieve our objectives. We then proceed through numerous stages of analysis that enable us to *measure* the return and risk characteristics of a property being studied. In the decision stage we *evaluate* all the data gathered and arrive at an investment decision that may commit us to buy, sell, exchange, or finance a property. Critical to this process is a feedback mechanism that will provide constant data updates that will enable us to make better investment decisions and outperform the competition.

Investment is defined to include the original commitment of capital by the investor, management of the investment to maximize returns, and disinvestment or liquidation. A capital asset is purchased by an investor and financed via a combination of debt and equity sources. While the investor has traditionally sought to maximize the debt/equity ratio using fixed-rate long-term mortgages, lenders have become more defensive, primarily because of inflation pressures, and are requiring more substantial amounts of equity capital and various types of flexible-rate shorter-term mortgages. The equity investor's primary financial objective is to make capital investments that will maximize wealth; that is, the investor seeks to identify, structure, and purchase projects that will maximize the return/risk ratio relative to his or her preferences. Also emphasized is the need to develop techniques for better management and control of risks.

Feasibility analysis, in contrast with investment analysis, focuses on the development of new projects and explicitly considers the numerous nonfinancial objectives of investors. It seeks to test the marketing, legal, political, physical, and social dimensions of a project as well as its financial dimensions. A complete feasibility study is extensive and can be broken down into seven separate types of studies: strategy studies, legal studies, compatibility studies, market analysis, merchandising studies, architectural and engineering studies, and financial/economic studies. The investor should be able to distinguish between investment and feasibility studies and other types of studies such as appraisals.

We examined also the importance of three types of life cycles that affect the return/risk relationships on which the investor bases a decision. The property life cycle encompases all the development and ownership periods of a property, from the idea inception stage through its demise. In contrast, an ownership life cycle encompasses only the purchase, operation, and termination of a property for one equity ownership group, and an investor life cycle tracks one investor's return/risk behavior over different stages of his or her life.

3

Decision-Making Approaches to Real Estate Investment

Real estate investment literature has historically been dominated by the "how to" experts in real estate. Such best-selling titles as *How I Turned $1,000 into Five Million in Real Estate,*[1] *How Real Estate Fortunes are Made,*[2] *How to Wake Up the Financial Genius Inside You,*[3] *How to Make One Million Dollars in Real Estate in Three Years Starting with No Cash,*[4] and *How You Can Become Financially Independent by Investing in Real Estate*[5] have flooded the marketplace during the last two decades. More recently, sophisticated investors have sought to increase their decision skills through the application of modern management and financial techniques. Although internal-rate-of-return and present value techniques were virtually unheard of in the real estate field during the 1960s, they became the accepted decision approaches in the 1970s. Today all students enrolled in college and university courses, as well as in trade organization courses leading to professional designations such as GRI, CCIM, CRE, MAI, SRPA, SREA, CPM, and CMB,[6] now study discounted cash flow approaches to decision making.

---

[1] William Nickerson, *How I Turned $1,000 into Five Million in Real Estate* (New York: Simon and Schuster, 1980).

[2] George Bockl, *How Real Estate Fortunes Are Made* (Englewood Cliffs, N.J.: Prentice-Hall, 1972).

[3] Mark Oliver Haroldsen, *How to Wake Up the Financial Genius Inside You* (Salt Lake City, 1976).

[4] Tyler G. Hicks, *How to Make One Million Dollars in Real Estate in Three Years Starting with No Cash* (Englewood Cliffs, N.J.: Prentice-Hall, 1976).

[5] Albert J. Lowry, *How You Can Become Financially Independent by Investing in Real Estate* (New York: Simon and Schuster, 1977).

[6] The designations and their granting organizations are, respectively, Graduate Realtors Institute (GRI), awarded by state associations of REALTORS; Certified Commercial Investment Member (CCIM), granted by the Realtors National Marketing Institute (RNMI), a subsidiary of the National Association of

EXHIBIT 3-1. Decision-Making Approaches

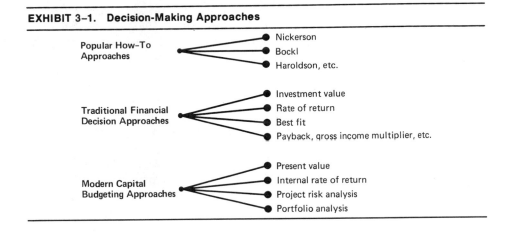

Exhibit 3–1 provides an overview of the investment decision approaches discussed in this chapter. In Chapters 8–17, we will show how many of the theories and approaches developed here should be applied. While many textbooks ignore or disparage many of the popular and traditional approaches, we recognize that each approach has merits and can offer an important perspective to the investor. There is as much to learn from successful school-of-hard-knocks entrepreneurs as there is from more sophisticated real estate managers who have completed their degrees in real estate studies and work for large, successful real estate companies.

POPULAR "HOW TO" APPROACHES

Popular real estate investment literature concentrates on "how to get rich" formulas, plans, schemes, strategies, and manuals. Real estate investing is portrayed as an activity that can be accomplished successfully in one's spare time and offers the individual investor the best opportunity available in this country today to "get rich quick." Although it is possible that some of the authors of these how-to books make considerably more money selling their books and seminars to the public than they do investing in real estate, there are millions of investors who believe in the "how to" approaches to real estate investing. They couldn't all be wrong—or could they?

The Nickerson Approach

When William Nickerson was 25 years old, he worked for the telephone company for a meager salary. Twenty years later, he had pyramided a small real estate

REALTORS (NAR); Counselor of Real Estate (CRE), granted by the American Society of Real Estate Counselors (ASREC); Member of the Appraisal Institute (MAI), granted by the American Institute of Real Estate Appraisers (AIREA); Senior Real Property Appraiser (SRPA), granted by the Society of Real Estate Appraisers (SREA); Senior Real Estate Analyst (SREA), granted by the SREA; Certified Property Manager (CPM), granted by the Institute of Real Estate Management (IREM), a subsidiary of the NAR; and Certified Mortgage Banker (CMB), granted by the Mortgage Bankers Association of America (MBA).

investment into a net worth of over $1 million. In 1959 he wrote *How I Turned $1,000 into a Million in Real Estate—In My Spare Time.*[7] Two revisions later, the book has become the most popular how-to-make-money-in-real-estate book published in this country. The author and his associates offer seminars on his wealth-pyramiding techniques in every major city in the United States, and they attract capacity crowds.

Pyramiding with Other People's Money   The key element of the Nickerson approach is *pyramiding with other people's money.* Nickerson observed that most millionaires had borrowed most or all of their investment capital from others. Probably the world's most outstanding pyramider, according to Nickerson, was Henry Ford. Ford's billion-dollar enterprise is said to have grown faster than any other in history and eventually outstripped all except the Rockefellers', although Ford himself had invested nothing in the business. One hundred percent of the investment capital was borrowed from others. Thus, the road to riches is paved with other people's money. "Big-time" operators buy millions of dollars' worth of property without investing a cent of their own money, and "big deals" are made by borrowing as much as possible from mortgages and the balance on personal and collateral notes.

The Wealth-Pyramiding Process   The Nickerson formula spells out a ten-step wealth-pyramiding process, beginning with the purchase of a single-family home. The leading example illustrated by Nickerson assumes an initial investment of $2,500, 75 percent leverage, *average* luck and market conditions, and investment in income-producing property, beginning with residential properties. The first step is to buy a somewhat run-down house that needs some "cosmetic" work. The purchase price is $10,000; the mortgage is $7,500 and the equity investment $2,500. The second step is to invest $600 from savings each year for two years to paint and renovate the house, thereby increasing the income and sales value of the property so that it can be sold at a profit. The third step is to sell the house for $14,000 (a 25% gross profit of $2,800 on the total investment of $11,200), paying the 5 percent sales costs of $700, which leaves a $2,100 profit *plus* the return of the original $2,500 investment capital *plus* the return of the $1,200 renovation capital. At the end of the second year the investor has accumulated $5,800 of investment capital ($2,100 + $2,500 + $1,200 = $5,800).

The fourth through tenth steps repeat the first three: Invest $5,800, borrow three times that amount (75% leverage), buy a larger property, renovate, hold two years, then sell for a 25 percent gross profit. By the end of the twentieth year the net worth or "estate" of the investor is $1,187,195, as shown in Exhibit 3–2. In theory, this pyramiding of income-producing property can be accomplished without substantial tax consequences through tax-free exchanges and tax sheltering by means of depreciation write-offs.

Clearly, the pyramiding formula is simply a mechanism used to generate high rates of return on the investor's equity through turnover operations. The rest is left to the theory of compound interest. In the case cited, the investor earns a com-

---

[7] Nickerson, op. cit.

EXHIBIT 3–2. The Wealth Pyramiding Process

Year	Net Worth (Estate)
0	$ 2,500
2	5,800
4	11,575
6	21,681
8	39,363
10	70,548
12	124,884
14	219,972
16	386,376
18	677,583
20	$1,187,195

pound rate of interest on successive investments of approximately 33 percent annually. This compounding factor, when applied against the original $2,500 investment (plus the two $600 renovation investments), results in an estate of over $1 million in twenty years. These results may appear miraculous to the novice investor, but they are quite elementary to a student who understands geometric progressions. There is absolutely no magic involved, only the well-known powers of compound interest and, according to Nickerson, average luck and market conditions.

Cardinal Principles   There are four cardinal principles of the Nickerson formula that, if followed, are said to produce (at least) the turnover profits just described:

1. Borrow the maximum that can be safely repaid.
2. Buy only property that needs improvement.
3. Make selective improvements that increase value.
4. Keep selling at a profit and reinvesting.

The base of the pyramid is built with rental housing properties, on the theory that sustained growth of metropolitan areas promises a continually increasing demand for rental housing and, consequently, an ever-expanding choice of real estate investment opportunities. Nickerson's formula assumes (implicitly) that the market will not be overbuilt and that the local economy will not contract.

The Bockl Approach

Like the Nickerson approach, the Bockl approach focuses on achieving high degrees of leverage and on the ability of the investor to raise income substantially and to capitalize that increased value over a relatively short period and thus achieve high rates of return. In his book, *How Real Estate Fortunes Are Made,* the author presents "sure-fire ways for any imaginative person to begin building a fortune that will provide a steady automatic flow of lifetime income."[8] Bockl's key to success is creating high rates of return with low risks through entrepreneurial ability and creativity—by applying *conduit theory* and *entrepreneurial leverage theory* to the investment decision process.

Conduit Theory   This theory assumes that youth is a valuable commodity and that a young person should learn to sell youth in a manner that will maximize investment returns. A young investor can serve as a "conduit" for money to flow through from real estate projects. The young investor with management skill and time, but no money, finds elderly property owners who seek security and convinces them to sell their real estate with nominal down payments and, usually, very generous financing terms. If the sale is structured correctly, both partners benefit and satisfy their personal investment goals. For the young investor, the objective is typically to build a multimillion dollar net worth rapidly with nominal down payments, while for the older investor the objective is security, certainty of income, and peace of mind.

Entrepreneurial Leverage Theory   This theory argues that the formula for buying and keeping a real estate fortune is youth, management skill, and imaginative borrowing. Any young person who becomes skilled in property management and learns how to borrow imaginatively will be worth at least as much as can be borrowed after debts are amortized. Through entrepreneurship an investor who can arrange to borrow a million dollars on real estate at age 30 will be worth $1 million at age 55–60. It's that simple! If loans cannot be obtained from financial institutions, partners should be found to finance the cash needs. In addition, the entrepreneur/investor should develop good credit relationships with banks and other lending institutions. This results in the ability to act quickly when opportunities arise and in situations in which a seller needs cash in a hurry.

The Four-Way Benefit Test   Bockl advocates the use of a rate-of-return analysis, called the *four-way benefit test,* in which the investor analyzes the different sources of income that make up the full rate of return:

1. Cash flow return—before tax, after debt service
2. Amortization return—annual loan reduction
3. Gain from tax shelter—sheltering income through accelerated depreciation
4. Return from inflationary gains—increase in property value

Although the Bockl rate-of-return approach contains the same basic return elements as modern financial rate-of-return methods, no adjustments are made for the time value of money, or for changes in rents, vacancies, and expenses over time. In essence, it is a one-year accounting rate-of-return method that includes both realized and unrealized returns and some tax shelter variables; no provision is made for tax liabilities arising at the time of sale. Bockl's key example shows a 44 percent annual return, which he claims is not an exaggerated representation of "typical" real estate returns.[9]

---

[8] Bockl, front jacket.
[9] Ibid., pp. 170–171.

The Haroldsen Approach

Mark Haroldsen, a former investment banker, claims to have accumulated almost $2 million in properties as an investor in less than four years, beginning with no real estate knowledge and an investment of $4,600. His goal was to double his net worth every twelve months, a goal that seems highly unrealistic until he presents his example of compound interest, in which one penny compounded at 100 percent per day is worth over a third of a billion dollars ($339,456,652.80) on the *thirty-fifth day*. The example is admittedly exaggerated; however, Haroldsen maintains that the use of compound interest is virtually the only way to make millions today.

Control—The Important Ingredient of Success   In his book, *How to Wake up the Financial Genius Inside You,* Haroldsen advises us to thoroughly understand interest rates, compound interest, and leverage and then find investments that we can control.[10] Control is the critical ingredient of successful investing, a management tool that Haroldsen claims is not possible with stocks and bonds but is possible with real estate. The small investor is said to have some distinct advantages in real estate investing. Having only a small amount of money, the small investor can compound money at higher rates of return by finding investments that larger and more sophisticated investors are not interested in. Additionally, small investors don't generally have a vast amount of experience or knowledge, so with a little extra effort you can surpass your competition.[11]

Clearly, the argument developed earlier—that real estate can be structured to increase the rate of return while minimizing risk—is supported by Haroldsen and the other "how to" authors. There are many imperfections in the real estate market, and decisions are often based on emotions and short-run distress situations, resulting in underpriced property that can be readily financed with small down payments and favorable terms. Haroldsen claims that through "brain compounding" (the ability to increase returns by developing increased mental capacity, real estate knowledge, and expertise) the investor can consistently take advantage of these "holes in the market" and build a portfolio at consistently high rates of return. Also because of "brain compounding," rates of return on investment do not necessarily fall as the smart investor increases the size of his or her portfolio.

The Formula for Financial Success   Investment success rests on the decision to plan, save, invest, and compound, as is shown in the Haroldsen formula:[12]

$$\text{Financial success} = P + S + I + C$$

The *planning phase (P)* of the Haroldsen formula requires "dreaming big" and then turning the financial dream into a plan, giving the plan details, making alternative plans if the first one fails, and putting the plan into action and making it come true. Haroldsen speaks with the zeal of an evangelist as he tells us that all the

[10] Haroldson, op. cit.
[11] Ibid., p. 7.
[12] Ibid., p. 11.

famous millionaires—Conrad Hilton, Aristotle Onassis, Rockefeller, and so on—
were big dreamers, planners, and very persistent people.

The decision to *save* (*S*) is explained by Haroldsen's *10 percent rule.* "You
must save a minimum of 10 percent of your gross earnings. The second part of the
rule is that you never, never, never spend that savings. Your capital is your
savings, and your capital must never be disturbed."[13] The *invest* (*I*) and *compound* (*C*) stages of the decision are the same as those presented by Nickerson.

Achievable Rates of Return on Equity   The rate of return on real estate equity
investments is the key to the compounding process and the source of wealth. The
rate of return on equity is measured by Haroldsen in the manner shown by Bockl
in the four-way benefit test—cash flow, equity buildup, inflation, and tax shelter.
What annual rates of return in real estate are achievable, when measured in this
way? Haroldsen's answer is 25–225 percent:

Type of Return	Annual Percentage Rate of Return on Original Equity
Cash flow	10–25%
Equity buildup	3–45
Inflation	10–105
Tax advantage	2–50
	25–225%

While Haroldsen claims that his own *overall* annual return has not exceeded
160 percent, he has reached the 225-percent mark on individual investments and
cites others who hit that mark consistently. However, an investor who achieves
only a 25–30 percent return—but keeps on investing—can become a millionaire
within eighteen years provided that he or she starts with $10,000 of initial equity
capital. Not bad, but what about the risks?

Risks in Real Estate Investment   The risks in real estate investment are negligible, claims Haroldsen, if you invest in housing. First, housing is a necessity; most
other investments, such as stocks, bonds, motels, hotels, and most businesses, do
not have this advantage. There is a constant demand for housing caused by
new-family formation through marriage and individuals setting up their own
households. In addition, there is in-migration into many regions of the country,
resulting in increased demand for housing in those regions. Finally, there is increased demand due to the great American dream—every person wants to move
into a nicer home. This constant demand is said to *only move upward.*

Leverage and Superleverage   Leverage is claimed to be the most important
tool in the investor's bag. The *OPM* (other people's money) formula is a formula
for using leverage. Haroldsen's example of the effect of leverage on the investor's
return is a 90 percent leverage situation in which inflation raises the total property
value by 10 percent each year. A $20,000 rental house is purchased with $2,000

---

[13] Ibid., p. 25.

(10 percent down). If the property value rises by 10 percent annually, or $2,000 (a reasonable amount, Haroldsen claims), the investor's rate of return is 100 percent annually. Not bad for a small, unknowledgeable investor, but the effect is the same for large investments. The ultimate in leverage is *superleverage*—you buy a property and at the closing, or shortly thereafter, mortgage out and perhaps generate extra cash, which you "pocket" in "Hip National Bank."[14] This is most often achieved by finding a "bargain" and refinancing, or by doing "cosmetic" work on a property, thereby raising both income and value, and refinancing on the basis of the higher value.

Bargains + Fixup = Wealth   The Haroldsen investment strategy, like those of most of the other "how to" authors, rests on searching for and finding "bargains" in the marketplace. Six types of property are viewed as bargains:

1. Property that is undervalued
2. Property that can be upgraded
3. Property where rents are too low
4. Property where expenses are too high
5. Property whose basic use can be changed
6. Property that can be purchased with little cash

The key to achieving the goal of 100 percent compounded annually lies in finding "bargains" and then improving the real estate in some way. Raising rents or decreasing expenses has a tremendous multiplier effect, as is illustrated by the 100 times formula. Using this formula simplifies the process of doubling one's net worth annually. The formula says that, *on average*, a $1 increase in rent per month adds $100 to the property value (if the gross rent multiplier is 8.34):

The 100 Times Formula

$1 × 12 months =

12 × 8.34 gross rent multiplier =

$100 added value

Thus, improvements to a property that result in rental increases or expense decreases can easily raise property values and compound equity by 100 percent per year. With a 10 percent down payment, it takes only a 10 percent increase in value to make a 100 percent return on investment.

A Critique of "How to" Approaches

The three approaches presented here are representative examples of the "how to" approach. They place great emphasis on the upside of real estate

---

[14] Ibid., p. 70.

investments—the tremendous rate-of-return potential available from shrewdly purchased, creatively financed (highly leveraged), and imaginatively managed properties. The powers of compound interest are believed to ensure an exponential rate of growth in the value of an investor's portfolio. The investor's primary goal is to create a monopoly, if only for a short while, and in so doing to increase cash flow. In addition, the concept of taking advantage of imperfections in the marketplace is illustrated by these authors' strategies for finding bargains and using entrepreneurial leverage and conduit theory to keep the rates of return high and the estate growing at a pyramiding rate.

Extraordinary rates of return *will* be available for some real estate entrepreneurs as long as "other" investors make irrational property decisions—decisions based on emotions rather than on economic analyses backed up by thorough analyses of the facts. More than one nationally known real estate consultant has observed that the majority of real estate transactions are based on the emotions of individuals, and not on economics.[15] Consequently, if an investor can structure real estate solutions to solve the personal and emotional problems of the seller, he or she can frequently raise the rate of return and simultaneously reduce the investment risks and the amount of cash necessary to acquire a property.

Risk appears to be a forgotten dimension in the "how to" approaches. Investors who employ these approaches might fit into our previously defined category of "risk ignorers." Real estate investment risks are assumed to be minimal if the formula is followed religiously. Any problem that arises can be solved through entrepreneurial effort. Market cycles, competition, and life cycles are perceived not as risks but, rather, as opportunities. In fact, with rent-producing property you are said to have negligible risks, and the chance of success is said to be 1600 times better than your chance of success if you start a new business.[16] Nickerson calculates this 1600-times-safer factor from Department of Commerce statistics showing that four out of five new businesses fail within eight years, so that the overall odds are four to one that a new business will not survive. In contrast, mortgage statistics show that only one in every 400 properties is foreclosed, so that the odds are 400 to 1 in favor of succeeding in real estate. By combining these statistics Nickerson comes up with odds of 1600 to 1 (4/1 × 400/1) for success in income-producing property. Can you think of any reason to question these statistics or the conclusion that follows?

The central theme of *this* book is that sound investment decision making based on thorough return *and* risk analysis is the best strategy for maximizing one's wealth over the long run. In the "how to" approaches little emphasis is placed on the development of analytical techniques for forecasting rates of return. High rates of return are presumed to occur if the formulas are followed. The approaches develop no theoretical framework for decision making but, rather, assume that practical step-by-step formulas that have worked for the authors can be applied anywhere, at any time, and by anyone of average intelligence. The real

---

[15] Robert W. Steele, *15 Ways to Buy-Sell-and-Control Real Estate Without Using Cash* (Medford, Ore.: Newport, 1975), p. 18.
[16] Nickerson, p. 13.

estate investment calculation is simple, and thorough financial analysis is not required.

TRADITIONAL FINANCIAL DECISION APPROACHES

In contrast with the "how to" approaches, both traditional and modern decision-making approaches concentrate on the development of decision models that measure the financial dimensions and provide quantitative data on which real estate investment decisions can be based. In the following sections we will look briefly at traditional and modern approaches to investment analysis. In later chapters we will examine these concepts in depth and apply them to various types of real estate decisions.

Traditional methods of analysis can be classified as (1) investment value (income capitalization) models, (2) rate-of-return models, (3) best-fit models, or (4) other models, such as payback and gross income multiplier models. In the past, because the field was dominated by appraisers who were trained to measure market value, real estate analysts preferred income capitalization models. Recent years have seen a shift to the rate-of-return approach because it more accurately reflects the thinking of many investors and provides data that is more directly comparable. In contrast with modern approaches, traditional approaches tend to be mathematically unsophisticated, contain few financial variables, and give little consideration to income taxes, changing cash flows over time, and the time value of money.

The Investment Value Approach

Investment value is the present worth to the investor of expected future net returns capitalized at a rate of return that reflects the perceived investment characteristics of the property.[17] Investment value is contrasted with *investment cost* (e.g., total purchase costs or total capital assets), which is the total amount of money the investor has spent, or expects to spend, to acquire a new or existing property. Investment value is also contrasted with the *market value* and *most probable selling price* of a property, as discussed in Chapter 2.

The Investment Value Decision Rule   The investment value approach requires the investor to estimate the investment value and investment cost for each project being considered. The decision rule is to accept projects if the investment value is equal to *or* greater than the investment cost:

$$
\begin{array}{l}
\textit{The Investment Value Decision Rule} \\[4pt]
\text{Invest if} \qquad\qquad V \geqslant C \\
\text{Reject or modify if} \quad V < C \\[4pt]
\text{where } V = \text{investment value} \\
\phantom{\text{where }} C = \text{investment cost}
\end{array}
$$

---

[17] Richard N. Ratcliff, *Real Estate Analysis* (New York, McGraw-Hill, 1961), p. 119.

If numerous projects are considered simultaneously, a *profitability index* for each project can be computed by dividing investment value by investment cost. Projects can then be ranked using profitability indexes, with the highest indexes indicating the most desirable projects and the lowest indexes the least desirable ones. Profitability indexes of less than 1.00 are unacceptable.

The Generalized Model of Investment Value   The basic model for computing the investment value of a real estate project is the basic appraisal capitalization model ($V = I/R$), with the variables redefined to reflect the individual investor's viewpoint.

The Generalized Model of Investment Value

$$V = I/R$$

where V = investment value (present worth of future rights to income)
I = net operating income before depreciation and debt service (rental income less operating expenses)
R = capitalization rate (required rate of return to induce investment)

All the traditional valuation models (including direct capitalization, land residual techniques, building residual techniques, and property residual techniques) are variations of this basic model.[18] The assumptions underlying the model are very restrictive, and most investors should use it only in a preliminary evaluation of a project. At best, it produces a quick-and-dirty method or ballpark estimate. The assumptions of the generalized investment value model are the following:[19]

1. All cash outflows occur at one time.
2. Productivity is defined as the annual net operating income from property before debt service and income taxes.
3. Income is often a "stabilized amount" derived from an assumption of declining or increasing income over the projection period.
4. The projection period is for the full useful life of the improvements. There is no consideration of the ownership life cycle.
5. Capital is recaptured from income, except for land value, which is assumed to be constant. No explicit consideration is given to resale price changes or transaction costs.

The Equity Cash Flow Valuation Model   Another basic model for computing investment value—to be discussed more fully in Chapter 10—is the equity cash

---

[18] A comprehensive analysis of these techniques is presented by the American Institute of Real Estate Appraisers, *The Appraisal of Real Estate* (Chicago, 1978), pp. 392–413.
[19] James A. Graaskamp, "Recent Trends in Real Estate Investment Valuation," in Arthur M. Weimer, Homer Hoyt, and George Bloom, eds., *Real Estate,* 6th ed. (New York: Ronald Press, 1972), p. 356.

flow capitalization model, which more fully parallels the orientation of most investors.

The Equity Cash Flow Valuation Model

$$V_E = \frac{CFBT}{RROE}$$

$$V_P = V_E + V_M$$

where V_E = equity value
      $CFBT$ = cash flow before tax
      $RROE$ = required rate of return on equity investment before
         tax (before-tax "cash on cash" return)
      V_P = project value (investment value)
      V_M = mortgage amount

Like the generalized model of investment value, the equity cash flow valuation model is a one-year model that does not explicitly consider the time value of money, equity buildup, changing revenues and expenses, income taxes, or property value increases or decreases over time. Nevertheless, as a "basic economics" testing model and preliminary evaluation technique this model can be quite valuable.

The Ellwood Valuation Model   Another well-known technique for measuring investment value is the *mortgage–equity technique*. Developed by L. W. Ellwood, formerly chief appraiser of New York Life Insurance Company, and referred to as the *Ellwood technique*,[20] it is the most sophisticated of the traditional models and is the forerunner of the modern present value approach. Originally developed for use in market value appraisals, it has become popular with brokers and investment counselors as a tool for investment analysis and marketing.[21]

The Ellwood model calculates investment value, given the mortgage terms, expected holding period, average annual income, future property value, and investor's required before-tax equity yield. It differs from the previously discussed techniques in four important respects:

1. Income projections are made over the holding period of the investment rather than its economic life. Since the average period of property ownership is eight to ten years, this assumption is more realistic.

---

[20] L. W. Ellwood, *Ellwood Tables for Real Estate Appraising and Financing, Part I*, 3rd ed. (Chicago: American Institute of Real Estate Appraisers, 1970).
[21] See, e.g., Irvin E. Johnson, *Selling Real Estate by Mortgage-Equity Analysis* (Lexington, Mass.: Lexington Books, 1976).

2. Mortgage financing and mortgage terms, including equity buildup through loan amortization, are explicitly considered. Traditional capitalization methods tend to ignore the direct impact of mortgage financing on value.
3. The residual value of the investment (property value at the end of the holding period) is estimated rather than ignored or fixed by the underlying mathematical assumptions of the model.
4. The time value of money is considered in discounting resale proceeds and mortgage flows. Also, net operating income is allowed to vary but must be converted into a stabilized annual amount before the value formula can be · applied.

In the Ellwood technique, value is calculated using the basic appraisal capitalization model, $V = I/R$, where I is the stabilized net operating income of the property. Since I is assumed to be constant, the capitalization rate (R) is the critical variable in the Ellwood method and includes adjustments for all of the complications just noted.[22] An overview of the Ellwood approach is presented in Exhibit 3–3. While the formula for computing R (denominator in equation 3) looks complicated, in practice it is greatly simplified by the use of precalculated tables and programmable calculators. It has been shown by Wendt that the answer produced by the Ellwood model is identical to that produced by the discounted cash flow present value model if identical input assumptions are used and a before-tax profile is assumed.[23]

Investment analysts have focused on three deficiencies of the Ellwood model: (1) It does not consider the income tax effects of real estate ownership; (2) it ignores relative changes in rents, vacancies, and operating expenses over the ownership period; and (3) it does not consider selling expenses and loan prepayment penalties when a property is sold. As a result, most investment analysts prefer the more flexible present value model, which can explicitly consider all of the variables just discussed.

The Rate-of-Return Approach

The rate-of-return approach is an alternative to the investment value approach for evaluating a real estate investment. Although the two approaches use the same basic formula and usually result in the same accept/reject investment decision, their application and use in practice has differed. Traditional rate-of-return models avoid many of the complexities of the income capitalization models. The concepts are simple. Land and building returns do not have to be separated, and investment alternatives can be compared and ranked without first estimating the investor's required rate of return (capitalization rate). We saw that in the value ap-

[22] An excellent overview of the Ellwood approach is presented by Peter F. Colwell and Philip J. Rushing in "To Ellwood and Beyond," *The Appraisal Journal,* July 1979, pp. 352–358.
[23] Paul F. Wendt, "Ellwood, Inwood and the Internal Rate of Return," *The Appraisal Journal,* October 1967, p. 563.

EXHIBIT 3–3. A Brief Overview of Ellwood

Ellwood's first premise is that value (V) equals the amount of the loan (L) plus the present value of equity (E).

$$V = L + E \qquad (1)$$

Ellwood's second premise is that the present value of equity is the present value of before-tax cash flow plus the present value of the future selling price minus the present value of the balance due on the mortgage at the time of the sale.

$$E = \sum_{t=1}^{m} \frac{d - VMf}{(1 + y)^t} + \frac{V(1 + app) - VM(1 - P)}{(1 + y)^m} \qquad (2)$$

where:

> d = stabilized net operating income (NOI) and VMf = mortgage payment. Therefore, $d - VMf$ = stabilized before-tax cash flow (BTCF)
>
> y = equity yield rate
>
> m = number of periods until property will be sold
>
> app = proportion by which property is expected to appreciate during holding period
>
> $V(1 + app)$ = projected selling price
>
> P = proportion of loan paid off. Therefore, $(1 - P)$ = proportion not paid.
>
> M = loan to value ratio
>
> VM = loan size
>
> $VM(1 - P)$ = balance due at time of sale

Substituting equation 2 into equation 1 and solving for V yields the familiar Ellwood basic equation:

$$V = \frac{d}{y - My + Mf - MP(1/s_m) - app(1/s_m)} \qquad (3)$$

SOURCE: Peter F. Colwell and Philip J. Rushing, "To Ellwood and Beyond," *The Appraisal Journal* (Chicago: American Institute of Real Estate Appraisers), July 1979, p. 353.

proach projects could not be ranked without first estimating the required rate of return and then capitalizing net income to find value. This is one of the practical drawbacks of the value model for an investor who is unsure of his or her required rate of return.

The Rate-of-Return Decision Rule   The rate-of-return decision approach requires three steps to arrive at a go/no-go decision for a project. First the investor must estimate the expected rate of return. Second, the investor estimates the rate of return necessary to justify the investment and compensate for the risks involved. Third, the expected and required rates of return are compared and a go/no-go decision is made. If the expected rate of return (ROI) is equal to or greater than the required rate of return (RROI), then the investor should invest because the project meets his or her financial criteria.

The Rate-of-Return Decision Rule

Invest if ROI ≥ RROI
Reject or modify if ROI < RROI

where   ROI = expected rate of return on investment
RROI = required rate of return necessary to induce investment

---

Rate-of-Return Calculation Models   The expected rate of return can be measured in a variety of ways, and no one method seems to be universally accepted. Four of the more popular "accounting" or rule-of-thumb measures are shown here:

Traditional Rate-of-Return Calculation Models

1. $\text{Rate of return} = \dfrac{\text{net income before depreciation and debt service}}{\text{total capital invested (purchase price)}}$

2. $\text{Rate of return} = \dfrac{\text{annual cash flow after debt service}}{\text{cash equity investment}}$

3. $\text{Rate of return} = \dfrac{\text{annual cash flow } plus \text{ debt principal amortized}}{\text{cash equity investment}}$

4. $\text{Rate of return} = \dfrac{\text{annual cash flow } plus \text{ debt principal amortized } plus \text{ property appreciation}}{\text{cash equity investment}}$

These measures can be computed on a before- or after-tax basis. While most investors use these measures to calculate the rate of return for a one-year period only, they can (and should) be computed each year over a projected holding period, as we will illustrate in Chapters 11 and 13. However, the simplicity of calculating a rate of return for one year only, using adjusted or normalized income and cash flow figures, appeals to many people. The Bockl approach, for example, advocates the calculation of the fourth rate-of-return measure just shown, using after-tax cash flows. Probably the most widely used return measure is the second one, cash flow relative to equity investment, measured on a before-tax basis. This is often referred to as the *cash-on-cash return,* the *cash throw-off rate,* or the *equity dividend rate.*

A less widely used rate-of-return measure is the *equity yield* (rate of return) calculated by the Ellwood model (*see* Exhibit 3–3). Using that formula, the investor solves for the equity yield rate y instead of the value of the property V. As is true with most investment value (income capitalization) models, redefining the dependent variable in this manner converts the model from an investment value model to a rate-of-return model. The reverse is also true.

Estimation of the Required Rate of Return   Estimation of the required rate of return, against which the investor measures expected return (and which is used as the capitalization rate in the investment value model), is a subjective judgment that the investor makes on the basis of experience, the rates of return available on alternative investment media, inflation expectations, and the riskiness of the deal. The required rate of return should include (1) a real return—a return for deferred consumption, (2) an inflation premium, and (3) a risk premium. In other words, the investor requires that the expected cash flows from a project compensate him or her for deferring consumption, for the expected rate of inflation over the holding period, and for the chance that he or she may not receive the expected cash flow.[24] Definition and quantification of the investor's required rate of return has long been a central problem in investment analysis. Not surprisingly, the subject of required rates of return is ignored by the "how to" authors.

The Best-Fit Approach

Although the traditional investment value and rate-of-return approaches are widely used by investors and analysts, the assumptions associated with some of the models are unacceptable to many investors and do not reflect current investor objectives and motivations. Most of the models give inadequate consideration to important variables, such as the time value of future cash flows, uneven cash flows, the after-tax value of proceeds from the sale of property, annual tax shelter benefits from depreciation, financing and refinancing alternatives and costs, inflation, possible holding periods, and risk.

Because traditional rate-of-return and value models exclude many important variables from consideration, their use as decision models is limited. Investors can overcome the limitations of the traditional models in three ways. First, they can use more sophisticated discounted cash flow models and incorporate more of the relevant variables into a decision model. Second, they can develop a *best-fit* model, which involves a multiple-criteria analysis that considers both nonfinancial and financial variables. Using the best-fit model, an investor analyzes alternative investments and chooses those that best fit the multiple objectives and constraints given. Third, investors can employ a combination of the two approaches, which

[24] Mike E. Miles and Arthur S. Estey, "The Relevant Required Rate of Return," *The Appraisal Journal,* October 1979, p. 513.

involves the use of discounted cash flow models in conjunction with a best-fit model.

Consider the use of a best-fit model by an investor who identifies eleven basic value factors that are believed to affect the financial success of a property:[25]

1. Proper location
2. High-quality construction
3. Professional property management
4. Good maintenance
5. Amenities desired by tenants in the market area
6. Attractive architecture and good land planning
7. Good interior layout
8. Property selected market to appeal to
9. Competent and reputable developer and/or owner
10. Sufficient cash from the project to cover operating costs and debt service
11. Careful analysis and verification of income and expense figures of the project and determination of their reasonableness in light of recognized standards

The investor is interested only in existing income properties. Each of the factors is weighted according to its relative importance to the investor, and each property analyzed is reviewed with respect to each factor listed.

After the basic value factors have been defined and analyzed, potential returns and risks can be analyzed in terms of *financial* benefits. These benefits might include the following:

1. Amount and stability of future equity cash flow
2. Equity buildup from loan amortization
3. Tax shelter benefits
4. Mortgage refinancing benefits
5. Net proceeds from sale or termination of property

Again, each of the factors is weighted according to its relative importance, and each property is reviewed with respect to each of the potential financial benefits. No sophisticated cash flow models are used. Rule-of-thumb investment criteria can be established on the basis of investment experience for each of the financial variables considered.

Projects that have a reasonable or best fit when the project characteristics are compared to the multiple investment criteria will be accepted by the investor.

Evaluation of the Best-Fit Model Many of the investment criteria in the best-fit model are *underlying* value (return and risk) factors that influence the investor's cash flow projections and financial yield calculations. Previously we argued that an

[25] William R. Beaton and Terry Robertson, *Real Estate Investment,* 2nd ed. (Englewood Cliffs, N.J.: Prentice-Hall, 1977); see also Lloyd D. Hanford, "Rating Guide for Real Estate Investments," *Journal of Property Management,* March-April 1972.

investor should buy the assumptions that create the yield rather than the yield itself. The best-fit model provides a vehicle for directly assessing the underlying assumptions that affect yield. This approach is intuitively appealing to many investors because it is easy to use and can incorporate a significant number of complex financial and nonfinancial variables into an understandable decision format. However, two criticisms of these models are (1) that it is difficult to identify the relevant investment criteria and (2) that the process of assigning relative weights to investment criteria is highly subjective.

Other Traditional Approaches

Two other popular models include the gross rent multiplier model and the payback period model. The gross rent multiplier approach advocates acceptance of projects in which purchase prices relative to gross rents are favorable. The payback period approach advocates acceptance of projects in which the cash flows are adequate to pay back the investor's original capital in less than some required number of years. Both of these approaches will be illustrated in Chapter 11.

MODERN CAPITAL BUDGETING APPROACHES

Modern capital budgeting approaches include present value models, internal-rate-of-return models, risk analysis techniques, and portfolio analysis techniques. Many variables that are not explicitly dealt with in traditional models are incorporated in these more advanced capital budgeting models, and many of the models have been adapted for computer systems and desk-top calculators to make them more convenient for students and practitioners.

The Present Value Model

The present value model, also called the discounted cash flow (DCF) valuation model, shifts attention away from measurement of the capitalization rate, assuming a constant net income, and emphasizes (1) redefining income returns as after-tax cash flows, (2) placement of returns in specific time periods, (3) accounting for each type of return to reflect exposure to income taxes, and (4) reliance on simple compound interest, reversion discounts only, rather than all-encompassing but fictional annuity factors.[26] Following is the basic after-tax present value model.

[26] James A. Graaskamp, "A Practical Computer Service for the Income Approach," *The Appraisal Journal*, January 1969, p. 51.

The After-Tax Present Value Model

$$PV_E = \frac{CF_1}{(1+R)^1} + \frac{CF_2}{(1+R)^2} + \cdots + \frac{CF_n}{(1+R)^n} + \frac{SP}{(1+R)^n}$$

$$PV_P = PV_E + PV_M$$

where

PV_P = present (investment) value of property

PV_E = present value of equity returns

$CF_1, CF_2, \ldots, CF_n$ = equity cash flow; annual after-tax cash flow to investor over the holding period (n)

SP = after-tax cash flow from sale of property (reversion cash flow)

PV_M = amount of debt borrowed to finance property (present value of mortgage)

R = required rate of return (IRR) on equity investment

n = holding period of investment

The after-tax cash flow received in each period $(CF_1, CF_2, \ldots, CF_n)$ is discounted back to the point of initial investment at the required (internal) rate of return on equity. The series of discounted cash flows is then totaled to measure the present value of the equity returns (PV_E). The present value of the property (PV_P) is then computed as the present value of the equity returns (PV_E) *plus* the amount of debt borrowed to finance the property (PV_M). If the present value of the property (PV_P) is *equal to or greater than* the total investments costs (C), then the project is acceptable using the decision rule described earlier. If $PV_P < C$, the project should be rejected or modified to either raise PV_P or lower C.

This basic present value model may be used to find the *net present value* of any series of cash flows by subtracting the present value of the project (PV_P) from the total investment cost (C). As long as the net present value is zero or greater $(NPV \geq 0)$, the project is considered acceptable. Also, the model can be redefined for before-tax cash flow analysis if an investor chooses to ignore tax ramifications.

The Internal-Rate-of-Return Model

In recent years internal-rate-of-return (IRR) models, or discounted cash flow rate-of-return models, as they are sometimes called, have become popular for evaluating and comparing real estate investments. This rate-of-return measure, or some modified version of it, is preferred by many sophisticated investors and analysts as the proper yardstick for comparing returns between real estate and other investment opportunities, such as bonds, stocks, and annuities.[27]

The internal rate of return (IRR) is the rate, expressed as an annual percentage, at which the present value of the cash flows $(CF_1, CF_2, \ldots, CF_n + SP)$ equals the present value of the equity investment (E_0). IRR can be calculated on a before- or after-tax cash flow basis on either total capital or equity capital invested. If it is computed on a *before-tax* basis on the equity invested and net operating

---

[27] For an exposition of some of the common methods of measuring the internal rate of return, see Stephen D. Messner, Irving Schreiber, and Victor L. Lyon, *Marketing Investment Real Estate: Finance, Taxation, Techniques* (Chicago: National Association of Realtors, Realtors National Marketing Institute, 1975), pp. 42–52.

income is held constant, it is identical to the *equity yield rate* y using the Ellwood approach. However, most sophisticated investors prefer an *after-tax* model, in which IRR is computed on the amount of *equity* investment. The basic model for performing this calculation is as follows:

The After-Tax IRR on Equity Model

$$E_0 = \frac{CF_1}{(1 + IRR)^1} + \frac{CF_2}{(1 + IRR)^2} + \cdots \frac{CF_n}{(1 + IRR)^n} + \frac{SP}{(1 + IRR)^n}$$

Solve for IRR
where

IRR = DCF (internal) rate of return on equity capital invested

E_0 = amount of equity investment

$CF_1, CF_2, \ldots, CF_n$ = annual after-tax equity cash flows

SP = after-tax cash flow from sale of property

n = holding period of the investment

The after-tax return on equity is generally recognized as the most significant measure of real estate returns because it explicitly considers the time value of money and the investor's ability to leverage the yield to a high degree and then shelter the return from income taxes.[28]

The suggested decision rule for investing is the same as that applied earlier, that is, to accept projects whose IRRs are equal to or greater than the investor's required IRR.

Risk Analysis Models

The internal-rate-of-return and present value models presented here are said to be *deterministic* in nature. A value for each input variable is entered into the model by the investor; then the desired output is calculated. In contrast, a risk analysis model is said to be *probabilistic;* that is, the values of many of the input variables are uncertain. The uncertain variables must be defined as ranges with associated probability distributions, rather than as single-point estimates. A risk analysis model thus generates a range of possible returns rather than a single value, and ideally will also compute the probability or chances of receiving different rates of return, depending on how the uncertain future unfolds.[29]

Real estate decision makers have always claimed to take calculated risks, but

---

[28] Paul F. Wendt and Alan R. Cerf, *Real Estate Investment Analysis and Taxation* (New York: McGraw-Hill, 1979), p. 53.

[29] Stephen A. Pyhrr, "A Computer Simulation Model to Measure the Risk in Real Estate Investment," *The Real Estate Appraiser,* May–June 1973, p. 18. (Also published in *American Real Estate and Urban Economics Association Journal,* June 1973, p. 57.) See also Steven D. Kapplin, "Financial Theory and the Valuation of Real Estate under Conditions of Risk," *The Real Estate Appraiser,* September–October 1976, pp. 28–37.

few of them have made it clear just how they calculate those risks. Traditionally, because of the difficulties, dislike, or lack of knowledge about how to deal explicitly with risk in making decisions, most people have concentrated on a few key assumptions about the future, examined a few rules of thumb, mulled over the situation, and then made a decision. Although some of the risk considerations were explicit, the mathematics of risk was left largely to the four horsemen of the implicit decision-making apparatus: judgment, hunch, instinct, and intuition.

In contrast, financial theory has attempted to make risk analysis more explicit and to suggest some improved procedures. Common methods used to analyze risk are (1) the payback decision rule, which focuses on how long it takes an investor to recover the initial cash investment; (2) the risk-adjusted discount rate, which attempts to account for risk by adding some premium to the required rate of return demanded (i.e., to the investor's capitalization rate); and (3) conservative forecasts, which deal with risk by reducing forecasted returns to some more conservative level. These three methods have been subject to increasing criticism. While they are simple and familiar, they contain assumptions that are not clearly understood, are erroneous, and could lead to decisions at odds with the decision maker's own objectives and preferences. In addition, these procedures ignore or lump together much information that could be valuable in sharpening the decision process.

Ratio and Sensitivity Analysis   Additional project risk information can be calculated using the techniques of ratio and sensitivity analysis. Ratios can be used to measure the level and trends of risk by comparing output data from a cash flow analysis. Popular ratio measures of risk are the debt coverage ratio (the ratio of net operating income to annual debt service) and the breakeven point (the ratio of operating expenses and debt service to gross possible income). In contrast, sensitivity analysis measures risk by assigning different values in a cash flow model to input variables that are believed to be uncertain, and then measuring their relative impact on the rate of return (or other important) output variables. With either ratio or sensitivity analysis techniques, if the data indicate a level of risk that is not commensurate with the expected level of return, the project is rejected or modified.[30]

The Direct Utility Approach   In a classic article Ratcliff and Schwab suggest that an investor can specify preferences for return and risk in the form of a utility, or preference, curve.[31] This curve can then be used to directly determine the desirability of an investment opportunity on the basis of the possible outcomes and the likelihood of their occurring. In calculating possible outcomes three estimates are used for each variable—high, most probable, and low—with corresponding probabilities of 10 percent, 80 percent, and 10 percent.[32] The outcomes

---

[30] For a complete discussion of ratio and sensitivity analysis, see Chapters 11 and 12.
[31] Richard U. Ratcliff and Bernard Schwab, "Contemporary Decision Theory and Real Estate Investment," *The Appraisal Journal*, January 1970, pp. 165–187.
[32] Ibid., p. 176.

produced are used as input into the preference curve to determine the acceptability of an investment.

The Monte Carlo Risk Simulation Approach   The most sophisticated probabilistic approach developed in real estate is known at the Monte Carlo risk simulation model. As the name implies, this approach attempts to imitate how the variables that influence the investor's rate of return could combine as the future unfolds. That is, probability distributions must be estimated for each uncertain factor that affects an investment decision, and the possible combinations of the values for each factor are then simulated in order to determine the range of possible outcomes and the probability associated with each.

A general model synthesizing much of the earlier discussion on return/risk measurement and evaluation, as well as the material on modern techniques of investment analysis, is shown in Exhibit 3–4. Risk analysis models usually incorporate a present value or internal-rate-of-return model as a basis for measuring possible investment outcomes. The generalized model is important because it provides a framework for comparing risk measurement with other aspects of an investment decision.

In the exhibit the real estate investment decision process is described as five distinct stages or steps:

1. *Model Specification.* The model uses a discounted cash flow procedure, such as the IRR on equity or total capital described previously. Input variables are defined as *control variables* or *state variables.* State variables are measured as probability distributions, while control variables are measured as single-point estimates.

2. *Information and Estimation.* At this stage the decision maker's uncertainty about the future is quantified by the estimation of probability distributions for the state variables. This requires forecasting possible values for each variable, together with their associated probabilities. It is difficult to meet this requirement with the poor quality of data available in real estate at this time. Factors and considerations that cannot be quantified (e.g., personal preferences or legal and environmental constraints) are placed in the *intangibles* category and explicitly considered in the final stage of the decision process.

3. *Calculations Using Monte Carlo Simulation.* In this step the probablistic information on state variables and the values of control variables are combined to produce a probability distribution for the expected rate of return on total capital (IRR_{TC}) and equity invested (IRR_E). In addition, liquidity or other measures (breakeven point, payback, etc.) can be computed from yearly cash flow data generated during the simulation process.

4. *Project Evaluation.* The information that has been generated enables the investor to compare projects in a number of ways. Projects can be ranked and compared through the use of risk profiles, probability-of-loss statistics, or desired liquidity measures. The measures used are a matter of personal preference.

EXHIBIT 3–4. A Risk Simulation Model of the Investment Decision Process

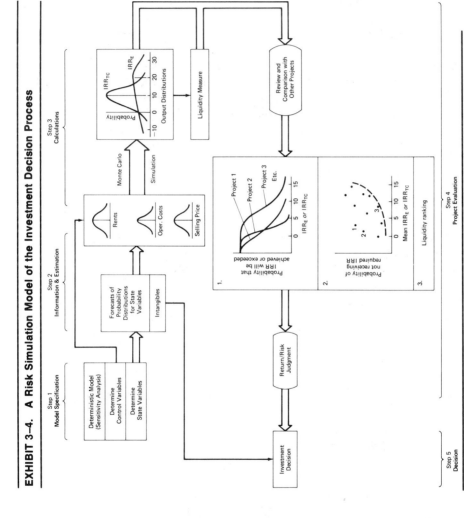

SOURCE: Stephen A. Pyhrr, "A Computer Simulation Model to Measure the Risk in Real Estate Investment," *American Real Estate and Urban Economics Association Journal*, June 1973, p. 57.

5. *The Investment Decision.* This is the final step in the investment decision process. On the basis of all the information generated, including intangibles that could not be quantified or were overlooked, the investor makes a decision to accept or reject the project. At this stage, the investor must weigh all the data on risk and return against his or her personal preferences (utility function) for various combinations of risk and return.

It is hoped that a formal procedure like the one developed here will help the investor make better and more profitable decisions over the long run. Even if the procedure is not actually used (or a simplified version is used), understanding how to systematically approach risk-and-return analysis and evaluation should materially increase an investor's ability to base decisions on more educated judgments, hunches, instincts, and intuitions. Note, however, that investment situations often call for immediate action by the investor, precluding a lengthy period of analysis. In cases in which a market advantage can be gained, and perhaps a monopoly position created or a "bargain" taken advantage of, a decision maker must learn to apply the principles and concepts discussed here without the benefit of extensive analysis. Analytical overkill has killed many a deal for would-be investors.

Portfolio Analysis Risk analysis in real estate may be divided into two categories: individual project risk and portfolio risk. Individual project risk analysis, as shown in the Monte Carlo model, considers a single project and implicitly assumes that the risk associated with it can be considered independently of the risk in other investments. Portfolio risk analysis is concerned with the interrelationships among various investments. For example, the overall risk profile of a portfolio of diversified real estate projects with different cyclical characteristics may be significantly less than the average of the risks of the individual projects that make up the portfolio. Although the portfolio rate of return is the average (mean) of the individual project returns, the portfolio risk (return variance) is less than the mean of the project risks because of the stabilizing effects of the contracyclical return patterns of the projects in the portfolio.

Harry Markowitz developed the basic framework for portfolio analysis in the early 1950s.[33] By taking into account the extent to which returns from investments vary jointly, Markowitz developed a measure of the overall risk in a portfolio of investments. In the area of real estate, however, portfolio analysis is still in its infancy. While mathematical portfolio analysis techniques have been applied to real estate by a number of researchers, including Pellatt,[34] Friedman,[35] and more recently Findlay, Hamilton, and Messner,[36] it has not yet developed to a stage at

---

[33] Harry M. Markowtiz, *Portfolio Selection: Efficient Diversification of Investment* (New Haven, Conn.: Yale University Press, 1959).

[34] Peter G. K. Pellatt, "A Normative Approach to the Analysis of Real Estate Investment Opportunities Under Uncertainty and the Measurement of Real Estate Investment Portfolios," Ph.D. dissertation, University of California, Berkeley, 1970.

[35] Harris C. Friedman, "Real Estate Investment and Portfolio Theory," *Journal of Financial and Quantitative Analysis,* April 1970, pp. 861–874.

[36] M. Chapman Findlay, Carl W. Hamilton, Stephen Messner, and Jonathan S. Yormark, "Optimal Real Estate Portfolios," *Journal of the American Real Estate and Urban Economics Association,* Fall 1979, pp. 298–317.

which practical applications are feasible. In the near future great advances in the state of the art will be forthcoming and institutional applications may be possible. The topics of portfolio planning and analysis will be addressed in depth in Chapters 26 and 27.

SUMMARY

The primary goals of this chapter were to examine and contrast (1) popular "how to" approaches, (2) traditional financial decision approaches, and (3) modern capital budgeting approaches to investment decisions. "How to" approaches tend to discount risk and to oversimplify decisions. They all stress pyramiding, in which the investor borrows the maximum that can be repaid, makes selective improvements to increase property value, and then sells at a profit and reinvests in larger properties to start the process over again.

Other related theories and strategies include (1) conduit theory, which shows how to take advantage of investor age differences; (2) entrepreneurial leverage theory, which argues that the formula for creating a real estate fortune is youth, management skill, and imaginative borrowing; (3) the four-way benefit test, which advocates that investment returns be analyzed in terms of their component parts; (4) control of property, the key to raising the rate of return; (5) brain compounding, or the ability to increase returns by developing increased knowledge and expertise; (6) superleverage, in which the investor uses the multiplier effects of increasing rents to increase value and then refinances the property; and (7) finding bargains in the marketplace and improving them in some way.

Traditional and modern decision approaches concentrate on the financial and quantitative dimensions of real estate investment and the application of rate-of-return, present value, and risk analysis theory. We saw that accept/reject decision rules could be developed for the investment value and rate-of-return approaches, and that these were valid regardless of the level of sophistication of the formula used. The decision rules apply to one-year accounting models, the Ellwood mortgage equity technique, and the internal-rate-of-return (IRR) and present value (PV) models. While before-tax accounting rate-of-return models are used by the majority of investors, after-tax models are preferred by sophisticated investors because they explicitly consider more of the variables that affect investment returns and risks. A best-fit decision model is recommended for use when the investor has multiple investment criteria and constraints, and views nonfinancial (as well as financial) variables as important investment considerations.

Finally, we discussed how risk analysis and portfolio models could be used to sharpen the decision process, to make investment risk considerations more explicit, and to measure the interrelationships among projects over time. Real estate portfolio analysis and portfolio planning are emerging topics that are addressed in the final part of this book.

II

Analyzing Real Estate Markets Under Changing Conditions

MARKET (MACROMARKET) ANALYSIS

1. Determine national and international trends, and monetary and fiscal policy impacts on real estate
2. Select the target SMSAs
3. Delineate market and trading area for intended uses
4. Perform supply and demand analysis
   - for SMSA
   - for selected market area
   - for specified neighborhood and use
5. Project future rent schedules, prices, and space needs

MARKETABILITY (MICROMARKET) ANALYSIS

6. Neighborhood analysis
7. Site analysis
8. Preliminary merchandising and management strategy
9. Competitive surveys
10. Estimates of market absorption rates, gross possible income, and vacancy rates

11. Revenue forecasts for alternative economic scenarios over projected ownership cycle

Input data to investor's return/risk analysis

Although careful market studies are essential in the real estate investment process, they are too often neglected or their importance is shortchanged by real estate investors. Even when market studies are performed, they may be incomplete, lack logical consistency, or fail to provide defensible input data upon which the investor can base the return and risk analysis. Consequently, in this section we focus on real estate market analysis topics, including the subjects of inflation and real estate cycles.

On the preceeding page we provide a conceptual model for analyzing real estate markets under changing conditions. The various steps of a *market analysis* (macro market study) and *marketability analysis* (micro market study) are outlined. The output of such analyses is a revenue forecast for a projected ownership life cycle under alternative economic scenarios that will provide input data into the investor's return and risk analysis. Observe that the process begins at a very macro (general) level converging to the micro, project-specific level at the end of the tenth step.

In Chapter 4 we discuss the process and patterns of growth and decline in metropolitan areas in order to choose target locations for investment. In Chapter 5 we outline the various steps involved in a market analysis, beginning with the analysis of national and international trends and ending with neighborhood comparisons. Marketability analysis, Chapter 6, begins with a neighborhood analysis and proceeds through a series of steps to generate specific revenue forecasts for a property. Finally, in Chapter 7, we tackle the very difficult topics of inflation and real estate cycles, and study their complex effects on real estate investors and properties.

4

Searching for the Target Metro Area: Evaluating the Growth and Decline of Metropolitan Areas

I'd target to build a luxury apartment complex on the Alaskan North Slope if I could get the loan. 'Cause I could mortgage out to a syndicate of rock stars, bone surgeons, and football stars before rent up.

—*Anonymous developer*

Successful real estate investors understand the process of urban growth and decline in metropolitan (or metro) areas. They are aware of the various stages of growth, the rate of growth, the prospects for continued growth, and the nature of the basic employment mix in the metropolitan area they are considering.

Successful real estate investors also understand that metropolitan areas compete for jobs and people, and in the way they use their land areas. While some areas are undergoing periods of rapid growth, others are maturing or stable, and still others are stagnating or declining. Technological changes, shifts in government expenditures, urban planning, and energy costs are among the factors that can affect the rate of growth and decline in a particular metro area.

It is, therefore, not necessarily wise for a real estate investor to follow the bandwagon to Sun Belt metro areas. Below-average returns are the result when investors bid up prices in attractive areas. Instead, the investor should focus on areas that offer better investment opportunities.

In this chapter we discuss the process of urban growth and decline and the principles of comparative advantage in order to enable us to select the best real estate investment opportunities.

Before one embarks on a market study or marketability analysis for a given metropolitan area, the area itself should be the target of a careful selection process. Because time and budget constraints usually require that an investor use a great deal of secondary data generated by government agencies and reporting services when evaluating metro areas, we must first define some of the terms used by such sources.

WHAT IS A METROPOLITAN AREA?

A metropolitan area is an integrated economic and social unit with a large population nucleus. The current criteria for defining a *standard metropolitan statistical area (SMSA)* were adopted by the Bureau of the Census in March 1976.[1] Each SMSA must include one central city with 50,000 or more inhabitants. In addition to the central city, the SMSA must include the county in which the central city is located and adjacent counties that are determined to be metropolitan in character and economically and socially integrated with the county of the central city. An SMSA may include other cities of 50,000 or more inhabitants in addition to its central city, and may include territory in more than one state. In New England the definition is slightly different because cities and towns, rather than counties, are used as the basis of the definition.

A *standard consolidated statistical area (SCSA)* includes two or more SMSAs with integrated and contiguous urbanized areas. Often SCSAs cross state lines. An example is the Chicago, Illinois– Gary, Indiana SCSA.

An *urban population* comprises all persons in an *urban place* with 2,500 inhabitants or more that is incorporated as a city, village, or borough, but excludes persons living in the rural portions of extended cities. An *urbanized area* consists of a central city (or twin cities) with a total of 50,000 or more inhabitants, together with a contiguous, closely settled territory known as the *urban fringe*.

Finally, a *city* is defined as a political entity with clearly delineated boundaries in accordance with its charter of incorporation. There are approximately 18,000 cities in the United States, and there may be dozens of cities within a single SMSA. The city of Atlanta (population 425,000), for example, is a political subsection of the Atlanta SMSA (population 1.8 million).

Exhibit 4–1 shows the number of metropolitan areas in the United States in 1976. The differences in size between metropolitan areas are significant in evaluating their function in the national economy, since the size of a metropolitan area is closely related to the feasibility of certain types of real estate investments. For example, high-rise combination use (mixed-use) buildings are seldom profitable in cities with populations under 1 million because of cost/revenue relationships and other reasons not discussed here.

Trends in growth and size are not irreversible, however. Metropolitan areas compete in terms of the way they satisfy basic human needs, and the quality of life they provide affects their rate of growth or decline. The Northeast and North Central states, the traditional destinations of migrants from other parts of the country, have become net exporters of population. Since 1970 the populations of

[1] U.S. Department of Commerce, Bureau of the Census, *Statistical Abstract of the United States,* (Washington, D.C.: GPO, 1978), pp. 2, 3, 935.

EXHIBIT 4-1.   Number and Population of SMSAs, 1976

Number	Population Class
7	3,000,000 or more
28	1,000,000–3,000,000
37	500,000–1,000,000
10	250,000– 500,000
112	100,000– 250,000
25	Less than 100,000
279	156,000,000 total population

SOURCE: U.S. Department of Commerce, Bureau of the Census, *Statistical Abstract of the United States, 1978* (Washington, D.C.: Government Printing Office, 1978). This annual publication is an inexpensive source of statistics about urban places.

New York, Pennsylvania, Rhode Island, and the District of Columbia have actually declined. Fifteen states, eight of them in the South, that exported people during the 1960s have gained in population since then. Maine, New Hampshire, and Vermont have also gained in population as a result of out-migration from lower New England.

PATTERNS OF METROPOLITAN GROWTH

Cities are places of central tendency for human activities. Since the earliest civilizations, cities have been centers of political power, seats of religious influence, and the focus of scientific and artistic development. People congregate in cities not only to engage in economic activities but for recreation and cultural pursuits as well. A city puts enormous numbers of diverse households, business firms, and other decision units face to face so that they may interact in fruitful and efficient ways.

Historically, the growth of cities has been related to the available modes of transportation and communication. This explains the vast differences in building-to-land ratios and lot sizes, for example, between Boston—which was built around its dock facilities and railheads—and Houston, which was built in the age of the automobile. (See Exhibit 4–3.) In the past limited resources led to the concentration of industry and commerce in relatively high-density areas. However, the centralization of manufacturing and distribution would never have occurred without the parallel development of improved modes of transportation.

Even today urban areas tend to concentrate some types of land use in order to minimize transportation or communication costs. Although workers often seek to minimize their journey to work, other space users in the same households, such as the shopping population or the school-attending population, may substantially affect the location of the family dwelling. Indeed, even the theater-going and library-using populations affect this choice.

Where goods rather than people are being moved, or where production serves local needs, such as the need for daily newspapers or bread, transportation costs are influential and affect the selection of the site for activities. Indeed, over time, as transportation and communication modes change, a metropolitan area may restructure itself into an entirely different setting.

The Maximum Distance to Daily Activities

The structure of metropolitan areas is affected by the maximum distance that users of the site would be required to travel to carry out daily activities. However, in selecting a location for a real estate investment one should be aware that travel time and convenience are usually more influential than actual distance. Exhibit 4–2 illustrates ideal maximum distances to daily activities for residential users.

Land Use in Metro Areas

Real estate practitioners have developed five descriptive categories to classify the types of land use that exist in any metropolitan area. These are as follows:

1. The CBD or central business district
2. Manufacturing and industrial sites
3. Housing (which, with its attendant services, is known as the residential area)
4. Regional shopping centers and other retail-service-oriented complexes
5. Open land and recreational areas

All of these uses tend to be organized around transportation facilities. Some writers suggest additional classifications for transportation, utility, and public land use.

EXHIBIT 4–2.   Ideal Maximum Distance to Daily Activities

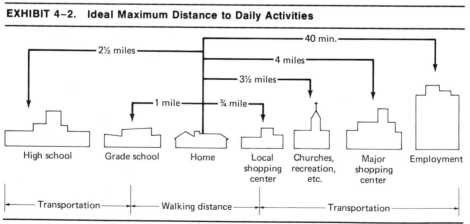

SOURCE: Reprinted with permission from *The Community Builders Handbook,* 1968 (out of print), p. 33, published by the Urban Land Institute.

Through the years real estate practitioners and land economists have sought to explain how categories of land use have developed. Many theories—multiple-nuclei, concentric zone, axial star pattern, sector, geophysical—are discussed in the literature.[2]

Multiple-Nuclei Theory

This concept of spatial patterns appears to recognize best many of the realities of contemporary metropolitan land use. In discussing the multiple-nuclei hypothesis, Harris and Ullman[3] identify four factors that tend to account for separate nuclei in urban land use patterns:

1. The interdependence of certain types of activities and their need for close proximity to one another.
2. The natural tendency of certain types of activities to find it mutually profitable to cluster together. For example, retail centers, medical centers, and outlying office building centers tend to cluster.
3. The third factor is the converse of the second, that is, centers that accommodate activities that have no particular affinity to one another but are incompatible with other uses by virtue of the quality of traffic generated. These include activities such as airports and their ancillary services, gas and fat-rendering complexes, railroads, large truck-loading facilities, and farmers' market areas.
4. High rents or land costs, which have the effect of attracting or repelling certain types of uses.

Increasing urbanization and the outward sprawl of metropolitan areas have complicated the land use patterns associated with smaller as well as larger metropolitan cities. Random observations of typical cities show that central business districts still attract multistory buildings and intensive uses. While in the past factory sites and industrial uses were frequently located near the central business district, these activities increasingly are moving to outlying areas to gain improved access to highways, provide parking facilities, and convert to single-story materials-handling processes. Commercial uses tend to follow the major arterial streets that flow out of the central business district; neighborhood shopping centers often are developed along these streets; and the areas between the major streets seem to be used primarily for residential purposes. Land use patterns may or may not be following the multiple-nuclei hypothesis. Aerial views of the outlying suburbs of many large metropolitan areas show the clustering of hierarchies of uses similar to those found in the central cities.

---

[2] Chapin, Stuart, *Urban Land Use Planning* (Champaign, Ill.: University of Illinois Press, 1965), pp. 7–21.
[3] Chauncy D. Harris and Edward L. Ullman, "The Nature of Cities," *The Annals*, 242 (1945). See also James R. Cooper and Karl L. Guntermann, *Real Estate and Urban Land Analysis* (Lexington, Mass.: Lexington Books, 1974).

Urban Cartography

Vast improvements in aerial photography have resulted in a much better way to study the structure of a metropolitan area and its probable growth patterns than any of the hypotheses developed in the past.

With the permission of the Association of American Geographers, we reproduce here maps showing generalized land use patterns for 1970 in the metropolitan areas of Atlanta (pop. 1,805,000); Houston (pop. 2,423,000); Washington, D.C. (pop. 3,037,000); and Boston (pop. 3,535,000). (See Exhibit 4–3.) Keeping in mind that these maps are all to the same scale, do you find the differences in geographic area surprising? Careful study will reveal the appropriateness of the multiple-nuclei hypothesis for describing the structure of metropolitan areas. It should also indicate that urban land use patterns are substantially affected by topographical conditions, the age of the city, and the differing economic functions that these metropolitan areas are known to serve.

In addition to generalized land use maps, urban geographers have adapted aerial photography to show economic and demographic data for metro areas. These maps can provide useful insights into urban land use patterns. For example, they can show housing broken down by such characteristics as age, location of mobile homes, range in value and in rent per month, or location of single-family detached housing. Information can be provided on such socioeconomic characteristics as occupation, income, and household size. Maps showing population density and age distribution, the locations of ethnic enclaves, and other significant characteristics can also be found.

Comparing land use maps from one point in time to another will help the real estate investor determine the path of growth in a metro area. Most regional planning commissions provide, at very low cost, maps that indicate their current estimates of growth trends.

Computer mapping techniques. The value of computer mapping lies in its ability to give a graphic presentation of complex statistical or other quantitative data. Computer mapping techniques are used to delineate the spatial variations in such characteristics as age, income, and residential density. After an investor has analyzed patterns of land use over an entire metropolitan area, computer mapping techniques are especially useful in analyzing one sector of the SMSA.[4]

All of the foregoing mapping techniques are relatively low-cost tools for identifying regional and community-wide growth trends and patterns of land use. They are extremely valuable for identifying a location within an SMSA that would be appropriate for a certain land use, or for locating the geographic area in which a particular land use is most likely to occur. However, maps provide little data about the current state of economic health of a metro area, nor do they enable the real

[4] Jack S. Wolf, "SYMAP, Computer Graphics for Marketing Management," *Journal of Marketing Research,* August 1969, p. 357. Wolf describes SYMAP, a computer mapping system, as "ideally suited for one concerned with any form of aerial analysis in which raw data are dispersed spatially with the aim of visually ascertaining their geographic presence."

estate investor to project supply and demand for a particular real estate use. These kinds of market studies will be discussed in Chapter 5.

Dominant Factors in Land Use

Economic specialization is a common phenomenon in today's world, and SMSAs tend to specialize in the industrial goods or business services that they provide to the national economy. The areas that specialize in producer durable goods are probably the most unstable; those that specialize in producer and consumer non-durable goods are relatively more stable. A local economy is an atypical jumble of industries, and the rise and fall of business activity in a given metro area does not necessarily follow the national business cycle.

The Principle of Comparative Locational Advantage

Within an SMSA some areas tend to concentrate on a limited number of goods or service activities in order to maximize the efficiency of the use of a parcel of land. As Raleigh Barlow states, "Comparative advantage stems from natural endowment, and involves favorable combinations of production outputs, location in relation to transportation costs, favorable institutional arrangements, or other desirable amenity factors."[5]

Industrial Locations

Industrial uses require sites that minimize materials-processing and transportation costs. Industries may be classified as follows:

Materials-Oriented Industries   Some materials-oriented industries, such as outdoor recreation, agriculture, fishing, lumbering, and mining, are bound to the location of the basic natural resources on which they depend. Another group of materials-oriented industries involves processes that require large quantities of fuel, power, or water. Examples are steel, aluminum, and synthetic nitrate. Another group processes material to eliminate bulk and excess weight. An example of this is sugar beet processing. This group tends to press for locations near its raw materials. Chemical producers need both to be near their raw materials and to be able to dispose of hazardous or bulky waste materials.

Market-Oriented Industries   These industries are the reverse of the raw materials-oriented industries in that they produce a good that becomes progressively more fragile, more cumbersome to pack and handle, more valuable in relation to its weight, and more differentiated in terms of weight and size. This tends to encourage location near the market, the ultimate user. Examples of this type of industry are home building, baking, and brewing.

Footloose Industries   These are the service or "clean" industries. They are neither pulled by the magnet of raw materials nor controlled by the need for

[5] Raleigh Barlowe, *Land Resources Economics*, 3rd ed. (Englewood Cliffs, N.J.: Prentice-Hall, 1978), p. 283.

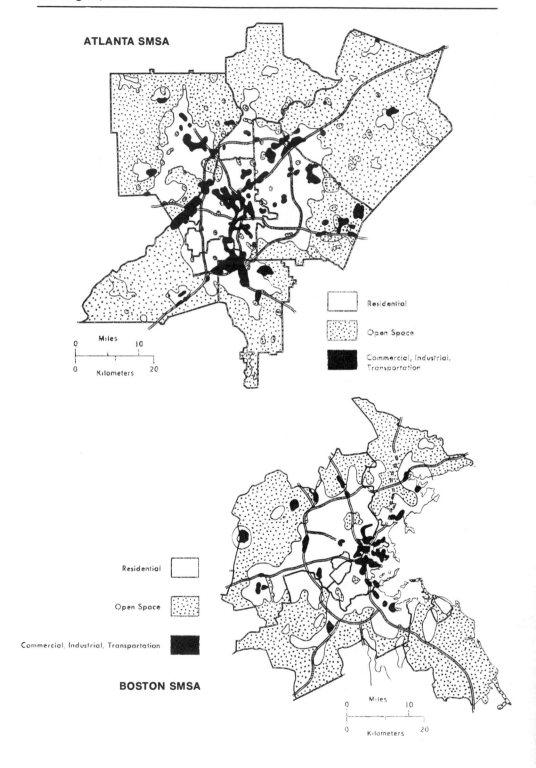

ATLANTA SMSA

Residential

Open Space

Commercial, Industrial, Transportation

Miles 10

Kilometers 20

Residential

Open Space

Commercial, Industrial, Transportation

BOSTON SMSA

Miles 10

Kilometers 20

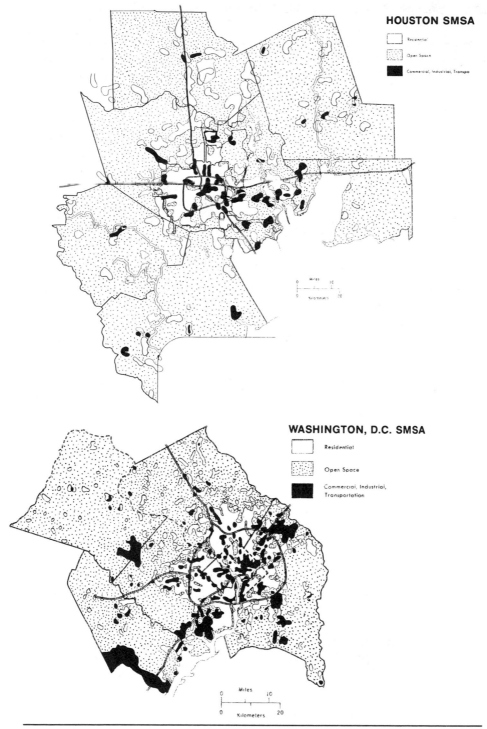

HOUSTON SMSA

☐ Residential

▨ Open Space

■ Commercial, Industrial, Transpo

WASHINGTON, D.C. SMSA

☐ Residential

▨ Open Space

■ Commercial, Industrial, Transportation

SOURCE: John S. Adams, ed., *A Comparative Atlas of America's Great Cities: 20 Metropolitan Regions* (Minneapolis: University of Minnesota Press and the American Society of Geographers, 1976), pp. 22, 198, 248, and 257. Reproduced with permission.

maximum access to the market. Labor is the most important ingredient in their process. Much of the growth in the United States since World War II has been in the service sector. Examples of these industries are computer software producers, research laboratories, and insurance companies.

Service industries usually prefer to locate near transshipment points or in locations that favor low production costs. Their location may be substantially affected by personal (psychic) and other noneconomic considerations. The quality of life that a metropolitan area can provide for its executive and essential technical personnel can be highly influential in affecting the choice of a location.[6] Service industries have often been attracted to industrial parks or to locations near large universities and cultural activities. Such industries often find it logical to locate near similar or complementary industries in metropolitan regions where they can draw upon the local pool of managerial and consultant talent. The availability of banking and ancillary services and the prospect of providing goods and services to complementary establishments are other attractions.

Heavy Industries   These still tend to locate near water, railroads, or highway transportation routes. There has been a distinct tendency for heavy materials-oriented and market-oriented industries to locate around the periphery of cities, where land is less expensive, taxes are lower, and large areas are available for parking and ancillary uses.

Environmental Impact   Today all industries must be concerned about finding acceptable solutions for the impact of an industrial location on its environment. Consideration must be given to effects on land, water, air, traffic congestion, sewage, and the aesthetics of the surrounding area and the metropolitan community.[7]

Commercial Locations

The percentage of a metropolitan area that is used for business and commercial sites is usually small. However, business districts represent some of our most valuable land because of the high intensity and rent-paying capacity of such use. Commercial sites usually provide access to the greatest number of potential customers for a particular retail use. Commercial districts are usually found at the hub of a city's traffic and transportation network or at axial points of major arterial highways. Sites near the "100-percent spot" offer the greatest opportunity for profitable use and are usually occupied by prestige department stores and high-rent tenants such as apparel shops, restaurants, and variety stores.

However, rents per square foot of leasable area tend to decline very rapidly as one moves toward surrounding areas. Sites located only a few blocks away from

---

[6] Lewis Mandell, "Quality of Life Factor in Business Location Decisions," *Atlanta Economic Review,* January–February, 1977. See also Elbert Hubbard, "Commentary on Site Selection," *Atlanta Economic Review,* April–May, 1978.
[7] Jane A. Silverman, *Environmental Factors of Real Estate Development: An Approach for Achieving Acceptable Solutions,* Real Estate Review Portfolio no. 17. (Boston, Mass.: Warren Gorham & Lamont, 1978.)

the 100-percent corner may have only a small fraction of the income-producing value of a ground floor location near the 100-percent corner.

Consumer buying preferences also affect the nature of real estate improvements, the way goods are displayed, and the type and volume of goods sold. In contrast to convenience goods, articles such as pianos and automobiles represent sizable purchases that can easily be postponed until the buyer has done some comparison shopping. Because buyers are willing to shop for big-ticket items at some distance from their primary location, it is often economically feasible to locate such establishments outside high-rent central business districts and regional shopping areas.

In addition to providing access to transportation facilities and adequate parking, a commercial site must be large enough to create a mix of shops and services that will maximize the number of potential customers. Success almost invariably calls for the presence of one or more *generative businesses* (anchor stores), such as branches of department stores and large food markets, which have active advertising programs that continually attract customers to the location both for themselves and for others.

Marketing models have been developed to determine the extent of a trading area. An example is Reilly's law of retail gravitation. This model defines the trading area boundary (point of equal probability) between two retail centers as the function of the distance between the centers and their size:

$$\text{Trade area boundary from the smallest center} = \frac{\text{distance between centers}}{1 + \sqrt{\dfrac{\text{size of largest center}}{\text{size of smallest center}}}}$$

This approach, of course, is simplistic because it assumes many things to be constant that are in fact variable. However, it does serve as a basis for many more realistic models. For example, Huff adapted Reilly's classic model to include a broader concept of consumer choice behavior.[8] There are many examples of techniques of retail store location analysis in marketing literature.[9] Economic–demographic profile reports for a trading area may now be obtained for less than $150. These sophisticated techniques, such as CACI's Site Potential,™ may also be used for other real estate products. Chapter 6 contains a discussion of market data models and shows how they can be accessed from computer terminals.

Residential Locations

The typical householder wants convenience as well as space and a pleasing environment. Consumer satisfaction and personal preferences play a bigger role

[8] David Huff, "A Programmed Solution for Approximating an Optimum Retail Location," *Land Economics*, August 1966, pp. 294–295.
[9] Robert F. Zaloudek, "Practical Location Analysis in New Markets," *Stores*, November 1971, pp. 40–41; J. D. Schneider, "Retail Competition Patterns in Metropolitan Areas," *Journal of Retailing*, Winter 1969–1970, p. 68; Robert A. Peterson "Trading Area Analysis Using Trend Surface Mapping," *Journal of Marketing Research*, August 1974, pp. 338–341; Charles T. Moore and Joseph B. Mason, "A Note on Interchange Location Practices of Developers of Major Retail Centers," *Land Economics*, May 1972, p. 199.

and economic considerations a smaller one in residential location decisions. The would-be buyer is significantly influenced by the residential amenities provided by a location. Access to schools, hospitals, shopping facilities, parks, and churches tends to take priority over the journey to work. However, what people want in a residential location and what they finally get is a product of compromise, and understanding this will help the real estate equity investor evaluate older neighborhoods in older metropolitan areas.

Before the advent of modern transportation, residential sites were almost always near the worker's place of employment. Today, most workers can locate almost anywhere within a large commuting distance, depending on their willingness and ability to pay the costs associated with the location decision. Of course, some families are subject to racial or ethnic discrimination, which segregates them out of certain markets, and others prefer to live near people with similar cultural values. Virtually every American metropolitan area has experienced growth patterns that demonstrate the ability of commercial and industrial establishments to outbid housing for the use of particular sites. With more urban growth, new residential developments normally tend to occur farther and farther from the downtown centers and industrial-use locations. High-cost residential neighborhoods frequently have first choice of the available sites for new residential subdivisions and developments because they can outbid lower-income families for the best package of amenities.

THE PROCESS OF URBAN GROWTH AND DECLINE

Urbanization can be defined as a concentration of both people and economic activities into political units called cities. The process is dependent primarily on jobs, and we can no longer assume that the general trend of rural-to-urban migration plus natural population increase will guarantee the continued growth of any single metropolitan area. Inter- and intraregional shifts are common as people respond to economic opportunities. Individuals and households consume much of our service-oriented gross national product; automated processes are capital intensive and reduce the number of manufacturing workers needed; technological changes in the service, computer, and communication industries will reduce the labor intensity of these industries from past trends. Institutional investors and conglomerate transnational corporations have little loyalty to any particular place. Thus, dynamic change will result in significant alterations in the pattern of urban growth.

A metropolitan area's growth cycle tends to reflect the regional as well as local mix of industries and services, in addition to the area's locational position within the region. By influencing the rate of growth of the local economy, local industrial characteristics also act indirectly to shape the level and pattern of local incomes. A local export sector that emphasizes either new products or income-elastic products will tend to experience greater-than-average expansion and will reach outward in its demand for labor.

Limits to Urban Growth

It is possible for a local economy to grow too large. The long-range viability of any metropolitan area rests on its capacity to innovate or in some way acquire a new export base to replace older industries as they decline. It has been suggested, for example, that New York and Chicago may have exceeded the limits of growth. Diseconomies of scale appear to have occurred in their provision of certain labor-intensive municipal services, such as garbage removal and police and fire protection. On the other hand, the rich diversity of the greater New York economic base, coupled with a demonstrated capacity for innovation and change, suggests that New York may simply be in a period of transitional stagnation while it works out a new direction.

Stagnation and Decline

Since the 1920s, services, trade, finance, real estate, business, and government have been the nation's main growth industries. During the same period, automobiles, trucks, and airplanes have replaced the railroad as the main mode of transportation. As a result, many older industrial cities in the Northeast and North Central regions are no longer primary job producers. For example, Pittsburgh thrived as the center of activity between the East and the continental interior, and then it prospered as long as it manufactured heavy industrial products. After World War II, when services and consumer goods became the main growth industries, Pittsburgh headed toward stagnation. Cities whose economies were more diversified, such as Cincinnati, have been able to make a more orderly transfer from a declining economic base to a growing one.

The recent development of computer networks and telecommunications is likely to have a substantial impact on regional growth and business and industrial relocation.

Indicators of Stability

Some metropolitan areas have a rich infrastructure that facilitates adjustment to change by providing the socioeconomic institutions and physical facilities needed to initiate new enterprises, convert capital from old forms to new ones, and retrain labor. These more stable economic bases are usually in the larger metropolitan areas (i.e., those with more than 250,000 inhabitants). Such areas have been able to restructure old and dying bases to new and growing ones through activities that are not usually found in smaller urban areas. Universities and research parks, sophisticated engineering firms and financial institutions, public relations firms and advertising agencies, transportation networks and utilities systems—all provide a much more diversified economic base than is found in the one-industry town. A diversified economy softens the shock of exogenous change by minimizing the impact of a dying industry on the metro area.

There appears to be a "ratchet" in urban growth that favors medium-sized and larger SMSAs. Once the larger size has been achieved, population decline is unlikely except in the largest SMSAs—the megalopolises—where diseconomies seem to occur.

Competition and Interdependence of Metropolitan Areas

The metropolitan areas of the United States compete with and at the same time depend on one another. Paradoxically, specialization is the key to both competition and interdependence. The past, present, and future roles of metropolitan areas are evident in their interdependence on their surrounding SMSAs. A city usually sends its largest outflows of travelers and information to the city on which it relies most heavily for specialized services that are not available locally. For instance, when one maps the interflow of telephone calls and air passengers, one finds a clear indication of New York's premier position among the twenty largest metropolitan areas. Only Detroit, St. Louis, Minneapolis/St. Paul, and Seattle are more closely linked to another one of the twenty metropolitan regions.[10]

Chicago is clearly the nation's second most dominant metropolis, with Minneapolis/St. Paul, St. Louis, and Detroit dependent on it. Los Angeles, the nation's second most populous metropolis, had captured only Seattle's primary attention by the late 1960s.

The connection or subordination of major metropolitan areas to surrounding SMSAs is a subject worthy of continued study. Atlanta is rapidly becoming the metropolis of the Southeast. Dallas, because of its links with both Oklahoma and Texas, is also profiting from the South's rapid urban growth. On the other hand, places like Hartford, Philadelphia, Baltimore, Pittsburgh, Cleveland, and St. Louis have lost potential client cities to stronger or later arrivals, partly because of the shift in transportation and communication modes. The future promises slow growth or stagnation for these cities, since with few client cities and no distinctive environmental amenities the opportunities for expansion in specialized employment, which would attract more people, are limited. Boston, New Orleans, Seattle, and Detroit seem to face a similar future because their peripheral location reduces the number of subordinate SMSAs that they might attract. San Francisco, formerly in a dominant position in West Coast affairs, is increasingly ceding to Los Angeles. Minneapolis/St. Paul has only one metropolitan subordinate (Duluth), but it serves a large and prosperous agrarian hinterland. Miami, Houston, and Washington, D.C., are unusual cases. Miami is peripheral to much GNP activity and has few subordinates, but it has valuable climatic amenities and possible relationships with Latin American countries. Washington, D.C., is almost fully a creature of the federal government. It seems to be insulated from typical metropolitan competition and is capable of self-sustained growth in a way that no other city could be. Houston's prosperity and rapid growth are based on complex petrochemical and aerospace industries that should provide sustained growth in the decade ahead. Thus, knowledge of the industrial mix and the way jobs,

[10] John S. Adams, ed., *A Comparative Atlas of America's Great Cities: Twenty Metropolitan Regions,* (Minneapolis: Association of American Geographers and the University of Minnesota Press, 1976). A good source of information on competition and interdependence among metropolitan areas.

people, and land can cluster in any and every metropolitan area is essential to rational real estate investment.

SEARCHING FOR A TARGET METRO AREA

America is undergoing evolutionary population trends, most of which will have a profound effect on the nation's real estate markets. Migration, changes in birth and fertility rates, increasing affluence, a shifting age distribution—all create changes in household size and composition. Local published population forecasts are often affected by political considerations, such as the desire to increase local shares of federal and state grants. As a result, while the investor must use the best available population statistics to select investment SMSAs, he or she must also use judgment in choosing a demographic forecast.

Some basic trends are apparent. Rapidly declining birth and fertility rates and slowly declining death rates herald the approach of near-zero or even negative increases in population. Among the expected results will be an aging population and vast shifts of resources—away from industries serving youth-oriented markets and toward those serving age-related markets. One can expect a further reduction in the size and composition of households, with resulting changes not only in the demand for housing and other goods and services but also in the role of the family in American life. The United States is not unique in these respects. Similar patterns are clearly emerging throughout the postindustrial economies of northern and western Europe and Japan.[11]

Since a real estate asset has a long ownership cycle, one should take care in selecting the SMSA in which the investment is to be located. For many general real estate uses, such as offices, retail space, or housing, most SMSAs will provide investment opportunities. However, for more specific uses great care must be taken to be sure the SMSA is large enough and can provide the essential transportation, communication, specialized utilities, climatic conditions, and natural endowments required by that use.

In Part IV of this book we provide specific data sources for such uses as shopping centers, office buildings, industrial parks, and apartments. At this stage, however, we are using metro area statistics to compare and evaluate SMSAs in order to choose the most likely target for further market studies and marketability analyses.

Sources of Secondary Data

There are many sources of data that can be used at this preplanning stage. Following is a brief summary of some that provide valuable, low-cost materials:

Governmental Agencies   The U.S. Department of Commerce publishes many indicators of economic activity. For example, the Bureau of Economic Analysis publishes material on the investment and legislative climate in each of the fifty

---

[11] George J. Stolnitz, "Current Population Trends," *MGIC Newsletter*, April 1979.

states and in Washington, D.C. The regional offices of the departments of Commerce, Transportation, and Housing and Urban Development and the Federal Reserve banks are rich sources of very low-cost data on the level of economic activity and trends in their regions.

The various state departments of commerce, community affairs bureaus, housing and finance agencies, and industrial development authorities continually monitor economic activity and can provide at low cost many technical reports that are useful for comparative analysis of the SMSAs in their regions.

Regional and local planning commissions and agencies and county and city planning bodies are often an excellent source of data. In addition to supplying raw data, many agencies also do economic base analyses and prepare transportation studies, master plans, and community renewal studies that are useful sources of data—if they are up to date. Much can be accomplished by contacting these sources by telephone. Many public employees will treat such a contact as an opportunity to display their knowledge of the metro area.

Other Sources   In addition to governmental agencies, there are private sources that can be of significant assistance at low cost. Local newspapers and television and radio stations often have on file excellent material concerning their trading areas. These data are usually available to interested individuals who visit their offices.

A list of various sources of data is provided in an appendix following Chapter 7.

This is not the right place to discuss statistical methodology and reliability. However, it is worth noting that, as a rule, federal, state, and local agencies provide technical appendixes to their statistics that explain the nature of their methodology and its reliability.

Major Indicators of Change

Generally, we seek SMSAs with growth rates in excess of the national rate or, better yet, in excess of those of other SMSAs. We compare rates of employment, population gain, migration in and out, growth in bank deposits, job formation rates, and quality of life indexes in order to select those with the greatest promise. To put it another way, we use *measures* of urban growth and stability as *investment screening criteria* to improve the probability of achieving the desired rate of return while minimizing risks.

Population Changes   Population changes mirror the growth, stability, or decline of a metropolitan area. They reflect the net natural increase (or decrease) in births relative to deaths, as well as in- and out-migration. However, it should be recognized that the impact of population change on real estate investment tends to lag. Small children boost sales of baby food and rattles, but they create little, if any, immediate demand for real estate—except possibly for day care centers and tot lots.

Exhibit 4–4 projects the U.S. population from now to the year 2050. The four series are the results of different underlying assumptions concerning immigra-

EXHIBIT 4–4.   U.S. Population, Projections to 2050

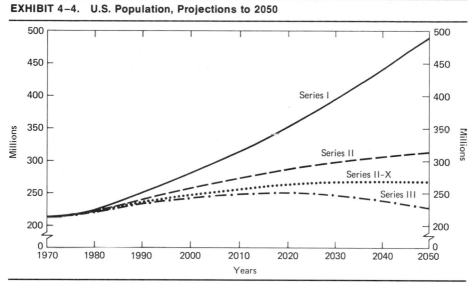

SOURCE: Bureau of the Census, *Statistical Abstract of the United States, 1978* (Washington, D.C.: Government Printing Office, 1978), p. 5.

tion, household size, birth rates, death rates, and fertility rates. Note that even in the relatively short forecast period to the year 2000, the population forecasts range from a low of about 240 million to a high of about 285 million. The current rate of natural increase—about 6 per 1000—is somewhat skewed. It is affected both by the fact that the children born during the postwar baby boom are now having children of their own and by the fact that the current overall death rate is also weighted by the large number of people in the 20–35-year-old category.

Birthrates   Today's birthrate is about 15 per 1000, which is substantially lower than in recent decades. Even so, it is greatly inflated by the fact that females born during the baby boom (1945–1960) have reached reproductive age (20 to 35). Therefore, during the 1980s we will face a sharp temporary increase in the underlying demand for housing and other goods as the generation born in the 1950s produces record rates of household formation.

Fertility Rates   Fertility seems to be on the decline. During the 1950s the U.S. birthrate was 60 percent higher than it is today. Even as recently as 1970 it was 20 percent higher. According to the latest surveys, Americans now expect to have just over two children; that's a full child less than the three-plus expectation of the mid-1960s. The odds currently strongly favor subreplacement fertility. The skyrocketing costs of raising and educating children, a chronic expectation of job insecurity among younger workers brought on by the arms race and the resulting inflation, and the rapid increase in the number of two-income families all signal smaller families. With large numbers of women now giving equal billing to having a career and raising a family, there is a tendency to postpone and reduce childbearing.

Death Rates From the standpoint of mortality, too, we seem to be entering an era that breaks sharply with previous trends and expectations. Death rates for people below age 50 have become so low that further declines are unlikely. For example, if all male and female death rates between birth and age 50 suddenly dropped to zero, the gain in life expectancy from the current level of about seventy-three years would be only about four years—a change of less than 6 percent. Future declines in death rates are likely to come only through major breakthroughs against old-age diseases—heart attack, cancer, and stroke.

Immigration Natural increase is not alone in making demographic history. In recent years immigration has also been setting records. Legal net migration, involving some 300,000– 350,000 people annually, accounts for 20 percent of the country's reported 1.7 million total annual growth. In addition, the net number of illegal immigrants is far higher than the number of legal immigrants. If we conservatively estimate illegal immigration to be about 500,000, and add that number to legal immigration, the ratio of total net migration to total growth doubles to nearly 40 percent. This is a greater level than that reached at the peak of European immigration a century ago.

An Aging Population As a result of these changes in birth, fertility, and death rates, changes are occurring in the age composition of the population. Exhibit 4– 5 illustrates the changes in population between 1960 and 1976, by age group.

We are entering unknown demographic territory, with implications for retirement policy, old-age care and dependency, and social security requirements. Certainly, new demands for extended-care facilities of various kinds are to be expected.

The Changing Composition of Households All the changes noted so far are having an impact on the size and composition of the average household. Statistically, if demand is measured by dwelling units, a decrease in average household size should stimulate the demand for houses. For example, with 240 million people living in households, 80 million dwelling units would be needed if the average number of persons per household were three, but 120 million would be needed if the average dropped to two—as long as income levels remained adequate to fulfill aspirations.

EXHIBIT 4-5.   U.S. Population Age Composition, 1960–1976

Age	Percent Change 1960–1976
0–15	(−) 6.1
15–30	(+) 67.0
30–45	(+) 3.3
45–60	(+) 19.4
60+	(+) 35.9

SOURCE: George J. Stolnitz, "Current Population Trends," *MGIC Newsletter,* April 1979. Reprinted with permission of Mortgage Guaranty Insurance Company, 1981.

The fact that more and more households are being headed by single people is also implicit in Exhibit 4– 5. The notion that housing is for families is waning. With a life expectancy of 73 years and a fertility rate indicating only two children per family, it appears likely that even if one becomes a parent, one can expect to live in a housing unit with children present for only about half of one's lifetime. The children will spend eighteen years with their parents and perhaps another eighteen with their own children—assuming, of course, no divorce.

Changes in Employment Rate and New-Job Formation   Since industrial and service employment are the key to economic base analysis, this is an important and useful set of statistics. Comparative statistics on the rate of unemployment, the level of employment, and the rate of new-job formation are very useful in evaluating the health and vitality of an SMSA. However, these statistics are substantially affected by short-run changes in activity that do not necessarily affect the need for long-term real estate assets.

Bank Deposits   Comparing data over time on the levels and rates of change of bank deposits in an SMSA may provide useful information. For example, a younger SMSA might show a substantial increase in the rate of growth of bank deposits, which would suggest that it is moving up in the hierarchy of SMSAs. In this age of electronic transfers of bank funds, we suggest that not much can be deduced from this indicator. However, for many of the service industries it is useful as a secondary statistic.

All of the foregoing indicators should be used together when one is subjectively selecting the SMSA that is to be the target of one's investment strategy.[12]

The Age of Migration

Population movements are the key to understanding the underlying demand for land use in a metro area. Theoretical economists correctly argue that households are consumers and not producers. However, this theoretical position is of very limited usefulness to a real estate investment decision maker. Dell Webb's Sun City, Arizona, and the growth around Tampa-Sarasota, Florida, are due to retirement, not new jobs. Billions of dollars of real estate assets are dependent on income and credit flows that are not related in any way to migration in search of job opportunities. In an era of increasing uncertainty there are substantial difficulties in forecasting population trends even using the best-available economic and demographic statistics. Therefore, investors find that they must be knowledgeable about the causes of population movements so that they can make their own demographic forecasts.

Migration as an Indicator of Change in the Demand for Real Estate   In- and out-migration are expressions of individual and family decisions to seek better economic and cultural opportunities. People move for many reasons—to begin a new career, to find a better climate for their retirement years, to leave an area

---

[12] *Planning Ahead—Trends in SMSA Population Forecasts* (Washington, D.C.: American Planning Association, annual).

where a plant has closed for another where their skills are in demand. In a market economy migration is an interesting statistic. People generally do not choose to leave friends, relatives, church, and familiar surroundings unless they believe it is necessary to do so in order to fulfill their aspirations.

Each year about two out of ten Americans move from one state to another. In 1971 over 36 million people moved, two-thirds of them within the same county. The most frequent movers, apart from college students, are young families in which the parents are 25– 34 years old. For many of these families, an intrastate move reflects an increase in family size. Older people are more inclined to stay put. This is especially true of those 65 years old and over, unless they are seeking a change at retirement time. Middle-aged parents with high school children move less often than younger families. However, younger families, middle-aged parents, and young singles seeking career opportunities all tend to move from one metropolitan area to another where economic opportunities appear to be greater.[13]

The U.S. Bureau of the Census reports that, in general, the Sun Belt states are growing more rapidly than other areas of the nation, while the Northeast and North Central states are experiencing a net out-migration. A countertrend is evident in New England, where Maine, New Hampshire, and Vermont have grown faster than the United States as a whole since 1970. Florida's growth has slowed to one-third its rate during the early 1970s. States with declining populations in the 1960s, such as West Virginia, the Dakotas, Mississippi, and Arkansas, are now experiencing some in-migration. A slowing of the growth rate has occurred in many states, including New Jersey, Virginia, Colorado, Massachusetts, Connecticut, and Maryland.[14]

Another study by the Census Bureau showed that in 1977, 73 percent of Americans were living in the same houses in which they had been living in 1975. Thirteen percent had moved within the same metropolitan area, and about 4 percent had moved from one metropolitan area to another. Only 1.6 percent had moved from *outside* a metropolitan area *into* a metropolitan area. More significant, a study conducted by the University of Wisconsin indicated that rural counties experienced a net gain of 1.8 million during the 1970– 1975 period, compared with a net loss of 3 million during the 1960s. This kind of population shift could pose particular challenges for the construction industry, which is not well developed outside metropolitan areas.[15]

This brief recital of population trends should make it clear that identifying an SMSA that would be a good place for a real estate investment requires some knowledge of the past, present, and future of that area compared with others. In the short run, an SMSA's age and the time during which it experiences its most rapid growth are the major determinants of how many problems it has and how serious they are. Similarly, one must identify its growth prospects and make a

[13] Morton J. Shussheim, *The Modest Commitment to Cities* (Lexington, Mass.: Lexington Books, 1974).

[14] Census Bureau Report no. P-25 (Washington, D.C.: GPO, 1972).

[15] *Buildings,* January 1977, Census Bureau Report no. P-20 (Washington, D.C.: GPO, 1977); *Urban Land Digest,* 11 (1978).

good forecast of how well it can cope with its problems. Human and environmental problems are likely to be more intractable in stagnating places than in those where opportunities are expanding. One should keep in mind, however, that choosing a growing SMSA is merely a risk management technique. It is quite possible to find good-quality investments at well-selected locations in some slow-growing SMSAs. Indeed, a mature, stable SMSA should have high-quality real estate investments that could be virtual "cash cows" with a minimum of risk over the ownership period. Obviously, choosing a prime location in slow-growing or stagnating SMSAs requires more careful judgment than would be the case in a faster-growing SMSA where external conditions provide growth to offset errors in decision making. The ways growth and status are translated into a metropolitan area's collective feelings about itself, the confidence the average resident has that problems are solvable, and the decision to stay rather than move elsewhere are important nonquantitative psychic factors used by residents and investors in evaluating an SMSA's future.

THE GROWTH DERBY

The *Statistical Abstract of the United States* reports on population changes for the 163 SMSAs with estimated populations of more than 200,000.[16] In addition, it reports on the 13 standard consolidated statistical areas (SCSA). Exhibits 4–6 and 4–7, derived from the 1978 edition, show population changes for the latter for the years 1970–1976, the most recent updates. To emphasize the overriding importance of up-to-date market studies, we have chosen to classify these larger metropolitan areas into categories that represent their relative growth potential or decline based on migration. They are labeled (1) *winners,* (2) *gainers,* (3) *laggards,* (4) *losers,* and (5) *also-rans.*

Note that we have avoided rates of growth. Instead, our emphasis is on the actual number of people involved in the migration from one SMSA to another. This is because we feel that amounts are more significant to the real estate investment decision maker than rates of change. In effect, using rates of change could lead one to a small SMSA with a high percentage change when the demand for units of real estate product may in fact be much higher in a slower-growing but larger SMSA. Similar evaluations could be made using other economic indicators, such as changes in employment, new-job formations, or bank deposits.

The questions here are, Why did some SMSAs gain and others lose? Why are some more attractive than others, as measured by levels of migration by people seeking new and better opportunities?

Analyzing the Growth Derby

Too much can be read into migration statistics. First, they do not represent the magnitude of population change. Second, they conceal important intra-SMSA movements. For example, Los Angeles lost 43,000 inhabitants by net migration,

[16] U.S. Department of Commerce, Bureau of the Census, *Statistical Abstract of the United States* (Washington, D.C.: GPO, 1978), pp. 20–22.

EXHIBIT 4–6.   The Growth Derby

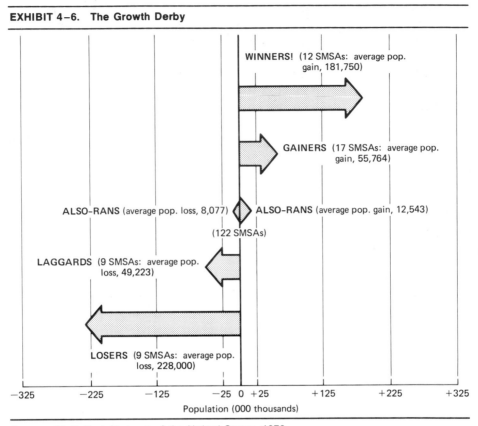

Population (000 thousands)

SOURCE: *Statistical Abstract of the United States, 1978*

but its Anaheim component gained 200,000. Following are comments on each of the categories of the growth derby.

The Winners   The twelve winning SMSAs are, in rank order, Houston, Tampa-St. Petersburg, Anaheim-Santa Ana-Garden Grove, Ft. Lauderdale-Hollywood, San Diego, Phoenix, Miami, Denver-Boulder, Atlanta, West Palm Beach-Boca Raton, Orlando, and Dallas-Fort Worth. In terms of annual demand for real estate, the range was from a high of 47,833 to a low of 17,166 in average population gain per year. In 1976 the range in population for these areas was from 465,000 to 2,611,000. Finally, we observe that five of the SMSAs are in Florida, two in Texas, two in California, and one each in Georgia, Arizona, and Colorado. The dominance of the Sun Belt is apparent. Some of these SMSAs are within SCSAs; therefore, the gain is intraregional.

The Gainers   The sixteen gainers are in rank order: San Jose; Riverside-San Bernardino-Ontario; Tucson; Austin; Sacramento; Portland, Oreg.-Wash.; Nassau and Suffolk Counties, N.Y.; Las Vegas; Oxnard-Simi Valley-Ventura, Calif.; San Antonio; Albuquerque; Daytona Beach; Jacksonville; Raleigh-Durham;

EXHIBIT 4-7. Standard Consolidated Statistical Areas (Alphabetical Order)

		POPULATION (thousands)		
Metropolitan Area	1970	1976	Amount Change	Net Migration, 1970–1976 (+) In; (−) Out
1. Boston-Lawrence-Lowell, Mass.-NH	3,526	3,525	−1	(N/A)
2. Chicago-Gary, Ill.-In.	7,611	7,637	29	−269
3. Cincinnati-Hamilton, Ohio-Ky.-In.	1,611	1,611	−2	−62
4. Cleveland-Akron-Lorain, Ohio	3,000	2,903	−97	−191
5. Detroit-Ann Arbor, Mich.	4,669	4,654	−15	−209
6. Houston-Galveston	2,169	2,611	442	+299
7. Los Angeles-Long Beach-Anaheim, Calif.	9,983	10,466	485	−71
8. Miami-Fort Lauderdale, Fla.	1,888	2,296	408	+382
9. Milwaukee-Racine, Wis.	1,575	1,591	16	−38
10. New York-Newark-Jersey City, NY-NJ-Conn.	17,035	16,638	−397	(N/A)
11. Philadelphia-Wilmington-Trenton, Pa.-Del.-Md.-NJ	5,628	5,639	11	−129
12. San Francisco-Oakland-San Jose, Calif.	4,423	4,648	222	+81
13. Savannah, Ga.	208	212	4	−27
14. Seattle-Tacoma, Wash.	1,837	1,839	−2	−57

SOURCE: U.S. Department of Commerce, Bureau of the Census, *Statistical Abstract of the United States, 1978* (Washington, D.C.: Government Printing Office, 1978), p. 22.

Santa Rosa; and Lakeland-Winter Haven, Fla. Among the gainers, the range of net in-migration was from 6,667 to 14,167 per year on an average annual basis. The Sun Belt still dominates, but the locations are more widely distributed than among the winners.

The Also-Rans For these 122 SMSAs, the net migration statistics were not meaningful for the six-year period. The range of population was from 200,000 for Lubbock, Texas to 2,144,000 for Baltimore. These metro areas are apparently stable, some might say stagnant. Migration statistics say little about these SMSAs as investment opportunities; other indicators should be used.

Some meaningful information may be derived from the regional location of these SMSAs. Grouped by state and classified according to their regional location, it appears that their population distribution is similar to that of the U.S. population as a whole. (See Exhibit 4–8.)

The Laggards The nine SMSAs included in this classification appear to be showing early signs of decline, and out-migration seems to be proceeding at a significant pace. The laggards, in rank order, are Cincinnati, Dayton, Buffalo,

EXHIBIT 4-8.   Distribution of Also-Ran SMSAs by Region and State

New England	No. of SMSAs in State	Middle Atlantic	No. of SMSAs in State	West South Central	No. of SMSAs in State
Maine	1	New York	7	Arkansas	1
New Hampshire	1	New Jersey	4	Louisiana	3
Vermont	0	Pennsylvania	6	Oklahoma	1
Massachusetts	5			Texas	4
Rhode Island	1				
Connecticut	8				
				Mountain	
East North Central		**West North Central**			
				Montana	0
Ohio	8	Minnesota	3	Idaho	0
Indiana	4	Iowa	2	Wyoming	0
Illinois	2	Missouri	0	Colorado	0
Michigan	6	North Dakota	· 0	New Mexico	0
Wisconsin	2	South Dakota	0	Arizona	0
		Nebraska	1	Utah	1
South Atlantic		Kansas	1	Nevada	0
Delaware	1				
Maryland	1				
Washington, D.C.	1			**Pacific**	
Virginia	4	**East South Central**		Washington	1
West Virginia	2			Oregon	2
North Carolina	2	Kentucky	3	California	6
South Carolina	3	Tennessee	5	Alaska	0
Georgia	3	Alabama	3	Hawaii	1
Florida	2	Mississippi	1		

SOURCE: *Statistical Abstract of the United States 1978*

Seattle-Everest, Jersey City, Kansas City, Boston, Milwaukee, Akron, and San Francisco-Oakland. The average annual loss in population ranges from 4,333 to 9,000. These metro areas range in population from 573,000 to 3,158,000. Six of the nine are in the Atlantic and Central regions. Five are SCSAs, an indication that Americans are moving from larger population centers to the SMSAs in the winner, gainer, and also-ran categories, and to a lesser extent to rural areas. Migration statistics cannot be taken at face value, however. Although Seattle-Everest is listed as a laggard, the Boeing turnaround has dramatically changed the picture for this SMSA.

The Losers   Except for St. Louis, the nine losing SMSAs are all components of SCSAs. The extent of their population loss ought to be seen as a national problem of adjustment. Much of the movement to the winning and gaining categories is out of these metro areas, which are in need of both reindustrialization and restructuring of their economic base. In rank order, these areas are New York, Los

Angeles-Long Beach, Chicago, Detroit, Cleveland, Philadelphia, Pittsburgh, Newark, and St. Louis.

New York is a statistical anomaly. Although out-migration goes off the chart at −663,000, actual population loss is considerably less. Nor are more serious problems revealed by these statistics: Chicago, for example, shows an out-migration of −246,000, but its population has actually increased by 18,000 for the period. Children are being born to the poor; the able-bodied are leaving; and the proportion of elderly is rising because of falling death rates. Furthermore, in all such cities the local tax base is declining On the other hand, a substantial part of our national wealth is built into permanent structures in these cities (e.g., the Metropolitan Museum of Art).

These 1970–1976 statistics are expressive of cycles of growth and change in a highly mobile society. Good investment opportunities exist in loser metro areas because many investors avoid them in favor of the winners and gainers. The task of analysis is more difficult, but possibly more rewarding as well.

SUMMARY

Finding the target SMSA is the first step in investment analysis. Investors need to understand the nature of growth and decline in metro areas in order to choose a target for investment analysis. Metropolitan areas compete for jobs, for people, and in the way land is used. While some metro areas may be in a period of rapid growth, others are mature and stable, and still others are in a period of decline.

The process of urban growth and decline may be observed through a study of metro area economic and demographic trends and the indicators of stability, growth, and decline. One must understand the concept of comparative locational advantage and how it affects land use. Population trends also profoundly affect demand for real estate assets. For the near- and long-term future migration statistics can help us analyze the trends of growth and decline, and our "growth derby" pinpoints the SMSAs that are most likely to grow and provide investment opportunities. Our emphasis is on the actual numbers of migrants because amount is more significant to real estate decision makers than rate of change.

An important observation in our growth derby is the clear indication that people do not move solely in pursuit of economic opportunities. The data suggest that Americans are moving from the larger urban agglomerations to medium-sized SMSAs. However, it should also be observed that the population of the New York SCSA exceeds the total population of all the winners. New York is, indeed, still the "big apple." The Chicago and Los Angeles SCSAs are also so large that comparisons with these "big three" are difficult to make.

The next step is to gain a better understanding of the economic base that supports a real estate market. Our strategy has enabled us to select a specific SMSA that appears to provide investment opportunities. In the next two chapters we will show how the economic base of a metro area is analyzed.

5

Market Studies

Real estate development is a function of the availability of money. And the availability of money is a function of the stupidity of those lenders who don't pay any attention to market demand.
—a young Atlanta builder who requested anonymity because he wants to remain in business

Real estate market analysis is an absolutely essential management tool for decision making in the capital-budgeting process of equity real estate investment. Although current tax policy favors investing equity funds in real estate, few real estate investors make good use of market analysis. It is not uncommon to make a market study *after* the decision to buy has been made. But careful market studies and marketability analyses done *prior* to investment are the essential conditions of success in real estate investment: "The process of investing, as contrasted to gambling, presupposes a gathering, forecasting, and structuring of data upon which reasons for conclusions or decisions can be based."[1]

Of course, the investor must keep in mind that any market study is a forecast of an uncertain future based on past trend data. In interpreting such information the investor must recognize the limitations of the data as well as the sometimes loose interrelationships among the factors studied. Real estate market analysis should be based on a probabilistic rather than a deterministic approach.

[1] Robert J. Wiley, *Real Estate Investment Analysis and Strategy* (New York: Ronald Press, 1977), p. 3.

Real estate market analysis is a generic term that covers many kinds of technical reports. Generally, these reports use demographic and economic trends to evaluate the present match or mismatch between the existing stock or inventory of facilities, on the one hand, and the demand for their use, on the other. The essential components of any competent real estate market study are the following:

1. A preliminary but careful analysis of national and international economic conditions to determine whether current macroeconomic conditions are favorable, or at least neutral, to entering into a real estate investment.
2. A report on current economic, social, political, and demographic trends in the *region* and in the targeted *metro area*. This is a selective report of economic base data that are relevant to the investment opportunity under consideration.
3. A delineation of the trading area to identify the area in which specified real estate facilities will be competing with one another to satisfy some market demand. This is the *location* of the real estate investment.
4. An analysis of the potential demand for the specified real estate facilities within the trade area.
5. An inventory report on existing competitive uses in the trading area.
6. An *analysis of the potential competition* should be provided to assess the nature of the various real estate products being offered to tenants in the would-be trading area.
7. Where appropriate, a study might then compare the target parcels with other parcels within the trading area to see whether or not it is likely that the gross possible rent schedules would be produced by the parcel under analysis.

As Dasso and Graaskamp have stated, market analysis applies to three types of situations: (1) a site or property looking for an appropriate use, (2) a use looking for an appropriate site or property that will provide certain types of improvements to capture the projected income stream, and (3) an investor looking for the best property opportunity available to him or her, given the goal objectives and risk/return constraints.

Our underlying bias is that the individual investor must cope with the constraints of time and budget limits in carrying out this critical function. Thus, we emphasize the use of existing published reports, secondary data, and professional real estate market analysts. The following discussion is intended to provide the small investor with a sufficient understanding of how to perform market studies and marketability analyses for his or her own purposes (or how to evaluate such studies when performed by professional analysts). Where appropriate, discussion of how to use statistical analyses or do consumer surveys will be covered in Part IV of this book.

Professional real estate market analysts tend to be specialists, for example, in the retail trade, the motel/hotel industry, industrial space needs, multifamily rentals, or single-family subdivisions. Because real estate is so heterogeneous and the markets so highly stratified, the analyst should be thoroughly knowledgeable about the urban area chosen by the investor and market conditions in the competitive trading area.

A number of factors influence the nature, scope, and intensity of market analyses. For example, is the development an existing one or a proposed one? Existing developments already have an identifiable occupancy level and a rent-paying capacity that will cover (or not cover) the debt service. On the other hand, a proposed development involves projecting and analyzing future demand. User profiles, competitive forces, site conditions, and so on must all be identified and analyzed. Another factor influencing the scope and depth of the market analysis is the size of the investment opportunity. Obviously, the expenditure allocated for a multimillion-dollar project is vastly larger than would be appropriate for a $100,000 investment. Finally, there is a great deal of difference between a preliminary analysis to start negotiations and a detailed market and feasibility analysis conducted after a basic meeting of minds has been reached with the seller.

REAL ESTATE MARKETS

A real estate market is an imperfect competitive model. In simple terms, a real estate market is the composite of negotiations between buyers and sellers (including lessors and lessees), who communicate with one another to acquire or dispose of individual real estate products that, by their nature, are in some degree of competition with each other. Real estate markets operate through the scattered transactions of owners, brokers, and users; their activities have no organized focus. Instead, unequally informed participants engage in a series of negotiations aimed at bringing about real estate transactions.

Location

Everyone seems to know that *location, location, location* is the essence of successful real estate investment. Unfortunately, many equity investors and lenders do not fully comprehend the meaning of this homily.

For the equity investor, a *location* is defined as the available site, which the negotiation process has selected from alternative parcels offered by the marketplace, that is most likely to achieve the buyer's minimum acceptable rate of return, given the buyer's stated assumptions regarding limits on available equity capital, financing terms, tax-planning considerations, ownership cycles, managerial skills, liquidity preferences, and personal, nonpecuniary psychic objectives.

While all real estate locations may be considered to be available for purchase if the price is right, at any point in time real estate markets deal only with a small fraction of the total supply of different types of land uses that are, in a sense, in production. Not more than 5 or 6 percent of residential locations, for example, are actively offered for sale in any given year. Also, although real estate brokers frequently find it possible to sell *comparable* types of property, a piece of real estate is never standardized in the sense that an automobile, a typewriter, or a can opener is. Brokers can't quote real estate prices fob point of production origin.

The real estate market is also very limited geographically. Real estate products are locations that must be sold where they are found, and unlike many commodities, new real estate products are the exception rather than the rule. Most of the sites that are capable of producing a rent schedule have benefited from some development work by previous owners. The location may even have passed through a succession of land uses—from grazing to crop production to mining, industrial, commercial, or residential use. The average residential property that is placed on the market is a second-, third-, or even fourth-hand structure that has been occupied by a succession of owners. Although new development may result when a location is converted to a higher and better use, the typical location on the market is a used product.

The Trading Markets

The competitive forces affecting the value of a particular type of real estate delineate the competitive market area. Investment locations may be regarded as links in a chain of substitutability. Thus, the market may be thought of as consisting of clusters of substitutes that are cross-linked in complex patterns related to buyer—seller behavior.

The lack of geographic focus and the absence of an organized exchange have caused some confusion in the minds of real estate investors as to the nature of real estate markets. To clarify this matter, we will draw a distinction between trading markets, where prices are established and actual real estate transactions take place, and real estate locations, where gross possible rents are generated, land use is determined, and, as a result, available space contracts or expands through changing conditions.

Understanding the nature of the trading market for real estate products helps us identify and find buyers and sellers. Trading markets are concerned only with carrying out the transaction; they are not concerned with the quality of the product, which is a result of the interaction of supply and demand for the actual use of space.

It is useful to classify the real estate trading markets as national, regional, and local in nature. Although there is considerable overlap at the margins of these markets, these categories enable us to identify the likely buyers and sellers for a particular transaction. More important, characterizing the market for a property as national, regional, or local helps to identify the kind of lender or investor who would be likely to assist in the transaction.

National/International Markets   These consist of high-rise office buildings, industrial parks, large luxury apartment complexes, warehouse parks, recreational complexes, regional shopping centers, flagship hotels, and nationally franchised motels. The potential lenders are large institutions such as transnational banks, mortgage bankers, life insurance companies, REITs, foundations, pension funds, and savings and loan associations.

Regional Markets   These include community and neighborhood shopping centers, medium-rise office buildings, industrial buildings, professional buildings, fast-food franchises, smaller garden apartment complexes (fewer than 100 units), many warehouse projects, free-standing commercial buildings and others. The potential lenders are regional institutions such as banks, savings and loan associations, and pension funds.

Local Markets These markets offer small, low-rise apartment buildings, small professional and commercial office buildings, free-standing retail locations and older areas, rehabilitation projects, and others. The potential lenders are purchase money mortgagees, second mortgagees, and local banks and savings and loan associations that are knowledgeable in the specific area. In international markets buyers and sellers may come from virtually anywhere in the world by phone, letter, or airplane. At the other extreme, the local market for a small low-rise apartment building caters to the few buyers and sellers who are knowledgeable about neighborhood conditions and the prospects for loan commitments.

WHAT IS A MARKET STUDY?

A real estate market study is a form of *macro* market analysis. Fundamentally, a market study involves the projection and analysis of the determinants of demand. Market analysis is demand oriented; it is concerned with the existing economic base of a specified market area (region, SMSA, or urban area); its future; and the potential for new, rehabilitated, or converted units of use in that area. It is important to note that, although a market study is demand oriented, it would be meaningless to project demand without making some provision for matching these projections with supply, taking into consideration current or potential changes in the inventory, or stock, of available real estate units. Determination of supply is essentially an inventory process that is carried out by planning agencies, departments of labor and industry, local assessors, or consultants.

The extent to which demand exceeds supply can provide insight into the opportunities for development, rehabilitation, or conversion in terms of type, size, and appropriate timing. This, however, is an aspect of marketability analysis, which will be discussed in the next chapter.

A study of all supply and demand indicators is invaluable in analyzing rent levels, probable absorption rates, occupancy levels, and, to some extent, the potential appreciation or depreciation of a property over its ownership cycle. The *supply* of real estate product is influenced by the availability of competing sites and land costs, the existing inventory of competing projects, demolitions and building permits, the volume of new construction, plans for comparable projects, building costs, and the availability of financing. The *demand* for real estate is found by gathering data on sales volume and rents, vacancies and turnover, and consumer preferences and real estate prices. Careful consideration should be given to the need for expansion demand and replacement demand, that is, whether there is demand for new facilities or whether there is continued demand for the use of existing facilities.

A market study is a review of aggregated data. Aggregated data, regardless of source, usually must be broken down or reduced to more usable units in order to measure the effective change within the broader category. For example, aggregated employment data may be further refined by type of industry (basic or nonbasic) or by relating historic and projected levels of employment in the area under study to national and state averages.

A market study is not merely a set of economic projections and ratio analyses but also uses the planner's art of evaluating the ability of a metropolitan area to cope with its problems of growth and decline. Investors cannot assume that political, legal, sociological, and physical forces will remain unchanged. Growth potential cannot be projected from analyses that are limited to economic activities. By its nature, investment in real estate is long term and illiquid, and reversals of trends in a neighborhood can prove disastrous to an unwary buyer—or highly profitable to a more careful one. Investors need to know what the metro area's priorities are. Where it stands on growth issues and zoning? What kind of capital improvement program it has?

The ideal macromarket analysis not only generates a basic fund of information about the urban economy but also examines how the area intends to attack and solve its local problems. It asks what decisions the area has made in order to achieve orderly growth.

ECONOMIC BASE ANALYSIS

An essential part of any market study is the economic base analysis. Demand analysis for an SMSA and sector (market share) analysis cannot be made without a study of the metropolitan area as a functioning economic unit.

The economic base of a metropolitan area consists of the activities that provide the basic and nonbasic employment for income on which the rest of the local economy depends. The primary focus of an economic base analysis is on employment and income-generating activities. Basic activities are those that produce goods or services for export outside the urban area. Nonbasic activities are primarily supportive in nature. Theoretically, nonbasic activities would not be there except that they are associated with the basic activities. Thus, economic base technique is simply a multiplier approach to urban economic and population relationships.

The primary objective of an economic base study is to develop a fund of information that will provide a factual basis for an attempt to measure the economic potential for future growth as related to past trends. It is hoped that economic base techniques will provide the user with an understanding of the sources and levels of employment and income in the SMSA. These data will improve the user's ability to evaluate the area's stability and risk factors. Unfortunately, many economic base forecasts merely extrapolate the past into the future; such studies are of doubtful value to a metropolitan area that is subject to eventful change.

At a minimum, economic base analysis should delineate the market area and classify economic activity into basic and nonbasic activities. It should then project the economic trends along with appropriate ratio analyses. A full-fledged market study will also provide an inventory of land uses, determine the physical capabilities of targeted sites, and mention jurisdictional limitations, political climate, conditions in the local capital markets, and the degree of community organization. This should be coupled with interpretative commentary on the metropolitan area's ability to achieve the implicit economic potential set forth in the economic base projections.

Although critics have successfully attacked the validity of the techniques used, economic base analysis is still the best available tool for short-run forecasts.[2]

Economic Base Ratio Analysis

Economic base ratio analysis assumes that, having identified the export base segment of the delineated SMSA, one can then quantify, by some appropriate standard of measure, the contribution of that basic activity to the urban economy. That is, it assumes that a ratio, or economic base multiplier, can be drawn between total base operations (e.g., total local sales dollars or employment) and the service sector of the economy. In this way one can calculate not only the growth trends of basic employment but also the trend of growth in the service sector of the SMSA. For example, after determining the ratio between basic and nonbasic employment, the analyst can calculate the ratio of total employment to total population to project population trends.

The usefulness of such projections depends largely on the skill and judgment of the analyst, for the trends are subjective rather than objective. A full-fledged economic base analysis done, for example, for a large-scale development such as a satellite new town would require the market analyst to interview employers in the basic and nonbasic industries and then make a judgmental estimate—taking into account past trends—of the probable future number of employees in order to forecast population trends.

After calculating the growth trends for basic and nonbasic employment, one can proceed to other useful ratio analyses to estimate future population trends and the potential demand for various types of land use. These calculations are essential for estimating market absorption rates.

Demand Indicators for Urban Space Use

In the absence of better data one can use population and employment estimates for SMSAs to make other useful market demand estimates:

1. *Total employment* for the metropolitan area at the end of the forecast period can be estimated by applying the ratio of basic employment to total employment *now existing.* Then, by adjusting this ratio for expected changes and conditions and using some selected percentage rate of growth based on information about basic employment in the area over the forecast period, this derived ratio of future basic employment can be used to arrive at the trend line of total future employment.
2. The *future population* of the entire metropolitan area may be estimated by applying the percentage of employment to the population that prevails in

---

[2] Ralph Pfouts, *Techniques of Urban Land Analysis* (Chandler-Davis, 1962). This is a classic compendium of articles on economic base analysis techniques, which have not been improved in recent years.

the base year and then using the selected percentage rate of growth for the forecast period.

3. The *potential need for housing* is estimated by dividing the estimated total population increase by the projected average family size, taking into account, of course, adjustments for trends in fertility, birthrates, in-migration, and so forth.

4. To *estimate the growth of any segment of the metropolitan area,* one should allocate a percentage of the total growth to that particular geographic segment on the basis of new highways, new sewer and water extensions, new industries, vacant lands that may be available for residential use, and expected rates of growth in that area. The probability of the projected use for the area will affect the estimates.

5. To calculate the *amount of land needed for new housing and retail service growth,* one would estimate the number of people to be added through population growth. This item would be separated into the need for ownership versus rental housing and, finally, into subclassifications such as apartments, row houses, detached single-family homes, and small estates. From this, one can estimate the land areas that would be necessary for each of the required types of residences.

    One can estimate the amount of land required for a new retail service center by calculating the square feet of floor area required for each type of store. This is done by estimating the volume of sales created by the buying power of the additional population in the trading area and allowing a 4-to-1 ratio between the parking and selling areas.

6. The *amount of industrial space* required for the new growth can be estimated by ascertaining the amount of factory and yard space required for each employee in each of the specified types of industry. On the basis of the total increase in employment expected in each industry, one can then multiply the average number of employees per industry by the average space now used by each employee in modern factories, warehouses, assembly areas, and other productive facilities, along with parking requirements.

Since jobs plus people result in land use, what we have done is to convert employment and population growth into gross crude indicators of the overall demand for land use in the appropriate residential, retail, and industrial categories.

The quality and usefulness of market studies depends largely on the skill and expertise of the person who produces the study. The gross indicators set forth in the preceding list can be used by investors to spot-audit the estimates made by the market study. Failure to synchronize expansion of urban land use and replacement of worn-out stock with actual population growth has resulted in serious local real estate depressions. Some foreclosures and bankruptcies can be attributed in part to the unwarranted enthusiasm of the population projections made in market studies done for developers and public agencies. Since investors must use secondary data and market studies prepared by and for others, they should treat them with a healthy skepticism and do some preliminary analysis before accepting the forecasts.

Classification Problems

In classifying the local metropolitan economy into its basic export sector and its nonbasic residual or service sector, we prefer market studies in which the structural parts have been formalized into the standard industrial classifications (SIC) defined by the Bureau of the Census. This will enable the investor to compare SMSAs and evaluate their potential. In the SIC system the economic activity is first classified as agriculture, mining, construction, manufacturing, transportation, wholesale and retail trade, finance, services, or government. Each of the divisions is broken down into major groups, which are assigned standard industrial classification numbers. Exhibit 5–1 is a table of the groupings with their SIC numbers. The two-digit designations of the major groups are broken down step by step to the four-digit level. Each successive digit represents a deeper level of specialization within the group. When employment and sales data are classified by SIC numbers, investors can compare rates of change from one metropolitan area to another. Unfortunately, in these federal economic projections there is a strong bias toward import and export products based on manufacturing, agriculture, mining, and other extractive industries. When one realizes that over 50 percent of employment is in the service sector, one can understand the need to extend the analysis to the subclassifications of the SIC. Obviously, basic activities encompass both the production of goods and the provision of services to users outside the metropolitan area; thus, both an automobile manufacturer and a state capital complex are basic producers. Another reason for preferring market studies that use SIC codes is that the Bureau of Economic Analysis publishes economic projections, called OBERS reports, that project personal income, business earnings, and employment for the entire nation, for 173 BEA economic areas, for water resource regions, for states, for all SMSAs, and for other significant areas. These reports break down their data according to SIC groups.

Problems of Area Delineation

As is true of many other social studies, economic base analysis has difficulty establishing the geographic limits of the economic base. For convenience, market analysts choose SMSAs because of their rich statistical base. However, such geographic limits are not necessarily realistic.

Another method of market area delineation that can be used is the *labor market area* delineated by the U.S. Department of Labor. This concept relies heavily on transportation facilities and commuting time limits. A labor market is defined as an area with an average radius from the center of the market area of 30 to 40 miles, and with a maximum travel time limit of about 90 minutes.

A third possibility is primary–secondary–tertiary retail trading areas. These are defined by the U.S. Census of Business. Data are available from any federal or regional Department of Commerce office and are usually on file at the local area's regional planning commission. Some state departments of community affairs provide reports on population and employment trends for economic development areas within the state that can be quite useful. In any event, great care must be taken to evaluate the acceptability of the method of delineating the market area.

EXHIBIT 5-1. Industrial Groupings with Standard Industrial Classification Codes

All-Industry Total	SIC Code No.
Agriculture, forestry, and fisheries:	
Agriculture	01, 07
Forestry and fisheries	08, 09
Mining:	
Metal	10
Coal	11, 12
Crude petroleum and natural gas	13
Nonmetallic, except fuels	14
Contract construction	15–17
Manufacturing:	
Food and kindred products	20
Textile mill products	22
Apparel and other fabric products	23
Lumber products and furniture	24, 25
Paper and allied products	26
Printing and publishing	27
Chemicals and allied products	28
Petroleum refining	29
Primary metals	33
Fabricated metals and ordnance	34, 19
Machinery, excluding electrical	35
Electrical, machinery and supplies	36
Motor vehicles and equipment	371
Transportation equipment, excluding motor vehicles	37, except 371
Other manufacturing	21, 30–32, 38, 39
Transportation, communications, and public utilities	
Railroad transportation	40
Trucking and warehousing	42
Other transportation and services	41, 44, 47
Communications	48
Utilities (electric, gas, sanitary)	49
Wholesale and retail trade	50, 52–57, 59
Finance, insurance, and real estate	60–67
Services:	
Lodging places and personal services	70, 72
Business and repair services	73, 75, 76
Amusement and recreation services	78, 79
Private households	88
Professional services	80, 81, 82, 84, 86, 89
Government:	
Civilian government:	
Federal government	91, except fed. military
State and local government	92, 93
Armed forces	part of 91

SOURCE: Executive Office of the President, Bureau of the Budget, *Standard Industrial Classification Manual* (Washington, D.C.: G.P.O., 1967).

The Need for Realistic Population Projections

As indicated in Chapter 4, the Census Bureau periodically publishes several national population projections that reflect current population and birthrates, assumed birth and death rates, and levels of international migration. The OBERS projections discussed here are based on the Bureau's series E projections, which assume a birthrate that will eventually result in no further population growth except for migration, and projects a population of 264,430,000 in the year 2000.[3]

In our opinion the series E assumptions used by OBERS are higher than the figures that will probably result if the high rates of inflation experienced in the 1970s continue. In that event, we believe that OBERS projections should be based on a series that projects a national population of about 245 million.[4]

It should be clear that the underlying assumptions concerning population projections have a critical effect on market absorption rates for urban land use. We think the OBERS projections should be based on three alternatives. The first is the series D projection (285 million), which would be treated as "optimistic." The second is the series E projections (264,430,000), which would be described as "most likely." The third is a series F population projection (240 million), which could be labeled "pessimistic." This would enable planners, lenders, government agencies, and investors to have relatively high-quality data on which to base their own judgments about the future.

The OBERS projections should in no way restrict regional planners from full consideration of alternative rates and patterns of economic growth. Indeed, the maximum usefulness of the baseline projections will be achieved only with careful study of alternative sets of projections. Of course, such projections ought to be based on realistic attitudes. Some regional real estate market studies use population projections that are a product of the rich imagination of community boosters seeking to realize self-fulfilling prophecies.

In summary, the methods used in real estate market studies are mature. The problem—a very real one—is to find forecasts that are realistic and not motivated by ulterior objectives. In the long run, it is hoped that those who are interested in rational real estate investment decision making will press for more thorough OBERS projections and encourage the regional development agencies to be more realistic. In the meantime, we must live with the over- or underbuilding that results when developers fail to perceive actual rates of growth. A good market study using realistic assumptions can be worth substantially more than the 1 percent of project costs that might be incurred in obtaining the information.

A Checklist for Metro Market Economic Base Analysis

So far our discussion of real estate market studies has emphasized the economic and demographic components of demand. In addition, one must consider physical, social, legal, and political elements. Exhibit 5−2 is a checklist for a metro

---

[3] Census Bureau Report no. P-25, December 1972 (Washington, D.C.: GPO)
[4] The Census Bureau's population reports and OBERS projections for the area under consideration are generally available from the regional offices of the Department of Commerce.

EXHIBIT 5-2. A Checklist for Metro Market Economic Base Analysis

INTRODUCTORY INFORMATION
  History
  Climate, geography, geology
  General factors

EXISTING LAND USE MAP
  Commercial, industrial, residential
  Boundaries
  Comments on existing conditions (blight, deterioration)

POPULATION STATISTICS AND TRENDS
  Total
  Households (size, number)
  Sex ratio, fertility ratio
  Age distribution
  Income distribution (per capita, per household)
  Trends; compare SMSA, state, national
  Comments and evaluation

EMPLOYMENT STATISTICS
  Male, female
  Skills
  Ratio (manufacturing, commercial, service)
  Compensation levels for subclasses
  Unemployment (structural, seasonal)
  Comparison of employment levels, trends
  Comments and evaluation

ECONOMIC TRENDS
  Basic (primary)—classification, description, available statistics (sales)
  Basic (secondary)—classification, description, available statistics (sales)
  Nonbasic (tertiary)—classification, description, available statistics (sales); retail
    sales per capita; subclasses
  Trends of sales and payroll statistics for each SIC classification
  Trends; compare SMSA, state, national
  Comments and evaluation

COMMUNITY FACILITIES ANALYSIS
  Hospitals
  Water, sewage, utilities (adequacy, age)
  Fire, police (adequacy, age)
  Schools (adequacy, age)
  Recreational: parks, libraries, cultural, other
  Comments and evaluation; compare SMSA, state, national
  Traffic patterns
  Parking facilities
  Streets
  Lighting
  Refuse collection
  Comments and evaluation

(continued)

EXHIBIT 5-2. *(Continued)*

TAX BASE STATISTICS AND TRENDS
  Assessed valuation
  Other taxes
  Capital improvement program indebtedness
  Revenues/expenditures
  Comments and evaluation

POLITICS AND JURISDICTIONAL LIMITATIONS
  Urban economy vs. political boundaries
  Stability of government (responsiveness to need, technical competence of
    officials, capacity and willingness to carry out plans)
  Comments and evaluation

COMMUNITY ORGANIZATION
  Degree, quality, scope of community organization
  Nature of civic organization (degree of awareness of problems, ability to mobilize,
    apathy)
  Comments and evaluation

SOURCE ATTRIBUTION (this relates to the credibility of the report)
  Adequacy

FORMAT, STYLE, APPEARANCE OF ACTUAL REPORT
  Superior, excellent, good, fair, poor

Note: City planning departments, councils of government, regional and state planning
agencies, etc., provide information on these subjects at very low cost. It is the user's task
to evaluate the quality and reliability of such reports. *Caveat emptor.*

market economic base analysis. It should serve as a useful review of all the
components of a competent market study of the economic and demographic
characteristics of an SMSA.

CASE STUDY

Using Economic Base Analysis to Forecast Growth in Atlanta, Georgia

To be useful for investors, market studies must be based on reliable statistical data.
The Atlanta SMSA, which is one of the winners in the Growth Derby set forth in 4,
provides an interesting case for examining the reliability of reports available from
others.

Atlanta showed a net migration of 115,000 for the 1970–1976 period, yet it
is also generally known that the Atlanta region suffered one of the worst real estate
depressions in the country at the time of the 1973–1974 energy crisis. One
reason for the great deflation in real estate assets in the Atlanta region during that
period was that market absorption rates were exceeded by construction in almost
every conceivable category of land use development. There is good reason to

believe that during the 1975–2000 period the economy of the Atlanta SMSA will continue to grow at a relatively rapid rate. However, there is considerable controversy, even litigation, surrounding the reasonableness of the projected rates of growth.

Exhibit 5–3 is an OBERS projection for the Atlanta region for the years 1950–2020. The Atlanta Regional Commission (ARC) used the same series E projections as the Bureau of Economic Analysis. However, the ARC made a significant departure from OBERS in estimating the Atlanta SMSA population for the year 2000. OBERS forecasts a population of 2,465,300, while ARC believes 3.5 million people will reside in the area. Obviously, there are significant differences in the resulting projections for employment; OBERS projects 400,000 *fewer* new jobs in the Atlanta region over the next twenty years than ARC does.

The real estate investor is forced to make a choice between these widely differing opinions about the growth possibilities of the Atlanta SMSA. Since real estate investment should be a risk-aversion process, with due consideration for risk management principles, the conservative approach would be to simply accept the OBERS projections. Those who take such a position might well argue that the ARC is forecasting enthusiastic gains in population and jobs in order to maximize federal and state grants for public facilities like sewers, water, and transportation. However, as with most other social sciences, this would be a simplistic approach. Further study is necessary, and we must look to the underlying assumptions of the ARC and OBERS projections.

The Atlanta SMSA represents a relatively new kind of postindustrial city. The OBERS projections are built around an economic base theory that emphasizes manufacturing, mining, agriculture, and the extractive industries. Although Atlanta is not viewed nationally as a manufacturing center, manufacturing is an important activity in the region. In fact, Atlanta is the largest manufacturing employment center in the Southeast. Manufacturing is projected to receive the largest numerical share of employment in the region, with 290,900 jobs by the end of the century.

While a substantial amount of growth is anticipated in manufacturing employment, this industry group is not expected to grow at a very high rate. In fact, two components, transportation equipment and textiles, are forecast to show declines over the period. The obscure outlook for the local aircraft industry (Lockheed) clouds the future of the transportation equipment sector, and new technology is expected to take its toll on the oldest employer in the Southeast: textiles. Thus, manufacturing will continue to decline in relative importance, and will decline at a faster rate in the Atlanta region than in the nation as a whole.

When compared with national and southeastern profiles, the industrial mix of the Atlanta SMSA will continue to be dominated by wholesale trade, followed, in order, by transportation/communication/utilities and financing/insurance/real estate. Since Atlanta is not only a state capital but also a regional capital in the federal bureaucratic system, government employment also constitutes an important part of its total employment. Finally, services are a more significant part of the total employment picture of the Atlanta SMSA than is true of many other regions studied by OBERS.

EXHIBIT 5-3. Population, Employment, Personal Income, and Earnings by Industry for the Atlanta SMSA, Historical and Projected, Selected Years, 1950-2020

	1950	1970	1980	1985	2000	2020
Population, midyear	729,821	1,393,929	1,690,800	1,887,700	2,465,300	3,119,800
Per capita income (1967 $)	2,185	3,816	5,100	5,800	8,500	13,500
Per capita income, relative (U.S. = 1.00)	1.06	1.10	1.08	1.07	1.04	1.02
Total employment	296,071	596,990	808,700	895,900	1,178,600	1,433,500
Employment/population ratio		.43	.48	.47	.48	.46
			In Thousands of 1967 Dollars			
Total personal income	1,594,708	5,319,106	8,719,900	10,965,900	21,013,800	42,192,600
Total earnings	1,349,771	4,803,628	7,852,700	9,747,100	18,033,600	35,138,500
Agriculture, forestry, and fisheries	15,881[a]	6,899[a]	8,600	8,600	9,500	11,900
Agriculture			8,100	8,100	8,900	11,100
Forestry and fisheries			(S)	(S)	(S)	(S)
Mining	[b]	3,919[b]	7,700	8,500	11,700	16,700
Metal			(S)	(S)	(S)	(S)
Coal						
Crude petroleum and natural gas			(S)	(S)	(S)	(S)
Nonmetallic, except fuels			7,000	7,700	10,600	15,200
Contract construction	96,468	280,693	502,400	611,400	1,058,300	1,880,700
Manufacturing	254,919	988,225	1,453,500	1,739,100	2,870,800	4,923,300
Food and kindred products			145,000	160,800	215,200	300,000
Textile and mill products			39,700	43,600	57,800	80,900
Apparel and other fabric products			62,500	72,500	109,600	170,900
Lumber products and furniture			51,800	58,400	83,300	126,400
Paper and allied products			76,800	90,600	145,400	243,300
Printing and publishing			125,400	155,400	279,600	506,800
Chemicals and allied products			83,400	106,800	211,000	422,100
Petroleum refining			3,700	4,800	9,100	16,500
Primary metals			28,800	31,900	42,000	56,900
Fabricated metals and ordnance			86,100	107,300	194,100	354,100
Machinery, excluding electrical			63,900	77,200	128,800	219,100
Electrical machinery and supplies			65,100	86,700	186,500	396,300
Motor vehicles and equipment			235,200	286,700	496,700	882,200
Transportation equip., excl. mtr. vehs.			259,900	293,400	409,200	592,600
Other manufacturing			125,400	159,700	301,800	554,500
Trans., comm., and public utilities	167,898	559,949	956,800	1,180,400	2,128,800	3,985,900
Railroad transportation			42,400	43,600	44,900	43,200
Trucking and warehousing			248,900	310,200	574,700	1,095,600
Other transportation and services			367,400	447,500	770,300	1,357,100
Communications			199,300	256,900	525,100	1,103,800
Utilities (elec., gas, sanitary)			98,600	121,000	213,500	385,900
Wholesale and retail trade	360,648	1,163,986	1,856,900	2,242,800	3,878,100	6,970,300
Finance, insurance, and real estate	91,691	367,700	657,800	837,600	1,693,300	3,688,100
Services	184,065	723,834	1,339,800	1,760,900	3,785,100	8,411,300
Lodging places and personal services			115,900	132,900	195,200	296,800
Business and repair services			307,200	409,800	912,500	2,056,900
Amusement and recreation services			43,100	53,100	94,000	168,500
Private households			57,100	60,100	69,200	82,400
Professional services			816,200	1,101,500	2,514,000	5,806,500
Government	175,959	705,271	1,068,800	1,351,400	2,597,600	5,249,900
Federal government	89,326	265,514	373,400	462,300	825,100	1,629,100
State and local government	62,256	375,067	645,600	832,900	1,694,900	3,498,300
Armed forces	24,377	64,693	49,700	55,500	77,500	122,300

a—represents 80.0 to 99.9 percent of the true value.   b—represents zero to 19.9 percent of the true value.
SOURCE: U.S. Department of Commerce, Bureau of Economic Analysis (BEA), Regional Economic Analysis Division, *OBERS Projections for SMSAs,* 1972-E projections (Washington, D.C., G.P.O.).

One might seek to justify the difference between the ARC and OBERS projections as a difference in the underlying assumption regarding the nature of the industrial mix. However, this does not account for the extraordinary difference between the population projections produced by these two important public agencies. To a risk-averse equity investor, such discrepancies can have a substantial impact on the return/risk trade-off.

ARC may be seeking to maximize its state and federal grants by way of its forecast. Conversely, OBERS may be serving the federal Office of Management and Budget by seeking to minimize federal grants to SMSAs. Unfortunately, the real estate investor seeking data in this controversial and contradictory atmosphere may feel that no reliable estimate can be made. However, one should keep in mind that the investor's problem is in the short- or medium-term, with a time horizon of perhaps three to ten years. During that time both sets of projections can be more reasonably evaluated.

It appears that in the case of Atlanta, population and employment are falling short of ARC's predictions. The annual increase in Atlanta's population in 1979 was approximately 38,000, which lends little credence to ARC's 1980 forecast of 55,430. The OBERS projections would seem to be much more useful. In any case, great care must be taken by an investor to find some basis of agreement between his or her own judgment and the underlying assumptions of the projections in the studies selected for use.

MARKET STUDIES—A DESCRIPTIVE ANALYSIS[5]

While an economic base analysis will provide reasonable estimates of the rate of growth or decline of a metropolitan area, the market must then be stratified to identify the zones in which a certain kind of real estate venture is likely to be successful. Such a market study ought to be conducted by an experienced analyst. Our purpose here is to provide a description of such a study in order to enable the investor to evaluate both the analyst and the report.

Since the investor's budget is often quite limited, market studies should be done either for a specified use or for a set of alternative sites. The major phases of a typical real estate market study follow. They can be expanded and contracted, depending on the availability of data and the size and type of decision being made.[6]

1. Market area delineation
2. Economic base analysis abstract
3. Supply and demand analysis for a specified use
4. Report and interpretative analysis of current market conditions
5. Projections of future rent schedules, prices, and space needs
6. Summary of salient facts and conclusions

[5] See Anthony Downs, "Characteristics of Various Economic Studies," *The Appraisal Journal,* July 1966, p. 336. The definitions of market study and marketability analysis were adapted from Stephen D. Messner, Bryl N. Boyce, Harold G. Trimble, and Robert L. Ward, *Analyzing Real Estate Opportunities* (Chicago: National Association of Realtors, 1977), pp. 40–43.
[6] See John B. Bailey, "Market Analysis," *The Appraisal Journal,* October 1972, pp. 644–649, and J. B. Bailey, P. F. Spies, and M. K. Weitzman, "Market Study + Financial Analysis = Feasibility Report" *The Appraisal Journal,* October 1977, pp. 550–577.

Market Area Delineation

For a market study, the key objective in market area delineation is to identify all the competitive geographic areas that will affect rent levels, vacancies, and prices, and effectively represent alternative sites for the users of the prospective investment. The difficulty of the problem centers on the fact that market area locations are influenced not only by economic elements but also by physical, social, and legal constraints.

The geographic zones that are appropriate for investment are affected by the journey to work and access to essential community facilities. Consumer preference patterns may tend to produce social and economic groupings in certain areas of the SMSA. Unfortunately, racial discrimination may result in dual markets for housing, with separation of groups representing the same economic and social class. In stratified housing markets competitive forces may operate to establish widely separated neighborhoods that are more or less equidistant from a major place of work. On the other hand, the market study area for a retail service use, such as a grocery, drug, or apparel store, might well be limited to a specific trade area or neighborhood. The use of thematic maps developed by urban geographers, as well as analyses by organizations like CACI, Inc., will be discussed in greater detail in the chapter on marketability analysis that follows.

Economic Base Analysis Abstract

When doing economic base analysis, OBERS projections should be used for population, employment, personal income, and earnings for the metro area. However, the investor should expect more than a mere copy of primary data produced by others. Instead, this section of the market study should provide an abstract of the data that are pertinent to the specific use or investment contemplated. It requires skill and judgment to select from the mass of data on the metro area's economic base only that which is relevant to the projected real estate product. For example, in industrial uses there is more concern about the adequacy and availability of water, electricity, and gas, and the rates for these utilities. On the other hand, hotels and motels may be quite concerned about crime rates, frequency of air travel schedules, and the nature and quality of local public transportation. In effect, the abstract of the economic base analysis should focus on the economic, legal, social, and physical factors in the market area that constitute services that are necessary to maximize the rent-producing capacity of the defined geographic area.

Supply and Demand Analysis for a Specified Use

Different real estate products tend to have unique sets of determinants of supply and demand. This brief discussion will outline the basic supply and demand determinants. Chapters 18–24 provide a more detailed discussion for a variety of important real estate products.

The primary determinant of *supply* is the existing inventory of space for a given use. Often the existing inventory stock is assumed to be equal to the inventory stock as defined in the last decennial census, modified by additions (based on building permits) minus removals (based on demolition permits). Unfortunately, in reality the quality of the building and demolition permit data is generally so poor that this primary source should be supplemented with data from the utility companies and local planning commissions.

Real estate markets are highly stratified. Therefore, a careful study of new construction permits should be made in order to identify how competitive forces are responding to the marketplace. Finally, a survey of lenders, utility executives, and city officials should be done in order to discover competitive additions to the inventory for which building permits have not yet been issued.

It is possible that the market absorption rate has already been exceeded by developments that are not yet visible. In the event that the investor is considering establishing a new real estate product, information should be provided on the availability and cost of land, utilities, materials, labor, and the availability and cost of mortgage financing in the area.

The function of supply and demand analysis is to relate the type and amount of economic activity in the delineated market area to the specific type of space or use that is the target of the study. The spending patterns of the area's population provide a means of relating population, income, and land use, and are, therefore, the primary determinant of the demand for most kinds of space use. The market study must analyze and characterize the values, tastes, attitudes, income levels, and other attributes of the population of the market area in order to determine the type of space use that will be demanded.

Current Market Conditions

This section of the report is an extension of the supply and demand analysis for the specified use. The skills of the market analyst are critical because the timing of the investment depends largely on the report's accuracy.

If demand is strong, unsold inventory, rental vacancies, and mortgage defaults should be at a low level. If demand is weak, then the indicators should be pointing in the opposite direction. The ratio of unsold inventory to the stock of space for a specified use is a useful indicator of the market absorption rate. It has been said that vacancies are the equivalent of unsold inventory. This is imprecise. Some vacancies are necessary for normal turnover in income properties. The report should stratify vacancies by rent levels and income classes in order to discover the vacancy level for the appropriate market. Overall vacancy rates for a particular category, such as housing or industrial uses, are inadequate for the real estate investor; the investor needs to know the vacancy level in the target market.

In addition, analyses of the *nature* of the unsold inventory may prove quite helpful in evaluating the values, tastes, and attitudes of would-be users. Poor location is not the only reason for market rejection. Sometimes the developer has built or is maintaining inappropriate improvements.

Current conditions in the mortgage market are also good indicators of the state of health of real estate markets. Usually, a small percentage of mortgages is in default because of death, divorce, or other difficulties of mortgagors. On the other hand, if current market conditions indicate an above-average level of defaults and foreclosures, this is a clear indicator of a market that is in trouble. The report should provide an analysis of the current building cycle and relate it to economic indicators for the region and the nation in order to provide the necessary information for the feasibility research to be done by the investor at a later date.

Projection of Future Rent Schedules, Prices, and Space Needs

Here one should find the long- and short-run analysis of supply and demand converted into projected rent schedules, prices, and space needs. This part of the report should establish the relationship between buying power and the competitive forces seeking to meet the needs of the space user. A key economic indicator that must be derived from the available data is the *market absorption rate*. This is a product of supply and demand analysis, and considers population movements, job formation, and other factors in order to estimate current demand, which is then compared with the standing stock to consider the number of units that will ordinarily become available during the forecast period. In this way the gap between supply and demand can be estimated and one can forecast the rate at which the market is likely to absorb any additional space—or the vacancy rate in the submarket in question.

The Census Bureau provides periodic reports on market absorption rates for sales and rental housing in most SMSAs, but the rate they supply is an aggregated gross rate, which is not very useful for a decision maker who is concerned with a targeted submarket.

Generally, the market absorption rate is stated in units per month (seasonally adjusted), or sometimes in units per year. For example, in 1974 condominiums appeared to be a good buy in Atlanta on the basis of gross rent multipliers, sales price per square foot, and similar indicators of comparability. However, a real estate market analysis would have reported the following:

1. New-household formations in the Atlanta SMSA, based on in-migration, population increases, and other factors, had slowed to about 18,000 households per year.
2. Though national averages indicated that about 10– 20 percent of the new-housing market would constitute a demand for condominium living, in recent years the demand for condominiums in the Atlanta area had been only about 6– 8 percent. Therefore, it seemed reasonable to expect demand for condominiums (in *all* price ranges and sizes) to be about 1080– 1450 units annually.
3. A recent survey of building permits, building starts, plans of developers, loan commitments, and vacant standing stock indicated that by the end of 1974 the vacant condominiums available for sale (*ignoring* turnover of presold units!) would be between 6000 and 7000 units in all sales and size ranges.
4. Therefore, using the optimistic annual market absorption rate of 1450 condominium units, the indication is that the lenders and developers had exceeded demand by four to five years. (Although it would be possible to calculate a more precise rate, uncertainty about the future compels us to

use the more judgmental market absorption rate of four to five years.) In any event, the overbuilding that had already occurred was certain to depress gross rent multipliers, square foot selling prices, and market values as owners desperately worked themselves out of this excess construction. Even superior locations and particularly well-designed condominium units would fail to gain in value at a normal rate. Clearly, the overall market absorption rate and the absorption rate of the targeted submarket could have been key indicators of the occupancy experience (vacancy) and the overall economic health of the condominium market.

Investors, thus, should press for market absorption rates, sometimes called turnover rates, and also require that the report divulge how they have been calculated or derived.

In the event that a specific site has been located within the SMSA, the report must relate the overall demand for the specified use to the demand for that use in the target location. This is a form of sector analysis in which demand for the specified use (e.g., housing for a specific income class) is allocated to the specific site in accordance with the demographic characteristics of that neighborhood. (In Chapter 6 we will indicate how to obtain such data for analysis.)

Four specific indicators of market demand should be analyzed:

1. The current financing practices of local lenders toward that kind of use in the neighborhood.
2. The vacancy rate for the specific use within the area.
3. The absorption rate of competitive units that are currently available in the existing stock.
4. The stability of tenure of users of the specified kind of use within the neighborhood—in effect, how long have they occupied the competitive unit.

In addition, although it is difficult to generalize, one should gather information on the income characteristics of the neighborhood; the lease terms, if any; and other indicators of comparative locational advantage or disadvantage.

Field surveys should be conducted in order to provide a competitive analysis of the existing stock and plans for the construction of new projects in the market area during the forecast period. This usually entails a visit to individual projects to determine the detailed characteristics of the competition, including type of unit, price, size, financing, maintenance, amenities, and value ratios. Comparative data should be assembled to evaluate the nature of annual absorption, that is, which are the best-selling units in the market area and which amenity and product packages seem to be most attractive to potential users.

It should be observed that there is an obvious overlap between a real estate market study and a marketability analysis of a specific site. Recommendations about amenity packages and product features may seem more appropriate for a marketability analysis than for a macromarket study. However, in projecting future rent schedules, prices, and space needs, it is obvious that gathering information on competitive projects is quite useful. Indeed, information about projects in the planning stage, including status, size, and probable marketing plan, could be even more useful because projects on the drawing boards probably will be directly competitive with the units in which the investor is interested. The planned location is also a good indicator of other decision makers' opinion of the direction of growth of the SMSA.

In addition, an inventory of other vacant land in the market area is useful to determine the availability of sites that may compete in the future with the use under study. All of the foregoing will supply supporting data for the important conclusions on the real estate outlook that the report is expected to provide.

In summary, this part of the market study ultimately should be a blend of the short- and long-run market outlooks for the specified targeted use. Since projected rent schedules, prices, and space needs provide the basis for projecting cash flows and sale prices, the conclusions are critical to the advisability of proceeding with the investment. However, even if the market is overbuilt, strong growth in demand may well absorb the excess space within the forecast period, and if the price is right, an investor with staying power may reap significant gains. Of course, if the market outlook is one of decline or no growth, then real estate needs will tend to fall off and property is not likely to appreciate in value. Indeed, it may even decline in value during the projected ownership cycle.

Elaborate market studies like these may appear to be beyond the time and budget constraints of the ordinary investor. Obviously, small investors in small projects should find a way to obtain market studies that have been done for other investors. On the other hand, it ill behooves a developer or purchaser of large projects to avoid this expenditure.

Summary of Salient Facts and Conclusions

This final component of a market study should be self-explanatory.

Some market studies also provide a feasibility analysis, which is a study of the profit potential of the proposed project or investment that takes into account market, physical, locational, legal, social, governmental, and financial factors. However, this book separates market studies from marketability analyses and financial feasibility analyses. Our objective is to clarify and isolate the functions of these distinctly different types of studies. In the next chapter we discuss marketability analysis, which is a *micro* market analysis of the neighborhood and the specific site under study. While the foregoing discussion has made it clear that a neighborhood analysis could well be part of a real estate market study, we have chosen to place it within the framework of the marketability analysis because it is normally the starting point of such a study.

SUMMARY

Careful market analysis is essential to success in real estate investing, but too often this step is neglected in the capital budgeting process. Generally, a market study should include a careful analysis of current economic, social, political, and demographic trends in both a national and a regional context. The trading areas in which demand for specific real estate facilities are likely to occur are then delineated, and potential supply and demand are analyzed. Aerial photography and computer mapping (which were discussed in Chapter 4) can significantly aid the real estate investor in understanding the growth and structure of a metro area over time.

An essential part of any market study is economic base analysis. Although it is an old method for gathering and analyzing statistical data, economic base analysis is still the best available tool for real estate decision makers. It enables one to forecast changes in employment, population, and in demand for housing, retail and industrial space. Primary economic base analysis is expensive but the OBERS projections prepared by the Bureau of Economic Analysis for all metro areas are easily compared with economic projections prepared by regional commissions, which are also available at very low cost. Thus, the real estate market analyst has access to good-quality secondary data. However, its use must be tempered with discrete judgment before decisions are made.

The skills of the market analyst are critical because the timing of the invest-ment in relation to real estate building cycles will depend largely on the accuracy of the report. The investor should require the analyst to provide projections of future rents, prices, and space needs. The report should relate the type and amount of economic activity in the delineated market area to the specific type of space or use that is the target of the study. The ratio of unsold inventory to the stock of space for a given use is a useful indicator of the market absorption rate. The gap between supply and demand should be estimated and a forecast pro-vided regarding the rate at which the market is likely to absorb any additional space, or whether excessive vacancies exist in the submarket in question. Ideally, the market study will provide information on current financing practices, turnover rates in the specified use, the stability of the neighborhood, and competitive activities.

It should be apparent that as one moves from the macromarket level (i.e., the region and the metro area) down to the various trading areas in which the specific use to be analyzed is located, we get closer and closer to a location-specific micromarket analysis. The overlap occurs at the neighborhood level. At that point a more intensive analysis is appropriate. In the next chapter, therefore, we con-sider marketability analysis, which takes place at the neighborhood or site level.

APPENDIX

Comment on Regional Planning Models

Our purpose here is to provide the equity investor with some insight into the current state of the art of regional planning models. Many real estate analysts, planners, and public officials feel that these models are ready for use as predictors of economic growth or decline in a metropolitan area. Although we believe that the models are technically mature in conceptual terms, we feel that there are significant political and sociological reasons why they are not yet entirely de-pendable.

For about two decades scholars and public agency planners have been using computer models designed to simulate the urban economy of a large metropolitan area. A good example is BASS (Bay Area Simulation Study) III.[7] BASS was designed to forecast land utilization and related waste disposal problems in thirteen counties of northern California (the San Francisco Bay area) for the period 1965–2020. The model was in a class referred to as *impact* models; that is, it was designed to show the impact of changing assumptions with respect to employment, income, household travel, spending behavior, public and private investment, and other variables that affect land absorption and utilization. Under the direction of Paul Wendt, the goal of BASS was to forecast land use, employment, and residential site locations for the years indicated. All indications are that it was a well-designed model that, if adequately financed, properly monitored, and refined to reflect experience during its use, would have been a useful predictor of land use for the Bay area. However, the BASS model was not adequately funded, and hence it cannot be said that it was properly used. Generally, this has been the history of regional planning models.

Another model that is relatively popular in the United States is EMPIRIC.[8] The EMPIRIC model is referred to as an activity allocation model. It was designed to allocate projected region-wide population and employment and land use growth among a set of smaller subregions or districts within an SMSA. On the surface the model is designed to serve both as a straightforward forecasting device and as a tool for policy consideration. It consists of a series of mathematical relationships relating changes over time in the distribution of subregional population, employment, and land use to each other and to the original distributions in some selected base year and, as a result, to the projected effect of the original planning policy on these subsets. "Activities" are defined by the model as classified, smaller amounts of population and employment, supplemented by parallel estimates of land use acreages broken down by type of use. Future planning policies are, ostensibly, expressed in terms of projected changes in regional highway and transit system service, land use and zoning control, and the availability and suitability of land for development, public open space, conservation control, industrial and residential location policies, regional housing policies, as well as the projected location of specific major developments and so forth. Currently, EMPIRIC is used by a number of regional planning commissions, such as the Atlanta Regional Commission (ARC), for the purpose of testing the impact of policy changes on the model's output. The output is currently reserved primarily for internal use of the planning staff.

None of the output data produced by the available planning models is sufficiently reliable to be used by real estate equity investors with relatively short time horizons. Population projections tend to be extrapolations from past trends that are occasionally judgmentally interrupted in accordance with one individual's expectations, which may or may not be reasonable. If such models were adequately funded and operated by an objective professional staff, and adequate data collection routines were required, it is quite likely that they could produce more reliable results. However, the models are often used for purposes of regional

[7] *BASS, Jobs, People, and Land,* Bay Area Simulation Study, Special Report no. 6, Center for Real Estate and Urban Economic Studies (Berkeley: University of California at Berkeley, 1968).
[8] Atlanta Regional Commission, *EMPIRIC, Studies for Design of Activity Allocation Model,* Final Report (Atlanta: Peat, Marwick & Mitchell, 1972).

boosterism in the game of grantsmanship, and the resulting outputs are designed to promote state highway appropriations, federal water resource and sewage grants, and the like.

At present, the state of the art is such that the best available data for the short-term analysis necessary for an equity investor is still generated by the rather crude tool of conventional economic base analysis.

6

Marketability Analysis

"I get people to invest by selling them the depreciation"

a nationally known syndicator

WHAT IS MARKETABILITY ANALYSIS?

A marketability analysis is a micromarket study. The micromarket is the specific site that is being considered for possible investment.

The marketability of a particular unit of space implies the ability of the market to accept the transfer, sale, or exchange of some or all of the rights in that space. A marketability study usually considers a specific use or uses of the space. This use may or may not represent the highest and best use, but focuses on what is *marketable*.

A marketability analysis has been defined as a

study to determine to what extent a particular piece of property can be marketed or sold under current or anticipated market conditions. It is inclusive of a study (analysis) of the general class of property being considered. Thus, a marketability analysis goes one step further than a market study by identifying the number of units that can most probably be absorbed within that specific trading area (market) and over a specified time period. Thus, the marketability analysis is not a project feasibility analysis in that it does not take into consideration development costs or profitability. In effect a marketability study is sandwiched in between the market study, on the one hand, and a basic financial feasibility analysis on the other.[1]

The usual conclusions of a marketability analysis are the following:

1. *Quality,* which in economic terms means the price or rent levels at which the market might accept the space.
2. *Quantity,* or absorption schedule within the defined time period.
3. *Specific conditions,* such as terms of financing, sales techniques, and amenities, which will enhance the acceptance of the property or encourage its acceptance by the market.[2]

A marketability analysis should forecast gross cash revenue and project the market share to be captured. Specifically, in an existing property situation (rather than development) the market analyst must project the gross possible income and vacancy rate under different economic scenarios for each year of the ownership life cycle. Preliminary property value and operating expense estimates might also be derived as an output of a marketability analysis; although this is cost efficient, it is not commonly done.

Location, Neighborhood, and Site

In Chapter 5 we noted that the location of an investment is influenced by the investor's overall philosophy and strategy, by the negotiation process, by the state of the capital markets, and even by nonpecuniary objectives. For the purposes of marketability analysis, a *location* is defined as the geographic area within which a real estate product could produce adequate income without suffering undue loss because of the absence or inadequacy of some particular factor that is usually necessary for such a use. Obviously, this is a pragmatic recognition of the imperfect efficiency of real estate markets. The same practical approach is taken in defining the limits of a neighborhood when doing a site analysis.

GUIDELINES FOR A MARKETABILITY ANALYSIS

As we have noted before, the investor is a coordinator of a process designed to maximize returns and accumulate wealth. Since micromarket analysis is quite location specific and requires extensive field survey work, the investor will most likely contract with a qualified real estate appraiser or counselor, such as an SREA or MAI, to perform the marketability analysis. One of the most valuable qualities of such an expert is the fact that he or she may have access to data that are not generally available. Especially for out-of-town investors, it is important that whoever performs the marketability analysis be knowledgeable about the local real estate markets.

[1] Bryl N. Boyce, *Real Estate Appraisal Terminology* (Cambridge, Mass.: Ballinger, 1975), p. 137.
[2] Stephen D. Messner, Bryl N. Boyce, Harold G. Trimble, and Robert L. Ward, *Analyzing Real Estate Opportunities* (Chicago, Ill.: National Association of Realtors, 1977), p. 43.

Because the uncertainty in much real estate investment is greater than one encounters with ordinary business risks, we believe that a marketability analysis should generate "optimistic," "most likely," and "pessimistic" levels of data.

The following is a list of the components of a thorough and complete marketability analysis:

1. Establishing the boundaries of the neighborhood
2. Neighborhood analysis
3. Site analysis
4. Survey of competition, with interpretative analysis
5. Marketing strategy and management plans
6. Capture and absorption rate analysis
7. Revenue and operating expense forecasts
8. Summary and conclusions

All of these components are interrelated: The economic–demographic profile, the competitive survey, the analyses of market absorption and capture rates, and the revenue and expense forecasts are based on the marketing strategy and management plans that the investor expects to adopt for the specific site use.

Establishing the Boundaries of the Neighborhood

As we have noted, a location may have more than one neighborhood within its boundaries. Since time and budget constraints do not permit an analysis of all the possibilities, the market study should provide sufficient information to select the neighborhood that best conforms with the investor's philosophy and strategy.

Neighborhood boundaries are often established by *natural barriers,* such as hills or bodies of water, or *legal/political barriers,* such as city limits, zoning boundaries, or school districts, or other *artificial buffers,* such as highways, rail lines, or green belts. The key to practical neighborhood delineation is to keep in mind that it is the competitive forces of users and lenders that establish and change neighborhoods, and not the decisions of analysts, planners, or statisticians. On the other hand, time and budget constraints compel the investor to define a neighborhood to fit available primary data, such as census tracts, blocks, or ZIP code areas.

In summary, one should delineate the neighborhood with due regard for natural and political barriers, competitive forces, and the best available fit to data sources.

Neighborhood Analysis

Neighborhood analysis should provide detail on the quality of access to public transportation, utilities, shopping centers, schools, religious and civic organizations, hospitals, community facilities, and recreational facilities, to the extent that they are pertinent to the use contemplated. Detailed information should be provided on the socioeconomic level of the neighborhood by income, education, occupation, age, and population trends. There should be descriptive data on geological, topographical, climatological, and other environmental influences. There should be a narrative description of the history and nature of the neighborhood, how it came into being, and past, present, and future trends. It is reasonable for the investor to require a map pinpointing the location of the neighborhood (and the site) within the metro area (locality map). Generally, the report should provide the following:

1. A statement of *what type of use predominates in the area, the degree of* conformity or diversity, and the extent of inharmonious uses.
2. *An evaluation of the area's reputation.*
3. *The representative range of sales and rentals,* and the *quality of improvements* relative to competitive and comparable submarkets.
4. An *informed opinion on the general remaining economic life* of the *typical* properties in the neighborhood area. Signs of spot blight should be observed.
5. A comment on the *extent of neighborhood maturity and degree of neighborhood sprawl.* Is the location built up? Is it stable? Is it on the decline? Is it being rehabilitated? Is there pride of ownership? What is the quality of routine maintenance?
6. A report on the typical source of financing and refinancing in the neighborhood. An evaluation of the attitude of lenders toward the future of the neighborhood.
7. An evaluation of *how accessible the neighborhood is* to the municipal infrastructure, the urban economy, and essential services and amenities.
8. A report on *planning, zoning, and code controls.* Are there any restrictive covenants? Are occupancy permits required for new owners? Is code compliance activity adequate or overzealous? Is there any illegal or nonconforming use in the area? Is a zoning variance, exception, or change necessary for the contemplated use?
9. An analysis of the *nature and adequacy* of available utilities and necessary amenities and other essential facilities *for the planned use.*
10. A report on the *vacancy and occupancy rates* that exist in the neighborhood as a result of current and/or long-term conditions. This report should be stratified as to tenure (owner/renter) and price/income categories.
11. A report on the *turnover rate* of ownership and/or occupancy.
12. A comment on any known hazards, nuisances, noise, air or water pollution, traffic congestion, etc.
13. A *comment on possible positive or negative effects of nearby major facilities,* such as schools, major complexes, regional shopping centers, convention facilities, stadiums, and industrial districts.
14. An evaluation of future trends for the neighborhood. The analysis should provide a factual and objective opinion of both positive and negative influences, free from speculative bias based on prejudices of any sort.

Site Analysis

Site analysis is an in-depth extension of neighborhood analysis. However, it focuses more narrowly on physical and geological conditions and terrain. It reviews zoning, land use controls, and other economic, legal, political, and sociological factors that might affect the use and, hence, the value of the site. If the neighborhood analysis has made some reference to hazards, nuisances, amenities, and the like, then this part of the report should discuss their effect on the site.

Generally, one should expect a site analysis to contain the following site-specific commentary:

1. The dimensions, shape, and area of the site.
2. Topography.
3. Soil and subsoil conditions.
4. Quality of drainage.
5. Quality and adequacy of utilities.
6. The nature of on-site landscaping, paving, etc.
7. Is the site typical and representative in nature? If not, what is the extent of its nonconformity?
8. Quality, adequacy, and level of maintenance of the municipal infrastructure (streets, curbs, sidewalks, etc.). (*Note:* The neighborhood analysis should have provided information on the quality and level of police and fire

Engineers Testing Laboratories, 1960

"...and we can save 700 lira by not taking soil tests."

protection, urban transportation, and sanitary hauling and sewage. However, some special comment may be necessary for a specific site. In a built-up area, the very reason for nondevelopment may often be the inaccessibility of some such service.)

9. Time and distance to urban services and amenities.

10. Comparison of the site with other competitive sites, using appropriate units of comparison (i.e., ratios such as real estate taxes per square foot or rents per square foot).

In addition to the foregoing, the investor must continuously assess potential users' and lenders' attitudes toward all of these factors, for user preferences have the greatest influence on current and future values. Exhibit 6–1 shows a segment of the appraisal form developed by the Federal Home Loan Mortgage Corporation (FHLMC) and the Federal National Mortgage Association (FNMA), which effectively summarizes neighborhood/site characteristics as evaluated by a skilled appraiser.

Site analysis can be extended by the use of *earth science maps*.[3] Covering anything from a city block to the entire planet, the calibrated scales of these maps are appropriate for urban applications. (The camera resolution is so high that one can see even the height of curbs.) These maps provide the investor with valuable information on, for example, ease of excavation, landslide susceptibility, slope stability, seismic susceptibility, percolation rates, mineral potential, and solid waste disposal. Neglect of site condition variables can be dangerous.

The Environmental Impact Statement

Today developers and investors must also keep in mind the need to comply with environmental laws and regulations, for the cost of such controls can make a large difference in profit potential. A site analysis, therefore, should consider the effect of such regulations. Under the National Environmental Policy Act (NEPA), Section 102 (2)(c), environmental impact statements must be filed on some projects that set forth, among other matters, the following:

1. The environmental impact of the proposed project.

2. A report on its adverse consequences.

3. Alternative uses that might be made of the environment.

4. Methods by which the proposed use can be better adapted to the environment.

5. The impact of the proposed use on long-term efforts to maintain or enhance the environment.

6. A report on the irreversible and/or irretrievable commitment of resources required to carry out the project.[4]

---

[3] G. D. Robinson and A. M. Spieker (eds.), *"Nature to be Commanded . . . ,"* Earth-Science Maps Applied to Land Use and Water Management, Geological Survey Professional Paper no. 950 (Washington, D.C.: GPO, 1978).

[4] Jane A. Silverman, *Environmental Impact of Real Estate Investments,* Real Estate Review Portfolio no. 17 (Boston, Mass.: Warren, Gorham & Lamont, 1974).

EXHIBIT 6-1.   A Portion of an FHLM/FNMA Residential Appraisal Form

NEIGHBORHOOD					Good	Avg.	Fair	Poor
Location	☐ Urban	☐ Suburban	☐ Rural	Employment Stability	☐	☐	☐	☐
Built Up	☐ Over 75%	☐ 25% to 75%	☐ Under 25%	Convenience to Employment	☐	☐	☐	☐
Growth Rate ☐ Fully Dev.	☐ Rapid	☐ Steady	☐ Slow	Convenience to Shopping	☐	☐	☐	☐
Property Values	☐ Increasing	☐ Stable	☐ Declining	Convenience to Schools	☐	☐	☐	☐
Demand/Supply	☐ Shortage	☐ In Balance	☐ Over Supply	Adequacy of Public Transportation	☐	☐	☐	☐
Marketing Time	☐ Under 3 Mos.	☐ 4–6 Mos.	☐ Over 6 Mos.	Recreational Facilities	☐	☐	☐	☐

Present Land Use ___% 1 Family ___% 2–4 Family ___% Apts. ___% Condo ___% Commercial
___% Industrial ___% Vacant ___%
Change in Present Land Use ☐ Not Likely ☐ Likely (*) ☐ Taking Place (*)
(*) From _____ To _____
Predominant Occupancy ☐ Owner ☐ Tenant _____% Vacant
Single Family Price Range $ _____ to $ _____ Predominant Value $_____
Single Family Age _____ yrs to _____ yrs Predominant Age $_____ yrs

Adequacy of Utilities
Property Compatibility
Protection from Detrimental Conditions
Police and Fire Protection
General Appearance of Properties
Appeal to Market

Note: FHLMC/FNMA do not consider race or the racial composition of the neighborhood to be reliable appraisal factors.
Comments including those factors, favorable or unfavorable, affecting marketability (e.g. public parks, schools, view, noise) _____

SOURCE: Federal National Mortgage Association, Form no. 1004, rev. 7/79.

Highest and Best Use

Many investors feel that a highest-and-best-use analysis should be part of the site analysis. This concept, developed by appraisers, is a useful method for preliminary site use analysis. Since an investor seeks the most profitable use of capital, the site use should meet the following criteria:

1. It is *reasonably probable*.
2. It is *legally permissible*.
3. It is *physically possible*.
4. It is adequately and appropriately *supported by the market*.
5. It is *financially feasible*.

A properly executed marketability analysis must address each of these preliminary determinations regarding the feasibility of the contemplated site and use, except for financial feasibility.

Is the Site Use Reasonably Probable?   The determination of what is reasonably, prudently, and likely to succeed is largely dependent on the separation of fantasy from what is likely to occur. Many raw land deals have been sold at exorbitant prices because buyers failed to consider when in the immediately foreseeable future urban fringe land would actually be converted into suburbs. In effect, whether the use contemplated is likely to occur is determined largely by its current accessibility to the essential services of the metro area. The determination of what is reasonably probable depends on the screening tests to be set forth shortly. The key to successful highest-and-best-use analysis is to select the use that is *the next most probable* profitable use in the short-term future.

Is the Site Use Legally Permissible?   Do subdivision regulations and zoning, housing, and building codes permit the use intended for this location? Even if the codes do permit that use, is it the most productive for that location? If the intended use is now illegal, should zoning changes be sought? What is the estimated cost of obtaining the change, and what is the probability of success?[5]

Is the Proposed Use Physically Possible?   Architects, builders, and engineers have developed construction technology to a point at which almost anything can be built anywhere at any time. But what is economically feasible to the investor may be a quite different thing.

The investor needs architectural, planning, and engineering services for many situations. Engineers and architects can estimate the cost of siltation management, which might require the removal of trees and ground cover and the construction of water retention ponds. Subsoil conditions can be estimated prior to purchase. Engineering studies also are often useful in determining the quality and adequacy of heating plants, air conditioning, elevators, and roofs. Failure either to have the seller cure defects or to take them into consideration in price negotiations can prove disastrous to the investor.

Is the Site Use Appropriately Supported by the Market?   The market for any use—a new development or improvements at an existing location—must be thoroughly known to the investor, or else the supply and demand characteristics of the contemplated use must be thoroughly explored. A site may be in the path of growth, but expansion of the urban fringe or the filling in of urban sprawl may take another ten years before it reaches the site. For example, in one case county planners had zoned an area near a regional airport for industry, but the acreage available constituted a 200-year supply at the expected rate of growth. In another type of situation, there may in fact be a demand for 2000 additional units of multifamily rental housing in the $250–350 per-month range, but a survey would reveal that ten developers were already building 2000 units *each* for the forecast period. During the 1970s most major SMSAs had begun to signal obvious potential distress due to overbuilding long before the overbuilding itself occurred.

Is the Proposed Use Financially Feasible?   Since all investors seek profitable use, an investigation of financial feasibility is mandatory. An appraiser makes such a study part of a highest-and-best-use analysis. However, this book defers discussion of financial feasibility until Chapters 10–13, since we feel that it warrants a separate study.

Economic and Demographic Profile of the Neighborhood/Site

Markets can be delineated in various ways: geographically, by political jurisdiction, or by time and distance radii. However, because of time and budget constraints we feel that the preferred choice is geographic delineation. A geographically oriented, areal, economic–demographic data base report can be conveniently

---

[5] Hinds, Dudley, et al., *Winning at Zoning* (New York: McGraw-Hill, 1979).

produced at low cost by using a proprietary, computer-based, data retrieval system like CACI's. We will use CACI's Siteline® and Site · Potential™ systems to demonstrate the type of marketability report that is now available.[6]

In 1970 the Census Bureau provided the Census of Population Housing Summary in computer readable form for the first time. Several organizations were formed to process the tapes and make them available to users.

In the Siteline system 98 key variables were selected. They include:

- Total population
- Population by race, age, and sex
- Family income
- Median income
- Home values and rental prices
- Major appliances
- Occupation
- Units in structure, including mobile homes
- Automobiles
- Education
- Household and family composition

The system provides a demographic data base covering 63,000 unique administrative or political units. In addition, special computer programs provide geographic cross-reference files for very small areas, such as block groups, census tract districts, and ZIP code identifiers, thereby enabling users to define areas of any size and shape required. To use a program, the user selects a *site*. A site is a physical landmark, such as the intersection of two streets, that serves as a reference point around which a number of area boundaries may be geometrically defined. The populations of these subareas, called *cases,* are equal in sum to the total population of the site area. CACI enables the user to define up to 20 possible cases in any one computer run. Exhibit 6–2 illustrates a few of the ways in which a market might be defined. In addition, the user can define a market as composed of one or more of the following: (1) the entire United States, (2) states, (3) counties, (4) SMSAs, (5) ZIP code districts in SMSAs, (5) census tracts, or (6) minor civil divisions.

CACI provides another example of proprietary data retrieval system with Site · Potential™. With this system, users simply define a trading area of any size or shape. The system scans the CACI demographic base to determine the demographic characteristics of the residents of the trading area and then computes sales potential information. Though the Site · Potential™ system is most useful for retail

[6] We gratefully acknowledge the cooperation of George Moore, Vice-President, CACI. 1815 Fort Myer Drive, Arlington, Virginia, 22209, for making this CACI material available.
    Scholarly sources for the concepts imbedded in models such as CACI's are: David E. Bell, Ralph L. Keeney, and John D. C. Little, "A Market Share Theorem," *Journal of Marketing Research,* (May 1975), pp. 136–141; Thomas J. Stanley and Murphy A. Sewal, "Image Inputs to a Probabilistic Model: Predicting Retail Potential," *Journal of Marketing,* (July 1976), pp. 48–53; and Stanley and Sewall, *Metro Markets* [with teaching notes and program listings] (Boston, Mass.: Intercollegiate Case Clearing House, 1977).

EXHIBIT 6-2. Defining Geographic Market Boundaries

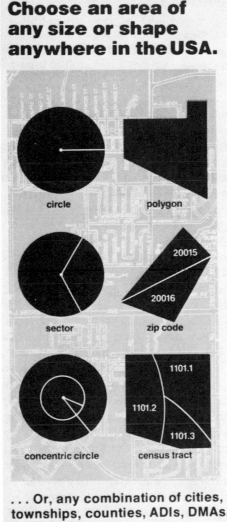

Choose an area of any size or shape anywhere in the USA.

circle   polygon

sector   zip code

20015

20016

concentric circle   census tract

1101.1

1101.2

1101.3

... Or, any combination of cities, townships, counties, ADIs, DMAs, and SMSAs.

SOURCE: Courtesy of CACI, Inc., Arlington, Va.

or commercial investments, the methods and techniques of analysis are appropriate, with modifications, for all kinds of real estate investments.

The older, now outmoded, methods of developing such sales potential for an area were of only marginal value for smaller trading areas because the procedures did not take into account many factors that influence expenditures, such as ethnicity, occupation, income, family size, education, household composition, and regional effects. CACI and other computer data retrieval systems, however, analyze the relationship between consumer expenditures and their demographic and socioeconomic characteristics. The Site · Potential™ system can generate both a market growth index (MGI) and a market potential index (MPI) for the trading area, as well as for each line of merchandise. The market growth index compares the growth rate of total sales potential in the trading areas with the growth rate of the economic region in which the trading area is located. This is very similar to the technique of economic base analysis. If the MGI of the trading area is 106, then the total sales potential of the area has grown at a rate that is 6 percent *greater* than the potential for the economic region. The market potential index compares weekly per capita sales potential of the trading areas with that of the economic region in which the trading area is located. When, for example, the market potential index is 123, the potential of the area is 23 percent higher than the average potential of the economic region. This information, covering over 74 lines of merchandise, is currently organized into 29 standard reports. (See Exhibit 6–3.)

The presentation of the CACI information systems has enabled us to review the nature of economic–demographic data base profiles and provided a brief study of how they are developed and made available. Obviously, proprietary systems of this kind are relevant primarily to commercial and service real estate uses. However, once a neighborhood and site have been selected, such data retrieval systems can provide the demographic and socioeconomic characteristics that must be reviewed for any contemplated use within that geographic area.

In addition to site evaluation, such data retrieval services might be used for market share analysis, customer profiling, and tenant mix decisions, and as an aid in forecasting market absorption and capture rates. The Siteline® reports are available by phone, and access to various subsidiary programs such as Site II™ and Site · Potential™ is available on nine time-sharing networks.

Keep in mind that such services do not offer only simple linear projections. The projections are controlled by the most recent estimates for census tracts and minor civil subdivisions. Some projections are adapted for information from utility companies, the construction industry, and environmental groups.

A major shortcoming of such profiles must also be kept in mind. The projections provided are based on past activities; they are not predictions of what will *actually* occur. No model can take into consideration changes like the following:

1. Rapid changes to higher and better land uses as a result of private or governmental action, such as demolition, highway construction, construction of public facilities, new industry in the area, conversions from old to new uses, etc.
2. Changes in technology or material shortages that are not yet reflected in consumption activities like mass transit, energy use, etc.
3. Rapid changes in consumer buying patterns, such as those brought about by Kentucky Fried Chicken and MacDonald's.
4. On an individual case basis, such statistics are necessarily silent on the effects of competitors' plans.

Field Survey of the Competition

This is a survey, by competent professionals, of *existing and planned* real estate that will compete with the investment under consideration. Before proceeding with an acquisition, it is essential for an investor to discover how competitors are currently serving the area and how *additional* competitors are *planning* to serve it in the immediate future. With this information the investor can refine and improve the merchandising plan during the preacquisition stage. It is also possible that an investor will find that new construction contemplated is of such quantity and quality that interest in the particular site should be abandoned. An investor must verify the accuracy of information gained from competitors' representatives. Such information can be cross-checked with utility engineers, other building contractors, mortgage lenders, and government agencies.

The data gathered from an appropriate competitive survey will provide direct market comparisons with alternative sites that are being offered to the tenants the investor seeks to capture. Competitive data will sharpen the investor's definition of customer profiles, potential rents, vacancies, and expenses, and can test the kinds of amenity packages that competitors are providing. These critical data will enable the investor to test his or her plans against what the market is already providing to tenants, and make it possible to identify what lenders have recently approved.

The following are factors that should be covered in various kinds of competitive field surveys.[7]

Residential Competitive Survey

1. Map showing location of various competitive projects.
2. Number of existing or planned units in project.
3. Unit mix (i.e., number of bedrooms).
4. Square feet per unit (including balconies, patios).
5. Amenities of unit (carpets, drapes, appliances, security).
6. Nature and quality of project amenities (recreational facilities, clubhouse).
7. Price or rental range (sales price per square foot, expenses per square foot).
8. Tenants' lease terms.
9. Sales and financing terms of recent sales.
10. Vacancy and occupancy rates (stratified by unit mix).
11. Quality and nature of management and merchandising strategy (advertising, models, signs).
12. Rate of absorption of new or vacant units in recent months.
13. Nature of occupants (income, occupation, place of employment).
14. A judgmental rating of the overall competitiveness of the project on a scale from 0 to 10.
15. Date of field survey.

[7] These guidelines were adapted from ideas presented by John McMahan, *Property Development* (New York: McGraw-Hill, 1976). A recommended book.

EXHIBIT 6-3.   CACI Standard Market Reports

Choose any of 29 standard reports.

Demographic Reports:
1. Income Forecast
2. Demographic Forecast
3. Income Update
4. Demographic Update
5. Demographic Profile
6. Demographic Summary
7. Columnar
8. Comparison
9. Growth
10. Component Area

Sales Potential Reports:
11. Shopping Center
12. Grocery
13. Drug
14. Apparel
15. Footwear

16. Department Store
17. Automotive Aftermarket
18. Home Improvement
19. Optical Center
20. Hair Salon
21. Bakery
22. Dry Cleaners
23. Photo
24. Appliances
25. Ice Cream
26. Restaurant
27. Commercial Bank
28. Savings & Loan
29. Consumer Finance

*. . . or call us if you
have a requirement
not listed here.*

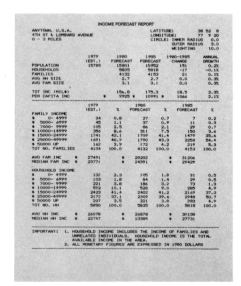

1   2

EXHIBIT 6–3. *(Continued)*

ANYTOWN, U.S.A.
4TH ST & LOMBARD AVENUE
0 - 3 MILES

DEMOGRAPHIC PROFILE REPORT

	DEG	MIN	SEC
LATITUDE	38	52	8
LONGITUDE	77	9	20

CIRCLE:	
INNER RADIUS	0.0
OUTER RADIUS	3.00
WEIGHTING PCT	10%

	LATEST	CHANGE FROM 70
1980 POPULATION	15801	291
1980 HOUSEHOLDS	5835	584
1980 PER CAP INCOME	$ 9925	$ 5145
ANNUAL COMPOUND GROWTH	0.2%	

1970 CENSUS DATA

POPULATION		
TOTAL	15510	100.0%
WHITE	14711	94.8%
NEGRO	666	4.3%
OTHER	133	0.9%
SPAN	501	3.2%

AGE AND SEX	MALE		FEMALE		TOTAL
0-5	780	10.5%	739	9.1%	9.8%
6-13	1153	15.6%	1072	13.2%	14.3%
14-17	615	8.3%	593	7.3%	7.8%
18-20	294	4.0%	376	4.6%	4.3%
21-29	1108	15.0%	1289	15.9%	15.5%
30-39	894	12.1%	921	11.4%	11.7%
40-49	941	12.7%	1144	14.1%	13.4%
50-64	1261	17.1%	1373	16.9%	17.0%
65 +	349	4.7%	607	7.5%	6.2%
TOTAL	[illegible]		8114		
MEDIAN(AGE)	27.9			29.9	29.0

FAMILY INCOME (000)		
$0-5	285	6.8%
[illegible]	[illegible]	[illegible]
$7-10	578	13.8%
$10-15	1045	24.9%
$15-25	1436	34.2%
$25-50	532	12.7%
$50 +	45	1.1%
TOTAL	4193	
AVERAGE	$16056	
MEDIAN	$14598	

HOME VALUE (000)		
$0-10	13	0.5%
$10-15	45	1.7%
$15-20	217	8.3%
$20-25	518	19.9%
$25-35	978	37.5%
$35-50	637	24.4%
$50 +	198	7.6%
TOTAL	2606	
AVERAGE	$32430	
MEDIAN	$30215	
% OWNER	50.7	

OCCUPATION		
MGR/PROF	2616	40.3%
SALES	513	7.9%
CLERICAL	1881	29.0%
CRAFT	563	8.7%
OPERTIVS	260	4.0%
LABORER	99	1.5%
FARM	5	0.1%
SERVICE	479	7.4%
PRIVATE	69	1.1%

RENT		
$0-100	307	12.1%
$100-150	1141	45.0%
$150-200	807	31.8%
$200-250	179	7.1%
$250 +	104	4.1%
TOTAL	2538	
AVERAGE	$ 147	
MEDIAN	$ 142	
% RENTER	49.3	

EDUCATION	ADULTS > 25	
0-8	935	10.7%
9-11	1062	12.1%
12	2874	32.8%
13-15	1509	17.2%
16 +	2380	27.2%

AUTOMOBILES		
NONE	513	9.8%
ONE	2530	48.3%
TWO	1875	35.7%
THREE+	324	6.2%

HOUSEHOLD PARAMETERS		
FAM POP	14034	90.5%
INDIVIDS	1392	9.0%
GRP QTRS	84	0.5%
TOT POP	15510	

UNITS IN STRUCTURE		
1	3199	60.9%
2	42	0.8%
3-4	240	4.6%
5-9	427	8.1%
10-49	825	15.7%
50 +	510	9.7%
MOBILE	7	0.1%

HOUSEHOLDS WITH:		
TV	4838	92.1%
WASHER	3275	62.4%
DRYER	2436	46.4%
DISHWSH	2188	41.7%
AIRCOND	2625	50.0%
FREEZER	1245	23.7%
2 HOMES	94	1.8%

NO OF HH'S	5251
NO OF FAM'S	4189
AVG HH SIZE	2.9
AVG FAM SIZE	3.4

5

COMPARISON REPORT

ANYTOWN, U.S.A.	4TH STREET & LOMBARD AVE	LOTA STREET & JACKSON ST	BENCHMARK SITE
1980 POP	15801	15309	10060
1970 POP	15510	15295	10152
1980 HH	5835	5628	3507
1970 HH	5251	5109	3109
ANNUAL GROWTH	0.2%	0.0%	-0.1%
1980 PER CAPITA INC.	$ 9925	$10191	$10583
1970 PER CAPITA INC.	$ 4780	$ 4875	$ 4956
MEDIAN			
FAMILY INCOME	$14598	$15220	$17702
HOME VALUE	$30215	$31094	$34045
MONTHLY RENT	$ 142	$ 141	$ 162
AGE	29.0	29.6	30.9
POPULATION			
TOTAL	15510 152.8%	15295 150.7%	10152 100.0%
WHITE	14711 150.4%	14624 149.5%	9782 100.0%
NEGRO	666 237.0%	535 190.4%	281 100.0%
OTHER	[illegible]	[illegible]	89 100.0%
SPAN	501 193.4%	468 180.7%	259 100.0%
FAMILY INCOME (000)			
$0-5	285 185.1%	278 180.5%	154 100.0%
$5-7	272 277.6%	251 256.1%	98 100.0%
$7-10	578 230.3%	518 206.4%	251 100.0%
$10-15	1045 182.4%	982 171.4%	573 100.0%
$15-25	1436 145.3%	1410 142.7%	988 100.0%
$25-50	532 96.2%	618 111.8%	553 100.0%
$50 +	45 65.2%	64 92.8%	69 100.0%
TOTAL	4193 156.1%	4121 153.4%	2686 100.0%
AVERAGE	$16056	$16934	$19350
MEDIAN	$14598	$15220	$17702
OCCUPATION			
MGR/PROF	2616 136.6%	2640 137.9%	1915 100.0%
SALES	513 158.8%	511 158.2%	323 100.0%
CLERICAL	1881 191.4%	1792 182.0%	983 100.0%
CRAFTSMEN	563 204.0%	533 193.1%	276 100.0%
OPERATIVES	260 220.3%	244 206.8%	118 100.0%
LABORERS	99 190.4%	92 176.9%	52 100.0%
FARMERS	5 83.3%	6 100.0%	6 100.0%
SERVICE	479 182.8%	454 173.3%	262 100.0%
PRIVATE	69 106.2%	73 112.3%	65 100.0%
ADULT EDUCATION			
0-8 YEARS	935 198.9%	915 194.7%	470 100.0%
9-11 YEARS	1062 189.0%	1026 182.6%	562 100.0%
12 YEARS	2874 173.4%	2751 166.0%	1657 100.0%
13-15 YEARS	1509 144.7%	1481 142.0%	1043 100.0%
16 + YEARS	2380 116.7%	2528 124.0%	2039 100.0%
MEDIAN	11.8	11.9	12.6

8

SHOPPING CENTER SALES POTENTIAL REPORT

ANYTOWN, U.S.A.
4TH ST & LOMBARD AVENUE
0 - 3 MILES

MARKET POTENTIAL INDEX = 145.7

MARKET GROWTH INDEX = 98.7

		CHANGE FROM 1970
1980 POPULATION	15801	291
1980 HOUSEHOLDS	5835	584
1980 TOT INC (MIL $)	157	83
1980 PER CAPITA INC $	9925	5145
ANNUAL COMPOUND POP GROWTH		0.19%
ANNUAL COMPOUND HSHLD GROWTH		1.06%
ANNUAL COMPOUND INCOME GROWTH		7.50%

TYPE OF EXPENDITURE	MPI (BASE=100)	WEEKLY TOTAL (THOU $)	WEEKLY $ PER HSHLD	WEEKLY $ PER CAPITA
1980 DEPT STORE MERCHANDISE	163.3	325.0	55.70	20.57
1970 DEPT STORE MERCHANDISE	163.8	178.2	33.93	11.49
ANNUAL GROWTH RATE 1970-1980		6.19%	5.08%	6.00%
1980 DRUG STORE MERCHANDISE	133.8	196.9	33.75	12.46
1970 DRUG STORE MERCHANDISE	134.1	97.4	18.55	6.28
ANNUAL GROWTH RATE 1970-1980		7.29%	6.17%	7.09%
1980 GROCERY STORE MERCHNDSE	137.1	588.8	100.90	37.26
1970 GROCERY STORE MERCHNDSE	138.2	319.1	60.76	20.57
ANNUAL GROWTH RATE 1970-1980		6.32%	5.20%	6.12%
1980 RESTAURANTS (FOOD ONLY)	189.8	150.4	25.78	9.52
1970 RESTAURANTS (FOOD ONLY)	191.0	70.8	13.49	4.57
ANNUAL GROWTH RATE 1970-1980		7.83%	6.70%	7.63%
1980 APPAREL STORE MERCHNDSE	173.4	155.5	26.65	9.84
1970 APPAREL STORE MERCHNDSE	174.5	85.4	16.26	5.50
ANNUAL GROWTH RATE 1970-1980		6.18%	5.07%	5.98%
1980 FOOTWEAR STORE MRCHNDSE	117.5	17.6	3.02	1.11
1970 FOOTWEAR STORE MRCHNDSE	117.7	9.3	1.77	0.60
ANNUAL GROWTH RATE 1970-1980		6.60%	5.48%	6.40%
1980 HOME IMPROVEMENT STORE	125.0	11.0	1.89	0.70
1970 HOME IMPROVEMENT STORE	126.3	5.4	1.03	0.35
ANNUAL GROWTH RATE 1970-1980		7.42%	6.29%	7.22%
1980 AUTO AFTERMARKET	128.7	42.0	7.20	2.66
1970 AUTO AFTERMARKET	129.4	18.1	3.45	1.17
ANNUAL GROWTH RATE 1970-1980		8.77%	7.63%	8.57%
1980 HAIR SALON SERVICES	126.1	23.9	4.10	1.51
1970 HAIR SALON SERVICES	126.7	11.3	2.15	0.73
ANNUAL GROWTH RATE 1970-1980		7.80%	6.67%	7.60%

11

APPAREL STORE SALES POTENTIAL REPORT

ANYTOWN, U.S.A.
4TH ST & LOMBARD AVENUE
0 - 3 MILES

MARKET POTENTIAL INDEX = 173.4

MARKET GROWTH INDEX = 98.7

		CHANGE FROM 1970
1980 POPULATION	15801	291
1980 HOUSEHOLDS	5835	584
1980 TOT INC (MIL $)	157	83
1980 PER CAPITA INC $	9925	5145
ANNUAL COMPOUND POP GROWTH		0.19%
ANNUAL COMPOUND HSHLD GROWTH		1.06%
ANNUAL COMPOUND INCOME GROWTH		7.58%

TYPE OF EXPENDITURE 1980		MPI (BASE=100)	WEEKLY TOTAL (THOU $)	WEEKLY $ PER HSHLD	WEEKLY $ PER CAPITA***
TOTAL APPAREL MERCHANDISE		173.4	155.5	26.65	9.84
MENS' APRL: (AGE 18+)	DRESS CLOTHES	190.4	21.0	3.59	4.25
	CASUAL CLOTHES	164.1	15.5	2.66	3.15
	SPORTS CLOTHES	212.6	4.5	0.77	0.91
	OTHER CLOTHING	168.0	8.0	1.37	1.61
BOYS' APRL: (AGE <18)	DRESS CLOTHES	167.1	3.3	0.57	1.28
	CASUAL CLOTHES	159.5	4.2	0.72	1.63
	SPORTS CLOTHES	87.7	0.6	0.10	0.22
	OTHER CLOTHING	176.3	1.4	0.24	0.54
LADIES' APRL: (AGE 18+)	DRESS CLOTHES	180.3	45.0	7.71	7.73
	CASUAL CLOTHES	155.3	15.0	2.57	2.58
	SPORTS CLOTHES	170.8	2.3	0.39	0.39
	OTHER CLOTHING	140.8	22.9	3.93	3.95
GIRLS' APRL: (AGE <18)	DRESS CLOTHES	173.6	4.6	0.80	1.90
	CASUAL CLOTHES	176.9	3.6	0.62	1.48
	SPORTS CLOTHES	185.1	0.7	0.11	0.27
	OTHER CLOTHING	172.9	2.9	0.50	1.18
1970 APPAREL MERCHANDISE		174.5	85.4	16.26	5.50
CHANGE 1970-1980			70.1	10.39	4.34
ANNUAL GROWTH RATE 1970-1980			6.18%	5.07%	5.98%

NOTES:
1. THESE EXPENDITURES REPRESENT THE ESTIMATED SPENDING OF CONSUMERS IN THE DEFINED AREA FOR APPAREL MERCHANDISE IN ALL TYPES OF RETAIL STORES AND NOT EXCLUSIVELY IN APPAREL STORES. TO ESTIMATE THE TRADE AREA POTENTIAL FOR YOUR PARTICULAR STORE, ADD UP THE LINES OF MERCHANDISE WHICH YOUR STORE CARRIES.
2. MARKET POTENTIAL INDEX (MPI) MEASURES THE RELATIVE SALES POTENTIAL OF THE DEFINED AREA. IF THE MPI OF YOUR AREA IS 123, THIS MEANS THAT THE PER CAPITA SALES POTENTIAL IN YOUR AREA IS 23% GREATER THAN THE AVERAGE POTENTIAL IN THE ECONOMIC REGION IN WHICH YOUR AREA IS LOCATED.
3. MARKET GROWTH INDEX (MGI) MEASURES THE RELATIVE GROWTH RATE IN SALES POTENTIAL OF THE DEFINED AREA. IF THE MGI OF YOUR AREA IS 106, THIS MEANS THAT THE TOTAL SALES POTENTIAL OF YOUR AREA HAS GROWN AT A RATE OF 6% MORE ANNUALLY THAN THE ECONOMIC REGION IN WHICH YOUR AREA IS LOCATED.
4. SEE APPENDIX VI OF THE SITE POTENTIAL USERS MANUAL FOR A DETAILED DESCRIPTION OF THE ABOVE ITEMS.

*** 'WEEKLY $ PER CAPITA' REFLECT PER CAPITA EXPENDITURES WITHIN EACH AGE AND SEX GROUP.

14

SOURCE: Courtesy of CACI, Inc., Arlington, Va.

Retail/Commercial Competitive Survey

1. Map showing location of competitive projects (including time and distance indicators).
2. Gross leasable area (GLA) of competitive projects, broken down into major categories of goods and services.
3. Parking index—number of parking stalls or square feet of parking area per square foot of GLA.
4. Sales or rents per GLA, broken down into categories of goods and services.
5. Identification of major anchor tenants and competitive stores.
6. An evaluation of directly competitive users (comments on stores, appearance, personnel, advertising, and promotional techniques).
7. Opinion of the overall quality of the competitive center. This should be a consideration of merchants' association, maintenance, shopping atmosphere, etc.
8. An analysis of the area surrounding the center (presence of buffers, nearby uses, transportation, type and quality of nearby uses, growth trends). A rating scale of 0–10 should be used.
9. Date of field survey.

Office Competitive Survey

1. Map showing location of competitive office buildings; the name of the office activity nodes where office uses cluster in the SMSA.
2. Gross building area, net rentable area, net rented area, net occupied area of competitive buildings.
3. Schedule of rents per square foot, broken down by tenant and floor location of tenant categories.
4. Minimum lease duration.
5. Items normally included in tenant finish allowance (partitions, utility outlets, lighting, carpets, drapes).
6. Lease terms (building services included in base rent, escalation clauses, maintenance duties, risk of loss in the event of casualty).
7. Parking (provided, how, monthly charge).
8. Other building amenities (function rooms, restaurants).
9. General profile of major and minor tenants.
10. An evaluation of the overall competitiveness of the project (maintenance and management, appearance, locational advantages/disadvantages). A rating scale of 0–10 should be used.
11. Date of survey.

Industrial Land Use Competitive Survey

1. Map showing location of competitive projects.
2. Accessibility to various transportation modes (air, highway, rail, public transit), with time, distance, and frequency indicators.

3. Nature, quality, adequacy of various utilities (capacity, limits on utilization, surcharges, tap-in charges).
4. Development controls imposed.
5. Alternative site developments permitted (build-to-suit, general purpose only, sale/leaseback).
6. Acreage sold or rented to date, with annual absorption rate.
7. Acreage vacant or remaining to be sold or rented.
8. Profile of major and minor occupant firms.
9. Price or rental terms, per square foot, for various uses.
10. Lease terms (duration, escalation clauses, risk of loss in the event of casualty, renewal options).
11. Project amenities provided by owner (landscaping, street maintenance, snow removal, lighting, conference facilities, recreational facilities, restaurants).
12. An evaluation of the overall relative competitiveness of the project. A rating scale of 0–10 should be used.
13. Date of survey.

The material listed here is schematic in nature and lacks detail. In Part IV we provide detailed definitions of many of the technical terms plus greater detail on the techniques of competitive analysis.

Sound marketability analysis requires the development of a logical merchandising plan early in the preplanning stage. A better competitive survey will result if the marketing strategy and management plan have been developed, at least on a preliminary basis, for the contemplated site use. This will lead to greater accuracy in the market absorption and capture rate analyses.

Marketing Strategy and Management Plan

Each of these terms covers a separate, but essential, management function.

Marketing Strategy   Marketing strategy is defined as the investor's policy concerning the merchandising of the property. This policy is designed to achieve or maintain an adequate level of occupancy within acceptable market absorption rates, and to produce a minimum rate of return at an acceptable level of risk. Although this definition differs from many, it is our belief that investment strategy, marketing strategy, property management, and so forth are all parts of a continuous process directed toward the goal of maximizing returns relative to risks. The functions should not be separated.

The original market study identified market areas in an SMSA where possible investment opportunities could be found. Once the site has been targeted for the contemplated use, a merchandising program must be devised to exploit the opportunity at the site.

A merchandising program varies with the neighborhood/site, the nature of the location, the degree and nature of the competition, special advantages or disadvantages of the subject site, and the investor's evaluation of the effectiveness of other merchandising programs. Although a market analyst is sometimes asked to develop the merchandising program, generally the investor devises the plan with the assistance of a qualified property manager and/or real estate broker.

In order to develop a merchandising plan, the characteristics and preferences of the target market must be described as precisely, simply, and definitively as possible. For example, the target market for an industrial park may be small business firms, young or mature, that require a combination of office space and/or warehousing, nonpolluting manufacturing, or a laboratory. An apartment building might be aimed toward singles and empty-nesters earning $20,000 or more who are interested in security, limited health facilities, and close proximity to hospitals and shopping. The target market for a boutique shopping center may be described as young executives and older couples with high disposable income who are interested in gourmet foods, art objects, high-fashion clothes, and other specialty items.

Definition of the target market early in the preacquisition stage forces the investor to ascertain whether or not the market currently exists in the targeted SMSA market area. Clear characterization serves another valuable function in that it requires the investor to formulate a merchandising plan that is consistent with the needs and resources of the target market. When purchasing an existing project with apparently adequate gross rents, this exercise is quite useful as a way of evaluating the representations made by the seller regarding the occupation, income, and the like of the users.

Although we cannot fully develop a general model of a merchandising plan here, we will note various decision points that are important in evaluating and estimating market absorption and capture rates, given the merchandising plan.

1. Once the typical space user has been defined, a shopping service might be engaged to compare the target with its competition.
2. Having considered the comparative advantages and disadvantages of the targeted use, one might consider what design, repairs, or improvements might be necessary. This could require amendment of the capital budget or renegotiation with the seller.
3. Every real estate project tends to develop an image in the marketplace, even if it is so desirable that it is rented by word of mouth. Generally, however, it is necessary to promote a project in order to maintain high occupancy levels throughout the building cycle.
4. Careful attention should also be given to the signage program, to the way prospective user traffic will be handled, how sales models will be shown, and to the sales/lease closing rooms.

The Management Plan A management plan is defined as the tactical system that implements investment, marketing, and merchandising strategy in accordance with the investor's philosophy. It is the investor's supervisory control system over the property manager.

In Chapter 16 there is a detailed discussion of the property management function. Here we simply list the functions of the property manager, who acts as an agent of the owner. In general, the supervisory control system requires the property manager to provide the following:

1. Space use planning to meet user preferences
2. Market promotion policies, merchandising, tenant selection
3. The maintenance and replacement policy
4. Policies for control of major construction and contractors
5. Accounting policies and control of reserves
6. Management policies for operation of the property

The investor separates management of the property from investment management, which is concerned with acquisition, investment, and market analysis; risk/return evaluation; financing and refinancing; tax planning; and disposal, or terminating the property interest. Although the investor may use an independent property manager to manage the property, control of the investment function should be retained.

The Market Absorption and Capture Rates

The Market Absorption Rate   This is the rate at which the market is capable of using space for a specified use. Sometimes the market absorption rate is stated as a percentage, but more often it is given as the ratio of the number of units absorbed over the time it will take to absorb them into the market. Since real estate is relatively inelastic in the short run, it is quite possible that a market absorption rate of 100 units per month could result in a queue of eager customers until new units were built and brought on the market to satisfy the demand. For example, at 100 units per month the absorption rate for 1200 units for the entire year (including both new and previously sold units coming back onto the market) would be 8.5 percent. But to say that the absorption rate is 100 units per month or 1200 units per year is not enough. To be practical, the market absorption rate should be related to both demand and supply. In addition to knowing the standing inventory for any given period, one needs to know how many units are expected to come onto the market during the same period.

A marketability analysis should provide absorption rates for *stratified* markets in small geographic areas, and should do so with a low rate of error. Because users can exercise a wide choice as to location—which is loosely defined as time and distance from home to work—the market absorption rate for, say, apartment space for an entire SMSA can be forecast with more accuracy than the effective demand for apartment space within a small geographic area. Under such conditions the usefulness of a proprietary type of demographic/economic data base profile for small areas is apparent, since it provides the means for matching estimates of absorption rates with historical trend comparisons. Since the estimation of market absorption rates is more an exercise in human judgment than an objective process of quantification, the investor should forecast data under: optimistic, most likely, and pessimistic conditions.

Capture Rates A capture rate is an estimation of market share. An *existing* capture rate is the percentage of the total potential market that is *currently retained* by existing competition. A *potential* capture rate is the percentage of the total potential market represented by an excess of demand over supply. To the extent that the existing capture rate is less than the total demand for space, there exists an opportunity for the development of a real estate product to serve the need.

Existing capture rates can be determined by comparing the total potential for the market area with the total number of existing units for the specified type of activity. An existing capture rate of less than 100 percent in retail sales, for example, indicates that consumers are traveling outside the local market to acquire the necessary goods or service. This leakage can be captured by an attractive local retail source. Using the *summation estimating technique,* the marketability analysis would first establish the potential of dollar expenditures for the particular use that would be originated in the market area. To estimate a reasonable market share for an existing site, one would allocate the appropriate share of potential dollars expenditures among the existing and planned competitive uses. The balance, divided by the site's revenue units (e.g., apartment units or gross leasable area of retail space), will provide an estimate of the reasonableness of achieving this level of market share.

A variation of this technique uses information produced by the field survey of the competition. Having identified the number of competing facilities within the market area, one proceeds to estimate the share of the market that the target site and the competitors have captured and/or are expected to capture in the case of new facilities. This is a judgmental estimation; it takes into account competitive locational advantage, attractiveness of facilities, and the like. At this point the capture rates can be multiplied by the expenditure for this type of consumption activity to provide an estimate of the sales that could be captured in this market area. When compared with estimates produced by the competitive survey, this acts as a check on the reasonableness of estimates.

In the case of a planned facility, the best available means of estimating a capture rate is to conduct primary behavioral research to supplement information on consumer expenditure patterns arising out of the data base profile. This is accomplished through personal interviews, phone interviews, or mail questionnaires. Attitudinal surveys of this kind are fraught with the possibility of error when conducted by amateurs. Such surveys probably should be done by a market research analyst because of the special skills required. A crude measure of the potential demand for the contemplated use can be provided by an enumeration of how the respondents would want to use the facility. With a scientific sample, it is possible that an adjusted capture rate can be derived for the total projected population during the rent-up or sell-off period. Certainly such projections should be judgmentally adjusted for the effects of competitive changes. One should also keep in mind that consumer surveys are an expression of wishes and desires; they are not measures of actual demand for the real estate product.

Unfortunately, formal methods for the determination of capture rates have yet to be developed. Therefore, the investor should use more than one of the methods indicated here. In addition, a range of capture rates should be estimated so that the reasonableness of the estimates can be assessed more effectively.

Revenue and Expense Forecasts

For existing properties the conclusion of a marketability analysis is a forecast of (1) gross possible rental income and (2) vacancy rates for each year over the expected holding period of the investment. Risk is taken into account by projecting data for alternative economic scenarios, defined above as optimistic, most likely, and pessimistic conditions. These data outputs from the marketability study will be used as input to the investor's return and risk analysis. We noted previously that some investors also seek additional information from a marketability analysis: estimates of future property value, and expected range of operating expenses (as inferred from the study of comparable properties). Estimating property value is an especially crucial issue in investment analysis and is addressed more thoroughly in Chapter 7.

SUMMARY

A marketability analysis is a micromarket study of the specific site being investigated for possible investment. Generally, marketability analysis requires the services of people who have technical qualifications beyond those of the typical equity investor.

The components of a marketability analysis include definition of the boundaries of the neighborhood, neighborhood analysis, site analysis, survey of the competition, development of a preliminary marketing strategy and management plan, identification and estimation of the market absorption and capture rates, and revenue and expense forecasts.

A careful, subjective analysis of the highest and best use of capital at the site must be made. To carry out such an analysis the investor can use proprietary data retrieval computer services that generate economic–demographic trends for a chosen site. While such data are essential, the dynamics of the urban environment are such that field surveys are also an essential part of a marketability analysis. Competitive surveys should be tailored to the type of site use contemplated and must discover not only existing but also planned competition. Because competitive surveys generate comparative data, the investor should develop a preliminary marketing strategy and management plan so that decisions can be made about how the site will be used.

Though the techniques for estimating market absorption and capture rates are still crude, the investor should press the analyst for such data for the specific submarket. Capture rates should be stratified by user profile and limited to appropriate time and distance radii.

In conclusion, a real estate marketability analysis estimates the amount of a specific real estate use that will be needed by the localized market within the forecast period. Much judgment enters into the making of marketability analyses because the techniques, concepts, and applications are not yet well developed, and because they deal with the uncertain future.

7

Inflation, Deflation, and Real Estate Cycles

THE WIZARD OF ID — By Parker

By permission of Johnny Hart and Field Enterprises, Inc.

Inflation and inflation cycles have been a strong underlying reason for the financial successes and failures of real estate investors in recent history. Inflation has dramatically increased rents and selling prices and, hence, the (nominal) rates of return of most existing properties. But inflation has also dramatically increased interest rates, construction costs, and operating costs, and thus has decreased the (nominal) rates of return for many new and some existing properties. In many cases inflation has created severe short-run solvency problems for investors, although the long-run prospects for high returns were excellent if the short-run crises could have been weathered. In short, inflation and inflation cycles have a complex impact on real estate returns, risks, and investment values—an impact that should not be ignored or oversimplified.

Acknowledgment: This chapter was prepared with the able assistance of Waldo Born, Ph.D. candidate, The University of Texas at Austin.

In previous chapters the subjects of inflation and real estate cycles have been treated only in a very broad sense. For example, in Chapter 5 we concluded that market studies and marketability analysis must ultimately be translated into forecasts of cash inflows—sales and rent schedules, vacancy rates, absorption schedules, and the *possible variability* of these cash inflows. Inflation and real estate cycles have a dramatic effect on these variables, which the investor must recognize in his or her investment analysis. The investor should also explicitly include inflation and cycle variables throughout the other steps of the analysis.

FRAMEWORK FOR ANALYZING INFLATION AND CYCLES

In this chapter we develop a normative framework for incorporating inflation and inflation cycle variables into the real estate investment analysis and financial structuring process. In developing such a framework we will seek to (1) identify the important inflation and real estate cycle variables that influence investment returns and risks, (2) develop a basic understanding of the dynamics of inflation cycles, (3) suggest a methodology for predicting inflation cycles and trends and their impact on investment variables, and (4) suggest specific strategies for coping with inflation cycles. In addition to examining the effect of inflation, we will look at other types of cyclical impacts on real estate. International and national business cycles, construction and mortgage cycles, city and neighborhood cycles, and social change cycles are too often ignored or misinterpreted in investment analyses. Although they are difficult to analyze and forecast, these variables should be explicitly considered in the investor's cash flow projections and decision-making process.

Two major themes will evolve during this chapter. First, inflation and volatile real estate cycles will continue in the future. However, they are relatively predictable, and investors can take advantage of their ability to predict these cycles to increase investment returns while decreasing risks. Second, timing is a key ingredient of successful investing. As pointed out earlier, investors must be willing to make considerable changes in their portfolios over time in order to take advantage of constantly changing business and market conditions. Different assets will have different performance characteristics in the various stages of a real estate cycle. Thus, while there is no real estate asset for all seasons, there is a season for all real estate assets.

The Unanalyzed Factor

Various researchers have developed theoretical models to analyze the impact of inflation on asset values. Fama and Schwert compared U.S. government bills, U.S. government bonds, real estate, human capital, and common stocks as hedges against inflation, and concluded that private residential real estate was the only asset that provided a complete hedge against both expected and unexpected inflation.[1] Lusht used a discounted cash-flow present-value model to demonstrate

[1] Eugene F. Fama and G. William Schwert, "Asset Returns and Inflation," *Journal of Financial Economics,* 5 (November 1977), 115–145.

that the value of highly leveraged, nondepreciating assets benefited most from inflation.[2] Spellman analyzed the impact of inflation on the value of home ownership, with emphasis on the results created by changes in government policy (e.g., taxes and mortgage loan structure).[3]

Numerous articles and books address the subject of inflation's impact on real estate returns and values. As early as 1973 Cooper and Pyhrr showed the impact of growth and inflation factors (rents, expenses, property values) on the investor's IRR on equity for various holding periods, loan terms, and depreciation methods.[4] Since then many real estate textbooks have incorporated discussions of inflation.[5] However, most of those discussions summarize and analyze historical data, with only limited treatment of the development of strategy and operational models for coping with inflationary effects.

In general, these authors place very little emphasis on real estate cycles.[6] There is almost no literature on how to develop a strategy that takes advantage of various types of real estate cycles, yet successful management of assets over various real estate cycles is the key to consistently above-average returns. Unfortunately, most investors tend to capitalize the present situation into perpetuity when forecasting cash flows and making investment decisions. History has proved that such projections are more often wrong than right.

Perhaps the greatest competitive advantage for investors in the future will be gained by those who develop a systematic approach to incorporating inflation and cycle variables into their investment decision process.

Return/Risk Framework for Analyzing Inflation and Cycles

The impact of inflation and real estate cycles should be an explicit consideration in the investor's analysis of specific properties, as well as the entire investment portfolio. The investor must learn to understand the inflation and cyclical factors that influence the value of investments and the events that cause those factors to change. If the investor cannot develop such an understanding, his or her percep-

---

[2] Kenneth M. Lusht, "Inflation and Real Estate Investment Value," *Journal of the American Real Estate and Urban Economics Association,* 6 (Spring 1978), 37–49.

[3] Lewis J. Spellman, *Anticipated and Unanticipated Inflation, Housing Prices and the Return to Homeownership,* research monograph prepared for the Department of Housing and Urban Development, HUD-1321-78, July 15, 1978.

[4] James R. Cooper and Stephen A. Pyhrr, "Forecasting the Rates of Return on an Apartment Investment: A Case Study," *The Appraisal Journal,* July 1973, pp. 312–337.

[5] Chris Mader, *The Dow Jones-Irwin Guide to Real Estate Investing* (Homewood, Ill.: Dow Jones-Irwin, 1975), pp. 3–15; John McMahan, *Property Development—Effective Decision Making in Uncertain Times* (New York: McGraw-Hill, 1976), p. 83; Maury Seldin and Richard H. Swesnik, *Real Estate Investment Strategy* (New York: Wiley-Interscience, 1977), pp. 157–165; Paul F. Wendt and Alan R. Cerf, *Real Estate Investment Analysis and Taxation* (New York: McGraw-Hill, 1979), pp. 29–43; James C. Downs, *Principles of Real Estate Management* (Chicago: Institute of Real Estate Management, 1975), pp. 70–78, 113–117; Stephen E. Roulac, *Modern Real Estate Investment— An Institutional Approach* (San Francisco: Property Press, 1976), pp. 18, 82, 284; Sherman J. Maisel and Stephen E. Roulac, *Real Estate Investment and Finance* (New York: McGraw-Hill, 1976), pp. 181–183, 327–329; Michael Sumichrast and Maury Seldin, *Housing Markets* (Homewood, Ill.: Dow Jones-Irwin, 1977), pp. 157–165.

[6] Notable exceptions to this rule are provided by James C. Downs, pp. 104–117. Also by Michael C. Halpin, *Profit Planning for Real Estate Development* (Homewood, Ill.: Dow Jones-Irwin, 1977), pp. 101–115.

tions of the risks and returns involved are likely to be influenced greatly by the wrong media—the daily newspaper headlines, the opinions of the six o'clock newscasters, and other highly subjective and shortsighted analyses. As a result, the investor is more likely to follow the crowd and buy and sell properties at precisely the wrong times.

The key to understanding how inflation and cyclical activity affect investment returns and risks is to understand how these macroeconomic variables interact to change the microeconomic real estate variables, namely, (1) property values; (2) rental income; (3) vacancies and credit losses; (4) operating expenses; (5) debt/ equity financing alternatives, amounts, and terms; and (6) the investor's required rate of return on investment. If the investor can project the values of these variables over time, using conventional discounted cash flow, sensitivity analysis, and risk analysis techniques, investment decisions can be made that will maximize returns relative to risks over time (i.e., maximize wealth). Furthermore, if such forecasts can be made for a wide variety of real estate investments, as well as non-real estate assets, the investor can begin to develop a strategy for shifting the portfolio to take advantage of cyclical developments.

It is our contention that economic history tends to repeat itself.[7] Rapid inflation and volatile real estate conditions are frequent in the United States. High rates of inflation have characterized over 20 percent of the period since the start of the century. Falling business activity has been almost as frequent, occurring in over 15 percent of the period since the mid-1800s. While history never repeats itself exactly, most real estate and business factors have shown consistent patterns for centuries. The serious real estate investor should study these patterns and consult others who have experienced many years of real estate inflation cycles. The first step toward understanding the impact of inflation on future real estate returns and risks is to understand their history.

Measures of Inflation

Various statistical data on prices and inflation rates are available to the real estate investor and are critical to the investment analysis. Much of the aggregate data is collected and published by various federal, state, and local government agencies, or by industry trade associations like the International Council of Shopping Centers and the National Association of Realtors.

Measures of General Economic Inflation   Three commonly used measures of inflation (called *series*) are published by the federal government. The most comprehensive measure of the overall price level is the implicit price deflator (commonly known as the gross national product price deflator). This measure encompasses the behavior of prices paid by consumers, business, the government, and purchasers of U.S. exports. Less complete measures of inflation include the con-

---

[7] The same line of reasoning is pursued by Beryl W. Sprinkel and Robert J. Genetski in *Winning with Money: A Guide for Your Future* (Homewood, Ill.: Dow Jones-Irwin, 1977), p. 248, and by Roger Klein and William Wolman, in *The Beat Inflation Strategy* (New York: Simon and Shuster, 1975). The authors develop a series of policies and rules for winning at the inflation game, although very little emphasis is placed on real estate investment alternatives.

sumer price index (CPI), which tracks prices paid by consumers, and the producer price index (PPI), formerly called the wholesale price index (WPI). There is no single correct measure for inflation on which economists are agreed. Each measure covers a different scope of activity, and each is subject to various measurement problems and inaccuracies that bias the information it provides.

The most common and most popular measure of inflation among investors is the consumer price index (CPI) or some variation of it. The CPI provides a monthly measure of the cost of living (expressed on an annual basis) for the "average urban American." It is based entirely on the retail prices of consumer goods and services, and is insensitive to changes in income or living standards. The U.S. Department of Labor is responsible for collecting and analyzing CPI data. About 400 consumer items are priced and weighted each month (for 85 geographic sampling areas in cities across the U.S.) in order to produce the *market basket* consumed by the average American.[8] From this data monthly or bimonthly indexes are published for 28 cities, and regional indexes are available for urban areas of different populations.[9]

The most pertinent CPI information for the investor is *percent changes* in the CPI over time. (See Exhibit 7−1.) The annual *rate of inflation* is the comparative yardstick that is used to measure "real" returns relative to "nominal" returns. However, some problems with the CPI should be recognized and understood. First, only "typical moderate-income urban families" are included in the sample from which the inflation data are collected. Investors who do not purchase the typical "market basket" will be subject to different inflation rates depending on their life style. Second, the index makes assumptions that may be unrealistic from a particular investor's viewpoint. For instance, the CPI component for home ownership assumes that everyone buys and refinances a home every month. Thus it tends to overstate inflation because it doesn't allow for the fact that an increase in housing prices to the buyer is offset by capital gains received by the seller.[10] Also, a family that remains in its home and has a constant debt service on a mortgage loan does not experience a rise in its cost of living, as reflected in increases in the CPI index due to rising home prices and interest rates.

Measures of Real Estate Inflation   Real estate prices and values do not automatically move with the CPI. At best, the CPI gives the investor a general yardstick against which specific real estate inflation data can be compared. In many cases there is a low or negative correlation between the CPI and real estate values. Regional and local supply and demand often produce real estate prices and values that defy comparison with nationally based statistics like the CPI. For example, apartment rents in overbuilt metropolitan areas are not sensitive to changes in the prices of other goods in the short or medium run. The CPI may be increasing at 12

---

[8] U.S. Department of Labor, Bureau of Labor Statistics, *The Consumer Price Index: Concepts and Content over the Years,* Report 517 (revised) (Washington, D.C., May 1978).
[9] This information can be obtained directly from the *CPI Detailed Report* (month, year), Bureau of Labor Statistics, U.S. Department of Labor, Washington, D.C.
[10] "Which Inflation Rate Should Business Use?" *Business Week,* April 7, 1980, pp. 94−97.

EXHIBIT 7-1.   Consumer Price Inflation

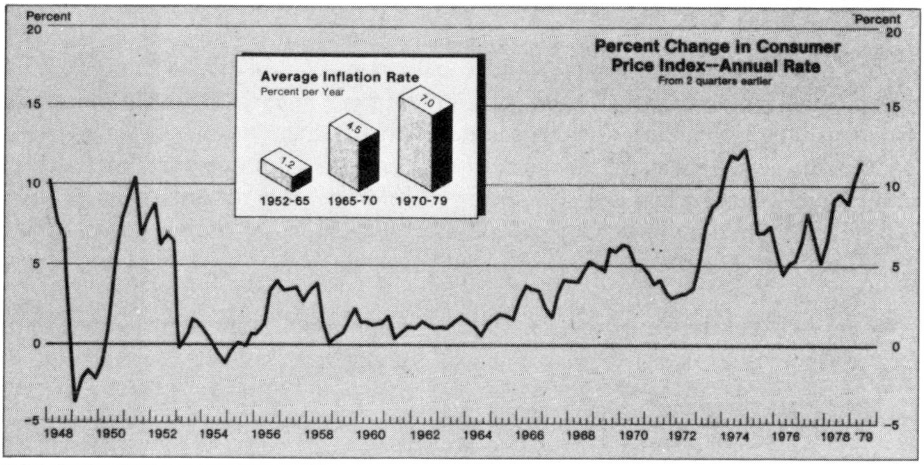

SOURCE: *Economic Road Maps* (published monthly), The Conference Board, June 1979, p. 1.

percent while landlords in such areas are lowering rents in order to increase occupancy and compete effectively in the overbuilt market. Until the excess supply of units has been absorbed, there may be little or no relationship between CPI movements and rent levels. Thus, local microeconomic factors can easily overpower macroeconomic factors.

Common Measurement Pitfalls   Investors are easily lured into making two mistakes when using published data. The first, mentioned earlier, is to assume that macroeconomic data apply directly to the micro situation. Usually much adjustment is necessary to develop project inflation rate assumptions from aggregate data series such as price, rent, and expense indexes. Certainly, *regional* and *city* data from the government-published series, if obtainable, would be far more appropriate (than national data) as a starting point for project cash flow projections.

The second classic mistake is to use *simple interest* rates of increase as a basis for projections that assume *compound interest* rate factors. Most cash flow model builders program in compound increase (decrease) factors for rents, expenses, and property values in their pro forma projections. Direct application of *ex post* trends (noncompounded) into the investor's *ex ante* model (assuming compounding of values) will seriously overstate (or understate) the cash flow returns and other financial data. This error is commonly observed in cash flow projections by students and practitioners alike. The obvious solution is to convert all inflation data used in the analysis to a common statistical base. Frequently this requires the conversion of an index number to a compound interest number. For example, the purchase price of an existing single-family home increased by 96 percent from 1971 to 1980 (nine years). This is an average noncompounded annual increase of

10.6 percent. The compounded annual rate, however, is only 7.8 percent. Using 10.6 percent instead of 7.8 percent in a projection would lead to a substantial overstatement of investment return.

Real Versus Nominal Returns   As with many aspects of life, the returns that an investor sees are not necessarily what he or she gets. Investors see nominal rates of return and interest rates, since these rates measure change in the dollar value of investments. But because of inflation (or deflation), dollar rates of return seldom reflect economic reality. Only real rates of interest (and return) measure real changes in an investor's economic well-being. Surprisingly, most investors never measure their real rates of return.

The classic work on the subject of real and nominal returns, Irving Fisher's *Theory of Interest,* was published in 1930.[11] According to Fisher, the relationship between nominal returns, real returns, and the expected inflation rate is

Nominal return = real return + inflation rate

or, if we rearrange the equation,

Real return = nominal return − inflation rate

Using this equation, consider the plight of investors who held government savings bonds or invested money in savings accounts that yielded nominal interest rates of 5–6 percent in the late 1970s. With inflation rates of 10–13 percent, the real rates of return (before tax) were a negative 4–8 percent. In retrospect these were very poor investments.

While the Fisher formula explains well the theory and concept of real versus nominal returns, it is mathematically correct only in a simple interest world. If the investor uses a compound interest model (any discounted cash flow model), the formula must be adjusted as follows:[12]

$$\text{Real rate of return} = \frac{1 + \text{nominal rate}}{1 + \text{inflation rate}} - 1$$

For example, if a proposed office building investment was expected to yield an internal rate of return (IRR) of 18 percent annually over a five-year holding period and the investor expected the average annual inflation rate to be 10 percent (compounded) over the period, the *real* IRR would be 7.27 percent, computed as follows:

$$\text{Real rate of return} = \frac{1 + .18}{1 + .10} - 1 = 7.27\%$$

[11] Irving Fisher, *The Theory of Interest: As Determined by Impatience to Spend Income and Opportunity to Invest It* (Philadelphia, Pa.: Porcupine Press, reprint of 1930 edition).
[12] Frank K. Reilly, Raymond Marquardt, and Donald Price, "Real Estate as an Inflation Hedge," *Review of Business and Economic Research,* Spring 1977, p. 3.

The investor will receive a real rate of return of 7.27 percent in addition to receiving a rate (10 percent) sufficient to compensate for losses in purchasing power due to price inflation.

The investor should use this measure of "real" rate of return for evaluating investment proposals or as a basis for establishing a required nominal rate of return. The formula can be rearranged to calculate the nominal rate of return (e.g., IRR after tax), given (1) the investor's required "real" rate of return (sufficient to compensate for the use of his or her money and the risks involved) and (2) the expected rate of inflation:

Nominal rate of return $= (1 + \text{real rate})(1 - \text{inflation rate}) - 1$
$= \text{real rate} + \text{inflation rate}(1 + \text{real rate})$

If, for example, our office building investor desired a minimum *real* IRR of 12 percent, the required nominal IRR would be 23.2 percent [.12 + .10(1 + .12)]. Investment proposals would not be acceptable unless the calculated IRR was 23.2 percent or greater.

IMPACT OF INFLATION ON INVESTORS AND PROPERTIES

Inflation does not necessarily destroy a nation, nor does it destroy investment opportunities. In fact, in many countries continued price inflation at a high rate is accompanied by a high savings rate, increasing productivity, a substantial rise in real economic output, and a rising standard of living for the average worker. Numerous researchers have concluded that factors other than inflation have a far more powerful effect on a country's growth rate than inflation.[13] If a country can adapt to inflation and simultaneously stimulate investment and productivity (as Japan and Brazil have), the investment outlook can be quite favorable.

Winners and Losers

While inflation may not by itself hurt a country or its investors in the aggregate, it does change the rules of the investment game and help determine who wins and who loses. Inflation may not destroy wealth or income, but it does redistribute it among competing elements through relative changes in asset prices. The winners receive the rewards of the redistribution, but largely at the expense of the losers. The successful investor learns to correctly predict inflation trends and to adjust his or her financial position so as to benefit from the redistribution.

During the 1970s inflation was generally higher than most equity investors and lenders expected. As a result, certain types of investors and economic groups gained while others lost, as shown in Exhibit 7-2.

Borrowers gain because they borrow money at interest rates that reflect inflation premiums that are underestimated by lenders. They pay off their debts with dollars that are worth less than was anticipated by the lenders. For each dollar

---

[13] For examples, see Sprinkel and Genetski, *Winning with Money*, pp. 99-101. Also, Klein and Wolman, *The Beat Inflation Strategy*, pp. 50-53.

EXHIBIT 7-2.   Inflation's Impact in the 1970s

Winners	Losers
Borrowers	Lenders
Investors in real estate	Investors in financial assets
Individuals with high skills or job mobility	Individuals on fixed incomes and those with no job mobility
Individuals employed in growth and high-technology industries	Individuals in mature and energy-inefficient industries
Government tax collectors	Most taxpayers and savers

gained by the borrower, a lender is losing a dollar. When we examine the mathematics of this process in the next section, we will see that when this process reverses itself, which occurs when the inflation rate falls, the process is reversed and borrowers end up on the losing team.

Empirical evidence shows that the prices of real and personal property (real estate, equipment, commodities, diamonds, gold, silver) increase during inflation while financial assets (currency, bank deposits, securities) lose value. Also, investors who have job mobility and are highly skilled are in a position to benefit from inflation while those on fixed incomes and those with little job mobility tend to lose. Similarly, there is a transfer of income and wealth from investors who work in industries and professions in which prices are rising more rapidly. Consequently, individuals employed in growth and high-technology industries do far better, on average, than individuals in mature and energy-inefficient industries. And finally, inflation raises nominal incomes and pushes more individuals into higher tax brackets, even if real incomes are declining. The beneficiary in this process is the federal government, which ends up with increased income and spending power at the expense of taxpayers and savers, in aggregate. Despite periodic "tax cutting" by the federal government, the percentage of personal income paid in federal taxes has climbed significantly over the last fifteen years.[14]

In 1985 this tax picture will change because the Economic Recovery Act of 1981 indexes the federal government's tax rates to the benefit of taxpayers.

The Mathematics of Wealth Transfer

When the inflation rate increases, the prices of real assets increase. For example, as the inflation rate increased in the 1970s and early 1980s, average home prices increased with (or exceeded) the inflation rate. However, the mortgage claim (a financial asset) against this real asset did not change in value (as long as the mortgage was not indexed to inflation in some way, as is currently the case). The homeowner owes the same number of dollars, but those dollars purchase less for the lender. Consequently, the homeowner's net worth increases by the entire amount of the increase in asset value. In this manner inflation has worked to

[14] Alfred L. Malabre, Jr., "As Salaries Climb with Prices People Pay More of Income in Taxes Despite Rate Cuts," *The Wall Street Journal,* November 28, 1979, p. 38.

transfer wealth from the *net monetary creditor* (the mortgage lender) to the *net monetary debtor* (the homeowner).[15] To illustrate the process, consider the plight of Mr. Conservative versus Ms. Aggressive. Before inflation increases, their balance sheets are as follows:

BEFORE INFLATION

Mr. Conservative (Net Monetary Creditor)				Ms. Aggressive (Net Monetary Debtor)			
Cash	$ 50,000	Mortgage	$ 25,000	Cash	$ 10,000	Mortgage	$ 75,000
Real estate	50,000	Net worth	75,000	Real estate	90,000	Net worth	25,000
	$100,000		$100,000		$100,000		$100,000

Mr. Conservative keeps half his money in cash and owes only $25,000 on his $50,000 parcel of real estate. He can be called a net monetary creditor, since his monetary assets (cash) exceed his monetary liabilities (mortgage). In contrast, Ms. Aggressive is a net monetary debtor, since her mortgage of $75,000 far exceeds her cash assets of $10,000. Ms. Aggressive owns $90,000 of real estate compared with Mr. Conservative's $50,000. Total assets in both cases are $100,000. Keep in mind that the important distinction is between the *relative* amounts of cash and mortgage, since neither will increase with inflation.

Now consider the impact of inflation. Assume that real estate prices double and the overall price level doubles, a relatively true assumption for the decade of the 1970s. For purchasing power to remain constant, the net worth of each individual must double. However, as we can see, Ms. Aggressive wins at the inflation game while Mr. Conservative loses.

AFTER INFLATION

Mr. Conservative (Net Monetary Creditor)				Ms. Aggressive (Net Monetary Debtor)			
Cash	$ 50,000	Mortgage	$ 25,000	Cash	$ 10,000	Mortgage	$ 75,000
Real estate	100,000	Net worth	125,000	Real estate	180,000	Net worth	115,000
	$150,000		$150,000		$190,000		$190,000

Ms. Aggressive (net monetary debtor) has increased her total net worth from $25,000 to $115,000, which far exceeds the doubling of the general price level. In contrast, Mr. Conservative (net monetary creditor) has increased his net worth from $75,000 to only $125,000. While his money wealth has increased substantially, his real wealth has declined by $25,000, the amount of additional money he would need to maintain a constant level of purchasing power.

[15] The following discussion is a modified version of the one presented by Klein and Wolman, pp. 56–59.

Although our illustration is oversimplified (because Mr. Conservative could put his cash into interest-bearing money market funds), it does illustrate how net monetary debtors increase their wealth during periods of rising inflation rates. They maintain adequate cash reserves to protect against short-run liquidity problems, but invest a large proportion of their wealth in real property or other real assets (gold, diamonds, art, commodities, etc.). The investors who became wealthy during the 1970s had balance sheets of this type. They kept up with inflation because they borrowed a large percentage of their assets from lenders who charged interest rates that did not fully reflect inflation. The 1970s were a period in which most lenders and equity investors underestimated the inflation rate. As a result, equity investors experienced windfall (unanticipated) gains at the expense of lenders who experienced windfall (unanticipated) losses.

The wealth transfer process works in reverse when inflation rates decrease after lenders have incorporated higher inflation expectations and premiums into the interest rates they charge. In addition, the wealth transfer process may not be evident in very strong or weak real estate markets, in which supply and demand are in substantial disequilibrium and dominate the inflation effects. Furthermore, the process for new properties differs substantially from that for existing ones, as we will show later.

Impact on Leverage Strategy

The first key impact of inflation on real estate is rising interest rates. Because real estate generally is a highly leveraged asset, small changes in financing conditions or terms have a substantial impact on project returns and risks. Rising interest rates have several important effects on investors who seek an adequate return on their investment by building or purchasing existing real estate:[16]

1. *Reduction in the amount of loan that can be supported by a project.* As more of a project's income stream must be used to pay for higher interest costs, the amount of loan must be reduced to compensate. Also, lenders tend to *reduce* the loan-to-value ratio that they will accept when interest rates are high, as a means of rationing funds and controlling risks. As a result, other things being equal, additional equity must be raised to finance a purchase, or the project must be rejected.
2. *More debt service and less cash flow.* Given a certain income stream from a property, more debt service to the lender means less cash flow to the equity investor. Not only is the return decreased, but the short-term risk is increased as a result of the additional fixed financial obligation to the lender.
3. *Operating costs rise faster than rents.* While operating costs have generally

---

[16] See Anthony Downs, "Interest Rate Rise Erodes Leverage and Appreciation," *The National Real Estate Investor,* September 1974, pp. 31, 98–99; also, Downs, "Inflation: A Two Edged Sword for Realty Investors," *The National Real Estate Investor,* November 1974, pp. 31, 113; also, Richard D. Marshall, "Inflation Partially Negates Risk Position Yields," *Mortgage Banker,* December 1975, pp. 48–53.

kept pace with inflation and increase immediately when inflation increases, rents tend to lag inflation and cause a profit squeeze for the investor when inflation increases. Rents are generally fixed by contract for various periods and prevent landlords from keeping up with cost increases by raising rents. In real terms rents actually decreased from 1967 through 1980.[17]

4. *Soaring construction loan costs.* Prime rates increase dramatically and raise the cost of construction. At the same time, high mortgage rates reduce the effective demand for real estate and tend to depress the prices people are willing (or can afford) to pay for real estate, as well as causing slower absorption rates for real estate in general.

These are primarily short-run effects, yet they can have a devastating impact on an acquisition or development program. In the long run, higher interest costs are like any other business cost and must be passed on to the consumer in the form of higher rents and asset prices. However, it must be remembered that one must live through the short run to get to the long run.

Another indirect effect of high interest rates is a reduction in the funds available for mortgage loans because of disintermediation. When short-term interest rates on money market instruments increase to high levels as a result of inflation or monetary restraint, savings are removed from savings institutions, where deposit rate ceilings are applicable, and placed directly into money market instruments that yield competitive rates. The result is a sharp decline in the amount of lendable funds available for new construction or for the financing or refinancing of existing projects, resulting in a reduced turnover of existing properties.

Impact on New Properties

As a result of rapidly rising land and construction costs and rising interest and capitalization rates, the difference between project sales prices and total development costs becomes intolerably small and new development ceases or is significantly curtailed. While higher construction and land costs can eventually be covered by higher sales prices and rental incomes, market prices do not respond immediately. Thus, the developer may have to survive an adjustment period until the market recovers and the product can be sold at a higher price. Unfortunately, with interim interest rates at a record high, holding costs increase and profitability declines rapidly.

Impact on Existing Properties

While high interest rates and decreasing new construction hurt builders and developers, it has resulted in good times for owners of most existing properties. Decreasing construction starts reduces the supply of competing new products and, given a constant or rising demand for space owing to population and income increases, vacancies will decrease and rents will be raised. In this situation rent

---

[17] *Real Estate Investing Newsletter,* November 1980, p. 1.

increases may keep up with inflation or in many cases exceed the inflation rate. Subsequently, as long as expenses increase at the same rate or slower than rental income, the project's net operating income will increase and property values will increase (assuming a constant or falling market capitalization rate).

The effects of the relationship among the inflation rate, the vacancy rate, and relative increases in rents and expenses are illustrated in Exhibit 7–3. We have assumed an overall inflation rate of 10 percent and two representative inflation situations. The point of departure is the base case, which assumes a gross possible income of $100,000, a vacancy rate of 5 percent, operating expenses of $40,000, and a capitalization rate of 10 percent, which is used to capitalize the net operating income into an estimate of market value. Case A represents a marketplace in which supply and demand are balanced, vacancy remains at 5 percent, and rents and expenses keep up with the 10-percent rate of inflation. Case B represents the impact of a tight market caused by a rise in interest rates, reduced construction starts, and an increase of demand over supply. The vacancy rate drops to 3 percent over a two-year period; rents rise at 12 percent; and expenses increase at the 10-percent inflation rate. Investors shift their dollars away from the purchase of new properties and into existing properties, resulting in the capitalization rate's falling from 10 to 9 percent.

In case A the investor has increased the operating income by $11,500 over two years, and the property value has increased by $115,000. In case B, however, the income has increased by over $18,000 and the property value has increased by over $264,000. Clearly, in case B the owner of the existing property,

---

EXHIBIT 7–3.   Effects of Inflation on Existing-Property Economics (10% General Price Inflation)

CASE A: **Balanced supply and demand market:** vacancy = 5%; rental income increase = 10% annually; expense increase = 10% annually; capitalization rate = 10%.

CASE B: **Expanded demand over supply market owing to unexpected inflation forces:** vacancy = 3%; rental income increase = 12% annually; expense increase = 10% annually; capitalization rate = 9%.

RESULTS:	TODAY	TWO YEARS LATER[a]	
	Base Case	Case A	Case B
Gross rental income	$100,000	$121,000	$125,440
Less: vacancy	−5,000	−6,050	−3,763
operating expenses	−40,000	−48,400	−48,400
Net operating income	$ 55,000	$66,500	$ 73,277
Divided by: capitalization rate	÷.10	÷.10	÷.09
Market value of property	$550,000	$665,000	$814,187

[a] All increases in rents and expenses are compounded annually.

who has experienced these market shifts, has benefited from a windfall profit that was produced by unexpected inflation and decreasing construction starts. Many owners of existing properties benefited from these favorable market conditions during the 1976– 1981 period.

Such increases in market value and income stream are not automatic, nor do they accrue to all owners of existing property in all cities. A number of factors affect the extent to which the owners of existing property enjoy rising operating income and property values during a period of inflation like the one just described. Among the most important are the following.

1. *Strength of the real estate market.* Demand and purchasing power grow relative to the increase in supply. A very strong market would have significant pent-up demand; a market in equilibrium would have supply and demand increasing at about the same rate; while a weak market would have significant overbuilding or, simply, a supply of available space in excess of the demand.[18]

2. *Nature of lease contracts.* To take advantage of inflation pressures, owners do best by having short-term leases, in which rents can be increased frequently, or long-term leases indexed to the rate of inflation. Long-term leases with fixed rates, or short-term leases with options to renew at fixed rates, are usually undesirable and have an adverse impact on property values.

3. *Favorable financing rates and terms.* Owners who financed properties with high-leverage loans at fixed rates before high inflation premiums were included in the interest rate, and who can provide these favorable loans to the next buyer of a property, have fared best. A seller who is willing to provide secondary financing to a buyer, where existing favorable loans can be assumed, can achieve the highest sales prices for property. Situations that require new financing have a negative impact on the selling price and marketability of the property.

The relationship between these factors and income property values during a period of price inflation can be viewed in Exhibit 7– 4. The ideal situation for maximizing property values while minimizing inflation (purchasing power) risk is found in a very strong real estate market, with either (1) short-term leases or long-term, inflation-indexed leases or (2) favorable loans that are assumable or (3) where the seller is willing to provide financing to the purchaser. In contrast, the most undesirable situation is found in a weak market, with long-term, fixed-rate leases (or short-term leases with fixed price renewals) and a selling situation that requires new financing at prevailing high interest rates. While there are many exceptions to these general rules (e.g., in rent control situations), they do provide a guideline for understanding how inflation helps or hurts existing properties on a *relative* scale.

---

[18] A comprehensive rating system for supply and demand factors for real estate markets throughout the country has been developed by Al Gobar, a California-based market analyst. See, e.g., "Housing Demand Index, Fourth Quarter, 1980," *Housing,* October 1980, pp. 59– 64.

EXHIBIT 7-4. Key Factors Affecting Property Values and Inflation Risks

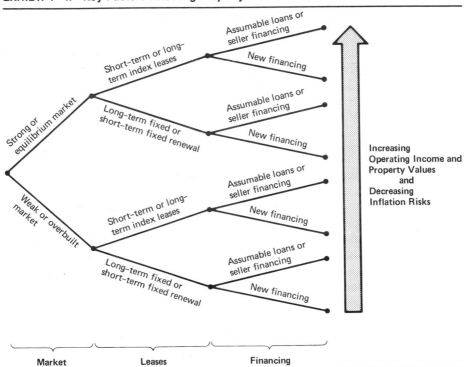

Impact on Unimproved Land

It is important to distinguish between two types of unimproved land when inflation impacts are analyzed: (1) urban land that will be developed with property in the future, and (2) agricultural and forest land.

    Urban Land Inflation produces adverse short-run and positive long-run effects on well-located unimproved land in urban areas. In the short run, increasing construction costs and higher interest rates are quickly reflected in lower residual returns to developable land investments, and in lower land prices.[19] In the long run, however, if taxes and holding costs are a small percentage of profit when the land is finally developed, price appreciation can make the investment quite attractive.[20] The investor should consider the facts that most types of land will not produce income until they are developed and that there are carrying costs as well as opportunity costs in holding a nonproducing asset. Rapid appreciation of property value owing to inflation pressures may not produce an attractive after-tax yield when all of the costs and risks over the holding period are considered.[21]

[19] Paul F. Wendt, "Inflation and the Real Estate Investor," *The Appraisal Journal,* July 1977, p. 345.
[20] Ben E. Laden, "The Impact of Inflation on the Investor," *Trusts and Estates,* January 1975, pp. 22–25.
[21] See J. Bruce Lindeman, "Is the Land Boom Coming to an End," *Real Estate Review,* Fall 1974.

Agricultural and Forest Land   Farm, ranch, and forest lands represent special types of investment in vacant land and have traditionally provided an excellent hedge against inflation. Exhibit 7–5 shows the relationship between the inflation rate and the increase in the average value per acre of farm real estate as reported by the U.S. Department of Agriculture. In every year from 1963 through 1979, except 1970 and 1971, the increase in land values exceeded the inflation rate. In numerous years the increase in land values more than doubled the rate of price inflation. Some land prices in specific states and regions increased at even more dramatic rates. From 1970 to 1977 the average price per acre of grain farm land in Iowa increased at an annual rate of 40 percent.

There is considerable evidence that farm land values will not continue to outpace inflation by such dramatic margins in the future. Much speculation by both Americans and foreigners occurred during the 1970s as investors shifted from financial to real assets as a hedge against inflation and foreigners sought to protect their assets from political turmoil. As a result, the gross income per acre has increased at a much slower rate than land prices. This, combined with high operating costs and financing costs, has resulted in severe cash flow problems for many farmers and ranchers. Over the long term, land prices cannot continue to increase rapidly if they cannot be supported by adequate production yields each year to cover operating costs, financing costs, and a small profit to the operator.

Impact on the Homeowner

Exhibit 7–6 shows the comparison for each year between the annual inflation rate and increases in the median price of new and existing single-family homes. The only years in which housing prices did not increase significantly faster than the inflation rate were the recession years of 1969–1970, 1974–1975, and 1980. Also, it can be observed that new-home prices decline faster in bad years but

EXHIBIT 7–5.   Increases in Farm Real Estate Values Relative to Inflation

Year	Inflation Rate[a]	Annual Increase in Value[b]	Year	Inflation Rate[a]	Annual Increase in Value[b]
1963	1.2%	5.5%	1972	3.3%	8.2%
1964	1.3	6.5	1973	6.2	13.6
1965	1.7	4.9	1974	11.0	24.7
1966	2.9	8.1	1975	9.1	13.9
1967	2.9	7.5	1976	5.8	13.6
1968	4.2	7.0	1977	6.6	16.9
1969	5.4	5.6	1978	7.7	8.8
1970	5.9	3.5	1979	11.3	14.0
1971	4.3	4.3	1980	13.5	15.1

[a] Calculated from annual percent change in the annual index CPI, adjusted annual rate, U.S. Department of Commerce, *Survey of Current Business.*
[b] Index number increases in average value per acre, U.S. Department of Agriculture, *Farm Real Estate Market Developments,* CD-84.

EXHIBIT 7–6. Percentage Increase in Prices of Single-Family Homes

Year	New Homes[a]	Existing Homes[b]	Inflation Rate[c]	Year	New Homes[a]	Existing Homes[b]	Inflation Rate[c]
1964	5.0%	n.a.	1.3%	1972	8.5%	7.7%	3.3%
1965	5.8	n.a.	1.7	1973	17.8	8.2	6.2
1966	7.0	n.a.	2.9	1974	10.5	10.7	11.0
1967	6.1	n.a.	2.9	1975	9.5	10.3	9.1
1968	8.8	n.a.	4.2	1976	12.5	7.9	5.8
1969	3.6	8.5%	5.4	1977	10.4	12.6	6.6
1970	−8.6	5.5	5.9	1978	14.1	13.5	7.7
1971	7.7	7.8	4.3	1979	13.8	14.4	11.3
				1980	11.0	11.7	13.5

[a] Median price of new single-family residences, U.S. Department of Commerce, *Characteristics of New Housing,* Construction Reports, C25-78-13.
[b] Median price of single-family homes, calculated from National Association of Realtors, Economics and Research Division, *Monthly Report.* Data not available for years prior to 1969.
[c] Calculated from the annual percent change in the annual index CPI, adjusted annual rate, U.S. Department of Commerce, *Survey of Current Business.*

increase faster in good years. Since new-home prices are a product of wide fluctuations in home construction activity each year, existing home prices are probably the best indicator of how most homeowners have fared. Even so, there are wide variations in prices in different parts of the country, in different seasons of the year, and in different neighborhoods within a particular SMSA. The data shown should be used only as a very general guideline for the investor.

· Studies have shown that owner-occupied homes have been a good financial investment and yielded a high after-tax rate of return on the equity capital invested. For example, R. Bruce Ricks concluded that a typical Los Angeles homeowner would have realized an after-tax rate of return of 18.5 percent annually on an original equity investment of $6,000 over a ten-year holding period on a $26,500 home purchased in 1965. And this study was completed before rapid inflation rates came into play.[22]

The average income property investor has also recognized the potential of the single-family home as a viable investment medium. Syndicators throughout the country have bought groups of single-family homes, have rented them, and have sold participation shares to equity investors. Single-family homes are said to be more marketable, are easier to finance, require relatively small down payments, and have more price growth potential than investments in other income properties, such as apartments, office buildings, and shopping centers. However, such acquisitions have generally been accomplished in a fixed-rate mortgage market in which interest rates did not fully reflect the inflation rate. As discussed previously,

[22] R. Bruce Ricks, "Managing the Best Financial Asset," *California Management Review,* Spring 1976; See also B. Jerrimad, "The Best Real Estate Investment Ever?" *Real Estate Review,* Fall 1977, pp. 62–64.

the lenders have been the losers. If, however, the interest rate is increased to fully reflect higher rates of inflation, or the mortgage is indexed to inflation (e.g., through a variable-rate mortgage), the equity investor's benefits are decreased.[23]

Impact on Multifamily Income Properties

Apartments have had a turbulent history compared to single-family homes. Although many analysts have concluded that apartments have outperformed many other types of investment media over a long period,[24] other experts remind us that apartment investing is subject to wide cyclical fluctuations characterized by periods of overbuilding and underbuilding that are tied to construction cycles. In strong apartment markets prices rise faster than inflation, but during overbuilt periods prices rise slowly or actually decrease. Thus, the ability of an apartment investment to provide an inflation hedge depends to a substantial extent on the ownership period chosen relative to the apartment construction cycle.

During the period 1977–1981 apartment construction was slow; the supply of existing apartments decreased as a result of condominium conversions; rents often rose faster than expenses; and capitalization rates fell as more investors shifted to real estate assets. As a consequence, price appreciation was exceptional, and investors who bought apartment properties after the real estate depression of 1974–1976 did exceptionally well, on average. In contrast, the 1974–1976 period was characterized by rapid expense increases owing to inflation and the impact of the energy crisis, high vacancies, and inability to raise rents until vacant units were absorbed. As a result, many investors became insolvent and distress sales and foreclosures were widespread.[25]

Many institutional investors and large syndicators exclude apartment properties from consideration for two main reasons. First, they view apartments as management intensive. Second, they are afraid of the political effects of inflation on apartments. Landlords must raise rents frequently in order to cover higher operating expenses, rising interest rates, and higher loan amounts when properties are sold or refinanced. At the same time, inflation has been consistently outpacing the after-tax incomes of tenants. They protest by demanding rent controls, and in many cases they get them. This has been happening in an increasing number of large cities and urban counties, and even throughout whole states.

As long as we have rapid inflation and renters outnumber landlords in local elections, rent control will be a definite long-run risk for apartment owners. In some nations, such as Brazil, which has experienced prolonged inflation, no

---

[23] For a discussion of the relative impact of inflation on lenders and equity investors, see David Rystrom, "Inflation and Real Estate Investment Value: A Comment"; also, Kenneth M. Lusht, "Inflation and Real Estate Investment Value: A Reply," *AREUEA Journal,* Winter 1980, pp. 395–403.

[24] See, e.g., the following studies: Paul F. Wendt and Sui N. Wong, "Investment Performance: Common Stocks Versus Apartment Houses," *Journal of Finance,* December 1965, pp. 633–646; Dennis G. Kelleher, "How Real Estate Stacks Up to the S&P 500," *Real Estate Review,* Summer 1976, pp. 60–65; Sheldon M. Blazar and Hugh G. Hilton, "Investment Opportunities in Existing Apartment Buildings," *Real Estate Review,* Summer 1976, pp. 47–52.

[25] A vivid account of the dynamics of the downside of the apartment cycle is provided in Howard W. Stevenson, "The Reason Behind the Real Estate Crash: A Case Study," *Real Estate Review,* Summer 1976, pp. 35–46.

developer builds residential rental property in the private sector of the economy. All new multifamily units are sold as condominiums.

Impact on Commercial Income Properties

Commercial income property, in the form of retail and shopping center investments, office buildings, and industrial buildings, has been the focus of activity for major institutional investors and sophisticated individual investors. Such property is regarded as an excellent hedge against inflation and, in addition, avoids the management intensiveness and political problems associated with residential rental properties.

Shopping centers were especially popular in the 1970s and early 1980s because of their excellent and well-publicized financial track record with lenders (a very low foreclosure rate) and the rapid expansion in consumer sales experienced during this period. Even during periods of economic downturn and overbuilding for other types of property, the rate of new shopping center development has progressed steadily. Shopping center leases have been well indexed to inflation through percentage-of-sales rent clauses, so that as inflation has pushed up retail prices, the rental income (in established shopping centers) has increased immediately. In addition, shopping center investors and managers have been very successful in negotiating net lease contracts so that rising energy and other operating costs are passed directly on to tenants.

The demand for space in commercial income properties tends to be more sensitive to general business conditions and cycles than the demand for space in residential properties. While consumers can easily delay purchases of new automobiles and durable goods, and businesses have less need for office and industrial space when economic activity declines, every family needs a place to live; new-family formations continue regardless of economic conditions.

INFLATION CYCLES AND INVESTMENT STRATEGY

The discussion so far has focused on rising inflation rates and their impact on investors and properties. We addressed both a short-term rise in inflation rates and its impact on new and existing properties, and the long-term effects of a rising inflation rate on property values and rates of return. A closer examination of inflation data (Exhibit 7–1) reveals the presence of short-term cycles around a rising long-term trend line. This distinction has important strategy implications, which should be examined.

A history of inflation provides the investor with a framework for understanding the relevance of short-term cycles and long-term inflation trends. For example, there were four (short-term) inflation cycles from 1964 through 1981, although the long-term inflation trend line reveals an increase in the average inflation rate from about 2 percent to 10 percent.

1. *Second quarter 1964 – first quarter 1967.* The acceleration phase of the cycle lasted about two years, while the deceleration phase lasted about one year.

2. *First quarter 1967 – first quarter 1972.* The acceleration phase lasted almost three full years and the deceleration almost two years.
3. *First quarter 1972 – second quarter 1976.* The acceleration phase of the third cycle lasted almost three years and reached double-digit figures in the fourth quarter of 1973. The deceleration phase occurred during 1975 and early 1976.
4. *Second quarter 1976 – third quarter 1981.* The most recent cycle increased from 1976 to 1979 and peaked at the end of 1979. We currently (fall 1981) appear to be in a deceleration phase.

The inflation rate fell during 1980 and 1981. If the present and future administrations are successful in curtailing increases in government expenditures, increasing the savings rate and productivity, and stabilizing money supply growth in relation to real economic output during the coming years, the long-term trend of inflation may be reversed and short cycles will trend downward during the 1980s. While the 1970s were a period in which investors consistently underestimated inflation rates, the 1980s may become a period in which investors consistently overestimate inflation rates in their analysis of real estate investments.

An Inflation Cycle Strategy

Changes in the inflation rate will affect the relative prices of real and financial assets, as noted previously. Generally, in periods of rising inflation rates real assets are the star performers, while financial assets like stocks and mortgages are the relatively best performers during a period of falling inflation rates. As a result, an investment strategy should dictate various portfolio changes over time. In order to understand why the portfolio should change, we must first analyze the dynamics of the inflation cycle itself.

Exhibit 7 – 7 illustrates the various stages that might make up a hypothetical

EXHIBIT 7-7. Stages of the Inflation Cycle

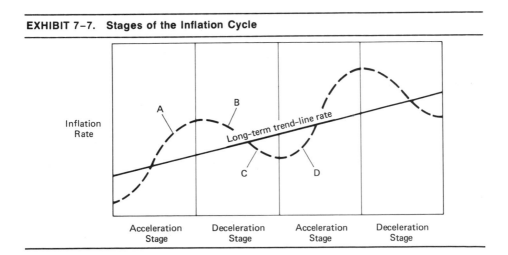

inflation cycle. At each point of the cycle changes are taking place in the economy, and the investor should be making shifts in his or her investment portfolio in order to maximize wealth. While the conservative investor will base investment strategy on the long-term trend line rate of inflation, the aggressive investor will shift some or all of the portfolio to take advantage of accelerating and decelerating rates of inflation.

Klein and Wolman advocate a relatively simple and straightforward strategy for benefiting from inflation cycles.[26] Their major tenet is that the prices of real assets, such as commodities and gold, rise when the prices of financial assets, such as stocks and bonds, fall; and vice versa. (Real estate assets are not considered.) The investor's general rule is to concentrate on investments whose prices are out of line with the expected long-term inflation trend. Consider, for example, the four points shown on the inflation cycle and the investment rules that might be applied:

- *Point A.* The actual inflation rate is still increasing but is near its peak and well above the long-term trend line rate. The stock market is depressed; interest rates are high; and bond prices are at an all-time low. Investors have been shifting into real assets for some time (the masses are jumping on the inflation bandwagon) and have bid those prices up. At this stage of the cycle the investor should sell real assets and buy short-term money market instruments. He or she should be prepared to shift into financial assets such as stocks and bonds.
- *Point B.* The inflation rate is still above the long-term trend line rate, but is decreasing. The investor has completely liquidated real assets and is selling short-term money market instruments and investing in a portfolio of stocks and bonds in order to take advantage of the falling inflation rates that will characterize the deceleration stage. As inflation rates fall, interest rates will decline, bond prices will increase, and the stock market will be revived as profit expectations increase.
- *Point C.* The inflation rate is below the trend rate and is beginning to bottom out. The process now reverses itself. The investor is selling stocks and bonds and investing in liquid assets, and preparing to reinvest in real assets, which will ride the upward swing of the inflation cycle.
- *Point D.* The inflation rate is in the initial stages of acceleration. The investor has liquidated all the stocks and bonds, and is converting the liquid assets to real assets, such as commodities and gold.

For the real estate investor, this strategy may be of limited use. Because real estate assets are illiquid and involve high transaction costs, rapid trading of assets is often not technically possible or financially feasible. While some of the real estate portfolio can be shifted over the inflation cycle, many investors prefer to develop a strategy that primarily takes advantage of the long-term trend line of inflation. As long as the long-term trend line is upward sloping, real estate investments become

---

[26] Klein and Wolman, p. 162. The examples given do not include real estate alternatives. The emphasis is placed only on bonds, stocks, commodities, and foreign currencies as investment media.

an increasing part of the portfolio. When a downward shift in the trend line occurs or is expected, real estate investments become a decreasing part of the investment portfolio. Most real estate acquisitions would logically take place between points C and D of the cycle, where interest rates are low and low inflation expectations result in lower asset prices. On the other hand, when the long-term trend line turns downward, most of the sales would logically take place between points A and B, where expectations of high inflation rates are incorporated into optimistic cash flow forecasts and result in high asset values and prices.

The real estate investor can therefore use both long-term trend line and short-term inflation cycle data as the bases of an investment strategy. The trend line projection results in shifts in the ideal mix of real estate and other assets in the portfolio, while inflation cycle projections are used to implement the actual changes desired. Thus, correct timing of a real estate portfolio can be a product of both long-term trend line analysis and shorter-term inflation cycle analysis.

The Performance of Real Versus Financial Assets   The inflation strategy just described is based on the assumptions that (1) volatile inflation cycles will continue and (2) financial and real asset prices and returns are negatively correlated with the inflation rate. The evidence presented by numerous researchers supports the thesis of a negative relationship between the returns on common stocks and inflation, and a positive relationship between inflation and real estate values (e.g., the value of farm land and private residential real estate, for which there are relatively good historical data).[27] However, the evidence does not clearly support the thesis that *all* types of financial assets do well in periods of moderate inflation or that *all* types of real assets do poorly in periods of moderate inflation.

Many investors will choose to remain fully invested in real estate assets over all phases of the inflation cycle. If such a strategy is adopted, then the investor should seek property types and locations that will perform *relatively* well over the downward swing of the inflation cycle. Also, acquisitions should be structured to benefit from this phase of the cycle. For example, an acquisition might be financed with a variable-rate mortgage that calls for a reduction in the interest rate and debt service when market interest rates fall as a result of lower inflation rate expectations. When the debt service declines, the investor will experience an increased cash flow and a higher investment value, other factors remaining constant.

A Capital Budgeting Approach to Inflation Cycle Strategy

A capital budgeting approach can be used in carrying out the inflation cycle strategy presented in the last section. Theoretically, the use of present value or internal-rate-of-return models would enable an investor to identify points A, B, C,

---

[27] Eugene F. Fama and G. William Schwert, "Asset Returns and Inflation," *Journal of Financial Economics,* November 1977, pp. 115–146; John Lintner, "Inflation and Security Returns," *Journal of Finance,* May 1975, pp. 259–280; Jeffrey Jaffe and Gershon Mandelker, "The 'Fisher Effect' for Risky Assets: An Empirical Investigation," *Journal of Finance,* May 1976, pp. 447–458; Zvi Body, "Common Stocks as a Hedge Against Inflation," *Journal of Finance,* May 1976, pp. 459–470; Charles R. Nelson, "Inflation and Rates of Return on Common Stocks," *Journal of Finance,* May 1976, pp. 471–483; Reilly, Marquardt, and Price, op. cit.

and D on the inflation cycle. The investor must first complete three steps in analyzing each investment alternative:

1. Forecast inflation trends and cycles.
2. Forecast the impact of these variables on project income, expenses, property value, and the required rate of return (hurdle rate) over the projected holding period.
3. Use an NPV or IRR model to process the data, using sensitivity and risk analysis to incorporate the impact of alternate possible economic scenarios, and arrive at an acceptable composite measure of return and risk.

The capital budgeting model should be rejecting many real estate alternatives between points A and B and accepting them between points C and D, and vice versa for many financial assets, if the cycle strategy presented is indeed correct. Stated simply, as point A is approached, the expected IRR on a real estate project should be falling relative to the required IRR (NPV approaches 0). At point A they should be equal (NPV = 0), and between points B and C the expected IRR should be less than the required IRR (NPV <0). The reverse should occur at the bottom of the inflation cycle.

A Framework for Forecasting Inflation   Inflation must be analyzed on several levels before it can be translated into estimates of changes in project rents, expenses, property value, and required rates of return, as shown in Exhibit 7–8. The investor begins with a forecast of general inflation, then moves to region, city, and neighborhood forecasts, in which an analysis of the history of rents, expenses, and property values allows the investor to make inflation forecasts under different assumptions about the future. Finally, all of the information analyzed must lead to a project-specific set of financial assumptions. The bottom line, and the most important part of the process, is an estimate of an inflation-adjusted required rate of return, plus forecasts of rents, expenses, and property value. Sensitivity and risk analysis techniques are used to test various possible inflation scenarios on the project's return and risk parameters.

The translation of national inflation trends and expectations into project-specific assumptions is difficult because price inflation is only one of many important supply and demand factors affecting a project's rent, expenses, and property value over time. Inflation analysis must be considered and structured as an integral part of the market and marketability analysis process described in the previous chapters if meaningful input assumptions are to be estimated.

An Example of an Inflation Forecast   Exhibit 7–9 illustrates a hypothetical example of an income property purchased at the beginning of 1981. The investor assumed an inflation rate falling from 10.5 percent in 1981 to 9.5 percent in 1986. Operating expenses are assumed to change at the same annual rate as inflation. Rental income, however, is assumed to lag changes in inflation and expenses on both the downside and the upside of the cycle. Instead of directly forecasting property value changes each year, the investor prefers to forecast the market capitalization rate each year and to determine property value by capitalizing the

EXHIBIT 7–8.   Framework for Predicting Impact of Inflation

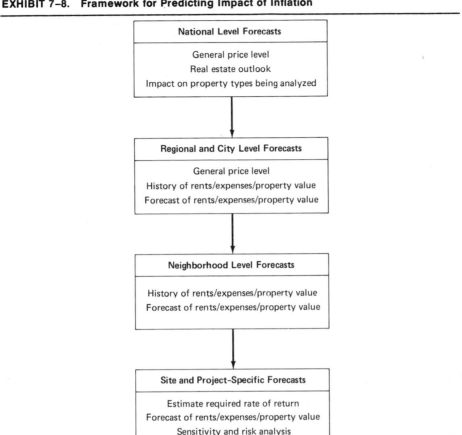

| **National Level Forecasts** |
| General price level |
| Real estate outlook |
| Impact on property types being analyzed |

| **Regional and City Level Forecasts** |
| General price level |
| History of rents/expenses/property value |
| Forecast of rents/expenses/property value |

| **Neighborhood Level Forecasts** |
| History of rents/expenses/property value |
| Forecast of rents/expenses/property value |

| **Site and Project-Specific Forecasts** |
| Estimate required rate of return |
| Forecast of rents/expenses/property value |
| Sensitivity and risk analysis |

residual NOI produced in the annual-cash-flow analysis.[28] The investor's local market data indicate a rising (current NOI) capitalization rate during periods of falling inflation rates, and falling capitalization rates when inflation increases. In effect, when inflation rates decrease, investors demand higher rates of return from current operations, since less property value appreciation is expected. While an investor's required nominal IRR may fall as the inflation rate falls, the NOI capitalization rate increases to reflect the shift in emphasis from future to current returns.

The annual cash flows would then be calculated each year on an after-tax basis and evaluated using an inflation-adjusted (nominal) required IRR. If the investor desired a 15 percent "real" IRR to compensate for the use of money plus various perceived investment risks, the "nominal" required IRR would be that

[28] The resulting estimate of property value becomes cash flow input data in the DCF analysis and is discounted at the investor's required IRR (or, using the IRR method, the estimated IRR is calculated from the cash flow input data and compared to the required IRR).

EXHIBIT 7–9. Most Likely Forecast of Critical DCF Input Variables Under Inflation Cycle Conditions

	Compound Annual Increase					
	1981	1982	1983	1984	1985	1986
Rental income	12%	12%	8%	6%	7%	8%
Operating expenses	12%	10%	8%	8.5%	10%	11%
NOI capitalization rate	8%	9%	10%	9.5%	9%	8.5%

rate adjusted for the expected inflation rate of 10 percent (average) over the six-year holding period, or 26.5 percent:

Nominal rate of return required
= real rate + inflation rate (1 + real rate)
= .15 + .10(1 + .15)
= .265

An investor would invest in a project alternative only if its expected after-tax IRR on equity exceeded 26.5 percent. If real estate alternatives consistently fail to meet the investment criteria, the investor should seek other, more profitable asset alternatives (or reconsider the criteria themselves).

Sources of Information and Data   The appendix following this chapter lists the many sources of essential data for real estate investors, from whom they can be obtained, and their cost. At the national level, the most important sources of information on inflation are the major New York City banks (e.g., Chase's *Business in Brief*) and the Federal Reserve Bank of St. Louis. The latter has led the way in compiling useful data and analyses on monetary growth rates, short- and long-term interest rates, and growth in output and asset prices. Especially useful are its free publications, *Monetary Trends, U.S. Financial Data, Review,* and *Annual U.S. Economic Data,* which can be obtained by writing to the Federal Reserve Bank and requesting them. Magazines like *Business Week* and *National Real Estate Investor,* and monthly newsletters like *Real Estate Investing Letter* and *The Mortgage and Real Estate Executives Report,* also contain many articles and ideas on inflation and its many effects on real estate investments by property type, location, and so forth.

At the regional and city levels, published information is disseminated by state, county, and city departments and agencies, and by the business research departments of universities and local and state planning commissions and agencies. In the private sector, state and local realtor organizations, banks, savings and loan associations, and land title companies and associations publish newsletters and information reports that are available to investors. In many cases the researchers and writers for these organizations can be contacted directly and consulted for various inflation-related information that does not appear in the published documents.

At the neighborhood and project-specific levels, great reliance must be placed on individual contacts with brokers, appraisers, and property managers who are intimately familiar with the history and trends of properties comparable to the property being analyzed, and who collect data on individual properties. Without data and information from these individuals on project-specific trends in rents, expenses, vacancies, and property values, accurate projections for a property being analyzed will be difficult to make.

OTHER REAL ESTATE CYCLES

The most important cycle affecting real estate investors in recent years has been the inflation cycle. However, from the individual investor's viewpoint many other cycles significantly affect rental income, vacancies, expenses, property values, and the cost and availability of mortgage financing. Some of these cycles are closely related to inflation, while others are not. Some are related primarily to new properties while others tend to affect existing properties. Some are not very important for investors operating on a national scale but are critical for individual investors operating in only one or a few local market areas.

In the following section we will discuss the various types of cycles that can affect the investor. We will begin with the macroeconomic cycles and work toward the microeconomic location- and property-oriented cycles. From a decision-making viewpoint, the local cycles are generally the most critical ones affecting particular investment decisions, and therefore deserve the most attention from the investor.

The Macro Real Estate Cycle

Long Cycles   The most general form of real estate cycle that is of interest to historians and some investors is called the *long cycle* and is based on total real estate transactions or sales recorded in real estate markets throughout the United States. Roy Wenzlick, publisher of the famous, but now defunct, journal *The Real Estate Analyst,* charted long cycles from 1795 through 1973 (when his publication was sold). In *The Coming Boom in Real Estate,* Wenzlick pointed out that the average duration of the long cycle from peak to peak (or trough to trough) averaged 18 1/3 years.[29] Exhibit 7–10 shows Wenzlick's index, which was based on the number of voluntary transfers of property in relation to the number of families.

[29] Alan Rabinowitz, *The Real Estate Gamble* [New York: AMACOM (a Division of American Management Association), 1980], p. 238.

EXHIBIT 7-10. The 18-1/3 Year Real Estate Cycle, 1795–1973

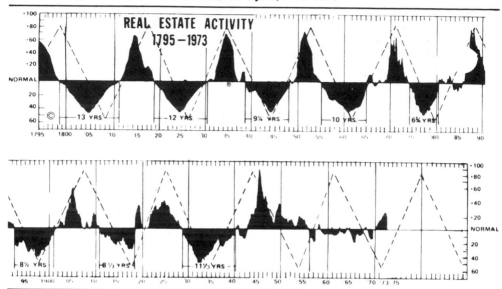

SOURCE: *The Real Estate Analyst,* November 1973.

A similar long cycle of real estate activity was charted by Fred Case for Los Angeles County from 1850 to 1972.[30] Case's real estate cycle is a report of deed recordings per 1000 population in Los Angeles County. On average, the Los Angeles real estate cycles were found to occur every 18 to 20 years, with a statistical average of 18 2/3 years. However, the cycles were longer or shorter on many occasions, and such deviations appeared to be tied to important historical events, such as wars, depressions, and major technological innovations like the automobile and railroads. Admittedly, since such historical events are difficult to predict, and since they disrupt the cycle for many years, precise forecasting methods may never be developed.

Short Cycles In contrast to long cycles, short cycles last up to five years and are caused by shifts in the money markets, the availability of mortgage funds, and government housing programs like FHA and VA.[31] In his recent book on real estate cycles, Rabinowitz notes that most attempts to involve the general public in income-producing real estate ventures (through security offerings) have been a failure and have resulted in five-year cycles of market acceptability. The examples cited are 1926–1931 for the sale of guaranteed mortgages, 1952–1957 for the great days of urban redevelopment finance, 1957–1962 for the first wave of publicly offered syndicate shares, 1960–1965 for the early land development securities, 1965–1970 for interest by big business in land development, and 1968–1974 for the Section 236 syndicates, REITs, and new communities.[32]

[30] Fred E. Case, *Real Estate Economics: A Systematic Introduction* (Los Angeles: California Association of Realtors, 1974), pp. 102–105.
[31] Ibid., p. 102.
[32] Rabinowitz, p. 237.

The Causes and Dynamics of a Real Estate Cycle

A real estate cycle is caused by shifts in supply and demand. Exhibit 7– 11 shows the important relationships between the supply and demand forces that affect real estate activities. It is critical that investors understand the flow and sequence of those activities if they hope to understand the dynamics of the real estate cycle and learn how to cope with it.

Let us begin by setting out the various stages of a real estate cycle and follow through a typical sequence of activities that might occur to produce that cycle.[33] The starting point is the beginning of a new real estate upswing after the trough has passed and there is significant pent-up demand.

Stage One   There is an imbalance between demand and supply. The unemployment rate is high, but the general business economy is expanding; government monetary and fiscal policies are expansionary; inflation is moderate; and mortgages are available at relatively low interest rates. Population and family size are increasing; incomes are rising; and better employment results in increased demand for housing. The price of housing has not increased rapidly, and construction starts have been in the basement for some time. Thus, the supply of housing and other real estate is relatively fixed over the short run, with demolitions and removals offsetting completions of new space to some extent.

It should be noted that housing activity dominates the real estate market cycle, since the volume of housing activity is far greater than that of commercial property activity. Thus, most discussions of real estate cycles emphasize the role of the residential sector. Also, we will see that single-family residential construction activities generally lead multifamily and commercial property construction.

Let us continue. As a result of increased demand, vacancies decrease as existing vacant homes are sold and apartments are rented. Home prices and apartment rents rise sharply relative to operating and development costs. Builders of single-family homes become optimistic; profits are rising; and the construction of new single-family homes picks up and dominates the market. Ample construction mortgage credit is available at favorable rates, and builders respond by providing medium-priced housing in large quantities in subdivisions. As subdividers respond to increased homebuilding activity, vacant land near the city begins to disappear and subdivisions move further out. Land prices begin to rise as a result. New apartment complexes have been planned, but the planning and construction cycle for them is much longer than that for single-family homes.

Stage Two   Sales activity rises sharply and the market is very active. The selling prices of homes are increasing, as are the costs of construction, and businesses of all types are expanding. Homes are sold very soon after they have been completed, and builders are building actively in all price ranges. Investors and speculators begin to enter the market to capitalize on the residential construction boom and the availability of mortgage credit at low rates. Multifamily housing projects begin to take off rapidly, followed by increasing numbers of commercial

---

[33] The stages of activity discussed here are based on a presentation by Fred E. Case, op. cit., pp. 107– 109; see also Sherman J. Maisel and Stephen E. Roulac, *Real Estate Investment and Finance* (New York: McGraw-Hill, 1976), pp. 183– 188.

EXHIBIT 7-11. Forces Affecting Real Estate Cycles

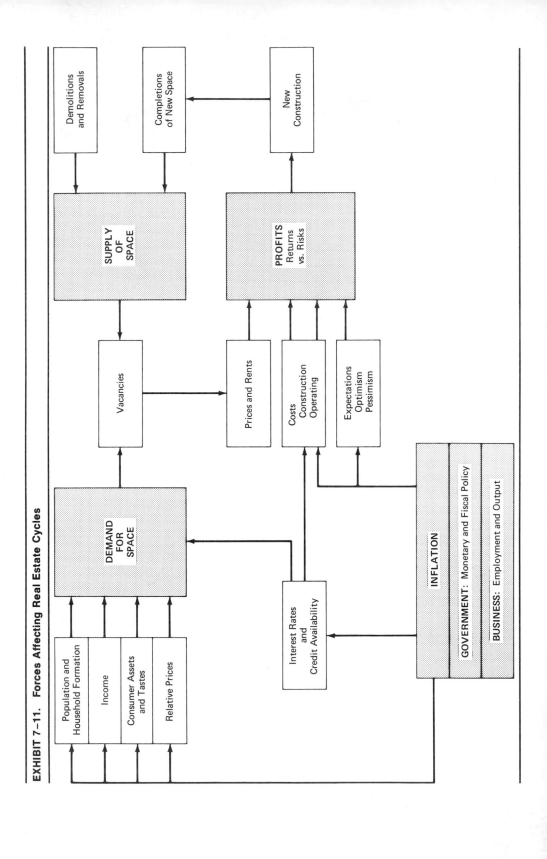

and industrial projects, which are developed to service the expanded residential areas. The demand for all types of space is high, and supply is increasing rapidly to meet the pent-up demand. All market indicators, rents and prices, mortgage recordings, building permits, and deed recordings increase to record levels. Inflation and interest rates are also rising, but building profits are still high and expectations are still optimistic. Investors are actively buying existing properties of all types and bidding up the selling prices of those properties.

Stage Three   Although demand increases at a steady rate, new construction tends to come onto the market all at once. Too many builders getting the same idea at the same time eventually cause an oversupply of space as projects are completed. Home markets become saturated; unsold inventory builds up; profits decrease; and builders begin advertising campaigns and offer additional amenities and financial inducements to buy at higher prices. Apartment projects and commercial properties are completed in large numbers and appear on the market. Inflation has increased rapidly, and the Federal Reserve is now applying the monetary brakes, causing interest rates to rise further. Some disintermediation is occurring in savings institutions, credit controls reduce the available supply of loanable funds, and effective demand for homes is decreased. With high home prices, high interest rates, and greater difficulty in qualifying for loans, the attitude toward homeownership changes and rentals become preferable. The prices of older homes begin to fall; the average time between listing and sale increases; and builders become pessimistic. Rising land and interest costs further decrease profit expectations and building feasibility. Overexpansion of new apartment space results in higher vacancy rates, and rental income levels off or decreases as landlords compete for tenants.

Stage Four   General business activity is being curtailed as the Fed continues to use monetary brakes to fight inflation. A decline in real estate activity is beginning, although the supply of commercial space is still increasing at a relatively strong pace. Builders are having trouble selling their properties and are taking second mortgages and offering concessions to facilitate sales. Holding costs are extremely high, as prime lending rates have increased to record levels. The apartment developers have overbuilt the market. As a result, renters are getting better services as landlords compete to avoid vacancies and turnover costs. Vacancies increase overall, however, and in overbuilt locations reach levels as high as 20–30 percent. Cash flows and profitability decline; builders and owners have difficulty meeting mortgage obligations; and foreclosures become more frequent. Lenders become pessimistic and cease to make new permanent loans on properties, and interim lenders demand repayment of loans with accrued interest. Disintermediation continues.

Stage Five   Business activity is slowing, unemployment increasing, and inflation continuing at a record pace and causing real incomes to fall. Credit is tight; interim and permanent mortgage interest rates are at record highs. Consumers and producers are pessimistic. The real estate cycle begins a rather sharp decline. High unemployment occurs, especially in the building trades; renters double up to save money; and the rate of new-household formation slows. Effective demand for all types of space is decreasing while substantial amounts of new space are being completed or are still under construction. How far down the real estate cycle goes depends on the degree of overbuilding that has taken place, what changes take place in restrictive monetary policies and lending practices, the degree to which lenders will work with developers and property owners to avoid foreclosures, and the degree to which real estate demand is decreased by the general economic recession. Stage five will end and a new stage one will begin only when there is an improvement in income and employment in the general business economy and consumers become more optimistic.

The Real Estate Cycle and the General Business Cycle

Clearly, there is a close (but not necessarily synchronized) relationship between the general business cycle and the real estate cycle. The character of the national real estate cycle is determined primarily by business conditions in the overall economy. Likewise, the character of local real estate cycles is determined by business conditions in local real estate markets. Basic business conditions influence real estate cycles directly. Real estate market activity increases when general business conditions become more favorable, and decreases when business activity slows. As we have seen, when the general economy is in an upswing, employment and income are up, consumption is up, and there is increased demand for all types of real estate space. The result is rising rents, sales prices, and expected profits and returns. The same is true in reverse. But this should be no great surprise to most students of real estate economics, who know that real estate demand is a derived demand and, hence, depends on other economic activity for its substance.

The Real Estate Cycle Is More Volatile   Real estate market activity tends to lag upward movements in business activity but goes to higher levels. During the downswing, real estate market activity tends to lead business activity, and it declines faster and goes down lower. Typically, business cycle changes are 20 percent above and below the long-term trend line of activity. In contrast, real estate cycles average 40 percent above and below the trend line.[34] It is no wonder that the real estate business is considered a boom and bust, rags or riches business.

One underlying reason for high volatility in real estate is imperfect markets. Developers, equity investors, and lenders consistently misjudge market demand and overproduce space. Unlike the industrial sector, which can curtail production schedules and reduce output to the level of demand relatively quickly, the amount of real estate space in production cannot be curtailed easily, and once it is on the market it is too permanent. Also, like any durable good, real estate is subject to wide demand fluctuations because consumers can postpone the decision to buy when economic conditions are poor and pessimism prevails.

The Increasing Importance of National and International Cycles   In the past, real estate investors could largely ignore national and international business de-

[34] Case, p. 109.

velopments and concentrate on the analysis of general business activity and trends in the particular SMSA or urban areas in which they operated and on the investment projects under consideration. However, because so many investors and developers have experienced serious setbacks in their local market areas as a direct results of actions at the national and international levels, more importance is being attached to the national and international outlook in evaluating projects.

The booms and busts in new and existing properties will increasingly result from conditions outside of the immediate market area, such as inflation, wide fluctuations in the availability and cost of mortgage funds, and the cost and availability of foreign crude oil. Luckily, the investor does not have to be a trained economist to understand the implications of national and international events, since analyses and interpretations of those events are readily available through publications like the *Wall Street Journal, The Kiplinger Report, Business Week, Money,* and *Forbes.* However, the investor must learn to translate national trends and the forecasts of economists into usable information at the local level. Their implications with respect to the risk and return parameters of specific property alternatives must be analyzed and understood.

Other Cycles

There are nine other types of real estate cycles that may directly or indirectly affect investor returns and risks.

The Construction Cycles[35]   When money is plentiful and interest rates are low, builders build to satisfy pent-up demand from the period of low construction activity. This is the most significant factor in housing construction. Many builders enter the market at the start of the cycle. Their success induces others to enter the market until supply equals or surpasses demand. Unless builders monitor supply and the absorption rate, they end up overproducing, which is precisely what occurred in the apartment and office building markets in 1973– 1975.

The go-stop-go from all-out production to overbuilding and a construction halt creates a kind of ratchet effect. Demand increases rather smoothly, but supply tends to increase in steps, as Exhibit 7– 12 shows. This step effect is most easily identified and certainly more pronounced on a local level. Temporary oversupply is caused by the large number of small firms involved that are not very sophisticated in supply and demand research. Production is usually based on their demonstrated construction skill, the availability of manpower, and their ability to obtain financing. If their bankers do not question the construction feasibility, the projects are built. Often a number of builders simultaneously initiate the same types of projects for completion in the shortest possible time, with little communication among them. Thus, the potential for continuation of this cyclical phenomenon seems to be built into the free-enterprise construction business.

The Mortgage Money Cycle   As noted previously, the mortgage money cycle is highly correlated with the business and construction cycle. During the contrac-

[35] Rabinowitz, pp. 240– 243; Clarence D. Long, *Business Cycles as a Theory of Investment* (Princeton, N.J.: Princeton University Press, 1940); Homer Hoyt, *The Urban Real Estate Cycle — Performance and Prospects,* Technical Bulletin no. 38 (Washington, D.C.: Urban Land Institute, June 1960).

EXHIBIT 7-12.   Construction Supply/Demand Relationship

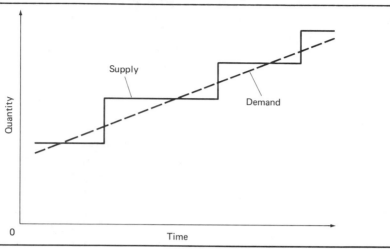

tion phase of the business cycle, Federal Reserve monetary controls almost always include credit controls in addition to tightening the money supply, which places upward pressure on interest rates. Credit controls mean that fewer buyers are able to come up with the increased equity required to compensate for reduced loan-to-value-ratio mortgages. Also, rising interest rates result in higher mortgage payments and lower income-to-debt-service ratios, which in turn result in smaller loans on income property and reduced project feasibility. Also, rising interest rates and debt service payments result in fewer qualified homebuyers because their incomes are too low to service the debt.

Two additional mechanisms that historically shut off permanent mortgage lending for single-family housing are disintermediation and usury ceilings. Disintermediation seems to have been moderated significantly by the introduction of money market certificates as a deposit vehicle for financial intermediaries. The federal government has taken steps toward rescinding state usury laws. If these two mechanisms become inoperative in the future, the historic mortgage boom—bust cycle will have been moderated considerably.

Urban Area and City Cycles   In Chapters 4–6 we discussed at great length the growth and decline of metropolitan areas, the analysis of market area fluctuations, and strategies for dealing with these factors. We saw that the character of the local real estate cycle is determined by business conditions in the local real estate markets. The driving force for increased real estate activity is the vitality of the business sector of the local economy, which is especially dependent on the basic industries that export products and services out of the metropolitan area and cause a multiplier effect throughout the service sectors.

The local business and real estate cycles can be substantially different from the national business and real estate cycles. To the extent that the mix of basic and nonbasic industries differs from the mix in the national economy, a city's cycles will have different characteristics and timing. Indeed, some local cycles will be countercyclical to the national cycle and those of other cities. In the middle of the energy crises of 1974–1976, which created serious economic problems for Frostbelt cities on the East Coast and in the Midwest, cities like Houston and Midland-Odessa, Texas, and Anchorage, Alaska, all of which are oil cities, were experiencing strong upswings in economic activity, population growth, and real incomes. Cities dominated by industries that produce consumer and producer durable goods experience the widest business and real estate fluctuations, while cities that specialize in consumer necessities and services have the most moderate fluctuations. As a city grows and its industrial mix becomes more diversified, its cycles begin to approximate the behavior of the national cycles.

Neighborhood Cycles   Each neighborhood has its own specific land use life cycle that affects real estate activity. Exhibit 7–13 shows a life cycle scenario for a typical neighborhood or urban area. The public sector events that characterize the cycle are shown in lowercase letters on the outside of the cycle, and the private sector real estate activities are shown in capital letters on the inside of the cycle. Keep in mind that this is a typical sequence of activity; each neighborhood is unique and differs to some degree in its development characteristics.

The best opportunities for increases in value appear in the early stages of neighborhood development, when new uses come into existence and the neighborhood is characterized by a high level of building and construction activity. The risk is also relatively high during these stages because of potential competition

EXHIBIT 7–13. Stages in the Land Use Life Cycle

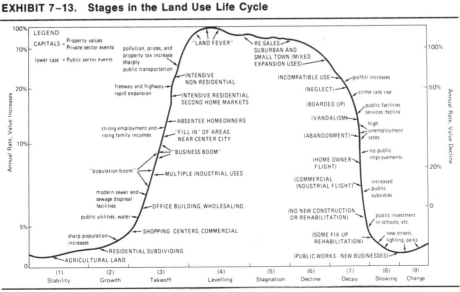

SOURCE: From the book *Investing in Real Estate* by Fred E. Case. © 1978 by Prentice-Hall, Inc. Published by Prentice-Hall, Inc., Englewood Cliffs, New Jersey 07632.

from other vacant sites and other builders and investors. As the neighborhood matures (the leveling stage) and vacant land becomes scarce, the risk tends to decline, but so do the returns. Depending on the investor's return/risk preferences, he or she should choose to invest during one of the first four neighborhood stages. Real estate values will increase during these periods, although the rate of increase will fall as the neighborhood approaches the stage of stagnation. As a general rule, most real estate advisers tell investors to avoid investing in neighborhoods that are in the declining stages. On the other hand, new real estate opportunities appear for the high-risk-oriented investor at the end of the cycle, when the neighborhood enters a period of change and renewal.

The investor should be careful to choose neighborhoods within a city that are consistent with his or her return and risk objectives. Ideally, one should rank-order acceptable neighborhoods and search for investment opportunities accordingly.

Property-Specific Cycles   Different types of properties are subject to different demand and supply relationships. As a result, each city has a unique set of property-specific cycles in apartments, office buildings, retail and shopping center properties, industrial buildings, and so on. While the office building market in city A is becoming overbuilt this year and will remain so for the next two years, the market for shopping centers in city A may be characterized by relatively well-balanced supply and demand and prospects for continued high absorption over the next two years. The exact reverse may be true in city B. It is for this reason that diversification by property type and location is popular among portfolio builders.

Halpin identifies two common types of property-specific cycles that result in market overkill cycles:[36]

1. A *new concept/market overkill cycle.* A good example of this is the booming cycle of the swinger apartments in the 1970s. When first introduced they offered a new concept in living to singles and were very popular. They became a good place for the single man or woman to get in the swing and "body snatch." However, as time passed, too many developers jumped into this market. The quality of the residents deteriorated; management problems developed; and swinger apartments gained a negative image in many markets. Swinger apartments often became problem properties.

2. A *hot market/overkill cycle.* When more and more large corporations were getting into real estate in the late 1960s and early 1970s, they reshaped industry patterns and economics. The trend was toward large, multimarket producers and investors who were anxious to expand into new markets. Expansion-minded companies systematically researched regional and local statistics throughout the country and attached growth labels to certain cities. Unfortunately, many of the resulting corporate strategies tended to be first self-fulfilling and then self-destroying. The cycle, thus, is as follows: Forecasts reveal an opportunity; investors and developers rush in to exploit it; and competitive overkill follows and destroys profit opportunities.

[36] Michael C. Halpin, *Profit Planning for Real Estate Development* (Homewood, Ill.: Dow Jones-Irwin, 1977), pp. 105–108.

Seasonal Cycles The timing of real estate transactions with respect to the month or season significantly affects a property's marketability, selling price, and terms of purchase and sale. It was common before the Tax Reform Acts of 1978 and 1976 for real estate tax shelter syndication activity to increase sharply before the end of the year, when wealthy investors realized that they had too much taxable income and needed to shelter some of it. Many syndicators who specialized in tax-shelter-oriented investments geared their operations for frenzied activity in the weeks leading up to December 31, hoping to take advantage of the often emotional tax avoidance syndrome that developed at this time of the year. While tax reforms have reduced the number of allowable year-end deductions, this seasonal trend persists in some areas.

Most real estate investment activity shows some seasonal tendencies. For example, investors in single-family homes (in most areas) are aware that both marketability and price will tend to be most favorable during the spring and summer months. While the seasonal fluctuations differ by region and are most notable in the Northeast, median home prices tend to rise through the summer months and decline toward the end of the year.

Property, Ownership, and Investor Life Cycles In Chapter 2 we discussed these three concepts at some length. Property life cycles were conceptualized by an eight-stage pyramid that encompassed the entire development and holding period—from the idea inception stage through the demise or abandonment of the project at the end of its useful economic life. The ownership life cycle is a particular period within the property life cycle encompassing the holding period experienced by one ownership group, from the day the investment is purchased through the disposal of the property at the end of the holding period. The investor life cycle is related to the types and amounts of returns and risks sought by the investor at different stages of life (usually related to age). As we have emphasized repeatedly, the analysis of every real estate investment should recognize and reflect these life cycles, which affect the return/risk relationships on which investment decisions are based.

The Popularity Cycle Also referred to as the bandwagon or herd cycle, this cycle typically occurs during boom-and-bust periods of real estate activity and is stimulated by the news media. If investors are currently successful in a particular type of property, location, or field, many others are attracted until the market becomes glutted. After a while those who cannot compete successfully drop out of the market. A new cycle begins when another attractive opportunity occurs. Central to the existence of this cycle is the effect of the news media on the attitudes and emotions of consumers and investors. During the upswing of the cycle, the news media exaggerate information on investment opportunities and potential profits, creating many false expectations and much unwarranted enthusiasm. On the downside the reverse occurs.

The bandwagon tendency is evident even among sophisticated investors. The rise and fall of the firms in the REIT business in the early 1970s are testimony to this fact.

Social Change Cycles A real estate investor must continually analyze the basic social and cultural changes occurring in society and their possible effects on changing real estate needs, returns, and risks. Increasingly, investors and developers are designing properties for flexible use as a method of coping with rapid social change. Minitheaters are constructed in shopping centers. Their seating capacities are relatively small and they are built on a level floor. If such use becomes unprofitable, the lease can be canceled and the space converted into a store.

Rapid social change creates cycles in property values. One study was performed concerning the impact of so-called hippies on property values.[37] It concluded that hippies affect values both negatively and positively. "Good" hippies spend money, do not destroy property, and cause property values to increase. However, they are often followed by "bad" hippies, who are panhandlers, do not spend money, and steal to support their drug habits, thereby causing property values to decline. This property value cycle can occur within a very short time, as it did in areas like Wells Street and Old Town in Chicago in the late 1960s.

Strategies for Dealing with Cycles

Many of the strategies developed early in the chapter for coping with inflation cycles apply equally well to all of the cycles discussed here. Among the basic tenets are the following:

1. *Identify important cycles.* Which cycles affect your investments? The investor must be constantly on the alert to identify new cycles and their implications.
2. *Research their effects on investment variables.* What short- and long-run impacts will these cycles have on rents, expenses, property values, financing variables, and capitalization rates? Be careful not to project trends indefinitely or use assumptions that are static and do not allow for change.
3. *Develop an investment strategy to cope with them.* Their possible impact can be included in the investor's cash flow projections and the resulting measures of investment return and risk. The concepts of designing a flexible portfolio, diversifying to reduce risk, timing investments correctly, and choosing investments that will let you sleep at night apply to all real estate cycles.

It is important that the investor learn to develop his or her forecasting abilities and then have a systematic and logical method of processing the information developed. Too many variables must be dealt with to leave this process to intuitive management techniques.

Sensitivity to the Law of Contrary Opinion   Successive investors recognize that they are operating in a highly cyclical environment in which most average investors guess wrong a large percentage of the time. What appears to be right to the average investor often has a high probability of being wrong, for the many reasons

[37] Anthony Downs, "Current Economic Trends: Impact upon Appraisal of Real Estate," *The Appraisal Journal,* April 1971, pp. 169– 170.

that have been given throughout this chapter. Excellence can be achieved only by those who are strong enough to follow a path contrary to that of the masses. To remain with the masses and do what everyone else is doing is to be mediocre at best. To achieve excellence, the investor must be sensitive to real estate cycles at all levels of the economy and have the courage to venture away from the consensus and lead the masses. Investments must be bought and sold before cyclical trends are fully reflected in real estate prices and activity.

Surviving the Downside, Preparing for the Upside At a minimum, every investor should be financially prepared to survive a serious real estate recession. The keys to such survival are liquidity and tight accounting controls. Cash and cash resources, including prearranged lines of credit, should be sufficient to avoid insolvency. Unnecessary spending can be reduced to a minimum. If the investor correctly forecasts a serious real estate recession, properties can be sold at the top of the cycle, before the market reflects the downturn. The wise investor knows when to slow an aggressive investment expansion program and begin a consolidation period in which emphasis is placed on planning for the next upside of the cycle; he has a cool head and a sense of balance, and acts in moderation.[38]

An Art, Not a Science The process described here is not simple and cannot be mastered quickly. Much like mastering the art of karate, developing and implementing a successful real estate cycle strategy requires much study, time, and effort, and an aggressive approach to the problem. But the expected returns relative to the risks may be great.

SUMMARY

In this chapter we introduced the complex subjects of inflation and real estate cycles. The many facets of each were arranged in a logical framework consistent with the techniques and concepts developed in the previous chapters. Important aspects of that framework include (1) identifying the inflation and other real estate cycle variables that influence returns and risks; (2) measuring their short- and long-run effects on rents, vacancies, operating expenses, financing costs and terms, property values, and the investor's required IRR; (3) processing the data through conventional DCF, sensitivity, and risk analysis models; and (4) developing an investment strategy that will provide decision rules for shifting the investor's portfolio over the cycle. The analysis presumes that investors wish to maximize their investment returns relative to risks; that real estate cycles do exist, can be predicted, and do have a dramatic impact on investment returns and risks; that investors can develop forecasting ability which will enable them to measure the relationships between specific cycles and cash flow variables; and that shifting between real and financial assets over the cycle is a viable investment alternative.

Since inflation is perceived to be the most important variable influencing investment returns and risks, primary emphasis is placed on the development of strategies for coping with it. Nine other types of real estate cycles were analyzed in

[38] Halpin, p. 114.

later parts of the chapter, including long and short real estate cycles, construction cycles, neighborhood cycles, seasonal cycles, popularity cycles, and social change cycles. Since most real estate activity is cyclical in nature, the investor's decision-making process must explicitly consider the nature and dynamics of these other real estate cycles. Failure to successfully cope with any one of these cycles can result in financial disaster.

Sources of Market Data for Real Estate Investors

I. NATIONAL TRENDS

(*Note:* For trends relating to specific property types, see end of chapter bibliographies in Part IV.)

Government and Quasi Government Publications

1. *Annual U.S. Economics Data*
Federal Reserve Bank of St. Louis
P.O. Box 442
St. Louis, Missouri 63166
(monthly, free)

2. *Census of Population and Housing* (1980)
(Population and housing characteristics of cities by census tracts, published by the U.S. Department of Commerce, Bureau of Census)
Superintendent of Documents
U.S. Government Printing Office
Washington, D.C. 20402
(request by state, $.85/copy)

3. *Construction Review*
Superintendent of Documents
U.S. Government Printing Office
Washington, D.C. 20402
(monthly, $19.00/year, $2.25/copy)

4. *Economic Indicators*
Office of Economic Research
U.S. Department of Commerce
Washington, D.C.
(monthly, free)

5. *Economic Report of the President*
Superintendent of Documents
U.S. Government Printing Office
Washington, D.C. 20402
(annual, $1.50/copy)

6. *Federal Reserve Bulletin*
Publication Services
Board of Governors of the Federal Reserve System
Washington, D.C. 20551
(monthly, $20.00/year, $2.00/copy)

7. *Housing Characteristics*
(U.S. Department of Commerce, Bureau of Census)
Superintendent of Documents
U.S. Government Printing Office
Washington, D.C. 20402
(irregular, $6.00/year)

8. *HUD Newsletter*
Superintendent of Documents
U.S. Government Printing Office
Washington, D.C. 20402
(weekly, $23.00/year)

9. *MGIC Newsletter*
MGIC Plaza
Milwaukee, Wisconsin 53201
(monthly, free)

10. *Monetary Trends*
Federal Reserve Bank of St. Louis
P.O. Box 442
St. Louis, Missouri 63166
(10 times/year, free)

11. *Monthly Review*
Federal Reserve Bank of San Francisco
P.O. Box 7702
San Francisco, California 94120
(monthly, free)

12. *Review*
Federal Reserve Bank of St. Louis
P.O. Box 442
St. Louis, Missouri 63166
(monthly, free)

13. **Survey of Current Business**
U.S. Department of Commerce
Washington, D.C.
  (monthly, $27.00 – $46.00/year,
  depends on classification)

14. **U.S. Financial Data**
Federal Reserve Bank of St. Louis
P.O. Box 442
St. Louis, Missouri 63166
  (monthly, free)

Publications by Financial Institutions

1. **Business in Brief**
Economics Group
The Chase Manhattan Bank, N.A.
New York, New York 10015
  (bimonthly, free)

2. **Credit and Capital Markets**
Bankers Trust Company
P.O. Box 318, Church Street Station
New York, New York 10015
  (periodic, free)

3. **Life Insurance Fact Book**
American Council of Life Insurance
1850 K Street, N.W.
Washington, D.C. 20006
  (annual, free upon request)

4. **Savings and Loan Sourcebook**
  (formerly *Savings and Loan Fact
  Book*)
U.S. Savings and Loan League
111 East Wacker Drive
Chicago, Illinois 60601
  (annual, single copies free upon request)

Magazines

1. **Architectural Forum**
2160 Paterson Street
Cincinati, Ohio 45214
  (ten times/year, $14.00/year;
  $2.00/copy)

2. **Business Week**
McGraw-Hill, Inc.
1221 Avenue of the Americas
New York, New York 10020
  (weekly, $34.95/year; $1.75/copy)

3. **Changing Times**
The Kiplinger Washington Editors, Inc.
Editors Park, Maryland 20782
  (monthly, $12.00/year;
  $1.25/copy)

4. **Forbes**
Forbes, Inc.
60 Fifth Avenue
New York, New York 10011
  (biweekly, $30.00/year,
  $2.50/copy)

5. **Fortune**
Time, Inc.
3435 Wilshire Blvd.
Los Angeles, California 90010
  (biweekly, $30.00/year;
  $2.50/copy)

6. **Housing**
McGraw-Hill, Inc.
1221 Avenue of the Americas
New York, New York 10020
  (monthly, $20.00 – $32.00/year,
  depends on classification;
  $3.00/copy)

7. **Money**
Time, Inc.
3435 Wilshire Blvd.
Los Angeles, California 90010
  (monthly, $21.95/year;
  $2.00/copy)

8. **Mortgage Banking**
  (formerly *Mortgage Banker*)
Mortgage Bankers Association of
America
P.O. Box 37236
Washington, D.C. 20013
  (monthly, $20.00/year;
  $2.50/copy)

9. **Multi-Housing News**
Gralla Publications
1515 Broadway
New York, New York 10036
  (monthly, free to qualified real
  estate professionals, otherwise
  $30.00/year; $3.50/copy)

10. *National Real Estate Investor*
Communication Channels, Inc.
6285 Barfield Road
Atlanta, Georgia 30328
  (monthly, $38.00/year,
  $3.50/copy)

11. *The Financial Planner*
International Association of Financial
Planners
5775 Peachtree Dunwoody Road,
Suite 120-C
Atlanta, Georgia 30342
  (monthly, $24.00/year)

Newsletters, Newspapers, Special Reports, Other

1. *Real Estate Investing Newsletter*
H.B.J. Newsletter, Inc.
1 East First Street
Duluth, Minnesota 55802
  (monthly, $72.00/year)

2. *Real Estate Investment Planning*
Institute for Business Planning, Inc.
IBP Plaza
Englewood Cliffs, New Jersey 07632
  (twice monthly update looseleaf
  service, $296.85/year)

3. *Real Estate Report*
Real Estate Research Corporation
72 West Adams Street
Chicago, Illinois 60603
  (quarterly, single copies free upon
  request)

4. *The Kiplinger Washington News-letter*
The Kiplinger Washington Editors, Inc.
1729 H. Street, N.W.
Washington, D.C. 20006
  (weekly, $42.00/year)

5. *The Mortgage and Real Estate Executives Report*
Warren, Gorham & Lamont, Inc.
210 South Street, Boston, Massachusetts 02111
  (twice monthly, $78.00/year)

6. *Wall Street Journal*
Dow Jones & Co., Inc.
200 Barnett Road
Chicopee, Massachusetts 01021
  (five days per week, $77.00/year,
  $.35/copy)

II. REGIONAL DATA

(*Note:* For trends relating to specific property types, see end-of-chapter bibliographies in Part IV. Some sources cited above have regional, area, and city reviews and information, e.g., *National Real Estate Investor, Housing*).

General Sources

1. Business research bureaus
2. Financial institutions—individual commercial banks, savings and loan associations, land title companies
3. Office of the Governor
4. Regional Council of Governments (COGs)
5. Regional real estate newspapers (e.g., *Southwest Real Estate News*)
6. Regional and state universities
7. State builders associations
8. State employment commissions
9. State associations of land title companies
10. State mortgage bankers associations
11. State Realtors® associations
12. State saving and loan league associations

13. *The Kiplinger Newsletter* (state editions)
14. U.S. government state and regional offices, and quasi-public organizations (e.g., FHA, FNMA, FHLMC)

Specific Examples

Business Review
Wells Fargo Bank
Economics Department
P.O. Box 44000
San Francisco, California 94144
(monthly, free)

California Savings and Housing Data Book
California Savings and Loan League
P.O. Box R
Pasadena, California
(annual)

Community Guides
(various California counties and cities)
Economic Research Division
Security-First National Bank
P.O. Box 2097, Terminal Annex
Los Angeles, California 90051
(irregular)

Economic Report of the Governor
Office of the Governor
Sacramento, California
(annual)

Western Business Forecast
(a survey of businessmen's opinions)
The Prudential Insurance Company
Western Home Office
5757 Wilshire Boulevard
Los Angeles, California 90036
(quarterly, free)

III.   CITY AND NEIGHBORHOOD INFORMATION

Location Analysis

1. Survey of business conditions and real estate activity in the area	Research department of banks
2. Business conditions and real estate markets	Banks; Federal Reserve Banks; land title companies
3. Planning reports	Planning commissions
4. Population, housing, and employment	U.S. Bureau of the Census; state departments of finance, state departments of employment, state chambers of commerce
5. Deeds recorded; building permits	County recorder; departments of building and safety
6. Locational analysis guides	Urban Land Institute, Washington, D.C.; research departments of financial institutions; chambers of commerce; large businesses
7. Population, markets, family income	Research departments of local newspapers

Site Analysis

1. Field surveys	Own resources or consulting groups
2. Tax assessments and amounts	Tax assessor
3. Building codes	Departments of building and safety
4. Zoning, planning, land uses	Planning commissions
5. Traffic and traffic patterns	Departments of highways or streets; automotive clubs
6. Land use maps	Planning commissions; map companies; Sanborn maps
7. Sales, sales prices, terms	Land title insurance companies; ownership map and book service companies
8. Census maps and reports; block books	U.S. Bureau of the Census
9. Rents, expenses, property values, vacancies	Property management companies, brokerage companies, appraisal firms

III

The Investment Analysis and Financial Structuring Process

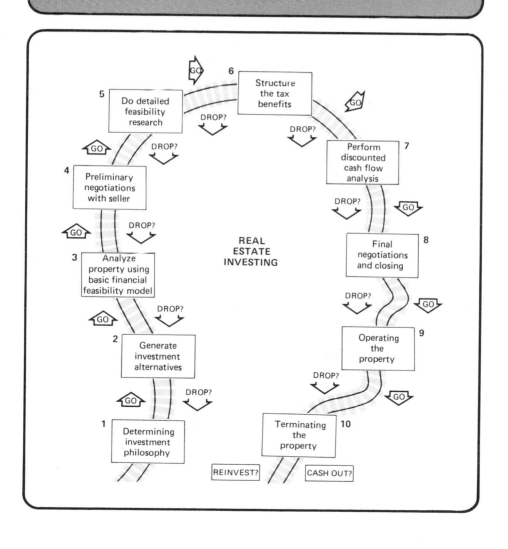

This part of the text develops a normative methodology for investment analysis and financial structuring that considers the efficient allocation of human, as well as financial, capital resources. A brief synopsis is illustrated on the preceding page. Unfortunately, most investment theories ignore the time resource problems of the decision maker—the time allocation problems associated with performing investment analysis and making accept/reject decisions. Furthermore, most theories implicitly and naively assume a one-shot investment analysis process which results in a "go/no go" decision.

In contrast, we advocate a stepwise investment analysis procedure which recognizes that knowledgeable investors develop "drop-continue on" points, and that they have multiple investment objectives and constraints that are applied at different time stages in the project evaluation process. Also, different procedures and levels of analysis are appropriate for different types of property and different sizes of projects. A "quick-and-dirty" analysis may be appropriate for a six-unit apartment project or a wealthy investor (given the return/risk trade-off preferences), while the professional documentation and standards of quantitative and qualitative analysis for a pension fund investing in a $500 million combination-use building would be very sophisticated.

The chapters in this part generally follow the steps outlined on the preceding page:

Chapter 8:   Investment Strategy
Chapter 9:   Selecting the Ownership Entity
Chapter 10: The Basic Financial Feasibility Model
Chapter 11: Discounted Cash Flow and Ratio Analysis
Chapter 12: Risk Analysis and Risk Management
Chapter 13: Tax Planning and Detailed Financial Analysis
Chapter 14: Financing and Refinancing Techniques
Chapter 15: The Art of Negotiations
Chapter 16: Property and Venture Management
Chapter 17: Termination of the Investment

A comprehensive case study, the 86-unit Aspen Wood Apartments, is presented at the end of each chapter and illustrates the application of the concepts and techniques discussed.

8

Investment Strategy

Many real estate investors are motivated to develop a sound investment strategy only after they have experienced financial troubles. Even many of the major financial institutions and corporate giants that entered the real estate investment business during the last two decades have poor performance records. There is considerable evidence that these disappointing results and unrealized expectations can be traced largely to deficient investment strategies.[1]

In this chapter we will define a framework for a real estate investment strategy and examine the elements of that strategy for various types of investors. A normative methodology will be developed to guide the investor through the investment analysis and financial structuring process, one that focuses on existing projects from the viewpoint of a managing equity investor. In the final section of the chapter a case study, Aspen Wood Apartments, is used to illustrate the concepts and principles discussed. This case study will be reintroduced in each chapter of this section as we proceed through the various facets of the ownership life cycle—acquisition, operation, and termination. The Aspen Wood Apartments case provides a well-documented practical application of strategic planning and its successful implementation to achieve return expectations.

We have argued that an investor's primary financial goal should be to maximize financial wealth over the long run. Real estate investment is thus viewed as a process of identifying and structuring projects in order to maximize expected

---

[1] Stephen E. Roulac and Donald A. King, Jr., "Institutional Strategies for Real Estate Investment," *The Appraisal Journal,* April 1978, pp. 257–258.

returns relative to risks. As we have shown previously, the first step of that investment process is to develop a strategy—to define the nature and level of the returns and risks that are to be evaluated by the investor and how they can be achieved through the purchase of real estate. The strategy framework is shown in Exhibit 8–1.

Strategy can be defined as "skillful management in getting the better of an adversary or attaining an end."[2] Strategy can also be defined as forging investment goals, setting objectives for the investor's organization in the light of external and internal forces, formulating specific policies to achieve objectives, and ensuring their proper implementation so that the basic purposes and objectives of the investor will be achieved.[3] Strategy thus implies that we develop our management skills in order to outperform our competition, skills that will "put us in the winner's circle." Such a strategy demands that we clearly identify and define four important elements: (1) overall investment philosophy, (2) objectives and decision criteria, (3) plans and policies, and (4) a strategy of analysis.

Successful investors are fully aware that real estate investment strategies are carried out in an atmosphere in which "gut feelings," experience, and judgments about the impact of external events greatly affect the decision-making process and investment results. A formal planning system would seem to clash with the style of brilliant intuitive planners like William Zeckendorf, the flamboyant financial and entrepreneurial genius who remodeled whole sections of New York, Denver, Washington, Montreal, and Dallas, and moved the headquarters of the United Nations to New York.[4] A formal planning system, however, might have helped to avoid the "surprises" that destroyed some of Zeckendorf's visionary plans and eventually drove him into bankruptcy. A formal planning system is simply an effort to replicate and fully disclose intuitive planning, not to eliminate intuition and judgment.

A formal, systematic strategic planning system can improve on intuitive and judgmental planning and reduce the number and severity of decision-making mistakes. It will result in a strategy that considers the interrelationships among the external environment, social mores, investor resources, and personal values. As can be seen in Exhibit 8–2, only a relatively small number of strategies, as shown by the darkened area, will be successful. It is the interplay among "might do," "should do," "can do," and "want to do" that determines a successful strategy, one that over the long run will result in high returns relative to risks.

The Terminology of Real Estate Investment Strategy

Real estate investment can be a confusing area of study for many people because no standard terminology is accepted by all the various disciplines involved. Appraisers, tax accountants, attorneys, lenders, investors, and brokers all use special-

---

[2] *American College Dictionary* (New York: Random House, 1966), p. 1195.
[3] For examples, see John B. Miner and George A. Steiner, *Management Policy and Strategy* (New York, Macmillan, 1977), pp. 91–121; K. J. Redford, *Strategic Planning: An Analytical Approach* (Reston, Va.: Reston Publishing, 1980), pp. 1–21; and C. Robert Coates, *Investment Strategy* (New York: McGraw-Hill, 1978), pp. 543–544.
[4] William Zeckendorf, *Zeckendorf* (New York: Holt, Rinehart and Winston, 1970).

EXHIBIT 8-1.   A Framework for an Investment Strategy

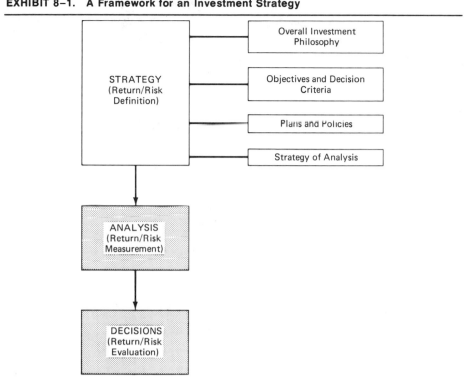

ized vocabularies, and some words tend to have many aliases. "Cash flow return" is also called "cash flow before tax on equity return," "equity dividend yield," or "cash-on-cash return." There are large gaps between the disciplines, and a modern decision-oriented approach to real estate investment is yet to be developed. Such an approach would begin with the acceptance of some basic decision terminology, including the following terms:

- **Investment strategy.** A definition of the nature and level of returns and risks that are to be evaluated by the investor and how they can be achieved through real estate ownership. An all-encompassing term that includes as its subparts the determination of an overall investment philosophy, objectives and decision criteria, plans and policies, and a strategy of analysis.
- **Investment philosophy.** A set of general principles and personal beliefs that guide the investor's behavior. An investment philosophy reflects the investor's financial and management resources and real estate knowledge and skills, the nature of the involvement sought, time availability, and so on. The philosophy determines the nature of the returns and risks that are acceptable to the investor.

EXHIBIT 8-2.   Determination of a Successful Strategy

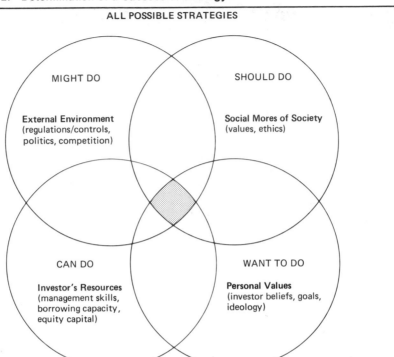

ALL POSSIBLE STRATEGIES

MIGHT DO

External Environment
(regulations/controls,
politics, competition)

SHOULD DO

Social Mores of Society
(values, ethics)

CAN DO

Investor's Resources
(management skills,
borrowing capacity,
equity capital)

WANT TO DO

Personal Values
(investor beliefs, goals,
ideology)

- **Investment objective.** A goal or end toward which investment efforts are directed consistent with the investment philosophy. Investors usually have multiple objectives: general and specific, financial and nonfinancial, short run and long run. Plans and policies are developed to achieve objectives.
- **Investment criteria.** A standard by which to test whether a proposed course of action will achieve the investment objective. An investment criterion can be stated as a decision rule.
- **Plan.** A course of action or procedures that seeks to achieve agreed-upon objectives. Contingency plans are made in case the original plans do not result in the desired outcome.
- **Policy.** A rule or course of action used to control plan implementation. Policies are decision rules used during the investment process and are applied after the objectives have been established but before the investment criteria are applied. They act as screening devices that reduce the number of alternatives for consideration and analysis.
- **Strategy of analysis.** A coordinated group of plans and policies that will guide the investor's behavior throughout the investment process.

Some of these terms are not used in the real estate investment literature; others are misused, not clearly defined, or used interchangeably. Agreement on essential terminology will greatly simplify the communication process and facilitate a systematic approach to investment strategy.

THE INVESTMENT ANALYSIS AND FINANCIAL STRUCTURING PROCESS

How should the investor proceed to acquire, operate, and terminate investment properties? An investor must learn to manage the investment process effectively in order to consistently achieve objectives with a minimum commitment of time and other resources. In short, each investor should have a strategy of analysis that outlines step-by-step procedure for acquiring, operating, and terminating a property. (See Exhibit 8–3.)

Basic Assumptions

This particular strategy of analysis was designed for a managing equity investor. It focuses on existing income property or properties bought from developers on a turnkey basis. No development period risks are present. The busy investor wishes to minimize the time commitment required for the acquisition and operation of properties, but also wishes to do thorough and systematic analyses. The strategy of analysis must therefore consider how human as well as financial capital can be allocated effectively. In addition, over the long run the investor is interested in achieving varying degrees of return from each of the four cash flow sources: (1) operations, (2) tax savings, (3) equity buildup from loan amortization, and (4) appreciation of property value. Thus, the investor will be searching for leveraged properties that will be evaluated and compared on an after-tax basis. While some investors may purchase on a before-tax and debt-free basis, most notably in the case of some pension funds, these situations are examined elsewhere. In any case, the basic principles and procedures are the same.

The Investment Process

The investment analysis and financial structuring process can be viewed as ten sequential stages, as shown in Exhibit 8–3. While the separation of these activities is somewhat arbitrary because the stages are highly interrelated, it does represent a typical sequence of events that many experienced, knowledgeable, and successful investors follow. More important, it is a "normative" decision model that describes how a rational investor should behave in the situation given, rather than a "descriptive" model that explains how most investors actually behave. There is little reason to perpetuate the naive and intuitive models that are actually used by many investors in the marketplace if our objective is to "do better than the competition."

The model covers the period from an investor's initial interest in a real estate investment through the purchase, operation, and termination of a property. The output from each step feeds into the next. If at any time during the process the investor reaches a point at which the investment being analyzed is no longer attractive in terms of increasingly stringent criteria, the project can be dropped at that point or the information concerning its shortcomings can be used as feedback

EXHIBIT 8-3.   A Model of the 10-Step Investment Analysis and Financial Structuring Process

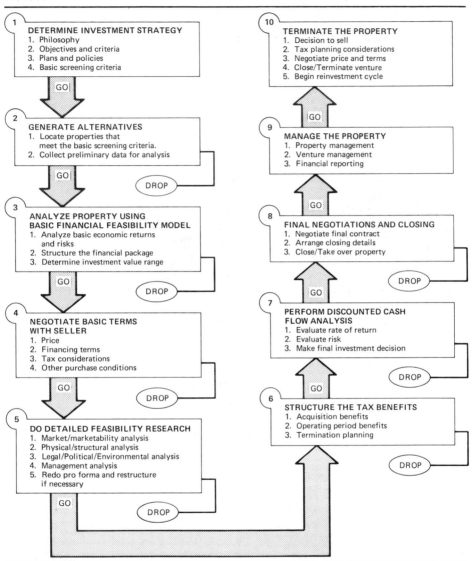

to restructure the deal. Then, after changes have been made in the assumptions and expected outcomes, the analysis is resumed several steps earlier.

The model describes a general process that is important to most equity investors in income property in any price range. Clearly, the purchase of a single rental house may not entail the explicit exercise of each step, but the thought process is basically the same. The ten steps may be summarized as follows:

Step 1: Determine an Investment Strategy   The investor determines his or her overall investment philosophy, objectives and criteria, plans and policies. From the list of investment criteria and policies, the investor specifies those that will serve as initial screening criteria. These criteria are used to disqualify from further investigation properties that have no reasonable chance of meeting the investor's objectives. Other investment criteria are applied at different stages of the process. Generally, the criteria become more specific and demanding as the investment analysis progresses. Also, it is common during this process for the criteria to be in a continual state of change as a result of new information (feedback) acquired and changing investor perceptions. Many investors will make their form-of-ownership decision (see Chapter 9) at this stage of the investment process.

Step 2: Generate Alternatives   The investor attempts to locate properties that meet the basic screening criteria. This activity can be time-consuming, frustrating, and unproductive. A 1976 study of professionally managed investment programs by Roulac showed that for every property purchased, 46 property submissions are considered.[5] Furthermore, for each property submission, many properties must be located and analyzed. Generating alternatives is a very creative and intuitive process, one that becomes more efficient as the investor gains experience in a variety of markets. In Chapters 5 and 6 we provided a general model for locating investment opportunities. In Part IV we will apply the process to specific types of properties.

Step 3: Analyze the Property Using the Basic Financial Feasibility Model   The basic financial feasibility model (discussed in detail in Chapter 10) utilizes a one-year cash flow projection, and inputs data on the investor's return/risk requirements as well as the lender's basic loan underwriting requirements. The model is used to structure and test the basic economics of the project, the available financing alternatives, and the investment value range for the property. Properties that do not meet the investment criteria imposed at this stage of the analysis are dropped from further consideration or modified until the criteria are met. An acceptable financial structure can often be achieved through negotiation.

Step 4: Negotiate Basic Terms with the Seller   The buyer begins to discuss and negotiate the basic parameters of the deal with the seller, including price, terms, and tax considerations. The preliminary offer and negotiations are based on the objectives defined in step 1 and the analysis performed in step 3. The objective at this stage is to achieve a basic meeting of the minds before valuable time is spent on detailed feasibility research.

Before doing more work on the property, action must be taken to tie up the property. Later chapters will deal with options, real estate contracts, letters of intent, and other ways of legally binding sellers while the buyer makes further investigations. In some situations it may require only a handshake for the buyer to obtain the seller's commitment to hold the property off the market until the feasibility research has been completed and negotiations can continue. Chapter 15 is devoted to the art of negotiation.

[5] Stephen E. Roulac, *Modern Real Estate Investment* (San Francisco: Property Press, 1976), p. 477.

Step 5: Do Detailed Feasibility Research   The investor collects and analyzes information in four areas: (1) market and marketability factors affecting the property; (2) the physical and structural condition of the property; (3) legal, political, and environmental considerations; and (4) management and operation of the property. Evaluation of these data, along with expectations regarding inflation and real estate cycles, will enable the investor to make cash flow forecasts over the entire ownership life cycle. In most cases the new information results in a reevaluation of the basic economics of the project (step 3) and, often, renegotiation of some of the basic parameters of the deal with the seller. Often projects are abandoned at this point because the new information places the property in an undesirable return/risk category.

Step 6: Structure the Tax Benefits   The investor must structure the tax package before a discounted cash flow after-tax analysis of the property can be performed to determine its complete rate-of-return and risk characteristics. Three different time periods produce differing tax consequences and should be carefully analyzed and structured to meet the investor's objectives: (1) Front-end write-offs produce a tax shelter in the year of acquisition; (2) operating-period write-offs produce a tax shelter during the period of ownership; and (3) the termination period produces a mixed bag of results, including favorable capital gains treatment, recognition of accrued tax liabilities, possible recognition of deferred income through exchanges and installment sales, and so on. These subjects are discussed in Chapter 13.

Step 7: Perform a Discounted Cash Flow Analysis   The investor combines all the information and data generated from the previous steps and performs a discounted cash flow after-tax analysis of the property. A thorough analysis of the important rate-of-return and risk parameters of the project is performed, including a sensitivity analysis of key financial variables, and the results are compared to the most stringent investment criteria developed in step 1. At this point the investment has successfully passed the hierarchy of other tests imposed at each step of the process and a final investment decision is made—either the project is abandoned or the investor enters final negotiations with the seller. These subjects are discussed in Chapters 11– 13.

Step 8: Engage in Final Negotiations and Closing   At this point the investor knows what trade-offs affect the returns and risks associated with the property, and what he or she can give up and must try to get at the final bargaining session. The investor is in a good position to increase expected returns relative to risks as a result of a final negotiation process that takes advantage of the personal preferences and biases affecting the positions of both the buyer and the seller. Ideally, the final purchase contract is drawn and closing details are arranged at this point. The buyer, the seller, and their attorneys go to a closing, review the final documents, sign the necessary papers; deeds are recorded and moneys disbursed. If the process goes smoothly, the investor has legally acquired the property. In many cases, however, the process does not follow the desired scenario: Disputes and arguments arise; tempers flare; and the deal falls through. Buyers and sellers should be prepared for "surprise negotiation tactics" at the closing. Coolheaded people can still make good deals, in keeping with the investment strategy, through effective confrontation and conflict resolution. These concepts are discussed in Chapter 15.

Step 9: Manage the Property   After the acquisition, competent property management becomes the critical aspect of successful ownership. Property management should have both authority and accountability for achieving the cash flow projections on which the investment decision was based. Venture management is responsible for managing the property manager, reporting to the investors, monitoring the performance of the property, and refinancing the property when such action is advantageous. The smaller investor may perform all management functions; larger institutions and syndicators often delegate responsibility to a number of specialists and professionals. These considerations are discussed in Chapter 16.

Step 10: Terminate the Property   Eventually the property is sold or exchanged, or is the subject of an involuntary conversion or foreclosure. The timing of a sale is critical if the investor is to obtain the most favorable price and terms. Like the original acquisition, the negotiations and the closing process can be problematic. After the closing, the venture is dissolved and final reports are issued to the investors. If an involuntary conversion, tax deferred exchange, or installment sale takes place, the process is somewhat altered and deserves special consideration. Chapter 17 discusses these subjects in depth.

The ten-step process just described is the subject of the next nine chapters. The greatest emphasis in this process is clearly on the acquisition phase of investment, which involves steps 2–8. While excellence in all phases of the investment process is important for long-run success, this is especially true for the acquisition process. It is at this stage that the returns and risks are analyzed and structured and the character of the investor's portfolio is established. If the process of acquiring properties is poorly structured and executed, good return/risk performance is unlikely to follow.

Although the ten-step process is dynamic and should be modified to fit each situation, it does provide a checklist of essential considerations for the investor who wishes to participate in the real estate investment process. Like an airline pilot's preflight preparation, the ten-step investment checklist is a risk management and control device.

DEVELOPING AN INVESTMENT STRATEGY

In the following sections we will elaborate on the various elements of an investment strategy, which was described previously as step 1 of the investment process.

Investment Philosophy

An investment philosophy must address the nature and degree of the investor's involvement in real estate activity, including the following alternatives:

1. *Direct or indirect involvement.* Will we buy properties outright or own shares of a company that owns real estate? If we choose indirect involvement, we can buy shares of an REIT, a development company, or a syndicate, or we can invest in companies that provide services to the real estate industry, such as brokerage and appraisal.
2. *Time investment.* How much time will we devote to investment activities? Perhaps it will begin as a part-time venture and later become a full-time pursuit.
3. *Investor role.* Will we be passive equity investors, managing equity investors, or joint venture partners? On occasion we might choose to become mortgage lenders by selling a property and financing the sale in order to achieve installment sales treatment. A desire for a well-balanced portfolio may require us to take on numerous roles simultaneously or to shift the roles to take advantage of real estate cycles.
4. *Management style and functions.* Will we hire professional managers or manage the property ourselves? Who will manage the financial affairs of the venture that owns the property? Will some or all of the tax, accounting, and legal work be done in-house or by outside consultants? Will management be a freewheeling one-man show, or will the investor seek to build a management team that gives continuity to the investment program?

The answers to these questions will be important aspects of the investor's overall investment philosophy. In addition, the investor should consider the types of returns and risks sought, given his or her financial resources and constraints, and whether the focus will be on portfolio analysis (estate building) or project analysis. Many astute investors have observed that portfolio values are created at the project level; the greatest emphasis, therefore, should be on project analysis, not portfolio analysis.[6] As our discussion in Chapter 3 emphasized, if projects are bought and sold in such a way as to generate, on the average, high compounded yields, then the theory of compound interest will take care of the portfolio over the long run. While the ultimate goal may be to produce a multimillion-dollar estate or portfolio, the key to the accomplishment of this goal is analysis and control of individual properties.

Investment Principles

An important part of the investor's philosophy should be a set of principles like the following, which were developed by the Coldwell Banker Company:[7]

1. *"The buyer should buy the assumptions that create the yield rather than the yield itself."* Real estate investment is seen as a process of validating key assumptions, such as income, expenses, and resale. The investors who most thoroughly validate assumptions are the most successful.

---

[6] Fred E. Case, *Investing in Real Estate* (Englewood Cliffs, N.J.: Prentice-Hall, 1978), p. 50.
[7] Robert M. Ellis, *Real Estate Investment Analysis* (Los Angeles, Calif.: Coldwell Banker Company, 1976), p. 5.

2. *"The investor should be as concerned about what to offer the next buyer as with what he is buying."* Often real estate investment is based on speculation and reliance on the "greater fool theory." Sound investment philosophy is based on the assumption that the next investor, as well as the present one, will value the property on an economic basis using realistic economic assumptions.

3. *"The investor should price the property apart from the tax advantages."* The project should make sense from a "basic economics" viewpoint—cash in and cash out. In general, a project should not be purchased on the basis of tax advantages *alone*. Over the entire ownership life cycle, real gains are more important than tax gains produced by artificial tax losses. Ultimately, most tax losses turn into real losses if a project is not supported by real economic gains (e.g., price appreciation and cash flow from operations).

4. *"The investor should compare alternatives."* Investment analysis is the process of comparing assumptions and property alternatives. A real estate investment is good only to the extent that its assumptions are better than other alternatives. If the assumptions are analyzed incorrectly, the rate of return and risk projections will be incorrect.

5. *"The investor should understand the potential profit and risks in terms of dollars and cents."* Investors should not leave the measurement of return and risk to intuition and hunch. They should attempt to quantify their judgments and measure the impact of investment uncertainties on the expected after-tax profits of each venture. The final investment decision requires a comparison of project returns and risks with the investor's objectives, constraints and resources, and relative returns on other types of investments.

Profitable real estate investing, thus, is seen as a process of finding properties that produce higher returns with more realistic assumptions. Profitable real estate investing is a critical balance among assumptions, alternatives, and yields.

Investment Objectives

While the overall investment philosophy is a set of general principles that guide the investor's behavior, objectives are ends toward which that behavior is directed. (The terms *goals* and *objectives* are often used interchangeably.) Investors generally develop a hierarchy of objectives, some long term and others short term, some financial and others nonfinancial, some very simplistic and others very sophisticated.

Each investor's objectives are unique to his or her personal, financial, and tax situation. As discussed in Chapter 1, investors have many general goals and objectives.[8]

[8] See also Paul F. Wendt and Alan R. Cerf, *Real Estate Investment Analysis and Taxation* (New York: McGraw-Hill, 1969), pp. 333–334; James R. Cooper, *Real Estate Investment Analysis* (Lexington, Mass.: Lexington Books, 1974), p. 10; Mary Alice Hines, *Real Estate Investment* (New York: Macmillan, 1980), pp. 187–191.

1. protection of purchasing power
2. diversification
3. tax shelter
4. regular return
5. capital gain
6. retirement income
7. estate building
8. investment for use
9. minimum equity
10. rapid recovery of equity
11. entrepreneurial profit

A specific investor's objectives would logically be some subset of the ones in this list. For example, consider the objectives of the pension investment fund founded in 1970 and administered by the Prudential Life Insurance Company. In 1980 the PRISA (Prudential Property Investment Separate Account) fund owned more than 900 properties with a value in excess of $2.75 billion.

> The objective of PRISA is to obtain an attractive rate of current income from the property investments which offer prospects of long term growth, in order to enhance the resources of participating pension plans to provide benefit payments. To fulfill that objective, Prudential invests PRISA funds primarily in the purchase of income producing real property including office and industrial buildings, shopping centers, other retail stores, apartments, hotels, and motels. Suitable diversification is maintained as to type of property and location. Particular attention is given to properties which are located in growth areas, may be leased on a basis permitting suitable rent revisions, and are considered to have good appreciation potential.[9]

Thus, PRISA's most important objectives are regular return, capital gain, and diversification, with the ultimate objective being retirement income to be provided by the individual pension plans around the country that participate in the PRISA fund. Little attention is paid to tax shelter because the pension plans themselves receive favorable tax treatment and because tax losses cannot be passed through to the individuals who contribute to the pension plans. In contrast, as one of their main objectives many limited partnership syndications seek to create a high degree on tax shelter for the participating investors, and to allocate tax losses that can be used to shelter other income earned by the investor.

Written Objectives The investor should carefully develop his or her objectives and commit them to writing. Experienced investors do not deviate from their written objectives. They do, however, review those objectives frequently in order to determine whether they are still valid and attainable in light of changing market conditions and changing personal net worth. If they are not, they are revised.

[9] "A New Dimension in Pension Funding. PRISA—The Prudential Property Investment Separate Account."

The Short Run Versus the Long Run   Historically, many individual and institutional equity investors have relied on one-year cash flow pro formas for their decision analysis. Syndicators and brokers have packaged investments and received all or most of their fees at the time of purchase rather than according to a formula based on property performance. Inadequate feasibility analysis of future trends and probable events has precluded the use of long-term forecasts as a basis for decision making. Nevertheless, successful real estate investing requires active, continuing, and prolonged involvement, and the responsibility should be delegated accordingly.

While short-run solvency is necessary, overall long-run profitability is the paramount objective. In the ten-step model developed here, both short- and long-term objectives are addressed. For example, short-run return and risk criteria are used in the basic financial feasibility model (step 3) while long-term (ownership-period) return and risk criteria are applied in the discounted cash flow model (step 7).

Unrealistic Objectives   Research studies have shown that real estate investors may be unrealistic in their return expectations. Most investors and managers indicate that they expect to outperform historical investment results. A survey by the Department of Housing and Urban Development, for example, found that 83 percent of the respondent investors expected an average annual return of 12 percent when, in fact, they had historically received only 10.5 percent.[10] Also, Roulac has concluded that most investor objectives and criteria are little more than irresponsible hearsay and are totally lacking in trustworthiness.[11] The less-than-impressive real estate performance record is striking evidence of the broad gap between expectations and realizations. Investors must learn to eliminate this gap and to be more precise and realistic in establishing their objectives.

Financial Versus Nonfinancial Objectives   Investors consider numerous nonfinancial as well as financial objectives when developing an investment strategy. A HUD study of 137 investors located in major cities around the nation analyzed both financial and nonfinancial objectives for different types of investors. In rating financial objectives, all the investors ranked annual cash return (before-tax from operations) as their most important objective. (See Exhibit 8–4.) Tax shelter, capital appreciation, financial leverage, and low risk of loss were also ranked high, but were of secondary importance. Liquidity and cash fees were consistently ranked lowest for all investor types.

The results of this classic study are outdated, and the relative importance of financial criteria have probably changed substantially as investors have become more inflation conscious. What would be the relative rankings of financial criteria in today's investment marketplace? While no data are currently available, it is clear that the rankings are based on current market perceptions, which are constantly in a state of change and evolution.

---

[10] U.S. Department of Housing and Urban Development, *Study on Tax Considerations in Multi-Family Housing Investments* (Washington, D.C.: GPO, 1972), p. 43.
[11] Roulac, p. 89.

EXHIBIT 8–4. Rating of Financial Objectives

	Insurance Companies	REITs	Real[a] Estate Subsidiaries	Real[b] Estate Groups	Individuals[c]
Annual cash return	9.2	9.8	9.0	8.7	8.7
Tax shelter	5.8	5.8	6.8	7.7	8.0
Liquidity/ease of sale	3.8	5.7	5.7	4.7	4.9
Financing leverage/minimum equity	7.5	3.5	7.7	7.8	6.6
Low risk of loss	7.0	8.8	7.0	6.5	6.7
Cash fees	1.4	1.0	5.6	3.9	2.4
Capital appreciation	9.2	8.2	6.8	6.9	7.6
Investors in sample	6	6	6	89	27

SOURCE: U.S. Department of Housing and Urban Development, *Study of Tax Considerations in Multi-Family Housing Investments* (Washington, D.C.: GPO, 1972), p. 28.
Ranking scale: 10 highest, 1 lowest.
[a] Subsidiaries of major corporations whose primary business is not real estate.
[b] Investors actively engaged in real estate on a full-time basis.
[c] Primarily passive partners in real estate partnerships.

Nonfinancial objectives vary widely and are substantially different for active investors than for passive ones. The passive investors in the HUD study ranked builder's reputation and location as more important than pride of ownership and meeting social needs; in contrast, active investors (full-time real estate practitioners) ranked location, demand and supply conditions, and mortgage financing as the most important objectives. Commenting on the overall importance of nonfinancial factors, investors thought that location was the most important item, but that if any one of these factors was out of line the project might not be feasible.

Ranking Objectives The investor must devise a ranking system when financial and nonfinancial objectives are numerous. A model must be developed for finding a "best fit" between property characteristics and investor objectives. Since all of the objectives cannot be achieved with equal success, the investor must decide the order in which they should be achieved and the relative importance of each. For example, in a period of rising inflation investors must look increasingly to long-run capital gains and sacrifice some current income from operations. For most types of property it is difficult, if not impossible, to achieve both simultaneously.

Decision Criteria

Explicitly stated financial and nonfinancial objectives reveal the complex nature of the return/risk trade-off that the investor is willing to accept and the unfolding of his or her investment philosophy. The process of developing objectives provides insight into what types of real estate investments the investor will consider, how much to invest, what kind of financing will be acceptable, how much liability can be assumed, what the best legal form of ownership is, where in the property and real estate cycles the investor will invest, and how long the investment will be held. Objectives also provide insight into the things the investor will not do and does not want. The investor may not want an investment that is so risky or so dominant that it could jeopardize the entire portfolio and perhaps ruin the investor's credit and reputation. Or the investor may not want an investment that requires too much time.

Once the investor has specified the nature of the risks and returns that are acceptable, criteria are developed for judging the magnitude of the returns and risks measured. In short, objectives define where the investor is going while the criteria signal when he or she has arrived. For example, if the objective is tax shelter, the criteria will pinpoint an amount of tax shelter that will be acceptable in a given situation. The criteria might be that an apartment complex should offer a 50 percent tax write-off per dollar of investment during the year of acquisition, with tax losses continuing each year for a minimum of five years.

Exhibit 8– 5 illustrates various types of financial and nonfinancial criteria that have been used by investors in the past. Be aware that these will be different for each investor and investment situation, and will be modified as the investment process produces new information.

Some of the criteria relate primarily to the rate-of-return dimension; others relate primarily to the risk dimension; while still others are indirect measures of both. The internal rate of return is clearly a measure of return, whereas a break-even point is clearly a measure of risk. A purchase price maximum of $70 per square foot for a shopping center, on the other hand, is a rule-of-thumb criterion experience might show to be a reasonable maximum to pay in order to achieve an acceptable return/risk ratio for a specific investor operating in a local market. The nonfinancial criteria also relate, usually indirectly, to returns and risks. A "structurally sound" building with good "curb appeal" is presumed by some investors to have a more favorable return/risk ratio than one that lacks these characteristics. Dealing only with reputable sellers increases the probability of closing a deal, thereby reducing the risk of loss.

The various criteria will be applied at different stages in the investment process. Curb appeal may be an initial screening criterion, while the internal-rate-of-return objective is applied many steps later. Also, each criterion should be ranked according to the importance of the investment objective it represents. Curb appeal may not be as important as the location of an office building: If a property has an excellent location, a relatively unimpressive façade may not be important enough to eliminate the project from consideration during the initial screening process.

Plans and Policies

Every investor should have an investment plan that defines a step-by-step procedure for achieving objectives. The ten-step investment process that we have described is a master plan that guides the investor's behavior throughout the

---

EXHIBIT 8-5.   Examples of Investment Criteria

FINANCIAL CRITERIA

A. *Measures of Rate of Return*
1. A cash-on-cash return (cash flow/equity investment) of at least 6%.
2. A cash flow and equity buildup of at least 10–12%.
3. Appreciation of property value of at least 6–8% annually.
4. Front-end tax write-offs of at least 20% of each dollar invested.
5. Holding-period write-offs that shelter all cash flow.
6. An internal rate of return on the equity investment of at least 20%.
7. A net present value greater than or equal to zero.

B. *Measures of Risk*
1. A break even point (operating expenses plus debt service divided by the gross possible income) less than 86%.
2. A coverage ratio (net income/debt service) not less than 1.20.
3. No all-bills-paid complexes; utilities pass through to the tenants.
4. A leverage ratio (debt/purchase price) not higher than 80% or, for a speculator, not less than 90%.
5. A strong rental occupancy history.
6. Payback period: all cash back within 5 years.

C. *Measures That Combine Risk and Return*
1. A gross rent multiplier less than 6.0.
2. A purchase price per unit maximum of $35,000 for apartments.
3. A purchase price per square foot maximum of $70 for shopping centers.

NONFINANCIAL CRITERIA

1. Structurally sound building.
2. Aesthetically pleasing design.
3. Age of building: 5–7 years, no new buildings.
4. Size: more than 100 units for managerial efficiency, fewer than 20 for individual investor/managers.
5. Tenants: no special-use buildings; must be multi–tenant, general use.
6. Leases: must have good escalation clauses and be of relatively short duration.
7. Management burden of an acceptable level.
8. No flat roofs or gas air conditioners.
9. Neighborhood: location must be promising—in path of growth and near major traffic arteries.
10. Must be able to obtain clear title with no complex legal problems.
11. Environment must be acceptable; pleasing landscape, no threat of floods.
12. Trustworthy seller with good reputation.
13. Type of property must be desirable and marketable.

---

investment and financial structuring process. At each stage of analysis the investor should also have a plan that will guide him or her through the maze of alternatives and, after the property characteristics have been compared to the investor's criteria at that stage, result in a logical decision to go on or to drop the project from consideration. Thus, an investment plan outlines how the investor is to proceed to achieve his or her objectives and apply the investment criteria. They should be flexible rather than rigid, and should provide for contingencies that could occur.

Investment policies are used to control plan implementation and act as a screening device to reduce the number of alternatives for consideration and analysis, as well as the amount of time required of the investor. For example, consider the statement of purchasing policy developed by two full-time investor–developers in Washington, D.C., who started with a combined net worth of $60,000 and thirteen years later had a combined net worth of over $2 million.[12] Their purchasing policies are shown in Exhibit 8–6.

Basic Screening Criteria

From the full set of investment criteria and policies, some basic screening criteria can be designated that will disqualify a property early in the process without further exploration. These criteria are used to evaluate the properties located during step 2 of the investment process. For example, some investors will not look at any property that is more than an hour's drive from their home, or will not consider student, military, or low-income housing. Other investors will not consider apartments because they are management intensive; they prefer commercial properties that are relatively new, are well located, and have plenty of "curb appeal" to impress limited-partner investors who are employed in the medical profession. Such preferences, and others, can be so overriding to a particular investor that they serve to eliminate many possible choices at the outset. Basic screening criteria should be foremost in the investor's mind as alternatives are located. Otherwise much time will be spent investigating properties that have no chance of meeting the investor's needs.

Once investment properties have been located (step 2), the screening criteria will serve to differentiate among them. If weights have been assigned to financial and nonfinancial criteria, potential acquisitions can be ranked according to the initial likelihood that they can fulfill investor objectives. The investor will want to continue investigating only the best opportunities.

Objectives and criteria developed in step 1 are used to judge acceptability throughout the investment process. At each step in the process the project is evaluated against increasingly more demanding criteria. A project that proceeds through all the steps has met the investor's criteria in many ways and has a higher probability of achieving the investor's objectives.

SUMMARY

Disappointing investment results and negative experiences with real estate have often been caused by deficient investment strategies. In this chapter we developed a framework for determining a sound investment strategy and presented a norma-

---

[12] Maury Seldin and Richard H. Swesnik, *Real Estate Investment Strategy* (New York: Wiley-Interscience, 1979), pp. 5–6.

EXHIBIT 8-6.   A Statement of Purchasing Policy

A. *Large Properties Only*
   1. Office buildings having a minimum net rental area of 80,000 square feet.
   2. Shopping centers in excess of 80,000 square feet of net rentable space or prime leasebacks.
   3. Industrial leasebacks such as warehouses and research laboratories to AAA-1 tenants.
   4. Apartment buildings having a minimum of 100 rental units.
   5. Vacant ground to accommodate any of the structures listed above.

B. *New or Relatively New Properties Only*
   1. To ensure an attractive property for loan purposes at the outset and for refinancing purposes after acquisition. This policy recognizes that many lenders, especially insurance companies, avoid making loans on older properties.
   2. To ensure that amortization exceeds depreciation (*actual* wear and tear) so that the investor's equity is constantly increasing.
   3. To provide a desirable property for sale after depreciation is no longer attractive enough in its tax consequences to produce tax-sheltered income. (This policy should not rule out properties that have been or may be completely restored through the installation of new mechanical, electrical, and air-conditioning equipment.)

C. *Large Equities, Never Thin*
   The payment of sufficient equity capital above a conservative first deed of trust (mortgage) to ensure servicing of nonfluctuating debt service even in periods of economic recession.

D. *Limited to Washington, D. C., and Surrounding Area*
   With approximately 50% of the employees in the metropolitan area employed by the Federal and District Governments, and the other 50% occupied in providing goods and services for these personnel, the chances of a prolonged economic recession in the metropolitan area in Washington appear remote. We believe that Washington provides an atmosphere of economic stability enjoyed by extremely few metropolitan areas.

(Only very impressive factors concerning other metropolitan areas may dictate a variance from this policy.)

E. *No Speculative-Type Business Properties*
   We do not buy any real property whose major source of income is derived from the operation of speculative-type business ventures such as hotels, motels, swimming pools, golf links or country clubs, amusement parks, bowling alleys, or stadiums; nor single-purpose buildings, such as funeral homes, garages, or automobile retail locations.

SOURCE: Maury Seldin and Richard H. Swesnik, *Real Estate Investment Strategy* (New York: Wiley Interscience, 1979), pp. 5-6.

tive model of the investment analysis and financial structuring process that focuses on existing projects.

The first step of that process is to develop a strategy that defines the nature and measurement of the returns and risks that are acceptable to the investor. Such a strategy requires the investor to systematically identify and define four important elements: (1) overall investment philosophy, (2) objectives and decision criteria, (3) plans and policies, and (4) a strategy of analysis.

The investment analysis and financial structuring process consists of ten sequential steps that require the investor to perform increasingly complex analyses. The ten steps are (1) determining an investment strategy, (2) generating alternatives, (3) analyzing the property using the basic financial feasibility model, (4) negotiating basic terms with the seller, (5) doing detailed feasibility research, (6) structuring the tax benefits, (7) performing a discounted cash flow analysis, (8) engaging in final negotiations and closing, (9) managing the property, and (10) terminating the property. Emphasis is placed on the acquisition phase, since the return and risk characteristics of an investment are largely established at this stage of the property life cycle. Emphasis is also placed on a project rather than a portfolio approach, since ultimately wealth accumulation is accomplished through the analysis and control of individual properties.

A comprehensive case study, Aspen Wood Apartments, is introduced on the following page. This 86-unit apartment complex will be discussed at the end of each chapter in this part of the book as we analyze the next nine steps of the investment process.

ASPEN WOOD APARTMENTS

INTRODUCTION AND INVESTMENT STRATEGY

Good theory is good practice! If we are to prove this statement, it is important to illustrate how the framework developed in this chapter unfolds into practice when applied to real-world situations. Therefore, we have chosen to illustrate the model of the investment analysis and financial structuring process by applying it to a case history of a typical investment property. Aspen Wood Apartments was purchased in 1974 and sold in 1981. Good data are available, and the history of the purchase, operation, and termination of the property is complete. At the end of each of the chapters in this part of the book the Aspen Wood case study will be reintroduced and the principles discussed in the chapter will be applied. It should be noted that the case study is based on actual fact; however, some of the names and information have been disguised to maintain the anonymity of the individuals involved.

The Aspen Wood property was syndicated in November 1974 under a joint venture (general partnership) form of ownership by a Texas-based real estate firm known as D&B Associates. The firm engages in consulting, development, brokerage, syndication, and management of income properties in central Texas. In this case the firm's primary role is that of managing equity investor.

The use of D&B Associates and Aspen Wood Apartments as a case study is not meant to imply that our investment model is useful only to syndicators of apartment complexes. Rather, it is felt that D&B Associates is a typical equity investor and that Aspen Wood Apartments is an understandable project of reasonable proportions. The general principles, concepts, and mechanics described in this study apply equally well to all types of residential and commercial properties.

DESCRIPTION OF THE PROPERTY

Aspen Wood Apartments is an 84-unit complex built in two phases in 1966 and 1967 in Austin, Texas, the state capital. The structure is approximately 75 percent masonry, with built-up roofs and about 55,000 square feet of rentable space. Aspen Wood is a well-designed, three-story walk-up, with a swimming pool in the middle of each phase and adequate parking surrounding the structures. The complex is situated in an excellent location for both students and state workers; it is adjacent to the University of Texas intramural fields and near the university campus and other state institutions.

General descriptive data are summarized in Exhibit 8–7. Additional information on Aspen Wood Apartments and its purchase will be presented as the case study develops.

OVERALL INVESTMENT PHILOSOPHY

D&B Associates, as a firm of real estate consultants, brokers, investors, and property managers, has a basic business objective of building a portfolio that will maintain growing profitability through all phases of real estate and economic cycles. In 1974 its investment philosophy focused on a plan to list or acquire income properties, package them, and offer shares to clients and members of the firm with the intention of maintaining control as partial owners, managers, and consultants. Substantial commissions on the purchase and sale of properties are expected to be forthcoming in times of high real estate turnover, but D&B relies heavily on the income from property and venture management agreements written into syndicated and other offerings, to carry it through downturns. At present (1974), the firm manages over 2500 apartment units, of which a majority were syndicated using a joint venture (general partnership) ownership vehicle. Also, its investment program includes purchases of shopping centers and office buildings. As a developer–investor, the firm engages in the development of apartments, shopping centers, condominiums, and condominium conversions.

In 1974 D&B Associates was looking for apartment investments. It recognized the need for portfolio diversification, and an apparent overabundance of office space, shopping centers, and adult apartment projects in Austin led it to consider student apartment complexes. This market had been strong during the period from 1965 to 1972; only recently had overbuilding and expense increases, among other factors, disrupted the student market. D&B had substantial management expertise in this area. It saw an opportunity to increase its control of apartment units, reap economies of scale in its property and venture management efforts, and develop an inventory of projects to meet clients' needs as well as provide inventory for future condominium conversions.

The principals of D&B Associates are Charlie Davidson and Clyde Boomer. Davidson has been an active broker, investor, and syndicator for over twenty years. He is forty-five years old and is responsible for the company's brokerage and syndication activities and venture management, including investor relations. Boomer, thirty-five years old, used to be an executive with a major computer manufacturer and has been an active real estate investor for ten years. He has been with D&B Associates for the past five years and is responsible for the company's property management and administrative functions. He recently installed a computer system that handles all the firm's management and accounting reports and provides a sophisticated software package for the financial analysis of income properties. The firm employs over fifty people, including professional and resident property managers, maintenance and repair personnel, and administrative and secretarial employees. Two of the property managers are CPMs (certified property managers, Institute of Real Estate Management), and the firm has recently achieved the professional designation of AMO (Approved Management Organization, Institute of Real Estate Management).

EXHIBIT 8-7. Aspen Wood Apartments

PROPERTY DESCRIPTION

Apartments:

	Type	Monthly Rental (1974)	
		Fall/Spring	Summer
64	1 Bedroom–1 Bath	$149.00	$129.00
14	2 Bedroom–1 Bath	$199.00	$159.00
6	2 Bedroom–2 Bath	$209.00	$179.00

Tenants pay electricity in individual units. Owner pays common electricity, gas heating, and hot water for all units.

Location: 4539 Guadelupe Street

Lots A and B in Huntington Place, a subdivision in the City of Austin, Travis County, Texas, according to the map or plat thereof as recorded in Plat Book 29, page 21, of the Travis County Plat Records.

Parcel size: Lots A and B of Huntington Place are rectangular in shape. Both average 208 feet in width and 131 feet in depth. Lot A contains 27,361 square feet and Lot B contains 27,374 square feet.

Year built: Phase I 1966; Phase II 1967

Construction: The complex is composed of two phases almost identical in structure, with built-up roofs and approximately 75 percent masonry construction.

Square footage:

	Floor		
	1	2	3
Phase I	7,463	10,367	10,367
Phase II	6,453	10,417	10,417

Real estate taxes (1974):

	Phase I	Phase II
City	$2,745.69	$2,740.45
School	$3,922.41	$3,914.93
County	$1,275.92	$1,414.54

7 Reasons Why You Should Live In Aspen Wood:

1. The Price The price of gasoline has gone up 5¢ in 5 months. When you live in Aspen Wood, you're miles closer to Highland Mall, UT, nightclubs and the airport. And, Aspen Wood is on the Shuttle Bus Route.

2. The Price The average cost of a one bedroom luxury apartment in Austin is $165/month. Our price is only $149.

3. The Price The average cost of a two bedroom luxury apartment in Austin is $230/month. Our price is only $199.

4. The Price Most other places can't boast a backyard with baseball diamonds, football fields and dozens of tennis courts. But we can! Aspen Wood wasn't built near the UT Intramural Fields by accident.

5. The Price Even with our low prices, we don't believe in wasting your time and money with long-term contracts. So, our contracts are for 6 months or 9 months.

6. The Price With the cost of eating out rising so rapidly, it's getting tough to find an inexpensive charcoal-grilled steak. Our price includes two outdoor fireplace grills for those special dinners with special friends. (It also means saving $15 to $20 on a new hibachi.)

7. The Price Our price includes furnished and fully carpeted apartments, two swimming pools, free cable hook-ups and landscaped courtyards. When you think about it, living at Aspen Wood *is* luxury. At the best price.

1 Bdr. $149.

2 Bdr. $199.

Davidson and Boomer take great pride in their professional approach to real estate investment. They use modern capital-budgeting techniques to analyze proposed ventures. Projects are analyzed on a before- and after-tax basis, using a discounted cash flow computer model. Extensive research and analysis is undertaken before the company commits itself to a project. This approach has apparently been successful, since the company has grown rapidly over the last five years and enjoys an excellent reputation in the community.

INVESTMENT OBJECTIVES AND CRITERIA

Davidson and Boomer sell shares in their joint ventures on the basis of three general objectives: (1) a regular cash flow from operations that can be distributed quarterly to investors, (2) a substantial tax shelter over the ownership period, and (3) substantial capital appreciation, to be realized through periodic refinancing or sale of the property at the end of a four- to seven-year holding period.

The specific investment criteria used by D&B in 1974 included the following financial and nonfinancial criteria:

Rate of Return. Most of D&B's investors seek a minimum 10 percent cash-on-cash return during the first year of ownership, increasing thereafter. D&B agrees that a property can be structured to offer that return to investors. In addition, to achieve its long-term rate-of-return objective D&B seeks a minimum 18 percent internal rate of return (after tax). While the investors did not specify this criterion (most are wealthy individuals who are not familiar with the IRR criteria), D&B believes that this is the single most important financial criterion to be utilized in the analysis of properties. Tax shelter criteria are also important both to D&B and to its investors: A project should be structured to generate front-end tax write-offs amounting to 25–50 percent of the equity investments and significant tax losses over the holding period by using component depreciation to increase tax deductions. (Note that component depreciation was eliminated by the Economic Recovery Tax Act of 1981.)

Risk. D&B feels that it has a fiduciary responsibility to establish risk constraints on its syndicated projects. Its ventures must have a breakeven point of less than 85 percent, a coverage ratio greater than 1.25, and a minimal chance of negative equity cash flows (cash calls). In addition, full multiperil insurance coverage must be established on each property, and the firm seeks mortgage loans that do not require the personal guarantees of the investors.

Leverage. Secondary or wraparound financing must be available at an acceptable interest rate. In financing the property, the leverage ratio could be 75–90 percent, but debt service must be reasonable—as evidenced by a coverage ratio greater than 1.25.

Location. The project must be visible, surrounded by a high-quality neighborhood, and close to shopping, transportation, and recreation.

Structure. The building must be well designed and appealing to an investor, structurally sound, usually less than ten years old, with more than 40 units (the most desirable size being 75– 150 units). Tenants must pay their own utilities, and a strong rental history must evidence the attractiveness of the complex as a living environment.

These financial and nonfinancial criteria were initially chosen by D&B Associates to be used in selecting properties that would satisfy the explicit as well as implicit objectives of its clients. D&B has as an objective earning commissions and management fees by pleasing clients. To do this, it must understand investor motivations and objectives and translate them into explicit investment criteria to be applied at various steps in the investment process.

PLANS AND POLICIES

D&B's investment plans and policies are action-oriented guidelines that reflect the investment philosophy and criteria enumerated earlier. Davidson and Boomer will use the ten-step investment analysis model as a guideline for their actions and will apply increasingly more demanding and stringent criteria as the investment analysis continues. Only properties that pass all the important hurdles will be acquired. We will see in later chapters how specific plans and policies evolve at each step of the investment process.

BASIC SCREENING CRITERIA

In the search for potential acquisitions the nonfinancial criteria just noted tended to become the basic screening criteria, although the list was altered and refined over time. It is easy to determine by inspection whether a property meets these criteria. The financial criteria specified, on the other hand, call for more detailed analysis that is best performed later in the process. One financial criterion is of initial importance, however. This is the availability of secondary or wraparound financing. In 1974 very few deals were feasible without financing from a seller. New-mortgage money was extremely difficult to obtain, and interest rates on new mortgages were too high to achieve economic feasibility. At the same time, with overbuilding prevalent in scattered locations around Austin and rent levels depressed, expenses were rising rapidly as a result of the energy crisis and general inflationary pressures.

After selecting the basic screening criteria, D&B have completed step 1 of the ten-step investment analysis process.

9

Selecting the Ownership Entity

In almost any new real estate venture, one of the critical decisions that the investor is confronted with concerns the form of business organization that should be used. Should the property be acquired and owned by the individual, by a general or limited partnership, or perhaps by a corporation or trust established by the investor? This decision is extremely important because it has a direct impact on the investor's ability to achieve his or her objectives. The type of entity chosen and the way it is structured affects the investor's rate of return and risk, and it often defines the nature of his or her involvement and the degree of control that can be exercised over the venture and the property purchased.

The ownership entity decision will often be an integral part of step 1 of the investment process, in which the investment strategy is determined. For example, an investor who seeks a high degree of tax shelter, flexibility, and complete control of a property may use the individual form of ownership for property acquisitions. The entity is thus an extension of the investor's basic philosophy and objectives. Many syndicators use *only* the limited partnership form in their business—no other alternatives are considered. In contrast, the ownership decision may be delayed until the tax-structuring step is reached (step 6), or even later in the process if lenders and other investors can influence the decision.

OWNERSHIP ALTERNATIVES

The ownership vehicles that can be used to acquire and own real estate may be classified as follows:

- *Noncorporate forms of ownership*—individual, joint tenancy, tenancy in common, general partnership, limited partnership, family partnership, and joint venture.
- *Corporations and trusts*—regular (Subchapter C) corporation, Subchapter S corporation, REIT, pension trust, and other types of trusts.
- *Syndication*—Although syndication is not a legal form of entity, it is commonly classified as a form of ownership as well as a method of financing and marketing real estate investments.

Of all the forms of ownership used in real estate investments in recent years, the limited partnership is said to be the most commonly used because it offers investors the limited legal liability that a corporation offers, together with the tax benefits achieved from the pass-through of tax losses and capital gains that a general partnership offers.[1] However, other ownership forms are appropriate for different situations, transactions, and investors. No single type of entity is the best. The purpose of this chapter is to examine the various types of entities available and develop a general framework for evaluating the alternatives.

OWNERSHIP DECISION MODEL

To facilitate the choice of the ownership form that best fits an investor's return and risk objectives, a decision model for ranking alternatives has been developed. Since the objectives of an equity investor will vary over time, the investment portfolio must be reviewed and revised periodically. Thus, the optimal ownership form must be able to accommodate possible changes in the investor's strategy over the expected ownership period.

Exhibit 9–1 is a flow chart of the ownership decision model. It begins with a restatement of the investor's objectives as developed in Chapter 8. Next the investor develops specific ownership selection criteria and ownership alternatives. Finally, the alternatives are compared and ranked according to their relative ability to satisfy investment objectives. This step requires the investor to assign relative weights to the selection criteria and, through analysis, determine the degree to which each ownership alternative satisfies the defined criteria. Only then can the investor choose the optimal form of ownership—the one that best fits the return/ risk criteria. Whether this process is intuitive or uses a model like the one presented here, the essential elements are the same.

In the following sections of the chapter we will analyze the various selection criteria and ownership alternatives listed in Exhibit 9–1. The last section of the chapter will illustrate the application of the ownership decision model to the Aspen Wood case study. While the discussions may seem technical at times, they barely scratch the surface of the highly complex federal and state laws that govern the various forms of ownership. Before reaching any ownership entity decision, the investor should seek the advice and counsel of qualified legal and tax experts.

[1] Jack Kusnet and Lee J. Holzman, *How to Choose a Form of Ownership for Real Estate,* Part 1, *Explanation and Practical Guide,* Portfolio no. 14 (Boston: Warren, Gorham & Lamont, 1977), p. 1.

EXHIBIT 9-1. Ownership Decision Model

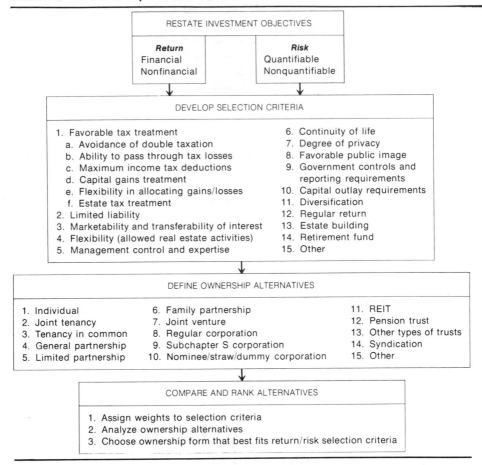

OWNERSHIP SELECTION CRITERIA

Criteria Defined

Tax Considerations   Tax considerations are usually critical in determining the best form of ownership for a real estate venture. The basic choice here is between a form of ownership that offers the advantage of a single tax on income and a corporate form of ownership, in which income is subject to double taxation—first at the corporate level and again at the stockholder (investor) level. In addition to double taxation, other important tax considerations that should be evaluated are the following:

1. *Ability to pass through tax losses.* With some forms of organization, such as partnerships, tax losses can be passed through directly to the individual investor and used to shelter other income. With other forms of

organization, such as a corporation or REIT, this ability is limited or does not exist.

2. *Maximum income tax deductions.* Some forms of organization are better suited to an aggressive tax shelter structure and can take liberal tax deductions without being disallowed or questioned by the Internal Revenue Service. For example, liberal amounts of medical and dental expenses can be deducted for corporate officers, but a partnership cannot deduct such expenses for partners.

3. *Favorable capital gains treatment.* With some forms of organization, it is easier to achieve capital gains treatment on a sale, distribution, or liquidation of an interest in the entity, or a sale or other disposition of the real estate itself.

4. *Flexibility in allocating gains and losses.* Investors may choose to allocate different items of taxable income and losses in a manner that meets their individual needs for tax shelter, capital gain, and cash flow. Special allocations are possible with some entity forms but not with others.

5. *Estate tax treatment.* A burden could be placed on an investor's estate by having to pay taxes on an interest in an entity that may be difficult to turn into cash.

To focus only on taxes, however, and overlook other important business, legal, and practical considerations can lead to financial disaster. The price for tax savings is too high if the chosen form of ownership makes it difficult to operate profitably or dispose of the ownership interest.

Limited Liability   The extent and probability of exposure to liability are important. Limited partnerships offer limited legal liability to the investor with respect to the capital contribution, but are subject to close government scrutiny. This can result in greater tax liabilities when the partnership is audited if tax deductions are challenged or disallowed.

Marketability and Transferability of Interest   A corporate share is generally more marketable than a partnership interest in the same property. With some forms of ownership, transfering an interest in real estate, or the real estate itself, is difficult if timely disposition with a minimum of legal hassle and expenses is desired.

Flexibility and Allowed Real Estate Activities   REITs and pension trusts are very limited in the scope and extent of real estate activities in which they can engage without jeopardizing their favorable tax status. In contrast, individuals have almost complete flexibility with regard to real estate activities.

Management Control and Expertise   The number of people required to run an entity, the type of management and expertise required, and the degree of control exercised by the investor over the property vary for different forms of ownership. A substantial number of experienced people may be required to organize and operate an REIT, where the investor has very little direct control over the properties purchased. On the other hand, a general partnership may consist of only a few investors who each choose to exert considerable influence over the operations of the venture and the property.

Continuity   Some ventures are organized with a limited holding period in mind and would cease to exist if any of the key investors died. Other ventures can span the lifetimes of many projects and investors.

Degree of Privacy   Some investors seek privacy in their real estate activities and choose not to have their names appear in public records, such as recorded partnership agreements, or on deeds, deeds of trust, and so on. Use of certain types of trust devices and partnership agreements can easily accommodate such objectives.

Favorable Public Image   Some forms of organization have better public images than others. In general, the corporate form of organization inspires public confidence. In contrast, the REIT and limited partnership forms of organization, because of widespread misuse in past years, are sometimes questioned or misunderstood by investors.

Government Controls and Reporting Requirements   Investors seeking to experience a minimum of government scrutiny and controls might favor the individual or tenancy in common form of organization, as opposed to a limited partnership, REIT, or corporate form of organization. The latter are more closely regulated and controlled, and the reporting requirements are significantly more complex and onerous.

Capital Outlay Requirements   Some forms of organization are significantly more costly to organize than others. It is not uncommon for a limited partnership to spend 20 to 30 percent of the total equity raised on organization, promotion, and legal fees. In contrast, a joint venture or a tenancy in common might limit such expenses to 5 to 10 percent of equity raised. Some forms of organization require large equity contributions (pension funds), while others seek to maximize the leverage ratio.

Diversification   Diversification by location, property type, management burden, and so forth can be achieved within one entity (REIT, corporation), or diversification can be prohibited by the entity agreement, as in the case of a joint venture agreement that limits activity to the ownership and operation of a single property.

Regular Return   Some forms of ownership are more conducive to regular distribution of returns than others. Investors seeking a regular current return may prefer an REIT over a corporation that accumulates earnings and reinvests them in real estate equities.

Estate Building   An investor who seeks to maximize the total value of real estate holdings over the long run, and is not seeking substantial current income and tax savings, may prefer a corporation or family trust form of organization.

Retirement Fund   Many investors seek to build equity during their younger years so that property is owned free and clear at retirement. Often the individual form of organization best suits this objective. For a self-employed individual, a Keogh or other pension plan for retirement may be the best alternative.

Other Selection Criteria   There are many other criteria that may become important in individual situations. For example, an investor seeking to avoid double taxation and generate fringe benefits for his or her family, may choose a Subchapter S corporate form of organization. If prestige is desired, the investor may choose to organize under the regular corporate form, elect himself or herself chairman of the board and president, and have an advertising firm develop an impressive corporate logo and business cards that can be distributed to family, friends, and business associates.

Assigning Relative Weights to the Selection Criteria

The importance of any given criterion in selecting a form of ownership may depend on the number of participants, their respective goals, the requirements imposed by the lender, and the nature of the transaction or operation. A tenancy in common, for example, might be desirable for two people. But this form of organization becomes less attractive with each additional person because of title problems. Even when a lender does not dictate the type of entity, a demand for personal guarantees will reduce the desire for a form of organization that shields the investor from personal liability.

How much weight is placed on any criterion is also influenced by the type of real estate investment. For example, new apartment projects usually are characterized by substantial risk in their early stages, yet they present an excellent opportunity for tax losses to the investors. On the other hand, the purchase of a hotel that generates substantial *taxable* cash flow returns (i.e., relatively little tax shelter) presents a different situation and suggests an entity that can serve to keep its taxable income separate from the investor's taxable income. Thus the investor must determine whether the profits of the venture must be distributed to the investors or whether there may be a valid business purpose for accumulating the income. Obviously, if there is no valid business reason for the accumulation of income, a corporate entity that is subject to double taxation is a disadvantage to the investor. Clearly, the assignment of weights to selection criteria is a highly subjective process. In the Aspen Wood case at the end of this chapter we will illustrate the dynamics of this process.

NONCORPORATE FORMS OF OWNERSHIP

Seven noncorporate forms of organization are discussed in the following paragraphs: individual, joint tenancy, tenancy in common, general partnership, limited partnership, joint venture, and family partnership. They have in common one important characteristic: They are all single-tax ownership entities that provide a flow-through of economic and tax benefits directly to individual investors. In general, they also lack continuity of life.

Individual Ownership

An individual ownership (sole proprietorship) exists when a single investor acquires a property solely in his or her own name and is taxed on the income just once. The taxable income from the property each year is added to other sources of income, and the investor is taxed at ordinary rates on total income for the year. If the property generates tax losses, they are used to reduce other income.

Several distinct advantages characterize the individual form of ownership. First, this form is advantageous if the individual's tax rate is lower than the corporate tax rate. Second, tax losses from the property can be used to shelter other income earned by the investor. Third, the individual has complete control over the property and is free from the interference of managers, trustees, and a board of directors. Fourth, it may be easier to liquidate an entire property rather than a fractional share. Finally, individual ownership is the most confidential form available.

The most significant disadvantage of this form of ownership is that the owner is subject to unlimited liability. Many investors choose not to subject themselves to this level of risk. Also, before choosing individual ownership, the investor should have decided that there would be no advantage in the limited legal liability and the possibility of fringe benefits offered by a closely held corporation, taking into account the double taxation aspect of the corporation and the cost of organizing and operating under the corporate structure. Frequently a closely held corporation entity is preferred. In any case, individual ownership is usually recommended only for relatively small-scale real estate investments.

Joint Tenancy

A joint tenancy exists when several people own the entire real estate. Each investor has the same ownership interest in a single parcel of real estate. Each owns an individual interest in the entire property, and the survivor takes the entire property (the survivor gets all!). The treatment of joint tenancy varies considerably from one state to another, so that it is difficult to make specific statements about this form of ownership. In some states there is a presumption that a joint tenancy is created when real estate is acquired by two or more people. Each joint tenant reports, for tax purposes, his or her share of income or loss generated by the property; but if one pays more than a pro rata share of the costs, the full amount of the payment may be claimed as a deduction. In contrast, some forms of organization (e.g., a tenancy in common) limit such deductions to the pro rata share of ownership.

The main advantage of joint tenancy is that it vests in the survivor. Thus, property does not go through probate when the investor dies, and much time and expense can be saved. On the other hand, each joint tenant is personally liable for all expenses incurred on a property. Consequently, the joint tenancy does not usually afford the insulation from liabilities created by co-venturers that is found in a tenancy in common.

Tenancy in Common

The ownership of real estate by two or more people, each of whom has an undivided interest in the property with no right of survivorship, is called a tenancy in common. While each tenant in common has an undivided interest in the entire property, their interests can be unequal; each investor can have any share of ownership that is agreed upon. When a tenant in common sells his or her interest (interest is freely transferable unless an agreement specifies otherwise), the buyer becomes a tenant in common with other tenants in common. When a tenant in common dies, the heirs—and not the other tenants in common—receive the ownership share. In many states there is a presumption that, in the absence of a written ownership agreement or provision to the contrary, a tenancy in common is created whenever real estate is acquired by two or more people.

Since each tenant in common owns an undivided interest in the property, difficult problems can arise when the tenants in common disagree and want to go their separate ways. A tenant in common is entitled to sue for partition of the property; if the property cannot be divided fairly, the court can order it to be sold and the proceeds divided among the investors according to their percentage interests.

A tenancy in common is considered by many investors to be a viable form of ownership only for a small project with relatively few investors. The property may not be sold, mortgaged, or even leased without the consent of all the investors. If the property is sold, all the investors must sign the deed to transfer the property. If one investor refuses, the others must enter into a costly legal process to enable the transfer to take place with a clear title.

Tax Treatment   Each tenant in common reports income, gain, or loss from the property according to his or her share of ownership. One tax advantage of this form of ownership, as compared with a partnership, is that each investor reports only his or her share of gains and losses to the Internal Revenue Service each year. No partnership return (Form 1065) need be filed; the IRS must audit the investor and the property records if it wishes to scrutinize the depreciation and other tax methods and assumptions used. Furthermore, it is argued that since there is no formal record of partners in the property, privacy is maintained and the probability of a *linked audit* is reduced. Thus, one investor will not be audited as a result of owning a property with another partner who is being audited. Further, since a tenancy in common is not recognized for tax purposes, income and losses are divided according to agreement and each investor can choose a depreciation method that suits his or her objectives and tax preferences. In contrast, each investor in a general partnership must accept the depreciation method chosen by the partnership entity.

In recent years the IRS has challenged the use of the tenancy in common as such for tax purposes. When the tenants in common are actively carrying on a trade or business (such as renting space and providing special services to tenants), the IRS may treat the entity as a partnership.[2] Consequently, a tenancy in common might be reclassified as a general partnership for tax purposes and be required to file a partnership return.

General Partnership

The general partnership is the most common form of noncorporate business association. It is very similar to a tenancy in common except for two major characteristics: (1) A partnership should have a partnership agreement; in numerous states a tenancy in common or other legal form is presumed to exist in the absence of such an agreement. (2) A partnership must file a federal tax return (Form 1065), in contrast to a tenancy in common, which does not usually file a tax return. Later we will see that some partnerships (which are entities formed under state law) can elect to avoid the partnership classification for federal income tax purposes.

According to the tax code, a partnership is a syndicate, group, pool, joint venture, or other unincorporated organization that carries on a business, venture, or other financial operation and that is not a corporation, trust, or estate.[3] The tax courts have ruled that a partnership exists if there is a voluntary association of the parties with the intent to carry out a business and each of the parties contributes property or service and shares in the profits of the organization. For federal income tax purposes, therefore, a partnership can be an entity that is not recognized as a partnership under state law. The concept of a partnership is much broader under federal law than under state law, which in most states is patterned after the Uniform Partnership Act.

The Primary Advantage Is Flexibility   Despite the problems that can arise from the unlimited personal liability of the members of a general partnership, the limited transferability of their interest in the partnership, and the limited continuity of the partnership, the partnership form of organization is popular because of its great flexibility. The investors have the freedom to structure an agreement that matches the rights and responsibilities of each partner to his or her particular risk/return objectives and areas of expertise. The partnership agreement may give more voting rights to some partners, delegate responsibility for property management to certain partners, and provide preferential returns to partners who require a return on capital before others get theirs.

Flexibility is an important advantage, but it underscores the importance of a well-written partnership agreement that clearly defines the terms used and the rights and obligations of the investors. Terms like *cash flow, profits,* or *proceeds from sales or refinancing* all mean different things to different investors. These and similar terms used should be defined clearly so that little ambiguity remains and costly disputes can be avoided.

Tax Advantages   Partnerships have distinct tax advantages over corporations. First, the partnership form avoids double taxation: No tax is imposed at the

[2] Gerald J. Robinson, "Setting Up the Real Estate Venture: An Overview," *The Journal of Real Estate Taxation,* Fall 1975, pp. 36–37.
[3] IRS §761.

partnership level. Second, the partnership can pass through tax losses to the investor, while the corporation cannot. In a partnership, the very substantial tax deductions that real estate can generate (e.g., depreciation, interest, maintenance and repair, tax credits) are passed through directly to the investors and serve as a tax shelter for them. Each partner picks up the income and losses of the partnership as ordinary income or losses, or as capital gains or losses, depending on their nature when realized by the partnership. Thus, a third tax advantage is the ability to pass through favorable capital gains treatment to the investor. Ordinarily, this advantage is available to corporate stockholders under very limited circumstances involving dissolution of the corporation.

The Tax Basis Problem The amount of partnership losses that may be deducted on a partner's tax return is limited to his or her *basis*. A partner's basis is the sum of two amounts: (1) the basis of his or her partnership (equity) interest and (2) his or her share of partnership mortgages and other liabilities. For example, if an investor contributes $10,000 cash to the partnership and his or her pro rata share of liabilities is $40,000, the basis is $50,000. However, if property with a tax basis different from market value is contributed, the allowable depreciation deduction is based on the tax basis and not on the market value. For example, if a property with a tax basis of $30,000 and a five-year life is contributed at a market value of $50,000, the allowable deduction is $6,000 annually for five years ($30,000 ÷ 5) rather than $10,000 annually ($50,000 ÷ 5). If the contributing partner gets credit for the contribution at market value, the other partners will receive a reduction in tax benefits as a consequence. The tax disadvantage to investors who contribute cash rather than property may be rectified somewhat by allocating a larger depreciation deduction to those who contribute cash than to those who contribute appreciated property. Such an arrangement is called a special allocation.

Partnership Special Allocations.[4] Special or disproportionate allocations are made when investors receive different amounts of cash flow, income, losses, deductions, or proceeds of sale or refinancing. Under the 1976 and 1981 tax acts these types of allocations are valid for income tax purposes only if the allocations have "substantial economic effect" and their primary purpose is not tax avoidance or tax evasion. For example, the IRS will not permit one partner to receive the benefit of all the partnership's depreciation deductions if that partner, regardless of whether there are profits or losses, will receive cash flow and sale proceeds from the partnership as if no special allocation has been made.[5]

The ability of a partnership to make special allocations, despite the problems involved, is an advantage of a partnership (or a tenancy in common). A partner in a high tax bracket who needs substantial tax shelter is often willing to reduce other benefits (cash flow, proceeds of sale or refinancing) in return for a larger allocation of deductible items such as depreciation. Set up correctly, special allocations can

---

[4] An analytical and historical treatise on the subject is presented in David Victor Eck and Stephen A. Pyhrr, *Analysis of Income-Producing Real Estate Investments: Partnership Special Allocations,* Technical Monograph no. 3 (College Station: Texas Real Estate Research Center, 1979).
[5] Kusnet and Holzman, p. 13.

result in higher rates of return for some or all of the partners. Limited partnerships, as well as general partnerships, can make special allocations.

Disadvantages   The three main disadvantages of a general partnership are said to be (1) unlimited liability, (2) limited transferability of interest, and (3) lack of continuity. In practice, these may or may not be disadvantages. For example, the members of a general partnership are personally liable for the debts and obligations incurred by the partnership, and each partner is jointly and severally liable for those debts and obligations. In practice, such unlimited liability can be limited through property and liability insurance; exculpatory clauses in mortgages, which relieve investors of personal liability; indemnification clauses, which relieve certain partners of liabilities assumed by other partners; and so on. Consequently, a general partnership entity can be structured to have de facto limited liability, as in the case of a limited partnership. Also, with respect to transferability of interest and continuity of life, a partnership agreement can be tailored to achieve almost any degree of continuity and transferability desired by the partners.

While a substantial degree of limited liability, continuity, and transferability of interest may be desirable attributes of an ownership entity, a substantial risk of tax reclassification exists. If the partnership takes on too many "corporate characteristics," it may be reclassified as a corporation for tax purposes and taxed twice—once at the entity level and again at the investor level. While this problem is usually associated with the limited partnership form of organization, it can also be a problem with a general partnership.

Yet another disadvantage of the general partnership, and other partnership forms, is the general lack of legal certainty associated with this ownership form. While corporate law is highly developed in most states, partnership law is subject to a mixed bag of legal precedents and case law. In short, the legal risk with a partnership form of ownership is somewhat higher than with a corporate form in most states.

Family Partnerships

Family partnerships can be established to lower the overall tax burden of owning income properties that produce substantial taxable gains. One method of doing this is to divide the income from the property among low- or no-income members of the family (e.g., the children); they become the partners of the parent–investor, who is in a high tax bracket and is subject to tax rates that reach 50 percent on income (70 percent on unearned income prior to 1982). Simply stated, the parent makes a gift of property to the children (or other family members), pays any applicable gift taxes, and effects a shift of tax brackets from his or her relatively high tax bracket to the lower tax brackets of the children. For example, if the marginal tax bracket of the parent is in the 40–50 percent range while the children's brackets are in the 0–25 percent range, a substantial reduction in the total tax burden can be achieved.

The IRS scrutinizes family partnerships very closely to see if there is a genuine arrangement or merely a tax avoidance scheme or sham that should not be recognized for tax purposes. To prevent shams, the tax code defines three requirements whose thrust is to ensure that donee partners actually own and control their interests in the partnership and that a family partnership is not merely a way of dividing among family members income for actual work that one person has performed.[6]

Limited Partnership

The limited partnership form of ownership is often preferred by a real estate professional because it gives the investor an opportunity to combine the financial resources of passive equity investors with his or her own skills in an organization that allows flexibility of operation, limited liability for the investors, and direct pass-through of tax benefits to the investors. However, limited partnerships have a number of disadvantages, including a sometimes poor image owing to past misuse of this ownership vehicle, tax basis problems, and the possibility of reclassification as a corporation for tax purposes. As a general rule, limited partnerships also draw a considerable amount of attention from various federal and state agencies, and are subject to numerous controls and regulations (e.g., security laws) that are not usually imposed as rigorously on other types of partnerships.

As defined under the Uniform Limited Partnership Act (ULPA), a limited partnership consists of at least one general and one limited partner. While the general partner (or partners) manages the affairs of the partnership and is personally liable for the debts and obligations of the partnership, the limited partners, who are passive investors, are not liable for partnership debts and obligations.

A limited partnership is actually a hybrid of a corporation and a general partnership. Like that of a corporate shareholder, the limited partner's liability is limited to his or her equity investment, and the status of limited partner does not allow him or her to control or actively participate in the affairs of the partnership. (A limited partner who actively participates in management legally becomes a general partner.) The general partner's roles and functions are very similar to those of corporate officers and directors. Just as a corporation must file a certificate of incorporation, a limited partnership must file a certificate of limited partnership with the appropriate state authority. This certificate must contain the names and addresses of all the partners and the major provisions of the partnership agreement. Thus, the limited partnership form of ownership does not generally afford a high degree of privacy to the investors as compared to a general partnership, tenancy in common, or individual form of ownership.[7]

In some respects, however, a limited partnership resembles a general partnership more closely than a corporation. In general, the rights and liabilities of the general partners in a limited partnership are similar to those of partners in a general partnership. Limited and general partnerships have similar problems with respect to continuity and transferability of interest.

---

[6] For further discussion of this subject see Institute for Business Planning, *Real Estate Investment Planning* (Englewood Cliffs, N.J., 1981), ¶56,240– 56,245.
[7] If a high degree of privacy is desired by a limited partner, various types of trust arrangements can be established to conceal the identity of the investor.

Limited Liability Considerations   Contrary to popular belief, limited partners may be liable for debts and obligations beyond their initial cash contribution. For example, limited partners are liable to the partnership for contributions that they have agreed to make to the partnership and for damages incurred owing to any breach of the partnership agreement. On occasion, for example, a partnership agreement may require partners to make staged payments over several years (also called split down payment), or can place a capital contribution limit on the partners that is significantly above the cash down payment required in the year of property purchase. Although both situations impose so-called limited liability, they nevertheless impose considerable liability on the investors beyond their initial capital contribution.

Under the Uniform Limited Partnership Act, limited partners can perform certain limited management duties without incurring the taint of a general partner and unlimited liability. They can (1) elect or remove the general partner or partners, (2) have a voice in determining whether the partnership agreement should be amended, and (3) determine whether and when the partnership properties should be refinanced or sold. On the other hand, the more rights that are granted to the limited partners, the greater the probability that they will be deemed by the courts to have the unlimited liability of general partners. Most important, however, limited partners should refrain from any active role in the day-to-day management of the partnership if they choose to maintain their limited liability status.[8]

Continuity and Transferability of Interest   While all partnerships have limitations with respect to these two characteristics, a limited partnership is usually structured to provide relatively more continuity and transferability than a general partnership. The death of a limited partner does not result in dissolution of the partnership. The recipient of the limited partnership interest (trustee or heir) has all the rights of the original partner, along with any additional liabilities. With regard to transferability of interest, the limited partner usually has more rights than a general partner. A limited partner's interest may be assigned at will, and the new partner has the same rights and obligations as the selling partner. While the partnership agreement may place some restrictions on the transfer to avoid too many corporate characteristics, the right to assign an interest is unrestricted.

The Problem of Too Many Corporate Characteristics   If a partnership has too many corporate characteristics, it will be taxed as a corporation. The so-called *Kintner regulations* are used to determine when a group will be treated as a partnership and when it will be treated as an *association* (corporation) for tax purposes. In short, the IRS will classify a group as a partnership for tax purposes if it avoids *at least two of these four* corporate characteristics:

1. Continuity
2. Centralization of management

---

[8] Recently, limited partners have been able to enter into the day-to-day management of "distressed property" threatened with foreclosure and have retained their limited liability status as long as there was a clear and unambiguous understanding with third-party creditors.

3. Limited liability
4. Free transferability of interests

In the past, tax experts have claimed that most limited partnerships qualify for partnership status because they lack the corporate characteristics of continuity and limited liability (the general partner always has unlimited liability). In addition, tax experts have successfully defended the limited partnership status in several instances, on the basis that centralization of management and free transferability of interest were not present.[9] Consequently, it is usually possible to structure an agreement so that the entity created will be classified as a partnership for tax purposes. A problem may occur, however, when a corporation is set up as the sole general partner, thus appearing to limit the liability of the general partner and giving the partnership entity the corporate characteristic of limited liability.

Use of a Corporate General Partner   The use of a corporation as the sole general partner of a limited partnership has become a popular technique in limited partnership syndications. The advantage of this arrangement is that it provides continuity of management that will survive the active managerial years of the individual general partner. A corporate general partner is not subject to ill health, death, insanity, or other human frailties. Specific requirements, known as the *Safe Harbor rules* (Revenue Procedure 72-13), have been set forth by the IRS for a partnership that seeks to avoid the limited liability characteristic:

1. *Net worth requirements.* If the equity contributions to the partnership total less than $2.5 million, then at all times during the life of the partnership the corporate general partner must have a net worth equal to 15 percent of the total contributions, or $250,000, whichever is less. If the total contributions are $2.5 million or more, the corporate general partner must have a net worth equal to 10 percent of total contributions.
2. *Ownership requirement.* The limited partners cannot own, directly or indirectly, more than 20 percent of the stock of the corporate general partner.

Thus, the corporation must have substantial assets of its own in order to pass the limited liability test.

Satisfying Investment Objectives Through Special Allocations   In a typical real estate limited partnership, the general and limited partners prefer to allocate items of taxable loss (e.g., from depreciation deductions) in a different manner than they would allocate taxable income. This might also apply to cash flow, refinancing proceeds, and sale proceeds. For example, tax losses incurred by the partnership in the early years of the investment might be allocated 95 percent to limited

[9] For a general discussion of these and other tax factors, see Sheldon Schwartz, "Tax Factors in the Limited Partnership," chap. 10, *Real Estate Securities and Syndication, a Workbook,* ed. Stephen E. Roulac (Chicago: National Association of Real Estate Boards, 1973), pp. 91–101; also Theodore S. Lynn, Harry F. Goldberg, Daniel S. Abrams, *Real Estate Limited Partnerships* (New York: Wiley-Interscience, 1977), pp. 20–26.

partners who require tax shelter and 5 percent to the general partner, while future taxable income would be divisible 50– 50. Also, it is common to give a preferred cash flow return to the limited partners (say, 6– 8 percent), while the general partner seeks to obtain substantial compensation if the property performs well by taking a disproportionate share of the sale proceeds (say, 20 percent of the sale proceeds after the limited partners receive their invested capital back plus a 6 to 8 percent noncompounded cumulative return on invested capital).

These allocations must, as previously stated, have economic substance and not be motivated principally by the desire for tax avoidance or evasion. If the allocation does not have "substantial economic effect," it will be disallowed and each partner will receive taxable income (loss), cash, and so forth according to his or her partnership interest.

Basis Problems and Other Disadvantages   Deductions generated by the depreciation of improvements are usually based on the *full cost* of the improvements to the owner, including the amount of any mortgage loans. A building purchased with a $100,000 down payment and subject to a mortgage loan of $900,000 produces $1 million of depreciable basis. The owner has purchased $1 million of depreciation with a $100,000 cash investment, thereby generating substantial amounts of tax shelter relative to a small down payment.

A problem that is peculiar to the limited partnership form of ownership is that the partner's basis in real estate is limited to the equity investment plus that partner's share of liabilities of the partnership for which no partner (general or limited) is *personally liable* (nonrecourse liabilities). For example, if the $900,000 loan were made by a local savings and loan association and contained personal guarantees by the general partner, only $100,000 of losses could be written off by the partnership. After the property basis reaches zero, no losses can be passed through to investors. In a tax-shelter-oriented investment, this might occur in two to three years, thus severely limiting the tax shelter benefits of the partnership. To correct the situation, the partnership should have negotiated a nonrecourse mortgage (an esculpatory clause in the mortgage) or bargained for personal liability on only the top 10– 25 percent of the mortgage (thereby removing from the basis only 10– 25 percent of the loan amount). In contrast, a proprietorship, tenancy in common, or general partnership can add the amount of *all* mortgage loans and liabilities to the basis for tax purposes, regardless of their personal-liability status. The problem of allocating mortgage amounts to the basis for tax depreciation purposes is unique to the limited partnership form of organization.

Another problem of the limited partnership is government regulation. Because limited partners are often unsophisticated and therefore are at the mercy of the general partner, and because the limited partnership form has been abused extensively by greedy and unscrupulous syndicators, the government sector has steadily increased its surveillance and regulatory controls over limited partnership syndications. The Securities Exchange Commission and state securities boards, as well as the IRS, have enacted numerous laws and regulations that seek to control the activities of promoters of real estate syndications. While the laws apply to all legal forms of ownership, the focus is on the limited partnership form. Syndication is discussed in Chapter 14.

Joint Venture

A joint venture is a special type of general partnership formed by investors for the purpose of owning a specific property or set of properties. While a joint venture is similar in most respects to a general partnership, as described, and is usually treated as such in many states, there is no intention on the part of the investors to enter into a continuing partnership relationship or to assume general partnership obligations and liabilities. It is usually formed for projects that require large amounts of capital and specialized experience. Thus, it might be an ideal form for a managing equity investor who is short on investment capital or doesn't want to risk all his or her money in one project. (The Aspen Wood case study involves a joint venture form of ownership in which the designated managing partner, i.e., the managing equity investor, is both syndicator and property manager, and the investor's liability is limited by a nonrecourse wraparound mortgage.)

Tax Treatment   A joint venture is treated as a partnership for income tax purposes unless it is deemed to be a corporation, and therefore is taxed at both the entity and investor levels; *or* the joint venture elects not to be taxed as a partnership and qualifies for such treatment under the IRS guidelines. The IRS has set forth four conditions that must be met if investors choose not to be taxed as a partnership [Regulation 1.761-2(a)]:

1. They must own the property as co-owners (undivided interest deeded to each of the investors).
2. They must reserve the right to own and sell their joint venture interest separately.
3. They cannot at any time actively conduct a business.
4. One of the investors cannot irrevocably authorize the sale or exchange of the property.

If the joint venture qualifies for the election, it must report its election in a statement to the IRS before the end of the first taxable year of the joint venture. As a result, the venture will not file a Form 1065 partnership return each year; rather, each venture partner will report only his or her pro rata share of income and losses on an individual tax return, and each investor can choose different accounting and depreciation methods for computing income and losses. The related benefits of this election were discussed in the section on tenancy in common. The risk of this tax election is that the IRS will disallow it and impose a penalty on the venture for not filing a partnership return.

In recent years the IRS has discouraged the use of this tax election and has defined and interpreted more narrowly the four conditions above. Consequently, to avoid the risks and costs described, many joint ventures are electing to report as partnerships for income tax purposes.

The Fiduciary Relationship Among Investors   Members of a joint venture, like partners, have a fiduciary relationship to each other that requires a significant degree of good faith and trust. As in all fiduciary relationships, each investor must fully disclose to the other investors all his or her dealings with the property and the venture. To prevent misunderstandings, a binding written agreement is necessary that outlines all the rights and obligations of each investor and the housekeeping rules of the venture. Typically, the investors appoint one member to be responsible for venture management and property management while the others remain relatively passive except for participating in major financial policy decisions.

CORPORATIONS AND TRUSTS

Regular (Subchapter C) Corporation

The corporate form of ownership is not normally used as an investment vehicle by equity investors because of three tax disadvantages. The first is double taxation—corporate income is taxable first to the corporation when it is received or accrued and again to the shareholders when it is distributed to them in the form of dividends. The second disadvantage is the inability of the corporation to pass through to its shareholders any tax losses generated by depreciation, interest, or other deductions. Third, it is difficult for a corporation to pass through capital gains income because dividends paid to stockholders are normally treated as ordinary income for tax purposes. Unlike a partnership or joint venture, a corporation is a legal entity that exists separately and apart from its stockholders. It files its own tax return, as do the investors who own stock in the corporation. Despite these disadvantages, there are many advantages of the corporate form, and in some situations these advantages make the corporate entity the ideal choice.

Advantages of the Corporate Entity

Some of the advantages of using the corporate form of ownership flow from the basic corporate characteristics discussed earlier in the chapter:

1. *Continuity.* A corporation continues until dissolved by law (unless limited by state statute).
2. *Limited liability.* Stockholders have no individual liability for corporate debts and liabilities; a stockholder's losses are generally limited to his or her equity investment.
3. *Centralization of management.* Stockholders are not responsible for management; authority is vested in a board of directors; corporate officers are hired as agents of the board and are paid to run the day-to-day operations of the corporation.
4. *Free transferability of interests.* Stock can ordinarily be sold or otherwise transfered at will. However, such transferability may be limited purposely by the organizers (e.g., a closely held or family corporation). Also, there may not be an active market for the stock.

Other advantages of the corporate form that are often cited by investors who use a corporate entity for their investments are the following:

1. *Diversification.* The corporation form allows the combination of several distinct properties into one entity so as to create diversification and a spreading of the risks involved in investment properties.
2. *Favorable public image and legal certainty.* Lenders, investors, and the general public tend to view the corporation favorably. This gives an aura of solidity, strength, and continuity to the operations of the entity. In addition, a well-developed body of law regulates corporate activity and lends a high degree of legal certainty to this form of ownership.
3. *Control of large properties with minimum capital outlays.* Small investors can pool their money and buy larger properties through the corporation than they could individually, while maintaining limited liability.
4. *Estate building or retirement fund.* A corporation can be used as a vehicle for building a portfolio of real estate assets by reinvesting accumulated earnings of the corporation. At the same time, the tax consequences to the corporation can be minimized by offsetting tax-loss properties with tax-gain properties, and through deductions allowed, such as salaries to stockholder-officers. Years later, when the stockholder-officer retires, the corporation can be liquidated or shares of stock sold and the capital gains income will pass directly through to the officer-stockholder without a tax at the entity level.
5. *Fringe benefits.* Principals, as officer-stockholders or employee-stockholders, can have a tax-favored retirement or pension plan set up for them. A corporation can carry insurance on the lives of employee and officer-stockholders at a reduced annual tax cost and then, without any further income tax burden, realize the proceeds and make them available to pay estate taxes. Other fringe benefits could include group life insurance, full medical and dental insurance coverage for employee and officer-stockholders and their families, disability insurance, pension plans, and death benefits to beneficiaries—all paid for by the corporation. These deductions are not generally available to the other forms of organization discussed.
6. *Financial and tax planning.* The corporate form can facilitate saving income and estate taxes by means of gifts to children or a family foundation. Corporate stockholders can often control the dividend process, dictating the year in which they will receive income and choosing years that yield the most favorable tax results. Frequently multiple corporations will be established, one for each property purchased, to limit liabilities and reduce the investor's overall tax burden. As we will see in Chapter 13, however, there are strict controls on corporations formed primarily for tax avoidance purposes.

In conclusion, the corporate entity may provide an ideal ownership entity for investors who seek wealth accumulation and can minimize or avoid the problems of double taxation and limited tax shelter.

Problem Areas for Corporate Entities   There are certain problem areas that should be considered by the investor who is considering the corporate form as a vehicle for building real estate equities.[10] In most cases careful tax planning can circumvent these problems before they occur.

The first is the *accumulated-earnings tax*. When a corporation accumulates earnings instead of distributing them as dividends to stockholders, it runs the risk of a penalty tax.[11] The penalty is intended to discourage formation of a corporation for the purpose of avoiding double taxation by "unreasonably" accumulating earnings. This penalty tax becomes operative only when accumulated earnings exceed $250,000 ($150,000 prior to the 1981 tax act), and the excess is taxed at 27½ percent on the first $100,000 and 38½ percent on the remainder. The investor can avoid the penalty tax by showing "reasonably anticipated needs of the business" as the purpose of the accumulation.[12] For example, if accumulated earnings are to be used to make mortgage payments, to buy additional properties, or as a reserve fund for the renovation of older properties, the accumulation problem can be avoided.

A related penalty tax problem occurs if the corporation is classified as a *personal holding company*.[13] Prior to the establishment of the personal holding company tax provision, a tax loophole called the *incorporated pocketbook* existed whereby an investor in a high tax bracket would form a corporation to furnish services to the investor. The corporation would then accumulate the income and obtain the benefit of the lower tax rates of the corporation. This tax shelter vehicle was closed by imposing a 50 percent penalty tax (70 percent prior to the 1981 tax act) on all undistributed personal holding company income in addition to the regular corporate taxes. There are numerous tests and regulatory definitions involved in the personal holding company problem, and careful analysis should be performed if the investor anticipates problems in this area.[14]

Multiple and Collapsible Corporations   A real estate investor may choose to operate with a separate corporation for each property (i.e., multiple corporations). If the legal entities are separate, the debts and obligations of one property will never be the responsibility of another. If one property becomes insolvent, creditors cannot look to the other properties for satisfaction of the debts. Investors also set up multiple corporations for tax purposes. Since the corporate tax rate in 1982 is only 16 percent (15 percent after 1982) on the first $25,000 of taxable income, increasing gradually to 40 percent on amounts of less than $100,000, it pays to spread the income from an investment program over as many low-tax-rate entities as possible. However, under current tax law this procedure may be disallowed if a major or principal purpose is to avoid income taxes. Special attention and scrutiny

---

[10] An excellent discussion of special corporate tax problems is provided in Arthur Anderson & Co., *Federal Taxes Affecting Real Estate*, 1978, pp. 382–399.

[11] IRC §531–537.

[12] IRC §537.

[13] IRC §541.

[14] See Institute for Business Planning, ¶56,315–56,320. Also, Coopers & Lybrand, *Tax Planning for Real Estate Transactions* (Jerome Y. Halperin et al.), prepared for the Farm and Land Institute of the National Association of Realtors (Chicago, 1978), pp. 45–46.

are given to the corporate form whenever multiple corporations are controlled by one person or by related individuals.[15]

Collapsible corporations can also create serious tax problems. When investors sell the property owned by a corporation, they can wind up with ordinary income rather than a capital gain if the corporation has held the property less than three years. The collapsible corporation rule, as it is called, was enacted to prevent investors from setting up a corporation to purchase or construct real estate with a view to selling the property or stock of the corporation before the corporation realizes any substantial ordinary income from the property. Generally, the collapsible corporation rule can be avoided if most of the corporate property is depreciable property, and provided that owners of the corporate stock are not "dealers" in real estate. The dealer classification and problem are discussed in Chapter 13.

Salaries of Stockholder Employees If corporate profits are distributed to shareholders as payments for services rendered to the corporation, the moneys are deductible by the corporation as expenses rather than being dividends to the shareholders and subject to a double tax. For example, investor-officers often attempt to adjust their bonuses or salaries at the end of each year in order to minimize corporate taxes. However, the IRS allows salaries and bonuses to be deducted by the corporation as an ordinary business expense only if they are "reasonable." If it is considered unreasonable, the purported salary or bonus cannot be deducted by the corporation. In addition, it will also be taxed as ordinary income to the shareholder as a "disguised dividend." The IRS uses a relatively elaborate set of principles and tests to ascertain reasonableness; basically, reasonable compensation is defined as that amount which would ordinarily be paid for like services by like enterprises under like circumstances.[16] As with other potential tax risks that we have discussed, the salary reclassification risk can be reduced or minimized through good tax planning.

Subchapter S Corporation

The Internal Revenue Code, Subchapter S, allows certain small business corporations to avoid corporate taxes. When a qualified corporation properly elects Subchapter S treatment, most of the tax consequences of its operations pass through to its shareholders. Thus, the investors enjoy the benefits of having a corporate entity offering them the usual corporate advantages—limited liability, continuity, centralized management, fringe benefits, good public image—and at the same time they enjoy many of the tax advantages of a partnership. Tax losses are passed through to stockholders, and each stockholder receives a pro rata share of those losses. Likewise, capital gains realized by the corporation are passed through to the shareholders. No tax is levied at the corporate level. Also, the corporate problems of the accumulated earnings tax and the personal holding company tax are avoided.

[15] IRC §1561 and 1563. See also §385.
[16] Kusnet and Holzman, pp. 37–38.

A corporation can elect Subchapter S treatment only if it meets *all* of the following requirements:[17]

1. It must be a domestic corporation incorporated in the United States.
2. It must have no more than twenty-five shareholders (fifteen prior to the 1981 tax act).
3. All stockholders must be individuals, estates, or special types of trusts.
4. Shareholders must all be U.S. citizens or resident aliens.
5. There may be only one class of stock.
6. The corporation cannot be a member of an "affiliated group" of corporations; it cannot own 80 percent or more of the stock of another corporation.
7. No more than 20 percent of the corporation's gross receipts can be derived from passive income, which includes, among other things, income from residential and commercial rents. Some types of rental income are not considered passive—such as that derived from hotel and motel operations, parking garages and lots, equipment rentals, and similar rents with regard to which the lessor renders "substantial services" to the tenant.

The Subchapter S election is made, assuming that the corporation meets all the requirements, by filing an election with the consent of all the stockholders. Once made, the Subchapter S election is effective for the taxable year of the corporation for which it is made, and for all subsequent tax years, unless the IRS revokes the election or the stockholders terminate it.

Use of Subchapter S in Real Estate Investment   Subchapter S treatment for real estate investors is severely limited by the provision that not more than 20 percent of the corporation's gross receipts for any taxable year can be derived from passive investment income. Despite this limitation, real estate investors can qualify for Subchapter S treatment by owning motels and hotels; shopping centers for which the corporate owner provides substantial promotional, maintenance, security, or other services; a real estate brokerage or development company; or any other business in which the investment income from property will represent less than 20 percent of gross income. An active real estate investor who owns and manages several properties might create a Subchapter S corporation to manage and lease properties, since the income of such a company is not from passive rents but from management services and leasing commissions.

A Subchapter S corporation may not be a wise choice for an investor, even if it can qualify. For example, a lender may insist that shareholders be personally liable for the amount of financing advanced to the corporation. Where this occurs, the legal advantage of limited liability is largely eroded. Under these circumstances the investor might prefer a partnership form of ownership. Also, a Subchapter S corporation does not provide the ease of transferability of stock or the flexibility of an ordinary corporation because of the limitations on the number and types of

---

[17] Mason J. Sacks, *Modern Tax Planning Checklists* (Boston: Warren, Gorham & Lamont, 1977, cum. supp. 1980), pp. 7–31, S7–4.

shareholders and classes of stock. These limitations, when added to the facts that (1) tax losses can be deducted only to the extent of the shareholder's basis of *shares* (corporate debt is *not* included in that basis) and (2) special allocations of particular loss items are not possible, may result in a decision against the Subchapter S corporation as an ownership entity.[18]

Nominee, Dummy, and Straw Corporations[19]

A nominee, dummy, or straw corporation (the three terms are synonymous) can be organized to achieve a number of objectives, including the following:

1. Limiting the personal liability of the beneficial owners of the property.
2. Privacy—concealing ownership of property.
3. Simplifying the transferability of interest when there is a large number of beneficial owners.
4. Raising money to finance a property on which the rate of interest charged would be usurious if the loan were made to an individual.

The tax and legal consequences of setting up a nominee corporation must be analyzed. From a tax standpoint, the corporate entity may be disregarded (not subjected to a corporate income tax) if it is the mere alter ego of its shareholders and beneficial owners, provided that it serves no other function and engages in no significant business activity.[20] For example, a corporation that is created and used as a mere "dummy" to take title to property and hold that title blind in order to deter the creditors of a shareholder may avoid taxation at the corporate level; the income is taxed only at the shareholder level. On the other hand, if the corporation is not completely inactive, its income may be subject to double taxation. For example, if it engages in such real estate activity as executing leases, collecting rents, making improvements, maintaining a bank account, or negotiating sales, it may be treated as a taxable entity.

Avoiding the Taint of Usury When a nominee, straw, or dummy corporation is used to avoid the taint of usury (paying an interest rate exceeding that which can be legally charged to individuals), the corporation takes title to the property, executes the mortgage loan documents, and then immediately transfers title to the investor-stockholders subject to the mortgage loan. Since the corporation is a mere shell and performs no real business functions, the investors want its existence to be ignored for tax purposes and to pay taxes only at the investor-stockholder level. Thus, the individual investors, rather than the corporation, report any tax losses generated by the property.

[18] H. Reed Wasson, "Real Estate Investment Vehicles: A Comparison of Partnership, Affiliated Subsidiary, Subchapter S Corporation, and Ordinary Corporation as the Form of the Vehicle," *Journal of Real Estate Taxation,* Winter 1976, p. 176.
[19] See Kusnet and Holzman, pp. 45–46. Also, P. Bruce Wright, "Owning Real Estate Through Shams and Nominees," *Real Estate Review* (Boston: Warren, Gorham & Lamont, Spring 1976), pp. 53–59.
[20] For a summary of the leading cases dealing with the subject, see Institute for Business Planning, ¶56,310–56,315.

Unfortunately, the history of court cases reveals a general uncertainty concerning such corporate arrangements. Careful planning and structuring can only reduce the risks of double taxation, not eliminate it. These risks should be weighed against the returns before such an ownership vehicle is used.

Real Estate Investment Trust

A real estate investment trust (REIT) is a specialized form of trust ownership created by congressional action, and its basic structure is defined by the Internal Revenue Code. Qualified REITs do not pay any federal income or capital gains tax on income or gains distributed to shareholders. The purpose of this favorable tax treatment is (1) to give small investors the chance to participate in large-scale real estate investments with professional management on a scale that was formerly available only to a few wealthy individuals, and (2) to stimulate the financing of the large-scale real estate developments needed in metropolitan areas.

REITs can own real estate, interests in real estate, and real estate mortgages. Some invest directly in real estate mortgages; others engage in a combination of investments and are known as hybrid trusts.

- *Equity REITs:* invest in real estate equities on a long-term basis, with their principal sources of income being rents. They invest in real properties such as apartment buildings, office and industrial buildings, and shopping centers.
- *Mortgage REITs:* frequently finance every phase of a real estate venture, including acquisition of the land, its development, and construction of the building and other improvements. They also invest in permanent mortgages on residential and commercial properties.
- *Hybrid REITs:* make a combination of equity and mortgage investments in real estate.

The REIT is managed by trustees who hold title to the property for the benefit of the shareholders. The trustees usually retain the advisory company that originally organized the real estate investment trust and selected the trustees. REITs have been organized by commercial bankers, mortgage bankers, real estate brokers, real estate managers, and others with real estate experience. A large percentage of REITs have been sponsored and are advised by major commercial banks.

Advantages Offered by REITs   The REIT is sometimes referred to as the mutual fund for real estate investors. In addition to the advantage of being a single-tax entity, REITs enable small investors to invest in large real estate enterprises and spread risk among many investors, and they provide diversification, professional management, and liquidity in the form of a public market for their shares. They are organized to earn immediate income and distribute that income to investors and, in equity and hybrid REITs, to achieve appreciation in the value of their investment. REITs enjoy the corporate attributes of centralized management, limited liability for their investors, continuity, and transferability of shares. At the same time, for income tax purposes the investor-shareholders are treated in a manner similar to the treatment of partners, with the limitation that tax losses cannot be passed through to them and used to shelter other income.

The REIT has generally been accepted by the investing public and, because of its broad base of shareholders and nationally recognized sponsoring agents, has established a reasonably good market for its shares. In the past the market for these shares has been stronger than the market for limited partnership shares or other forms of ownership. Even large investors may find the REIT an attractive vehicle because of features that are not available in other forms of ownership. A REIT can be organized to acquire a property that has limited market appeal as a single property but can be marketed more easily through the sale of shares. Thus, the unique advantages of the REIT may be attractive to investors who can adapt these advantages to their return and risk objectives.

Eligibility Requirements for Conduit Tax Treatment

Unless the REIT meets *all* the requirements of the Internal Revenue Code, it will not receive the conduit tax treatment just described. Furthermore, the REIT may be disqualified if it does not continue to meet these requirements each year; in some cases it may be assessed a penalty tax. These requirements include the following:

1. *Corporation or trust.* The REIT must be a corporation or a common law trust. It cannot be a limited partnership.
2. *At least 100 beneficial owners.* The REIT must have at least 100 beneficial owners, who can be individuals, trusts, estates, partnerships, or corporations. It cannot be more than 50 percent owned by five or fewer individuals. The shares must be transferable.
3. *No real estate dealer activities.* The REIT may not be a dealer in real estate; that is, it may not hold property primarily for sale to customers in the ordinary course of business. Consequently, the REIT must not be an active participant in a real estate business such as development, property management, leasing, or brokerage. Any income from dealer properties is subject to a 100 percent penalty tax but does not result in disqualification.
4. *Passive income tests.* The REIT must derive at least 90 percent of its gross income from passive sources (e.g., dividends, rents from real estate, gain from the sale of real estate, stock, and securities) each year and at least 75 percent of its gross income from specified real estate sources. Instead of being disqualified, a 100 percent penalty tax is charged on income that exceeds these limits.
5. *Dividend test.* A REIT loses its favored tax status and is treated like a corporation unless it distributes 95 percent (formerly 90%) or more of its income in the year the income is earned or in the following year.
6. *Asset tests.* There are a series of asset tests related to the relative proportions of real estate assets, corporate securities, government securities, cash, etc., that a REIT has in its portfolio. Failure to meet these tests, results in the REIT's losing its status.

Disadvantages of the REIT The REIT did not become a popular form of ownership until the early 1970s. Unfortunately, many REITs, especially the mortgage types specializing in construction and development loans (sponsored largely by commercial banks), grew too fast and raised too much capital, which was required by law to be placed in real estate assets within a relatively short period. Billions of new dollars entered the real estate financing marketplace from 1970 to 1974, and many properties were built and financed regardless of their financial and market feasibility. The management teams that ran many of the REITs were incompetent. The subsequent real estate crash of 1974–1976 was disastrous to the REITs, and they quickly fell from public favor. As late as 1979–1980, some REITs were still recovering from their losses and attendant mismanagement. Much of the investment public continues to question the REIT as a desirable investment vehicle, despite the excellent track record of many of the well-managed mortgage and equity REITs.

Other disadvantages of the REIT form, which preclude it from consideration by many investors, are the following:

1. *Strict rules and regulations.* A REIT must comply with many federal and state regulations in addition to the ones cited earlier. There is not much freedom or flexibility in the real estate investment program; the accounting and legal requirements are onerous and entail substantial expense for the REIT.
2. *Probability of losing REIT status.* There is a significant risk of losing REIT status or incurring heavy penalty taxes. If a REIT loses its status, it is treated as a regular corporation and incurs double taxation. Regaining the REIT classification is difficult.
3. *Limited tax shelters.* A REIT can shelter all cash flow produced by its properties, and therefore distribute "tax-free" cash, but it cannot pass through tax losses to the investor. Consequently, the REIT is not a practical entity for investors who seek to shelter income earned from other sources.
4. *Limited growth potential.* A REIT cannot significantly accumulate income and reinvest in properties. Thus, it is a relatively poor estate-building vehicle.
5. *Limited use for syndication of a single property.* A REIT is not usually the best form of organization for acquiring a single property due to the substantial costs involved and the long time period required to organize it.

In most real estate transactions time is of the essence. For an entrepreneur who must quickly tie up property, set up an ownership form, and raise the required equity with a minimum of expense and hassle, the REIT is not a desirable form of ownership. The REIT is better suited to a larger, institutional type of organization that can effectively manage the relatively cumbersome process of organizing and operating such an entity. In recent years well-managed equity and hybred REITs have experienced increasing earnings per share and asset values and have been excellent investments for their shareholders.

Other Types of Trusts[21]

The common types of trusts provide popular and flexible devices for indirectly controlling property while transfering the financial benefits to the beneficiary, without taxation at the entity level. The important feature of any trust, including the REIT, is that legal title to property is held by trustees for the benefit of the shareholders or beneficiaries who possess rights to share the income from the property and/or the proceeds from the sale of assets. The authority of a trustee to purchase and sell real estate is established by a recorded deed to the trustee from the grantor. Then a trust agreement is drawn up that spells out the rights and responsibilities of the beneficiaries and the trustee. Almost every trust agreement has control in the trustee, transferability of shares, and continuance beyond the death of a participant. Therefore, it closely resembles a corporation and may be reclassified as a corporation by the IRS if it does not meet certain tests.

Revocable and Irrevocable Trusts A *revocable trust,* sometimes called a *living trust* or *grantor trust,* may be terminated by the grantor during his or her lifetime. This type of trust is desirable in that real estate placed in the trust may avoid probate procedure upon the death of the grantor. Also, the trust provides a measure of privacy and protects assets from outside creditors. It provides for continuity of management if the grantor becomes incapacitated. On the other hand, the revocable trust has the least favorable tax effects. The income is taxable to the grantor each year, and all real estate transfered to the trust is included in the grantor's gross estate for inheritance tax purposes. Thus, a high-tax-bracket owner is not able to shift taxable income to lower-bracket beneficiaries.

An *irrevocable trust,* in contrast, cannot be terminated by the grantor once it has been established and all property interests have been transfered to the trustee. This is the favored vehicle for tax planning of large estates because, if set up correctly, it provides more flexibility than a revocable trust and the income is not taxed to the grantor. It is often used (as are family partnerships) to redistribute income from real estate ventures among family members who are in lower tax brackets. Also, the property value can be deducted from the gross estate of the grantor. One disadvantage of the irrevocable trust is that it usually triggers a gift tax at the time of the transfer.

Clifford Trusts A Clifford trust is a trust established for ten years or the life of the beneficiary, whichever is less, after which the property interests revert to the grantor. For example, assume that an investor owns an apartment building (land and building) that generates significant depreciation deductions. The deductions are used to shelter other income that is taxed at a high rate. The investor transfers the land, a nondepreciable asset, to a Clifford trust for the benefit of his child who is attending college. The investor retains ownership of the building and agrees to pay rent to the trust for the use of the land. As a result, the grantor's tax shelter increases because the rent payment is deductible for tax purposes. At the same

---

[21] A complete discussion of trusts is provided in the looseleaf service *Estate Planning* (New York: Institute for Business Planning), vol. 1, ¶16,901–17,200. This service is updated monthly.

time, the college student receives an attractive cash flow that is taxable at a low tax bracket. The reverse situation can also be desirable if the child has taxable income but the grantor has too many tax losses; if he transfers the building and retains the land, he generates ordinary income (land rent) that can be sheltered. The child receives tax losses that are used to shelter his or her income.

A Clifford trust can also be an excellent vehicle for supporting elderly family members. For example, the grantor can transfer income property to the trust to provide income to an elderly parent for his or her lifetime or ten years, whichever is shorter.

Offshore Trusts   The ownership vehicle used in most "tax haven" (avoidance) strategies is an offshore trust set up in a low-tax country by a wealthy investor who wishes to accumulate profits and provide a channel for large deductions against U.S. taxation.[22] This device is frequently used by foreign corporate investors who seek to avoid paying taxes on operations conducted in the United States. If the trust is properly established in a country that has favorable tax treaties with the United States (e.g., Bermuda or the British Antilles), the income from operations is taxed at a relatively low rate (not subject to the regular graduated income tax) and the capital gains is not subject to any federal income tax. To qualify for these tax exclusions, the foreign trust must not be in a "U.S. trade or business" and its trustees cannot be physically present in the United States for 183 days or more during the taxable year.

In recent years the Internal Revenue Service has been discouraging the use of these vehicles to avoid taxes in the United States, especially if any of the beneficiaries are U.S. citizens. For example, the 1981 Economic Recovery Tax Act contains several foreign investment provisions designed to close loopholes and correct certain tax inequities, thus putting foreign investors more on a par taxwise with domestic investors.

Pension Trusts   A pension trust is established for the benefit of employees and is similar to a tax-exempt foundation in that the beneficiaries (employees) are taxed on distributions of income that they receive while the trust itself is exempt from income taxes. Pension funds are becoming a significant factor in real estate investment markets, although they have traditionally restricted their purchases to publicly traded marketable securities. Because they have grown substantially over the past ten years, and because of the stock market's dismal performance in the 1970s, pension funds have been required by law to diversify into real estate, investing in real estate equities as well as mortgages. Pension funds can commingle their funds with other pension funds and other entities, which allows them to invest in projects that are too large for a single pension fund, and to diversify their portfolios. Pension funds that invest in real estate are usually managed by banks, life insurance companies, and other financial institutions that have developed the real estate expertise required for such an investment program. Two of

---

[22] An excellent article on offshore trusts and other types of tax haven vehicles is Adam Starchild and John T. Kosarowich, "Using Tax Havens for U.S. Real Estate Investment," *Journal of Property Management,* January-February 1978, pp. 12–15.

the largest commingled real estate funds in the United States are operated by the Prudential Life Insurance Company (the PRISA fund) and The First National Bank of Chicago (Fund F). In Chapter 26 we discuss this form of ownership in greater depth.

One significant problem that may be encountered by a pension fund in real estate is known as the "unrelated business income" problem. The use of debt to finance a property creates "unrelated business taxable income," which may result in loss of tax-exempt status for a portion of the trust's income. As a result of this problem, many pension trusts have a policy of buying only debt-free properties. Fund F, for example, requires that all mortgage debt be retired before legal title is transferred to it. Other pension funds choose to buy mortgaged property and pay some taxes in exchange for the substantial benefits expected from leverage and the ability to diversify and control more properties with fewer equity dollars invested.[23]

Individual Retirement Accounts and Keogh Plans   The 1981 revisions to the Employee Retirement Income Security Act (ERISA) allows all individuals to set up their own individual retirement accounts (IRAs) or other qualified pension plans. Contributions to a qualified retirement plan are deducted from the individual's annual taxable income. In effect, individuals can build equities with before-tax dollars and defer taxation until distributions are made during retirement, when the tax bracket may be lower. Both the capital contributions and the earnings on the amounts invested in IRA accounts are tax free until distribution. An individual can contribute and deduct up to a maximum of $2,000 a year.

IRA contributions must be invested in one or more of three ways: (1) an IRA with a bank or other qualified organization as trustee, (2) a qualified individual annuity contract, or (3) a retirement bond issued by the U.S. government. Under the present law the amount of contributed funds that can be invested in real estate is very limited.

A self-employed person can set aside money for retirement in a *Keogh* plan instead of an IRA. This type of plan often is more desirable because it allows individuals to contribute up to $15,000 each year (instead of $2,000 as in an IRA) or 15 percent of earned income, whichever is less. In addition, ERISA offers an alternative to the $15,000 or 15 percent limitation: Contributions can also be made on a sliding percentage scale based on age and income level. The latter choice may result in substantially more tax-free contributions to a retirement plan and a larger portfolio of real estate assets and securities at the time of retirement. A Keogh plan provides significantly more flexibility than an IRA in choosing real estate investments to build the retirement portfolio. However, the ERISA rules and regulations are very strict and cumbersome to administer with regard to real estate investments; thus, careful tax planning is necessary.

Numerous other types of pension plans can be established and used to channel before-tax dollars into real estate investments. For example, professional

---

[23] Stephen E. Roulac, *Modern Real Estate Investment* (San Francisco: Property Press, 1976), pp. 273–275

people (doctors, dentists, lawyers) can purchase real estate through the properly qualified plans of self-employed professional corporations that they administer. This can provide a very flexible vehicle for real estate investments compared with the IRA or Keogh plans. One should be forewarned that the tax act provides that *qualified* plans may not properly receive *unrelated business income* without risking heavy tax penalties. Distributive shares of capital gains, or taxable income arising out of debt-financed properties, may be characterized by the IRS as unrelated business income.

REAL ESTATE SYNDICATION

Syndication can be defined as a device by which a real estate professional—the syndicator or sponsor—obtains investors who provide the funds required to engage in a real estate enterprise.[24] Some people consider it to be a legal form of ownership while others view it as a type of financing—one that offers smaller investors the opportunity to invest in real estate ventures that would otherwise be beyond their financial and management capabilities.

A syndicate can be formed to acquire, develop, manage, operate, or market real estate, or to perform any combination of these functions.[25] For example, a real estate syndicate might be organized to acquire income property and hold it for the cash flow and tax shelter it generates, or to acquire and hold real estate primarily for capital appreciation over a period of years, or for a combination of these objectives. Syndicates are often formed to construct buildings or develop land, which is then sold to other investors. They can be formed to do virtually anything that any real estate enterprise might do. Syndicators benefit from the fees for their services, the interest they may retain in the syndicated property, and the ability to manage and profit from several ventures at the same time and thereby spread the risk. If a syndicator is also a real estate broker, he or she benefits from the increase of the market for the properties handled.

The subject of syndication is discussed at length in Chapter 14, since we consider it primarily a financing vehicle. However, to the extent that syndication is a form of ownership, it utilizes the selection criteria and legal entities discussed in this chapter.

SUMMARY

In this chapter we examined the various ownership alternatives available to investors, and developed a general framework for evaluating those alternatives in relation to the investor's selection criteria and return/risk objectives. We noted that no single type of entity is necessarily best for a wide range of investment

---

[24] Alvin L. Arnold and Jack Kusnet, *The Arnold Encyclopedia of Real Estate* (Boston: Warren, Gorham & Lamont, 1978), pp. 804–807.
[25] A complete discussion of real estate syndication is presented in *Portfolio Number 11: How to Syndicate Real Estate; Explanation and Practical Guide* (Boston: Warren, Gorham & Lamont, 1977). The portfolio, which includes a book of forms, was prepared by the staff of *Real Estate Review* with the assistance of Alan Parisse, a real estate consultant.

activities, and it is possible for an investor to have a variety of ownership entities in his or her portfolio.

We examined numerous ownership selection criteria. While favorable tax treatment is of paramount importance to most investors, many nontax considerations should also be taken into account in the ownership decision, including the cost of formation, the number of investors, the type of management needed, the degree of flexibility required, the extent and probability of exposure to liability, the ease and transferability of interests, and so on.

Next we analyzed various types of ownership entities, their important characteristics, their advantages and disadvantages, and how they might be used in order to achieve the investor's return/risk objectives. Ownership vehicles were analyzed in three broad categories: (1) noncorporate forms of ownership, (2) corporations and trusts, and (3) syndication. While syndication is not technically a legal form of ownership entity, it is commonly classified as such by investors.

An ownership decision model is developed as part of the Aspen Wood case study. Such a model is developed in matrix form and is used to compare and rank the ownership alternatives being considered.

ASPEN WOOD APARTMENTS

APPLICATION OF THE OWNERSHIP DECISION MODEL

In the preceding pages we have discussed a wide variety of selection criteria and ownership alternatives. From the list of possible selection criteria, an investor must define those that are most important given overall return and risk objectives, and then weight the relative importance of each. The investor must also be able to quickly evaluate the basic characteristics of each form of ownership and narrow the choices down to a manageable number. Normally this process is performed intuitively by experienced investors. However, a formal process using a decision model will make explicit all the variables being considered and increase the rationality of the process. This should lead to more consistent and profitable decisions.

THE DECISION MATRIX

The decision matrix developed for Aspen Wood Apartments is shown in Exhibit 9–2. The managing equity investor-syndicator, D&B Associates, use twelve of the criteria listed in Exhibit 9–1, plus a thirteenth—ability to control the property, earn commissions, and retain the property management. After the desired holding period D&B would, in most cases, form a new joint venture to buy the property from the existing joint venture and begin a new ownership and tax cycle. In many cases some of the old joint venture investors would also become partners in the new joint venture.[26] In this manner the property management company and the syndicator could assure themselves of repeat business and clients as long as the properties performed up to the expectations of the investors.

Each selection criterion is weighted according to its relative importance as perceived by the managing equity investor. The managing partners of the firm, Charlie Davidson and Clyde Boomer, have placed the greatest weight on five criteria that are extensions of the investor objectives developed in Chapter 8: (1) ability to pass through tax losses, (2) ability of the syndicator to control the property, (3) avoidance of double taxation, (4) limited liability, and (5) favorable image of the entity form among the target investor group. Of least importance to the investor are continuity and marketability of interest, which are assigned three and two points, respectively. The investors who invest with Davidson and Boomer are expected to commit their capital for the entire ownership period, at the end of which, and as determined by a

---

[26] Under current (1981) tax law up to 80 percent of the owners of the selling entity can be partners in the buying entity without the IRS challenging the validity of the sale transaction.

EXHIBIT 9–2. The Ownership Decision Matrix

SELECTION CRITERIA	POINTS AVAILABLE	OWNERSHIP ALTERNATIVES					
		Tenancy in common	General partnership	Limited partnership	Joint venture	REIT	Regular corporation
1. Avoidance of double taxation	10	10	10	9	10	8	0
2. Ability to pass through tax losses	15	15	15	14	15	0	0
3. Maximum income tax deductions	8	8	7	6	8	4	4
4. Capital gains treatment	5	5	5	5	5	3	2
5. Limited liability	10	8	8	10	8	10	10
6. Marketability of interest	3	0	1	2	1	3	3
7. Flexibility/Allowed activities	7	7	7	4	7	0	4
8. Ability to participate in management	6	6	6	2	6	1	1
9. Continuity of life	2	0	0	1	0	2	2
10. Favorable image—good track record	10	3	8	4	10	4	6
11. Minimum govt. controls and reporting	5	5	3	1	5	0	1
12. Minimum capital outlay	5	5	5	5	5	3	3
13. Ability of syndicator to control property	14	8	9	14	10	14	13
TOTALS	100	80	84	77	90	52	49

majority of the investors (who participate in major management decisions), the ownership entity will cease to exist. The investors will usually achieve a high degree of limited liability, regardless of the ownership entity chosen, through the use of a nonrecourse mortgage and substantial liability insurance coverage. Consequently, all of the entity forms shown can be characterized by a high degree of limited liability.

When analyzing each ownership form, Davidson and Boomer assign to each some of the total points allocated for each selection criterion (10 for avoidance of double taxation, 15 for ability to pass through tax losses, etc.) If an ownership form meets the criteria perfectly, in their opinion, it is given the full number of points. If it does not meet the criteria to any significant degree, it receives no points. If the ownership form partially meets the criteria, it is allocated points accordingly. For example, with respect to avoidance of double taxation, three forms of ownership—tenancy in common, general partnership, and joint venture—are believed to meet this criterion competely and are therefore allocated the full ten points. In contrast, a corporation will be double taxed, and is therefore assigned 0 points. Both a limited partnership (9 points) and a REIT (8 points) are subject to reclassification as corporations and, hence, to double taxation. While this is not highly probable, these forms do not meet the criteria as well as the other forms do.

THE CHOICE OF A JOINT VENTURE VEHICLE

After evaluating each of the ownership alternatives in terms of their selection criteria, Davidson and Boomer find that the joint venture entity accumulates the most points, given their return/risk criteria and their subjective evaluation of each ownership entity. Keep in mind that the joint venture is a type of general partnership formed for the purpose of owning a single property—Aspen Wood Apartments. This explains why the general partnership form of ownership ranks second in the model, since it received an identical number of points in most categories.

Davidson and Boomer know their targeted investor market well and have consulted with their tax attorney in evaluating the alternatives and assigning weights. As with most models, the results are only as good as the input assumptions (garbage in, garbage out!). D&B has had excellent experiences with the joint venture form of ownership as a syndication vehicle in the past. The firm has experienced relatively few problems with this entity form, and by insisting on nonrecourse mortgages and full-coverage liability insurance it has achieved a high degree of limited liability for the investors. Thus, the joint venture has a very favorable image among their investors and is readily accepted; in contrast, some of the investors have experienced poor results with limited partnership investments formed by other syndicators in past years, and some of them would prefer not to invest in such a vehicle again. When economic adversity struck in the mid-1970s, many limited partnerships quickly depleted their cash reserves and were unable to raise additional capital through the partners, who were not required to contribute moneys beyond their original capital contribution. Consequently, many good properties suffering from short-run difficulties were foreclosed or deeded back to lenders in lieu of foreclosure.

In contrast, joint venturers under D&B's direction were usually able to jointly decide on the merits of the property. If the joint venturers decided to save the property from foreclosure, they approved the necessary "cash calls" to support operations until the real estate market improved.[27] In these

---

[27] The same procedure can be achieved by a limited partnership in which the general and limited partners agree to such cash calls. Thus, the partnership agreement can be amended in a distress situation in order to solve such a financial problem.

instances the joint venture form has proven to be more flexible than a limited partnership and has allowed the investors to play a significant role in the investment decision process. These advantages have proved to be a good marketing tool in the selling of the joint venture shares. Most of D&B's investors are local and enjoy the opportunity to periodically evaluate their property's performance and make suggestions to the management.

10

The Basic Financial Feasibility Model

In Chapter 9, as step 1 of the investment analysis and financial structuring process, we developed a methodology for determining the form of ownership that would best fit the return and risk objectives of the investor. We are now ready to proceed to steps 2 and 3 in that process, which involve the following activities:

- *Step 2: Generate alternatives.* Locate properties that meet the basic screening criteria, and collect preliminary data for analysis.
- *Step 3: Analyze the property using the basic financial feasibility model.* The model is used to test and structure the basic economics of the project, the financing alternatives available, and the investment value range for the property.

Our primary focus will be on analyzing and structuring the basic economics of a project using a one-year cash flow pro forma model. While such a model has numerous shortcomings, most investors prefer to use a simple model before spending valuable time researching a property in depth. An investor needs to understand the basic return and risk parameters of the property and know *about how much it is worth* before entering into negotiations with a seller or mortgage lender. After preliminary negotiations have been completed, the investor will proceed to more sophisticated forms of analysis.

IMPORTANT CONCEPTS, PRINCIPLES, AND TECHNIQUES

In working through the investment analysis process, we must be proficient in the basic mathematics involved in that process.[1] We must know how to prepare an accurate cash flow statement, the basis of all investment; we must know how to work with a mortgage constant table and debt coverage ratios; we must know how to compute rates of return on investment; and finally, we must master the concepts of positive leverage, negative leverage, and risk.

The Cash Flow Statement

Consider an existing sixteen-unit apartment complex that is for sale. Each unit is a 400-square-foot efficiency with central heat and air conditioning paid for by the tenant. The complex is twelve years old and the asking price is $180,000. The investors are seeking to refinance the property with a $144,000 loan (80% of the purchase price) from a local savings and loan association at 9 1/4 percent interest for 28 years, resulting in a mortgage constant (K) of 10 percent. The required amount of equity is $36,000 ($180,000 − $144,000). On the basis of the past performance of the project, the cash flow is estimated as shown in Exhibit 10–1.

   Note that the cash flow statement does not consider tax shelter factors, equity buildup through loan amortization, or property appreciation. These items would be added in a more sophisticated analysis, as we will see later. Note also that the cash flow statement is a one-year statement in which we estimate the *most likely* outcome. In a more sophisticated analysis we would attempt to measure cash flows for *each year* over the expected holding period of the investment. Also, we may want to vary our assumptions to simulate a *pessimistic* and an *optimistic* set of outcomes, as we will see later when the subject of risk analysis is discussed.

   Despite all its shortcomings, the one-year cash flow pro forma is widely used

---

EXHIBIT 10–1.   Cash Flow Pro Forma for Sixteen-Unit Apartment Building

Gross rental income (16 units × $175/mo. × 12 mo.)	$33,600
Plus: vending income (16 units × $1.50/mo. × 12 mo.)	288
Gross possible income (GPI)	33,888
Less: vacancy and credit loss (7% of GPI)	(2,372)
Gross effective income (GEI)	31,516
Less: operating expenses (45% of GPI)	(15,250)
Net operating income (NOI)	16,266
Less: debt service (10% × $144,000)	14,400
Cash flow	$ 1,866

---

[1] This discussion was largely developed in an earlier application by Stephen A. Pyhrr entitled "Mathematics of Real Estate Finance," in James A. Britton, Jr., and Lewis O. Kerwood, eds., *Financing Income-Producing Real Estate—A Theory and Casebook* (New York: McGraw-Hill, 1977), pp. 312–324.

for investment analysis by equity investors, lenders, brokers, and developers throughout the nation.

Working with Mortgage Constants and Debt Coverage Ratios: Understanding the Lender's Viewpoint

The mortgage constant (K) is defined as the amount of annual debt service that is necessary to pay interest at some stated rate and the entire principal over the amortization period. It is stated as a percent. The mortgage constant is used to compute the annual debt service (principal plus interest) on a loan, as shown by the following formula:

Annual debt service = loan amount × mortgage constant

In the example given earlier the loan amount was $144,000 and the mortgage constant was 10 percent, resulting in debt service of $14,400. We found K by referring to the mortgage constant chart (Exhibit 10–2). Going down the left side of the chart to 9 1/4 percent, and across to 28 years, resulted in a K of 10.01 percent, or roughly 10 percent.

Now suppose the interest rate rises to 11 percent and the lender will allow only a 25-year term. What happens? The mortgage constant increases to 11.77 percent. Debt service increases from $14,400 to $16,949:

Annual debt service = loan amount × mortgage constant
$16,949 = $144,000 × .1177

As a result, the cash flow decreases by $2,549 and the value of the property will decrease by a multiple factor, as we will see later.

EXHIBIT 10–2.   Mortgage Constant (Constant Annual Percent), Monthly Payments

Interest Rate	21 yr	22 yr	23 yr	24 yr	25 yr	26 yr	27 yr	28 yr	29 yr	30 yr		35 yr
9.00	10.62	10.46	10.32	10.19	10.08	9.97	9.88	9.80	9.73	9.66	. . .	9.41
9.25	10.82	10.66	10.52	10.39	10.28	10.18	10.09	10.01	9.94	9.88		9.64
9.50	11.01	10.86	10.72	10.60	10.49	10.39	10.31	10.23	10.16	10.10		9.86
9.75	11.21	11.06	10.93	10.81	10.70	10.60	10.52	10.44	10.38	10.31		10.09
10.00	11.41	11.26	11.13	11.01	10.91	10.82	10.78	10.66	10.59	10.54		10.32
10.25	11.62	11.47	11.34	11.22	11.12	11.03	10.95	10.88	10.82	10.76		10.55
10.50	11.82	11.68	11.55	11.43	11.34	11.25	11.17	11.10	11.04	10.98		10.78
10.75	12.03	11.88	11.76	11.65	11.55	11.46	11.39	11.32	11.26	11.21		11.02
11.00	12.23	12.09	11.97	11.86	11.77	11.68	11.61	11.54	11.48	11.43		11.25
11.25	12.44	12.30	12.18	12.08	11.98	11.90	11.83	11.77	11.71	11.66		11.48
11.50	12.65	12.51	12.40	12.29	12.20	12.12	12.05	11.99	11.94	11.89		11.72
11.75	12.86	12.73	12.61	12.51	12.42	12.35	12.28	12.22	12.16	12.12		11.95
12.00	13.07	12.94	12.83	12.73	12.64	12.57	12.50	12.44	12.39	12.35		12.19
12.25	13.28	13.16	13.05	12.95	12.87	12.79	12.73	12.67	12.62	12.58		12.43
12.50	13.50	13.37	13.26	13.17	13.09	13.02	12.96	12.90	12.85	12.81		12.67
12.75	13.71	13.59	13.48	13.39	13.31	13.24	13.18	13.13	13.09	13.05		12.91
13.00	13.93	13.81	13.71	13.62	13.54	13.47	13.41	13.36	13.32	13.28		13.15
13.25	14.14	14.03	13.93	13.84	13.77	13.70	13.64	13.59	13.55	13.51		13.39
13.50	14.36	14.25	14.15	14.07	13.99	13.93	13.87	13.83	13.79	13.75		13.63
13.75	14.58	14.47	14.37	14.29	14.22	14.16	14.11	14.06	14.02	13.99		13.87

SOURCE: David Thorndike, *Thorndike Encyclopedia of Banking and Financial Tables,* Rev. ed. (Boston: Warren, Gorham & Lamont, 1980), p. 1-3.

In summary, the mortgage constant, which is determined by the mortgage term and interest rate granted by a lender, is used to compute the debt service on a loan and thus affects the cash flow generated by the project. For each dollar increase in debt service, cash flow decreases by one dollar and the value of the project declines. An equity investor attempting to maximize cash flow—and, hence, the investment value of the property—would logically bargain with a lender for the longest term and lowest interest rate possible, thus keeping K to a minimum.

Two other useful formulas are the following (both are derived from the debt service formula):

$$\text{Loan amount} = \frac{\text{annual debt service}}{\text{mortgage constant}} \tag{1}$$

$$\text{Mortgage constant} = \frac{\text{annual debt service}}{\text{loan amount}} \tag{2}$$

The first formula is used to determine the amount of the loan that a lender can grant, if the amount of debt service that the project can support is known. The second is used to compute the mortgage constant on an outstanding loan when the debt service and the loan amount are known.

Note that the mortgage constant will increase each year as a loan is amortized, since the denominator of the mortgage constant formula (loan amount) is decreasing as loan amortization occurs. In other words, while the interest rate and the amount of the debt service remain constant, the amount of the loan decreases because a portion of each debt service payment represents principal paid on the loan. From the equity investor's viewpoint, a rising K means an increase in the effective cost of borrowed money each year; it explains why investors periodically seek to refinance their properties, thereby raising the loan amount and term to more desirable levels.

Impact of New Mortgage Instruments   Be aware also that the mortgage constant can change periodically if a *variable rate* or *renegotiated rate* mortgage is used to finance the property. In either case, both the interest rate and term can be adjusted depending on market interest rate conditions and the particular provisions of the mortgage instrument used. If such changes do occur periodically, the debt service and cash flow will change accordingly. For our purposes here, we will ignore these complexities; they will be addressed at length in Chapter 14.

The Debt Coverage Ratio   Most large institutional lenders now favor the debt coverage ratio (DCR) as the primary financial underwriting criterion for granting loans:

$$\text{Debt coverage ratio} = \frac{\text{net operating income}}{\text{debt service}}$$

Many institutional lenders have developed minimum acceptable coverage ratios for different types of property. For example, a lender may require a minimum coverage ratio of 1.3 for an apartment project and a coverage ratio of 1.5 for a motel (which is usually considered more risky). As the perceived risks associated with the property increase, the lender demands compensation in the form of a higher coverage ratio, and perhaps a higher interest rate and mortgage constant. Thus, the lender wants a cushion or buffer in case net income in any year should drop owing to a rise in vacancies, expenses, and so forth, and this cushion should increase as the risk increases.

To illustrate, take our example of a sixteen-unit apartment complex for which the expected net operating income (NOI) was $16,266 and the equity investor was seeking a loan of $144,000 at 9 1/4 percent for 28 years. The lender does not make loans that result in a coverage ratio less than 1.3. Can the loan be granted? Obviously not, because the resulting coverage ratio is less than 1.3 and such a loan would be too risky:

$$\text{Coverage ratio} = \frac{\text{net operating income}}{\text{debt service}} = \frac{\$16,266}{\$14,400} = 1.13$$

In order to raise the coverage ratio, and thus make the loan acceptable, a combination of three things can be done:

1. The mortgage constant and debt service can be reduced by increasing the amortization term of the loan.
2. The mortgage constant and debt service can be reduced by lowering the interest rate (which is generally the least desirable alternative for the lender).
3. The amount of the loan can be reduced, thereby decreasing the debt service.

A fourth possibility for raising the coverage ratio would be to raise the estimated net operating income by finding some realistic method for raising rental income, or reducing vacancies or expenses. For example, utilization of a professional property management company with a proven track record might convince a lender that *better-than-market* operating results are consistently possible and that such inputs should be reflected in the net operating income estimate.

The Maximum Loan Formula   Once the loan terms have been established, the following formula can be used to determine the maximum loan that a lender can grant while maintaining the desired coverage ratio:

$$\text{Maximum loan} = \frac{\left[\dfrac{\text{net operating income}}{\text{desired coverage ratio}}\right]}{\text{mortgage constant}} = \frac{\text{maximum debt service}}{\text{mortgage constant}}$$

$$= \frac{\left[\dfrac{\$16,266}{1.3}\right]}{.10} = \frac{\$12,512.31}{.10}$$

$$= \$125,123$$

In our example, the project can support a loan no greater than $125,123 if the desired coverage ratio is 1.3. The loan request was for $144,000.

The numerator of the formula ($16,266/1.3) indicates what the maximum amount of debt service can be in order to achieve a coverage ratio of 1.3. The maximum amount of debt service is simply the net operating income divided by the desired coverage ratio, and is derived from this formula: Coverage ratio = net operating income/debt service. The loan amount is then computed by our previous formula: Loan amount = annual debt service/mortgage constant. In summary, the maximum loan formula is derived by combining and manipulating the coverage ratio and loan amount formulas.

Consider the effects of a reduced mortgage constant on the maximum loan. Assume that K falls from 10 percent to 9.3 percent. (What loan terms will produce this result?) The result is that the lender can make a loan of approximately $134,541:

$$\text{Maximum loan} = \frac{\left[\frac{\$16,266}{1.3}\right]}{.093} = \$134,541$$

If the lender will reduce the desired coverage ratio to 1.25, the loan can be increased to approximately $139,923, which is near the amount requested:

$$\text{Maximum loan} = \frac{\left[\frac{\$16,266}{1.25}\right]}{.093} = \$139,923$$

On the other hand, if interest rates increase to the levels seen in recent years and the mortgage term stays the same, the loan amount decreases significantly and equity investors are forced to invest more cash to purchase the property. For example, if the interest rate rises to 12 percent and the term of the loan is 25 years, the mortgage constant (K) rises to 12.57 percent and the maximum loan falls to $103,523. The equity required to purchase the property rises from $36,000 (80 percent loan) to $76,477, which is an increase of 112 percent from the original loan request.

$$\text{Maximum loan} = \frac{\left[\frac{\$16,266}{1.25}\right]}{.1257} = \$103,523$$

$$
\begin{aligned}
\text{Equity investment required} &= \text{purchase price} - \text{loan amount} \\
&= \$180,000 - \$103,523 \\
&= \$\ 76,477
\end{aligned}
$$

Rising interest rates thus result in more conservative leverage ratios unless (1) a longer amortization term is negotiated, (2) a lower coverage ratio is accepted, (3) some form of secondary mortgage financing is used, or (4) sellers are willing to reduce the price of their property. In most market situations a combination of all four tends to occur as interest rates rise. For example, in 1980 and 1981 numerous lenders increased their loan amortization terms from 25– 30 years to 35– 40 years to partially offset the effects of rising interest rates. In some foreign countries amortization terms of 50– 75 years are acceptable. An increase in the mortgage term from 25 to 35 years in the case described earlier will decrease the K from 12.57 percent to 12.19 percent; the maximum mortgage loan that can be justified increases from $103,523 to $106,750.

In summary, we can use the maximum loan formula to compute how much of a loan a lender should be willing to grant if we know the desired coverage ratio, the mortgage constant the lender will accept (this is to some degree negotiable), and the net operating income figure the lender will accept.

Risk and the Debt Coverage Ratio   Although other financial ratios may also be used (e.g., break-even ratios, loan per square foot, etc.), the debt coverage ratio tends to be the primary financial criterion used by most institutional lenders and, therefore, is the key to creating acceptable financial packages.

Risk is explicitly considered by the lender in establishing the minimum acceptable coverage ratio and mortgage constant. If a lender feels that a project is relatively risky but still wishes to make the loan, the lender can compensate by raising the desired coverage ratio and mortgage constant. As a result, the amount of the loan offered will decrease. Conversely, anything the equity investor can do to convince the lender that the risks have been decreased should result in more favorable loan terms. For example, lease insurance or longer term leases, evidence of a successful track record, strong anchor tenants with substantial preleasing, and a good feasibility study and mortgage submission package are factors that will decrease the perceived risks for the lender and increase the maximum loan amount for the equity investor.

The Break-even Ratio (Default Point)   Another ratio that many lenders look at when evaluating a loan proposal is the break-even ratio:

$$\text{Break-even ratio} = \frac{\text{operating expenses} + \text{debt service}}{\text{gross possible income}}$$

In our original example, in which a loan of $144,000 was requested, the break-even ratio is

$$\frac{\$15,250 + \$14,400}{\$33,888} = 87.5\%$$

In the restructured case, which resulted in a mortgage loan of $125,123, the break-even ratio falls as a result of reduced debt service:

$$\frac{\$15,250 + \$12,512}{\$33,888} = 81.9\%$$

A break-even ratio of 82 percent means that a project can have a vacancy rate of up to 18 percent before net operating income will not cover debt service payments. Thus, there is an 18 percent cushion for the lender before the possibility of default arises. Alternatively, the project must be 82 percent occupied in order to *break even*. After the break-even point has been reached, a positive cash flow will occur.

As with the coverage ratio, the break-even point can be used as an underwriting ratio by the lender. For example, many lenders will not make a loan on a general use income property for which the resulting break-even ratio is greater than 82–84 percent. The higher the break-even ratio, the higher the risk, and vice versa. Risk can be reduced by structuring a loan that reduces the break-even point.

The Equity Investor's Strategy An equity investor must be aware of the "golden rule" (those who have the gold make the rules) and seek to understand the lender's viewpoint when developing a mortgage finance structure. Although the equity investor usually negotiates for the highest loan amount, the lowest interest rate, and the longest amortization term possible, the minimum objectives of the lender must simultaneously be achieved or exceeded. A mortgage loan proposal that does not explicitly meet the lender's interest rate, amortization term, coverage ratio, and break-even criteria has a low probability of succeeding.

The equity investor, like the lender, can use the coverage ratio and break-even point as measures of risk. High coverage ratios and low break-even ratios indicate a low degree of risk (i.e., a lower probability of default on debt service obligations), while low coverage ratios and high break-even ratios indicate a high degree of risk. If the equity investor wishes to control the degree of risk as evidenced by these ratios, he or she can structure the project price and loan terms to achieve the desired coverage and break-even ratios. Later we will see how this can be achieved using the basic financial feasibility model.

Computing Rates of Return on an Investment

Two important rate-of-return measures are critical for evaluating the debt and equity structure of a project. The first is the rate of return on total capital (ROR), sometimes referred to as the *free and clear return* or the *overall rate*:

$$\text{Rate of return on total capital (ROR)} = \frac{\text{net operating income}}{\text{total capital investment}}$$

This rate-of-return measure focuses on the productivity of the total capital invested, including both debt and equity capital. As presented here, it is used in conjunction with a one-year cash flow pro forma and should not be confused with the internal rate of return (IRR), which considers the cash flow for the entire ownership period.

The second important rate-of-return measure is the rate of return on the investor's initial equity investment (ROE), sometimes referred to as the *cash-on-cash return* or the *equity dividend rate*:

$$\text{Rate of return on equity (ROE)} = \frac{\text{cash flow}}{\text{equity investment}}$$

The ROE is probably the measure that investors use most frequently to evaluate proposed income property investments during the early stages of the investment process.

Using our original example, in which net income is $16,266, cash flow is $1,866, the total capital investment (asking price) is $180,000, and the equity investment is $36,000, ROR and ROE can be computed as follows:

$$\text{ROR} = \frac{\$16,266}{\$180,000} = 9.04\%$$

$$\text{ROE} = \frac{\$1,866}{\$36,000} = 5.18\%$$

This situation is generally undesirable for the equity investor unless net operating income can be raised over time (by increasing rents or decreasing expenses) and the ROE can be supplemented through property value appreciation and tax shelter. We noted previously that this situation is also unfavorable for the lender because the resulting coverage ratio is only 1.13. The basic problem here is negative leverage.

Positive and Negative Leverage

Leverage exists whenever debt is present in the capital structure.[2] Simply stated, leverage means use of debt financing. The greater the use of debt financing relative to equity financing, the greater the leverage.

The situation described here is unfavorable because the ROE is only 5.18 percent while total assets are earning at a rate (ROR) of 9.04 percent. The problem is that $K = 10$ percent. The equity investor can earn only 9.04 percent on the assets, but must pay 10 percent to the lender. Only 5.18 percent is left for the equity investor. In this case leverage works against the investor; we have negative (or reverse) leverage.

Negative leverage exists whenever the ROR is less than K (ROR $< K$). In contrast, whenever ROR is greater than K (ROR $> K$), leverage works for the equity investor; then we have *positive* leverage.[3] In other words, the rate of productivity for the total amount of money invested in a project must be greater

---

[2] This definition refers to *financial* leverage, rather than *operating* leverage, as it is described in the business finance literature. See, e.g., Eugene F. Brigham, *Fundamentals of Financial Management* (Hinsdale, Ill.: Dryden Press, 1978), pp. 373–383.

[3] A number of authors have criticized this definition and approach to positive and negative leverage. One author has argued that this approach must be rejected on both theoretical and practical grounds because it does not consider "the interrelationship among the interest rate, the loan/value ratio, expected reversion value and the tax considerations involved, which determines the favorability of a given leverage situation. A complete discounted cash flow analysis is necessary to properly evaluate the effects of those relationships on return to equity"—Kenneth M. Lusht, "A Note on the Favorability of Leverage," *The Real Estate Appraiser*, May–June 1977, pp. 41–44. It should be recalled, how-

than the cost of debt financing in order to create a favorable leverage position for the equity investor. An equity investor should beware of any financing situation that is expected to create a situation of negative leverage for an extended period. In Chapter 11 we will see how positive or negative leverage can be measured using an internal-rate-of-return model that considers all sources of after-tax cash flow over the expected ownership period. Keep in mind that the model presented here is a one-year, before-tax, cash flow model that seeks to test the short-run economics of a property.

In summary, comparing K with ROR tells us whether we have positive or negative leverage. Remember, whatever net operating income is earned by the project goes to the lenders or to the equity investors. If too much is given to the lenders (ROR $< K$), there will be little left for the equity investors (ROE $< K$). As we saw in our example,

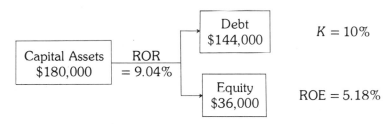

Another method of defining positive and negative leverage is by directly comparing the equity investor's return (ROE) to the lender's return (K). Whenever the equity investor is earning less than the lender (ROE $< K$), negative leverage is present; whenever the situation is reversed (ROE $> K$), positive leverage is present. The relationships can be expressed as follows:

1. *Conditions for positive leverage:*
    Whenever   ROR $> K$
    Then   ROE $> K$
    And   ROE $>$ ROR
2. *Conditions for negative leverage:*
    Whenever   ROR $< K$
    Then   ROE $< K$
    And   ROE $<$ ROR

Another possibility is that of break-even leverage. Break-even leverage occurs when ROR is equal to K (then ROE $= K$ and ROE $=$ ROR).

---

ever, that most investors are concerned with short-run as well as long-run risk and return objectives; short-run solvency is necessary to achieve long-run profitability. Consequently, an investor can logically utilize short-run cash flow models as well as longer-run ownership period (DCF) models to determine investment feasibility. Each has its proper place in the investment analysis process. As discussed in Chapters 11 and 13, the final measure of leverage favorability should be determined by comparing after-tax yields for the leveraged and unleveraged capital structure. See also Robert H. Zerbst, Charles E. Edwards, and Phillip L. Cooley, "Evaluation of Financial Leverage for Real Estate Investments," *The Real Estate Appraiser,* July–August 1977.

The situation we have illustrated (an ROE of 5.18% and a K of 10%) would not be acceptable to most knowledgeable investors except over a relatively short-run period when inflation is expected to bail out the project over the long run by increasing rents and property values.[4] Basic economics are working against the investor and have resulted in a relatively high-risk (coverage ratio = 1.13) and low-return (ROE = 5.18%) venture. What we need to do is to raise ROR and/or lower K in order to achieve positive leverage. The desired result can be achieved using the basic financial feasibility model.

THE BASIC FINANCIAL FEASIBILITY MODEL

The basic financial feasibility model incorporates all the concepts discussed up to this point and allows us to program in an acceptable ROE level, a leverage advantage for the equity investor, and a coverage ratio that will satisfy both the lender and the equity investor. The investor's return/risk criteria are the inputs: The output is a financial structure that will satisfy both the equity investor and the lender. The feasibility model presented in Exhibit 10–3 allows us to manipulate the numbers in order to structure the economics of a project and simultaneously achieve the financial objectives of both the equity investor and the lender.

The final outputs of the model are estimates of (1) the maximum loan amount, (2) the maximum equity investment, and (3) the maximum project value or purchase price. The inputs are (1) estimates of rents, vacancies, and expenses; (2) the debt coverage ratio and mortgage constant desired by the lender and/or equity investor; and (3) the desired rate of return on equity.

To understand the use of the basic financial feasibility model, consider again the sixteen-unit apartment building, along with the following information:

- The total leasable area in the buildings is approximately 6,400 square feet. The gross possible income per net leasable square foot is 44.13¢ per month, or approximately $5.30 annually (actually $5.295).
- Vacancy and operating expenses are 52 percent of gross possible income (45% operating expense ratio and 7% vacancy ratio, as shown in Exhibit 10–1).
- The required debt coverage ratio is 1.3 and the mortgage constant (K) is 10 percent (9 1/4% for approximately 28 years). The investors are seeking a loan of $144,000.
- The equity investors require a 12 percent ROE. In the proposed sale of the property, a $26,000 equity price is asked.

The feasibility model (Exhibit 10–3) indicates that the project is worth approximately $156,400, not $180,000. If a coverage ratio of 1.3 is to be maintained, annual debt service cannot exceed $12,512, and a loan greater than $125,120 is not acceptable. With regard to the equity value, the investor cannot

---

[4] The current investment climate is precisely the one described. Investors are accepting low or even negative ROEs on a current operating basis; they believe that continued inflation at high rates will result over the longer run in higher rents and property values. In common parlance, they are "betting on the come."

EXHIBIT 10-3. The Basic Financial Feasibility Model

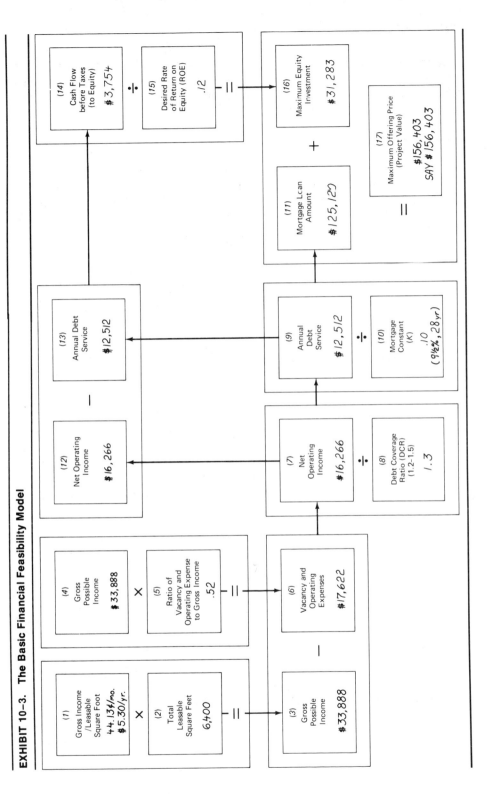

(1) Gross Income / Leasable Square Foot
$.44.13¢/mo.
$5.30/yr.

×

(2) Total Leasable Square Feet
6,400

=

(3) Gross Possible Income
$33,888

(4) Gross Possible Income
$33,888

×

(5) Ratio of Vacancy and Operating Expense to Gross Income
.52

=

(6) Vacancy and Operating Expenses
$17,622

−

(3) ...

(12) Net Operating Income
$16,266

−

(13) Annual Debt Service
$12,512

(7) Net Operating Income
$16,266

÷

(8) Debt Coverage Ratio (DCR) (1.2-1.5)
1.3

(9) Annual Debt Service
$12,512

÷

(10) Mortgage Constant (K)
.10
(9½%, 28 yr.)

(14) Cash Flow before Taxes (to Equity)
$3,754

÷

(15) Desired Rate of Return on Equity (ROE)
.12

=

(16) Maximum Equity Investment
$31,283

+

(11) Mortgage Loan Amount
$125,129

=

(17) Maximum Offering Price (Project Value)
$156,403
SAY $156,403

257

pay more than $31,283 if the goal is to achieve a 12 percent return and thus maintain a positive leverage position. Using this model, the investor dictates the ROE necessary to make the investment and then capitalizes the cash flow to determine the equity value.

Illustration of the Model[5]

Box 1: Gross Income per Leasable Square Foot   This figure should be based on the history of comparable projects if the subject property is new. If the subject property is already in existence, its rental history will provide the number, *but rents on existing projects should be adjusted to reflect current market conditions.* Other income in addition to rents (e.g., vending income, income from laundry, etc.) should be included. In the example it is assumed that gross income per leasable square foot is $5.30.

Box 2: Total Leasable Square Feet   This includes only the *leasable* square footage. It does not include, for example, the laundry room, foyers, lobbies, the manager's office space, and so forth. The example assumes 6,400 leasable square feet.

Boxes 3 and 4: Gross Possible Income (GPI)   This is the product of box 1 times box 2: $5.30 × 6,400 = $33,888.

Box 5: Ratio of Vacancy and Operating Expense to Gross Income   As with income, expenses as a percentage of gross income can, for new properties, be estimated on the basis of the history of comparable properties. For existing projects, expenses can be based on historical data *as long as the figures are adjusted for anticipated changes.* Note that both a vacancy and bad-debt allowance (usually 5–10%) *and* operating expenses (usually 35–55%) are included. Here the sum of vacancy and bad-debt allowances and operating expenses, as a percentage of GPI, is 52 percent.

Box 6: Vacancy and Operating Expenses   This is the product of box 4 times box 5: $33,888 × .52 = $17,622.

Box 7: Net Operating Income (NOI)   This is the remainder of box 3 less box 6: $33,888 − $17,622 = $16,266.

Box 8: Debt Coverage Ratio (DCR)   In most situations the lender will indicate a minimum debt coverage ratio. In our example the DCR is assumed to be 1.3. As indicated earlier, the DCR may also be calculated as DCR = NOI/DS.

Box 9: Annual Debt Service (DS)   This is the product of box 11 times box 10: $125,120 × .10 = $12,512.

If the NOI (box 7) and DCR (box 8) are known, the maximum available debt service can be computed as follows:

Maximum DS = NOI/DCR

[5] Prepared with the assistance of Russell Welch, J.D., Murray State University, Murray, Kentucky.

In our example the NOI = $16,266 and the DCR = 1.3; therefore, DS = $16,266/1.3 = $12,512.

Box 10: Mortgage Constant (K) Given the terms of the loan (assumed as 9 1/4%, 28 years), K can be obtained from a table of mortgage constants. In our example $K = 10$ percent.

Box 11: Mortgage Loan Amount The maximum may be predetermined by the lender (e.g., as a percentage of appraised value) or calculated if the maximum debt service and mortgage constant are known. In our example the maximum loan amount is calculated as follows:

$$\text{Loan amount} = DS/K = \frac{\$12,512}{.10} = \$125,120$$

Box 12: Net Operating Income (NOI) From box 7

$$NOI = GPI - \text{vacancy and bad debt allowance} - \text{operating expenses}$$
$$= \$16,266$$

as before.

Box 13: Annual Debt Service (DS) From box 9: $12,512.

Box 14: Cash Flow Before Taxes (CF) This is calculated as

$$CF = NOI - DS$$

or, if the maximum equity investment and desired ROE are known, as

$$CF = \text{equity} \times ROE$$

Here, CF = $16,266 − $12,512 = $3,754.

Box 15: Desired Rate of Return on Equity (ROE) The desired ROE may be predetermined by the investor on the basis of the return available from alternative investments. The actual ROE is calculated as

$$ROE = CF/\text{equity investment}$$

Assume that an ROE of 12 percent is required.

Box 16: Maximum Equity Investment The investor may be willing or able to invest only a given amount. If the price of the project is fixed and the maximum loan amount is known, the equity investment equals price less loan amount. Here, however, it is calculated as

$$\text{Maximum equity} = CF/ROE = \$3,754/.12 = \$31,283$$

Box 17: Maximum Offering Price   This is the sum of box 11 plus box 16: $125,120 + $31,283 = $156,403.

The significance of box 17 is that it illustrates that mutual equilibrium can be achieved. The lender has specified loan terms and a satisfactory debt coverage ratio and hence, presumably, is satisfied. The investor has determined that the desired rate of return on the equity investment (ROE) should be achievable and has calculated the maximum offering price for the property. Obviously, if the asking price is less than the maximum offering price, the property is more attractive. The equity investor should not offer *more* than the asking price.

The preceding example has assumed that the equity investor wishes to work forward through the model to determine the investment value of the project by capitalizing the cash flow. The model can actually be used in a combination of ways. For example, if the price is known, the investor can work backwards to determine intermediate values, such as coverage ratios and mortgage constants, or even beginning values, such as rents and expenses required to satisfy investor objectives. Thus, if the investor knows the basic formulas used in the model, the dependent variable can be changed and desired output data and values can be calculated. The various formulas used in the basic financial feasibility model are presented in Exhibit 10–4.

Restructuring the Financial Package

The financial model indicates that the apartment project is worth approximately $156,400, not the $180,000 asking price. If a coverage ratio of 1.3 is to be maintained, annual debt service cannot exceed $12,512 and a loan greater than $125,120 is not acceptable. Furthermore, we saw that the equity investor cannot pay more than $31,283 for the equity if the goal is to achieve an ROE of 12 percent and maintain a positive leverage position.

The value of a project to both the equity investor and the lender is highly sensitive to the terms of the financial package, including the desired debt coverage ratio, and the required K and ROE. The model allows us to manipulate the numbers easily and to restructure the financial package in order to achieve a more desirable solution. Also, sensitivity analysis can be performed quickly to test the impact of changes in input variables on the investment value or other desired investment parameters.

Let us assume that the financial package and solution shown in Exhibit 10–3 are not acceptable to the seller. The seller demands a minimum selling price of $175,000, and the current interest rate on new loans has risen to 14 percent. Is there a solution that is acceptable to the seller, the buyer, and the lender?

Clearly, with interest rates of 14 percent or more, conventional refinancing through an institutional lender is not feasible. However, in many cases, for existing properties seller financing can be provided in tandem with the assumption of existing notes. Assume that two mortgage notes exist on the sixteen efficiency units in our example. One of the notes is from an institutional lender and one is from a previous owner. The interest rates are 7 1/2 percent and 8 3/4 percent, respectively, but have relatively short maturities (12 and 18 years, respectively). The balances on the two notes total approximately $117,000.

EXHIBIT 10–4.   Formulas in the Basic Financial Feasibility Model

---

1. Gross possible income = gross income per net leasable square foot × total leasable square feet

2. Vacancy & operating expenses = gross possible income × ratio of vacancy & operating expenses to gross income

3. Net operating income = gross possible income − vacancy & operating expenses

4. Debt coverage ratio $= \dfrac{\text{net operating income}}{\text{annual debt service}}$

5. Annual debt service = 12 × (monthly interest + principal payment)

$$= \frac{\text{net operating income}}{\text{debt coverage ratio (DCR)}}$$

$$= \text{mortgage loan amount} \times \text{mortgage constant}$$

6. Mortgage constant $(K) = \dfrac{\text{annual debt service}}{\text{mortgage loan amount}}$

7. Mortgage loan amount $= \dfrac{\text{annual debt service}}{\text{mortgage constant } (K)} = \dfrac{\left[\dfrac{\text{net operating income}}{\text{debt coverage ratio}}\right]}{\text{mortgage constant}}$

8. Cash flow before tax = net operating income − annual debt service

9. Rate of return on equity (ROE) $= \dfrac{\text{cash flow}}{\text{equity investment}}$

10. Maximum equity investment $= \dfrac{\text{cash flow}}{\text{desired rate of return on equity (ROE)}}$

11. Rate of return on total capital (ROR) $= \dfrac{\text{net operating income}}{\text{total capital investment}}$

We can arrive at an acceptable solution if we can assume or "wrap around" the existing notes and take advantage of their low interest rates.[6] At the same time, we wish to negotiate a relatively long mortgage term on the wraparound note in order to reduce the debt service payments and thus increase cash flow and the value of the project to the equity investors. There is no due-on-sale clause in either

---

[6] A wraparound mortgage, in this instance, is a form of third-lien financing in which the face amount of the third (wraparound) loan is equal to the balance of the first and second loans plus the amount of new financing. Because the interest rate on the wraparound loan normally is greater than that on the first mortgage, upside (positive) leverage is achieved on the new lender's return. In our case the new lender *is* the seller.

of the two underlying mortgage notes that would prevent this transaction and result in the underlying notes being called (escalated) when the property is sold.

Assume that we negotiate the following solution: The seller takes a 10 percent, 30-year note for $145,000 on the property, and this note "wraps around" the two existing liens. A third-party trustee receives debt service payments on the $145,000 note, pays the debt service on the two underlying mortgage notes, and then pays the seller what is left over. In effect, the seller provides $28,000 of debt financing to the buyer ($145,000 − $117,000) and receives 10 percent on the entire $145,000 note while the underlying notes bear interest rates of 7 1/2 percent and 8 3/4 percent. The seller's effective yield on the $29,000 financing is significantly greater than 10 percent; in addition, the seller qualifies for installment sales treatment for tax purposes.[7]

Assume further that a preliminary market, marketability, and management analysis of the property reveals the following:

1. Apartment rents are low and have not kept pace with competitive properties in recent years. The investor believes that rents can be raised to an average of $.50 per square foot per month next year from a previous average of $.4413.

2. Past management practices have resulted in a vacancy ratio of 7 percent annually. The investor forecasts 5 percent in the future, thereby decreasing the vacancy and expense ratio from 52 percent to 50 percent.

3. The overall risk of the property is perceived to be lower than originally estimated owing to the excellent location and physical condition of the building. The investor is willing to lower the desired coverage ratio from 1.3 to 1.25 and the required return on equity from 12 percent to 11 percent to reflect this lower risk level.

Exhibit 10−5 shows the new solution, which produces a purchase price above the $175,000 minimum desired by the seller, satisfies the explicit financial objectives of the buyer-investor, and shifts the burden of some of the financing to the seller. The investor can compute the actual expected ROE by calculating the equity investment and dividing it into the expected cash flow. The equity investment is $30,000, or the purchase price of $175,000 less the seller's wraparound loan of $145,000. The expected ROE is 12.8 percent:

$$\text{ROE} = \frac{\text{cash flow}}{\text{equity investment}} = \frac{\$\ 3,840}{\$30,000} = 12.8\%$$

This example illustrates the pronounced effect of changes in the investor's perceptions of the market, in conjunction with changes in the financial package, on the investment value of a property. Further feasibility research will allow the

[7] For examples see Richard T. Garrigan, "Wrap-Around Mortgage Enhancing Lender and Investor Wealth," *Real Estate Issues*, Summer 1979, pp. 20−38; also, Donald J. Valachi, "Installment Sales of Mortgaged Real Estate and the Wraparound Mortgage," *The Appraisal Journal*, January 1980, pp. 9−14.

EXHIBIT 10–5. Basic Financial Feasibility Model, Revised

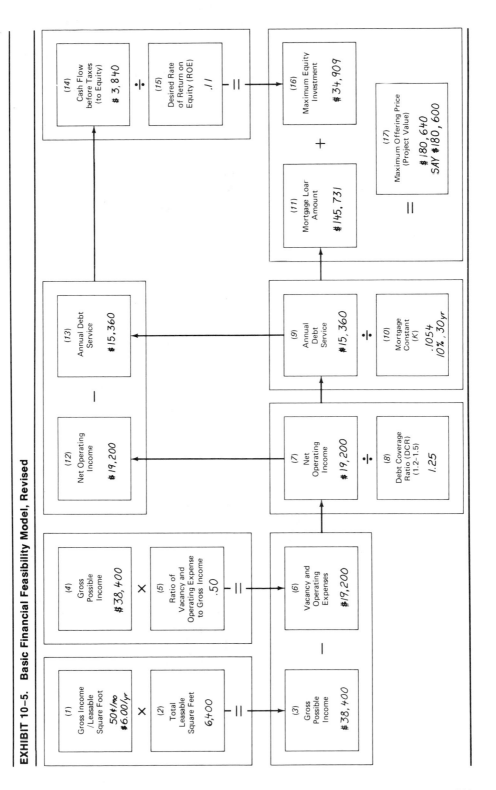

(1) Gross Income /Leasable Square Foot
50¢/mo
$6.00/yr

×

(2) Total Leasable Square Feet
6,400

=

(3) Gross Possible Income
$38,400

(4) Gross Possible Income
$38,400

×

(5) Ratio of Vacancy and Operating Expense to Gross Income
.50

=

(6) Vacancy and Operating Expenses
$19,200

(3) Gross Possible Income
$38,400

−

(6) Vacancy and Operating Expenses
$19,200

=

(7) Net Operating Income
$19,200

(7) Net Operating Income
$19,200

÷

(8) Debt Coverage Ratio (DCR) (1.2–1.5)
1.25

=

(9) Annual Debt Service
$15,360

(9) Annual Debt Service
$15,360

÷

(10) Mortgage Constant (K)
.1054
10%, 30-yr

=

(11) Mortgage Loan Amount
$145,731

(12) Net Operating Income
$19,200

−

(13) Annual Debt Service
$15,360

=

(14) Cash Flow before Taxes (to Equity)
$3,840

(14) Cash Flow before Taxes (to Equity)
$3,840

÷

(15) Desired Rate of Return on Equity (ROE)
.11

=

(16) Maximum Equity Investment
$34,909

(11) Mortgage Loan Amount
$145,731

+

(16) Maximum Equity Investment
$34,909

=

(17) Maximum Offering Price (Project Value)
$180,640
SAY $180,600

263

investor to refine further the input estimates and measure their possible effects on project value. It is not uncommon to use the basic financial feasibility model over and over again to analyze and restructure the project so as to achieve a solution that is acceptable to all the parties involved in the transaction.

Shortcomings of the Basic Model

Substantial criticism can be levied against the use of the basic financial feasibility model for project evaluation. It utilizes a single net operating income and cash flow figure that purports to represent the productivity of the property for each year in the future over the useful life of the property; thus, it can be called a capitalization-into-perpetuity model. Many investors and appraisers have contended that real estate works on this normalized or stabilized net income statement, and have successfully convinced most lenders, brokers, and syndicators to adopt these measures of return. However, a stabilized income measure ignores the complexities of real estate investments and thus ignores many important variables that affect investment value and loan quality. Specifically, the basic financial feasibility model does not explicitly consider eight variables:

1. Inflation of rents, expenses, and property value, which causes the income and cash flow to change each year.
2. Equity buildup over time through loan amortization.
3. The expected holding period of the investment.
4. The investor's income and capital gains tax position, and investor logic and motivation.
5. Start-up and transaction costs.
6. The uneven and erratic nature of NOI from year to year and, thus, the "riskiness" of the investment. As we will see later, the debt coverage ratio is a relatively static measure of risk.
7. The time value of money—the fact that a dollar promised in the future is worth less than a dollar today.
8. Innovations in mortgage market instruments, such as variable- and renegotiated-rate mortgages and other hybrid financing instruments that are products of our current inflationary environment.

These shortcomings can be overcome through the use of discounted cash flow models and the application of modern capital budgeting techniques, as discussed in Chapters 11–13. While the basic feasibility model can be used effectively during the early stages of project analysis, negotiation, and financial structuring, the more sophisticated capital budgeting techniques should be employed before the final investment decision is made.

APPLICATION OF THE BASIC FINANCIAL FEASIBILITY MODEL

The financial feasibility model can be used to structure the basic economics of a property to achieve an acceptable return/risk ratio for the investor. In the last section we used the model to achieve three sets of short-run objectives:

1. *Equity investor objectives*—by achieving the investor's required ROE and DCR criteria and positive leverage.
2. *Lender objectives*—by providing an acceptable mortgage loan amount, mortgage constant, interest rate, amortization term, and debt coverage ratio.
3. *Seller objectives*—by structuring an acceptable combination of sales price and terms that satisfy the seller's return/risk criteria.

Such a model, while it has numerous limitations, can be a tremendous aid to a managing equity investor by providing a framework for engaging in preliminary negotiations with the seller, discussing loan parameters with a potential lender, counseling passive equity investors or partners who do not understand more sophisticated financial techniques, and understanding basic return-and-risk trade-offs involved in a potential property purchase. The return/risk trade-off is the relationship between the return on equity (ROE) and the debt coverage ratio (DCR). Whenever the two are out of adjustment, the investor can revalue the property using more desirable ROE/DCR combinations.

In the following examples we will show some applications of the model to situations that frequently occur in the early stages of analysis. As we have argued previously, valuable time can be saved if the "dogs and alligators" are identified and discarded early in the investment process.

Analyzing Rent and Expense Variability

Consider a five-year-old retail center consisting of 14,000 square feet of leasable space located on a major throughfare. It is being offered for sale at $600,000. The facts are presented in Exhibit 10–6.

Using the data in the exhibit, and assuming a 5 percent vacancy and collec-

---

EXHIBIT 10–6.   Retail Strip Center: Facts

• *Facility:* 14,000-square-foot building, good location, high traffic count.

• *Asking Price:* $600,000. Owner says he has a commitment for a new mortgage at $450,000, 10 1/2 percent, 30-year amortization term, no personal liability ($K = 10.98\%$).

• *Tenants:* regional chain furniture store, national chain drug store, beautician, and dentists. Lease rates average $.60 per sq. ft./month, or $7.20 per sq. ft./year.

• *Occupancy:* present owner warrants that building is 100 percent leased on new five-year leases signed recently.

• *Operating Expenses:* owner warrants that all tenants pay their own utilities and that escalation clauses allow for passing through all increases in operating expenses to tenants. Thus, property can be operated on about $2.16 per sq. ft./year, or about a 30 percent expense ratio.

EXHIBIT 10-7.   Retail Strip Center: Solution

- Gross possible income = 14,000 × 7.20 = $100,800

- Vacancy and operating expenses = .35 × 100,800 = $35,280

- Net operating income = 100,800 − 35,280 = $65,520

- Maximum debt service = 65,520/1.25 = $52,416

- Maximum loan possible = 52,416/.1098 = $477,377

- Cash flow = 65,520 − 52,416 = $13,104

- Equity value = 13,104/.08 = $163,800

- Maximum offering price = 163,800 + 477,377 = $641,177

---

tion loss factor in the future, a minimum debt coverage ratio of 1.25, and an equity investor who is willing to purchase the center at an 8 percent ROE, the value of the center is approximately $641,000, as shown in Exhibit 10−7. The proposed $450,000 loan appears to be achievable and perhaps could even be increased to the $477,000 level calculated in the model.

The investor is willing to accept an 8 percent current ROE and negative leverage (ROE < K) because of the expected potential for raising rents in the future and because of the potential for increases in property value. A quick analysis of the effect of increasing rents and expenses, illustrated in Exhibit 10−8, demonstrates that a 25 percent rise in existing rents and expenses over the next five years will increase the equity value from $163,800 to $368,550 at the end of five years.

On the basis of this analysis and a thorough sensitivity analysis of the financial variables, the investor entered into a contract with the seller to purchase the property for $600,000, contingent on obtaining a loan of $450,000, bearing interest at 10 1/2 percent for 30 years, or better, and contingent on inspection of the seller's financial records and leases, and a physical inspection of the building. During the following two weeks of inspections, data collection and analysis, and other feasibility research, a number of important facts were discovered that substantially changed the data base used in the original analysis and cast doubt on the

---

EXHIBIT 10-8.   Retail Strip Center: Value Five Years Hence

- Gross possible income (100,800 + 25%) = $126,000

- Vacancy and operating expenses = 35,280 + 25% = $44,100

- Net operating income = 126,000 − 44,100 = $81,900

- Cash flow = 81,900 − 52,416 = $29,482

- Equity value = 29,482/.08 = $368,550

EXHIBIT 10-9.   Retail Strip Center: New Data

• *Utilities:* Actually paid for by the owner, not the tenants. The seller had apparently confused this property with another one.

• *Major lease:* The major furniture store lease (65% of total space leased) was actually a two-year lease with one-year options. Discussions with the owners of the store and friends of the owners revealed that they were negotiating to build their own store and would most likely leave the center within two years. They were unhappy with the access to the property and the parking facilities.

• *Lease escalation clause:* A thorough reading of each lease revealed only partial escalation clauses.

---

reliability of the seller's information and the value conclusions reached. This new information is shown in Exhibit 10–9.

On the basis of the new data the investor adjusted the inputs into the model and discovered that neither the proposed loan nor the purchase price was attainable. Vacancy was adjusted upward to 10 percent to account for the apparent certainty of losing the major tenant and the subsequent costs of re-leasing and remodeling the space. Estimated operating expenses were increased from $2.16 to $2.88 per square foot per year, or to 40 percent of gross possible income to account for rising utilities and other operating expenses that were not covered by the tenant escalation clauses. To compensate for the increased risks of the venture, the coverage ratio was increased to 1.30, the interest rate on the loan was increased to 10.75 percent and the term lowered to 25 years ($K = 11.55\%$), and the equity investor increased his ROE requirement to 11 percent. As a result of all these changes, the property value dropped nearly $200,000, from approximately $641,000 to almost $441,000, as shown in Exhibit 10–10.

Even extensive sensitivity testing, restructuring, and subsequent negotiations failed to provide a possible solution that would be acceptable to both the seller

---

EXHIBIT 10-10.   Retail Strip Center: Revised Solution

• Gross possible income (unchanged) = $100,800

• Vacancy and operating expenses (.50 × 100,800) = $50,400

• Net operating income = 100,800 − 50,400 = $50,400

• Maximum debt service = 50,400/1.25 = $38,769

• Maximum loan possible = 38,769/.1155 = $335,662

• Cash flow = 50,400 − 38,769 = $11,631

• Equity value = 11,631/.11 = $105,736

• Maximum offering price 105,736 + 335,662 = $441,398

---

and the investor. The investor was forced to drop the project and go on to the next-best alternative. Nevertheless, he had been able to identify an unacceptable project before spending substantial time gathering additional data and proceeding through a discounted cash flow analysis. There was simply no way of meeting the short run economic criteria.

Multiple Loans and Joint Ventures

The basic financial feasibility model and concepts can also be applied to sophisticated multiloan packages and joint venture situations. For example, consider a high-rise 40-story luxury apartment-hotel under construction in downtown Chicago, with 11 floors of office space pre-leased to AAA-rated corporate tenants. The apartment-hotel is a relatively unique special-use concept catering to business people and travelers who wish to combine hotel services with the typically larger size and cooking facilities of a residential apartment. A customer might stay one week or three months; the cost would be significantly less per night than luxury hotel accommodations, yet would not require the relatively inflexible lease contract required for a normal luxury apartment rental in downtown Chicago.

The joint venturers and lenders agreed on the following pro forma and financial structure for the property, as shown in Exhibit 10–11.

The total cost of the project was $10 million and included a development fee and general contractor's profit to the developer-investor. Thus, the $49,626 cash flow left after all obligations were paid was a pure investment profit. The net

---

EXHIBIT 10–11.   Financial Pro Forma for Luxury Apartment–Hotel Property

Rate of Return	Income/Cash Flow	Cost	Source of Financing
12.00% (ROR)	$1,200,000	$10,000,000	Total cost to be financed
10.83% (K)	682,290	6,300,000	First loan on building
13.99% (ROE)	517,710	3,700,000	Remaining equity
			REIT second loan
11.00% (K)	275,000	2,500,000	(for furnishings)
20.23% (ROE)	242,710	1,200,000	Remaining equity
			Third loan by joint venture
16.00% (K)	160,000	1,000,000	partner
41.30% (ROE)	82,710	200,000	Remaining equity
			Joint venture investment
16.54% (ROE)	33,084	200,000	(life insurance co.)
∞ (ROE)	$ 49,626	$ 0	Remaining equity

ROR = 12%
Weighted average DCR = 1.07
Weighted average K = 11.40%
ROE to joint venture partner = 16.54%
ROE to investor/developer = ∞

operating income was conservatively projected to be $1,200,000; all parties to the transaction felt that actual operations would exceed this projection. A first mortgage loan of $6,300,000 (conservative by most standards) was negotiated at a mortgage constant of 10.83 percent and required debt service of $682,290. After this loan had been deducted from the total project cost, $3,700,000 remained to be financed, and a cash flow of $517,710 remained after servicing the first loan. This resulted in a ROE of 13.99 percent ($517,710/$3,700,000). A second loan ($K = 11\%$) was arranged with a REIT to cover furnishings, and the joint venture partner, a national life insurance company, provided a third mortgage of $1 million with a K of 16 percent. The joint venture partner also invested the final cash equity of $200,000 and received 40 percent of the remaining cash flow, or $33,084 ($82,710 × 40%).

The project risk was high, as is evidenced by the low overall coverage ratio (1.07) and the nature of the proposed real estate activity, which remained untested in the Chicago marketplace. Nevertheless, there was positive leverage at all stages of financing, and the remaining ROE was always greater than the K of the next loan. The weighted-average K was 11.40 percent (all loans), and the project ROR was 12 percent, again showing positive leverage. The joint venture partner received a 16 percent guaranteed return on the third-mortgage loan and an expected ROE of 16.54 percent on the $200,000 equity investment. The developer-investor had no cash equity; thus, the ROE was not meaningful as a decision criterion.[8]

The *value* of the equity can be computed should the developer-investor decide to sell his interest, if he knows what ROE is required by potential equity investors for a project like this one. If the required ROE were 17 percent (slightly above the joint venture partner's ROE), the equity could probably be sold for approximately $292,000:

$$\text{Equity value} = \frac{\text{cash flow}}{\text{required ROE}} = \frac{\$49,626}{.17} = \$291,918$$

In sum, with the return/risk relationship apparently in balance, all parties agreed to the transaction as proposed. The developer-investor structured the project to receive a handsome development and contractor's profit, in addition to a holding-period investment return of over $49,000 annually. Actually, it was believed that the property would perform significantly better than the pro forma indicated, and the returns shown here would most likely improve as a track record was established.

Competition and Changing Property Usage

As the steel superstructure of the apartment-hotel project was being erected, the owners were approached by a major international hotel chain. The chain was

---

[8] Actually, as the equity investment approaches zero, the ROE approaches infinity. In mathematical terms, when the equity is zero the ROE is an "undefined" number.

seeking a site in the immediate area for a luxury hotel, but because of the strong competition for prime sites it was unable to locate one that met its criteria. After months of negotiations, the owners agreed to lease to the hotel chain the entire space that was not already committed to office usage. The chain would guarantee a net rate (with possible future escalations) that would raise the NOI from $1,200,000 to $1,590,000. The total cost of the project would remain approximately $10 million. The $2.5 million of furnishings would not be needed, but about $2.5 million of structural changes and facility upgrading were required to meet the hotel chain's luxury standards.

The immediate result was a significant reduction in risk for all the parties involved in the project. Consequently, the owners renegotiated the first- and second-mortgage loan constants (Ks) to reflect the reduced risk of AAA leases on the entire building. The net result is shown in Exhibit 10– 12.

The return to the investor increased to $299,850 annually with no cash equity investment; the debt coverage ratio rose to 1.46; the entire net operating income was guaranteed by AAA credits; and profit potential was present as a result of escalator clauses in the long-term hotel chain contract and periodic renewals in the office space contracts. The joint venture partner's return on his $200,000 equity investment rose from 16.54 percent in the previous case to 99.95 percent, and his risk was reduced significantly. In addition, the joint venture partner continued to received a K of 16 percent on the $1 million third loan, which was (at the time) significantly above the loan rates on competitive mortgages in a similar risk classification. If the equity investor-developer chose to sell his interest at this point, what would its value be? What would the required ROE be?[9]

Conclusion

Through their knowledge and expertise these managing equity investors have seemingly achieved the ultimate goal of investing: to identify and structure projects that produce maximum rates of return relative to the risks.

The vehicle used for analyzing these projects was the basic financial feasibility model. While we recognize its limitations, we also need to recognize its advantages. It is easy to use; it is understandable; and it allows the investor to quickly test various combinations of economic variables. Most important, it appears to work in most income property situations in which investors have short-run positive cash flow objectives. Most sophisticated investors around the country are using this type of model in conjunction with the discounted cash flow models discussed in Chapter 11.

Postscript   A number of years after the project was completed and operating, the hotel chain encountered financial difficulties and defaulted on its lease. Soon thereafter the project became insolvent and went bankrupt. Ultimately, a second hotel chain took over the operation of the building at a reduced rental. The project

---

[9] The required ROE would probably drop significantly owing to the reduction in risk as compared to the original case. If the ROE dropped from 17 percent to 12 percent, the value of the developer's equity would be $299,850/.12 = $2,498,750.

EXHIBIT 10-12. Revised Financial Pro Forma for Luxury Hotel/Office Property

Rate of Return	Income/Cash Flow	Cost	Source of Financing
15.90% (ROR)	$1,590,000	$10,000,000	Total cost
10.50% (K)	661,500	6,300,000	First loan (10.75 to 10.5%)
25.09% (ROE)	928,500	3,700,000	Remaining equity
10.75% (K)	268,750	2,500,000	Second loan (11.02 to 10.75%)
54.98% (ROE)	659,750	1,200,000	Remaining equity
16.00% (K)	160,000	1,000,000	Third loan (same K)
250.00% (ROE)	499,750	200,000	Remaining equity
99.95% (ROE)	199,900	200,000	Joint venture investment
∞ (ROE)	$ 299,850	$ 0	Remaining equity

ROR = 15.9%
Weighted average DCR = 1.46
Weighted average K = 11.12%
ROE to joint venture partner = 99.95%
ROE to investor–developer = ∞

never reached its long-run projected cash flow return to the original equity investors. While the overall projected coverage ratio (1.46) appeared to provide adequate protection, it was based on assumptions that proved to be unsupported in the marketplace.

DEVELOPING A DETAILED ONE-YEAR PRO FORMA

The most critical number in any financial analysis of income property is the amount of net operating income (NOI) expected for the first year of operation. The first-year NOI projection, which includes estimates of gross possible income, vacancy and credit losses, and operating expenses, is the basic productivity estimate on which all financial structuring and rate-of-return estimates are based. Since all future-year projections are generally based on this first-year estimate, any mistakes made in it will usually be compounded in future years and result in multiple errors in the final property value estimates and rate of return calculations.

In the basic financial feasibility model we used rules of thumb and aggregate estimates of income and expenses based on the investor's knowledge and experience, and on records for comparable properties that were available in-house or from property management firms. At some point in the investment process, however, a detailed income and expense statement must be constructed to verify the estimates used in the basic financial feasibility model. Investors who have ready access to management records for similar properties usually build this statement early in the investment process, before negotiating the basic purchase price and terms with the seller. Other investors choose to enter preliminary negotiations with the seller and collect the necessary data to build a detailed statement only if preliminary purchase negotiations are successful. This procedure is said to minimize the investor's time commitment and data collection costs, but it can lead to many surprises after a "meeting of the minds" between the investor and seller has been reached.

Most books on real estate investment skim over the subject of developing a detailed pro forma, despite its great importance in the real-world investment environment. Most investors also skim over the importance of these calculations because they are time consuming and require much detail work and patience. As a result, many investors buy a property on the basis of one set of numbers and then find that it operates on the basis of a completely different, more onerous set of numbers. Many surprises occur, and many unexpected risks are taken as a result of these miscalculations.

We go on now to develop some general ideas about the development of a detailed pro forma and the data sources that are required for its development. In Part IV of this book detailed information will be presented on estimating income and expenses for each type of property.

How Current NOI Can Be Distorted[10]

The financial records kept by an owner are the primary source of information about a property's NOI, but reading these records is an art in itself. In a variety of ways, and either deliberately or inadvertently, property records can mislead a prospective investor. There are many different ways in which the current NOI from a property can diverge from the property's true earning power, and many defenses that an investor should develop against problems of this nature. Here are eight such divergences, with the appropriate defense against each.

1. *Deferred maintenance.* One of the most frequently met problems, deferred maintenance, refers to inadequacies in maintenance and repair of the property. Simple examples include failure to paint at proper intervals and failure to periodically maintain the boiler and inspect and repair the heating, electrical, and plumbing elements. A owner may defer maintenance because the necessary cash flow is lacking, or in a deliberate attempt to show the highest possible operating income to prospective purchasers.

   Investor's defense: A thorough inspection of the property by a competent engineer is the most obvious defense against this problem. Experienced investors also will have developed rules of thumb concerning the percentage of rental income that should be devoted to maintenance and repair each year (e.g., 10 percent of rental income). A financial statement that shows a much smaller percentage devoted to this purpose is suspect.

2. *Substantial capital improvements needed.* In addition to deferring necessary maintenance, the owner may have postponed needed capital

---

[10] Major sections of this discussion were excerpted from Warren, Gorham and Lamont, *The Mortgage and Real Estate Executives Report* (bimonthly).

improvements (thereby causing physical or functional depreciation). Capital improvements (e.g., a new roof) may be required to keep the property in good condition or may be necessary so that the building can remain competitive (e.g., an apartment building may require a swimming pool and other amenities in order to avoid losing tenants to newer buildings).

Investor's defense: Again, a complete inspection of the property is a must. In addition, the purchaser should do whatever market research is necessary to ascertain what the property needs to maintain its competitive position.

3. *Inadequate replacement reserves.* When personal property is a significant factor (as in the case of motels or apartment buildings offering furnished units), adequate cash reserves should be maintained to replace short-lived items (furniture, carpets, etc). A new investor may be forced to invest a substantial amount of additional capital soon after acquiring title to the property in order to replace short-lived items.

Investor's defense: The investor should deduct the amount necessary to fund the reserves to their proper level from the price he or she initially is willing to pay for the property.

4. *Improper capitalization of expenses.* The first three items all relate to actual inadequacies. But even when the owner has properly maintained the property, the financial records can be misleading if, in order to increase net operating income, the owner has capitalized (i.e., added to the capital account) expenditures that properly should have been deducted currently from gross rental income. In other words, by shifting actual expenditures (e.g., carpet repair and painting expenses) from the operating statement to the capital account statement, an owner can present an inflated net operating income and cash flow picture.

Investor's defense: While the distinction is sometimes difficult to make in practice, the general rule is that costs that do not increase the value of the property are to be regarded as expenses rather than capital expenditures. As already noted, experienced investors usually have their own rules of thumb as to the percentage of gross income that should be devoted to repairs and maintenance. They substitute this figure for the one in the owner's financial statements.

5. *No provision for vacancies.* An owner whose property is 100 percent rented will not hesitate to show gross rental income based on full occupancy. Indeed, in their flyers (offering statements) many brokers assume full occupancy even though this is not the fact (the gross rental income is then called *scheduled net*).

Investor's defense: Astute investors normally reduce rental income to some extent to provide a cushion against future vacancies, perhaps 4–10 percent. This certainly should be done if there is a current oversupply of space in the neighborhood and any leases in the particular building will expire in the near future. For this purpose the investor should prepare a lease expiration schedule showing the precise dates on which each lease expires and the number of square feet that will become available.

6. *Special concessions in leases.* In order to fill up a new building, or during periods of market weakness, many tenants are given leases with rent concessions (e.g., one rent-free month for each year of the lease) or step-down renewal options (the right to renew at a lower rental in the future). This may mean a substantial decline in rental income in the next few years.

    Investor's defense: The investor requires the owner to provide a list of all leases and a summary of their rental provisions. The owner should also represent that there are no side agreements with tenants that contravene the lease terms. In addition, the purchaser or an attorney should read all leases to verify this information.

7. *Bona fide tenants.* Years ago, when high vacancy rates were the rule, unscrupulous landlords would "pack" a building with short-term tenants or people paying no rent at all to give the appearance of full occupancy. While this is much less common today, it remains a possibility that should be guarded against when dealing with unknown sellers. Another way for a landlord to defraud an investor is to enter into side agreements with some tenants, giving them free rent in the future in exchange for an immediate cash payment to the landlord. This is called milking the property.

    Investor's defense: An investor who has doubts about the ethics of a seller should personally interview some or all of the tenants to verify their rent obligations. A more formal way to do this is to have the tenants execute *estoppel statements* in which they acknowledge their continuing obligation to pay rent according to the written lease terms.

8. *Management duties performed by the investor.* Property management and related expenses are often omitted or grossly understated if the seller performs property management and administrative duties. It is common for an investor-manager to render extensive property management and administrative services but never receive payment for them. Consequently, operating expenses will be understated by the value of the services rendered by the owner.

    Investor's defense: To reflect the real cash flow generated by the property, the investor's financial projections should include a complete cost estimate for management services rendered, including resident and professional property management duties, accounting, payroll taxes, and other administrative expenses. Although these items may not be treated as expenses for income tax purposes, they should be included in the investment analysis.

The seller's financial records, thus, are subject to much distortion. These records may provide a beginning basis for an NOI pro forma, but the investor must obtain data from other sources and make income and expense estimates that best represent how the property will perform for him or her during the first full year of operation.

On the other hand, historical data provided by the seller on rent rates, vacancies, and expenses can be a reliable basis for projections if consistent accounting practices have been followed and a professional property management firm has been employed. While NOI estimates are easily distorted in the short run, trend data for a period of years are less likely to be distorted significantly. These data, along with data from other sources, can provide an accurate basis for forecasting future income and expenses.

Other Sources of Data

- *Management firms in the area.* Locate property managers that operate a substantial number of properties similar to the one being analyzed. Sharing information and expertise with other firms that have good data bases will solve many problems of data collection and forecasting. A professional property manager may be quite willing to share information and aid the investor in developing the one-year pro forma or budget if a fee or management contract may result from the services and expertise rendered.
- *In-house data on similar properties.* Ideally, an experienced investor develops in-house accounting systems and data that are easily accessible for the purpose of analysis. Income and expenses are commonly kept on percentage and square-foot bases, and historical trends are figured on a line-item basis for a detailed one-year pro forma analysis.
- *Personal interviews with owners.* Personal contacts with other owners or through ownership associations can provide much needed information, as well as a format for discussions of market trends and changes that will directly or indirectly affect a property's performance.
- *Published data.* Numerous national and regional trade associations publish data on income and expenses for apartments, office buildings, shopping centers, hotels and motels, industrial buildings, and so on. The submarket data classifications are often useful in comparative and trend analysis. These will be discussed in detail in Part IV.
- *Market and marketability studies.* These studies can be undertaken periodically by the investor as a source of information and data for analyzing potential investments as well as evaluating existing properties in the portfolio. These studies were discussed in Part II and will be studied in detail again when individual property types are analyzed in Part IV.

SUMMARY

In this chapter we developed a financial model to (1) analyze the basic economics of the project with respect to the return and risk characteristics of a property, (2) analyze the leverage alternatives and structure or restructure the financial package, and (3) determine an investment value or range of value after having worked through the model with alternative assumptions. The model allows the investor to structure the economics of a project so as to simultaneously achieve the financial objectives of the equity investor, lender, and seller.

The basic financial feasibility model is a one-year cash flow model that incorporates a number of important relationships. The primary return measure used by the equity investor is the before-tax cash-on-cash return (ROE), while the primary measure of return to the lender is the mortgage constant (K). Both the equity investor and the lender can measure the risk level by computing a coverage ratio and a break-even point, and by analyzing the degree of positive or negative leverage. The most important overall measure of return is the ROR (net operating income/total capital invested), since it measures the overall productivity of the property. If the ROR is adequate, proper financial structuring can guarantee a mutually beneficial relationship between the equity investor and the lender.

We noted a number of weaknesses in the model, the most important ones being that it utilizes a single net operating income and cash flow figure to represent the productivity of the property over its useful life and that it ignores tax factors that affect the investor's return and risk. While the model is easy to understand and the concepts are widely employed by real estate professionals, it is best used only in the early stages of analysis. If the basic economic criteria are met, a discounted cash flow after-tax analysis should follow.

After applying the basic model to a number of investment situations, we focused our attention on developing a detailed one-year pro forma.

In the Aspen Wood case study that follows the basic financial feasibility model is used to generate financing alternatives for the proposed apartment building investment.

ASPEN WOOD APARTMENTS

GENERATING ALTERNATIVES AND APPLICATION OF THE
BASIC FINANCIAL FEASIBILITY MODEL

In 1974, D&B Associates was seeking apartment, office, or retail properties
that met their various investment criteria. In Chapter 9 we saw that the firm's
basic apartment screening criteria included (1) location—apartment
properties that were highly visible, located in high-quality, stable
neighborhoods, and close to shopping, transportation, and recreation; (2) a
minimum of forty units, less than ten years old, well designed and appealing
to the local investors as well as the renters, with utility charges paid by
tenants on individual meters; (3) a good rental income track
record—consistently high occupancy in recent years; (4) availability of
secondary or wraparound financing to create a relatively high (75–85%)
leverage position at a time when new financing was expensive and
unavailable; and (5) tax'shelter—ability to structure the property in such a
way as to generate a relatively high degree of tax shelter during the year of
purchase.

Locating desirable properties proved to be a difficult task for Charlie
Davidson and Clyde Boomer, the owners of D&B Associates. As we have
noted, the years 1974–1976 have often been described as the great
post-World War II real estate depression. The problems included (1) rapidly
rising utility expenses as a result of the energy crisis, (2) low rents and high
vacancy rates owing to excess inventory of apartment properties, (3) high
interest rates and reluctance on the part of institutions to make any
apartment loans in the city, and (4) a general economic recession, which,
along with the depressed real estate conditions, discouraged investors from
participating in syndication programs. Real estate became a buyer's market
characterized by widespread mortgage defaults and negative cash flows.

Two members of D&B Associates spent nine months researching the
desirable apartment areas in the city, writing down addresses, looking up
ownership records, and contacting property owners. They also maintained
active communication with other commercial brokers, commercial bankers,
trust officers, tax attorneys specializing in real estate, builder-developers,
owners of large properties in the city, and principals of other property
management firms. After over one hundred properties had been analyzed,
only two were purchased for D&B's syndication program. Locating
properties that passed the basic screening criteria was not difficult, but few
were able to pass the more rigorous return/risk criteria imposed in the basic
financial feasibility model (step 3). In even fewer cases could successful
negotiations be held with the seller (step 4).

In July 1974 Aspen Wood Apartments was located and appeared to
meet the basic screening criteria (basic information was presented in
Chapter 9).

1. It is adjacent to the Intramural Fields (40 tennis courts, track, baseball fields) and on the University's shuttle bus route. The neighborhood is pleasant and attractive to local workers as well as to students. The site is within three miles of two regional shopping malls, is visible from the intersection of two major traffic arteries, and is within one mile of numerous state office buildings.

2. Aspen Wood has eighty-four units, an acceptable number for managerial efficiency.

3. The building is durably constructed and well designed, including two swimming pools, laundry facilities, and adequate parking. The complex would appeal to investors and prospective tenants.

4. Electricity is paid for by the tenants.

5. The project had just undergone a complete refurbishing, including new drapes, carpet, furniture, and repainting inside and out. Over $100,000 was spent on these capital improvements in 1973–1974.

6. The seller was willing to accept a wraparound mortgage or secondary financing on the project. There was $650,000 of underlying liens and the asking price was approximately $1 million, depending on how the purchase was structured.

7. The seller was willing to offer tax benefits in the form of write-offs for 1974. This was important because the purchasing investors were tax-oriented professionals.

8. The project (allegedly) was 95 percent occupied and had an excellent occupancy record.

9. The seller was willing to sell on the basis of a 10 percent cash-on-cash yield (ROE) to buyers. (Recognize that current market standards might dictate a ROE of 5–8% on such a property.)

The seller of Aspen Wood Apartments was a limited partnership syndication consisting of three general partners and numerous limited partners. The general partners were representing the syndication in the sale of the property. The limited partnership syndication had originally overpaid for the complex and had borrowed (short term) $120,000 from local banks for the recent refurbishing program. The banks were now putting pressure on the general partners to repay the notes. The general partners had no experienced professional property manager on their staff; property records were practically nonexistent; and the current resident manager had stolen the last month's rental income and disappeared. Clearly, the sellers were motivated to sell.

THE SELLER'S OPERATING PRO FORMA

Exhibit 10–13 shows the seller's operating pro forma. The rent schedule presented seemed reasonable to the buyer, but the so-called scheduled net income figure was distorted by a large "net deposits" figure and a 3 percent vacancy allowance. (Note that correct titles are given after the seller's terms.) Net deposits of such a large amount are usually a result of poor

---

EXHIBIT 10–13. Seller's Operating Pro Forma, 9/1/74–8/30/75

INCOME

Scheduled gross rentals	$156,552	
Net deposits	3,000	
Net concessions	1,200	
Parking (18 spaces × $7.50)	1,620	$162,372
Less 3% vacancy		4,871
Scheduled net income (gross effective income)		157,001

OPERATING EXPENSES

Labor expense			
Resident manager	$ 3,600		
Maintenance	2,700	6,300	
Payroll taxes and insurance		1,194	
Electrical expense			
Materials and supplies	285		
Lamps	240		
Equipment maintenance	300		
Electricity	4,200	4,860	
Heating and air-conditioning expense			
Materials and supplies	285		
Equipment maintenance	600		
Gas	2,685		
Water	2,100	5,680	
General building expenses			
Materials and supplies	180		
Maintenance supplies	240		
Trash removal	816		
Exterminating	180		
Management fee (4.5%)	7,092		
Telephone	300		
Swimming pool	250		
General building maintenance	600		
Appliance repair	240		
Painting maintenance	480		
Plumbing maintenance	285		
Carpet repairs and replacement	120		
Cable television	1,560		
Advertising	1,800		
Legal and professional fees	800		
Miscellaneous	600	15,543	
Other expenses			
Real estate taxes	16,135		
Insurance	2,640	18,775	
Total expenses (33.2%)			52,342
Net cash flow before debt service (net operating income)			105,259
Debt service			66,591
Net cash flow before taxes (cash flow before tax)			$ 38,668

management, indicating a questionable policy of not returning rent deposits to tenants who move, allowing too many tenant "skip-outs," or not requiring tenants to clean up their units at the termination of their leases. A 3 percent vacancy rate is not realistic for a long-run projection; few landlords in a student apartment market collect more than 95 percent of gross possible income even when physical occupancy is 97–100 percent much of the time.[11]

Operating expenses were itemized in elaborate detail, but totaled to only 33.2 percent of gross possible income. This figure is unrealistically low; one might suspect that some bills were unpaid or "lost," maintenance was being deferred, expenses were being capitalized instead of expensed, or a combination of these. In addition, the seller's expense statement represented "last year's" expenses while the income represented next year's expectations.

Revision of these figures was necessary so that the buyer would have reliable data to feed into the basic financial feasibility model. A check of comparable well-managed properties led Davidson and Boomer to believe that rental rates were in line with the market, but that the vacancy allowance should be 5 percent and expenses about 40 percent.

SALE STRUCTURE PROPOSALS

The general partners made two initial presentations to D&B regarding sale structures that might be acceptable to both general and limited partners:

1. *Straight-sale proposal.* The asking price, which was derived by capitalizing the projected NOI of approximately $105,000 by a 10 percent capitalization rate, was $1,050,000. The buyer would make a total down payment of $414,000, to be paid $164,000 at closing (1974) and $250,000 one year later (1975). The buyer would assume the three existing notes on the property in the total amount of $636,000.
2. *Owner-financed sale proposal.* The asking price remained at $1,050,000, but the total down payment was reduced to $164,000. The remaining amount of the purchase price was to be financed by the seller using a wraparound mortgage bearing an interest rate of 8.875 percent, an amortization term of 20 years, and a 15-year balloon (remaining principal balance to be paid at the end of 15 years). The seller was willing to accept over $100,000 of the down payment in the form of prepaid interest, points on the wraparound mortgage, and other fees that the buyer could deduct for income tax purposes (see

[11] Because of tenant turnover, broken leases, and collection losses, economic occupancy tends to be less than physical occupancy. Inexperienced investors often overestimate the amount of gross effective income (economic occupancy) that a property will produce because they underestimate the amounts of real vacancy and collection losses.

Chapter 13). This proposal provided attractive tax shelters for the buyer.

The seller provided elaborate five-year projections of after-tax cash flows for each proposal. Both were reviewed carefully by Davidson and Boomer.

VALUATION USING THE BASIC FINANCIAL FEASIBILITY MODEL

In D&B's opinion neither of the seller's presentations was realistic. But the two presentations and some discussion provided useful information on which to base an offer. D&B felt that the general partners representing the property had two principal concerns: (1) appeasing the limited partners with a respectable selling price of approximately $1 million and (2) receiving an equity down payment of at least $160,000 to cover repayment of outstanding refurbishment loans. (The general partners had revealed that their creditors were pressing for repayment of about $120,000 in furniture liens and another $40,000 in other debts, for a total cash requirement of $160,000.)

With this knowledge, D&B began to work the basic financial feasibility model both forward and backward, utilizing a $1 million minimum sales figure and an equity investment of $200,000– $220,000 ($160,000 plus a $50,000 commission to D&B).

Exhibit 10– 14 shows a solution developed by Davidson and Boomer after numerous iterations. While the maximum equity investment was somewhat less than the target amount of $210,000, the total project value of $1,036,000 was greater than the $1 million minimum specified; thus, the numbers were "in the ballpark" from the point of view of the seller.

Gross rents were calculated on the basis of the seller's figures, but the vacancy and expense figures were adjusted as previously mentioned. As a result, the net operating income decreased to $89,305 from the $105,259 projected by the seller. Having specified the beginning and end values for the model, D&B began to specify values for other variables. A debt coverage ratio of 1.3 was felt to be minimum, as was a 10 percent desired (before-tax) rate of equity return (ROE). With a debt coverage ratio of 1.3, the maximum debt service that the project could support was $68,695 ($73,067 ÷ 1.3); with a debt amount of $830,000, the mortgage constant could be no greater than 8.3 percent. For this solution to be achieved, the seller had to be willing to provide wraparound financing of $830,000 with an interest rate and amortization term that would result in a mortgage constant no greater than 8.3 percent. In effect, the seller must buy the high selling price with favorable mortgage terms.

At this point the seller has made a presentation regarding what he would like to receive if a sale were consummated, and D&B (the buyer) has completed a basic economic analysis of what it can offer. Now both parties must go over the facts and figures together to determine their bargaining positions and judge whether further efforts will be worthwhile. There is no

EXHIBIT 10–14. The Basic Financial Feasibility Model—D&B's Solution

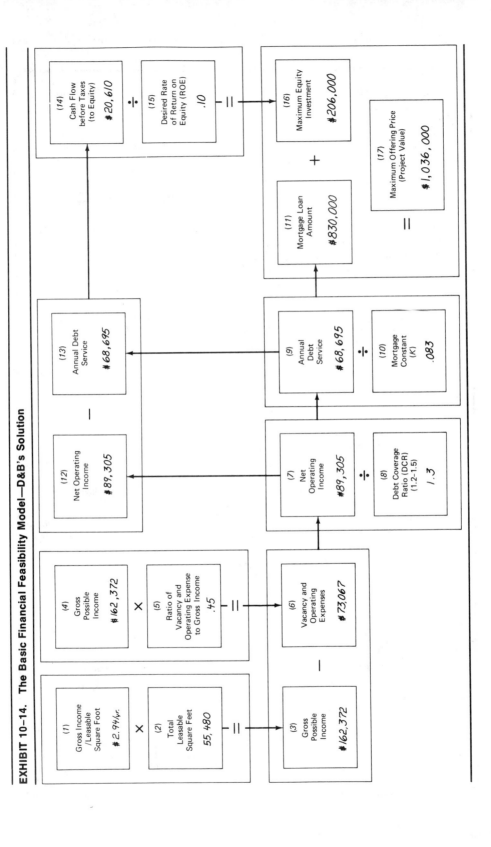

reason to begin the exhaustive research and analysis called for in steps 5–7 (feasibility research, tax analysis, DCF analysis) if it appears that no agreement can be reached on the basic parameters of the sale.

In the following chapter we will follow Davidson and Boomer as they proceed through steps 4–7, beginning with negotiations with the seller and ending with a discounted cash flow analysis of the Aspen Wood property.

11

Discounted Cash Flow and Ratio Analysis

The use of the basic financial feasibility model to evaluate the performance of income-producing real estate was discussed in Chapter 10. Recall that our objections to the model focused on its inability to consider changes in economic variables over time. We concluded that the investor can use *present value* (PV) and *internal rate of return* (IRR) models, commonly known as discounted cash flow (DCF) models, to overcome many of these limitations. Indeed, the DCF models should be used extensively in the latter stages of the investment process, as described by our ten-step model, before a final investment decision is made.

Chapters 11 and 12 will provide an integrated framework for return-and-risk analysis using modern capital-budgeting techniques. Chapter 12 should be considered a continuation of this chapter. We will first review the mathematics and economics of discounted cash flow methods, including tax shelter impacts on cash flow. Then we will develop a complete after-tax cash flow analysis model using the DCF methods and analyze a project over a seven-year holding period. Third, we will review various types of annual financial ratios that can be utilized for evaluating the investor's rate of return, risk, and the quality of the underlying assumptions used in the analysis. Then, in Chapter 12, we will develop the concepts of sensitivity and risk analysis, and show how a computer simulation model can be utilized to evaluate the return/risk trade-offs in a real estate investment. Finally, we will again introduce the Aspen Wood case study and see how the concepts in both chapters were applied by D&B Associates in its investment analysis process.

Be aware that the Economic Recovery Tax Act of 1981 (which became effective after this chapter was in print) has changed the rules of the investment game. In a number of places in the chapter, the financial calculations are based on tax assumptions that apply to properties purchased before the 1981 tax act became effective. These situations are noted throughout and the reader should refer to Chapter 13 for a complete discussion of the provisions of the 1981 tax act and their impact on real estate investments.

PRESENT VALUE AND INTERNAL RATE OF RETURN

The Time Value of Money[1]

We have all heard the cliche, A bird in the hand is worth two in the bush. Clearly, this refers to the time value of birds, but the concept involved is equally applicable to money and real estate. If we were offered a choice between a dollar today and a dollar a year from now, most of us would choose a dollar today. Why is this so? We might reply that immediate pleasure is preferable to postponed pleasure.

However, we must look at this problem from the point of view of the real estate investor, who prefers a dollar today not because an immediate pleasure can be gained but because the dollar can be put to work to earn a return. Should the investor choose to receive the dollar a year from now, it will mean forgoing the money that might be earned over the course of the year on the present dollar; that is, there is an *opportunity cost* to passing up the cash flow that could be obtained by putting the present dollar to work in an income property for a year.

Actually, a dollar received in the future can be less valuable for three reasons:

1. *Opportunity cost*—earnings forgone, or the return that could have been earned if the amount to be received in the future had been available for immediate investment.
2. *Inflation*—the purchasing power of a sum to be received in the future may be diminished by intervening increases in the price of goods and services.
3. *Certainty of payment* (risk)—uncertainty associated with receiving the payment in the future. For example, obligations of the U.S. government (e.g., Treasury bills) are considered free from the risk of loss. On the other hand, a lottery ticket bears a high degree of uncertainty. Most real estate investments fall somewhere between these extremes.

When determining the present value of future income, all three considerations must be evaluated in estimating a discount rate. A *discount rate* is simply the investor's required rate of return (or rate of interest), taking into account opportunity cost, inflation, and certainty of payment (risk).

Present Value[2]

Perhaps the easiest way to understand *present value* (PV) is to first consider future value. If an individual has $1.00 and deposits it in a savings account that pays 6

[1] A good early discussion of this topic can be found in Robert Johnson, *Financial Management* (Boston: Allyn and Bacon, 1962), pp. 182–193.
[2] This discussion was developed with the assistance of Russell Welch, J.D., Murray State University, Murray, Kentucky.

percent interest (compounded annually), at the end of one year the depositor will have $1.06 (the original $1.00 plus $.06 interest). If the $1.06 is left in the savings account, at the end of the two years it will have grown to $1.1236 (the $1.06 at the beginning of the second year plus $.0636 interest earned during the second year). After three years the original $1.00 will have increased to $1.191. So the *future value* of $1.00 at 6 percent interest for three years is $1.191. The future value of any amount can be calculated as follows:

$$FV = A(1 + i)^n$$

where FV = future value
$\quad\quad\quad A$ = original amount (here, $1.00)
$\quad\quad\quad i$ = the rate of interest earned (here, 6%)
$\quad\quad\quad n$ = the number of periods in the future (here, 3 years)

If $1.191 is the future value of $1.00 at 6 percent for three years, then the *present value* of $1.191 to be received in three years, to someone whose opportunity cost or discount rate is 6 percent, must be $1.00. After all, if the $1.00 were available today, in three years it would increase to $1.191. The present value of any amount, thus, can be calculated by the reciprocal of the future-value equation:

$$PV = A \left[\frac{1}{(1 + i)^n} \right]$$

where PV = present value
$\quad\quad\quad A$ = amount to be received in the future ($1.191)
$\quad\quad\quad i$ = the rate of interest that could have been earned, or the discount rate (6%); also called the required rate of return
$\quad\quad\quad n$ = the number of periods in the future (3 years)

Fortunately, tables for the term inside the brackets in this equation are widely available, so long calculations are rarely necessary. (See Appendix B.) Present value tables are fast becoming obsolete, however; today most students and analysts buy financial calculators (at a cost of $10–$100) that generate the present-value factors internally.

Using the 6 percent *annual* compounding table, the present-value factor for three years is 0.839619. Multiplying this times the amount to be received in the future ($1.191) gives $1.00: $1.191 × 0.839619 = .99998623, or very close to $1.00. The difference is due to insignificant rounding. Again, to calculate the present value of an amount to be received in the future, multiply the amount by the present-value factor from the table, using the appropriate discount rate and the number of periods in the future.

Unequal Cash Flow Streams   The application of the notion of present value to real estate investment can be illustrated with another example. Suppose that a real estate investor has an opportunity to buy an income-producing property that is projected to provide an after-tax cash flow of $10,000 in the first year, $11,000 in the second year, and $15,000 in the third year.[3] The investor has determined that 12 percent is the appropriate discount rate for investments with risk levels comparable to that of this property. What is the present value of these cash flows? Clearly, it is *not* $10,000 + $11,000 + $15,000 = $36,000. Rather, it is calculated as follows:

Year	Cash Flow	)(	PV Factor at 12%	=	Present Value
1	$10,000		0.892857		$ 8,928.57
2	11,000		0.7971		8,769.13
3	15,000		0.711780		10,676.70
			Total present value		$28,374.40

An analysis that valued the cash flows at $36,000 would obviously be misleading, since the calculated present value is almost $8,000 less. The calculated present value can be viewed as the maximum offering price for a project on which a 12 percent discount rate is used. Alternatively, if $28,374.40 is paid for the project, a rate of return of 12 percent can be expected.

Equal Cash Flow Streams   Occasionally a real estate investor may be presented with a situation in which an income stream will remain constant for several years (e.g., under a fixed-rate lease). Rather than applying a separate factor to each year's cash flow, the investor can refer to a table that *accumulates* these factors and permits determination of the present value of a constant income stream with a single calculation. Such tables are known as *ordinary annuity* or *present value of one per period* tables. (See Appendix B.) For example, suppose an investor wants to determine the present value of a five-year net lease paying $1,000 per year. One way to find the present value would be to discount each year's lease payment at, say, 10 percent:

Year	Payment	×	PV factor at 10%	=	Present Value
1	$1,000		0.909091		$ 909.09
2	$1,000		0.826446		826.45
3	$1,000		0.751315		751.32
4	$1,000		0.683013		683.01
5	$1,000		0.620921		620.92
			Total present value		$3790.79

---

[3] By convention, all cash flows are assumed to be received at the end of the year. This obviously is slightly misleading, but it reduces the number of calculations by a factor of 12 and is a well accepted practice among financial analysts. However, if cash flow is received continuously, monthly, quarterly, or semiannually, other tables can be used. The present-value formula does not change, but all the terms in the formula are redefined in terms of the relevant cash flow period. For example, if we desire to discount cash flows on a monthly basis, i is the monthly interest rate and n is the number of months.

A much simpler method is simply to multiply the amount by the table factor for the present value of one *per period* (10% column, Appendix B).

$$PV = \$1,000\ (3.790787)$$
$$= \$3,790.79$$

Note that the factor for the present value of one per period is simply the sum of all of the years' factors for the present value of one.

Now, what if the lease called for payments to be increased to $2,000 for years 6 to 10? How can the present value of this income stream be calculated? Obviously, we could laboriously multiply each year's payment by the present-value factor and sum the resulting amount. However, use of the table can greatly reduce the computational effort. One way to determine the present value of this second stream of income would be to recognize that years 6 to 10 are another five-year period. Using the present-value-one-per-period factor for five years (again at 10%) yields

$$PV = \$2,000\ (3.790787)$$
$$= \$7,581.57$$

However, this is the value of the income stream at the end of the *fifth* year (or the beginning of the sixth). Finding the *present value* necessitates discounting this amount by the five-year, *present-value-of-one* factor:

$$PV = \$7,581.57\ (0.620921)$$
$$= \$4,707.56$$

The same result can be reached by subtracting the present-value-of-one-per-period factor for *five* years (since the $2000 payment will not be received until years 6 to 10) from the present-value-of-one-per-period factor for *ten* years, and multiplying the difference times the amount of the income stream:

$$PV = A\ (\text{tenth-year factor minus fifth-year factor})$$
$$= \$2,000\ (6.144567 - 3.790787)$$
$$= \$2,000\ (2.35378)$$
$$= \$4,707.56$$

The Present-Value Decision Rule   The present value of an investment is the maximum amount an investor should pay for the opportunity of making the investment. If the calculated present value is *equal to* or *greater than* the investment cost, the decision rule is to *invest,* since there are net monetary benefits to be gained. If the calculated present value is *less* than the investment cost, the decision rule is reject or modify the investment, since the investment will not produce the required rate of return.

Let us illustrate the process. Assume that our required rate of return is 20 percent. The cash flows from a $100,000 investment have been estimated at

$50,000 per year for three years. Using Appendix B, we find that the present value of this stream of cash flows, discounted at 20 percent, is $105,324:

$$2.106481 \times \$50,000 = \$105,324$$

The proposed investment is worthwhile because the present value of the cash flows ($105,324) is greater than the cost of the investment ($100,000). Our expected rate of return will be higher than 20 percent, since a 20 percent rate of return will allow us to pay $105,324. Whenever the present value is greater than the investment cost, the expected rate of return is higher than the required rate of return. The reverse is also true.

Net Present Value (NPV)   Exactly the same analysis can be carried out by subtracting the investment cost from the present value of the cash flows. If this difference is greater than zero, a net gain will be realized from the investment.

Present value of cash flows	$105,324
Investment cost	−100,000
Net present value	$ 5,324

The proposed investment is worthwhile because the net present value ($5,324) is positive). By computing NPVs for other investments, we can rank them in order of desirability, from highest to lowest.

The Profitability Index (PI)   When comparing or ranking investments of different sizes and costs, some investors prefer to calculate a profitability index rather than NPV, that is, the present value of cash flows divided by the cost of the investment. For example, the profitability index for the $100,000 investment would be 1.05:

$$PI = \frac{\text{present value of cash flows}}{\text{investment cost}} = \frac{\$105,324}{\$100,000} = 1.05$$

By computing profitability indexes for other projects, we can rank them in order of desirability, as shown in the following table. (A project with an index of profitability of less than 1.00 would be undesirable; that is, its expected rate of return would be less than the 20 percent required rate of return.)

	Investment Cost	Present Value of Cash Flows	Net Present Value	Profitability Index
Investment C	$ 80,000	$128,000	$48,000	1.6
Investment A	20,000	30,000	10,000	1.5
Investment B	100,000	130,000	30,000	1.3

Note that while investment B has a net present value greater than that of investment A, its profitability index is less than that of investment A. Thus, on a *relative* cost and profitability basis, investment A is more desirable than investment B; it produces higher net returns for each dollar invested.

Given this conflict, which investment should be accepted if only one can be chosen? Stated another way, is it better to use the NPV or the PI approach? The general rule is that, barring capital-rationing constraints, the NPV method is preferred.[4] There are exceptions to the rule, and there remains some debate on the issue. Keep in mind, however, that both methods produce the same accept/reject answer; investments that are acceptable under NPV are also acceptable under PI.

Internal Rate of Return[5]

The internal rate of return (IRR) was defined in Chapter 3 as the rate of return that equates the present value of the expected future cash flows to the initial capital invested. Alternatively, the IRR may be defined as the interest rate equivalent to the cash flows that the investment will yield *in addition to* returning the original investment cost. The IRR is also the discount rate that results in an NPV of zero. The internal-rate-of-return formula is simply the present-value formula solved for the particular value of the discount rate that results in an NPV of zero; the same basic equation is used for both methods.

Calculation of the Internal Rate of Return   In our earlier discussion we knew the required interest rate, or IRR, and were trying to calculate the present value of expected cash flows at that IRR. Now we know the expected cash flows and the investment cost required to achieve those cash flows, but we would like to calculate the IRR.

Let us apply this technique to determine the rate of return on our $100,000 investment that produced cash flows of $50,000 per year for three years. We can estimate the IRR through a series of successive approximations, that is, by making guesses at its value. We wish to find the one rate that will equate the $50,000 cash flows for three years with the $100,000 initial investment cost. We know that a 20 percent rate produced a present value of $105,324:

$$2.106481 \times \$50,000 = \$105,324$$

This tells us that if we were to invest exactly $105,324 in return for $50,000 each year for three years, the annual IRR would be 20 percent. But we do not need to invest this much money; our investment is only $100,000. Therefore, the true IRR that we will receive will be more than 20 percent. Let us try 25 percent. Using the present-value tables again, we find that the present value of $50,000 received annually for three years and discounted at 25 percent is $97,600:

$$1.952 \times \$50,000 = \$97,600$$

---

[4] J. Fred Weston and Eugene F. Brigham, *Managerial Finance* (Hinsdale, Ill.: Dryden Press, 1978), pp. 327–329.

[5] An excellent survey of the literature on the IRR concept and its problems and limitations is provided by Austin J. Jaffe, "Is There a 'New' Internal Rate of Return Literature," *AREUEA Journal,* Winter 1977, pp. 482–502.

This calculation tells us that if we were to invest $97,600 in return for the $50,000 cash flows, the IRR would be 25 percent. Because we actually must invest more than $97,600, the IRR must be less than 25 percent but more than 20 percent. Moreover, it must be closer to 25 percent, because the actual required investment of $100,000 is closer to $97,600 than to $105,324. We can approximate the actual rate by interpolation:

Rate of Return   *Present Value*

$$5\% \left[x \left[\begin{array}{l} 20\% = \$105,324 \\ \text{IRR ?} = \$100,000 \\ 25\% = \$\ 97,600 \end{array} \right| \$5,324 \right] \$7,724$$

$$\frac{x}{5\%} = \frac{\$5,324}{\$7,724}$$

$$x = \frac{(5\%)\$5,324}{\$7,724} = 3.45\%$$

$$\text{IRR} = 20\% + 3.45\% = 23.45\%$$

Observe that the calculated rate is, as we expected, closer to 25 percent than to 20 percent. In other words, a net cash inflow of $50,000 at the end of each year for three years is equivalent to an interest rate of about 23.45 percent *compounded annually* on an initial investment of $100,000.[6]

Actually, the internal-rate-of-return calculation using this interpolation method is only an approximation of the true mathematical solution. If one uses a mathematically preprogrammed calculator, IRR is found to be 23.38 percent. The formula programmed into the calculator is the one presented in Chapter 3:

$$\text{Investment cost} = \frac{CF_1}{(1 + \text{IRR})^1} + \frac{CF_2}{(1 + \text{IRR})^2} + \cdot \cdot \cdot + \frac{CF_n}{(1 + \text{IRR})^n}$$

$$\$100,000 = \frac{\$50,000}{(1 + .2338)^1} + \frac{\$50,000}{(1 + .2338)^2} + \frac{\$50,000}{(1 + .2338)^3}$$

Most calculators, as well as most computers, are programmed to find the IRR in a manner similar to ours—a process of trial and error. The process begins by choosing some discount rate as a starting point and computing the present value of the cash flows (CF, CF_2, CF_3, etc.). If the resulting PV on the left-hand side of the equation is greater than the investment cost ($100,000 in this case), a higher

---

[6] Observe also that the investor receives a *return* of the original $100,000 investment *in addition to* an annual interest rate of 23.45 percent. If the investment did not yield cash flows of at least $100,000 over three years, the calculated IRR would be negative; if the investment yielded exactly $100,000 over three years, the calculated IRR would be zero. Thus, an investment must produce cash flows that total *more than the initial investment cost* in order for the IRR to be a positive number.

discount rate is chosen and the process is started again. This process is continued until the present value of the cash flows is just equal to the investment cost. In our example this occurs when the discount rate is 23.38 percent. *By definition, we have found the IRR when the present value of the cash flow benefits are equal to the investment costs.* Over a period of three years we will receive a return on our original $100,000 investment plus a compounded annual return of 23.38 percent on that investment.

When IRR is computed by hand through the interpolation process, rather than by a preprogrammed calculator or computer, it should be recognized that errors exist because it is a *linear* estimation that can only approximate a *geometric* progression. If the discount rates are far apart when the interpolation process begins, the resulting IRR approximation will have a relatively substantial error. As the discount rates come closer together, the error decreases and the IRR comes closer to the actual IRR using the formula shown. For accurate results, 5 percent is the maximum spread between discount rates that should be used for interpolation calculations.

Unequal Cash Flow Streams   Suppose that we are presented with an opportunity to purchase a property that requires an equity investment of $10,000. The projected cash flow for year 1 is $2,000, for year 2 is $2,500, and for year 3 is $3,000. We anticipate selling the property at the end of the third year for a price that would result in net sale proceeds of $7,500. What is the IRR?

The true IRR is 17.43 percent using a programmed calculator, and the solution is as follows:

$$\$10,000 = \frac{\$2,000}{(1+.1743)^1} + \frac{\$2,500}{(1+.1743)^2} + \frac{\$3,000}{(1+.1743)^3} + \frac{\$7,500}{(1+.1743)^3}$$

If we were to guess at the IRR, however, and end up interpolating between 15 and 20 percent, the resulting IRR would be 17.53 percent:

Year	Cash Flow	Sale Proceeds	PV Factor at 15%	PV
1	$2,000		.869565	$ 1,739.13
2	2,500		.756144	1,890.36
3	3,000		.657516	1,972.55
3		$7,500	.657516	4,931.37
			Total PV	$10,533.41

As before, the benefits are not being discounted at a high enough rate. Using a rate of 20 percent gives the following:

Year	Cash Flow	Sale Proceeds	PV Factor at 20%	PV
1	$2,000		.833333	$1,666.66
2	2,500		.694444	1,736.11
3	3,000		.578704	1,736.11
3		$7,500	.578704	4,340.28
			Total PV	$9,479.16

The total PV of the benefits to the equity investor is now *less* than the required equity, so the IRR lies somewhere between 15 and 20 percent. Interpolating as before, we get

$$\text{Rate of Return} \qquad\qquad \text{Present Value}$$

$$5\% \left[x \left[\begin{array}{l} 15\% = \$10,533.41 \\ \text{IRR ?} = \$10,000.00 \\ 20\% = \$\ 9,479.16 \end{array} \right. \$533.41 \right] \$1,054.24$$

$$\frac{x}{5\%} = \frac{\$533.41}{\$1,054.24}$$

$$x = \frac{(5\%)\$533.41}{\$1,054.24} = 2.53\%$$

$$\text{IRR} = 15\% + 2.53\% = 17.53\%$$

The Internal-Rate-of-Return Decision Rule   The calculated IRR is then compared with the required IRR. If, for example, we determined that a 20 percent IRR was the lowest acceptable rate for a particular real estate investment, the project would be rejected or restructured until the calculated IRR was above the 20 percent required IRR. The suggested decision rule for investing is to accept projects that have IRRs equal to, or greater than, the investor's required IRR. Be aware that projects that are acceptable under the IRR method are also acceptable under the PV, NPV, or PI methods; they will all produce the same accept/reject answer for specific properties.[7]

The Modified (Adjusted) Internal Rate of Return (MIRR)

Although IRR is widely used as a measure of investment return, there are a number of problems connected with reliance on IRR as an investment criterion.[8] Two of the commonly cited problems are the following:

1. *The multiple-rate-of-return problem.* Mathematically, the internal rate of return is calculated by solving an equation called an nth-degree polynomial [created by the denominator terms in the equation, $(1 + \text{IRR})^n$]. In practice, what this means is that a project can have more than one IRR under certain conditions. In most situations there is only one IRR solution. However, if during the forecast period the expected cash flow changes from a positive to a negative and back to a positive number, more than one IRR solution may exist.[9]

[7] See, e.g., Weston and Brigham, p. 299.
[8] See Stephen D. Messner, Irving Schreiber, and Victor Lyon, "Problems with the Use of IRR," *Marketing Investment Real Estate* (Chicago: National Association of Realtors, Realtors National Marketing Institute, 1975), pp. 46–48.
[9] For additional insights into the multiple-solution problem, see Donald J. Valachi, "The Internal Rate of Return: A Note on the Arithmetic of Multiple and Imaginary Rates," *The Real Estate Appraiser,* March–April 1977, pp. 39–42; see also the classic article on the subject, William H. Jean, "On Multiple Rates of Return," *Journal of Finance,* March 1968, pp. 187–191; also, James C. T. Mao, *Quantitative Analysis of Financial Decisions* (New York: Macmillan, 1969), chap. 6.

2. *Assumed reinvestment at the IRR.* The IRR is an *internal* rate of return on capital *within* an investment. No mention has been made of a rate of return on reinvested capital after it has been withdrawn from the investment. However, there is an implicit assumption that the cash proceeds from the investment can be reinvested at the calculated IRR. If the timing of the cash flows differs among the investments being compared, and if the investor is choosing between mutually exclusive investment alternatives, the IRR may provide a misleading indicator of investment desirability. While the go/no-go decision (accept/reject) will be the same using both the PV and IRR approaches, the two may *rank* projects differently. In the PV approach, cash flows are assumed to be reinvested at the required IRR (discount rate); this is considered to be a more conservative and consistent assumption by many analysts.[10]

One solution to these two IRR problems is to assume a reinvestment rate equal to the required IRR or some other, more realistic rate. Thus, annual cash flows (including sale proceeds) are equated with the original equity at the *modified* (*or adjusted*) *internal rate of return*. This MIRR is referred to as the *terminal-value IRR* by some analysts.

For instance, in our previous example, in which we had an investment of $100,000 and annual cash flows of $50,000 for three years, we calculated a true IRR of 23.38 percent (23.45% using interpolation methods). But what if our realistic reinvestment rate for projects of similar risk levels is only 15 percent, rather than 23.38 percent? What is the MIRR if we assume reinvestment at 15 percent? Obviously, the calculated IRR of 23.38 will fall to some number between itself and 15 percent, making the project somewhat less attractive:

END-OF-YEAR CASH FLOWS

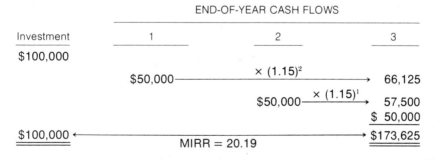

Investment	1	2	3
$100,000			
	$50,000 $\xrightarrow{\times \, (1.15)^2}$		66,125
		$50,000 $\xrightarrow{\times \, (1.15)^1}$	57,500
			$ 50,000
$100,000 $\longleftarrow$		$\longrightarrow$	$173,625
	MIRR = 20.19		

The MIRR procedure involves compounding forward to a terminal period (usually the year in which a property is sold) all the periodic cash flows at the required IRR (or some other appropriate rate), and then finding the compound interest rate that equates the terminal value and the initial investment cost. In the example, the $50,000 cash flows received in the first and second years are compounded forward at 15 percent for two and one years, respectively. The $50,000

[10] See Eugene F. Brigham, "Conflicts between NPV and IRR," *Fundamentals of Financial Management* (Hinsdale, Ill.: Dryden Press, 1978), pp. 277–284.

received in the third year is received at the terminal point, so no adjustment is needed. The *total terminal value* of the investment three years hence is therefore $173,625. The annual compound interest rate that causes the $100,000 investment to grow to $173,625 is 20.19 percent.

As we can see, the IRR falls from 23.38 percent to 20.19 percent when cash flows can be reinvested at only 15 percent instead of the calculated IRR. If the holding period of the investment were longer or the calculated IRR higher, the difference between the IRR and the MIRR would be greater. Nevertheless, the project is still acceptable, since the MIRR is above the required 15 percent return.

The Financial Management Rate of Return (FMRR)[11]   Suppose there is more than one reinvestment rate for cash flows received during the investment holding period. If cash flows must be invested at a "safe (low) rate" for a period until they can accumulate to an amount sufficient to reinvest in a real estate project earning a higher rate, then a more complicated reinvestment rate IRR model must be developed. Such a model has been developed by M. Chapman Findlay, III, and Stephen D. Messner and is sometimes referred to as the *Findlay-Messner rate of return.*[12]

The FMRR is a specialized form of the MIRR in which it is assumed that

1. Only cash flows after financing and taxes from the property under evaluation are considered.
2. Funds can be invested at any time in any amount at a safe after-tax rate of i_L, and withdrawn when desired.
3. Funds can also be invested in "run of the mill" real estate projects of comparable risk at an after-tax rate of i_R. Such funds must be in minimum quantities of R dollars, however, and may not be withdrawn during the period to meet other requirements.

From these assumptions the FMRR is computed as follows:

1. Any positive cash flows that precede in time negative flows are employed (including compounding at i_L) to offset such negative flows. All remaining negative flows, including the initial outlay, are discounted to the present at i_L and added to become $D_0{}^*$.
2. The remaining positive flows are compounded at i_L until they sum to R, and they are then compounded at i_R. Subsequent flows continue the process toward a second investment of R. The compounded sum of these flows at the end of the project's life (year n) becomes $T_n{}^*$.
3. The basic FMRR is then defined as follows:

$$\text{FMRR} = n\sqrt{\frac{T_n{}^*}{D_0{}^*}} - 1$$

[11] Stephen D. Messner and M. Chapman Findlay, III, "Real Estate Investment Analysis: IRR Versus FMRR," *The Real Estate Appraiser,* July–August 1975, pp. 5–20.
[12] Michael S. Young, "FMRR: A Clever Hoax," *The Appraisal Journal,* July 1979, pp. 359–369.

4. Modifications of this technique can also be employed to determine optimal holding periods, select among mutually exclusive investment alternatives, and even deal with simple cases of rationing. [13]

The FMRR technique is taught widely in investment courses throughout the country; furthermore, at least one study has demonstrated mathematically that the reinvestment rate must be considered a major determinant of a project's rate of return and risk, especially when a long holding period is anticipated. [14] On the other hand, the technique has been criticized as a measure of investment performance that bears "a striking resemblance to the development of ancient cosmology." [15] In short, both the FMRR and the MIRR are said to be cases of mathematical overkill. The investor might better spend his or her time worrying about the underlying economic and market assumptions of the analysis than worrying about multiple reinvestment rate assumptions that will rarely change an investment decision in the real world. As we have already indicated, the IRR (or PV) is only one of many pieces of information that will be used to make the investment decision. Too exclusive a focus on any single investment criterion is generally a mistake.

Summary

Present-value and internal-rate-of-return methods are adaptable to almost all income property situations. They can be utilized to evaluate cash flows on a before- or after-tax basis. They can be used to evaluate mortgage investments as well as equity investments. And they produce values that permit comparisons between projects and with other forms of investments.

The internal-rate-of-return approach seems to be preferred by real estate practitioners because (1) it is simple to understand and compute; (2) the calculated solution appears to be unique and unambiguous; (3) the measure is the "standard" among most financial institutions and has been widely used for mortgage loan rates, bond rates, and the like; and (4) the measure provides a solution in a convenient form—a rate—that can be readily used as the criterion for comparisons with alternative investments. [16] In contrast, the present-value approach is preferred by many financial analysts and theorists because of the more conservative reinvestment rate assumptions that underlie the model and because it is said to be more consistent with the investor's primary financial goal of long-run wealth maximization.

In the following sections we will see both approaches applied to income property analysis. Like most "tools," they must be applied properly and accurately if they are to benefit the investor.

---

[13] Guilford C. Babcock, M. Chapman Findlay, III, and Stephen D. Messner, "FMRR and Duration: Implications for Real Estate Investment Analysis," *AREUEA Journal,* Winter 1976, pp. 49–50.
[14] George W. Gau and Daniel B. Kohlhepp, "Reinvestment Rates and the Sensitivity of Rates of Return in Real Estate Investment," *AREUEA Journal,* Winter 1976, pp. 69–83.
[15] Young, p. 359.
[16] Messner and Findlay, p. 6.

DISCOUNTED CASH FLOW AFTER-TAX ANALYSIS

Discounted cash flow analysis focuses on valuation of the cash flows expected over some holding period of the investment. We generally consider three primary sources of after-tax cash flows:

1. Annual cash flow from operations (as measured previously).
2. Annual cash flow from tax savings (or taxes paid).
3. Cash flow from the sale of property after debts and capital gains taxes (reversion).

A fourth source, cash proceeds from refinancing the property, is also possible but is not generally considered in most cash flow projections.

The Aspen Wood Case*

To demonstrate a typical DCF analysis we turn once again to our Aspen Wood case. We are interested now in analyzing the effects on the property's total investment value and rate of return of increasing rentals and expenses, loan amortization, accelerated depreciation, investor tax considerations, price appreciation, transactions costs, and the time value of money.

The analysis incorporates the following assumptions:

1. The first-year gross possible income of $166,980 increases by 4 percent annually (compounded). There are 84 units; the average unit, approximately 659 square feet, brings in $165.65 of gross income monthly (including other income).
2. The vacancy and credit loss allowance is expected to be 5 percent of gross income.
3. Total operating expenses are estimated to be 40 percent of gross possible income during the first year of operations, or $66,792. Thereafter expenses increase at 7 percent per year (compounded).
4. The total cost of the project is $1 million. The land is valued at $100,000 and the improvements at $900,000. Since there are 55,356 leasable square feet in the building, the per-square-foot cost of the improvements is approximately $16.26.
5. A mortgage debt of $825,000 was negotiated at 7 1/2 percent for 28 years. This results in annual amortization payments (debt service) of $70,574 and a mortgage constant of 8.55 percent. Recall that our time frame is 1974 and the loan wraps around two underlying mortgage notes that bear interest at 6 1/2 percent and 7 1/4 percent, respectively.
6. The improvements will be depreciated at the 125 percent declining-balance rate, and the remaining economic life of the improvements is 22 years. This economic life is an estimate of the average useful life of the building

---

* In other chapters the Aspen Wood case is presented as a separate section. Here, we follow Aspen Wood as part of the chapter itself.

components, which have in fact been separated and individually depreciated by the investors, as we will see in the next chapter. (Under the provisions of the Economic Recovery Tax Act of 1981 the depreciation deductions would approximate the 175 percent declining-balance rate, and the allowed cost-recovery period (useful life) would be 15 years for the building and 5 years for personal property.)

7. The project value is expected to grow at 3 percent compounded annually, based on the original $1 million cost of the project. A selling expense (brokerage commissions and closing costs) of 5 percent is anticipated.

8. The investor's marginal income is taxed at 50 percent, and capital gains on the sale of the property are taxed at 25 percent. While the actual capital gains rate would be 20 percent under the ordinary method using the 60 percent exclusion rule, the investor anticipates some rise in tax bracket during the year when the gain from sale is reported. Also, there may be some minimum tax on the gain. Consequently, the investor prefers to use the more conservative 25 percent effective capital rate for the financial analysis.

9. An after-tax (internal) rate of return on equity investment of 18 percent is sought. This is the IRR necessary to induce the investor to commit equity funds.

This analysis will provide information on the most likely consequences of the investment. As illustrated in Exhibit 11– 1, our cash flow model incorporates five sets of input variables: investment outlays, operations, financing, reversion, and tax assumptions. The output of the analysis includes annual cash flow projections, discounted cash flow information, and various types of rate-of-return, risk, and assumption base information. Assumption base information consists of annual financial ratios that are used to test the underlying economic and market assumptions and relationships that have been presumed in the analysis but not explicitly tested.

Calculation of Cash Flow Data

The seven-year cash flow analysis illustrated in the following sections has been generated for us by a computer model known as RE001.[17] This model is one of many that are available to students and practitioners for use on mini, desktop, and main-frame computers. Section 1 (Exhibit 11– 2) is simply a recap of the data already given.

---

[17] RE001 is a basic discounted cash flow computer model developed by Stephen A. Pyhrr at the University of Texas, Austin. The computer software is available from the Texas Real Estate Research Center at Texas A&M University, College Station, Texas 77843. The monograph that describes this model and the advanced model, RE004, is also available from the Research Center. The monograph, authored by Stephen A. Pyhrr and James A. Baker, is entitled *Computer Models for the Financial Analysis and Tax Planning of Income-Producing Real Estate Investments,* TRERC Technical Monograph no. 2. These models are used in real estate courses at numerous universities, and by practitioners throughout the nation.

EXHIBIT 11-1.   Project Analysis—Discounted Cash Flow Return Model

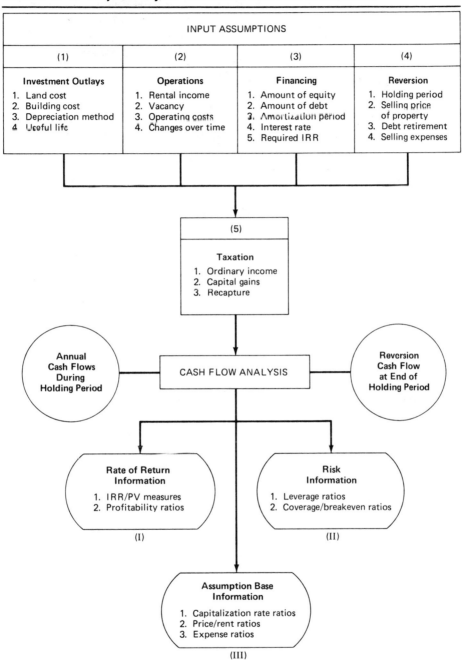

EXHIBIT 11-2.   Aspen Wood Apartments: Computer Analysis—Section 1

1. RECAPITULATION OF INPUT DATA (SEPTEMBER 1974)

1. Type property (0. = residential, 1. = commercial)	1.
2. Total land cost	100,000.00
3. Number of units in project	84.
4. Average square feet per unit	659.00
5. Square foot cost of all improvements	16.26
6. Depreciable life of improvements (years)	22.00
7. Depreciation method	1.25
1.00 = straight line 1.75 = 175 percent	
1.25 = 125 percent 2.00 = double declining	
1.50 = 150 percent	
8. Average monthly income per unit	165.65
9. Expected occupancy rate	.9500
10. Operating cost (percent of gross possible income)	.4000
11. Annual growth rate of gross possible income	.0400
12. Annual growth rate of operating costs	.0700
13. Annual growth rate of property value	.0300
14. Holding period (cash flow projection period)	7.
15. Selling expense (percent)	.0500
16. Ordinary income tax rate	.5000
17. Capital gains tax rate	.2500
18. Required rate of return (IRR) on equity	.1800
19. Amount of loan 1	825,000.00
20. Effective interest rate on loan 1	.07500
21. Amortization term of loan 1	28.00
22. Does this project involve secondary financing	no

Property Information (Section 2)   This section (Exhibit 11–3) shows our balance sheet as of the purchase date. Also calculated is the *leverage position* as of the date of purchase, which is simply the total debt ($825,000) divided by the total property cost ($1 million). The project has a debt ratio of 82.5 percent. The equity investment of $175,000 thus represents 17.5 percent of the total property cost.

EXHIBIT 11-3.   Aspen Wood Apartments: Computer Analysis—Section 2

2. PROPERTY INFORMATION

Total square feet of improvements   55,356

Total property cost $1,000,000

Assets		Liabilities and Net Worth	
Land	$ 100,000	Total debt	$ 825,000
Building	900,000	Equity invested	175,000
Total	$1,000,000	Total	$1,000,000

Leverage position (debt/property cost) = .825

EXHIBIT 11–4.   Aspen Wood Apartments: Computer Analysis—Section 3

3. DEPRECIATION INFORMATION

Year	Beginning Basis	Depreciation Claimed	Undepreciated Balance	Straight-line Basis	Excess Depreciation
1	900,000	51,136	848,864	859,091	10,227
2	848,864	48,231	800,633	818,182	17,549
3	800,633	45,490	755,142	777,273	22,130
4	755,142	42,906	712,236	736,364	24,127
5	712,236	40,468	671,768	695,455	23,686
6*	671,768	39,516	632,253	654,545	22,293
7	632,253	39,516	592,737	613,636	20,899

* Straight-line depreciation amount exceeds accelerated depreciation amount, switched to straight-line depreciation.

Depreciation Information (Section 3)   (See Exhibit 11–4.) The depreciation coefficient used to calculate annual depreciation expense is the following:

$$\text{Depreciation coefficient} = \frac{1}{\text{useful life}} \times \text{depreciation method}$$

$$= \frac{1}{22} \times 1.25$$

$$= .056818$$

Depreciation for each year is calculated by multiplying the depreciation coefficient by the *beginning basis*. For example, the amount of *depreciation claimed* in year 1 is $900,000 × .056818 = $51,136. The beginning basis is $900,000 and declines each year by the amount of *depreciation claimed* the previous year. The *undepreciated balance* at the end of the year is found by deducting *depreciation claimed* from the *beginning basis*. At the end of year 1, for example, the *undepreciated balance* is $900,000 − $51,136 = $848,864. Note that each year the depreciation declines until it becomes advantageous to switch to straight-line depreciation, which occurs in year 6.[18]

---

[18] Each year the computer calculates the actual amounts of straight-line and accelerated depreciation. When the amount of straight-line depreciation, which changes each year as the remaining basis and useful life change, exceeds the amount of accelerated depreciation, the depreciation method is changed. A simple formula can also be used to indicate when an investor should switch from declining-balance to straight-line depreciation:

$$CP = n - (n \div f)$$

where CP = crossover point (period) in years;
   n = total useful life;
   f = the declining-balance factor as a ratio of 100 (1.25, 1.50, 2.00)

The optimum crossover point is the optimum time at which to switch from the declining-balance method, assuming a zero salvage value. For further details see J. Warren Higgins and David Scribner, Jr., "A Simple Formula for Switching from Declining Balance to Straight-Line When Depreciating Real Property," *The Real Estate Appraiser*, July-August 1976, pp. 36– 37.

The *straight-line basis* calculation is made to determine the amount of *excess depreciation*, which is said to be *recaptured* and is subject to taxation at ordinary income tax rates. The *straight-line basis* is calculated by taking 1/22 of the *beginning basis* (1/22 × $900,000 = $40,909) and then subtracting this result each year from the *straight-line basis*. For example, *straight-line basis* at the end of year 1 is $900,000 − $40,909 = $859,091; at the end of year 2, $859,091 − $40,909 = $818,182; and at the end of year 3, $818,182 − $40,909 = $777,273.

The amount of *excess depreciation* each year is simply the difference between the *straight-line basis* and the *undepreciated balance* for that year.

Impact of the 1981 Tax Act. If the Aspen Wood property had been purchased *after* December 31, 1980, the building could be depreciated according to statutory percentages that approximate the 175 percent declining-balance method over a recovery period (useful life) of 15 years. Qualifying personal property (e.g., furnishings) could be depreciated according to statutory percentages that approximate the 150 percent declining-balance method over a recovery period of 5 years. Using a basic DCF computer model, such as the one shown, in which only a single depreciation method is permitted, the analyst can input a weighted-average method and recovery period if both real and personal property components are present; the result will *approximate* the actual depreciation schedules for the two components. These concepts and tax provisions will be explained and discussed further in Chapter 13.

Loan Information (Section 4)   (See Exhibit 11–5.) The amortization payment of $70,574 is calculated by multiplying the mortgage constant (8.55442%, shown as 8.55% in the output) by the loan amount ($825,000). Allocations are made each year to interest and principal, but are based on monthly payments (this assumes monthly compounding). The *remaining principal* is calculated by taking

---

EXHIBIT 11–5.   Aspen Wood Apartments: Computer Analysis—Section 4

---

4. LOAN INFORMATION

Loan 1 information

Amount	$825,000
Rate	.0750
Term	28.00
Mortgage constant	.0855

Year	Amortization Payment	Interest Expense	Amortization of Principal	Remaining Principal	Effective Mortgage Constant
1	70,574	61,570	9,004	815,996	.08649
2	70,574	60,871	9,703	806,293	.08753
3	70,574	60,117	10,457	795,836	.08868
4	70,574	59,306	11,268	784,568	.08995
5	70,574	58,431	12,143	772,425	.09137
6	70,574	57,488	13,086	759,339	.09294
7	70,574	56,472	14,102	745,237	.09470

the amount of *remaining principal* at the end of the previous year and deducting the *amortization of principal* during the current year. For example, *remaining principal* at the end of the year 1 is $825,000 − $9,004 = $815,996; and at the end of year 2, $815,996 − $9,703 = $806,293. Note that the year 1 calculation begins with the original loan amount of $825,000. Various methods of calculating amortization schedules are illustrated in Chapter 14.

The *effective mortgage constant* is calculated by the following formula:

$$\text{Effective mortgage constant} = \frac{\text{amortization payment}}{\text{remaining principal}}$$

While the mortgage constant is originally 8.55 percent (70,574 ÷ 825,000), it increases to 9.47 percent (70,574 ÷ 745,237) in year 7 as the loan is paid down from $825,000 to $745,237. Thus, the effective cost of borrowing rises for the equity investor as equity build-up (loan amortization) takes place.

Note that, like depreciation, interest deductions decrease as the loan is paid down, and that this, as well as declining depreciation deductions, results in loss of tax shelter benefits.

Cash Flow Analysis (Section 5) (See Exhibit 11–6.) The calculation of net operating income, columns A–E, is self-explanatory.

Observe the changes in net operating income over the projection period. NOI increases each year despite the fact that operating expenses are increasing at 7 percent while income is increasing at only 4 percent. This somewhat surprising result is not intuitively obvious to most people. But the explanation is quite simple: 7 percent of the operating expenses (a relatively low dollar amount) is less than 4 percent of gross possible income (a relatively high dollar amount). However, the *rate* of increase of NOI is *decreasing* each year. Eventually, as the expense ratio rises above a certain point, 7 percent increases in expenses will be greater than 4 percent increases in gross income, and NOI will begin to decrease. This is expected as a property gets older, and will usually occur until a property renovation is undertaken.

Taxable income (column H). This is calculated by deducting depreciation and interest expense from the NOI estimate each year. In this case we generate tax losses (negative taxable income) for five years and thus can shelter other income earned by the equity investor. In addition, all cash flows generated by the project (column I) are being sheltered as long as tax losses occur.

Equity cash flow before tax (column I). This is computed by deducting the amortization payment from the NOI estimate. For example, in year 1 the cash flow before tax is $91,839 − $70,574 = $21,265; in year 2 it is $93,509 − $70,574 = $22,935; and so on.

Equity cash flow after tax (column J). This is different from the cash flow before tax by the amount of tax saving or taxes paid. In our example, during the first five years tax losses generate a tax saving equal to the tax rate *times* the amount of tax losses. For example, in year 1 the tax saving is 50% × $20,867 =

EXHIBIT 11–6.   Aspen Wood Apartments: Computer Analysis—Section 5

5. CASH FLOW ANALYSIS

Year	(A) Gross Possible Income	(B) Vacancy Allowance	(C) Gross Effective Income (A − B)	(D) Operating Expenses	(E) Net Operating Income (C − D)
1	166,980	8,349	158,631	66,792	91,839
2	173,659	8,683	164,976	71,467	93,509
3	180,606	9,030	171,575	76,470	95,105
4	187,830	9,391	178,438	81,823	96,615
5	195,343	9,767	185,576	87,551	98,025
6	203,157	10,158	192,999	93,679	99,320
7	211,283	10,564	200,719	100,237	100,482

Year	(F) Interest Expense	(G) Depreciation Expense	(H) Taxable Income (E − F − G)	(I) Equity Cash Flow Before Tax (E − Amor. payment)	(J) Equity Cash Flow After Tax [I − (tax rate × H)]
1	61,570	51,136	−20,867	21,265	31,699
2	60,871	48,231	−15,593	22,935	30,731
3	60,117	45,490	−10,503	24,531	29,783
4	59,306	42,906	−5,596	26,041	28,839
5	58,431	40,468	−874	27,451	27,888
6	57,488	39,516	2,316	28,746	27,588
7	56,472	39,516	4,494	29,908	27,661

Year	(K) Cash Flow to Total Capital After Tax	(L) Cumulative Cash Flow Before Tax	(M) Cumulative Cash Flow After Tax	(N) Property Value at End of Each Year
1	71,488	21,265	31,699	1,030,000
2	70,870	44,200	62,430	1,060,900
3	70,298	68,731	92,212	1,092,727
4	69,761	94,773	121,052	1,125,509
5	69,247	122,224	148,940	1,159,274
6	69,418	150,970	176,528	1,194,052
7	69,999	180,878	204,189	1,229,874

$10,434. Added to the $21,265 cash flow from operations, the after-tax cash flow is $31,699. In year 2 the tax loss declines to $15,593 and the cash flow before tax rises to $22,935 as a result of rising net income, but the *net result is a decrease* in the cash flow after tax to $30,731 [$22,935 + (.50 × $15,593)].

Of course, the underlying assumption in computing tax savings in this manner is that the investor has a substantial amount of taxable income from other sources to shelter and that these *artificial accounting losses* can be applied against the investor's other income, which is taxable at the rate assumed. In practice tax rates are difficult to estimate because all items of income and loss affect the marginal tax bracket. A wealthy individual may have numerous projects that completely shelter income from other sources, and a substantial loss from a particular project can substantially lower the marginal tax bracket below that assumed in the analysis.

Under these conditions, what are the proper tax bracket assumptions for analyzing any one specific project in the investor's portfolio? We will address this problem in Chapter 13.

After year 5 *taxable income* (column H) turns positive and the investor must pay taxes instead of receiving a tax saving. From this year on, unless the project is restructured to increase the tax shelter, *equity cash flow after tax* (column J) will be less than *equity cash flow before tax* (column I). In the example shown, the decline in tax shelter outweighs the increase in NOI from increasing rentals each year. The final, *bottom-line* result is a declining cash flow figure: *Equity cash flow after tax* declines from $31,699 in year 1 to $27,661 in year 7.

Cash flow to total capital after tax (column K). This is computed in exactly the same way as *equity cash flow after tax,* but the former eliminates all leverage factors; it can be called the unleveraged cash flow after tax. If the project were 100 percent equity financed, *equity cash flow after tax* would be identical to *cash flow to total capital after tax*. The reason for computing this cash flow figure is to show the unleveraged after-tax return on the total capital investment. In the internal rate-of-return analysis, it will be used to calculate the unleveraged IRR on the $1 million total capital investment, which is useful for comparison purposes (and certainly would be an important rate-of-return figure to institutions that buy un-leveraged properties). The formula used to calculate the *cash flow to total capital after tax* is the following:

Cash flow to total capital = equity cash flow after tax
    + annual amortization payment
    − (ordinary tax rate × interest expense)

For example, in year 1 the cash flow to total capital after tax is $31,699 + $70,574 − (.50 × $61,570) = $71,488; in year 2 it is $30,731 + $70,574 − (.50 × $60,871) = $70,870; and so on.

Cumulative cash flow before tax and after tax (columns L and M). These are calculated by adding the annual cash flow figures in columns I and J for the number of years specified. These estimates are useful for determining when the equity investor gets the *payback*. On a before-tax basis, we will get our original $175,000 back during the seventh year. On an after-tax basis, our payback occurs during the sixth year. Some investors use this measure as one criterion for evaluating the investment. For example, an investor might reject a project if it has a payback greater than five years.

Property value at end of each year (column N). This is the final set of computations made in section 5 of the cash flow analysis. Each year the property value increases at a specified compounded annual rate based on the original total property cost. For example, at the end of year 1 the property value is assumed to be $1,030,000 [$1,000,000 × (1.03)^1]; at the end of year 2 the property value is assumed to rise to $1,060,900 [$1,000,000 × (1.03)^2]; and so on. The annual increase in property value is assumed at 3 percent—somewhat less than the increase in rents and expenses for reasons to be explained later.

Calculation of Proceeds from Sale of Property (Section 6)   This is also called the *reversion* cash flow and is shown in Exhibit 11–7. The selling expense is calculated at 5 percent of the selling price. The property is sold at the end of year 7 for $1,229,874. The remaining debt principal at this time is $745,237 (Section 4, Exhibit 11–5) and taxes on the sale of the property amount to $124,136.

The *tax on the sale of the property* is computed by adding the capital gain tax to the ordinary income tax on excess depreciation. The four-step process for computing tax liability on the sale of this property is shown in Exhibit 11–8. The capital gain rate (25%) is applied to the difference between the *net selling price* and the *straight-line basis,* while the ordinary rate (50%) is applied to the difference between the *straight-line basis* and the *accelerated basis.*

The cash flow that remains in the investor's pocket after all has been said and done is $299,007. We assume that it is received at the end of year 7 (in its entirety) when the property is sold. This cash flow will be used in computing the internal rate of return and present value of the investor's equity, and is indeed the largest cash flow received during the holding period in this example. In an inflationary economy in which demand for real estate is strong, the reversion cash flow is the single most important factor affecting the internal rate of return and present value of the project.

Internal Rate-of-Return and Present-Value Analysis (Section 7)   So far, our equity investor expects to receive a total of eight cash flows during the seven-year holding period (Exhibit 11–9).

Present value. To find the *total present value of equity investment* (Exhibit 11–10) we take the equity cash flows shown in Exhibit 11–9, multiply them by the present-value coefficients for each year at 18 percent (the required IRR), and add up the resulting present-value figures. The sum will be $206,895.

EXHIBIT 11–7. Aspen Wood Apartments: Computer Analysis—Section 6

---

6. CALCULATION OF NET PROCEEDS FROM SALE OF PROPERTY

Selling price of property at end of holding period	$1,229,874
Less: Selling expense	61,494
Less: Remaining debt principal	745,237
Net proceeds from sale of property (before tax)	423,143
Less: Tax on sale of property at end of holding period	124,136
Net proceeds from sale of property (after tax)	$299,007

EXHIBIT 11–8.   Computation of Taxes on Sale of Property

---

1. COMPUTE BASIS OF PROPERTY USING 25% METHOD (END OF YEAR 7)

Undepreciated balance of improvements	$592,737
Plus: land value	100,000
Accelerated basis of property	$692,737

2. COMPUTE BASIS OF PROPERTY USING STRAIGHT-LINE METHOD (END OF YEAR 7)

Undepreciated balance of improvements	$613,636
Plus: land value	100,000
Straight-line basis of property	$713,636

3. COMPUTE NET SELLING PRICE

Gross selling price	$1,229,874
Less: selling expenses (5%)	61,494
Net selling price	$1,168,580

Tax Situation Graphically

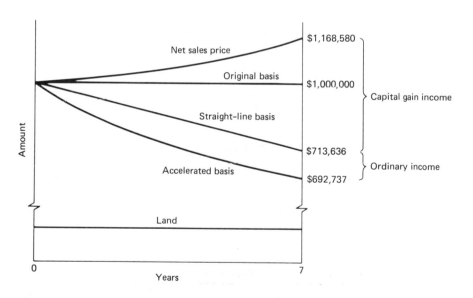

4. COMPUTE TOTAL TAX ON SALE OF PROPERTY

Capital gains tax = ($1,168,580 − $713,636) × .25 =	$113,686
Ordinary income tax = ($713,637 − $692,737) × .50 =	10,450
Total tax on sale of property	$124,136

EXHIBIT 11-9. Aspen Wood Apartments: Summary of Project Cash Flows

Year	Equity ($175,000) Cash Flow After Tax	Total Capital ($1,000,000) Cash Flow After Tax
1	$ 31,699	$ 71,488
2	30,731	70,870
3	29,783	70,298
4	28,839	69,761
5	27,888	69,247
6	27,588	69,418
7	27,661	69,999
7	$299,007	$1,044,244*

* The reversion in this case simply eliminates the debt principal repayment of $745,237. Tax liability is not affected by eliminating leverage factors. Consequently, this cash flow can be calculated by deducting selling expenses and taxes from the selling price ($1,044,244 = $1,229,874 − $61,494 − $124,136).

Shown mathematically, the result is as follows:

$$\text{Present value} = \frac{\text{cash flow}}{(1 + \text{RIRR})^1} + \frac{\text{cash flow}}{(1 + \text{RIRR})^2} + \cdots + \frac{\text{cash flow}}{(1 + \text{RIRR})^n}$$

$$= \frac{\$31,699}{(1 + .18)^1} + \frac{\$30,731}{(1 + .18)^2} + \frac{\$29,783}{(1 + .18)^3} + \frac{\$28,838}{(1 + .18)^4}$$

$$+ \frac{\$27,888}{(1 + .18)^5} + \frac{\$27,588}{(1 + .18)^6} + \frac{\$27,661}{(1 + .18)^7} + \frac{\$299,007}{(1 + .18)^7}$$

$$= \$206,895$$

Next, if we add the original mortgage balance (which already is a present-value figure) to the present value of the equity, we arrive at an estimate of the total project value. The total project value is therefore $206,895 + $825,000 = $1,031,895.

The project is acceptable, using the present-value criterion, because its value ($1,031,895) is greater than its cost ($1,000,000). Likewise, the *equity value*

EXHIBIT 11-10. Aspen Wood Apartments: Computer Analysis—Section 7

7. INTERNAL RATE OF RETURN—PRESENT VALUE ANALYSIS

Total present value of equity investment	$ 206,895
Plus: original mortgage balance	825,000
Total project value	$1,031,895

Internal rate of return
On total capital invested   .0820
On initial owners equity   .2214

($206,895) is greater than the *equity cost* ($175,000). Comparing *equity value* to *cost equity,* the resulting *net present value* is positive and the *profitability index* is greater than 1. Thus, the investor will exceed the minimum criterion of an 18 percent IRR by investing in this project.

Internal rate of return. Since the project cost is less than the project value, we know that the actual IRR is greater than 18 percent. To compute it, we must use the trial-and-error process described previously and the *equity cash flows after tax* just given. If we do this, we find the IRR to be about 22 percent. Using the same trial-and-error process, but to a much higher degree of accuracy, the computer calculated the IRR to be 22.14 percent. At 22.14 percent, the *present value* of the equity cash flows *just equals the cost* to acquire the equity ($175,000).

If we performed an IRR calculation on the total capital invested ($1,000,000) using the cash flows shown previously, we would find that rate to be 8.2 percent:

$$\text{Investment cost} = \frac{CF_1}{(1 + \text{IRR})^1} + \frac{CF_2}{(1 + \text{IRR})^2} + \cdots + \frac{CF_n}{(1 + \text{IRR})^n}$$

$$\$1,000,000 = \frac{\$71,488}{(1 + .082)^1} + \frac{\$70,870}{(1 + .082)^2} + \frac{\$70,298}{(1 + .082)^3}$$

$$+ \frac{\$69,761}{(1 + .082)^4} + \frac{\$69,247}{(1 + .082)^5} + \frac{\$69,418}{(1 + .082)^6}$$

$$+ \frac{\$69,999}{(1 + .082)^7} + \frac{\$1,044,244}{(1 + .082)^7}$$

The 8.2 percent rate is the only rate that results in a present value of $1 million; thus, by definition we have found the IRR on total capital invested.

It is important that the unleveraged IRR is substantially *below* the leveraged (equity) IRR. That is, the effect of using leverage here is to raise the after-tax IRR from 8 percent to 22 percent. Assuming that we actually receive the equity cash flows projected, a 22% equity IRR is equivalent to putting money in a savings and loan association or bank, earning a 44 percent interest rate compounded annually, and then paying the federal government taxes equal to 50 percent of this return. Said differently, it is equivalent to putting money in a tax-free municipal bond that pays a 22 percent annual interest rate.

FINANCIAL RATIO ANALYSIS

In section 8 of our DCF analysis we calculate data for thirteen financial ratios. These are simple accounting ratios, calculated annually, with no consideration given to the time value of money. The ratios are shown in Exhibit 11–11.

We are interested in using financial ratios for three primary purposes. First, they tell us more about the nature of the *profitability* of the project—that is, how much of the IRR (relatively speaking) is from cash flow from operations, from tax savings, from equity buildup, and from appreciation—and the trends in profitabil-

EXHIBIT 11–11. Aspen Wood Apartments: Computer Analysis—Section 8

8. FINANCIAL RATIO ANALYSIS

Profitability Ratios

Year	(A) NOI/Total Property Cost	(B) Cash Flow Before Tax/ Initial Equity	(C) Cash Flow After Tax/ Initial Equity	(D) Cash Flow After Tax + Equity Build-up/ Initial Equity	(E) Cash Flow After Tax + Equity Build-up + Appreciation/ Initial Equity
1	.092	.122	.181	.233	.404
2	.094	.131	.176	.231	.408
3	.095	.140	.170	.230	.412
4	.097	.149	.165	.229	.417
5	.098	.157	.159	.229	.422
6	.099	.164	.158	.232	.431
7	.100	.171	.158	.239	.443

Risk Ratios

Year	(F) Debt Coverage Ratio	(G) Break-even Point	(H) Loan Balance (End of Year) as a Percent of — Original Cost	(H) Loan Balance (End of Year) as a Percent of — Property Value
1	1.301	.823	.816	.792
2	1.325	.818	.806	.760
3	1.348	.814	.796	.728
4	1.369	.811	.785	.697
5	1.389	.809	.772	.666
6	1.407	.809	.759	.636
7	1.424	.808	.745	.606

Assumption Base Ratios

Year	(I) NOI to Property Value	(J) Gross Rent Multiplier	(K) Operating Expense Ratio — Gross Possible	(K) Operating Expense Ratio — Gross Effective
1	.089	6.168	.400	.421
2	.088	6.109	.412	.433
3	.087	6.050	.423	.446
4	.086	5.992	.436	.459
5	.085	5.935	.448	.472
6	.083	5.877	.461	.485
7	.082	5.821	.474	.499

ity over time.[19] Second, they give us additional information about the *riskiness* of the project and trends in the future; included are ratios that help us analyze our leverage position each year and indicate when refinancing may be advantageous. Third, financial ratios are used to test the *underlying assumptions* used in the analysis, and to suggest when we have used assumptions that are inconsistent with conditions in the marketplace.

Profitability Ratios

NOI to Total Property Cost This ratio is the same as the ROR profitability measure described in Chapter 10, but it is calculated each year. As discussed earlier, whenever this ratio is less than the ROE (and therefore greater than the initial mortgage constant, K), a *positive leverage* situation from operations exists, and vice versa.

Year 1	91,839/1,000,000 = .092
Year 4	96,615/1,000,000 = .097
Year 7	100,482/1,000,000 = .100

Our analysis here shows the ROR rising from 9.2 to 10 percent in year 7, with the basic productivity of the property rising each year relative to the total capital investment. Because the initial mortgage constant is 8.55 percent, a positive leverage situation exists in each year; also, the ROE is greater than the ROR each year, as the following calculations show.

Cash Flow Before Tax to Initial Equity This ratio is identical to the ROE profitability measured used in Chapter 10, but it too is calculated each year. The cash flow increases each year and rises to 17.1 percent in year 7, indicating a very profitable situation for the equity investor; the initial level and trend are favorable.

Year 1	21,265/175,000 = .122
Year 4	26,041/175,000 = .149
Year 7	29,908/175,000 = .171

Cash Flow After Tax to Initial Equity This profitability ratio takes the cash flow before tax, adds the amount of tax saving (or deducts the amount of taxes paid), and then compares the result to the initial equity invested. Alternately, it is the amount of *cash flow after tax* divided by the *initial equity investment*. It is sometimes referred to as the *ROE after tax*.

Year 1	31,699/175,000 = .181
Year 4	28,839/175,000 = .165
Year 7	27,661/175,000 = .158

---

[19] The investor should not attempt to use ratios as substitutes for the IRR measure. A discussion of this subject is provided by Kenneth M. Lusht, "Measuring Rates of Return: Two Rules of Thumb v. Internal Rate," *The Appraisal Journal*, April 1978, pp. 245–256.

Our analysis shows that cash flow *after tax* is decreasing each year because the declining tax shelter outweighs the effects of increasing cash flow from operations. Thus, while cash flow before tax *increases* from 12.2 percent to 17.1 percent in year 7, cash flow after tax *decreases* from 18.1 percent to 15.8 percent. After year 5 the investor must pay taxes (instead of receiving a tax saving) and the after-tax return falls below the before-tax return. Whenever taxable income is positive, the cash flow after tax will be less than cash flow before tax, and vice versa.

This ratio helps the investor understand the net impact of tax shelter items on the after-tax return, and can be used to indicate when a sale or refinancing of the property should be considered in order to achieve tax shelter objectives. For example, some equity investors would consider refinancing and/or selling after year 5, when taxable income turns positive and tax liabilities result.

Cash Flow After Tax Plus Equity Buildup to Initial Equity   This ratio adds to the preceding one the impact of equity buildup (loan amortization). While the cash flow after tax is decreasing each year, the equity buildup is increasing because a larger part of each amortization payment represents amortization of principal.

Year 1   (31,699 + 9,004)/175,000 = .233
Year 4   (28,839 + 11,268)/175,000 = .229
Year 7   (27,661 + 14,102)/175,000 = .239

The net effect is that profitability, measured this way, decreases for four years and then levels off and starts increasing. Obviously, the effects of declining tax shelter are greater than the effect of increasing equity buildup in the early years. Then the situation is reversed. For all practical purposes, we might say that profitability remains fairly stable at 23 percent during the holding period, using this measure of return.

It is important to recognize that while the equity buildup adds to the investor's return, it is an unrealized gain until the time of sale or refinancing; consequently, the time value of money is ignored in its measurement.[20] The next ratio can be criticized for the same reason. Nevertheless, the ratio just presented can help us understand the *relative* impact of tax shelter and equity buildup on the investor's rate of return.

Cash Flow After Tax Plus Equity Buildup Plus Appreciation to Initial Equity   This ratio adds to the preceding one the impact of property value appreciation (or depreciation) that occurs each year. Property value appreciation is calculated as the difference between the property value at the end of the year and the value at the beginning of the year, as shown in column N of Exhibit 11–6.

[20] This point raises an interesting question. If "equity buildup" is not realized until the time of sale or refinancing, neither is the return of the *original* equity, on which these ratios are based. Thus, in making these ratio calculations we presume that the original equity investment *will in fact* be realized. If it is not, then the ratios do not fully represent a return *on* the original equity investment, and they may be misleading.

Year 1   [31,699 + 9,004 + (1,030,000 − 1,000,000)]/175,000 = .404
Year 4   [28,839 + 11,268 + (1,125,509 − 1,092,727)]/175,000 = .417
Year 7   [27,661 + 14,102 + (1,229,874 − 1,194,052)]/175,000 = .443

Measured in this fashion, the total return rises from 40.4 percent to 44.3 percent in year 7, as contrasted with a 23 percent return before this factor is included. Property value increases add 17−20 percent to the investor's rate of return and further offset the effect of declining tax shelters.

We should note that this return measure makes no deductions for taxes and expenses resulting from the sale of the property. If, however, we deducted these expenses and then applied the time-value-of-money discount, we would arrive at our IRR on equity of 22 percent. Thus, our 40−44 percent *accounting rate of return* over seven years falls to a 22 percent *true yield* when we add these important economic variables.

Risk Ratios

Debt Coverage Ratio   Analysis of the debt coverage ratio indicates decreasing risk and increasing project liquidity over the seven-year holding period. Each year, as net income increases, debt service remains constant.

Year 1   91,839/70,574 = 1.301
Year 4   96,615/70,574 = 1.369
Year 7   100,472/70,574 = 1.424

Break-even Point   Like the debt coverage ratio, the break-even point is used to analyze the risk and liquidity profile of a project. Risk is said to decrease as liquidity increases. Over each year of the seven-year projection period, a lower occupancy level is necessary to pay operating expenses and service the debt. In our example both the initial level and the trend of the break-even point are favorable.

Year 1   (66,792 + 70,574)/166,980 = .823
Year 4   (81,823 + 70,574)/187,830 = .811
Year 7   (100,237 + 70,574)/211,283 = .808

Loan Balance as a Percent of Original Cost and Property Value   These two leverage ratios allow us to measure the impact of a declining loan balance relative to our original cost and property value.

Remaining Principal/Original Cost
Year 1   815,996/1,000,000 = .816
Year 4   784,568/1,000,000 = .785
Year 7   745,237/1,000,000 = .745

Remaining Principal/Property Value
Year 1   815,996/1,030,000 = .792
Year 4   784,568/1,125,509 = .697
Year 7   745,237/1,229,874 = .606

On a cost basis, our leverage ratio declines to about 75 percent in year 7; on a value basis, to about 61 percent. To the extent that the loan is a decreasing percentage of either cost or value, the riskiness of the investment tends to decrease over time. In addition, the potential benefits of refinancing after the property has been held for a number of years is readily apparent from the ratios.

Assumption Base Ratios

NOI to Property Value   This critical ratio is used to test the underlying assumptions used in the analysis. It is better known to students of appraisal as the *overall capitalization rate*. Specifically, this ratio tests our assumption of increasing property value over time. It is measured by dividing the NOI (column E) by the property value (column N) each year (from Exhibit 11–6).

Year 1	91,839/1,030,000 = .089
Year 4	96,615/1,125,509 = .086
Year 7	100,482/1,229,874 = .082

Our analysis shows the capitalization rate falling from 8.9 percent to 8.2 percent in year 7. This might be a realistic assumption in a period of rising inflation rates (as explained in Chapter 7) but is highly suspect in a period of stable or falling inflation rates when capitalization rates tend to rise. Also, as a property gets older and uncertainties increase, this ratio tends to increase to reflect the increasing risk associated with most older properties. We probably have property value rising too fast relative to net income. If this is true, then we have seriously overestimated the IRR on equity and total capital, and any other return measure that includes capital appreciation. We might try another analysis with a more conservative property value assumption, or we might want to reassess our assumptions affecting NOI increases each year.

The capitalization rate data should be compared to data from comparable property sales. This information can be obtained from local appraisers. Such comparisons will enable the investor to determine whether the assumptions used in the analysis are realistic or whether adjustments should be made to the assumption base and the analysis redone. Remember that the output information is only as good as the input assumptions.

Gross Rent Multiplier   Like the expense ratios, the primary purpose of the gross rent multiplier is to test the underlying assumptions of the analysis. The ratio is calculated by dividing the property value at the end of each year by the gross possible income from the corresponding year.

Year 1	1,030,000/166,980 = 6.168
Year 4	1,125,509/187,830 = 5.992
Year 7	1,229,874/211,283 = 5.821

Generally, in a stable economic climate we might expect this ratio to decline over time as a structure gets older and becomes more expensive to maintain. An investor should be willing to pay more to acquire a dollar of rent from a new structure than from an older structure, other factors remaining the same. Since most experienced income property appraisers keep extensive data on gross rent multipliers, it is easy to make comparisons to see if the forecasts are realistic. If not, the analysis should be redone.

The assumption on property value increases has a very substantial impact on the equity investor's IRR. We have already questioned the validity of our property value appreciation assumption. In fact, comparative sales data from 1974 (the date of the Aspen Wood analysis shown in the example) suggests that a 5.5– 5.8, rather than 6.1, gross rent multiplier in year 1 might have been more appropriate for the most likely data set.

Operating Expense Ratios Two operating expense ratios are calculated; one based on gross possible income, the other on gross effective income. These ratios are used primarily as comparative tools to test the underlying assumptions. As a project ages, the expense ratio usually increases, and the ratio that results should be consistent with ratios experienced by operators of comparable properties and with the statistics published by property owners' associations throughout the nation.

Operating Expenses/	*Operating Expenses/*
Gross Possible Income	*Gross Effective Income*
Year 1 66,792/166,980 = .400	Year 1 66,792/158,631 = .421
Year 4 81,823/187,830 = .436	Year 4 81,823/178,438 = .459
Year 7 100,237/211,283 = .474	Year 7 100,237/200,719 = .499

The many data sources that may be useful to investors in analyzing specific property types are discussed in Part IV.

SUMMARY

The concepts and mathematics of discounted cash flow and financial ratio analysis were developed in this chapter. We began by reviewing time-value-of-money concepts, and saw how present-value and internal-rate-of-return models are logical extensions of time-value-of-money and compound interest formulas. While the PV and IRR models usually result in the same accept or reject investment decision, they can rank projects differently owing to their differing assumptions about reinvestment rates. Various analysts have developed formulations, such as the modified internal rate of return (MIRR) and the financial management rate of return (FMRR), to overcome problems with the IRR, but there is still disagreement regarding the proper formula and approach to be used in evaluating proposed investments.

The second section of the chapter presented a full-scale after-tax cash flow model using the DCF methods developed in the first section. Using the Aspen Wood property as an example, we developed a seven-year projection that included inflation estimates of rents, expenses, and property value and used the price structure and wraparound mortgage package negotiated by the sellers in Chapter 10. Various types of annual financial ratios were then calculated, explained, and used for further analysis of the project's profitability and riskiness. In addition, and perhaps most important, the ratios were used to analyze the underlying assumptions and economic relationships on which all the output data and return/risk measures are based.

The next chapter addresses the subjects of risk analysis and risk management, and presents a sophisticated risk analysis model based on the DCF concepts presented here.

12

Risk Analysis and Risk Management

As we can readily see, a DCF model provides valuable information that is not provided by the basic financial feasibility model. It explicitly considers (1) changes in rents, expenses, and property value over time; (2) equity buildup through loan amortization; (3) income taxation; (4) transaction costs; (5) expected holding period; and (6) the time value of money. As we have observed, all of these variables affect the risk and return parameters of a proposed investment.

However, an important variable that is not adequately measured by the DCF model is risk—the probability that the expected net income and cash flows will not be received. While financial ratios, such as the debt coverage ratio and the breakeven point, provide some information about the risk profile of a project, they do not provide information about the probable deviations from the *most likely* values used in the analysis. A complete risk analysis should provide information about (1) the magnitude of possible deviations in cash flows that can occur under varying market and economic conditions, and (2) the probability associated with each of these projections.[1] None of the ratios presented provides this information adequately.

In the following sections concepts and techniques are presented that attempt to harness the risk dimension and provide the investor with a better understanding of the possible consequences of risk and uncertainty. At the end of the chapter we

[1] This statement refers only to the analysis of *project risk* as addressed in this chapter; it does not treat risk from a portfolio perspective. The relationship between the two is explained by Steven D. Kapplin, "Financial Theory and the Valuation of Real Estate Under Conditions of Risk," *The Real Estate Appraiser,* September–October 1976, pp. 28–37. Also see Chapter 25.

show how the concepts and techniques developed here and in Chapter 11 are applied in our Aspen Wood case.

RISK ANALYSIS

The Nature and Definition of Risk

Risk exists in real estate because investors are unable to make perfect forecasts.[2] If they could, they would never make an investment that would yield them less than their required rate of return, and they would plan to meet all financial obligations with precision. Real estate investors and entrepreneurs would cease to play their vital role as bearers of risks associated with economic, social, and political change.

Risk Versus Uncertainty Many economists distinguish between risk and uncertainty. One basis for this distinction is whether or not the probability distribution of outcomes (for rents, expenses, selling price, etc.) is known or can be estimated.[3] If the distribution is known or can be estimated, *risk* exists; if it is not known or cannot be estimated, *uncertainty* prevails. Such a distinction, however, has little meaning in most business situations today. Most real estate decision makers have *some* feeling about the probability of future events occurring, ranging from a high degree of confidence to a vague and ill-defined feeling. They neither are *completely ignorant* nor feel that they *completely know* the probabilities of future events.[4] In real-world decision making, the terms *uncertainty* and *risk* are used interchangeably. We will use both words to mean situations in which real estate analysts can assess the probabilities (objectively or subjectively) of future events.

Definitions of Risk Risk can be defined in a variety of ways. Here are five popular definitions:

1. The probability of loss.
2. The probability of not receiving what is expected.
3. The difference (or potential variance) between expectations and realizations.
4. The possible variance of returns relative to the expected or most likely return.
5. The chance or probability that the investor will not receive the expected or required rate of return that is desired on the investment.

The last of these is probably our best operational definition. For example, assume that an investor with a required IRR of 10 percent is analyzing two

[2] G. David Quirin, *The Capital Expenditure Decision* (Homewood, Ill.: Richard D. Irwin, 1967), p. 199.
[3] Famous for making this distinction are F. H. Knight, *Risk, Uncertainty and Profit* (Boston: Houghton Mifflin, 1923), and J. A. Schumpeter, *The Theory of Economic Development* (Cambridge, Mass.: Harvard University Press, 1934).
[4] C. Jackson Grayson, Jr., "The Use of Statistical Techniques in Capital Budgeting," *Financial Research and Management Decisions,* ed. Alexander A. Robichek (New York: Wiley, 1967), p. 91.

apartment projects, both of which have an expected *mean* IRR of 20 percent. Owing to the possibility of changes in the economy or competition in the future, while project A has a 30 percent chance, project B has only a 5 percent chance of returning less than the required 10 percent IRR. Clearly, if the investor is concerned with *downside* risk, project A is more risky than project B because there is a higher probability of not achieving the required 10 percent IRR. A probability distribution can be used to describe this hypothetical situation. (See Exhibit 12–1.) The distribution simply shows the possible IRRs that could occur in the future, and the probability associated with each. Later we will show how these distributions can be generated through computer simulation.

Types of Risk

Risk can be classified in several ways. One useful scheme is shown in Exhibit 12–2. The first distinction is between business and financial risk. Business risk can be static or dynamic; financial risk can be internal or external.

Business Risk   Business risk is the underlying asset risk—the probability that the expected level and pattern of productivity returns will not be received, or the uncertainty of the prediction of productivity; that is, business risk is the *probability that the expected or required rate of return on total capital (IRR$_{TC}$) will not be realized.* Business risk is related to expected changes over time in five variables: capital expenditures, gross possible income, vacancy and credit losses, operating expenses, and property value. (It ignores financing variables.) The greater the potential variance in the five variables, the greater the business risk. Also, if an after-tax cash flow model is used, income and capital gain tax variables affecting the property (excluding all financing impacts) will be among the business risk considerations.

Business risk can be further divided into static and dynamic categories. *Static risk* is related to physical cause and effect, occurs at random, and is beyond the

---

EXHIBIT 12–1.   Distributions of Probable Rates of Return for Each of Two Projects

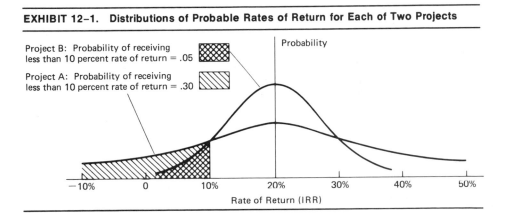

EXHIBIT 12-2.   Classification of Risk

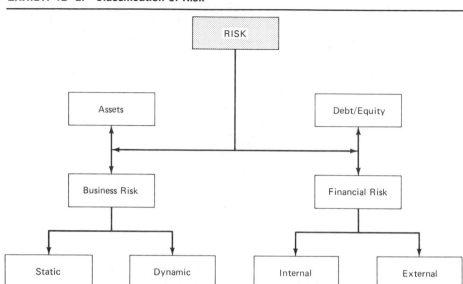

control of the investor.[5] Static risk always results in a loss. Examples include damage to property caused by fire, storm, or flood, or losses caused by personal injury, theft, or "malicious mischief." Normally, these risks can be insured against because they are predictable over the long run. Consequently, most investors shift these risks by entering into an insurance contract with a property and casualty insurer.

Dynamic risk, on the other hand, can mean either profit or loss. Dynamic risk is related to changes in general business conditions and the physical condition of the property. It is related to market demand and supply conditions, the age of the property, the quality of the property management, changes in the economic base and the environment, tax reforms, and so on. Changes in these factors could cause changes in the purchase price, the net operating income, the value of the property, and related tax benefits, and thus would change the IRR_{TC}.[6]

Financial Risk   Financial risk refers to the extra risks to the investor created by debt financing. Financial risk is additional to the underlying business risks and increases whenever the amount of debt service or related charges increase. Otherwise stated, financial risk is the *probability of not receiving the expected or*

---

[5] James A. Graaskamp, "An Approach to Real Estate Finance Education by Analogy to Risk Management Principles," *Real Estate Issues,* Summer 1977, p. 55.
[6] A somewhat different approach to risk classification is taken by other authors. See, e.g., Herman Kelting, *Real Estate Investments* (Columbus, Ohio: Grid Publishing, 1980), pp. 71–75. Our classification scheme closely follows those that are commonly presented in business and corporate finance textbooks.

required rate of return on equity (IRR$_E$) owing to the investor's inability to meet fixed financial obligations created by debt financing.

Since financial risk is essentially a cash liquidity or solvency problem that can be created by either internal or external factors, the investor must consider two types of financial risk. *Internal financial risk* relates to the ability of the project to generate enough cash to pay the monthly or yearly debt service. For example, if the debt coverage ratio is low because of a high leverage ratio or mortgage constant, the project is characterized by high internal financial risk. If this ratio increases, internal financial risk decreases. The second type of financial risk, *external financial risk,* is related to the investor's ability to obtain cash in the money markets or from other external sources. For example, if an investor can readily finance a cash need of a property using funds from external sources, such as bank loans or additional equity cash investments, the project is said to be characterized by low external financial risk. If funds from external sources become more difficult to obtain, external financial risk increases.

Relationship Between IRR and Business and Financial Risk   The relationship between financial risk and the IRR on equity (IRR$_E$) is not quite as simple as the relationship between business risk and the IRR on total capital (IRR$_{TC}$). We cannot simply say that financial risk is the probability of not receiving the expected IRR$_E$, since the IRR$_E$ depends both on basic productivity factors (IRR$_{TC}$) *and* on financing factors. The IRR$_E$ is directly related to both business and financial risk; an increase in both types of risk can be directly linked to fluctuations (variance) in the IRR$_E$. Therefore, we can think of fluctuations in the IRR$_E$ as a measure of *total* project risk, while fluctuations in the IRR$_{TC}$ are a measure of business risk only.

One final, but important, relationship between business and financial risk should be noted: Business risk should be the prime determinant of the amount of debt financing employed. The degree of business risk that is inherent in a project and the degree of financial risk incurred by the investor in financing the project should be inversely related. For example, if an investment is made in a neighborhood shopping center characterized by very high business risks (high vacancy rates, unstable neighborhood), the investor should use a relatively low degree of leverage financing so that total debt service will remain relatively low. Following this rule will reduce the probability of insolvency in any given year and thus will reduce financial risk. In situations in which there is less business risk, the investor might prudently justify higher degrees of leverage financing.

This normative relationship between business and financial risk was illustrated in Chapter 10 when we worked with the basic financial feasibility model. If we compensated for higher business risk (first-year NOI deviations) by raising the desired debt coverage ratio (DCR), the amount of debt service and the loan amount declined. In contrast, when using a DCF model we measure the degree of total project risk by simulating the possible variations in cash flows and IRR$_E$ under different states of nature and different capital (financing) structures. After analyzing the results, we determine the particular capital structure that best fits our return and risk preferences. Such a procedure for determining an optimal balance between business and financial risks is presented in Chapter 14.

Levels of Risk Analysis

There are numerous levels of risk analysis that can be performed by the investor. The investor should begin by applying simple one-year cash flow techniques and then apply more rigorous forms of analysis as the investment analysis proceeds. We can define five levels of risk analysis.

First Level: The Basic Financial Feasibility Model Using this one-year cash flow model, the investor analyzes risk by analyzing the debt coverage ratio and the positive/negative leverage situation. A low debt coverage ratio indicates high risk, as does the presence of negative leverage. No attempt is made to analyze the *probability* of different rate-of-return outcomes at this stage. At best, these are crude measures of total project risk.

Second Level: DCF Most-Likely Output At this stage we generated annual data on the debt coverage ratios and break-even points. By viewing these ratios over time, we could further analyze the level of risk, as well as the trends in risk over time. Also, by comparing IRR on total capital (IRR_{TC}) and IRR on equity (IRR_E), we could evaluate the long-run, after-tax, positive/negative leverage situation. If $IRR_E > IRR_{TC}$, a long-run, positive leverage situation is achieved.

Third Level: IRR Partitioning and Risk Absorption Analysis Using DCF data, Valachi[7] and Zerbst[8] have presented methods for analyzing risk by partitioning the IRR into various components using present-value techniques. Three basic components of return are partitioned: annual cash flows, tax shelter, and cash proceeds of sale. The rationale for this type of analysis is that investors place different risk weights on different sources of return. The partitioned IRR can be used to determine whether the sources of expected returns from a particular property are consistent with their investment objectives. The more refined the categories (sources) of investor benefits, the more the partitioned IRR can add insight into the riskiness of an investment.

Exhibit 12–3 shows the results of a component analysis of the IRR. The IRR on equity was calculated to be 18.5 percent. The results of simple partitioning, having discounted each of the dollar amounts of return, indicate that total cash proceeds of sale represent 69.9 percent of the total 18.5 percent IRR (column 4). Of that 69.9 percent, *recapture of original equity* accounts for 51 percent, equity buildup through *loan amortization* for 5.5 percent, and *expected net appreciation* for 13.4 percent of the total return. The concentration of returns in the *total cash proceeds* from sale emphasizes the dependence of investment returns on the project's selling price and clarifies the relative sources of risk associated with the total IRR return.

Another DCF measure of risk is called the *risk absorption (RA) ratio*. This ratio, introduced by Wofford and Gitman, measures the amount of risk a project can absorb while still remaining acceptable to the investor.[9] The calculation of the

---

[7] Donald J. Valachi, "The Three Faces of IRR," *Real Estate Review,* Fall 1978, pp. 74–78.
[8] Robert H. Zerbst, "Evaluating Risks by Partitioning the Internal Rate of Return," *Real Estate Review,* Winter 1980, pp. 80–84.
[9] Larry E. Wofford and Lawrence J. Gitman, "Measuring a Project's Ability to Survive Adversity," *Real Estate Review,* Spring 1978, pp. 91–94.

EXHIBIT 12–3.   Component Analysis of the Internal Rate of Return

(1) Components of Total Return	(2) Present Value of Components	(3) Component as Percentage of Total	(4) Results of Simple Partitioning
Year 1 level of cash flow	$ 11,165	12.5%	
Growth in cash flow	9,075	6.7	
Total cash flow			19.2%
Tax savings	11,505	10.9	10.9
Recapture of original equity	53,848	51.0	
Loan amortization	5,809	5.5	
Expected net appreciation	14,265	13.4	
Total cash proceeds	$ 73,922		69.9
Total return	$105,666	100.0%	100.0%

SOURCE: Robert H. Zerbst, "Evaluating Risks by Partitioning the Internal Rate of Return," *Real Estate Review*, Winter 1980, p. 83.

risk absorption ratio is illustrated in Exhibit 12–4. The ratio is based on the concept of annualized net present value (ANPV). The ANPV determines the maximum amount by which the cash flow each year could be reduced without reducing net present value below zero, that is, to a level that makes the investment unacceptable. The RA ratio is created by dividing the annualized net present value of equity cash flows by the equity investment required to initiate the proposal. Like the profitability index, the RA ratio is a relative measure used to compare projects of different sizes. *The RA ratio measures risk-absorbing ability per dollar of investment.* If all other risk and return measures are equal, the investment with the greatest risk-absorbing capacity will be preferred.

Fourth Level: Sensitivity Analysis   Sensitivity analysis is a technique that attempts to test the impact of uncertainties on the investment decision. We can perform sensitivity analysis by varying the values of the input variables in the basic financial feasibility and DCF models to show how they affect the project value, the ROE, the IRR, the debt coverage ratio, or other relevant output data.

If, through sensitivity analysis, it is discovered that certain variables have values that are uncertain but do not have a significant impact on rates of return, debt coverage ratios, or other outcomes, the investor can stop worrying about those uncertainties; there is no reason to worry about variables that "don't count." Equity investors are often surprised to discover which uncertain variables are important and which are not. This is because it is difficult to predict the results of the interaction among many complex economic and market interrelationships.

Exhibit 12–5 illustrates the final results of a sensitivity analysis on a 287-unit apartment property using computer model RE001. Through the analysis it was discovered that the four most important determinants of the investor's IRR on equity and coverage ratio over a ten-year period analyzed were (1) the growth rate of gross possible income, (2) the growth rate of operating costs, (3) the

---

EXHIBIT 12–4.   Calculation of the Risk Absorption Ratio

Investment A has the following equity cash flows:

Year	Cash Flow	Present Value of Cash Flow @ 15 Percent
0	($25,000)	($25,000)
1	10,000	8,700
2	9,500	7,182
3	9,100	5,988
4	8,700	4,976
5	12,000	5,964
	Net present value	$ 7,810

The investor has a required IRR of 15 percent. The net present value of $7,810 can be annualized by dividing this amount by the factor for the present value of a five-year annuity discounted at 15 percent (i.e., by 3.352). The resulting annualized net present value is $2,230 ($7,810 ÷ 3.352 = $2,330). This means that if the investor experienced a reduction in annual cash inflows of $2,330, the investment would still be acceptable since its net present value would then be zero. Any reduction in annual flows below $2,330 would leave the net present value positive. The risk-absorption ratio (RA ratio) is defined as follows:

$$\text{RA ratio} = \frac{\text{annualized net present value}}{\text{initial equity investment}}$$

$$= \frac{\$2,330}{\$25,000} = .093$$

The RA ratio thus is a *relative* measure of risk-absorbing capacity. The higher the RA ratio, the greater the risk-absorbing capacity of the investment. RA ratios for competing projects can also be computed and ranked from high to low.

SOURCE: Larry E. Wofford and Lawrence J. Gitman, "Measuring a Project's Ability to Survive Adversity," *Real Estate Review,* Spring 1978, p. 93.

expected occupancy level, and (4) increases in property value. Exhibit 12–4 shows the effect of changes in these four variables on (1) IRR on equity investment, (2) IRR on total capital investment, (3) net operating income, (4) the breakeven point, and (5) the debt coverage ratio.

The investor should conclude a sensitivity analysis with a set of computer runs representing optimistic, most likely, and pessimistic assumptions, as shown in Exhibit 12–5. This provides data that represent the possible range of results that can be reasonably expected if the inputs have been measured accurately. Clearly, the most crucial aspect of the whole process is generating accurate input information through market research.

In the example presented, the IRR on equity was acceptable to the investor, with the most probable IRR being 21.24–22.63 percent, depending on the hold-

EXHIBIT 12–5. Summary Table of Sensitivity Analysis Calculations, 287-Unit Apartment Complex

	I Optimistic	II Most Probable	III Pessimistic
A. INPUT VARIABLE ASSUMPTIONS			
1. Growth rate of gross possible income	5%	3%	1%
2. Growth rate of operating costs	3%	4 5%	6%
3. Growth rate of property value	5.5%	3%	0%
4. Expected occupancy level	96%	93%	87%
B. IRR ON EQUITY INVESTMENT (IRR$_E$)			
1. Year 3	31.64%	21.24%	5.75%
2. Year 7	31.24%	22.63%	7.67%
3. Year 10	30.10%	22.05%	6.94%
C. INTERNAL RATE OF RETURN ON TOTAL CAPITAL INVESTMENT (IRRTC)			
1. Year 3	11.46%	9.07%	6.01%
2. Year 7	11.69%	8.96%	5.54%
3. Year 10	11.89%	8.95%	5.23%
D. NET OPERATING INCOME			
1. Year 3	$426,577	$369,336	$293,389
2. Year 7	$544,742	$395,583	$236,800
3. Year 10	$651,901	$414,931	$181,332
E. BREAK-EVEN POINT			
1. Year 3	.728	.768	.812
2. Year 7	.639	.754	.893
3. Year 10	.581	.747	.967
F. DEBT COVERAGE RATIO			
1. Year 3	1.686	1.459	1.159
2. Year 7	2.152	1.563	.936
3. Year 10	2.576	1.640	.717

ing period of the investment. The coverage ratio averaged 1.4– 1.6, considerably above the investor's desired 1.3 minimum. Only in the pessimistic case for seven- and ten-year holding periods does the coverage ratio drop below 1.0, where project revenues are insufficient to meet all expenses, and cash flow before tax is negative. The IRR on equity drops to the 6– 7 percent range. In the optimistic case, the IRR on equity increases to 31.64 percent for the three-year holding period and falls to 30.1 percent for the ten-year holding period, with a coverage ratio above

1.6 in all cases. If the financial structure is perceived to be too conservative, the investor can increase the degree of leverage and raise the IRR on equity, as long as the coverage ratio and breakeven points remain within acceptable limits.

Fifth Level: Monte Carlo Risk Simulation.[10]   Sensitivity analysis is not a complete form of risk analysis. While it can provide the investor with ranges of possible returns, it does not indicate the probability that the different returns will actually occur. A risk analysis simulation model attempts to overcome this problem. Such a model is pictured in Exhibit 12–6. It measures the probability of various rates of return and liquidity positions being achieved if we can measure the probability distributions for uncertain variables. The basic theory and concepts underlying the model were explained in Chapter 3.

The first step in using the risk simulation model is to designate the *control variables* (single-value estimates) and the *state variables* (probability distribution estimates). In the exhibit there are six control variables: (1) the square-foot dimensions of the property, (2) the equity investment ratio, (3) the depreciation method and useful life of improvements, (4) the existing tax structure, (5) the holding period of the investment, and (6) the loan amount and the terms of the loan.

The remaining state variables are assigned probability distributions by the analyst. Several methods for estimating these probability distributions have been developed and are used extensively in fields other than real estate. Some of these methods require that the real estate forecaster understand probability concepts; some do not. Some allow the forecaster to estimate his or her own probability distributions, others employ interview techniques. While space does not permit us to discuss these methods in depth, it is important to recognize that recent experiences with probability estimation are encouraging and reinforce the credibility of its use as a technique for quantifying risk. Experience has shown that decision makers and experts can realistically estimate probability distributions for variables and, after some practice, become comfortable with the concept and process involved.[11]

Given the values of the control variables and the probability distributions for

[10] See Stephen A. Pyhrr, "A Computer Simulation Model to Measure the Risk in Real Estate Investment," *American Real Estate and Urban Economics Association Journal,* June 1973, pp. 48–78; reprinted in *The Real Estate Appraiser,* May–June 1973, pp. 13–31. See also Richard U. Ratcliff and Bernard Schwab, "Contemporary Decision Theory and Real Estate Investment," *The Appraisal Journal,* April 1970, pp. 165–187. Also, an application in urban housing by James R. Cooper and Cathy A. Morrison, "Using Computer Simulation to Minimize Risk in Urban Housing Development," *The Real Estate Appraiser,* March–April 1973, pp. 15–26. Also, Michael S. Young, "Evaluating the Risk of Investment Real Estate," *Real Estate Appraiser,* September–October 1977, pp. 39–45. An operational risk simulation model for classroom use has been developed by George W. Gau and Daniel B. Kohlhepp. Entitled *OUPROB: A Discounted Cash Flow Model for Real Estate Investment Analysis* (User Guide and Instructor's Manual), it is available through the Center for Economic and Management Research, University of Oklahoma, Norman, Okla. (73019).

[11] For examples see Carl S. Spetzler, "The Development of a Corporate Policy for Capital Investment Decisions," *IEEE Transactions on Systems Science and Cybernetics,* September 1968, pp. 279–300; Donald H. Woods, "Improving Estimates That Involve Uncertainty," *Harvard Business Review,* July–August 1966, pp. 91–98; David B. Hertz, "Risk Analysis in Capital Investment," *Harvard Business Review,* January–February 1964, pp. 95–106. For a complete treatment of the subject, see Larry Wofford, *A Simulation Approach to the Appraisal of Income Producing Real Estate,* Ph.D. dissertation, University of Texas, June 1977.

EXHIBIT 12–6.   Project Analysis—Probabilistic Rate-of-Return Model

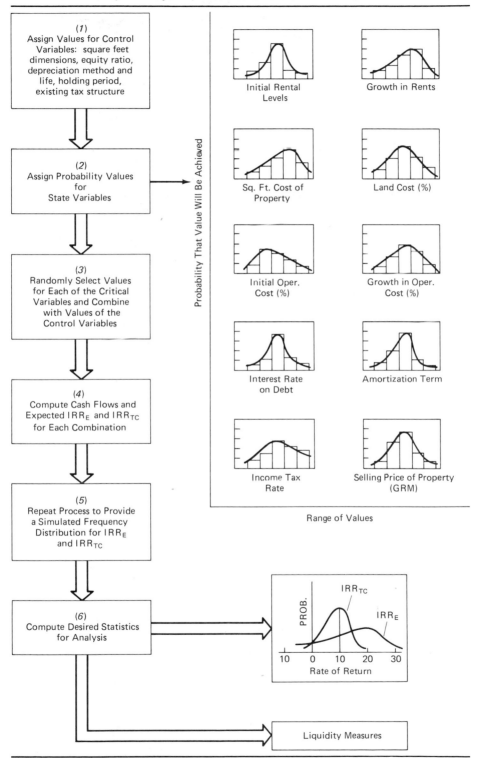

(1)
Assign Values for Control Variables: square feet dimensions, equity ratio, depreciation method and life, holding period, existing tax structure

(2)
Assign Probability Values for State Variables

(3)
Randomly Select Values for Each of the Critical Variables and Combine with Values of the Control Variables

(4)
Compute Cash Flows and Expected IRR_E and IRR_{TC} for Each Combination

(5)
Repeat Process to Provide a Simulated Frequency Distribution for IRR_E and IRR_{TC}

(6)
Compute Desired Statistics for Analysis

Probability That Value Will Be Achieved

Initial Rental Levels

Growth in Rents

Sq. Ft. Cost of Property

Land Cost (%)

Initial Oper. Cost (%)

Growth in Oper. Cost (%)

Interest Rate on Debt

Amortization Term

Income Tax Rate

Selling Price of Property (GRM)

Range of Values

IRR_{TC}

IRR_E

PROB.

10   0   10   20   30
Rate of Return

Liquidity Measures

the state variables, the Monte Carlo simulation procedure is used to generate cash flows, DCF rates of return, and other statistical data. As shown in step 3 of the exhibit, a value for each of the ten uncertain variables is randomly chosen from the respective probability distributions and combined with the values of control variables. Then, in step 4, annual cash flows and the rates of return on total capital and equity are computed for that particular combination of input values.

This process is repeated a large number of times and a count is kept of the number of times various rates of return are computed. When the computer runs have been completed, the probability that various rates of return will occur can be calculated and plotted as shown at the bottom of Exhibit 12– 6. Exhibit 12– 7 is a detailed example of a cumulative probability distribution (risk profile) curve of the rate of return on equity (IRR_E) plotted from one hundred simulations. The vertical axis is the probability of IRR_E being achieved or exceeded, and the horizontal axis reflects IRR_E. For example, there is a 98 percent chance that a 7.5 percent rate of return will be achieved or exceeded over the ten-year holding period. Moving down the cumulative distribution curve shows that there is a 50 percent chance that a 10.3 percent rate of return will be achieved or exceeded. In this case the analyst desired to know the probability of receiving less than an 8 percent rate of return. As can be seen on the graph, the computer specifies that there is a 5

EXHIBIT 12–7.   Cumulative Probability Distribution Curve of the Rate of Return on Equity (IRR_E)

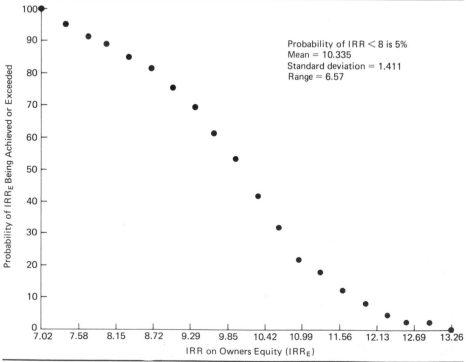

Probability of IRR $<$ 8 is 5%
Mean = 10.335
Standard deviation = 1.411
Range = 6.57

percent chance of this occurring, and also gives mean, standard deviation, and range.

Additional information can easily be generated in whatever form the investor seeks. For example, liquidity measures can be computed from yearly cash flow data generated during the simulation process. If the investor is concerned with the probability of negative equity cash flows and their respective amounts for consecutive years, a summary statistical measure of these two dimensions can be specified and computed. Suppose an investor specifies that a negative cash flow of $25,000 in two or more consecutive years would cause insolvency. A measure of liquidity might be defined as the probability of receiving negative equity cash flows exceeding $25,000 in two or more consecutive years during the holding period. Instructions are given to the computer to calculate this liquidity measure.

Will probabilistic models like the one just described be utilized in the future? Psychologists and sociologists have demonstrated repeatedly that most people are reluctant to adopt new ideas that they find to be at variance with currently held beliefs. The successful development of a risk simulation model into a production model depends on acceptance of the model for planning and decision making and on the investor's ability to forecast and estimate probability distributions for uncertain variables. It may take considerable time before confidence in such a model evolves in the real estate field.

RISK MANAGEMENT AND CONTROL

Many investors manage money, but the really successful ones manage risk, the idea being not to avoid risk but to be skilled at identifying it, coping with it, and living with it.[12] Real estate investors who remain in business never risk more than they can afford to lose, never risk a lot for a little, and always consider the odds. Before committing capital, investors should seek answers to the following questions:

1. What situations create the risk of loss?
2. Can they be avoided or eliminated?
3. Can the remaining risks be controlled?
4. How can losses be minimized?
5. Is there a need to shift the risk to others?
6. What are the trade-offs and costs involved?

Although there is some overlap, there are three general techniques for managing business and financial risk: avoiding or eliminating risk, transferring or shifting risk, and reducing the remaining risk.

---

[12] From J. Thomas Montgomery, "Real Estate Investment Risk—Basic Concepts," *The Appraisal Journal*, January 1976, pp. 9–22; revised and reprinted in James A. Britton, Jr., and Lewis O. Kerwood, *Financing Income-Producing Real Estate* (New York, McGraw-Hill Book, 1977), pp. 18–36. See also Graaskamp, op. cit.

Avoiding or Eliminating Risk

The most basic risk management technique is "Don't make the deal." If the expected returns from a property do not compensate for the risks involved, and restructuring cannot correct the problem, reject the investment. Other examples are the following:

1. *Playing the real estate cycle.* The market is overbuilt and we are in a general economic recession. Avoid making the real estate investment in a shopping center; instead, wait until the time is right, when the bottom of the cycle has ended and conditions are beginning to improve. This eliminates a dynamic business risk.
2. *Nonrecourse mortgages.* An esculpatory clause in a mortgage will avoid the possibility of a lawsuit and a judgment if the property is unsuccessful. This eliminates an internal financial risk.
3. *Avoiding specific types of property.* To avoid insolvency due to rent controls, the investor can avoid apartment projects in certain communities. This eliminates a dynamic business risk.
4. *Avoiding market-indexed loans.* By avoiding the use of variable- or renegotiated-rate mortgages, or similar types of market-indexed financing techniques, the investor can eliminate a dynamic business risk associated with inflation and other uncontrollable economic variables.

Transferring or Shifting Risk

As another risk management technique, the investor refuses to invest unless all or part of the risk can be shifted to someone else. Here are some examples:

1. *Insurance policy.* Fire and extended coverage, flood, rent loss, liability, mortgage, and title insurance are vehicles for shifting static business risks—but at a certain cost to the investor.
2. *Limited partnership form of ownership.* The limited partners shift the risk of unlimited liability and cash calls to the general partner. This shifts an external financial risk to the general partner.
3. *Long-term leases with escalation clauses.* A long-term lease shifts the vacancy risk to the tenant, while contribution and rent escalation clauses shift inflation risks and expense uncertainties from the investor to the tenant. A dynamic business risk is thereby shifted to the lessee.
4. *Land contract.* This shifts a dynamic business risk by ensuring that, in the event that the buyer defaults on the installment contract, possession of the property will revert quickly to the seller at a minimal cost.

Reducing the Remaining Risks

The investor can attempt to minimize any remaining risks through a variety of tactics. The following are examples:

1. *Loan amount and terms.* Reducing the amount of the loan and improving the mortgage terms, lowering prepayment penalties, eliminating the

due-on-sale clause, and reducing origination costs are methods of controlling internal financial risks.
2. *Purchase price.* The investor can increase the expected rate of return and lower his or her equity investment exposure by negotiating better purchase terms. A dynamic business risk is reduced in this way.
3. *Diversification.* Risk can be spread through diversification with respect to size, type, and location of investments within a given portfolio. As a result, business risk is reduced.
4. *Good accounting controls and reporting system.* If problems are identified when they first occur and partners informed, corrective actions can be applied faster and expenses reduced. In this way partners will be better informed, more content, and less likely to create trouble for the managing equity investor.
5. *Better financial feasibility research.* Better information will reduce perceived risk, since many uncertainties and financial surprises are due to ignorance of the facts rather than to any inherent unpredictability. More accurate pro formas can be developed, thus reducing the perceived business risks.
6. *Better property management and venture management.* A professional property management firm with skilled personnel should be able to generate a higher NOI from a property over a longer period. More skillful negotiations by the managing equity investor should also raise the returns relative to the risks of investment.
7. *Superior location.* Attracting and keeping good tenants who pay "top-of-the-market" rents through the purchase of superior locations will reduce the dynamic business risks associated with rent collections and vacancy losses.

The risk management and control techniques described here should be an integral part of the investment decision process. Different types of risk management techniques can be applied at different points in the ten-step investment analysis process.[13] Using the basic financial feasibility model to structure acceptable return/risk parameters is a risk management technique. Developing an efficient investment analysis process, such as our ten-step process, will reduce the amount of time expended to successfully locate and purchase a property that satisfies the investor's objectives. Clearly, risk management is critical to successful investing.

SUMMARY

Various concepts and techniques of sensitivity and risk analysis are discussed in this chapter, and we show how at different stages of the investment analysis process the investor can apply risk management and control techniques to avoid, transfer, or reduce risk. Successful investors are generally good risk managers.

[13] A comprehensive strategic planning framework for managing and controlling risk at various stages of a real estate decision process is presented by Mahlon Apgar, IV, "Commitment Planning: An Approach to Reducing Real Estate Risks," *The Appraisal Journal,* July 1976, pp. 412–427. While the framework is applied to the real estate development process, the major elements and techniques of structuring and phasing apply equally well to equity investment.

Turning to the Aspen Wood Apartments case, we shall see how the concepts presented in the chapter are applied by D&B, as well as how the basic negotiations with the seller were handled. In the next chapter we will develop further the topics of tax planning and structuring, and present a more detailed financial model for analyzing income properties.

ASPEN WOOD APARTMENTS

NEGOTIATION, FEASIBILITY RESEARCH, AND
RETURN/RISK EVALUATION

In Chapter 10 Charlie Davidson and Clyde Boomer arrived at a proposed
structure for the acquisition of Aspen Wood Apartments using the basic
financial feasibility model. Among the major purchase parameters calculated
were the following:

Estimated NOI	$ 89,305
Minimum acceptable debt coverage ratio	1.3
Maximum acceptable mortgage constant	8.3%
Minimum acceptable ROE	10.0%
Maximum mortgage loan amount	$ 830,000
Maximum equity investment	$ 206,000
Maximum offering price	$1,036,000

Davidson and Boomer planned to approach the seller with a $1 million
purchase price offer, including an equity down payment of $175,000, from
which a brokerage commission of $50,000 would be paid to D&B
Associates for handling the transaction. The seller would be asked to provide
wraparound mortgage financing in the amount of $825,000 at 7 1/2
percent, 28 years, no personal liability, with a balloon (escalation-of-
principal clause) at the end of ten years. Also, Davidson and Boomer
would negotiate for the following mortgage clauses: prepayment of the
note, without penalty and at the option of the buyer; and elimination of
the standard due-on-sale clause. Elimination of the due-on-sale clause
would give the purchasing joint venture the flexibility to sell the property in a
future year and "wrap the wrap," that is, finance the next buyer by
wrapping around the existing wraparound note and the underlying three
mortgage notes.

Our DCF analysis in Chapter 11 was based on the preceding
assumptions. We found that the IRR_E was 22.14 percent, based on growth
rate assumptions of 4 percent for rents, 7 percent for expenses, and 3
percent for property value. Although we noted some possible inconsistencies
in the assumption base relationships (a falling overall capitalization rate over
seven years), all of the risk and return ratios look favorable and are expected
to improve each year over the seven-year projection period.

The ten-step investment process identifies three steps between
application of the basic financial feasibility model and application of the DCF
model:

• Step 4: Negotiate basic terms with the seller.
• Step 5: Do detailed feasibility research.

- Step 6: Structure the tax benefits.
- Step 7: Perform DCF analysis.

In the following sections we will take the Aspen Wood project through these four steps, showing the activities and thought processes leading up to the DCF analysis already presented, and the subsequent "surprises" that necessitated many reiterations of these steps.

NEGOTIATIONS WITH THE SELLER

D&B Associates presented its offer to the seller and was prepared to trade off various elements of price and terms as the negotiations proceeded. Davidson and Boomer began with an offer that maximized their returns relative to the risks, knowing that numerous concessions would be necessary. Using the basic financial feasibility model, they had performed an extensive sensitivity analysis on the price, mortgage package, and other terms of the purchase, and knew how different combinations of price and terms affected their before-tax return/risk position. Armed with this knowledge, they could bargain for a purchase structure that would simultaneously satisfy the personal needs and financial problems of the sellers and maximize the returns relative to risks for D&B. In addition, a number of preliminary DCF analyses were performed to test the after-tax consequences of the investment.

Mortgage Terms. Davidson and Boomer specified a maximum mortgage constant of 8.3 percent. What interest rate and term would be acceptable? A review of the K table shows that many combinations of rate and term will produce a K of .083—say, from 6.75 percent/25 years to 7.5 percent/30 years. A K of less than 8.3 percent would not produce enough debt service on the wraparound to cover the debt service on the underlying three loans. A K of more than 8.3 percent would reduce the buyer's ROE to less than 10 percent, which was unacceptable. The sellers maintained that they would not accept less than the average interest rate (approximately 7%) on the three underlying loans and would prefer a higher rate to create a positive interest spread for their investors. A 7.5 percent interest rate was eventually agreed upon. Also, the sellers agreed to a nonrecourse loan that provided for prepayment without penalty at the buyer's option.

Basic Tax Structure. In addition to negotiating a desirable price and mortgage package for the investors, Davidson and Boomer sought to create a tax package that would maximize tax shelter during the year of purchase and for each year during the expected holding period of four to seven years. Their basic objective, as will be detailed in Chapter 13, was to create the maximum degree of tax benefits over the ownership life cycle: acquisition, operation, and termination.

It is important for both parties to consider the tax package during the early negotiation stages. If both the buyer and the seller are aware of and investigate all tax planning alternatives, concessions can be made that cost one party little but provide a sizable benefit to the other. These benefits will be reflected in the subsequent DCF analyses and negotiations leading to the final purchase contract.

Letter of Intent. A series of negotiations between the seller (general partners of the selling syndicate) and buyer (Davidson and Boomer, representing the buying syndicate) resulted in the September 30, 1974 letter of intent (see Exhibit 12–8), which was written by Davidson and itemized the intended terms of purchase. Numerous other versions had preceded this one, and some changes had been made by both parties, but the offer reflected the price and terms outlined earlier. Total consideration (net price) to the seller was set at $980,000, which, with the $50,000 commission and syndication fee to D&B Associates, brought the total project cost to $1,030,000. The $980,000 cash paid to the seller was divided into cash, financing points, and prepaid interest. The buyer would be able to deduct the latter two items as expenses in the current tax year (1974). (These benefits were subsequently eliminated by the 1976 Tax Reform Act.)

Although it was the end of September, the parties were hoping to close the project *as of* September 1, 1974, and prorate all income and expenses as of that date. The seller was to guarantee the cash flows equivalent to a 95 percent occupancy through the remainder of the calendar year but was allowed to refinance the wraparound obligation after five years, provided it could be accomplished within set mortgage constants of a magnitude that leave the buyer indifferent. The last paragraph of the letter of intent spells out the contingencies of the agreement and calls for a rent roll, a profit and loss statement, and an on-site inspection, in addition to other evidence and reassurances. Upon accepting this offer, the seller was required to lay bare the records and property for inspection, enabling the buyer to pursue the detailed feasibility research that would be required before additional return/risk analysis could be undertaken.

DETAILED FEASIBILITY RESEARCH

The purpose of the detailed feasibility research is to gather the information required to structure the tax package and perform the discounted cash flow analysis. The negotiation process and the detailed feasibility research interact to a significant degree. If new inputs into the investment analysis result in a change in the investor's valuation of the property, more negotiation ensues. Seldom are everyone's cards laid on the table at one eventful meeting. The letter of intent, for example, only summarizes the negotiations as far as they've gone; it is not usually an enforceable contract. The buyer may inspect, research, interview, and otherwise collect information until there are adequate feasibility data on which to base projections and a final return and risk analysis of the property. In Chapter 19 we provide a detailed analysis and checklist of apartment feasibility factors.

EXHIBIT 12–8.   Provisions of the Letter of Intent—September 30, 1974

This letter will set forth the term of my offer to purchase the Aspen Wood Apartments complete with furniture,
fixtures and equipment on behalf of the investor clients
whom I represent:

1.   Total consideration of $980,000.00, computed as
follows:

$160,000.00	Cash to sellers at closing
820,000.00	Wraparound mortgage, 7 1/2%, 26 1/2 years, balloon at end of 10 years
$980,000.00	Total consideration

2.   The cash paid to sellers at closing will be accounted
for as follows:

$ 86,000.00	Equity cash invested
12,500.00	Financing points
61,500.00	Prepaid interest, 1 year, 7 1/2% x 820,000
$160,000.00	Cash to sellers at closing

3.   Closing as of September 1, 1974. Seller to provide
title policy to buyer, all rental and damage deposits to
be transferred to buyer. All project income expenses,
taxes, and insurance shall be pro-rated as of the closing
date.

4.   The initial payment on the wrap-around mortgage note
will be due on September 1, 1974, provided, however,
such payment shall be applied in full to the reduction
of principal.

5.   Seller will retire all loans and encumbrances existing on the property except the three mortgage loans which
underlie the wrap-around loan. The wrap-around loan will
have original principal of $820,000.00 at 7 1/2% interest
rate amortized over a period of 26 1/2 years with an
accelerated maturity (balloon) at the end of 10 years
from the date of execution thereof. Said note shall provide that it is prepayable without penalty at any time
after the expiration of one year following consummation
of this transaction. Said note shall also provide that
neither the maker, nor any other party interested in the
subject property, shall have any personal liability for
the repayment of such note but that the holder thereof
shall look solely to the security for satisfaction of said
obligation in the event of default.

EXHIBIT 12–8. (*Continued*)

6. We will agree that after the expiration of five years, the seller can obtain refinancing of this obligation and tender it to purchaser and purchaser will be obligated to refinance provided the refinancing is at a 9.3 constant or less and such refinancing can be accomplished at no cost to the buyer. This obligation will extend until 7 1/2 years following consummation. From 7 1/2 to 10 years following consummation, seller shall have the further right to obtain refinancing of such obligation and tender the same to purchaser and purchaser shall be obligated to accept the same provided it can be accomplished at no cost to buyer but during this period buyer will be obligated to accept such financing if it is at a 10.0 constant or less.

7. The payee named in the promissory note secured by the wrap-around mortgage shall be The Town National Bank, Trustee, and a trust agreement will be entered into between purchaser, seller and The Town National Bank, as trustee, which shall provide for the bank to receive all payment due on such promissory note as well as payments for a reserve for taxes and insurance, to make all payment on all notes secured by mortgages which underlie the wrap-around mortgage, to pay all taxes and insurance premiums as and when the same become due, and to disburse any remaining monies in accordance with the instructions of seller.

8. As above provided, this transaction is going to be consummated as of September 1, 1974. The seller shall, however, be obligated to guarantee the income from such property for the remainder of the calendar year, 1974, at a rate equal to 95% of the monthly gross scheduled rents ($13,616.00) or a monthly guaranteed income of $12,935.00. To insure seller's performance in this regard, seller will deposit in an escrow account suitable to purchaser, at the time of consummation of this transaction, the cash sum of $10,616.00. Purchaser shall be allowed, for the months of September through December of 1974 to draw from such escrow account, monthly, an amount sufficient to raise the gross rents collected during such month to the sum of $12,935.00. In the event such sum deposited in escrow by seller is insufficient to accomplish this obligation, seller shall be obligated to make such additional contributions into escrow as may be necessary to maintain the gross rents at such 95% level. By the same token, as additional units are rented, and no vacancies occur, seller shall be entitled to withdraw from such escrow account an amount equal to the rental of such newly rented apartments multiplied by the remaining rental months of 1974. On December 31, 1974 such escrow shall be resolved and all monies remaining therein shall be delivered to buyer.

(*continues*)

EXHIBIT 12–8.   *(Continued)*

9.   This offer, and buyer's obligation to perform hereunder, is expressly contingent upon the following:

a.   Seller tendering to buyer, within ten days from the
date hereof, a title policy commitment showing good and
marketable title in seller with no encumbrances other than
those which are to be wrapped around or released at the
time of consummation and with no other exceptions other
than for utility easements which must be satisfactory to
buyer and for restrictions which likewise be satisfactory
to buyer.
b.   Seller furnishing to buyer, within ten days from
the date hereof, the current monthly profit and loss
statement (and such other profit and loss statements as
buyer may request) which shall reflect a performance
satisfactory to buyer.
c.   Seller furnishing to buyer, within ten days from
the date hereof, a current rent roll certified to be
correct, which rent roll must be satisfactory to buyer.
d.   Seller making the premises available to buyer,
within ten days from the date hereof, for a complete on-
site inspection.
e.   Seller furnishing to buyer, within ten days from
the date hereof, an itemized, verified inventory of all
personal property, including furniture, fixtures and
equipment, situated on the subject property.
f.   Seller furnishing to buyer evidence satisfactory to
buyer that all mechanical equipment situated on the subject premises is now and will be at the time of closing in
good working condition.
g.   Seller furnishing to buyer, within ten days from
the date hereof, a survey of the subject property showing
its area, boundaries, the location of all improvements
thereon and that there are no encroachments.
h.   Seller furnishing to buyer, within ten days from
the date hereof, copies of all notes and deeds of trust
which will underlie the wrap-around mortgage, the terms
of such notes, obligations and mortgages to be satisfactory to buyer.

If any of the foregoing, upon the examination by buyer,
prove to be unsatisfactory in buyer's sole judgment, then
buyer shall have the right to terminate this contract and
all monies deposited hereunder by buyer shall be returned
to buyer.

Feasibility Results. Davidson and Boomer have managed approximately eight hundred apartment units within a two-mile radius of Aspen Wood. Past experience and analysis had convinced them that there was a strong market for this complex and that the location was favorable now and into the foreseeable future. Aspen Wood appealed to them because of its location, sound structure, and good floor plans and amenities. It was for these reasons that the problems that arose when they researched the various items identified in the letter of intent were deemed worth working out.

On-site inspection revealed many inconsistencies. The "total refurbishment" program that allegedly had been completed had obviously missed many of the apartments. The flat roof had a number of serious problems, and the swimming pool filters and other major equipment were in questionable operating condition. The sellers were unable to produce an accurate rent roll, an inventory account, or other relevant details. The resident manager had recently been fired, and records were in disarray or missing. Vacancies, after freeloaders were evicted, amounted to 29 percent, not the reported 3 percent. The parking spaces shown in the seller's pro forma were seldom rented and deposits were unaccounted for. The management of this complex was clearly incapable of meeting any of the seller's projections.

The buyers also had questions concerning the legal and political efficacy of the transaction. A thorough reading of the note and deed of trust revealed that one of the underlying lienholders had an option to accelerate the loan, calling all remaining principal due when the property changed ownership. Securing the lender's permission to wrap around the existing mortgages took an unknown amount of politicking and financial compensation. To consummate the sale, all the limited partners had to agree to sign the contract. This was difficult to arrange because the three general partners representing the limited partners disagreed among themselves regarding certain parameters of the sale.

Davidson and Boomer thus discovered that they were not going to receive the economic entity assumed in the analysis thus far; the complex, as represented to them, did not exist. Some of the adverse facts discovered during the research process were surprises to the general partners as well, and their bargaining position dwindled. As a result, Davidson and Boomer drew up a new operating pro forma that incorporated lower rental rates, a higher expense ratio, and no income from deposit forfeitures. They also required guarantees and escrows, to be described in the sales contract. Their revised selling price reflected the new information:

	Revised Purchase Structure	Structure as per Letter of Intent
Note	$ 793,400	$ 820,000
Down payment	160,000	160,000
Commission	50,000	50,000
Selling price	$1,003,400	$1,030,000

These revised figures and expectations were used for the remaining analyses of Aspen Wood.

DCF ANALYSIS

The DCF analysis was rerun to reflect the adverse changes that had occurred as a result of the feasibility research and subsequent negotiations.

1. *Price reduction:* from $1,030,000 to $1,003,400.
2. *Debt reduction:* from $820,000 to $793,400.
3. *Gross possible income reduction:* by approximately $3,000 per year to reflect the drop in rent required to attain 95 percent occupancy.
4. *Expense ratio increase:* from 40 percent to 42 percent to reflect the increased operating expenses necessary to improve and maintain the building in good condition.
5. *More detailed tax package:* to increase the front-end tax benefits and the annual depreciation write-offs, within the framework of the 1974 tax law.
6. *Increased IRR requirement:* from 18 percent to 20 percent on equity, owing to the increase risk perceived as a result of the feasibility research.

    Return/Risk Evaluation. The main output data for the most likely run (assuming a five-year holding period) included the following:

- IRR on equity invested = 24.01%
- IRR on total capital invested = 8.43%
- ROE before tax = 9.9%, increasing to 15.1% over 5 years
- ROE after tax = 20.1%, decreasing to 18.3% over 5 years
- Debt coverage ratio = 1.23, increasing to 1.35 over 5 years
- Break-even point = 85.2%, decreasing to 82.3% over 5 years

All of the ratios indicate improving returns and decreasing risk over time and an acceptable IRR over a five-year period. Subsequent sensitivity and risk analyses confirmed this conclusion. The project, on average, met all the basic parameters set by the investors.

    Some of the primary risk management tools used by D&B were revaluation and renegotiation of the purchase price and terms, the use of a nonrecourse wraparound loan with favorable terms and conditions, and an increased IRR requirement to compensate for higher risk. In addition, aggressive tax planning in conjunction with the renegotiated purchase price and terms increased the IRR on equity (after tax) from about 22 percent (see Chapter 11) to 24 percent after the process was complete, thereby offsetting the increased IRR requirement.

    Although three months had passed since the initial screening process identified Aspen Wood apartments (it is now late November 1974), it appeared that the time spent would eventually pay off for D&B and the investors.

13

Tax Planning
and
Detailed Financial Analysis

In the days of the Indians there were no taxes—no debts—and the women did all the work. The white man thought he could improve on this system.

Death and taxes will always be with us; but there is a difference . . . death cannot get any worse.[1]

The tax laws in our country have become so complex and perplexing that more than one observer has exclaimed that "it takes more brains to make out income tax reports than it does to make the income." Tax laws, regulations, procedures, and guidelines become significantly more understandable when placed in an investment analysis framework and analyzed over the entire ownership life cycle. We are interested not in tax factors themselves, but, rather, in how they work through real economic variables and affect a property's investment value and expected rate of return and risk profile over both the short and the long run. We are especially interested in how we can manage and control tax variables within the framework of tax laws, regulations, and guidelines in order to increase or maximize the investor's after-tax IRR relative to business and financial risks.

During the development of our ten-step model of the investment analysis process, we noted that tax considerations are important in many of the steps. In fact, taxation considerations will play an important role in each step (except step 3) as illustrated in Exhibit 13–1.

In this chapter we will emphasize step 6 of the investment process, beginning our discussion by examining the various provisions of the federal income tax law

[1] Hugo H. Lowenstern, *Tax Facts* (Amarillo, Texas: Tax Facts, 1972), pp. 117, 118.

EXHIBIT 13–1.   Overview of Tax Considerations in the Investment Analysis and Financial Structuring Process

Step in the Investment Process*	Description of Relevant Tax Considerations
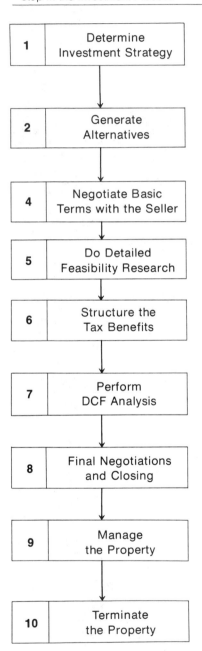 **1** Determine Investment Strategy	Tax objectives and criteria are defined at this stage; plans and policies are developed to achieve these objectives. Basic screening criteria may be oriented toward achieving tax objectives.
2 Generate Alternatives	Properties are located that meet the basic tax criteria. The investor might seek properties with low land-to-improvement ratios, sellers who are willing to take low down payments, with interest-only financing terms, and so on.
4 Negotiate Basic Terms with the Seller	The basic tax parameters of the purchase are negotiated with the seller. The purchase price, down payment required, and financing arrangements all have related tax impacts.
5 Do Detailed Feasibility Research	Basic data for arriving at the tax assumptions will be utilized to structure the tax package in step 6.
6 Structure the Tax Benefits	Detailed analysis and structuring of tax benefits is undertaken. A tax package that considers all ownership phases—acquisition, operations, and termination—is developed.
7 Perform DCF Analysis	The impact of tax variables as they interact with other economic and financial variables is analyzed. The tax results are compared to tax criteria established in step 1 and a final investment decision is made.
8 Final Negotiations and Closing	Final negotiation of the contract and closing details are arranged, locking in all tax ramifications produced by the price/terms/timing factors of the acquisition.
9 Manage the Property	Decisions regarding expensing or capitalizing cash expenditures, preventive maintenance programs, periodic refinancing and renovation, and leasing policies, among other factors, have important tax impacts each year.
10 Terminate the Property	Tax planning considerations include recognition of gain, installment or outright sale, tax-free exchanges, income averaging, and balancing off gains or losses from other sources.

* Step 3 (Analyze the Property Using the Basic Financial Feasibility Model) is excluded because tax factors are not considered at this stage.

as it affects real estate investors. Then we review numerous tax planning alternatives and discuss issues that affect a property's return and risk parameters. Finally, a tax strategy framework and checklist will be developed, incorporating many of the complexities discussed. Then, the Aspen Wood case is used to illustrate the principles presented, with detailed financial and tax analysis of that property.

The Economic Recovery Tax Act of 1981[2]

In August 1981 Congress passed the most comprehensive revision of the tax law since it was amended in 1954. The intended purpose of the Economic Recovery Tax Act of 1981 (ERTA) is to reduce the federal income tax burden on individuals and businesses, thereby placing more dollars into the private sector in the hope that capital will be reinvested in business enterprises to revitalize the American economy. For individuals, ERTA provides across-the-board income tax rate reductions phased in over the years 1981–1984. After 1984, individual tax rate schedules will be adjusted annually for inflation. Also, the maximum tax rate on all income is reduced from 70 percent to 50 percent, and the top rate on long-term capital gains is reduced from 28 to 20 percent.

For real estate investments the former system of tax depreciation has been eliminated and a completely new, simplified system called the accelerated cost recovery system (ACRS) has been adopted. In general, real estate investors will write off depreciable assets at a much faster rate than under prior law. (Appendix E at the end of the book contains the 1981 ACRS tables for real estate assets.) Also, on certain types of savings certificates interest received will be tax exempt, thereby encouraging deposits in financial institutions.

The vast scope of the changes in the tax law in 1981 will result in a reevaluation of many traditional tax planning ideas. While some of the particulars of the new tax law have not yet been resolved by Congress or the IRS, we incorporate here as many of the known variables and provisions as possible, show how these compare to the provisions of the prior law, and indicate how they are likely to affect real estate investment decision making.

As an investor you should consult tax planning literature to ascertain the current status of the new tax law as it is refined by the IRS and tested in the marketplace and through the federal court system.

THE TAX LAW

Real estate is taxed by all levels of government—federal, state, and local. The federal government taxes real estate investments through the income tax, the estate tax, and the gift tax. Our main emphasis here is on the federal income tax,

---

[2] For an excellent summary of the 1981 Act, including implications for tax planning from the investor's viewpoint, see Peat, Marwick, Mitchell & Co., *The Economic Recovery Tax Act of 1981*, August 5, 1981, 47 pp.; a similar publication is available from Arthur Andersen & Co. For a detailed analysis of the new tax law, including the text of the law and relevant commmittee reports, see Commerce Clearing House, Inc., *Economic Recovery Tax Act of 1981; Law and Explanation*, August 1981, 496 pp. Special thanks is given to James Flieller of Peat, Marwick, Mitchell & Co. who read the revised manuscript of this chapter and provided constructive and thoughtful criticism.

since it has by far the most important influence on real estate investment decisions. As we saw in Chapter 11, federal income taxes are levied on two forms of income: ordinary income and capital gain income. Gift and estate taxes are also relevant, but they will be discussed in Chapter 17.

In contrast to the federal government, most state governments do not rely on real estate as a primary source of revenue. Most states share in property taxes collected at the local level, and many states have an income tax, but the rates are quite low compared with federal rates. At the local level, the primary form of taxation is the real (ad valorem) property tax. For investment property such taxes are treated as operating expenses and, therefore, are deductible for purposes of federal income taxation.

The Income Tax Formula

Real estate investments, as contrasted with other investment media, generally receive relatively favorable tax treatment. One of the keys to understanding real estate taxation is to understand the general income tax formula. For individuals, this is encompassed by Form 1040—the individual income tax return. While the details of the 1040 statement are extremely complex, the basic formula contained therein is quite simple, as shown in Exhibit 13–2.

All Income   The income tax formula begins with the total income to the individual, including the following:

1. Wages, salaries, and tips
2. Interest income
3. Dividends
4. Capital gain or loss
5. Rents, royalties, partnerships, estates, or trusts
6. Scholarships, gifts, inheritances

For the real estate investor, items 4 and 5 are the key elements in generating tax shelter. In effect, the investor reports (1) the *net* amount of capital gains and (2) ordinary tax losses or income from each property and partnership. Under current tax law only 40 percent of the total long-term capital gain is considered taxable income at this stage of the formula. Also at this stage, income earned by the investor from other sources is sheltered by tax losses generated from real estate investments. Income is thus sheltered *before* personal deductions are itemized or before taking the standard deduction. (Under current tax law the standard deduction is called the "zero bracket amount.")

Adjusted Gross Income (AGI)   Deductions *for* AGI are subtracted from *Gross Income* to arrive at the *Adjusted Gross Income.* Deductions *for* AGI include items such as moving expenses, business expenses, and payments to an IRA or Keogh retirement plan. After the investor has determined AGI, he or she must choose between itemizing personal deductions or taking the standard deduction. If the investor has substantial mortgage interest and property tax deductions on a *per-*

EXHIBIT 13–2.   The General Income Tax Formula (Individual Taxpayer)

	All income
Less:	Exclusions
Equals:	Gross income
Less:	Deductions FOR adjusted gross income (AGI)
Equals:	Adjusted gross income (AGI)
Less:	Deductions FROM adjusted gross income (which consist of):
	1. The larger of:
	·A standard deduction, OR
	·Itemized personal deductions, PLUS
	2. Personal and dependent exemptions
Equals:	Taxable income
Times:	Applicable tax rate(s)
Equals:	Gross tax
Less:	Tax credits and prepayments
Equals:	Net tax payable

SOURCE: Raymond M. Summerfeld, Hershel M. Anderson, and Horace R. Brock, *An Introduction to Taxation* (New York: Harcourt Brace Jovanovich, 1979), p. 5–1.

sonal residence, these will be deducted as itemized personal deductions. Deductions related to a personal residence are therefore adjustments *from* AGI, while tax losses on other types of real estate investments are adjustments in arriving at *All Income*.

Taxable Income and Taxes   The tax rate is applied to *Taxable Income,* which is the net amount remaining after all exclusions and deductions have been taken. For example, the tax table for married individuals filing joint returns for years 1981–1984 is shown in Exhibit 13–3. The basic theory underlying the tax table is that the tax rate increases proportionately with the investor's income and wealth. In real estate the system sometimes works in reverse. For the investor who structures properties to produce tax losses, the tax benefit is directly related to the marginal income tax rate of the individual. If a married investor reports taxable income in excess of $215,400 (Exhibit 13–3), the marginal income is taxed at 50 percent (70 percent in 1981) and tax losses are used to shelter income that would otherwise be taxed at that rate.

For example, assume that a married investor has a taxable income of $109,400 in 1982 and subsequently purchases properties that produce tax losses of $109,400. By using these losses to offset the $109,400 in taxable income, the investor reduces net taxable income to zero.[3] Instead of paying $42,149, the investor receives a tax benefit of $42,149, and income through all the tax

---

[3] For the moment we will ignore the minimum tax provision, which may increase taxes payable.

EXHIBIT 13–3.   Tax Rate Schedules for Married Individuals Filing Joint Returns

Taxable Income	1981*		1982		1983		1984	
	Pay +	% on Excess**	Pay +	% on Excess**	Pay +	% on Excess**	Pay +	% on Excess**
0– $3,400	0	0	0	0	0	0	0	0
$3,400– 5,500	0	14	0	12	0	11	0	11
5,500– 7,600	$294	16	$252	14	$231	13	$231	12
7,600– 11,900	630	18	546	16	504	15	483	14
11,900– 16,000	1,404	21	1,234	19	1,149	17	1,085	16
16,000– 20,200	2,265	24	2,013	22	1,846	19	1,741	18
20,200– 24,600	3,273	28	2,937	25	2,644	23	2,497	22
24,600– 29,900	4,505	32	4,037	29	3,656	26	3,465	25
29,900– 35,200	6,201	37	5,574	33	5,034	30	4,790	28
35,200– 45,800	8,162	43	7,323	39	6,624	35	6,274	33
45,800– 60,000	12,720	49	11,457	44	10,334	40	9,772	38
60,000– 85,600	19,678	54	17,705	49	16,014	44	15,168	42
85,600–109,400	33,502	59	30,249	50	27,278	48	25,920	45
109,400–162,400	47,544	64	42,149	50	38,702	50	36,630	49
162,400–215,400	81,464	68	68,649	50	65,202	50	62,600	50
215,400–	117,504	70	95,149	50	91,702	50	89,100	50

SOURCE: Reproduced with permission from *Economic Recovery Tax Act of 1981: Law and Explanation*, published and copyrighted by Commerce Clearing House, Inc., 4025 W. Peterson Ave., Chicago, Illinois 60646.
* The rate schedule shown above for 1981 is the same as that applied for 1980 taxes. A taxpayer may use this schedule to find the approximate taxes due for 1981 by computing the tax under the schedule and reducing the result by 1.25%. The IRS is expected to issue an official 1981 rate schedule that will incorporate the 1.25% tax cut.
** The amount by which taxable income exceeds the base of the bracket.

brackets (from 50 percent down to zero) has been sheltered. The greatest benefits, of course, are received at the higher tax brackets; lower tax brackets produce lower amounts of tax saving. In this example, the *effective marginal* tax rate used to calculate the tax savings (assuming that the tax situation shown remains unchanged over the holding period) should have been approximately 38.5 percent:

$$\text{Effective marginal tax bracket} = \frac{\text{taxes saved}}{\text{income sheltered (amount of tax loss)}}$$

$$= \frac{\$\ 42,149}{\$109,400}$$

$$= 38.52\%$$

The investor must always consider the impact of new investments on the marginal tax bracket. In the case above, the marginal bracket went from 50 percent to zero, with the net impact being an *effective marginal bracket* of 38.5 percent for investment analysis calculations. If the original 50 percent marginal tax bracket were used (instead of 38.5 percent), the resulting cash flow projections (after tax) would overstate the amount of annual tax savings.

Net Tax Payable The Gross Tax minus tax credits and prepayments equals the Net Tax Payable. Investment tax credits have played an increasing role in real estate investments in recent years. Tax credits are often preferred by Congress when it seeks to stimulate capital investment, since individuals in lower tax brackets benefit equally with those in higher brackets. On the other hand, liberalizing investment expense deductions favors individuals in higher tax brackets. An increased depreciation deduction of $10,000 is worth $5,000 to an individual in the 50 percent bracket, but only $2,500 to a person in the 25 percent bracket. An investment tax credit is thus a direct tax subsidy, while increased expense deductions are an indirect subsidy that works through the investor's tax bracket and favors persons in high tax brackets.

Corporations Corporations use an abbreviated form of the tax formula to compute taxable income. They go directly from Gross Income to Taxable Income, with deductions allowed for all ordinary and necessary business expenses. Under the 1981 Tax Act the top corporate income tax rate is 46 percent; a graduated rate structure is provided for corporations with taxable income of less than $100,000, with minor changes over tax years 1981–1983:

CORPORATE TAX RATES

Taxable Income	Tax Rate (%)		
	1981	1982	1983
0–$25,000	17	16	15
$25,000–50,000	20	19	18
$50,000–75,000	30	30	30
$75,000–100,000	40	40	40
over $100,000	46	46	46

Capital Gain Versus Ordinary Income

In our DCF analysis in Chapter 11, we measured two types of income:

1. *Ordinary income.* Rents, vending machine income, deposit forfeitures, and so on. After operating expenses, interest, and depreciation were deducted, these income sources became *Taxable Income* and were taxed at ordinary income tax rates. In the case of tax losses, tax savings were generated at the ordinary income tax rates.
2. *Capital gain income.* When realized upon the sale of the property, this type of gain, except for the amount of excess depreciation, was taxed at the lower long-term capital gain tax rate—assumed to be 40 percent of the ordinary income tax rate.

Capital Gain Taxation of Individuals　Unlike ordinary income, there is no published tax table for capital gain income. The ordinary method of handling a long-term capital gain is to take 40 percent of the capital gain, add it to ordinary income, and then apply the ordinary income tax rate as provided in the tax tables. For purposes of investment analysis this has the effect of placing the maximum tax on long-term capital gain at 20 percent after 1981 (40 percent times the highest individual tax bracket of 50 percent). However, this ignores the effects of the alternate minimum tax on capital gains and the impact of a sale on the investor's ordinary income tax bracket, all of which can significantly raise the effective capital gain rate and adversely affect projected after-tax returns.

Exhibit 13–4 illustrates how the realization of a large capital gain can raise the marginal ordinary income and long-term capital gain tax brackets. In the example, Smith will experience an increase in capital gain tax bracket from 13 to 20 percent without the aid of income averaging or an installment sale to spread a $200,000 gain realized over a period of years.

The alternate minimum tax on capital gains and its impact on the investor's tax bracket will be discussed in a later section.

Capital Gain Taxation of Corporations　The corporate capital gain rate is 28 percent, *or* a corporation can treat the whole gain as regular income, taxable at the graduated corporate tax rates. A corporation chooses the method that results in the lowest tax liability.

Necessary Conditions for Long-Term Capital Gain Treatment　There are four conditions that must be met to achieve favorable long-term capital gain treatment on the sale of property. If they are not met, some or all of the gain recognized will be considered ordinary income.

1. The property must be considered a *capital asset* or *Section 1231 property* under the tax code definition.
2. The property must be owned for a period greater than twelve months.
3. The investor cannot be considered a *dealer* in real estate.
4. The straight-line depreciation (cost recovery) method was used.

EXHIBIT 13-4. Example of the Impact of a Capital Gain on an Investor's Income Tax Bracket

Smith, a midwestern farmer, sold a tract of land in 1982 for $300,000 cash. The original cost of the land in 1970 was $100,000 and taxable income from farming operations is $30,000. Since Smith files a joint return, the marginal tax bracket from ordinary income is 33 percent. (See Exhibit 13-3.) However, the realization of the $200,000 capital gain raises the marginal tax bracket from 33 percent to 50 percent, computed as follows:

Taxable income before sale	$ 30,000
Plus: 40% of capital gain	80,000
Total taxable income after sale	$110,000
Marginal tax bracket after sale (married, filing joint returns)	50%
Effective capital gain bracket after sale (40% × 50%)*	20%
Marginal tax bracket before sale was	33%
Effective capital gain bracket before sale (40% × 33%)	13%

Smith's effective capital gain bracket rises from 13 percent to 20 percent as a result of the additional gain reported.

---

* Ignores alternative minimum tax considerations, which will be discussed later.

Many real estate assets (e.g., raw land investments) are considered *capital assets* by the tax code. However, a special provision of the tax code—Section 1231—allows for favorable long-term capital gain treatment for real or depreciable property used in a trade or business, provided that the property has been held for more than twelve months and the net total of the transactions for the year for those properties shows a gain. Surprisingly, most rental property (e.g., apartments, office buildings, shopping centers) is classified as Section 1231 property for tax purposes. Exhibit 13-5 illustrates how gains and losses are netted in the various categories of capital assets and 1231 property. Only the net amount, long-term capital gain (LTCG), is eligible for favorable capital gain tax rates. If the final netting process results in a long-term capital loss (LTCL), a short-term capital loss (STCL), or a short-term capital gain (STCG), taxes are levied or benefits provided according to the taxpayer's classification, either corporation or individual, as shown.

Note that the sale of Section 1231 property (most income property) can result in even more favorable tax treatment than that given to capital assets because (1) the net gain is taxed as a long-term capital gain if held more than 12 months, and (2) a net loss is fully deductible against other income without the limitations imposed on the deductibility of a loss on a capital asset.

The third requirement for capital gain treatment is that the investor avoid the taint of *dealer.* A dealer is defined as one who holds property primarily for sale to

EXHIBIT 13–5. Taxation of Real Estate Asset Transactions*

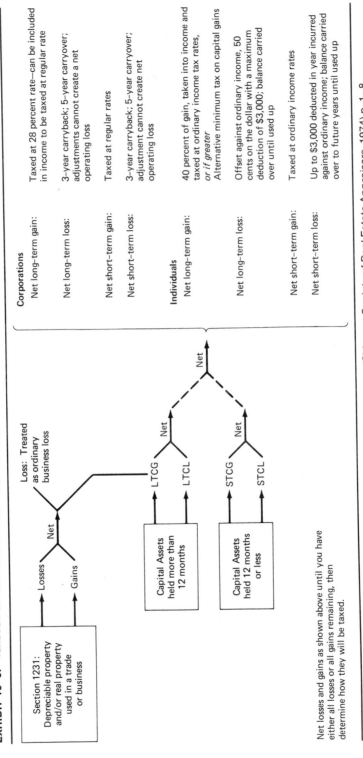

SOURCE: J. Warren Higgins, *Tax Considerations in Real Estate Transactions* (Chicago: Society of Real Estate Appraisers, 1974) p. 1–8.
*Updated through the Economic Recovery Tax Act of 1981.

customers in the ordinary course of a trade or business. A holder of property for long-term appreciation and/or income production is not a dealer. Many factors are considered in distinguishing a real estate dealer from an investor. They include the following:

- The seller's purpose in acquiring the property—whether for long-term investment or short-term resale.
- The purpose for which the seller actually used the property.
- The length of the holding period.
- Whether the property was promptly replaced with similar property, as is a dealer's inventory.
- Segregation of the investment property from business property on the owner's books.
- The extent of promotional or developmental activity—dealers, not investors, promote and develop their holdings.
- Whether the owner's intent at the time of sale was the liquidation of an investment, rather than turnover of inventory.
- The frequency of sales of the particular type of property sold—numerous sales point to a business rather than an investment.
- Whether the gain realized resulted from the owner's development activities or was a long-term appreciation in value.
- The manner in which the property was sold and the purpose for which it was held at the time of sale.[4]

The IRS will often contest the capital gain treatment if the investor is a real estate salesperson, broker, or developer, or has sold several properties within a reasonably short time. While real estate practitioners are especially vulnerable to IRS scrutiny of capital gains reported, other professionals and business executives are also frequently challenged. For example, the following situations will militate against favorable capital gains treatment for any investor: (1) Several properties are sold in one tax year, (2) the net gains from property are a large part of the investor's total income, (3) the investor actively advertises and sells the properties he or she owns without using a broker, and (4) a large percentage of the investor's time is devoted to real estate investment transactions.

Investors can take an aggressive position on the classification of their property. If an investor is not successful in having the property classified as investment property, the risk is that the IRS will reclassify the property and charge the difference between the ordinary and capital gain taxes, plus interest (which is deductible) on the deficiency.[5] Even developers have been permitted capital gains treatment by the courts, provided they have been careful to segregate their books and

[4] Mason J. Sacks, *Real Estate Tax Shelter Techniques,* Portfolio Number 13 (Boston: Warren, Gorham, & Lamont, 1977), p. 36.
[5] Coopers & Lybrand, *Tax Planning for Real Estate Transactions,* Jerome Y. Halperin et al., eds., prepared for the Farm and Land Institute of the National Association of Realtors, 1978, p. 186.

list their investments separately from property suitable for development. Carefully kept books and records are essential to a successful investor defense.[6]

The fourth condition for complete capital gain treatment requires that the investor have used only straight-line depreciation (cost recovery).[7] To the extent that depreciation on residential and commercial properties is taken in *excess* of straight line, the excess is taxed as ordinary income rather than capital gain income. Also, where an accelerated method is used for commercial properties, the total amount of depreciation (cost recovery) deductions taken is taxed as ordinary income. One notable exception to these rules occurs when a qualified government-sponsored housing project is owned (as explained below).

Capital Gain and Depreciation Recapture   The amount of *total gain* recognized on the sale of real estate is equal to the difference between the depreciated basis of the property and the net selling price of the property (see Exhibit 13–6). If the owner used the straight-line method of depreciation and the property qualifies for long-term capital gain tax treatment, the entire difference $(B - D)$ is taxed as a capital gain. However, if accelerated depreciation was claimed and the property is *residential* in character, the difference between accelerated and straight-line depreciation (called *excess depreciation* or *depreciation recapture*) is taxed as ordinary income.

Under the 1981 Tax Act the recapture rules have been modified for nonresidential (commercial) properties where the investor has elected an accelerated depreciation (cost recovery) method. In such cases, not only will the amount of excess depreciation $(D - E)$ be treated as ordinary income, but the total amount of straight-line depreciation taken $(C - D)$ will also be treated as ordinary income. Thus, for commercial properties such as buildings and shopping centers, the total amount of depreciation taken $(C - E)$ will be taxed as ordinary income when the property is disposed of. The investor can avoid such onerous recapture treatment only if the depreciation method is limited to straight line; if the straight-line depreciation method is used, then the entire gain $(B - D)$ is a capital gain.

The recapture rules are also modified for government-qualified, low-income residential properties. For such properties, if the holding period is less than 100 months (8 1/3 years), all excess depreciation is recaptured as ordinary income. For each month thereafter, a 1 percent credit is given toward capital gain treatment. After 200 months (16 2/3 years), all excess depreciation has been converted to capital gain income. This phase-out provision for depreciation recapture is intended to provide a tax incentive for investment in low-income housing.

Exhibit 13–6 assumes purchase of a building (no land) at a cost of $100,000

---

[6] A strategy for avoiding dealer-investor problems is provided by Richard P. Sills in, "The Dealer-Investor Problem Revisited: Charting a Course to Avoid the Pitfalls," *Journal of Real Estate Taxation*, Fall 1976, pp. 24–40; see also the author's earlier article on the subject, "The 'Dealer-Investor' Problem: Observations, Analysis, and Suggestions for Future Development," *Journal of Real Estate Taxation*, Fall 1974, pp. 51–67.

[7] Under the 1981 Tax Act the term *cost recovery* is introduced to distinguish pre-1981 depreciation rules from post-1981 depreciation rules. Since the term *depreciation* is ingrained in tax planning literature, it is unlikely to be completely replaced by the term *cost recovery*. Throughout our discussions we will use the terms interchangeably.

EXHIBIT 13-6.   Taxation of Total Gain upon Sale of Property

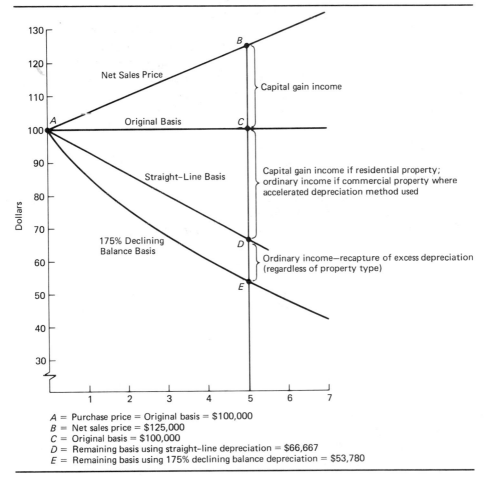

A = Purchase price = Original basis = $100,000
B = Net sales price = $125,000
C = Original basis = $100,000
D = Remaining basis using straight-line depreciation = $66,667
E = Remaining basis using 175% declining balance depreciation = $53,780

with a depreciable life (recovery period) of fifteen years; the building appreciates at the rate of 5 percent (noncompounded) per year. At the end of five years the property has a market value of $125,000 and is sold at that price. Line AB shows the annual market value of the property. Line AC shows the original basis of the property. Line AD shows the annual depreciated basis for the property assuming the investor used straight-line depreciation. The amount of gain represented by the distance between points B and D will be taxed as a capital gain, except in the case of a commercial property where an accelerated depreciation method was used. Line AE shows the annual basis for the property, assuming the investor uses the 175 percent declining balance method. The amount of gain represented by the distance between points D and E is the portion subject to recapture and will be taxed as ordinary income, regardless of the property type.

Depreciation and the Accelerated Cost Recovery System

Certainly the most significant variable that creates tax shelter benefits for the investor is the allowance for depreciation. From the beginning, the federal tax laws recognized an investor's right to deduct from taxable income an amount representing the *using up* of assets. In essence, this is a recognition that a portion of the net operating income from a property represents not true income but a recoupment of the capital investment, measured by the depreciation of those assets.

Prior to the Economic Recovery Tax Act of 1981, there were six factors to be considered in calculating the amount of depreciation that could be deducted by the investor each year:

1. *Depreciable basis* — the amount of capital expenditures allocated to improvements, less salvage value.
2. *Salvage value* — the amount that will be realized upon disposing of the property at the end of its useful life.
3. *Method of depreciation* — straight-line, declining-balance, sum-of-the-years' digits, sinking-fund,[8] or other allowable methods.
4. *Useful life* — the number of years over which the asset will be depreciated for tax purposes.
5. *Component depreciation* — the separation of total improvements into component parts and the calculation of depreciation schedules for each.
6. *Special depreciation provisions* — such as bonus depreciation on personal property purchased, and accelerated write-offs for rehabilitation expenditures.

The 1981 tax act simplifies the depreciation determination using these six variables and should greatly reduce depreciation controversies between investors and the IRS. In general, the 1981 act provides a more rapid depreciation system — the *accelerated cost recovery system (ACRS)* — which is intended to provide incentives for increased real estate and other capital investment, higher national productivity, and a lower inflation rate during the 1980s. The new depreciation deductions under the ACRS are called *recovery deductions* and apply to all real estate assets acquired after 1980. The concept of ACRS eliminates the need to determine the depreciation method used for each asset, its useful life, and its salvage value. As we will see, these determinations are greatly simplified and allow the investor fewer choices. (In the following sections, the terms *depreciation* and *cost recovery* will often be used interchangeably.)

Depreciable Basis and Salvage Value   What capital expenditures can be depreciated over time? In general, if a property expenditure is capitalized, everything except land and salvage value can be depreciated. For most properties purchased prior to 1981, investors were allowed to ignore salvage value and write the basis of improvements down to zero over the expected useful life of the asset.[9] Under the 1981 act, salvage value is to be disregarded altogether. With regard to allocations between land and improvements, tax shelter maximizers are motivated to

---

[8] David A. Diegelman, *The Tax Shelter of Real Estate* (Menlo Park, California: Master Sales Institute, no publication date), p. 7.
[9] Arthur Andersen & Company, *Federal Taxes Affecting Real Estate* (1978), pp. 96–97.

allocate the maximum amount of basis to improvements and a minimum to land, thereby maximizing the amount of potential depreciation over time.

The problem of allocations between improvements and land is especially difficult when land and improvements are acquired together for a lump sum. The IRS regulations are silent on the issue of how the respective values are to be ascertained. While a professional appraisal is one approach to solving the problem, few investors are anxious to incur the expense of a professional appraisal for this purpose alone. Other approaches used successfully by investors include the establishment of land and improvement values based on (1) the local tax assessor's allocation, (2) allocations specified by the seller and buyer in the purchase contract, and (3) valuation of the building from an investment viewpoint by capitalizing its cash flow.[10]

When does depreciation begin? Since depreciation is allowed on property that is assumed to be decreasing in value because of physical wear and tear, depreciation of an asset should begin when the asset is placed in service. Depreciable property usually is considered to be placed in service when it has been completed and is ready to be occupied by renters.

On properties purchased prior to 1981 numerous methods for calculating depreciation charges for a property purchased during the middle of a tax year were allowed.[11] However, the 1981 tax act eliminates any choice of method and prescribes that *real property* be depreciated from the first day of the month in which the property is acquired or placed in service. In contrast, *personal* property must use the *half-year convention*—50 percent of the first year's depreciation is deducted regardless of when during the year the asset is acquired.

Depreciation (Cost Recovery) Methods Traditionally, the tax law permitted real estate investors to use one of three depreciation methods: straight line, sum-of-the-years' digits (SOYD), and declining balance. Exhibit 13–7 shows the depreciation method limitations applicable to various categories of real assets acquired before and after 1981. The personal property category (Section 1245 property) includes assets such as furniture, drapes, refrigerators, stoves, individual room air conditioners, coin-operated vending machines, maintenance equipment, and carpets not permanently attached to the floor. Thus, numerous items in both residential and commercial properties qualify as personal property.

For properties acquired prior to 1981, the tax law authorized *maximum* depreciation-rate methods based on property type, age, and remaining useful life. In addition to those shown, other methods could be chosen by the investor, provided that the accumulated depreciation deductions were not greater than those that would have resulted using the maximum depreciation method authorized. The taxpayer was free to switch from any one of the rapid depreciation methods to the straight-line method when it became advantageous to do so. In contrast, the accelerated cost recovery system greatly simplifies the depreciation calculation by providing statutory percentages that dictate a schedule of accelerated cost recovery deductions for personal and real property. (Appendix E at the end of the book contains the ACRS tables for real estate assets.)

---

[10] For examples, see Sacks, pp. 10–11.
[11] Coopers & Lybrand, p. 128.

EXHIBIT 13–7. Depreciation (Recovery) Method Limitations Applicable to Real Estate Assets

Type of Property	Property Acquired Before 1981 Maximum Depreciation Method Authorized*	Property Acquired After 1980 Maximum Cost Recovery Method Authorized under ACRS**
PERSONAL PROPERTY (Section 1245 property)		
A. If the property is new	200% declining balance if life is greater than three years	Statutory percentages approximate the 150% declining balance method for years 1981–1984, the 175% method for properties acquired in 1985, and the 200% method for properties acquired after 1985. No new/used distinction. Assumes switch to straight-line or sum-of-the-years' digits method.
B. If the property is used	150% declining balance	
REAL PROPERTY (Section 1250 property)		
A. If residential rental property is		
(1) Acquired new	200% declining balance or sum-of-the-years' digits	Statutory percentages approximate the 175% declining balance method with switch to straight line for all property except low-income rental housing. Low-income rental housing is permitted deductions based on the 200% declining balance method with switch to straight line. No new/used property distinction is made.
(2) Acquired used with an estimated life of twenty years or more	125% declining balance	
(3) Acquired used with an estimated remaining life of less than twenty years	Straight line	
B. If commercial property is		
1. Acquired new	150% declining balance	Statutory percentages approximate the 175% declining balance method with switch to straight line. No new/used property distinction is made.
2. Acquired used	Straight line	

* Using a declining balance method, any rate *less than* that shown can be used in computing depreciation deductions.
** The investor can also choose a method of cost recovery based on the straight-line depreciation method. Other methods are not permitted.

In the case of *personal property,* the statutory percentages provide deductions that approximate the 150 percent declining-balance method for the early years, with a switch to the straight-line method in later years when it becomes advantageous to do so.[12] The "half-year convention" is used for the year of acquisition. After 1984, the recovery deductions are accelerated in two steps. In 1985 the statutory percentages reflect the 175 percent declining-balance method, with a change to the sum-of-the-years'-digits (SOYD) method. After 1985, the statutory percentages reflect the 200 percent declining-balance method, with a change to the SOYD method when that becomes advantageous. As an alternative, investors can elect to use a method of recovery based on the straight-line depreciation method.

For *real property* other than low-income rental housing, recovery deductions approximate the benefits of using the 175 percent declining-balance method for the early years, with a switch to the straight-line method. The recovery deductions permitted in the years of acquisition and sale take into account the number of months the property was held, in contrast to the use of the half-year convention for personal property. Low-income rental housing is permitted recovery deductions based on the 200 percent declining-balance method with a switch to straight line. Under the 1981 Act, there is no longer a depreciation-method distinction between new and used property, nor is there an important distinction between ordinary residential and commercial property. As with personal property, the investor can elect to use a straight-line recovery system for real property instead of the accelerated method.

Again recall that if the investor owns commercial property purchased after 1980 and uses an accelerated method, *all* recovery deductions taken will be treated as ordinary income when the property is sold. Only appreciation of property value will be treated as a capital gain. Consequently, the law provides a strong incentive for owners of commercial property to use the straight-line method. In comparison, owners of residential rental property are treated favorably—gain on the sale of property is ordinary income only to the extent that the accelerated deductions taken exceed those using the straight-line method (see Exhibit 13– 6).

The term *residential rental property* includes single-family and multifamily housing, apartments, and similar structures used to provide living accommodations on a rental basis. To qualify, at least 80 percent of the gross rental income must be from dwelling units. Hotels, motels, inns, or other similar establishments are not treated as dwelling units if more than one-half the units are used on a transient basis. If the investor owns a multiuse property, at least 80 percent of the gross income must be from the residential portion in order to qualify.

Low-income housing rehabilitation projects receive special treatment under the 1981 Act cost recovery rules. Such expenditures qualify for a special 60-month amortization period for up to $40,000 per unit. To qualify, however, such projects must meet strict criteria that may appear onerous to potential investors.[13]

---

[12] See Chapter 11, footnote 18 for a formula that can be used to determine the optimum time to switch from the declining-balance to the straight-line depreciation method.
[13] Commerce Clearing House, §343, p. 105.

EXHIBIT 13–8. Determination of Appropriate Recovery Period

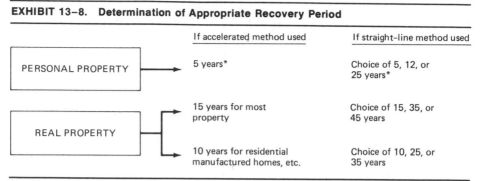

	If accelerated method used	If straight-line method used
PERSONAL PROPERTY	5 years*	Choice of 5, 12, or 25 years*
REAL PROPERTY	15 years for most property	Choice of 15, 35, or 45 years
	10 years for residential manufactured homes, etc.	Choice of 10, 25, or 35 years

* Some assets purchased as part of a real estate transaction, such as automobiles and equipment acquired in a hotel or motel purchase, may qualify for a 3-year recovery period.

Useful Life Determination   Traditionally, a popular technique for increasing depreciation deductions was to select the shortest possible useful life for the asset being depreciated. Although the choice of a useful life had a substantial impact on the amount of depreciation deductions claimed, and thus on a project's investment value and IRR, it was a highly subjective determination and disputes with the IRS were common.[14] Consequently, the 1981 tax act sought to simplify the system by defining only six useful lives, called *recovery periods*, that apply to real estate. These recovery periods are different for real and personal property, and are shown in Exhibit 13– 8.

If the investor uses the accelerated method of cost recovery for *personal property,* a 5-year recovery period must generally be used (some real-estate-related items, such as automobiles used in connection with a motel investment, will qualify for a 3-year recovery period). No shortening of this period is allowed for used property, as was possible before 1981. On the other hand, if a straight-line recovery method is elected, the investor can choose a recovery period of 5, 12, or 25 years. If rapid deductions are desired, the investor will always choose the 5-year alternative for personal property. As under the prior tax law, on the sale of personal property the portion of the gain that represents recapture of recovery deductions is treated as ordinary income; that is, all recovery deductions are recaptured as ordinary income. Using the straight-line recovery method limits the amount of recapture to the amount of straight-line deductions taken.

For most classes of *real property* a 15-year recovery period must be used by the investor who chooses an accelerated method of cost recovery. However, if the straight-line method is elected, then a recovery period of 15, 35, or 45 years can be chosen. A few types of real property, such as residential manufactured homes, will qualify for a 10-year recovery period.

[14] For elaboration on these points see John B. Corgel and Paul R. Goebel, "Choosing Depreciable Lives: Weighing Gains vs. Risks," *Real Estate Review,* Summer 1979, pp. 80– 84; Jerry S. Williford, "Selecting Useful Lives in Depreciation of Buildings," *Real Estate Review,* Fall 1977, pp. 31– 37; and Alvin L. Arnold, *Tax Shelter in Real Estate Under the Tax Reform Act of 1976* (Boston: Warren, Gorham & Lamont, 1977), pp. 21– 28.

Component Depreciation   A widely used technique for maximizing depreciation deductions prior to 1981 was the component depreciation method. When this method was used, each item (or group) of building components and equipment was depreciated separately, based on its own useful life. The effect of using component depreciation was to reduce the overall effective useful life of the improvements and increase depreciation deductions during the early years of ownership, thereby increasing a project's after-tax IRR.[15] Component depreciation was permitted on both new and used property, but often was not viewed enthusiastically by the IRS.[16]

Under the 1981 tax act, component depreciation is no longer available for real property; real property must be written off on a *composite* basis using the appropriate recovery period shown in Exhibit 13–8. Note, however, that personal property is treated separately. Thus, for a purchase involving both real and personal property, two components will be written off by the investor. Furthermore, as substantial additions or improvements are made to real or personal property subsequent to project acquisition, the investor will treat each as a separate purchase and establish a cost recovery schedule for each, using the prescribed cost recovery method and period. In effect, then, there is a limited form of component depreciation allowed when the entire project holding period is considered.

Special Depreciation Provisions   Prior to 1981, an investor could claim a special first-year depreciation allowance, known as *bonus depreciation,* for personal property for the first year in which it was placed in use. The allowance was 20 percent of the cost of the personal property, with a maximum deduction of $2,000 per individual or partnership in any tax year. The 1981 act repeals this bonus depreciation provision but does allow an investor to take a special deduction, known as a *Section 179 deduction,* on qualified personal property in the year of acquisition. The investor can expense qualified personal property to the extent of certain annual dollar limitations, as follows:

Acquired in Tax Year	Annual Dollar Limitation
1982, 1983	$ 5,000
1984, 1985	$ 7,500
1986 and thereafter	$10,000

For a married individual filing a separate return, the amounts are reduced by one-half. In the case of a partnership, both the partnership and each partner are subject to the annual dollar limitation. Unlike the bonus depreciation rule, which

[15] Robert W. Wyndelts and Joseph M. Davis, *Component Depreciation: A Likely Option For Real Estate Investments* (College Station, Texas: Texas Real Estate Research Center, Texas A & M University, 1978), 27 pp.; see also Davis and Wyndelts, "Component Depreciation for a Shopping Center," *The Appraisal Journal,* April 1979, pp. 209–217.

[16] For example, see Sheldon Schwartz and Richard J. Livingston, "What Price Accelerated Depreciation," *Journal of Real Estate Taxation,* Fall 1978, pp. 32–45.

allowed many personal property items to qualify, the Section 179 deduction applies only to property that qualifies for the investment tax credit. As we will see later, residential properties do not contain many items that qualify for investment tax credits.

Another special depreciation provision is the five-year (60 month) write-off for low-income housing rehabilitation expenditures, as noted previously. This provision is intended to be a stimulus to investors to rehabilitate low-income rental housing.

The Minimum Tax

Thus far, the minimum tax has not directly entered into our cash flow computations. The minimum tax is a result of congressional desire to create more "tax equity" by ensuring that no taxpayer can use a combination of long-term capital gain exclusions and other *tax preferences* to reduce tax liability to zero or a nominal amount. The 1978 Revenue Act made the minimum tax an extremely complex calculation for the investor. The net impact is to impose additional taxes on real estate investors who rely heavily on two *tax preference items:* (1) accelerated depreciation (cost recovery) on real property in excess of straight-line depreciation and (2) the 60 percent untaxed portion of an investor's long-term capital gain.[17] The amount of accelerated depreciation, as well as other tax preference items created by investments such as oil and gas, is taxed under a provision called the *add-on minimum tax;* the untaxed portion of a capital gain is taxed under a provision called the *alternate minimum tax on capital gains.*

The Add-on Minimum Tax   The add-on minimum tax is payable in addition to the investor's regular income taxes. Each year the investor adds together all tax preference items (except capital gains), subtracts the greater of $10,000 or one-half the regular income taxes due, and multiplies the result by 15 percent to determine the tax payable. Assume that an investor has property that results in excess depreciation of $100,000 each year, and has a regular tax liability of $40,000. Assuming that no other tax preference items are present, the add-on minimum tax would be calculated as follows:

Amount of excess depreciation	$100,000
Less: Exemption (greater of $10,000 or one-half the regular tax—1/2 of $40,000)	−20,000
Equals: Taxable excess depreciation	$ 80,000
Times: Add-on minimum tax rate	.15
Equals: Add-on minimum tax payable	$ 12,000

[17] The 1981 tax act defines a new item in the list of tax preference items—the excess of the cost recovery deduction for each leased property (other than 15-year real property) over the straight-line depreciation deduction that would have been allowable if it were computed in accordance with the following recovery periods: (1) five years in the case of 3-year property, (2) eight years in the case of 5-year property, and (3) fifteen years in the case of 10-year property. Simply stated, the investor is required to compute the cost recovery deductions under two recovery periods for each class of asset; the difference is a tax preference item. For elaboration, see Commerce Clearing House, §135, p. 54. Also, note that our discussion here pertains to individual investors, not corporate investors. A corporate entity is subject to an *add-on minimum tax* but not to an *alternative minimum tax on capital gains.*

The effect of the add-on minimum tax provision is to raise the investor's effective ordinary income tax rate, and should be considered when estimating inputs for a DCF analysis.

Alternative Minimum Tax on Capital Gain   The 1981 tax law allows an investor to exclude 60 percent of capital gain income from taxation. However, the excluded portion may be taxed under the minimum tax provision, thereby raising the investor's effective capital gain rate. The taxable base subject to the alternative minimum tax is computed by adding (1) regular taxable income, (2) capital gain excluded from taxable income, and (3) the tax preference for "excess itemized deductions." This amount is subject to the following alternative minimum tax rates:

Amount	Rate
Zero to $20,000	0%
$20,000 to $60,000	10%
Over $60,000	20%

The alternate minimum tax on capital gain actually comes into play *only* when it exceeds the investor's regular tax liability *plus* the add-on minimum tax. And since the first $60,000 is taxed at less than a 20 percent rate, it takes a very large amount of capital gain to approach an effective rate of 20 percent. Because the highest regular capital gain tax rate for individuals is now 20 percent, this means that the alternative minimum tax rate will usually be lower and thus not apply to the typical investor.[18]

Investment Tax Credits

The investment tax credit provisions allow an investor to take a direct credit against regular tax liability for a maximum of 10 percent of an investment in equipment and other related personal property. Although the credit is not designed primarily for the benefit of real estate equity investors, many types of real estate property components will qualify. The credit effectively reduces the amount of equity investment in a property, thus increasing the expected IRR. Currently the investment credit is 10 percent of the *total cost* of a property if it has a recovery life of five years or more; an investment credit of 6 percent is applicable to some assets with a three-year life.

Qualifying Property and Credit Limitations   Except for a few special items— vending machines, washers and dryers, and window air-conditioning units— residential properties, in general, do not qualify. In hotels and motels, furniture, TV sets, drapes, elevators and escalators, and wall-to-wall carpeting qualify for the credit. In other commercial types of real estate, office equipment, pollution control

[18] See, for example James B. Kau and C. F. Sirmans, *Tax Planning for Real Estate Investors* (Englewood Cliffs, N.J.: Prentice-Hall, 1980), p. 142. An excellent analysis of the relationship between depreciation, the minimum tax, and the maximum tax on earned income, under the pre-1981 tax law, is presented in Gailen L. Hite and Anthony B. Sanders, "Excess Depreciation and the Maximum Tax," *AREUEA Journal,* Summer 1981, pp. 134–147.

equipment, display racks and shelves, refrigerators, neon signs, dehumidifiers, and pumps qualify. There is no apparent logic as to which properties qualify and which do not; furthermore the list of qualified properties changes periodically.[19]

Investment credits can be used to offset the first $25,000 of the investor's current-year tax liability. Thereafter, 90 percent of the investor's tax liability over $25,000 can be offset with additional credits. All unused credits can be carried back and/or forward fifteen years. Only $125,000 of used property will qualify for the credit each year ($150,000 after 1984), thereby limiting the total credit on used property to 10 percent of $125,000, or $12,500 annually.

One potential pitfall in using investment tax credits is the possible recapture tax that may be imposed if the property is disposed of before it has been held for its full ACRS period. For example, the percentage of the original credit claimed that must be recaptured for 5-year property (and added on to the investor's tax liability for the year) is shown below:

	For property that is not held at least				
	1 year	2 years	3 years	4 years	5 years
Percent recaptured	100%	80%	60%	40%	20%

Special Provision for Rehabilitation Expenditures   A special tax credit is provided to investors for rehabilitating qualified commercial buildings and for rehabilitating qualified historic structures (residential or commercial). The investment tax credit percentage is 15 percent for structures at least 30 years old, 20 percent for structures at least 40 years old, and 25 percent for certified historic structures. These provisions are substantially more favorable than those existing prior to 1982 and will provide a stimulus to real estate investment in older neighborhoods and central business districts of the cities throughout the country. Several limitations exist with respect to these special investment credits and they should be carefully researched when their use is considered.[20]

Investment Interest Limitations

Investors view the deductibility of interest payments on loans as one of the key advantages of owning real estate. However, there is a noteworthy limitation on such deductions under the current tax law—the limitation on *excess investment interest*. The primary purpose of the limitation is to restrict the amount of the interest deduction to the amount of investment income the taxpayer receives in the same year; interest on loans to carry property that has the potential of producing future capital gains, but generates little current income, is not deductible until the gains are in fact realized. Thus, income and expenses are to be matched; this is a basic tax principle that has often been cited by the IRS and the tax courts.[21]

---

[19] For example, in a recent ruling (Rev. Rul. 81–133, IRB 1981-18,5), owners of duplexes, apartment buildings, and similar investments were allowed to take an investment tax credit on furniture that is leased directly to tenants.

[20] See, e.g., Commerce Clearing House, #141–142, pp. 56–57.

[21] Arnold, p. 35.

Properties Subject to Investment Interest Limitations The limitation on the deductibility of interest applies only to interest paid or accrued on property "held for investment." For real estate investments this term can be classified and analyzed as follows:

1. *Trade or business property.* The limitation has little application to most rental property (e.g., an apartment or office building *owned and operated* by the investor). Such property is considered trade or business property rather than investment property.
2. *Net leased property.* This is the most significant type of real estate affected by the limitation. In general, property will be considered subject to a net lease if business deductions are less than 15 percent of the rental income from the property. Business deductions do *not* include ground rents or expenses for which the taxpayer is reimbursed by the lessee.
3. *Undeveloped land.* Another type of property that is ordinarily considered to be investment real estate is raw land held for speculation. Thus, interest on loans used to finance such land may be subject to the excess interest limitation. Suppose an investor acquires land with the intention of erecting commercial property on it? If the land remains undeveloped, it may be difficult to prove it is not investment property, unless the investor can show a history of maintaining an inventory of such property for development.

Limitations Imposed Under the current tax law excess investment interest can be deducted only to the extent of:

• An initial exemption of $10,000, *plus*
• "Net investment income" from rents, royalties, interest, dividends, and so forth, *plus*
• An additional $15,000 annually if the investor incurs indebtedness related to the purchase of certain partnership interests or corporate stock.

Interest deductions disallowed under these rules can be carried over indefinitely until they are used up. Furthermore, these interest limitations apply only to investors other than regular corporations—individuals, partners, Subchapter S shareholders, and trusts.

As a practical matter, the problem occurs most often with investments in raw land and net leased property. However, income property syndications where the seller or syndicator *guarantees* a return to the investors or where investors are passive rather than active management participants, can also be subject to these limitations.[22] When one is planning any transaction involving large amounts of interest to be paid, it is important to consider these limitations and seek professional advice.

---

[22] See J. Warren Higgins, "Limitation on Investment Interest Deduction," *The Real Estate Appraiser,* January–February 1978, p. 55.

TAX PLANNING ALTERNATIVES AND ISSUES

Among the more interesting tax-planning alternatives and issues an investor may encounter are: (1) timing of income as influenced by the choice of a tax year and accounting method, (2) operating deduction issues, including the great debate about capitalizing or expensing cash expenditures, and (3) the IRS audit. Each of these subjects will be addressed in the following pages. Since tax issues related to form of ownership were discussed in Chapter 9 they will not be discussed here.

Timing of Income: The Tax Year

When do you report your taxable income or losses to the IRS? Of course, you do so at the end of the tax year, which cannot exceed twelve months. But the tax year can be different for different ownership entities:

- *Individuals and partnerships* usually report at the end of the calendar year. Under certain conditions, a tax year other than the calendar year can be elected.
- *Corporations* often choose a fiscal year that is different from the calendar year. For example, a corporation may choose to be a "February 28 corporation," whose fiscal year runs from March 1 to the following February 28 (except for leap year!).

A primary reason for having a fiscal year that is different from the calendar year is to reduce or postpone taxes. For example, assume you have a "January 31" consulting and appraisal corporation. On January 15 you pay yourself a $20,000 bonus from the corporation, thereby reducing corporate earnings and taxes reported for the year ended January 31. When do you as an individual report the taxable income? For most individual investors, not until April 15 of the following year, 14 1/2 months later.

If income flows evenly during the year, it may be advantageous to close the first tax year at the point when income begins, especially if start-up losses can be passed through to individual investors. If income is seasonal, the tax year can be ended just prior to a normal high-income period in order to obtain recurring deferral of tax payments.[23]

The IRS does limit the ability of the investor to change the tax year to accommodate tax planning objectives. A corporate investor can change a fiscal year with IRS permission, or without permission under certain restrictive conditions. In either case, the change must be supported by a sound business purpose other than tax reasons.

Cash Versus Accrual Accounting   Real estate investors basically use two methods of reporting income—the cash method and the accrual method. The cash basis investor reports income when cash is actually or constructively received and expenses when actually paid, as shown in Exhibit 13–9 and the following examples.

[23] Coopers & Lybrand, pp. 69–70.

EXHIBIT 13-9. Accounting Methods

CASH METHOD

Income: Reported when actually or constructively received.
Expenses: Deducted when actually paid.

ACCRUAL METHOD

Income: Reported when earned (an unconditional right to receive it exists),
Expenses: Reported when they are incurred (a legal obligation to pay exists).

Example 1: An investor is holding a rental income check for $5,000 on December 20 and trying to decide whether to deposit the check this year and report it as taxable income, or wait until January to deposit the money and report the income the following year. Under the *constructive receipt* doctrine, the investor should report the income in the current year.

Example 2: An investor does "creative" year-end tax planning by writing a large number of checks to vendors and employees to increase current-year tax deductions. The investor does not actually have enough cash in the bank account and will not be able to cover the checks until January rents are received and deposited. The checks are placed in the top drawer of the desk until January 5, and then are mailed. Are these expenditures valid deductions for the current year? Upon audit, the deductions will be disallowed if they are discovered. There was no actual payment.

Example 3: You invest in a warehouse property on December 30 and prepay three years of property insurance to a local insurance carrier. The cash basis taxpayer can write off the whole expense in the current year. The one primary exception to this is where the deduction "distorts income." The IRS has the unconditional right to challenge *any* accounting method or deduction if, in its opinion, the reported income or expense distorts net income.[24] There are no definitive rules regarding what constitutes distortion of net income; consequently, significant tax risks may be created if the investor is aggressive in making accounting method decisions.

The cash method of accounting is generally preferred by most real estate investors because it is simple to understand, easy to use, and usually allows higher tax deductions and more flexible tax-planning alternatives. Because accrual accounting for real estate investment transactions is complex, it is usually avoided except by large corporations whose accounting policies require that all activities be reported on a consistent accrual basis. Also, if inventory is a substantial income-producing factor in the investor's business (e.g., the investor is a merchant homebuilder), the IRS will require the use of the accrual method.

Actually, most real estate investors use a hybrid method of accounting: They

---

[24] For example, see Arthur Anderson, pp. 88–89.

use the cash method to report operating income and expenses, but the accrual method when reporting depreciation, which is an accrued expense. Whichever method the investor chooses, the election must be reported to the IRS in the first tax return after the property is purchased. Once adopted, the method must be consistently applied and cannot be changed without the consent of the IRS.

Operating Deductions

In the cash flow examples presented throughout this book, we assume that we are cash basis taxpayers and thus record expenses when they are paid. Clearly, the advantage of deducting expenses when they are paid, such as prepaying vendors, taxes, and insurance on December 31, is to produce the greatest possible tax write-off in the year in which it is needed the most. In most cases investors prefer to take higher deductions sooner rather than later, except when taxable income is expected to rise sharply in future years. In the latter case the investor might prefer to capitalize operating expenses and produce deductions in the years in which they will produce the greatest tax benefit.

The Great Debate: Operating or Capital Expense?   The great debate, which continues without end, is whether a cash expenditure should be expensed in the current year or capitalized and written off over a period of years.

Investor strategy. The tax-shelter-oriented investor will expense as much of the purchase price and as much of every cash expenditure each year after the property is purchased as can be justified. Such an investor might like to expense all new carpets and drapes; new air conditioning units, roofs, water heaters, and refrigerators; parking lot repaving, and so on. Immediate tax benefits are preferred to depreciation write-offs in future years. Most investors recognize the time value of money!

IRS position. The IRS, on the other hand, tends to be very conservative and would like the investor to capitalize most of the items listed above. The IRS defines a capital expenditure as anything that adds value to, lengthens the life of, or changes the use of the property. Prior to the 1981 Tax Act, if the useful life was greater than one year and was a significant dollar amount, the IRS required that the expenditure be capitalized. The minimum recovery period under the 1981 Act is three or five years, and it has not yet been determined how this capitalization rule will be administered.

Realistic position. The many court rulings dealing with the distinction between operating and capital expenditures are not consistent. Since policy seems to change from one regional IRS office to another, the investor should research the policies used by other ethical and aggressive investors who have been audited to determine the optimal strategy. For example, by being aggressive and writing off all minor capital items, the worst thing that will happen is that the investor may be audited and required to pay back taxes plus interest. As more than one investor has stated, "You don't get what you don't ask for!"

In most cases, the best plan is to keep the property in excellent physical condition through regular repairs and maintenance.[25] The related expenses are deductible in the year in which they are incurred, and result in a higher property value when the property is sold; this additional property value becomes a capital gain for the investor and should qualify for the 60 percent long-term capital gain exclusion.

Debatable Deductions   Over the years many court cases have identified specific *tax traps* and problem areas relating to operating deductions. Some of the more important ones involve lease-purchase contracts, security deposits, and a transaction involving a purchase price in excess of market value.

Lease-purchase contracts. The investor normally expects lease payments to be fully deductible as expenses for tax purposes. However, they may not be if a property purchase is structured as a lease with an option to purchase at a nominal price at the end of the lease term. Under this type of arrangement, the IRS will claim that a portion of the lease payment is actually a principal payment covering the cost of purchasing the property, and will disallow part of the lease payment as a deduction for tax purposes.

Security deposits. For a cash basis taxpayer, the IRS may argue that security deposits received are taxable income in the year received and tax deductions in the year paid back to tenants. The problem occurs most notably when the investor commingles security deposit funds with the bank accounts for operating income and expenses, and can usually be avoided if the investor keeps security deposits in a separate bank account and treats them as legally separate from the operating funds.

Price in excess of market value. Real estate tax shelter syndicates will often negotiate a price exceeding the *fair market value* of a property in compensation for high-leverage seller-created mortgage terms and a high property basis that allows liberal depreciation deductions. The courts have denied depreciation and interest deductions that are based on a purchase price far in excess of and having no relationship to the value of the building and land purchased.[26]

Other problem areas relating to expense deductions will be discussed later in the chapter when the concepts of tax shelter and tax shelter strategies are fully developed.

The IRS Audit

Investors are subject to periodic audits by the IRS. What is the strategy to be employed when the IRS audits your property returns? Experienced investors who are frequently defendants in the audit arena suggest that the development of a strategic plan that focuses on good records and a systematic, clear, and logical defense of all tax assumptions used in the property returns are the essential ingredients in successfully surviving an IRS audit. If the investor is unsuccessful, he or she will receive a tax deficiency statement from the IRS and must remit addi-

---

[25] Kau and Sirmans, p. 73.
[26] Arthur Anderson, p. 91.

tional taxes, plus interest, and a penalty tax in some cases. Under the 1981 Tax Act, the interest rate on deficiencies are established annually at the average prime rate and penalty taxes have been significantly stiffened.

Upon receipt of a deficiency statement, the investor has five basic decision alternatives:

1. Pay the additional taxes and interest requested.
2. Go to Appellate Conference and argue the case. If you lose, pay the taxes or choose among alternatives three, four, or five.
3. Pay the additional taxes requested; sue the IRS for a refund in the Federal District Court. (The investor can request a jury trial if this appears to be more advantageous than a trial by judge.)
4. Don't pay the additional taxes requested; go to the Tax Court and argue the case.
5. Don't pay the additional taxes requested; go to the Court of Claims and argue the case.

Ultimately, the case could be appealed up to the Supreme Court of the United States.

An investor should seek experienced legal and tax counsel when weighing the pros and cons of these alternatives, and should recognize that each regional IRS office differs somewhat in its orientation and audit practices. As with any investment decision, the basic question is, Are the returns worth the risks? The time involved and the "hassle" experienced by the investor are the key variables to be considered when measuring the risk associated with this decision.

TAX SHELTER STRATEGY

In this and previous chapters, we have made frequent reference to tax shelters. We have discussed the mechanics of tax shelters from the standpoint of both financial leverage and depreciation; and we have analyzed the strategy of expensing cash payments instead of capitalizing them and the debatable deduction items that frequently result in IRS challenges. However, the term *tax shelter* has not been explicitly defined or analyzed as a concept. In this section of the chapter we will develop the concept of tax shelter and present a decision-making framework for analyzing tax shelter strategy.

The Concept of Tax Shelter

Tax shelter can be defined in a number of ways and there appears to be little agreement on the proper definition to be used by investors. Here are a few possible definitions:

1. Any deduction or credit against income that is available only to a special category of taxpayer.
2. Any favorable tax treatment providing preferential tax relief of a particular investment under the Internal Revenue Code.
3. Transactions or investments that have one or more of three objectives: tax deferral, leverage benefits, and the conversion of ordinary income into capital gain.
4. Tax shelter exists whenever taxable income is negative; that is, when tax losses are generated and can be used to shelter other earned income.
5. Tax shelter exists whenever the depreciation expense is greater than amortization of principal. As long as this condition exists, at least part of the investor's cash flow from operations is sheltered.

The first two definitions are general in nature. Each definition thereafter becomes more specific. The fifth definition is the most useful one for understanding the nature and mechanics of tax shelter over the ownership period; this concept is based on the difference between the cash flow and the taxable income statements.

Comparison of Cash Flow and Taxable Income Statements   Consider the accounting statements shown in Exhibit 13–10. We will assume that the investor is a cash basis taxpayer and that all cash operating income and expense items are allowable revenue and expense items in the statement of taxable income. As noted previously, some investors use a different method of accounting for income and expenses, although these methods may not be acceptable for tax pur-

EXHIBIT 13–10.   Statement of Cash Flow and Taxable Income

	Cash Flow	Taxable Income
Gross possible income	$ 200,000	$ 200,000
Less: Vacancy and credit losses	− 20,000	− 20,000
Gross effective income	180,000	180,000
Less: Operating expenses	− 80,000	− 80,000
Net operating income	100,000	100,000
Less: Interest	− 80,000	− 80,000
Amortization of principal	− 10,000	0
Depreciation	0	− 70,000
Cash flow before-tax	$ 10,000	
Taxable income (loss)		$ − 50,000

poses. For example, a capital expenditure that is deducted as an expense in the cash flow statement may be disallowed in the tax statement. In our example, we assume an NOI of $100,000 in both statements and no difference between income and expense reporting policies.

As shown, the cash flow from operations is a positive $10,000. This amount can be distributed to the investor "tax free"; it is *not* reported to the IRS as income (contrary to the belief of some investors) because it is considered to be a recoupment of invested capital. At the same time, taxable income is negative, so we have an artificial accounting loss of $50,000 that can be used to shelter the investor's other income. In effect, we keep two sets of books—one real economic set of books and one for tax purposes.

The only difference between the two statements is in depreciation and amortization of principal. Therefore, the key to the tax shelter concept must be the relationship between these two variables, which in algebraic form can be expressed as follows:

$$CFBT = TI + dep - amort \quad or \quad TI = CFBT - dep + amort$$

where   CFBT = cash flow before tax (cash flow)
         TI = taxable income
         dep = depreciation
         amort = amortization of principal

For example, if depreciation is equal to the amortization of principal ($10,000), both cash flow and taxable income will equal $10,000. Every dollar of cash flow will be taxable; thus, there is *no tax shelter*. If depreciation is greater than amortization, then at least part of the cash flow is tax sheltered. When depreciation exceeds amortization by the amount of cash flow (10,000), taxable income is zero and the cash flow is completely sheltered. The investor receives a $10,000 cash distribution but reports no taxable income from the property. Once again, the IRS treats the $10,000 cash flow as a return *of* original capital to the investor; thus it is not a taxable transaction. Finally, if depreciation is greater than amortization *by more than* the cash flow, a tax loss is produced and can be used to shelter other income.

Game Plan of the Investor   The game plan of the investor with respect to tax shelter is to generate cash flow from operations (CFBT) and at the same time produce tax losses that are as high as possible for as long as possible. The goal is to produce artificial tax losses, not real economic losses. All "real losers" produce good tax shelter. Unfortunately, if tax losses are maximized through reduced rental income or increased operating expenses, real cash flow dollars are reduced commensurately; effectively, an investor in the 50 percent tax bracket must lose $1.00 to receive a $.50 tax saving. While most rational investors consider this a poor economic trade-off, history has suggested that many investors purchase property without sufficient regard for its *real* economic performance.

Tax shelter should be considered from an investment analysis viewpoint.

Such a viewpoint presumes that investors seek to maximize overall returns relative to risks, and that tax savings is only one of four cash flow benefits that can result from ownership: cash flow from operations, tax savings, refinancing proceeds, and net proceeds from disposition. To focus too much on tax shelter aspects is usually a mistake. In their recent book, *Tax Planning for Real Estate Investors,* Kau and Sirmans offer several words of caution in this regard:

1. Tax shelters generally have high risk. Does the expected rate of return compensate the investor for the increased risk?

2. Tax shelters may be the last outpost of *caveat emptor* (let the buyer beware). Investors should know with whom they are dealing and should read all relevant documents carefully. They should not be misled by the short-run benefits but should determine the total impact of taxation on the investment decision.

3. Most tax shelters have a sponsor–manager of the project. The ability, reputation, and past experience of the sponsor is a critical factor. Full and complete disclosure of the investment should be demanded by the investor.[27]

Stages of Tax Shelter   A distinct pattern of tax shelter emerges if a property has a stable or increasing cash flow from operations, there is a relatively high degree of mortgage financing, and an accelerated form of depreciation (cost recovery) is used. This tax shelter pattern can be described in five distinct stages:

Stage 1: Excess tax shelter. In the early years of ownership the entire cash flow from operations is sheltered from the payment of any income taxes, and there is *excess* tax shelter left over. Taxable income is negative; that is, a tax loss situation exists. At this stage depreciation exceeds amortization by an amount *greater than* the cash flow from operations.

Stage 2: Complete tax shelter. The entire cash flow from operations is sheltered from income taxes, but there is no excess. Taxable income is zero. At this stage, which occurs at a point in time during a tax year, depreciation exceeds amortization by the amount of cash flow.

Stage 3: Partial tax shelter. After a period of years the property shows a taxable income and part of the cash flow from operations must be used to pay income taxes. Depreciation is still greater than amortization, but by an amount less than the cash flow.

Stage 4: No tax shelter. Taxable income is equal to the cash flow. Thus every dollar of cash flow generated through rentals is taxable. At this stage depreciation is equal to amortization.

Stage 5: Negative tax shelter. Because of ever-decreasing amounts of mortgage interest and tax depreciation, the IRS begins taxing the project on income that exceeds the cash flow generated by the property. Amortization, which

[27] Kau and Sirmans, p. 23.

is a cash expense but is not deductible for tax purposes, is now greater than depreciation. Most investors feel very uncomfortable in this stage and take some action to correct the situation, if they have not done so prior to reaching this stage.

As the investor proceeds through the five stages, tax shelter declines and equity builds up through loan amortization. As more dollars are tied up in the property, leverage and tax savings decrease and opportunity costs rise. At some point, usually during the third stage, an investor will take one of several actions to correct the tax shelter problem that is developing. First, the investor can refinance the property and start a new interest cycle on the property. The refinancing proceeds are tax-free and can be reinvested in other properties. Second, the property can be sold and the equity reinvested in other properties, thereby creating new interest and depreciation cycles on the properties purchased. Third, a major renovation program can be undertaken to create a new depreciation cycle and increase tax shelter. Fourth, a tax-free exchange can be structured to raise the investor's depreciable basis and interest deductions, thereby increasing tax shelter. Finally, the investor can combine any two or more of the four actions. As always, the returns must be carefully weighed against the risks, since each action is a complex investment decision in itself.

Tax Shelter Pitfalls   The key to the tax shelter concept as presented above is depreciation working through the leverage magnification process. While many other variables influence the investor's taxable income and taxes payable, as we have discussed throughout this chapter, the two most important variables are depreciation and leverage. The investor should consider the following tax shelter pitfalls related to these variables, in addition to the general statements made earlier:

1. *Depreciation write-offs create future taxable gains.* For each dollar of depreciation write-off taken during the holding period, a dollar of gain is realized upon the sale of the property. If the property value has increased and an accelerated depreciation method is used, some of the gain will be taxed at the capital gain rate (if all the necessary capital gain conditions are met) and the remaining gain will be taxed at the ordinary rate. The net benefits are: (a) the time value of money and (b) the conversion of ordinary income into capital gain income if the property is not commercial in nature.
2. *Some tax depreciation is real economic depreciation.* Tax depreciation is an artificial accounting loss, but it may also be a real economic loss if the property is actually declining in value. Even if the monetary value of the whole property is increasing as a result of price inflation, components wear out and must be replaced periodically. To the extent that depreciation is equal to actual wear and tear, no *net* benefit is created by the depreciation process.
3. *Greater leverage creates greater financial risks.* Tax shelter benefits are magnified through (a) the use of leverage and (b) periodic refinancing to balance the relationships among depreciation, amortization, and the

amount of equity value tied up in the project. As we saw in our basic financial analysis, additional leverage also lowers the coverage ratio, raises the break-even point, and increases the probability of insolvency and the risk of ruin.

4. *Tax law reforms often reduce shelter benefits.* The structure upon which most tax shelter rules are built is very fragile. The laws are changed every two to five years, and the trend during the last two decades until the 1981 Tax Act, has been to chip away at the favorable tax treatment offered to real estate investors. The investor should test the impact of changing tax laws through sensitivity analysis of the tax variables. If such changes have a substantial impact on the investor's IRR and other investment criteria, the risks of tax reform should be weighed carefully.

Another problem that is often overlooked is the relationship among the amount of debt remaining, the market value of the property, and the tax basis of the property. Consider, for example, a property that is purchased for $1,000,000 and sold ten years later for $2,500,000. The depreciated tax basis at the end of ten years is $500,000. One year prior to the sale, the property was refinanced with a $2,000,000 loan. The "tax-free" refinancing proceeds were reinvested in other properties. Assuming, for simplicity, that the $2,000,000 loan is interest only, the situation at the time of sale can be described as shown in Exhibit 13–11.

Simply stated, the investor cannot afford to sell the property. The total taxable gain ($1,900,000) is more than four times the cash proceeds realized from the sale ($400,000); in addition a substantial portion of the total gain may be recaptured recovery deductions subject to taxation at ordinary rates. Those "tax-free" refinancing proceeds and "tax-free" cash flows during the holding period have come back to haunt the investor. They have become tax liabilities at the time of sale. Investors frequently overlook these common pitfalls and risks when they are designing tax shelter packages.

Tax Shelter Strategy Checklist

The investor should develop a tax shelter strategy within the framework of the ownership life cycle: acquisition, operations, termination. Assuming that we would like to design an aggressive tax shelter package for a high-tax-bracket investor that

---

EXHIBIT 13–11.   Relationship Among Sales Price, Loan Balance, and Tax Basis

Sales price	$2,500,000	
Less: Commissions and closing costs (4%)	100,000	
Net sales price	$2,400,000 ⌐A	
Loan balance	$2,000,000 ⌐⌐	B
Depreciable basis of property	$ 500,000	

A = Net sale proceeds received equals $400,000 ($2,400,000 − $2,000,000)
B = Total taxable gain equals $1,900,000 ($2,400,000 − $500,000)

will maximize the after-tax IRR over the holding period, which tax variables can be structured and controlled to achieve the goal? The following checklists will prove useful to the investor.

Acquisition Period   The objective in designing an aggressive front-end tax package is to create the maximum possible amount of tax deductions and tax credits in the year of acquisition. The effect will be to reduce the after-tax equity investment, since immediate tax benefits produce an immediate return of a portion of the investor's equity capital. In the past, investors have looked to the following variables to create tax shelter during the acquisition period:

	Available under Previous Tax Law	Available under 1981 Tax Law
• Prepaid interest	Yes	No
• Financing points	Yes	No
• Consulting fees	Yes	Very limited
• Organization and legal fees	Yes	No
• Prepaid management and leasing fees	Yes	No
• Construction period interest and taxes	Yes	Limited
• Prepaid taxes and insurance	Yes	Yes
• Bonus depreciation (or special first year expenses)	Yes	Yes
• Investment tax credits	Yes	Yes

Generally, the strategy was to convert "hard" dollars into "soft" dollars—to convert as much as possible of the purchase price into tax deductible dollars. This could be accomplished by reducing the contract purchase price for the property and substituting various fees and expenses that would be paid to the seller. Unfortunately for the investor, tax reforms during the 1970s eliminated most of the acquisition period write-offs. Except for the last three items on the list (prepaid taxes and insurance, bonus depreciation, and investment tax credits), the IRS now requires that most or all of these amounts be capitalized and written off over the appropriate recovery period. Since few alternatives remain for acquisition structuring, emphasis has shifted to the operating period.

Operating Period   The objective in designing an operating-period tax package is to create the maximum possible amount of tax deductions and tax benefits, *relative to the amount of cash flow and risk*. For example, although increasing the interest rate or prepayment penalties on a loan will create more tax deductions, it will also create *real* cash flow losses. Such actions are not usually worthwhile in the long run.

There are four categories of operating-period tax variables that are subject to some control by the investor:

1. *Depreciation deductions*
   • Basis of improvements—as high as possible
   • Salvage value—none under the 1981 act

- Useful life (recovery period)—as low as possible (fixed cost recovery classes under ACRS)
- Depreciation method—maximum allowed by law (ACRS defines statutory percentages for property types)
- Component depreciation—use whenever possible (very limited after 1981)
- Bonus depreciation (special first year expenses)—use on new expenditures that qualify
- Change depreciation method—when advantageous (very limited because ACRS defines statutory percentages to be used)

2. *Interest deductions and leverage variables*
- Amount of debt—as high as possible within risk constraints
- Interest rate—as low as possible generally (if too low, IRS will impute)
- Term of loan—as long as possible, interest-only is ideal
- Refinancing—periodic refinancing is usually desirable
- Prepayment penalties—as low as possible

3. *Operating expenses and revenue*
- Expensing policies—expense rather than capitalize where possible
- Shift expenses and reserve to years in which needed most
- Repairs and maintenance—keep property in good condition to maximize capital gain

4. *Investment tax credits*
- Amount—as much as possible
- Timing—as soon as possible, can carry back or forward 15 years

5. *Marginal tax rate of investor*
- Level—higher bracket receives more tax loss benefit
- Stability—change variables above to take advantage of possible tax bracket changes

Since the overall investment objective is to maximize return relative to risk, the investor should try various combinations of these tax shelter variables in order to best fit his or her objectives and risk-taking abilities.

Termination Period   At the end of the holding period the objective generally shifts to minimizing the tax consequences of the property disposition. Some of the more important variables to consider are:

- *Price and terms of sale*—obtaining the highest price will create more capital gain
- *Installment sale treatment*—to defer the taxable gain to the future
- *Income averaging*—to spread the taxable gain over past years and reduce marginal tax rate in year of sale
- *Tax free exchange*—to defer the taxable gain, increase depreciable basis and leverage
- *Allocation of sales price among components*—shift to components that have the least depreciation recapture potential
- *Gift or trust*—to minimize capital gains and estate taxation

Since termination period strategy is covered in Chapter 17, further discussion of these variables will be deferred to that chapter.

SUMMARY

Taxation and tax planning should be understood from an investment analysis viewpoint. The investor can learn to manage and control many of the important tax variables, thereby increasing a property's value and its rate of return relative to business and financial risks. The primary emphasis in this chapter was placed on the federal income tax and its impact on the investor over the entire ownership life cycle—acquisition, operations, and termination.

In the first section of the chapter, we analyzed various aspects of the tax law, including the general income tax formula that determines the investor's tax liability, ordinary and capital gains taxation, depreciation and the accelerated cost recovery system, the minimum tax, investment tax credits, and investment interest limitations. Then, we turned our attention to tax planning alternatives and issues, such as the choice of a tax year and accounting method and the great debate about capitalizing or expensing cash expenditures. Tax shelter strategy was the third major subject discussed. The ideal tax shelter game plan is to generate positive cash flow from operations while at the same time producing tax losses that are as high as possible for as long as possible. At the end of the holding period the investor seeks to have most of the taxable gain treated as long-term capital gain and taxed at favorable long-term capital gain rates.

After reviewing the various stages, pitfalls, and risks of tax shelter, a detailed plan for developing an aggressive tax shelter package was presented. We noted that tax laws are fragile and periodic changes in the laws tend to have substantial impacts on the investor's after-tax return.

In the final section of the chapter, we will return to the Aspen Wood Apartments case study and develop a more sophisticated DCF model that includes the many tax and financial variables discussed throughout this chapter.

ASPEN WOOD APARTMENTS

DETAILED FINANCIAL AND TAX ANALYSIS

In this chapter we have sought to develop many of the tax concepts that influence investment returns and risks. A more sophisticated DCF model must now be developed to handle the many variables discussed. While it need not be computerized, the analysis presented here was performed on a computer model known as "RE004: Detailed Financial Analysis and Tax Planning Model."[28] The project analyzed is the 84-unit Aspen Wood Apartments. Recall that the analysis was prepared in the fall of 1974 and the acquisition (closing) date was projected to be November 1, 1974. Charlie Davidson and Clyde Boomer, the managing equity investors, projected a holding period through 1979, or roughly five years plus two months of 1974. (The property was not actually sold until the end of 1981, as we will see in Chapter 17.)

CAPITAL EXPENDITURES (SECTION ONE)

The total cost to acquire the property, including all commissions, closing costs, and legal fees, was expected to be $1,003,400 (as negotiated in Chapter 11). The total equity cash required was $210,000, with a wraparound mortgage of $793,400. The detailed financial picture is shown in Exhibit 13–12.

For tax purposes, Charlie and Clyde sought to convert as much of the total purchase cost as possible into "soft" dollars, deductible in the year of acquisition. One full year's prepaid interest ($59,505) on the wraparound loan was negotiated with the seller; two financing points ($15,868) were paid to the seller; and a consulting fee of $15,000 was paid to D&B Associates by the joint venture partners. The total expensed items amounted to $90,373. (Note that under current tax law all three deductions would be capitalized. The consulting fee would be capitalized as part of the depreciable basis of the property and written off over the recovery period of the two components (real and personal property), rather than expensed in the year of acquisition. However, prepaid interest and points on the wraparound loan could be capitalized as a separate component and amortized over the 10-year balloon period of the loan, rather than written off over the recovery period of the property.)

---

[28] Stephen A. Pyhrr and James Arthur Baker, *Computer Models for the Detailed Financial Analysis and Tax Planning of Income-Producing Real Estate Investments*, TRERC Technical Monograph No. 2 (College Station, Texas; Texas Real Estate Research Center, Texas A & M University, 1979.) The computer software is available through the research center.

EXHIBIT 13–12.   Aspen Wood Apartments: Capital Expenditures

SECTION ONE: CAPITAL EXPENDITURES

Total Cost to Acquire Property

Total equity cash required	$ 210,000
Total debt	793,400
Total cost	$1,003,400

Allocation of Total Equity Cash Required for Tax Purposes

Expensed items		
Prepaid interest	$59,505	
Financing points	15,868	
Consulting fee	15,000	
Total expensed items		$ 90,373
Capitalized items		
Total capitalized items		119,627
Total equity cash required		$210,000

Balance Sheet at Date of Closing

Total cost to acquire property	$1,003,400
Less expensed items	90,373
Total assets	$ 913,027

Assets		Liabilities and Net Worth	
Working capital	0		
Land	$ 84,027	Total debt	$793,400
Total improvements	829,000	Net worth	119,627
Total	$913,027	Total	$913,027

Allocation of Total Improvements for Tax Purposes

Item	Percent of Improve- ments	Amount (Basis)	Percent Depre- ciation	Useful Life (yrs.)	Depre- ciation Method	Bonus Depre- ciation Appli- cable
Structure	55.5	$460,095	100	25	125	No
Paving, pool, etc.	5.5	45,595	100	4	100	No
HVAC	7.3	60,517	100	5	100	No
Appliances	5.3	43,937	100	3	150	No
Carpeting	2.4	19,896	100	4	100	No
Electrical and plumbing	19.0	157,510	100	9	100	No
Drapes and personal property	5.0	41,450	100	6	150	Yes
Total	100.0	$829,000				

At the date of closing, which was moved back to November 1, 1974 as a result of the problems that developed, the book assets were estimated to be $913,027, which is the total cost of the property less all expensed items. Of the total book assets, about $1,000 per unit was allocated to land and the remaining amount to depreciable improvements. As a result of the expensed items, *net worth* is shown to be only $119,627 at the date of closing. Net worth is simply the total equity cash investment ($210,000) *less* the amount expensed for tax purposes ($90,373). Each year the *book* net worth will decline by the amount of tax losses produced by the property; eventually it will become negative. At the same time, the investor expects the actual market value of the net worth (equity) to rise substantially.

The component depreciation method was used (as noted, this has been limited under the 1981 tax act), with no salvage value attributed to any component. Seven components are defined: six real property components and one personal property component. The basis allocations and useful lives were based on Charlie and Clyde's previous experience with such allocations, including numerous audits and negotiations with the IRS agents at the appellate conference level. At the time of acquisition, minimum tax provisions were less rigorous than they are now; therefore, D&B made greater use of accelerated depreciation methods. The maximum accelerated depreciation rates were taken on all components. Bonus depreciation was taken only on the drapes and personal items, although appliances could have been included. In 1974 each partner could receive up to $2,000 of bonus depreciation, or $4,000 for a joint return. Under the 1981 tax act these items could not be deducted; they do not qualify for the special Section 179 expensed deduction.

No property components qualified for investment tax credits, and no major capital expenditures were expected during the projected five-year holding period. The recent renovations were expected to maintain the property until the end of 1979, at which time a major renovation would probably be required. Increasing maintenance and repair costs would be expensed annually and would compensate for the increasing amount of wear and tear over the holding period. Also, to compensate for the aging of the building, property value would be increased at a slower rate (3 percent) than gross possible income (4 percent) and operating expenses (7 percent).

DEPRECIATION SCHEDULES (SECTION TWO) AND LOAN SCHEDULES (SECTION THREE)[29]

A depreciation schedule was computed for each of the seven components for two months of 1974 and annually thereafter for five years. If capital expenditures during the holding period and investment tax credits had been applicable, these schedules would have been generated at this point.

A loan amortization schedule was computed for the wraparound loan. Payments for the partial year 1974 as well as five full operating years were

[29] Because of space limitations these schedules are not shown.

computed. If refinancing or secondary financing were expected, then these schedules would also need to be included at this point of the analysis.

OPERATING ASSUMPTIONS (SECTION FIVE)[30]

During the mid-1970s, inflation was averaging 5–7 percent. In their operating assumptions (Exhibit 13–13) Davidson and Boomer projected growth rates in rental income at 4 percent annually beginning in 1975, based on the assumption that rents in an aging building generally lag behind inflation rates. Occupancy was held constant at 95 percent, while increases in operating costs were projected at 7 percent. The growth rate in property value was projected at 3 percent annually. Actual experience during those 5+ years reveals the following comparison:

	Projected	Actual
Growth rate in revenue	4%	8%
Projected occupancy	95%	96%
Growth rate in operating cost	7%	10%
Growth rate in property value	3%	7%

In general, investors during the 1970s underestimated inflationary trends; D&B were no exception.

The ordinary income tax rate was assumed to be 50 percent and the (effective) capital gain rate was 25 percent. (Only a 50 percent exclusion for capital gains was available in 1974.) Sensitivity analysis was also performed on the tax rates to test the impact on the different partners' IRRs. Surprisingly, varying the tax rates between 30 to 70 percent had minimal impact on the IRR. (Note that the top tax rate for individuals after 1981 is 50 percent.) Little further thought was given to placing investors with different tax brackets in the same joint venture, a problem previously of concern to D&B.

CASH FLOW ANALYSIS (SECTIONS SIX AND SEVEN)

Cash flow analysis is undertaken for the year of acquisition and five full tax years through 1979, as illustrated in Exhibit 13–14. With the very substantial expensed items in the year of acquisition, Davidson and Boomer thought the expected return, including the excellent year-end tax shelter, would attract many wealthy investors to the joint venture.

The annual cash flow projection shows a steadily increasing cash flow before tax and tax losses each year through 1979. As a result of the rapidly decreasing amounts of depreciation and mortgage interest, the cash flow

---

[30] Note that Section Four, which is a summary of capital expenditures and financing transactions over the holding period, has been omitted in this discussion because, in this case, no additional financing or capital expenditures are expected.

EXHIBIT 13–13.   Aspen Wood Apartments: Operating Assumptions

SECTION FIVE: OPERATING ASSUMPTIONS

Year

1974	Gross possible income	$ 26,620
	Operating expenses	$ 10,648
	Occupancy rate	95%
	Growth rate in property value during year	0%

1975	Gross possible income	$159,720
	Operating expenses	$ 63,888
	Occupancy rate	95%
	Growth rate in property value during year	3%

	Growth Rate in Revenue	Projected Occupancy	Growth Rate in Operating Costs	Growth Rate in Property Value
1976	4%	95%	7%	3%
1977	4%	95%	7%	3%
1978	4%	95%	7%	3%
1979	4%	95%	7%	3%

Cash flow projection period	6 years
Selling expense (percent of sales price)	5%
Investors required IRR on equity	18%
Ordinary income tax rate	50%
Capital gains tax rate	25%

after tax decreases each year. Nevertheless, we will see that the IRR actually increases each year over the holding period as a result of property appreciation.

NET CASH POSITION ANALYSIS (SECTION EIGHT)

This is a summary of all capital and operating transactions affecting the cash position of the investor each year—cash flow from operations, refinancing proceeds or deficits, capital expenditures, tax savings or taxes paid, and investment tax credits, as shown in Exhibit 13– 15. Since the Aspen Wood Apartments analysis contained no capital expenditures, financing transactions, or investment tax credits during the period analyzed, the *net cash position after taxes* is identical each year to the *cash flow after tax* figures shown in Sections 6 and 7 (Exhibit 13– 14). Consequently, the complete schedule of *net cash position after tax* is not shown here. The *net cash position after-taxes* amount is used each year to calculate the IRR and PV outputs. Essentially, we have expanded the concept of cash flow so as to accommodate the additional variables shown in Exhibit 13– 15.

EXHIBIT 13-14. Aspen Wood Apartments: Cash Flow Analysis

SECTION SIX: CASH FLOW ANALYSIS FOR CURRENT TAX YEAR (2 months, 1974)

Gross possible income	$ 26,620	Gross possible income	$26,620
Less: Vacancy	1,331	Less: Vacancy	1,331
Effective gross income	25,289	Effective gross income	25,289
Less: Operating		Less: Operating costs	10,648
costs	10,648	Net operating income	14,641
Less: Expensed		Less: Debt service	5,752
items	90,373	Less: Lease payment	0
Net operating income	−75,732	Cash flow before tax	8,889
Less: Depreciation	18,802	Plus: Tax savings (taxes)	49,746
Less: Interest	4,959	Plus: Investment tax	
Less: Lease payment	0	credit	0
Taxable income	$−99,493	Cash flow after tax	$58,636

Taxable income (loss) as a percent of total equity cash required = 47.38%

SECTION SEVEN: CASH FLOW ANALYSIS FOR FUTURE TAX YEARS

PROJECTED CASH FLOWS

	1975	1976	1977	1978	1979
Gross possible income	$159,720	$166,109	$172,753	$179,663	$186,850
Less: Vacancy	7,986	8,305	8,638	8,983	9,342
Effective gross income	151,734	157,803	164,115	170,680	177,507
Less: Operating costs	63,888	68,360	73,145	78,266	83,744
Net operating income	87,846	89,443	90,970	92,415	93,763
Less: Depreciation	98,380	85,723	81,267	68,355	51,716
Less: Interest	59,109	58,340	57,511	56,617	55,654
Less: Lease payment	0	0	0	0	0
Taxable income	−69,643	−54,619	−47,808	−32,558	−13,607
Plus: Depreciation	98,380	85,723	81,267	68,355	51,716
Less: Principle payment	9,913	10,682	11,511	12,405	13,368
Cash flow before tax	18,824	20,421	21,948	23,393	24,741
Plus: Tax savings (taxes)	34,822	27,310	23,904	16,279	6,803
Plus: Investment tax credit	0	0	0	0	0
Cash flow after tax	$ 53,646	$ 47,731	$ 45,852	$ 39,671	$ 31,545

EXHIBIT 13-15. Net Cash Position Analysis for Years 1974-1975

SECTION EIGHT: ANALYSIS OF NET CASH POSITION

	1974	1975
Cash flow before tax	$ 8,889	$18,824
Plus: Net refinancing proceeds*	0	0
Minus: Capital expenditures	0	0
Net cash position before taxes	$ 8,889	$18,824
Plus: Tax savings (taxes)	49,746	34,822
Plus: Investment tax credits	0	0
Net cash position after-taxes	$58,636	$53,646

* Includes net loan transactions, less loan points and penalties, plus any recaptured prepaid interest.

PROJECTION OF NET SALE PROCEEDS (SECTION NINE)

For purposes of comparison, the project is assumed to be sold at the end of each tax year over the projection period. In essence, six possible holding periods are analyzed, 1974 through 1979. Transaction costs are deducted, loans are repaid with prepayment penalties, and the investor pays the capital gain and ordinary income taxes due on the sale. This analysis is shown in Exhibit 13- 16.

DCF ANALYSIS (SECTION TEN)

For each possible holding period, 1974 through 1979, the investor calculates the present value of the property and the IRR after tax on total capital and equity invested (Exhibit 13- 16). The IRR on equity, considered to be the most important investment criteria by Davidson and Boomer, declines each year through 1979, reaching a low of about 34 percent. Clearly, the aggressive tax packaging paid off financially. The DCF analysis in Chapter 11 (using RE001) resulted in an IRR of 22 percent. Both analyses used the same NOI and growth rate assumptions (see Exhibit 11- 2). When compared to the 18 percent required IRR, the project looked very desirable.

RATIO ANALYSIS AND FINAL INVESTMENT DECISION (SECTION ELEVEN)[31]

Ratio analysis using the more sophisticated model turned out results consistent with those presented in Chapter 11. All the ratios indicated

[31] This section of the computer output is not shown.

EXHIBIT 13-16.   Aspen Wood Apartments: Sale Proceeds and DCF Analysis

SECTION NINE: PROJECT NET RESALE PROCEEDS

	1974	1975	1976	1977	1978	1979
Gross resale price	$1,003,400	$1,033,502	$1,064,507	$1,096,442	$1,129,336	$1,163,216
Less: Transaction costs	50,170	51,675	53,225	54,822	56,467	58,161
Net resale price	953,230	981,827	1,011,282	1,041,620	1,072,869	1,105,055
Less: Loan principle	792,607	782,694	772,012	760,501	748,096	734,727
Less: Loan penalty	0	0	0	0	0	0
Plus: Prepaid interest	29,753	29,753	29,753	29,753	29,753	29,753
Proceeds from sale before tax	190,376	228,885	269,022	310,872	354,526	400,080
Less: Ordinary tax	1,268	7,657	7,717	6,770	6,834	6,409
Less: Capital gain tax	14,117	42,667	71,431	99,806	124,675	145,863
Net proceeds from sale	$ 174,990	$ 178,561	$ 189,874	$ 204,296	$ 223,016	$ 247,807

SECTION TEN: DISCOUNTED CASH FLOW ANALYSIS

	1974	1975	1976	1977	1978	1979
Present value if held until year indicated	$ 227,269	$ 248,471	$ 267,266	$ 282,717	$ 293,565	$ 300,450
Plus: Original mortgage	793,400	793,400	793,400	793,400	793,400	793,400
Total project value	$1,020,669	$1,041,871	$1,060,666	$1,076,117	$1,086,965	$1,093,850
Internal rate of return						
On equity	89.6%	41.7%	38.3%	36.7%	35.4%	34.2%
On total capital	22.2%	11.2%	10.4%	10.2%	10.0%	09.8%

improving returns and decreasing risk over time. Front-end tax shelter was a substantial *sweetener* and effective sales tool. Because the project continued to meet or substantially exceed all the investment criteria set by D&B, few problems were anticipated in selling shares to investor clients, even in the depressed real estate market that characterized their city at that time. They believed they had found their "hole in the market," and then further capitalized on the situation through financial structuring and the application of appropriate risk management techniques. As a result, returns had increased and risks had been reduced.

The decision was reached to proceed to final negotiations and closing. Various delays occurred, but the property was finally closed and deeds delivered on December 30, 1974. The effective date of closing remained November 1, 1974.

14

Financing and Refinancing Techniques

Financing and refinancing decisions have become critical aspects of the investment process in recent years. Because the availability of mortgage loans has fluctuated widely and their costs and terms have become more onerous, equity investors are being forced to rethink their financing and refinancing strategies. The historically high interest rates of 1980 and 1981 have caused many institutional lenders to abandon fixed-rate, long-term mortgages in favor of short-term mortgages, variable- and renegotiated-rate mortgages, and equity participations. In general, high inflation rates have encouraged all investors to shift their portfolios out of fixed-rate and long-term debt investments and into short-term and equity types of investment vehicles.[1]

While the equity investor has traditionally viewed financing as a problem of raising sufficient debt capital, today emphasis is increasingly being placed on the process of raising sufficient equity capital and negotiating creative financial structures that "make the numbers work." In this chapter we emphasize both debt and equity financing techniques, along with the many creative financing techniques that have evolved recently.

After presenting a model of the financing decision process, we devote the two major sections of the chapter to debt and equity financing alternatives. Syndication is included as an equity financing alternative, and the various state and federal government laws regulating syndicate operations are discussed. The Aspen Wood

[1] See Anthony Downs, "With Inflation Rising, Does It Really Pay to Be a Lender?" *National Real Estate Investor,* October 1978, pp. 34–36.

case study is used to illustrate the analysis of various debt/equity alternatives using a DCF model.

THE FINANCING DECISION MODEL

The financing decision can be viewed as a submodel of the ten-step investment process model, as shown in Exhibit 14–1. Assuming that the investor has well-defined objectives and decision criteria, the financing process can be completed in four steps:

1. Identify a project with an adequate NOI stream. The most difficult aspect of the financing process is identifying a project that will produce an NOI stream that is sufficient to support a high level of debt financing. The NOI stream must be high enough to service the debt and must increase over the ownership period to protect the investor from loss of purchasing power due to inflation.

EXHIBIT 14–1.   The Financing Decision Model

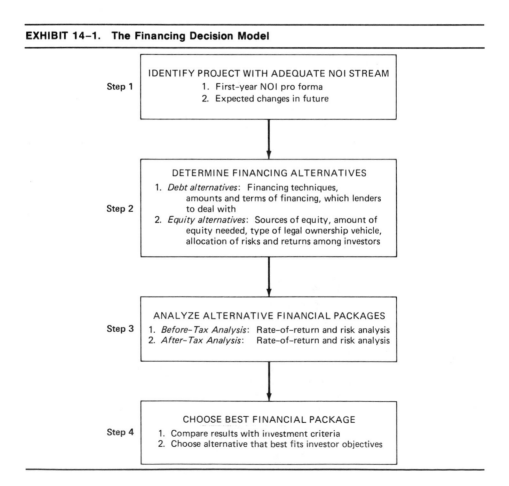

Step 1
IDENTIFY PROJECT WITH ADEQUATE NOI STREAM
1. First-year NOI pro forma
2. Expected changes in future

Step 2
DETERMINE FINANCING ALTERNATIVES
1. *Debt alternatives*: Financing techniques, amounts and terms of financing, which lenders to deal with
2. *Equity alternatives*: Sources of equity, amount of equity needed, type of legal ownership vehicle, allocation of risks and returns among investors

Step 3
ANALYZE ALTERNATIVE FINANCIAL PACKAGES
1. *Before-Tax Analysis*:   Rate-of-return and risk analysis
2. *After-Tax Analysis*:   Rate-of-return and risk analysis

Step 4
CHOOSE BEST FINANCIAL PACKAGE
1. Compare results with investment criteria
2. Choose alternative that best fits investor objectives

2. Determine the financing alternatives. Alternative financial packages must be defined and analyzed. A financial package can be defined as any combination of debt and equity sources that is used to finance a project. Debt alternatives include the types of financing to be employed (first-mortgage loan, sale-leaseback, wraparound loan, etc.), the amounts and terms of financing, and which lenders to deal with. Equity alternatives include the various sources of equity (individuals, institutions, syndication, etc.), the amounts of equity needed, the type of legal ownership vehicle, and the allocation of returns and risks among investors. Discussions with mortgage bankers and other lenders and equity investors will often narrow the alternatives to a workable number. Further screening can be accomplished using the basic financial feasibility model.

3. Analyze alternative financial packages. The basic financial feasibility model can test the before-tax return and risk profile for each alternative financial package. Alternatives that do not meet certain minimum requirements are dropped from consideration. The remaining alternatives should be analyzed using an after-tax model (such as the IRR models described in Chapters 11 and 13). After-tax rates of return, ratio and sensitivity analysis, and risk analysis will provide the investor with sufficient data for making the financing decision.

4. Choose the best financial package. The best combination of debt and equity financing is the package that best fits the investor's financial and nonfinancial objectives and risk-taking capacity. To a substantial degree the equity investor has control over the financial package created and can therefore manipulate the return/risk relationship. However, the investor should also be aware that many external factors cannot be controlled, including changes in the money supply, reserve requirements, and open-market activities, which can markedly change the cost and availability of debt financing in the short run.[2]

DEBT FINANCING ALTERNATIVES

The first basic question of debt financing is, How much leverage should be employed? The leverage decision is a subject of considerable debate. In the following section we will take a closer look at the leverage decision and then discuss debt financing techniques and the variables to be negotiated as an integral part of the debt financing package.

The Leverage Decision

Thus far we have analyzed leverage on a before-tax "operations" basis, using the basic financial feasibility model to structure a loan package that met desired DCR and ROE criteria. Leverage was positive if the return on total capital was greater than the mortgage constant (ROR > *K*; when this occurs, ROE > ROR). However, it is important to recognize that over the holding period the relationship

---

[2] See, e.g., Halbert C. Smith and Carl J. Tschappatt, "Monetary Policy and Real Estate Values," *Appraisal Journal,* January 1976, p. 20.

among ROR, *K,* and ROE will change as rent and operating expenses change; leverage can be positive in some operating years and negative in others. Therefore, in addition to analyzing leverage on a year-by-year, before-tax basis, one should test it on an after-tax basis using the IRR or *PV* formulations.[3]

Actually, three types of financial leverage should be considered:

1. *Operations leverage.* ROR, *K,* and ROE should be compared each year over the operating (holding) period.
2. *Tax leverage.*[4] Interest and depreciation deductions produce tax benefits that generally increase the investor's return on equity. While interest deductions are based on the entire mortgage value and depreciation deductions on the entire improvement value, the tax benefits accrue only to the equity contribution.
3. *Appreciation leverage.* Increases in property value work through the leverage factor to raise the investor's return on equity. For a 90 percent leveraged property, a modest 5 percent annual increase in value will result in a 50 percent annual appreciation return on the investor's equity investment.

Only through analysis of tax and appreciation leverage can one explain the recent widespread phenomenon of negative leverage from operations (ROE < ROR). Properties are being purchased with low or negative ROEs on the basis of expectation of rising NOI and property values and the continued existence of liberal tax shelter benefits for real estate investors. While the short-run risk of such investments is high (i.e., low coverage ratios and high breakeven points), investors expect to be "bailed out" of negative-leverage situations over the long run.

The effects of the three types of leverage can be illustrated by comparing before-tax and after-tax data for a property. For example, consider our analysis of Aspen Wood Apartments in Chapter 11. Ratios and IRRs were calculated for a seven-year holding period, as shown in Exhibit 14–2. The before-tax analysis compares ROR with ROE. Each year the leverage is positive, and as NOI increases, it becomes more favorable. The after-tax analysis compares IRR on total capital (unleveraged position) with IRR on equity capital (leveraged position). The analysis shows that the net impact of leverage is to increase the IRR_E from 8.2 percent to 22.1 percent; this is a 170 percent increase in the investor's return as a result of the leverage structure.

Whenever positive leverage exists (on either a before- or an after-tax DCF basis), increasing the loan-to-value ratio will increase the ROE, the IRR on equity,

---

[3] Various approaches and techniques are presented and compared in the following articles: Kenneth M. Lusht, "A Note on the Favorability of Leverage," *The Real Estate Appraiser,* May– June 1977, pp. 41– 44; William Dennison Clark, Jr., "Leverage: Magnificent Mover of Real Estate," *Real Estate Review,* Winter 1972, pp. 8– 13; Raymond L. Erler, "Rejoinder on Leverage," *Real Estate Review,* Summer 1972, pp. 81– 82; T. D. Englebrecht and Travis P. Goggans, "Leverage and After-Tax Returns," *Real Estate Review,* Summer 1980, pp. 15– 18.
[4] An in-depth analysis of tax leveraging is provided by Ted L. Fisher, "Tax Leveraging and Real Estate Tax Shelters," *The Appraisal Journal,* July 1980, pp. 414– 422.

EXHIBIT 14–2.   Aspen Wood Apartments: Summary of Financial Results

| | BEFORE-TAX ANALYSIS | | AFTER-TAX ANALYSIS | |
| | ANNUAL FINANCIAL RATIOS | | DISCOUNTED CASH FLOW MEASURES | |
Year	Net Income to Property Cost (ROR)	Cash Flow Before Tax to Initial Equity (ROE)	IRR on Total Capital Invested (IRR_{TC})	IRR on Equity Capital (IRR_E)
1	9.2%	12.2%		
2	9.4	13.1	Seven-year	
3	9.5	14.0	holding	
4	9.7	14.9	period	
5	9.8	15.7		
6	9.9	16.4		
7	10.0	17.1	8.2%	22.1%

and the present value of the property. In contrast, if negative leverage exists (ROE < ROR; IRR_E < IRR_{TC}), increasing the loan-to-value ratio will decrease the ROE and the IRR on equity. Furthermore, it is quite common to have negative operations leverage each year (ROE < ROR), yet positive leverage over the long run when tax and appreciation leverage are considered (IRR_E > IRR_{TC}).

In sum, the leverage decision should probably be based on a combination of before- and after-tax DCF criteria. The investor should increase the leverage ratio until either short-term risk constraints (annual coverage ratio minimum, break-even point maximum, etc.) or long-term risk constraints (excessive variability of IRR) are exceeded. Finally, the investor should be aware that as the debt ratio approaches 100 percent, the amount of equity investment approaches zero and the rate of return on equity (ROE and IRR_E) approaches infinity. Since a *mortgaged-out* project cannot be evaluated by a rate-of-return-on-equity measure, other investment criteria must be used in the decision-making process; in such cases the NPV approach is usually preferred.

Erosion of Leverage Benefits   The benefits of financial leverage that used to be available to equity investors are no longer readily available.[5] Because lenders have limited the availability of traditional, nonrecallable, fixed-rate, long-term mortgage loans, the degree of leverage on operations and on appreciation has diminished. For example, a rising ROE due to increases in net operating income might be offset by the rising K in a variable-rate mortgage; or the appreciation benefits might be diminished by a lender's participation in net sale proceeds. As a result, a property's expected IRR_E might be diminished substantially; also, its financial risk increases because of the cash flow uncertainties created by the lender's variable rate or participation requirement.

[5] Wayne E. Etter, "The Investor Loses His Leverage," *Real Estate Review*, Spring 1981, pp. 92–97.

Debt Financing Variables

The optimal amount of debt financing (leverage) involves not only the *amount* of financing but the *terms* as well.[6] As we saw when negotiating the wraparound mortgage on Aspen Wood Apartments (Chapter 12), an important trade-off exists between the amount of financing and the mortgage constant (interest rate and amortization term). Better financing terms allow the investor to increase the amount of loan without adversely affecting the amount of debt service and the coverage ratio. In addition to these variables, many other financing terms affect the return/risk profile of a property.

A loan package typically includes two *term* provisions, a method of loan amortization, and compound or simple interest. For example, a first mortgage at 12 percent interest may be payable monthly, fully amortizing over a 30-year *amortization term,* with a *loan term* (balloon) of 5 years. While the lender is willing to base the payback of principal on a 30-year period, it wants to be able to call in the remaining mortgage balance at the end of 5 years so that the money can be reinvested elsewhere if a higher return can be achieved.

Interest Rate   There are two kinds of interest: simple and compound. Simple interest is earned and immediately paid out. Compound interest is earned and reinvested; it is interest plus "interest on interest." When interest is compounded more frequently than once a year, it produces an effective rate in excess of the nominal rate. On the other hand if a lender seeks a certain effective interest rate, more frequent compounding (e.g., monthly instead of annual payments) will reduce the mortgage constant and annual debt service payments (more interest on interest can be earned by the lender), as shown in Exhibit 14–3. Note that for

---

EXHIBIT 14–3.   The Annual Mortgage Constant Factor (*K*), Assuming Different Compounding Periods

MORTGAGE CONSTANT FACTOR: 12% INTEREST RATE

Term of Loan (Years)	Annual Payments (Annual Compounding)	Semiannual Payment (Semiannual Compounding)	Monthly Payments (Monthly Compounding)
1	1.120000	1.090874	1.066176
5	0.277410	0.271736	0.266928
10	0.176984	0.174370	0.172164
15	0.146824	0.145298	0.144012
20	0.133879	0.132924	0.132120
25	0.127500	0.126888	0.126384
30	0.124144	0.123752	0.123432
35	0.122317	0.122066	0.121860
40	0.121304	0.121146	0.121008

---

[6] For a comparative analysis of loan terms by major lenders, see James R. Webb, "Terms on Loans for Eleven Types of Income Property: A Comparative Analysis for 1967–1977," *The Real Estate Appraiser and Analyst,* July–August 1980, pp. 40–45.

short amortization terms (5–10 years), the method of payment makes a substantial difference in the mortgage constant (K); for longer terms, K does not decrease significantly when the method of payment is changed.

The investor's strategy might be to choose more frequent payments (monthly rather than annually) in order to reduce debt service payments and raise the coverage ratio. This strategy would be incorrect, however, if the investor could invest intermediate funds at a rate greater than 12 percent. In this case the best strategy would be to negotiate infrequent mortgage payments and make interim investments of the funds. In most cases, however, long-term mortgage lenders (especially institutional lenders) require monthly mortgage payments when a property generates revenue on a monthly basis. Tying debt service to the timing of the revenue stream is a risk control device. The conventional lender wants its money when the investor gets it (yet another example of time value of money!).

Amortization Method Loan amortization schedules can be customized in an endless variety of ways to meet the objectives and constraints of both lenders and equity investors. The equity investor will seek to negotiate repayment terms that will have the most favorable effect on cash flow and the IRR, relative to the risk imposed by such repayment terms.

Ideally, an investor would like a mortgage calling for no repayment of principal (a cash payment that is not deductible for tax purposes), that is, *interest-only* for the entire term of the mortgage. Better yet, the investor would prefer no payments of principal *or* interest. Zeckendorf describes such an arrangement as a *dormant mortgage,*[7] which is a form of second-mortgage financing. Neither interest nor principal is paid until the first mortgage on the same property is paid in full, at which time the owner of the dormant mortgage takes a first-lien position and begins to receive debt service payments. The maker of such a mortgage would possibly be an individual who seeks no current income but wishes to generate retirement income in the future or for his or her children.

Despite the many possibilities for creativity, most mortgage amortization arrangements fall into one of three basic categories:

1. *Straight-term mortgage (also referred to as an interest-only or standing loan).* This calls for no amortization during its term; the entire principal becomes due at maturity. Prior to the Great Depression, most real estate loans took this form: They had a term of five years and were expected to be automatically renewed at the end of each five-year period.
2. *Partially amortizing mortgage (also called a balloon loan).* The most common arrangement today, this calls for some, but not complete, repayment of the principal during the loan period. At maturity the borrower will have a substantial sum (balloon) still to be repaid, but less than the full amount. In a typical situation a loan might bear a 14.5% interest rate, with monthly payments based on a thirty-year amortization period, but with the term of the loan limited to a five- or ten-year maturity date.

[7] William Zeckendorf, *Zeckendorf* (New York: Holt, Rinehart and Winston, 1970), p. 147.

3. *Fully amortizing mortgage.* Historically, this was the most common type of financing used for residential and commercial properties in the United States. Also called a self-liquidating loan, it employs periodic payments that provide for the full repayment of the principal (over 20 to 40 years) along with interest payments based on the balance of the principal. With the gradual reduction in the principal balance, the proportion of the debt service that represents interest declines over time.

Commitment Fees and Points   From the equity investor's viewpoint, commitment fees and points are the same. A first-mortgage loan commitment, for example, might require one point (1 percent of the loan balance) as a commitment fee and two discount points. The financial effect is the same: 3 percent of the loan balance must be paid in cash to secure the new loan. Typically, the commitment fee is paid when the lender issues the loan commitment (*take-out letter*) and the discount points are paid at the loan closing. If some flexibility is permitted by the lender, the investor will negotiate payment of all three points at closing, or post a letter of credit in lieu of immediate payment of the commitment fee. A letter of credit guarantees payment of the fee to the lender, whether or not the loan is funded.

The investor should treat loan points and fees as a capital investment. They increase the investment cost and the tax basis of the property. Under the provisions of the Economic Recovery Tax Act of 1981 they can be capitalized as a separate component and amortized over the term of the loan (the balloon period rather than the amortization period), thereby creating a tax shelter effect over the holding period. If the property is refinanced before the loan fees and points have been fully amortized, any remaining basis can be written off during the year in which the refinancing takes place. Frequently investors overlook this potential tax shelter; they simply forget to take these tax deductions in the year of refinancing.

Another way to treat loan points and fees is to consider them as an increase in the effective cost of financing. If the total dollar amount of fees and points is deducted from the loan amount (to arrive at the net loan proceeds received), the effective interest rate (yield) on the mortgage can be computed by solving for the interest rate in the internal rate-of-return formula.[8]

Degree of Personal Liability   Other things equal, the investor will always prefer to design a loan with no personal liability, commonly referred to as a nonrecourse loan. Such a loan, which is achieved through the *exculpatory clause* in the mortgage instruments, prevents the lender from seeking a personal judgment against the borrower when the borrower defaults and a deficiency remains after the sale of the mortgaged property.[9] Such a provision clearly is desirable from the investor's viewpoint, and many lenders are willing to provide such a clause.

---

[8] The effective interest rate is the discount rate that equates the debt service payments over the term of the loan (or the holding period) with the net loan dollars received by the investor. The mortgage yield calculation is simply an application of the internal-rate-of-return procedure. As the amount of loan fees and points increase, the net loan proceeds decrease and the true mortgage yield (IRR) increases.

[9] An excellent article on the subject is Emanuel B. Halper, "People and Property: Mortgage Exculpation Clauses," *Real Estate Review,* Summer 1978, pp. 35–40.

Indeed, a limited partnership syndication must have some degree of relief in this respect in order to allocate the loan amount to the depreciable basis (see Chapter 9).

Many lenders have discovered that in many states deficiency judgments are difficult and expensive to obtain and collect. As a result, some lenders avoid litigation and write off their loan losses immediately; it is hoped that they learn from their mistakes. Other lenders, however, require personal liability on mortgage loans and look to both the property and the borrower as security for the loan. For example, in cases in which property performance is highly dependent on the borrower's performance (e.g., special use properties) or the loan is underwritten by local savings institutions, personal signatures are almost always required. If personal liability is a requirement of the lender, the investor should seek to limit the liability to a fixed amount (say the top 10 or 20% of the loan amount). In some cases a higher interest rate might be required to limit liability; this will decrease the project IRR to some degree.

Prepayment Provisions   Prepayment provisions are very important to the equity investor. An investor who can refinance a loan at the right time can substantially increase cash flow and IRR or decrease the risk profile of the project. For example, the investor might increase the amount of the loan, reduce the debt service, or decrease the interest rate. When a mortgage is structured with a variable interest rate, the importance of the prepayment provision is increased. It is important to recognize that if no prepayment provision is provided in the loan agreement, the borrower has no right to prepay the loan.[10] Such an omission might be disastrous for the investor.

The following are five prepayment provisions, many or all of which are subject to negotiation:

1. *Initial no-prepayment period.* This is also referred to as a *closed* or *lock-in* period. Frequently the lender insists that the loan remain on its books for a minimum period (say, five or ten years), during which no prepayments are allowed. Obviously, the investor would like to avoid a closed period if possible. If it cannot be avoided, the investor should negotiate for a provision that allows for a sale of the property in which the existing loan can be assumed or wrapped around with a junior-lien form of financing.

2. *Prepayment penalty.* If the lender is forced to retire the mortgage investment (beyond the closed period), compensation is in order. Penalties may be stepped up or down; the latter is more common. For example, a prepayment clause may provide that no prepayment is permitted for the first five years of the loan and that the prepayment penalty in the sixth year is 5 percent and declines by 1/2 percent per year thereafter until it reaches 1 percent, at which point no further decline occurs. In practice, many

---

[10] Also, the borrower cannot force prepayment by defaulting on the loan and then arguing that the acceleration clause comes into play and allows repayment of the principal balance. The relevant legal case on the subject is *Peter Fuller Enterprises* v. *Manchester Savings Bank,* 152 A. 2d 179 (Vt. 1959).

lenders are willing to waive prepayment penalties if the borrower refinances the loan with them.

3. *Dates when prepayment can be made.* The investor should be sure that prepayments can be made at the time of closing of the property (if sold) or when a new loan closes.

4. *Notice of prepayment.* The lender often requires advance notice of prepayments and specifies the manner in which notice must be given.

5. *Partial prepayments.* The investor may wish to reduce the debt if a better rate of return on capital cannot be earned elsewhere. Lenders are frequently willing to accept small prepayments of principal, without penalty, at any time during the mortgage term.

Some lenders have standard *boilerplate* clauses with respect to the five considerations just listed and are not willing to negotiate terms to suit the borrower; others are willing to negotiate on some or all of the points. Sellers who are taking back mortgages to facilitate the sale are generally most willing to negotiate on these and other terms.

Required Escrow Accounts   A lender often requires the borrower to maintain tax and insurance escrow accounts with them. While this requirement is common for small residential properties, it becomes a negotiable item for larger commercial properties. Ideally, the investor would like to pay his or her own taxes and insurance, keeping all interim funds invested in money market instruments until tax and insurance payments are due. In such cases the lender will usually require evidence that tax and insurance payments are made in a timely manner.

Due-on-Sale Clause   A due-on-sale clause is commonly written into mortgage instruments today, permitting the lender to accelerate the mortgage debt (call the remaining balance due and payable immediately) in the event that the borrower sells the real estate (or otherwise transfers it). During the 1960s this clause was often absent from mortgage agreements. When inflation and interest rates rose during the 1970s, owners were able to sell property on the basis of loan assumptions (without interest rate acceleration) and wraparounds at favorable financing terms. In recent years such investor flexibility has been reduced, if not completely eliminated, by most mortgage agreements.

When frequent ownership turnover is contemplated, the investor should negotiate provisions that facilitate a sale between owners. Various compensation schemes can be provided to the lender to permit flexibility in this regard.[11] In any case the investor should check the legality of due-on-sale clauses in his or her state; these clauses are being challenged and rendered invalid in some situations.

Due-on-Encumbrance Clause   This is a clause in the mortgage that permits the lender to accelerate the outstanding loan balance in the event that the borrower negotiates other financing on the property. The argument in favor of such a clause states that other financing weakens the security for the first mortgage because the

[11] For examples see Alvin Arnold, *Real Estate Financing Techniques,* Portfolio no. 5 (Boston: Warren, Gorham & Lamont, 1974), pp. 38–39.

borrower, with less equity in the project, has less inclination to maintain it properly. Also, the burden of the additional debt financing increases the likelihood of default.

Other Acceleration Clauses   In reality, any event that the lender is able to put in the contract may be cause for acceleration. Such events may include

1. Failure to make required debt service payments.
2. Condemnation of any part of premises.
3. Bankruptcy of property owner.
4. Failure to maintain the property in good physical condition.

While the acceleration clauses may not be exercised by the lender even when one or more of the required conditions exist, they nevertheless limit the flexibility of the investor and to some degree present an element of risk that might be avoided.

Foreclosure   If the investor defaults on the mortgage payments, or if a condition exists that allows the lender to otherwise invoke an acceleration clause, the principal balance of the loan becomes due and payable (i.e., is *accelerated, called,* or *ballooned*). The investor will want to be given sufficient time to cure any default before the lender is entitled to foreclose. If the condition is incurable, the investor will not want the lender to have the right to foreclose unless the default is a material one. For example, if the debt service payment does not reach the lender's office on or before the due date (or within some *grace period*) as a result of a mistake at the local post office, a lender might be able to accelerate the entire loan. The investor should have negotiated a more reasonable acceleration clause allowing for minor delays and mistakes. For example, late-payment penalties are frequently charged by lenders in lieu of exercising an acceleration clause.

Participations   Also known as *equity kickers,* equity participations give the lender a share of the equity returns in addition to the normal debt service on a mortgage loan. Faced with inflation and tight money in the late 1960s, lending institutions often insisted on some form of equity participation. The lender's position was strong and equity kickers became the rage. Many different types were developed:

1. Extra interest as a percent of gross income.
2. Extra interest as a percent of net profit.
3. Extra interest as a percent of overages (shopping centers).
4. Extra interest based on fixed step-ups, reappraisals of the property, or cost-of-living or similar index changes.
5. Participation in refinancing proceeds; a percent of the new mortgage loan over the old one.
6. Participation in net sales proceeds; a percent of the net cash realized when the property is sold.
7. Option to purchase an interest in the investor's real estate, stock, or partnership.

Equity investors have always resisted equity participations. They do not want lenders to be partners in profits but not in losses. They also fear that, because of the adverse effect on investment value, resale value will be hurt when a lender has an equity participation. In fact, lenders had serious problems with equity kickers in the 1970s. They were difficult to administer; usury problems developed; and the lenders received less overall return than expected. As a result, equity kickers lost much of their appeal and joint ventures began to replace them. In a joint venture the lender contributes some of the equity investment and assumes a risk of loss. Lenders also began to prefer the subordinated land leaseback, which gave them a preferred equity position and participation in future growth of income and property values. This technique is discussed later in this chapter.

Despite the problems just noted, equity kickers regained popularity among lenders in the early 1980s and will probably remain popular in the future. If so, the investor must be careful to measure the effects of such participations on projected cash flows and expected IRRs; often lender participations make a proposed investment infeasible.

Generating a Mortgage Amortization Schedule

There are a number of methods for calculating interest and principal breakdowns over time: (1) interest rate method, (2) mortgage constant method, (3) present-value method, (4) tables, and (5) financial calculators.

The Interest Rate Method   Exhibit 14–4 illustrates the calculation of interest, principal, and mortgage balance for a $100,000 loan at 12 percent with a 30-year amortization term, payable annually over a five-year holding period. Each year the amount of interest is calculated by multiplying the interest rate times the loan balance at the beginning of the year (for year 1, .12 × $100,000 = $12,000). The principal reduction is found by taking the difference between the amount of interest and the annual debt service (for year 1, $12,414.40 − $12,000 =

EXHIBIT 14–4.   A Mortgage Amortization Schedule with Annual Payments— Interest Rate Method

	(1)	(2)	(3)	(4)	(5)
Loan amount	$100,000.00	$99,585.60	$99,121.47	$98,601.65	$98,019.45
Interest rate	×.12	×.12	×.12	×.12	×.12
Interest	12,000.00	11,950.27	11,894.58	11,832.97	11,762.33
Principal	+414.40	+464.13	+519.82	+582.20	+652.07
Debt service	$ 12,414.40	$12,414.40	$12,414.40	$12,414.40	$12,414.40

Debt service $= K \times$ loan amount
$\qquad = .124144 \times \$100,000$
$\qquad = \$12,414.40$

Loan balance, end of fifth year $= \$98,019.45 - \$652.07 = \$97,367.38$

$414.40). The loan balance at the end of year 1 (beginning of year 2) is the beginning-of-the-year balance minus the principal reduction during the year (for year 1, $100,000 − $414.40 = $99,585.60). The process continues until the interest and principal amounts have been calculated for each of five years. At the end of the fifth year, the loan balance is $97,367.38. If monthly instead of annual payments were specified, this procedure would require performing these calculations each month for five years, using a monthly interest rate of 1 percent. The calculations would become quite laborious.

The Mortgage Constant Method   Computer models generally use the interest rate method for calculating mortgage schedules. Another method that arrives at the same result, which is frequently used when monthly payments are required and calculations must be performed by hand, is the mortgage constant method shown in Exhibit 14–5. The methodology is based on the loan formula introduced in Chapter 10:

$$\text{Loan amount} = \frac{\text{debt service}}{\text{mortgage constant}} \quad \text{or} \quad L_t = \frac{DS}{K_t}$$

where t = remaining term of the loan

For example, if the investor wants to know the mortgage balance of the $100,000 loan at the end of the third year, he finds the mortgage constant for a 27-year term at 12 percent, annual payments. The effective mortgage constant is .125904. The balance of the loan at the end of the third year is computed as follows:

$$L_{27} = \frac{DS}{K_{27}} = \frac{\$12,414.40}{.125904} = \$98,602.11$$

The loan amount at the end of each year is computed using the formula just presented. Then the amount of principal amortized during the year is computed

---

EXHIBIT 14–5.   A Mortgage Amortization Schedule with Annual Payments— Mortgage Constant Method

	(1)	(2)	(3)	(4)	(5)
Debt service	$12,414.40	$12,414.40	$12,414.40	$12,414.40	$12,414.40
Effective K	÷.124660	÷.125244	÷.125904	÷.126652	÷.127500
Loan amount, end of year	99,586.07	99,121.71	98,602.11	98,019.77	97,367.84
Loan amount, beginning of year	100,000.00	99,586.07	99,121.71	98,602.11	98,019.77
Principal	413.93	464.36	519.60	582.34	651.93
Interest	+12,000.47	+11,950.04	+11,894.80	+11,832.06	+11,762.47
Debt service	$12,414.40	$12,414.40	$12,414.40	$12,414.40	$12,414.40

by taking the difference between the loan balances at the end and beginning of the year. Finally, the interest amount is computed by taking the difference between the debt service and the principal amortized. Note that this method produces a slightly different answer than the first method. This is solely because of rounding errors in the mortgage constant factor. (The interest rate method produces a more technically accurate mortgage schedule because it avoids rounding errors.)

Also, if monthly payments are required, the mortgage constant factors for *monthly* payments must be used, which will result in lower annual debt service payments and lower annual interest expenses. The procedure shown remains the same; however, only five sets of calculations are required for a five-year projection as contrasted with sixty using the interest rate method. Appendix D presents mortgage constant factors for monthly and annual payments (rounded to four places) for interest rates ranging from 4.00 to 20.75 percent.

The Present-Value Method   The present-value method for calculating a mortgage amortization schedule recognizes the fact that the loan balance is simply the present value of the remaining debt service payments discounted at the mortgage interest rate. For example, the present value of a $100,000 loan with 27 years remaining, annual payments of debt service of $12,414.40, and a 12 percent interest rate, can be computed as follows:

$$L_{27} = \$12,414.40 \times 7.942554 = \$98,602.04$$

where   7.942554 is the present value of an ordinary annuity for 27 years, 12%, annual compound interest

The mortgage balance can be computed in this manner at the end of each year over the holding period. The amortization schedule can then be calculated by taking the difference between the loan balances for consecutive years and deducting the result (principal amortized) from the debt service to find the amount of interest.

The Tables and Financial Calculator Methods   The amortization schedule can also be calculated from tables published by numerous companies. Remaining-balance tables and interest and principal amortization schedules can be obtained at most bookstores, or free from many local financial institutions. As is usual in the use of tables, rounding errors will occur frequently. Furthermore, many debt service tables are biased in the lender's favor. For example, mortgage constant factors are rounded up rather than to the closest significant digit. In many cases the methodology for rounding is not explained by the publisher.

By far the easiest and best way to calculate an amortization schedule by hand is to use a programmed calculator that can generate technically accurate amortization information for use in cash flow projections. Such calculators are widely available at a modest price.

First-Mortgage Financing Alternatives

We have recognized that high inflation and uncertainties about interest rate fluctuations have caused many lenders to seek investment alternatives such as equity participations and joint ventures. Lenders have also developed various forms of alternative mortgage instruments (AMIs) in order to shift inflation and interest rate risks.[12]

1. *Variable-Rate Mortgage (VRM).* A VRM provides that the interest rate charged will be increased or decreased periodically on the basis of some predetermined interest index. Some versions of the VRM give the borrower the option to extend the term of the mortgage in the event of an interest rate increase in order to minimize the effects of the increase on the debt service payments.

2. *Renegotiated-Rate Mortgage (RRM).* Also called a Canadian rollover (CRO), the purpose of an RRM is to achieve some of the benefits of a VRM without departing substantially from the provisions of a conventional mortgage loan. The amount of debt service is fixed for a specific period, but at each renegotiation the interest rate is adjusted to a rate near the current market rate.

3. *Graduated-Payment Mortgage (GPM).* A GPM provides for periodic payments that increase one or more times during the term of the mortgage. During the early years of the mortgage, the amount of debt service may not be enough to pay the contractual interest rate (i.e., the mortgage constant is *less than* the contractual interest rate), resulting in an increase in the loan balance over time. The GPM is attractive to some borrowers because as time passes, the increased payments will be matched by the property's or borrower's increased income (at least in theory).

4. *Price-Level-Adjusted Mortgage (PLAM).* A PLAM provides for periodic increases or decreases in the loan amount on the basis of some price level index. The interest rate and term remain fixed. The debt service consequently will change when the loan balance changes. The PLAM approach has been adopted in several foreign countries that have experienced wide variations in inflation rates (e.g., Brazil).

5. *Reverse Annuity Mortgage (RAM).* The RAM is designed primarily for owner–occupants who have large amounts of equity tied up in their property and seek annuity income. For example, an investor borrows the equity in her property, but instead of receiving a lump-sum loan she receives a monthly payment (annuity) from the lender. In such a case the cash inflows and outflows of the RAM are the reverse of those of a conventional mortgage. The borrower receives monthly payments and contracts to repay the lender the amount loaned, plus interest, at the

---

[12] For further discussion of the first five, see James H. Hammond, Jr., "Alternative Mortgage Instruments," *Mortgage Banker*, October 1978, pp. 44, 46, 50, 52, 54–56, 58.

maturity date of the mortgage or upon the death of the borrower (through settlement of the estate), whichever is sooner.

6. *Shared Appreciation Mortgage (SAM).* An old idea with a new name, the SAM allows the borrower to pay a below-market fixed rate of interest in exchange for giving the lender a percent of the property appreciation. This is identical to the equity participation mortgage loan discussed before, and is nothing more than an institutionalized version of the equity kicker.

The VRM, RRM, and GPM are being used in home ownership situations in many states. While they are not widely used in multifamily and commercial lending, these and similar techniques are becoming more common in the 1980s as high inflation and interest rate fluctuations continue. Cash flow forecasts will become more difficult as interest rate and purchasing power risks are shifted from the lender to the equity investor through the use of these new mortgage instruments. [13]

Government-Sponsored Loan Programs

All levels of government have been active participants in providing loan assistance (first-mortgage loans and related subsidies) for residential and commercial properties. [14] Most of the local, state, and federal programs have focused on providing housing loan assistance, although assistance to owners of commercial property is also available (e.g., through the Small Business Administration). The investor should be aware of these programs, since they may provide viable alternatives to financing properties for which conventional financing sources are limited.

At the local, county, and state government levels, there has been a surge in moneys loaned for the creation of single-family and multifamily units in recent years. Through the use of tax-free bonds, government agencies are able to grant loans at a lower effective rate than is possible through private sources. However, it is at the federal level, within the Department of Housing and Urban Development (HUD), that the great majority of loan programs are available.

Congress enacts a new housing statute, or amendments to one, every year, and HUD determines which section of the population or area of the country is being overlooked. As a result of constant changes in the top HUD post and pressures from various interest groups, programs gain or lose priority over time. It is important for real estate investors to know what the priorities and funding capabilities of various programs are. An investor can spend countless hours and dollars learning to operate within a government subsidy program, and then have his or her entire investment plan undermined overnight by a congressional dictate. On the other hand, investments in a particular government-sponsored housing program that is subsequently eliminated could provide certain monopoly advan-

---

[13] The question of shifting interest rate risk through the use of such mortgages is addressed by Ravindra Kamath and Russell B. Raimer, "Do VRMs Transfer Interest Rate Risk," *Real Estate Review,* Spring 1981, pp. 102–108.

[14] For a thorough discussion of government involvement in financing real estate investments and the myriad of related government programs, see "Financing" in the looseleaf service *Real Estate Investment Planning* (Englewood Cliffs, N.J.: Institute for Business Planning, 1980), paras. 55,450–55,500.

tages to the investor who owns such properties. In any case the risks are high, and to compensate for them most investors require higher rates of return.

Active programs in recent years have included the following:

1. *The Section 8 Housing Program.* This program is designed to stimulate privately constructed and financed housing. The principal thrust of Section 8, unlike previous housing programs, is to provide a direct subsidy to the tenant rather than to the owner of the project.[15] New and existing single-family houses, mobile homes, multifamily structures, and apartment hotels can qualify. However, preference is given to projects for the elderly and handicapped, and to projects with fewer than fifty units. Section 8 projects can be financed by conventional as well as FHA loans, and through public housing finance agencies.

2. *Community Development Block Grants/Urban Development Action Grants.* Federal support for these programs has been strong. The attraction of these funds ($950 million in 1980) is that they provide seed money for urban redevelopment, which reduces the private capital required to redevelop property that will be owned by private investors.

3. *Title V Farmers Home Administration (FmHA) Rural Housing.* Houses, condos, and rental properties can be financed through this program in small rural communities and cities with populations under 20,000. In the multifamily housing program, direct loans are made to the investor at subsidized interest rates and a forty- or fifty-year amortization term. The equity investor is limited to an 8 percent ROE (cash flow return) on the initial equity invested.

4. *Section 202 housing program.* Section 202 is a mortgage loan program to stimulate investment in housing for the elderly and handicapped. This program has increased in popularity, with Congress providing a cumulative loan authority of $4.8 billion in 1981 and $5.8 billion in 1982.

Junior Mortgage Financing Alternatives

Various methods of junior mortgage financing have always been popular with real estate investors who seek a high degree of financial leverage. There are many possible reasons for using secondary financing, including the following:

• To generate tax-free dollars while retaining favorable existing financing.
• As an alternative to syndication, a joint venture partner, or other forms of equity.
• As an alternative to refinancing, when the current K exceeds the combined K that could be obtained by using junior lien financing.
• As a tax shelter vehicle, with lease rental payments, wraparound interest, or second-mortgage interest sheltering taxable income, while borrower's equity increases through first-mortgage liquidation.

---

[15] Jerome Y. Halperin and Michael J. Brenner, "Opportunities Under the New Section 8 Housing Program," *Real Estate Review,* Spring 1976, pp. 67–75.

• Larger loans may be obtained through unregulated commercial sources or through institutions if they grant a junior mortgage via "basket" funds—a device that allows them to exceed statutory or internal policy loan-to-value limits.
• Prepayment penalties are avoided, and the payment of financing fees is limited only to the new funds obtained through the junior mortgage or leaseback.[16]

The essential advantage of secondary financing is to increase the "upside leverage" that exists. As long as the marginal cost of the additional debt is less than the rate of return on total capital invested, the additional debt will increase the rate of return on equity. However, as pointed out earlier, there may be a split effect from the extra debt. On a before-tax operations basis the debt may cause severe negative leverage, while an after-tax DCF analysis may show very favorable positive leverage.

The majority of junior mortgage financing alternatives can be grouped into the following categories: (1) commercial second mortgages, (2) institutional second mortgages, (3) purchase money junior mortgages, (4) wraparound mortgages, and (5) subordinated land leasebacks.

Commercial Second Mortgages   REITs, commercial finance companies, and mortgage companies have provided most second-mortgage loans in recent years. These loans are relatively short term (three to five years), are priced on a floating-rate basis (4–5 percent over the prime), and usually allow prepayment without substantial penalties. Commercial second lenders usually operate without any statutory limitations and can accept higher loan-to-value ratios and lower debt coverage ratios than conventional institutional lenders. Combined first and second mortgages of 85 percent of appraised value are often acceptable. The lender's historical rule of thumb for such loans is "five times the bottom line"; that is, the amount of secondary financing is equal to the project's NOI, minus the debt service on the first mortgage, multiplied by five.

Institutional Second Mortgages   If available, the investor will usually prefer a second loan from a life insurance company, a pension fund, or a wholly owned subsidiary company that operates outside of insurance industry regulations. The interest rates charged are usually lower than with commercial second mortgages, and the amortization term is usually longer. On the other hand, depending on statutory limitations imposed on a particular lender, the loan-to-value ratios may be more conservative than those offered by commercial lending sources, and the prepayment privileges are likely to be more onerous.

Purchase Money Junior Mortgages[17]   Probably the most common form of junior lien financing is the purchase money mortgage, often termed *seller financing*. Purchase money mortgages become especially critical in real estate transactions when institutional financing is unavailable at a price and terms that are

---

[16] William L. Ward et al., "Junior Lien Financing—Five Varieties and the Advantages They Offer," *The Mortgage Banker*, May 1978, p. 41.
[17] See Robert Bell, "Negotiating the Purchase-Money Mortgage," *Real Estate Review*, Spring 1977, pp. 51–58.

acceptable to the investor. Instead, the seller provides financing to the buyer and takes back a mortgage on the property. The mortgage can be a conventional second (or junior) or wraparound mortgage.

Sellers are often motivated to provide purchase money mortgages for one or a combination of the following reasons:

1. *Installment sale tax treatment.* The seller wants to spread the taxable gain over a number of tax years.
2. *Facilitating the sale.* The buyer may not be able to qualify for an institutional loan; institutional mortgages may not be readily available; the interest rate and terms can be negotiated and the loan closed with few delays.
3. *Higher selling price and lower selling costs.* Providing favorable mortgage terms can create more value, which will receive favorable capital gain treatment. The requirements for appraisal, legal fees, and so forth are generally less than for institutional mortgages.
4. *A viable investment alternative.* The effective yield on the mortgage can be attractive to a seller who wishes to shift some of his or her portfolio into lower-risk investment vehicles. The loan may provide the seller with a comfortable annuity during retirement or with liquidity to protect other high-risk investments that have substantial negative cash flow possibilities.

The investor (buyer) also finds the purchase money route attractive. A high degree of leverage might be achieved with very favorable mortgage terms. Also, the mortgage clauses (timing of payments, personal liability, prepayment options, etc.) can be negotiated to fit the investor's needs and requirements. In many cases little flexibility is permitted in the mortgages and notes drafted by institutional lenders. Thus, the key advantage of this type of financing is flexibility.

A problem that often develops in purchase money mortgage situations could make a wraparound more desirable than a conventional second mortgage. The investor may not want to assume the first or other senior mortgages on the property for two reasons: (1) The effective mortgage constant may be too high to create positive leverage, and (2) the payments may have an unfavorable interest/principal ratio, thereby creating tax problems. A wraparound mortgage can solve both problems.

Wraparound Mortgages[18]   A wraparound is simply a junior mortgage loan that permits a second lender (e.g., a seller or institutional lender) to finance a borrower by lending an amount over and above the existing first-mortgage balance, which is not disturbed or paid off. (Note that if there are numerous senior mortgages already in existence, a wraparound could legally be a third, fourth, or fifth lien against the property.)

The important feature of a wraparound is that the face amount of the loan is

[18] See Alvin L. Arnold and Jack Kusnet, *The Arnold Encyclopedia of Real Estate* (Boston: Warren, Gorham & Lamont, 1978), pp. 893–896. Also, Arnold Leider, "How to Wrap Around a Mortgage," *Real Estate Review,* Winter 1975, pp. 29–34.

equal to the balance of the first loan plus the amount of new financing. The wraparound loan (usually) calls for a higher interest rate than the first loan, and that higher interest rate covers the entire amount of the loan, even though the wraparound lender provides only a relatively small amount of new money. For example, in the Aspen Wood case a note for $793,400 *wraps around three* underlying notes totaling $636,000 (Chapter 12). In effect, the seller was providing junior lien financing (fourth mortgage) of $157,400 ($793,400 − $636,000). The investors paid debt service on the entire $793,400 note to the seller (actually, a trustee who was appointed to administer the loan), and the seller (trustee) sent to the senior lenders the debt service on the three underlying loans. The wraparound note carried an interest rate of 7 1/2 percent, while the underlying liens had interest rates in the 6 1/2− 7 percent range. The effect is to leverage the wraparound lender's return on the $157,400 investment. The seller received not only the 7 1/2 percent on his $157,400 investment but also a 1/2− 1 percent spread on the $636,000 underlying liens.[19]

Four other situations might suggest the use of a wraparound mortgage:

1. The first-mortgage lender refuses to refinance, and prepayment is either prohibited or subject to heavy penalties.
2. The first-mortgage lender is unable to refinance (because of lending restrictions) and is not willing to allow prepayment.
3. The investor wants to reduce the debt service on an existing loan and cannot recast the first mortgage, and looks to the wraparound lender to refinance on a longer-term basis.
4. The borrower does not want to prepay a very favorable first mortgage, but needs additional short-term financing.

Probably the least understood aspect of wraparound financing is that in most situations, while the underlying loan balance is amortizing, the wraparound loan balance (net funds loaned) actually increases. This is because the loan amortization term on the wraparound is (usually) long compared to the remaining term on the underlying loan. Very little principal is being amortized on the wraparound, but a substantial portion of the debt service on the underlying lien represents amortization of principal.

The wraparound can present a serious tax problem to a seller who takes it back. If a substantial portion of the wraparound interest received is used to amortize the principal on the underlying lien, the resulting tax liability on the net interest received by the seller (wraparound interest minus underlying loan interest) may approach or even exceed the amount of cash received by the seller.

As noted previously, wraparound mortgages are often used as the financing vehicle of buyers and sellers, and thus are a common form of purchase money mortgage. However, as a result of the gradual deregulation of financial institutions that has occurred in recent years, most federally and state-chartered financial

---

[19] The computation of IRR before tax and after tax on a wraparound mortgage is illustrated by Egon H. Kraus in "Tax Advantages of Wraparound Financing," *Real Estate Review,* Spring 1981, pp. 11− 17.

institutions now have the authority to make wraparound loans. Many S&Ls and mortgage companies aggressively seek opportunities to make such loans. Numerous life insurance companies, commercial banks, and REITs also make wraparound loans.

Subordinated Land Leasebacks A subordinated land leaseback arrangement is created when an investor sells the land under an income property and then leases it back from the buyer on a long-term basis. Although the land fee is transfered to the new buyer, the investor retains ownership of the improvements, control of the property, and the benefits of depreciation, equity buildup, and any operations related to the improvements. It is important that the equity investor (the owner of the improvements) negotiate a subordination clause with the land buyer to allow an institution to place a first mortgage on the improvements. Without a subordination clause, the fee owner of the land would hold the senior claim on the property and a subsequent mortgage loan placed on the property would be in a second-lien position. Mortgage financing on the improvements would be difficult to obtain and would require second-lien rates and terms.

The cost of the leaseback to the investor comes in the form of land rent, which is fully deductible for tax purposes. Land rent payments are normally payable monthly and have three principal components:

1. *Fixed rent.* This is typically a fixed percentage of the selling price of the land; sometimes fixed rental increases are required during the life of the lease. Since subordinated land leasebacks are junior mortgages, the fixed percentage rates are generally from 1 percent to 4 percent above first-mortgage constants.
2. *Inflation hedge or percentage rent.* This is generally pegged to the income stream generated by the property and is often around 10–15 percent of all gross rents collected over a certain base level. If the bargaining power of the land buyer is strong, a share of the refinancing or sale proceeds may also be demanded.
3. *Reimbursement for taxes.* Since the new owner of the land will be assessed for property taxes once the fee has been transfered, the leaseback agreement will usually provide for reimbursement by the lessee.

Sources of subordinated land leaseback financing include REITs, some pension funds and life insurance companies, and individuals who seek a relatively high level of current income but have no need for depreciation deductions. The financing criterion for land leasebacks is often stated as a land rent coverage ratio—the ratio of cash flow (left after debt service) to the land rental. The coverage ratio may be anywhere between 1.30 and 2.00. The normal range for the term of the lease is 50 to 99 years.

Two particular areas of concern for the equity investor who is buying a property that is subject to a land leaseback arrangement are (1) refinancing restrictions in the land lease that disallow refinancing the first mortgage on the improvements and (2) land rent escalations that are not limited to increases in the property's operating income or cash flow. Both may restrict the investor's flexibility and have severe negative effects on future cash flows over time.[20] In solving such problems, extensive cash flow simulations should be undertaken to test the impact of various alternatives on the investor's return and risk. In many cases land leaseback arrangements will dramatically increase the risk and reduce the marketability of the property. For this reason, many conservative investors avoid properties with land lease arrangements.

Other Creative Financing Techniques

Other financing techniques also allow an investor to leverage a small equity position. These techniques include (1) sale-leaseback of an entire property or building, (2) sale-buyback, (3) sandwich lease, (4) collateralized or personal loan, and (5) high-credit lease loan.

Sale-Leaseback of Property or Building   The most frequent sale-leaseback situation involves the entire property. A developer sells to an institutional investor and simultaneously enters into a long-term net leaseback. Sale-leasebacks are also used by businesses and commercial firms that use real estate but do not wish to own it and have the related asset and debt shown directly on the balance sheet. The most important benefit to the seller of the property is that 100 percent (or greater) financing is attained and the investment is converted into cash. On the other hand, the seller loses all the depreciation deductions and the right to any future appreciation in the value of the property; also, the arrangement usually includes escalation clauses that periodically raise the lease payments and reduce cash flow. Normally, the lease will run anywhere from 25 to 99 years.

A sale-leaseback of the *building only* occurs where the seller-lessee retains title to the land while selling and leasing back the building that is on the land. Normally, the purchaser of the building is an investor who is interested primarily in tax shelter (100% of the property purchased can be depreciated) rather than cash flow or long-term appreciation.

Sale-Buyback   A sale-buyback, like a sale-leaseback, allows the investor to mortgage out (100% financing). The investor sells the property to a lending institution with an agreement to buy it back under a long-term installment contract. The lending institution retains title, but the investor has an *equitable interest* in the title and therefore is entitled to take the depreciation deductions on the improvements. Whereas the investor in effect achieves 100 percent debt financing, the lender receives a fixed contract payment (interest and principal) and a contingent payment in the form of a percentage of the cash flow (or some other income figure).

A sale-buyback arrangement with a lender, like a sale-leaseback, is possible only if the investor has strong credit and a good track record. Both are relatively high-risk, high-return alternatives and are rarely used by conservative investors.

Sandwich Lease   A sandwich lease is a double-lease arrangement in which the investor creates a return without an equity investment. Simply stated, the investor leases an income property for a relatively long period, at a relatively low

---

[20] An excellent discussion of the subject, including proposed solutions and examples, is provided by Arnold, *Real Estate Financing Techniques,* pp. 56–63.

lease payment rate, and with the right to sublet the property at a profit. For example, an investor negotiates a twenty-year net lease on a vacant office building for $100,000 annually. The space is then sublet on the same net terms to numerous tenants (or, preferably, one high-credit tenant) at rentals that total $125,000. The investor, if successful, will receive a $25,000 cash flow each year for twenty years (or more, if escalations are present). The investor is "sandwiched" in the middle, at a profit. Alternatively, the present value of the leasehold income can be estimated and the leasehold interest can be sold or mortgaged, or both, to equity investors.

The Empire State Building was syndicated under such an arrangement in 1961; the promotors sold $26 million of equity interests to investors at $10,000 per share. In essence, the investors bought a leasehold interest in the land and building, which was owned by Prudential Life Insurance Company, and then created a sublease that guaranteed them a minimum ROE of 9 percent plus overages.

The primary risk for the owner of the leasehold interest is that some or all of the sublessees will default on their obligations. Ideally, the investor would seek a single high-credit sublessee on a lease term concurrent with that of the master lease, which would minimize the financial risk and management burden associated with such a financing technique.

Collateralized and Personal Loans If a high-ratio loan exceeding the normal lending limit is sought by the investor, the lender can secure such a loan by taking a first mortgage on the property and a pledge of marketable securities (or some other collateral) for the amount that exceeds the normal lending limit. In this manner the investor can achieve a high leverage ratio from a single lending source. The same result can be achieved with a personal (unsecured) loan if the borrower has a substantial financial statement and good credit. For example, some equity investors will enter into syndications of property with equity investments that are 100 percent financed through short-term loans from their local commercial banks. In effect, they achieve 100 percent debt financing at the time of purchase.

High-Credit-Lease Loan One key method of achieving a 90–100 percent loan is available when the investor has long-term, high-credit tenants occupying the property. A lender looks primarily to the credit of the tenants, and unless legal restrictions exist, a low debt coverage ratio (1.05–1.20) and a high loan amount are acceptable. In general, the higher the credit of the lessee and the better the lease terms, the greater the loan amount that will be permitted. For example, a major food chain store on a triple net lease for thirty years, with periodic rent escalations based on the CPI, would provide an investor the maximum opportunity for high leverage.

THE REFINANCING DECISION

The rapid inflation of property values over the last decade has directed considerable attention to the subject of refinancing existing mortgages on residential and commercial properties. While historical data on the refinancing of mortgage loans on investment properties are not generally available, surveys of large U.S. life insurance companies and savings and loan associations indicate that their activity in refinancing mortgage loans has increased substantially.[21]

For many investors, refinancing is the preferred alternative to selling the property when the objective is to realize the benefits of increased property values. Many investors believe that a profitable property should never be sold. Rather, properties should be refinanced periodically and the refinancing proceeds used to achieve the investor's other objectives—expanding the portfolio, tax shelter, and so on.

Objectives of Refinancing

The specific objectives of financing can take numerous forms, including the following:

1. *Increasing liquidity.* Tax-free capital is obtained, since borrowing entails no ordinary or capital gains. The proceeds can be used to increase the liquidity of the investor's financial statement or to purchase consumer products and services.
2. *Expanding the portfolio (pyramid properties).* The refinancing proceeds are used to purchase other properties and begin new cycles of cash flow, tax shelter, and appreciation.
3. *Diversifying the portfolio.* The tax-free cash is invested in other types of property, at different locations, using different ownership forms, investment interests, and so forth. The objective is to reduce the overall riskiness of the portfolio.
4. *Increasing cash flows.* A lower interest rate or extended term will increase the investor's cash flow from operations.
5. *Increasing tax shelter.* Refinancing will begin a new interest cycle, minimizing the amortization while maximizing the interest portion of the debt service. Also, an increased loan amount may substantially raise interest deductions and tax shelter. Moreover, any prepayment penalties and unamortized loan expenses on the original financing can be taken as deductions in the year of refinancing.
6. *Improving marketability and selling price.* Creating an attractive, high-leverage financial package for a potential buyer will make a property more salable and usually increase its market value. The risk of financing the property has been eliminated for the buyer, and a lower capitalization can be justified.
7. *Funding a renovation or refurbishing program.* Periodically a property must undergo major renovations or refurbishing. Refinancing an existing first mortgage may provide an attractive alternative to securing secondary financing for this purpose.

While refinancing is attractive in many situations, timing is critical. Too often refinancing proceeds are not available when the investor needs them. High inter-

[21] Perry Hayes, "Making the Right Refinancing Choice," *Real Estate Review,* Summer 1978, p. 92.

est rates and tight money conditions often prohibit refinancing. Tight money conditions will generally result in more conservative leverage ratios, higher points, higher interest rates, and more severe prepayment penalties. Also, substantial prepayment penalties on existing mortgages, or the presence of a *closed period,* may make a refinancing infeasible or unprofitable in relation to the risks involved.

A new loan may take a substantial amount of time to arrange, require personal liability, have substantial prepayment penalties, and contain other onerous mortgage clauses. The tax-free refinancing proceeds may be difficult to reinvest at a high IRR. Finally, as we illustrated in Chapter 13, the refinancing may create a serious tax problem at the time of sale if the net proceeds are small but the tax liability from the sale is large.

Refinancing Alternatives

The key to solving a refinancing problem is the investor's ability to define or create alternatives. The number of possible alternatives is limited only by the creativity and imagination of the investor, as shown in Exhibit 14–6.

Impact on Returns and Risks

The frequently stated principle, "Refinancing should be undertaken when cash flow becomes subject to tax as a result of the interplay between lower depreciation deductions and rising mortgage amortization," is incorrect for many, perhaps

---

EXHIBIT 14–6. Twenty Techniques an Investor Can Use to Refinance Property

---

1. Sell the land and lease it back.
2. Obtain secondary financing to generate cash.
3. Pyramid with a second mortgage to gain buying power.
4. Refinance the existing financing into a new first mortgage.
5. Sell the entire property, lease back with an option to buy.
6. Renegotiate the existing financing to lower the mortgage constant.
7. Seek a moratorium on the existing financing for either interest or principal or both.
8. Refinance with use of real estate bonds.
9. Bring in a partner through a syndication or joint venture.
10. Plan addition and refinance total package.
11. Buy adjoining property and refinance total package.
12. Discount existing financing for cash.
13. Sell chattels (personal property) and lease them back.
14. Seek unsecured financing.
15. Refinance with a blanket mortgage adding other security.
16. Rent to cover expenses and debt service.
17. Prepay rent or mortgage to obtain better terms.
18. Sell only a portion of the property or interest.
19. Sublease a portion of the property or interest.
20. Look to a wraparound mortgage to generate required capital.

SOURCE: From the book *Complete Guide to Real Estate Financing* by Jack Cummings, © 1978, by Prentice Hall, Inc., Englewood Cliffs, N.J., 07632. Published by Prentice-Hall, Inc.

most, investors in most situations. Rather, the existing market environment and the expected returns and risks should determine the best refinancing strategy.

Various techniques for evaluating the refinancing decision have been proposed, including application of net present value and internal rate-of-return models on both an after- and a before-tax basis.[22] Both techniques require that a proposed refinancing strategy be evaluated by comparing cash inflows and outflows assuming refinancing with those assuming no refinancing (hold strategy). If the returns relative to the risks are greater under the refinancing strategy (NPV > 0, or IRR > required IRR), then refinancing should be undertaken; otherwise, it should be rejected or modified.

EQUITY FINANCING ALTERNATIVES

Thus far we have focused on the methods of debt financing that can be used to achieve the optimal or desired combination of returns and risks. Now we will turn our attention to the equity portion of the capital structure decision. It will become obvious that many of the alternatives, like debt financing, are actually hybrid structures that mix elements of pure debt and pure equity.

Whenever a real estate project is organized under a multiperson form of ownership, it can be considered a syndication. In the following sections we treat syndication as simply one form of equity financing alternative. Therefore, be aware that much of the general material on equity financing alternatives applies equally well to individuals, institutions, and syndicates. Our later presentation on syndication offerings will extend this discussion and focus on security laws, regulations, and issues, and specific types of syndicate offerings.

Form of Ownership

To a substantial extent, the form of ownership chosen defines the legal and economic relationships between the parties involved in the equity structure. The various ownership alternatives were discussed in Chapter 10, but it is important to reiterate a few points. First, we noted that the form of ownership significantly affects the nature and level of returns and risks. Limited partners have limited liability, but they must sacrifice some of the property returns to the general partner, who is thereby compensated for accepting unlimited liability for the partnership. A joint venture partner shares in the major management and financial decisions of the venture, but a corporate stockholder or limited partner has very limited ability to affect ongoing management decisions.

We also noted that the form of ownership chosen affects the ability of the managing equity investor (syndicator) to raise equity capital in the marketplace. For example, in comparison to a joint venture or tenancy in common, a limited partnership is generally a far superior pass-through tax vehicle for raising large

[22] Ibid, pp. 92–96. See also Donald L. Valachi, "Analysis for Refinancing Decisions," *The Real Estate Appraiser and Analyst,* September–October 1978, pp. 42–47, and "Should You Refinance," in *15 New Real Estate Opportunities,* ed. John T. Reed (New York: Real Estate Investing Newsletter, 1980), pp. 25–27.

amounts of equity capital from unrelated individuals over a wide geographic area. Finally, we showed that if the investor could define and weigh objectives and investment criteria, an ownership decision model can be developed to choose the best ownership form.

Sources of Equity Financing

Most equity real estate investments are sold to individuals or to groups of individuals. Increasingly, however, major industrial and manufacturing corporations seek involvement through joint ventures and other partnership arrangements with developers and institutional lenders. Likewise, major institutional lenders are increasing their investments in equity or hybrid positions as inflation continues to erode the traditional fixed-debt position. It is estimated that by the year 2000, 50 percent of all commercial real estate in the United States will be owned by institutions.[23]

In addition to the various forms of equity participations discussed earlier, lenders are developing new debt-equity combination vehicles. One of these is the convertible mortgage. Designed as permanent financing, the convertible mortgage progressively increases the lender's equity interest in the mortgaged real estate in lieu of cash amortization payments by the borrower.[24] The mortgage interest of the lender is converted into equity ownership over the amortization term of the financing. In effect, the convertible mortgage is a new kind of joint venture between the equity investor and the lender. Other combination debt-equity vehicles that are employed by lenders have been discussed throughout this chapter.

Institutional investors and developers are also seeking to increase their investments in long-term equity interests through joint venture ownership arrangements. As a result, large projects can be planned, developed, and owned over the long term without any participation by outside equity investors or syndicators.[25] Pension funds and foreign investors are competing with traditional investment groups and individuals. Local markets are disappearing as investor groups play an arbitrage game in which money is moved from lower-return investments in one part of the country to higher returns in other geographic areas, including smaller towns, which heretofore have been overlooked by both individuals and institutions. Slowly the market is becoming more efficient as information flows and competition increases, and as the investment process becomes more systematized. Creative equity structures are becoming commonplace and today offer investors a wider variety of equity alternatives than ever before. Public ownership of real estate through passive equity investment vehicles (primarily equity REITs

---

[23] William S. Reiling, "Lenders Seek New Financing Alternatives," *Mortgage Banker,* March 1981, pp. 36–39. Reiling presents an excellent overview of financing alternatives for the 1980s.

[24] Lois A. Vitt and Joel H. Bernstein, "Convertible Mortgages: New Financing Tool," *Real Estate Review,* Spring 1976, pp. 33–37.

[25] As institutional lenders gain more expertise in equity participations and development joint ventures, it is likely that many will choose to perform all the development and equity investment roles as well as the traditional lending roles. The developer may become an employee of the lender in these situations, working on a fee-plus-bonus basis. See Walter L. Updegrave, "Joint Venture: The Boom That's Reshaping the Industry," *Housing,* August 1980, p. 48.

and limited partnerships) is becoming a standard practice as most of the major stock brokerage houses in the country develop real estate securities offering divisions.

In short, the amount of equity money from all sources has increased dramatically, while the amount of pure debt financing has decreased. Managing equity investors need to tailor their financing structures to take advantage of these emerging trends.

Creative Equity Structures

Investors in corporate securities have a wide variety of choices that define particular return and risk classifications—common stock, preferred stock, bonds, puts, calls, and so on. Only recently have various classes of real estate equity interests been similarly developed.

Multiclass Equity Structures   In a multiclass equity structure, the benefits and risks are divided to coincide with different investor objectives. For example, some investors might receive a disproportionate allocation of the tax benefits, while others receive a preferred cash flow and still others appreciation returns. In earlier chapters we concluded that such allocations would be disallowed for tax purposes if their principal purpose was found to be the avoidance or evasion of federal income taxes. Consequently, the equity ownership vehicle must be carefully structured to achieve the desired tax and economic benefits.

A multiclass equity structure should increase the total returns to the investors and, thus, the investment value of the property.[26] The packager can pass along this increase in value to the investors by offering equity shares with higher returns. Or, when the sum of the parts offered separately is greater than the price the property would bring if offered as a whole, the packager can take the benefits by selling different components. This concept of fractionalizing investment interests was pioneered by William Zeckendorf and is called the Hawaiian technique.[27]

Three general approaches to multiclass equity structures can be used:

1. *Different classes of ownership interest within the same ownership vehicle.* Two classes of interests are offered to investors, class A and class B. Class A is entitled to a preferential cash flow until a specified annual yield has been achieved, after which cash is distributed according to some formula between the two classes. Class B is entitled to a preference in the allocation of tax benefits in a similar fashion.
2. *The leasehold approach.* Two partnerships are created to own one property. Partnership A buys the property and leases it to partnership B for a rent equivalent to the mortgage payments on the property. Thus, partnership A investors realize a return consisting essentially of the tax deductions from depreciation on the property. Partnership B investors

---

[26] Stephen E. Roulac, "What's in Those Shiny New Syndication Packages," *Real Estate Review,* Summer 1972, p. 79.
[27] Zeckendorf, pp. 143–148.

operate the building and enjoy a high (and perhaps increasing) cash return but little or no tax shelter.

3. *The loan approach.* This approach is similar to the leasehold approach except that partnership B (cash-flow-oriented investors) make a loan to partnership A (tax-shelter-oriented investors who own the depreciable assets). Payments on the loan, rather than rent payments, are made to partnership B, including some form of participation in the cash flow from the property.

In all three approaches tax and legal problems, as well as conflicts of interest, can arise. For example, during an economic downturn the tax-shelter-oriented investors may have increasing returns (more tax losses) while the cash flow investors have decreasing returns (less rents and cash flow). On the other hand, management decisions that result in increased cash flow may decrease the amount of tax shelter. Great care must be taken to clearly define the financial implications of the equity structure for all parties involved.

Compensation Schemes for Investors

In most equity investment structures the managing equity investor (who may be referred to as the general partner, the operating partner, the promotor, the syndicator, or the project sponsor) will seek compensation in the form of fees and commissions, as well as participation in the various forms of property return. Considerable debate has arisen in recent years regarding the compensation schemes used. Syndication sponsors have often been accused of structuring investments that benefit them handsomely, regardless of the economic consequences to the passive investors. Such structures are said to lack "goal congruency." An equity structure that has goal congruency is one in which the economic consequences to the sponsor closely parallel the economic consequences to the passive investors. That is, if the project does poorly, the sponsor receives a minimum return; if it does well, the sponsor is compensated proportionately (or more) for a job well done.

Various types of compensation schemes have been used or suggested.[28] The three in Exhibit 14–7 show varying degrees of goal congruency.

The first scheme, which is used by many real estate syndicators, is characterized by a high front-end load, including commissions and fees that are paid regardless of a property's performance. The sponsor also takes a subordinated interest in both the cash flow and the proceeds of sale. Scheme II is similar, but the front-end fees and market/organizational costs are regulated by the amount of equity investor dollars going into the project (rather than being a percentage of the total purchase price, as in scheme I). Scheme III provides the most goal congruency; it has a low front-end load and market/organizational costs, but allocates

---

[28] See Gary K. Barr, "Compensation Schemes of Real Estate Securities," *The Real Estate Appraiser,* May–June 1974, pp. 4–9. Also, Stephen E. Roulac, "The Promoter's Participation Interest as a Form of Compensation in Real Estate Syndication," *The Real Estate Appraiser,* May–June 1973, pp. 33–40.

EXHIBIT 14–7. Investment Sponsor Compensation Schemes

Compensation scheme I: 6% real estate commission
Front-end load = 27.5% of money raised (6% sales commission)
Marketing and organizational costs = 1.7% of money raised
Subordinated cash flow = 10% of cash flow above an annual return of 6% on
   money raised. (cash return)
Subordinated interest at sale = 10% of proceeds after a return of capital plus 6%
   annual return. (cash return)

Compensation scheme II: Using guidelines recently adopted by the Midwest Securi-
   ties Commissioners
Front-end load = 18% of money raised
Marketing and organizational costs = 15% of money raised
Participation = 10% of cash flow from operations
Participation at resale = 9% of proceeds after a return of capital plus a 6% annual
   return. (cash return)

Compensation scheme III: Suggested method to provide goal congruency
Front-end load = 10% of money raised
Marketing and organizational costs = 10% of money raised
Participation in operation = 50% of cash flow above a 7% annual return. (cash
   return)
Participation at resale = 45% of net proceeds after a return of capital plus a 7%
   annual cumulative return. (cash return)

SOURCE: Gary K. Barr, "Compensation Schemes of Real Estate Securities," *The Real Estate Appraiser,* May–June 1974, p. 6.

---

a large sale participation interest (45%) to the sponsor if the property is successful. This scheme requires the promoter to maintain a continued interest in the operation and resale of the property, since the promoter's substantial profits are received only after the property has performed well for the passive investors.

Guaranteed and Nonguaranteed Returns Equity investors often seek to limit the risks they take through some form of guarantee from the seller of the property. This guarantee can take many forms, including the following:

1. *Rent-up guarantee.* The seller agrees to guarantee against a negative cash flow, or promises some positive cash flow for a specified period after purchase.
2. *Subordination of management fee.* The seller agrees to manage the property and subordinate the management fee until some specified cash flow is received by the investors.
3. *Minimum cash-flow-through leaseback arrangement.* A minimum cash flow rate is assured by a leaseback agreement with the seller for a limited period.

Clearly, the reduction of risk is proportionate to the type of guarantee, the length of the guarantee, and the quality of the guarantor. Also, it should be clear that while guarantees are desirable in many situations, they are usually paid for in the purchase price of the property. The risk reduction achieved in this manner usually results in some loss of returns to the investors.

Staged Equity Investment Techniques In many purchases the investor negotiates a staged down payment arrangement in which the total equity is paid to the seller over several years. Thus, during the early years of ownership the relative returns are greatly magnified when measured by a cash flow (or tax shelter) to equity ratio, and the marketability of the investment is increased substantially. For example, consider a highly leveraged property that can be purchased for an equity investment of $100,000 and is structured to produce tax losses of $50,000 in the year of acquisition. This structure provides the investor with a potential 50 percent tax write-off for each dollar of equity investment in the year of purchase. If, however, the equity down payment can be split into two equal payments, one this year and one next, the equity investor's tax shelter write-off doubles to 100 percent in the year of acquisition. The property becomes considerably more attractive to tax-shelter-oriented investors.

A staged equity investment can also result when the exact purchase price is not known at the time the property is closed because it is based on the property's performance (or some other event) after the closing. In this case modifications in the equity (and debt) structure may take place as the property does, or does not, perform according to the seller's pro forma guarantees.

SYNDICATION OFFERINGS

In the past, most real estate syndications involved a single property and a single class of investors, each of whom received a pro rata ownership interest in the syndicate. Purchasers of partnership units expected to hold their units until the property was sold and the partnership terminated. Today, managing equity investors frequently use a variety of new syndication concepts and vehicles. Syndications are becoming much larger in scope and size, are being offered through the public media, and consequently are being closely scrutinized and regulated by federal and state securities agencies.

Types of Syndication Offerings

Single- or Multiple-Property Offerings An increasingly popular syndication concept is the multiple-property offering, or the fund approach, as it is often called. This type of syndication is said to offer investors the following advantages:

1. *Diversification of risk and type of return.* The syndicate may diversify by size and type of property purchased, geographic location, and so forth. Also, high cash flow properties on net leases can be combined with appreciation-oriented investments.
2. *Economies of scale in the origination phase.* These reduce marketing, legal, and administration costs (on a per-unit basis). Only one prospectus needs to be developed, instead of many.

3. *Economies of scale in operations.* Management and accounting costs can be reduced on a percentage-of-revenue basis as a result of operating efficiencies.
4. *Tax and cash flow planning among properties.* More control can be exercised to achieve the investment objectives.

If a syndicator offers shares to the public and must register the offering under federal and state laws, it makes sense to seek fewer registrations and raise more money per syndication. The minimum cost for a registration with the SEC is about $50,000 and may run as high as $300,000– 500,000 for large syndications that register and sell shares in a large number of states.

The proponents of single-property offerings believe that the best theory is to "put all your eggs into one basket, then watch the basket like a hawk." They argue that it is more difficult to structure a multiple-property offering to meet the specific cash flow, tax, and other requirements of the investor. Furthermore, using this approach, investors can achieve some diversification by investing in several single-property offerings to fit specific needs and requirements.

Specified or Nonspecified Property Offerings   When an offering specifies its properties, it can be evaluated on the basis of the investment quality of the real estate itself; also, the exact amount of the sponsor's front-end compensation is known before the passive investors make their decision. Thus, assuming that projections are available, the investor can directly assess whether the investment is viable. In the nonspecified investment offering, also called a *blind pool* or *blank check* offering, investors do not know which properties will be owned by the partnership. Consequently, they must rely solely on the general statement of the syndicate's objectives and investment criteria, and on the reputation and track record of the syndicator.

Both approaches have advantages and disadvantages. Proponents of the nonspecified type feel that they can obtain better buys if they have the money in hand when they are negotiating. Also, the syndicator does not have to use personal funds to tie up a property for an extended period of time while putting together a prospectus, going through the registration process (if necessary), and raising the funds for acquisition. On the other hand, there is the danger that a syndicator who is motivated to produce tax benefits before the end of the current tax year, will be pressured to rush out and invest the money before year-end. Having to invest money quickly is not usually a negotiating advantage, and may result in a higher purchase price and more onerous purchase terms.

Open- or Closed-End Offerings   Historically, most investment offerings have been closed. Partnerships were formed to own, operate, and sell real estate, and the partnerships were dissolved once the assets were sold. While some provision may have been made for new partners, issuance of new shares on a continuing basis was not usually allowed. However, a relatively new form of syndicate, called the open-end fund, has developed.

An open-end fund, like a common stock mutual fund, includes provisions to issue new ownership units on a continuing basis. These syndicates can acquire additional properties over time or, when a property is sold, replace it with another. Although the concept is relatively new, it will become more popular as increased government regulation and control drive up the costs of registration and legal compliance procedures. Furthermore, if the fund builds a track record, name identification can substantially aid in further marketing efforts.

An investor should be careful to evaluate the liquidity of the shares purchased in an open-end fund, since no orderly method of termination is provided. It is important to be able to dispose of shares to realize any appreciation in property values. The ability to trade shares in an organized marketplace and through organized exchanges and brokerage houses will be a key factor in evaluating such investments in the future.

The Master Prospectus[29] This concept combines the economies of the multiple-property offering and the advantages of the single-property syndication. Investors buy partnership interests, which can later be converted into ownership shares in separate partnerships formed to hold each property. In one type of offering, for example, the investor specifies his or her investment objectives in the syndicate's subscription agreement. The syndicator then allocates the investor's dollars to various individual partnerships according to the objectives and instructions contained in the subscription agreement. Another variation of the master prospectus approach occurs when the investor purchases a participation interest and then selects a particular partnership.

Federal and State Regulation of Syndicates

The government imposes direct controls and regulations on real estate transactions whenever they are deemed to be "security" transactions. Many investors and syndicators have been surprised to learn that over the years their real estate transactions have actually been securities transactions and that they have not been complying with federal and state laws. Considering the many civil and criminal penalties that can be imposed, a syndicator today must begin with the assumption that all syndication activities are security transactions. Only by meeting certain exemption provisions will the syndicator be relieved of the onerous reporting requirements and procedures imposed by the Securities and Exchange Commission and, in most cases, state securities agencies.

A real estate interest is considered an "investment contract," and hence a security, if the "investors are induced to invest in a common enterprise in the expectation of profits which are to result solely from the efforts of the promoter or a third party other than the investor."[30] Most real estate syndications are therefore within the securities law, since passive investors receive investment interests in return for the funds they put into a common pool and are led to expect profit from the efforts of the syndicator.

The definition of "security" is constantly expanding, and can be interpreted

---

[29] Roulac, "What's in Those Shiny New Syndication Packages," p. 80.
[30] *How to Syndicate Real Estate*, Portfolio no. 11, prepared by the editorial staff of *Real Estate Review* with the assistance of Alan Parisse (Boston: Warren, Gorham & Lamont, 1977), p. 57.

to include almost every real estate investment and brokerage activity.[31] In general, whenever a syndicator (regardless of the type of ownership form used) *sells* the ownership units and *management* of the property is an essential part of the transaction, there is a sale of a security. Thus, the crucial determinant of "security" is the manner in which the real estate asset is *marketed* and *managed*.

The Securities Acts of 1933 and 1934   The Securities Act of 1933 defines the basic federal law governing the sale and offering of securities. For this law to apply, the securities must be offered and sold in interstate commerce. However, interstate commerce is very broadly defined, and even the use of a telephone (which is regulated at the federal level) can mean that the offering will fall under the interstate commerce classification.

The regulation provisions call for the following:

1. *Registration*—to be filed with the SEC (form S-11) before the securities are distributed.
2. *Full disclosure*—a prospectus disclosing all relevant information needed by an investor to make an assessment of the security and all risks involved.
3. *Discouragement of fraud*—provides statutory remedies that are broader than those available under common law to discourage misrepresentation.

Under the Securities Exchange Act of 1934 securities exchanges are required to register with the SEC or to obtain an exemption from registration as a prerequisite for doing business. Before securities can be traded they must be registered with the SEC.

Fortunately, the federal government offers exemptions from full registration for certain classes of securities, including private offerings, intrastate offerings, and offerings aggregating under $1,500,000 (Regulation A).

Private Offerings. To qualify for this exemption, the securities must be offered only to people who are believed to be financially strong enough to bear substantial investment risks. These offerees should be capable of making intelligent investment decisions or have access to an adviser who can assist in such a decision. The issuer and investor should be in direct contact so that questions can be answered, and no solicitation (e.g., advertising) that would attract an unsophisticated investor is permitted.

The private-offering exemption language in the Securities Act of 1933 was vague. However, in 1974 the SEC issued Rule 146 (known as the Safe Harbor Act), which specifically sets forth the exemption requirements. Under Rule 146 a private-offering exemption is achieved if *all* the following conditions are met:

1. The number of purchasers must be less than thirty-five.
2. General solicitation and advertising to sell or offer securities are prohibited.

---

[31] For a complete discussion of securities laws in real estate, see *How Securities Laws Affect Real Estate Offerings,* Portfolio no. 12, prepared by the editorial staff of *Real Estate Review* and Jackson L. Morris (Boston: Warren, Gorham & Lamont, 1977), p. 72.

3. The offeree must be a knowledgeable investor, or be able to bear substantial economic risks.
4. A private offering memorandum is required—the offeree must be given the same information that the formal registration statement would contain.

Although SEC Rule 146 clarified the guidelines for the private-offering exemption, many questions and issues still remain. For example, one might ask, What is a "knowledgeable" investor?[32] What constitutes being "able to bear substantial economic risk"? In any case, a syndicator who wants a private offering exemption should proceed with caution and under the direction of experienced legal counsel.

Intrastate Offerings. The Securities Act of 1933 exempted the issues of securities sold only to residents of the state in which the issuer is a resident and doing business. This exemption can be lost if even one offeree is an out-of-state resident. SEC Rule 147 (Safe Harbor for Intrastate Exemption) was adopted to implement the intrastate exemption; the requirements are very strict, and the exemption cannot be relied upon unless *all* of its qualifications are met. These include the following:

1. The issuer is a resident and doing business (at least 80% of total assets) in the state in which offers are being made.
2. No part of the issue is offered or sold to nonresidents, or resold to nonresidents until nine months from the date of the last sale.
3. All documented precautions are taken against interstate distribution.

Offerings Aggregating Under $1.5 Million (Regulation A). Regulation A is a "short form" registration available for offerings under $1,500,000. The major benefit of this exemption is that the offering document is simplified and review is done at the regional SEC office, rather than in Washington, D.C. Theoretically, the processing time is less and the costs are reduced. The exemption has not been used frequently because the previous equity limit was $500,000. Also, syndicators of relatively small offerings tended to rely on the intrastate and private-offering exemptions. The raising of the equity amount to $1,500,000 should substantially increase the use of this vehicle in the future.

Consequences of Failure to Qualify for an Exemption. When an exemption is lost, it is lost for the entire issue. While there are no specific penalties against the syndicate, the syndicator must offer all investors a refund, and no sales can take place until the issue is registered. As a consequence, the syndication may be abandoned, or substantial costs and delays must be incurred to register the syndication. However, if a syndicator has made untrue statements or has materially misrepresented the property or has misled the investor, then both civil and criminal penalties can be imposed.

---

[32] A study of investor profiles and attitudes is presented by Wayne E. Etter and Donald R. Levi in "Investors' Views of Real Estate and Limited Partnerships," *The Appraisal Journal,* January 1978, pp. 112–121.

State laws   State "blue-sky laws" have basically the same objectives as federal laws. Some states can even disqualify investments that are found lacking in merit under so-called *merit review* procedures. Satisfaction of the federal registration requirement does not automatically satisfy the state requirements. The toughest hurdle is often compliance with state regulations and "administrative" procedures. Each state has a distinct and usually different set of regulations. Thus, full registration in all fifty states can be expensive, ranging in cost from $400,000 to $600,000, and time-consuming. For this reason, some syndicates register only in states in which they believe their potential investors reside, and in states where the reporting requirements are not too stringent.

SUMMARY

In this chapter we designed a methodology for the financing decision process. That process begins with the identification of a property that will produce an adequate NOI stream. Next, the investor determines the financing alternatives, including debt and equity, that are possible. Third, the alternative financial packages are analyzed on a before- and after-tax basis. A financial package is defined as a particular combination of debt and equity sources used to finance a project. Finally, the results for each alternative are compared with the investment criteria, and the alternative that best fits the investor objectives is chosen.

The bulk of the chapter was devoted to analyzing debt and equity alternatives. The analysis of debt alternatives included a discussion of the leverage decision, debt financing variables that can be negotiated, the calculation of mortgage amortization schedules, senior and junior mortgage financing techniques, creative debt financing techniques, and various government-sponsored loan programs. The refinancing decision was also discussed.

Later in the chapter equity financing alternatives were considered. This involved a discussion of forms of ownership, sources of equity financing, creative equity structures, and syndication. The various federal and state laws regulating syndicates have become major factors in the design of syndicate marketing and management techniques.

The Aspen Wood case study is introduced again to illustrate the many principles and concepts developed in this chapter. Using the DCF model presented in Chapter 11, a variety of simulations are undertaken to measure the impact of alternative financial packages on risk and return parameters.

ASPEN WOOD APARTMENTS

NEGOTIATING THE FINANCIAL PACKAGE

The financial package negotiated for Aspen Wood Apartments by syndicators Charlie Davidson and Clyde Boomer of D&B Associates is shown in Exhibit 14–8.

Recall that the basic parameters of the package were determined using the basic financial feasibility model. Given the basic return objective (ROE = 10%) and risk level constraint (DCR = 1.3), along with our best estimate of NOI ($89,305), D&B proceeded to determine an acceptable debt and equity structure. The original solution shown at the end of Chapter 10 included a maximum loan of $830,000, with a mortgage constant not to exceed 8.3 percent, a maximum equity of $206,000, and a maximum purchase price of $1,036,000. Later (Chapter 12), with additional information obtained during the feasibility research stages, the NOI dropped and a more conservative financial package was structured using a DCF model to test the after-tax impact of various financing alternatives. The complete and final financial package is illustrated in Exhibit 14–8.

INPUT ASSUMPTIONS FOR FINANCIAL PACKAGE ANALYSIS[33]

The basic project data for the DCF analysis (using computer model RE001) were presented in Chapter 11. At that stage of analysis the total purchase price was $1 million, with debt of $825,000 and equity of $175,000. Using this data Davidson and Boomer analyzed the impact of various financial packages on the expected returns in different economic scenarios to determine the most desirable package. The critical financing variables tested were as follows:

1. *Leverage ratio:* 75%, 85%, and 95%
2. *Interest rate:* from 6% to 12%, with 1 1/2% increments
3. *Amortization term:* 20, 25, and 30 years
4. *Economic scenarios:* most likely (base case), pessimistic, and optimistic

The three economic scenarios involved variations in vacancies, rents, expenses, and property value, as follows:

	Most Likely (Base Case)	Pessimistic	Optimistic
Occupancy rate	.95	.90	.975
Income growth rate	.04	.02	.08
Expense growth rate	.06	.10	.06
Property value growth rate	.03	.00	.08

[33] This analysis is patterned after a case study presented by James R. Cooper and Stephen A. Pyhrr, "Forecasting the Rates of Return on an Apartment Investment: A Case Study," *The Appraisal Journal,* July 1973, pp. 312–337.

EXHIBIT 14–8.   Aspen Wood Apartments—Financial Package

DEBT STRUCTURE

1. *Amount of debt:* $793,400.
2. *Lender:* Seller (a limited partnership syndication).
3. *Type of mortgage:* Wraparound, junior to three existing mortgage loans.
4. Interest rate: 7.5% annually, payable monthly with principal.
5. *Amortization method:* Fully amortizing, level payment.
6. *Amortization term:* 26.5 years.
7. *Loan term:* Balloon at end of 10 years. First payment due one month after closing.
8. *Commitment fees/points:* Two points paid to lender (seller) at closing.
9. *Degree of personal liability:* None (seller remains liable on underlying notes).
10. *Prepayment provision:* Seller can prepay at any time.
11. *Prepayment penalty:* Pay only specified penalties in underlying notes when they are prepaid.
12. *Required escrow accounts:* No escrows for taxes and insurance. Tax and insurance paid receipts to be provided to lender. Trustee account (for buyer and lender) is established and receives debt service on wraparound loan, pays debt service on underlying loans, sends overage to wraparound lender (seller).
13. *Due-on-sale clause:* None. Owners can sell subject to a wraparound loan.
14. *Due-on-encumbrance clause:* No restriction on additional financing. Lender (seller) can refinance the wraparound loan at terms that leave the owners financially indifferent. Approval will not be unreasonably withheld by owner.
15. *Other mortgage clauses:* No adverse clauses affecting buyer. One-month grace period on debt service payments before loan balance can be accelerated by lender.

EQUITY STRUCTURE

1. *Amount of equity:* $210,000.
2. *Form of ownership:* Joint venture (general partnership, essentially).
3. *Source of equity:* Private participation by individuals and syndicators.
4. *Allocation of returns/risks:* All partners share equally in cash flow, tax benefits, refinancing and sale benefits, according to their percentage ownership.
5. *Property management:* D&B Associates (syndicators); 5% fee.
6. *Venture management:* D&B Associates. Attorney and tax accountants retained by venture. All direct costs paid by the joint venture.
7. *Registration:* None. Venture relies on private and intrastate exemptions under federal and state laws.
8. *Tax status:* No 1065 filed. Venture elects out of partnership tax reporting.

Especially important to D&B was the impact of the financial package on cash flow during an economic downturn (pessimistic case). Could the joint venture survive through bad times? The concern was to structure a financial package that would result in "tolerable" cash flow losses during such a period. It was clear to Davidson and Boomer that as the leverage ratio and interest rate increase and the loan term decreases, the debt coverage ratio falls and eventually negative cash flows occur. What are the relationships among these changes, the IRR_E, the debt coverage ratio, and other risk and return ratios?

OUTPUT DATA AND ANALYSIS

Altogether, the investor would need to perform 135 cash flow simulations to generate all the data required under the variations just described.[34] Exhibit 14–9 presents the financial data for the most likely case only, using only the IRR_E and DCR range as financial criteria.

The results show IRR_E ranging from a high of 67 percent (95% leverage, 6% interest, 30 years) to a low of 11.8 percent (75% leverage, 12% interest, 20 years). The coverage ratios range from a high of 1.70–1.96 (75% leverage, 6% interest, 30 years) to a low of .73–.84 (95% leverage, 12% interest, 20 years). The results are not surprising, but they do show the relative magnitude of changes in the return parameter (IRR_E) and risk parameter (DCR) as the financing variables change. As expected, more aggressive leverage positions require the assumption of higher risks and increase the probability of negative cash flows (DCR $<$ 1). However, in all cases there is positive leverage after tax in the long run, as evidenced by a comparison of the IRR_{TC} and the IRR_E. In all cases $IRR_E > IRR_{TC}$.

An analysis of the output data for the pessimistic economic scenario provided important information but is not presented here. As expected, all the data look substantially worse. The returns and the coverage ratios are consistently lower.

THE FINANCIAL PACKAGE DECISION

The investor's strategy is to negotiate a financial package that will produce the highest returns (IRR in this case) relative to the risks (DCR range in this case).

The financial analysis should provide enough data for two important determinations:

1. *Trade-off decisions.* What can be gained and lost during the negotiation process in order to leave the investor financially indifferent? The goal is to gain more than you lose, yet leave the negotiation table with the seller believing that he or she has done the same thing.

---

[34] Three leverage ratios, five interest rates, three amortization terms, and three economic scenarios will produce 135 simulations ($3 \times 5 \times 3 \times 3 = 135$).

EXHIBIT 14–9.   IRR$_E$ and DCR Data for Financial Package Analysis, Most Likely Scenario

	75% LEVERAGE			85% LEVERAGE			95% LEVERAGE		
	20 Years	25 Years	30 Years	20 Years	25 Years	30 Years	20 Years	25 Years	30 Years
6%	18.0 (1.42–1.64)	18.9 (1.58–1.83)	19.5 (1.70–1.96)	25.0 (1.26–1.45)	27.0 (1.40–1.61)	28.5 (1.50–1.73)	49.3 (1.12–1.30)	59.5 (1.25–1.44)	67.0 (1.34–1.55)
7.5%	16.6 (1.27–1.46)	17.3 (1.38–1.59)	17.8 (1.46–1.68)	22.7 (1.12–1.30)	24.4 (1.22–1.41)	25.6 (1.29–1.49)	43.8 (1.00–1.15)	52.6 (1.09–1.26)	58.9 (1.15–1.33)
9%	15.1 (1.13–1.31)	15.6 (1.22–1.40)	16.0 (1.27–1.46)	20.2 (1.00–1.16)	21.6 (1.07–1.24)	22.5 (1.12–1.29)	37.7 (0.90–1.03)	44.8 (0.96–1.11)	49.8 (1.00–1.16)
10.5%	13.5 (1.02–1.78)	13.9 (1.08–1.25)	14.1 (1.12–1.29)	17.5 (0.90–1.04)	18.5 (0.95–1.10)	19.2 (0.98–1.14)	31.1 (0.81–0.93)	36.4 (0.85–0.98)	40.1 (0.88–1.02)
12%	11.8 (0.93–1.07)	12.0 (0.97–1.12)	12.1 (0.99–1.15)	14.6 (0.82–0.94)	15.3 (0.86–0.99)	15.7 (0.88–1.01)	24.1 (0.73–0.84)	27.6 (0.77–0.88)	29.9 (0.78–0.90)

Investment criteria:
1. Internal rate of return on equity (IRR$_E$) for 7-year holding period (top number shown in each box).
2. Debt coverage ratio range (DCR), years 1 and 7 (numbers in parentheses). In all cases the DCR increases each year for seven years; thus, the two DCR figures show the level and trend over the holding period.

Internal rate of return on total capital (IRR$_{TC}$): 7.64% in all cases. Variations in the financing variables do not affect the IRR$_{TC}$.

2. *Minimum-cutoff-point decisions.* Certain financial packages are not acceptable to the investor and therefore should not be considered.

   In the Aspen Wood situation Davidson and Boomer were not able to negotiate a high leverage ratio owing to the seller's cash requirements, as explained in Chapter 10. However, a favorable interest rate and term were negotiated, along with very favorable mortgage clauses. All of the minimum financial requirements of the venture were achieved, and the expected IRR$_E$ was substantially above the required IRR$_E$.[35]

[35] Note that the required IRR$_E$ might change for each financial package analyzed. The investor's required IRR$_E$ should be increased when riskier financial packages are designed (e.g., higher leverage ratios and interest rates) and lowered when more conservative financial packages are designed.

15

The Art of Real Estate Negotiations

Handling other people's mistrust is the skilled negotiator's stock-in-trade.
. . . . In a successful negotiation, everyone wins.[1]

Gerard I. Nierenberg

In Chapter 8 strategy was defined as skillful management in getting the better of an adversary for attaining an end. Strategy implies that one develops a plan to outperform the competition and maximize financial wealth. In purchasing a specific piece of real estate the investor is seeking to achieve certain strategic goals and objectives. However, the seller is also seeking to maximize his rate of return. Thus, negotiations should be seen as a cooperative enterprise between wary parties; common interests must be sought.

The ideal negotiator has developed skills useful in many careers and tasks. In *How Nations Negotiate,* Fred Charles Ikle stated that

> The compleat negotiator, according to seventeenth and eighteenth century manuals on diplomacy, should have a quick mind but unlimited patience, know how to dissemble without being a liar, inspire trust without trusting others, be modest but assertive, charm others without succumbing to their charm, and possess plenty of money and a beautiful wife while remaining indifferent to all temptation of riches and women.[2]

[1] Gerard J. Nierenberg, *Fundamentals of Negotiating* (New York: Hawthorne Press, 1973), p. 1.
[2] Fred C. Ikle, *How Nations Negotiate* (New York: Harper & Row, 1964).

This sexist definition may be archaic, but certainly skilled negotiators are rare. Negotiation is a useful tool of human behavior and, as such, can be mastered with study and experience. Negotiations for the acquisition of a real estate investment involve an exchange of ideas. Gathered at the conference table is a heterogeneous group of individuals with varying educational backgrounds, personalities, and levels of experience. Each of them will be influenced by his or her own subconscious emotional drives.

Our ten-step investment analysis process requires us to begin to negotiate the basic parameters of the deal, including price, financial terms, and tax considerations, as early as step 4, in which the buyer seeks an early meeting of minds with the seller. By step 8, the final negotiations, the buyer should be in a position to take advantage of both the buyer's and the seller's perceived preferences and biases to increase returns. An investor should not proceed to final negotiations without knowing what he or she is willing to give up in return for what can be gotten at the final bargaining session. The final purchase contract and the closing of the deal should conform to both the buyer's and the seller's expectations.

The success or failure of real estate negotiations depends on following the strategic plan, knowing all the underlying assumptions, being fully prepared, spotting the effects of human behavior on the process, and finally recognizing that negotiation is the process of need fulfillment. Gerard I. Nierenberg, a master negotiator, has provided a description that should prove instructive. (See Exhibit 15–1.) See if you can spot the elements of human behavior, preparation, assumptions, strategy and tactics, and need fulfillment.

THE ROLE OF NEGOTIATIONS

When we buy a six-pack of beer, we don't dicker over the price at the checkout counter. Nor do we negotiate with the broker over the price of a common stock on the New York Stock Exchange. Real estate, however, is a different kind of commodity. When a parcel of real estate is placed on the market, the price and terms of sale can only be estimated. Thereafter, buyers and sellers dicker within a range of values and terms to arrive at the selling price. This uncertainty over price is a result of the unique attributes of real estate as an economic good. The buyer is contemplating a purchase that will provide cash flow benefits over a relatively long period. The seller is terminating an ownership period and seeks to maximize the final returns. Both parties are operating in a market in which the quality of information is poor. Real estate markets are highly stratified, and even in a seller's market, buyers are few and not easy to find. The one major advantage that buyer and seller have is that they have found each other.

The buyer is concerned with such matters as price, down payment requirements, required escrows, financing, closing costs, personal liability, the timing of the closing, and other items that affect the nature of the deal and the costs of the transaction. But the nature of real estate markets is such that the buyer must also be concerned with the location and marketability of the property. Since it takes time to uncover such information, the seller, if he or she is in a hurry, must be

---

EXHIBIT 15-1. A Masterly Negotiation

A plain postcard is not usually the most interesting item in a stack of mail. However, a real estate associate and I discovered an exception one morning when we were reviewing offers of properties submitted by brokers. On a postal card was a broker's offer to sell an $800,000 property. If the broker had meant to attract our attention he certainly succeeded. We had to know more about the property.

We investigated. My associate, Fred, and I discovered a most interesting situation. The property was controlled by a trust company, and under ordinary circumstances the land itself would probably have been worth $800,000. But these were no ordinary circumstances. A fire had virtually destroyed the building on the property, leaving only a shell that was in danger of collapsing. The building department had already served the trust company officers with a summons demanding immediate action to make the property safe. Instead of the staid day-to-day routine of administering the property, the trust company was confronted with an unfamiliar and threatening situation, one it seemed unable to cope with. The only solution the officers could come up with was to sell immediately. Fred and I decided to relieve them of their dilemma, but of course on our terms.

We submitted our offer: $550,000 if they would take back part of the purchase price in a twenty-year mortgage, or, as an alternate proposal, $475,000 in cash. The property manager at the trust company refused even to entertain our written offer. Fred then called him and requested an appointment, which was reluctantly granted.

Fred came to the point at once. He told the property manager that the board of directors would have to make the ultimate decision whether to sell or not, that the manager was only their agent. Therefore, if the manager refused to act, Fred would bypass him and submit the offer to the board himself. This threat—to his *security*—worked. Our offer was submitted to the board.

The board, being concerned with the dangerous condition of the property, had limited themselves to a single strategy—to accept the first firm offer they received. Our cash offer was accepted. Quite naturally the property manager was extremely unhappy when he notified us by phone. He said the contract would be ready at five o'clock Friday and we had better be there at five o'clock sharp. When Fred and I arrived, we were presented with a carefully worded thirty-page document. The manager, still unhappy, scowled. "Here is the contract. Don't dot an *i* or cross a *t*. Take it or leave it just as it is." After reading it, we decided to take it. Thirty minutes after arrival, we left the manager's office. We were now the contract owners of the property. Only the formality of the title closing remained before we became full legal owners.

As so often happens in negotiations, a "mere formality" became the springboard for still further discussion and adjustment of the agreement. Incredibly, a few hours after we signed the contract, a second fire swept the building, completely demolishing the damaged structure. The next morning I hurried to my office and spent the weekend deep in legal research. By Monday morning I had completed my "homework." Fred and I waited in my office for a phone call from the trust company. The telephone rang at nine o'clock. We arranged a meeting that morning at the offices of a prominent Wall Street law firm.

The senior partner of the law firm was very cordial as he ushered us into his private office suite, and opened the discussion: "We are not here to discuss law,

(*continues*)

EXHIBIT 15-1. *(Continued)*

but merely to get rid of a very difficult situation." I nodded in agreement. He went on to explain what we already knew, that the streets around the property were closed because of the dangerous condition, and that the trust company was more anxious than ever to be rid of the property. The company and its lawyers insisted we take over the property immediately and eliminate the hazard.

I countered with the statement that Fred and I had not had a chance to discuss the matter thoroughly and that we would need a little time. A large conference room was put at our disposal, but before he left us alone the attorney took me aside. "Remember," he said, "in this contract your client waived all the statutory protection." The statute he referred to would have placed the fire loss on the seller. By waiving it, the loss would be ours.

"You're absolutely correct," I said carefully. "We waived all our statutory rights. But," I added, giving him the benefit of my weekend research, "that means we have only the right that existed under common law before the statute was passed." The common law generally had placed a fire loss before the closing on the purchaser, but the courts had made many exceptions to this rule of law. I reminded the attorney of an exception applicable to our situation. In the event something specific, such as a building, was sold with the land, the building was damaged by fire, the loss would be the seller's. The seller must deliver exactly what he contracts to sell or there must be an adjustment in price.

"Now," I continued, "that wonderful contract that you drew up made it extremely clear what we were purchasing. It made it so clear that not once but four times it stated we were buying a *partially* damaged building. Now it is completely demolished. We are entitled to a partially damaged building or an adjustment in price."

In the conference room, Fred and I put ourselves in the trust company's position. If the matter went into litigation, it would take at least two years to determine the equities involved. During that time the trust company would have to pay $25,000 a year in taxes on the property and would lose an equal amount in interest to be earned on our purchase price. According to our conservative estimate, the company would lose at least $100,000 even if it won the case.

We went back with our proposal: We would take over the property immediately instead of two or three weeks later if they reduced the purchase price by $100,000. A stunned silence was followed by an outburst from the property manager. But in a few minutes we agreed to a reduction of $50,000 and immediate possession of the property.

Thereupon, Fred and I became "fee title absolute owners" of a valuable piece of land and, of course, a completely demolished building—requiring far less expenditure for clearing the land.

willing to provide representations and warranties concerning zoning, existence of adequate utilities, highway access, land and roads, absence of condemnation or other adverse proceedings, and other critical matters that affect value.

The seller and his or her counsel need assurance that once the terms of the contract have been agreed upon, it will be fully executed and binding on the parties. The seller usually prefers to limit exposure to contracted contingencies, subsequent to closing.

In effect, although the negotiation for the purchase and sale of a parcel of real estate is an adversary relationship, both buyer and seller should realize that there is mutual benefit to be derived from minimizing conflict and seeking mutual accommodation to achieve a successful acquisition and sale.

Cooperative Bargaining Versus Confrontation   Real estate negotiation is an interpersonal process. Ideally, each negotiator works both for the opponent's needs as well as his or her own. We all have an urge to win, but the win/lose approach should be replaced by creative alternatives. There are many solutions to a problem—some better and some worse—but they all should be examined by each of the parties concerned in order to find the one that provides the greatest mutual advantage. Using computer software programs to pretest "what if" scenarios and doing sensitivity analyses *prior* to holding negotiating sessions is good preparation. A well-prepared negotiator can change defensive behavior into supportive, communicative action and thus improve interpersonal relations across the bargaining table.

During the negotiations you may reduce the defensiveness of your opposer by communicating your willingness to experiment with your own behavior, attitudes, and ideas. Questions often produce defensiveness. A person who appears to be taking a tentative attitude rather than taking sides on an issue may seem to be problem solving rather than debating the questions. Fact finding is also an adaptive procedure.

Jack R. Gibb cites six pairs of defensive and supportive categories:[3]

Defensive Behavior	*Supportive Activities*
1. evaluation	**1.** description
2. control	**2.** problem orientation
3. strategy	**3.** spontaneity
4. neutrality	**4.** empathy
5. superiority	**5.** equality
6. certainty	**6.** provisionalism

Keep in mind that *negotiating provides room to bargain and compromise.* Confrontation freezes positions, which can put an end to bargaining and result in loss of the deal.

Satisficing Versus Maximizing   Though some scholars claim that businesspeople always seek to maximize profits, Herbert Simon argues that they are really

---

[3] Jack R. Gibb, "Leadership and Interpersonal Behavior," (L. Petrullo and B. M. Bass, 1961).

"satisficing" or seeking to satisfy many different needs. Thus, although our objective in real estate investing is to maximize wealth, we are more likely to achieve that long-term objective by following a "satisficing" strategy.

A Basic Meeting of Minds   The basic financial feasibility model (Chapter 10) structures and tests the basic economics of the project. Thus, as we enter step 4 ready to negotiate the basic terms with the seller, the preliminary need of the investor is to achieve a basic meeting of the minds in which the seller can be trusted to allow the time to do detailed feasibility research, perform the discounted cash flow analysis, and structure the tax package.

Listening   The key to successful negotiation is to use the preliminary meeting to gain information as well as satisfy objectives. Listening is as much a persuasive technique as speaking. A successful listener keeps an open mind and strives to be free from bias and preconceived notions. Sandor S. Feldman mentions many common mannerisms of speech and nonverbal communications that can be important in negotiations.[4]

For example, a person who says, "Oh, by the way . . ." may want to give the impression that what he or she is about to say is spontaneous. But usually it is very important and the person is only pretending to be nonchalant. When a person begins a sentence with words like "To be honest, "To tell the truth," "Frankly," or "Honestly," the chances are that he or she is *not* being frank or honest. These speech mannerisms have psychological significance, and they give us a clue to what is going on in the mind of the opponent. Listen attentively and always be alert to spot the hidden motives and needs revealed by seemingly innocent phrases.

Watching   Besides listening, you should clearly observe your opponent's gestures. We must watch not only gestures but also simple body motions. Frequent coughing has significant implications. Facial expression is an obvious means of nonverbal communication. Blinking and other gestures may be significant. The skilled negotiator always keeps eyes and ears fastened on the opponent.

Parties to a negotiation should meet at an early stage in order to evaluate the trustworthiness and credibility of the opponent in the negotiating process. Keep in mind that much of the data used in real estate investment emanates from opposing parties. Alternatively, one would be forced to trust no one and generate hypothetical information based on theoretical assumptions. In certain situations, when a good property is owned by a bad negotiator, this may be the best available approach to achieving a basic meeting of the minds.

Keys to Successful Preliminary Negotiations   As one approaches the negotiation table, tension normally increases. Since the negotiations are the culmination of a long screening process, there is a natural tendency for emotions to override reason. The prospect of having to drop the target property and search for another one will tend to cause one to want to make a deal. Thus, it is wise to keep in mind the systematic rules of the investment strategy process. Following are some control mechanisms that will tend to make negotiations more successful:

[4] Sandor S. Feldman, *Mannerisms of Speech and Gesture in Everyday Life* (New York: International Universities Press, 1959).

1. *The strategic plan should control the investor's behavior.* The strategy is to achieve the investment objectives. Although the basic screening criteria were used to target the property, preliminary negotiations may indicate that one should drop consideration of this property. On the other hand, be aware of and open to creative alternatives.

2. *Use the basic financial feasibility model.* This model structured and tested the basic economics of the project, the financing alternatives that appeared to be available, and the investment value range for the property. Don't permit the opposer to seduce you into accepting terms outside the basic investment value range that you have developed unless hard facts indicate that your preliminary analysis was inaccurate. New information produced by the negotiation process may require that you reanalyze the property using the basic financial feasibility model. If you are prepared to do some on-the-spot calculations, you may be able to determine whether or not you should continue to negotiate for this particular property.

3. *Careful preparation.* Earlier we explored the necessity for understanding the political, legal, economic, and sociological assumptions built into the detailed feasibility research. Many other kinds of unconscious assumptions are part of the negotiating process. Too often they are ignored and the venture fails during the ownership cycle because the property was purchased under different assumptions than were consciously realized. Any psychiatrist will tell you that people rationalize, project, displace, and role play, or they unconsciously repress things, react to externalities, and engage in other behavior that affects the negotiations.

   The more alternative ways you have for handling the needs of the opposing party in a negotiating situation, the greater your chances of success. Understanding those needs is essential to success as a negotiator. You must combine the scientific attitude of the financial analyst with the cunning of a gumshoe detective to dig up facts and figures; you should contact bankers, brokers, attorneys, and property managers to find out what your opponent's personality is like *prior* to negotiating.

   Investigate the opponent's previous real estate sales. Is the opponent litigious? Does he or she keep promises? Contacts in the community may provide information on deals that the opponent has failed to consummate successfully. If you carefully analyze why certain deals fell through, you will probably get a good understanding of the opponent's thought processes and approach to negotiating.

   Careful preparation also requires a reappraisal of yourself. Unconscious drives have a powerful effect on individual actions. Irrational drives, such as the need for status, pride of ownership, or wanting to win the game, can subvert your conscious investment strategy. Just as you have carefully considered the opponent's needs, you should reconsider why you want the target property. If the opponent has prepared more carefully than you have, he or she may have the advantage during the negotiations.

4. *Be prepared for mutual accommodation.* The imperfect markets of real estate produce data in an inefficient manner. Thus, the rational mind is applying logic to a perceived reality that may be inaccurate. Being able to

come up with creative alternatives is basic to successful negotiation. If a proposed change in position can be supported by subsequent feasibility studies compromise and concessions are not necessarily a loss.

THE PSYCHOLOGY OF NEGOTIATIONS

Like corporate acquisitions, mergers, and tender offers, real estate transactions are similar to a high-stake game. Equity positions are usually highly leveraged. Negotiations are carried out in an emotionally charged atmosphere. It should be the objective of both parties to convert a potentially antagonistic atmosphere into a cooperative enterprise. In order to do so, the opposing parties must know human nature, be able to analyze the roles being played by the negotiating parties, and seek to have even the site of the negotiations conducive to good bargaining. The buyer and seller should control the use of brokers, CPAs, and attorneys, and great care should be taken to effectively use other team members, such as partners, in the negotiating process. The use of negotiating strategies must be carefully thought out.

The decision to buy is a product of a forecasting mind. Many recent studies have shown that the process of human thought consists of both logical thinking and intuitive inspiration. It takes the different sections of the brain, all working together, to forecast the future for which we plan and make decisions.

Master negotiators have learned to effectively use both the right and the left hemispheres of the brain in the process of negotiation. For convenience, left-brain thinking can be seen as predominantly rational, while right-brain thought is essentially intuitive. Left-brain thinking is well represented by the ten-step process of investment strategy set forth in Chapter 8. This portion of the brain, which can be called the conscious mind, is involved primarily with analytical, logical thinking and with verbal and mathematical functions. Of fundamental importance in terms of forecasting, it processes information sequentially.

The right side of the brain is primarily nonverbal, and is linked to human feeling for spatial relationships and the arts and crafts. If the left hemisphere is primarily analytical and sequential in operation, then the right hemisphere is holistic and more simultaneous in its mode of operation. Right-brain functioning tends to be more unconscious than left-brain functioning.

Some people rely more on left-brain rationality, others on right-brain intuition. Most of us, however, draw to some extent from both halves, although not consciously. It is the function of the forebrain to monitor the left and right sides of the brain. From these two sources information bearing on the future flows into the forebrain, distinguishes sense from nonsense, and decides what action should be taken—or not taken—in the negotiating process.

As you can see even from this brief overview, a master negotiator must be a serious student of how human beings interact with information and with each other.[5]

---

[5] David Loye, *The Knowable Future: A Psychology of Forecasting and Prophecy* (New York: Wiley, 1978), and Abraham Maslow, *Motivation and Personality* (New York: Harper & Row, 1954).

Know Human Nature and Cultural Traits

Earlier in the chapter we noted the importance of nonverbal communications in discovering the facts about the opposing party. It is important also to acknowledge differences arising out of cultural heritage and social stratum. For example: In the New York area it is customary to get down to business immediately and bother very little with the "nonsense" of social niceties. Southerners, however, take time to discuss the weather, family, and friends before proceeding to bargain. To them, social interaction is part of the negotiating process. In the United States a man generally places himself 18 to 20 inches away when conversing face to face with another man. When talking with a woman, he usually backs off an additional 4 inches. In contrast, Hispanic–American men may feel quite comfortable at 13 inches. In the north central part of the United States, unacceptable offers are usually rejected promptly and emphatically in an unambiguous manner, but in the Southeast many real estate negotiators will respond with an indirect, soft response designed to avoid hurt feelings. It is not uncommon for negotiations to break down because of cultural difference. While local brokers and/or attorneys may be quite useful in bridging these cross-cultural differences, a showing of congenial good will and a sense of humor will often go far to restore a cooperative attitude to the bargaining process.

Roles Played by Negotiating Parties

Every person has an image of herself or himself, and personal decisions are often made either to protect the self-image or to enhance it. It would seem that if we knew how a person regarded himself or herself, we could make some assumptions about that person's underlying motivations and how he or she would react to the negotiation process. Role playing should be expected by both parties in the negotiating process. The kinds of behavior shown in acting out a role are usually based on previous experiences and on the extent to which they succeeded.

Robert Ringer, in his book, *Winning Through Intimidation,* holds that there are only three types of roles played by negotiators. Ringer's theory seems to see the negotiating process as a struggle for dominance and control rather than as mutual accommodation, and seems to be based on the useful but too simplistic premise that no one can be trusted.[6]

Type one is a person who lets you know from the outset that he or she is out to get all your chips, and follows through by attempting to do exactly that. In our experience, many people who play this role do it in a very smooth, sophisticated, and friendly manner; others, apparently uncomfortable in projecting such an image, do it in a hostile and too-aggressive way.

Type two assures you at the outset that he or she is interested only in getting a fair share. However, the person's actions are clearly directed toward getting as much as possible. Careful preparation prior to negotiating may indicate whether

[6] Robert J. Ringer, *Winning Through Intimidation* (Los Angeles: Los Angeles Book Publishers, 1974); William A. Thau, *Negotiating the Purchase and Sale of Real Estate,* Real Estate Review Portfolio no. 8 (Boston: Warren, Gorham & Lamont, 1975); Alvin Arnold and Owen Smith, *Negotiating the Commercial Lease,* Real Estate Review Portfolio no. 1 (Boston: Warren, Gorham & Lamont, 1972, 1973).

this type of person is unethical and dishonest or simply a hard bargainer. Unfortunately, good properties may on occasion be owned by bad and dishonest bargainers. These slippery people should be controlled during every step of the bargaining process with legally enforceable language in signed and initialed documents. On the other hand, one should not irritate an ethical hard bargainer by trying to document every move prior to final settlement. With such people everything will be aboveboard, but it can be a fast track, and the losers are usually the parties who are poorly prepared.

Probably the most difficult opponent to negotiate with is Ringer's *type three*. Unfortunately, the large majority of people probably fall into this class. Although a type three person assures you that he or she is not interested in getting *any* of your chips, the person's conduct indicates that he or she is trying to get *all* of your chips. The reasons for this contradictory conduct are myriad. Lack of self-knowledge and lack of familiarity with good business conduct are among them—or the person may sincerely make a deal that is not legally binding and then be persuaded by a professional to reopen negotiations. Such people may be difficult to deal with, but it is not uncommon for them to own real estate that you may want to buy.

The mutually accommodative bargaining process that we have described is more likely to bring about successful negotiation with all three types of opponent than any other method—including trying to win by intimidation.

The Negotiation Site

Should you meet in your office, or should you go to the opponent's home ground? (Banks and savings and loan associations often make meeting rooms available without charge as a courtesy.) Should you meet in neutral territory? There are advantages to meeting on your own ground: (1) It enables you to get approval on problems that you did not anticipate; (2) it makes it discourteous for the other side to terminate the negotiations abruptly or prematurely by leaving; (3) you can take care of other matters and have your own facilities available while you are handling the negotiations; (4) it gives you a psychological advantage; and (5) it saves you money and traveling time. On the other hand, going to your opponent's home base also has advantages: (1) You can devote your full time to negotiation without the distractions and interruptions of your office; (2) you can withhold information, stating that it is not immediately available; (3) you might have the option of going over the opponent's head to someone in higher management; and (4) the burden of preparation is on the opponent, who will not be free from other duties.

The physical arrangements of the room, such as the lighting, the color, and the seating, also have a potential affect on the negotiations. Some people still consider the head of the table the leadership seat and will listen more intently to or accede to suggestions made by the person who occupies that seat. Some people find an advantage in intentionally sitting on the opponent's side of the table in order to minimize the adversary atmosphere.

Other physical requirements are (1) a telephone; (2) an adequately sized room large enough to hold all the participants comfortably; (3) adequate ventilation; and (4) chairs that are comfortable but not too comfortable. It has been suggested that negotiations tend to be more successful in cheerful, bright-colored rooms. Although most of us have heard of deals made on the back of an envelope, or scribbled on a napkin at a cocktail bar, we believe that care and preparation in the selection of the site of negotiations will improve the chances of success.

Using Professionals to Assist in Negotiations

Professionals can be useful in negotiations. There are times when it is desirable simply to increase the number of participants on your side of the negotiating table. But real estate investment is a complex, multifaceted process, and the typical general practice lawyer, CPA, or broker is not necessarily qualified to handle all phases of it. Indeed, many investors use one lawyer for investment tax planning and to put real estate deals together, and another to handle closings. A CPA may be competent in the field of tax planning but is not necessarily well trained in real estate financial analysis. Many brokers are real estate marketing specialists but have little knowledge of the intricacies of real estate investment analysis. The key to using professionals is to carefully define the limits of the function you want the selected professional to serve.

Brokers can serve a vital function. They can be your antenna in the field for improving your market data base; they can provide information on new or alternative sources of financing; they can assist in gathering the documents that are necessary to close the transaction. When tempers flare, the broker can act as an intermediary and aid in reestablishing a negotiating atmosphere. Because of their professional stature, attorneys and CPAs can lend credence to hard positions that must be taken concerning tax and legal considerations such as zoning, occupancy permits, and code violations. The investor should make an effort to use attorneys and CPAs who specialize in real estate.

Using Other Partners in Negotiations

Obviously, on both sides of the transaction someone should be in charge of the negotiations. If there are partners, it is wise to give one of them the authority to negotiate within carefully thought out parameters. If other partners are to be present, their roles should be carefully defined and arrangements should be made so that they can leave the room and settle any differences they have during the bargaining session.

HOW TO ACHIEVE THE OBJECTIVES OF THE NEGOTIATING PARTIES

In order for both the buyer and the seller to estimate the appropriate range of offers and counteroffers, they must, prior to negotiations, properly characterize the submarket for the property. In order for both parties to get what they are bargaining for, they must be prepared to make assurances to each other that will result in a final settlement and closing.

The main objective of any negotiations is a legally enforceable contract at mutually acceptable terms. A legally enforceable contract is merely a written expression of the mutually acceptable terms arrived at by buyer and seller. It is essential that both parties know the limits of their bargaining power. The negotiation tactics for bringing about an exchange are quite different from those used in a foreclosure. Negotiating long-term leases requires intensive bargaining because each clause may vary the economic returns of the package. The negotiator's aim should never be to get the last possible dollar; the danger of going too far is not worth the risk.

Proper Characterization of the Market for the Property   Is it a buyer's market or a seller's market? There are cyclical swings in buyer or seller dominance of the marketplace. In preparing for negotiations, both the buyer and the seller should satisfy themselves that their market information is current. Good characterization of the marketplace can aid greatly in estimating the appropriate range for offers and counteroffers.

GRM, Cap Rates, and Square-Foot Prices   Many real estate markets are influenced by rule-of-thumb pricing. Obviously, if transactions in a submarket are frequently based on gross rent multipliers, negotiations are going to be significantly influenced by the multiplier for the target property. On the other hand, properties in some regions are traditionally exchanged on capitalization rates. Under no circumstances, though, should a prudent investor pay more than an investment value that will produce the minimum acceptable rate of return. A buyer should not be pressured to pay a price that is excessive by financial analysis even if it can be justified by recent comparable sales. Irrational gross rent multipliers, square-foot prices, or cap rates may indicate that negotiations should be dropped because the property does not conform to one's investment philosophy. Holding funds in short-term liquid notes is better than making a bad investment.

Unique Predicaments of Buyers and Sellers   Buyers and sellers may be willing to go outside the range of acceptable prices because of special circumstances in order to bring about a sale or acquisition of a property. However, there is grave danger in asking the seller why he or she is selling. The danger is that you are likely to believe the reason given and not investigate the situation as thoroughly as you should. Even if the seller shows you a doctor's report saying that he or she must sell the property now, the real reason could be that impending changes in zoning will substantially diminish the area's growth possibilities. Sellers may need to raise cash for taxes; buyers may be under time pressure to invest funds or to make a real estate investment within the tax year; public agencies exercising eminent domain may be under time pressure to gain possession of the property. Careful investigation prior to negotiating may reveal information that can increase one's resistance to unreasonable demands by the opposing party.

Using Market Value, Most Probable Selling Price, and Investment Value   Swings in the economic base, business cycles, and other external factors cause substantial disequilibrium in real estate markets. A careful and imaginative negotiator can put the variance among most probable selling price, market value, and investment value to use. The buyer prefers to negotiate on the basis of investment value. By discussing its relationship to the current market and most probable selling price, the opposing parties are more likely to gain an understanding of the underlying economics of the proposed deal. However, buyers should be aware that there are other investors who lack financial sophistication and therefore are willing to offer a higher price. This competitive activity cannot be ignored.

Estimating the Range of Offers and Counteroffers

Preliminary offers should be within the range developed by the basic financial feasibility model. It is strongly urged that before entering into negotiations you use sensitivity analysis to determine the effect of variances in price, financing terms, tax planning, and other factors on the acquisition offer. Such information can prove very helpful in setting minimum and maximum offers. One should also estimate the effect of nonprice concessions on the return/risk relationship. Some of the possibilities to be considered are the following:

1. The seller agrees to defer the date of settlement without changing the price, thereby absorbing some interest costs and other cash outlay.
2. The seller agrees to finance all or part of the debt at terms better than those obtainable in the marketplace.
3. The seller provides warranties that are better than normal expectations.
4. Leases provide better-than-expected escalation clauses for such items as real estate taxes, insurance, etc.
5. The seller accepts an exculpatory clause minimizing the risk for the buyer.
6. The seller agrees to assume more than a prorated share of the transaction costs and fees.

Having estimated the range within which an acceptable offer can be made, one should proceed to unfold the negotiating strategy. Certainly it is easier to deal with an experienced negotiator than with an inexperienced one, but it is rare to discover that your opponent is eager, intelligent, reasonable, well informed, and experienced. Even if the opponent is all these things, he or she may have limited authority, and therefore your negotiations should be treated as preliminary. One must be prepared to educate an inexperienced negotiator to see your needs as well as his or hers. If you reveal your position too quickly, it can be interpreted as excessive eagerness to buy. It is a better strategy to present the facts as you see them before moving into an offer position.

Occasionally you will encounter an opponent who quotes a price that is outside the range of acceptable offers. If it is a good property and intuition suggests that this is only a preliminary position, it may be appropriate to make a counteroffer that is also below the range of reasonable offers. The function of this sort of tactic is to enable you to turn the discussion toward a reasonable consideration of both your and the opponent's minimum needs. Keep in mind that the seller is taking the time to negotiate with you. In all probability, then, he or she is seeking a successful sale.

Some people feel that the party who initiates the negotiations should set the price of the first offer. Many sellers feel that they should entertain an offer but not make a counteroffer. It is probably most advantageous to let the opposer begin by attempting to sell you on why you should accept a certain proposition. This has the advantage of gaining more information on the property as well as demonstrating an accommodating attitude. In many successful negotiations the initial asking price is simply set aside and negotiations are shifted to nonprice concessions in order to clarify the underlying structure of the deal.

Getting What You Bargained For

As negotiation proceeds to the final contract and the closing, the understanding is that the deal has been structured for most favorable tax consequences and an acquisition price that fits the investment strategy. A real estate sales contract is designed to make a closing a certainty. Obviously, the purchaser wants as many agreed-upon conditions in the contract as possible to ensure that at the closing the property will meet his or her requirements in every respect. On the other hand, the seller will generally not want any conditions whatsoever limiting the sale. The negotiations at this point should focus on limiting unilateral exit clauses for either party.

On the whole, we urge that a real estate sales contract not be unconditional, because the costs of examining title and preparing the closing documents should be deferred until the acquisition appears to be a reasonable certainty. On the other hand, since most loan officers will not review an application without an executed sales agreement in hand, in most cases the parties will find it mutually beneficial to enter into a legally enforceable contract.

At the end of this chapter (Exhibit 15–2) you will find the closing statement for Aspen Wood Apartments. Its format and mechanics should be reviewed carefully.

Following are some of the conditions that the negotiating parties normally expect to be made part of a real estate sales contract.

Conditions Required by the Seller   The seller has less need for conditions than the buyer. His or her primary objective is to seek a firm price with clearly specified time and method for receipt of the cash. The closing documents can provide the remedies for any default. Usually the seller seeks to avoid any further obligation after the date of final settlement. It is appropriate for the seller to seek assurance that the buyer (individual, partnership, or corporation) has the legal power to close the transaction and that the person or persons acting on behalf of the buyer have been duly authorized to do so.

Conditions Required by the Purchaser   Objective standards should be set forth to define the purchaser's right to terminate. In order for a purchaser to use nonoccurrence of a condition precedent as a reason for not closing the contract, he or she must prove due diligence in attempting to make the condition come about. For example, if the purchaser wants to retain the right to withdraw because of an unsatisfactory feasibility report, he or she must make a "best effort" to investigate the location, market, and legal and political environment of the property. Other cases that require the purchaser's best effort include seeking a building permit, a soil engineer's report, FHA approval of the development plan, and the like.

If possible, the purchaser should obtain seller's representations and warranties for conditions that must be fulfilled prior to or at the time of the closing of the transaction. Some typical representations and warranties are the following:

1. The property will not be threatened or adversely affected as a result of acts of God or municipal authorities, disaster, condemnation, and so forth on the closing date. This is a self-operating condition that can serve as an exit clause.

2. The seller shall provide for inspection prior to the closing date of all executed tenants' leases, along with their phone numbers and places of employment. Such leases are to be properly assigned at the closing.

3. The seller shall provide at the time of the closing a bill of sale for all personal property, furniture, fixtures, and equipment that are *not* attached and affixed to the realty. The seller shall also provide an adequate description of the structure, describing all fixtures attached, affixed, dedicated, and annexed to the realty and made part of the transaction.

4. The seller should warrant the adequacy and availability of all utility services. (This may be critical in commercial and industrial installations.)

5. The seller should warrant the structure to be sound and in good operating condition.

6. The seller should warrant any unique attributes of the property that are essential and prerequisite to the property's gross possible income.

7. The seller should provide an affirmative covenant to assure the purchaser's right to use the property for the purposes intended. On occasion occupancy permits are required by local law.

8. The seller should acknowledge that he or she continues to bear the risk of loss due to damage to the property through acts of God, casualty, or acts of the government or private parties during the period prior to the closing of the transaction. The seller should warrant that all special assessments and existing liens and taxes will have been paid prior to the closing. (In contrast to item 1, this is a guaranty clause that the buyer may exercise subject to litigation.)

9. The buyer should have protection against any defects in title to the property. Some kind of warranty deed is typically required.

10. The purchaser should be provided with covenants that will limit the effect of the doctrine of merger by deed. Otherwise, in many jurisdictions, the warranties and representations of the seller made prior to the conveyance will be a nullity and no longer enforceable immediately after the deed of conveyance has been recorded. The buyer should have the right to physical inspection of the property without waiver of the enforceability of the warranties and representations made by the seller and without eliminating the right to justifiable reliance under the doctrines of fraud, deceit, and misrepresentations.

Since some jurisdictions require time-is-of-the-essence clauses in real estate contracts unless the parties have stipulated otherwise, and since many of the requirements in the preceding list require time and effort, the contract should provide for an orderly way to handle delays and postponement of the closing date.

Conditions Required by Both Parties   Both parties should provide for a specific fixing of liability for all closing costs, rather than depending on vague customs and traditions that vary from one local area to another. The purchase contract should also define who is to pay finder's fees, broker's commission, points, and so forth, and should provide for the proration of real estate taxes, rents, interests, insurance, and expenses relating to the property as of a specified date. It is not desirable in many cases to use the closing date as the date of proration, although it may be preferred by the attorneys, because delays in the closing date act to the disadvantage of the seller and can cause a carefully negotiated deal to fall through.

Both parties will find it desirable to provide for severability of good contract clauses in the event of amendments to the contract in the event of a material mutual mistake or other specified surprise events, such as a national emergency, credit rationing, or unexpected condemnations. One should keep in mind that one purchases investment properties for economic return and not to win a contest. Therefore, it is better to provide for specified remedies and liquidated damages for breach of contract than to consume management skills in frustrating litigation. In some jurisdictions it may be preferable to consider an arbitration clause to handle such disputes.

Both parties should be willing to agree to specify the nature of the seller's duty to deliver a good and marketable title. In some jurisdictions certain entities are barred by law from using a general warranty deed that provides conditions tantamount to a good and marketable title, free and clear of all liens and encumbrances. It is recommended that the contract include a so-called Mother Hubbard clause to the effect that the description includes all the property owned by the seller at the location or, if appropriate, that it includes all real property owned by the seller in the particular city or county.

An accurate description of the property should be obtained and included in the contract. Appropriate sources of legal description include current surveys, copies of the seller's warranty deed or title policy, a current title report, or binders. The purchaser should not rely blindly on the description of the property furnished by the seller. To be enforceable, a contract must furnish a means of determining with reasonable certainty the property intended to be conveyed by it.

Both parties should mutually agree upon and enumerate the duties that the purchaser is to assume at the time of the closing (e.g., the duty to pay the price in cash).

Some transactions use complex, creative forms of financing, such as purchase money mortgages, purchase-leasebacks, and so forth. Since such clauses shift the risk of loss and gain back and forth, they are critical to the implementation of the investment strategy and should be negotiated carefully.

No one can prepare a real estate sales contract that will anticipate every possible surprise event. However, you should not use a mortgage document or other contract form as part of your negotiations without being fully knowledgeable regarding the duties and obligations assumed by the parties and their economic effects on your investment, and one should be particularly wary of a switch to another document as negotiations progress, because the so-called fine print may actually be effectively changing the understanding between the parties.

ENDING THE NEGOTIATIONS—FINAL SETTLEMENT AND CLOSING

We believe that our ten-step investment analysis model should enable you to reach the final negotiation and closing stage with greater likelihood of success than a less orderly approach to real estate acquisition. However, we are fully aware that the opposing parties are human beings who may arrive at the closing not fully prepared to complete the transaction. It is not uncommon for one or the other of the parties not to have fulfilled certain conditions. However, if one is to make a successful acquisition, the contract documents should be a guide to final settlement and not a tool for litigation. Being unable to compromise is one of the handicaps of many real estate entrepreneurs. One should not accommodate a bad and unethical bargainer; one should not deviate from the investment strategy and go outside the range of acceptable prices and terms; nor should one hesitate to abort a closing and reset the closing date if the other party has failed to fulfill some essential condition, even though it is claimed to be trivial. Many unethical bargainers, operating under the premise that anything is worth a try, use this tactic to squeeze the deal for an extra few dollars. The opposing party must defend by quietly insisting on fulfillment of the contractual obligations. This can be done in an amiable but firm manner.

In a complex transaction, phone communications may be necessary to complete the transaction. It is not uncommon for the purchaser to require that the seller provide an agent so that a simultaneous inspection of the premises can be made to verify that all personal property, furniture, and equipment are present on the site on the closing date. The seller should be willing to notify all tenants in writing of the change in ownership, and direct them to pay future rents to the purchaser. Keys to the property should be transferred before witnesses. The parties should proceed to change over the utilities with dispatch, and the buyer should in fact take possession by means of an actual personal inspection as soon as possible after the closing.

Finally, both parties should immediately deposit all cash and checks. Many sellers will not even permit checks to be drawn on out-of-state or out-of-town banks, and require that they be either cashier's or certified checks.

A successful legal closing often depends on the particular skills of an attorney who specializes in such transactions. Even attorneys who are knowledgeable in syndication and complex financing transactions often are not very well qualified to handle the complexities of a closing in a particular jurisdiction, and an investor is well advised to bear the costs of the services of a closing attorney recommended by trusted advisers.

SUMMARY

Real estate transactions are complex because each parcel is unique, and negotiation priorities vary from one deal to the next. To be a successful negotiator, you should be able to find and define the issues, evaluate the opponent's position to determine strengths and weaknesses, engage in mutual accommodation, and justify your position in reasonable terms. You should also be thoroughly prepared so that you are in control of the compromises and concessions that are necessary to produce the agreement.

The following is a convenient checklist for the real estate negotiation process.

CHECKLIST

Guide to Real Estate Negotiations

The Role of Negotiation: Satisfying Needs

1. Engage in cooperative bargaining rather than confrontation.
   a. Try to satisfice, not maximize
   b. The goal is a basic meeting of minds.
2. The strategic plan should control one's behavior.
   a. Use the basic financial feasibility model.
   b. Fact finding is essential to defining the issues.
   c. Careful preparation means understanding the assumptions.
   d. Determine the strengths and weaknesses of both sides.
3. Be prepared for mutual accommodations.

The Psychology of Negotiation

1. Know your "audience."
   a. Who are you trying to please?
   b. Who is the opponent trying to please?
   c. To whom are the negotiating parties accountable?
   d. Know relevant human and cultural traits.
2. Be aware of the roles played by negotiating parties.
   a. Be wary of rigid types.
   b. Be wary of high rollers.
   c. "Don't trust me—I'm out to get you."
   d. "Trust me—I'll be fair."
   e. "Trust me—I only want what's coming to me."
3. Know your self-concept.
   a. Control the desire to control others.
   b. Be aware of the need to win and achieve.
   c. Avoid being overly trusting/suspicious.
   d. Avoid being manipulative and exploitive.
4. Be informed about the opponent's self-concept.

5. Physical factors can affect negotiations.
   a. The location—your place or mine or a neutral place?
   b. The set up—where to sit, colors, air conditioning, and other comfort factors.
   c. What are the time limits?
6. Use professionals to assist in negotiations.
7. Be wary of using other partners in negotiations.
   a. Who's in charge here?
   b. What are the limits on each partner's authority and flexibility?

Arriving at Mutually Acceptable Terms

1. Properly characterize the market activity.
   a. Is it a seller's market?
   b. Is it a buyer's market?
   c. Is it a normal market?
2. Be careful in using GRMs, cap rates, square-foot prices, etc.
3. Be aware of unique predicaments of buyers or sellers.
4. Make effective use of the market value, most probable selling price, and investment value concepts.
5. Estimate the range of your offers and counteroffers in advance.
6. Consider in advance the nonprice factors that can affect your return/risk relationships.

Getting What You Bargained For

1. For the buyer: What are the necessary conditions?
2. For the seller: What conditions do you require to close?
3. Identify the conditions both parties need for reassurance.
4. Provide for specified remedies and liquidated damages, if possible.

Ending Negotiations—Final Settlement and Closing

1. Be prepared to compromise within the strategic plan.
2. Cordially and respectfully demand fulfillment of return/risk expectations within any contract provision.
3. Use an attorney who has experience in closings within the jurisdiction.
   a. Require inspection.
   b. Require lease assignments.
   c. Do not waive essential warranties and representations that must survive the closing.
   d. Take hard positions in cases in which rights and duties were unmistakably clear in the real estate contract.
   e. Cooperate with your closing attorney, but make your own business policy decisions.
   f. Don't be afraid to abort and reschedule a closing if *essential* terms are not being fulfilled.
4. Don't squeeze for the last buck! If it's still a good deal, be willing to close.

ASPEN WOOD APARTMENTS

THE FINAL SALES CONTRACT

Previous chapters have described various stages of negotiation that occurred from July 1974 to November 1974, when the final purchase structure was established. The bargaining position of the seller had been substantially reduced over time as a result of severe property management and operating problems and pressure from local commercial banks to repay short-term loans used to finance capital improvements and operating losses. The sellers readily accepted the major parameters of the restructured financial package described in Chapter 14, including a selling price of $1,003,400 and a favorable wraparound mortgage, and substantial tax shelter in the year of purchase.

The final sales contract was signed on December 6, 1974 and reflected the outcome of extensive negotiations and compromises by both parties. It included the following provisions:

Description of Parties and Property. Charlie Davidson, trustee, was the designated purchaser acting on behalf of the joint venture, and the three general partners of the limited partnership acted on behalf of the seller. Davidson and Boomer were concerned that the designated general partners did not have the legal authority to sign the sales contract, and demanded a copy of the limited partnership agreement for review and verification by their attorney. In addition, the real and personal property items involved in the sale were carefully described to prevent any misunderstandings. Nevertheless, subsequent to the signing of the contract a disagreement arose over numerous pieces of expensive furniture in the sales office that the seller claimed were the personal property of an employee of one of the general partners. Negotiation and compromise ensued to resolve the disagreement.

Consideration for the Transaction. The total amounts of equity and debt and the timing of all payments were detailed. The purchaser was to pay $10,000 as earnest money to a local title company to secure the contract, and the additional equity cash at closing. Because of the depressed local investment economy, as well as the occupancy and operating problems that developed in the fall of 1974, Davidson and Boomer were not able to raise the full $150,000 in cash that was due the seller at closing (equity of $210,000 less $10,000 earnest money and $50,000 commission). To solve the problem, the seller agreed to accept a non-interest-bearing, nonrecourse note of $10,500 for one year, representing a one-half-share equity interest in the property. It was agreed that the note would be retired as soon as D&B sold the remaining half-share. The provisions of the wraparound mortgage note of $793,400 were to be administered by a local commercial bank that would act as a trustee for both the seller and the purchaser; the bank would be empowered to collect all payments on the wraparound note, make the debt service payments on the underlying mortgage notes, and deposit the remaining balance in the seller's account.

The total project cost also included two mortgage points (2% of the original loan balance), $59,505 of prepaid interest, and a real estate commission of $50,000 to D&B Associates. D&B would not receive the $50,000 commission until all remaining equity shares were sold, which occurred in April 1975.

Provisions of the Wraparound Mortgage. The contract specified that the sellers were to obtain any consents or waivers of provisions in any of the underlying notes and deeds of trust that would restrict in any manner D&B's ability to purchase the property or to transfer the title at some future time. While the sellers bargained for a due-on-sale clause in the wraparound mortgage, Davidson and Boomer insisted on waiver of such a clause; in return for that concession, it was agreed that the seller had the option to substitute another mortgage for the wraparound mortgage after five years, under specific conditions that would leave the new owners in an unchanged financial condition. A trust agreement was to be entered into by the buyer, the seller, and the bank trustee; Davidson and Boomer, who were in the driver's seat at this stage, appointed their bank as the designated trustee.

Proration of Closing Costs. The seller was to furnish the buyer, at its cost, a title policy in the full amount of the purchase price, a survey, and a set of building plans and specifications within fifteen days of the contract signing. Taxes and insurance were to be prorated as of the date of closing, and based on year-end actuals rather than estimated amounts. Legal costs and recording fees related to the closing were divided equally between seller and buyer (see the closing statement, Exhibit 15–2).

Conditions Necessary to the Purchaser. D&B was obligated to consummate the purchase only if (1) the seller provided an acceptable title policy and survey and (2) all mechanical equipment was in good working condition at the time of closing. For any other reason, D&B could terminate the contract and lose only its $10,000 earnest money. The final draft of the contract explicitly recognized defective roof conditions and water heater malfunctions that could not be corrected prior to closing. Additional moneys were to be escrowed by the seller to guarantee payment for roof repairs and provide a warranty fund for one year on the project's four central hot water heaters. The risk of any loss or damage was not to pass to D&B until delivery and recording of the general warranty deed, and until the insurance policies were transfered to the buyer. Also, D&B required a specific performance clause in the contract requiring the seller to deliver the property to the purchaser at closing. Finally, the seller was to provide to the buyer at closing a general warranty deed and bills of sale for all personal property involved in the transaction.

EXHIBIT 15–2. Aspen Wood Closing Statement

CITY TITLE COMPANY, INC.
500 GRANDE
AUSTIN, TEXAS 78767

PURCHASER/BORROWER'S STATEMENT

Purchaser/Borrower Charlie Davidson, Trustee	
Seller/Contractor Sellers Ltd.	
Address of Property Aspen Wood Apts.	**Closing Date** 11/1/74
Lender _____ **Closer** Smith	**GF** _____

Purchase/Contract Price		$878,027.00
CLOSING COSTS:		
Appraisal or Examination Fee	$ _____	
Credit Report	$ _____	
Photographs (for Mortgage Company)	$ _____	
Loan/Finance Fee	$ _____	
Survey	$ _____	
Attorney's Fees		
Preparation of Note and Deed of Trust	$ 70.00	
	$ _____	
Recording Fees to County Clerk	$ 16.00	
Interim Construction Title Policy Binder	$ _____	
Owner's Title Policy	$ _____	
Mortgagee's Title Policy	$ _____	
Transfer Fee	$ _____	
Processing Fee	$ _____	
Tax Information	$ _____	
2% of Note	$ 15,868.00	
One-year's Prepaid Interest	$ 59,505.00	
Total Closing Costs		$ 75,459.00
PREPAID ITEMS:		
Hazard Insurance (one year in advance)	$ _____	
FHA Mutual Mortgage Fee (one month in advance)	$ _____	
*_____ Taxes	$ _____	
*_____ Hazard Insurance	$ _____	
Interest (for balance of current month)	$ _____	
Total Prepaid Items		$ —0—
TOTAL CLOSING COSTS AND PREPAID ITEMS		$ 75,459.00
TOTAL DUE FROM PURCHASER/BORROWER		$953,486.00
CREDITS		
Downpayment held in escrow by	$ _____	
Loan from Seller	$793,400.00	
Second lien	$ _____	
Loan balance assumed at	$ _____	
Tax proration	$ _____	
Note	$ 2,125.00	
Rent deposit and expense adjustment as per attached statement	$ 12,487.64	
Total Credits		$808,012.64
BALANCE PAID to/by PURCHASER/BORROWER		$145,473.36
Amount paid as per contract (balance pd. by Seller)		$ _____

* Deposited in escrow account with above-mentioned Mortgage Company. Tax deposit based on estimated annual taxes of $_____ and is subject to future adjustment. Pro rata taxes collected from Seller in the sum of $_____ and deposited in Purchaser's escrow account.

This is to certify that the foregoing is a true and correct statement of fees and charges to Purchasers herein named.

Received of _____ the above mentioned sum of $_____ representing loan to me/us; and I/we hereby approve payment of the items charged above.

I/We further certify that the above purchase price is the true and correct consideration paid to the Seller for this property.

CITY TITLE CO., INC.

By *Fred N. Route* _____
    Closing Officer/Attorney

Estimated monthly payment:
Principal & Interest:
Tax escrow:
Insurance escrow:

First payment due:

Conditions Necessary to the Seller. The main consideration of the seller/general partners was to get to a closing, receive as much of the $150,000 cash payment as possible, retire the bank loans, and get the limited partners off their backs. As described in Chapter 14, they did insist on a refinancing clause that would allow them to substitute another loan for their wraparound loan, thereby releasing to them the equity remaining in the wraparound loan. This clause was necessary if certain limited partners were to approve the sale.

Closing Date. The final contract specified a closing date on or before December 10, 1974, but all prorations of income and expenses were to be made effective November 1, 1974, in order to achieve the desired financial results for the new investors. In fact, the closing was not completed and deeds fully recorded until December 28, 1974, because of additional problems that occurred in mid-December. The on-site property management was so poor that tenants were deserting their units, suing the owners for property damage due to failure to make necessary roof repairs, and discouraging potential renters from signing leases. Under threat of contract termination, the seller reluctantly agreed to guarantee rents and expenses at the pro forma projection levels for the months of November and December. Despite these problems, D&B believed it could re-lease most of the units by the middle of January, the following month, and achieve the projected pro forma results in 1975.

Another source of delay was the requirement that the general partners receive the consent of a majority of the limited partners regarding the essential terms of the sale. Owing to the complex and dynamic nature of the changes taking place and the negotiations that ensued, that consent was difficult to obtain and was discouraging to all the parties in the transaction. Persistence and patience on the part of all concerned resulted in a closing on December 28. The property management (the subject of the following chapter) took over the property on the afternoon of that day and was expected to salvage a near-disaster occupancy and tenant morale situation.

16

Managing the Property

FRANK & ERNEST

Reprinted by permission. © 1978 NEA, Inc.

WHAT IS PROPERTY MANAGEMENT?

Property management is a service designed to maintain the greatest possible net cash flow from a given real estate investment using a socially responsible plan to conserve the value of the asset for resale at the end of the ownership cycle.

Managing the property is an essential cost of operation during the ownership years of a real estate investment cycle. Even raw land has risks—it may be an attractive nuisance; squatters may have to be ejected; the neighborhood must be investigated for socioeconomic changes—that could imperil the estate of the investor.

Acknowledgment: The authors gratefully acknowledge the assistance of William M. Weisiger, CPM, Urbana-Champaign, Ill., who reviewed this chapter.

Property management performs the following functions:

1. *Space use planning,* which involves obtaining market information on revenues and costs, user profiles, and competitive projects.
2. *Market promotion,* which involves implementing the merchandising strategy and selecting tenants.
3. *Operating the property,* which involves maintaining accounts; administering the maintenance plan and supervising maintenance and administrative employees; public relations, tenant relations; evictions; and replacement of tenants and employees.
4. *Counseling the investor* on how to enhance the value of the property and on refinancing, capital improvements, and selling.

A property manager is any person—an owner, an employee, an agent, or an independent contractor—who has the power to direct, control, or advise the investor with respect to management of the real estate.

Professional Property Management Our bias here is toward professional management by third-party contractors. Even investors who prefer to manage their properties themselves will find that to achieve their objectives they must meet the professional standards of the Institute of Real Estate Management (IREM).[1] The reasons for using professional management include the following:

1. Property management requires extraordinary attention to detail and following through. This can interfere with the investor's primary career or other objectives.
2. Property management includes such tasks as trash removal, repairing stopped drains, and fixing roof leaks, tasks that many investors consider beneath their dignity but must be done promptly.
3. By nature many investors prefer to be passive investors (REITs are required to be by law). Seeking to be an idle capitalist conflicts with the need for attention to detail noted earlier.
4. The investor could more profitably devote the time required to adequately perform the property management function to venture (investment) management functions such as new acquisitions and refinancing.
5. Many investors are lulled into a sense of security by 100 percent occupancy and achievement of budget objectives, but an agent with an eye on market trends could warn that it is time to sell or raise rents before market trends have fully developed.

Whoever accepts the responsibility for management should be able to meet the performance projections on which the investor's purchase decision was based. David W. Walters[2] has analyzed how changes in certain variables can affect a

[1] James C. Downs, Jr., *Principles of Real Estate Management* (Chicago: Institute of Real Estate Management, 1975), p. 25.
[2] David W. Walters, "Just How Important Is Property Management," *Journal of Property Management,* July-August 1978, pp. 164– 168. See also Don W. Carlson, "Professional Property Management: The Real Estate Key to a Successful Real Estate Venture," *Journal of Property Management,* November-December 1977, pp. 295– 297.

typical apartment project's IRR. Although Walters' analysis deals with only one project, it appears that the investor should give high priority to competent, creative property management.

Good property management cannot be taken for granted. Good management can have a significant impact on rate of return,[3] and a good manager can do much to obtain optimal market rents, maintain tenant satisfaction, achieve lower turnover, and provide up-to-date financial information. While a low purchase price can do much to improve returns, an experienced property manager will not overlook the need for capital improvements, deferred maintenance, and similar problems. Seeking a property manager's judgment during the preacquisition stage could prove invaluable during negotiations and development of the management plan and merchandising strategy.

WHO NEEDS PROPERTY MANAGEMENT

Individual Investors   One argument for self-management cites the advantage of collecting the management fees rather than paying them to third parties. Some even include the management fees produced by equity investor "sweat" as part of the return on investment! Beginning investors are often forced to take on the burdens of self-management in order to gain entry into real estate investing. Because of diseconomies of scale, it is difficult to justify professional, independent property management for any real estate investment with less than twenty units or a gross effective income of $50,000. The authors suggest group equity investing as a good alternative because it spreads the risk to more than one location and provides the opportunity for third-party professional management. Indeed, one possibility is to invest in a project in which a professional manager has bought a share as part of the syndicate and has also made a commitment to act as the manager, as is the case for Aspen Wood.

Institutional Investors   Too often, institutional investors like REITs and life insurance companies view the property management function as akin to bond "coupon clipping"—as though rents were simply interest payments. Independent professional management should be the policy of institutional investors unless they hold a large enough portfolio within one SMSA to justify a separate management subsidiary with *independent,* semiautonomous authority.

THE PROPERTY MANAGEMENT PROCESS

Planning for the Use of Space

Planning for space use is a crucial first step in developing an appropriate management plan. The investor must clearly identify the user in order to match the property management services with the users' needs. Property managers, who

---

[3] James R. Cooper and Stephen A. Pyhrr, "Forecasting the Rates of Return on an Apartment," *The Appraisal Journal,* July 1973, pp. 312–337; see also Austin J. Jaffe, "The Property Manager: Foremost Among the Decision-Makers," *Journal of Property Management,* November-December 1977, pp. 288–290.

work daily in the users' market, are best equipped to advise the investor, once the user profile has been identified, on the best estimates for market rent schedules. In addition, property managers are often consulted on such questions as whether or not a property should be modernized, rehabilitated, converted to another use, or conceivably demolished to minimize taxes. It is worth noting that to the skilled property manager, *modernization, rehabilitation,* and *conversion* are technical terms with specific meanings:

1. *Modernization* (remodeling) is designed to *overcome functional obsolescence* and extend the economic life of a building by replacing worn out equipment. Generally, there is no change in use. However, room layouts may be improved and outmoded heating equipment, lighting fixtures, and plumbing may be replaced.
2. *Rehabilitation* is the process of restoring a structure to like-new condition and giving it a new economic life, but without significant change in the design or present use.
3. *Conversion* is succession to a higher and better use. Some conversions are physical in nature, for example, changing an old warehouse into a shopping complex. Others may be primarily a change in concept, for example, converting from rental to condominium ownership.

The property manager's skills are sometimes used (1) to estimate the revenue and expenses likely to be produced from the highest and best use, (2) to estimate the cost of conversion and the return/risk relationships implicit in such a change, or (3) to evaluate the existing design, layout, and physical condition of a prospective investment.

The Institute of Real Estate Management has designed a management plan[4] that provides a comprehensive economic analysis of an income property. Much of the work performed by Certified Property Managers (CPMs) is similar to that performed by MAIs (Member, Appraisal Institute), Senior Real Estate Analysts (SREAs), or other appraisers. The CCIM (Certified Commercial Investment Member) designates of the National Realtors Marketing Institute (RNMI) may also do such work. Whoever does such a survey should relate the use of the space to a preliminary operating statement, the marketability analysis, and competitive surveys. This will enable the investor to develop a rational plan for capital additions and a maintenance policy, both of which may affect the acquisition price or the decision to purchase.

Operating statements differ depending on the type of property. In our Aspen Wood Apartments case at the end of this chapter we show a representative statement that includes items typically budgeted for property management. In Part IV of this book, operating statements for other types of properties are shown in various chapters.

Exhibit 16–1 demonstrates how an operating statement can be analyzed to

---

[4] James Downs, pp. 157– 167.

EXHIBIT 16-1. Identifying the Break-Even Point

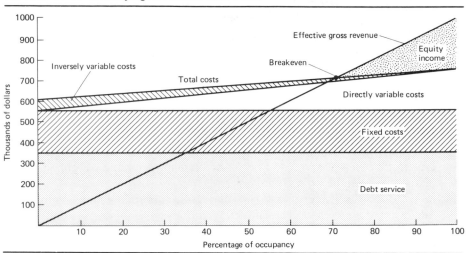

SOURCE: John McMahan, *Property Development,* (New York: McGraw-Hill, 1976), p. 365.

identify the break-even point and the amount of cash throw-off (equity income) that can be generated by an efficient manager.

Developing the Maintenance Plan

Most well-managed business enterprises are aware of the need for a policy on capital additions. It is also recommended that as part of the management plan a policy be developed for replacing short-lived items. Crisis management with emergency repairs as a daily routine is inefficient and costly. To avoid the high costs of emergency repairs, provision should be made for annual and seasonal inspections and for routine repairs. If small-cost, short-lived items, such as exhaust fans and disposals, are replaced throughout the project on a sequential cycle, this will enable the enterprise to benefit from volume discount purchases and speciali-zation of labor for installation. High-cost items, such as reroofing and repaving, should also be anticipated during the ownership cycle.

There is no clear line that can be drawn between a capital addition and a repairs expense for budget purposes. Both are intended to extend the ordinary operating efficiency of an asset over its useful life. (See Chapter 13.) According to the Internal Revenue Service, a capital addition is an item done or installed to add value, extend the useful life, or adapt the asset to a different use. Maintenance, on the other hand, is generally continuous and routine, and is done to prevent disruption in service. Repairs are a form of maintenance that is done as a result of disruption of service. A few examples may explain why the IRS and taxpayers often disagree on whether an item is a repair to be expensed and deducted, or a capital addition to be capitalized and depreciated:

Type of Expenditure	Repair	Capital Addition
Plumbing	Mending; parts replacements	Major replacements
Roofing	Patching leaks; replacing a limited number of shingles	Addition of new roof; major area replacements

Obviously, careful accounting records must be kept in order to prove the distinction between maintenance and capital additions.

Capital Additions Policy

A capital additions policy is necessary to guide the property manager. An excellent budget control is an early agreement between the property manager and the investor regarding the limits of the former's authority to undertake a capital addition. For example, installation of smoke alarms in each unit of a 400-unit project is a matter over which the investor should retain control. A practical guideline is to agree on a list of items (or, alternatively, on a dollar limit for any single expenditure) that cannot be replaced without the approval of the investor.

Marketing and Merchandising the Space

Real estate investors are operating a business, and marketing or merchandising the product is an essential function of that business. An empty building can be managed by a janitor or a watchman. The real test of a property manager's skill is whether he or she can fill the space with appropriate users at market rents, and keep it filled with a minimum of turnover and bad debts.

Selling Versus Merchandising   Generally, the manager of a real estate product need not "sell" in the sense that a salesperson creates a need and then closes the lease transaction. An exception would be someone who is introducing a new concept of space use (e.g., office condominiums, time sharing of a recreational facility). As a merchandiser the property manager has three functions: (1) getting the customers targeted by the marketability analysis *to see the property,* (2) getting these prospective tenants to *prefer that space* over competitive alternatives, and (3) *selecting good tenants.*

Promoting the Project   Getting the prospective tenants to see the project is the objective of advertising, public relations, and other promotional activities.

A thematic image. A thematic image is essential for successful promotion. This can be achieved by capitalizing on architectural style, or it can result from consistency in the use of a name, symbols, and signs in the promotional materials and activities designed to get prospects to the site. For example, a property manager in a northern city, confronted with a foreclosed project with extremely low occupancy, decided that he had something other than a lemon on his hands. He named it the Lemontree, created a warm, sunny image with sunshine colors, and got free newspaper publicity by putting maintenance people in bright yellow golf carts and yellow uniforms and calling them "Lemon Aides"! The result was strong word-of-mouth advertising that picked up on the other advertising and promotion and increased the flow of potential tenants.

A carefully thought out and implemented merchandising strategy can be developed for any real estate product, although obviously time and budget constraints will vary depending on the type, size, and location of the property. For example, having identified his market as college students, nurses, and white-collar technicians, the owner of a six-unit building simply required his tenants to provide 60 days' notice and posted the vacancies on bulletin boards at nearby hospitals, universities, and computer facilities. He also offered any tenant who was leaving a bonus for helping to show and rent the apartment. The result was no vacancies for five years, in spite of occasional softness in the market.

Once the thematic image has been selected, the property manager should establish a promotional program, of which the most important elements are signs and advertising.

Signs. Promotional, directional, informational, and permanent identification signs must be prepared. Competent sign artists should be instructed to maintain the selected thematic image.

Brochures and collateral materials should be brief; written in clear, simple language; and inexpensive. They serve to keep the address and phone number in the hands of the prospect, but they should not be expected to sell the space. Brochures can be important selling tools in the case of a condominium, a new office complex, or new industrial space because some of the decision makers may not visit the point of sale.

Advertising. The best advertisement is the project itself and a point-of-sale vacancy or For Sale sign. Over 50 percent of the people who sign leases do so because they liked what they saw when they drove by. The only reason for advertising is to obtain prospects. A rule-of-thumb suggests that, on the average, about five prospects are required for every lease.

When to spend for advertising depends on the level of occupancy. *How much* to spend is a function of the size of the project and how well established the thematic image is in the target market. A budget of 3–5 percent of gross effective income for overall promotional activities (including advertising) is a guideline.

Location has a great influence. Some projects are so located that they are their own best billboard; others are in such remote locations that advertising is necessary to build prospect traffic. The choice of advertising media is wide: radio; television; daily, weekly, and neighborhood newspapers; direct mail; yellow pages; classified ads; billboards; bulletin boards (e.g., in nearby supermarkets); and so forth. Whatever advertising medium is used, a careful count should be made of the number of prospects generated per dollar expended. To make each advertising dollar effective, either the investor or, preferably, the property manager should be expert in the use of the promotional budget.

Other traffic builders. Examples of other appropriate traffic builders would include apartment guides, handbills and flyers, newsletters, airport displays, apartment locator services, brokers, and so on. A grand opening may be a good time to use a celebrity as a traffic builder, along with giveaways, street theater, and the like, but such techniques can be overdone. Giveaway premiums for signing leases should be avoided because they encourage retaliatory competition that can substantially reduce net operating income.

Selecting Tenants

On the one hand, a tenant is potentially a stable and adequate income stream— that is, a person who will continue to pay the rent, possibly renew the lease, and use the property in accordance with the terms of the lease as long as the landlord is socially responsible, competent, and honorable in meeting the standards of the lease. On the other hand, a tenant may be a source of bad debts, pilferage, vandalism, ignorant or irresponsible usage of the premises, discord among the other tenants, litigation costs due to eviction, and other problems that will diminish the owner's cash flow.

The task of tenant selection requires the skills of a credit manager, a personnel manager, and a psychotherapist. Generally, no tenant should be approved by the property manager without a personal interview during which the nonverbal communications and oral assurances made by the would-be tenant are evaluated. All prospects say they will be good tenants; the interviewer should both evaluate the credibility of the prospect and elicit other necessary information.

Ideally, the real estate product is sufficiently competitive so that one has some choice and can select tenants in such a way as to minimize bad debts and other problems. The Institute of Real Estate Management and competent local property managers have application forms that can be used as checklists to be sure sufficient data are obtained to make a prompt evaluation after the tenant has made a deposit and the lease has been partially executed (by the tenant only). Finally, one must keep in mind that the tenant selection process occurs during the marketing/merchandising phase. The individuals who receive calls, interview tenants, show the premises, and take applications should be well trained in telephone etiquette, courtesy, and good public relations. Even those who are turned away should have a good image of the real estate product. Traffic building requires great care in handling relations with the public.

The following are some general criteria that can be used to evaluate the quality of would-be tenants:

1. *Creditworthiness.* The credit rating of a prospective tenant is essential. Employment, sales volume, or sufficient other income should be substantiated. The current landlord is often a poor reference source, especially for deadbeats. He or she may even be paying the first month's rent at your location in order to get rid of a bad-debt tenant. Since more than 90 percent of tenants pay rent voluntarily, you are really checking on the stability of the tenant's income and seeking to avoid slick, dishonest deadbeats.

   Reluctance to meet rent and security deposit obligations at the time of lease execution are red-flag warnings against going ahead with would-be tenants. Inability to meet your needs for rent and property security at the time of lease execution is a harbinger of trouble.

In the case of a commercial or industrial tenant, one must take care to avoid the problem of the AAA name, that is, the practice of using a newly formed, thinly capitalized corporation to insulate assets from lease responsibility.

2. *Compatibility of tenants.* Property managers are not social arbiters or gatekeepers, but they are entangled in the legal, cultural, and social problems of human equality and distributive justice. In making qualitative judgments the manager's difficulties are very real, especially when it comes to housing and shopping centers. It is imperative that a property manager thoroughly understand compliance obligations under the civil rights and equal employment opportunity acts, and various Supreme Court decisions under the antitrust laws. Membership in an appropriate owner/manager association is an efficient way of keeping up with changes in federal, state, and local laws and regulations.

The property manager is in charge of a small unit of society. The personal satisfaction of tenants is, in part, dependent on the ability of the group as a whole to be congenial and live with a minimum of discord. As a result, the person interviewing the prospect must consider compatibility. In housing, for example, mixing elderly empty-nesters with swinging singles may be threatening to both groups. Mixing students with working couples is another example of potential incompatibility. In an industrial park, placing a small foundry next to an electronics manufacturer could produce hostility. One of the important reasons for the prospect interview is to be sure the would-be tenant realizes his or her duty to comply with the lease obligations.

3. *Permanence potential.* Some luxury apartments experience twice the turnover of their competitors, and some industrial parks have much more rapid turnover than others. Generally, this is because the property manager has failed to carefully evaluate the staying power of prospects. A good apartment application form can reveal frequency of moves, frequency of job changes, and other indicators of nomadic conduct. In the case of commercial/industrial prospects, bank references and business associates can usually be relied upon to provide the necessary information. One should be particularly aware of the need for special service requirements and possible expansion.

Obviously, since turnover is impossible to prevent, rent schedules should be set high enough to anticipate vacancy rates. Large projects usually allow for a 2–5 percent vacancy rate, which covers refurbishing and any changes required by new tenants.

Lease Negotiations and Lease Terms

The skilled property manager is fully aware that the lease terms establish the rules of the game for a continuing relationship with the prospective tenant. Although it is a matter of judgment as to when the manager should make an issue of specific lease clauses, a discussion of lease terms is an excellent technique for eliciting prospect responses and can be a way of revealing true motives.

In the case of commercial/industrial properties, negotiating skills are essential because lease clauses can be used to shift risk between investor-owners and the user-lessee.

The following is a brief discussion of some of the more typical lease terms that affect return and risk.

The Lease   A carefully conceived, fair, and equitable lease is essential to a good image and efficient property management. It encompasses the rights and obligations of the owner and tenants within the law of the jurisdiction. In the United States there is a wide range of judicial decisions and statutory laws, with the result that there is great variance in the terms that are enforceable locally. The standard-form leases of *local* owner/manager associations are a good starting point for choosing and developing a lease that is appropriate to the real estate product. Such leases may even be preferable because they have passed the test of local litigation. The advice of a lawyer and a property manager may be necessary in choosing the proper vehicle for controlling the landlord-tenant relationship.

Gross versus net leases. Traditionally, all residential leases have been of the kind in which the tenant pays a flat rate and the landlord is responsible for all costs. Such leases are called *gross leases*. In recent years inflationary conditions have produced such uncertainty that residential property managers have been changing to a fixed base rent with a schedule of base operating expenses (e.g., sanitation fees, common area utilities, water and sewage, real estate taxes), with the tenant required to pay for any increases over the base that occur during the lease. In areas where there is tenant resistance to this technique, property managers have been changing to shorter-term (six-month) leases.

The fixed-base lease with proportional share of the operating increases approach is also being applied in retail, office, and industrial leases where occupancy levels are high.

The term *net lease* is a confusing misnomer, although the concept itself is simple. Under a net lease, some operating costs are shifted to the tenant. It is necessary to look at the specific lease to determine its *netness*. Usually the landlord receives a fixed rent, which is adjusted annually on the basis of an index, from the base period; the tenant pays for all increases in real estate taxes, insurance, and for specified maintenance and repair costs above the base-year amounts. Some leases require that the tenant also pay for *all* interior and exterior structural repairs and/or replacements of building improvements in the event of their destruction by fire or other casualty.

The investor should be aware, however, that the greater the burden of management, leasehold improvement, and capital additions placed on the tenant, the greater the likelihood that the IRS may deem the relationship a sale rather than a lease, or the net lease an "investment" rather than the operation of a business. This may have an adverse impact on the investor's rights to deductions for depreciation and favorable tax treatment. Net leases are usually made with lessees who have strong credit ratings, and are often for long terms.

Percentage leases. Many leases, particularly those for commercial tenancies, provide for a *base* rent related to a specified level of gross receipts, to be paid on a monthly basis for the rights of possession. Whenever gross sales rise above the base rent threshold point, a percentage clause automatically takes effect and the rent due is based on the formula set forth in the clause. The amount by which the percentage rent exceeds the base rent is the *overage*. Some rules of thumb may be useful in making effective use of this powerful clause:

1. Although landlords are generally reluctant to admit it, percentage clauses are negotiable and may vary within the same class of tenants.
2. In establishing the base rent for new leases, it is probably mutually beneficial to negotiate a fair, average ratio of base rent to typical gross sales per square foot for the gross leasable area (GLA) for that type of retail use, rather than driving a hard bargain. The gross sales and rents per square foot of GLA can be found in the current reports of *Dollars and Cents of Shopping Centers,* published by the Urban Land Institute. By taking a conservative approach to the base rent, you should not trigger the overage rent until sales are above the retailer's breakeven point. This could help minimize turnover. At the same time, the marginal tenant is required to pay a sufficient base rent to fairly share occupancy expenses and amortization costs.

The landlord should clearly spell out the right to audit the tenant's operating records for business at that specific location. Percentage leases based on "net profits" or "gross margins" are potentially troublesome because of the difficulty of proof. It is preferable for the percentage to be based on gross receipts. Since disputes do arise, we urge insertion of an arbitration clause, which costs less than court litigation, as a means of conflict resolution.

Escalation clauses. Escalation clauses provide a formula for adjusting the rent on the basis of a change in a specified economic indicator. They maintain the yield on the lease by adjusting for changes in monetary values and costs. The most commonly used indicators are the wholesale commodity index and the consumer price index. It is preferable to use a regional index in order to minimize distortions.

Recent inflationary trends have made it essential to include this clause in any lease. On the other hand, the high rate of inflation is causing resistance to using actual index changes without negotiation.

Reappraisal clauses. The negotiation of a long-term relationship between the lessor and the lessee often embroiders the lease with special clauses, such as options to purchase, renewal options, and lessee's right to first refusal in the event of sale during the term. Since the parties to the negotiation of the original lease are usually conversant with the relationship of gross rents to the yield and to the value of the property, it is best to include a reappraisal clause triggered by such contingencies as renewal and exercise of options. Indeed, if the rent has been calculated on the basis of a percentage of property value, the clause should call for adjustment of that value at periodic intervals through reappraisal by independent fee appraisers. The typical appraisal clause provides for the lessor and the lessee to each appoint qualified appraisers, who then seek to agree on the value. In the event that they cannot agree, the clause provides that the appraisers appoint a third appraiser to arbitrate the value. Though this will not eliminate disputes, it does provide for orderly resolution of the conflict.

Tenant's rights and obligations. The tenant has a right to possession and use of the property. Most leases contain a provision that a tenant who pays rent and abides by the terms of the lease has a right not to be disturbed by the landlord except for reasons of fire, safety, sanitation, panic, and prevention of water damage. Leases should provide the property manager with the limited right of access for repairs, inspection, and showing the premises to prospects at times that are not inconvenient for the tenant.

Provision should be made for tenants' right to remove trade fixtures or leasehold improvements when they have declared their intent to retain title. The right of removal should be conditioned on the duty to restore the property to its original condition. Failure to remove should, by the terms of the lease, vest the title to the abandoned property in the landlord.

Since the tenant is in possession with broad rights of private use and enjoyment in accordance with the lease terms, it is best for the liability for dangerous conditions to be imposed on the party in possession. Recent changes in landlord-tenant law for urban rental housing in most jurisdictions have given tenants some limited rights to cure defective conditions and make repairs related to habitability. The cost of the repairs can be charged to the landlord. The property manager's authority to deal with such matters and solve such problems should be clear and unequivocal.

Generally, landlords should require the right of prior written approval before any sublet or assignment takes legal effect. Since use involves personal habits, attitudes toward responsibility, and creditworthiness, it is unwise to give tenants unilateral power of assignment or sublet. Most leases provide that in the event of a sale a tenant retains all rights and duties under the existing lease. However, some jurisdictions give tenants a unilateral right to terminate the lease in the event of a sale, as long as it is a term-of-lease contract and even though it may result in some inequity.

Finally, the landlord should be acquainted with the possible effects of antitrust laws, building codes, land use controls, crime and security regulations, and pollution controls on the rights and duties of the parties to the lease relationship.

Managing and Operating the Property

The key skills in managing and operating a property require that the property manager be a generalist rather than a specialist. Although it is not uncommon for CPAs, engineers, and commercial real estate brokers to become property managers, they must develop new and demanding skills if they are to fulfill the role of property manager for a large complex or for many different projects. The following are some of the primary duties of the property manager.

Tenant Move-ins and Move-outs   It is essential to provide for inspection and inventory of the premises when a tenant takes possession or vacates. Appropriate inventory forms and inspection sheets should be developed, and the tenant should initial them to acknowledge that all items are in good operating order and on the premises at the time of taking possession or vacating. This procedure fixes responsibility for abuse or neglect; it helps avoid false claims of ownership and minimizes disputes. It can act as the tenant's acknowledgment that there were no building violations and that the premises were habitable or, in the case of retail and industrial uses, that utility entrances were adequate.

Maintenance and Repairs   Assuming that the lease places the responsibility for maintenance of the building, fixtures, equipment, and other improvements on the owner, this duty requires prompt and competent action. The legal responsibility for fire prevention, sanitation, panic control, and security, if not properly fulfilled, can turn ownership of property into a catastrophic invasion of the capital assets of the investor. This function is one that requires skill in managing employees and/or selecting and supervising independent trade contractors. Attention to detail is necessary to be sure that all complaints are attended to with dispatch.

Some investors minimize maintenance and repair and "milk" the property to maximize net operating income. In most cases this practice results in less capital gain when the property is terminated. A responsible maintenance program is necessary to conserve and enhance the value of the real estate product. Of course, if political rent controls eliminate net cash flow, the owner may be forced to defer maintenance or shift the duty to the tenants.

Following are the basic elements of a *general* maintenance plan:

1. *An inventory of mechanical equipment and physical components.* The objective is to develop an annual maintenance schedule that can act as a calendar of activity for the maintenance personnel. The strategy is to avoid a continual stream of crises and, instead, to program periodic maintenance tasks. It is possible that a list of mechanical and physical equipment was produced while preparing the schedule for ACRS personal property depreciation. Manufacturers' instruction booklets are quite helpful in determining when maintenance should be done on mechanical equipment. Be sure to take advantage of guarantees for such items as roofs, pumps, appliances, and air conditioning.
2. *Periodic "eyes on" inspection of the property.* Every six months—more frequently in large installations—one should supplement the periodic maintenance schedule with a field inspection of the structural components. September and March are good checkpoint intervals. One is looking for components that require attention because of wear and tear, such as roofs, eaves, gutters or downspouts, stairs and railings, sewers and drains, screens, windows, brickwork, painted surfaces, and pavements. At this time one should also check on the need for yard maintenance.
3. *Maintenance equipment, service contracts, supplies, and parts.* Depending on the size and nature of the real estate product, appropriate tools must be on location for adequate maintenance. Buy supplies like paint and cleaning

materials in bulk (10-gallon cans) to obtain discounts and minimize pilferage. Underqualified personnel should *not* be used for roofing, plumbing, electrical work, and other repairs that require special skills. Service contracts may be appropriate if they are cost effective. The manager will usually assign such equipment and supplies to a named person in order to assign accountability.

Every effort should be made to avoid "cannibalization" because, by its very nature, it takes two repair jobs to correct one problem. Parts that are needed frequently should be kept on hand or be readily available from a nearby source. Skyscrapers and other high-rises require highly skilled stationary engineers, computer technicians, mechanical engineers, and the like. Maintenance of such buildings is a profession in and of itself. Large apartment projects require maintenance crews and supervisory personnel to monitor performance and set up work schedules. Competent managers must continuously monitor maintenance needs and keep abreast of changes in technology and conservation practices.

Accounting and Record Keeping   These are essential aspects of property management. The budget provides a plan for meeting revenue and expenditure goals. Accounting provides the investor with the most effective tool for monitoring management performance and the operating income and expenses of the project.

Small investors prefer to use a single-entry cash basis form of accounting to minimize the time devoted to this function. Banks offer checking account services that can act as the entire accounting system for the investment when paid invoices are stapled to the nonnegotiable duplicate of the check that remains in the book as it is written. One husband-and-wife-team who own over 400 apartment units at 28 different addresses avoid all accruals and simply maintain a separate checking account for each address. Of course, careful and complete notations must be made for depreciable items purchased or sold, capital distributions, refinancing income, short-term loans by the owners to a project, and other items that affect the balance sheet but are not necessarily part of the current operating statement. Even simple checkbook accounting requires periodic consolidation and analysis in order to produce an operating statement and balance sheet. However, one can expect that the advent of microcomputers will soon make it even easier for small investors to maintain cash basis books.

At the other extreme are real estate projects with thousands of tenants and a full-time property manager on the site. Some large properties have access to a computer, and using a uniform chart-of-accounts and accrual accounting system, can provide not only monthly but daily reports on income and expenditures. Investors in such properties can expect to receive such services as money management of funded reserves, regular reports on escrow accounts, and supervised handling of security deposits and rental adjustments.

Skill in promptly preparing and interpreting operating results and budgets is expected of competent property managers. Many CPAs, having proven their worth as accountants for property investors, have chosen to become full-time property managers. Certified property managers (CPMs) can obtain valuable statistics on regional income and expense experiences for various kinds of property from the Institute of Real Estate Management.[5] More important, an independent property manager who deals with many clients has access to information that can serve as a basis for reasonable budget projections.

A monthly cash flow statement, which reflects expenditures and charges such as real estate taxes, insurance, or seasonal utility bills in the months in which they occur, will permit planning for spending needs. The monthly cash flow statement should also reflect debt service payments to enable the investor to monitor cash flow returns to the equity investment. (See the Aspen Wood Apartments case at the end of this chapter.)

The operation of a real estate business also requires separate, carefully maintained records for the following items, among others:

- Antidiscrimination laws
- Lease contracts and tenant files (especially evictions)
- Building code violations
- Mandatory licenses and notices (elevators, worker compensation, etc.)
- Occupational Safety and Health Act (OSHA) requirements
- Correspondence concerning the property

Supervising Major Construction Work   The property manager is often the appropriate person to assure the investor that contractors are complying with material and job specifications. The manager should have the power to approve or disapprove payments in order to control the costs of improvements. The nature of real estate construction is such that many sins can be covered by paint, plaster, and other exterior coatings. Since a property manager is seldom an engineer or an architect, for major construction he or she should have the authority to obtain consulting and inspection services from qualified personnel.

SELECTING THE PROPERTY MANAGER

Defining the Scope of Management Services

The property manager is an agent of the owner; he or she may be an employee, a general agent, a special agent, or an independent contractor. Usually the relationship between the owner and the manager is that of principal and agent.

The authority of the property manager and the scope and nature of the services to be performed for the specific property should be carefully defined. Likewise, the authority of the investor over venture management and other functions specifically reserved to him or her should be clearly understood. For example, an eight-unit apartment building probably needs no more than a part-time resident manager whose payment takes the form of a reduction in rent. The investor would do the budgeting, accounting, and other administrative tasks, with

---

[5] Edward N. Kelley, *Practical Apartment Management* (Chicago: Institute of Real Estate Management, National Association of Realtors, 1976), pp. 210–259; John W. McMahan, *Property Development: Effective Decision Making in Uncertain Times* (New York: McGraw Hill, 1976), pp. 333–353.

the manager collecting rents, selecting tenants, and handling tenant complaints. As we moved up the scale in terms of property size, we could eventually justify contracting for an independent property manager (at, say, 24 units) as well as a person on the site. Some large investors have enough projects within one SMSA to justify an in-house property management organization.

Since we have already urged that investors seek professional property managers unless they have enough real estate assets to profitably operate an "in-house" full-time property management division or have the skill and desire to self-manage, in the balance of this chapter we will assume that most investors will seek independent property management. Generally, the relationship between an independent property manager and the investor would be covered by a written contract that would provide the following:[6]

1. *A description of the property to be managed is essential.* A legal description, or an address with a reference to the number of units, is certainly insufficient. The description should detail the improvements to the site (landscaping, paving); describe the exterior shell and major structural improvements; and provide a list of the furniture, fixtures, appliances, equipment, and special appointments in the revenue units. The description should specifically disclaim any property owned by the tenants.

2. *The exact names of the owner and manager.* Since the management agreement may well be the basis of future litigation, regardless of the intent of the parties, legally correct names should be used in all communications to protect the rights of the parties.

3. *A clear statement of the nature, scope, and extent of the manager's authority and any limitations on his or her power to operate the property.* This is an essential enabling clause and should set forth a statement of delegation of authority that is sufficient in scope and detail to make it clear that the manager is the steward of the asset and the custodial caretaker of it as long as he or she is the agent, independent contractor, or employee.

Generally, the investor will find it practical to establish a limited power of attorney. The full-time property manager should also have the following: (a) the right to execute and terminate leases; (b) the right to meet the requirements of state and federal filing requirements for tax payments (e.g., withholding, FICA), OSHA standards, worker compensation, civil rights, building codes, and litigation regarding the property; (c) the power to distribute net operating income to debt service and periodic cash distributions to the various owners (the manager should require all owners to agree in writing to the cash distribution instructions); (d) the authority to deal with third-party contractors in making repairs, obtaining supplies, and making cash disbursements to pay for such work; (e) the authority to deal with any emergency involving fire, panic, safety, sanitation, electricity, plumbing, water, or heat; and (f) the power to hire, fire, and supervise personnel.

---

[6] David W. Walters, "Negotiating the Property Management Agreement," *Journal of Property Management,* November-December 1977, pp. 291–294; John McMahan, *Property Management* (New York: McGraw Hill, 1976).

In addition, it is not uncommon for the manager to provide certain *consulting functions,* such as

- periodic review of insurance coverage to ensure that the owner is continuing to receive cost-effective insurance against fire, casualty, public liability, and other risks of loss.
- periodic review of real estate taxes to be sure they are fair, not disproportionate, and nondiscriminatory as to the property.
- periodic review of the quality, adequacy, and remaining economic life of all short-lived items.
- periodic review of the neighborhood, competitive properties, and tenants' profiles and activities.
- in some cases, although not typically, venture management functions such as filing partnership information returns and forwarding K-1s to partners. (More often, these functions are performed by others in order to protect performance auditing prerogatives.)

Though consulting services are valuable, an owner should not expect them to be performed as part of the ordinary management duties for the usual compensation. We suggest that per diem compensation be agreed upon in advance for such work, or that it be left for negotiation when the request for service is made.

4. *Adequate protection from the risks of agency should be provided.* Depending on the size of the project, one should provide fidelity bonding, errors and omissions insurance, and so forth. In addition, a mutually agreeable, save-harmless (or, *hold*-harmless) clause should be negotiated. No contract can provide for all contingencies and risks; however, a long-term manager must feel free to exert his or her best good-faith effort without fear of reprisal for honest errors of judgment.

5. *The method of compensation and incentives should be performance oriented.* The owner seeks to maximize rents, minimize expenses in a socially responsible way, and conserve the asset so as to protect and enhance its value. The percentage commission for management should be based on gross effective income (actual rent receipts).[7] Incentives may then be paid for new leases, renewals, and achieving a level of rent receipts that exceeds budgeted expectations. Some useful generalities for fixing compensations are as follows:

- When the service requires a regular expenditure of a predictable amount of time and money (e.g., maintaining 95 percent occupancy), the fee could be a fixed salary or a percentage fee (say, 5%).
- When the service is of a variable nature in terms of time and money, the fee could be a percentage of the rents produced (e.g., a lease-up fee of, say, $40 for producing a moved-in lessee on a new annual lease of $3,600) or a per diem for consulting services.

---

[7] On the other hand, a strong argument can be made for basing management commissions on a property's net operating income (NOI). For example, see Austin J. Jaffe, "A Reexamination of the Problem of Management Fee Assessment," *Journal of Property Management,* January-February 1979, pp. 339–347.

Information on appropriate fees and commissions is usually available through local lenders, appraisers, and other investors. One should expect to negotiate compensation; uniform fee schedules are a violation of antitrust laws.

6. *Length of agreement, resolution of disputes, termination, and enumerated causes for discharge should always be considered in advance.* To the extent possible the specific circumstances that will result in termination (or the right to terminate) and the method of termination should be carefully spelled out in the agreement. Often no actual duration is set forth in the property management contract, but each party retains the right to terminate with adequate notice (e.g., 30–90 days). However, property managers who take over special problems need time to achieve occupancy and cash flow objectives. Provision should be made for the owner to have the right to terminate in the event that specified profit or occupancy objectives are not met.

The property manager and the owner should both have the right to terminate in the event of foreclosure, insolvency, bankruptcy, or deterioration of the financial condition of either party below tolerable levels. Usually both parties prefer to have the right to terminate the relationship in the event of a change in ownership.

Because property management is usually an ongoing relationship, provision should be made for extralegal resolution of disputes. One frequently used method is arbitration. Another effective method is to agree in advance to submit the dispute to a previously appointed impartial, named third party. Careful consideration must be given to whether both parties really want to make the final award of this informal process binding on the parties. In any case, when the parties feel that the specific issue merits the heavy expenses of litigation, the right to take the dispute to court ought to be preserved.

Since the nature of the property management relationship is one of personal service, provision should be made for termination in the event of the death, insanity, or permanent disability of the owner or manager. A taking of the property or its destruction may also be a specified cause of unilateral termination by either party.

In the end, it is not possible to cover all the reasons why one or the other party may wish to end this important relationship. Both parties should recognize the fact the property management is the kind of relationship in which ethics, trust, and other intangible elements are just as important as contractual clauses. Sound owner-manager relations are dependent on compassionate understanding of each other's problems and concerns. No contract can substitute for good reports, timely written communications, explanatory phone calls, and a mutually accommodative attitude.

Selecting, Negotiating with, and Contracting for the Manager

Personal direct negotiations with the person who will in fact manage the property is a *sine qua non* of good selection. The investor should look for personality attributes that are compatible with the property management functions (i.e., one must evaluate both right-mode and left-mode brain function). The property manager should have the following skills and characteristics:

1. Capacity to handle many small details.
2. Ability to negotiate with suppliers, subcontractors, owners, tenants, and employers.
3. Assertiveness, decisiveness, and energy.
4. Entreprenuerial skills, coupled with the ability to work within an organizational structure.
5. Professional commitment to truth, purpose, responsibility, and trust, coupled with a continuing interest in professional education.
6. Capacity to be an officer: to supervise employees, to give direction to the business, and to enhance the value of the investment.

In *The Practice of Property Management* William Walters, Jr., provides job descriptions that can help the investor match the necessary behavioral attitudes with the kind of property managership required by a specific investment.[8]

Property management is a relatively new profession. Through the Institute of Real Estate Management, individuals can now become Certified Property Managers upon completion of a course of study, examinations, and proof of experience. In addition, IREM accredits on-site managers with the Accredited Resident Manager (ARM) designation; business organizations can be designated as Accredited Management Organizations (AMOs). All members are expected to meet standards of professional conduct. The code of ethics of IREM members is regulated by local chapters and the national organization. If at all possible, an investor should obtain up-to-date comments on the competence of prospective managers from local lenders, appraisers, bankers, and other investors.

EVALUATING THE PERFORMANCE OF THE PROPERTY MANAGER

Most competent, ethical property managers welcome a systematic review of their performance. Institutional investors will find that some sort of performance auditing system is necessary if they are to efficiently manage their portfolios. Small investors would be wise to have a system for making periodic checks of a manager's performance.

The management agreement should provide for certain reports to be furnished by the manager:

1. physical conditions and maintenance problems
2. vacancy and bad-debt experience
3. changes in tenant profiles and tenant relations

---

[8] William Walters, Jr., CPM, *The Practice of Property Management* (Chicago: National Association of Realtors, Institute of Real Estate Management, 1979). See also William M. Shenkel, *Modern Real Estate Principles* (Dallas: Business Publications, 1977), chap. 18; Alfred A. Ring and Jerome Dasso, *Real Estate Principles and Practice,* 9th ed., (Englewood Cliffs, N.J.: Prentice-Hall, 1981), chap. 25–26; Alvin L. Arnold, Charles H. Wurtzebach and Mike E. Miles, *Modern Real Estate* (Boston: Warren, Gorham & Lamont, 1980), chap. 11; Albert J. Lowry, *How to Manage Real Estate Successfully in Your Spare Time* (New York: Simon and Shuster, 1977); C. W. Bailey, "Do You Need a Professional Management Company?" *Journal of Property Management,* May–June 1976, pp. 150–154.

4. reports on competitive properties—recent comparable sales
5. report on the economic outlook of the SMSA and mortgage market conditions
6. recommendations for capital additions, replacements, selling, refinancing, etc.

In the Aspen Wood Apartments case at the end of this chapter we show an operating statement summary, a cash information report, a statement of operations, and a balance sheet (see Exhibits 16-3– 16-6 in the Aspen Wood case.)

In order to promote trust and mutual accommodation, the investor should fully disclose to the manager that he or she will use a performance audit system that includes periodic inspection of the property and interviews with tenants. (See Exhibit 16– 2.) These audit functions should be performed at least annually. If third-party contractors are to perform these functions, the property manager should know who they are and approximately how often the audits will take place.

Annual Conference with the Manager on Goals and Budget Objectives[9]

The annual conference between the investor and the manager is based on two management principles: management by objectives and the exception principle. Management by objectives is a system for motivating the property manager by using the principle of goal setting. Management by exception is a control technique that gives the property manager the full authority of the investor, *except* in clearly defined areas that have been agreed upon in advance.

The management agreement, operating budget, and previously adopted policies and goals may be used to guide discussion at the annual conference. The investor should have been directly involved in the development of the original

---

EXHIBIT 16–2. A Performance Audit Checklist for Evaluating the Property Manager

---

1. Periodic inspection of the physical condition of the property by the investor— review of turnaround time of maintenance complaints, direct reports from selected tenants.
2. Periodic reports on tenants' level of satisfaction—review of tenant activity reports and interviews with selected tenants.
3. Periodic review of neighborhood and metromarket conditions—this might be performed by a third-party consultant, such as an appraiser or another independent property manager. It would include a report on employment rates, the economic outlook, a comparative analysis of competitive projects, and reports on rent level changes, utility rates, etc.
4. An independent audit of all cash reserves, such as security deposits, debt service reserves, cash on hand, petty cash, spot audits of invoices for repairs and supplies, etc.

---

[9] Peter F. Drucker, *Management* (New York: Harper & Row, 1974); John B. Miner and George A. Steiner, *Management Policy and Strategy* (New York: Macmillan, 1977), pp. 260– 262.

budget and all subsequent annual budgets. The budget should be supplemented by a narrative statement of goals to be achieved. The goals must be realistic, measurable, and specific, and a reasonable timetable for their achievement must be included.

Application of the exception principle should free the manager to take action and free the investor from worry about problems that do not exist.

The conference itself should be conducted in a businesslike atmosphere and should consider the following subjects:

1. a comparison of yield experience with budget objectives
2. a discussion of goals and objectives for the forthcoming year
3. decision making on major changes (e.g., capital additions, refinancing, possible sale or exchange, changes in management agreement, changes in marketing strategy or management plan, etc.)
4. mutual agreement on the budget for the forthcoming fiscal year

SUMMARY

Property management is an essential service designed to maintain the greatest possible net cash flow using a socially responsible plan to conserve the value of the asset for resale at the end of the ownership cycle. Studies have indicated that the property management function, if properly carried out, will have a favorable impact on the rate of return.

Property management involves space planning, market promotion, operation of the property, maintaining accounts, administering the maintenance plan and the capital improvements policy, public relations, tenant relations, evictions, and providing counseling and consulting services for investors.

Early consultation with a local property manager will enable the investor to develop a rational plan for management, merchandising, and first-year maintenance so that important capital-budgeting decisions can be made prior to acquisition.

Independent property managers, such as Certified Property Managers, can apply their expertise to designing a project's thematic image, signs, promotion, and tenant selection patterns to fit the profile of the intended space user. Property managers should be experts in lease administration.

The investor should carefully define the scope of the property manager's authority, and the management contract should fit the size of the property and the nature of the tenant–lessee's duties. There should be methods for resolving disputes, enumeration of the grounds for discharge, a limit on the duration of the agreement, and an agreement on methods for evaluating the performance of the property manager.

Property management is a wide-ranging, complex endeavor that is critical to the success of the real estate investment.

ASPEN WOOD APARTMENTS

MANAGING THE PROPERTY

The Aspen Wood joint venture agreement empowers D&B Associates to provide complete venture and property management services. Although Charlie Davidson is designated as the manager of the venture, in actual practice Clyde Boomer is in charge of day-to-day management. They have the following privileges, duties, and obligations:

1. The manager shall open and maintain a bank account upon which he shall be authorized to draw checks and into which all joint venture moneys shall be deposited.
2. The manager shall maintain or cause to be maintained true and accurate books of account of the joint venture operations, which books of account shall be readily available to the co-owners for inspection and/or audit.
3. The manager shall cause to be rendered monthly a statement reflecting income and expense for the month, such statements to be in the hands of the co-owners by the twentieth day of the following month. He shall, after accumulating a reasonable contingency reserve, issue and disburse with each such monthly statement the excess of cash income over expenses for the previous month, if any, to the participating parties in accordance with their proportionate interests.
4. The manager shall cause to be rendered annually a statement reflecting the financial operations of the joint venture for the previous year and the current financial condition of the joint venture. Such statements shall cover the calendar year, or part thereof, and shall be in the hands of the co-owners by March of the succeeding year.
5. The manager is authorized and obligated to manage the operation of the project, including obtaining tenants, collecting rents, depositing rents and deposits, paying bills and obligations, and handling repairs, maintenance, cleaning, and any other matter concerning operation. He is expressly authorized to hire (and discharge) resident managers of the apartment projects and to delegate to them such duties as he may desire, and shall determine the salary to be paid resident managers.
6. The manager shall be paid monthly for his services an amount equal to 5 percent of the gross income of the joint venture for the previous month. All other expenses, including advertising, of the project are classified as those of the joint venture.
7. Neither the manager nor resident managers shall be held liable to the joint venture or any co-owner for any loss or expense incurred by them in connection with the prudent discharge of their duties.

THE MANAGEMENT ORGANIZATION

One of the keys to D&B's success in real estate syndication is its excellent property management and maintenance services. A property management division handles all details of preventive and rehabilitative maintenance, including landscaping, gardening, refurbishing, and furnishing. The availability of maintenance personnel on a day-to-day basis ensures prompt attention to emergency problems, which is a major contribution to resident satisfaction and low vacancy rates.

A computer data management system is used extensively to analyze property performance. The system not only assists in coordinating and controlling the property management activities but also provides a data base for financial analyses of proposed new ventures. The D&B investment division works closely with the property management division to establish operating and capital expenditure budgets. After the cash flow budgets have been established, the property management division is held accountable for delivery of the amounts projected.

PROPERTY MANAGEMENT AT ASPEN WOOD

On December 20, 1974, D&B's property management division officially took charge of all property management activities at Aspen Wood. Before that date D&B worked closely with the on-site manager to arrange all the details of the takeover and design a leasing and maintenance program to turn the property around. On December 28 there were twenty-four vacancies, and the leasing, maintenance, and financial records were a disaster. The roofs were leaking; the central hot-water heaters were malfunctioning; and the utility company was threatening to shut off common-area electricity owing to payment delinquencies. The university students had left town for the holidays, and it was not certain how many would return on January 10 to honor their lease contracts, which expired on May 31, 1975.

Despite these problems, the 1974 operating performance was guaranteed through rent/expense provisions in the contract (described in Chapter 15). As a result, the cash flow and tax losses realized by the investors for the remainder of 1974 were close to pro forma projections:

	Amounts Projected (RE004 Analysis)	Amounts Realized (2 months, 1974)
Cash flow	$ 8,889	$ 8,163
Tax loss	$99,493	$106,229

While the cash flow realized was about $800 less than projected, tax losses exceeded projections by almost $7,000. Because of the operating problems that the property would be facing in 1975, Davidson and Boomer chose not to disburse the cash flow realized; it would be used as working capital to weather the early-1975 storm.

MONTHLY REPORTS TO INVESTORS

Several reports are sent to the joint venture partners each month, including (1) an operating statement summary, (2) a cash information report, (3) a detailed statement of operations and capital expenditures, and (4) a balance sheet. These are illustrated in Exhibits 16-3 – 16-6. Exhibits 16 – 3 and 16 – 4 are investor-oriented reports that provide summaries of the cash flow from operations, taxable income, and the sources and uses of cash. Exhibits 16 – 5 and 16 – 6 are full information reports used for analysis by property managers. All income and expense items in the detailed reports are shown as dollar amounts, percentages of gross possible income, dollars per square foot of leasable area, and actual versus budget amounts. This presentation method permits easy comparison between projects managed by D&B Associates and data published by trade associations.

Each month Boomer prepares a cover letter with the accounting reports, highlighting the developments of the past month and discussing items that may affect future performance. Periodically, Davidson includes a letter discussing important partnership matters, developments in the marketplace, and current activities of the investment division. Major decisions that must be made by the venture, such as capital expenditures, refinancing, and sale, are also presented to the partners by Davidson.

OPERATING HISTORY OF THE PROPERTY

During 1975 Aspen Wood Apartments did not achieve its cash flow return objectives. The roofs were repaired and the central hot-water heaters were replaced. The building and the individual apartments were gradually brought up to higher standards. The resident managers were replaced, and marketing efforts were made to change the poor image of the complex. Nevertheless, it required more than a year for occupancy to reach the projected 95 percent level, and a working-capital loan was arranged from a local bank to finance unbudgeted capital expenditures. Operating expenses for the first three years ran in the range of 47 – 50 percent of gross possible income, as contrasted with the 42 – 45 percent budgeted amount.

The operating history of Aspen Wood from 1974 through 1980 is shown in Exhibit 16 – 7. Actual amounts realized are compared to the 1974 – 1979 financial forecast (which was presented in Chapter 13).

The first three years were disappointing from an operating viewpoint but produced favorable tax shelter results. The next three years were excellent from the standpoint of cash flow but produced declining tax shelter. In 1980 the property produced a taxable income of $22,431 and the investors became anxious to take some action to relieve the rising income tax burden and realize some of their appreciation gains. In 1981 various alternatives for the disposition of Aspen Wood Apartments were considered; these are analyzed in the next chapter.

EXHIBIT 16–3. Aspen Wood Operating Statement Summary, period ended December 31, 1980

	% Month	% YTD	December	To Date (12 Months)
STATEMENT OF CASH FLOW				
Gross Possible Income				
Gross possible rent	95.7	95.9	$22,290.00	$239,560.00
Other income	4.3	4.2	1,009.40	10,373.99
Gross possible income	100.0	100.0	$23,299.40	$249,933.99
Vacancy and collection loss	.5	3.6—	113.11	8,999.77—
Gross effective income	100.5	96.4	$23,412.51	$240,934.22
OPERATING EXPENSES				
Tax and ins accrual/expense	8.9	9.9	$ 2,071.00	$ 24,852.00
Maintenance and repairs	12.5	12.9	2,911.47	32,226.59
Gas	6.4	4.3	1,497.61	10,858.44
Electricity	.0	1.0	.00	2,535.07
Water/waste water	.0	3.1	.00	7,804.65
Other utilities	1.4	1.7	322.40	4,145.89
Professional management	5.0	4.8	1,170.63	12,046.71
Resident management	5.9	6.0	1,363.11	15,080.28
Advertising and promotion	.1	1.0	26.20	2,417.86
Other	1.3	1.1	290.24	2,689.67
Total operating expenses	41.4	45.9	$ 9,652.66	$114,657.16
Net Operating Income	59.1	50.5	$13,759.85	$126,277.06
DEBT SERVICE				
Principal & interest payment	24.7	27.6	$ 5,751.83	$ 69,021.96
Total debt service	24.7	27.6	$ 5,751.83	$ 69,021.96
Cash Flow from Operations	34.4	22.9	$ 8,008.02	$ 57,255.10
STATEMENT OF TAXABLE INCOME				
Net operating income			$13,759.85	$126,277.06
Interest expense			4,502.00—	54,525.85—
Depreciation/amortization			3,806.41—	45,676.92—
Depreciation/current year improvements			28.64—	725.65—
Taxable Income			$ 5,422.80	$ 25,348.64

EXHIBIT 16–4. Aspen Wood Cash Information Report, period ended December 31, 1980

	December	To Date (12 Months)
Beginning Cash Balance	$2,338.43	$ 1,336.62
Cash flow from operations	8,008.02	57,255.10
Accounts payable	.00	185.00
Prepaid rent	.00	445.00–
Owner withdrawals	4,000.00–	28,206.00–
Capital expenditures	286.39–	7,256.35–
Reversal and tax & ins accrual	2,071.00	24,852.00
Tax and insurance escrow payment	1,657.79–	19,848.48–
Tax and insurance cash payments accrued	3,021.09–	3,930.71–
Cash to/from investment acct	1,000.00–	21,066.93–
Employee advances	29.65	23.42–
Net change in cash	143.40	1,145.21
Ending Cash Balance	$2,481.83	$ 2,481.83

Note: Sources are plus; uses are minus

EXHIBITS 16–5 and 16–6. *(See following pages)*

EXHIBIT 16–7. Aspen Wood Operating History

	CASH FLOW DISTRIBUTED		TAXABLE INCOME (LOSS)	
	Forecast	Actual	Forecast	Actual
1974	$ 8,889	0	($99,493)	($106,229)
1975	18,824	0	(69,643)	(104,650)
1976	20,421	0	(54,619)	(63,853)
1977	21,948	0	(47,808)	(47,208)
1978	23,393	$20,000	(32,558)	(32,653)
1979	21,741	21,176	(13,607)	(4,136)
1980*	N.A.	28,206	N.A.	22,431

* Financial projections assumed a holding period ending in 1979.

EXHIBIT 16-5. Statement of Operations, Aspen Wood, 12 Months Ended as of December 31, 1980

	% Month	% Y-T-D	MONTH December	MONTH Budget	MONTH November	YEAR TO DATE December	YEAR TO DATE Budget	YEAR TO DATE 12-31-79	Per Month	Sq. Ft. Y-T-D
RENT ANALYSIS										
Gross possible	100.0	100.0	$22,290.00	$19,953	$22,290	$239,560.00	$239,436	$209,705	$5.01	$4.49
Vacancy	1.1	3.5–	250.00	600–	250–	8,342.88–	7,200–	5,074–	.06	.16–
Collection losses	.6–	.3–	136.89			656.89–			.03–	.01–
GROSS EFFECTIVE INCOME										
Rent collections	100.5	96.2	$22,403.11	$19,353	$22,040	$230,560.23	$232,236	$204,630	$5.04	$4.32
Attorney collections	.0	.1	.00			281.53		56	.00	.01
Parking	.8	.8	167.00		157	1,845.83		1,500	.04	.03
Forfeited deposits	.5	.3	100.00			671.72		721	.02	.01
Vending concessions	1.3	1.4	290.95		296	3,249.50		2,717	.07	.06
Special charges	.4	.2	80.00		5	353.75		300	.02	.01
Interest income	1.7	1.5	371.10		299	3,680.74		1,715	.08	.07
Other income	.0	.1	.35			290.92		19–	.00	.01
Gross effective income	105.0	100.6	$23,412.51	$19,353	$22,797	$240,934.22	$232,236	$211,170	$5.27	$4.52
OPERATING EXPENSES										
Taxes and Insurance										
Personal property tax accrual	.3	.4	$ 75.00		$ 75	$ 900.00		$ 840	$ .02	$ .02
Real property tax accrual	7.1	8.0	1,590.00		1,590	19,080.00		17,220	.36	.36
Property insurance accrual	1.8	2.0	406.00		406	4,872.00		3,600	.09	.09
Total taxes and insurance	9.3	10.4	$ 2,071.00	$ 2,071	$ 2,071	$ 24,852.00	$ 24,852	$ 22,860	$ .47	$ .47
Maintenance and Repairs										
Maintenance wages	4.6	4.0	$ 1,018.00		$ 818	$ 9,591.86		$ 6,859	$ .23	$ .18
Maintenance overhead	.8	.7	182.35		152	1,585.66		1,145	.04	.03
Pest control	.4	.5	84.00		84	1,105.10		525	.02	.02
Grounds	.1	.2	30.00		45	549.83		1,422	.01	.01
Buildings and exterior	.2	.6	33.66		41	1,447.36		1,188	.01	.03
Heating and air conditioning	.7	1.7	161.25		510	4,007.24		4,056	.04	.08
Plumbing	2.3	1.9	514.78		329	4,653.89		3,999	.12	.09
Appliances	1.3	.6	298.59		358	1,492.99		1,870	.07	.03
Doors, windows, locks, and keys	.1	.3	19.33		4–	661.04		1,207	.00	.01
Pool cleaning and supplies	.1	.2	26.20		110	515.99		1,001	.01	.01
Pool repair	.0	.1	.00			183.62		523	.00	.00
Electrical	1.9	.9	425.00		54	2,033.22		1,078	.10	.04
Supplies	.1	.1	30.64			310.24		534	.01	.01
Fire prevention	.0	.1	7.72			143.85		97	.00	.00
Signs	.0	.1	.00			161.75		102	.00	.00
Total maintenance and repair	12.7	11.9	$ 2,831.52	$ 2,100	$ 2,497	$ 28,443.64	$ 25,200	$ 26,137	$ .64	$ .53

Unit Make Ready										
Cleaning	.0	.1	$ .00		29	$ 171.00		121	$ .00	$ .00
Painting and patching	.2	.5	52.01		91	1,274.62		1,655	.01	.02
Carpets and drapes	.0	.3	.00		46	1,887.45		1,243	.00	.04
From deposit account	.1	.0	27.94			5.12		824	.01	.00
Total unit make ready	.4	1.4	$ 79.95	$ 420	$ 166	$ 3,338.19	$ 5,040	$ 4,411	$ .02	$ .06
Furniture expense										
Moving furniture	.0	.1	$ .00		$ 11	218.01		218	$ .00	$ .00
Furniture repair	.0	.1	.00			226.75		109	.00	.00
Total Furniture Expense	.0	.2	$ .00	$ 84	$ 11	$ 444.76	$ 1,008	432	$ .00	$ .01
Utilities										
Gas	6.7	4.5	$ 1,497.61	$ 1,050	$ 1,021	$ 10,858.44	$ 12,600	10,520	$ .34	$ .20
Electricity	.0	1.1	.00	250	183	2,719.06	3,000	2,555	.00	.05
Water	.0	2.1	.00	378	441	4,905.56	4,536	4,348	.00	.09
Waste water	.0	1.6		372	369	3,710.21	4,464	3,214	.00	.07
Trash	.8	1.0	181.00	190	201	2,281.00	2,280	1,887	.04	.04
Telephone	.1	.1	27.52	25	23	311.97	300	250	.01	.01
TV cable	.6	.7	129.45	130	129	1,558.40	1,560	1,422	.03	.03
Long distance	.1–	.0	15.57–		6	5.48–		49	.00	.00
Total utilities	8.2	11.0	$ 1,820.01	$ 2,395	$ 2,373	$ 25,339.16	$ 28,740	24,245	$ .41	$ .49
General and Administrative										
Managers wages	3.4	3.3	$ 752.35		$ 571	$ 7,840.72		7,360	$ .17	$ .15
Employee bonus	.2	.2	34.44		138	558.31		164	.01	.01
Rental allowance	1.8	1.7	390.00		390	4,168.00		4,200	.09	.08
Employee taxes	.5	.3	75.16		65	800.33		788	.02	.01
Employee insurance	.5	.4	111.16		97	949.39		795	.03	.02
Manager electricity	.0	.2	.00		30	586.62		590	.00	.01
Manager training	.0	.1	.00		21	207.50		242	.00	.01
Management fees	5.3	5.0	1,170.63		1,139	12,046.71		10,604	.26	.23
Locator fees	.6	.3	130.00			741.25		1,330	.03	.03
Advertising	.1	.9	26.20		74	2,254.54		1,488	.01	.04
Promotion	.0	.1	.00			163.32		68	.00	.00
Legal and accounting	.6	.7	125.00		125	1,660.88		1,352	.03	.03
Dues and subscription	.0	.0	10.00			10.00		85	.00	.00
Office supplies	.1	.1	24.29			276.59		325	.01	.01
Bank charges	.0	.0	.95			.95		9	.00	.00
Total general & admin.	12.8	13.5	$ 2,850.18	$ 2,772	$ 2,650	$ 32,265.11	$ 33,264	$ 30,053	$ .64	$ .60
Total Operating Expenses	43.3	48.3	$ 9,652.66	$ 9,842	$ 9,768	$ 115,682.86	$ 118,104	$ 108,138	$ 2.17	$ 2.17
NET OPERATING INCOME	61.7	52.3	$ 13,759.85	$ 10,011	$ 13,029	$ 125,251.36	$ 120,132	$ 103,032	$ 3.09	$ 2.35

(continues)

EXHIBIT 16-5. (Continued)

	% POSSIBLE		MONTH			YEAR TO DATE			Per Month	Sq. Ft. Y-T-D
	MO.	Y-T-D	December	Budget	November	December	Budget	12-31-79		
INTEREST AND DEPRECIATION										
First mortgage interest	20.2	22.8	$ 4,502.00			$ 54,525.85			$1.01	$1.02
Depreciation allowance	17.1	19.1	3,806.41			45,676.92			.86	.86
Depreciation/current year improvements	.1	.3	$ 28.64			725.65			.01	.01
Total interest/depreciation	37.4	42.1	$ 8,337.05			$100,928.42			$1.88	$1.89
TAXABLE INCOME	24.3	10.2	$ 5,422.80			$ 24,322.94			$1.22	$ .46
CAPITAL IMPROVEMENTS										
Capital replacement	.0	.1	$ .00			$ 157.93			$ .00	$ .00
Furniture purchase	.0	1.3	.00			3,081.95			.00	.06
Appliance replacement	.4	.1	77.50			112.50			.02	.00
Drape replacement	.0	.2	.00			431.64			.00	.01
Hot water heater replacement	.0	.7	.00			1,642.76			.00	.03
Casualty loss/recovery	.0	.1–	.00			334.90–			.00	.01–
HVAC replacements	.9	.9	208.89			2,164.47			.05	.04
Total capital improvements	1.3	3.0	$ 286.39			$ 7,256.35			$ .06	$ .14

EXHIBIT 16-6. Aspen Wood Balance Sheet, as of December 31, 1980

	Balance 12-31-80	Balance 12-31-79	NET CHANGE December	NET CHANGE To Date
ASSETS				
Owners cash balance	$ 1,456.13	$ 1,336.62	$ 143.40	$ 119.51
Taxes and insurance escrow	22,008.81	2,160.33	1,657.79	19,848.48
Operating invested cash	35,156.21	14,089.28	1,000.00	21,066.93
Employee advances		23.42—	29.65—	23.42
Land	84,027.00	84,027.00		
Buildings, 5–7 years	173,619.60	173,619.60		
Buildings, 8–10 years	155,047.93	155,047.93		
Buildings, 25–30 years	461,239.50	461,239.50		
Equipment	68.75	68.75		
Personal property	59,174.21	59,174.21		
Accumulated depreciation	453,030.70—	406,628.13—	3,835.05—	46,402.57—
Total Assets	$538,767.44	$544,111.67	$1,063.51—	$ 5,344.23—
LIABILITIES AND EQUITY				
Liabilities				
Prepaid rent		$ 445.00		$ 445.00—
Accounts payable		185.00		185.00—
Taxes and insurance payable	$ 20,921.29		$ 950.09—	20,921.29
First mortgage payable	719,069.49	733,565.60	1,249.83—	14,496.11—
Total liabilities	$739,990.78	$734,195.60	$2,199.92—	$ 5,795.18
Equity				
Owner's equity	$210,000.00	$210,000.00		$28,206.00—
Owner's withdrawals	69,377.01—	41,171.01—	$4,000.00—	17,066.59
Retained earnings	341,846.33—	358,912.92—	5,136.41	$11,139.41—
Total equity	$201,223.34—	$190,083.93—	$1,136.41	$ 5,344.23—
Total Liability and Equity	$538,767.44	$544,111.67	$1,063.51—	$ 5,344.23—

477

17

Termination of the Investment

Terminating the investment is the last step in the ownership cycle. Methods of disposal are limited only by the imagination, the law, and economic and financial feasibility. The transfer of ownership rights may be brought about by, among other things, sale, exchange, gift, will or intestacy, condemnation, foreclosure, and casualty loss.

Here, for convenience, the terms *disposal, disposition,* and *termination* will be used interchangeably, even though some terminations are voluntary and others involuntary.

Generally, an investor disposes of real estate because his or her investment goals and objectives have been achieved, because of failure to achieve those goals, because the good fairy has fulfilled the investor's wildest dreams of profitability, or for personal reasons. Since a strategy for investing requires that disposal—whether voluntary or involuntary—be planned, the first objective of this chapter is to discuss the role of disposal in real estate investment analysis.

DISPOSAL AS PART OF THE INVESTMENT CYCLE

Disposal of the investment produces a net reversion to equity (net sales proceeds). In the case of a raw-land investment, this may be the only significant capital inflow during the entire ownership cycle. In the case of an abandonment, it may staunch the flow of operating losses but yield no capital inflow. In our strategic planning process (see Chapter 8) we define terminating the property as (1) making the decision to sell, (2) reviewing tax considerations, (3) negotiating price and terms, (4) closing the venture, and (5) beginning the next investment cycle. This chapter is limited to the mechanics of selling, pertinent tax planning, the closing transaction, and other techniques for terminating the investment.

Effect on Rate of Return   To monitor investments during the ownership cycle, the investor looks at the sources of the returns and the certainty or uncertainty of projected future net income flows in order to be sure that the property will continue to meet investment goals and objectives. In addition, if the investor's personal financial position changes, this too could affect the pattern of returns. If a detailed sensitivity analysis indicates that a greater return would be gained from disposing of the property, care must be taken to arrange the disposition so that the internal rate-of-return objective is achieved.

The Effect of Transaction Costs   Transaction costs diminish the net equity reversion realized from the disposal. Ignoring termination transaction costs overstates the net reversion.

Although transaction costs vary, depending on the nature of the disposition, some typical ones are proration of real estate taxes, insurance, and final month's interest; the deed preparation fee; special assessments; seller's points to the lender; the transfer tax; releases from record; title insurance; and the broker's commission. These costs may amount to 8–10 percent of the total selling price. Since the typical transaction produces a net cash flow only after payment of the mortgage balance and federal and state income taxes, in a marginal situation transaction costs may cut deeply into the net cash reversion.

Effects on Exposure to Risk   Disposition, of course, ends risk. Acquisition planning projects earnings from operations, but actual experience in the market may be quite different because of the dynamics of the economy, the neighborhood, and the location. Thus, all real estate investors must regularly monitor the timing of the disposition. Adherence to a preconceived plan can be disastrous. The investor must be prepared to respond to changes in market conditions as they affect both the timing of the disposal and the most probable selling price.

The Need for Liquidity   Wise investors provide a liquidity reserve in assets other than real estate in order to avoid forced disposition. Adverse changes in interest rates, droughts in mortgage credit, threats of condemnation, and other external factors can prevent a planned disposition, or at least throw off its timing. Real estate investors are well advised to expect the actual time of disposition to be subject to considerable variance, diverging by many months (or even years) from the planned termination date.

Trading on the Equity   Trading on the equity is a speculative technique by which a buyer contracts to purchase real estate with the intention of selling and assigning the contract rights to a third-party purchaser before the date of closing. The buyer is "trading on the equity" in his or her good-faith earnest money deposit and attempting to profit from superior knowledge of market value trends. Obviously, the risk is that the buyer will not find a third party and will have to forfeit his or her rights in the down payment. Dealing with such speculators can waste valuable time for the investor and even result in the loss of a good transaction. Careful credit checks and lenders' references may help investors avoid such abortive transactions.

GUIDELINES FOR DISPOSITION STRATEGY

The factors that impel investors to dispose of property are many; some are voluntary, others involuntary. Efforts should be made to anticipate possible reasons for disposition and to respond with the appropriate sell or hold decision.

Generally, the reasons for *voluntary* disposition are optimizing the ownership or property life cycles, and portfolio adjustment.

- Financial analysis may indicate that it is time to convert amortized equity buildup into cash. Analysis may demonstrate that taxes are having a negative effect on profitability.
- A neighborhood may be changing, either for the better or for the worse.
- An owner may have "milked" a property because of financial difficulties, only to find that overcoming the conditions of deferred maintenance are beyond his or her resources.
- Realization of a gain or loss may be necessary in order to adjust the portfolio and reinvest in another opportunity. This could result from an unexpected offer.

Estate and family planning considerations may result in transfers for reasons of love and affection, charitable gifts, or arm's-length "bargained" sales within the family with the goal of effectively conserving accumulated equity. Sales may also be made for personal reasons, such as the desire to end a self-management role.

The reason for *involuntary* disposition is generally forced liquidation because of default on the mortgage, condemnation, or insolvency or bankruptcy from external causes. Also, a primary-career change may force a move to a remote location and the investor may be unable to find competent management. In other cases divorce, health problems, resignation, or death call for liquidation.

Evaluating the Decision to Sell

Our model of the investment analysis and financial structuring process makes it clear that through step 9 the investor is monitoring the property through financial reporting and the application of investment management principles. Therefore, before reaching a decision to sell, an investor should, generally, consider the urgency of the need to sell relative to optimizing the ownership cycle; consider the alternatives; analyze the "ripeness" of the market; consider the tax effects; and evaluate whether or not the time is right for beginning another reinvestment cycle.

Optimizing the Ownership Cycle   The results of a disposition are greatly affected by the timing relative to tax planning considerations. Consideration must be given to problems arising from recapture of *excess depreciation*, the investment tax credit, and capital gains, any of which may trigger the minimum tax provisions.

Friedman rates eleven important variables that can affect the so-called optimum holding period of a property.[1] They are as follows:

1. The overall rate of return, or the ratio of net operating income to the selling price at the time of purchase and resale.
2. The loan-to-value ratio. This ratio will change over time.
3. The mortgage interest rate.
4. The amortization term of the mortgage(s).
5. The owner's marginal income tax bracket.
6. The minimum tax on preference income.
7. The improvement ratio and cost of various assets.
8. The depreciation method used.
9. The depreciable life (or lives) claimed for income tax purposes.
10. Forecast changes in net operating income.
11. Forecast changes in property value.

The number of possible combinations and permutations of these variables is astronomical. Thus, it is dangerous to use any general rule to identify the optimum time to end the ownership cycle of a property.

Friedman suggests that the powerful, combined effects of depreciation charges and mortgage principal payments create two turning points in the ownership cycle that should be carefully observed. His study indicated that a property might be held at least until principal payments exceed depreciation charges. Before that time, the amount of taxable income will be less than the amount of the cash flow and at least some of the annual cash flow will not be subject to tax.

Friedman's second turning point seems to indicate that property should be sold when after-tax cash flows from operations turn negative, for at that point the owner is paying cash to retain the property. While greater after-tax proceeds may be realized from a sale if property is held beyond this point, the fact that annual outlays continue pending the sale may make deferral of disposition a poor choice because of the effects of the time value of money.

However, as Friedman points out, distress situations, the need to settle estates, and the *rate of return of alternative investments,* among other circumstances, impinge on the question of when to sell. Cooper and Pyhrr believe that appreciation in value, the need to renovate, and the "opportunity to pyramid" may be more powerful influences on the time to sell than those listed by Friedman.[2] The decision to sell or hold should rest on the anticipated future income (a subjective forecast) compared with alternative investment opportunities (another subjective judgment).

Individual investors must also consider whether or not a sale, at the time in question, is appropriate in view of personal objectives and obligations. Disposition

[1] Jack Friedman, "When Should Real Estate be Sold," *Real Estate Issues,* Summer 1979, pp. 68–77; see also Austin Jaffe, "Critique," *Real Estate Issues,* Summer 1979, pp. 79–82; and Reply to Jaffe," *Real Estate Issues,* Summer 1979, pp. 82–83.
[2] James R. Cooper and Stephen A. Pyhrr, "Forecasting the Rates of Return on Apartments: A Case Study," *Appraisal Journal,* July 1973, pp. 312–337.

usually requires time for preparing the property, negotiations, marketing, and preparing to reinvest in the next ownership cycle. Some people prefer to pay the opportunity costs of a lower overall rate of return rather than suffer the burden of selling at an inconvenient time. In effect, although a hold strategy may be irrational on the basis of financial analysis, it may be appropriate in view of overall life objectives.

Considering the Alternatives to Selling   Intelligent tax planning considers the many alternative ways of disposing of a property other than a cash sale. Planning for termination should include an evaluation of refinancing, installment sales, exchanges, gifts for reasons of love and affection, charitable contributions, and short-term trusts. In the case of a corporate owner, merger, liquidation, or reorganization of the corporation are alternatives. An option may enable the seller to effectively use the time and energy of a diligent would-be purchaser to achieve the seller's desired price with a minimum of personal effort.

Analyzing the "Ripeness" of the Market   Is the market ready for this property? There may be a drought in mortgage credit; interest rates may be at a peak; the dynamics of neighborhood change may have a significant effect on the readiness of the market; and construction cycles in relevant submarkets must be evaluated for the impact they may have. If the investor has been complying with good investment management principles, continual monitoring of the property management and financial reports should indicate the external factors that might affect a sale.

Exhibit 17–1 shows a simple technique for making an annual analysis of whether or not it is time to sell.

Tax Planning

Investors in real estate consider the effects of taxes in relation to the potential capital gain or loss arising out of a disposition.

For example, if the property value has appreciated as a result of inflation and the tax basis has been significantly reduced by depreciation deductions, one might want to consider a proper tax deferral technique, such as an exchange. On the other hand, realization and recognition of a capital gain tax should not be thought of as unwise if the disposition produces substantial cash after taxes.

It is also possible, with good timing, for a capital loss to be advantageous. For example, the owner of a Section 1231 business property that has an unrecognized loss would be wise to dispose of the property, recognize the loss, and take the deduction from ordinary income in a year in which he or she has experienced a surge in earned income from other activities. (See Chapter 13 for a discussion of dealer versus investor status.)

Timing the Closing

Sellers today do not necessarily seek the highest price obtainable in the market. Instead, their objective is to retain the largest number of after-tax dollars, or possibly the equivalent in other things of measurable worth. They will seek to time

---

EXHIBIT 17–1. Annual Analysis of Conditions That Could Call for Sale of a Property

1. ANALYZE THE CURRENT RATE OF RETURN ON THE PROPERTY

Since IRR is a projected average return over a future period, each year one should analyze the marginal return/risk relationships:

$$\frac{\text{Current annual cash flow (cash throw-off)}^*}{\substack{\text{Current-year equity investment} \\ \text{(original equity + equity buildup}^*)}} = \text{\% current annual rate of return}$$

---

* These analyses ignore appreciation or depreciation of value.

2. CONSIDER ALTERNATIVE TERMINATION OR HOLD STRATEGIES

Should you hold, sell and reinvest, refinance and disburse, refinance and rehabilitate, exchange, make an installment sale, sell and liquidate, or give to a trust? Make after-tax cash flow projections for each alternative. Computer simulations that consider projected appreciation or depreciation for a future holding period should be used. Do a sensitivity analysis.

3. CONSIDER THE RESULTS OF THE ANALYSIS OF ALTERNATIVES

Choose the alternative that seems to best suit the objectives and appears to maximize returns relative to risks.

---

the sale so that they pay the lowest tax on any profit; alternatively, they may seek to maximize the tax benefit from a loss. The most widely accepted view is that a sale is a consummated event for tax purposes when there has been substantial performance by both parties to the agreement. Passage of title is usually the significant event.[3] The holding period begins on the day *after* the property is purchased and ends *on the day* the property is sold.[4] Normally, the IRS will follow state law. It is necessary to check the local jurisdiction, however; a minority of states have held that execution and delivery of the contract of sale results in a consummated sale.

Defining the Nature of the Gain or Loss

A sale of real property may result in any one of the following:

- An ordinary gain or loss
- A gain or loss from disposition of an asset used in a trade or business (Section 1231 asset)
- An involuntary conversion (casualty or condemnation)
- A capital gain or loss

---

[3] Comm'r v. Segall, 114 F. 2d 706 (1940); see also Donald Borelli, T. C. Memo 1972–178.
[4] Arthur Andersen & Co., *Federal Taxes Affecting Real Estate,* 4th ed., supp. (1978), p. 144.

Investors must maintain good documentation to support the kind of classification they intend to use at the time of disposition. Separate records should be maintained for property held for investment, for business, for personal use, for inventory, or for development purposes.

Computation of the Selling Price   The gross selling price is generally the sum of the following:

- The cash received
- Any other amounts received (e.g., notes on mortgages)
- The fair market value of any other property received
- Any liens against the property that the buyer has assumed[5]

The net selling price is arrived at by deducting the expenses of the transaction. State and local transfer taxes are usually deductible in the year of the sale rather than being considered a reduction of the selling price.

Calculating the Gain or Loss   Gain and loss are two separate and distinct concepts. First, one must calculate taxable gain or loss to determine the capital gain tax, if any. Second, one must determine the *after-tax cash flow* resulting from the sale. The latter is usually called *net equity reversion* or *net sale proceeds*. Under current law, computation is relatively straightforward when there is no recapture of either excess depreciation or investment tax credits. (See Chapter 13.)

Basis

In order to determine the tax effects of a sale, it is necessary to understand the adjustments to *basis* that have occurred. The gain or loss upon sale or other disposition of realty is calculated on the basis and not on the difference between the selling price and the mortgage balance. Using accelerated forms of depreciation to maximize the tax shelter effects in the early years of ownership rapidly decreases the basis. Thus, the artificial losses that provide attractive tax savings in the early years may also substantially increase capital gains and the taxes on ordinary income at the time of disposition. Real estate investors should understand both original basis and adjustments to basis for effective tax planning.

Original Basis   The original basis of property is its historical cost. Cost is usually the price paid plus any acquisition expenses. Note that the actual cash paid at the time of purchase includes items that are not part of the acquisition price but, instead, are of an expense nature; for example, prorated real estate taxes, prepaid insurance, and utility deposits. On the other hand, the following charges *are* added to the purchase price and capitalized: broker's commissions, appraisal fee, survey costs, attorney's fees, title charges, tax stamps, option payment, the cost of outstanding leases, and costs of condition precedent zoning changes.

---

[5] Crane v. Cobb, 331 US 1 (1947).

Adjusted Basis   To calculate adjusted basis, sum the following:

- Original purchase price (or fair market value, whichever is lower)
- Miscellaneous acquisition costs
- Additional paid-in capital
- Any capital improvements to the property

From this figure, subtract depreciation (by chosen method) and distributions of capital to owners. (Note: The depreciation allowable under the tax laws reduces the basis *whether or not it is actually taken.* When allowable depreciation is not taken, the straight-line method is used to determine the actual adjusted basis at the time of sale. The tax benefit of depreciation allowed but not taken is lost unless the prior years' returns can be amended.) Under the Economic Recovery Tax Act of 1981 the IRS would probably impute the appropriate 35-year or 45-year life rather than ACRS.

In addition, whenever there is an acquisition of improved real estate, it is necessary to allocate the total purchase price between depreciable items and the nondepreciable (e.g., land) portion of the property. The evidence that is most acceptable to the IRS is value as determined by independent third parties, such as qualified appraisers. In certain cases it is possible to establish the market value of the land in the contract of sale. However, one should keep in mind that artificial values with unrealistic tax results will not pass an IRS audit.[6]

When Mortgage Is Greater Than Basis   This is a situation that requires expert legal advice and tax counseling. It usually arises when accelerated depreciation has reduced the basis of the property below the outstanding mortgage, which is being amortized according to a long-term schedule. However, it can also happen with straight-line depreciation if a property's value has appreciated and refinancing has occurred.

The tax trap in such situations is the possibility of a "phantom" taxable gain. For example:

1. When the investor is personally liable on the mortgage debt, a transfer to the mortgagee with a release of liability will give rise to a gain or loss equal to the difference between the mortgagor's basis and the amount of mortgage discharged.
2. On the other hand, if the investor has no personal liability, the loss will be limited to the adjusted basis in the property and is deductible in the year of the foreclosure. If the sales price of the property exceeds the adjusted tax basis on the property, there will be a realized gain. This is so even though such excess was paid directly to the mortgagee in reduction of the debt.

Before a debtor decides to give up a troubled project and allow the mortgagee to foreclose, both parties should consider the possibility of taxable

---

[6] Institute for Business Planning (IBP), *Real Estate Investment Planning* (reporting service), vol. 1, paras. 55,010.1, 55,010.2.

recognition of a phantom gain. (Review the discussion of abandonment and reduction and cancellation of a mortgage as alternatives to foreclosure; see also Foreclosure discussion in this chapter.)

Generally, adjustments to the debt structure may be a way to work out of this tax trap. Extending the mortgage term, adding unpaid interest to the mortgage balance, a moratorium on principal payments, or a more liberal amortization schedule all are ways of avoiding foreclosure and phantom gains. Of course, this assumes a viable project for which sound management, favorable urban economic conditions, and increasing demand will produce a turnaround.

DISPOSING OF PROPERTY

Disposition by Sale

A sale is a contract by which a seller transfers real property or an interest in real property to a purchaser. To constitute an enforceable sale, the agreement must meet the usual requirements of contract law in the *local* jurisdiction.

The interest in the real property subject to the sale may be fee simple absolute or any fractional interest permitted by public policy and the law. A sale may be absolute or conditional. It may be a voluntary agreement, fairly bargained and entered into by mutual assent of the parties, or it may be under judicial decree (e.g., sheriff's sale, receiver's sale). The seller should try to avoid warranties and representations that may survive a closing. It is best to plan the disposition.

Is the title insurable to the purchaser? Can the seller convey a good and marketable title, free and clear of all liens and encumbrances, except for the assumable mortgage and acceptable easements? One must make a judgment as to whether any clouds on the title should be satisfied in some way before negotiations are commenced.

Is the property physically ready for inspection by a buyer? One should avoid providing negotiation ammunition for the opposing party. Painting, fixing, cleaning, trimming, pruning, and so forth should be done to give the property a facelift. The books should be in good order. The tenants' lease files should be up to date. Warranty certificates on appliances and termite and pest control guarantees should be readily assignable.

Are market conditions favorable? Will mortgage market conditions support your intended sale, or will it be necessary to provide financing for the would-be purchaser? Since seller financing will reduce the cash produced by the sale, there should be sufficient liquidity reserves to handle the tax impact.

Straight Sale   Sales contracts, deeds, and all the other symbolic rituals that are absolutely necessary to the disposition of an interest in real estate are adequately discussed in most principles textbooks.[7] (See the latter for examples of closing documents and settlement statement transactions.)

---

[7] See e.g., Alvin L. Arnold, Charles H. Wurtzebach, and Mike E. Miles, *Modern Real Estate* (Boston: Warren, Gorham & Lamont, 1980), pp. 92–122.

In a straight sale, the investor receives the equity interest in the year of the sale. The taxable gain or loss on the sale is also recognized in the year of the sale. Whether or not there are any cash proceeds, of course, depends on the size of the equity interest.

Conditional Sale   Generally, in a conditional or contingent sale title will not pass until one or more specific future events have occurred. Examples are rezoning, delivery of financial statements, delivery of leases, ratification by probate court, submission of engineering studies proving physical feasibility of the proposed use, and so forth. In such a sale, the contract may even make the price subject to specified adjustments depending on the occurrence of future contingencies.

Buy–Sell Agreement   A buy-sell agreement provides the remaining participants in a business venture with an opportunity to purchase the interest of a retiring or deceased participant. Generally, the agreement does not force a sales transaction but, instead, provides for the retiring participant to offer the fractional share to the remaining participants, who may or may not buy.

A typical agreement will provide for the price to be an appraised "most probable selling price," with the appraisers selected according to a specified method. (The American Arbitration Association provides model contracts.) Insurance programs are sometimes set up to provide the necessary cash to carry out the agreement.

Sale and Leaseback   Although it is generally thought of as a form of real estate financing, this may well be a means of disposal of important rights of the investor. Sale-leasebacks of improvements are used by developers who are willing to sacrifice future appreciation in value, equity buildup, and depreciation and interest deductions in order to cash out their equity interest and move on to other developments while still retaining controlling possession of the site. Such users as commercial, industrial, and other business concerns will sell the leaseback property to institutional investors in order to free up working capital and obtain the 100 percent deductibility of rent payments rather than the partial deductibility of debt service. (See Chapter 14 for more details.)

Financing the Purchaser to Facilitate the Sale

Even though some foreign investors prefer tangible assets to American dollars, and thus pay cash for real estate assets—and some institutional investors do likewise—most investors finance a large proportion of the total purchase price. When market and economic conditions are good, most sellers can expect a creditworthy buyer to obtain his or her own financing. Sometimes, however, there are tax benefits to be realized by not receiving all the cash proceeds in the year of the sale.

Purchase Money Mortgages

A purchase money mortgage may or may not be a first mortgage. Because a purchase money mortgage is considered to be an intrinsic part of the sales transaction, in some jurisdictions it may take priority over previous money judgments. In some states purchase money mortgages are not subject to usury ceilings on mortgage interest rates, and the interest rate and the principal amount are subject to negotiation between the buyer and the seller. Those who use purchase money mortgages should take care to be knowledgeable about the special characteristics of such seller-to-buyer mortgages within the *local* jurisdiction.

Purchase money mortgages are a valuable tool in three particular circumstances:

1. Under conditions of mortgage drought.
2. When neighborhood or site conditions cause institutional lenders to reject loan applications, although such conditions may be tolerable to a buyer, for example, when the use is an illegal one under zoning regulations but it is known that the government authorities are doing nothing about it.
3. When the interest rate that can be obtained on the purchase money mortgage makes it an attractive long-term investment. Someone who is retiring, for example, might prefer a purchase money mortgage to cash.

Land Contracts

A land contract is a method of sale by which the seller finances the purchaser. The key element is that, until the purchase price is fully paid, the seller retains title and provides the purchaser with the right of possession *only*. In the event that the buyer defaults in making installment payments or in the performance of other mandatory duties, such as paying real estate taxes or insurance, or maintaining the assets, the seller declares the contract forfeited and may simply evict (eject, in some states) and re-enter and take possession without the use of foreclosure proceedings or judicial sale, as would be the case with a purchase money mortgage.

Some states have passed remedial legislation to make the repossession and forfeiture more equitable. Land contracts have become more popular in recent years for raw-land sales, recreational sites, properties to be rehabilitated, and farms, and in urban areas where lenders are reluctant to provide conventional financing.

Installment Sales

An installment sale is a method of disposal that provides for tax minimization under Section 453 of the IRS Code. Installment sales allow sellers to finance buyers.

In an installment sale a designated portion of the purchase price is paid when title is transfered; then the unpaid balance is paid to the seller by means of installment notes or purchase money mortgage financing. The seller must elect to use the installment method of reporting gain on the tax return for the year in which the real estate is sold.

The installment sales method provides an attractive advantage to both dealers and investors because taxes on a gain can be spread over future years rather than being paid in full in the year in which the sale occurred. The objective is to avoid calls for cash, particularly when a large profit results from the sale but the buyer will not provide the necessary funds. Since installment payments tend to level out the receipts there is an additional advantage for cash method taxpayers of lowering the marginal tax rates as compared with the ascending effect of a large receipt in the year of the sale. Also, by spreading the gain out over the years, it reduces the amount that is subject to tax preference and minimum tax computations.

In the past, taxpayers encountered serious problems in planning the handling of installment sales. However, the IRS Code was changed in 1980. Starting with sales made in that year, the initial-payment limitation was eliminated; there is now no restriction on the size of the payment that may be received in the year of the sale. The 1980 law also eliminated the restriction on installment reporting if more than 30 percent of the total sale was received in the year of the sale. Another significant change is the elimination of the "two-payment rule." A sale is eligible for installment reporting even if the purchase price is paid in a single lump-sum amount, provided that the payment is made in a year subsequent to the taxable year in which the sale is made. Thus, no installments are actually required. Another important change is that installment sale reporting is automatic for qualified sales, *unless* the taxpayer elects not to have the provision apply with respect to the deferred-payment sale. A seller may avoid installment reporting by electing to have the entire gain taxed in the year of sale in which he or she has capital losses, a net operating loss, or loss carryovers to offset the gain.

The 1980 change has placed greater restrictions on sales between related parties. In sales of depreciable property to a spouse or controlled party, all installment payments are treated as received in the year of the sale unless it can be demonstrated that the sale was not made for purposes of tax avoidance. Second sales of nondepreciable assets between family members may be treated as sales to the original seller when the second sale occurs.

It is worth noting that an investor may subsequently borrow against the buyer's installment obligation, using the notes as collateral, thereby realizing cash without accelerating the deferred installment payments.

Exhibit 17–2 is a simple example of a sale by the installment method. Note the economic consequences:

1. The series of payments represented as interest at $16,600 are taxed as ordinary income in the year of receipt.
2. The principal payments as received represent a complex mix of (a) a return of adjusted tax basis; (b) tax effects of the recapture of excess depreciation, if any; (c) tax due on the capital gain due as a result of the sale; and (d) the net profit, if any, received. Assuming that the sale qualifies and installment reporting is elected, the seller must report as gain (subject to the set-aside for recapture of excess depreciation) the portion of the installment payment that is actually received in the year that the *gross profit* bears to the total contract price.

The IRS concept of *gross profit* requires some explanation, because the gross profit portion of the cash that is received each year as principal will be taxable as a

EXHIBIT 17-2. An Example of a Sale by the Installment Method

Selling date: December 1, 1979
Price: $100,000; adjusted basis: $27,000
Down payment: $10,000
Contract interest rate: 8% per annum on remaining balance, due with
  principal payment
Installments due: end of year 1—$10,000
                 end of year 2—$40,000
                 end of year 3—$40,000

Schedule of Receipts by Seller Pursuant to the Contract

Year	Unpaid Balance, Beginning of Year	Interest on Unpaid Balance	Principal Payments Received	Total Received at End of Year, Principal + Interest
0	$100,000	0	$ 10,000	$ 10,000
2	90,000	$ 7,200	10,000	17,200
3	80,000	6,400	40,000	46,400
4	40,000	3,200	40,000	43,200
		$16,600	$100,000	$116,600

Analysis of Yearly Income from Sales

Each year the interest on the unpaid balance constitutes ordinary income as actually received. Thus, the $16,600 indicated above will all be ordinary income.

Allocation of principal payment as received:

$$\frac{\text{Gross profit}}{\text{Total contract price}} = \frac{\text{price} - \text{adjusted basis}}{\text{total contract price}}$$

$$= \frac{\$100,000 - \$27,000}{\$100,000} = .73$$

Gross profit percentage ratio (.73) × $10,000 received first year = $7,300, which is taxed as capital gain. The remaining part of the principal received ($2,700) is not taxed, for it is a return of capital. All other things being equal, the capital gain tax will be:

$7,300 × .40 × individual's effective income tax rate

capital gain. The IRS defines the *gross profit percentage* as the amount resulting from dividing realized gain (gross profits) by the contract price. Realized gain is the selling price minus the adjusted basis minus costs of sale. The contract price is the selling price minus the amount of any mortgages assumed by the buyer. Remember, if a buyer assumes a mortgage that is greater than the adjusted basis, the *excess* must be added to the basis.

In Exhibit 17– 2 we illustrate a scheme for determining (1) whether or not the sale qualifies for installment reporting and (2) how much of the installment received represents reportable capital gain to be taxed in the usual way. In our example calculations for adjusted basis are simplified in that the annual depreciation deductions have been deleted. In a typical case accumulated depreciation would be deducted to arrive at the adjusted basis.

Open-End Sales Contracts

When the entire price is contingent on future events, such as the success of a development, the parties should avoid the installment sales method and consider using an open-end or contingent-price sales contract. These methods are useful, for example, for a subdivider who is selling lots to a builder in a situation in which the price may vary, depending on the degree of success of speculative building. In this way the seller can recover the entire cost basis before reporting profits because the fair market value of the contingent sale is priced indeterminately. Sellers using this method should consult tax experts.

Deferred-Payment Sales

This is another means of postponing recognition of gain on a sale. Under this method no gain is recognized until payments received plus fair market value of other property received, including obligations of the buyer, *exceed* the adjusted basis.[8]

The key to determining whether or not this method is useful is to analyze the spread between the face value and the fair market value of the buyer's obligation. Only the spread can be deferred. Deferred-payment sales are beyond the scope of this book. Therefore, one should seek legal and tax counsel for further information concerning its nature and its appropriateness for terminating a property.

The Problem of Imputed Interest

Some sellers have attempted to manipulate the principal and interest in artificial ways in order to avoid taxes. In effect, if by increasing the price, the seller could report what would have been interest as a capital gain, the buyer would also benefit from a higher basis. Because some uncommonly low interest rates were appearing on purchase money mortgage transactions, the IRS persuaded Congress to stop this form of so-called avoidance. Under present law, with respect to contracts under which some or all of the payments are due more than one year from the date of sale, the contract must specify an interest rate of no less than 9 percent or, in the absence thereof, the IRS may use tables that result in imputing an interest rate of 10 percent (1981 tax act). It is expected that these tables will be revised to permit the IRS to use higher imputed interest rates. A sale by a dealer does not come under the imputed-interest rule. However, the rules against tax evasion would apply if evidence of fraud existed.

[8] See Caruth, 411 F. Supp. 604 (1976).

Auctions

Auctions are frequently used to dispose of hard-to-sell properties, farms, and other rural land, although this technique is being used more frequently in urban areas. An auctioneer does not make offers; bids are invited from those present, but no bid becomes binding until it has been accepted by the auctioneer. The seller may by preannouncement reserve the right to reject unsatisfactory offers.

In real estate auctions, since sales usually require substantial deposits, the seller must be in a position to prove good and marketable title and have the documentation on hand immediately after the auction in order to make settlement. Federal and state laws dealing with full disclosure and consumer protection must be complied with.

Partial Dispositions

Fractional Interests   Generally, it is difficult to find a market for stock in a small, closely held corporation, for a partnership interest, or for a tenancy in common when it constitutes less than a controlling interest in the property. On the whole, those who buy a fractional interest in a real estate investment should understand at the outset that they are in it to stay. Liquidation of a fractional interest prior to disposition of the entire property will be done in a buyer's market. The use of buy-sell agreements is a relatively efficient way to facilitate such a withdrawal.

Subdivision Lot Sales   Subdivision development is beyond the scope of this book. However, a few comments are worthwhile.

A land developer is similar to a manufacturer or a retailer in that profit generated by selling lots is usually taxed as ordinary income. However, developers face a longer cash flow cycle, and as a result they can apportion acquisition and improvement costs and report sales according to special IRS rules. They also can write off some expenses against ordinary income or choose to capitalize certain expenses.

Section 1237. This is a special provision of the tax code designed to protect investor status in a few subdivision situations. The regulations permit taxpayers who qualify under it to sell real estate from a single tract for investment without the income being treated as ordinary income merely because of the subdivision of the tract or because of active efforts to sell it.[9] Generally, the investor must have held the property for five years (unless it was acquired by inheritance) and may not make improvements that will substantially enhance its value. Surveying, clearing, construction of all-weather access roads, filling, and draining are not considered substantial improvements. However, construction of hard-surface roads and installation of utilities and street lighting are considered substantial improvements. Competent tax and legal advice should be sought by investors who want to meet the requirements.

---

[9] See Malat v. Riddell, 383 US 569 (1966), for an important discussion of dealer versus investor status; see *esp.* Biedenharn Realty Co., Inc. v. US 526 F. 2d 409 (5th Cir. 1976) in re subdivision sales.

Air and Subsurface Rights and Profit à Prendre   A partial disposition can also be accomplished by severing the fee into fractional interests—air and subsurface rights and/or mineral and timber rights. In some cases, conveyance of a fractional interest makes possible the highest and best use of the property. The Pan Am building in New York City, for example, is an outstanding example of the use of air rights. In other cases, such partial disposition is for all practical purposes a disposition of the economic value of the property for the foreseeable future (e.g., deep strip mining in Wyoming).

Disposition by Exchange

An exchange of real property can defer federal and state income taxes on all or part of the capital gain resulting from a disposition. Under IRS rules no gain or loss is recognized if property held for productive use in a trade or business or for investment is exchanged solely for property of a like kind. In addition to tax-free treatment, an exchange can result in a step-up of basis for depreciation purposes for some of the parties. In theory, a series of exchanges could defer taxable gain indefinitely, and if the exchange cycle lasted until the investor's death, a "stepped-up basis" could be achieved for the heirs and the tax on the basis at death might be permanently avoided.[10] In any event, exchanges are an inviting disposal alternative. (Exchanges are discussed in greater detail later in this chapter.)

Charitable Contributions

Some taxpayers may reap much more substantial tax shelter benefits from a charitable contribution than could be realized from a sale. When a property is located in a declining neighborhood, putting it on the market may not attract a buyer except at a sharply reduced "distress" price that would probably result in a long-term capital loss, but a transfer by gift to a charity may have much more profitable tax effects. A fair and ethical appraisal may indicate a market value far in excess of the current most probable selling price. In such a case, and assuming that the property is producing some cash throw-off after debt service, a charity may be willing to accept a gift and assume the mortgage.[11] Tax counseling should be sought in such cases.

Sale of a Personal Residence

Since the tax effects of the disposition of a personal residence are adequately discussed in most principles textbooks, we will not discuss them here. It is as-sumed that the reader is acquainted with the partial rollover rights that permit

[10] See IBP, para. 55,150.10. See also *Taxation and Exchange Techniques,* 2nd rev. ed. (Chicago: National Institute of Real Estate Brokers, 1972), and *Real Estate Tax Shelter Techniques,* Real Estate Portfolio no. 13 (Boston: Warren, Gorham & Lamont, 1977), pp. 45–53; Donald J. Valachi, "The Tax-Deferred Exchange: Some Planning Considerations," *Appraisal Journal,* January 1979, pp. 76–85; William J. Tappan, *Real Estate Exchanges* (Englewood Cliffs, N.J.: Prentice-Hall, 1979); M. W. Weinstein, "Tax Ideas—How to Approach Real Estate Exchanges," 4 *Real Estate Law Journal* 306 (1976).
[11] IRC §1011 (b).

deferral of capital gain when a home is sold. (Recently a yacht with bath and cooking facilities qualified as a replacement residence.) There is also a one-time, post-age 55 rule that permits exemption of up to $125,000 of gain from the capital gain tax. This tax policy is intended to promote home ownership. In general home ownership will continue to be preferable to renting as long as owners can deduct interest expense and real estate taxes from their personal income taxes.

Disposition by Will or Descent and Transfers for Reasons of Love and Affection

As noted earlier, there are many disposition methods, some voluntary, others involuntary. In every case the impact of state and federal tax laws and IRS rules and regulations, which may differ in important respects, must be considered.

Gift   A gift is a transfer of property by a donor to a donee without the receipt of value or other consideration in return. The two essential elements of an effective gift are the intention of the donor to make the gift and delivery of the property constituting the gift. In the case of real estate and other large items, for which physical delivery is impossible or impractical, delivery is made by means of a document of title (e.g., a deed).

Gift in contemplation of death. Under the 1981 Economic Recovery Tax Act any gift in excess of the annual $10,000 exclusion made within three years of a decedent's death is no longer to be included in the decedent's estate for tax purposes, regardless of whether or not the gift was made in contemplation of death.

Trust   A trust is an arrangement by which the party creating the trust (the settlor-grantor) places legal title to property (*the corpus*) in the hands of a *trustee* with the objective of having the property administered for the benefit of the *beneficiary,* who has the rights to the benefit of the property during the term of the trust. (Various kinds of trusts are discussed in Chapter 9).[12]

Gift–Trust/Leaseback   This method of disposing of property may be used by an upper-bracket taxpayer to benefit members of the taxpayer-settlor's family. The gift or trust is coupled to a leaseback of the property to the settlor. The rent payments made by the settlor-taxpayer become a necessary and ordinary deductible business expense and are income to the beneficiaries of the trust (presumably at lower marginal rates). Although the IRS will threaten litigation, the tax courts have found for the taxpayers as long as the gift met four tests:

1. The settlor must not retain the same control over the property prior to the gift.
2. The leaseback should require market rents. An independent appraiser's opinion may be desirable for IRS audit purposes.
3. The leaseback must have a bona fide business purpose such as the use by the lessee-settlor in his profession or business.

---

[12] See also E. William Carr, *Short-Term Trusts* (Englewood Cliffs, N.J.: Prentice-Hall, 1973).

4. The settlor must not retain during the lease term a disqualifying "equity" in the property, such as a vested right to regain ownership.[13]

Options

Options are an extremely important technique in both acquisition and disposal. An option is a written contract by means of which an optionor grants, for good and valuable consideration, the optionee the exclusive right to buy, sell, or lease a particular parcel of real estate at a specified (or determinable) price during a specified period. In effect, the property is sold on a condition to be performed.

Options allow the option holder to tie up the property until financial analysis and market research have been completed. An option holder can control large parcels of property with only small cash outlays at risk. Agreements of sale may also be used for this purpose.

An optionor should take care to provide that the cash consideration to be forfeited is sufficient to pay for the time value of the investment and the loss of other opportunities during the option period. This, of course, is a matter of negotiation.

Options may take several forms. The simplest is the *fixed option,* which entitles the optionee to buy the property for a fixed price during the option period. *Step-up options* require the purchase price to increase periodically over time, often at the time of renewal. Step-up options are frequently used in rolling and long-term options.

Rolling options are commonly used by developers of subdivisions. The option normally covers a number of contiguous tracts, rolling from one tract to another as the developer progresses with the building of the subdivision. The option price usually steps up over time so that the landowner can share in the success of the venture, and to protect against loss in value due to inflation and the passage of time.

A *full-credit option* credits the optionee with 100 percent credit for the consideration paid for the option against the purchase price of the real estate when the option is ultimately exercised. A *declining credit* option provides an inducement for early exercise of the option because the percentage of the option consideration that may be applied to the purchase price declines over time in accordance with a negotiated schedule until it is extinguished by forfeiture at the end of the term.

Receipt of the proceeds from granting an option is not a taxable event for either the buyer or the seller.[14] No sale or purchase has been made. On the other hand, if an option is exercised, the seller treats the option proceeds as part of the selling price of the property and the purchaser adds the consideration paid to the basis.

The distinction between a contract of sale and an option is critical. If the

---

[13] *The Arnold Encyclopedia of Real Estate* (Boston: Warren, Gorham & Lamont, 1979), p. 853. See also IRC §§1239 (a), 267 (annotated), and Mathews, 61 TC 12 (1973). *Caveat:* Some Circuit Courts of Appeal disagree.

[14] Lucas v. North Texas Lumber Co., 281 US 11 (1930); Rev. Rul. 69–93, 1969–1 CB 139.

option consideration is substantial and full credit is granted toward the purchase price, the IRS may argue that the date of the sale was the date on which the option was granted, and this could adversely affect installment sale rights. It is important to take care that title remains in the seller until settlement.

If an option expires, the payments retained by the optionor become ordinary income in that tax year. For the optionee, the forfeiture of the option price is considered a sale of the option and, if it is a capitalized asset, will result in a capital loss. If it is a Section 1231 asset, it can be treated as an ordinary loss. Dealer status requires that the loss be treated as an ordinary loss.

An option holder may sell or exchange an option for a gain. If it was held for more than twelve months, it is a long-term gain (unless the holder was a dealer, in which case it would be an ordinary short-term gain). This can be an exceptionally profitable method of disposal for a promoter who sells to a syndicate.[15]

Abandonment

Abandonment is the act by which an owner voluntarily relinquishes all right, title, and interest in a property. Under federal income tax laws abandonment may give rise to an abandonment loss that may be used to offset ordinary income.

Abandonment is an important risk-avoidance tactic of disposition for distressed debtors. Recently some lenders have encouraged the formation of "take-out" partnerships, which take over the ownership of troubled projects with the intention of abandonment after a few years. This action may provide the lender with a respite until conditions change; however, it may be labeled a sham, abusive tax shelter by the IRS. Abandonment may also be viewed as an unethical desertion by the mortgagee.

Although the law on the subject is too complex for this book, it should be noted that abandonment is more than simply a failure to pay real estate taxes. There must be evidence that the owner vacated the property with no intention of ever returning to claim it.

A carefully planned and executed abandonment can successfully terminate a property with a deductible loss without the risk of "mortgage forgiveness," which is a dangerous tax event. The key is to achieve abandonment without a discharge of the indebtedness. One way to abandon is by means of a voluntary conveyance of title without consideration to the mortgagee. A quitclaim deed may suffice. In effect, it must be a surrender of the property without a discharge of the debt.[16]

Tax Deeds

Tax deeds are generally a result of abandonment by an owner of land. The usual procedure is to enter a lien for unpaid taxes on the public record of the local jurisdiction. If the lien is not satisfied within a specified period, the land is sold at a public auction. The buyer pays the bid price to the sheriff or other public official

---

[15] See IBP, para. 55,070.2; IRC § 1234-1.
[16] Crane, 331 US 1 (1947); Aberle, 121 F.2d. 1726 (1941); Tanforan Co., Inc., US 313 F. Supp. 766 (1970).

and receives a tax deed, which may or may not ripen into a title. The defaulting taxpayer is given a specified period in which to redeem the property by paying the purchase price plus costs, penalties, and interest. (It is important to understand that such tax liens are state and local jurisdiction claims. The federal tax lien is a general lien, and although it applies to all the delinquent taxpayer's property, liens for real estate taxes and assessments specific to the property usually have priority over all other liens, including the federal lien.)

Investors who buy at such tax sales often seek quitclaim deeds from the former owners for a nominal sum and then file for quiet title action in order to clear title and bring the property to marketable condition. Investment in tax deeds can be quite profitable, but it is akin to speculation and requires a thorough knowledge of local law and custom.

Involuntary Conversions

An involuntary conversion may occur when property is condemned or destroyed by casualty. An involuntary conversion may result in a loss, a gain, or a partial loss or gain. The gain or loss is computed on the excess of the proceeds over the adjusted basis of the property at the time of the conversion. Since the owner of such property has little or no control over the conversion, special rules are provided to alleviate the inequity of recognizing a gain under the circumstances in which replacement property is obtained.

The law has partitioned the rules in relation to involuntary conversions. Those resulting from condemnation or threat of condemnation are treated differently than other involuntary conversions.

Condemnation or Threat of Condemnation Condemnation is defined as an exercise of legal power by government to take privately owned property for necessary public use with or without the owner's consent but upon payment of a reasonable price (fair market value) to the owner.[17] Mere notice by a public official that a decision has been made to acquire the property is deemed a sufficient threat, as long as the property owner had reasonable grounds to believe it would result in a condemnation.

Disposition as a result of condemnation results in a much more liberal interpretation of the kinds of property that are eligible for replacement. In general, for properties subject to the threat of eminent domain or its occurrence, the investor can elect to invest in a wide variety of "like-kind" properties.

The replacement period for property subject to condemnation ends three years after the date on which the converted property was disposed of or the date of imminence of condemnation, whichever comes earlier.[18]

Other Forms of Involuntary Disposition The possibilities for the occurrence of an involuntary disposition are virtually unlimited. A squatter's adverse possession

---

[17] U.S. Department of the Treasury, "Condemnation of Private Property for Public Use," Publication 549 (Washington, D.C., rev. to date).
[18] Rev. Rul. 63-221, 1963-2 CB 332; Creative Solutions, Inc., 3-20 F. 2d 809 (5th Cir. 1963); S&B Realty Co., 54 TC 863 (1970).

in a remote rural area such as Alaska may ripen to a proper claim of title; a disgruntled co-tenant may force a judicial partition; divorce, death, insanity, disabling accident, or illness may terminate the ownership cycle; financial problems may result in a judicial sale.

Casualty losses. The rules as to the nature of the replacement property for casualties and the duration of the replacement period are more restrictive for involuntary conversions other than condemnation.[19] Generally, for an owner to successfully elect nonrecognition of a gain, the proceeds of an involuntary conversion (e.g., insurance proceeds from a fire) must be reinvested either in replacement property "similar to or related in service or use" to the property converted or in acquisition of the controlling stock interest of a corporation holding such property. The *replacement period* generally ends two years from the close of the taxable year in which *any* gain from the involuntary conversion is realized. Extensions may be applied for, however.

The long ownership period characteristic of real estate requires contingency planning. Preplanning can change a crisis-producing event into an orderly transition of ownership. Involuntary conversions are seldom the disasters they appear to be at first glance. Even if the property was an ideal "cash cow" with a stable future, conversion permits commencement of a new ownership cycle with the substitute property without the impact of capital gains taxes.[20]

Foreclosure

Foreclosure is the process of law by which a mortgagee, or others with an interest in the debt instrument, may compel a mortgagor-debtor who has violated one of his or her mortgagor duties to promptly redeem the pledge of payment or eventually forfeit right to the property. In many states the mortgagee may sell a property under a power of sale contained in the mortgage itself. In other states the mortgagee must apply to courts of equity for a court-supervised process resulting in a decree of foreclosure and a sale.

Generally, the proceeds of a sale of mortgaged property are applied first to indebtedness secured by the mortgaged property—assuming that it has priority on the record—and to foreclosure expenses, and then, in order of priority, to junior lien holders, with the remaining balance, if any, paid to the mortgagor-debtor.

If foreclosure is insufficient to satisfy the secured debt, the mortgagee may proceed to seek satisfaction of the deficiency from other assets of the mortgagor. However, it is unusual for mortgagee-creditors to pursue satisfaction of a deficiency. In fact, it is not uncommon for the mortgagor and the mortgagee to have agreed at the time of origination to a nonrecourse loan. Although foreclosure is deemed a creditor's remedy by the law, debtor-mortgagors may force the creditor to act, thus using foreclosure as a tactic for disposition of unwanted property.

Mortgage foreclosure presents a variety of tax consequences for both the mortgagor and the mortgagee. Even though the mortgagor-investor suffers the loss of property, a foreclosure sale is treated as a sale-disposition for tax pur-

[19] Rev. Rul. 76–319, 1976-2 CB 242.
[20] See Arthur Andersen & Co., pp. 233–243.

poses. Thus, it may result in a gain or loss to the mortgagor as well as to the mortgagee. The nature of such a gain or loss depends on the character of the property—capital asset, business asset, dealer property, or personal residence—and is measured by the difference between the net proceeds of the transaction and the mortgagor's adjusted basis in the mortgage debt.

To avoid ordinary income resulting from the reduction or cancelation of the mortgagor's indebtedness, the investor must carefully plan the transaction to qualify it under one of the following exceptions:[21]

1. The cancelation or reduction is made pursuant to the orders of bankruptcy or reorganization proceedings.
2. A purchase money mortgagor voluntarily reconveys to the mortgagee, or the purchase money mortgagee voluntarily reduces the original price of the property.
3. The mortgagee makes a gift of the reduction to the mortgagor.
4. The mortgagor can prove insolvency both before and after the debt is discharged.
5. The mortgagor *ex ante* elects to have the amount of the debt cancelation reduce the basis of the property and thus be excluded from income.
6. The mortgagor abandons the property to the mortgagee without discharge of the debt. Thus, there is no sale or exchange.

Foreclosure is usually thought of as an ancient remedy encrusted by embellishments resulting from debtor-creditor battles through the centuries. Under the commerce clause, Congress could pass remedial legislation to simplify and unify legal precedent instead of allowing mortgage and foreclosure procedures to be peculiar to local jurisdictions.

There are many ramifications of foreclosure, such as equity of redemption, statutory redemption, foreclosure by sale, and deeds in lieu of foreclosure. Any real estate investor with a substantial portfolio should be knowledgeable about mortgage law in appropriate jurisdictions.[22]

An important note of caution concerns the possibility of phantom gain resulting in ordinary income for partners in real estate investments. Generally, an increase in a partner's share of partnership liabilities will increase the basis of his or her interest.[23] The opposite result will occur when the partner is relieved of a personal obligation.[24] Partnerships may anticipate some of these problems by mutual agreement as to special allocations of capital gains and losses.[25] In most

---

[21] Foreclosure as sale: Hamel, 311 US 504 (1941); discharge or reduction as phantom gain: Regs. 1.61-12; debt reduction as gift: Liberty Mirror Works, 3 TC 1018 (1944) (Acq.); purchase money mortgage reduction: Killian Company, 128 F.2d 433 (1942); insolvency: Dallas Transfer, 70 F.2d 95 (1934); election to reduce basis: Regs. 1,108(a) 1, 1.1017-1(a); also Hotel Astoria, 42 BTA 759 (1940) (Acq.); for Abandonment, see note 18.

[22] See Robert Kratovil and Raymond J. Werner, *Real Estate Law,* 7th ed. (Englewood Cliffs, N.J.: Prentice-Hall, 1979); see also Kratovil, *Modern Mortgage Law and Practice* (Englewood Cliffs, N.J.: Prentice-Hall, 1972).

[23] IRC §752(a) (annotated).

[24] IRC §752(b) (annotated).

[25] IRC §704(c)(2) (annotated).

cases limited partners may increase their basis and still limit their liability by using nonrecourse debt, an obligation that can be satisfied only by partnership assets. However, since partnership allocations of income gains, losses, deductions, or credits will be followed for tax purposes only if they have a "substantial economic effect," reduction and cancelation of mortgage debt must be carried out with great care by an attorney and an accountant.[26]

EXCHANGES

Taxes act as a deterrent to many people who want to dispose of their property. The Internal Revenue Code allows an escape from this binding situation for those who wish merely to exchange investment properties rather than converting property into cash or other assets. If two or more owners exchange like-kind properties of equal value, all taxes from the transaction are deferred until there is an actual sale. When the properties are not of equal value or the parties' equities in their properties are unequal, the parties balance out the exchange with cash or other property (the so-called *boot*), with an existing mortgage on one of the properties, or with a combination of these adjustments. Although exchanges of this type are frequently referred to as "tax free," this is inaccurate, since

1. taxes on the realized gains are merely deferred until the occurrence of a taxable event.
2. to the extent that unlike assets (such as cash) are included in the deal to offset unequal property values, a portion of the transaction will be taxable.
3. in multiple exchanges, some parties to the transaction may not be eligible for tax deferment.

A tax-deferred exchange may occur any time two or more investors with real property decide to change their holdings. As long as the intention of the parties is exchange (rather than liquidation), a transaction that is eligible for tax deferment may take any of several forms.

Section 1031 Exchanges   Generally, a broker identifies opportunities for multiple transactions among his or her current listings. Nationwide, computerized, multiple listing services like the NAR National Property Exchange Section of the Realtors Marketing Institute may facilitate the setting up of multiple exchanges.

The advantage of a multiple exchange is the greater probability that all parties will achieve their particular objectives in the transaction. For example, a developer may trade a completed project to the owner of raw land, who exchanges the project for a more mature income-producing property. Even more flexibility is introduced by the fact that some parties in the exchange may qualify under Section 1031 even though others do not. Although an owner who wants to liquidate an investment may receive no direct tax advantages, he or she may benefit by receiving a higher price than would be possible from a straight sale (i.e.,

---

[26] See Arthur Andersen & Co., p. 354; see also S. C. Orrisch, 55 TC 395 (1970), aff'd per curiam, 31 AFTR2d 73-1069 (9th Cir. 1973) for related matter.

the property may be more valuable to a purchaser involved in an exchange than otherwise).

Why Exchange?

Tax benefits may be achieved if a property disposition is arranged as an exchange. For the transaction to make sense, however, there must be some economic advantage besides tax savings to the parties making the exchange.

Changes in Investor Objectives Provided that a transaction for a desirable parcel can be arranged, an exchange can permit an investor to improve his or her portfolio without loss of equity or investment continuity. For example,

1. An investor who wants to reduce management responsibilities may exchange property used in his or her business for income property upon retirement.
2. A property owner who is relocating to another city may want to find a replacement investment close at hand.
3. An investor who wants to sell or refinance may find that the present parcel is not ideally suited to these purposes. An exchange, however, may be used to acquire another parcel that can be sold outright.
4. An investor may want to exchange non-income-producing real estate (e.g., raw land) for income-producing property.
5. Changes in an investor's ordinary income may increase the need for tax shelter. If an exchange increases the depreciable basis of a property, it also increases depreciation deductions. Exchanges may be arranged so as to obtain properties with higher debt (to increase interest expense and total value), a higher building-to-land allocation, or a shorter useful life, or of a type that is eligible for accelerated depreciation methods.

Changes in Investment Performance Risk, income, and other investment features may change dramatically over the ownership cycle. Therefore, investors may want to replace properties that no longer satisfy investment objectives. For example:

1. A developer may want to exchange a completed project for new development sites.
2. A farmer may want to exchange land that is suitable for development for new farm land.
3. A large-scale developer may want to consolidate land inventory into one contiguous parcel.
4. An investor may want to improve cash return by leveraging accrued equity buildup and value appreciation.
5. An investor may want to convert a portion of equity into cash.

Advantages of Exchange If an exchange can be arranged, much or all of the capital gains tax levied on a sale may be postponed. This tactic provides several benefits:

1. *Conservation of equity.* The portion of capital gains that is not taxed in an exchange is forwarded to the new property in the form of a reduced tax basis. Therefore, when property received in an exchange is eventually sold, more of the gain will be capital gain than if the property had been purchased. Moreover, since this tax is not due until eventual sale, an investor may use the entire amount of the increasing equity to acquire new investments.

Postponing the taxes benefits in two ways: in the income production and value appreciation of a larger project and, when the taxes eventually come due, payment with less valuable future dollars. In effect, Section 1031 provides an interest-free loan from the time of exchange until the time of eventual sale.

2. *Continuity of investment.* Since an exchange is consummated as one transaction, the investor may keep funds continually active over the transaction period; thus, loss of income during the time required to dispose of one property and acquire a new one is avoided.

3. *Estate building.* Exchange can be an effective means of estate building. Contributions to the investment program may be confined to carrying costs (debt service and property taxes) and occasional broker's fees. Capital gains taxes may be deferred indefinitely, with the investor receiving the full benefits of an expanding equity. Of course, cash may be necessary to balance the equities of the transaction.

Taxes deferred through exchange may be escaped entirely upon death and transfer of the estate to devisees, when the basis of the inheritance could be adjusted to current market value. Thus, if the property were sold at the right time, capital gains would be zero.

Disadvantages of Exchanges   While exchange can be a useful procedure, it should be entered into with a full understanding of its repercussions. Treatment under Section 1031 cannot be elected. A transaction with the characteristics of a tax-deferred exchange must be treated as a 1031 exchange. Therefore, an investor who does not desire tax deferment must be careful to structure the deal to avoid designation as an exchange.

Why avoid 1031 status? Section 1031 provides for nonrecognition not only of gains but of losses as well. Should one of the parties in an exchange dispose of property at a value below the basis, the loss could not be written off.

An investor who wants to increase depreciation deductions for maximum cash flow may also wish to avoid Section 1031. Under the law the basis of acquired property is reduced by an amount equal to the unrecognized (deferred) gain. A taxpayer may prefer to pay capital gains taxes immediately in order to start a new property life cycle and thus a new depreciation cycle.

Basic Considerations in Structuring an Exchange

In most exchanges only a technically qualified broker can arrange the deal to the satisfaction of all parties. Sometimes it is necessary to find additional property owners to enlarge the number of exchanges and provide each participant with the best available match.

In any exchange transaction the following points should be considered:

1. The transaction must be intended as an exchange and must comply with Section 1031. This test must be applied to each party, since some may achieve tax deferment while others do not.
2. In order to minimize taxable gains, properties should be matched so as to minimize the necessity for exchanging unlike properties (boot).
3. Parties who realize a capital loss must be isolated from the transaction in order to allow recognition of the loss.
4. The property received by each party should represent a sound investment vis-à-vis his or her own objectives.

Legal Qualification for Section 1031 Treatment   Exchange transactions must follow both the letter and the spirit of the law. It is not uncommon for exchanges to be disqualified on technicalities. In *Halpern* the court upheld a disqualification with the remark that "there is no equity in tax law; conformity to the law is the requirement."[27]

Actual Exchange of Properties   For an exchange to occur, the parties in the transaction must simultaneously convey properties to which they hold title in exchange for other properties that they did not originally own. A bona fide exchange need not be as simple and pure as the case in which several property owners agree to swap. Often what begins as a sale may be converted into an exchange. However, the conversion must be handled precisely to avoid disqualifying results. For example, in *Alderson*[28] a sale was converted into an exchange by requiring the purchaser to acquire a new property (chosen by the Aldersons) to trade for their property. This arrangement was ruled acceptable on the grounds that the Aldersons *stipulated* their preference for an exchange and the potential buyer actually took title to the new property prior to the exchange.

The procedure used in the exchange can be crucial. In the case of *Carlton*[29] a development company that wanted to acquire the taxpayer's property agreed to find a replacement property for exchange. To save title transfer taxes, however, the company merely assigned the contract to the taxpayer at the closing. The transaction was ruled a separate sale and purchase, since the company never took title to the new property.

In a multiparty exchange, it is often necessary to require some party to temporarily take title to property and pass it on to another party. It is important that these "conduits" actually take title and that each part of the exchange be made contingent on all other parts. In *Halpern*[30] these procedures were not explicitly followed and resulted in a transaction separated into an exchange and a consequent sale.

Timing is also important for an exchange to be valid. Under Section 1031

[27] B. Halpern, 286 F. Supp 255 (1968).
[28] Alderson, 317 F.2d 790 (1963).
[29] Carlton, 385 F.2d 238 (5th Cir. 1967).
[30] See Halpern (note 27).

there is no provision for a reinvestment period. The exchange usually must be simultaneous. However, this requirement was successfully circumvented in *Starker II,*[31] in which an exchange of property for a promise to deliver property in the future was found to qualify because it was pivotal to the transaction's occurrence. Subsequent tax cases are supporting this precedent.

Relationship of the Parties   If one of the parties in the transaction is acting as an agent of another party, any exchange between the two does not qualify for Section 1031 treatment. The key test of this agency relationship is *who bears the risk of loss* for the new property *prior* to exchange. If a second party in the exchange arranges for property to be used in the transaction *but bears no ownership responsibility,* he or she may be deemed an agent. The courts, however, have made clear that for the exchange to be invalid, the agency relationship must exist in the particular transaction at hand. In *Baird*[32] a broker participated in an exchange by providing a replacement building. This was ruled valid, since the broker was not acting for Baird in the acquisition of the replacement property. In *Coupe*[33] the taxpayer's attorney participated, but the exchange was upheld since the attorney was not acting in an agency capacity.

Qualifying Properties in an Exchange   Section 1031 applies to only two classes of real property: that held for productive or business use (e.g., a farm, office space, factory, or resort) and that held for investment (both income-producing and non-income-producing property). Property held as inventory to be sold is not eligible.

For the transaction to qualify as a tax-deferred exchange, both the property conveyed and the property received must be eligible. Trading business property for investment property is permissible.

Disqualification of a property occurs when it is judged to be held primarily for sale. It is the owner's intention, as indicated by his or her actions, that determines disqualification. This judgment is based on two factors: the use of the property while it is held by the taxpayer and the timing of its consequent sale. Both points were used to uphold disqualification in *Bernard.*[34] The court upheld the IRS because Bernard did not use the land but listed the property for sale immediately after the exchange.

Property acquired in exchange frequently has been purchased by the other party solely for the exchange. This practice does not jeopardize qualification for the receiving party if that party intends to hold the property for an eligible purpose. Thus, in *Alderson* the taxpayer retained eligibility even though the other party had acquired the property solely for the transaction.

Exchange of Like-Kind Properties   Section 1031 applies only to exchanges of like-kind properties. This does not mean that each property must be of the same type or grade, nor that they must be held for the same purpose. The like-kind

---

[31] Starker II, 602 F.2d 1341 (1979).
[32] Baird Publishing Co., 39 TC 608 (1962), (Acq.) CB 1963-2, 4.
[33] Coupe, 52 TC 394 (1969), (Acq.) CB 1970-1 XV.
[34] Bernard, TC Memo 1967-176

criterion refers to the type of ownership rights in the realty. Thus, a fee title in any eligible property may be exchanged for a fee title in any other eligible property.

In most cases a less than fee title may be exchanged for a similar interest. Some examples of interests that must be exchanged for similar interests are leaseholds, life estates, and partnership interests. (A general partnership and a limited partnership are not of like kind.) In *Starker* we have an exchange of 1,843 acres of timberland for the recipient's promise to provide Starker with suitable real estate within five years or pay the balance at that time in cash. Thus, Starker exchanged for future rights to transfers of entitlement to property

Some partial interests have been ruled to be of like kind with fee titles. The following qualify:

1. long-term leaseholds (greater than 30 years)
2. leased fee interests (long or short term)
3. mineral and water rights

Boot Often some form of unlike-kind property is included in an exchange to balance the equities exchanged. This property, which may be cash, equipment, other personal property, or relief from mortgage obligations, is termed *boot*. The presence of boot does not disqualify the entire transaction from Section 1031 treatment. It does, however, affect the amount of realized gain that may be deferred, and may result in some capital gains tax on the exchange. The mechanics of calculating this effect are presented at the end of this section.

Effect of Disqualification of One or More Participants Failure of all parties to qualify does not affect the ability of any one party to claim benefits. Indeed, if this were not true, very few exchanges would be practical.

In multiparty exchanges it may also be possible that part of the transaction will qualify as a Section 1031 exchange while other parts are judged to be sales. This may be so even though one of the parties is involved in both transactions. In *Halpern* one exchange was converted by the IRS into a sale and exchange. Although the exchange portion qualified under Section 1031, Halpern was forced to pay taxes on the boot.

Valid Purpose Even though one follows the letter of the regulations in conducting an exchange, the transaction may still be disqualified if the procedure lacks a valid business purpose. If an actual sale is arranged to appear as an exchange purely for tax benefits, this is viewed as a sham use of Section 1031, and the courts have upheld the IRS's attempts to invalidate it. An example is *Smith*.[35] Smith sold his interest in one property primarily to purchase a second property. The transaction, though procedurally correct, was disallowed. Somewhat similar situations can qualify, however, as long as they are correctly labeled and occur in the proper order. In the *Alderson* exchange, after the contract on a straight cash sale had been made, Alderson found land that he preferred. The putative cash buyer (Alloy) agreed to amend the agreement, prior to settlement,

---

[35] Juhl Smith, 76-2 USTC 9541 (8th Cir.) 1976.

to provide that Alloy would acquire the land and exchange it for Alderson's property. If the exchange did not take place as contemplated, the original cash sale would be carried out as previously planned. Ultimately, Alloy took title to the property bought for Alderson, paid the balance of the purchase price in cash (boot), and exchanged (traded in) the property acquired to Alderson to acquire his land. The Ninth Circuit Court relied on *intention* and legal obligation. It found that Alderson's intent from the beginning had been to make a tax-free exchange transfer if possible. (Such intent must be provable from the record.) In addition, it found that Alloy was legally bound, by the amendment prior to closing, to pay cash or its equivalent (i.e., the property sought by Alderson). The court made it clear that acquiring property solely for the purposes of facilitating an exchange transaction was perfectly proper. As in *Coupe,* mentioned earlier, an outsider who was not acting as an agent arranged the exchange.

Generally, it is more conservative to arrange for the exchange property prior to the closing, although *Starker II* has raised new possibilities. Since finding exchange properties is so critical, interested parties have organized exchange clubs in many metroareas. The Realtors National Marketing Institute (RNMI) has an International Traders Club that lists exchanges.

Evaluating the Exchange

Evaluating an exchange entails determining the taxable gains and the adjusted basis of the new property. Taxable gains will result for at least one of the parties if unlike-kind properties are included in the exchange. Gains that are not taxed but deferred affect the basis of the new property and, consequently, future depreciation deductions and capital gains at a future sale. The entire process is simplified by the use of readily available forms. (See Exhibit 17–3.)

Calculating Realized Gain   The gain realized from an exchange is determined in exactly the same manner as for a sale. The gain is the difference between market value (as indicated in the transaction) and adjusted basis. Transaction costs—commissions and loan fees—may be capitalized by being added to the adjusted basis.

Balancing Equities   When properties that are unequal in value are exchanged, additional consideration must be included to balance the transaction. This "boot" is equal to the difference between the values of the two properties represented by the owners' equity. For unencumbered properties, the equity is the market value subject to the exchange. Commonly, the properties are exchanged subject to or by assumption of existing mortgages. Therefore, equity is market value minus the outstanding mortgage balance.

As an example, assume that properties A and B are exchanged. Both are valued at $100,000, but A has an outstanding mortgage of $50,000 while B has one of $40,000. The owner of property A, with an equity of $50,000, must provide boot of $10,000 in exchange for the $60,000 equity in property B. The $10,000 boot may expose the owner of B to a capital gains tax on the exchange. (Boot may be eliminated by either party's adjusting the outstanding debt prior to the exchange.)

EXHIBIT 17–3. Worksheet for Basis Adjustments and Calculations

Exchange Basis Adjustment

Name _____ Date_____

Property Conveyed_____

LINE NO		(1) PROPERTY		(2) PROPERTY		(3) PROPERTY		(4) PROPERTY	
INDICATED GAIN	1	Market Value of Property Conveyed							
	2	Less: Adjusted Basis							
	3	Less: Capitalized Transaction Costs							
	4	INDICATED GAIN							
	5	Equity Conveyed							
	6	Equity Acquired							
BALANCE EQUITIES	7	Difference							
	8	Cash or Boot Received							
	9	Cash or Boot Paid							
	10	Old Loans							
	11	Less: New Loans							
DETERMINE RECOGNIZED GAIN	12	NET LOAN RELIEF							
	13	Less: Cash or Boot Paid (L9)							
	14	Recognized Net Loan Relief							
	15	Plus: Cash or Boot Received (L8)							
	16	TOTAL UNLIKE PROPERTY RECEIVED							
	17	Recognized Gain LESSER OF L4 or L16							

Transfer of Basis

	LINE		(1)		(2)		(3)		(4)	
TRANSFER OF BASIS	18	Adjusted Basis (L2)							
	19	Plus: New Loans (L11)							
	20	Plus: Cash or Boot Paid (L9)							
	21	Plus: Recognized Gain (L17)							
	22	Total Additions							
	23	Less Old Loans (L10)							
	24	Less: Cash or Boot Received (L8)							
	25	NEW ADJUSTED BASIS							

New Allocation and Depreciation

	LINE									
ALLOCATION	26	Land Allocation							
	27	Improvement Allocation							
	28	Personal Property Allocation							

			PP	IMP	PP	IMP	PP	IMP	PP	IMP
DEPRECIATION	29	Estimated Useful Life in Years								
	30	Depreciation Method								
	31	ANNUAL DEPRECIATION IMPROVEMENTS								
	32	ANNUAL DEPRECIATION PERSONAL PROPERTY								

SAMPLE

The statements and figures presented herein, while not guaranteed, are secured from sources we believe authoritative. Prepared by_____

SOURCE: Courtesy of Realtors National Marketing Institute

Calculating Recognized Gain   Each party to the exchange is subject to capital gains taxation on recognized gain. *The gain recognized is either the realized gain or the total unlike-kind property received, whichever is less.* Therefore, a taxpayer who either realizes no gain or receives no unlike-kind property pays no tax on the exchange.

Unlike-kind property includes both net mortgage relief and boot. Net mortgage relief is the amount of the old mortgage minus the amount of the assumed mortgage. Negative mortgage relief is ignored. The total value of unlike-kind property is arrived at by subtracting any boot paid out and adding any boot received. The result is recognized gain if this figure is less than the gain realized. It is important to note that someone who is "trading up" in an exchange cannot offset the recognition of boot received by taking on a greater amount of mortgage debt.

Adjusting the Basis of the New Property   Taxes that are deferred in the exchange offset the basis of the new property. Property owners generally desire as high a basis as possible, since this increases depreciation deductions and recognized gains on sale. Therefore, the cost of deferring taxes is a reduced basis.

The starting point for determining the basis of the acquired property is the adjusted basis of the old property. To this are added the assumed mortgage, the boot paid out, and any recognized gain. From this figure are subtracted the old mortgage and the boot received. A good general rule when analyzing basis in an exchange is that the aggregate basis of all qualifying and nonqualifying property, other than cash, received in the exchange should equal the basis of all qualifying and nonqualifying property and cash transferred.

To demonstrate how the deferred gains are deducted from the basis, consider a simple exchange involving no boot and, therefore, no recognized gain. All realized gains are deferred.

	Property A	Property B
Market value	$30,000	$50,000
Basis	25,000	35,000
Mortgage	20,000	40,000

The equities are identical, $10,000, so no boot is required. If each property were sold, the recognized gain on A would be $5,000 and that on B would be $15,000. The new owners could take as basis the market value of the properties. No gain is recognized in the exchange of the properties, but the basis to the new owners must be adjusted as shown in Exhibit 17–4. The diminished basis for each property equals the gain deferred through the exchange.

Allocation of the New Basis   Before the adjusted basis of the new property may be used for depreciation, it must be allocated between the land and depreciable assets. This is done by allocating the new basis in the same proportions as the old basis. For example, assume that one received property A in the preceding example. The old basis of $25,000 was allocated $15,000 (60 percent) to the building and $10,000 (40 percent) to the land. The new basis, $15,000, is allo-

EXHIBIT 17-4. Basis Calculations in a Real Estate Exchange

	A	B
Basis of old property	$25,000	$35,000
+ New mortgage	40,000	20,000
+ Boot paid	0	0
+ Recognized gain	0	0
− Old mortgage	20,000	10,000
− Boot received	0	0
New basis	$45,000	$45,000
Basis if purchased	30,000	30,000
Deferred gain	$ 5,000	$15,000

cated in the same proportions: 60 percent, or $9,000, to buildings and 40 percent, or $6,000, to land. If one receives several properties in one exchange, one must first split the unallocated basis among the properties (in proportion to their old basis) and then allocate each piece to land and buildings.

Recapture in an Exchange Provisions for recapture of excess depreciation apply to exchanges as well as to sales. Even if accelerated depreciation has been used, however, there will be *no* recapture unless (a) there is some recognized gain or (b) the deferred gain in the exchange exceeds the market value of the property received. In either case, the extent of the gain that may be treated as ordinary income due to recapture is limited to the recognized gain. Thus, to some extent the recapture event has been deferred.

A Final Note on Exchanges

Exchanges epitomize the strategic objective that dispositions of real estate should be structured to benefit each party to the transaction. However, at present exchanges are so complex that many people are discouraged from using this technique. The development of conversational computer software programs should do much to make it easier to evaluate exchanges. In addition, professional assistance from a broker, attorney, or CPA can be cost effective. Careful documentation and proper labeling of each step along the way are essential to a successful exchange. The key is to accept the rigid reality of Section 1031 and to comply strictly with its requirements.

SUMMARY

Competent investors are familiar with the wide variety of techniques used to facilitate sale and maximize returns, such as conditional sale contracts, buy-sell agreements, sale-leasebacks, land contracts, auctions, installment sales, and exchanges.

The accumulation of wealth over an investor's life cycle is difficult under current tax policy. To succeed, the investor must work closely with CPAs and attorneys who are knowledgeable about transfers for love and affection, the use of trusts, and the use of wills in real estate and tax planning.

Many of the techniques discussed in this chapter require that the investor be knowledgeable about local law and the Internal Revenue Code. Options, tax deeds, foreclosures, involuntary conversions, and air and mineral rights all pose risk and return trade-off opportunities that can greatly affect the success or failure of a transaction.

Exchanges are one of the major areas of opportunity for wealth accumulation in real estate investing. Although Section 1031 transactions are complex, exchanges give the investor an opportunity for deferral of capital gains tax, offer some investors a chance to acquire a stepped-up basis with a minimum cash outlay, and provide an opportunity to replace a property that no longer satisfies investment objectives.

Although this chapter discusses different disposition techniques, only one will be used for any given transaction. The choice of a method depends on the investor's goals and objectives. In effect, terminating the property interest is part of the investor's overall strategy. As indicated in Chapter 16, one aspect of disposition is to keep your house in order—in real estate investing one should always be ready to move to negotiation rapidly when the right offer comes along.

Finally, once the termination process starts, the principals should agree to keep the lines of communication open. One should seek solutions rather than emphasizing problems.

ASPEN WOOD APARTMENTS

TERMINATION OF THE INVESTMENT

In 1980 the taxable income from Aspen Wood Apartments turned positive. In May 1981 Charlie Davidson and Clyde Boomer projected a taxable income of $30,500 for the year. Cash flow before tax was expected to increase to over $68,791 in 1981; however, the property needed substantial capital improvements to replace components that were nearing the end of their useful life. Boomer undertook a five-year capital budget study. The results showed a five-year schedule of capital expenditures as follows:

Year	Required Capital Expenditures
1982	$63,500
1983	62,500
1984	36,000
1985	10,500
1986	0

D&B commissioned a local MAI appraiser to estimate the current market value of the property at the end of 1981. On the basis of local market conditions, the most probable selling price was estimated at $1,600,000 if the majority of the capital improvements shown above were made prior to sale. Alternatively, a refurbishment reserve of approximately $100,000 would have to be deducted from the $1,600,000 selling price to arrive at an "as is" selling price, under the assumption that the new owner would prefer to undertake the capital expenditure program. The net proceeds from the sale of the property for investors in the 50 percent and 70 percent tax brackets were estimated as shown in Exhibit 17–5. Also shown is an IRR and present-value calculation based on historical cash flows and a required IRR of 20 percent.

If a sale with the assumptions shown in Exhibit 17–5 were negotiated, the investment in Aspen Wood would prove to be a highly profitable one. The focus now, therefore, must be on marginal additional return.

TERMINATION ALTERNATIVES

Since nothing can be done to alter past events, the focus should be on possible future occurrences over which the investor has some control. On the basis of prevailing economic and logistic conditions as well as physical and locational characteristics specific to the Aspen Wood Apartments

EXHIBIT 17-5. Analysis of Sale: December 31, 1981

	50 Percent Tax Bracket	70 Percent Tax Bracket
Estimated selling price	$1,600,000	$1,600,000
Less: Refurbishment reserve	100,000	100,000
Selling expenses	90,000	90,000
Net selling price	1,410,000	1,410,000
Less: Capital gains tax	168,936	236,510
Recapture tax	5,997	8,395
Mortgage balance	718,853	718,853
Net Proceeds from Sale	$ 516,214	$ 446,242

Internal Rate of Return/Present-Value Analysis

Equity investment, December 1974	$210,000	$210,000
Cash flows after tax		
1974 (Nov.–Dec.)	$53,115	$74,360
1975	52,325	73,255
1976	31,927	44,697
1977	23,604	33,042
1978	36,326	42,857
1979	23,244	24,071
1980	16,990	12,504
1981	20,752	14,653
Net proceeds from sale, December 1981	$516,214	$446,242
Internal Rate of Return	34.2%	45.1%
Net Present Value (@20%)	$106,241	$144,106

complex, five alternatives that were generally appealing to the partners were isolated for consideration:

1. Sell the property and reinvest the proceeds in another investment that would earn the required IRR.
2. Sell the property on an installment basis, providing the new buyer with a wraparound mortgage.
3. Refinance the property; then sell the property on an installment basis and encourage the selling investors to participate in a new venture.
4. Make required capital improvements; continue to hold.
5. Refinance the property; make required capital improvements; continue to hold.

Although refinancing a property was not generally a viable alternative in the 1981 mortgage market (interest rates of 15-19%), recall that the existing wraparound mortgage (at 7.5%) on the Aspen Wood property could itself be wrapped. A local savings and loan association was willing to provide wraparound financing to the present venture if they agreed to continue to hold the property, or if D&B agreed to become partners in a new venture that bought the property. This made possible alternatives 3 and 5 above.

An investment time horizon of five years was chosen for the analysis of all the alternatives. The amount of equity investment available for any alternative was considered to be the amount of after-tax dollars that could be realized from a straight sale of the property as described; that is, the investor's opportunity cost was measured in terms of the net proceeds of sale: $516,214 for the 50 percent-tax-bracket investor and $446,242 for the 70 percent-tax-bracket investor (from Exhibit 17-5). Only if an alternative produced an IRR greater than 20 percent on these equity dollars would that alternative be considered superior to a straight sale.

ANALYSIS OF THE ALTERNATIVES

A complete rate-of-return, ratio, and risk analysis was performed for each of the alternatives listed above. The techniques described throughout Chapters 9–17 were utilized to weigh the risk and cash flow return characteristics of each alternative, and to systematically consider the nonfinancial objectives of the investors in the aggregate. The financial analysis resulted in a ranking of the alternatives as follows:

1. Refinance; sell on an installment basis; encourage the selling investors to buy shares in a new venture.
2. Sell on an installment basis; provide the new buyer with a wraparound mortgage.
3. Refinance; make required capital improvements; continue to hold.
4. Make required capital improvements; continue to hold.
5. Sell the property; reinvest the proceeds in another investment that would earn the required IRR (this is the "base case" against which other alternatives are compared).

Alternatives 1–4 all produced IRRs greater than the required IRR of 20 percent and therefore were superior to the straight-sale alternative, in which the funds would be reinvested at the required IRR. Davidson and Boomer recommended these alternatives to the investors in the order shown, sending each investor a copy of the investment analysis and supporting documentation.

THE TERMINATION DECISION

Davidson and Boomer called a partnership meeting in August 1981. As expected, few of the investors had studied or understood the elaborate analysis provided or the performance measures on which the analysis was based (IRR, FMRR, and NPV were calculated for each alternative). Although the explanations were clear, the investors needed to have each alternative explained again, and the pros and cons summarized and debated again. A five-hour evening meeting concluded with the investors approving D&B's recommendation to accept the first alternative—refinance and sell.

[On January 5, 1982 the project was sold (closed) to a new joint venture created by D&B. About 90 percent of the investors in the selling venture chose to become investors in the purchasing venture; they purchased a 75 percent interest in the new venture. The other 10 percent of the investors chose to utilize their refinancing and sale proceeds in other ways.]

CONCLUSION

The Aspen Wood investment has now passed through each of the investment phases—origination, operation, and termination—as described in our ten-step investment analysis and financial structuring process. Through the use of this case study we have illustrated the many principles, concepts, and techniques that the investor must understand and systematically apply in order to be a successful managing equity investor in a dynamic and cyclical real estate environment.

IV

Property Selection

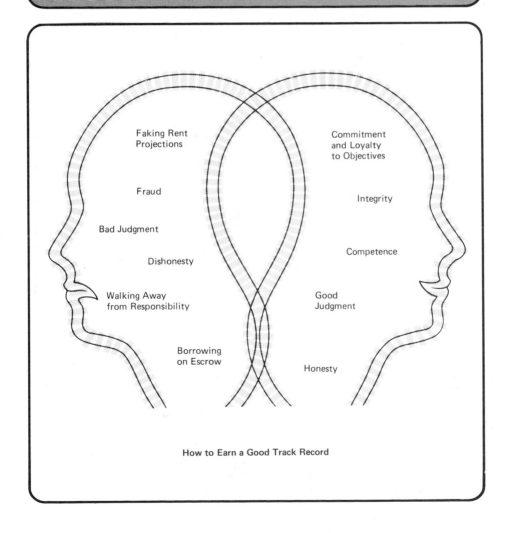

Faking Rent Projections	Commitment and Loyalty to Objectives
Fraud	Integrity
Bad Judgment	
Dishonesty	Competence
Walking Away from Responsibility	Good Judgment
Borrowing on Escrow	Honesty

How to Earn a Good Track Record

Different Property Types

LAND

Raw acreage
Recreational acreage
Subdivided lots
Farms, ranches and groves
Oil and timber lands

RESIDENTIAL PERMANENT FACILITIES

Houses
Apartments
Townhouses
Condominiums
Cooperatives
Mobile homes
Nursing homes

RESIDENTIAL TRANSIENT FACILITIES

Motels
Hotels
Resorts
Spas
Recreational condominiums
Convalescent homes

OFFICE PROPERTY

General use buildings
Office parks
Professional buildings
Trade centers
Condominiums

RETAIL AND SHOPPING CENTERS

Stores
Restaurants
Fast food franchises
Gas stations
Supermarkets
Strip centers
Neighborhood, community, regional
  centers
Merchandise marts
Airport concessions
Parking lots and garages
Car washes
Laundry facilities

INDUSTRIAL

Warehouses and mini-warehouses
Factories
Industrial parks

ENTERTAINMENT AND RECREATIONAL

Theaters
Bowling alleys
Golf courses
Golf driving ranges
Miniature golf courses
Arenas
Museums
Convention centers
Marinas
Target practice ranges
Baseball batting ranges
Tennis clubs
Racketball clubs
Massage parlors
Gymnasiums
Health spas

COMPREHENSIVE DEVELOPMENT

Subdivisions
Skiing facilities
Amusement parks
Retirement communities
Urban redevelopments
Rehabilitating existing projects
New communities
New towns

PUBLIC SERVICE

Hospitals
Schools
Public buildings

OTHER

Churches
Islands
Foreign investments
Exotic properties

18

The Property Selection Process: A Plan for Earning a Good Track Record

You're not worth much of anything in real estate until you owe at least a million dollars. . . . Lenders seem to base much of their decision on an investor's track record.

—*Anonymous*

No book can make a novice the equal of an experienced real estate decision maker. However, a beginning investor can build a good track record by using the analytical property selection process outlined in this book.

In earlier chapters we presented an overview of the investment decision-making process. In Exhibit 18–1 we present a general scenario designed to generate the best available data for identifying, analyzing, selecting, and rejecting or accepting a property. This is the *application* of the strategic process set forth in Exhibit 8–3.

Investors who have succeeded at intuitive investing might sneer in derision at our elaborate process of market and investment analysis. However, they are probably not aware that their experience has trained them to go through the same process intuitively, and that they have, in fact, accumulated a great deal of knowledge about the SMSA, the markets, and the neighborhoods in which they operate.

Such intuitive ability is of little value to an investor who is trying to succeed in an unfamiliar metro area. In the case of Hilton Head, South Carolina, for example, superior financial analysis could not overcome inadequate market analysis for a recreational resort whose success depended on capturing a high percentage of second-home buyers and retirees from distant urban areas who had unusually

---

EXHIBIT 18-1. Scenario for the Property Selection Process

INTRODUCTION (specific as to property type)

Definitions
Track record and trends
Advantages and disadvantages of investment
Types of investors and investor motivations

MARKET AND MARKETABILITY ANALYSIS

Demand analysis
Supply analysis
Projection of rents, expenses, and vacancies
Risk management and control techniques (market oriented)

PHYSICAL, LEGAL, POLITICAL, AND ENVIRONMENTAL ANALYSIS

Physical analysis—site, structural, improvements
Legal, political, and environmental factors
Risk management of selected factors

ANALYSIS OF OPERATIONS

Property management and leasing
Analysis of current operating expenses
Analysis of trends and uncertainties
Projection of expenses
Risk management and control techniques

FINANCING AND REFINANCING

Sources of funds
Rates, terms, and conditions
Estimating the costs of financing
Risk management and control techniques of lenders

TAXATION PLANNING AND TAX STRUCTURING

The nature of tax shelter effects (property specific)
Identification of variables to be structured in planning
Tax problems and uncertainties

DISCOUNTED CASH FLOW ANALYSIS

Rate-of-return analysis
Ratio and risk analysis

THE INVESTMENT DECISION

Footnotes, data references, and additional bibliography

---

long trip times. The financial institutions that put their faith in developers who had operated successfully by rule of thumb during the wild days of 1972–1974 seemed unaware that those good track records were more a result of rapidly rising rents coupled with level-payment debt service than of skill in market or project financial feasibility analysis.

During the 1970s major SMSAs throughout the United States experienced titanic disasters because an overabundant supply of mortgage credit was made available to developers who ignored economic and demographic trends. For example, the Omni-Mega structure in Atlanta, Georgia, a combination-use building (hotel, restaurants, offices, retail outlets), although now fully occupied, is capable of amortizing only about $47 million. Unfortunately, this is about $55 million less than was actually expended on the project.

DEFINING THE CONCEPT OF A MODERN TRACK RECORD

In these uncertain times, as a result of major changes in financing, such as the renegotiable note, to earn a successful track record one has to be a sophisticated investor. Lenders will rely on an investor's track record when they believe the investor can manage a property in such a way as to achieve a fair and reasonable rate of return.

What we are suggesting, of course, is that a modern track record will be based on a sophisticated form of trust. *Trust is a human judgment based on the belief that the person you are dealing with has integrity, competence, judgment, and commitment.* Not everyone has all of these qualities to the degree required by different types of real estate projects. *Funds for real estate should not be entrusted to a person who cannot provide definite evidence, such as character references and reputation, that he or she has integrity.* For example, the selection of a property manager who will handle the rent roll and pay expenses should be based on such evidence. Another reason for evaluating integrity arises out of the poor quality of the underlying data in real estate. Fraudulent tinkering with operating expenses and other variables can make a bad project look good. Unfortunately, honesty and integrity are not enough; a poorly executed, inadequately analyzed marketability analysis may be honestly done.

Trust is also based on an evaluation of competence. Investors must be satisfied that the people who evaluate the rate-of-return and risk relationships for a particular project have the necessary skills and technical training. Different types of property require unique data sources, references, and, to some extent, special analytical techniques. Whether or not an equity investor who proposes to buy and manage a project has the competence to do it is an important separate evaluation. However, even honest investors with technical knowledge about a particular kind of investment may lack good judgment regarding the timing of the investment.

Trust is based on a track record of good judgment. This a psychic quality, but it is very real. Because of a combination of intelligence, training, intuition, risk-taking capacity, and ability to evaluate other people, some investors make fewer mistakes than others. John Portman, Trammel Crow, and Robert McNeil, among others, appear to have these qualities. Informed judgment, based on fragmentary data and opinion, must often be relied upon to make many of the estimates that are part of real estate decision making. The investor must be able to discount and weight the information received on the basis of his or her opinion of the quality and bias of the source. Bias is often based on self-interest, lack of good market knowledge, or exaggeration of the significance of past events. For example, one must exercise judgment in choosing the appropriate population projection from the available U.S. Census trend lines, and one must use judgment in specifying the minimum acceptable rate of return by which to discount cash flows. It is judgment that decides whether to buy, sell, or hold. Data analysis provides a working hypothesis for a targeted project at the time of decision; the course of action is set by the use of judgment.

Interestingly, it is often true that the same people who have the quality of good judgment often have the final essential component of trust—commitment.

Trust is also based on the confidence that the investor has the commitment and loyalty to achieve the promised objectives. Some call this the guts to follow through when the going gets rough or, more politely, staying power. Investors and lenders need to satisfy themselves that the would-be investor has the will to fight for solvency and survival should externalities—mortgage drought, neighborhood decline, energy shortage—create difficulty. Exculpatory clauses are a desirable device for avoiding risk, but they aren't meant to be escape hatches for those who would abandon ship at the first sign of trouble. An ownership cycle is planned for a number of years; real estate investing requires patience and the willingness to be loyal to the goals and objectives of the commitment.

To develop a successful track record, investors must know the extent of their ignorance of the market and be willing to pay professionals to aid them in the decision-making process. Yet often an investor will make a $100,000 decision on the advice of a broker who is, in fact, the agent of the seller! Multimillion-dollar projects have been built based on market forecasts performed for incredibly low budgets of $5,000. It should be clear that the investor must properly allocate management time and budget for market, financial feasibility, and rate-of-return and risk analyses.

There are those who believe that the selection of an investment property is so different from one kind of property to another that it is not susceptible to a formal statement or definition like that in Exhibit 18– 1. During interviews with representatives of thirty-five successful equity REITs, each was asked to provide the forms and procedures used to rationalize and control the real estate acquisition process. Only a few used such processes. We will describe three of the replies here because they provide some insight into why a systematic process should be followed in selecting properties.

The first was from the operations chief of a REIT with one of the best records of profit stability in the field. He expressed annoyance with academics who try to make square pegs fit into the round holes of the analytical techniques they develop. He felt that three decades of buying and selling had taught him that there is no common analytical technique, that desk-bound analysis is dangerous, and that there is no substitute for field work in the neighborhood and physical inspection of the buildings. He felt that the investment decision process is intuitive.

The second reply was from the largest of the REITs, as measured by assets. Headquartered in Florida, it was a glamour stock in the early 1970s. The letter from the court-appointed receiver in charge of the remaining assets was tragic. In essence, he said that whatever the acquisition policy might have been, it was useless because 90 percent of the assets held are now in default and foreclosure. This REIT had suffered a 60 percent deflation of its assets in less than four years.

Finally, a small equity REIT in the San Francisco area provided us with an acquisition policy appropriate to its size of operations. There were two people on the staff. Generally the firm had $300,000 in equity per year. Its policy demonstrates awareness of the need to allocate management time efficiently, to minimize the number of properties to be investigated, and to control risk by way of the property selection process. In brief, the printed statement forwarded to its network of brokers, lenders, and developers set forth the following policy:

> This REIT is interested in purchasing office buildings valued at about $1,300,000. We will consider equity participations with qualified principals for not less than a 20 percent interest in larger buildings. All buildings proposed must be professionally managed by independent property managers and have no less than a three-year earnings record of achieving budget with 93 percent or better occupancy. The age of the building shall be no more than ten years. All records offered for inspection shall have been audited by a reputable accountant. The building shall be substantially occupied by a national or regional insurance company as the major tenant. Other buildings substantially occupied by financial institutions will be considered. The buildings should be located in the financial center of a growing SMSA of 300,000–500,000 population, preferably one with a viable and dominant CBD.

The two managers indicated that they don't get many proposals—which saves them travel time. They do devote time to keeping up with changing conditions in the SMSAs that they have chosen as their niche. They have a good track record.

SOURCES OF COMPUTER SOFTWARE

As you read the following chapters you will find that we have not strictly adhered to the outline in Exhibit 18–1, but instead have adapted it to the problem being analyzed. Furthermore, one should keep in mind that since these chapters deal with generalized types of property, the discussion is at the national, macroanalytic level. In your own use of the process you will be doing project-specific microanalysis.

These chapters should be useful in analyzing case problems. The authors strongly urge the investor to obtain training and experience in the use of computer software designed for real estate investment. The key to useful computer simulation of an investment is careful development of the input assumptions, for which the scenario property selection process is designed. Sensitivity analysis using discounted cash flow analysis (after taxes) will be especially rewarding. Note that rate-of-return, risk, and ratio analyses are the last step in the scenario process.

Good-quality computer software is available at low cost from the following sources among others:

1. **REIG, USA**™. Microcomputer software for a variety of desktop computers. Provides investment analysis for individuals, corporations, partnerships, Ellwood analysis, depreciation schedules, mortgage amortization schedules, and drills in the use of compound interest tables. (Proprietary: James R.

Cooper, 106 Peachtree Battle Ave. NW, Atlanta, Ga. 30305; $250 with documentation; limited license trade secret)

2. **RE001 and 004-Pyhrr—mainframe computer models.** Illustrated in Chapters 12 and 14 of this text; Fortran IV; batch processed; developed on Control Data and IBM equipment; attractive format; superior ratio analysis. [Contact: Texas Real Estate Research Center, Texas A&M, College Station, Texas (713-845-2036). For more information on this and other Pyhrr models, call 512-471-4368.]

3. **Educare/Radio Shack.** Both mainframe and microcomputer models. The mainframe models are centered on Mr. Cap, a sophisticated investment analysis model with versatile capabilities. Available through Educare network for time-sharing terminals. [For additional information: Prof. James A. Graaskamp, University of Wisconsin, Madison, Wisc. (608-238-8542)]

4. **GSU-Williams.** Mainframe computer model. Language: Basic; conversational for CRT or paper roll terminals. Developed as a successor to the Illini-Cooper Model by John E. Williams and James R. Cooper. Not as powerful as Mr. Cap, but performs well as an introduction to mainframe computer analysis for college students. (Contact: Prof. James R. Cooper, Department of Real Estate and Urban Affairs, Georgia State University, Atlanta, Ga. 30303)

5. **Gau-Kohlhepp OUPROB.** A probabilistic and deterministic investment analysis model using Monte Carlo simulation. (For additional information: Prof. George Gau, University of British Columbia, Vancouver, B.C., Canada)

6. **Value Analysis System (VAS)**℠ and **The Appraisal Plant**℠. CP/M and Wang microcomputer programs with consultation and continued support. Packaged and customized client-oriented systems: data storage, word processing, financial analysis, basic accounting, Freddie Mac/Fannie Mae preparation, office management, balance sheets, spread sheets. [For additional information: Don Dorchester, MAI, Society of Real Estate Appraisers, Tulsa, Oklahoma, (918)-583-9191), or Charles Nash, Valuation Systems of Georgia, 390 Courtland St., N.E., Atlanta, Ga. (404-875-0044).]

Of course, whatever computer program is used and no matter how carefully one applies the knowledge gained in this book, all expenditures of time and budget on a project are a wager on the future. Real estate markets are so uncertain that, given the state of the art, an investor cannot expect analyses to produce precise estimates.

Indeed, one of the most valuable functions of an entrepreneur is to discover that the time is ripe for a new type of equity real estate development. For example, in 1490 a Genovese sailor proposed that if he sailed west he would ultimately arrive in the East. The Spanish monarch directed a panel of the country's sages to evaluate the project. The experts provided the king and queen with six reasons showing that the scheme was impossible. As we well know, the speculative venture of Ferdinand and Isabella reaped returns that no one could have expected.

Of course, one should not confuse speculation with systematic investing. We believe that when competent, honest analysis is done by a person of good judgment who has the loyalty to carry out a project, the venture has more chance of success than a simple bright idea with money behind it.

19

Apartments

Free market, for-profit, rental housing [development] cannot survive a prolonged inflation. From an investor's view, rentals must support not only the increased cost of construction and the financing but also a continuous rise in the market value of the property to match the continuous fall in the value of the dollar.

—*Martin Mayer,* The Builders

Prior to World War II, less than 45 percent of all American households owned their residences. By 1976, almost two-thirds of American households occupied their own dwellings. (See Exhibit 19–1.)

From 1970 to 1976 we added 8 million new single-family homes and only 2.5 million additional rental units, in spite of a surge in construction of apartments due to government rent subsidies. Rental housing has tended to serve as transitional housing for most Americans until they can finance a home of their own.

In spite of inflation in the costs of home ownership, Americans continue to vigorously pursue one-family home ownership. However, changing demographic characteristics suggest that multifamily apartments may continue to be a significant investment opportunity.

Concern must be expressed about rates of return, however, for a variety of reasons. Operating costs have been increasing at a faster rate than rents. In

Acknowledgment: The authors gratefully acknowledge the valuable assistance of Georgia State University students John E. Williams and Jim Hunter.

EXHIBIT 19–1.   Occupied Housing Units, by Tenure (U.S. Total, 1890–1977)
(Units in Thousands)

Year	Total Occupied Units	Owner Occupied		Renter Occupied	
		Number	Percent	Number	Percent
1890	12,690	6,066	47.8	6,524	52.2
1900	15,964	7,455	46.7	8,509	53.3
1910	20,256	9,301	45.9	10,954	54.1
1920	24,352	11,114	45.6	13,238	54.2
1930	29,905	14,280	47.8	15,624	52.2
1940	34,855	15,196	43.6	19,659	56.0
1950	42,826	23,560	55.0	19,266	45.0
1960	53,024	32,797	61.9	20,227	38.1
1970	63,450	39,855	62.9	23,565	37.1
1973	69,337	44,653	64.4	24,684	35.6
1974	70,830	45,784	64.6	25,046	35.4
1975	75,523	46,867	64.6	25,656	35.4
1976	74,005	47,904	64.7	26,101	35.3
1977	75,280	48,765	64.8	26,515	35.2

SOURCE: *Savings and Loan Fact Book* (Chicago: United States League of Savings Associations, 1980), p. 37.

particular, utility costs, real estate taxes, and repairs and maintenance have been rising at a rate greater than that of rent increases. Gross rent revenues have increased at a much slower rate than household expenses and home amortization costs throughout the 1970s. Landlords have been under pressure not to increase rents, partly as a result of municipal rent controls (now in over 80 cities) and partly because of excessive construction at the height of the residential building cycle in 1972– 1975.

At the time of this writing (1981), adequate profitability is largely dependent on tax shelter benefits and expected appreciation of the equity reversion over the ownership cycle. The cash throw-off rate (before-tax cash flow) from apartments is substantially below the conservative interest rate on savings. If the market economy is permitted to operate without political intervention, supply and demand relationships indicate sharp rental increases during the early 1980s, which should produce another cycle of apartment construction. On the other hand, social and political forces may discourage investors, and an increase in the apartment supply may not occur. Construction and rehabilitation should be undertaken with caution; metro areas with a political climate favoring rent controls should be avoided.

Definitions[1]

There are five general types of apartment complexes:

Garden apartments. These usually consist of 2- to 2 1/2-story buildings with a wide range in the number of units per building. The garden apartment provides

[1] For more complete definitions see Urban Land Institute, *Residential Development Handbook* (Washington, D.C., 1978).

access to a semipublic front yard and a semiprivate backyard. The buildings are usually constructed of wooden studs and brick veneer (or low-maintenance siding), are stick-built (built on-site by construction tradespeople), and have carpeted floors. Party-wall construction provides lower heating and cooling costs, usually paid directly by metered tenants. Terrain varies greatly. Sloping sites are preferred because the second story may be situated in such a way that the tenant does not have to climb a flight of stairs.

In the 1970s developers of new apartments preferred densities of twenty to twenty-five per acre where land acquisition costs were not prohibitive. Recently, interior public corridors have been eliminated in favor of direct outside entrances. Large windows and sliding glass doors opening onto patios, terraces, or balconies are being used to integrate indoor and outdoor areas. Planned-unit developments (PUDs) are preferred. These group units into clusters, minimizing site development costs (streets, utility supply lines) and providing recreational amenities that are shared by the tenants. The provision of a clubhouse, laundromat, swimming pool, and other such amenities varies, depending on the rental range. In recent years drainage and other environmental management problems have made site development more complex and dwelling-unit costs higher.

Walk-up apartments (low rises). These usually consist of four- or five-story buildings. Generally, there is no elevator, or a hydraulic elevator provides limited service. The first floor may have a patio. Tenants on other floors are provided with a balcony with sliding glass doors. Such low-rise apartments usually provide few amenities compared with suburban garden-type apartments. A laundry room, a storage locker, bicycle storage, and an occasional game room are all that is provided. In large metro areas where land costs force higher density, some walk-ups have been constructed with middle-income amenities, often stacking the apartments as two-tiered (lower tenant—ground floor/second floor; upper tenant—top two or three floors).

Mid-rise apartments. These usually have six to nine stories. They may be in the inner city or the suburbs. Hydraulic or cable-lift elevators are used, with a service core area containing the elevator, the trash depository, meter rooms, the stairwell, and some utility runs. Usually a common hallway provides access to each tenant's apartment. The building may contain up to 150 units. Amenities range over varying rent levels, and may include club and exercise rooms, a swimming pool, and a sun deck, as well as laundry and storage facilities. Parking is on site. In larger metro areas the parking may be integral to the building, above or below ground. The complexity of the building construction may require personnel with engineering capabilities; professional property management is a virtual necessity.

High-rise apartments. These are typically 20- to 30-story buildings. Such complexes average about 240 units, although some may have over 750 units. High-speed elevators (computer programmed) are used, with a ratio of about one elevator to every eight floors. Operating and maintaining the utility, elevator, and service equipment requires special technical training. The same basic service core as in the mid-rise building is provided with a greater number of apartments per floor. The supporting amenities are larger in size and scope, and include receiving rooms (tenant package-delivery rooms), maid and valet service, doormen, garage attendants, retail outlets, and other convenience amenities. Some tier arrangements are provided as amenities, and custom work is not uncommon in room layouts for long-term tenants. There is some competition with townhouse complexes, luxury garden apartments, and single-family mansions. The occupants are usually upper-income empty nesters, professional couples, or families.

Townhouse complexes. These consist of row houses with party walls; masonry or wood stud with brick veneer construction is common. There are usually 2 or 2 1/2 stories. Party-wall construction provides savings in energy costs compared with single-family detached dwellings (which are to some extent competitive). Young families are attracted to townhouses as a stepping stone to eventual ownership of a single-family detached dwelling. Major features are separate entrances and private patios; the illusion of a private detached house is created, with ample parking and shared recreational amenities. Townhouses cost less to manage than other types of complexes. Often interior upkeep is left to the occupants. The appliances provided are usually mass-produced national brands. Use by families is more typical than in other types of apartments, resulting in more maintenance problems due to the presence of young children. Individual ownership of apartment units is becoming an option in many cases.

Condominiums. In this form of ownership the occupants buy rather than lease the dwelling units. The deed and mortgage provide for fee ownership of the apartment (or townhouse), with a patio or balcony and some other interest in the common areas, streets and sidewalks, parking areas, recreational amenities, and clubhouse. State enabling legislation controls how the board of governers of the complex is set up. Management control rests with the homeowners' association, which has responsibility for yard maintenance, recreational facilities, the exteriors of the buildings, real estate taxes and insurance, water and sewage, and other common-area amenities. In large projects day-to-day management is typically delegated to an independent property management organization.

Condominiums are competitive with single-family dwellings and townhouses and with garden-type rental housing. They provide relatively maintenance-free living with a clubhouse-like atmosphere that is attractive to working couples and empty nesters. They are also a popular form of ownership for retirement living in resort areas where time-sharing rental may be offered.

Cooperative housing projects. These provide apartments within multiunit structures. The owner obtains the right to occupy a dwelling unit by purchasing a required number of shares in a nonprofit housing corporation organized to comply with both state and federal enabling legislation. To qualify as a cooperative under IRS rules, 80 percent or more of gross income must be derived from payments by the tenant–shareholders. In a qualified co-op real estate taxes, insurance, and interest expense payments can be passed along through a proration among the tenant–shareholders. Management is in the hands of a board of directors elected by the shareholders under the provisions of the constitution and bylaws. Actual management is usually delegated to independent organization or, in larger projects, a full-time management office with maintenance personnel. This type of ownership is not uncommon in the Northeast and North Central sections of the country. It is unusual in the Sun Belt and the Southwest.

It is conceivable that this type of ownership may flourish in the future. Some geographic areas (e.g., Pittsburgh, Detroit) have discovered that it produces relatively low-rent housing that is well maintained, particularly after the first mortgage has been amortized. Further, it can also produce a steady stream of home buyers who are good underwriting risks because they have built equity and a sense of property management responsibility during their short-term experience as co-op owners.

TRACK RECORD AND TRENDS

The future productivity of an existing apartment project is not usually related to the past. From 1975 to 1979 an excess supply of units in many SMSAs deflated the rental market. Many complexes went into foreclosure; although others survived, it was at the cost of extensive deferred maintenance. The managers of some properties leased units to tenants who literally destroyed the units. And even when a property may appear to be holding its own, the surrounding neighborhood may be deteriorating or undergoing a radical change.

The demand for apartments is derived from the total demand for housing. The sum total of all the services that a household requires is the utility or amenity package and convenient linkages to municipal services, shopping, and so forth.

In simple terms, the relevant housing market (neighborhood) is the area where lessors and lessees communicate with each other for the leasing of individual dwelling units. In a metro area there may be a number of geographic submarkets that compete for the same set of lessees.

In broad terms, housing market analysis is concerned with the following:

1. Delineation of the market area within which dwelling units compete with one another.
2. The area's economy—principal economic activities, basic resources, economic trends.
3. Demand factors—employment, incomes, population, family size.
4. Supply factors—residential construction activity, housing inventory, conversions, demolitions.
5. Current market conditions—vacancies, unsold inventory, marketability of sales and rental units, prices, rents, building costs, mortgage defaults and foreclosures, disposition of acquired properties.
6. Quantitative and qualitative demand—prospective number of dwelling units that can be absorbed economically at various price and rent levels under conditions existing on the "as of" date.

The demand for housing has been substantially affected since the end of World War II by the government's policy of promoting ownership of single-family houses. Occupancy of apartments is dominated by one- and two-person households.[2] The apartment market now seems headed for prosperity. With the continued growth in the rate of household formations, the slowdown in sales of single-family houses, and the relative rigidity of the supply of apartments, rents are currently being increased by 10 to 20 percent annually and occupancy of most rental projects is approaching 96 percent.

Currently, rental supply is affected by the number of units being converted into condominiums. Generally, the best units in the submarkets are the better candidates for this process.

The recent high rate of increase in house prices, the increase in construction

[2] U.S. Department of Commerce, Bureau of the Census, *Annual Housing Survey* (Washington, D.C., 1975 to date); see 1975 ed., Tables V,53,45.

costs, and the high cost of mortgage money may tend to make apartment living a prime substitute for single-family detached housing. A projection by the Rutgers University Urban Policy Research Center indicates that the demand for apartments through 1980 was 5,388,000, with demand for an additional 9,356,000 units projected through the year 2000.[3]

A large percentage of new units in the 1975– 1980 period were built under the Section 8 housing program authorized by the Housing and Community Development Act of 1974, which is designed to subsidize both new and existing housing. The principal thrust of the Section 8 program is that the subsidy goes to the tenant rather than to finance the project. It is significant that new construction or substantial rehabilitation qualify only if HUD determines that the existing housing supply in the community is inadequate. If HUD determines that the supply is adequate, the only opportunity for a developer under the program would be a Housing Assistance Planning (HAP) contract to subsidize new tenants because occupancy is low. This vehicle may be used to salvage a troubled project.

HUD annually establishes a fair market rent for each community and each type of housing. This figure includes all property charges, including utilities. HUD may accept a contract rent that exceeds the fair market rent by up to 20 percent. If a contract unit is not leased on the effective date of the contract, the owner is entitled to housing assistance payments totaling 80 percent of the contract rent for a vacancy period not exceeding sixty days.

The provisions of the contract are designed to assure that HAPs will be increased on a timely basis to cover cost increases. Automatic adjustments are to be determined by HUD at least annually, while interim revisions may be made as market conditions warrant. On each anniversary date of the contract, the contract terms will be adjusted by a published adjustment factor.

ADVANTAGES AND DISADVANTAGES OF INVESTING IN APARTMENTS

Well-located multifamily units in good physical condition and controlled by good management can produce a substantial cash flow and significant tax shelter benefits. In addition, the units may be sold for condominium conversion, or the apartments can be held for future appreciation during a three- to ten-year ownership cycle.

The primary disadvantage is the intensity of management needed to keep the property stable. Another negative factor is the intensity of use by the average tenant, requiring redecorating, repair, and rehabilitation of units as they are vacated.

TYPES OF INVESTORS AND INVESTOR MOTIVATIONS

The basic motivating factor in this type of investment is the availability of tax shelter. Therefore, they are attractive to individuals or groups of individuals with substantial taxable incomes. There is a tendency to prefer limited partnership as the ownership entity.

Recently a second factor has been the desire to convert apartments into condominium units. This procedure has been highly profitable in the past, but there is some concern that the next cycle of conversion may be marginal and that

---

[3] Rutgers University, Center for Urban Policy Research, *Future Demand for Rental Housing— 1980– 2000* (New Brunswick, N.J., Spring 1978).

the number of units offered may exceed market absorption rates. Great care must be taken to avoid dealer status on the sales. It is best to sell to a condominium converter/developer.

A third factor causing investors to buy and hold apartments for resale is the recent phenomenon in which the value of an existing apartment [capitalized net operating income (NOI)] is considerably less than the reproduction cost. Newer apartment units have been costing more than comparable older ones. Although new units provide greater utility for the tenant, investment in such units has become less attractive. Therefore, there is a reasonable expectation of more appreciation in the value of older apartments.

A final motivating factor is the Section 8 rent subsidy program. Since HUD will accept both new and rehabilitated units in this program, some developers have been purchasing older buildings and building new developments. The profit in this activity is in the mortgager–developer fees that are built into the original rehabilitation cost and then realized by mortgaging out at high prices.

THE NATURE OF THE RETURNS AND RISKS

In the recent past apartment investors have expected a cash-on-cash return of 10 percent over a ten-year period. Additional benefits were the excellent tax shelter provided to apartment owners. Under provision of the Economic Recovery Tax Act of 1981, apartments are a type of income property permitted to utilize accelerated depreciation, both for original owners and for purchasers of used apartments. A factor that augments the benefit is the higher ratio of improvement to total costs than exists in other types of investment.

Since the proportion of land cost to value is generally lower for apartments, the result is that more of the investment can be depreciated. The ratio of land to building might be as low as $1:6$, while an office building in the same area might show a ratio of $1:3$. Recently investors have bid up the prices of apartments to produce merely breakeven returns.

The primary source of risk is the quality of management of the property. Although other forms of risk are present, poor management can produce an immediate disaster.

Another risk factor that currently concerns owners is the escalation of property expenses. The high occupancy level of apartments indicates that the supply curve is moving to a position approaching perfect inelasticity. Therefore, owners should be able to recover their increases in property expenses through similar increases in rents. However, divergence in the timing of these events can drastically alter the cash flow.

A third type of risk is changing tastes and preferences of renters and deterioration of the neighborhood. The short duration of leases creates another risk. If the market is characterized by an oversupply of units, then leases are necessary to hold tenants. If a high demand for units predominates, lease terms become a hindrance in raising rents to allow owners to recover escalating expenses.

MARKET AND MARKETABILITY ANALYSIS

Demand and Supply Analysis. The targeted submarket for apartment investment will be a result of stratification of income, geographic segmentation of the market, and identification of the appropriate occupational mix in order to identify the profile of user preferences that the investor wants to serve.

When the targeted submarket has been identified, the techniques set forth in summary fashion here would be applied to the location. Generally, the analyst will gather and process the following supply and demand data for the selected apartment submarket:

1. Data on the trends and characteristics of the local housing stock—tenure, types of structures, rents and values, quality and condition (including age and physical conditions)—must be collected. The analyst will then proceed to identify short-run changes, such as losses to inventory due to demolition (public and private) or casualty; conversions and mergers, such as remodeling large houses into apartments or the reverse; and new construction activity, both actual and planned, that is or will be occurring within the forecast period.

2. It is necessary to evaluate the quality of access and the availability of urban services. This is done by estimating time—distance radii and the quality and adequacy of such facilities as hospitals, shopping centers, cultural and religious activities, and schools. The adequacy and availability of police and fire protection, sanitary services, utilities, and parks and recreation, and accessibility to highways and arterial roads, must also be considered. It is desirable to evaluate the nature and quality of neighborhood organizations, such as civic clubs and neighborhood planning organizations. Such activities tend to promote stability and harmony, and to enhance values. One should consider the quality of code compliance.

3. Stratified vacancy estimates must be obtained. Useful vacancy data generally are not available except by field survey. Vacancy data should be stratified by rent-per-month classes and geographically zoned to target the appropriate submarket. In addition to the vacancy rate, information should be gathered on its causes. It will be necessary to make a judgment on the rate of vacancy necessary for normal market turnover. Variance is based on the market absorption rate and related to the rate of growth of the local urban economy.

4. Economic—demographic data must be gathered for evaluating the quantity and quality of demand for apartments in the target neighborhood (see Chapter 6 for details on computer-assisted data retrieval systems). In order to understand the user profile, the analyst will obtain information on such population characteristics as age distribution, race, ethnic origin, and religion. (*Note:* The U.S. Justice Department objects to the gathering of some of this information about neighborhoods.) It is also necessary to know the number of households and families in the neighborhood; household size, mobility, and turnover; household and family income per dwelling unit; and occupation mix. The nature of households should be analyzed. Are they families? congregate living? singles? In effect, are there any unique characteristics or attributes of the occupants of the target or surrounding neighborhood that will have an impact on demand. This information should enable the analyst to evaluate the relevant competitive sales and rental housing markets.

5. The boundaries are delineated and the scope of the pertinent target housing market is analyzed. Consideration is given to the distribution of ready-for-sale houses among the various price classes. In effect, a quantitative and qualitative analysis is made of the existing competitive sales inventory, including units that are due to come on stream during the

forecast period, to identify the sales housing units that would be viewed as competitive for would-be apartment dwellers who are considering the homeownership alternative. Only a small fraction of the sales housing inventory actually competes with rental housing.

6. The analyst is now ready for a detailed analysis of the targeted rental housing market for apartments. It is necessary to identify the range of rents (per month) and make a quantitative analysis of the spread of the dwelling units over the range of rents per month. Since gross rents usually vary as to the expenses (e.g., utilities) included, an in-depth analysis must be done. An effort must be made to identify the typical amenity package provided to the tenant in the representative dwelling unit. A summary is developed covering the quality, quantity, vacancy, turnover, occupational mix, and so on of the most comparable competitive apartment projects. (See the discussion of competitive survey techniques in Chapter 6.) Consideration should be given to the possible impact of special government housing programs and the rate of conversion of private housing units in the target neighborhood. The analyst is striving to make a best-available estimate of the market absorption rate of the new and planned rental units, and to determine whether the investment will capture its share of the market during the early years of the ownership cycle.

7. The investor should expect the analysis to relate supply and demand to current overall market conditions, such as prevailing construction costs, the nature and quality of financing, recent selling prices, current operating experiences, development activities, deed and mortgage activities, and foreclosure rates.

This may appear to be an elaborate process; however, much of the information required is available either free or at low cost from regional or city planning commissions, appraisal firms, and other local agencies and private bodies. (See appendix to Part II.)

Although completely reliable current surveys are rarely available for local neighborhoods and metro-wide data produce errors that discourage their use for neighborhood investment decisions, the best-available information can aid in evaluating risk/return trade-offs. The most likely sources of data from the field include local associations of apartment managers and owners (AOMA), builder–developers, commercial real estate brokers, utility engineers, mortgage lenders, university real estate departments, chambers of commerce, and planning departments. For detailed research, classified newspaper advertising and utility meter and telephone hookup data are excellent sources of current trends. (Unfortunately, utility companies are not generally cooperative.) Building permit and demolition data are also useful. A few SMSAs (e.g., Dallas) have organized nonprofit research organizations to generate such data.

Any investor who intends to specialize in apartments should obtain a copy of *FHA Techniques of Housing Market Analysis.* [4]

Projection of Rental Income and Vacancies. Estimates of rents and miscellaneous income and expenses should be taken from the most current operating statements for the property. Rents should be calculated on a per-square-foot-per-

---

[4] *FHA Techniques of Housing Market Analysis* (Washington, D.C.: Government Printing Office, 1978).

month basis and compared with figures for comparable apartments. Shop the market by going to the competitive units and enquiring about vacancies and rental rates. It is difficult to project income by applying a simple growth factor—a weighted-average growth rate would be more realistic.

A vacancy rate factor should be based on the historical experience of comparable properties. Income from other sources, such as laundry income and income from vending machines, should be added. Generally, occupancy cannot be better than 95 percent, which translates into 18 vacant days per unit per year. Units must be vacant for cleaning, painting, and normal turnover. Another source of loss is evictions, which take time. Although collection efforts will minimize bad debts, a bad-debt reserve is necessary.

Expenses should be examined on the basis of reasonableness and completeness. If the property appears to be in poor condition, inadequate funds are going toward maintenance. Some items, such as management salaries and fees, may not appear on financial records, particularly if the current owner is managing the property. Another item that too often is not included is a reserve for replacement of short-lived items like carpet. See the case study at the end of Chapter 16 for a model statement of operations.

Risk Management and Control Techniques. The primary risk is the quality of management of the property. Other risks are functional obsolescence and neighborhood deterioration. The effect is the same—loss of high-quality tenants as the filtering-down process begins and the chain of moves brings in lower-income users.

PHYSICAL, LEGAL, POLITICAL, AND ENVIRONMENTAL ANALYSIS

Physical Analysis—Site and Structural Improvements. The physical condition of the units must be thoroughly inspected. Certain items, such as carpet, heating and air-conditioning units, drapes, and appliances, have rather short useful lives, and generally some portion is replaced each year. Roofs and exterior walls should be inspected to determine how much maintenance has been deferred. Flat, built-up roofs often leak and require repair.

If the exterior of the units is wood, extensive maintenance is required. For example, some developers use 3/8-inch plywood sheets although architects and manufacturers recommend 5/8-inch sheets. Investors often prefer brick exteriors, even though wood can be superior from the standpoint of both construction and energy conservation.

A good complex should have as an amenity package a swimming pool, a clubhouse, tennis courts, laundry facilities, good landscaping, playground equipment if it is a family complex, and adequate parking. There should be at least 1.5 parking spaces per unit, preferably two.

After a good location has been found, the functional design of the apartment building is of maximum importance to potential demand. The living space should be roomy and well closeted, with neatly arranged kitchens and bathrooms and exterior exposure and balconies wherever possible. Architectural expertise in the arrangement of the living quarters and central placement of the lobby, elevators, corridors, and laundry rooms so that these services are readily accessible are vital. Amenity factors have a bearing on the value of apartment buildings, just as they do on that of individually owned residences.

Legal, Political, and Environmental Factors. Adequate and convenient municipal services are essential to the profitability of apartment projects. More than one
foreclosure has occurred because promised bus schedules never materialized. A
rating system should be developed for evaluating the adequacy and availability of
municipal services. Consideration should be given to police and fire protection,
sanitary hauling, the quality of local schools, water, sewage, parks, recreation,
hospitals, shopping, urban transportation, and highway access. Property taxes
should be compared to taxes in other localities on a per-unit or per-square-foot
basis.

One should review the quality of local government, its capital improvement
program, and how it handles its budgets. Crisis financing by inept local governments can result in increases in assessments and real estate taxes. An investor
should be wary of the political attitudes in a locality. Some local governments are
very responsive to the demands of apartment dwellers. For example, some cities
have passed laws prohibiting all-adult apartment projects, condominium conversions, and tenant assessments. Others have enacted rent control measures that do
not allow for increases in owners' expenses.

Developers and rehabilitators are facing increasing per-unit costs because of
environmental regulations. For example, developers are being required to install
water retention basins to control runoff. Rehabilitators are finding that compliance
with building codes is not enough. Often room layouts, closets, entries, and the
like must be changed to meet the standards of stringent housing codes.

ANALYSIS OF OPERATIONS

Property Management and Leasing. One of the key management functions is
leasing. This task is complicated by the need to screen out low-quality tenants who
may create immediate problems, including nonpayment of rent, annoyance of
other tenants, and illegal activities, thereby driving away more stable tenants. This
problem is prevented by careful selection of prospective tenants. Tenants pay for
comfort, safety, and quiet enjoyment of the premises. Good occupancy means
that the rents collected are normally budgeted for 95 percent of the scheduled
gross income.

Rents should be kept in line with those of competitors.

While many investors prefer to act as their own property managers, with the
trend toward larger projects, professional management may become essential.
Some of the important functions provided by the professional manager are the
following:

1. Selection and training of on-site personnel.
2. Tenant selection and leasing.
3. Rental collection and evictions.
4. Timely maintenance and repairs.
5. Cleanliness of improvements and grounds.
6. Providing tenant rules and regulations.
7. Budget and expense control.
8. Record keeping and reporting to the owner.

The rates charged for professional management vary widely by locality and by
project size, but range from 2 1/2 percent of gross effective income up to 7
percent. (See Chapter 16 for more on managing the property.)

Analysis of Current Operating Expenses. Apartment operation generally involves the following expense items:

1. Maintenance, which includes redecorating; appliance repair; repair of the structural, electrical, and plumbing systems; maintenance of grounds and recreational facilities; and exterminating.
2. Payroll for on-site staff; the cost of management-used apartments.
3. A pro rata portion of other administrative, office, professional, advertising, and travel expenses.
4. Utilities, including trash removal.
5. Fixed expenses, including real estate taxes and insurance.
6. Capital repair and replacement reserves (usually estimated).

The remaining balance, net operating income, is the amount available for debt service, income taxes, and cash flow. A realistic method to estimate the expense statement is to compare it with expenses for similar properties in the same market. Generally, expense statements are divided between fixed and variable expenses.

Utility expenses are based on the consumption of these services for common facilities and/or employee units. In some older apartments all utilities are provided to the tenants. As utility costs have skyrocketed, however, apartment managers have sought to pass the cost on to the tenant, either by going to separate meters or by allocating utility costs (in high-turnover apartments it is difficult to put tenants on separate meters). In most garden units the owner is responsible for water, sewage, and trash removal for the tenants.

Real estate taxes and insurance are fixed in nature, but a new owner may successfully appeal the assessment. Insurance costs can be reduced if the risk of one unit can be pooled into a blanket policy over several properties.

Capital additions and replacements often are not included in current operating expenses, since they are generally controlled by the investor's policy and occur only with the owner's approval.

Depreciation is not included, since it is a noncash accounting item.

Amortization and interest expense generally should not be included in the operating portion of the expense statements because the manager has no control over them. Including them reduces the comparability of expense statements and clouds the measurement of management effectiveness.

Generally, apartment managers can be relatively successful in projecting expenses through a budget. With experience, managers can predict timing of repairs and maintenance and staff levels. Utilities, taxes, and insurance can be estimated, although at a different level of confidence. Generally, the apartment manager will include in the annual budget capital funds for major repairs or renovations that will be funded during that year. (See the case study at the end of Chapter 16 for a sample operating statement.)

The NAR's Institute of Real Estate Management does an important annual research study—*Income/Expense Analysis: Apartments.*[5] The study, which is a

---

[5] National Association of Realtors, Institute of Real Estate Management, *Income/Expense Analysis: Apartments* (annual research report); see also Edward N. Kelley, *Practical Apartment Management* (Chicago: National Association of Realtors, Institute of Real Estate Management, 1976), and William Walters, Jr., *The Practice of Real Estate Management* (Chicago: National Association of Realtors, Institute of Real Estate Management, 1979).

useful source of comparable data, is broken down into regions, SMSAs, size, age, type of construction, and so forth, and is a valuable reference. The Aspen Wood case in Chapter 16 is a computer-assisted operating statement.

Analysis of Trends and Uncertainties. The major current trend is cost-push inflation. Labor costs are increasing sharply. Utilities, property taxes, and insurance are similarly escalating. The apartment manager must pass these costs on to tenants if a fair rate of return is to be maintained. The biggest current uncertainty is the ability of apartment managers to maintain full occupancy while passing along cost increases

In normal times, the fact that apartments provide basic shelter affords some protection against business cycles. However, residential construction cycles have caused serious imbalances in the market, with adverse effects on occupancy rates. In such times the older apartments have tended to have an advantage because of favorable mortgage constants based on lower interest rates. In addition, the apartment market has experienced oscillations in mortgage credit availability. As a result, on occasion investors may experience financing conditions that make conventional mortgage financing unavailable when they are planning to sell or refinance, with the result that illiquidity may defeat tax-planning objectives.

Risk Management and Control Techniques. The apartment manager desires to maximize cash flow, and to this end he or she works to minimize expenses. Through his or her efforts units are leased, tenants qualified, rents and late charges collected, vacancies minimized, and, it is hoped, tenant turnover reduced. In controlling expenses the manager may reduce the level of some expenditures—say, by deferring maintenance, cutting down on amenities, or lowering the level of staffing on site—but at a risk of potential future cost and tenant turnover.

FINANCING AND REFINANCING TECHNIQUES

Prices, Terms, and Conditions. Apartment loans are considered to be somewhat riskier than loans for commercial, office, and industrial properties. Consequently, most long-term lenders will require an interest rate about half or three-quarters of a percent higher than rates on other types of properties. In addition, most lenders require shorter loan terms and will often hold back about 20 percent of the loan funds until the complex attains a required level of rental achievement (say, 85 percent).

Commercial banks have recently made equity money available for a limited term (generally five years) for purchase of good apartment complexes. However, these loans are usually based on the personal security of the borrower and not on the value of the real estate.

Generally, the government has not been active in direct financing of apartment units. Its efforts are centered on the Section 8 rent subsidy program, and not on mortgage lending. However, that program is dependent on the purchase of these mortgages for the GNMA and FNMA portfolios. Renegotiable-rate mortgages with balloons in three to five years are becoming more common. Higher equity requirements (20–30%) are being required.

Estimating Financing Costs. When projecting the expense of financing, include finder's fees, if any; the first or partial month's interest; origination fees; discount points for construction and permanent loans; equity participations as required; legal and organization expenses; and accounting records and reports as required.

Know the Risk Control and Management Techniques of Lenders. Many mortgagees were forced to foreclose on apartments during the 1975 recession. One consequence is that lenders have acquired hard-earned experience in the process of working these properties out of distress. Many lenders now are more knowledgeable than some developers about successful apartment management and will critically evaluate requests for apartment loans. Today a developer is fortunate to secure 75 percent financing; large equity contributions are generally necessary and equity participations are common.

In evaluating the financing available for an apartment project, it is useful to consider debt coverage ratios (say, 1.25) and default ratios (say, 0.80). One should make a direct comparison of the amortization term with the remaining economic life of the project. If the project life is shorter than the mortgage payout period, serious doubts should be raised about feasibility unless succession to a higher and better use is contemplated as part of the strategy. If balloon payments, refinancing, or junior financing are contemplated in order to replace major short-lived items, the investor must consider the possibility that such financing will not be available when needed. Finally, one must consider the financing situation for the next buyer. Will the physical conditions of the project and neighborhood conditions be good enough to enable the person who buys the project from you at the end of the ownership cycle to obtain the necessary financing?

The primary risk control technique used by lenders is discretion in selecting the properties on which they will make loans. However, long-term lenders have acted to shift almost all of the initial development risk to the construction lender. Although the terms of all long-term lenders include loans of 75 percent of value, the 20 percent holdback on rental achievement for new developments minimizes the risk of loss to them if they refuse to take out the property before it becomes effectively leased.

The construction lender will act to minimize the risk of advancing funds on an incomplete project when the owner cannot obtain permanent long-term financing. This risk is controlled primarily through analysis of the developer's creditworthiness and ability to complete the project.

Today banks provide construction financing only for the minimum loan amount approved. They extend funds on a periodic basis as work progresses and as subcontractors and suppliers of materials are actually paid.

TAXATION AND TAX STRUCTURE

The Nature of the Tax Shelter. Compared with other types of nonresidential properties, apartments usually offer better tax benefits. These include accelerated depreciation on both new and used units, deduction of interest on mortgages, and potential capital gain treatment of sale. Investment tax credits and expensing are not available to any significant degree.

Identification of Variables to Be Structured. Low-income housing may use the 200 percent declining-balance method as its maximum rate. Or, low-income and other housing may depreciate the improvements at the statutory 175 percent declining-balance method which switches over to straight line at about the ninth year according to the IRS schedule. All apartments may use the 15-, 35-, or 45-year straight-line recovery periods for the improvements. The use of the shorter ACRS lives of three years and five years is limited to carpets, elevators, escalators, and personalty, such as furnishings, not attached and separately leased to the tenants.

Tax Problems and Uncertainties. If accelerated depreciation methods are used, the tax deduction may result in the apartment project generating lower or even negative taxable income, which could shelter other taxable income while still generating a positive cash flow. Use of accelerated depreciation lowers taxes in early years but causes them to be higher than pretax cash flow in the later years of ownership. In effect, profitable projects using accelerated depreciation methods simply defer taxes to later years. Depreciation may rapidly reduce adjusted basis below the mortgage balance.

The possibility of recapture of depreciation at ordinary income marginal rates, and the resulting increase in taxes, requires planning and action. The techniques that can be used are (1) avoiding accelerated depreciation by using ACRS composite straight-line depreciation; (2) refinancing, thereby withdrawing funds and deferring the impact of recapture; (3) making a like-kind exchange; (4) leasing the property to a prospective buyer with appropriate options to the buyer for purchase; and (5) selling the property on an installment basis.

Under the 1981 tax act the disposition of apartments will result in gain, if any, being recaptured as ordinary income only to the extent that the deductions under the accelerated method exceed those that would have been allowable under the straight-line 15-year method. Use of the 15-year straight-line ACRS may result in a large gain based not only on appreciation in value but also on the extent to which the mortgage exceeds basis. Such a situation may result in a call for cash.

DISCOUNTED CASH FLOW ANALYSIS

Rate-of-Return Analysis. When analyzing an apartment complex, it is readily apparent that since income and expenses change constantly, the traditional valuation method of capitalizing the first year's net income or using a stabilized income is misleading. The most accurate estimate may be derived by estimating income and expense for the expected holding period of the property and discounting to the present value, using IRR/PV methods of analysis. Currently investors are buying apartment projects for exceptionally low cash-on-cash returns of 0–6 percent. Analysis indicates that their IRR on after-tax cash flow may be only 12–15 percent unless rental increases exceed the rate of inflation. Apparently, many apartment investors are wagering that apartment rent increases will be quite high in the next five years. Current indications are that the competition for quality projects is such that investors will be fortunate to obtain an after-tax IRR on equity of 6–8 percent above the necessary inflation premium.

Ratio and Risk Analysis. Sensitivity analysis should be applied to determine the effects of rental increases, the rate of growth of expenses, and the effect of vacancies on the viability of the investment.

After targeting a property using the basic screening criteria, one should use the basic financial feasibility model and obtain an interest in the apartments through preliminary negotiations. We recommend the use of computer software to simulate the investment and for sensitivity analysis. Such simulation models generate many useful ratios for comparing the subject project with data on comparable projects.

THE INVESTMENT DECISION

Currently apartment investors seem to be seeking well-constructed, well-located units to purchase on a cash-on-cash break-even or even worse solvency basis. Their usual objective is conversion to condominiums or holding for short-term appreciation. The major risks are management or market oriented.

Many investors seem to be buying as a hedge to protect capital against erosion by inflation. Such investors are running the risk of general deflation. Cautious application of the productivity analysis is essential, and apartment investors should avoid projects for which profitability is based largely on tax effects and the impact of inflation on rents. In the past, apartments have been a relatively stable lower-risk investment medium. Because competition for good-quality projects is intensifying, returns are becoming lower. Therefore, if substantial rental increases do not occur in the short run, apartment investments will become riskier.

Selected References

"Apartment Market Outlook." *National Real Estate Investor* [annual].

Brown, Gordon T., and Robert W. Dunham. "America's Planned-Unit Developments: Do They Accomplish Their Purpose?" *The Real Estate Appraiser,* September-October 1973, pp. 21–28.

Buck, Gordon H. "The Case for the Planned Unit Residential Development." *Real Estate Review,* Summer 1976, pp. 104–107.

Burchell, Robert W., and James W. Hughes. "Financial Aspects of Planned Unit Development." *The Appraisal Journal,* July 1974, pp. 372–390.

"Checklist for a Residential Lease." *Real Estate Investors Report,* June 1974, pp. 2–5.

Etzel, W. T., Jr. "Good Data In, Good Loans Out." *Savings and Loan News,* October 1972, pp. 74–80.

Fantle, Chuck. "Leasing Can Be Successful If." *Journal of Property Management,* May-June 1974, pp. 126–128.

Fisher, Roy R. "A Viewpoint on Condominiums." *The Real Estate Appraiser,* September-October 1977, pp. 62–64.

"Five Recreation-Oriented Projects." *House and Home,* February 1973, pp. 84–97.

Friedman, Edith J. *Real Estate Encyclopedia,* rev. ed. Englewood Cliffs, N.J.: Prentice-Hall, 1978.

Gerardi, N. "Apartments: There's One Way to Win the Numbers Game, Raise Your Rents." *Housing,* August 1978, pp. 52–57.

———. "Apartments: Is It Time to Rethink the Product." *Housing,* April 1979, pp. 60–66.

Gibbons, James E. "Apartment Feasibility Studies." *The Appraisal Journal,* July 1968, pp. 325–332.

Graybeal, Ronald S. "Condominium Computerized Feasibility Analysis." *Appraisal Journal,* October 1973, pp. 526–534.

Hanford, Lloyd D., Sr. "Condominium Feasibility Study: Planning from the Ground Floor Up." *Journal of Property Management,* May-June 1969, pp. 130–133.

Hiban, Arthur W., and James T. Derry. "Ten Biggest Budgeting Mistakes Made by Community Associations." *Journal of Management,* January-February 1978, pp. 33–35.

"Is This Apartment Necessary." *Savings and Loan News,* March 1972, pp. 28– 34.

Jaffe, A. J. "Evaluating Rules of Thumb (Apartment Complexes)." *Real Estate Today,* October 1978, pp. 22– 25.

Jerremad, B. "The Best Real Estate Investment Ever." *Real Estate Review,* Fall 1977, pp. 62– 64.

Jones, James. "The Apartment Project: Development and Financing." *The Appraisal Journal,* January 1972, pp. 96– 102.

Kelley, Edward. *Cost, Rent and Profit Computer* (handbook). Chicago: Institute of Property Management, 1978.

Kozuch, James R., and Andrew G. Shank. "Management of Funds Is Key to Successful Condo Conversions." *Mortgage Banker,* November 1974, pp. 5– 12.

Leventhal, K. "Easier Financing Sparks New Interest in Coops." *Professional Builder and Apartment Business,* January 1979, pp. 62.

Liebman, John R. "Can Condominium Time-Sharing Work." *Real Estate Review,* Fall 1973, pp. 40– 45.

Lum, Tan Tek. "Feasibility Analysis of Condominiums." *The Appraisal Journal,* April 1972, pp. 246– 252.

Macousky, S. J. "Apartments: What $500 Will Rent in St. Louis, Boston, Dallas, Los Angeles, Atlanta." *Money,* June 1978, pp. 77– 81.

Manheim, Uriel. "Condohotels: Promise Versus Performance." *Real Estate Review,* Fall 1977, pp. 23– 29.

Mylod, Robert J. "Housing Boom Threatens to Outpace Supply of Lots." *Mortgage Banker,* February 1978, pp. 76– 78.

Opelka, F. Gregory. "Appraisal Report: How to Analyze Project Feasibility." *Savings and Loan News,* October 1977, pp. 113– 115.

———. "FHLMC's Condo Form: Tell It All, Tell It Like It Is." *Savings and Loan News,* November 1977, pp. 98– 99.

"Preventative Apartment Maintenance Keeps Lid on Repairs." *Professional Builder and Apartment Business,* June 1979, pp. 39f.

Ratcliffe, Philip E., Jr. "The Apartment Building Feasibility Study: Its Needs, Components and Production." *Journal of Property Management,* July-August 1967, pp. 161– 171.

Ritley, Roger D. "Measuring Demand for Multi-Unit Housing." *Journal of Property Management,* November-December 1972, pp. 269– 276.

Rowlson, John. "The Feasibility and Appraisal of Garden-Type Condominiums." *The Appraisal Journal,* July 1973, pp. 338– 349.

Sachar, Roger, A. "The Art of Merchandising." *Journal of Property Management,* September-October 1973, pp. 220– 225.

Schmidt, John L. "Density, Permitted Uses Complicate PUD Ordinance Writing." *Savings and Loan News,* March 1972, pp. 64– 65.

Starr, John O. "Guidelines for Mobile Home Park Development." *The Appraisal Journal,* January 1971, pp. 41– 51.

"Study of a Proposed Mobile Home Park." *The Appraisal Journal,* January 1971, pp. 52– 56.

"Tale of Two Subdivided Projects." *Professional Builder and Apartment Business,* January 1979, pp. 220– 223.

Train, John. "A Good Investment, but a Bad Business." *Forbes,* November 15, 1977, p. 206.

Wagner, Percy E. "Analyzing and Appraising Condominium Projects." *The Appraisal Journal,* October 1971, pp. 576– 582.

The shopping center industry has become increasingly important since World War II. Whereas there were only 100 centers in the United States in 1950, by 1977 there were an estimated 19,190, with retail sales of over $250 billion (1979). In the mid-1970s a softening in shopping center development occurred, with most major retail markets saturated. Some supersaturation is occurring as superregional centers vie for more market share. Attention is now being focused on small centers in the smaller SMSAs, on rehabilitation of stable older centers, and on regional centers designed to draw customers from a number of small urban areas.

Although the overall risks are increasing because of greater and more skillful competition, shopping centers are considered blue-chip investment properties by foreign and institutional investors, equity REITs, and large public syndicates. In recent years competition has resulted in lower capitalization rates as more investors are willing to pay higher prices to obtain ownership of a site where rents are tied to retail prices (through percentage rate overage clauses), thus providing the investor with some protection against erosion of principal by inflation.

Definitions

Throughout this section many specialized terms are used. Some of these are defined here.

Shopping center. A shopping center is a group of commercial establishments that are planned, developed, owned, and managed as a unit and are related in

Acknowledgment: The authors gratefully acknowledge the valuable assistance of Georgia State University students Peter Hotine, John E. Williams, and C. Jackson Harris.

terms of location, size, and type of shops to the trade area served by the unit. Shopping centers typically include as part of the site area (the gross area within the property lines) sufficient space to provide for customer and employee parking, in proportion to the types and sizes of shops required by the local planning agency.

A shopping center's type is usually determined by the nature of its major tenant or tenants. Neither site area nor square footage alone determines the type of center.

There are four basic types of shopping centers:

1. *Neighborhood center.* A neighborhood center provides for the sale of goods (foods, drugs, and sundries) and personal services (laundry and dry cleaning, barbering, shoe repair, etc.) for the day-to-day needs of the immediate neighborhood. It is usually built around a supermarket and/or drugstore as the principal tenant. The typical neighborhood center has a gross leasable area (GLA) of about 50,000 square feet and is the smallest type of shopping center.

2. *Community center.* In addition to the convenience goods and personal services of the neighborhood center, a community center provides facilities for the sale of soft lines (wearing apparel for men, women, and children) and hard lines (hardware and appliances). It is built around a junior department store, variety store, or discount department store, although it may have a strong specialty store. The typical size of about 150,000 square feet of gross leasable area makes this an intermediate type of center, which is difficult to estimate for appropriate size and pulling power.

3. *Regional center.* A regional center provides general merchandise, apparel, furniture, and home furnishings in depth and variety, as well as a range of services and recreational facilities. It is built around one or two full-line department stores of generally not less than 100,000 square feet. A typical size is about 400,000 square feet of gross leasable area. The regional center is the second-largest type of shopping center. As such, it provides services that are typical of a business district, yet is not as extensive as a superregional center.

4. *Superregional center.* A superregional center provides an extensive variety of general merchandise, apparel, furniture, and home furnishings, as well as services and recreational facilities. It is built around at least three major department stores of generally not less than 100,000 square feet each. While by definition the typical size is about 750,000 square feet of gross leasable area, in practice the size ranges from 1 million square feet up.

Exhibit 20–1 summarizes the characteristics of the four types of shopping centers.

Specialty or theme center. As the number of shopping centers has grown in recent years, developers have sought to build centers that would compete more effectively. The result has been the development of specialty or theme shopping centers.

Since, by definition, each specialty or theme center is different, they defy categorization and analysis as a group. Typically, they have a concentration of imported goods and gift specialty shops. They may also have one or more restaurants and specialty food shops, boutiques, jewelers, high-fashion clothiers,

EXHIBIT 20–1.   Characteristics of Shopping Centers

Type	Leading Tenant (Basis for Classification)	Typical GLA	General GLA Range	Usual Minimum Site Area	Minimum Support Required
Neighborhood	Supermarket or drugstore	50,000 sq. ft.	30,000–100,000 sq. ft.	3 acres	2,500–40,000 people
Community	Variety, discount, or junior department store	150,000 sq. ft.	100,000–300,000 sq. ft.	10 acres or more	40,000–150,000 people
Regional	One or more full-line department stores of at least 100,000 sq. ft. GLA	400,000 sq. ft.	300,000–1 million sq. ft. or more"	30–50 acres or more	150,000 or more people
Superregional	Three or more full-line (sometimes free-standing) department stores of at least 100,000 sq. ft. GLA	1 million sq. ft.	750,000–2 million sq. ft.	85 acres or more	1 million or more people in primary–tertiary trading area

SOURCE: *Shopping Center Development Handbook* (Washington, D.C.: Urban Land Institute, 1978).
*" Centers with more than 750,000 sq. ft. GLA usually include three or more department stores and hence are super-regionals.

and artisans. The shoppers tend to be affluent and well informed, and spend more time making the purchase decision. Generally, such centers have no anchor tenant, but instead consist predominantly of independent merchant tenants. Examples of such theme centers are Ghiardelli Square in San Francisco, the Galleria in Houston, Trolley Square in Salt Lake City, and Reading Station in Philadelphia.

Another dominant characteristic of the specialty or theme center is architectural design, and they often have an unusual structural configuration (e.g., a renovated factory or trolley barn) or a dominant architectural theme, or use extensive gardens and landscaping to create a special environment.

Anchor tenant. The anchor tenant is the key tenant (or tenants), the one that gives the center its stability and drawing power. The commitment of a well-known anchor tenant is generally required before construction financing can be arranged.

Convenience goods. These are items, such as groceries, shampoo, dry cleaning, and hardware, that are needed immediately and often, and are purchased where it is most convenient for the shoppers.

Impulse goods. These goods are not actively sought by shoppers. Impulse goods have an indefinite trade area and are placed so as to get them into the customer flow created by other businesses or within a store where people are passing by on their way to find a specifically sought item.

Major tenants. These are tenants with high credit ratings and substantial net worth (over $1 million). They add stability to the center.

Mall. A mall is a pedestrian way between two facing strips of stores. The mall area may be enclosed or open.

Market trading area. The geographic area from which customers for a given class of goods or services are expected to be drawn is called the market trading area. The *primary* area is the immediately surrounding area, in which few competitors exist and a high market share is expected. The *secondary* area may be shared with competitors. The *tertiary* (peripheral) area is expected to supply only customers who cannot find satisfactory goods in more convenient locations.

Merchants' association. An effective merchants' association makes a significant contribution toward the objective of a stable, profitable shopping center. The association can promote the shopping center on a collective basis more effectively than separate actions by individual tenants. It is also a forum for tenant–management relations, and is helpful in formulating policies for the center and enforcing regulations that affect all tenants.

All U.S. superregional centers have merchant's associations; 99 percent of the regional centers have them; 71 percent of the community centers have them; but only 27 percent of the neighborhood centers have them.

Tenants are assessed by the association for working funds for such services as trash pickup, snow removal, air conditioning of common areas, parking area maintenance, security, and so forth.

In 1977 a typical superregional center assessment was $0.23 per square foot of GLA, with department stores contributing about 26 percent of the total, or $0.05 per square foot, and other tenants contributing $0.11 per square foot, or about 48 percent of the total. The shopping center's management typically contributes $0.04 per square foot of GLA, or 20 percent of total contributions.

Regional shopping centers have merchant's associations with department stores and other tenants contributing 25 percent, others contributing 49 percent, and center management typically contributing 22 percent.

The merchant's association in community shopping centers typically raises $0.10 per square foot of GLA. Junior department stores and variety stores typically contribute $0.02 per square foot, or about 16 percent of the total, and other tenants 66 percent.

Neighborhood shopping centers typically raise $0.08 per square foot of GLA, with center management contributing about $0.02, or 22 percent.

Multiuse center. A multiuse center is a development that incorporates residential, office, and recreational uses with commercial retail shops.

Satellites. Satellites are small, localized tenants attracted to the center by the potential spillover of customers drawn by major tenants. Satellites are expected to pay higher rentals than majors and receive lower allowances and concessions.

Shopping goods. These are larger-ticket items that generally are subject to comparison shopping. Examples are pianos, appliances, stereos, microcomputers, and lawnmowers.

Specialty goods. These are highly differentiated by brand and style and are generally purchased after considerable shopping effort; examples are jewelry, fashion clothing, imported cheese, and wine.

Strip center. A strip center is a line of stores tied together by a canopy over the sidewalk running along the fronts of the stores.

Vertical center. This is a center with more than one level.

TRACK RECORD AND TRENDS

The development of the shopping center industry has closely followed the major population and economic trends at work in the country. In the 1950s and 1960s, when the suburban and fringe areas of most large cities were growing rapidly, large regional, and later superregional, centers developed to serve these new markets. In recent years there has been a slowdown, and most major metropolitan areas are saturated. Community resistance, expressed through restrictive zoning and environmental controls, has limited the available sites for development and has raised the cost of suitable land. Today most of the growth is shifting to the growing southern and western states and, within those states, to the smaller market areas.

The industry has developed innovations to deal with the problems imposed by land and economic constraints. There is more interest in development of downtown centers, often as part of urban renewal efforts. Also, renovation of older centers in profitable locations is a major trend. The introduction of the multilevel center is another attempt to minimize land costs (e.g., the three-level Galleria in Houston and Chicago's Water Tower Place, with six stories.) For an excellent example see the photographs and data for the Cumberland Mall on pages 546–547.

Rising energy costs add to the appeal of multiuse developments in which retail shops are combined with residential and office uses to form a self-sufficient minicity (e.g., Allegheny Center in Pittsburgh). Special shopping needs are now being catered to with the development of discount centers (where the anchor is a major discount store) and fashion/specialty centers (e.g., Northridge Fashion Center in Northridge, Calif.). The Urban Land Institute (ULI) Project Reference Files provide additional information on some of these projects, such as costs of construction, financing, design, tenant mix, and expense/revenue units.

The demand for shopping center investments remains high. Concern about inflation has led lenders and investors to seek equity positions in well-located centers. The associated high cost of debt financing has caused developers to invite greater equity participation as an alternative to highly leveraged financing techniques. Institutional lenders are participating.

Prior to projecting future income, the investor should answer the following questions:

1. What is the historical trend of net income from the center? the trend of rental income from individual stores?
2. Has the trade area recently been invaded by other centers offering similar merchandise? Is the area's potential, as measured by population and income, growing or declining?
3. When will existing leases expire, and do renewal options preclude raising rental rates?
4. What possibilities exist for expanding the center or changing the tenant/product mix? How would such changes affect the sales of existing stores?
5. What plans do the municipal or state governments have with regard to changing highway services?

ADVANTAGES AND DISADVANTAGES OF INVESTING IN SHOPPING CENTERS

A well-located center can provide a relatively stable and secure return with adequate growth potential to ward off losses of real income due to inflation. Security is provided by the generally high credit ratings of major tenants and the minimum rent schedules in most leases. Growth potential is afforded by provisions for overages and the ability to pass along increases in expenses to the tenants through net leases and pro rata sharing of common expenses. Prospects for resale and refinancing are also good because of the appreciation in land values and the strong investor demand for profitable centers. Formerly, shopping centers had an advantage of strong depreciation write offs due to a shorter economic life as a result of functional and locational obsolescence (median life equalled 26 years). However, the ACRS lives of 15, 35, and 45 years have virtually equalized depreciation rates for different types of property. However, centers that are more than 30 years old have gained a great advantage by way of special rehabilitation tax credits that are now available.

However, because of strong investor demand and the difficulty of developing new centers, locating a profitable center at a price that will provide suitable returns may be difficult. The most likely candidates are smaller centers in relatively untapped market areas, such as medium-sized cities, and centers that are ripe for rehabilitation and are located in stable trading areas. Generating a competitive return depends to a great extent on the negotiating skill of the manager and his or her ability to obtain leases with provision for income growth and tenant participation in expense increases. The negotiating power of the owner may be restricted by the ability of major tenants to extract favors and concessions. The value of a center is also dependent on dynamic features, such as attractiveness of design, convenience of layout, population distribution, and the quality of surrounding development. Other disadvantages are, of course, found in the complexity of the management and economic factors that most frequently affect centers. These factors, in order of impact, are set forth in Exhibit 20–2.

TYPES OF INVESTORS AND INVESTOR MOTIVATIONS

Shopping centers have been attractive investments for major institutions, wealthy individuals, and development firms alike. The motivations of the investors differ, with individuals and development firms interested in near-term income and tax shelter. Institutions, which are willing to accept lower, but stable, initial returns, have sought their return over the long term through general appreciation. Quite often these two groups are not in direct competition. The developers and equity partners are generally first investors. The institutions become second-user investors or buyers after the property has been established. This is changing, though: Institutions are now seeking immediate equity positions in order to enhance their returns. However, their risk-avoidance policies generally limit the effective returns for the developer/investor who is willing to assume greater risks.

EXHIBIT 20–2.   Factors That Cause Change in Shopping Center Rates of Return

---

- Competition entering the market
- Outdated design and layout
- Changes in trade area income levels
- Changes in population density
- Changes in highway network

Source: Institute for Business Planning, *Real Estate Investment Planning* (Englewood Cliffs, N.J.) 1, 57, 306.

CUMBERLAND MALL, Atlanta, Georgia

Project Data

Site: 72 net acres

Building area (gross leasable area):
Cumberland Mall: 325,000 sq. ft.
Four free-standing department stores:[1] 840,000 sq. ft.
Total gross leasable area: 1,165,000 sq. ft.

Existing parking: 5,800 spaces

Parking ratio: 5.7/1,000 sq. ft. of gross leasable area

Tenant information (other than department stores)

Classification	Number of Stores	Percent of GLA	Sq. Ft. of GLA
Food	9	13.1%	42,603
Food services	10	2.7	8,655
Clothing and shoes	52	49.6	161,147
Furniture and house furnishings	2	1.7	5,757
Other retail	48	31.4	101,807
Financial	2	.5	1,797
Services	3	1.0	3,154
	126	100.0%	325,000

Sales and rent information[2]
Total rent roll for Cumberland Mall: $4,990,000
Average rent/square foot: $8.25[3]
Operating expenses/square foot: $2.45[4]
Estimated retail sales/square foot of GLA: $199.00
Merchants' Association dues: $0.50/square foot

[1] Davisons: 160,000 sq. ft.; J.C. Penney: 195,000 sq. ft.; Richs: 285,000 sq. ft.; Sears: 200,000 sq. ft.
[2] Sales and rent information per tenant classification may be estimated from Urban Land Institute, *Dollars and Cents of Shopping Centers.*
[3] Department stores are self-owned in fee simple. A proxy rental income could be estimated from *Dollars and Cents of Shopping Centers.*
[4] Operating expenses do not include central administrative overhead for Carter & Associates.

Photos and data courtesy of Carter & Associates, Inc., Commercial real estate developers.

Mall Level

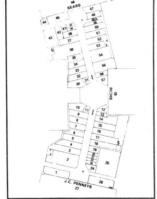

Upper Level

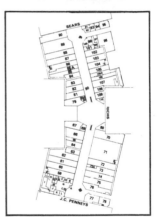

Foreign investors. The desire of foreign investors to place money in American real estate is motivated by the need for security from government confiscation, plus tax advantages and the lack of better investment opportunities at home. Immediate profitability appears to be secondary; furthermore, our lower rate of inflation invites investment here to conserve capital.

Institutional investors. Insurance companies and pension funds are seeking relatively secure investments with growth potential. To achieve this potential, these sources increasingly are seeking ownership participations.

Large public syndications. These investors have expressed interest in smaller centers in untapped markets in order to diversify their largely residential property portfolios.

Equity REITs. Some large equity REITs specialize in shopping centers (e.g., the Henry Miller REIT in Dallas and Great American Growth Properties in the Quad Cities [Iowa-Ill.] area) and are quite active in the market.

THE NATURE OF THE RETURNS AND RISKS

Compared to most other commercial real estate ventures, investments in existing shopping centers entail relatively lower risk. The high credit ratings required by lenders for major tenants, as well as pre-lease commitments, reduce the speculative aspects of development. The return/risk trade-off may be balanced by adjusting the tenant mix. Higher percentages of major tenants add to security by providing a dependable base of rental income and enhancing the drawing power of the center. However, their superior bargaining position can result in lower NOI and meager returns. Satellite tenants, on the other hand, add to profitability through the payment of higher rents and the requirement of fewer lease concessions.

Lenders often seek full amortization with modest debt coverage solely from the rent rolls of the major tenants. Enforceable leases requiring minimum level of rents when the center is in operation are typical for new centers and for renovations or refinancings of existing centers. Thus, the priority lien of the mortgagee shifts much of the primary source of returns for the equity investor to the satellite stores.

In less inflationary times investors were demanding 10– 12 percent (IRR) on total assets on the basis of after-tax cash flow analysis. The result was that rising sales volume coupled with a level annual debt constant soon produced high yields to equity for well-located centers. After-tax equity yield rates (IRR) of 20– 40 percent were reported. In 1981 the equity investor's situation became more uncertain. American equity investors in regional shopping centers are now seeking an 8 percent current yield on total assets (ROR), often with little if any cash flow before tax (ROE), in order to gain control of a property, with the growth potential coming from the overages. Foreign investors are bidding the prices up because they will settle for even lower returns (e.g., 5 percent on total assets in the initial year). Often the foreign investors are using no financing, budgeting 100 percent equity into the project. Even institutional investors like insurance companies, comingled funds, and equity REITs are buying at exceptionally low yields on equity in order to gain control of a high-quality shopping center's income stream. Motivations are diverse: The individual equity investors appear to be the already wealthy who are seeking to conserve assets; foreign investors are moving capital out of economies that have higher inflation rates than the United States and are less stable politically; life insurance companies are moving money out of utilities, bonds, and mortgages in an effort to protect principal against the pernicious erosion caused by inflation. Apparently, all of them believe that retail price levels will trigger rent increases by way of the overage clauses and thus make shopping centers one of the best hedges against inflation. Certainly, increases in the prices of food, clothing, hardware, and household items have been among the leaders in the market basket of goods on which the consumer price index is based. Unlike apartment tenants, shopping center tenants lack the political influence that might result in rent controls. Rents have been increasing much faster for shopping centers than for apartments.

Major sources of risk include the possibility of high vacancy rates for non-major tenants, lack of adequate growth in sales to provide overage income, bankruptcy of a major tenant, uncompensated but escalating operating costs due to rising tax and utility bills, and the opening of new shopping centers in the trading area without concomitant increases in consumer buying power.

MARKET AND MARKETABILITY ANALYSIS

Depending on the size and type of center and population density, the primary market (trading) area will vary from a few miles to twenty to thirty miles in radius. A survey of the delineated trade area will indicate trends in population and income that are important in determining the area's potential. The market area should also be segmented according to the product mix offered in the center. Convenience goods have a more immediate market range than shopping and specialty goods. Compare the tenant mix with the growth potential for each segment of the buying power for the market area.

An evaluation should also be made of factors that threaten the sales potential of the center. Existing and potential competitors should be examined for proximity, duplication of product, and design advantages. Changes in the location and upgrading of access roads may affect the convenience of the location. Impending disruptions in the basic industries of the local economy could soften sales in the near future. An examination of locally prepared planning reports may uncover these trends.

Demand Analysis. Commercial retail investments are based on derived demand. Although income is provided by leasing space to stores, the demand for this space is derived from customers' demands for goods and services. Therefore, demand analysis should focus on the retail sales potential of the center.

The first step is delineation of the *trading area*. Although market analysts use intensive survey methods to accurately measure market areas, a good approximation can be made by considering the size of the center, the type of goods offered, population density, and available transportation facilities. As a guide, neighborhood centers require a market of 2,500– 40,000 people within a 1 1/2-mile radius; community centers, 40,000– 150,000 within 3– 5 miles; and regional centers, 150,000 or more within 8– 10 miles. In densely populated areas with many competing centers, these trading areas are smaller; in rural areas with good high-speed roads, they may be expanded.

The core of the market is the primary area in which the center represents the most ready source of convenience goods. In urban areas the core may have a radius of no more than one mile. A larger, or secondary, market area is generally shared with other centers equally or slightly more conveniently located for customers. A peripheral (tertiary) area may exist for specialty and shopping goods, extending beyond the boundaries of the formal market area.

Once the market area is defined and segmented, an examination of population and income statistics within the area will reveal its potential. In Chapter 6 we reviewed the CACI Site POTENTIAL™ and SITE II™ as good examples of economic–demographic data retrieval systems available at reasonable cost for any defined size or shape of market area. Dense population and high incomes indicate a large capacity for generating sales, but trends in these two key indicators should also be examined. Growth potential provides opportunities for improving the performance of an existing center.

The attributes of the market area also indicate the type of center that is most needed in the area. A high-income area provides a good market for specialty and luxury goods, possibly a good setting for a specialty center. Low and moderate incomes call for discount stores. The type of merchandise should match the purchasing habits of the area.

Supply Analysis. After the potential of the trading area has been determined, an estimate of market penetration should be made. The key factors are the location and nature of competitors and any competitive advantages the subject center or location may command. The center will normally draw most of the business of the immediately surrounding area, depending on the existence of independent stores in the area. The center can expect no more than a fractional share of the secondary market area. In a multicounty or state area, a check of license plates in the parking lot may reveal the drawing power of the center. Any superior features of the center, such as covered parking, well-regarded stores, or excellent exposure and access, will add to the share of customers attracted. Potential for improving such features should be considered. Competitive surveys should be carried out and market share (capture rates) developed. (See Chapter 6 for the components of a retail competitive survey.)

Projection of Rental Income and Vacancies. Projections of trading area growth and market share provide an indication of the future sales potential at the site. These indicators are converted into shopping center income by examining existing and future lease provisions. Minimum rents provide the base for these projections. As the center becomes more profitable, fewer vacancies can be expected and minimum rents may be raised at the termination of existing short-term leases. Increased sales, moreover, make possible higher percentage rents, which should provide higher returns to the center's owners. To determine the minimum sales needed to trigger the percentage provision, divide the minimum rent by the percentage rate. For example, if the lease called for rent of $1,000 per month or 5 percent of sales, whichever is greater, sales of $1,000/.05, or $20,000 per month, would be the threshold point for percentage rent.

In projecting rental income it is important to consider any recapture provisions in the lease. Recapture allows for payment of shared expenses and pro rata assessments from the overage income, when it exists. Such lease agreements will reduce overage income in cases of rising expenses.

Risk Management and Control Techniques. The most effective internal control technique available to the shopping center investor is the tenant mix selection.

Generally, investors and managers of shopping centers should be knowledgeable about retail marketing business risks and consumer buying behavior patterns. For example, the power of the retailer to influence the actual decision to buy changes as one moves from convenience goods to shopping goods. The management skills of the tenants are more important with shopping goods than with convenience goods.

A certain proportion of high-credit-rated tenants will be required by the lenders in order to reduce risk. Such tenants, realizing their value to the investor, can often negotiate favorable lease terms. The satellites, while increasing the risks of turnover and bankruptcy, generally pay higher rents. This is especially true of first-time business enterprises. Reflecting the differences in risks are the lease terms offered to major and minor tenants. Majors generally enter long-term (10–20-year) leases while other tenants may obtain short-term (3–5-year) leases. Unilateral options of tenants to renew are risks that should be carefully negotiated.

Setting the level of minimum rents is another risk control measure, although it is highly restricted by relative market rents. Requiring low minimums with high percentages effectively shifts much of the risk of the tenant onto the investor, as the tenant pays high rents only when most able to do so.

The purchaser of an existing or newly built center may be able to get the seller to warrant the level of percentage rental income. This shifts some of the risk back to the seller. The manager may also control the ability of tenants to sublet space to other businesses, thereby controlling the entry of undesirable tenants.

PHYSICAL, LEGAL, POLITICAL, AND ENVIRONMENTAL ANALYSIS

Physical and Structural Factors. The center should provide design features that are comparable to the market standard in the area. Such features as mall enclosure, sheltered parking, attractive landscaping and façades, and mall ornamentation may add to the appeal of the center. The location of the anchors can affect their utility to other tenants in terms of attracting customers. Evaluate how easy and inexpensive it will be to maintain, clean, heat, air-condition, and light the center. This will depend on the location of janitorial facilities, the construction materials, the amount of insulation and glass surfaces, the heating/air-conditioning equipment, the type of fuel used, and the amount of natural lighting. Where appropriate, snow removal equipment, high-capacity air-conditioning equipment, and so forth should be checked. Consider the adequacy and quality of drainage facilities to handle rain and snow runoff.

Take note of how much space, if any, in the center is devoted to special uses, such as theaters, medical offices, and restaurants. Adequate parking should also be provided for both current and potential business. Look for adequate curb cuts and ease of legal access to and from major streets.

An inspection and evaluation should be made of all components that may need repair or replacement. This should be done by technically qualified personnel. Include in this estimate a provision for adding any improvements necessary to meet market standards. These expenditures should be considered in evaluating the purchase price.

Legal and Political Factors. A study should be made of the local attitude toward shopping center operation and development. In a hostile environment local communities may use zoning and other environmental controls and tax policy to restrict the growth profitability of the center. Compare assessed value to appraised value to consider the possibility of increased taxes. A field inspection of the taxing jurisdiction may be necessary to consider whether or not the schools, roads, sewage system, and so forth are adequate. Suburban communities often sharply increase tax assessments after the subdividers have phased out. Shopping centers often bear the brunt of delayed capital improvements. Also, differentials in the sales tax may affect sales volume if the rate is higher than in surrounding jurisdictions (with most of the impact on big-ticket shopping goods). An examination of existing leases should be made to uncover possible antitrust violations (primarily agreements to restrict competition with the center).

ANALYSIS OF OPERATIONS

Property Management and Leasing. Efficient operation of the center depends on competent management. The common areas should be well maintained and clean. The shops should be full of customers during peak shopping hours. Survey the parking areas to determine center use. Leases should be structured to provide for income growth. This will mean percentage rent agreements and the ability to raise minimum rents at the expiration of short-term leases. Look for an active merchant's association with an effective promotion campaign.

In addition to performing the normal tasks of property management— maintenance, sanitation, leasing, and bill paying—the shopping center manager is expected to collect and maintain sales records for each store in the center. Such information is important for determining overage rents and provides the owners with an indication of the economic health of the center. The manager is also expected to calculate and bill tenants for any pro rata share of the expenses, according to the lease provisions.

Three types of rent structures are commonly used in shopping center leases. The *percentage rent* structure provides that a tenant pays the *greater* of two amounts: a minimum rent or a percentage of gross sales, with the percentage subject to negotiation. Such an arrangement provides a stable minimum income and the potential for increases as sales volume expands. Examples of percentages used in such leases are shown in Exhibit 20–3.

For tenants that are not involved in retail sales, *graduated rents* may be used. In such cases rent payments usually follow an established schedule of steps during the life of the lease.

Major tenants often operate on *net leases*. Such leases usually provide a clause that makes the base rent amount subject to an index change. These arrangements require a *set base rent with a combination of additional charges* correlated with the costs of operating the center—pro rata shares of common-area maintenance, taxes, and utility bills and an administrative surcharge are typical. The rate of change may be dollar-for-dollar-true-cost related, or the base year may be subject to a specified index (e.g., a regional consumer cost index) and its rate of change.

A sufficient lease will include the following provisions, among others:

1. A description of the space to be leased.
2. The beginning and length of the lease term.
3. The rental agreement and payment procedures.

EXHIBIT 20-3. Representative Percentage Rent Structure for a Shopping Center

Type of Business	Percentage Rental	Type of Business	Percentage Rental
Auto parts and accessories	1–3	Haberdasher	6–8
Bakery	5–7	Hosiery	7–8
Beauty shop	8–10	Jewelry	5.5–8 (exclusive); 8–10
Bookstore	6–8	Laundromat	10–20
Camera shop	4–6	Men's clothing	6–7
Candy store	10	Men's hair stylist	10–12
Card and gift shop	8.5–10	Men's ties	10
Children's wear	6–8	Millinery	15–20
Cigars and cigarettes	8	Optometrist and optical instruments	10–17
Cleaning and dyeing	8–10	Parking lot	45–50
Cocktail bar	25 (and downward)	Piano	5
Coffee shop and luncheonette	8–10	Prescription pharmacy	8
Coins and stamps	9–10	Radio, TV, stereo	4–5
Cosmetics	10 (and downward)	Record shop	6–8
Cutlery	6–8	Restaurant and cafeteria	6–8
Currency exchange	15	Shoe repair	7–10
Department store	2–3	Shoe store	6–8
Drapery and dry goods	11 (and downward)	Sporting goods	4–5
Drugstore	4–5	Stationery	5–6
Fast food	8	Supermarket	1.5–2
Florist	7–10	Trunks and leather goods	8
Furniture	4–5	Variety shop	5–6
Furs	5–7	Watch repair	20
Greeting cards	7–10 plus	Women's wear	5–6 (exclusive)

4. Specific required sales reports and other necessary information on tenant experience.
5. Required membership in a merchant's association, and dues.
6. Restrictions on the use of the premises, including types of merchandise sold.
7. Fixing of responsibility for utility bills, repairs, insurance, and tax increases.
8. Restrictions on subletting space.
9. Conditions under which the landlord may cancel the lease.
10. Limits on tenant's right to constructive eviction (e.g., condemnation, fire or other casualty, lease violations by other tenants, loss of parking per square-foot ratio, etc.).
11. Duty to pay for share of common-area maintenance charges.
12. Requirements for security deposits.
13. Provisions triggering assessments for major center improvements, such as enclosure of the mall or renovation of the façade.
14. An arbitration clause to handle disputes in lieu of litigation.

Analysis of Current Operating Income and Expenses

Estimates of rents, vacancies, and expenses. Rents and vacancies can be estimated from the track record of the property (or comparable ones if new construction is involved). Average income, including overage, should be multiplied by total GLA to estimate total income. Expenses may be estimated in the same manner (subtract any expenses shared by tenants.)

An investor should have available the operating history of a center for the past three to five years. In a new development, projections should be based on realistic market shares (capture rates). A comparative analysis should then be undertaken to test the validity of the data prior to doing financial analysis.

Key ratios. Space/sales and income/expense data related to GLA are useful analytical tools for prospective shopping center investors. Longitudinal trends indicating percentage changes over time are useful indicators of the potential profitability of the targeted center.

The Urban Land Institute provides data that enable one to analyze the primary sources of income and expense for a shopping center. Exhibit 20–4 abstracts key ratios for median sales per square foot of GLA for different types of shopping centers.

Total rent is the income from tenants received as rent for the leased space, including the minimum guaranteed yearly rent, straight percentage rent (no minimum guarantee), and overage rent for the year.

EXHIBIT 20-4.   Space, Sales, and Rent Data for Shopping Centers, by Type

	MEDIAN GLA (FT.)			
	Super-regional	Regional	Community	Neighborhood
Department store	164,694	100,000	48,613	31,200
Variety store	*	*	18,000	8,716
Ladies' ready-to-wear	3,705	3,702	3,190	1,800
Men's wear	3,109	3,173	3,000	2,100
Family shoes	3,350	3,360	3,120	2,594
Cards and gifts	2,487	2,500	2,129	2,000
Jewelry	1,531	1,607	1,400	960
Medical and dental	1,460	1,080	1,000	1,120
	MEDIAN SALES VOLUME/FT² OF GLA			
Department store	*	$ 83.48	$ 79.94	$ 94.91
Variety store	*	*	43.67	40.87
Ladies' ready-to-wear	$117.86	116.43	94.62	81.56
Men's wear	115.16	130.85	105.03	110.50
Family shoes	130.98	103.57	76.44	64.04
Cards and gifts	117.78	95.78	66.17	44.82
Jewelry	321.13	271.59	166.93	126.95
Medical and dental	*	*	*	*
	MEDIAN RENT/FT² OF GLA			
Department store	$ .46	$ 2.07	$2.10	$2.70
Variety store	*	*	1.94	1.92
Ladies' ready-to-wear	7.31	6.49	5.00	5.42
Men's wear	7.92	7.00	5.28	6.00
Family shoes	9.45	7.40	4.94	4.79
Cards and gifts	10.00	· 7.99	5.76	5.49
Jewelry	18.23	14.37	8.10	7.00
Medical and dental	8.00	8.82	5.50	6.00

SOURCE: *Dollars and Cents of Shopping Centers: 1980* (Washington, D.C.: Urban Land Institute, 1981), pp. 27, 60, 78, 112, 128, 130, 178, 180, 186, 188.
* = no data

Common-area charges are collected from tenants for operating and mainte-nance items pertaining to the common areas. Shopping center leases usually contain a clause that requires the tenant to pay a share of operation and mainte-nance costs for common areas. Of the ways to prorate the charges among tenants, the most common are (1) a pro rata charge based on a tenant's leased area as a percentage of the total leasable area of the center or the linear exposure in store frontage, (2) a fixed charge for a stated period, or (3) a variable charge based on a percentage of sales. Some centers include a cost-of-living index to determine increases in common-area charges.

Other charges are income to the center under certain lease provisions, such as real estate tax and insurance escalator clauses and income from facilities like pay telephones, pay toilets, and vending machines. Full tax escalation without ceiling and recapture from overage rents is included where such lease clauses pertain after the initial year's assessment.

Total operating receipts are the total income received by the owner of the shopping center—all the money received from rentals, common-area charges, and other income described earlier. Total operating receipts do *not* include in-come from furniture and equipment sold to tenants, charges collected to be given to another organization (e.g., merchant's association dues), or any special situa-tions that are not directly related to the operation of the shopping center. (Total operating receipts are the same as gross receipts.)

For the cost side of the shopping center ledger, information is collected on the basis of functional categories and natural divisions of expenses. The functional expense categories are broad classifications that can be applied to all centers. They include expenses for building maintenance, the parking lot, the mall and other common areas, central utility systems, office area services, advertising and promotion, real estate taxes, insurance, and general and administrative functions. The definition of each functional category may be found in the *Standard Manual of Accounting for Shopping Center Operations* published by the Urban Land Institute.

The natural divisions of expenses are the breakdowns of operating costs used for recording items within a functional category. There is interchangeability among some of the natural divisions of expense, such as payroll, management fees, contracted expenses, and professional services. For example, some centers pay an agency for management services, while others are managed by the owner. In the latter case the management cost would be considered a payroll expense to the extent that the owner pays himself or herself a salary. It is not possible, therefore, to provide a uniform comparison of the natural divisions of expenses.

The following functional expense categories are the bases of developing comparative data on operating statistics per square foot of GLA:

- *Building maintenance*—includes such items as painting, repairs, and uncapitalized alterations to structures.
- *Common-area maintenance*—covers repair of paving and striping of the parking lot; cleaning, lighting, guard or police service, heating, ventilating, and air conditioning (HVAC) of an enclosed mall; servicing public toilets; power used for maintenance of signs (those for which the landlord is responsible); snow and trash removal; maintenance and landscaping of grounds; and so on.
- *Office area services*—include janitor service, lighting, and the like for the office areas occupied by office tenants.

- *Central utility systems*—include all costs of operating a central utility plant or total energy system in the center.
- *Real estate taxes.*
- *Insurance*—includes fire and other damage, public liability, plate glass, and rental value (use or occupancy).
- *General and administrative*—includes expenses not otherwise classified, such as management of the center, communications, and office staff.

Exhibit 20–5 shows some median values for operating statement analysis of various kinds of shopping centers. These figures can be used for comparison with a targeted property only for the data base year (1978).[1]

Analysis of Trends and Uncertainties. Unless the center is in need of major repairs or renovation, the greatest potential for increased expenses during the life of the investment is in utilities and taxes. Utility rates are tied to the cost and

EXHIBIT 20–5. Operating Statements for Shopping Centers (Median Values)

Item	SUPERREGIONALS		REGIONAL		COMMUNITY		NEIGHBORHOOD	
	$/ GLA	% of Re- ceipts	$/ GLA	% of Re- ceipts	$/ GLA	% of Re- ceipts	$/ GLA	% of Re- ceipts
GLA	366,018		261,203		162,262		53,911	
Operating receipts								
Minimum rents	4.75	67.6	2.98	64.5	2.09	77.6	2.41	83.1
Overage rents	0.68	9.8	0.86	13.4	0.39	12.0	0.33	11.3
Total rents	5.51	78.4	4.10	81.9	2.59	92.6	2.81	93.9
Common area charges	0.67	11.8	0.35	9.3	0.11	3.5	0.12	4.1
Rent escalation	0.33	3.7	0.17	2.5	0.09	2.8	0.16	4.5
Income from utilities sales	0.96	9.8	0.67	10.7	0.05	1.1	0.05	1.5
Miscellaneous	0.12	1.8	0.04	0.8	0.03	0.4	0.04	0.4
Total operating receipts	6.94	100.0	4.85	100.0	2.96	100.0	2.99	100.0
Operating expenses								
Building maintenance	0.08	1.3	0.04	1.0	0.06	2.1	0.06	1.9
Common area maintenance	0.57	10.0	0.48	11.8	0.15	5.6	0.13	4.6
Central utilities	0.35	8.4	0.35	9.4	0.09	3.0	0.08	2.9
Office area services	0.06	1.9	0.05	1.0	0.05	1.6	0.04	1.4
Advertising and promotion	0.05	0.8	0.05	1.1	0.03	1.0	0.03	0.7
Property taxes	0.57	9.0	0.44	10.4	0.31	11.3	0.34	10.7
Insurance	0.04	0.7	0.05	1.2	0.06	2.1	0.06	2.2
General and administrative	0.28	5.0	0.20	5.9	0.17	5.9	0.15	5.1
Total operating expenses	1.88	33.6	1.49	38.1	0.90	32.3	0.80	27.1
Net operating income	5.08	66.4	3.32	61.9	1.92	67.7	2.12	72.8
Minus finance costs[a]	2.69	43.3	1.34	30.7	0.77	30.7	1.08	36.9
Minus depreciation	0.81	14.1	0.71	16.4	0.54	19.5	0.57	18.2
Taxable income	1.60	14.7	1.21	16.6	0.60	20.6	0.60	20.1
Plus depreciation	0.81	14.1	0.71	16.4	0.54	18.5	0.57	18.2
Minus principal amortization	0.31	5.5	0.45	9.7	0.38	14.9	0.40	12.6
Cash flow before tax	2.09	21.5	1.54	21.0	0.71	24.9	0.76	23.7

SOURCE: *Dollars and Cents of Shopping Centers* (Washington, D.C., Urban Land Institute, 1978), Tables 3–1, 4–1, 5–1, 6–1.
[a] Includes mortgage interest, income participation, and ground rent.

[1] See later editions of Urban Land Institute, *Dollars and Cents of Shopping Centers,* for more recent comparable revenue/expense unit comparisons.

availability of fuels, with escalating prices expected in the future. The efficiency with which the center uses energy will help determine the impact of these higher costs. Property taxes may increase substantially in suburban areas faced with the prospect of building new infrastructures for development, and in large cities with increasing operating costs and a diminishing tax base. Popular movements for limitation of property tax increases may result in tax relief for residential properties only. Tax assessors may raise the assessed value of the center to reflect the increased value of the underlying land. Although there are appeal procedures to contest tax increases, a center is somewhat vulnerable to greater property tax charges, especially if it is successful in capturing a large market share.

Projection of Expenses. Dollars and Cents of Shopping Centers also provides useful data on current and historical cost trends for various types and locations of centers. Projection of these trends, with modifications for expected increases as described earlier, should provide good data for comparative analysis. For pro forma purposes, all expenses billed to the center should be shown on the expense side of the statement. Contributions by the tenants to offset these expenses should be included on the revenue side. By isolating these charges one may evaluate the impacts on individual stores as the charges and pro rata shares fluctuate.

Risk Management. Net lease provisions are the investor's protection against rising operating costs. Rapid increases, however, may outstrip the ability of many smaller tenants to pay pro rata shares and still maintain profitability. Such a situation will result in higher vacancy and turnover rates. Emphasis on energy efficiency, diligence in challenging tax increases, and more efficient maintenance and housekeeping procedures may hold down cost increases.

FINANCING AND REFINANCING TECHNIQUES

Sources. Large shopping centers generally receive funding from the major institutional lenders—insurance companies and pension funds. Large public investment syndicates are also entering the picture. The trend for all sources of funds is for greater equity participation as investors seek to protect yields against erosion due to inflation. Because of the nature of the risks to equity investment, shopping centers provide an ideal vehicle for regulated institutions to make equity investments.

Rates, Terms, and Conditions. The investor should expect to pay interest rates comparable to the market rate on commercial loans (i.e., ±13 percent in the 1981 market). The amount of the loan will generally coincide with the life of the anchor tenant's lease. Thus, renewal of major leases and increases in rental income from them provide opportunities for refinancing.

Because of the importance of income from major tenants, lenders require firm commitments from a certain number of tenants with substantial credit ratings and financial substance. In addition, lenders are seeking participation in the center's overage income or the proceeds of resale or refinancing.

Projection of Financing Costs. Debt service has generally been fixed over the investment period and could be accurately projected. If escalation provisions are involved, a judgment must be made about future interest rate trends.

Renegotiable-rate mortgages will introduce interest rate uncertainty. Simulation should be done over the expected range of rates to test the effect on IRR.

Debt Coverage Ratio and Mortgage Constant Desired by the Lender. If a loan is assumed, debt service continues from the existing loan. When refinancing, currently available rates should be used. Required debt coverage ratios for shopping centers are generally based on minimum rents, often from major tenants only. Estimates of the lender's share of income participation may be added to debt service. Some computer models make it necessary to treat such equity participation as an operating expense.

Ground rent payments may be projected in much the same way as debt service, especially if no graduated payments are involved. Participations should be proportioned according to the assumptions used for increases in income and resale value. Though variable-rate mortgages are still uncommon for commercial properties, such indexing of debt service to protect the lender against erosion of principal may be in the offing. If contractual obligations force consideration of variability of the annual mortgage constant, one must make key assumptions as to the range of such variability. Of course, variable-rate mortgages may be structured so that they simply vary the size of the final payment (balloon) rather than the annual debt service, thus shifting the impact from operating income to the net equity reversion. Whatever the case, the impact of such variation in mortgage payment obligations must be projected in the way in which it is likely to occur for useful financial analysis.

Know the Risk Control and Management Techniques of Lenders. Market financing usually requires a varying down payment, depending on the availability of mortgage credit, the quality of the shopping center's location, and the net worth of the buyer. Down payments may vary from 10 percent to 30 percent without overburdening the cash flow. Debt service should be compared to minimum rents to gauge the margin of coverage.

In general, requirements are that minimum rents from major tenants (those with a net worth greater than $1 million) should be sufficient to cover debt service and operating expenses, including property taxes. The remaining term of the mortgage should be at least ten years so that immediate financing is an option rather than a necessity. Examine loan terms carefully to detect any participation agreements that may be triggered by increased income. The loan agreement should be rigorously analyzed so that one can detect, for example, a possible due-on-sale clause that may trigger increased interest rates, and acceleration clauses based on external occurrences (e.g. condemnation). If assumption is a valuable right, it may be necessary to bargain aggressively with the lender as well as the seller concerning such clauses. Exhibit 20–6, averaged from loan commitments exceeding $100,000 by fifteen life insurance companies in 1979, may be used as a guide for evaluation.

Lenders attempt to control their exposure to risk through two mechanisms: (1) the ratio of the amount of the loan committed to the value and (2) requirements on tenants. The loan amount may be based on the capitalized value of income from major tenants, possibly 60–70 percent of the capitalized value of total income. In addition, a maximum may be set on a per-GLA basis, varying with the type and location of the center.

Lenders also require that a certain proportion of the space be leased to tenants with high credit ratings under triple net leases with overages.

EXHIBIT 20-6.   Shopping Center Financing Terms

Period	Average Interest Rate	Average Constant[a]	Average Term[b]
4th quarter 1978	9.85	11.0	21,3
3rd quarter 1979	9.70	10.7	22,2
4th quarter 1979	9.21	10.2	22,1

SOURCE: *The Appraiser,* June 1979, p. 12.
[a] debt service/loan amount
[b] years, months

Specialized financing techniques are used in shopping center ventures to manage risk and structure capital. Sale–leaseback and sale–buyback arrangements are used to reduce equity contributions and maximize depreciation deductions. Joint ventures may be formed with anchor tenants for the development of new centers and free-standing parcels within multitenant centers. Other recent trends worthy of observation are (1) the increased use of wraparound mortgages, mortgage assumptions, and various forms of lender participations, and (2) the increased use of creative financing techniques, such as junior mortgages, ground leases, and spreading of the risk through syndication of the equity interest.

TAXATION AND TAX STRUCTURE

The Nature of the Tax Shelter. Tax shelter benefits are derived from the ability to defer or avoid payment of taxes ordinarily due on current income. These benefits are garnered, in part, by claiming noncash deductions to offset depreciation of wasting assets.

Shopping centers are eligible for ACRS 15-year recovery periods; taxpayers may choose either the 35-year of the 45-year recovery period. Any substantial improvement is treated as a separate building depreciation schedule. Alternatively, centers may choose the 175 percent declining-balance method with statutory switch to straight-line depreciation at about the ninth or tenth year. However, there is a substantial recapture penalty of all depreciation for those who choose the latter election but then dispose of the property before it is depreciated by way of the 15-year ACRS schedule. The authors recommend serious consideration of the 15-year ACRS straight-line recovery method as a better strategy under current law.

(When purchasing an existing shopping center, it will be necessary to allocate a part of the price to the land. The services of a qualified appraiser are recommended to prepare for the IRS audit.)

The 1981 tax act allows certain business assets to be expensed instead of taking an ACRS deduction. The maximum amount subject to expensing is $5,000 in 1982, increasing to $10,000 in 1986 and thereafter. Such expensing will be treated as recapturable depreciation in the event of a premature sale and is subject to a "taxpayer" limit of no more than the allowable amount for each (e.g., for each partner). We do not recommend this method because of the nuisance effect.

Although buildings, their structural components, and items attached, affixed to, and made part of the realty are not eligible for investment tax credit, some personalty is eligible for the three- and five-year ACRS lives and the appropriate investment tax credit. Examples are snow-clearing equipment, mall furniture, artificial plants, and the like. Tax counsel should be sought when seeking to classify as personalty any separately maintained and movable items that might be property classified as equipment. Examples are carpeting, movable partitions, bank equipment, vending machines, fencing, window-washing equipment, leasehold improvements, and specially designed and installed HVAC and humidity control equipment.

In rehabilitating older shopping centers, care should be taken to design and carry out the rehabilitation so that it will be eligible for the investment tax credit incentive of 15 percent for structures at least 30 years old, 20 percent for structures at least 40 years old, and 25 percent for certified historic structures. There is no longer an investment tax credit for buildings less than 30 years old.

Improvements made for a specific tenant may enable the landlord to specify a certain portion of rental income as repayment for the improvement and deduct this amount from taxable income. Finally, if property improvements can be legitimately scheduled as periodic repairs, the expenditures may, to some extent, be expensed as current operating expenses rather than being added to the depreciable base.

For some expenditures for improvements to be eligible as deductible operating expenses, the improvement program might be *fractionalized* into routine repair operations, thus minimizing capital additions. Tax advantages should be weighed against any additional costs or inconvenience that may result from spreading the program over several tax years. To take advantage of the tax-deductible rent proceeds for repayment of tenant-specific improvements, a portion of rental income from the tenant must be identified as amortization of that expense in the lease. The portion identified as such must be based on some reasonable imputed discount rate. Such activities must have a sound business policy objective and not be carried out simply to evade taxes.

Disposition of shopping centers is also eligible for various tax deferment techniques, such as installment sales and tax-deferred exchanges.

Tax Problems and Uncertainties. Using the 175 percent accelerated depreciation method is more risky than using the 15-year straight-line ACRS method. When the former is used, the taxpayer must be aware of possible recapture effects upon premature sale of the property. All depreciation is recaptured at ordinary tax rates. Investment tax credits are also subject to recapture upon premature resale.

Determination of Tax Assumptions for Analysis. After structuring the venture for tax planning, the analyst must make assumptions about the ownership entity, marginal tax rates and changes in those rates, and probable resale value and proceeds. These assumptions are fairly standard for all types of property and should be done in accordance with principles and concepts set forth in earlier sections of this book.

DISCOUNTED CASH FLOW ANALYSIS

Rate-of-Return Analysis. To calculate internal rate of return, it is necessary to make assumptions about the length of the holding period and the probable resale value. Projections of income, expenses, finance costs, and taxes are extended to cover the assumed ownership cycle. The chart of accounts used for pro forma comparative analysis should follow the format shown in Exhibit 20–5.

Desired Rate of Equity Return. Equity investors in shopping centers ought to require a 10– 18 percent IRR return on cash invested based on after-tax cash flow, *plus* an appropriate long-term average inflation premium. This figure may be moderated by growth of the reversion expectations, the supply of investment alternatives, and competition from other investors. In recent years acceptable yields have been much lower, in spite of inflation, because of distortion caused by the influx of foreign investors with Eurodollars and petrodollars. See the discussion earlier in this chapter under the heading "Nature of the Risks and Returns."

When performing present-value analysis to determine target offering price, it is common to apply different discount rates to minimum and overage rates. While a rate of 9– 12 percent might be used for minimums, 15– 20 percent is used on overages to reflect the greater uncertainty of realizing those receipts.

Ratio and Risk Analysis. In analyzing risk, sensitivity analysis provides a good interpretative tool. Variations of average minimum rents, the growth rate of overages, vacancies, and operating expenses should be tested. Variables like net cash flow, rate of return, and debt coverage ratio should be used to test for risk sensitivity.

Evaluation of the Data. The key tests in the sensitivity analysis are the following:

1. The probability of negative cash flows and the ability to carry the project through such periods.
2. Dependence on overages for adequate rates of return.
3. The impact of foreseeable vacancies on the ability to cover debt service.

THE INVESTMENT DECISION

The analysis of risk and rate of return provides essential information for negotiating the purchase. The investor may use this information to negotiate the purchase price and request concessions from the seller, and when negotiating the loan with the lender and leases with major tenants. In the latter case, the investor should use the analysis to set limits on the amount of equity participation granted to a lender and the concessions granted to tenants.

Selected References

Trends

"A Swing to Multi-Use Centers?" *Chain Store Age Executive,* May 1977, pp. 73–75.
"Are Center Go-go Years Over?" *Chain Store Age Executive,* May 1977, pp. 51–55.
"Average Sales Now Top $100 per Square Foot." *Shopping Center World,* May 1979, pp. 38–40.
Enclosed Mall Shopping Centers. New York, International Council of Shopping Centers, 1965.
Gruen, Victor, and Larry Smith. *Centers for the Urban Environment: Survival of the Cities.* New York: Van Nostrand Reinhold, 1973.
Redstone, Louis G. *New Dimensions in Shopping Centers and Stores.* New York: McGraw-Hill, 1976.

Shopping Centers: The Next 15 Years. New York, International Council of Shopping Centers, 1975. (Many other publications available from this source.)
Shopping Centers, 1976. New York, Practicing Law Institute, 1976.

Investment Performance

Ellis, Robert M. *Real Estate Investment Analysis.* Los Angeles: Coldwell Banker, 1976.
Farber, Leonard. "Checks and Balances Make Shopping Centers Attractive Investments." *Mortgage Banker,* December 1977, pp. 34–39.
Garrett, Robert L., Hunter A. Hogan, and Robert M. Stratton. *The Valuation of Shopping Centers.* Philadelphia: Ballinger, 1976.
Shlaes, Jared, and Michael S. Young. "Evaluating Major Investment Properties." *The Appraisal Journal,* January 1978, pp. 101–111.
Weisinger, Lee. "Shopping Center Check List." *Real Estate Today,* February 1976, pp. 42–44.

Market Analysis

Nelson, Richard L. *The Selection of Retail Locations.* New York: McGraw-Hill, 1966.
Rams, Edwin, ed. *Analysis and Valuation of Retail Location.* Reston, Va.: Reston Publishing, 1976.
"Site Selection Methods Vary for Community Center Anchors, Specialty/Convenience Chains." *Shopping Center World,* April 1979, pp. 36–37.
"Why They Shop Some Centers." *Chain Store Age Executive,* May 1978, pp. 31–35.

Development and Renovation

Applebaum, William, and S. O. Kaylng. *Case Studies in Shopping Center Development and Operation.* New York: International Council of Shopping Centers, 1974.
Bell, Curtis C. *Shopping Center Development Guide.* Washington, D.C.: NAHB, 1975.
Teichin, Charles S. *How to Improve Developer/Tenant Planning and Construction Coordination.* New York: International Council of Shopping Centers, 1977.
"The Ten Most Common Problems in Renovation—And What to Do About Them." *Shopping Center World,* May 1979, pp. 138ff.

Operations

Callahan, William W. *Shopping Center Promotions: a Handbook for Promotion Directors.* New York: International Council of Shopping Centers, 1972.
Carpenter, Horace. *Shopping Center Management: Principles and Practices.* New York: International Council of Shopping Centers, 1978.
Dollars and Cents of Shopping Centers. Washington, D.C., Urban Land Institute, 1980 (published biannually).
Halpin, Emanuel. "People and Property: Insurance Changes in Shopping Center Leases." *Real Estate Review,* Fall 1977, pp. 72–78.
"Releasing: The Secret of Successful Older Centers." *Shopping Center World,* May 1979, pp. 102ff.
Standard Manual of Accounting for Shopping Center Operations. Washington, D.C., Urban Land Institute, D.C., 1971.

Taxation

Davis, Joseph, and Robert Wyndelts. "Component Depreciation for Shopping Centers." *The Appraisal Journal,* April 1979, pp. 204–217.
Touche Ross & Company. *Depreciable Lives of Shopping Centers.* New York: International Council of Shopping Centers, 1973.

General

"The Evolution of the Shopping Center Lease." *Real Estate Today,* August 1978, pp. 20– 23.

Lamm, Robert R. "Selling an Overpriced Shopping Center." *Shopping Center World,* February 1978, pp. 16– 66.

"New Opportunities in Shopping Centers." *The Mortgage and Real Estate Executives Report,* October 1, 1978, pp. 8– 10.

1978 Shopping Center Directory. Burlington, Iowa: National Research Bureau, periodic. (This series includes four regional volumes.)

"The Regional Mall from the Ground Up." *Real Estate Today,* August 1978, pp. 24– 28

"Retail Property Financing at Equitable." *Novicks Income Property Finance Report,* August 18, 1978, pp. 8– 10.

"Shopper Dining Habits: A Restaurant Business Survey." *National Mall Monitor,* July-August 1978, pp. 65– 67.

Woodward, Lynn W. "Modern Shopping Center Design: Psychology Made Concrete." *Real Estate Review,* Summer 1978, pp. 56– 63.

Periodicals

Chain Store Age Executive (monthly). Lebhar-Friedmann, Inc., 425 Park Ave., New York, N.Y. 10022.

Downtown Idea Exchange (twice monthly). Downtown Research and Development Center, 555 Madison Ave., New York, N.Y. 10022.

ICSC Newsletter (monthly). International Council of Shopping Centers, 445 Park Ave., New York, N.Y. 10022.

National Mall Monitor (bimonthly). National Mall Monitor, One Cherry Hill, Suite 806, Cherry Hill, N.J. 08034.

Percentage Leases (commercial rental survey, 1977). Realtors National Marketing Institute, 430 North Michigan, Chicago, Ill. 60611.

Shopping Center Leasing Opportunities (annual). International Council of Shopping Centers, 445 Park Ave., New York, N.Y. 10022.

Stores (monthly). National Retail Merchants Association, Inc., 100 W. 31st St., New York, N.Y. 10001.

Survey of Buying Power (annual). *Sales and Marketing Management,* 633 Third Ave., New York, N.Y. 10017.

Urban Land (monthly). Urban Land Institute, 1200 18th St., NW, Washington, D.C. 20036.

U.S. Bureau of the Census Reports

Advance Monthly Retail Sales
Annual Report, Retail Trade
County Business Patterns (annual, issued in separate reports by state)
Final Weekly Sales Estimates
Monthly Department Store Sales in Selected Areas
Weekly Retail Sales

21

Office Buildings

Much of the growth in GNP since World War II has been in the service sector. As the amount of paper work, computer use, and telecommunications increases, the demand for office space will also rise. On the other hand, word-processing and voice-actuated terminals will cause great changes in the nature of the need for office space during the next twenty years.

Office building construction tends to follow the path of growth of financial and other service centers within an SMSA. In picking a site for an investment in an office building, the investor seeks an area that scores high on accessibility and is near well-established traffic and business generators. The investor should weigh carefully the comparative advantage and disadvantage of the targeted site. Factors to be considered are parking, visibility, prestige, proximity to desired amenities and related uses, accessibility to surrounding streets, and accessibility to major traffic generators. In 1980 most office building investors are looking for a secure investment in a location with some growth potential, with stable returns providing about a 0– 6 percent cash flow return from operations. The investment would be leveraged through debt financing, appreciation of value, and tax benefits. Investors are taking the business risk that gross rents will increase at better than inflationary rates to improve the internal rate of return. They expect to use professional management, pay leasing commissions, and have a bare minimum of maintenance and repair responsibilities. Generally, office buildings are perceived as relatively conservative investments, although historical data indicate wide cyclical fluctuations in office building returns.

Acknowledgment: The authors gratefully acknowledge the valuable assistance of Georgia State University students Jim Hunter, C. Jackson Harris, and John E. Williams.

Definitions

Competitive building. A competitive building is a building that offers space to the public. The building may be completely competitive—that is, all space is under lease to nonowners—or, in an owner-occupied building surplus space may be leased on a competitive basis. The building may be identified with the name of the owner or management.

Gross building area. This is the aggregate area of the building, measured according to the exterior dimensions.

Office building. An office building is a structure devoted to nonretail business and service activities. A portion of the building may be used for ancillary activities, such as retail shops and food services.

Office park. Two or more office buildings arranged in a coordinated development, including parking and landscaping, make up an office park.

Owner-occupied building. This is a building in which the principal or exclusive tenant is the property owner. Owners typically are large financial institutions or corporations for which the building serves as national or regional headquarters.

Professional building. A professional building is an office building used exclusively by professionals, for example, CPAs, attorneys, doctors, and dentists. Such a building may also contain associated drug retailers and clinics.

Net rentable area. This is the total area available for occupancy by tenants. Net rentable area excludes stairwells, common areas, and mechanical areas.

TRACK RECORD AND TRENDS

The future productivity of the property is partially indicated by past trends. The experience in terms of comparative trends, relative rental rates, and credit standing of tenants will indicate whether the building is in the process of filtering downward toward eventual zero demand. Even if the property is holding its own, the surrounding area may be deteriorating in quality. Such trends promise difficulties in holding tenants when current leases expire. Environmental deterioration of the location also may limit the feasibility of modernization efforts.

The leasing structure of the property also influences its future profit potential. Gross, fixed-rate leases with long maturity dates obligate the owner to years of declining real income. Net leases with escalators and reasonable renewal options are preferred for maintenance of real returns.

Office properties are of two general types: the familiar highrise building common to downtown districts and the low or medium-rise buildings found in suburban locations.

As population spread to the suburbs, office development began to decentralize. Small buildings and groups of buildings arranged in attractive office parks offered shorter commuting distances, ample parking, quiet settings, and better opportunities for smaller tenants and investors.

Downtown office development continues to grow, however, even in cities with generally declining central districts. There remains a distinct demand for large, contiguous spaces and for the prestige of large-building ownership or principal tenancy.

EXECUTIVE PARK

Project Data

Site: 120 acres: 8 acres dedicated streets; 3 acres private streets; 2 acres leased land

Land value: $250,000 per acre[1]

Building area
Existing offices: 1,632,109 sq. ft.
Convenience commercial: 17,193 sq. ft.[2]
Floor area ratio: .3
Parking ratio: 5 spaces/1,000 sq. ft. of gross building area[3]

Tenant Information
Total, January 1981   165
Number with less than 20,000 sq. ft.   149
Number with more than 20,000 sq.ft.   16[4]

Lease information
Leases vary from 3 to 10 years based on negotiation with tenant. All leases include escalation clause for changes in operating and maintenance costs and ad valorem taxes. All covenants include provisions for relocation for expansions.

Rates 1981: $10.50-$12.00/sq. ft. net rentable area[5]

Operating expenses projected for 1981: $4.23/sq. ft.

Building developments costs
Typical cost during 1968-1970 for 5-story, 100, 000 sq. ft. building was $26.50.[6]
1981 cost is $60.00.

---

[1]Includes dedicated roads and private roads, street lighting, and signing, street landscaping, utilities to sites.
[2]Includes 2-acre bank site. Cafeteria in operation. Additional uses include retail establishments to meet needs of tenants' employees. Leases signed include dress shop, beauty and barber shops, copy service, etc.
[3]Early buildings were provided with three spaces/1,000 sq. ft. gross building area.
[4]American Mutual Liability; American Oil Co., Continental Can Co., Simmons, U.S.A., National Cash Register Co., Radio Corporation of America, American Express Co., Prudential Insurance Co., Service Bureau Corp., Southern Bell T&T Co., Procter & Gamble, Texaco, Union Carbide Corp., Sentry Insurance Co., Republic Steel.
[5]Typically includes janitorial services, building and grounds maintenance, heating and air-conditioning, parking, security, and all utilities except telephone. Where a tenant occupies an entire floor, rentals are based on total floor area rather than net floor area.
[6]During that period rents ranged from $4.75-$5.25 per net foot and net square footage averaged 82-87 percent of gross square footage.

Photos and data courtesy of Mr. Thomas Eldridge, Manager, Executive Park, Taylor Mathis Management Company

Executive Park

Both the national and the regional supply of office space has tended to follow a boom-and-bust cycle more dramatic than that of any other real estate sector. Builders and lenders typically overreact to demand by producing enough office space for a five-to-seven-year absorption period. This short-term oversupply results in periodic depression of rental rates, high vacancies, and significant rent concessions. A new wave of construction may not begin for another thirty years. On the other hand, in rapidly growing SMSAs it may resume in less than five years.

Functional and locational obsolescence is an important feature of office building investment. A superior location offering favorable public exposure and proximity to clients maximizes rent-producing capacity. Modern design and style features command premium rents and can maximize occupancy. (For an excellent example, see the photos and project information on pages 566–567 for Executive Park, Atlanta, Georgia.) Older buildings in good locations often compete successfully with new ones if they have been modernized to provide computer-assisted elevator service, heating and air conditioning, attractive appearance, and contiguity of space comparable to that provided by new buildings. Otherwise, a form of filtering takes place in which a building accommodates lower-paying tenants as it ages. Significant variations in rental rates usually coexist in each submarket, depending on location, age, obsolescence, and other functional characteristics of the particular property. The 1981 tax act may provide significant competitive advantage over new development for rehabilitating buildings that are more than 30 years old and have ample layouts and architectural amenities.

ADVANTAGES AND DISADVANTAGES OF INVESTING IN OFFICE BUILDINGS

Stable income streams are derived from well-located buildings. Standard leasing arrangements provide for periodic income increases and investor protection against rising expenses. Some buildings also provide opportunities for additional income from store rentals, vending and food service, and provisions for antennas, observation decks, and advertising. Demand is segmented, so older buildings may be profitable with low rental rates if purchased at appropriately lower prices, and modern buildings may command high rentals because of superior features. Office buildings may obtain debt financing in relatively higher ratios, especially when rented to high-quality tenants. The short ACRS lives of leasehold improvements and some equipment (e.g., office partitions) provide large tax deductions and credits.

The primary disadvantages are the large outlays needed to purchase major buildings and the nature of the competition. New high-rise buildings may cost $100 million or more. The resulting equity contributions, even with substantial leverage, are relatively large. Investors may scale down such problems by participating in investment ownership entities or, alternatively, by purchasing smaller suburban buildings. Competition from new development may not be synchronized to normal demand conditions, which are tied to local economic–demographic trends. For example, a major tenant may vacate to build its own building. Other owner–users may construct buildings and then lease excess space, or a government office complex may be developed to accommodate agencies that currently occupy competitive space. All may be acting without regard to current vacancy rates. This has resulted in destructive competition with serious adverse affects on profitability.

TYPES OF INVESTORS AND INVESTOR MOTIVATIONS

Many large organizations own their buildings and occupy them exclusively or lease out excess space competitively. Some of the reasons for such buildings go beyond pure economics; for example:

1. Control over operation, security, and maintenance.
2. Protection against loss of lease.
3. Advertising (being able to place the company's name on the building's façade).
4. Creating a monument to the organization's status and achievements.
5. Expression of architectural creativity or demonstration of the company's products.
6. Need for highly specialized facilities.
7. Lack of a high enough credit rating to command a "preferred" occupancy status in competitive buildings

Office buildings often involve complex split-ownership interests. A building may have been developed as a joint venture by a builder and a user or investor. The builder may derive profits through development and rental in the early years and eventually be phased out by the user. A ground lease may be involved, with the lessor seeking a stable, low-risk income stream and the building owner seeking residual cash flow and maximum deductions for tax purposes. Leasebacks are common.

Office buildings are popular vehicles for institutional investment because of the property's ability to offset inflation and the relatively low management burdens. Pension funds invest to diversify their portfolios in response to ERISA directives. Foreign investors favor office buildings for steady long-term returns that are safe from confiscation by their home government. For pension funds, diversification and management problems may be reduced further by participations offered by major financial institutions. Institutional investors have traditionally sought full ownership positions, but recently they have begun to purchase leveraged properties and shared interests as risks are better understood.

THE NATURE OF THE RETURNS AND RISKS

In normal times office building investors have sought a stable cash flow return of 8–12 percent plus an inflation premium over a ten-year period. However, the market is now fragmented by investors with diverse motivations (See the section on risks and returns in Chapter 20. Similar problems exist for office buildings.)

A well-located existing building designed so that it can be modernized periodically can be a relatively stable, low-risk investment. Leases generally are negotiated so that they are net of operating expenses; tenant turnover is low. Such properties enjoy high leverage possibilities and tax shelter, and internal rates of return (on after-tax cash flows) are often over 20 percent for seven to ten years.

The primary source of risk is competition from new and renovated buildings and overbuilding. The cyclical effects may be minimized by maintaining a stable core of long-term tenants and selecting the competitive advantage of a good location. New construction will generally force owners of older buildings to modernize, and what is considered a favorable location can vary over time. When this happens, chains of moves take place, with adverse effects on cash flow and returns. However, one factor that currently favors owners of existing buildings is the escalating cost of new development. In 1980 high-rise development cost $95– 105 per square foot, exclusive of site costs, requiring rentals of $19– 20 per square foot for reasonable returns. Such cost/benefit ratios provide opportunities for owners of old buildings, particularly those with favorable assumable financing. The 1981 tax act provides powerful tax credit incentives to rehabilitate older (30 years and over) buildings.

Since site location is such an important determinant of the rate-of-return/risk relationship in office buildings, great care should be taken to evaluate market risk. Being one city block away from the prime location can have great impact on the rate of return. (See Exhibit 21– 1.)

EXHIBIT 21–1.   Characteristics of a Good Office Building Location

---

CENTRAL CITY

Proximity to
  Other major office buildings
  Main railroad terminal
  Main suburban buses
  Mass transit stations
  Fashionable shops
  Department stores
  Good restaurants
  Government office buildings and courts
  Financial district
  Esthetically pleasing neighborhood
  Leading quality hotels
  No objectionable neighborhood activities

SUBURBAN

Proximity to
  Major highways to central city (e.g., frontage road*)
  Central location (relative to other major business centers such as shopping
    centers)
  Government buildings and courts
  Other new office buildings
  No objectionable neighborhood activities
  No heavy industrial buildings
  Banks
  Restaurants
  Bus service and other mass transit
  Parking
  Metropolitan airports*
  Industrial parks*

SOURCE: Sanders A. Kahn and Frederick E. Case, *Real Estate Appraisal and Investment*. (New York: Wiley, 1977), pp. 430–431.
* Added by author.

MARKET AND MARKETABILITY ANALYSIS

The demand for office space is derived from the needs of service-related industries and the administrative functions of all types of concerns. In general, areas with manufacturing-based economies generate relatively lower demand than areas with service-based economies. Therefore, the nature of the local economic base is a good indication of current and future needs for office space.

Occupancy rates are good indicators of current market conditions, although they may vary greatly for different types of buildings. Occupancy is better analyzed when buildings are segmented by location, age, and features. Rules of thumb, such as ratios of square feet of office space/population or service employment, may be applied to available projections to estimate future demand. Also, one should check recent building trends in the area to anticipate future additions to the competitive stock. Discussions with local construction lenders may also prove revealing.

Demand Analysis. The key to effective demand analysis is proper stratification of the office space market. There are five major segments of office demand.

1. *Major institutions.* Large financial and nonfinancial corporations seek large blocks of space in a building that they may use as a corporate symbol. While many of these organizations build their own buildings, others become key tenants under favorable lease conditions. Their primary concern is to have a prestigious location and building. The most prestigious locations are downtown and in the more fashionable suburban office parks near regional shopping centers.
2. *General commercial.* Smaller tenants are more interested in good access and favorable rates. These concerns are prime candidates for free-standing and park-based suburban buildings. Attorneys, engineers, accountants, and computer software firms are in this category.
3. *Medical/dental.* These professionals like to be located near one another and near major medical facilities. They have very specialized needs in terms of space and facilities. This segment is decreasing as more such users purchase space cooperatively or in condominium arrangements and as hospitals provide captive space at favorable rentals.
4. *Quasi-industrial.* Users whose business is related to manufacturing activities or who seek low-cost space in industrial parks may take advantage of excess space in parks where land use controls permit a mixture of uses.
5. *Industrial.* The administrative and engineering functions of manufacturing concerns often locate their space in close proximity to the factory. Such users generally will not seek competitive office space.

The first two segments are the chief target markets for competitive buildings, and the location and features of the subject property determine which segment is more appropriate.

An investor should identify the target market and the specific industry groups represented. Forecasts using standard industrial code classifications are generally available from BOMA (Building Owners and Managers Association International) regional offices, local planning agencies, commercial brokers, and regional U.S.

Department of Commerce offices. The forecasts may be combined with current ratios (office area occupied per employee) for each industry group to project space needs. An indication of expanding needs for space may indicate strong future demand for existing space as well as for any new space developed. BOMA reports are stratified by region, city (SMSA), and type of physical buildings, providing useful underlying data to aid demand analysis.

Supply Analysis. Just as demand is segmented, so is supply. A survey should be conducted of the existing stock of the appropriate market segment to determine rates, vacancies, and recent improvements. New construction will affect older buildings primarily as a result of the filtering process. Without new construction, and given constant demand, all existing space will tend to be at a premium.

The absorption rate for new space depends on the composite inventory of new space produced and occupied, the amount of old space vacated and converted, and the net change in vacancies. High absorption rates relative to new construction indicate continued good prospects for low vacancies and sufficiency of revenues. However, one should carefully monitor the process because, as noted earlier, office construction occurs in waves followed by long periods of oversupply.

Exhibit 21–1 lists factors to be used in evaluating the market risk for an office building location. (See also the technique for conducting a competitive survey of office locations presented in Chapter 6.) Within the types of activities an ideal site might have, an actual location could be rated on a scale of 1–10.

Local utility companies, lenders, and planning offices should be checked to measure the effects of the invisible competitive supply.

Projection of Rental Income and Vacancies. Information gathered from current operating statements for the property provide a good starting point for analysis. Multiyear leases and the lack of percentage rates act to stabilize the rent schedule to some extent. The assumed income stream should include scheduled tenant contributions to offset expense increases. Any contemplated rent increases should compare favorably with market rates in buildings of a similar class in the appropriate market.

Most office buildings are rented to a number of tenants, each with separate rental rates, lease provisions, and expiration dates. Therefore, it is not possible to accurately project income by applying a simple growth factor to current average contract rates. A rent roll should be constructed showing the current rental income and rate, tenant contributions to defray expenses, and renewal dates and options for each tenant. Realistic assumptions must be made concerning changes in market rents for space available for new leasing. Consider creditworthiness, amount of space occupied, duration of leasing arrangement, location in the building, and the "netness" of the lease. From this rent roll, market-oriented projections as an estimate of future gross rental revenues may be made.

A vacancy rate factor should be applied to this total and should be based on historical experience, comparable properties, and examinations of supply and demand conditions in the local market. Income from other miscellaneous sources, such as rental of retail space, vending income, parking, advertising space, and sale of utilities to tenants, is then added.

Risk Management and Control Techniques. The primary risks are loss of high-quality tenants and bad-debt losses from low-quality tenants. The first is hard to control except by providing good service and timely modernization. Some buildings make concessions to preferred tenants in the form of prime space, rent-free periods, and allowances for remodeling. One should attempt to get better tenants to sign longer-term leases with rent escalation provisions. The second problem is handled by investigating the credit histories of prospective tenants. The degree of insistence on high credit ratings, of course, depends on the age and quality of the building and market conditions.

PHYSICAL, LEGAL, POLITICAL, AND ENVIRONMENTAL ANALYSIS

Physical and Structural Factors. The desirability of office space to the tenant depends greatly on the physical features of the building. Convenience and comfort are valuable amenities. Tenants expect good elevator service, temperature control, ventilation, and lighting, and uncramped quarters. Deviations from the standards available in the most recently developed buildings will be penalized by lower rental rates unless offset by a superior location.

Some of the physical characteristics to check are the following:

1. *Poor soil conditions* or improper foundation work. The bearing qualities of the substrata are critical to the economic life of multistory buildings.
2. *Feasibility of modernization* at some future date. Can the elevator and heating/air-conditioning plant be readily updated or replaced? Can office space be internally redesigned? How adaptable is the electrical system to varying intensities of use and to changes in outlet locations?
3. *Availability of parking,* either on-site or publicly provided nearby.
4. *Floor space per floor.* Will a large tenant have to spread personnel over a number of floors?
5. *Preparation for contingencies.* Is there auxiliary power to run elevators during a power cutoff? Is there adequate fire protection and provision for rapid evacuation and emergency lighting?
6. Are there *unnecessary architectural features* that add to maintenance costs but contribute little to value?
7. *Space efficiency for the building.* One rule of thumb is the ratio of gross area minus net leasable area to gross area (GA − NLA/GA). Generally, it should be no more than 12 percent for a high-rise building. The newer the building, the lower this ratio is likely to be.

Legal and Political Factors. The primary legal concerns of the investor are local policies that affect operations and restrictions on the use of the property. Local-government policies may also affect the demand for space, for instance, by instituting tax programs or even rent control laws that reduce investment feasibility. Assessments favoring noncommercial land uses may add to operating costs and shift competitive advantage to other locations. Conversely, a local government can substantially improve the attractiveness of a location with strong law enforcement, good public service, and effective planning and capital improvement programs.

Restrictions on use may emanate from several sources. Deed restrictions from private covenants or liens may prohibit conversion or partial demolition. Public ordinances may restrict the height of a building, change parking requirements, prohibit certain types of business operations (e.g., sale of liquor), and limit outside advertising and signing. Clustering of office uses may be limited in order to control traffic congestion and pollution. An older building may be placed on the national historical register, which may or may not be advantageous to the owners.

Becoming familiar with local politics is probably the best way to evaluate the probability of such occurrences.

ANALYSIS OF OPERATIONS

Management of Leasing. The leasing of office space is complicated by the number of methods used to protect income against inflation and by the concessions offered to entice good tenants to the building.

Basically, three types of variable-rate leases are used. The first stipulates a fixed rental rate with pro rata contributions by the tenants to offset increased operating expenses—utilities, taxes, and insurance—which are paid by the management. Charges are made to tenants on the basis of the proportion of space occupied. The second type adjusts rental rates periodically according to changes in the consumer price index. (Regional indexes may more accurately reflect rates of change in office rents.) The third type of lease makes the tenant responsible for all expenses, including structural repairs. This takes the equity owner out of the landlord business; he or she becomes a purely passive investor.

Management. Good management is the key to maintaining high occupancy and minimizing operating costs. Large office properties generally have a professional property manager to handle leasing and overall administration and a building engineer to supervise upkeep of the mechanical apparatus in the building. Whether either employs a staff to assist in these duties depends on the size of the property. Larger buildings may have a permanent crew for maintenance and housekeeping, while small ones contract for such services. Large, modern buildings also utilize specialized computer systems to regulate heating and air conditioning, operate security systems, and perform other functions. The choice is largely a matter of economics, and the purchaser should evaluate the system from the standpoints of adequacy and efficiency.

Analysis of Current Operating Income and Expenses. Office building operation generally involves the following expense items: staff payroll, fuel for heating plant, utilities (electricity, water, and sewer); maintenance contracts, supplies and uniforms, repairs, insurance, real estate taxes, management, and reserves for mechanical replacements, alterations, tenant improvements, and lease commissions. Expenses for payroll and supplies vary, depending on whether an in-house crew is used for repairs and housekeeping. Payroll expenses also vary according to prevailing local wages and the presence of unions. Cleaning costs may be as low as $5.00/sq. ft. per year in the South and up to $9.40/sq. ft. per year in the mid-Atlantic states (1980).

When constructing a chart of accounts, one should include all income and expenses. Any pro rata payments from tenants may then be deducted from the expense total. Typically, management is expected to provide utility services, cleaning and janitorial service, elevator operation, and building security. It is becoming common for lease provisions to provide for tenant payments to offset increases in expenses over a base year figure.

The Experience Exchange Report of the Building Owners and Managers Association (BOMA) International. The BOMA International method of accounting is designed to provide the best available accounting breakdowns for effective fiscal management of office building properties.* Exhibit 21–2 illustrates the BOMA Chart of General Ledger Accounts for Office Buildings. Note that balance sheet accounts—assets, liabilities, capital—are represented by the sections numbered 100–499. The profit and loss income and expense accounts are grouped under sections numbered 500–999. For investment analysis purposes, the most useful items are 501–599 Income and 600–998 Expenses. Exhibit 21–3 depicts an Office Building Company Profit and Loss Statement based on the BOMA standard accounting method system. These national standards, adopted in 1972 and later refined, enable a real estate investment analyst to make more accurate comparisons for purposes of leasing and operations analysis.

BOMA's *Experience Exchange Report* provides comparative data on downtown and suburban office buildings on a national and regional, calendar year basis. The basic measure of comparison is cents/sq. ft., and the report provides a glossary of terms, thereby enabling an analyst to compare income and expense items as set forth in the report with the statement for a targeted investment. For effective computer simulation of an office building investment, one should categorize the income and expense items according to the BOMA standard accounting system, as follows:

• *Building total*—operating costs and income in cents per square foot for total rentable area, both office and nonoffice.
• *Office total*—operating costs and income in cents per square foot for total rentable office area.
• *Office rented*—operating costs and income in cents per square foot for the office space actually rented.
• *Operating cost breakdown*—wages, supplies, contract services, and other costs of operating the building.
• *Operating ratios*—the Exchange calculates a number of significant ratios to facilitate comparison of properties.

We recommend that those who are interested in office building investments analyze the Exchange reports. However, one must be careful in analyzing how income and expense items are allocated within the uniform chart of accounts. Significant distortions could occur if the data being used do not conform to the BOMA uniform method of accounting and the BOMA *Experience Exchange Reports*. Information is available from BOMA on the evolutionary changes in the reports for anyone who wants to make a comparison using past *Experience Exchange Reports*.

Analysis of Trends and Uncertainties. Like other properties, office buildings have the potential for significant increases in expenses. Buildings designed during

---

* Exhibits 21–2 and 21–3 are reproduced courtesy of the Building Owners and Managers Association International.

ASSETS

100 CURRENT ASSETS
101 Cash
102 Cash Fund-petty cash
110 Bank Accounts
111 General Account
112 Pay-Roll Account
113 Savings Account
119 Total Bank Accounts
120 Marketable Securities
121 Securities
(If a variety of securities are owned, individual accounts may be kept for each kind of security)
130 Accounts-Notes Receivable
131 Accounts Receivable-Rents and Services
132 Accounts Receivable-Alterations
133 Notes Receivable
134 Accrued Receivables
135 Reserve for Doubtful Receivables (credit)
139 Total Accounts-Notes Receivable
140 Inventory
141 Inventories-Materials
(There may be items, such as removable partition stock, which should be carried in Inventory Accounts; however, miscellaneous supplies which will be consumed within a short time should not be included in these accounts. See also Account 261.)

150 INVESTMENTS
151 Investment in Subsidiary Companies
152 Sinking Fund Investments
159 Total Investments
199 Total Current Assets

200 FIXED ASSETS
201 Land
202 Leasehold
20201 Reserve for Amortization of Leasehold
203 Building
20301 Reserve for Depreciation of Building
204 Equipment-Building
20401 Reserve for Depreciation Equipment-Building
(If desirable, separate accounts can be used for the various kinds of equipment numbering the accounts from 20402 to 20499 inclusive.)

31303 State Unemployment Insurance Tax
314 Accrued Property Taxes
315 Provision For Federal and State Taxes
316 Accrued Interest Payable
319 Total Accrued Liabilities
320 Other Current Liabilities
328 Total Current Liabilities
329 LONG TERM LIABILITIES
330 Bonds Payable
340 Mortgages Payable
350 Long-Term Notes Payable
358 Total Fixed Liabilities
359 DEFERRED INCOME
360 Deferred Income
361 Advance Rentals
362 Deferred Interest Income
363 Deferred Income/Credits
368 Total Deferred Income
369 Total Liabilities
370 RESERVES
371 Reserve for Contingencies

CAPITAL

401 CORPORATION
402 Preferred Stock
40201 Authorized
40202 Unissued
410 Common Stock
41001 Authorized
41002 Unissued
420 Surplus—Capital
430 Retained Earnings
450 Profit & Loss—Current Year
459 PROPRIETORSHIP OR PARTNERSHIP
(The following accounts should be used only in the event that the ownership of the building is in a partnership or sole proprietorship)
460 Capital (An account is provided for each partner)
470 Drawings. (An account is provided for each partner)
480 Profit and Loss—Current Year
498 Total Capital
499 Total Liabilities—Capital

620 Electrical
621 Wages
62101 *Social Security
62102 **Compensation Insurance
62103 ***Fringe Benefits
622 Supplies/Materials
623 Contract Services
628 Miscellaneous
629 Total Electrical

630 Heating
631 Wages
63101 *Social Security Taxes
63102 **Compensation Insurance
63103 ***Fringe Benefits
632 Supplies/Materials
633 Contract Services
638 Miscellaneous
639 Total Heating

640 Air Conditioning and Ventilating
641 Wages
64101 *Social Security Taxes
64102 **Compensation Insurance
64103 ***Fringe Benefits
642 Supplies/Materials
643 Contract Services
648 Miscellaneous
649 Total Air-Conditioning-Ventilating

650 Combined Heating, Ventilating and Air Conditioning
651 Wages
65101 *Social Security Taxes
65102 **Compensation Insurance
65103 ***Fringe Benefits
652 Contract Service
658 Miscellaneous
659 Total Combined Heating, Ventilating And Air Conditioning

660 Elevators
661 Wages
66101 *Social Security Taxes
66102 **Compensation Insurance
66103 ***Fringe Benefits
662 Supplies/Materials
663 Contract Service
668 Miscellaneous
669 Total Elevators

670 General Expense—Building
671 Wages (Watchman, Matron, Storekeepers, etc.)
67101 *Social Security Taxes
(If social security taxes are not charged to each expense group on the basis of the wages charged to each, charge the entire social secu-

70801 Business Association Memberships and Dues
70802 Donations, Subscription, and Gifts
70803 Other
709 Total Administrative Expenses

720 Energy (Building Operation Only)
721 Electricity
722 Gas
723 Oil
724 Steam
725 Chilled Water
726 Coal
729 Total Energy
730 Total Operating Expense

738 ALTERATIONS—PAINTING—DECORATE
740 Alterations—Tenants' Premises (Not Charged to Tenant)
741 Wages
74101 *Social Security Taxes
74102 **Compensation Insurance
74103 ***Fringe Benefits
743 Contract Services
748 Miscellaneous
749 Total Alterations—Tenant

750 Painting or Decorating—Tenants' premises (not charged to tenants)
751 Wages
75101 *Social Security Taxes
75102 **Compensation Insurance
75103 ***Fringe Benefits
753 Contract Services
758 Miscellaneous
759 Total Painting—Decorating—Tenant
760 Total Alterations—Painting—Decorating
(It may be desirable to segregate Accounts 740 and 750 between (a) Ground Floor Tenants (b) Office Tenants, in which case sub-accounts can be created.)

798 FIXED CHARGES
800 Insurance
801 Fire Insurance
802 Earthquake Insurance
803 Liability Insurance
805 Other Insurance
809 Total Insurance

810 Operating Taxes
811 Real Estate Taxes
812 Personal Property Taxes
819 Total Operating Taxes
829 Total Fixed Charges

830 Leasing Expense
831 Commissions

INCOME

501 RENTAL INCOME
502 Rental Income
503 Office Rent (Fixed)
50301 Office Rent Escalation
504 Store Rent (Fixed)
50401 Store Rent (Overage)
50402 Store Rent Escalation
505 Storage Area Rent
506 Rent of Special Areas
507 Loss on Uncollectible Accounts
509 Total Rental Income

510 SERVICE INCOME
511 Service Income
512 Energy Sales
513 Alterations and/or Decorating for Tenant
518 Other Services
519 Total Service Income
530 Service Expense
531 Service Expense
532 Energy Expense (For Resold Energy Only, Not Building Operating Energy)
533 Steam
537 Alterations—Decorating for Tenant (Billed)
538 Other Services
539 Total Service Expense
542 Total Net Service Income

545 MISCELLANEOUS INCOME
546 Miscellaneous Income
547 Interest Income
548 Other
549 Total Miscellaneous Income
599 Total Income (Including Net Services)

EXPENSES

600 OPERATIONS
610 Cleaning
611 Wages
61101 *Social Security Taxes
61102 **Compensation Insurance
61103 ***Fringe Benefits
612 Supplies/Materials
613 Contract Services
618 Miscellaneous
619 Total Cleaning

rity tax to this account and prorate to expense groups at the end of the year.)
67102 *Compensation Insurance
**Compensation Insurance (If compensation insurance is not charged to each expense group on the basis of the wages charged to each, charge all compensation insurance expense to this account and prorate to expense groups at the end of the year.)
67103 ***Fringe Benefits
672 Supplies/Materials
673 Contract Services
674 Decorating (Public Areas)
675 Plumbing
676 Sewer
677 Water
678 Miscellaneous
679 Subtotal General Expense Building

680 Security and Life Safety
681 Wages
68101 *Social Security Taxes
68102 **Compensation Insurance
68103 ***Fringe Benefits
682 Contract Services
683 Supplies/Materials
688 Miscellaneous
689 Total Security and Life Safety

690 Landscaping & Grounds
691 Wages
69101 *Social Security Taxes
69102 **Compensation Insurance
69103 ***Fringe Benefits
692 Supplies/Materials
693 Contract Services
696 Miscellaneous
697 Total Landscaping
699 Total General Building Expense

700 Administrative Expense
701 Salaries
70101 Management
70102 Clerical
70201 *Social Security Taxes
70202 **Compensation Insurance
70203 ***Fringe Benefits
703 Building Office Expense
70301 Supplies and Stationery
70302 Other
704 Management or Agency Fee
705 Advertising
706 Professional Fees (Legal, Etc.)
708 Miscellaneous

832 Other Leasing Expense
839 Total Leasing Expense
840 Tenant Alteration Amortization (or Expensed)
849 Total Tenant Alteration Amortization
850 Depreciation
851 Building
852 Building Equipment
853 Office Furniture and Fixtures
859 Total Depreciation
925 Total Fixed Charges

929 FINANCIAL EXPENSES
930 Ground Rent
931 Ground Rent/Air Rent
939 Total Ground Rent
940 Organization Expense
941 Amortization of Organization Expense
942 Amortization of Capital Stock Discount
949 Total Organization Expense
950 Interest Expense
951 Interest on Notes and Mortgages
952 Bond Interest Paid
953 Amortization of Bond Discount
959 Total Interest Expense
970 Corporate Taxes
971 State and Federal Taxes (except income taxes)
972 Income Taxes
979 Total Corporate Taxes
990 Other Financial Expenses
998 Total Financial Expenses

*Social Security Taxes should be charged to each expense group. Accounts 600 to 750 inclusive, on the bases of the wages charged to each group. If Social Security Taxes cannot conveniently be segregated in this manner each month, charge all such taxes to Account 67101, Social Security Taxes, in the General Expense—Building group expenses and prorate to the proper expense group at the end of the year.

**Compensation Insurance should be charged to each expense group on the basis of the wages charged to each. If compensation insurance cannot conveniently be segregated in this manner each month, charge all such insurance to Account 67102, Compensation Insurance, in the General Expense—Building group of expenses and prorate the proper expense group at the end of the year.

***Fringe Benefits should be charged to each expense group; 600 to 750 inclusive on the basis of wages.

©

205 Office Furniture and Fixtures
20501 Reserve for Depreciation Furniture-Fixtures
(If more than one building is operated, separate accounts should be kept for each building. Use a capital letter prefix with the account number to distinguish the separate properties, as: 203, 204, 205)
249 Total Fixed Assets

258 DEFERRED CHARGES
260 Deferred Charges
261 Supplies
262 Prepaid Insurance Premiums
263 Prepaid Taxes
264 Organization Expense
265 Unamortized Bond Discounts
266 Unamortized Capital Stock Discount
268 Other Deferred Charges
269 Total Deferred Charges

270 OTHER ASSETS
271 Other Assets
272 Utility Deposits
273 Deposit on Workmen's Compensation Insurance
279 Total Other Assets
299 Total Assets

LIABILITIES

300 CURRENT LIABILITIES
301 Notes and Accounts Payable
302 Notes Payable (Short Term)
303 Accounts or Vouchers Payable
306 Dividends Payable
309 Total Notes—Accounts Payable
310 Accrued Liabilities
311 Accrued Pay Roll
31101 Accrued Bonuses
312 Employee Pay-Roll Contributions
31201 Federal Old-Age Benefit Tax
31202 State Unemployment Insurance Tax
313 Employer Payroll Taxes Payable
31301 Federal Old-Age Benefit Tax
31302 Federal Unemployment Insurance Tax

SOURCE: Reprinted with permission from Building Owners and Managers Association International's publication, 1980 Downtown and Suburban Office Building Experience Exchange Reports.

EXHIBIT 21-3. BOMA Office Building Company Profit Statement

Office Building Company
PROFIT AND LOSS STATEMENT
Six Months Ending June 30, 19____

Acct.	DESCRIPTION	Detail	Subtotals	Total
	RENTAL INCOME			
503	Office Rent	XXXX.XX		
504	Store Rent	XXXX.XX		
505	Storage Area Rent	XXX.XX		
506	Rent of Special Areas	XXXX.XX		
	Total Rental Income		XXXX.XX	
	MISCELLANEOUS INCOME			
542	Total Net Service Income	XX.XX		
547	Interest Income	XX.XX		
548	Other	XX.XX		
	Total Miscellaneous Income		XXX.XX	
	TOTAL RENTAL AND MISC. INCOME			XXXXX.XX
	OPERATING EXPENSES			
619	Cleaning Expense (see schedule)	XXX.XX		
629	Electrical Expense (see schedule)	XXX.XX		
639	Heating Expense (see schedule)	XXX.XX		
649	Air Conditioning and Ventilating Expense (see schedule)	XXX.XX		
650	Combined HVAC (see schedule)	XXX.XX		
669	Elevator Expense (see schedule)	XXX.XX		
699	General Expense—Building (see schedule)	XXX.XX		
709	Administrative Expense (see schedule)	XXX.XX		
729	Energy Expense (see schedule)			
	Total Operating Expense		XXXXX.XX	
	ALTERATIONS, DECORATING, AND REPAIRS EXPENSES			
749	Alterations—Tenants' Premises (see schedule)	XXX.XX		
759	Painting or Decorating—Tenants' Premises (see schedule)	XXX.XX		
	Total Alterations and Decorating		XXXX.XX	
	FIXED CHARGES			
809	Insurance Expense (see schedule)	XXX.XX		
829	Operating Taxes Expense (see schedule)	XXX.XX		
849	Tenant Alterations—Amortization/Expensed	XXX.XX		
	Total Fixed Charges Expense		XXXX.XX	
	TOTAL EXPENSES			XXXX.XX
	NET OPERATING PROFIT			XXXX.XX
939	Ground Rent (see schedule)	XXXX.XX		
949	Organization Expense (see schedule)	XXX.XX		
959	Interest Expense (see schedule)	XX.XX		
979	Corporate Taxes (see schedule)	XX.XX		
990	Other Financial Expense	XX.XX		
	TOTAL FINANCIAL EXPENSE			XXXX.XX
	FINAL NET PROFIT			XXXX.XX

(Subsidiary schedules must be prepared for each expense group
indicated in this condensed statement)

Use of Operating Statement

The Profit and Loss Statement, as it appears above, is practically the same as the Operating and Service sections of the Experience Exchange report form. By adopting this standard breakdown for your monthly and annual statements, the extra effort involved in making out your Experience Exchange return will be eliminated and the procedure simplified throughout.

The reference, "see schedule," appearing in several places, calls for a supporting memorandum which will correspond with the Analysis of Operating Costs on the reverse side of the Experience Exchange form.

The great advantage of adopting this standard operating statement is that its use enables you to make accurate comparisons with local, regional and national unit cost figures, as compiled from industry experience, thus deriving practical benefit from the authoritative information contained in the Office Building Experience Exchange Report.

SOURCE: Reprinted with permission from Building Owners and Managers Association International's publication, *1980 Downtown and Suburban Office Building Experience Exchange Reports.*

periods of readily available, low-cost energy are especially vulnerable to substantial fuel and electricity cost increases. If curtailment of heating and air conditioning is necessary to maintain profitable operation, tenants may be irritated. Energy-efficient buildings have some market advantage. Computer-assisted energy-use control systems are producing major savings with rapid payback.

Another potential cost increase is in the area of local taxes. Some buildings have been developed under favorable tax assessments to encourage expansion of business. As these concessions expire, taxes may rise dramatically. The tax rolls should be studied for trends on other commercial properties. Tax appeal litigation may be necessary. Also, if the building is on a ground lease, check to see if any escalation clauses are included. Such costs should be reflected in the income and expense projections.

Projection of Expenses. The projection of operating expenses is straightforward. Better estimates are attained by applying different growth rates, according to recent trends, to each item of expense. Depending on the present condition of the building and the rate of anticipated new construction in the market area, capital expenditures should be estimated and allocated to amortization where necessary for modernization and renovation. Care should be taken to integrate this analysis with the data produced in the market study and marketability analysis.

Risk Management and Control Techniques. Skillful negotiation of leases to seek tenant absorption of the occupancy expenses is the best means of controlling operating expenses. The primary constraint on this technique is the market conditions surrounding the negotiations. Ultimately, the quality of the building will greatly influence the investor's ability to control expenses. A building that conserves energy is easier to keep clean and repaired, is likely to have cost-effective security, and may be more amenable to modernization. Features like omniflexible partition systems in open-space interiors, with zoned heating, ventilation, and air conditioning, should maximize the opportunity to control occupancy expenses. Architectural features that do not increase maintenance costs and are effective in producing revenue (i.e., are cost efficient) may well serve to reduce risk by making the building more attractive to tenants.

FINANCING AND REFINANCING TECHNIQUES

Sources. Large office buildings attract capital from sources like REITs, foundations, life insurance companies, and pension funds. Commercial banks and others may provide construction loans, permanent mortgages, and refinancing. Smaller buildings generally must rely on local sources such as savings and loan associations. Well-located buildings with quality tenants and net leases are popular investments for major institutions. A growing trend, however, is toward equity ownership (and income participation) by the funds, even extending to ownership of leveraged properties. For example, PRISA, a special commingled pool of pension funds, had over 30 percent of its portfolio in office buildings in 1980.

Rates, Terms, and Conditions. Office building loans are generally considered less risky than most other real estate loans as long as overbuilding doesn't occur. The borrower or lessee is often a prime, creditworthy client. Consequently, interest rates tend to be lower, terms longer, and loan-to-value ratios higher. In the fourth quarter of 1978 the average interest rate and term for office building loans made by a group of fifteen life insurance companies were 9.81 percent and 22.5 years, respectively. In contrast, average hotel/motel loans were at 10.29 percent for 17 years, 5 months.

Debt coverage ratio and mortgage constant desired by the lender. This information is obtained from existing loans. For new financing, debt coverage of 1.25–1.30 should provide a conservative estimate. Exhibit 21–4 shows the trend in mortgage constants required by a group of life insurance companies on loan commitments of $100,000 or more on office building properties.

Lenders prefer buildings with substantial lease commitments by high-quality tenants. They prefer leases at net or with pro rata expense sharing. The leases should be subordinated to the mortgage. This allows the lender to foreclose on a fully occupied building while requiring lessees to continue their lease obligations. Many lending sources are also amenable to sale-leaseback. (See Chapter 14.)

Projection of Financing Costs. When projecting financing expense, one should include the following: any participation charges required by the lender; financing adjustments necessary to fund renovations and modernization; ground lease payments (when appropriate); allocation of points and other front-end charges; balloons; and so forth. For simulation purposes one-time items may be capitalized; others may be treated as projected operating expenses.

Know the Risk Management and Control Techniques of Lenders. At one time, some new office buildings utilized bond financing, often under the sponsorship of the local government as part of the city's urban development program. Today most debt financing for competitive buildings is provided by financial institutions, especially insurance companies, although federal urban development assistance grants can favorably affect the financing. Owner-occupied buildings may carry no specific debt financing other than general-obligation debt instruments, such as debentures issued by the owner–organization. Thus, the purchase of an owner-occupied building may require new financing. Off-balance-sheet financing may be obtained through the use of purchase-sale-leaseback techniques where appropriate. Investors will negotiate to minimize their risk and will shift the risk of loss to the lender by seeking to raise the loan-to-value ratio; avoiding personal liability, at least on the top 20–25 percent of the loan; eliminating prepayment penalties; minimizing holdbacks for completion and rental achievement; eliminating due-on-sale clauses to permit wraparounds; and the like. Also, they will seek to prevent clauses that do not permit prepayment of the loan.

The keys to evaluating an assumable financing package are the adequacy of

EXHIBIT 21–4.	Average Annual Constants	
	1978	1980
4th quarter	10.1%	11.6%
3rd quarter	10.8	11.0
4th quarter	10.9	10.9

SOURCE: Based on data from *The Appraiser*, June 1980, p. 12, May 1980, p. 10.

the remaining life of the loan, the remaining economic life of the building, and special conditions associated with the mortgage. The remaining term should be sufficient to provide an opportunity to obtain refinancing at a time when it is advantageous to the owner. This, in turn, is dependent on the tax shelter situation and changes in monetary policy over the ownership period. Another factor is the relationship of the current contract mortgage interest rate to interest rate trends for office buildings, as affected by the office space construction cycle. An investor should not be backed into an assumed mortgage if he or she feels that rates and terms will improve in the short run. The new mortgagor should also become informed about possible special provisions in the mortgage that might limit changes in the physical design of the building or its use.

The primary risk control technique used by lenders is rejecting inferior loan proposals. For new buildings, 75–80 percent rental achievement with high-quality lease commitments is often required. Older buildings are judged primarily on the basis of existing leases and physical conditions. The lender is concerned with the continued ability of the building to produce adequate revenues to meet fixed obligations. Therefore, leases with escalation clauses and expense-defraying mechanisms are desired.

Two situations may occur that make financing and refinancing difficult. In the period following a wave of overbuilding, lenders will be reluctant to take on more office building commitments. This policy may persist even beyond the time when the excess space has been absorbed. The other situation is in the financing of a special-purpose building, such as a professional building. Such properties have limited market value, and their value may decline rapidly after foreclosure. Many of these buildings must rely on noninstitutional financing, such as sale to a cooperative or condominium arrangement, syndication, and a high ratio of equity contribution to loan, or possibly joint and several liability of the principals.

TAXATION AND TAX STRUCTURE

Nature of the Tax Shelter. Office buildings have available the same types of federal and state income tax advantages as other types of nonresidential properties. These include depreciation allowances, deduction of interest on the mortgage, and capital gains treatment. Office building investments often have less favorable tax effects from depreciation because of relatively high ratios of land to total property value.

Identification of the Variables to Be Structured. Under the Economic Recovery Tax Act of 1981 office buildings are eligible for ACRS 15-year recovery periods. However, the taxpayer may also elect to use a 35- or 45-year recovery period. The use of ACRS is expected to vary depending on the type of investor. Preliminary studies indicate that accelerated cost recovery at 15, 35, or 45 years is more generous—for office buildings, in particular—than was component straight-line depreciation because, under component depreciation, office buildings had to attribute 60 to 80 percent of cost to the shell.

Since many investors in office buildings expect holding periods of more than 15 years, the ACRS 175 percent declining-balance method can be chosen for the real property without fear of recapture. However, institutional investors holding property at superior locations may well prefer to depreciate slowly over 35-year or 45-year schedules, modernizing at the appropriate time. In existing buildings, since controversy with the IRS over the proper percentage to be allocated to land is anticipated, a qualified appraiser should be used.

Although buildings and their structural components, as well as items attached and affixed thereto, are all treated as realty and thus are not eligible for investment tax credits, there are items of personalty that are eligible for the ACRS three- and five-year lives and appropriate investment tax credits. Examples are window-washing equipment, computer-control systems, office furniture, sidewalk cleaning equipment, nonattached carpeting, fencing, vending machines, bank equipment, art objects, and (possibly) free-standing, specially designed and installed HVAC and humidity control systems for special uses. Taxpayers will probably elect to segregate leasehold improvements by special agreement and amortize them over the term of the lease rather than to depreciate them.

When planning rehabilitation under the 1981 tax act, one should take care that significant and substantial rehabilitation is eligible for the investment tax credit incentives of 15 percent for structures at least 30 years old, 20 percent for structures at least 40 years old, and 25 percent for certified historic structures. No credit is allowed any longer for buildings less than 30 years old. (See Chapter 13 for additional discussion of tax treatment.)

Tax Problems and Uncertainties. Through the use of sale-leaseback arrangements, the entity operating the building may shift ownership of some of the nondeductible assets, for example, by means of a land lease to another entity. The lessee may then deduct 100 percent of the rental payment. If the ground lessor is a tax-free organization, it may be indifferent to the tax implications of this shift.

Care must be taken in structuring the sale-leaseback. If the sale is based on a below-market price and the property is leased back at favorable rates with unlimited renewal options, the transaction may be interpreted as a mortgage by the IRS. This would mean that only some depreciation and a portion of rental payments may be deducted from taxes. The investor must be wary of shifting federal budget priorities which may result in large increases in state and local government taxes.

DISCOUNTED CASH FLOW ANALYSIS

Rate-of-Return Analysis. When older buildings are compared with alternative investments, some difference in results may occur from using rate-of-return versus present-value analysis. This is due to potential negative cash flows in years when modernization is expensed. In such cases net present value may be a more reliable technique. IRR/PV analysis should be based on at least a full building cycle. The desired rate of return should be competitive with those of comparable investments. In 1981 a well-located office building sought 9 percent plus an inflation premium, or a total of 20 percent.

Desired rate of equity return. The investor's desired rate of equity return will depend on yields on alternative investments and the age and condition of the building. Older buildings may require extensive renovation at some future date to remain competitive. This means possible future contributions by equity investors that are not accounted for in the basic feasibility model. For new buildings, equity investors may seek approximately 12 percent IRR discounted cash flow after taxes on equity, plus an inflation risk premium. The required shorter payback periods for older buildings may raise this figure to 15 percent or more, plus the inflation premium. Consideration should be given to adding risk premiums to the minimum acceptable rate of return to cover for specific problems (e.g., neighborhood, architecture, lease terms, etc.). Current conditions are so uncertain that the selection of minimum acceptable rates of return is problematical. We recommend scenario-type sensitivity analysis. In rehabilitations, the investment tax credit, with appropriate holding periods, may be so important that one should either use computer simulations that provide for tax credit inputs or opt for manual spread sheet analysis.

Ratio and Risk Analysis. Office properties tend to be lower in risk and steadier in income generation than many other real property investments, assuming that the difficult problem of cyclical overbuilding is kept under control. These facts should be reflected in ratios and cash-on-cash measures. Sensitivity analysis should be applied to determine the effects of varying vacancies (e.g., 5– 10%), expense growth rates (8– 14% annually), and rental rate increases (e.g., 6– 10% annually).

Evaluation of the Data. If the investor has prior investment experience both in office buildings and in the particular submarket of the specific SMSA, independent evaluation may be conducted successfully. Otherwise, an ethical local real estate counselor (e.g., an appraiser, lender, property manager, or commercial broker) should be engaged on a per diem basis to review the data, consult, and advise.

THE INVESTMENT DECISION

Office building investors tend to be more averse to risk and more patient than most real estate investors. Consequently, their returns are lower but on the other hand, more stable over time. Tenants are less volatile, and management is less onerous. Recently some investors have chosen to avoid the larger SMSAs. Instead, they are concentrating on well-located high-rise office buildings in SMSAs with populations of 300,000– 500,000 and a record of growth, which they believe are less likely to be threatened by new construction than building in more popular fast-growing SMSAs.

Selected References

Trends and Statistics

Downtown and Suburban Office Building Experience Exchange Report. Washington, D.C.: Building Owners and Managers Association, International, 1978. (Annual)
Rosenthal, Robert. "Competition Fierce for Prime Investment Properties: New Opportunities Expected for U.S. Developers." *National Real Estate Investor,* January 1978, pp. 26– 32.
———. "New Directions in Medical Office Building Development." *Real Estate Appraiser,* January-February 1978, pp. 5– 12.
Spencer, Jerry I. "The Future of High-Rise Office Buildings." *Journal of Property Management,* July-August 1976, pp. 181– 183.

Investment Performance

Reiss, Jerome L. "Office Buildings." *Real Estate Today,* April 1976, pp. 39ff.

Market Analysis

Detoy, Charles L. and Sol L. Rabin. "Office Space: Calculating the Demand." *Urban Land,* June 1972, pp. 4–13.

Lex, Richard A. "Marketing Studies for Office Buildings." *Real Estate Review,* Summer 1975, pp. 101–103.

Wurtzebach, Charles H. "Major Factors Affecting Selection of Office Facilities." *Journal of Property Management,* September-October 1976, pp. 221–224.

Operation

Basie, J. P. "Energy Survey and Money in Office Building Management." *Real Estate Appraiser,* July-August 1976, pp. 5–9.

Cunningham, Phillip J. "Some Suggestions from an On-Site Office Building Manager." *Journal of Property Management,* January-February 1979, pp. 10–16.

King, John. "Contracting for Standards of Service in Leased Office Space." *Administrative Management,* February 1977, pp. 63–68.

Levine, Mark. "Legal Aspects of Commercial Leasing." *The Appraisal Journal,* April 1977, pp. 229–241.

Reinhold, Hohl, *Office Buildings: An International Survey.* New York: Praeger, 1968.

Wimberly, Brooks. "True Office Lease Values." *Journal of Property Management,* September-October 1978, pp. 290–296.

Finance

Grubb, Robert C. "Release Provisions in Office and Industrial Park Development Plans." *Real Estate Review,* Winter 1979, pp. 77–80.

Smith, Charles C., and Harold A. Lubell. "A Lender Looks at Large Office Building Loans." *Real Estate Review,* Fall 1978, pp. 12–14.

———. "What Lenders Want in Leases." *Real Estate Review,* Winter 1977, pp. 11–14.

22

Industrial Buildings and Parks

Industry embraces all the activities involved in the production, storage, and distribution of tangible economic goods, as opposed to intangible services. Industrial real estate is where those activities are located.

Manufacturing has been defined as "the mechanical or chemical transformation of inorganic or organic substances into new products."[1] This includes all the activities involved in the creation of what economists call *form utility*. The relatively new process of recycling worn-out, discarded, or waste materials, which are then used in the manufacture of new products, is encompassed by this definition.

Industry also includes research and development activities that serve the needs of manufacturing. Moreover, the facilities of transportation companies that provide terminal space and maintenance facilities as a service to industrial firms come under this classification. Those facilities include public warehousing facilities, airport terminal services, stockyards, and packing and crating activities. Finally, such business services as publishing and printing, automobile and equipment repair, and cleaning establishments are regarded as industrial activities.

Definitions

Industrial building. There are three categories of industrial buildings: *general-purpose, special-purpose,* and *single-purpose.*

[1] U.S. Office of Management and Budget, *Standard Industrial Classification Manual* (Washington, D.C.: GPO, 1972), p. 37.

Acknowledgment: The authors gratefully acknowledge the valuable assistance of Georgia State University students Jim Hunter and John E. Williams.

General-purpose industrial buildings have a wide range of alternative uses. They are often constructed on speculation and generally are adaptable to light manufacturing, assembly, storage, research, or service.

Special-purpose buildings are those whose physical characteristics and facilities are suitable to a restricted range of industrial processes.

Single-purpose buildings are adaptable to only one kind of process, or perhaps to one particular firm. The more closely facilities are adapted to the particular needs of a given process or firm, the less readily they can be converted to other uses.

In addition to structural attributes, there may be other limits to industrial site uses. These arise from physical characteristics of the site itself, such as size, shape, slope, or bearing characteristics. The site may also be severely limited with respect to use by zoning or other land use controls, as well as by the availability of essential utility and transportation facilities.

Industrial plant. A plant is an establishment at a single location where industrial operations are performed. The total floor area of a plant includes all structures on the site, such as offices, power plants, repair shops, garages, warehouses, and laboratories.

Plant area. The United States of America Standards Institute has adopted a standard method of computing plant size: "The gross floor area of a plant is the sum of the areas at each floor level included within the principal outside faces of exterior walls, and neglecting architectural set-backs or projections." To qualify as part of the floor area, the clear, standing headroom must be at least 7 feet 6 inches. Balconies and mezzanines are included in the gross floor area if they form an integral part of the building and have a minimum width of 12 feet.

Certain other structures are not properly considered part of the gross floor area. Structures with unroofed floor areas, unenclosed roof spaces, light wells, connecting passageways, and various sheds, lean-tos, and unenclosed loading platforms and silos are all excluded from the gross floor area of the plant. Some authorities have suggested a minimum ceiling of 14 feet as a standard measurement, but because many older buildings have lower ceilings, industrial specialists have not yet agreed on a standard ceiling height. (Industrial real estate brokers generally prefer the term *floor* rather than *story* in describing plant levels.)

Plant site. The total land area within the property boundaries is expressed in either square feet or acres. The net land area excludes public easements or public roads that are not under private control.

Clear span. No columns or posts, all open space.

Fireproof building. This is a fire-resistant structure with no combustible materials used in its construction. The construction is usually masonry, concrete or concrete block, steel, and glass, with metal doors.

Floor loads. This is the weight that a floor can hold safely. In effect, it is the bearing capacity, usually measured in pounds per square foot of floor area.

Floor space per employee. This ratio is expressed in terms of square feet per employee. It varies considerably by industry, geographic region, size of firm, and age of plant. It is a useful measure for planning for the growth of a metro area.

Hoist (levelator). A hoist is an apparatus resembling a sunken elevator that moves up and down from the building's dock floor level to the truck's floor level to facilitate loading and unloading.

Loading docks. A loading dock is a platform built to truck or freight car floor height so that trucks or cars can be loaded and unloaded easily.

Loading well. A loading well is a ramp built to allow trucks and trailers to back down to the floor level of a building for easy loading and unloading.

Major-shift employment. This term refers to the number of employees working at the plant site during the largest daily shift and during periods of normal plant operation. In order to obtain an accurate estimate of needed parking space, the term covers *all* employees, whether they serve in administrative, maintenance, or operating capacities. Employment densities are figured by relating the number of employees on the major shift to the land area. They are expressed as the number of employees per acre of land, or per square foot of parking area required. In estimating parking requirements, however, an allowance for overlap in shifts, visitors, temporary contractors, and so forth is common.

Mill construction. This term refers to buildings with heavy wood beams and heavy wooden, brick, or steel upright members. This type of construction was common fifty years ago, and many such buildings are still in use. They are sometimes called slow burners because the knurled beams resist combustion.

Power wiring. Special heavy-duty wiring is brought in to service machinery that cannot be operated from average-size power lines. Power wiring usually involves high-cost switch boxes and fittings.

Sprinklered building. A sprinklered building is one with an overhead sprinkler system with shower heads that will be activated at a certain degree of heat. A sprinklered building is less expensive to operate because its fire insurance rates are substantially lower.

Structural density (floor area ratio). This figure is derived by dividing the ground area of structures by the total land area. The floor area ratio is the ratio of the *total* floor area of the plant to the site area. Thus, a three-story building containing 10,000 square feet per floor on a 50,000-square-foot site has a floor area ratio of 60 percent.

RECENT TRENDS

The most significant trend in industry has been a *migratory shift* in industrial employment and activity from the traditional concentrations in the northeastern and north central states to the southern, southwestern, south central, and Pacific regions. Simultaneously with the southward and westward movement, there has been a marked tendency for new establishments to locate in suburban or outlying communities rather than in central cities. The chief impact of obsolescence on industrial real estate owners and inventors has been the need to devise means to rehabilitate the old facility.

Transportation Changes. The development of highway and expressway travel has led to greater reliance on truck transportation. The American worker remains automobile oriented, and public transportation systems in metropolitan areas have not kept pace with the outward movement of population and industry. All of these developments have combined to accelerate the movement of freight-generating industries and large employers away from congested central districts.

Meanwhile, rail facilities have become less important to many industries. As we seek greater energy efficiency, the 1980–2000 period may see a revival of rail transportation for industrial purposes.

A rapid growth in air freight transportation has occurred in recent years, particularly in activities in which the speed of delivery of items with high value-to-weight ratios is critical. Locations that provide air transport facilities therefore have a great comparative advantage in attracting such activities.

Process Changes. The shift in location from central to more outlying areas has been accompanied by a trend toward one-story buildings in which goods flow horizontally rather than vertically. Most firms prefer single-story plants because the layout and flow of goods and materials is considerably more flexible than in multistory structures, and also because heating and ventilation can usually be handled more efficiently.[2]

For operations in which location is more important than process flows (e.g., high-fashion garment manufacturing), "vertical" industrial parks have emerged (or continue to operate) in central locations on a modest scale.

Both manufacturing and storage processes have been significantly influenced by new methods of materials handling, such as forklifts designed to handle multilevel pallets and containers with standardized sizes and shapes.

Containerization has necessitated redesign of docking and loading facilities. Sea–land and air–land containerized facilities are now relatively common.

Shifts in Demand. The United States has undergone a long-term shift in demand that has resulted in significant changes in employment patterns among major manufacturing industries. As new products have emerged, others have declined in market share.

Investors in industrial real estate must be students of the Census of Manufacturers, last done in 1977.[3] (The next such census will be in 1982.) These selected statistics, grouped by standard industrial classification, provide the investor with a better understanding of the pattern of change in the use of industrial facilities and sites. They also provide an early-warning system that permits rehabilitation and salvage of existing industrial real estate to prevent the waste of valuable assets. Succession to other uses, such as conversion of old warehouses and loft buildings into apartments or artisan villages is one imaginative example. Subdivision of old facilities into smaller areas (e.g., for microelectronics or plastic extrusion processes) is another.

Land Use Patterns and Controls. In the private sphere, the most important single development is the *planned industrial district* (PUD) or *industrial park,* where economies of scale allow concentrations of industrial establishments to take advantage of the locational amenities offered by outlying areas with excellent access.

The trend is toward wider use of zoning controls. Indeed, the private restrictions and covenants found in planned industrial districts have increasingly shifted from specific inclusions or exclusions to standards of performance.

---

[2] Detroit City Planning Commission, *Industrial Study,* Master Plan Technical Report, Second Series (Detroit, 1956), pp. 27–36.
[3] U.S. Department of Commerce, Bureau of the Census, *1977 Census of Manufacturers—Selected Statistics—Summary Series,* MC77-S-1(P) (Washington, D.C.: GPO, November 1979).

Industrial renewal and/or rehabilitation has been thrust upon many older cities because of a declining employment and tax base. The programs have emphasized new, efficient industrial spaces in central-city locations. Because of the legal problems and the expense involved, this has usually been carried out with federal subsidies, such as Urban Development Action Grants (UDAG), and state industrial development authority bonds.

Ecological Concerns. Industrial real estate is affected by the intense, almost frantic, concern of many public and private groups about the effects of some industries on the local environment. Although there is currently little agreement as to who should pay, it is clear that major steps are being taken by governments at all levels to "internalize" the costs of the more obvious and widespread forms of pollution by industrial firms. Many industrial firms have voluntarily acted to reduce pollution even before the imposition and enforcement of public regulations.

These pollution abatement activities result in more elaborate facilities and a tendency to segregate certain necessary but polluting uses. Tallow rendering and junkyards are examples of uses that most communities try to prohibit. Obviously, waste recycling must be provided for at some nearby place.

ADVANTAGES AND DISADVANTAGES OF INVESTING IN INDUSTRIAL BUILDINGS AND PARKS

The market for industrial space is actually national or international; competitive properties may be widely dispersed, and often several SMSAs may be involved. To reduce search costs, the investor may use an industrial relocation service, such as Fantus, a Dun and Bradstreet subsidiary; some local public utilities and railroads have developed competent real estate search departments and a few even maintain up-to-date reporting services on the supply of industrial real estate available in their service area.

The fixed location of industrial real estate means that investors (both equity and loan) must be attracted *into* the market area in most instances. This increases preacquisition planning and transaction costs. Also, since relatively large amounts of funds are required to effect an industrial real estate transaction, there is a tendency for investment funds to come from outside the local market area. The major centers of investment fund accumulations, such as New York City and Chicago, represent outstanding exceptions.

Industrial users are very reluctant to move both because of the actual cost of relocating machinery and equipment and because of the lost production time. Thus, even if an area is deteriorating, its effect on industrial concerns will lag. Industrial tenants are the least demanding of all; since many install large, bulky machinery and equipment, they are willing to sign long-term leases. Also, the cost of an industrial building is generally many times (say, 95%) the cost of the land, thus enabling the owner to take a higher depreciation base and generating relatively more tax shelter. The 1981 tax act has sharply increased the tax shelter opportunities on buildings and equipment for manufacturers and business corporations. In addition, because tenants usually manage their own facilities, a relatively high proportion of gross income is translated into net income.

Industrial buildings, particularly those designed for manufacturing purposes, are often highly specialized. The more specialized the building, the greater the difficulty of adapting it to the requirements of another user. Industrial real estate tends to be a relatively slow-moving commodity. Generally, the more specialized the facility, the less rapidly it turns over, which increases the liquidity risk. The value of the real estate itself typically is intimately interrelated with the profitability of the industrial process it houses. Therefore, once equipment has been installed, it is often difficult to separate the value of the plant from that of the equipment.

Industrial real estate exhibits a higher degree of sensitivity to local taxes and other government regulations. Therefore, a particularly good working knowledge of tax impacts (realty and personal), as well as the regulatory climate, is required. Industrial buildings also involve relatively high ratios of fixed charges (property taxes and insurance), whether occupied or not, which makes marketability or adaptability to other uses a major consideration.

TYPES OF INVESTORS AND INVESTOR MOTIVATIONS

Investors in industrial real estate may be categorized as follows:

Users. For users, the primary investment goal is to pay less than the prevailing competitive price for the space. Because funds are generally more productive as working capital, there is a financial advantage for the user to be a tenant rather than an owner, unless control of the location takes priority.

Equity investors. Equity investors in industrial real estate are usually very high-income individuals or groups seeking high returns through tax-sheltered income flows. Currently such investors are willing to forego current income for the sake of greater capital gains in the future. Historically, they have sought a turnover of ownership after seven to twelve years. Balloon mortgage loans are particularly popular with such investors.

The 1981 tax act changes provide an incentive for the formation of joint ventures between small- and medium-size, closely held corporate users and equity investors. Through such ventures users and investors can exploit the ACRS three-year and five-year lives and concomitant tax credits. Leasebacks between corporate parties provide a safe-harbor leveraged lease for those who comply with the strict provisions of Act Sec. 201 (amends Sec. 168f(8)).

Institutional investors. Life insurance companies, trusts, pension funds, and similar institutional investors make equity investments in industrial real estate, as well as mortgage loans. They are more inclined to make large, long-term investments in established industrial parks or buildings with proven good records. Short-term liquidity is rarely a primary objective. Instead, reduced investment portfolio turnover and increased average size of investment are sought in order to reduce operating and management costs per dollar invested.

Institutional investors normally are subject to lower income tax rates than private, profit-seeking individuals or groups. Some are tax exempt. Consequently, they have tended to emphasize the size and stability of the annual income flow rather than the prospect of capital gain. Thus, lower-risk, long-term leases with highly rated tenants are most likely to be found on the properties sought by institutional investors. Their lower tax liability and long-run orientation, together with their generally greater accumulations of funds seeking investment outlets, often permit them to outbid leveraged and tax-oriented investors.

Recently some life insurance companies have made equity investments in industrial real estate and then obtained the maximum mortgage loan available from another insurance company or bank. Thus, they are maximizing financial leverage and seeking an arbitrage between the overall rate generated and the loan rate that must be paid. Lease guarantee insurance companies, one-bank holding companies, pension funds, and commingled funds have increasingly invested in industrial real estate.

Corporate surplus. An important source of equity investment funds is the earned surplus of smaller business corporations. Both equity and loan investments in industrial real estate represent attractive alternatives for such corporations. Such investments and loans may also be used to facilitate production and/or distribution relationship with suppliers or buyers.

This section of the balance sheet may be substantially improved by the 1981 tax act change in carry backs and carry forwards. Taxes should be minimized, cash flow improved, and the collateral security of net worth enhanced by the fact that credits which cannot be used in any one year because of limitations can be carried back three years, including years before the 1981 enactment of the credits, and carried forward 15 years.

Public development agencies. Particularly for new firms that have been attracted to an area, local (and occasionally state) development agencies will often construct a plant and make it available on favorable lease terms. The incentive is to attract industry to an area that is seeking to expand or diversify its economic base. Often the plants must be general-purpose plants built on speculation, although they are built specifically for the tenant under a long-term lease arrangement.

Both public and private money is often found in industrial development commissions. However, they are much more likely to lend money or guarantee loans than to make equity investments.

MARKET AND MARKETABILITY ANALYSIS

Demand Analysis

The history of the property in terms of the credit standing of tenants, relative rental rates, and comparative trends will indicate a property's stage in the filtering-down process. Although industrial property is not as sensitive to neighborhood change as other types of income property, deterioration of the environment can cause difficulties in holding tenants when current leases expire and severely limits the feasibility of modernizing the property.

The structure of the lease also can influence the economic performance of the property. Gross, fixed-rate leases with long maturity dates and no expense stops may burden the owner with years of declining real income. Leases that share or shift the risk of rising expenses and index net income are preferred in order to maintain real returns from the property.

In analyzing demand one should understand the bases for site selection. The decision to move or expand an industrial plant is based on two factors: (1) The plant must remain competitively productive during the period of the investment, and (2) although production and distribution methods change over time, the fundamental economic rationale for the location must remain cost effective.

An *agglomerating* or clustering tendency results when one type of production tends to be concentrated in one place (e.g., air frame production). Industrial services expanding to meet the needs of the dominant industry create a complex that attracts other industries that require similar services. Substantial concentrations are usually necessary before related services and supporting facilities develop to a significant degree.

Deglomerating forces are factors that detract from otherwise favorable locational advantages. Temporarily high land prices resulting from increased demand as new industry impacts on an area illustrate deglomerating forces. Another example is plant obsolescence in the dominant industry.

Industrial users seek least-cost locations. The location selected will depend on such factors as (1) the location of competitors, (2) the importance of proximity to customers, (3) the importance of direct contacts with customers, (4) the extent of the market area, and (5) costs, including basic land prices, labor costs, community facilities, availability of housing, state labor laws, and the costs of materials, equipment, and transportation.

Locational orientation. There are five basic categories of industry: (1) mineral and agricultural extractive, (2) those most oriented to sales markets, (3) those most oriented toward transportation, (4) those most oriented toward labor, and (5) nonoriented industries.[4]

Demand for industrial space may come from entirely new establishments, from firms moving in from outside the metro area, from relocations within the metro area, or from on-site expansion of existing establishments.

The steps in estimating future space requirements for industry are as follows:

1. Determine the present number of manufacturing employees per gross acre by type of industry.
2. Estimate future industrial employment, by type of industry and size of firm.
3. Estimate future employee densities in the light of changing trends in industrial space requirements. As industries modernize plant and equipment, the result is usually greater output per square foot of floor space. Offsetting this is the trend toward one-story buildings on outlying sites that contain more parking area and more room for plant expansion.
4. Estimate future land requirements by multiplying the estimated square feet of land area required per worker (the industrial density) by the expected industrial employment for each use as of a given date. Employment estimates must relate to all industrial uses (rather than simply to manufacturing), or land needs for industrial purposes will be understated. A further adjustment may be necessary if nonindustrial uses are permitted in industrial zones. The estimate must also take into account the community's land use regulations. Employment density analysis will have limited applicability for many commercial uses that are permitted in industrial zones.
5. Compare the estimated demand for industrial land with an estimate of the future supply of industrial land. However, a survey of the industrial land supply must also consider the quality of the land that is expected to be made available. Future land requirements may, for example, be dominated by demand for space with a structural density of 20 percent or less. Yet the supply of available space may consist largely of scattered lots of odd sizes.

---

[4] William Kinnard and Stephen Messner, *Industrial Real Estate* (Washington, D.C.: Society of Industrial Realtors, 1976). See also Melvin L. Greenhut, *Plant Locations — Theory and Practice* (Chapel Hill: University of North Carolina Press, 1956), pp. 263–272.

Supply Analysis

Generalizations about supply analysis within a region are not useful because users of industrial land often consider sites scattered throughout a region and in more than one SMSA.

In a study by the American Trucking Association, the factors in plant location that were mentioned most often by industrial respondents, *in order of frequency,* were the following:

1. Proximity to good highways (interstate access—time lapse).
2. Abundant labor supply (industry specific).
3. Availability of suitable land.
4. Proximity to markets for product or services of user.
5. Availability of rail service, if relevant.
6. Availability of raw materials.
7. Favorable state and local tax structure.
8. Favorable leasing or financing.
9. Abundant water supply, if important.
10. Proximity to related industry.
11. Existence of building at site.
12. Community's cultural and recreational assets.
13. Nearby vocational training facilities.[5]

While many similar studies report that essentially the same factors are significant, *there is variation in the priority of factors, depending on the industry, the size of the firm, or the process.* For example, in a *Fortune* survey of over 400 of the largest manufacturing firms in the United States the following factors were mentioned most frequently (in order of importance):

1. Availability of workers of appropriate skill.
2. Proximity to customers (for minimizing transportation).
3. Proximity to raw materials, supplies, and services.
4. Ample area for future expansion.
5. A growing regional market.
6. Water supply.
7. Inexpensive power and other utilities.[6]

Analyzing Industrial Sites. The supply of industrial space is stratified or segmented by type. For example, some users are limited to sites with high-capacity, low-cost water, gas, and electricity. Others are strongly attracted to certain labor skills. In the event that improvements are already on the site, one should analyze physical, legal, political, and environmental factors in order to identify competitive sites that would be of interest to the appropriate users. Particular attention should be given to the structural characteristics of the buildings in order to match these to the needs of potential users.

---

[5] *Summary of Highways, Trucks, and New Industry Locations,* Hardeman, ed. American Trucking Association, Department of Research and Transport Economics (July 1963), p. 5.
[6] *Fortune Survey on Locating Plants, Warehouses, and Laboratories* (New York, Time Inc., 1963), p. 13. (Note: Only factors mentioned by at least 30 percent of the respondents are listed here.)

Centrally located sites. Land in older industrial areas is relatively scarce. Further, the sites are often small and irregularly shaped; there is a limited amount of land available for parking, off-street truck loading, or expansion. Traffic congestion is a common problem. Security may be perceived as a problem as well.

Available central sites may also be adversely affected by surrounding uses. Dilapidated buildings, smoke, smells, and the noise of the central district seriously limit prospects for modern industrial use. The utility service in older industrial areas may not be adequate for modern industry. Relatively high property taxes also are often encountered, partly because other central-district uses normally support higher land values.

To the extent that workers seek to live in suburban communities, the central location may be poorly situated with respect to commuting.

However, these disadvantages must be balanced against many advantages. For some industries, a central location may be of overriding importance. The potential savings in transportation costs may justify locating warehouses and other distribution facilities in the downtown fringe area. Where customer contact is highly important, as in job printing, space in the central area is often preferred. Thus, when delivery time and frequent customer contact are important, a central location is often preferred.

The central area may be better served by lower-cost utilities, and other municipal services, such as police, fire protection, snow removal, are often superior. Hence, an industrial firm located in the central area obtains more than space; it acquires the right to use a valuable municipal infrastructure. Though real estate taxes in such areas are high, they tend to rise at a slower rate than taxes in outlying areas.

A downtown site is often strategically located with respect to the supply of unskilled and semiskilled labor. The proximity of professional consultants, suppliers, and subcontractors helps explain why some firms prefer central locations.

Central industrial areas, though limited by traffic congestion, are often advantageously placed near major transportation terminals.

Finally, for certain industries a central location improved with older buildings provides a means of securing space at a lower cost than is possible in suburban areas.

Suburban sites and acreage. Industrial acreage and individual sites in rural or suburban areas are often used for agriculture before they undergo a transition to industrial use. The cost of many suburban sites consists of the cost of the vacant land plus the cost of land development. Topography and the load-bearing quality of the soil are important determinants of whether industrially zoned land can be made into an industrial site.

Large sites (100 acres or more) in outlying areas permit occupants to isolate their operations from those of adjoining landowners. The dangers of explosion, heat, glare, fire, or radiation and the nuisances of noise, smog, and smoke may be minimized by purchasing sufficient acreage. Enough land can be acquired to construct a one-story building, and still allow room for expansion and landscaping.

Though utilities are often lacking, large plants may prefer to install their own systems. In this manner a firm may avoid the limitations of inadequate existing water lines, sewer mains, gas lines, and power sources. Utility companies occasionally cooperate in providing the necessary capacity and connections.

Organized industrial parks. An organized industrial park is a tract of land under proprietary control that is reserved for the exclusive use of industry and supporting uses according to a master plan.

Sites in industrial parks are relatively expensive compared to industrial acreage. However, higher prices are often associated with better support services and superior location.

Industries that do not conform to the land use controls and lot sizes of the industrial district are unable to utilize such sites effectively. On the other hand, zoning and other land use problems are resolved by the park sponsor. Firms that locate in organized industrial districts avoid the time and expense necessary to negotiate and arrange for utility extensions with public authorities. Compared to uncontrolled industrial areas, the organized industrial district generally has superior highway access. Technology Park in Atlanta is an attractive example. (See pages 596–597.)

The organized industrial district represents a specialized source of industrial land that is useful primarily for (1) firms that require less than 10 acres and can adapt to the architectural and landscaping requirements imposed by the district; (2) distribution establishments that need superior market access; and (3) firms that require the special services and facilities of the organized industrial district.

Redeveloped land. The older areas of many cities—frequently those with mixed-use land, blighted sections, and dilapidated buildings surrounding downtown areas—are being redeveloped under federal or state urban renewal programs. In these areas privately owned land has been acquired by local public agencies and cleared, subdivided, and offered to industrial prospects for sale or lease. The sites are often oddly shaped, irregular, and uneconomical in size. While the land is generally expensive—at least in comparison with outlying sites—it is generally less so than competitive industrial sites in the same neighborhoods. Long-term land leases occasionally overcome the high cost. Prospects for renewal may be adversely affected by surrounding incompatible land uses that have not been eliminated.

However, urban-renewal space is generally more convenient to urban centers, with the attendant attractions of such locations. Such space is attractive to (1) industries and distribution firms that require centrally located space; (2) industries that emphasize customer service and convenience to downtown merchants, suppliers, and customers; (3) industries that must locate near labor supplies surrounding the downtown area; (4) small plants and industries that are ancillary to major industries located in the central area; and (5) firms that can afford relatively high land prices and comply with severe restrictions. The Urban Enterprise Zones, if adapted, will provide tax incentives for industry to occupy and use urban ghetto sites and train underemployed youths.

Projection of Rental Income, Expenses, and Vacancy Levels

In most cases industrial real estate occupancy is based on a long-term lease, usually ten or more years in duration. The typical industrial lease is more nearly net to the investor than is a commercial lease, with much of the risk of changing operating expenses (e.g., utilities and property taxes) assumed by the tenant. Gross income is the annual contract rental for the space, plus any service income (e.g., from sale of electricity). When there is a long-term lease on industrial property with a well-rated tenant, potential gross income and effective gross income often are equal.

TECHNOLOGY PARK, Atlanta Georgia

Project Data

Site: 340 acres: 277.5 acres platted; 35.4 acres right of way; 37.1 acres lake

Sales price per acre (parcel size 1 to 15 acres)
Interior: $65,000-$80,000
Lakefront: $80,000-$100,000

Building use (total area 850,000 sq. ft.): office, engineering production, warehouse

Open space ratio: .40; Floor area ratio: .026

Construction costs (without land)

	Sq. ft.	Built	Cost/sq. ft.
Office	27,000	1979	$40
Engineering production	40,000	1979	25
Office	44,000	1980	35

Rents and operating expenses per square foot (developer-owned buildings)

Rents
Office: $8.50-$14.00
Engineering production: $4.50-$8.00
Operating expenses: $2.75-$3.00

Photos and data courtesy of Technology Park/Atlanta, Georgia

Site Plan

TECHNOLOGY PARK | ATLANTA

The average tenant in an industrial building makes fewer demands for services than tenants in other types of income-producing properties. The landlord pays the property taxes, but the leases contain a tax stop clause so that each tenant pays a pro rata share of any increase. The landlord pays for fire insurance on the building, but the tenants pay for liability, equipment, and inventory coverage. The tenants pay for their own separately metered utilities. However, exterior lighting is usually paid for by the landlord and prorated among the tenants. Generally, the tenant is responsible for all interior maintenance and repair, as well as for replacing broken glass. The landlord's responsibility is limited to maintenance of the roof and exterior walls, and sometimes common areas. The landlord should set up a reserve account, e.g., $2.50 per building lineal foot, to take care of future roof and wall maintenance.

The cost of maintaining the parking lot and common exterior grounds is borne by the landlord but passed on to the tenants, also on a pro rata basis. When a vacancy occurs, the landlord should remember that, in addition to the loss of rental income, he or she assumes other expenses that the tenant would have paid. The landlord should take into account the administrative overhead for management of the property. This category includes office expenses, bookkeeping and accounting, legal fees, telephone charges, advertising expenses, commissions, and time to resolve tenant problems. When a good management company performs these services without the responsibility for leasing, the cost is in the range of 2–4 percent of gross income; with leasing responsibility, it is 7–10 percent.

Investor–tenant relations vary over such a wide range that it is difficult to show a typical industrial investment. However, Exhibit 22–1 is a sample analysis of a representative multitenant industrial building.

PHYSICAL ANALYSIS OF SITE AND IMPROVEMENTS

The Site

There has been a general trend toward low-density, single-story industrial buildings. Concrete block and prefabricated modules by Butler, Inland, Stransteel, and similar firms are common because of their low per-square-foot construction costs. The supply of industrial buildings is highly stratified by type of building and the specialized needs of various types of users. Custom adaptation of industrial structures may lead to conversion problems when there is a change in occupants.

Plant Layout and Construction. A plant may be laid out in various ways: In a *product layout* equipment is arranged according to the particular sequence of operations needed to produce a particular product. Plans that produce different but related products generally have a *process layout,* which centralizes certain production functions.

Three construction classifications, distinguished by degree of fire resistance and quality of materials employed, are generally used for fire insurance rating:

First-class buildings are usually constructed of nonflammable materials. Exterior walls, bearing partitions, roofs, floors, doors, and window frames are usually concrete, steel covered, or aluminum. Floors are hardwood, rubber blocks, or metal strips. Vibration and noise are minimized. Alteration, expansion, and demolition costs are relatively high for such buildings.

Second-class buildings are only partially fireproof. Here the exterior walls, which are usually solid brick and constructed to a height of five or six stories, as

EXHIBIT 22–1. Operations Report for a Multitenant Industrial Building

Subject property is a 42,000 sq. ft., multitenant industrial building located in the I-85 N corridor of Atlanta, inside I-285. In an area comprised solely of industrial users, the property's favorable access to Atlanta's interstate system renders it desirable for companies servicing larger industrial users in the metro area. The building has experienced few and short-lived vacancies since it was built in 1971.

The exterior walls of the building are precast concrete and the interior walls are drywall, with 3 1/2 inches of insulation between. The roof is of built-up design covered with corrugated steel and layers of felt finished with tar and gravel. The floor is of poured concrete and is constructed at dock height to permit level loading. The size of the lot is approximately 2 acres and is paved with asphalt.

The building is presently separated into seven bays, each separately metered with tenants paying their own utilities. The seven leases are detailed below:

Tenant	Area Leased	Base Year	Term	Commencement Date	Expiration Date	Annual Rental	Notes*	Per Square Foot
1	4,500 sq. ft.	1978	3	9/78	8/81	$ 9,675	1	$2.15
2	3,000 sq. ft.	1978	2 1/2	2/79	8/81	5,250	2	1.75
3	4,500 sq. ft.	1974	1	11/79	10/80	10,125	3	2.25
4	3,000 sq. ft.	1978	3	2/79	1/82	6,000		2.00
5	6,000 sq. ft.	1978	3	3/78	2/82	15,240	4	2.54
6	6,000 sq. ft.	1978	3	3/79	2/82	10,500	5	1.75
7	15,000 sq. ft.	1978	3	5/78	4/81	23,550	6	1.57
Totals	42,000 sq. ft.					$80,340		$1.91

* Notes	Options and Cancellation Rights
1	Right to cancel at end of 24 months.
2	Right to cancel at end of August 1980.
3	Option to renew for 5 years at rate not less than $2.25 per sq. ft.
4	Option to renew for 2 years at base rate of $1.65.
5	Option to renew for 3 years at agreed-upon market rate.
6	Right to cancel at end of 24 months with 90-day notice.

ANNUAL PROPERTY OPERATING STATEMENT (1980)

	(actual for 1980)	(Cost/sq. ft.)	
Gross rental income			$80,340
Expenses			
Taxes	$ 5,710	$.14	
Insurance	1,163	.03	
Management	2,400	.06	
Maintenance	2,100	.05	
Repairs	2,100	.05	
Landscaping	200	—	
Dumpster (paid by tenants)	—		
Leasing com.	1,562	.038	$15,235
Totals	$15,235	$.37	
Net operating income			$65,105

We gratefully acknowledge the assistance of W. M. Sellars, Jr., Vice-President, Ward Wight Company, Atlanta, Ga.

well as the bearing partitions, stairwells, elevator shafts, and doors, are fireproof. Such buildings are illustrated by the mill-type structures erected in the late 1800s or early 1900s. The floors, interior walls, columns and all other interior construction, and the roof are generally flammable. Consequently, these buildings must be served with overhead sprinkler systems (dry or wet), fire doors, fire walls, and exterior fire escapes. In general, they are suited to light or medium, multiple-product operations.

Third-class buildings are of wood frame construction and are more flammable than the preceding types. Light-duty construction of one or two stories, a relatively low floor loading—bearing capacity, and high maintenance costs are characteristic. Compared to those of first- and second-class buildings, construction costs are relatively low. Third-class buildings are inexpensive to alter, expand, or remove. Arsonists prefer them.

Architectural design. In judging the utility of a building, it is important to relate the uses to which the building is adapted to the demand for those uses. For example, high walls with few windows are highly desirable for warehouses and general storage. Steel or galvanized iron walls are often used where the climate is more moderate.

Floors elevated to railroad car or truck bed levels are important for distribution purposes. Street-level floors are best for fork-lift truck use. Shipping floors adapted to food processing are unsuitable for most manufacturing or storage uses.

Buildings with open ceilings and exposed rafters, trusses, and beams are more useful for warehousing because of their greater ceiling clearance.

Multistory plants are better adapted to processes in which gravity flow is required. Also, activities that should be isolated from major functions are often better located at a different level.

Adaptability. Where feasible general-purpose buildings are preferred because changes in industrial processes or products manufactured may be accommodated more readily. A general-purpose building usually is more salable, and most important, normally is easier to finance.

Manufacturing and processing plants are more likely to be special-purpose (or even single-purpose) buildings; wholesaling, distribution, and assembly activities (as well as related office and management functions) can usually be carried out in less specialized structures.

Building Analysis

As with site requirements, building characteristics tend to be specific to the needs of a particular user. Among the items to be considered, in addition to the required amount of square footage, the type of construction material, bearing capacity, and foundations, are the following:

Electrical, gas, water, sewage, and rail installations. The proper type of electrical installation is an example of what are termed *economic* standards as opposed to physical standards. Many production activities, for example, require not only high-voltage and heavy-wattage electrical service but also specialized levels or cycles of electric power. It is not sufficient to have enough power; a planned network of lines and circuits with adequate capacity for maximum load is needed. It is not uncommon for gas, water, sewage, and electrical service to be custom designed to adequately serve the industrial customer. The absence of such utility services makes a site unacceptable to many industrial tenants.

Protection (security) systems. This factor requires careful evaluation, preferably by an experienced specialist.

One potential pitfall is spending excessive sums to provide superadequate fencing and other devices. However, protection systems and devices can be quite expensive if they must be installed at a later date.

Fire protection and sprinkler systems. This varies with the type of activity and local or state codes. Many industrial users have special requirements that are mandatory.

Elevators, lifts, and conveyors. Because of the expense of both acquisition and installation of these items, as well as the space they absorb, extreme care must be exercised to make sure they suit the purpose for which they are intended. Correcting mistakes can be very costly. Allowance for future expansion must be made.

Heating, lighting, and ventilation. Electronics manufacturers may require a hermetically sealed environment, cooled, heated, and humidified to close tolerances. Many uses require special high-speed, high-capacity ventilators equipped with pollution abatement devices.

Ceiling heights. The adequacy of ceiling heights is directly related to the intended use of the structure. The shift from bow trusses to laminated or I-beam construction has made higher, clear-span ceiling heights financially feasible and has enabled users to take advantage of the economies of new materials-handling equipment. Spans and heights tend to be in multiples of six feet for palletizing. Recently, heights in excess of over 28 feet have been required.

LEGAL, POLITICAL, AND ENVIRONMENTAL ANALYSIS

Zoning and environmental-quality regulations must be analyzed before anything else. Everyone wants jobs, but few communities want industries with pollution management problems located within their boundaries. Some enlightened communities, however, are creating industrial districts that are zoned to provide land for inharmonious, but necessary, uses.

Urban renewal can actually create new industrial sites in areas that were previously devoted to other uses. Local industrial-development commissions can often be very helpful in overcoming opposition to the acquisition and holding of land (and occasionally buildings) by an industrial investor for future development and use. The failure of an SMSA to provide enough good locations for industry, or to protect industrial reserves, is starting to be recognized as a serious mistake.

There are economic opportunities for investors in proprietary industrial parks that provide adequate land use controls, including control of environmental degradation. In recent years militant opposition to establishing new industrial locations has given a quasi-monopoly market power to those who already own industrial land because such sites don't have to run the ecological gauntlet to qualify as a prospective site.

An environmental-impact analysis may be required for rehabilitation, expansion, or new-site development.[7]

---

[7] Jane A. Silverman, *Environmental Factors of Real Estate Development,* Real Estate Review Portfolio no. 17 (Boston: Warren, Gorham & Lamont, 1978). See also *Environmental Comment* (Washington, D.C., Urban Land Institute, series).

PROPERTY MANAGEMENT AND LEASING

The management of industrial properties is a separate specialty. Whereas maintenance and operating needs are comparatively simple (since most industrial tenants completely maintain the interior and often the exterior of their spaces), the
merchandising of industrial space requires substantial specialized knowledge
about the manufacturing and distribution problems of the various enterprises to
be housed.

Another reason for the specialization of industrial brokers is the national, even
international, nature of the trading markets, which ties brokers into a semiconfi-
dential communication network concerning the relocation plans of industrial
businesses. It is in a broker's self-interest not to disclose the intent of a would-be
tenant to change locations. Often the decision to seek an industrial site in a new
region is made at a corporate headquarters a great distance from the site. Even
local industries that are going to move usually seek to keep it quiet.

One of the most effective ways, therefore, for equity investors to tie into this
private network is to offer an industrial broker a joint venture or ask to join a
syndicate that the broker is putting together. One should expect the broker to
require that he or she be the property manager during the ownership cycle, as well
as requiring sales commissions and a share of the equity reversion. The extent to
which a broker shares in the responsibility for providing cash equity contributions
depends on negotiations, as well as the return/risk relationships implicit in the
particular project. Since the broker's involvement, as described here, is fraught
with possible conflicts of interest, it should be clear that equity investors should
carefully investigate the reputation of the would-be working partner.

The management of industrial real estate may or may not be tied to leasing. In
some areas, the management fee is included in the leasing contractor's obligations
and is part of the commission structure. In others, a separate management fee is
charged only when there are multiple tenants.

Whatever the arrangement, there is a distinction between the functions of
leasing—that is, merchandising the space—and managing the property, which
consists of collecting rents and maintaining the physical condition of the real estate
in accordance with the requirements and wishes of the owner. Management is an
important function that must be integrated with leasing so as to keep the building
completely and continuously occupied at appropriate rental levels.

A distinguishing characteristic of industrial real estate is that more of the
maintenance and operation of the building tends to be automated. The hours of
service of many facilities, such as heating and elevators, will be specified in the
lease contract. Also, owners of multiple-tenant industrial buildings often buy
utilities (especially electricity) at wholesale rates and resell them to their tenants at
retail rates. Since this may be an important source of income, the lease must be
analyzed to ascertain which party is responsible for services. Generally, one can
expect all but first-year operating costs to be borne by the lessee.

Leases and Tenant Arrangements. Landlords reduce leasing risk by attracting
high-quality tenants and negotiating net leases. Smaller local tenants may be able
to get lease guarantee insurance from the Small Business Administration; this
makes them comparable with top-rated credit risks.

On the revenue side, the investor can avoid the effects of inflation through a
lease provision for rent escalation based on a periodic evaluation of the cost of

living. Another method that is frequently utilized is to base future rental changes on a reappraisal of the property.

The four types of general leasing arrangements used to manage risk in industrial real estate practice are the following:

Straight lease. A straight or direct lease is used for a property that is already in existence or is being built as a general-purpose building.

Build-lease. This arrangement, also termed *build to suit*, refers to one of two situations. In the first a property owner-developer already owns a building site in which a prospective tenant is interested. The owner constructs a building to suit the tenant. In the second situation the investor may have an arrangement with a prospective tenant to construct a building specifically for the tenant, but must find and purchase a suitable site.

Frequently a build-lease building is a special-purpose or special-use structure. The lenders therefore consider the credit of the tenant-user. As in all credit-oriented industrial real estate transactions, the higher the credit rating of the tenant, the better the tenant's bargaining position. The lessor can utilize the credit of the tenant in negotiating more favorable mortgage financing. The lender will, of course, insist on an assignment of the lease from the lessor in the event of mortgagor default.

Sale-leaseback. In a sale-leaseback transaction the buyer-lessor is often a financial institution, pension fund, or wealthy individual seeking a tax shelter. It is not necessary for the lessor to be a tax-favored or tax-exempt organization, but such status adds considerably to the attractiveness of the leases that such investors are able to offer.

Institutional lessor-purchasers are more interested in "paper deals" that are susceptible to financial analysis than in complex real estate development transactions. Sale-leasebacks of existing facilities are readily understandable to them because the risk can be measured by familiar credit analysis methods.

Although emphasis is usually placed on high-credit transactions involving large financial institutions, the sale-leaseback can be an effective device for smaller industrial firms. It can be a real estate market analysis problem as well as a financial analysis transaction.

Ground lease. Under this arrangement the land is subject to a long-term lease and the lessee utilizes the leasehold estate to finance the construction of buildings on the land or as a way to partially refinance. In effect, leasing the site is similar to obtaining a loan equal to 100 percent of the land value. Recently industrial firms have been inviting investors to buy ground leases on established locations in order to generate working capital from an otherwise nonproductive asset.

RISK MANAGEMENT AND CONTROL TECHNIQUES

The market analysis for the industrial building and land is itself an application of a risk analysis technique. However, it must be remembered that voids on the supply side more frequently exist because the private sector has lacked the creativity to lead demand rather than because it has failed to meet a known consumer need. Assumptions regarding general lease parameters, tenant quality, and tenant mix will be based on the market study. Often ambitious SMSAs will zone a supply of industrial land far beyond the capacity of the market to absorb it in the near term.

This tends to deflate land values and may result in an oversupply of general-purpose industrial buildings built on speculation. A competent market study should forewarn equity investors of such an unfortunate phenomenon. Coordination of investment in new and used industrial buildings with an ethical and knowledgeable industrial broker is a good risk-avoidance technique because of the broker's closer ties to tenants and knowledge of competitive revenue/expense units. We strongly urge the use of competitive survey techniques like those delineated in Chapter 6. Consultation with a qualified, well-connected industrial realtor, such as a member of the Society of Industrial Realtors (SIR), will do much to minimize business risk.

FINANCING AND REFINANCING TECHNIQUES

Estimating Financing Costs. Debt service is generally fixed over the investment period and may be accurately projected. If loan call or escalation provisions are involved, a judgment must be made regarding future interest rates. In recent years rising construction costs and interest rates have resulted in such high annual amortization costs that industrial real estate investors have sought to lower the constant. Balloon payment mortgages have become common. Thirty-year and even 40- or 50-year amortization terms are used to establish the annual mortgage constant on which the payments are based, with the balloons typically due in 10 to 12 years.

Sources of Funds. The financing of industrial real estate is more diversified than the financing of any other type of property. Banks, pension funds, and insurance companies participate. Regulations and laws set the limits; within these limits, individual variation is found among different types of lenders, from one lender to another in the same group, and even from one loan to another by the same lender.

Pension funds are showing much greater interest in this type of real estate. Since they are not hampered by the laws and regulations that affect insurance companies and banks, as long as they comply with fiduciary responsibilities, they may lend on higher loan-to-value ratios.

Firms like Shell, U.S. Plywood, General Electric, and U.S. Steel, among others, have supplied funds and taken junior liens to facilitate good relations with suppliers who deal with them.

The Small Business Investment Companies (SBICs) are specifically authorized to make both equity investments and long-term secured loans. SBICs usually demand premium rates and equity rights, so they tend to serve borrowers who cannot qualify for conventional loans.

In addition, estates, private trusts, university endowment funds, REITs, and wealthy individuals have an interest in industrial real estate lending. Besides the more conventional loans, they may be willing to consider junior lien positions and subordinated land leases as well as convertible bonds. (See Chapter 14 for more details on the institutional lenders and financing techniques applicable to this market.)

Until recently public agencies at all three levels of government had industrial-development programs. Most public agencies, whether at the federal, state, or local level, generally offer advice and assistance to industrial firms and developers; however, they do not usually make loans.

An exception at the federal level is the Small Business Administration (SBA). Any manufacturing establishment with fewer than 250 employees is an eligible small business, and in some industries the limit is even higher. As a general rule, the Small Business Administration has extended long-term credit secured by industrial real estate only if such credit is not available from private sources. The SBA may make a direct loan to the borrowing firm, or it may participate in a loan by a private lender.

State and local industrial-development commissions frequently advance funds for plant construction and/or acquisition, particularly when private sources do not provide as much as is needed by the firm. This credit is commonly in the form of junior liens, with relatively low interest rates and very favorable amortization provisions.

Federal industrial-assistance programs are currently in a state of flux. A more conservative administration has indicated that such functions will be restructured. Perhaps more will be done locally. In the past assistance offered through state agencies and corporations differed considerably from federal programs.

There are no significant differences in financial or technical assistance programs among the various regions of the United States. It can be noted, however, that the industrial mortgage guaranty is aptly termed the New England plan, since it is concentrated heavily in the New England states. In contrast, tax concessions or inducements in some form are found in every state. The available programs range from exemptions to encourage research and development to excise tax exemptions.

Industrial Real Estate Bonds

Mortgage bonds are often issued by industrial corporations that are short of capital. Substantial limitations are usually placed on the issuing firm. The range of restrictive covenants that is possible is almost limitless; three of the most common provisions are (1) the "after-acquired clause" (dragnet), which states that any other real estate acquired by the corporation subsequent to the issuance of the mortgage bonds also becomes security for the bonds until they are retired; (2) a limitation on dividend payments until sufficient funds have been built up to assure continued payment of interest and principal on the bonds; and (3) a requirement that minimum working capital ratios be maintained. Offsetting these restrictions, the chief advantage of the mortgage bond to the issuing corporation is that bonds offer a way to avoid the legal limits on mortgages that affect some lenders. It may be possible to borrow 100 percent of the value of the property. The costs of a mortgage bond issue are considerably higher than those of placing a mortgage.

Debentures are simply full faith and credit promissory notes of a corporation, secured by a loan agreement. Two types of debentures can be used to finance real estate acquisitions. First, highly rated industrial corporations may utilize their own credit in the financial markets to issue debentures, the proceeds of which pay for the acquisition of real estate. In a strict technical sense, this is not real estate finance at all. It does have the advantage of being less expensive, because the interest rate on debentures of high-credit corporations is usually lower than that on mortgage bonds and even that on first mortgages in some capital markets.

Small corporations that need funds for physical expansion often issue convertible debentures. These carry the right of conversion into common or preferred stock of the issuing corporation. This "sweetener" is designed to overcome the

fact that the issuing corporation represents a relatively high risk. The chief difference is a legal one. Since debentures come under the heading of securities, one
must comply with the securities laws, whereas a mortgage is simply a loan. The
risk-taking investors or lenders that are most likely to be attracted to convertible
debentures are SBICs and REITs.

Equipment trust certificates are a rarely utilized alternative to financing
equipment and fixtures that technically may be regarded as part of the realty.
These certificates are a form of chattel mortgage and are unusual enough to
require the advice of a specialist in the Uniform Commercial Code and local law.

Major Bases of Credit. Although greater emphasis is placed on the status of
occupants in credit analysis by mortgage lenders, the financial status of the
investor–owner is not ignored.

Owner-occupant. An owner with blue-chip national credit will always command favorable terms. If the owner-occupant is a good local risk, some financial
covenants may be attached to the loan agreement, such as a limit on future
borrowing by the corporation until the mortgage is paid off; the establishment of
working capital ratio standards; or a limitation on the distribution of profits while
the mortgage loan is outstanding.

Owner-investor. Relatively little emphasis is placed on the credit standing of
the typical owner-investor, primarily because there is little effective recourse
against him or her in the event of default. The trend among institutional lenders on
industrial real estate is for the notes to be endorsed without personal liability on
the part of the owner. In the event of default, assignment of rents and receivership
are essential lender rights. Many institutional lenders who are precluded from
lending on unimproved property may lend on leaseholds without the land being
pledged. In this situation the real security for the mortgage is the credit of the
tenants.

Tenant-owner. Any lease on industrial real estate will ordinarily be condi-
tionally assigned to the lender. Therefore, the mortgagee will normally expect the
tenant to continue paying rent in the event of default by the mortgagor. As a
further safeguard, the loan agreement will normally provide for subordination of
any penalty clause or condemnation clause that the lease contains. Generally
speaking, the better the credit rating of the tenant, the more favorable the terms
that the borrower can receive and the greater the emphasis on credit rather than
real estate.

The lending institution normally pursues two avenues of investigation in
evaluating the risk of either the owner–occupant or the tenant–occupant. The
credit quality of either a tenant or an owner–occupant depends in part on the
industry in which it is operating and its place in that industry. Within the framework of its industry and its history, the credit quality of a tenant or owner–
occupant also depends on its financial characteristics and earnings record. The
future prospects of the firm, its earnings record, and the quality of its management
are all considered by the lender. A variety of ratios—working capital, dividend
payout, capitalization—are utilized to evaluate the stability and strength of the
company. Credit reports (e.g., Equifax or Dun and Bradstreet) are used to supplement earnings records. Bank references, competitors, customers, and outside
auditing firms may be interviewed if permitted.

Lease Guarantee Insurance. It is not surprising that one of the most important uses of lease guarantees has been to help obtain financing for new construction. The guarantee offers an excellent form of collateral to the lender, and is used to support the financing of industrial developments or investments that otherwise might not be acceptable risks to the mortgagee. Private lease guarantee companies usually insure up to 85 percent of the lease income in return for a lump-sum premium that is generally treated by developers as part of the cost of project development. The premium is usually equal to approximately six months' rent.

Debt Coverage Ratio and Mortgage Constant Desired by the Lender. Required debt coverage ratios vary significantly, depending on the owner's or tenant's credit credentials and on the location of the real estate. Generally, higher loan constants are used for industrial properties, unless there is a high-quality tenant with a "no-exit" lease permitting longer amortization than the normal 15 to 20 years.

Loan-to-Value Ratio. Conventional industrial real estate mortgages usually carry loan-to-value ratios of between 66 2/3 and 75 percent of estimated market value. There are certain exceptions; New York State insurance companies, for example, loan up to 90 percent of value on "adequately secured loans." A construction loan may be granted for 75 to 80 percent of certified construction costs. A development loan might go to 60 percent of development costs. In either case, the value of the land does not enter into the cost/value base. Alternatively, a "floor loan" arrangement may be employed, with the full loan commitment available when a specified level of income has been achieved.

Mortgage Loan Maturity. A new industrial building may carry a loan term of between 15 and 30 years, while an older existing building might command only a 10- to 15-year maturity.

To a large extent leases tend to set the maturity of the mortgage. Generally, the term of the mortgage will not run beyond the term of the lease. If underlying leases have really long terms (e.g., 35– 40 years), are noncancelable, and are made to high-credit tenants, the terms of the mortgage can and will be extended accordingly. When the real estate, rather than the credit of the occupant or tenant, is the fundamental collateral, shorter terms are usually dictated by the lender's desire for safety. State industrial-development authority guarantees are used to extend maturities.

TAXATION AND TAX STRUCTURE

Nature of the Tax Shelter. The Economic Recovery Tax Act of 1981 has provided ACRS lives of ten and fifteen years for industrial real estate property and three and five years for equipment as a stimulus to production. Industrial buildings are expected to use the statutory ACRS 175 percent declining-balance method over 15 years because long-term leases minimize concern over recapture on premature disposition.

Depreciable, tangible personal property that is used as an integral part of manufacturing, production, extraction, and related research and storage functions is generally eligible for the investment tax credit. Thus, if a building is properly classified as a general-purpose building and the owner is supplying such equipment as overhead cranes, counters, racks, gasoline pumps, signs, fencing, storage bins, and special heating or air conditioning to maintain a specific temperature or humidity, those items may be segregated out of the structural components and are eligible for the investment tax credit and accelerated depreciation.

Improvements made for a specific tenant may enable the landlord to use a certain portion of the rental income as repayment for the capital improvement, deducting this amount from taxable income. To take advantage of this opportunity, a portion of the rental income based on some reasonably computed discount rate must be identified *ex ante* as amortization of the expense in the lease. The cautious strategy is to have an actual written agreement with the tenant.

Disposition of industrial properties is also eligible for various tax deferment techniques—capital gains or losses may be eligible for Section 1231 asset treatment, exchanges, or installment method sales.

Depreciation. The use of ACRS composite depreciation requires that the depreciable asset be segmented into appropriate classes. Generally, the class life will be statutory or regulatory.

Although depreciation based on useful life has been eliminated, the ACRS lives are generous. An investor should consult an accountant, or a machinery and equipment appraiser, to determine the appropriate 3-, 5-, or 10-year life for items other than the real property. Trade and industrial fixtures that are not intended to be a part of the realty, even though apparently attached permanently, may be treated as personalty and thus eligible for the appropriately shorter life. (See also Chapter 13.) A significant percentage of the value of an industrial building may be correctly treated as personalty rather than being subject to the 15-year ACRS recovery period for real property.

Tax Problems and Uncertainties. The taxpayer should be aware of possible recapture effects upon sale of the property. *All* depreciation will be recaptured as ordinary income in the year of a sale if the property is sold prior to completing the statutory period for the class life.

A problem of a sale-leaseback arrangement is whether the transaction will be treated as a lease or a sale for income tax purposes. If it is truly a lease, the lessee is entitled to deduct the rental payments. The rent is ordinary income to the lessor, who is entitled to a deduction for depreciation and other expenses. On the other hand, if the transaction is treated as a sale, it may be taxed at ordinary rates, the sale may not be eligible for installment reporting, and the seller may have to report imputed interest income. The purchaser will receive deductions for depreciation and imputed interest. Merely calling an agreement a lease will not ensure its treatment as one. Similar problems exist for poorly drafted purchase–leaseback agreements, which may be classified as loans.

DISCOUNTED CASH FLOW ANALYSIS

Rate-of-Return Analysis. The most accurate estimate may be derived by estimating equity cash flows after taxes for the anticipated ownership cycle and discounting each to its present value, using IRR/PV methods of analysis.

Desired Rate of Equity Return. Equity investors in industrial properties generally have required an after-tax IRR of 10 percent or higher, plus an inflation premium. This expectation will be lowered significantly if the investor can purchase industrial property leased by a firm with strong national credit on a long-term lease. In recent years, as investors have tried to hedge against inflation, acceptable current cash flow yields (ROEs) have been much lower than the historic rule of thumb (10% ROE) plus the inflation premium on the best of the industrial properties leased to blue-chip tenants.

Ratio and Risk Analysis. Sensitivity analysis should be applied to determine the separate effects of individual expense increases, sudden vacancy, and potential rental increases as per the lease terms. In effect, an analysis should be made of the various escalator items to determine how effective they are in offsetting inflation and enhancing profitability.

THE INVESTMENT DECISION

Currently, investors seem to be aggressively seeking well-constructed industrial properties leased to strong-credit tenants on long-term net leases, or multitenant properties in established industrial parks. Also worth considering are properties for sale and leaseback to creditworthy owner–tenants. Warehousing, distribution facilities, and industrial park sites are the preferred risk investment. It appears likely that more industrial corporations are willing to sell and lease back land, plants, and equipment in order to put such assets to more productive use. As a result, one can expect more syndication of such industrial assets, and increased equity investments by institutional portfolio managers.

Selected References

Conway Publications. *Industrial Development Site Selection Handbook, 1980.* Airport Road, Atlanta, Ga., 30341.
———. *Industrial Development* (published six times annually).
Dodge Building Cost and Specification Digest, a summary of construction costs. New York: McGraw-Hill, annual (also a reporting service).
Dolman, John P. "Special Factors in Appraisal of Large Industrial Plants." *The Appraisal Journal,* January 1979, pp. 8–16.
Fullerton, Paul. "Appraisal of Industrial Property." In Edith J. Freidman, ed., *Encyclopaedia of Real Estate Appraising.* Englewood Cliffs, N.J.: Prentice-Hall, 1978.
Georgia Power Company, Industrial Development Department. *Cost Data: Industrial Buildings.* P.O. Box 4545, Atlanta, Ga. (annual).
Hartman, Donald J. "Industrial Real Estate—Estimating Value in Use." *The Appraisal Journal,* July 1979, pp. 340–350.
Industrial Development Handbook. Washington, D.C., Urban Land Institute, 1978.
Ordway, Nicholas. "Controlling Uncertainty Through Computer Applications of PERT/CPM to Real Estate Project Analysis." *AREUEA Journal,* Fall 1976, pp. 33–57.
Rubin, Marilyn, Ilene Wagner, and Pearl Kamer. "Industrial Migration: A Case Study of Destination by City-Suburban Origin within the New York Metropolitan Area." *AREUEA Journal,* Winter 1978, pp. 417–438.
Seymour, Charles F. "Appraising Industrial Parks." *The Appraisal Journal,* April 1979, pp. 165–176.

23

Other
Income-Producing
Properties

In this section of the book we have presented a technique for selecting suitable investments and have applied this scenario-type strategic planning specifically to apartments, shopping centers, office buildings, and industrial buildings. Although the generalized model provided in Chapter 18 has proved adaptable to many kinds of properties, it is clear that no model can serve for all types of property. However, it might be helpful to provide a brief analysis of three additional property types—single-family houses, condominiums, and small apartment buildings; and two types of special-purpose properties—hotels/motels and nursing homes. Our purpose is threefold: (1) to show how to simplify the analytical process presented by this book when selecting a simple investment such as a single-family home, a condominium, or a small apartment property; (2) in the case of hotels/ motels, we suggest that some real estate products are actually investments in a highly specialized primary business venture; and (3) we take a brief look at a real estate product—nursing homes—that is dominated by government regulations and special financing programs. Since none of these properties is analyzed in detail here, investors who are interested in pursuing the analysis further should consult the references provided at the end of the chapter.

Acknowledgment: The authors gratefully acknowledge the valuable assistance of Georgia State University doctoral students C. Jackson Harris and John E. Williams and University of Texas master's student Masa Scott Roberts. We also wish to thank John Poole, MAI, Atlanta, Georgia, who reviewed the nursing home materials.

SINGLE-FAMILY HOMES, CONDOMINIUMS, AND SMALL APARTMENT PROPERTIES

I told them in Washington that I didn't know all there was to be known about housing, but I certainly knew more than any of them did.

William Levitt (1948)

Definitions

Single-family homes. A *single-family* home may be a detached unit on a single lot providing primary shelter for one family, or it may be a *townhouse*, a residence that shares common walls with contiguous units. Setbacks of the units are often varied to avoid the monotony usually associated with the single setback line of older row houses.

Duplexes, triplexes, and *quadruplexes* are rental units on one site, usually sharing common walks and driveways, exterior walls, and sometimes common facilities. Among the advantages of this type of investment are the fact that (1) rental units can be clustered in one neighborhood, and (2) where the owner occupies one of the rental units, he or she is, in effect, a resident property manager. Offsetting this advantage is the fact that the owner is easily accessible for maintenance requests. Such complaints can be quite discouraging at 4:00 A.M. Also, being both landlord and neighbor can be a source of friction.

Condominiums. A condominium is a form of ownership; it can be any type of structure. Often condominiums are high-rise apartments; however, townhomes with four to six units are becoming very popular.

Timesharing is an increasingly popular way to secure guaranteed use of high-priced resort properties and facilities. There are two types of timesharing: (1) *interval* timesharing, in which an ownership position is taken in the property, and (2) on lease, with the right to use the property for a limited number of years. In ownership interval timesharing (here we are referring to tenancy-in-common ownership and time interval ownership), the investor acquires an equity position by purchasing an undivided interest in the property based on some predetermined percentage, usually in proportion to the length of the time period selected for personal use.

An investor in interval ownership timesharing has

1. An equity position.
2. Security (warranty deed and title insurance).
3. The right to sell, will, rent, lend, or transfer share of ownership in the living unit, within the limits set by the owner's association.
4. The right to sell at a profit.
5. The right to take a pro rata share of tax deductions from real estate taxes and interest, provided the property is owner-occupied for more than 14 days.
6. A greater say in building management (through the owner's association) but, in turn, is responsible for hiring a management firm and paying assessment fees.
7. Guaranteed use of the property for a set time period.

8. A limited obligation for taxes or maintenance, based on a pro rata share of ownership.

The buyer's privileges may be encumbered by outstanding debt (in most cases construction loans) on the property. The buyer should insist on a nondisturbance clause or a trust or escrow fund set up for the retirement of outstanding obligations if the property is purchased during the development stage, or on a mortgage payment certificate if the property is purchased after occupancy has commenced.

RECENT TRENDS

Investing in single-family (rental) houses, duplexes, small apartment buildings, and condominiums is one way to begin building a real estate portfolio. During the 1970s single-family detached houses were among the best investments in income-producing properties.[1] However, the future of this market is much more uncertain than the past.

The fixed annual mortgage constant may have had its last hurrah. Recent trends demonstrate the gradual abandonment by lenders of the fixed-rate 30-year mortgage. While lenders' money costs have soared with inflation, their income has increased more slowly because they hold portfolios of fixed-rate mortgages. By turning to various forms of adjustable-rate mortgages, they hope to pass on fluctuations in their cost of money to borrowers.

Another significant destabilizing factor is the change in the characteristics of homebuyers. In the past there was a clear separation between single-family houses, which on the whole were privately owned, and multifamily apartment buildings occupied by renters. The late 1970s saw more and more single-family homes taken over by investors whose intent was to "flip" the properties for a quick turnover profit. Other, more conservative investors sought tenants as interim users while they awaited market appreciation for a capital gain in the near-term future. Another major market change has been the decrease in the number of first-time home buyers. In 1977 over 50 percent of home buyers were first-home buyers; in 1978 such buyers accounted for 36 percent, while in 1979 they accounted for only 18 percent of the market.[2]

Furthermore, first-home mortgage applicants are seeking more modest homes. According to the National Association of Home Builders, first-time buyers are sharply reducing the square footage of living space they are willing to occupy. Energy costs are considered a primary factor by three out of five home mortgage lenders when evaluating mortgage applications. Appraisers are also giving energy efficiency important weight in their valuations.

It appears that young couples are making major changes in life style in order to achieve the old American dream. The traditional 25 percent of income allocated to housing has risen to 30–40 percent. Couples are postponing childbearing in order to permit both partners to work more years. Working couples are returning in the inner city because city homes are cheaper to own and maintain.

Bernard Freidan of M.I.T. feels that this "sacrifice" strategy to buy the first home may backfire. In particular, he feels that the two-income family is more

---

[1] R. Bruce Ricks, "Managing the Best Financial Asset," *California Management Review,* 18 (Spring 1976): 96–102.
[2] "For the First-Time Home Buyers: Despair, Sacrifice, Compromises," *The Wall Street Journal,* October 29, 1980, p. 31.

prone to divorce and to periods of high unemployment. Finally, half in jest, he adds that "prices are getting so high that husbands may need to go to polygamy to buy a house. They need two working wives."[3]

The National Association of Realtors® has reported that the average price of existing homes increased by 188 percent, from $25,700 in 1970 to $74,100 in June of 1980. (See Exhibit 23–1.) During the same period the overall consumer price index rose only 85.9 percent. It appears likely that residential construction costs will continue to rise faster than other consumer prices. Thus, the supply side cost of new production increases the value of existing stock. It appears likely that speculative buying of houses by people who already own a dwelling is a factor in driving up prices. Recently, the Federal Home Loan Bank Board in San Francisco had to threaten to stop the flow of mortgage credit because speculative fever in the southern California housing market had caused prices to soar beyond reason. Some purchasers seemed unaware that they were engaging in criminal conduct when they swore that they were buying as owner–occupants when in fact their intent was to find a tenant. Recent price deflation indicates the risk to any investor as a result of this churning of the market.

Forecasts of the types of structures that will be built in the 1980s seem easier to make. It is predicted that

1. There will be a fall in the size of homes from the current average of 1,750 square feet to around 1,500 square feet.
2. Lot sizes will decrease.
3. Cluster houses and townhouses with densities of from 15 to 30 units per acre may replace the detached house on a quarter-acre lot.
4. Owing to rising energy costs, there will be more insulation and fewer cathedral ceilings, central air conditioners, and other energy-consuming luxury items.

Rental units are expected to become increasingly expensive and scarce because of rent controls and other economic pressures working against increasing supply. Condominiums could be to the 1980s what single-family detached units were to the 1970s. It is expected that 2,614,000 units will be built in the 1980s. As their popularity increases, so will their unit prices.[4]

EXHIBIT 23–1. Selected Selling Prices of Existing Single-Family Homes for the United States and Each Region (Not Seasonally Adjusted)

Year	UNITED STATES Median	UNITED STATES Average (Mean)	North-east Median	North Central Median	South Median	West Median
1968	$20,100	$22,300	$21,400	$18,200	$19,000	$22,900
1972	26,700	30,100	29,800	23,900	26,400	28,400
1977	42,900	47,900	44,400	36,700	39,800	57,300
1980	63,400	74,100	61,000	52,700	59,900	91,800

SOURCE: Based on data from National Association of REALTORS.

[3] Ibid.
[4] *Fortune,* April 17, 1980, p. 1.

The increasing popularity of condominiums may be traced to their ability to achieve high unit densities on increasingly expensive land, as well as their appeal to first-time buyers and empty-nesters. Condos offer the same tax write-off advantages as single-family residences, and they offer lower monthly costs in comparison to renting or to buying and maintaining a single-family detached dwelling. However, the spread of rent controls and moratoriums on condominium conversions point to the growing recognition of tenant rights and increases the risk to the investor.

INVESTMENT ADVANTAGES AND DISADVANTAGES

The initial cash investment for this type of property is usually relatively low. Down payments may run from 5 to 20 percent of value. Some investors have assumed mortgages by having the seller provide a second mortgage that requires no initial cash investment. Such properties also offer the usual tax advantages, such as depreciation of the improvements; interest, real estate tax, and operating expense deductions; and capital gain treatment of profits from a sale.

Because they are based on an underlying demand for shelter and a broad market such investments are relatively secure. Moderately priced single-family homes are becoming scarce, demand remains relatively high, and vacancy rates usually are lower than for multifamily property. In growing metro areas rental houses are among the most liquid type of real estate property, and frequent, recorded sales of comparable properties allow the investor to establish a relatively reliable market value estimate.

Rental houses are a good starting point for the new real estate investor who wants to learn how to operate a property. The costs of *mis*management are relatively small, and such properties are easier to manage, sell, or buy than more complex investments. There is less governmental control than for large apartment complexes.

On the other hand, small rental properties can be quite time consuming. Where an investor owns several properties at scattered sites, hiring a professional management company is too expensive. Thus, the responsibility for renting the property, collecting rents, and maintenance falls directly on the investor. And, in a single-family home a vacancy can wipe out operating income while expenses continue.

It is also becoming increasingly difficult to find investments that will easily provide substantial returns or break even. Because of intensive competition, capitalization rates have declined in many metro areas.

THE NATURE OF THE RETURNS AND RISKS

The four types of returns from small rental properties are cash flow, tax shelter, equity buildup, and appreciation.

Cash Flow. Cash flow from small rental properties is, in most cases, either negative or negligible. The three determinants are as follows:

1. *Rental levels.* In recent times monthly rent multipliers have increased substantially (up to 150) because, although the prices of houses have risen, rental increases have lagged far behind. Lately rents have been increasing from 10

to 20 percent per year; therefore, the situation may ease to the point at which positive cash flows are no longer a rarity.

2. *Financial levels.* The amount of the mortgage constant, which is determined by the prevailing mortgage rate, constitutes the largest drain on cash flow from rental receipts. The loan-to-value ratio may be very high for single-family residences. Coupling these heavily leveraged positions with mortgage rates running from 12.5 percent to 16 percent will result in monthly mortgage payments causing negative cash flows, without even considering other fixed and variable costs. Liquidity reserves are virtually mandatory.

3. *Expense levels.* Maintenance, management, and repair expenses are escalating. Such out-of-pocket expenses can be held down when the owner provides these services personally and places a low value on his own time.

Investors have recently been satisfied with nonexistent to negative cash flow from operations because (1) they have little up-front equity in the investments; (2) the amount of negative cash flow is usually small and intelligent investors have already budgeted for this contingency; and (3) most investors realize that their major gains will come from property appreciation and tax shelter.

Tax Shelter. The IRS permits the investor to deduct depreciation, interest, and necessary and ordinary business expenses for Section 1231 property on the regular federal income tax return. Straight-line depreciation over 15 years was authorized in 1981.

Equity Buildup. A portion of each monthly mortgage payment applies to reduction of the principal on the mortgage note balance. As each loan payment is made, the investor's equity in the property increases. Since some, if not all, of the monthly payment is made from rentals, rentals may help pay for the equity gain. This depends, of course, on stable, or even increasing, value.

Appreciation. Because of the rising cost of housing and the ability to take a heavily leveraged position, appreciation is where the greatest returns have been made in small rental properties. Over the last decade the price of existing houses increased, on average, at a nominal rate of 17 percent a year.

The major sources of risk are (1) purchasing a property in a deteriorating neighborhood, (2) a 100 percent vacancy rate (if an investor owns one rental house, one vacancy represents a 100 percent vacancy rate), (3) liability for personal injuries that occur on the investment property, and (4) bad tenant relations. A poor tenant can easily cause more damage to the property than the security deposit will cover.

MARKET AND MARKETABILITY ANALYSIS

The best opportunity for substantial short-term gains in small rental properties occurs in rapidly growing cities. Timing is important. Metro areas do not grow evenly: Some sections expand rapidly; in some, only affluent people or only the poor live.

The best place for an investment in small rental properties is a section that is in the path of the area's outward growth in terms of residential use. Such neighborhoods are often on the outer fringes of metro areas.

Successful investments may also be found in older sections of the city that are experiencing new popularity. Such areas are characterized by a higher number of resales. Investors should be careful to buy into an upgrading neighborhood, not a deteriorating one. A visual inspection is the first step.

Demand Analysis. Demand analysis is the same as for apartment investments. (See Chapter 19.) A simplified comparative market analysis form is presented in Exhibit 23–2.

Locational check. A city's planning department will be able to tell you what services (parks, street improvements, water, etc.) are planned for the future.

It is important to determine the area's competitive rent level. This can be accomplished through discussions with professional management and realty

---

EXHIBIT 23-2. A Comparative Market Analysis Form

Subject Property Address ⸻ Date ⸻

Information on other properties which are located in the same general area and have the same approximate value as the subject property:

FOR SALE NOW	Bedrooms	Bath	Den	Sq. Ft.	Mtgs.	Price	Days on Market	Terms
SOLD PAST 12 MONTHS								
EXPIRED PAST 12 MONTHS								

Source: *Nothing Down.* Copyright © 1980 by Robert G. Allen. Reprinted by permission of Simon & Schuster, a Division of Gulf & Western Corporation.

companies or a survey of the leading city newspaper (the one with the largest classified ad section).

The school that area residents' children must attend is an extremely important factor. Residential housing also needs to be close to parks, shopping, and churches.

The investor must be thoroughly familiar with the neighborhood before purchasing a property. The best way is to consult a neighborhood Realtor®, other than the seller's agent.

Supply Analysis. Consulting an area Realtor, driving around the area, and keeping a record of offerings and sales should acquaint the investor with the properties that a neighborhood has to offer. If it is a developing area, conversations with builders will reveal what they will be bringing to the market. However, there are other procedures that the investor can follow in making a supply analysis. For a more detailed discussion see Chapter 19.

Developing working arrangements with area Realtors. When you work with a Realtor, you are paying a professional to stay on top of the market for you. The Realtor's business is to keep abreast of what is happening in the area, to know where lot locations are and what is selling, at what price, and how fast. A Realtor has access to the local multiple listing service. If your relationship with the Realtor is a good one, you may be able to learn about area properties before they are formally listed.

When working with a Realtor, always be very specific about the type of property you are looking for. The Realtor should be aware of your limits concerning the age, size, price, location, and amenities of the property. This can save valuable time.

If time is not of great concern, there are some alternative methods for finding properties in the target area:

1. Use the local newspapers. In addition to combing the classified ads, the investor can run an ad expressing interest in buying certain types of properties in certain areas.
2. Send out flyers to residents in the targeted area. This is the procedure that Realtors use to cultivate a listing contract.
3. Send out word to other area professionals (lawyers, CPAs, doctors, etc.) that you are interested in purchasing.

The buyer should purchase problem properties only after a detailed analysis has confirmed that the identified problems can be profitably solved.

Projection of Rental Income and Vacancies. Existing selling prices and rents provide the basis for projections. The investor can obtain these data through discussions with professionals in the area.

One method of projecting these data is to analyze the preceding five-year record for the area and calculate the yearly percentage increase in prices and rents. After taking into consideration new demand elements and noting recent trends, one can apply the derived growth figure to current sales and rent levels to determine what future levels might be.

Risk Management and Control. The greatest risk in small rental properties is nonappreciation of the property value. The major way to reduce this risk is to select a good neighborhood and purchase the property at or below the going market rate.

The next major risk is loss of marketability and, thus, liquidity. The best way to guard against loss of liquidity occurs during property selection. The investor should select only properties in stable, highly regarded neighborhoods that appeal to broad segments of the market.

PHYSICAL AND STRUCTURAL ANALYSIS

The property should appear neat, clean, and well kept. Avoid run-down or functionally obsolescent older homes, unless you plan rehabilitation.

Amenities can be locationally specific. Houses in the Sun Belt require air conditioning. If 90 percent of the houses in an area have large lots and enclosed garages, the investor should purchase only houses with these features. Some desirable amenities are dishwashers, garbage disposals, trash compactors, extra insulation, and electric garage door openers.

Exhibit 23–3 is a checklist for evaluating the physical and structural, as well as neighborhood, aspects of an investment property.

LEGAL, POLITICAL, AND ENVIRONMENTAL ANALYSIS

Taxation. The investor should be wary of an increasing real estate tax burden. Communities with inadequate streets, water and wastewater services, and parks might be faced with property tax increases to fund the delayed capital improvements. Compare market values to appraised values; properties with large discrepancies face the prospect of an equalizing property tax increase.

Zoning. Past trends and proposed zoning plans should be reviewed. The local planning department will provide this information.

PROPERTY MANAGEMENT

Finding competent property management firms for small rental properties is difficult. Therefore, most investors in such properties self-manage the properties. An investor-manager has a greater incentive to enhance the value of the property.

The two most important factors in managing a property are tenant relations and maintenance. Better tenants keep the property in good condition; to attract quality tenants, the property must be well kept and maintained. In the long run this can lead to considerable savings in maintenance costs.

Generally, selecting good tenants depends on the following:

1. *Previous references.* Make phone calls to verify the prospective tenant's statements.
2. *Steady employment.* Verify the existence of the claimed job and income level. A one-year record of steady employment is a good minimum cutoff point.
3. *Credit report.* Have the tenant list at least three credit references. Require the divulgence of credit card numbers.

EXHIBIT 23-3. A Small-Property Investment Checklist

NEIGHBORHOOD QUALITY

- Are property values rising?
- Are the other houses in the same price range?
- Are the property taxes in line with those in other areas?
- Is the neighborhood well maintained?
- Is there good access to public transportation?
- Is there adequate parking (on and off street)?
- Are all municipal services available and adequate?
- Is the quality of the schools good?
- Is there adequate shopping nearby?
- Are there any special noise problems?
- Are there any hazardous traffic patterns?

THE SITE

- Is the size of the yard adequate?
- Is the drainage away from the foundation?
- If the house has a septic tank, has it been serviced recently?
- Are there any dead trees?
- Is the general condition of the yard good?
- Are all fences, retaining walls, and walkways in good repair?
- Does any landscaping need replacement?

THE BUILDING (STRUCTURAL AND EQUIPMENT)

- Is there any problem that will require an immediate outlay of cash?
- Is there a 220-volt line for the range and dryer?
- Is the roof watertight? Will it be in the near future?
- Is the basement free from water marks, wet cracks, or other signs of moisture?
- Is the building structurally sound?
- Is the garage wide enough and long enough for adequate parking?
- Is the electrical service adequate?
- Are the range and oven included in the price?
- Are all floors and floor coverings in good repair?
- Is the furnace working properly?
- Does the water heater have a good remaining useful life?
- Is the condition of the exterior paint adequate?
- Is the condition of the interior paint adequate?
- Are walls and ceilings free from minor cracks?
- If there are any additions or alterations, were the necessary permits filed?
- Are kitchen countertops and cabinets in good repair?
- Do all windows have coverings or draperies, and are they in acceptable condition?
- Is there ample wall space for furniture?
- Is there adequate closet and storage space?

4. *Income-to-rent ratio.* The tenant must realistically be able to afford the rent payments. A good ratio is 3 1/2 or 4 to 1.

5. Other matters to be discussed and investigated are bank references, pet controls, age limits, and advance payment of rent and a security deposit against cleaning and damage. Resistance to any of these is a sign of potential trouble.

Another way to cut down on the maintenance burden is to pass on as much of the responsibility and cost as possible to the tenant through the lease agreement. For example, a clause like the following might be included:

MAINTENANCE, REPAIRS, OR ALTERATION: Tenant acknowledges that the premises are in good order and repair, unless otherwise indicated herein. Owner may at any time give Tenant an accurate written inventory of furniture and furnishings on the premises and Tenant shall be deemed to have possession of all said furniture and furnishings in good condition and repair, unless he objects thereto in writing within five days after receipt of such inventory. Tenant shall, at his own expense, and at all times, maintain the premises in a clean and sanitary manner including all equipment, appliances, furniture, and furnishings therein and shall surrender the same, at termination hereof, in as good condition as received, normal wear and tear excepted.

Tenant shall be responsible for all repairs required for exposed plumbing or electrical wiring and for damages caused by Tenant's negligence and that of his family or invitees or guests. Tenant shall not paint, paper, or otherwise redecorate or make alterations to the premises without the prior written consent of the Owner. Tenant shall irrigate and maintain any surrounding grounds, including lawns and shrubbery, and keep the same clear of rubbish or weeds if such grounds are a part of the premises and are exclusively for the use of the Tenant.

(*Note:* Shifting too much property management to the tenant may result in the investor losing Sec. 1234 status and being classed as a passive investor. See Chapter 13 for further discussion.)

Self managers should point out such a clause to the tenant and explain it. One should be firm in enforcing the requirements, although cooperation with reasonable tenants is important. For all *major* repairs, have the tenant call you so that you can arrange for them promptly. If the repair is required as a result of negligence or abuse, bill the tenant for it.

The owner should use a written property inspection report. Such reports can help to minimize disputes when a tenant vacates, or in the case of an eviction or casualty such as a fire. Forms are available from local managers.

ANALYSIS OF OPERATING INCOME AND EXPENSES

An analysis of potential cash flow, expenses, and taxes is essential to enable the investor to evaluate the debt-carrying capacity of the property and the stability and adequacy of the net operating income (NOI). Exhibit 23–4 is a representative cash flow statement for a rental house.

Capitalization rates based on net operating income in today's market are generally low (5–8%) because investors are looking to potential appreciation for

---

EXHIBIT 23–4.   A Cash Flow Statement for a Rental House

Location: 3310 Harpers Ferry, Austin, Texas
Type of property: 1 year old, 3 bedroom, 2 baths, single-family residence
Date: October 17, 1980
Financing: VA assumption, 9.87% interest, term 29 years
Price: $57,540
Loan balance: $47,500
Equity: $10,040

Gross possible income ($500 per month × 12)	$6,000	
Less: 5% vacancy allowance	300	
Gross operating income		$5,700
Expenses		
Taxes (102 × 12)	$1,224	
Insurance (20 × 12)	240	
Maintenance/repairs	250	
Other	100	
Total expenses		1,814
Net operating income (NOI)		$3,886
Mortgage payments ($415 per month × 12)		4,980
Cash flow		($1,094)
Monthly negative cash flow		($91.17)

Assumptions:
1. Management performed by owner.
2. Maintenance is a low 4.385% due to age of house and HOW (builder's Home-owners Warranty) still in effect.
3. Other includes supplies and advertising.
4. Tenant pays all utilities.
5. No allowance is made for owner's time and effort.

SOURCE: We gratefully acknowledge the assistance of Scott Roberts, graduate student, University of Texas at Austin.

virtually all of their return. Mortgage equity capitalization rates that take into consideration appreciation or depreciation in value are recommended instead.

Generally, there are three reasons that a property has a below-market (5% or less) capitalization rate: (1) Rents are too low; (2) expenses are too high; or (3) price is too high. The last is usually the case. However, an investor can buy a property with a low market-derived capitalization rate if he or she is confident that expenses can be lowered, that rents can be raised, or that values will increase sharply over the short term.

ANALYSIS OF LOCAL TRENDS AND UNCERTAINTIES

If we exclude the need for major repairs brought about by code compliance activity of the local governing body—which usually is the case only for older structures—the greatest potential for increased expense in small rental properties is in real estate taxes. Utility bills are usually paid by the tenant. Growing communities often raise property tax rates to pay for new municipal services and/or escalating service budgets. In addition, assessed values may be raised to reflect increasing market values. Conversations with local public officials can reveal the trend in taxes for a community.

FINANCING AND REFINANCING TECHNIQUES

With today's high inflation rates and unpredictable interest rate fluctuations, lenders are becoming less willing to make long-term fixed-rate loans, and the market is moving toward a type of variable rate by indexing. The Federal Home Loan Bank Board, FNMA, FHLMC, Federal Reserve Board, and others have left the choice of index that will control the periodic change in interest rates up to market negotiations and competition among buyers and sellers.

In today's world of highly appreciated prices for existing structures, owner–sellers are becoming an important source of real estate financing. This is accomplished through subordination. With wraparound mortgage financing, one must beware of a due-on-sale clause.

Sellers are willing to accept such arrangements because they enable them to take advantage of high interest rates and receive higher prices for their properties. Investors benefit because they can increase leverage.

In 1981 investors were paying interest rates of 12–17 percent on new conventional loans. FHA and VA rates run approximately 1 percent below the rates on conventional loans. The amount of the loan depends on the appraised value and the proposed use of the property. Lending institutions may make loans on new *owner-occupied* residential property for as much as 90–95 percent of the property's appraised value.

On *non*-owner-occupied (i.e., rental) property, loans will be made for only 75–80 percent of the appraised value. Currently, in order for an owner-occupant to qualify for a loan, the monthly income should be up to approximately three times the monthly debt service. The terms of the mortgages run up to thirty years. For assumptions, the term would be the remaining life of the underlying mortgage.

Conventional loans often present problems for the investor who is trying to assume them. There may be prepayment penalties for the seller, or the loan may contain a due-on-sale clause. The purchaser may have to sign an affidavit, under criminal penalties, that he or she will be an owner-occupant.

Questionable practices are sometimes used to increase leverage positions. For example, the investor may (1) time the closing date so that the down payment comes out of the first month's rent; (2) use the tenant's security and cleaning deposits to fund part of the down payment; (3) require the Realtor to lend his or her commission to the investor for the down payment in order to make the sale (the investor does not inform the seller of this deal); (4) use personal credit cards to purchase goods for the seller in lieu of a cash down payment; (5) stagger the down payment. Such practices should be avoided. They are not sound business practices if they create financial obligations that the investor cannot afford. Moreover, they are unethical and sometimes illegal or even criminal.

Projection of Financing Costs. For a fixed-rate mortgage, debt service is normally fixed over the life of investment; for a variable-rate mortgage, the investor must project future interest rate levels. With an assumable mortgage, the debt service may or may not be the same as the existing mortgage.

There are creative financing techniques that can be used to increase the leverage position and reduce the level of monthly debt service. These techniques require that the seller provide lenient, flexible, favorable terms for the buyer. Needless to say, this is sometimes difficult to achieve. Robert G. Allen suggests the following techniques:[5]

1. *Structuring a seller's note to match seasonal demand.* During months when expenses are usually high, payments would be below the negotiated level. In months when expenses are low, the difference would be made up with payments above the negotiated level.
2. *Requiring interest-only notes.* Here, the investor does not amortize the principal amount. The principal (in some cases principal and interest) comes due in one lump sum at the end of the note's duration.
3. *Lowering the amortization cost with a balloon payment.* The monthly debt service is calculated for a note with a long term (20– 40 years). However, the remaining balance—the balloon—comes due earlier, usually in the fifth to seventh year.
4. *Increasing the interest rate.* The interest rate in the initial years of the note is set low. In later years, after the project is established, the rate increases.
5. *Converting balloon notes into amortization notes on the due date.* When the lump-sum balance comes due, the investor negotiates a new amortization note for the balance due.

TAX PROBLEMS AND UNCERTAINTIES

Depreciation recapture problems exist only if accelerated depreciation has been used. In that case all excess depreciation is taxed as ordinary income, which can result in large tax liabilities in the year in which the property is sold. We recommend ACRS composite straight-line depreciation for 15 years. (See Chapter 13 for additional discussion of tax planning.)

RATE-OF-RETURN ANALYSIS

The key to successful investment in small rental properties is price appreciation and leverage. Cash-on-cash returns for these properties are very low or negative, making traditional methods of capitalizing income virtually worthless. The best method for ranking investments is an after-tax IRR/PV analysis. Most investors are currently assuming that short-term appreciation will be extremely high and therefore are specifying 20– 30 percent as the minimum acceptable after-tax IRR. This includes the inflation premium. It is believed that the changes in mortgage financing will lower such rates to 6– 9 percent plus an inflation premium.

RATIO AND RISK ANALYSIS

Sensitivity analysis will provide a useful measure of the risk associated with different properties. Key variables are operating expenses, repairs, vacancy rates, and appreciation. Careful attention should be paid to their effect on cash flow. Many

[5] Robert G. Allen, *Nothing Down* (New York: Simon & Schuster, 1980). See also Dave Glubetich, *The Monopoly Game* (San Luis Obispo, Calif.: Impact Publishing, 1978), and Maury Seldin and Richard Swesnik, *Real Estate Investment Strategy,* 2nd ed. (New York: Wiley, 1979), p. 189.

property foreclosures have been caused by the investor's inability to accommodate negative cash flows. Depending on appreciation to bail out poor productivity is risky.

THE INVESTMENT DECISION

Investors are buying small rental properties for short-term appreciation gains and as a hedge against erosion of capital by inflation. The investor should purchase property only in neighborhoods that are not expected to suffer any type of decline. The highest possible leverage position should be sought, but the investor should be sure that potential negative cash flows can be handled. Sufficient liquidity reserves must be maintained to meet unexpected contingencies. High minimum rates of return should be used in DCF and sensitivity analyses because of the difficulty of projecting the holding period and providing for an appropriate inflation premium.

SPECIAL-USE PROPERTIES

Success in special-use properties—hotels/motels, nursing homes, hospitals, recreational facilities, fast-food franchises, service stations—depends on specialized skills in business, marketing, promotional, and financial management related to the primary business for which the property is used. Space limitations permit us to review briefly only two types of special-purpose properties—hotels/motels and nursing homes—each of which has its own unique analytical tools.

A special-use property includes undeveloped land or an existing improved property that is used for a specific nonindustrial business. Buying an interest in a special-use property requires an equity investor either to become a serious student of the underlying business or to have blind faith and trust in others. In analyzing the investment viability of the special-purpose property, the investor should consider four questions: (1) What is an appropriate alternative use for the property? (2) What is the lender's equity investment requirement? (3) Does the operating management of the existing business pass sound management tests? (4) Will the lender require collateral beyond the security of the business, realty, and personal property at the location itself?

1. *Evaluating alternative uses for the property.* A building erected for a fast-food franchise in the shape of a hot dog with mustard and pickle would be difficult to adapt to another use in the event of business failure. Many special-use properties, however, can be adapted to alternative uses. A motel may be adaptable to a senior citizens' residence. A fast-food restaurant, with some cosmetic changes, might well be a good location for a microcomputer store. The flexibility, ingenuity, and imagination of the investor in showing the lender what the possibilities are may do much to improve the underwriting risks in the mind of the lender. Exhibit 23–5 may be helpful in this regard.

2. *Knowing the lender's equity investment requirements.* In spite of the fact that special-purpose properties are a speculation on the probability of success of the business operations, loans must be obtained with higher equity-to-loan ratios than are typical of ordinary real estate investments. Loans are usually not available for more than 70 percent of the cost of construction or capitalized value,

EXHIBIT 23-5. Table of Alternative Uses

Type of Property	Proposed Use	Alternate Use
Freestanding open construction	Catering hall	Supermarket or warehouse
Freestanding multirooms	Motel	Senior citizens' residence
Freestanding small shell construction	Diner	Gas station, bank, funeral home
Attached open construction	Restaurant	Office building
Attached multirooms	Office buildings	School

SOURCE: Sheldon Farber, "Financing the Specialty Property," *Real Estate Review,* Winter 1975, p. 106.

whichever is lower. However, the cushion of the higher debt coverage ratio for the lender, coupled with equity capital from outside investors, can enable a superior business manager to make a satisfactory return for everyone.

3. *Evaluating the operating management.* Investors who are going to risk equity capital in the belief that a business manager can deliver above-average returns should take the time to study the chart of accounts; find appropriate units of comparison to evaluate performance; and understand the threats, competition, and problems that are peculiar to the business in question. Each business has a literature of its own and its own trade periodicals.

Investors should require submission of pro forma and actual operating statements. Agreements that the business will operate according to strict accounting procedures and maintain minimum working capital ratios, with controls on dividends and disbursements, are essential. It is not unreasonable to require that certain key management personnel be insured against death, accidental injury, and disability. The costs for such insurance should be borne by the underlying business.

4. *Is additional collateral required?* When other sources of collateral are required by the lender, most investors are reluctant to burden their personal balance sheets with liens, pledges, and contingent obligations. On the other hand, greater risk may realize greater gain, especially with well-managed special-use properties. Borrowers will sometimes agree that if the property produces a deficiency at foreclosure, the lender has recourse to other assets of the investor. This pledge might be limited to, say, the top 20–30 percent of the loan. The agreement could also provide that the pledge of secondary collateral will be reduced in accordance with a specific schedule as the loan is reduced. Flexibility on the part of the investor may well overcome the lender's reluctance to fund an otherwise acceptable special-purpose property.

HOTELS AND MOTELS

The motel/hotel industry employs more than 5 million people. In many states it is one of the largest industries, although it is dependent on a derived demand that is strongly cyclical in nature and subject to externalities like gas shortages and transportation strikes.

A *hotel* can be defined as an establishment that provides transient lodging, and usually meals and entertainment, for the public. Reservation service by tele-communication is usually provided.

- *Convention hotels* cater to national, regional, and local meetings of business and other organizations. They are generally located in the central districts of major cities and at major highway intersections, and provide meeting rooms, accommodations for exhibits and expositions, and entertainment.
- *Resort hotels* are located near vacation-related activities such as skiing, swimming, golf, tennis, sailing, fishing, or simply relaxing in a pleasant climate.
- *Residential hotels* accommodate a significant number of long-term residents. Their rooms are sometimes leased for years.

A *motel* is an establishment that is located on or near a highway and is designed to serve the motor traveler. Although originally conceived of as providing only transient lodging, they now, more often than not, provide food, entertainment, and beverages as well. Reservation service by telecommunication is usually provided.

Budget motels, which are generally associated with a national chain, offer modest lodging at a low price. The management generally achieves economy by reducing room size and minimizing amenities.

In describing the characteristics of the successful hotel or motel, *location* has several different meanings:

1. The location must be an active point of interest for business and pleasure travelers or in a busy transportation corridor at a logical stopover point. Examples of the former are major convention cities, large universities, and tourist attractions like Disney World; an example of the latter is Lake City, Florida, located on Interstate 75 approximately one day's drive from Miami.
2. There should be convenient access to and from major transportation arteries, exhibit halls, auditoriums, and other points of local interest.
3. There should be good exposure to passers-by and out-of-town visitors.
4. There should be attractive, safe surroundings offering sufficient entertainment and sightseeing opportunities.

Industry experts project a growth in hotel/motel capacity of 60 percent in the next twenty years as various metro areas grow and new SMSAs come into being.

INVESTMENT ADVANTAGES AND DISADVANTAGES

The lodging industry tends to break even on a relatively low average-occupancy level, say, 60–65 percent. Thus, successful properties have a large potential for high profits when fully occupied. The industry also offers opportunities to add other profit-generating activities such as food, beverage, and valet services; retail sales; conference accommodations; and entertainment. Frequently such ancillary facilities are operated as concessions or leased units and thereby converted into rental rather than business operations. Large convention and resort properties (e.g., Disney World, Busch Gardens) also provide a certain measure of prestige and glamour for corporations.

Vulnerability to downside risk is enhanced by the cyclical and seasonal use of the properties, by changes in what is considered fashionable, and by the properties' short economic life. Expert and efficient management and promotion are vital. Location is of prime importance, but may be destroyed by changes in local economic conditions, the quality of tourist attractions in the area, and major transportation routes. Ownership of new and reviving properties requires sufficient cash reserves to cover low occupancies and heavy promotional expenses during the startup phase.

TYPES OF INVESTORS AND INVESTOR MOTIVATIONS

Independent, small-scale motel operators generally view their investment as a business opportunity providing self-employment. *Individual franchise holders* are attracted primarily by profit potential. *Institutional investors* seek to boost portfolio yields and add inflation-offsetting equity participations to the fixed returns on loans to hotel/motel properties. *Chains* participate by providing expertise in operation, construction, and promotion. Many operate management contracts for investors or partnership arrangements.

MARKET AND MARKETABILITY ANALYSIS

A property should be examined from the standpoint of the stability of its income stream, the would-be owner's position in the long-term life cycle of the property, and its neighborhood.

Demand Analysis. The key to a successful hotel/motel investment is a thorough analysis of the location's potential for attracting and holding clientele and how well the services offered are matched to the proper market segment. The following are important characteristics of demand: purpose of trips, duration of visits, seasonal variations, and demographic characteristics of travelers. Exhibit 23–6 presents important factors to consider when selecting hotel and motel locations. Exhibit 23–7 presents an analysis of various activities that result in "guest days." By comparing the attributes of the location to these activities, one may estimate the type of guest the property is likely to attract. Exhibit 23–8 suggests a format for comparing market segments to the features of a particular property. Activity descriptions are usually analytically adjusted to fit (attract) the most promising segment of the market.

Basic marketing strategies emphasize *differentiation* (attempts to point out the advantages of the property over competitors) and *segmentation* (attempts to direct an appeal to a given segment of the market). Situations that favor such emphases are shown in Exhibit 23–9.

Changes that may affect the advantages or disadvantages of certain locations should be considered when assessing future demand. (See Exhibit 23–10.)

Supply Analysis. A stratified analysis of competitive facilities should concentrate on the clientele attracted, competitive advantages of the subject property, and customer loyalty. Nearby facilities may be serving segments of the market that are inappropriate for the subject property. Where competitive properties serve the same segment, check room rates and occupancies. Several factors may be used to classify competitors: rates, size, type of accommodations, location, restaurant and meeting rooms. The competitive survey should include an evaluation of marketing strategy and management policies. Also important are proposed new facilities

---

EXHIBIT 23-6.   Important Factors to Consider when Selecting Hotel/Motel Locations

---

GENERAL CONSIDERATIONS

- Local, regional, and national economic trends
- Neighborhood characteristics and appearance
- Location and type of competitive lodging facilities: number of rooms, facilities, average rate, percentage of occupancy
- Availability of adequate utilities
- Location and transportation for labor force

DOWNTOWN LOCATIONS

- Traffic patterns—access and visibility
- Location of generators of visitation—offices, convention centers, tourist attractions, entertainment, etc.
- Availability of parking
- Availability of public transportation—taxi, bus, subway
- Location of restaurants and evening entertainment
- Location of convention center—size and types of events
- Effectiveness of convention and visitors' bureau
- Potential for weekend patronage
- Security of surrounding area and character of neighborhood

AIRPORT LOCATIONS

- Number of passengers per year (historic and future trends)
- Volume of airport cargo
- Number of airlines serving airport

- Usage of airport—origination, destination, transfer point
- Types of airport traffic—overseas, domestic, charter, long haul, short haul
- Purpose of airport travel—commercial, convention, vacation, etc.
- Layover point for airline crews
- Hours of airport operation
- Local weather conditions—potential for delayed flights
- Type and location of nearby business or industry
- Highway and traffic patterns
- Types of transportation to nearby hotels
- Distance of hotel from airport, travel time to downtown, convenience to terminal, restaurants, and entertainment
- Potential for weekend patronage

HIGHWAY LOCATIONS

- Traffic counts (historic and future trends)
- Highway patterns and type (interstate, U.S. highways)
- Access—both ingress and egress
- Visibility
- Origination and destination of traffic
- Types of travelers—commercial, vacation, etc.
- Periods of travel—weekly, monthly, seasonally
- Distance and travel time from major destinations
- Future changes in highway and travel patterns

SOURCE: William Eggbeer, "What Should You Do When Foreclosure Is Imminent on Your Hotel or Motel Property?" *The Mortgage Banker,* July 1978, p. 56.

---

and expansions. Construction in this industry tends to be highly cyclical; overbuilding often occurs.

Projection of Rental Income, Expenses, and Vacancies. Income projections are complicated by the instability of the revenue stream over seasons and years. Any

EXHIBIT 23-7. Activity Attributes of a Motel/Hotel Location

Activity	Example
Leisure	sun seeking, sightseeing
Recreation	sailing, golf, skiing, climbing, riding, spectator games, sports, displays
Culture	interests in art, history, archeology, pageantry
Religion	ceremonies, pilgrimages, festivals
Entertainment	theatres, concert halls, opera houses, casinos, night clubs
Convention	conferences, conventions, assemblies, meetings, exhibits, shows
Institutional	visitors to institutions, hospitals, universities
Business	business and commercial travel, executive meetings
Economic	promotional shows, exhibitions, trade displays
Medical	health, dietary, spa and convalescence facilities
Social	visits by relatives, friends' societies, clubs
Travel	overnight and staging requirements along route

SOURCE: Fred R. Lawson, *Hotels, Motels and Condominiums: Design, Planning and Maintenance* (Boston: Cahners, 1976), p. 19.

EXHIBIT 23-8. A Development and Design Criteria Matrix

Guest Requirements	MARKET SEGMENTS									
	COMMERCIAL–INDUSTRIAL				RECREATIONAL–PLEASURE					
	Independent		Group		Independent		Group		Independent	Local Group
	In-Transit	Terminal	In-Transit	Terminal	In-Transit	Terminal	In-Transit	Terminal		
LOCATION										
Accessibility	X		X		X		X			
Parking	X	X	X	X	X	X	X	X	X	X
Proximity	X	X	X	X	X	X	X	X	X	X
Visibility	X		X		X		X			
APPEARANCE										
Decor		X		X		X		X		
Design		X		X		X		X		
Landscaping						X		X		
Structure		X		X		X		X		
LODGING										
Capacity			X	X			X	X		
Equipment		X		X		X		X		
Rates	X	X	X	X	X	X	X	X		
Room Size		X		X		X		X		
RESTAURANTS										
Capacity	X		X	X			X	X		X
Diversity		X				X		X	X	X
Function Space				X				X		X
Hours of Operation	X	X	X	X	X	X	X	X	X	X
OTHER GUEST SERVICES										
Laundry		X		X		X		X		
Shops		X		X		X		X	X	
Valet		X		X		X		X		
ENTERTAINMENT AND RECREATION FACILITIES										
Active		X		X		X		X	X	X
Sedentary		X		X		X		X		

SOURCE: Clarence Peters, "Pre-Opening Marketing Analyses for Hotels," © *Cornell H&R Administration Quarterly*, May 1978, pp. 15–22.

EXHIBIT 23-9. Market Differentiation and Segmentation Decision Criteria

---

I. *A differentiation strategy will generally prove most appropriate where the following can be demonstrated:*
 1. The total market is demographically, geographically, and psychographically homogeneous.
 2. Market sensitivity to differences between establishments is high.
 3. The establishment is relatively new.
 4. The establishment is distinctive (e.g., architecturally, style of service).
 5. There are few competing establishments.
 6. Most competitors employ a differentiation strategy.

II. *A segmentation strategy is most appropriate when the following conditions prevail:*
 1. The total market is demographically, geographically, and psychographically diffuse.
 2. Market sensitivity to differences between establishments is low.
 3. The establishment has been in operation for several years.
 4. The establishment is not distinctive.
 5. There are several competing establishments.
 6. Most competitors employ a segmentation strategy.

SOURCE: Peter Yesavich, "Post-Opening Marketing Analysis for Hotels," © *Cornell H&R Administration Quarterly,* November 1978, pp. 70–81.

EXHIBIT 23-10. Possible Causes of Hotel/Motel Decline

Market Considerations	Changes
1. Individual customer needs	Changes in fashion, attitudes, requirements, and standards
2. Group needs	Changes in business and social functions and requirements
3. Surroundings	Changes in character of surroundings, deterioration of property values, increasing dilapidation, noise, vandalism
4. Economic	Decline of specific attractions or in the economic prosperity of the area generally
5. Transportation dependence	Increasing fuel costs and travel surcharges; changes in mode of transport
6. Access	Highway improvements and bypassing, new airports and expressways or motorway links, creating alternative destinations within competitive time–distance
7. Competition	Within the area and in newly created areas offering advantageous facilities

---

SOURCE: Fred R. Lawson, *Hotels, Motels and Condominiums: Design, Planning and Maintenance* (Boston: Cahners, 1976), p. 28.

projection by years should be based on weighted, seasonally adjusted, average guest days (occupancy) and room rates (considering off-season specials) during the year. For most properties, there will be several distinct sources of income. According to the *Uniform System of Accounts and Expense Dictionary for Motels/ Hotels* of the American Hotel and Motel Association, these sources are rooms, food, beverages, telephone, other department profits, and other income. Income from other sources, such as rental of retail space, is reported as a separate item.

Periodic recessions have a drastic impact on income. Travel for both business and pleasure is affected. The effects are generally immediate for smaller, transient motels but may be delayed for hotels that hold advance reservations for conventions. One can account for such disruptions by making pessimistic and optimistic projections and comparing the sensitivity of the rates of return generated.

PHYSICAL ANALYSIS

The physical design and condition of the property are important from two standpoints: (1) attracting and pleasing the clientele and (2) improving operating efficiency. Architectural design is a matter of taste but should be tailored to the target market. A design that is suitable for Miami Beach or Las Vegas might not be appropriate in Williamsburg or San Francisco. Chains that appeal to middle-class business and vacation travelers use a standard motif connoting modest but comfortable standard accommodations at a reasonable price. In addition to design appeal, features that add competitive advantage are protection from noise and nuisance light, logical layout, connections between buildings that are protected from the elements, and adequate security and fire protection. Operating efficiency is increased by design and materials that promote ease of upkeep and by well-designed work areas.

LEGAL, POLITICAL, AND ENVIRONMENTAL ANALYSIS

The primary legal liabilities of hotel/motel operation are laws regulating the sale and consumption of alcoholic beverages; efforts to control illegal activities, such as prostitution, sexual perversion, and gambling, within the facility; and laws governing reservations and the activities of travel agents. Most problems of this type may be avoided by using knowledgeable and experienced management.

PROPERTY MANAGEMENT

Effective management of operations is almost as crucial as location. The clientele must be made to feel welcome; a continuous effort must be made to maintain a good reputation and avoid erosion of return business. Signs of management problems in existing properties include (1) failure to adopt the uniform system of accounts; (2) high levels of accounts payable, indicating cash management problems, underfinanced operations, or shoddy account administration; (3) neglected maintenance; (4) a high turnover of managerial personnel; and (5) recent use of giveaway promotions to bolster sagging occupancy. Such promotions are properly used only in the off season in order to retain personnel and provide amortization income.

The Hotel Management Contract. While many hotel/motel properties are operated by individual owners, most larger establishments are run by management chains. Where the chain works under contract for a percentage fee, the cost of management is treated as a normal operating expense to the owner. However, many institutional investors prefer to lease the property to specialized operators. Lease terms provide for a minimum and an alternative percentage rate. Typical lease rates are 20–30 percent of room rental income, 5–7 percent of food income, and 10–15 percent of income from liquor sales. Leases are generally net of all operating expenses. Under this arrangement owners may treat the lease payments as income subject only to financing and taxation costs. The important details of such contracts are beyond the scope of this book; however, it should be noted that negotiations for such contracts require a thorough knowledge of both owner and operator concerns. During the 1970s leases on some distressed properties were negotiated that were extremely favorable to the hotel management companies in that they provided for, say, 10–15 percent of *gross* revenues with an *additional* incentive percentage of cash throw-off after debt service. The owner had 100 percent of the risk, including even china breakage and silver losses, with the only exception being malfeasance of top management at the management company's home office. Such is the price of bad marketing, overbuilding, and foreclosure to a lender who lacks the skills of hotel/motel business management.

ANALYSIS OF CURRENT OPERATING INCOME AND EXPENSES

Operating statistics from Pannell, Kerr, Forster's *Trends in the Hotel/Motel Business* provide useful insight into the ratio relationship of revenue and expenditure items.[6] (See Exhibit 23–11.)

Many components of income and expense fluctuate because of seasonal demand variations. Seasonally adjusted averages should be used as input into the basic model. These may be derived from recent experience of the property moderated by information from comparable properties. Be cautious in accepting projections of revenues and expenses for uses that have not been market tested at the location (e.g., PLATO franchise, disco lounge).

The main problem is estimating the trend of gross potential income on the basis of projections of seasonally adjusted guest-day units and ancillary income from other operations (e.g., bar/restaurant). Fixed costs (amortization of debt, real estate taxes, insurance, and necessary maintenance) tend to produce a breakeven point of about 60–70 percent. As guest-day units rise, fixed costs per unit fall. Variable costs per guest-day are subject to some significant economies of scale for large functions such as conventions, banquets, and balls. However, variable costs tend to be a relatively constant proportion of projected gross revenues. Promotional costs tend to be heavier during preopening, rehabilitation, and low-occupancy periods.

Some operating expenses are not subject to internal control. For example, energy costs, which doubled between 1973 and 1977, have accelerated much faster than room rates.

A substantial portion of the tax burden may be due to a personal property tax on furnishings and inventory. Investors should check local rates and the level of

[6] Harris, Kerr, Forster & Co. [Certified Public Accountants], *Trends in the Hotel/Motel Business, 1978* (New York).

EXHIBIT 23–11. Operating Statistics for U.S. Motels and Hotels—1981

| | | HOTELS | | MOTELS | |
Item	Full Sample	Transient	Resort	With Restaurant	Without Restaurant
Sample size	800	325	100	275	100
Occupancy	69.9%	70.1%	71.8%	69.2%	64.3%
Avg. daily rate/occ. room	$45.55	$49.52	$53.52	$32.61	$33.97
Avg. size/no. of rooms	263	359	329	185	98
Revenues					
Rooms	60.2%	60.6%	55.2%	61.2%	92.5%
Food	24.3	24.4	27.1	23.8	—
Beverages	9.0	8.8	9.3	10.2	—
Telephones	2.4	2.6	1.4	2.8	3.6
Other operated depts.	1.9	1.6	3.5	1.2	1.0
Rentals & other income	2.2	2.0	3.5	.8	2.9
Total	100.0%	100.0%	100.0%	100.0%	100.0%
Expenses					
Rooms	15.3%	15.0%	15.6%	15.0%	20.3%
Food & beverage	26.7	26.9	29.1	26.9	—
Telephone	3.1	3.4	2.0	3.2	4.0
Other operated depts.	1.3	1.1	2.8	.7	.7
Total	46.4%	46.4%	49.5%	45.8%	25.0%
Undistributed expenses					
Admin. & gen.	7.8%	7.8%	7.7%	8.2%	7.7%
Management fees	2.5	2.4	3.1	1.7	5.1
Market	3.6	3.7	4.2	2.6	3.3
Franchise fees	.5	.4	.2	1.2	1.4
Guest entertain.	.1	.0	.2	.0	.0
Property operation & maintenance	5.7	5.8	5.6	5.6	6.4
Energy costs	4.7	4.6	4.3	5.0	6.1
Total	24.9%	24.7%	25.3%	24.3%	30.0%
Property taxes and other municipal charges	2.6%	2.9%	1.8%	2.2%	4.4%
Insurance on building and contents	.5%	.5%	.4%	.6%	.7%
Income before other fixed charges	25.6%	25.5%	23.0%	27.1%	39.9%

SOURCE: *Trends in the Hotel Industry, 1981 U.S.A. Edition,* Pannell Kerr Forster (New York, 1981), pp. 10, 20, 37, 48, and 59.

compliance activity. Assurances should be sought that such taxes are paid in full, with the tax for the current year prorated at settlement.

Making projections requires knowledge of the local motel/hotel industry. Past earnings records for the property—assuming continuation of the marketing/management plan—may be useful. Competitive surveys may produce useful data. In the absence of usable current local data at the basic financial feasibility stage, one may make judgmental projections based on regional data in *Trends in the Hotel/Motel Business* and other sources. A field survey prior to purchase is essential.

RISK MANAGEMENT

When ownership is in the form of a partnership, one should be wary of abuses of ownership privileges by fellow partners. Free use of facilities for lodging, dining, and entertaining not only cuts into operating revenues but may have adverse effects on management and other personnel. Pilferage and embezzlement are chronic problems in this business.

FINANCING

Lenders generally limit loans to 50–60 percent on operations affiliated with a franchised management chain, preferably net leased. Recently participations on profits have been required, or the lender may obtain a partial equity interest. Hotel/motel operations lend themselves to splitting the equity contribution into several layers (the so-called Zeckendorf Hawaiian pineapple slices), with individuals, institutions, operators, and developers taking a cut, each with varying risk/return trade-offs.

Debt structure may also be leveraged by mortgaging separate components. Mortgageable assets may be separated into the management contract or lease, land, the improvements (through a junior mortgage), and furnishings (through a chattel mortgage).

Debt service projections should include provisions for participation payments (corresponding to projected income), ground rents (if any), and periodic refinancing. If the loan is short term or subject to a balloon, the remaining economic lives of the improvements should be carefully scrutinized.

NATURE OF THE TAX SHELTER

Hotel/motel properties are eligible for the usual special tax treatments: investment tax credits, the first-year depreciation bonus, depreciation deductions, capital gain treatment, and tax-deferred exchange. In addition, owners may elect to form a Subchapter S corporation, thereby avoiding double taxation while retaining limited liability. The provision prohibiting Subchapter S election for most real estate ventures is the limit of not more than 20 percent of "passive" income. Room rental income from lodging is not considered passive, since the hotel/motel operator must actively provide these services. However, rental income from space other than rooms (e.g., retail stores) should not exceed 20 percent of income. The Subchapter S corporation entity can be advantageous when no partner is willing to function as the general partner in a limited partnership.

Depreciation. Since a significant proportion of value is represented by equipment, furniture, and other components subject to ACRS three-year and five-year lives, the hotel/motel industry provides an opportunity for unusually short depreciation schedules for much of the overall value.

In addition, many parts of a hotel/motel may be considered tangible personal property and thus also be eligible for the investment tax credit. Examples are swimming pool equipment, vending machines, wall-to-wall carpeting, through-the-wall air conditioners, and elevators and escalators.

Most hotels and motels have a large investment in service assets such as linens and crockery. Often these assets are grouped into a single account with a useful life of three years. On occasion a good case has been made for expensing rather than capitalizing these items.

Finally, the 1981 Economic Recovery Tax Act has provided graduated tax credit percentages for substantial rehabilitation of older buildings. This is in lieu of the 60-month depreciation formerly provided.

Because of the substantial proportion of total property value represented by personal property, classifying some items (e.g., carpets and drapes) as personalty may be advantageous. The new law limits discretion (e.g., elevators and escalators must be included in the 15-year real property class). Component depreciation is no longer allowed. However, the 15-year ACRS life for real property should encourage investment. Recall that in Chapter 13 we discussed the risk involved in using accelerated depreciation methods.

CASH FLOW, RATIO, AND RISK ANALYSIS

This requires some knowledge of hotel/motel accounting, although uniform standards that permit useful comparisons have been adopted. After determining "house profit," the real estate analyst must allow for the effect of store rentals; financing costs; depreciation; fire insurance; and franchise, personal property, real estate, and income taxes *before* estimating net cash flow. See Exhibit 23-12 for an example of a statement based on uniform standards.

Of course, equity cash flows and tax effects must be divided among the ownership interests as agreed. In accordance with state laws and IRS regulations, disproportionate shares are a common practice. Investment analysis is conducted by assuming an average room rate and calculating profits on the basis of varying levels of occupancy. The level of occupancy at which cash flow to equity (cash throw-off) begins (i.e., equals zero) should be the breakeven point. Generally, it occurs at about 60-70 percent occupancy in normal markets.

THE INVESTMENT DECISION

Investors are generally interested in the same ratios as are applied to other businesses: liquidity ratio, collection period, inventory turnover, and return on total assets. During normal operating periods these ratios should compare favorably with those for other properties in the industry. Because the rate of return is very sensitive to cyclical and seasonal variations, careful consideration should be given to the way in which income and expense items are estimated.

These kinds of properties represent somewhat speculative ventures because high occupancy depends on prosperity in both the national and local economies. The downside risk is high. Location advantages may vanish as a result of shifts in transportation routes. A good reputation is difficult to cultivate and maintain. New competition is a constant threat; there is no income stability by way of long-term agreements, since rooms are rented on at most a weekly basis.

Considering the speculative nature of such properties and the extraordinary

EXHIBIT 23–12. Estimated Statement of Income and Expenses for an Average Year at an Average Daily Rate of $39.00

	ASSUMED OCCUPANCY LEVEL	
	70 Percent	80 Percent
Total sales and income		
Rooms (average daily room rate: $39.00)	$2,979,432	$3,405,173
Food	1,654,653	1,826,761
Beverages	534,944	627,540
Telephone	106,184	121,281
Other departmental profits	24,407	28,433
Other income	77,499	87,564
Subtotal	$5,377,119	$6,096,752
Cost of goods sold and departmental wages and expenses		
Rooms	$ 883,941	$ 996,415
Food and beverages	1,752,785	1,963,391
Telephone	152,482	172,863
Subtotal	$2,789,208	$3,132,669
Gross operating income	$2,587,911	$2,964,083
Deductions from income		
Administrative and general expenses (less management fee)	$ 272,253	$ 296,408
Advertising and sales promotion	125,810	125,810
Heat, light, and power	251,368	260,930
Repairs and maintenance	213,877	230,736
Subtotal	$ 863,308	$ 913,884
House profit	$1,724,603	$2,050,199
Plus: Store rentals	225,979	255,328
Gross operating profit	$1,950,582	$2,305,527
Less: Franchise taxes and fire insurance	22,155	24,030
Profit before real estate taxes and capital expenses	$1,928,427	$2,281,497
Less: Real estate taxes	385,000	455,000
Net cash flow to investors before provision for replacement of short-lived items	$1,543,427	$1,826,497

management capabilities required, ownership should demand relatively high rates of return—say, 20–25 percent—plus an inflation premium. If much of the return is dependent on tax benefits, the holding period may be short and the resale value lower than would otherwise be the case. Elimination of the 50–70 percent marginal tax brackets may well cause many equity investors to switch from special-use properties to less risky investments.

Much of the foregoing analysis applies also to fast-food and greeting card franchises, car washes, and similar properties. Each has unique business characteristics, its own chart of accounts, special locational characteristics, marketing problems, and the like. A potential investor must evaluate management, location, and marketing plans. Success depends on the quality of the primary business operation.

NURSING HOMES

A major growth sector in urban land use from 1981 to 2000 will be custodial and domiciliary nursing homes. Although there will be some tendency for new construction to concentrate in the Sun Belt states, one can expect nursing homes to be constructed or rehabilitated in both urban and rural areas throughout the nation.

Currently, the problem with nursing homes is that their feasibility is dependent on changing government programs. Because they are *not* generally economically feasible, we must subsidize them because we need them. A few nursing homes, which are located where there is strong demand from upper-income families and are blessed with strong management, can provide above-average returns. However, most analysts consider nursing homes to be speculative for the real estate investor because the yields are derived largely from tax effects, the cash flow is modest, and the capital gain from appreciation is uncertain. The recent change in marginal tax brackets, which lowers the maximum tax on investment income to 50 percent, makes equity positions even more speculative.

Definitions

A *nursing home* is a facility that offers living quarters, food, and skilled nursing care for convalescents, the chronically ill, and other people who need third-party domiciliary or custodial care. About 70 percent of nursing home beds are in *proprietary* (profit-seeking) organizations. The balance are operated by nonprofit organizations like counties, churches, and hospitals. Facilities used as homes for the elderly and specialized clinics (e.g., rehabilitation, diagnostic) are not included in this definition.

Medicare. In 1966 Public Law 89-97 amended the Social Security Act to provide a health insurance program for the aged. Nursing homes may receive financial assistance under this program. Designated state agencies determine the eligibility of a facility. A Utilization Review Committee functioning under federal guidelines and composed of the director of nursing, the nursing home administrator, and two licensed physicians reviews the record of every person seeking benefits under the Medicare program.

Medicaid. Medicaid is a program for the medically indigent. The benefits not only vary greatly from one state to another but are subject to manipulation as state budgets are formulated from year to year. Part of the Medicaid program provides nursing care for poor people, young and old. It is necessary to analyze the local jurisdiction's regulations and level of reimbursement to determine whether or not the state fully covers the costs (including profit) of nursing care. In some states the rates are so inadequate that Medicaid patients will substantially depress the investment potential of a facility.

Life Safety Code. Inspection and certification for fire, safety, and panic protection are the responsibility of a state fire marshal or other designated state employee. A copy of the Life Safety Code is available from the National Fire Protection Association in Boston. All nursing homes insured under the FHA or are receiving federal payments for patients must comply. Compliance activity is vigorous.

Accreditation and licensure. Every state and many political subdivisions have an active licensure program. Files of the state health department and other regulatory bodies should be investigated by a would-be investor to determine whether or not deficiencies or violations exist. In addition, accreditation or recognition of a nursing home is available through the Joint Commission on Accreditation of Hospitals and Long-Term Care Facilities in Chicago. Other important forms of official recognition are certification by Medicare and the Blue Cross organizations, and approval by the Veterans Administration. Exhibit 23–13 illustrates a request for a Medicare certificate and should provide some insight into the nature of nursing home facilities.

Nursing Hours. These are units of nursing care. An investor can compute nursing hours by dividing the total number of patient-days for a period

---

EXHIBIT 23–13.   HEW Form Requesting Medicare Certification

FORM APPROVED
OMB No. 0938-0100

DEPARTMENT OF HEALTH AND HUMAN SERVICES
HEALTH CARE FINANCING ADMINISTRATION

LONG-TERM CARE FACILITY REQUEST FOR CERTIFICATION
IN THE MEDICARE AND/OR MEDICAID PROGRAM

I. Identifying Information	NAME OF FACILITY	STREET ADDRESS		MEDICARE/MEDICAID PROVIDER NUMBER (N1)	STATE VENDOR NO.
	CITY, COUNTY, AND STATE	ZIP CODE	TELEPHONE NUMBER *(Including Area Code)* (N7)	STATE/COUNTY (N3)	STATE REGION (N4)

II. Eligibility	REQUEST TO ESTABLISH ELIGIBILITY IN (N13) 1) ☐ MEDICARE 2) ☐ MEDICAID 3) ☐ BOTH (N8)	RELATED PROVIDER NUMBER

III. Type of Facility *(Check one)* (N14)

01 ☐ Skilled Nursing Facility	04 ☐ Skilled Nursing Unit of Domiciliary Inst.	07 ☐ General ICF	12 ☐ ICF/MR Distinct Part of Hospital
02 ☐ Skilled Nursing Unit of Hospital	05 ☐ SNF Distinct Part of Skilled Nursing Facility	08 ☐ ICF Distinct Part of Skilled Nursing Facility	13 ☐ ICF/MR Distinct Part of SNF
03 ☐ Skilled Nursing Unit of Rehabilitation Center	06 ☐ Christian Science San.	09 ☐ SNF/ICF (Swing Bed)	14 ☐ ICF Distinct Part of Hospital
		10 ☐ ICF/MR	15 ☐ ICF Distinct Part of ICF
			16 ☐ ICF/MR Distinct Part of ICF/MR

IV. Type of Control *(Check one)* (N15)

Voluntary Non-Profit 1 ☐ Church	3 ☐ Proprietary	Government *(Non-Federal)* 4 ☐ State	6 ☐ City	Hospital 8 ☐ District
2 ☐ Other *(Specify)* ☐		5 ☐ County	7 ☐ City-County	

V. Services Provided: BY STAFF. Place a "1" in the block(s). If UNDER ARRANGEMENT, place a "2" in the block(s). (N16)

01 ☐ Nursing	08 ☐ Recreational Activities	14 ☐ Podiatry
02 ☐ Physical Therapy	09 ☐ Pharmacy	15 ☐ Ophthalmology
03 ☐ Outpatient Physical Therapy	10 ☐ Clinical Laboratory	16 ☐ Psychological Services
04 ☐ Occupational Therapy	11 ☐ Diagnostic X-ray	17 ☐ Other *(Specify)*
05 ☐ Speech Pathology	12 ☐ Administration and Storage of Blood	
06 ☐ Outpatient Speech Pathology	13 ☐ Dentistry	
07 ☐ Social Services		

VI. Number of Employees (Full-time equivalents) Please See Instructions

1. REGISTERED PROFESSIONAL NURSES		2. LICENSED PRACTICAL/VOCATIONAL NURSES		3. ALL OTHERS	
(N17) (a)	(b)	(N18) (a)	(b)	(N27) (a)	(b)

WHOEVER KNOWINGLY AND WILLFULLY MAKES OR CAUSES TO BE MADE A FALSE STATEMENT OR REPRESENTATION ON THIS STATEMENT, MAY BE PROSECUTED UNDER APPLICABLE FEDERAL OR STATE LAWS. IN ADDITION, KNOWINGLY AND WILLFULLY FAILING TO FULLY AND ACCURATELY DISCLOSE THE INFORMATION REQUESTED MAY RESULT IN DENIAL OF A REQUEST TO PARTICIPATE OR WHERE THE ENTITY ALREADY PARTICIPATES, A TERMINATION OF ITS AGREEMENT OR CONTRACT WITH THE STATE AGENCY OR THE SECRETARY, AS APPROPRIATE.

SIGNATURE OF AUTHORIZED OFFICIAL	TITLE	(N28) DATE

HCFA-1516 (10-80) Destroy Prior Editions

REGIONAL OFFICE-ORIGINAL

(month, year) by the total number of nursing personnel hours for the same period. One should keep in mind that nursing homes are stratified by level of care: (1) minimal, (2) normal, and (3) intensive. Nursing hours per patient-day differ under each mode of operation. State licensure laws generally provide for a minimum of two hours of nursing care per patient-day.

INVESTMENT ADVANTAGES AND DISADVANTAGES

Several trends fuel the expanding demand for nursing home facilities. They include the extended life span of the general population, the rapidly escalating costs of hospital care, and the establishment of government programs for people who need custodial and domiciliary medical care.

In spite of expanding demand, increased public regulation and scrutiny call for exceptionally skillful management if profits are to be realized from the investment. The 1982 federal budget reductions in Medicaid and the slowdown in Medicare payments threaten the solvency of many nursing homes.

However, knowledgeable operation may provide substantial returns. Opportunities exist to add profit centers that provide patient services beyond the necessities included in the basic fee.

This is a highly regulated business with few options in terms of design, operation, and rent structure. Paper work is an ever-expanding management burden, and the operator must have extensive, detailed, and current knowledge of the legal and regulatory procedures involved. Occupancy during the startup phase can be expected to be low, calling for substantial working capital in the early years. The facility is highly specialized, a fact that reduces its market value and discourages conventional financing sources. Working capital reserves are necessary to carry accounts receivable because of slow-paying insurance companies and government agencies.

SUPPLY AND DEMAND ANALYSIS

Most areas have publicly employed planning personnel who routinely conduct surveys and prepare plans for health care systems. Such reports may provide an adequate basis for market and marketability studies of specific facilities. The reports may show population trends that indicate increasing demand for extrahospital patient care. There may be a prepared projection of the number of beds needed, by county or by regional unit. If not, rules of thumb—for example, 45 beds per 1,000 over-65 population in urban areas—may be applied.

State agencies ostensibly attempt to control overbuilding through the issuance of certificates of need. Any proposed facility must obtain such a certificate before being qualified for assistance. For an existing facility, check the effectiveness of the program to prevent overbuilding. Unfortunately, some state planning agencies are "growth" oriented and have granted certificates far in excess of demand.

Given sufficient demand, an examination of current supply will indicate whether the facility has a chance of maintaining high occupancy. Inventories of current facilities are available from local and regional health planning agencies. These agencies may also have data on average occupancy rates. Ninety-five percent by the third year is considered a minimum to justify investment. Fieldwork should concentrate on the features offered by the competition. The age and design of the structure, staffing, and auxiliary services are important features. Also, a competitive survey should be conducted in order to evaluate the comparative advantage of the subject property in terms of location and staffing.

Projection of Rental Income and Vacancies. Revenues are derived from two types of patients: private and Medicare/Medicaid-assisted. Nationally, the average home has 45 percent private and 55 percent assisted patients. Reimbursed revenues, however, are controlled by federal and state government policies and may not equal 100 percent of the normal rate. In recent years, because some costs of operation are not allowable under accounting procedures of the Social Security Administration, it has been difficult to break even on Medicare patients. Therefore, nursing homes are reluctant to permit the ratio of Medicare patients to exceed 50–55 percent. A further problem is that reimbursements are subject to post-audit and delay in payment by the Social Security Administration. Therefore, the investor should discount expected income from Medicare patients by about 20 percent.

Compare private rates to those of comparable facilities to ascertain the market rate, and use this in projections. A conservative vacancy factor of 7–10 percent will cover losses due to bad debts and reimbursement delay. Daily rates generally include a fixed package of services. Additional services, such as therapy, medicine, haircuts, and outings, are billed separately and should be projected as additional income.

PHYSICAL ANALYSIS

The key points of structural design and maintenance are adequate space, fireproofing, emergency power provisions, and ability to maintain high hygienic standards. State licensing laws and the Fire Safety Code include an extensive list of specifications for design and upkeep. Do not assume, however, that the subject property adequately conforms to these requirements simply because it is licensed to operate. Some nursing homes operate under grandfather clauses with currently approved existing conditions that will be deemed nonconforming whenever a change in ownership occurs.

LEGAL, POLITICAL, AND ENVIRONMENTAL ANALYSIS

Although the industry is highly regulated, nursing home operation may be periodically subjected to public scrutiny concerning adequacy of care and level of profit. Some people feel that such operations should be a public service and that profit-seeking concerns have lower standards of sanitation and care. The investor should become aware of reports of past scandals exposing inadequate sanitation and fire prevention in the area, particularly any that are associated with the subject property.

Many homes operate under a special-use permit rather than the sanction of proper zoning. Such permits may be revoked at any time, causing the operation to be nonconforming.

PROPERTY MANAGEMENT

A premium should be placed on proven experience in operating successful homes. The manager must be able to provide satisfactory patient care and a good working environment for a qualified and efficient staff, and at the same time satisfy licensing and accreditation inspectors and the supervisory medical care committee.

In the operation of nursing homes, ownership of the physical facility and equipment is often separated from the business of operating the home. Allocation of returns may be disproportionate but, obviously, must allow a sufficient return to provide an incentive for the manager to remain on the job.

ANALYSIS OF OPERATIONS

Returns from operations ought to be segregated to permit better analysis. The ownership entity could control the real property and receive its return via a lease to the operating entity. Such leases are net and based on an annual rate per bed. The operating entity pays rent as an operating expense with the proceeds from patient fees, reimbursements, and additional income.

The expense breakdown shown in Exhibit 23–14 provides a tool for comparative analysis; the costs are for 1980. Before one determines the net cash flow to the investors in the real estate, deductions must be made for fire insurance, franchise taxes, and licenses, which pertain to the building and not to the nursing home operation; real estate and other local taxes; and financing costs, depreciation, and necessary reserves. Of course, disproportionate partnership allocations may be made in accordance with business risk principles that enable the equity investors to participate in income and loss from the nursing home operation.

TAX SHELTER VARIABLES

Nursing homes are eligible for investment tax credits, a first-year depreciation bonus, ACRS composite depreciation, capital gains, deferred-tax exchanges, and the installment sales method of allocation. Unfortunately, since the government does not yet recognize the residential nature of the use, accelerated forms of depreciation are not practical. However, it is felt that use of ACRS 15-year composite straight-line depreciation is appropriate. Very short lives for wall surfaces, floor coverings, and so on may be appropriate because to meet state and federal hygienic requirements such equipment must be replaced. However, to qualify for such treatment these items must be classified as equipment, which is debatable. In any event, the tax benefits would be minimized by the capital expenditures required. Finally, many items of equipment—perhaps as much as 15–20 percent of total value—may be properly classified as personal property and ACRS 3-year and 5-year lives can increase the amount of deductions in the earlier years.

First users should be aware that many states restrict resale of nursing home properties. Approval may be required. Such restrictions may force investors into longer-than-anticipated holding periods. Thus, capital gains, being deferred, may not contribute to the rate of return to the extent expected.

THE INVESTMENT DECISION

A primary requirement is a nursing home property with high occupancy. This is a high-overhead business, but one that offers good compensation to diligent and expert management. Specifically, the subject property should have a stable or increasing occupancy rate of at least 93 percent, have operating expenses amounting to no more than 70 percent of revenues, and provide a sufficient

EXHIBIT 23-14. Income and Expenses for a Large Nursing Home for a Twelve-Month Period

	Actual Income from Operations	Percentage of the Year's Revenue	Cost per Patient-Day[a]
Income: Patient-Days (Occupancy @ 89.7%)			
Routine services	$1,107,088	93.5	$34.40
Personal nursing (net)	8,916	0.7	.27
Incontinency care (net)	12,230	1.0	.38
Special diet	—	0.0	.00
Medical supplies (net)	17,595	1.4	.54
Pharmacy (net)	5,869	0.4	.17
Laboratory (net)	3,357	0.2	.09
Physical therapy (net)	12,321	1.5	.38
Beauty and barber (net)	1,015	0.0	.03
Equipment rental (net)	10,030	0.8	.31
Laundry and dry cleaning	6,017	0.5	.17
Other revenue (net)	(439)	0.0	(.01)
Total Revenue	$1,183,999	100.0	$36.73
Operating Expenses			
Nursing—salary and wages	$ 393,533	33.2	$12.22
Supplies and expense	4,587	0.3	.13
Professional nursing service	—	0.0	.00
Recreational therapy—salary and wages	10,491	0.8	.32
Supplies and expense	948	0.0	.03
Dietary—salary and wages	77,543	6.5	2.41
Supplies and expense	13,210	1.1	.40
Food	63,448	5.3	1.97
Housekeeping—salary and wages	23,967	2.0	.74
Supplies and expense	7,263	0.6	.22
Laundry—salary and wages	8,916	0.7	.27
Supplies and expense	1,750	0.1	.05
Linens	1,346	0.1	.04
Plant maintenance—salary and wages	27,014	2.2	.83
Supplies and expense	662	0.0	.01
Repair and maintenance	10,394	0.8	.32
Exterminator and trash	2,466	0.2	.07
Utilities—electricity	19,302	1.6	.59
Fuel	8,081	0.6	.24
Water and sewer	6,714	0.5	.20
Total Operating Expenses	$ 681,635	56.6	$21.06
Gross Operating Income	$ 502,364	43.4	$15.67

EXHIBIT 23–14. *(Continued)*

	Actual Income from Operations	Percentage of the Year's Revenue	Cost per Patient-Day[a]
Gross Operating Income	$ 502,364	43.4	$15.67
Administrative Expenses			
Salary and wages	$ 49,880	4.2	$ 1.55
Payroll taxes	ˋ44,286	3.7	1.37
Insurance employee	16,408	4.3	.50
Employee welfare	285	0.0	.00
Advertising and public relations	13,487	1.1	.42
Travel	2,611	0.2	.08
Professional fees	11,227	0.9	.34
Equipment rental	170	0.0	.00
Dues and subscriptions	2,119	0.1	.05
Telephone	3,303	0.2	.09
Supplies and printing	3,117	0.2	.09
Insurance business	5,521	0.4	.16
Employee recruiting	622	0.0	.01
Other administrative expense	2,862	0.2	.08
Total Administrative Expenses	$ 155,898	12.5	$ 4.74
Net Income Before Other Expenses	$ 346,466	30.9	$10.93
Other Income and Expenses			
Add: Other income	$ 1,160	0.0	$ 0.3
Deduct: Other expense	15,269	1.3	.47
Management fee	69,454	5.8	2.15
Medical writeoff	28,142	2.3	.82
Welfare writeoff	10,881	0.9	.34
Other writeoff	—	0.0	.00
Total Other Income and Expenses	$ 122,586	10.3	$ 3.81
Net Operating Income from Nursing Home Business	$ 223,880	20.6	$ 7.12
Property Expense			
Taxes—real estate	$ 36,003	3.0	$ 1.12
Taxes—personal property	1,553	.1	.04
Total Property Expenses	$ 37,556	3.1	$ 1.16
Net Income Before Taxes and Debt Service	$ 186,324	17.5	$ 5.96

[a] A patient-day is a 24-hour period during which a patient is in the nursing facility. The number of patient-days for the year is divided into the individual revenue and cost figures to determine the revenue and cost per patient-day.

before-tax cash flow return (ROE of 15–20% annually). The required IRR may be in the 22–30 percent range when an inflation premium is included.

Conventional debt coverage ratio and break-even analysis is not used because the feasibility of nursing home financing is controlled by the procedures of the Section 232 FHA-insured loan program. Such a technical analysis is beyond the scope of this book. But even risk and return analysis should not be undertaken without specialized knowledge of federal and state financing procedures and minimum property standards.

In 1981 it appears that, as a real estate investment, nursing homes are a speculative investment for only the very high marginal-tax-rate investor. The maximum tax rate reduction makes these properties even less attractive. Equity investors should be acutely aware that net cash flow is a *residual* after compensating management and is subject to politically inspired program changes that cause delays in payments and much uncertainty. We need nursing homes, but we haven't yet found a socially acceptable way to make them consistently viable as an investment of public or private funds.

Selected References

Houses, Condominiums, and Small Apartments

American Land Development Association. "Resort Timesharing." Resort Condominiums International, 1977.

Breckenfeld, Gurney. "A Decade of Catch-Up for Housing." *Fortune,* April 7, 1980.

Case, Fred E. *The Investment Guide to Home and Land Purchase.* Englewood Cliffs, N.J.: Prentice-Hall, 1977.

Davidson, Harold A. "The Impact of Rent Control on Apartment Investment." *The Appraisal Journal,* October 1978.

Downs, Anthony. "Inflation a Major Cause of Current Real Estate Boom." *National Real Estate Investor,* August 1979.

Edwards, Audrey. "A House Is Not the Only Home." *Black Enterprise,* October 1979.

Expense Analysis—Condominiums, Cooperatives, and PUDs. Chicago: Institute of Real Estate Management (annual).

Goodkin, Sanford. *Winning in Real Estate.* New York: McKay, 1977.

Harris, Marlys. "Moving In on the Condominium Boom." *Money,* June 1979.

Irwin, Robert. *Protect Yourself in Real Estate.* New York: McGraw-Hill, 1977.

Lowry, Albert J. *How You Can Become Financially Independent by Investing in Real Estate.* New York: Simon & Schuster, 1977.

————. *How to Manage Real Estate Successfully—In Your Spare Time.* New York: Simon & Schuster, 1977.

Meagher, J. P. "Flipping Surges: A View on House Prices." *Barron's,* December 17, 1979.

"Mixed Use Can Make Rental Numbers Work." *Housing,* 56 (October 1979).

Nicholson, S. "Rental Housing: Why Don't the Numbers Work." *Buildings,* December 1979.

"Real Estate: A Maturing Boom Calls for Caution." *Business Week,* December 25, 1978.

Residential Development Handbook. Washington, D.C.: Urban Land Institute, 1979.

Schubb, D. E., and J. M. Grubb. "Single Family Homes and the Novice Investor." *Real Estate Today,* August 1978.

Seldin, Maury, and Sumicharst, Michael. *Housing Markets.* Homewood, Ill.: Dow Jones-Irwin, 1977.

Sexrar, Suzanne. "Recession Proof Real Estate." *Money,* September 1979.

Shulman, Morton. "Getting Rich from Inflation." *Canadian Business,* May 1979.

"Special Issue on Income Property." *Mortgage Banker,* November 1979.

Spellman, Lewis, Jr., and A. Hughes Stephens. "The Limits of the Housing Price Boom." *Texas Business Review,* 51 (August 1977).

Tamarkin, Bob. "Condomania in Chicago." *Forbes,* November 13, 1978.

Weaver, R. C. "Rental Housing: An Endangered Species?" *Property Management,* Spring 1979.

Wood, Stephen F. "Refinancing: A Viable Option?" *Real Estate Today,* September 1980.

Yannacone, V. J., Jr. "Urban Comeback Opens New Vistas for Investors." *National Real Estate Investor,* September 1979.

Hotels and Motels

American Hotel and Motel Association, *Uniform System of Accounts and Expense Dictionary for Motels–Motor Hotels, Small Hotels.* New York, 1962.

Arbel, Avener, and Paul Grier. "The Risk Structure of the Hotel Industry." *Cornell H&R Administration Quarterly,* November 1978, pp. 15–22.

"A Bibliography: Hotel and Restaurant Administration and Related Subjects." *Cornell H&R Administration Quarterly,* August 1978.

Brener, Stephen W. *Census of the Motor Hotel Industry in the U.S.* New York: Helmsley-Spear, periodic.

———. "Factors Involved in Motel Site Survey." *Valuation,* (4) 1969, pp. 9–16.

Brener, Stephen W., and Stephen Rushmore. "Valuing Motels and Hotels in the Current Market." *Real Estate Review,* Fall 1972, pp. 59–62.

Coffman, Charles D. *Marketing for a Full House: A Complete Guide to Profitable Hotel/Motel Operational Management.* Ithaca, N.Y.: Cornell University Press, 1973.

De Marrais, Herbert. "6 Ways Motor Lodges Risk Financial Disaster." *Hotel and Motel Management,* January 1978, pp. 24–26.

Dittmer, Paul R., and Gerald R. Griffin. *Principles of Food, Beverage and Labor Cost Controls for the Hotel and Restaurant Industry.* Boston: Cahners, 1976.

Eyster, James J. "The Hotel Management Contract: Owner and Operator Concerns." *Real Estate Review,* September 1978, pp. 74–79.

Hall, Thomas H. "The Motor Hotel: Appraisals and Feasibility Studies." *The Appraisal Journal,* October 1971, pp. 568–575.

Horwath, Ernest B. *Hotel Accounting.* New York: Wiley, 1978.

Horwath and Horwath International. *Worldwide Operating Statistics of the Hotel Industry.* New York, 1978.

Laventhol & Horwath. *U.S. Lodging Industry.* New York, annual.

Lawson, Fred R. *Hotels, Motels and Condominiums: Design, Planning and Maintenance.* Boston: Cahners, 1976.

Lundberg, Donald E. *The Hotel and Restaurant Business.* Boston: Cahners, 1970.

Manheim, Uriel. "Condohotels: Promise Versus Performance." *Real Estate Review,* Fall 1977, pp. 23–29.

McConnell, Jon P. "Innkeeping and the Law of Antitrust." *Cornell H&R Administration Quarterly,* May 1977, pp. 18–21.

Peters, Clarence N. "Pre-opening Marketing Analysis for Hotels." *Cornell H&R Administration Quarterly,* May 1978, pp. 15–22.

Rushmore, Stephen. *The Valuation of Hotels and Motels.* Chicago: American Institute of Real Estate Appraisers, 1978.

———. "What Can Be Done About Your Hotel's Real Estate Taxes?" *Cornell H&R Administration Quarterly,* May 1977, pp. 78–81.

Waddell, Joseph M. "Hotel Capacity: How Many Rooms to Build?" *Cornell H&R Administration Quarterly,* August 1977, pp. 35–47.

"Where Will the Money Come From?" *Hotel and Motel Management,* May 1978, pp. 32ff.

Nursing Homes

Bachner, John P. *Public Relations for Nursing Homes.* Springfield, Ill.: Chas. C Thomas, 1974.

Coggeshall, John H. *Management of Retirement Homes and Long Term Care Facilities.* St. Louis, Mo.: C. V. Mosby, 1973.

Dunlop, Burton D. *The Growth of Nursing Home Care.* Lexington, Mass.: Lexington Books, 1979.

Hogan, John O. "The Valuation of Nursing Homes." *The Appraisal Journal,* April 1979, pp. 185– 195.

Journal of Nursing Administration Editorial Staff. *Nursing Home Administration.* 1976.

Koetting, Michael. *Nursing Home Organization and Efficiency: Profit Vs. Non-Profit.* Lexington, Mass.: Lexington Books, 1980.

McQuillan, Florence. *Fundamentals of Nursing Home Administration,* 2nd ed. Philadelphia: Saunders, 1974.

Mendelson, Mary A. *Tender Loving Greed: How the Incredibly Lucrative Nursing Home "Industry" Is Exploiting America's Old People and Defrauding Us All.* New York: Random House, 1975.

Miller, Dulcy B., and Jane T. Barry. *Nursing Home Organization and Operation.* New York: CBI Pub., 1979.

Nursing Home Fires and Their Cures. Boston, Mass.: National Fire Protection Association, 1972.

Posyniak, Henry. *Guide to Accounting Principles, Practices and Systems for Nursing Homes.* St. Louis, Mo.: Cath Health, 1978.

Rogers, Wesley W. *General Administration in the Nursing Home,* 2nd rev. ed. New York: CBI Pub., 1976.

Shipp, Audrey, ed. *The National Nursing Home Survey: 1977 Summary for the United States.* Hyattsville, Md.: National Center Health Stats, 1979.

Stevenson, Taloris, ed. *Charges for Care and Sources of Payment for Residents in Nursing Homes, United States National Nursing Home Survey August 1973–April 1974.* National Center Health Stats, 1977.

24

Land Investments

Buy land! They aren't making it anymore. Gene Autry believed that, and he's a very wealthy man today. . . . I knew a muleskinner, he was really big! . . . He had mule trains! . . . He believed that about land . . . Eventually he lost all his asses.

Anonymous land trader

Buying land to make a profit is like a game of Monopoly®. The buyer seeks a parcel that has the potential to quickly change from a lower use to a higher one with a minimum of holding costs and a maximum of financial leverage. Many people who buy land seem to expect the weedy ground cover to soon be replaced by a regional shopping center, or that they will be able to find some other person, who has such faith and hope, to whom they can sell the land.

Land developers and interstate land marketing companies came under severe attack and consequent regulation during the 1970s. Many groups have joined the battle against premature land development and land waste, and we can expect that socially responsible, ethical development will become the rule. In the 1980s the competent, successful land investors will be those who work with the environment and local planners in a cooperative way for orderly growth and development.

"Land always increases in value." Nevertheless, the application of strategic

Acknowledgment: The authors gratefully acknowledge the assistance of Charles Chandler, Atlanta, Georgia.

planning to investing in raw land will disclose implicit risks that can destroy many investors' expectations. Raw-land speculation and land investing is a field in which the unexpected spreads faster than the weeds; it is not for the risk averse. There is little chance of cash flow from operating the property. Your equity buys only the right to risk a capital gain by way of the reversion.

A respected scholar in real estate, Fred Case, has suggested that land requires a very high rate of price increase over the ownership cycle. Case attributes this primarily to the annual cost of holding the land and the earnings required on money invested in order to achieve the profit objectives. He provides an example in which he has converted these earnings objectives into percentages of the market price, assuming a one-year holding period:[1]

	Annual Rate Required
1. Earning on the down payment (10% earnings × 10% down)	1%
2. Interest on the loan (10% × 90%)	9
3. Real estate taxes	3
4. Improvements	2
5. Overall profit on total investment	12
6. Transaction costs (commission, legal, etc.)	11
	38%

Although transfer costs and improvements could be stretched out over a longer ownership cycle, whatever the assumptions, you will discover that land must earn, by way of higher prices, relatively high returns. Higher rates of return should be required for riskier investments.

Consider the following application, known as the rule of 72. If you divide your minimum acceptable rate of return into 72, the product will be the maximum number of years that may pass before you must sell to double your money and achieve the specified rate of return. (See Exhibit 24–1.)

Are you still ready to try land investing? Clearly, lack of interim income places a heavy burden on the reversion. Keeping in mind that no provision has been made for deducting the capital gain tax from the sale, it takes a real optimist to make a land investment. However, people can make fortunes with superior market knowledge and some good luck.

TRACK RECORD AND TRENDS

In the post-World War II period, farmers, developers, land bankers, and land investors have, in many instances, reaped large gains because of rising land values on the urban fringes of growing SMSAs. In less than forty years the population has grown by nearly 100 million and GNP has multiplied about five times (nominal dollars). The main problems now faced by a land speculator are two: (1) To what extent does the slower growth implicit in our lower rate of population growth imply slower rates of gain in land values? (2) To what extent has future growth already been capitalized in the asking price by the current owner?

[1] Fred E. Case, *The Investment Guide to Home and Land Purchase* [Englewood Cliffs, N.J.: Prentice-Hall (Spectrum Books) 1977], pp. 154–155.

Obviously, many factors other than these affect land value, such as interregional migration, the shift from manufacturing to service industries, the current trend of population movement away from the larger SMSAs to the smaller ones; the problems of energy use and efficiency; and the extent to which "back-filling," or the filling up of land that was skipped over, may occur in the targeted SMSA.

It appears that the period of rapid growth for this nation is over. We have "settled in." In general, we have selected the locations of all of our metro areas.

Many people who have studied the rate of suburban conversion relative to land prices feel that current land values have, to a large extent, already anticipated

---

EXHIBIT 24–1

EXAMPLE 1

Assumptions

You buy a "promising" parcel of raw land (gross original price)	$10,000
Your holding costs will be real estate taxes and insurance (per year)	$200
Your minimum acceptable rate of return is 6%	

1. 72/6.0 = 12 years to achieve 6% = $20,000 required (rounded)
2. Plus: accumulation of the $200-per-year holding costs at 6% per year = $ 3,277.11
3. Transaction costs at time of sale, say, 10% commission + legal costs of 1% (.11 × 23,000) = $ 2,560.48

To achieve your rate of return you must sell, at the end of the twelfth year, for no less than $25,837.60

Warning: You have made no provision for the effect of inflation on your principal. Therefore, if the annual rate of inflation exceeded your 6 percent rate of return you have actually lost money.

EXAMPLE 2

Assumptions

The same gross original price for land	$10,000
The same holding costs per year	$200
Change the rate of return required to 12%	

1. 72/12 = 6 years to achieve 12% = $20,000 required (rounded)
2. Plus: accumulation of the $200-per-year holding costs at 12% per year (8.115189* × $200) = $ 1,623.04
3. Transaction costs at 11% = $ 2,310.59

To achieve your rate of return of 12% you must sell, at the end of the sixth year, for no less than $23,315.93

Warning: Again, if the annual rate of inflation exceeds 1 percent, the rate of return diminishes pro rata; in effect, at an inflation rate of 12 percent you would achieve a 0 percent rate of return but your principal would remain intact.

(*continues*)

EXHIBIT 24-1 *(Continued)*

EXAMPLE 3

Assumptions

The same gross original price for land	$10,000
The same holding costs per year	$200
Change the rate of return required to 19%	

To provide a real rate of return of, say, 8 percent based on your subjective opinion of the investment, you must add an inflation premium of, say, 11 percent per annum.

1. 19%/72 = 3.789 years (we will round to 4.0) to
   achieve approximately 19%   = $20,000 required (rounded)
2. Accumulation of the $200-per-year holding
   costs at 19% = 5.291259* × $200   = $ 1,058.25
3. Transaction costs at 11%   = $ 2,316.41

To achieve your rate of return of 19% you must sell,
at the end of the fourth year, for no less than $23,374.67

---

* See Appendix B.

the next possible use, given the holding costs and the current discount rates.[2] Thus, opportunities for the above-average returns required by land speculation are unlikely to occur in most SMSAs in the near future—with the following qualified exceptions:

1. Speculators will continue to make large gains when they guess right on changes in zoning, master plans, and other government controls, and buy before the transition is generally known.
2. High profits will be realized by those who benefit from the "windfall" of improved highway access, mass transit, airport facilities, and rail and sea terminals. Caution: Sharp increases in the value of privately owned land tend to occur only for parcels that are very close to these uses and their corridors. Values drop sharply as one moves away from the immediate vicinity.
3. Speculative gains will be obtained by those who can anticipate the effects of the actions of OPEC and other commodity cartels on essential minerals, foods, and fossil fuels. For example, the oil shales of Colorado and the tar flats of Alberta, Canda, have been traded back and forth for years. When the time is right for actual development because the world price of oil has risen enough to justify the costs of extracting shale oil, the owner who is holding such land will probably make a large gain.
4. Speculators will perform a useful function by "taking out" landholders who are holding parcels that have been passed over by urban growth. The

---

[2] See Marion Clawson, *Suburban Land Conversion in the United States* (Baltimore: Johns Hopkins Press, 1971); *Real Estate Reports* (issued monthly) (Chicago: Real Estate Research Corporation), *The Wall Street Journal,* various articles.

current holder will need to cash out for some reason. The speculator will believe that the metro area will be ready to back-fill the site with an appropriate use in three to five years.

5. Speculators will obtain high returns when they can anticipate that a metro area has grown to the point at which it is ready to break through to more intensive land uses than it has supported in the past, *and* the speculator can forecast the most likely locations for those uses.

6. Population and employment will continue to have a heavy impact on some land values. In the United States we have seacoast, skiing areas, oil–gas lease land, crossover points of interstate highways, and other locations where speculative activity is appropriate because it is difficult to guess *when* the next most probable use will in fact take place. The demand for beach and lakefront uses will increase as more people compete to gain control of this desirable amenity. Caution is needed, however. One must be greatly concerned about travel time from metro areas to such recreational sites. There are beautiful seacoast areas in the United States that are simply not convenient to enough people to warrant sharp increases in land value in the short term. Hilton Head, South Carolina, was an example of such premature development. The capture rate was based on travel times and trip costs that did not anticipate the 55 mph speed limit and the rising cost of gasoline.

ADVANTAGES AND DISADVANTAGES OF INVESTING IN LAND

Investing in raw land may offer a higher potential for gain than investing in income property. Through the use of options and/or low down payments with purchase money mortgages or installment land contracts on favorable terms, the investor can gain control of the property at a relatively low cost. Some land investors couple this lower capital requirement with diversification of location to minimize market risk. They buy scattered sites in the area or systematically buy alternate parcels to achieve a checkerboard effect, in the hope that their "holdout negotiating power" over the next buyer will enable them to get a premium price. As long as investor status can be maintained, there is also the advantage of classifying profits as capital gain rather than ordinary income.

The problem of dealer status is very real for a regular trader in land. It is expected that as IRS auditors become more sophisticated, in part by way of computer searches of past income tax returns, more and more investors will suffer the penalty of being assigned dealer status in real estate.

There are other risks, too:

1. Throughout the ownership period there are cash outlays for real estate taxes, liability insurance, and property maintenance (removing weeds, preventing unattractive nuisances); mortgage principal and interest payments; and site improvement programs to create interest and promote sale.

2. Inflationary effects on price levels may or may not work to your advantage, depending on your mortgage/equity ratio and the rate of gain in value relative to the inflation rate.

3. Mortgage contract terms usually require loss of all equity in the event of default. Exercise of the equity of redemption, if available, is unlikely.

4. Lack of liquidity is pronounced with raw land and other rural properties.

5. The uncertainty of timing makes financial analysis quite problematical. If the market doesn't develop as expected, the time value of money, inflationary effects on the dollar, and additional cash outlays for carrying costs will quickly reduce the rate of return unless prices increase faster than expected.
6. Increasing public scrutiny makes the political, legal, and physical risks of land development greater than in the past.
7. The investment interest limitation applies to most land investment debts. It is difficult to classify land investments as a trade or business unless one is growing Christmas trees, or operating a driving range, farm, or ranch. In effect, an investment with no interim business use will encounter the problems of tax preference and minimum tax if investment interest from all such investments is equal to $10,000 or more per year.

TYPES OF INVESTORS AND INVESTOR MOTIVATIONS

Most investors lack the risk-taking aggressiveness, liquidity, and ability to handle uncertainty that land investment requires. As a general rule, land investing is for people who have already accumulated wealth. For the wealthy, under current tax laws, buying land as an investment for future generations makes sense. Of course, land speculation on a small scale in an overall plan may be a justifiable strategy, especially when one considers the current rate of inflation relative to typical rates of return from other investment forms.

Recently, another kind of land investor has come into the market. Large-scale developers cannot afford to have their borrowing capacity or working capital tied up in banking land at the current cost of money. On the other hand, they need to have the land inventory in "friendly hands" in order to do rational production scheduling. As a result, both individual and institutional investors are forming joint ventures with established developers to hold the property for the developer, who acts as a captive market. This niche in the market may open up to land syndications as the practice spreads to smaller, stable, well-capitalized developers.

MARKET AND MARKETABILITY ANALYSIS

Supply and Demand Analysis. A successful investor in land is an expert on the patterns of growth and land uses in the metro areas in which he or she is active. This knowledge makes it possible to forecast the next possible use for selected vacant parcels of real estate. The investor's task is to find *nodes* of activity just before they actually occur. This involves conducting market segmentation and geographic-zone analysis in an effort to find underpriced land that has the possibility of being developed within a relatively short time. An example is the general shift in the location of auto dealers during the past few decades away from the central business districts to the perimeter highways. Another example is the Hallmark Center in Kansas City. This successful office/retail/condominium was built about twelve blocks away from the older central business district. The area between is deteriorated, with mixed low-intensity uses. Eventually a higher-intensity corridor will create a dumbbell-shaped layout in which the central business district and Hallmark Center will be merged. The question for the investor is when. It is axiomatic that for a land buyer market analysis is a predevelopment decision process similar to that which a developer carries out when the right time for construction is some years away. Ideally, the investor will identify a use in search of a site and the site will be the targeted investment.

Experience indicates that speculators seldom do market sector and/or geographic-zone analysis in order to discover a site for a specific use. Instead, they monitor overall growth trends and respond to offers from the network of brokers and owners with whom they have working relationships. They then do an analysis of the offered site. We believe that better opportunities are produced by making systematic analyses and then seeking to buy a site that is well situated to satisfy the demand.

Holding Costs During the Land Ownership Period. During the market analysis stage it is appropriate to project any interim income and to estimate the expenses and other capital outflows that are likely to occur during the ownership cycle. These estimates are based on the investor's experience or, in the case of an inexperienced investor, on advice from knowledgeable professionals.

Income analysis. Generally, no income is anticipated from raw land except by way of sale of the asset at the end of the ownership cycle. However, an effort should be made to identify any interim use that could provide some income to help defray the expenses that are certain to occur. Examples of such uses include produce and Christmas tree stands, miniature golf courses, drive-in theaters, auction barns, nurseries, storage for builders' supplies and many more. Be imaginative! Think of a temporary use that is easily removed, and offer an attractive rent on a short-term lease. Keep in mind that renting the land may aid in protecting your investor, as opposed to dealer, status.

Expense analysis. This is an exercise in the estimation of annual cash outlays. Their nature and amount will vary from year to year, but projection is necessary in order to avoid surprises and unexpected invasions of liquidity reserves. Great care should be taken to estimate the probable length of the holding period.

Debt service costs. Of course, principal reduction is not a true cost, but our function here is to estimate cash outlays. Interest and principal reduction payments, if required, should be based on locally prevailing rates or the likely financing arrangements.

Real estate taxes. What are they now and what increases should be anticipated? How frequently does reassessment occur in the area? Will purchase by the investor, when recorded, trigger a much higher assessment? Are there any problems in the jurisdiction's municipal financing that might trigger a sharp increase? If one seeks a zoning change, will it result in a reassessment?

Additional assessments. Occasionally assessments for such items as new water and/or sewage lines can require large outlays. Local assessment authorities might accept installment payments. Persuading a utility company to move an easement that bisects a parcel to its boundaries may result in a sharp increase in value.

Site improvements. Often activity on a vacant parcel stimulates interest in it. Grading, planting, or demolition of existing improvements may be part of your program to make the land ready for the next user. The costs of such work should be estimated prior to purchase. It is an expense to be capitalized and must be anticipated.

Legal and engineering expenditures. Sometimes these are the key to producing a change in use. Obtaining a zoning change and surveying and platting are among the many things that might be done.

Contingency fund. A contingency fund is an essential in land investing.

RISK MANAGEMENT AND CONTROL TECHNIQUES

A good way to be a loser in land investment is to pay a little too much, slightly underestimate your holding costs per year, hold a year or two longer than expected, and sell for a bit less than you had anticipated. The investor must complete a thorough decision process by which the amount of growth, the rate of growth, and the areas where such growth is most likely to occur are identified. Assuming that one has identified several alternative parcels within a geographic zone—say, A, B, C, D, and E—there are techniques that will tend to minimize risk:

• *The checkerboard technique.* Instead of buying only C, buy A, C, and E.
• *The parimutuel technique.* Join with other speculators and buy fractional shares in C.
• *Combine the checkerboard and parimutuel techniques.* Join with other speculators in buying fractional shares in sites in a checkerboard pattern.

Of course, there are many variations on these techniques. Suppose analysis indicates that the next possible use may leapfrog to *one* of several submarkets in different neighborhoods. There are now a number of possible sites in each of several neighborhoods:

I—A, B, C, D, and E
II—F, G, and H
III—I, J, K, and L

The risk management strategy would be as follows:

Alternative 1: Buy I-C, II-H, and III-L.
Alternative 2: Join with other speculators in buying a checkerboard in each of the three areas.

Finally, in recent years some land traders have set up syndications in which they lay off the risk by acting as general partners for a number of separate syndications.

There is another way for risk-averse land investors to use reinsurance or the lay-off maneuver. When a land investment doesn't mature as rapidly as expected, it presents both time-value-of-money and liquidity problems. In such cases investors should consider selling off fractional interests. This both minimizes the opportunity for gain and loss and, more important, frees capital for another investment opportunity. Interestingly, the reinsurance tactic should be attractive to the buyer because his or her time horizon for the profitable sale of the land is shorter than that of the original investor. Thus, the buyer should realize higher returns.

Finally, negotiations should take into consideration the effect of time on price. The further into the future one expects the next probable use to occur, the more aggressive one must be in negotiations because of the time value of money and the uncertain timing of the resale.

PHYSICAL, LEGAL, POLITICAL, AND ENVIRONMENTAL ANALYSIS

Generally, the physical, legal, political, and environmental site analysis proceeds along the same lines as any conventional predevelopment site analysis *after* a proposed use has been appropriately identified by means of market analysis.

Physical Analysis—Site and Improvements. Physical factors are critical when evaluating the future potential of undeveloped land. The task is to match the existing and potential site conditions to projected needs. Access to municipal services, utilities, and transportation; subsoil conditions; and parcel size are of particular importance.

The capacity of and access to off-site improvements such as railroads, highways, utilities, and urban transportation should be adequate. Although there may be a railroad at the site, it may be scheduled to be abandoned next year. Conversely, it is possible that the urban transportation company might be persuaded to provide more frequent service than is currently scheduled. An otherwise attractive site may have been passed over by other investors because sanitary sewers are not available and the soil type does not permit adequate septic tanks. The water supply may be from an artesian well, and its future capacity may be questionable.

On-site conditions should be carefully evaluated by actual field inspection. Engineering studies may be essential. Is the topography appropriate for the projected use? What are the bearing characteristics of the subsoil? Are conditions so rocky as to make excavation expensive? Will the seller warrant the legal descriptions and boundaries? Is the site in a flood plain? Are there marshy areas, clay, or sand? It is possible that the present owner hasn't envisioned a change in the site that earth-moving equipment could produce by filling or recontouring.

Legal Considerations. Legal considerations constitute both opportunities and pitfalls for land speculators. Land traders know that it isn't enough to make a thorough investigation of the public record for easements, liens, zoning regulations, buildings code violations, unpaid taxes, mineral rights, and the like. One must inspect the site for unrecorded easements, encroachments, adverse possession, and other rights held by adjoining landowners, utilities, and the public. Certainly, one must make a careful analysis of the present state of land use controls. Requirements for open space, setback, building height, and so forth may be the reason that the parcel hasn't been developed according to its highest and best use. Recently a would-be buyer found that an otherwise attractive parcel had an unrecorded easement for an approach to an airport 2.5 miles away that limited building height to a range of 4–16 feet. The owner had failed to disclose that a few months earlier he had received a letter notifying him that the FAA would impose the easement in the near future. The only record of the intended easement that was available to the would-be investor was in the FAA regional office 150 miles away.

Political Factors. Political uncertainty as it affects land use may be one reason why real estate investment is more of an art than a science. Who makes the zoning and other land use control decisions in the jurisdiction? What are the prevailing attitudes toward development? Even in a "no-zoning" city like Houston there are powerful lenders and other influential groups who have much to say about the types of land use that are acceptable. The master plan may be ignored in one metro area while in another area planning and consumer groups may be ready to do battle whenever uses contrary to the master plan are proposed.

Rahenkamp and associates have provided a methodology by which one may predict the chances of getting approval of a zoning change.[3] Their assimilation capacity model moves from present zoning status through a number of decision matrices that consider the income level of the community, the ratio of existing to projected population in the area, the community's growth rate, the rate of political turnover, the size of the community's bureaucracy, and so forth, and provides a formula that enables one to calculate the probability of approval. The model also provides a way of measuring how long it may take to achieve legal approval of the proposed change.

Environmental Quality. Environmental quality is a prime concern of the public. Land investors make money on changes in the use of land. Removal of trees and other vegetation may destroy wildlife habitats. The new use may affect air or water quality in an adverse way (in a built-up area where buildings are being demolished, it might be argued that air or water quality is being improved).

The land investor must be environmentally sensitive. In fact, he or she should be well informed about which locations within the metro area are "officially" sensitive and avoid purchasing in those zones. Environmental-impact studies are quite expensive, and the delays they cause can substantially diminish the rate of return. Just as important, a land investor needs a good reputation with land regulators and leaders of environmentalist groups. The bad publicity and hostile feelings that can result from challenging groups that are seeking to preserve natural resources may have a negative effect on future requests for change.

FINANCING

The nature of raw land does not make it attractive to institutional lenders. Raw land generates no interim income. It is difficult to appraise because its potential use is, as a matter of routine, ignored by financial institutions as being too speculative.

Some land investors may be able to obtain funds from institutional investors if they have adequate liquidity reserves, good financial ratios, and substantial net worth, all of which must be pledged to secure the loan.

Although savings and loan associations are generally required by their charters and regulations to lend only on residential and improved income properties, they have some limited discretion to make land loans. Usually they limit such lending to land banking for well-capitalized customers seeking short-term inventory for forward planning of subdivisions. The Federal Land Bank makes loans on

---

[3] The Assimilation Capacity Model was developed by John Rahenkamp, Kathleen McLeister, and Robert Ditmer for the firm of Rahenkamp, Sachs, and Wells, Philadelphia; for reports on the models see *House and Home,* August 1972 and August 1976.

farmland. Therefore, if a land investor intends to continue a productive farm as an interim use, he or she may be able to get such a loan.

Commercial banks, particularly smaller country banks, may make land loans for periods of less than five years if the investor is willing to pledge personal credit as additional security. A no-recourse loan from a bank is unlikely.

Life insurance companies generally limit their land loans to farms and short-term land development loans that provide them with important lending opportunities for large-scale real estate development projects. Land investors per se are of little interest to them. On the other hand, a developer who is going to produce a large-scale property will be of interest to them if he or she has a well-established record. Recently life insurance companies have been interested in some joint ventures and other forms of direct participation.

Owner financing is usually the key to financial leverage in land investing. Sellers whose property has appreciated significantly in value will often provide financing in order to facilitate a sale. Indeed, if a seller insists on cash, it is usually a signal to sophisticated land investors that negotiations should produce a much lower price than the prices of comparable parcels. Creative financing techniques are common in land investing.

In theory, options provide the land investor with the greatest leverage and flexibility. However, to minimize the possibility of forfeiture, a sufficient time must be allowed to "ripen" the next use. Also, the investor must demand specific performance of deed transfer from the grantor. Optioning a parcel with an ironclad enforceable right to buy provides time to effectuate zoning changes, obtain institutional financing, and check environmental problems. However, it may also give the seller the power to bargain for unfair concessions after the land investor has diligently worked to bring about the necessary changes.

Installment land sale contracts provide the advantage of high leverage. However, the seller retains title until the final payment has been made. Thus, if the land investor defaults, the seller keeps all payments to date and is not required to foreclose but may simply repossess or use ejectment proceedings.

Land investors often prefer purchase money mortgages because they can obtain title as well as possession, can make improvements, and are in a position to negotiate with the seller in the event of financial difficulty because of their debtor's rights in foreclosure. Further, they can use balloon payments, interest-only loans, wraparounds, and other devices to increase leverage and minimize the burden of cash outlays during the holding period. High-leverage investors seek interest-only loans for three to five years with the goal of selling before the principal payments start.[4] Low-leverage investors, who are typically long-term landholders, often prefer to make a substantial down payment and start amortizing the loan immediately. Exculpatory clauses (nonrecourse loans) are commonly negotiated.

The financial arrangements are a crucial part of the risk profile of a land investment. They affect the holding costs and may have an effect on resale opportunities. Since it is more difficult to make financial arrangements in land than in income-producing properties, it is important to work with the seller's broker. Realtors who are members of the National Institute of Farm and Land Brokers of the National Association of Realtors are among the best qualified.

Some brokers have seen the risk management advantages of syndication for

[4] Jack Friedman, "How to Value Variable Payment Mortgages," *Real Estate Review,* Fall, 1975, 92–96.

the land investors who are working with them. Although purchase of a fractional interest will lower the dollar return on a successful land deal, it also spreads the risk and enables the investor to buy into more locations.

TAXATION AND TAX STRUCTURE

A prime attraction of land investment is that the payments made to hold the land are largely tax deductible, since they generally consist of real estate taxes, operating expenses, and interest. Of course, substantial improvements may have to be capitalized, and legal expenses, engineering services, surveying, and the like are generally considered to be capital expenditures.

Another problem is the investment interest limitation, which is applicable to most land investments.[5] Under the Economic Recovery Tax Act of 1981 the deductibility of interest from passive investment has been limited to an amount equal to $10,000 plus net investment income. No offset of investment interest against the long-term capital gain preference is permitted. Suffice it to say, holding land is much less attractive to an investor if there is a significant limitation on deductibility of interest. Keep in mind that calculation of the investment interest is cumulative within a tax year, in that one sums investment interest from all sources except personal residence interest and interest expenses on trade or business investments. There are carryover rights.[6] (See also Chapter 13.)

Another serious problem for land traders is the IRS position on dealer versus investor status for land traders. We discuss this important problem in Chapter 13. In brief, a real estate trader may preserve the right to a capital gain provided that he or she can prove that a particular parcel was bought primarily for investment purposes. Difficulties with the IRS arise when there are frequent sales, fast turnover, and prompt reinvestment of the proceeds into other properties. Exchanging is an ideal way of avoiding the dealer taint because there is no realization of gain. Of course, if one *is* classified as a dealer, income from the land deal is treated as ordinary income. It is expected that during the 1980s the IRS will become more aggressive in this area.

DISCOUNTED CASH FLOW ANALYSIS

A land investor deals in a simple future expectancy. Projected return is realized only if the land appreciates in price to produce the specified rate of return. The sole inflow for the land investor is what will be received as the net cash proceeds after selling the property. The significance of the rate of appreciation as it affects the target rate of return is best illustrated by the following example.[6]

The Anatomy of a Land Deal

Consider the Recreation Lakes Investment Properties, Ltd. offering (a limited partnership offering), which was publicly registered with the California Department of Corporations in 1970 and involved an

---

[5] IRS Sec. 93; see also Coopers Lybrand, *Tax Planning for Real Estate Transactions* (Chicago: National Association of Realtors, Institute of Farm and Land Brokers, 1978), pp. 92–95.
[6] See Stephen E. Roulac, "Anatomy of a Land Deal," *Real Estate Review,* Winter 1975, pp. 93–96, for a more complete exposition of this example. We gratefully acknowledge permission to use this material.

investment of $1,024,000 to acquire six parcels consisting of approximately 13,715 acres.

The proceeds of the $1,024,000 offering were used as follows:

Cash down payment	$540,000
Prepaid interest	450,300
Organization costs	33,700

The $4,340,000 total purchase price for the six parcels was financed by the $540,000 down payment and all-inclusive deeds of trust in the aggregate sum of $3,800,000 with interest at 7.9 percent. The note payment schedule called for interest-only payments from the close of escrow in 1970 through 1980.

The summary of the after-tax cost of the investment, as presented in the offering document, appears as Exhibit 24–2. The income (column 4) is derived from renting out certain existing structures on the land, as well as from "use rights" for fishing, hunting, and so forth. The depreciation deductions (column 5) relate to these structures, as well as to fencing and other improvements. It should be noted that the first-year after-tax cost of $765,150 is understated by $33,700, the amount of the initial organization cost.

For purposes of our analysis, it will be assumed that

- the property is sold in 1975.
- the investor seeks a 10 percent after-tax internal rate of return.
- the investor is in the 62 percent effective tax bracket.

EXHIBIT 24–2. Summary of After-Tax Cost of Investment

Year	(1) Principal	(2) Interest	(3) Taxes	(4) Income	(5) Depreciation
1970	$540,000	$450,300	—	—	—
1971		300,200	$17,000	$50,200	$33,195
1972		300,200	17,000	50,200	33,195
1973		300,200	17,000	50,200	33,195
1974		300,200	17,000	50,200	33,195
1975		300,200	17,000	50,200	33,195

Year	(6) (= 1 + 2 + 3 − 4) Net Dollars Invested	(7) (= 2 + 3 + 5 − 4) Tax Deductions	(8) (= 50% of 7) Tax Savings	(9) (= 6 − 8) After-Tax Cost
1970	$990,300	$450,300	$225,150	$765,150
1971	267,000	300,195	150,097	116,903
1972	267,000	300,195	150,097	116,903
1973	267,000	300,195	150,097	116,903
1974	267,000	300,195	150,097	116,903
1975	267,000	300,195	150,097	116,903

SOURCE: Stephen E. Roulac, "Anatomy of a Land Deal," *Real Estate Review*, Winter 1975, p. 95.

EXHIBIT 24-3. Discounted Costs of Holding Land

Year	After-Tax Cost	10 Percent Discount Factor	Present Cost
1970	$798,850[a]	1.000	$ 798,850
1971	116,903	.909	106,265
1972	116,903	.826	96,562
1973	116,903	.751	87,794
1974	116,903	.683	79,841
1975	116,903	.621	72,597
			$1,241,909

SOURCE: Stephen E. Roulac, "Anatomy of a Land Deal,"
Real Estate Review, Winter 1975, p. 95.
[a] $765,150 + $33,700 (initial organization cost) = $798,540.

The investor's initial contribution, as well as his subsequent contributions, will all be outflows. The calculations in Exhibit 24–3 show how the 1970 cost of the payments to hold the property for the years 1970–1975 (from Exhibit 24–2) are derived. It can be seen that the present cost (discounted at 10 percent) of the payments required to hold the property through 1975 is $1,241,909. The proceeds of sale, of course, will not be realized until 1975. Therefore, to compare the sales proceeds with the total cost expressed in 1970 dollars, it is necessary to discount the 1975 proceeds to 1970 value. Thus, for a 10 percent internal rate of return to be realized, the property must be sold in 1975 for a price that, when discounted at 10 percent for *five* years, is equal to $1,241,909. This price is calculated by dividing the needed "discounted value" of $1,241,909 by 0.621; the indicated "cash proceeds after taxes" is $1,999,853.

It should be emphasized that the $1,999,853 that the investors must receive in 1975 is the remainder after the costs of the sale (specifically, brokerage commissions), the outstanding indebtedness on the note, and capital gains taxes.

Computing the sales price to achieve target rate of return. The sales price may be broken down into the following components:

a. Transactions costs equal to 6 percent of sales price.
b. Tax liability.
c. Mortgage balance (in this case, $3.8 million).
d. Any remaining proceeds (in this case, we require after-tax cash proceeds of $1,999,853).

If we call the sales price X and tax liability Y, we may write an equation:

$$X = \underset{\text{(a)}}{.06X} + \underset{\text{(b)}}{Y} + \underset{\text{(c)}}{\$3,800,000} + \underset{\text{(d)}}{\$1,999,853}$$

This simplifies to

$$.94X = Y + \$5,799,853$$

To solve this equation we must determine the value of Y. Since we have assumed a 62 percent tax bracket, the appropriate tax rate on the gain is 25 percent. Thus, Y, the unknown tax liability, will be about 25 percent of the capital gain. The capital gain is the difference between the net selling price of 0.94X (as determined earlier) and the tax basis. The tax basis is computed as follows:

Purchase price	$4,340,000
Organization costs	33,700
Less: Depreciation (from Exhibit 24 – 2, column 5)	165,975
Tax basis	$4,207,725

Now, since the tax basis is known, it is possible to determine the capital gain:

Net selling price − tax basis = $.94X - \$4,207,725$
Capital gain tax liability @ 25% = $.25\ (94X - \$4,207,725)$
$= .23X - \$1,051,931$

With the value of Y expressed in terms of X, it is possible to substitute this amount for Y in our equation:

$$.94X = Y + \$5,799,853$$

The following is elementary algebraic manipulation:

$$.94X = .235X - 1,051,931 + 5,799,853$$
$$.94X = .235X + 4,747,922$$
$$.705X = 4,747,922$$
$$X = 6,734,641$$

Thus, an investor seeking a *10 percent internal rate of return on the venture in our example must anticipate the property will be sold for 155 percent more than the purchase price at the end of five years.* This represents an 11 percent simple annual rate of appreciation, or a 9.2 percent compounded rate.

Conclusion. While each land investment situation must be evaluated in terms of its unique financial and tax characteristics, the analysis illustrates the substantial rate of appreciation required to achieve merely a normal return. A very large return will require much more dramatic price increases. Indeed, the advice of the Red Queen to Alice is particularly apt as a basic principle of land speculation: "You must run as fast as you can just to stay in the same place. If you want to get ahead, you must run at least twice as fast."

Selected References

Benjamin, Gary L. "Can the Boom in Farmland Values be Sustained." *Real Estate Review,* Winter 1978, pp. 60– 63.

Case, Fred E. *The Investment Guide to Home and Land Purchase.* Englewood Cliffs, N.J.: Prentice-Hall, 1977.

Copp, Dana D. "Selling the Large Landholding." *Real Estate Review,* Summer 1975, pp. 46– 49.

Council on Environmental Quality, *The Costs of Sprawl.* Washington, D.C., 1974.

Friedman, Jack P. "Tax-Sheltering Opportunities in Real Estate Investments." *Atlanta Economic Review,* January-February 1973, pp. 19– 21.

Hubbard, Elbert W. "A Commentary on Site Selection: Is Quality of Life a Criterion?" *Atlanta Economic Review,* March-April 1978, pp. 52– 53.

Hubbard, Elbert, and Adriane Hubbard. "Taxing Land Value Gains to Public Land Banks." *Atlanta Economic Review,* November-December 1974, pp. 25– 27.

"Investing in Raw Land," Portfolio no. 3. In Warren, Gorham & Lamont, *Real Estate Review Portfolios.* Boston, 1974.

Kern, James A. "The Art of Buying Land." *Real Estate Review,* Winter 1974, pp. 38– 41.

Kirk, John E. *How To Build a Fortune Investing in Land.* Englewood Cliffs, N.J.: Prentice-Hall, 1973.

Miles, Mike. "Impact of the 1976 Tax Reform Act: A Real Property Tax Planner's Review." *The Appraisal Journal,* October 1977, pp. 485– 498.

Paulson, Morton C. *The Great Land Hustle.* Chicago: Henry Regnery, 1972.

Price, Irving. "Buying Country Property—Caveat Emptor!" *Real Estate Review,* Winter· 1972, pp. 62– 64.

"The Real Estate Analyst." *Real Estate Review,* Winter 1975, pp. 16– 18.

Seldin, Maury. *Land Investment.* Homewood, Ill.: Dow Jones-Irwin, 1975.

Sverdlik, Jerome S. "How to Buy Raw Land." *Real Estate Review,* Winter 1973, pp. 28– 33.

Thau, William A. "Turning Raw Land into Pay Dirt." *Real Estate Review,* Summer 1972, pp. 73– 83.

V

Portfolio Strategy and Investment Outlook

BUY		?	Utilities	?			SELL
Gold				Memora-bilia			?
	Blue-chip Stock	?	Cash		Fine Art		Oil Drilling
		Stamps	Industrial park / Shopping center / Apartments / Land / Hotel / Motel / Office building		?	Bonds	
?	T-Bills						Auto-graphs
Cattle Feeding		Silver	?			Mort-gages	
		Cable TV			CDs	?	Rare Coins
HOLD	?	Mutual Fund		Antiques			ACCUMU-LATE

The final section of this book is devoted to three important and emerging topics of interest: (1) institutional real estate portfolios, (2) developing a personal portfolio with real estate, and (3) the investment outlook.

Chapter 25 presents an overview of modern portfolio theory, its application to real estate investing, and its impact on large institutional real estate funds—pension funds, REITs, and public limited partnerships. Chapter 26 examines portfolio problems from the viewpoint of the individual who is seeking to accumulate wealth over his or her lifetime. Both of these topics often receive scant attention in most investment texts, possibly because there has been little academic research on the subjects and a lack of data on the performance of real estate portfolios.

Chapter 27 on the real estate investment outlook is the final chapter of the book. It presents our opinions on the inflation and market outlook, and our expectations for specific property types through the mid-1980s. Investors are urged to develop scenario planning techniques as a means of dealing with increasing levels of uncertainty, and to further their investment education through the use of case studies and computer applications.

Institutional Real Estate Portfolios*

INTRODUCTION

The emergence of the real estate investment trust, the enactment of the Employees Retirement Income Securities Act, and recent changes in general economic conditions have changed the focus of real estate investment. The change has been to concentrate less on the evaluation of individual real estate projects and more on the portfolio impact of real estate investment. The portfolio approach emphasizes the synergistic effects of a single investment on the total package of assets held by the investor. Before exploring further the concept of portfolio decision making, we will briefly examine how REITs, ERISA, and the changing economic climate have brought about this shift in investor attitudes.

Real Estate Investment Trusts

REITs were organized under a 1961 revision of the Internal Revenue Service code.[1] Originally they were authorized to provide a "real estate mutual fund" for small investors. The early REITs invested in real estate equities and provided their

[1] Public Law 86-779, which revised the Internal Revenue Service Code by adding Sections 856, 857, and 858 to include real estate investment trusts. For a good history of the REIT see Kenneth Campbell, *Real Estate Investment Trusts: America's Newest Billionaires* (New York: Audit Investment Research, 1971).

* Special thanks are due to Steven D. Kapplin, College of Business, University of South Florida, Tampa, who was the primary author of this chapter.

shareholders with higher-than-average dividend yields but lower appreciation potential. In the late 1960s REITs began to diversify into long-term mortgages, wraparound mortgages, sale/leasebacks, and construction loans. Through the increased use of debt, REITs grew substantially, offering shareholders high dividend yields and appreciation. When the REIT bubble burst in 1975, the industry had grown from $2.0 to $21.0 billion in five years.[2]

The equity REITs (EREITs), which invested almost exclusively in property ownership, with only a small proportion of assets allocated to mortgages, fared exceptionally well through the recession years. Many of the EREITs, such as General Growth, Real Estate Investment Trust of America, and Hubbard, continued to pay dividends throughout the recession. However, the mortgage REITs, especially short-term mortgage trusts (construction and development or C&D trusts), lacked the necessary diversification of assets and were seriously hurt when developers were forced to terminate projects prior to completion and defaulted on their construction loans.

Two important lessons can be learned from the REIT experience. First, real estate portfolios are not only practicable but even desirable commodities, as is evidenced by the relatively successful performance of EREITs. Second, real estate securities are not necessarily valued by the securities markets in the same way that real estate assets are valued by the real estate markets. The REIT experience has placed a new emphasis on the need for sophisticated project analysis and the need to evaluate project acquisition in terms of the entire portfolio, not simply at the project level.

The Employee Retirement Income Security Act (ERISA)

ERISA was enacted in 1974 as a sort of "centralization of regulation" of the management of pension funds. It directed pension fund managers to diversify investments in order to minimize the risk of large losses. Prior to ERISA very few pension funds had significant real estate holdings. The requirement of full diversification has been a major spur to the pension fund industry, which has expanded its holdings of real estate from less than 1 percent of assets to between 3 and 5 percent of assets since 1974.[3] Because federal regulation permits such funds to invest up to 10 percent of their assets in real estate, most funds are actively pursuing investment policies with that objective. During the recent period of high interest rates—substantially higher than at any time in the past—many funds suspended investments in all media save real estate.

Pension fund investing has brought a higher level of sophistication to the real estate business and a strong sense of competition for quality projects. The demand for investment-grade real estate of sufficient magnitude (large funds have minimum investment limits of around $1 million per project) continues to increase the need for sophisticated project analysis and for the development of methods for rapid evaluation and selection of suitable projects. As these funds approach their

---

[2] *REIT Fact Book, 1978* (Washington, D.C.: National Association of Real Estate Investment Trusts, 1978.)
[3] *Life Insurance Fact Book, 1977* (Washington, D.C.: American Council of Life Insurance, 1977).

statutory investment limit, the importance of a portfolio approach to solving the investment analysis and selection problems will increase.

Recent Changes in Economic Conditions

Since 1974 the U.S. economy has been through a topsy-turvy period of recession, increasing inflation and unemployment, rising interest rates and tighter money, and increasing governmental regulation. Characterized as a "stagflation" economy, it brought a new "type" of investor to the real estate market—one who is more concerned with future appreciation and capital preservation than with cash flow and current income. Properties have been purchased with low or even negative current yields, and for which the mortgage constant is much greater than the "free and clear" yield. In many instances the prices paid seem out of line with those estimated using conventional appraisal techniques.

These factors, together with many others, have changed the focus of real estate investment. There is a growing interest in a "portfolio" approach that emphasizes sophisticated methods of project analysis and selection in a multiproperty context. The balance of this chapter will be devoted to examining the theory and techniques of a portfolio approach to real estate investment.

PORTFOLIO CHOICE

At the simplest level the portfolio approach is the theory that you shouldn't put all your eggs into one basket (although there is a contradictory theory—that you should put your eggs into one basket and watch the basket very closely!). In simple terms, diversification means purchasing many investments instead of one, or purchasing several smaller projects rather than one large one. This approach is often referred to as *naive diversification* and is essentially a "safety in numbers" concept. Naive diversification lacks a theoretical justification, and in 1952 Markowitz challenged that approach in an article that has become the classic work of modern portfolio theory.[4] Markowitz distinguished among naive diversification, safety in numbers, and *efficient* diversification. The essence of efficient diversification lies in the trade-off between investment returns and risks. Modern portfolio theory stresses a scientific approach to the selection of portfolio assets that produces an efficient combination of assets—one that maximizes investment returns for a given level of investment risk.

Markowitz argued that little could be done to reduce the inherent risk of any single project, but a portfolio or combination of properly selected assets could be devised in which *portfolio* risk could, theoretically, be eliminated. To fully comprehend the impact of Markowitz's theory, it is important to understand, thoroughly, two elements: *expected* return and risk. Markowitz's theory is predicated on the proposition that all investors characterize their investment choices by two parameters—expected return and risk.

---

[4] Harry Markowitz, "Portfolio Selection," *Journal of Finance,* March 1952, pp. 77–91.

Definition of Expected Return and Risk   The expected return on investment, $E(R)$, is the most likely return where one is uncertain about the actual return the investment will produce. It is the *weighted average* of all possible returns, where the weights are the probabilities of occurrence.

As we observed in Chapter 12, risk may be defined in many ways: (1) as the probability of loss, (2) as the probability of not receiving what is expected, (3) as the difference (or potential variance) between expectation and realization, (4) as the possible variance of return relative to the expected or most likely return, and (5) as the chance, or probability, that the investor will not receive the expected or required rate of return. From a project viewpoint, it was argued that the best operational definition of risk is the last one. In contrast, the literature on portfolio theory and analysis has generally adopted the fourth definition—e.g., that risk is measured by the *variance of returns* (σ^2), or the standard deviation (σ) of possible returns about the expected return $E(R)$.[5]

Markowitz's theory of portfolio choice is based on the recognition that the returns on one asset are interrelated with those on other assets. The degree to which one asset's return varies with that of another asset is called *covariance*. Intuitively, one can see that if a decline in the return on one asset is offset by a rise in the return on another asset, the variance of the combination will be less than the variance of either asset held singly. This intuitive assumption is representative of efficient portfolio diversification. The combination of assets provides less risk in combination than when held singly. Efficient diversification, as opposed to naive diversification, can reduce or eliminate risk.

Covariance and Portfolio Characteristics   Covariance measures how one asset's return varies with that of another asset. Algebraically, covariance is found, in a two-asset case, by

$$\sigma_{ij} = \sigma P_{ij} \sigma_i \sigma_j \tag{1}$$

where σ_{ij} is the covariance
σ_i is the standard deviation for the ith investment
σ_j is the standard deviation for the jth investment
P_{ij} is the correlation coefficient

Calculating the covariance requires first calculating the standard deviations of each investment and then determining the correlation coefficient for the two investments. Correlation coefficients range from -1 to $+1$. A correlation coefficient of $+1$ means that the two assets are *perfectly positively* correlated—as investment A's return rises, investment B's return will also rise. A correlation

[5] For most portfolios models, the holding period return (HPR), IRR, or geometric mean return (GMR) are commonly used. As discussed in Chapter 11 some controversy exists concerning the "correct" measure of rate of return. For an excellent discussion of the IRR and FMRR, see Stephen Messner and M. Chapman Findlay, III, "Real Estate Investment Analysis: IRR versus FMRR," in *The Real Estate Appraiser*, July-August 1975, pp. 5–20. The use of HPR and GMR has received widespread attention in many portfolio texts, e.g., Harry Latane, Donald Tuttle, and Charles Jones, *Security Analysis and Portfolio Management* (New York: Ronald Press, 1975).

coefficient of -1 means that the two assets are *perfectly negatively* correlated; a rise in one investment's return will bring about a *decline* in the return of the other. A zero correlation means that the returns on the investments are not interdependent and a change in one will not cause a change in the other.

The portfolio's return and risk characteristics are a combination of the return, risk, and covariance of the assets based on the proportion of each asset held in the combination. The portfolio's expected return is the weighted average of the expected returns of all of the assets, where the weights are the proportion of each asset in the portfolio. Thus, for the two-asset case,

$$E(R_p) = W_A E(R_A) + W_B E(R_B) \qquad (2)$$

where $E(R_p)$ is the portfolio expected return

       $E(R_A), E(R_B)$ are the expected returns of assets A and B, respectively

       W_A, W_B are the proportions (for the two-asset case $W_A + W_B = 1.0$)

The portfolio's variance is defined as

$$\text{VAR}_p = W_A^2 \sigma_A^2 + W_B^2 \sigma_B^2 + 2 W_A W_B \sigma_{AB} \qquad (3)$$

where VAR_p is portfolio variance

       σ_{AB} is from equation 1, the covariance

       W_A, W_B are the proportions of assets A and B, respectively

A careful look at equations 2 and 3 will reveal that when the correlation coefficient is positive, the term $2 W_A W_B \sigma_{AB}$ in equation 6 will be positive and will add to the total variance of the portfolio combination. Where the correlation coefficient is zero, the last term drops off. Where the correlation coefficient is negative, this term becomes negative and *reduces* the total portfolio variance. Graphically, we can depict how the portfolio's $E(R_p)$ and VAR_p vary with changing proportions, W_A and W_B, for different assumptions about the correlation coefficient. Exhibit 25–1 depicts such relationships.

When the correlation coefficient is positive, the covariance will be positive. The portfolio combination becomes a linear combination of case A and B, as depicted by line AB in Exhibit 25–1. When the correlation coefficient is zero, then the covariance is zero and the portfolio combination is depicted as line ACB. It can be seen that a combination is found at point C which has a lower risk at a given level of return than a similar combination of positively correlated investments. Line ADB depicts the combinations in which the correlation coefficient is negative. Here it is seen that at D a combination exists that provides a positive $E(R_p)$ and a VAR_p of zero.

Exhibit 25–1 illustrates the importance of Markowitz's portfolio selection theory. By choosing negatively correlated assets the investor can design a portfolio that eliminates risk. Markowitz demonstrated that among all possible combi-

EXHIBIT 25-1.   Effects of Three Values of Correlation Coefficients on Portfolio Return and Variance

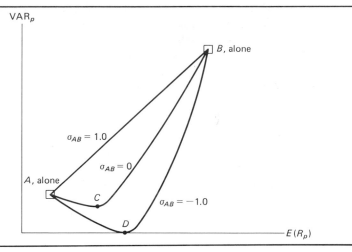

nations of risk and return only certain combinations are efficient, that is, maximize return for a given level of risk. Through efficient diversification, portfolios can be selected that include assets with low or negative covariances, thereby reducing the portfolio's overall risk, although the investor cannot affect the risk of any single project.[6]

Modern Portfolio Theory

In 1964 William F. Sharpe published his classic article, "Capital Asset Prices: A Theory of Market Equilibrium Under Conditions of Risk."[7] Sharpe provided an extension of Markowitz's portfolio theory to a general theory of market equilibrium. Sharpe theorized that inherent in the rate of return of an asset were two prices: the price of time and the price of risk. The price of time was awarded to all investors on the basis of the *maturity* of investments. The price of risk was the investor's premium for bearing the uncertainty associated with investments in capital. Sharpe proposed that risk entailed two aspects: market-related risk and business-related risk. Business-related risk is internal to the firm and reflects such elements as management, financial leverage, and production delays. Market risk refers to the impact of securities market activity on the prices of a firm's securities. In the Markowitz framework it is the covariance of a single security with the entire securities market.

Business-related risk, Sharpe argued, could be diversified away, as Markowitz demonstrated, by selecting securities with low or negative covariances. But some

[6] The illustration assumes only a two-asset portfolio problem. In the more general N-asset problem, the solution cannot be effected simply but requires computer assistance. Multiasset solutions are generally solvable using modern integer programming techniques.
[7] William Sharpe, "Capital Asset Prices: A Theory of Market Equilibrium Under Conditions of Risk," *Journal of Finance,* September 1964, pp. 425–442.

risk—market-related risk—would remain. In Sharpe's theory, therefore, only market-related risk was compensated for in the rate of return. Sharpe provided a method for evaluating market-related risk by measuring the covariance of an individual security with a "perfectly" diversified portfolio—the market portfolio.[8] The method is a two-asset portfolio analysis in which one asset is the individual security and the other is the perfectly diversified market portfolio. A measure of relative risk, called beta (β), is derived from this analysis. Beta quantifies the sensitivity of an individual security's return to the return of the market portfolio. Sharpe proved that the rate of return required for a risky security in equilibrium was a linear combination of the price of time, called the riskless rate, and a risk premium. The risk premium was the market portfolio's risk premium multiplied by the security's beta. Thus, the relationship between the required return on the security and the market portfolio return was a straight-line relationship, as is shown in Exhibit 25–2.

The line is called a characteristic line, and the security's beta (β) is the measure of the slope of the characteristic line. The equation that defines the line is of the form $Y = a + \beta X + e$, where Y is the required return on the risky security, X is the market portfolio's return, e is a random error term, with an expected value of zero, and a is the security's unique rate of return.

The importance of Markowitz and Sharpe's contributions to modern portfolio theory cannot be overstated. Modern theory considers that investor decisions (utility maximizing decisions) can be characterized essentially by two parameters: expected return and variance. Portfolio decisions are based on schemes that will maximize an investor's expected return at a given level of risk. That risk is com-

---

EXHIBIT 25–2.   The Characteristic Line for a Typical Security

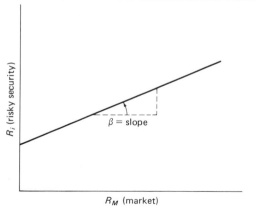

R_M (market)

---

[8] There has been some substantial criticism of the capital asset pricing theory that focuses on the market portfolio. For additional discussion see Stephen A. Ross, "The Current Status of the Capital Asset Pricing Model (CAPM)," *Journal of Finance*, June 1978, pp. 885–901, and Richard Roll, "A Critique of the Asset Pricing Theory's Tests: Part I: On Past and Potential Testability of the Theory," *Journal of Financial Economics*, March 1977, pp. 129–176.

posed of two elements: business-related risk (known as *unsystematic* risk) and market risk (called *systematic* risk). An asset's variance actually measures both risks. Because business or unsystematic risk may be eliminated through efficient diversification, *à la* Markowitz, only market risk is borne by the investor, and it is compensated for by additional return over the price of time (riskless rate of return), *à la* Sharpe. Market risk, an asset's beta coefficient, measures the amount of additional return required over the market return for risk taken. An investor may now select a portfolio that eliminates unsystematic risk through diversification and is equally tailored to provide maximum return for a given level of market or systematic risk.

The selection of an optimal portfolio is based on the individual investor's attitude toward risk and return. If all investors seek to maximize return for a given level of risk (or minimize risk at a given level of return), then selecting an optimal portfolio requires superimposing the investor's utility function on the curve that defines the set of all possible efficient portfolios (called the *efficient frontier*). The efficient frontier describes the set of efficiently diversified portfolios that provide maximum return at specified levels of risk. In Exhibit 25–1 the curve segment labeled *ACB* describes such a frontier for a two-asset portfolio. In general, the efficient frontier and total opportunity set may appear as illustrated in Exhibit 25–3. The segment labeled *ABCDEF* is the efficient frontier. All portfolios on this frontier dominate all other portfolios in the opportunity set in that they will provide either greater return at a given level of risk or less risk at a given level of return. The curves marked U_1, U_2, and U_3 are investor utility curves (called *isoquants*). By superimposing the investor's utility curves on the efficient frontier,

---

EXHIBIT 25–3.   Using Investor Utility Curves to Select an Optimal Portfolio from the Efficient Frontier

---

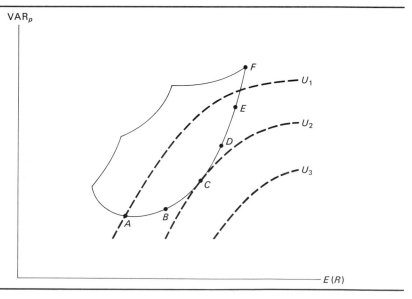

the investor may select a portfolio from the efficient set where one of his or her utility curves is tangent to the efficient frontier. This point, labeled C, is on utility curve U_2. By selecting that portfolio the investor can attain the level of utility defined by utility curve U_2.

REAL ESTATE INVESTING AND MODERN PORTFOLIO THEORY

The preceding discussion provides the background of modern portfolio theory, but the reader may have noticed that this theory has developed exclusively in the context of securities markets. There the assumptions of a "perfectly" diversified market portfolio and the efficiency of security markets are more acceptable. However, real estate markets are very different. They tend to be highly localized rather than national, so that information about transaction prices is lacking. Furthermore, there is a much lower incidence of transactions in real estate markets than in security markets. Real estate transfers are also usually characterized by complex financing structures, and often the participants lack the sophistication of securities traders. Despite these and numerous other contrasts, a growing interest has evolved in developing applications of modern portfolio theory to real estate investing. This interest has of course stemmed in part from the growing number of real estate portfolio investors—real estate investment trusts, pension funds, and large limited partnership offerings. Consequently, the informality that characterized real estate investment decision making in the past has given way to the sophistication of computerized project simulations that require the investor to "know" much more about projects and to make many more decisions than were required in the past.[9] As in the case of security investments, analyzing real estate investments in a portfolio context requires the ability to develop measures of expected returns and variances.

Developing Measures of Expected Return and Variance

Computer simulation models like the one presented in Chapter 12 permit an analyst to develop a sophisticated project analysis that can produce estimates of expected return and variance. Computer simulations of real estate projects typically follow one of two avenues. The model developed by Pyhrr and illustrated in Chapter 12 is based on the use of independent continuous probability distributions for input variables. These distributions are used in a Monte Carlo simulation process to generate output distributions for the expected equity IRR after tax, as well as other output parameters. From the output data generated, the analyst estimates the mean and standard deviation of the return.

The second avenue uses a Bayesian approach and assumes that the probabilities of certain future events (for, say, a multiyear project evaluation) are *dependent* on the outcomes of certain past events. Thus, if an analyst assumed that gross revenue in the *first* year of a project had a 40 percent chance of being

[9] *Study on Tax Considerations in Multi-Family Housing Investment* (Washington, D.C.: U.S. Department of Housing and Urban Development, 1972). See also Robert J. Wiley, "Real Estate Investment Analysis: An Empirical Study," *The Appraisal Journal*, October 1976, pp. 586–592.

EXHIBIT 25-4. Illustrative Components of a Typical Project Cash Flow Statement

Gross possible income	$10,000
Less: vacancy and collection loss	− 500
Effective gross income	9,500
Less: operating expenses	− 3,000
Net operating income	$ 6,500

$10,000, then the probability of gross revenue's being $10,000 in the *second* year would be dependent on whether gross revenue was $10,000 in the first year.

This approach, the use of Bayesian analysis, was initially demonstrated in a real estate simulation by Pellatt.[10] To demonstrate the essential difference between these approaches, we present a simplified example. Exhibit 25–4 depicts some assumptions about three components of a typical real estate cash flow statement: (1) gross revenue, (2) vacancy loss, and (3) operating expenses. For this analysis subjective estimates of the probabilities of occurrence are assigned to each variable. These estimates of low, median, and high values are shown in Exhibit 25–5, with the assigned probabilities in parentheses.

In the first type of simulation discussed, each year's pro forma would be derived by randomly selecting one value for each variable out of the specified distribution. For, say, 100 simulations, we could expect gross revenue to be $10,000 fifty times, $15,000 twenty times, and $7,000 thirty times. The expected value of gross revenue for 100 simulations is ($10,000 × .5) + ($15,000 × .2) + ($7,000 × .3), or $10,100. A similar result can be expected for each year of a multi-year forecast if one assumes that each year's results are independent of the results in the preceding period.

If we now assume that the outcomes in the second year are dependent on the outcomes in the first year, the problem takes on a different perspective. If gross revenue *is* $10,000 in the first year, then the likelihood of its being $7,000 in the second year may be less than the 30 percent probability previously assigned.

EXHIBIT 25-5. Subjective Estimates of Distributions and Assigned Probabilities for Typical Project Cash Flows

	Middle Value (Prob.)	Highest Value (Prob.)	Lowest Value (Prob.)
Gross revenue	$10,000 (.5)	$15,000 (.2)	$7,000 (.3)
Vacancy allowance	5% (.6)	10% (.2)	2% (.2)
Operating expenses	3,000 (.7)	5,000 (.2)	2,000 (.1)

[10] Peter G. K. Pellatt, "A Normative Approach to the Analysis of Real Estate Investment Opportunities Under Uncertainty and the Management of Real Estate Investment Portfolios," unpublished Ph.D. dissertation, University of California, Berkeley, 1970.

EXHIBIT 25-6. Tree Diagram Showing Distribution of Gross Revenue for Two Periods from Typical Project Cash Flows

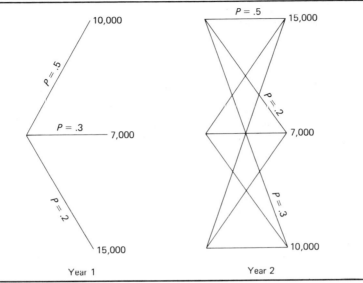

Year 1   Year 2

Exhibit 25–6 shows the branches specified for years 1 and 2. In year 1 the probabilities are as assigned in the original example. In the second year, however, the analysis presumes that if the $10,000 level of gross revenues is achieved in the first year, then revenues in year 2 would have the distribution illustrated for year 2. Now, the probability of achieving $15,000 in year 2 is higher than it was for year 1, while the probability of $7,000 in year 2 is *lower* than it was for year 1.

Insofar as simulation models of either type are actually extrapolations from reality, it may be difficult to argue that one approach is more correct than the other. Furthermore, it is possible to combine the best elements of both methods by designing a conditional probability distribution network between input variables over time using the Monte Carlo simulation framework. In such a model, for example, the probability distribution for gross possible income in year 2 would be dependent (conditional) on the outcome simulated in year 1. Although such a model is difficult to design and implement, it appears to be more theoretically precise than the two described.[11]

In addition to the stochastic models just described, there are *deterministic* models (described in Chapter 12) that use sensitivity analysis to evaluate risk. The latter technique is essentially one of deriving elasticities for certain important measures of project performance. Several models using sensitivity analysis have

[11] Such a model was developed by Mike E. Miles in "A Conceptual and Computer Model for the Analysis and Management of Risk in Real Property Development," Ph.D. dissertation, The University of Texas at Austin, August 1976. The model was subsequently refined and presented by Stephen A. Pyhrr and Mike Miles in a paper entitled, "A Framework and Computer Model for Risk Analysis and Risk Management in Real Property Development," for the annual meeting of the Financial Management Association, Montreal, Canada, October 1976 (available from the authors).

been developed by Wendt,[12] Hemmer,[13] Decisionex,[14] and Graaskamp and Robbins.[15] Although sensitivity analysis is of particular value for individual project analysis, the elements of modern portfolio theory as described earlier dictate the use of expected return and variance for developing efficient portfolios. Consequently, risk simulation models like Pyhrr's or Pellatt's lend themselves more specifically to portfolio selection and analysis.

Real Estate Portfolio Selection—An Illustration

By incorporating simulation models like those illustrated in the previous discussion with the basic framework proposed by Markowitz, it is possible to derive efficient real estate portfolios. The methodology has been amply demonstrated by numerous authors in the field.[16] There are four basic steps in the process of developing an efficient two-asset portfolio:

1. Derive estimates of rates of return and corresponding probabilities of occurrence of each project.
2. Compute expected returns, $E(R)$, and variances for each project.
3. Compute covariance for both projects.
4. Compute or graphically derive the optimal combination.

The derivation of such a two-asset portfolio might proceed as follows:

Step 1. Each project's cash flow data are analyzed through the use of a probabilistic model for the projected holding period, and estimates of rates of return and their corresponding probabilities of occurrence are derived. For simplicity, Exhibit 25–7 summarizes the results of such an analysis.

Step 2. The $E(R)$ for the project and variances are calculated. Exhibits 25–8 and 25–9 show the required format and computations. Project A has an $E(R_A)$ and variance of .14 and .00416, respectively. Project B has an $E(R_B)$ and vari-

---

[12] Paul Wendt, REAL III, described in Paul Wendt and Alan R. Cerf, *Real Estate Investment Analysis and Taxation,* 2nd ed. (New York: McGraw-Hill, 1979), pp. 63–88.

[13] Edgar H. Hemmer, "A Valuation Model for Investments in Real Estate," unpublished Ph.D. dissertation, Purdue University, 1972.

[14] Decisionex, Inc., QUICK, presented at the 1978 Colloquium on Computer Applications in Real Estate, Georgia State University, November 27–29, 1978.

[15] MRCAP, developed at University of Wisconsin by Dr. James Graaskamp and Michael Robbins. For additional discussion of these and other models, see Paul Wendt and Janet Tandy, "Evaluation of DCF Computer Models in Real Estate Investment Analysis," paper presented at the annual meeting of the American Real Estate and Urban Economics Association, Dallas, Texas, December 1975.

[16] Steven D. Kapplin, "Financial Theory and the Valuation of Real Estate Under Conditions of Risk," *The Real Estate Appraiser,* September-October 1976, pp. 28–37. See also Michael S. Young, "Comparative Investment Performance: Common Stock Versus Real Estate—A Proposal on Methodology," *Real Estate Issues,* Summer, 1977, pp. 30–46; Richard J. Curcio and James P. Gaines, "Real Estate Portfolio Revision," *Journal of the American Real Estate and Urban Economics Association,* Winter 1977, pp. 399–410; M. Chapman Findlay, III, Carl W. Hamilton, Stephen D. Messner, and Jonathan S. Yormack, "Optimal Real Estate Portfolios," *Journal of the American Real Estate and Urban Economics Association,* Fall 1979, pp. 298–317; George W. Gau, and Daniel B. Kohlhepp, "Estimation of Equity Yield Rates Based on Capital Market Returns," *The Real Estate Appraiser and Analyst,* November-December 1978, pp. 33–39.

EXHIBIT 25-7. Subjective Estimates of the Internal-Rate-of-Return Distribution for Two Projects

PROJECT A		PROJECT B	
IRR	Probability of Occurrence	IRR	Probability of Occurrence
−.05	.05	−.20	.05
+.05	.15	−.05	.15
+.15	.30	+.15	.30
+.20	.50	+.30	.50

ance of .2275 and .02987, respectively. Upon inspection, project B appears to be the riskier investment.

Step 3. The covariance between projects A and B can be calculated using equation 1 when the correlation coefficient is known. The format illustrated in Exhibit 25–10 can be used where the correlation coefficient is not known.[17] Because the covariance is positive, the optimal combination of projects A and B will not provide complete elimination of risk.

Step 4. Determine the optimal combination by graphing the risk vs. return of the portfolio combinations by using equations 2 and 3 to compute portfolio $E(R_p)$ and variance. Exhibits 25–11 and the accompanying graph in Exhibit 25–12 illustrate that no reduction in risk can be derived from any combination of projects A and B that would require portfolio risk below the risk level of the least risky project. This suggests that the correlation coefficient for projects A and B is significantly positive. In fact, the correlation coefficient can be calculated as $COV_{AB}/\sigma_A \times \sigma_B = .9285$.[17] Investors seeking to minimize risk could choose between a portfolio of A and B with a small amount of B or simply investing in

EXHIBIT 25-8. Computation of Expected Return and Variance for Project A

(1) Probability of Occurrence	(2) R_A	(3) Col. 1 × Col. 2	(4) $[R_A - E(R_A)]$	(5) (Col. 4)^2	(6) Col. 1 × Col. 5
.05	−.05	−.0025	−.1900	.0361	.00181
.15	+.05	.0075	−.0900	.0081	.00122
.50	+.15	.0750	.0100	.0001	.00005
.30	+.20	.0600	.0600	.0036	.00108
		$E(R_A) = .1400$			$VAR_A = .00416$
					$\sigma_A = .0645$

[17] See equation 1. Note that the sign of the correlation coefficient will be positive if projects have a positive covariance and negative if covariance is negative. Cf. Exhibits 25–10 and 25–14.

EXHIBIT 25-9.   Computation of Expected Return and Variance for Project B

(1)	(2)	(3)	(4)	(5)	(6)
.05	−.20	−.0100	−.4275	.18276	.00914
.15	−.05	−.0075	−.2775	.07701	.01155
.50	+.25	.1250	.0225	.00051	.00025
.30	+.40	.1200	.1725	.02976	.00893
	$E(R_B) =$	.2275		$VAR_B =$	.02987
				$\sigma_B =$	.17283

project A only. (This assumes that investments are made in cash and without debt.)

To illustrate the impact of selecting projects with low correlations, the preceding example is altered slightly. Project A's characteristics are modified as shown in Exhibit 25–13. The $E(R_A)$ and variance are recomputed and found to be .0425 and .0056, respectively. Exhibit 25–14 shows the calculation of covariance. In this example the covariance is *negative* and the calculation of the correlation coefficient shows a value of −.908. Projects A and B are now very negatively correlated rather than very positively correlated. Reconstructing Exhibit 25–11, the results are summarized in Exhibits 25–15 and 25–16.

In this example, project A is negatively correlated with project B and an optimal portfolio combination is found that contains approximately 75 percent of project A and 25 percent of project B. The combination has an $E(R_p)$ and variance of .089 and .0006, respectively. Exhibit 25–16 depicts how the proper selection of negatively correlated projects provides for the elimination of risk from the portfolio.

This section has presented a simplified illustration of optimal portfolio combinations for a two-asset case. Four basic steps for deriving the optimal portfolio were presented, together with an example of how positively and negatively correlated assets affect risk, return, and the efficient combination. The difference between the efficient combinations for positively and negatively correlated assets is starkly evident in the contrast between the efficient frontiers graphed in Exhibits 25–12 and 25–16.

EXHIBIT 25-10.   Computation of Covariance for Projects A and B

(1) Probability of Occurrence	(2) $[R_A - E(R_A)]$	(3) $[R_B - E(R_B)]$	(4) Col. 2 × Col. 3	(5) Col. 1 × Col. 4
.05	−.1900	−.4275	.08123	.00406
.15	−.0900	−.2275	.02048	.00307
.50	.0100	.0225	.00023	.00011
.30	.0600	.1725	.01035	.00311
			$COV_{AB} =$	.01035

EXHIBIT 25-11.   Computation of Portfolio $E(R_p)$ and Portfolio Variance for Various Combinations of Projects A and B

Proportions		Portfolio Return	Portfolio Variance
W_A	W_B	$E(R_p)$	VAR_p
.10	.90	.21875	.0261
.25	.75	.20563	.0209
.50	.50	.18375	.0137
.75	.25	.16188	.0081
.90	.10	.14875	.0055

EXHIBIT 25-12.   Graph of the Efficient Frontier Derived from Data in Exhibit 25-11

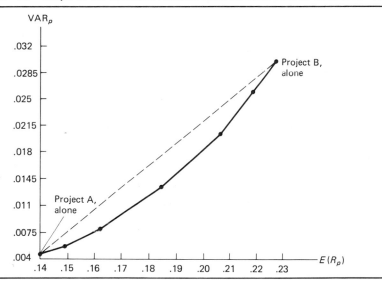

EXHIBIT 25-13.   The Revised IRR Distribution for Project A

R_A	Probability of Occurrence
+.20	.05
+.15	.15
+.05	.50
−.05	.30

EXHIBIT 25-14.   Computation of the Revised Covariance for Projects A and B

(1) Probability of Occurrence	(2) $[R_A - E(R_A)]$	(3) $[R_B - E(R_B)]$	(4) Col. 2 × Col. 3	(5) Col. 1 × Col. 4
.05	.1575	−.4275	−.0673	−.00337
.15	.1075	−.2275	−.0245	−.00367
.50	.0075	.0225	.00017	.00008
.30	−.0925	.1725	−.01596	.00479
				$COV_{AB} = -.01174$

EXHIBIT 25-15.   The Revised Portfolio $E(R_p)$ and Variance for Various Combinations of Projects A and B

Proportions		Portfolio Return	Portfolio Variance
W_A	W_B	$E(R_p)$	VAR_p
.10	.90	.2090	.0221
.25	.75	.1813	.0124
.50	.50	.1350	.0030
.75	.25	.089	.0006
.90	.10	.061	.0027

EXHIBIT 25-16.   Graph of Efficient Frontier Derived from Data in Exhibit 25-14

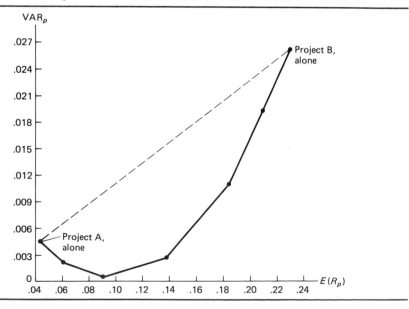

This illustration of portfolio development demonstrated both the formal pro-cess of portfolio design and the computational steps involved in that process. However, the discussion has been limited to the two-asset case. Although the two-asset case is a useful representation of modern portfolio theory and design, it is fairly unrealistic. Large real estate or mixed-asset portfolios are more likely to contain many assets than to contain only two. The illustration also points up some other problems in applying Markowitz portfolio theory to real estate portfolios. First, it is difficult to devise a real estate portfolio that consists of "75 percent investment A and 25 percent investment B," because real estate project acquisi-tions are usually an all-or-nothing proposition. Second, the discussion has ex-cluded any consideration of the use of leverage. Because an investor may lend (invest) or borrow, debt can be viewed as an alternative investment that has certain risk/return and covariance characteristics which would be positively corre-lated if they were acquired as an investment and, therefore, are negatively corre-lated when they are acquired as a debt. Third, multiasset selection models tend to be extremely complicated and difficult to implement.

AN EXTENDED DEVELOPMENT OF PORTFOLIO THEORY

Extending the two-asset portfolio analysis to the more general problem of the N-asset case is too complex for this discussion. The N-asset problem involves a linear-programming type of problem where the object is to maximize the differ-ence between expected portfolio return and variance. The functional form is that of calculus maximization of an objective function:

$$\text{Maximize } Z = \lambda E_p - V_p \tag{4}$$

$$\text{where} \quad E_p = \sum_{i=1} E(R_i) W_i$$

$$V_p = \sum_{i=1}^{N} \sum_{j=1}^{N} W_i W_j \sigma_{ij}$$

subject to

$$\sum_{i=1}^{N} W_i = 1.0$$

Adaptations of the *N*-Asset Calculus Model to Real Estate

Several adaptations of the calculus model above have been made in the area of real estate. These were developed to overcome some serious difficulties that are peculiar to real estate investment:

1. Real estate acquisitions usually involve all-or-nothing decisions. That is, one purchases either the entire project or nothing because there are no

fractional interests. (Limited partnerships, REIT shares, and so forth may present alternatives and ease the restriction of all-or-nothing acquisition.)

2. Real estate purchases are frequently leveraged. The inclusion of borrowed funds complicates the optimal selection inasmuch as debt tends to have the effect not only of increasing equity rates of return but also of increasing the variance of equity rates of return.

3. Most portfolio optimization models are single-period models. Real estate is a multiperiod commitment that usually doesn't permit the investor to restructure the portfolio at the end of the period.

One of the most interesting portfolio models for use with real estate was developed by Pellatt.[18] Pellatt's model incorporated several innovative design characteristics. It was designed to generate an efficient frontier for real estate assets that included financing decisions as part of the model's specification, permitted an all-or-nothing acquisition criterion, and was predicated on a multiperiod decision horizon. This was accomplished using net present value and the variance of NPV in lieu of rate of return and variance of returns. The general structure of the model is similar to that described in equation 4:

$$MAX\ E(NPV) = \sum_{i=1}^{N} (PVAL_i)W_i + \sum_{i=1}^{N} (MVAL_i)^{Y_i/P_i}$$

subject to

1. $CAP = \sum_{i=1}^{N} (W_i - Y_i)(COST_i) \le CAPMAX$

2. $VAR = \sum_{i=1}^{N} \sum_{j=1}^{N} W_i W_j\ \sigma_{ij} \le VARMAX$

3. $0 \le Y_i \le P_i W_i$ for all $i = 1$ to N

4. $0 \le W_i \le 1$ for all $i = 1$ to N

where

   $E(NPV)$ = expected NPV of portfolio
   N = number of properties being considered
   $PVAL_i$ = expected NPV of property i
   $MVAL_i$ = net present value of maximum mortgage allowable on property i
   Y_i = proportion of total cost of property i provided by mortgage funds

---

[18] Pellatt, op. cit.

P_i = maximum proportion of total cost of property i that can be provided by mortgage funds

CAP = required total investment capital

$COST_i$ = acquisition cost of property i

CAPMAX = externally imposed limit on size of portfolio

VAR = variance of NPV for investment portfolio

σ_{ij} = covariance of NPVs for ith and jth properties, respectively

VARMAX = externally imposed upper limit on portfolio variance

Note that Pellatt's model includes an optimal financing decision, Y_i/P_i, in which the model selects a proportion of total cost to be provided through mortgage debt subject to a stipulated maximum loan-to-value ratio, P_i. The efficient frontier is subject to maximum capital constraints, CAPMAX, and a maximum variance constraint, VARMAX. When one relaxes the VARMAX constraint, the entire efficient frontier is generated. The imposition of a VARMAX constraint limits the portfolio to that which is optimal within the VARMAX limit.

The model was designed to provide limits on the proportion of each investment selected such that the portfolio generated either included an asset or excluded it. No fractional part of an asset could be selected. This limitation could be relaxed by the user. Pellatt devised several overlapping computer programs that provided the means of generating efficient frontiers for up to four properties. Of course, a close look at Pellatt's model specification indicates that it is a specialized case of the calculus model that incorporates some of the unusual characteristics of real estate assets. Perhaps what is most unusual about Pellatt's model is that it was developed before 1970.

It was not until 1977 that another model was proposed. In that year Curcio and Gaines[19] proposed a model that was based on the general optimization model but modified slightly to provide for a multiperiod decision horizon. Curcio and Gaines assumed that in a pure "real estate" portfolio the initial optimal portfolio needed to be revised periodically. However, their model did not differ from Pellatt's, except that Pellatt's model maximized E(NPV) whereas Curcio and Gaines' maximized terminal wealth. Insofar as Curcio and Gaines' model was based on the concept of terminal wealth, the financing decision was external to their formulations, whereas Pellatt made the financing decision an explicit component of the model.

Most recently, Findlay, Hamilton, Messner, and Yormack (Findlay et al.) presented a model similar to Curcio and Gaines', but structured so as to be more easily solved using current computer programming technology.[20] More in keeping with the standard portfolio model, Findlay et al. use expected returns and variances rather than terminal-wealth or NPV criteria. To adapt their model to the multiperiod features of real estate investment, they proposed the use of the FMRR rather than IRR because FMRR incorporates reinvestment rate parameters and makes possible the inclusion of uninvested portions of capital in the optimal

---

[19] Curcio and Gaines, op. cit.; Findlay et al., op. cit. (footnote 16).

[20] Findlay et al., pp. 298–317.

portfolio. They claim that the ability to include uninvested portions of the total capital in the optimum portfolio makes the comparison of portfolios more legitimate. In their model the use of the FMRR makes possible an assumption that uninvested capital may be invested in a risk-free asset. This essentially makes each generated portfolio a combination of risky real estate assets with a risk-free asset.

The formulation of the Findlay et al. model is interesting and is presented here for comparison with Pellatt's model:

$$\text{MIN } Z = \frac{1}{b^2} \sum_{i=1}^{N} \sum_{j=1}^{N} W_i C_i \, \sigma_i \, P_{ij} \, \sigma_j \, C_j W_j$$

subject to

1. $r_0 + \dfrac{1}{b} \displaystyle\sum_{j=1}^{N} U_j W_j \geqslant Y$

2. $\displaystyle\sum_{j=1}^{N} C_j W_j \leqslant b$

3. $W_j = 0, 1, \; j = 1, 2, \ldots, N$

where

b = total capital funds constraint
Y = externally imposed minimum return constraint
C_j = acquisition cost for project j
W_j = proportion of capital invested in project j
σ_i, σ_j = standard deviations of expected FMRRs for projects i and j, respectively
P_{ij} = correlation coefficient of projects i and j, respectively (may be negative)
r_0 = risk-free rate

It is interesting to note the essential similarities among these portfolio models. Furthermore, all three are basically derivatives of the original Markowitz and Sharpe models. The critical elements of a real estate portfolio model—its multiperiod nature, the need for discrete project selection, and the need to include financing—are addressed in each model, but in a somewhat different fashion. Pellatt attempted to resolve the problem by using NPV rather than rate-of-return (e.g., IRR) criteria. Pellatt assumed that by so doing one makes the financing decision an explicit element of the designated cost of capital. Therefore, financing alternatives could be explored by noting their impact on the discount rate. Curcio and Gaines addressed the multiperiod nature of real estate by formulating the portfolio model to include balance sheet changes and the use of dynamic programming. However, they did not tackle the leverage problem. Findlay et al.

utilized the FMRR concept because they felt that its multiperiod formulation and ability to handle reinvestment and the inclusion of cash as a risk-free asset are well adapted to both the multiperiod and leverage problems. All three models utilized modern programming algorithms to handle the problem of multiple assets and discrete project selection.

A Simplified Approach to Portfolio Selection

A major stumbling block to the solution of portfolio models of the types illustrated in the previous section is the need to specify the correlation coefficients (the covariance matrix) for all project pairs in the set of projects from which the efficient frontier will be generated. All three of the models described require that these inputs be generated subjectively. In fact, the limitation of Pellatt's model to four properties was predicated in part on the difficulty faced by an analyst who must generate a matrix of subjective joint probabilities (i.e., generate the matrix of correlation coefficients or covariance).

Sharpe proposed an alternative formulation of the basic Markowitz model (on which the three real estate models are based), which he called the diagonal or single-index model.[21] Sharpe's formulation of a security's characteristics line was presented in Exhibit 25–2. The development of the characteristic line was predicated on the assumption that risk contains two distinct elements: systematic and unsystematic risk. The latter was eliminated through portfolio diversification, while the former was undiversifiable. Systematic risk was the risk associated with the impact of changes in the market for all securities on the return on any individual security. The measure of that risk was beta (β). The security's characteristic line was formulated as $Y = a + \beta X + e$, where Y is the security's forecasted return, a is the security-unique rate of return, and e is an error term. In the general terminology of portfolio theory, portfolio return was defined as follows:

$$E(R_p) = \sum_{i=1}^{N} W_i \, E(R_i)$$

where W_i is the proportion of the portfolio invested in the ith security and $E(R_i)$ the expected return on the ith security. From the equation for the characteristic line, $E(R_i)$ was defined as follows:

$$E(R_i) = a_i + \beta_i X + e_i$$

and therefore portfolio return was defined as follows:

$$E(R_p) = \sum_{i=1}^{N} W_i \, E(a_i + \beta_i X + e_i)$$

[21] William F. Sharpe, "A Simplified Model for Portfolio Analysis," *Management Science*, January 1963, pp. 277–293.

The term X is the return on the market as represented by some market index, for instance the index for the S&P 500 or the Dow Jones industrials. Carrying this one step further,

$$E(R_p) = \sum_{i=1}^{N} W_i(a_i + e_i) + \sum_{i=1}^{N} W_i(\beta_i X)$$

Sharpe redefined portfolio return as involving an investment in two components:

1. An investment in the "basic characteristics" of each security $(a_i + e_i)W_i$, and
2. An "investment" in the market index— $W_i(\beta_i X)$

The variance of this portfolio is as follows:

$$\text{VAR} (R_p) = \sum_{i=1}^{N+1} W_i^2 \text{ VAR}(R_i)$$

Sharpe's simplified model results in a covariance matrix that has zeroes in each position other than the diagonal. This simplifies the computational requirements and makes possible the generation of an efficient frontier with less difficulty than when using the Markowitz model. The data requirements are also simplified in that only periodic return data are required on each security and on the market index. Through the use of simple linear regression the values for a, e, and β can be generated.

Adaptation to Real Estate Portfolio Selection

The adaptation of Sharpe's simplified model to real estate portfolio selection is especially hampered by the lack of an index. Several studies have been done in which real estate assets were compared with an index. Kapplin illustrated the creation of an artificial index based loosely on state preference theory in which a project's expected performance was tied to the analyst's subjective opinion of how a change in economic conditions (state of nature) might affect a project's rate of return.[22] By using an analysis similar to that used for the two-asset portfolio problem, the covariance of the project's return with the "state of nature" could be calculated and a β estimated for the project.

Wofford and Moses used an interesting technique to create an index utilizing data on real estate investment trusts.[23] Using regression analysis and using the proportion of REIT assets invested in the type of project under consideration, they were able to generate estimates of the β coefficient for specific types of property

[22] Kapplin, pp. 28–37.
[23] Larry E. Wofford and Edward A. Moses, "The Relationship Between Capital Markets and Real Estate Investment Yields: Theory and Application," *The Real Estate Appraiser and Analyst,* November-December 1978, pp. 51–61.

investment. However, the range of the β estimates was quite substantial. In their example for shopping centers, β estimates ranged from .135 to .921 for an 80-percent confidence interval. Despite the statistical problems involved, the technique does offer a possible method of creating an index.

Friedman used GNP growth as a superindex in his innovative study of real estate, stock, and combined portfolios.[24] However, such an index may have questionable relevancy to real estate investment performance. When real estate returns are regressed against such an index, as would be required in the simplified portfolio model, there would be a low correlation between real estate and an index like GNP. Since unexplained variance is assumed to be unsystematic and, hence, diversifiable, the index may be erroneously interpreted as meaning low portfolio risk.

Young demonstrated the use of the NYSE index as a comparative index for evaluating the performance of a portfolio combining real estate assets and common stock.[25] His technique was essentially a replication of the Sharpe model using two assets, a real estate portfolio, and a security portfolio. Portfolio returns were regressed against the NYSE index to derive the appropriate data inputs.

These several studies all illustrate the general applicability of modern portfolio models to the problem of selecting optimal real estate portfolios. The index (diagonal) models are simplifications of Markowitz's model of portfolio selection that tend to reduce both data requirements and computational complexity. However, they all have certain limitations when applied to real estate. These include (1) inability to handle discrete project selection, (2) failure to incorporate optimal financing decisions, (3) inability to handle many projects, and (4) lack of an acceptable index for real estate. Each model adaptation, from Pellatt to the present, has addressed itself to resolving some area of limitation. But at this point in the state of the art there is yet no conclusive solution to the problem of deriving a comprehensive model for real estate portfolio selection.

THE IMPACT OF PORTFOLIO THEORY ON LARGE INSTITUTIONAL INVESTORS

Comparing the Performance of Real Estate and Stock Portfolios

Thus far our discussion has focused on the development of a body of theory and its application to a portfolio approach to investment. This section will focus on the performance of real estate portfolios in contrast with security portfolios. The focus will then shift to the investment criteria of large institutional real estate investors and the performance of their real estate portfolios.

Although there have been many studies of the performance of real estate vis-à-vis securities investments, a complete discussion of those studies would be out of place here.[26] Instead, we will concentrate on a few studies that are certainly

---

[24] Harris C. Friedman, "Real Estate Investment and Portfolio Theory," *Journal of Financial and Quantitative Analysis,* March 1971, pp. 861–874.
[25] Young, pp. 30–46 (footnote 16)
[26] An excellent article reviewing and comparing eleven studies of real estate returns is Stephen Roulac's, "Can Real Estate Returns Outperform Common Stocks?" *The Journal of Portfolio Management,* Winter 1976, pp. 26–43.

indicative of the trends, results, and problems of all such studies. The first significant study was "Investment Performance: Common Stocks vs. Apartment Houses," by Paul Wendt and Sui Wong.[27] This study, done in 1965, compared the performance of a randomly selected stock portfolio with that of a portfolio of selected FHA-subsidized apartment properties. It concluded that the real estate turned in a significantly better performance than the stock portfolio for the period covered by the study. However, the authors acknowledged that real estate's superiority was due almost entirely to the unusual tax advantages of real estate ownership. They also recognized that individual returns varied widely for both real estate and security issues, suggesting that individual property or security analysis was important.

Although this study suffered from certain defects, such as poor selection criteria for the real estate portfolio, inadequate cash flow measures, failure to account for the impact of financing, failure to deal with transaction costs, poor-quality data, and the geographic limitations of real estate properties, Wendt and Wong nevertheless were able to illustrate that real estate portfolios could have advantages that are not present in stock portfolios.

An interesting contrast to Wendt and Wong's study is provided by a study done by Harris Friedman in 1971.[28] Friedman compared a sample of fifty apartment properties to a sample of common stocks. The apartment properties were randomly selected from the portfolios of several large real estate trust holdings. Friedman used return on total investment rather than return on equity as the standard measure of return. The returns were holding-period returns, which assumed that the investments were sold at the end of each period. Using data from 1963 to 1968, Friedman generated portfolio returns for the real estate sample, the stock sample, and a combined portfolio using the Sharpe diagonal (index) model to generate efficient frontiers. On both a pre- and an after-tax basis, real estate dominated stocks both separately and when combined. This study was the first basic research illustrating the portfolio effects of combining real estate with other investment media. Friedman's study provided evidence that real estate portfolios dominate security portfolios and that real estate and common stock may have low correlations, making them ideal assets for combination in an investment portfolio.

In 1976 an interesting study by David Kelleher appeared in *Real Estate Review*.[29] Kelleher compares the rates of return on a select sample of prime apartment properties with Standard and Poor's 500-stock index. Kelleher's study utilized only fully owned properties (no mortgages) and compared them with the security index for 1960–1966 and 1967–1973. Like Friedman and Wendt and Wong, Kelleher used a rate of return on total capital, calculating IRRs for all investments using holding periods of from one to seven years. His study indicated that the real estate portfolio provided better and more stable returns than the S&P index. (It should be noted that a comparison of real estate to an index like the S&P index is a usual step in developing the beta measure for real estate.) Kel-

[27] Paul F. Wendt and Sui N. Wong, "Investment Performance: Common Stocks Versus Apartment Houses," *Journal of Finance*, December 1965, pp. 633–646.
[28] Friedman, pp. 861–874.
[29] Dennis G. Kelleher, "How Real Estate Stacks Up to the S.&P. 500," *Real Estate Review*, Summer 1976, pp. 60–65.

leher's study is interesting principally because he compares not individual properties, but an entire portfolio, with the index. His study is perhaps less indicative of real estate performance per se than of how a real estate portfolio responds to an index—it is in some part indicative of the degree of diversification of unsystematic risk.

As recently as 1978 several studies appeared that were similar to Kelleher's but had greater academic precision. These studies compared real estate returns to returns on other investment media. The first of these, "Toward a More Complete Investigation of the Correlation of Real Estate Investment Yield to the Rate Evidenced in the Money and Capital Markets," by Mike Miles and Michael Rice, sought to formulate a more precise index for comparing real estate returns and deriving betas.[30] Miles and Rice derived a comprehensive index consisting of three principal components: (1) real property, (2) common stock, and (3) human capital. This new index was regressed against farm real estate in eleven major farming states. The results indicated that farm real estate betas are more logical when using their index than betas derived using the S&P index. A major problem of the study was the lack of a test using developed urban investment property.

C. F. Sirmans and James R. Webb investigated real estate returns and their correlation with returns in other media in their article, "Investment Yields in the Money, Capital and Real Estate Markets."[31] Using loan data published by the American Council of Life Insurance Companies, they imputed equity yield rates using a technique originally described by Bruce R. Ricks in 1969.[32] These equity rates were then regressed against the periodic returns on several other investment media, namely, common stock, long-term government bonds, long-term T bills, and long-term corporate bonds. The study illustrates the extent to which real estate yields are correlated to the yields on other investments. Real estate returns were shown to be negatively correlated with common stock (a result that confirms Friedman's findings) but positively correlated to returns on bonds (government and corporate) and T bills. Attempts by the authors to use regression to base their forecasted real estate yields on the yields observed in the money and capital markets were inconclusive. The strongest predictive relationship existed between real estate yields and yields on T bills.

A similar study by Walter Chudleigh and Lawrence Brown compared real estate yields on "net leased" properties derived from 423 sales that occurred between 1971 and 1977 (most in California) with yields on corporate bonds and the prime rate.[33] The basis of their study is somewhat unclear, but the results were similar to those of Sirmans and Webb.

---

[30] Mike Miles and Michael Rice, "Toward a More Complete Investigation of the Correlation of Real Estate Investment Yield to the Rate Evidenced in the Money and Capital Markets: The Individual Investor's Perspective," *The Real Estate Appraiser and Analyst*, November-December 1978, pp. 8–19.

[31] C. F. Sirmans and James R. Webb, "Investment Yields in the Money, Capital and Real Estate Markets: A Comparative Analysis for 1951–1976," *The Real Estate Appraiser and Analyst*, November-December 1978, pp. 40–46.

[32] R. Bruce Ricks, "Imputed Equity Returns on Real Estate Financed with Life Insurance Company Loans," *Journal of Finance*, December 1969, pp. 921–937.

[33] Walter H. Chudleigh III and Lawrence E. Brown, "Real Estate Investment Yield as Correlated to the Rate Shown in Money and Capital Markets," *The Real Estate Appraiser and Analyst*, November-December 1978, pp. 47–50.

The studies that have been briefly reviewed here give an idea of the direction of research contrasting real estate with alternative investment media. The research spans the period from 1965 through 1978 and, although not exhaustive, is representative. Real estate has typically been found to provide better returns than other types of investments and to have low correlations with other investments.

When combined with other assets (i.e., in a mixed-asset portfolio), real estate tended to dominate the portfolio. Beta measures have been developed using both established and newly devised indexes, but have yet to be incorporated into a portfolio selection model. Although these studies are indeed interesting and informative, in one way they beg the issue. Certainly a low correlation between real estate portfolios and other media portfolios is desirable; however, these and other studies provide no evidence supporting any conclusion regarding the identification of negative or low positive correlations among real estate assets themselves. Indeed, the most efficient real estate portfolio (in the Markowitz sense) would contain assets selected for their low or negative correlations. Intuitively, one might say that real estate investments share so many similar characteristics that all returns may have relatively high positive correlation. The lack of evidence to the contrary has led the industry to assume that diversification of the real estate portfolio must be achieved through the acquisition of many different types of properties (apartments, shopping centers, motels) in many different locales (geographic as opposed to asset-type diversification). Geographic diversification has intuitive appeal as a means of reducing portfolio risk. However, current research provides no empirical evidence that geographically diversified real estate portfolios fare any better than local ones.

Institutional Real Estate Portfolios—Characteristics and Performance

The success of large investment funds is typically judged by how well the fund has met its stated goals and objectives. The fund's investment policies are stipulated with respect to several criteria: risk control, returns, diversification, consistency of performance, and maintenance of adequate but not excessive operating expenses. In this section we will provide a brief overview of the background and investment performance of the three major institutional real estate funds: pension funds, real estate investment trusts (REITs), and large, publicly offered limited partnerships.

Pension Funds   The largest institutional investors are pension fund accounts, which are managed principally by large insurance companies, but also include trust accounts of major commercial banks and a few non-institutionally managed closed-end investment funds. In addition to investing for pension funds, a few larger insurance companies (particularly Prudential and Equitable Life) are acquiring real estate for their own portfolios. The magnitude of the funds invested in real estate by the insurance companies currently runs from 3 to 5 percent of total assets, or around $12 billion.[34] Of this amount, approximately $3–3.5 billion is invested on behalf of pension funds.

[34] *Life Insurance Fact Book, 1977,* p. 83.

Pension funds and insurance companies are legally permitted to invest up to 10 percent of their assets in real estate equities. With insurance company assets exceeding $400 billion and pension fund assets exceeding $300 billion, this industry segment has only begun to move toward its potential of $70 billion in real estate equity.[35] The largest of the insurance company pension funds are Prudential's Property Investment Separate Account (PRISA), with assets exceeding $2 billion plus more than $1 billion for the company's own account, and Equitable Life Real Estate Account 8, with assets of nearly $1.1 billion. Total bank trust funds are estimated at around $1.25 billion, or nearly double their asset size at the end of 1978. A couple of closed-end noninstitutional funds, Coldwell Banker Fund and CB Institutional Fund II, reported assets of nearly $90 million at the close of 1979. Almost all of these funds were nonexistent before 1970. Thus, in a relatively short time institutional real estate funds have become a significant force in the equities market.

Pension fund performance has been quite successful. A study of two bank and two insurance company funds by Aldrich and Upton indicated compound yields of around 7 percent for the five-year period 1971– 1975.[36] In a more recent summary of pension fund performance for the year 1979 in *Mortgage and Real Estate Executives Report,* fourteen pension funds, twelve open-ended commingled funds, and two closed-end partnerships showed an average gain in portfolio value of 12.8 percent and income returns of 9.6 percent.[37] In another study Miles and Langford contrasted the performance of twelve commercial bank trust funds with the returns on two security indexes and a corporate bond index.[38] Over the study period, 1969– 1977, the bank funds consistently did better during down-market conditions, but not as well during up-market conditions. This suggests that real estate portfolios have less variance than securities portfolios. In addition, the real estate funds had average returns of 7.3 percent, in contrast to only 5.5 percent for the stock indexes and 5.3 percent for the bond index.

Exhibits 25– 17 and 25– 18 show the results of the Miles and Langford study; Exhibit 25– 19 depicts the portfolio characteristics of the nation's largest real estate portfolio, PRISA.[39]

Real Estate Investment Trusts REITs are perhaps the oldest group of institutional real estate investors. They date from before the 1960s, although their existence became formalized in 1960. The industry has had its booms and busts, and now appears to be settling down to a more conservative future. Originally realty trusts were organized to invest in equities through a vehicle that permitted most of the tax benefits of individual ownership while offering a fractionalized and

---

[35] It should be noted that the aggregate figures for insurance companies also include properties owned *and occupied* by the insurance companies.
[36] Peter C. Aldrich and King Upton, "The Pension Funds Finally Move into Real Estate," *Real Estate Review,* Winter 1978, pp. 30– 35.
[37] Alvin L. Arnold, ed., *Mortgage and Real Estate Executives Report,* June 15, 1980, p. 8.
[38] Mike Miles and Janelle Langford, "Bank Trust Department Operation of Commingled Real Estate Funds," *Real Estate Issues,* Winter 1978, pp. 62– 73.
[39] *PRISA, 1980 Annual Report,* The Prudential Insurance Company of America, Prudential Group Pension Funding, p. 31.

EXHIBIT 25–17. Annual Rates of Investment Return, Including Capital Gains and Income for Several Commingled Bank Trust Real Estate Funds

Year Ending 9/30	Commingled Real Estate and Mortgage Fund	Dow Jones Industrial Average	Standard & Poor's 500	Standard & Poor's High-Grade Bonds
1969	(6.5)%	(9.0)%	(9.0)%	(7.3)%
1970	6.9	(2.2)	(5.7)	(0.7)
1971	23.3	20.2	19.8	12.1
1972	11.3	10.7	15.2	8.9
1973	9.5	2.9	1.1	2.5
1974	0.9	(29.7)	(35.8)	(2.2)
1975	8.1	37.0	37.7	7.9
1976	0.5	29.5	30.0	15.3
1977	11.8	(10.2)	(4.0)	11.0
Average	7.31	5.47	5.48	5.28

SOURCE: Mike Miles and Janelle Langford, "Bank Trust Department Operation of Commingled Real Estate Funds," *Real Estate Issues,* Winter 1978, p. 69. Reprinted with the permission of the American Society of Real Estate Counselors of the National Association of Realtors.

fungible investment in the form of a share of beneficial interest (SBI). Small investors were able to obtain ownership in a diversified portfolio of real estate properties by purchasing shares in an REIT whose portfolio and objectives corresponded to those of the investors, but without the large cash outlay required for direct equity ownership.

At one time the industry's assets totaled over $21 billion, but this figure is now

EXHIBIT 25–18. Distribution of Investments of Several Bank Real Estate Funds

	Number of Funds Investing in This Type of Property	≤20%	21–39	40–59	60–79	80–99	100%
Office	6	3	3	—	—	—	—
Commercial retail	9	2	5	—	—	1	1
Industrial/warehouse	9	3	2	1	3	—	—
Residential	4	3	—	1	—	—	—
Raw land	3	3	—	—	—	—	—
Farm, forest, and mineral land	0	—	—	—	—	—	—
Hotel/motel	3	3	—	—	—	—	—
Other	4	—	—	—	—	—	—

SOURCE: Mike Miles and Janelle Langford, "Bank Trust Department Operation of Commingled Real Estate Funds," *Real Estate Issues,* Winter 1978, p. 68. Reprinted with the permission of the American Society of Real Estate Counselors of the National Association of Realtors.

EXHIBIT 25–19. Distribution of PRISA Portfolio: Property Values by Geographic Area and Class of Property

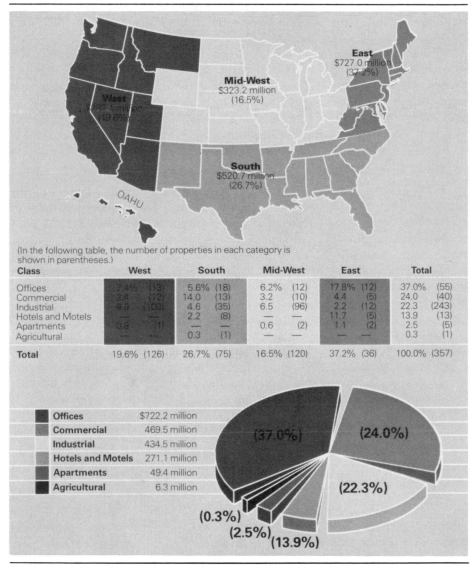

(In the following table, the number of properties in each category is shown in parentheses.)

Class	West		South		Mid-West		East		Total	
Offices	7.4%	(13)	5.6%	(18)	6.2%	(12)	17.8%	(12)	37.0%	(55)
Commercial	2.4	(12)	14.0	(13)	3.2	(10)	4.4	(5)	24.0	(40)
Industrial	9.0	(100)	4.6	(35)	6.5	(96)	2.2	(12)	22.3	(243)
Hotels and Motels	—	—	2.2	(8)	—	—	11.7	(5)	13.9	(13)
Apartments	0.8	(1)	—	—	0.6	(2)	1.1	(2)	2.5	(5)
Agricultural	—	—	0.3	(1)	—	—	—	—	0.3	(1)
Total	19.6%	(126)	26.7%	(75)	16.5%	(120)	37.2%	(36)	100.0%	(357)

Offices	$722.2 million
Commercial	469.5 million
Industrial	434.5 million
Hotels and Motels	271.1 million
Apartments	49.4 million
Agricultural	6.3 million

(37.0%) (24.0%) (22.3%) (13.9%) (2.5%) (0.3%)

SOURCE: *PRISA 1980 Annual Report.* Reproduced with permission of the Prudential Insurance Company of America.

closer to $15 billion as a result of the losses and bankruptcies that occurred after the 1974– 1975 recession.[40] Dividend yields have also improved sizably, averaging over 7.5 percent during the 1977– 1978 period. But performance has been spotty, with many short-term mortgage trusts still wrestling with large proportions

[40] *REIT Fact Book, 1979*, p. 8.

of their portfolios not earning income. Many of these trusts have not been paying dividends for several years, and their share prices are substantially depressed from the highs of 1973. Equity trusts have fared much better. Most are paying dividends averaging 10 percent and have recently been selling at over ten times earnings.

The somewhat mixed performance of REITs may be credited partly to the diversification policies of the various trusts. The trusts that sustained earnings and dividends throughout the recession years were more diversified, having investments in well-diversified equities and long-term as well as short-term mortgages. Short-term mortgage trusts committed the bulk of their assets to riskier construction and development loans, second mortgages, and wraparound loans. As a result, their portfolios were more susceptible to the short-term volatility of the construction cycle.

Limited Partnerships   Little is known regarding the aggregate size and results of the many limited partnership ventures in existence. The largest participants in the institutional markets are the limited partnerships that are sold publicly through major brokerage houses like Merrill Lynch, Oppenheimer, and E. F. Hutton. Many limited partnerships were originally intended for a predominantly tax-shelter-oriented market; hence, most of them involved subsidized housing ventures that promised large, attractive write-offs for high-tax-bracket investors. However, many limited partnerships are currently offered to investor groups seeking income and appreciation as well as tax shelter benefits.

Although no "industry" data are available, two large limited partnerships sponsored by Merrill Lynch have acquired more than $800 million of real property during the past ten years. A smaller offering through Merrill Lynch, called MLH Properties, proposes to raise up to $13.8 million of net proceeds to be used to purchase nearly $26 million of property. MLH Properties was proposed to begin with a portfolio of only five properties consisting of two apartment projects, one in California and one in South Carolina; a shopping center in Stuart, Florida; a multitenant warehouse facility in Texas; and a regional trade mart in Columbus, Ohio. The larger offerings from Merrill Lynch have been through a series of limited partnerships called JMB Properties, Ltd., and Carlyle Real Estate Limited Partnership. There have been seven JMB and eight Carlyle offerings. Several other offerings have also been made under different names. These offerings have raised nearly $1.5 billion in investment proceeds over the past ten years. The various partnerships have invested in most types of properties, with each partnership containing somewhat different mixes tailored to specific investors. The portfolios are also well diversified geographically.

Operating data on some older partnerships show that they have provided excellent tax shelter benefits, capital gains, and income. Over a ten-year period, one typical JMB partnership provided ordinary deductions of $2,770, capital gains of $361, and returns of capital of $765 for each $1,000 investment.[41]

A major benefit derived from limited partnerships is that investors are able to

---

[41] *Prospectus, JMB Properties, Ltd. — VII* (New York: Merrill, Lynch, Pierce, Fenner and Smith, 1980), p. 82.

extract maximum investment potential through leverage and tax benefits while having the ability to purchase small interests in large, diversified portfolios. Investors may diversify more by investing in the interests of several limited partnerships. REITs and pension funds find this advantageous and commit a portion of their investment funds for this purpose.

The decade of the 1970s, thus, has witnessed a phenomenal growth in the scope and dominance of major institutional investors in real estate markets. The scarce data on limited partnerships is inconclusive but is suggestive of a growing impact that already probably exceeds several billion dollars. REITs currently control over $15 billion in real estate assets, as do major pension funds. Donald Knab, senior vice-president in charge of real estate investments for Prudential, has been quoted as saying that pension funds are seeking to increase real estate equity holdings to the 10-percent-of-assets limit, up from the 3 – 5 percent currently held.

Present Problems and Future Prospects

The promotional brochures of funds like PRISA, the Bank of America Real Estate Fund, Connecticut General Mortgage and Realty Investments, and JMB, Ltd., are very similar in their statements of objectives and investment policies. Each intends to invest in income-producing real estate, usually commercial retail facilities, office properties, industrial properties, and residential properties across a broad geographic area in order to provide maximum portfolio diversification.

PRISA's portfolio is heavily concentrated in office buildings and industrial properties, while the several JMB, Ltd., partnerships were concentrated in shopping centers and the Carlyle partnerships were oriented toward apartment properties and mobile home parks. The industry appears to have assumed that diversification of the real estate portfolio can be obtained by acquisition of many properties (even if they are of similar types) scattered over a wide geographic area. However, it seems unlikely that an efficient portfolio would consist mostly of office buildings in one case, shopping centers in another case, and apartment/residential properties in a third. Even the general 10-percent-of-assets limitation that applies to the pension and insurance funds has no explicit rationale.

The research evidence has not shown what benefits of diversification may be derived in the real estate portfolio (viewed as a separate entity), but it certainly demonstrates that real estate assets reduce portfolio risk when combined with other assets, such as common stock. It would seem that portfolio managers and researchers should continue to focus on developing models of portfolio selection that concentrate on the real estate portfolio. The current lack of any definitive operational model leaves the portfolio manager with the intuitive appeal of a geographic dispersion and "safety in numbers" approach to asset selection and portfolio management, for lack of any better approach.

The application of portfolio theory to real estate has exciting implications, although it is currently in its infancy. The state of the art is very dynamic. In recent years much of what had been accepted into the traditional literature has come under question. Sharpe's capital asset theory of equilibrium was based on four assumptions: (1) investors choose portfolios that are perceived as mean–variance efficient; (2) all investors have similar *ex ante* beliefs vis-à-vis expected return and variance; (3) the "perfectly" diversified market portfolio is mean–variance efficient; (4) the risk premium for any asset is a linear function of its covariance with the market portfolio (as measured by beta). Recently these assumptions have been seriously questioned through empirical research.[42]

Real estate investment has only just entered the era of the portfolio approach to project analysis and selection; hence, the research available adapts past research in the securities arena rather than extending the current state of research. Although caution is appropriate when adapting academic research to investment practice, nevertheless real estate investors must become more decision oriented and develop greater sophistication by learning and using the newer analytical concepts and tools. The use of modern tools and concepts provides investors with a logical and consistent methodology for analysis that, when used properly, helps eliminate inconsistent, undesirable, or conflicting decisions.

SUMMARY

This chapter has presented an overview of modern portfolio theory, its application to real estate investing, and its impact on large institutional real estate funds. The contrast between individual project analysis and portfolio strategy was discussed, and the need to consider real estate in a portfolio context was stressed. The concept of diversification was presented, with a discussion of the difference between naive and efficient diversification. The concept of covariance was introduced, and we showed how efficient portfolios are developed through the proper selection of assets on the basis of their covariance. Assets that covary negatively enable the investor to develop a portfolio in which variance is eliminated or substantially reduced.

The application of portfolio theory to real estate investment was illustrated and the contrast between real estate markets and security markets stressed. The use of high leverage, the localized nature of real estate markets, the general lack of transaction information, and the lack of sophistication on the part of participants make it difficult to use modern portfolio theory in the development of real estate portfolios. Methods of developing input data were discussed, and an example of the use of a portfolio model was presented for the case of a two-asset portfolio. Four steps are required to develop a two-asset portfolio: (1) Derive estimates of rates of return and associated probabilities; (2) calculate E(R) and variance for each project; (3) calculate covariance; (4) calculate and graph the efficient frontier. Later, the arithmetic solution model for the case of a two-asset portfolio was expanded to the general case of N assets using the general calculus model. A brief overview of research on the impact of real estate on mixed-asset portfolios as well as research on the performance of real estate portfolios was presented. Current research, it was found, has not fully examined the problem of developing efficient

---

[42] See Ross, op. cit., and Roll, op. cit., for a full discussion of the current status of capital asset theory (footnote 7).

real estate portfolios, and diversification of modern real estate portfolios is still largely naive.

The characteristics of several institutional funds were examined to illustrate the level of performance of such portfolios and the apparent failure to use sophisticated models in their development. Although research in real estate portfolio modeling is still in its infancy, the impetus for further research is being provided by the rapid growth of large institutional investors. During the next decade research in this field will surely make dramatic progress, and the extensive use of portfolio selection models for real estate portfolio management is sure to become a reality.

Developing a Personal Portfolio with Real Estate*

There's no luck to professional portfolio investing. It is a craft, involving thousands of decisions a year. You can no more pile up a superlative record by luck or accident than you can win a chess tournament by luck or accident. . . . Go-go "performance" investors skate around like daddy long legs on a pond; pile too much weight on, and they sink. . . . If someone asks me what the best preparation is for the investment counsel profession, I usually reply: the classics. The vast tableau of century upon century of detailed analysis of discoveries, conflicts, statecraft, learning and human growth and turmoil offers a unique perspective on the problems we find so puzzling.[1]

John Train

This chapter considers the process of developing and implementing a strategy for a personal portfolio containing real estate properties. It does not pretend to tell you what your investment strategy and objectives should be, or even that real estate or any other particular type of investment should be included in your

[1] John Train, *The Money Masters — Nine Great Investors: Their Winning Strategies and How You Can Apply Them* (New York: Harper & Row, 1980), p. xiii.

* This chapter was coauthored by Dr. Larry Wofford, Associate Professor of Finance and Real Estate, University of Tulsa, Oklahoma, and Distinguished Professor and Visiting Chairholder in Real Estate, University of Hawaii, 1981– 1982. We also gratefully acknowledge the assistance of F. Lee Ring, a graduate student at Georgia State University.

portfolio. Your own philosophy, goals, objectives, and perceptions should ultimately determine your investment strategy and how it is implemented to build your personal portfolio.

Conventional financial wisdom has noted that all the attributes of any investment—prestige, liquidity, estate building, protection of purchasing power, diversification, tax planning, regular periodic returns, marketability, leverage, and capital gains—can be compressed into the two variables of return and risk. However, any spouse who has encountered the anger of the other spouse at the suggestion that the couple second mortgage their single-family house to buy another "investment" knows that the process of personal investing is not based on logic but, rather, on human experience. Unfortunately, as a result, many people also find it impossible to treat their personal financial affairs in a businesslike manner.

ADOPTING A PORTFOLIO-BUILDING STRATEGY

Everyone with surplus income available for saving or discretionary consumption has to make the same basic decision that a large corporation makes. What assets or services should be acquired? How should the purchase be financed? How much money should be spent on current consumption?

In Chapter 2 the reader was urged to adopt the goal of maximizing returns relative to risks. As we developed this concept, we saw that such an objective had to be achieved within the framework of various time-period constraints—the property life cycle, the ownership life cycle, and the investor life cycle. In this chapter these three life cycle concepts are integrated into the broader concept of a portfolio life cycle, and are examined from the viewpoint of an individual investor seeking to accumulate wealth through portfolio development. For strategic planning purposes, an individual's personal portfolio life cycle should be viewed as a business entity of limited duration—it produces income, pays expenses, and provides surplus funds for investment toward the objective of accumulating wealth.

Perhaps many people reject the idea of systematically planning their financial affairs because the problem is overwhelming. Exhibit 26–1 illustrates why this may be so.[2] It provides a framework for evaluating problems on the basis of three attributes: complexity, dynamism, and uncertainty. The easiest problems are those in corner 1. Such problems involve few variables; the values are known with certainty and do not change over time. As we move toward corners 2, 3, 4, 5, 6, 7, and ultimately 8, the problems become more complex, the environment is more dynamic, and there is more uncertainty. Portfolio building for an individual is similar to problem solving in corner 8.

The Portfolio Life Cycle

There are three stages in the life of a personal portfolio: the feeding stage, the growth stage, and the benefit stage. The *feeding stage* is the period during which

[2] Ronald A. Howard, "The Foundations of Decision Analysis," *IEEE Transactions on Systems Science and Cybernetics,* September 1968, p. 213.

EXHIBIT 26–1. The Problem Space

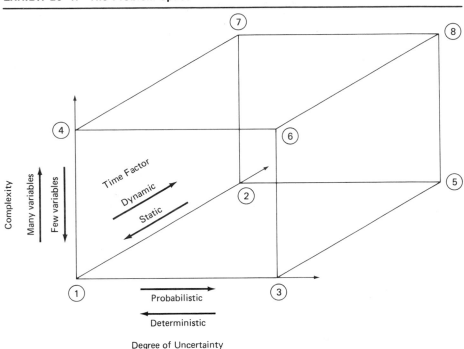

SOURCE: Ronald A. Howard, "The Foundations of Decision Analysis," IEEE *Transactions on Systems Science and Cybernetics,* September 1968, p. 213.

savings and money from other sources are used to create portfolio assets. This is somewhat like priming a pump. The emphasis at this stage is on a personal budget. Such a budget is essential in planning for the systematic savings that will provide the capital to be used in acquiring appropriate assets for the portfolio. The length of time one remains in this stage is directly related both to one's willingness to sacrifice immediate wants in order to maximize savings and to the success of the investments in producing expected returns.

The *growth stage* is achieved when the portfolio is capable of producing income (ordinary income or capital gains) in sufficient quantity so that investment and reinvestment goals become self-sustaining. At this point one may produce a synergistic effect by continuing to feed savings into the portfolio.

The *benefit stage* is achieved when the portfolio is generating current income sufficient to satisfy personal objectives and to provide for management costs, thereby allowing the investor to conserve the capital assets of the portfolio. In the case of retirement, for example, one might consider enjoying benefits in the form of both current income and an actual reduction in the asset value of the portfolio through use of the principal.

It should be emphasized that for any given stage there is no single best strategy. For example, some investors prefer a relatively low-risk strategy and are willing to accept a lower expected rate of return during the feeding stage. Such a person may prefer apartment investments, for example, to raw land. Another may feel that the feeding stage is an excellent time to take the risks involved in investing in raw land, trading on the high potential for gain.

Managing Risk in the Personal Portfolio

While modern portfolio theory stresses a scientific approach to the selection of institutional portfolio assets (see Chapter 25), such a normative framework is too elaborate and unwieldy for most individuals. It is generally accepted that business-related risk (*unsystematic* risk) for institutional investors may be eliminated through efficient diversification. Furthermore, it is presumed that market risk (*systematic* risk) can be tailored to a level that will provide the investor with a maximum return. However, it is felt that *individual* investors who are building personal portfolios will find the tools of modern portfolio management theory of limited use, for the following reasons:

1. It is rare for an individual investor at most stages of portfolio development to own the critical minimum number of assets necessary to ensure sufficient diversification.
2. The differences between stocks and securities, on the one hand, and real estate, on the other, discourage the use of common-stock-dominated portfolio models to control *systematic* risk in real estate assets.
3. The extensive data requirements of most portfolio models and the limited quantitative background of most individuals preclude their use in personal portfolio development.

As we saw in Chapter 25, Miles and Rice proposed a market index that, when fully developed, would sum the value of human capital, real property, and common stock into a new market index. This composite index would be much closer to reality than the inherently biased narrowly defined stock market indexes.[3] Unfortunately, more research is needed before such an index can be developed and put to practical use. The value of the human capital component must be revised to account for maintenance costs and quality variations. Attention must also be given to the problem of finding an acceptable source of national data on real estate market prices and rates of return.

Gau and Kohlhepp made an interesting attempt to develop beta coefficients for estimating the undiversifiable risk of real property.[4] In a lucid statement of the problem, they proposed three possible methods of estimating the value of beta (for real estate) in a capital asset pricing model: (1) the historical data of the specific property's value over time; (2) an estimation of beta (β) derived from comparable properties' values and earnings records; and (3) the beta of a publicly

---

[3] Mike E. Miles and Michael Rice, "Toward a More Complete Investigation of the Correlation of Real Estate Investment Yield to the Rate Evidenced in the Money and Capital Markets: The Individual Investor's Perspective," *Real Estate Appraiser and Analyst,* November-December 1978, pp. 8–19.
[4] George W. Gau and Daniel Kohlhepp, "Estimation of Equity Yield Rates Based on Capital Market Returns," *Real Estate Appraiser and Analyst,* November-December 1978, pp. 33–40.

traded real estate firm that specializes in investments similar to the subject property.

Assuming that the portfolio is large enough to overcome unsystematic risk, the latter method has some merit as long as great care is taken in matching the subject portfolio's assets with the publicly traded corporation's assets. Defining "similarity of investment," however, is no small problem. Gau and Kohlhepp also provide methods for calculating the betas for the historical-data approach and the comparable-property approach. It appears likely that further research based on their article may develop computer software that will enable portfolio investors to use such proxies for developing beta coefficients. However, calculating betas is still too laborious a task for the individual investor in terms of costs versus benefits realized. It is more likely that the individual investor will use IRR and PV analysis with Ellwood (mortgage equity) capitalization rates as a market proxy, when appropriate, to monitor the equity yield rates and investment values of real estate assets in the overall portfolio.

In summary, the apparently precise and objective standards for measuring performance of portfolio assets are based on the assumption that rational equity participants in real estate markets diversify sufficiently to eliminate unsystematic risk. This book rejects that premise for individuals because it is not achievable when the portfolio has a significant portion of its assets in real estate or other nonfinancial assets. Experience indicates that only in the late growth or benefit stage of a large individual portfolio could an individual real estate investor succeed in achieving the essential objective of sufficiently diversified assets in order to eliminate the diversifiable risk while selecting *nonrandomly* chosen real properties that meet such criteria as tax-planning considerations, marketability, cycles in the local economy, and debt service contractual requirements. While studies have indicated that eight or ten *randomly* selected securities are sufficient to eliminate *most* of the diversifiable risk in a portfolio,[5] it is improbable that most individual investors will achieve this minimum. In any case, the beta and other regression coefficients that might be used are too laborious to develop at this time, or the proxy for an appropriate beta (e.g., publicly traded real estate company) has characteristics and attributes that usually make it unrepresentative of the subject properties being analyzed for individual portfolio management purposes.

Here we are going to present a financial planning scenario that makes personal portfolio management part of a life plan. Its holistic nature will take the individual into many fundamental aspects of real-world involvement that are usually thought of as outside the scope of traditional financial planning.

BASIC STEPS IN DEVELOPING AND IMPLEMENTING A PERSONAL FINANCIAL PLAN

In Exhibit 26–2 we show a process for developing a philosophy and strategy for implementing a personal financial plan. The reader will note a strong congruence between the real estate investment strategy developed in Part III and the model

---

[5] J. Evans and S. Archer, "Diversification and Reduction of Dispersion," *Journal of Finance*, December 1968, pp. 761–767, and Robert Klemkosky and Robert Martin, "The Effect of Market Risk on Portfolio Diversification," *Journal of Finance*, March 1975.

EXHIBIT 26-2. A Strategic Framework for Personal Financial Management

---

1. Develop a personal philosophy.
2. Do a personal situation audit of
   • Current financial condition.
   • Personal attributes and aspirations.
3. Reassess philosophy in view of the personal situation audit.
4. Develop a master strategy for portfolio building to include real estate.
5. Assemble a team of professional advisers and consultants to assist in implementing the strategy.
6. Implement the strategy.
7. Monitor and periodically evaluate the plan's performance.
8. The plan should be flexible enough to adapt to
   • Changes in the environment (political, legal, economic, social, personal).
   • Opportunities and threats.
   • Individual strengths and weaknesses.

---

set forth here. Your plan should organize your financial and investment activities into a cohesive, internally consistent package.

Developing a Personal Philosophy

Whether you are a butcher, a baker, or a real estate investor, your personal philosophy should give purpose to your saving and investment plans. Most of us find that successful pursuit of a full-time career, while it produces the savings that "feed" a portfolio, leaves little time for portfolio building and management. Therefore, one needs a set of personal beliefs and values as they relate to saving and investing in order to achieve one's objectives.

The following are examples of a variety of personal plans, expressed as goals to be achieved. As you can see, there is no limit to the possible variations.

Short-range goals, for example, might include a vacation, a better car, jewelry, accumulating a down payment for the first real estate investment, having a savings account containing about six times monthly expenses as a liquidity reserve, or adequate life insurance to enable your family to maintain its present life style if you should die.

Long-range goals might be identified as an inflation-protected retirement income of $30,000 in 1980 dollars; a first-rate private school education for your two children, now aged 8 and 10; a cache of ten pounds of gold bullion; a camera safari to Kenya; an art collection containing a Chagall, a Miro, a Gauguin, a Dali, and similar works; a cellar of fine wines; or a major gift to your favorite university to establish a chair of real estate.

Ideally, such brainstorming will be a contemplative attempt to rein in your imagination and establish life-sized goals.

The Personal Situation Audit

A prerequisite to developing a strategy for building a personal portfolio containing real estate assets is a comprehensive analysis of your current financial condition and a qualitative assessment of your managerial skills and the income potential arising out of your primary career.

Estimating the Cost of Producing an Inventory of Assets

Quantifying the monetary costs of acquiring assets can be a very sobering experience for an ambitious young person with little in the way of current income or financial assets. Two simple examples should make the point. Assume that a young person, A, 25 years old, wishes to buy a home with a 40-year mortgage for $60,000 at an interest rate of 14 percent (monthly payments of $702.69). A is making a commitment to spend $337,291.20 of earning power to pay off that $60,000 mortgage, at which time A will be 65 years old.

Another person, B, decides to postpone the housing purchase for ten years. Instead of monthly payments of $702, B allocates the same amount toward debt service on a six-unit self-managed apartment building. Because the B family will occupy one unit, we must lower the rate of return on the investment to impute a charge for the value of the shelter. Using a rate of return of 7.5 percent, we find from the compound interest tables that B will have accumulated a fund of $124,907.10 at the end of ten years by way of equity build-up from the net operating income and the $702 monthly payments.

Assuming that home prices have risen 7.5 percent a year, a house equivalent to the one purchased by A for $60,000 would cost $133,000. However, B needs a mortgage of only $8,093. If the $8,093 were financed for thirty years at 14 percent with monthly payments of about $150 (we have used the same target age of 65), then over the years B would spend a total of $56,514 out of current income.

In effect, the propensity to save and invest would make an additional $280,777—the difference between A's commitment of $337,291 and B's total of $56,514—available over the forty-year period for investing or other important life cycle objectives. (Note: We realize that these examples simplify many assumptions concerning taxes, changes in value, and so forth. However, they illustrate the power of compound interest and the need for early identification of goals.)

By coupling the power of compound interest with estimates of the costs of various short- and long-range goals, you can easily estimate the assets that must be created by your portfolio:

Example. Ten years from now you want to be able to send your 8-year-old to a fine university for four years. Assume that in 1980 a university education costs $7,500 a year and the estimated inflation premium is 7.5 percent per year. Therefore, average costs for the years 1990—1994 are estimated to be $18,000 per year. You make the judgment to deduct from that amount the cost (adjusted for inflation) of supporting the child, on the assumption that you would be paying that amount anyway out of your 1990 income. This reduces the required four-year annuity to $14,000 per year. Your goal for 1990, then, is to have assets in your portfolio that will enable you to deposit a sum at a safe rate of 5.5 percent that will pay $14,000 per year for four years. The present value of that required annuity will be $49,072. Current investment opportunities indicate that you can either save at 7.5 percent in an insured account or, by taking more risk in a real estate investment, realize a return of 15 percent IRR over a ten-year period.

To save: To produce $49,000 in ten years at 7.5 percent, the calculation uses the sinking factor (column 3, Appendix B): .00562 × $49,000 = $275.38 per month saving rate.

To invest: One must invest $12,122 at a 15 percent IRR to have the $49,000 fund ready in ten years. The calculation uses the ten-year reversionary factor (column 4, Appendix B): .247185 × $49,000 = $12,122 at 15 percent per year.

This straightforward method of monetizing the size of the portfolio necessary to achieve your goals will set the stage for doing the personal situation audit.

During this evaluation stage one should stretch one's philosophical goals. Stage 3 (benefits) is the time to cut back and redefine personal goals. During the feeding stage one defers objectives to achieve a calculated lump sum or annuity at some time in the future. The authors would not presume to suggest what your investment philosophy should be. Thus, no detailed example is given.

Since this chapter recommends a conservative strategy toward risk taking, it is suggested that a minimum capital base to sustain one's primary career income potential is necessary before one risks assets on potential capital gains. Therefore, while preparing your statement of financial condition you should answer the following questions:

1. Are you, your spouse, and others of your choice adequately insured?
2. Are your insurable assets adequately insured against casualty loss?
3. Do you have sufficient savings in cash or its equivalent for *emergencies?*
4. Do you have in relatively *liquid reserves* the assets necessary to meet the "surprise" calls for cash arising out of leveraged investments?
5. Do you have seed money ready for investing? How large is this equity capital fund?
6. How do you rate the investment assets you currently hold in terms of liquidity, marketability, adequacy and stability of returns, protection against inflation, availability of financial leverage, tax shelter benefits, possible appreciation of value, and the burden of management? In effect, what is your current buy, sell, or hold position with regard to each investment asset?

Preparing a Statement of Financial Worth

In order to determine your current net worth (i.e., assets − liabilities = net worth) you should prepare a financial statement. In addition to the balance sheet, you will need supporting statements detailing all benefits—insurance, retirement, annuities, survivors' rights, social security, and death benefits—that would be realized.

A growing net worth is a way of measuring the effectiveness of one's financial planning strategy. We urge that an annual historical record of net worth be maintained as an incentive to portfolio building.

The first step in determining your net worth is to detail the types and relative amounts of your assets. The following is a typical list of personal asset accounts, with commentary:

Assets

- *Cash equivalent reserves:* Cash on hand, checking accounts, checks not yet deposited, U.S. treasury bills and notes, banker's acceptances, commercial paper, and other assets that can easily be converted into cash at par.
- *Notes receivable (one year)*: Principal and interest due within the next year on nonmarketable loans owed to you.
- *Liquidity reserves:* Time deposits (penalty for early withdrawal), high-quality common stock, preferred stock, bonds, money market funds.
- *Optional investment fund:* Stocks and other marketable securities held for growth (diversification objective).
- *Investment real estate:* See Chapter 17 for how to monitor current value and devise an appropriate buy– hold– sell– exchange strategy.
- *Home (market value)*: Obtain the range of current value from a broker who regularly sells in the area. This is not an appraisal but merely a curbstone valuation, usually done *gratis* in the hope of getting a listing later.
- *Home furnishings:* Do not list collectibles. Clothing should be omitted. More and more Americans are putting part of their wealth in this category. Use your judgment to determine whether you have value here. Get the items appraised and photographed about every three years. Place the photos and inventory with the value estimate in your safe deposit box for proof in the event of casualty loss.
- *Collectibles:* This item probably should be divided into two classes: (1) heirlooms and other items of sentimental value that one would be very reluctant to sell, and (2) collectibles, such as stamps, coins, gems, and works of art that were purchased because of their market value. Avoid the temptation to overvalue these items because of personal biases.
- *Other tangible personal property:* Automobiles, yard equipment, power tools, boats, trailers, musical instruments that were not included in home furnishings or collectibles.
- *Cash value of life insurance:* Easily calculated from the policy documents, or call your agent to obtain the current amount.
- *Vested pension and profit-sharing rights:* Avoid counting any value based on a nonvested right. Most funds provide annual reports on the current value of your vested right.
- *Prepaid taxes:* Federal, state, and local taxes paid prior to the due date.
- *Miscellaneous assets:* Any other assets that have market value and have not yet been entered on your balance sheet.

Liabilities   *Current liabilities* are usually defined as accounts that are payable within 30 to 90 days:

- *Current accounts payable:* Should include the total balance on all bills, even those not yet received, such as MasterCard, Visa, department store charge accounts, and the like, even though you may be paying only a small fraction each month along with the usual interest costs of 18–22% per annum. Be sure to list any other personal debts.

- *Short-term liabilities:* Installment loans on automobiles, furniture, and home improvements with payment periods ranging upward to seven to ten years are often listed in this category. They are usually loans from banks or credit unions. List them with their terms and abbreviated conditions. Some may pledge specified assets as collateral security; in such cases include an explanatory note.
- *Security deposits from tenants:* This is a fiduciary receipt. In some cases the law requires that this amount not be commingled with other funds. In any event, it is a liability against your current assets.
- *Taxes and assessment due:* Real estate taxes, income taxes, personal property taxes, license fees, and the like are all claims against your current assets.

Long-term liabilities include the following types of accounts:

- *Mortgage payable on home:* Show balance with abbreviated terms, conditions, and interest rate.
- *Mortgage payable on other real estate:* Balance, with terms, conditions, and interest rate in an explanatory note. Itemize the properties.
- *Insurance policy loans outstanding:* Itemize for each policy. Include interest and terms of repayment.
- *Miscellaneous liabilities*

Net Worth (Your Current Equity Position) Subtract your total liabilities from your total assets; the result is your current net worth. Enter this figure on your historical record. Compare with your previous year's net worth and consider your rate of progress. Accumulating the first $100,000 is the hardest!

Analyzing the Balance Sheet

Analyzing the balance sheet is an exercise in classification that will shed light on the quality of your assets and liabilities and your past practices in relation to portfolio building. You should prepare a supporting document to your balance sheet that classifies any significant asset according to the following characteristics:

- *Ownership.* Do you own it? Does your spouse own it? What is the nature of the title? This information is necessary for tax planning, estate planning, and so forth.
- *Nature of the asset.* Was the asset purchased for personal use or was it meant to be an investment that would produce income and/or appreciate in value? Assets held for personal use are usually excluded from the financial-planning strategy unless a sale is necessary to maintain solvency.
- *Quality and variability of income.* Is the income in American dollars? Are there problems of foreign exchange rates? How would you rate the income stream as to stability, periodicity, and predictability? What is the estimated date on which any appreciation in value might be realized?

• *Risk level.* The general level of risk of each asset should be assessed. Possible risk categories are "safe," "moderately risky," "risky," and "speculative." (For further discussion see Chapter 12.)

• *Return level.* Analyze each asset for the level of expected return on the capital invested. The same *after-tax* cash flow analysis should be used on all assets for purposes of comparison. There will, of course, be some uncertainty about expected cash flow where appreciation has not been realized. Improvements in conversational computer software will make available at lower cost more powerful methods for evaluating risk, rate of return, and ratio analysis.[6] Evaluation of future returns, however, is primarily a subjective process.

Record Maintenance

In addition to drawing up and analyzing one's balance sheet, it is essential that one maintain permanent records on assets—date of purchase, original basis, adjusted basis, and depreciation schedules arising from capital additions—in order to accurately estimate the tax consequences of a sale or other disposition. Finally, one should note any special or unusual characteristics of assets or liabilities. For example, some heirs are barred from selling or pledging certain assets; some liabilities may contain prepayment penalties; and so forth.

Some individuals may feel that they don't have sufficient insight to do a personal situation audit. Such individuals should at least try, and then seek advice from a trusted confidant who has the capacity to be totally honest. In this way realism will probably be achieved.

The Seven-Step Personal Audit

A personal audit can be as wide ranging or as narrow as you choose, depending on how you define your personal philosophy. The personal characteristics and attributes that should be defined and discussed are set forth in Exhibit 26–3.

While it may be difficult to relate your current capabilities to the goals and objectives of your philosophy, it is necessary to try to structure this analysis of your personal investment abilities and motivations. The learning curve for this exercise is sharply upward, and monitoring your personal situation will be easier each year.

Evaluating the Earnings Record

Past earnings records and sound judgment about opportunities for raises and promotions in the primary career produce the trend-line estimates. Some individuals may have sources of funds other than their primary career income.

Anticipating Extraordinary Expenses

Calls for cash to meet liability commitments can reduce the funds available for investment. In addition, there are items that a financial analysis will not reveal. Is a

---

[6] "Program for Personal Financial Planning," Educational Programming Systems, St. Louis, Missouri, 1980 ($199) (Apple); "Stockpak Program" (TRS-80), Standard & Poor; "Portfolio Master," Investors Software, San Francisco ($75.00); and many others are available. See also Herbert T. Spiro, *Financial Planning for the Independent Professional* (New York, Wiley, 1978), p. 3.

EXHIBIT 26–3. The Seven-Step Personal Audit

Step 1
- What is your personal earnings record for the past five years? Make a fair and reasonable projection of earnings from your primary career for the next five years.
- What is your current marginal income tax bracket (federal, state, and local combined)?
- What is your current maximum *effective* tax rate (federal, state, and local combined)?
- Do you have sources of funds other than primary career income?

Step 2
- Do you anticipate any extraordinary, nonrecurring, or semipermanent *increases* in personal expenses in the next three to five years?

Step 3
- Have you adopted and implemented a form for an annual budget of income and expenses? Will your current budget and balance sheet analysis produce the following information?
- *How much of your net worth is currently available for investment* in real estate and other investment media? This presumes systematic rather than impetuous investing, and sufficient liquidity reserves. An individual should not risk investing in real estate projects before such reserves have been established.
- *How much of an increment to net worth is expected* over the next three to five years? Will it become available for investment?
- *Are you adequately insured* against appropriate risks? For an individual five types of insurance are usually necessary: life, health, hazard, business and personal liability, and disability.
- Are your *cash equivalent reserves* adequate for personal emergencies?
- Are your *liquidity reserves* adequate for the risks associated with your current investments and those you contemplate in the next few years?

Step 4
- How do you rate yourself as a risk taker? How much risk you can handle emotionally and afford financially is a critical factor in this situation audit.

Step 5
- What is the main objective for the portfolio at this time?
- What is the desired ratio between periodic income and capital growth?

Step 6
- What is the minimally acceptable average annual rate of return (after taxes) for each of the following? (1) Cash equivalent reserves; (2) Liquidity reserves; (3) The optional investment fund; (4) Investment real estate; (5) Other investment assets

Step 7
- In real time, how many hours per week, per month, per year can you devote to implementing the portfolio-building strategy and monitoring the plan's performance?

personal relationship in trouble? Might you have to provide financial help to a family member? Will you be forced to buy out a business associate soon? Have you done adequate contingency planning?

Adopting an Annual Budget

The budget form shown in Exhibit 26– 4 may appear too detailed for you. In that event you may consolidate some of the accounts at the cost of becoming less explicit. However, it is worth noting that recordkeeping in the manner illustrated in Exhibit 26– 4 can be a great aid should the Internal Revenue Service audit your personal tax return. Opting for "intuitive" budgeting without record keeping is rarely workable. Few individuals can achieve savings and investment goals without structured plans. Software for personal microcomputers is making such planning more convenient.

How Much of the Net Worth Is Available for Investment?   This is a loaded question because it presumes systematic rather than impetuous investing. Only after allocating a sufficient base to liquid assets should an individual risk investing in real estate projects.

Maintaining Adequate Insurance   Adequate insurance is necessary for systematic financial planning. For an individual, five types of insurance are usually necessary: life, health, hazard, business and personal liability, and disability. Failing to provide adequate coverage against the usual risk of loss is poor risk management and may result in a financial plan that is self-destructing.

Life insurance needs vary, depending on life style and number of dependents. The objective within a real estate portfolio should be to provide (1) a source of funds for living expenses to replace the lost earning power of the deceased wage earner for a transition period and (2) another source of funds to pay the fees for management of the portfolio, including property management over a transition period.

In most cases decreasing term insurance is the contract of choice for those who are building portfolios. The forced-savings feature of whole life and other such policies do not seem appropriate for systematic portfolio builders because of the low rate of return, although one may want to consider their surrender value as a ready source of liquidity reserves. The new universal-life policies may be an appropriate compromise.

Do not ignore the term insurance provided for you at your primary place of employment. Another source of income protection for surviving dependents, which is much more liberal than most people realize, is the social security system. By taking into consideration these sources of income protection, one may minimize the current cost of insurance protection and thus increase the level of annual savings available for investing.

Health insurance has become a necessary protection against catastrophic costs that could destroy financial plans. Often the primary place of employment provides excellent coverage. However, it is of great importance to be knowledgeable about the nature and extent of that coverage. Recently, for example, Willy B.

EXHIBIT 26-4. Form for an Annual Personal Budget

CATEGORY	1. Monthly Budget	2. Jan.	3. Feb.		12. Nov.	13. Dec.	14. This Yr. Total	15. Last Yr. Total	16. This Yr. Est.
			←——THIS YEAR'S ACTUAL EXPENSES——→						
Deposits in savings accounts									
Vacation (or other) fund									
State Income Tax									
Federal Income Tax									
F.I.C.A. (Social Security)									
Property tax on home									
Medical insurance									
Life insurance									
Disability insurance									
Home insurance									
Auto insurance									
Home mortgage or rent									
Auto Licenses									
Church contributions									
Other contributions									
Domestic help									
F.I.C.A. for domestic help									
Electricity									
Water									
Gas									
Heating fuel									
Telephone									
Home maintenance & repair									
Gardener									
Garden supplies									
Pest control									
Supermarket									
Pharmacy									
Cleaners & laundry									
Clothing									
Bank credit cards									
Gasoline, etc.									
Auto repairs									
Auto club									
Local transportation & cabs									
Membership clubs									
Education									
Doctors & dentists									
Subscriptions									
Entertainment (est.)									
Liquor									
Safe deposit box									
Tax accountant									
Attorney fees (est.)									
Payments on other loans									
Cash gifts to children for birthdays & Christmas									
TOTALS									

Source: Richard K. Rifenbark, *How to Beat the Salary Trap—8 Steps to Financial Independence* (New York: McGraw-Hill, 1978), p. 59.

found it necessary to commit his son, who had a drug problem, to a psychiatric hospital. He wasn't worried because he believed he had $250,000 in major medical catastrophe insurance. However, the policy specifically excluded in-patient care in a psychiatric hospital. Result: a bill of over $85,000, which Willy paid by liquidating part of his hard-earned portfolio.

Hazard insurance provides protection against casualty losses arising out of certain enumerated perils. Because of the large pools over which the risk is spread, the costs of protection against loss from fire, burglary, larceny, wind damage, lightning, armed robbery, arson, and even flood insurance are generally low. (The federal government provides special flood and crime insurance for heavily affected areas, which further minimizes such risks.) Since many policies require full coverage or an 80 percent minimum co-insurance clause for full indemnification, one must be knowledgeable about insurance or have expert advice. There are rate-deviating companies, such as nonassessable mutual casualty companies, that pass on the benefits of insuring a preferred-risk-only pool. However, it may be worthwhile for the investor to instead pay full standard premiums in order to obtain the expert advice of an agent. An annual insurance review, which should be part of such an agent's service, is important.

Today multiperil policies provide coverage against tort and contractual liabilities of an ordinary business nature other than the risks of profit and loss from operations, as well as enumerated perils. Because these "excess coverage" policies usually require an underlying basic coverage, one may obtain multimillion-dollar coverage at very low cost.

Professional and business insurance is a low-cost way of shifting the risk of loss for errors and omissions and tort and contractual liabilities, as well as other forms of malpractice and negligence, to the insurance carrier. We list this type of insurance here, rather than under hazard insurance, to emphasize that good property management practices can reduce premium charges through good loss-experience ratings. If one is managing for a group that has the right to litigate, one should insure against the risks. Adequate landlord-tenant and public liability insurance is necessary for those who own and/or manage real estate. Recently rent interruption insurance has become available to replace income that has been interrupted by a casualty that has not destroyed the premises.

Disability insurance is virtually mandatory for high-income individuals who are also taking investment risks. We live in an age of high speeds and amazing medical advances. It is possible to live for many years after being permanently disabled by accidents, cancer, heart disease, stroke, and exotic diseases like multiple sclerosis. We recommend disability coupled with accident insurance, which covers death, dismemberment, and loss of sight. Often this may be purchased through payroll deductions at low cost at the place of employment.

It is worth noting that one can properly deduct the costs of various kinds of insurance, including term life, as necessary expenses of doing business for dealers and operators of Section 1231 assets, and even for the active managers of a business entity that manages investment assets. Corporations and partnerships are usually the appropriate vehicles.

Do You Have Adequate Cash Reserves?   Estimate the savings needed to provide a fund that would be adequate for six months of family expenses while you are in the feeding or early growth stage of building a portfolio. This may be reduced to a lower level (say, three months) when your investments are providing a steady stream to supplement primary earnings. One should invest such funds in an immediately accessible, insured savings account; the return could be maximized by putting a 30-day fund in the passbook account and placing the balance in a less liquid fund, such as a 180-day certificate with risk penalties for early withdrawal. The objective is safety of principal and instant liquidity. If the fund is large enough, one could invest $10,000 or more in U.S. treasury bills, which may be easily and promptly liquidated in the event of an emergency. Recently money market funds have provided prompt liquidity with relatively high interest rates; these investments, however, are not insured.

Building Liquidity Reserves The primary function of liquidity reserves is to provide immediate access to ready funds to meet the surprises caused by errors in investment judgment and external political, socioeconomic, and legal factors. In effect, this is a contingency fund. The goal is appreciation in value through higher yields with a minimum of investment risk. However, since the cash equivalent reserves are adequate for living expenses, we can invest in media with more potential risk, giving up some safety of principal, risking lower returns to seek higher yield, and concentrating on a high degree of marketability. We recommend that one maintain a liquidity reserve in *excess* of the cash equivalent fund (which should be about 5 to 10 percent of net worth).

Consider growth stocks rated A-minus or better by services like Standard & Poor. We recommend the strategies espoused by Benjamin Graham *if one can read financial statements, has patience, and has a bent for ratio analysis.*[7] In general, it is recommended that the following criteria be set up as standards for selection: (1) A stock should be bought for less than two-thirds of its net quick assets, then sold at 100 percent of current assets; (2) the company should owe less than its net worth; (3) the earnings-per-share yield should be twice the prevailing Aaa bond yield; and (4) the dividend policy should approximate two-thirds of the current Aaa bond yield. The rules for selling are as follows: (1) Sell if the stock market price of the stock has gone up 50 percent or after two years, whichever comes first; (2) sell if a dividend is omitted; and *finally* (3) sell if an earnings decline causes the market price of the stock to decline to less than 50 percent over your target price. Of course, implementing this strategy takes time and a data source like *Standard & Poor's Stock Guide.*

If one would rather play chess or bridge, then one must depend on the work of others. Standard & Poor's *Outlook* regularly lists stocks that are selling below working capital and at discounts from book value. The *Value Line Investment Survey* occasionally reports on stocks that are selling below net liquidating value. *Forbes* magazine has a famous annual report, "Loaded Laggards," that lists stocks selling below their stated book value. We recommend that you obtain the standard stock reports on the individual company and consider management, earnings record, market share, products and new products, nature of research and development, high and low prices in recent years, adequacy of trading volume, and so forth before deciding whether to buy.

If you want to invest in equity securities but lack enough time to monitor the

---

[7] Benjamin Graham, *The Intelligent Investor,* 5th ed. (New York, Harper & Row, 1978).

stock portfolio, you might consider a no-load mutual fund after carefully investigating its investment objectives, portfolio, earnings record, and capital appreciation over time.

Optional Investment Funding   Early in the portfolio life cycle the primary objective is to be conservative as reserves are created and insured against various risks. Safety of capital is more important than yield or appreciation. Then comes a transition stage in which the important planning objective is to create enough ready capital to invest in real estate. Later, after one has passed from the feeding to the late growth stage and the real estate in the portfolio is achieving cash flow goals, one can return to this step and make optional investments in other assets in order to diversify the portfolio.

The strategy adopted here should reflect your personality and risk-taking capacity. However, the key to creating a wealth-building optional investment portfolio is understanding the dynamics of economic change.

We do not recommend dealing in options or commodities, or even regularly trading in securities. Since real estate can be considered a speculation until the gross rent schedule, net operating income, and cash throw-off have proven to be up to expectations, portfolio diversification should tend toward more conservative investments. In fact, an important underlying objective is to create a fund that is "bankable" in the sense that the securities will be acceptable as pledges against bank loans to facilitate real estate investing. An aggressive investor should economize on time by buying fewer stocks, which can be carefully analyzed and monitored. A more conservative investor can simply spread funds among the blue-chip and growth stocks while seeking the time to purchase defensive and cyclical stocks with an eye to the peaks and troughs of the business cycle.

A major effort should be made to buy low and sell high. This is not a homily. Don't buy on a whim. Don't be an active trader. One should avoid buying at the feverish peaks of bull markets, and should use an overall holding period of from two to five years. Decide what your area of interest is and buy only after thorough study.

The stock market has a record of anticipating the end of a business recession. Maintain good records and make plans to respond to important signals. There are many different strategies for individual portfolio building.[8] You should select one that is suited to your own risk and return preferences. The securities market should be seen as a vehicle for appreciation and not a means of producing income during the early stages of your portfolio cycle. There are times when you may not want to invest in the market at all.

Investment Real Estate   How soon you embark on real estate investing depends on how you rate yourself as a risk taker. The *type* of real estate investment is also a reflection of how aggressive you are in relation to return/risk profiles. Residential real estate is usually the port of entry for most would-be real estate

---

[8] For complete treatment of this subject see Venita VanCaspel, *Money Dynamics for the 1980s* (Reston, Va.: Reston Publishing, 1980); John Train, *The Money Masters*, op. cit., and Richard Rifenbark, *How to Beat the Salary Trap* (New York: McGraw-Hill, 1978).

investors. Higher-tax-bracket investors may be more interested in office buildings, hotels and motels, or industrial buildings. The differences in investment and property management responsibilities between one type of real estate and another are detailed in Part IV of this book.

The Home as an Investment   Recently the effects of inflation have brought to the attention of nearly everyone the fact that the single-family home has gained in value faster than many other investments.

This book urges a conservative strategy. We suggest that the home as an asset should *not* be thought of as a source of funds for investing, unless one is willing to self-manage a duplex, triplex, quadraplex, or apartment building. The advantages of such a self-management arrangement are very real. For example, recreational amenities (shared with the tenants) can be made available at low cost. But individuals have aspirations other than wealth accumulation. Treating the home as an investment asset is fraught with the possibility of marital trouble unless you are absolutely certain that your *feelings* flow in the same direction as your logical thinking. It is suggested that equity in one's home be treated as something like a cash equivalent reserve—to be tapped only in an emergency.

In our opinion home furnishings should not be considered as part of the portfolio of a person who is investing in real estate. While they may have great value for personal use, it is difficult to find a market that will produce a fair value.

Collectibles   Though many people view gold, silver, gems, antique furniture, fine art, and other tangible goods as an important store of value, it is our opinion that those who are trying to build a portfolio and accumulate wealth will find such goods difficult to liquidate. No periodic income is produced, and appreciation is generally erratic. Until recently diamonds, gold, and bullion coins all performed well; now fine art is doing well. Those who have developed expertise in these specialized markets and can devote ample time to monitoring the market trends may continue to fare well. But be aware that these are markets with a limited utility function and subject to manipulation by arbitragers.

This review of various investment media sets the stage for the difficult task of evaluating yourself as a risk taker. It also will enable you to make some judgments about your minimally acceptable rates of return and the objectives of your portfolio.

Rating Yourself as a Risk Taker

How much risk can a person handle emotionally and afford financially? This may be the most difficult problem to answer.

Recently, a couple was presented with the opportunity to purchase a 34-unit student apartment building in a stable university community for $875,000. The building has been 94–100 percent occupied for over four years. The downpayment was to be $120,000, payable in two installments: $65,000 at settlement and the balance of $55,000 payable at the end of the first year.

The couple's combined income (after annual payments of $20,000 to their individual retirement accounts) was over $100,000. Thus, substantial shelter was needed.

Analysis indicated that over a five- to ten-year holding period an above-average return of 24–31 percent (IRR) based on after-tax cash flows might be realized. Depreciation and interest expense would provide over $35,000 of tax shelter benefits for each of the first two years. On the basis of apartment project analysis the recommendation was: *buy.* The couple had only a weekend to decide whether or not to make an offer because of competitive threats. There were some relevant personal factors to consider.

In order to make the downpayment of $65,000, the couple would be forced to exhaust their liquidity reserves, use up one month of their cash equivalent reserves, and borrow $10,000 against their optional investment fund, which was predominantly in high-grade municipal bonds. They were already facing calls in the total amount of $14,000 at the end of four months for final installment payments on purchases of two separate real estate partnership interests. Experience indicated that they normally saved about $20,000 per year out of take-home income. There was a high probability that in order to meet the second installment on the student apartment building they would be required to pledge more of the municipal bonds against a bank loan. So long as they remained in good health and were prepared to make some sacrifice, although the opportunity appeared risky, it was do-able.

On the other hand, one spouse was a physician who faced great stress and long hours, and had little time or energy to learn the subtleties of real estate investing. About 60 percent of their annual earnings came from the medical practice. The municipal bonds that would have to be pledged had been accumulated by this spouse prior to the marriage. As they discussed the opportunity, this spouse displayed great concern. Tempers flared.

In the end it appeared to the other spouse that the risk being taken was at a price of imposing great stress over the next few years until the cash-throw off, equity build-up, and appreciation of the property had proven itself. The ultimate decision was: *reject.* The anxious state of mind produced by the process of considering the investment had signaled to them that it was beyond their risk-taking capacities.

The evaluation of personal risk-taking capacity may be structured by considering the following factors:

What trade-off between return and risk are you willing to accept? for everyone there is a point at which the marginal possibility of greater returns no longer exceeds the possible costs. Some have suggested that there is an intuitive guide known as the "sleep factor." Accordingly, one continues to take on more investment risk until it starts to keep one awake at night, at which point one reduces the risk to a more comfortable level.

What degree of control must you have? There are good investments that require very little personal control or investment of time. The fiduciary responsibilities of the trustee preclude a high degree of control for individual retirement accounts (IRAs), profit-sharing plans, or defined-contribution plans under ERISA. One has little personal control over investments in national "blind pool" partnerships like the McNeil Real Estate Fund, Consolidated Capital Properties, Fox and Caskadon, and others.

If you feel that direct control is necessary, you may prefer to invest in self-managed real properties, special-purpose business properties in which you have a managing voice, land speculations, actively traded stocks, or collectibles. However, it is doubtful that anyone with a primary career would have the time or risk-taking capacity to invest in much more than one of these media at a time.

In structuring your risk-taking capacity you must consider your personal utility function, the degree of control you want, the degree of legal liability you are willing to assume, and the time you are willing to spend. An important part of the personal situation audit is gaining some insight into your own return and risk trade-offs and matching your investment philosophy with the current stage of your portfolio life cycle.

Identifying the Main Objectives of Your Portfolio

This exercise will crystallize the nature of the personal portfolio and convert intuitive thinking into the written goals of the portfolio-building process. By monetizing philosophical aspirations into wealth accumulation goals, you can estimate the size of the portfolio you must accumulate by the time you reach the benefit stage. Since we have already classified investment media as cash equivalent reserves, liquidity reserves, optional investment funds, real estate investments, and collectibles, in this step we review the balance sheet and identify the current stage of the portfolio life cycle.

By rating the assets according to quality and variablity of income, risk level, return level, and other such characteristics, you can evaluate whether or not the assets currently held match the stage in the portfolio life cycle. For example, in the feeding stage the current portfolio should not be dominated by assets designed to maximize current periodic income. A more appropriate strategy would be to move, in part, out of such assets and into assets that place more emphasis on appreciation in value and capital gains. Current income is predominantly a benefit-stage objective; in the growth stage one may work for more of a balance between assets that produce current income and assets selected primarily for appreciation.

Determining an Acceptable Rate of Return

What average annual rate of return (after tax) would be acceptable now and in the future for the following investments:

• Cash equivalent reserves: 5–9 percent?
• Liquidity reserves: 7.5–14 percent?
• The optional investment fund assets: 9–20 percent?
• Investment real estate assets: 11–35 percent?
• Your other investment assets: unknown?

The rates of return suggested above might be appropriate in the current monetary and fiscal climate; in the early 1960s they would have been astonishingly high.

Because investing, monitoring, and reinvesting take time and expertise, it makes sense to do only part of the portfolio management function yourself. For example, in the case of *cash equivalents* and *liquidity reserves* you can put funds in a time deposit account at a thrift institution and thereby avoid management costs. On the other hand, to maximize the return of this category one would have to invest in a go-go money market fund. This would require monitoring that portion of the portfolio. Similarly, in the optional investment fund some people prefer speculative appreciation while others would feel more comfortable with blue-chip stocks.

This exercise in identifying acceptable rates of return should enable you to focus on whether or not you have the skill or time to achieve the appropriate level of returns within each classification. In this way the skills you don't have will emerge and you are on the way toward identifying the people who must be added to the investment team to implement your strategy.

How Much Time Can You Devote to Portfolio Building?

This is a difficult decision. Few individuals with primary careers have the time to self-manage real estate investments. Whatever the case, an honest appraisal must be made of how much time—hours per day? days per week or month?—one is willing to give to implementing the portfolio strategy.

The situation audit is not yet complete. The next step is a "do" loop.

Reassessing the Personal Philosophy

For the most part, the process of reconsideration has been going on intuitively as we have proceeded through the steps of the personal audit. Perhaps it has become apparent that the proportion of earned income that you must allocate to savings is beyond your ability to sacrifice. Or it may be that the estimated size of the portfolio necessary for the benefit stage is such that you are now prepared to take more risk at the early stages than you had originally contemplated. Or you may realize that you will have to put in more time and effort than you were willing to give originally. You now know that the oceangoing yacht was merely a fantasy. Instead, you are willing to settle for a Sea Scout sailboat. Whatever the case, reappraise and clarify your philosophical objectives, for they will be the goals of your portfolio strategy.

Developing a Master Strategy

The foregoing process of settling philosophical objectives, reviewing one's financial status, and carefully considering one's situation enables one to develop a personal investment strategy. The solution to developing a portfolio strategy is found in the realization that perfectly naive and purely efficient strategies are end points on a continuum. By borrowing the basic concepts underlying the efficient approach, one may improve on the perfectly naive approach. Thus, a portfolio can be developed that will generally outperform a naive strategy, although it will not provide the risk reduction of the so-called efficient strategy.

The problem becomes more complex in a portfolio that contains real estate because of the nonrandom selection process and other factors affecting this heterogeneous commodity. One must consider both the real estate and the non-real-estate portions of the portfolio in order to achieve the overall objectives. The long-term strategy requires continuous monitoring and revision of the portfolio. Generally, you will find it necessary to consult attorneys, CPAs, stockbrokers, bankers, and experts in real estate and other subjects to establish the parameters of the overall strategy. You should use this opportunity to evaluate the skills and experience of such professionals and decide whether or not you want them on the team that will be helping you achieve your portfolio goals.

Personal financial planning is like planning a city; one is never finished. You should not be discouraged if important objectives change. If you find such a change necessary to fulfill important aspirations, then your strategy and plans should be changed to meet the new aspirations.

Naive Versus Efficient Portfolios

Diversification is the central concept of our personal portfolio management plan. The concept of modern portfolio theory, which was developed in depth in Chapter 25, defines an *efficient frontier* (see Exhibit 26–5) as the optimal combination of assets in which all risk and return trade-offs have been theoretically quantified.

EXHIBIT 26-5.   The Efficient Frontier

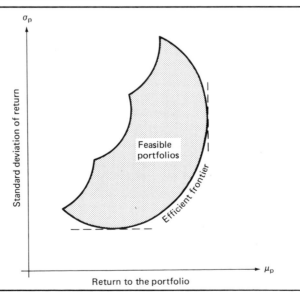

A naive approach, on the other hand, adopts the view that if one simply combines enough investments one can reduce portfolio risk. Any rational, risk-aversive investor will seek to be at the efficient frontier. Exactly where one will be at any given point in time depends on the perceived utility function. A naive portfolio strategy will produce a portfolio on the efficient frontier only by accident. We will seek a strategy between these two extremes.

An important concept from efficient portfolio management is that of minimizing risk for a given level of expected return. Another important concept is covariance. By applying these two concepts to the problem of individual portfolio management, even on a subjective basis, one may develop a better portfolio.

Individual portfolio management is constrained by the existence of subsidiary portfolios—cash equivalent reserves, liquidity reserves, optional investment funds, real estate investments, and possibly collectibles—whose risk should not exceed established levels. Thus, return and risk trade-offs must satisfy the requirements of these qualitatively different subsidiary portfolios.

The first step in deciding whether or not an investment asset should be added to the portfolio is to determine which of the subsidiary portfolios it is to become part of and whether its risk is suitable for that portfolio. At the subsidiary portfolio level, especially for the cash equivalent and liquidity reserves, the total risk of each asset may be more important, since these assets may have to be liquidated quickly. If the asset passes this test, then the nature of its covariance with the overall portfolio risk should be evaluated as the second step in the process. The decision rule would be to choose the asset with the lowest covariance. This would result in lowering overall portfolio risk. When removing an asset, the decision rule is to select the asset with the greatest covariance, unless it was satisfying a subsidiary-portfolio objective very nicely.

This basic concept is illustrated in Exhibit 26–6, in which the present portfolio is located at the intersection of the dotted lines. If one could revise the overall portfolio to reduce risk while keeping expected return constant, one would do so—assuming that a subsidiary portfolio was not affected unacceptably. The same holds true for the possibility of increasing returns while keeping risk constant.

Two areas, II and IV, in the figure are labeled "ambiguous." Whether you move your portfolio into these areas depends on your utility function, that is, on changes in your perceived willingness to take risk. It is presumed that as one moves from the feeding stage to the growth stage and into the benefit stage the proportions of the overall portfolio in relation to the various subsidiary portfolios will shift in response to these changed financial circumstances and personal needs. An example might be a shift from self-managed real estate into blue-chip common stocks with a record of stable cash dividends. Changes in risk must always be considered in relation to changes in expected returns.

To estimate whether or not the returns on two assets vary generally in the same direction, or to estimate the extent of covariance, it is necessary to return to basic investment analysis. For example, two potential office building investments will be affected by a major change in office employment in the market. Assuming that they are in close proximity to each other, they will also both be affected by the same competitive threats and environmental factors. A subjective analysis of the

EXHIBIT 26–6.   Portfolio Revision Decisions

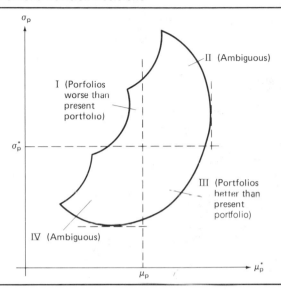

factors affecting the two office buildings would expect returns to be similarly affected. But further analysis might reveal that they have substantially different lease terms, dates of purchase, maintenance problems, and so forth, which in turn could cause expected returns to vary markedly. The important point is that one cannot take a purely naive approach to portfolio building. Although this is a subjective analysis, it has been structured to move portfolio decisions in the general direction of the efficient frontier.

While the preceding analysis is useful, it has assumed that the investor's objectives may be summarized in the two variables—expected return and risk. For those with a more mathematical bent, it may prove useful to consider a more complex portfolio decision function than the one illustrated in Exhibit 27–6. Such an analysis will indicate that the efficient frontier concept should have limited application in personal decisions.

Limitations on the efficient portfolio approach. Many investors have objectives that cannot be reduced to the two variables of rate of return and risk. Some real estate investors, for example, enjoy the prestige associated with ownership of a specific project, while others are quite willing to accept lower financial returns for a given level of risk to avoid the hassle of becoming familiar with a new property. Operating on the efficient frontier implies more property turnover and more frequent buy, sell, and hold decisions than usually occur in real estate.

To consider three variables, the efficient frontier concept must be changed from a curve to a multidimensional area. In Exhibit 27–5 this would mean extending another axis out of the paper toward you, resulting in a spherical surface. While real estate investors tend to seek satisfaction of multiattribute utility functions for the sake of efficiency, their investment calculus is usually dominated by rate-of-return and risk trade-offs. Personal aspirations will tend to cause efficient investment decision making to be interrupted by major changes in life situations. Divorce and property settlements are good examples.

Retirement and Tax Planning

It is now necessary to complicate the development of a realistic strategy even more by taking into consideration some very important laws concerning retirement rights and estate and inheritance taxes. It is possible to make the portfolio even more sophisticated, so that there are *two* portfolios within *each* subsidiary area. One is an individual subsidiary portfolio with the maximum flexibility that the law allows; the other is designed to conform to the special legal requirements of Keogh plans, individual retirement accounts (IRAs), defined-contribution (pension) and profit-sharing plans, or other ERISA pension plans. The attractive feature of these plans is that savings may be accumulated as a *deduction from taxable income.* The income tax is deferred until distributions are made, in accordance with the law, at the specified retirement age, which in some cases must be after age 59. The great advantage, especially for taxpayers in the upper marginal brackets, is that one is able to invest a portion of income that would otherwise be taxed away. In addition, interest earned—and to some extent capital gain—may be reinvested and compounded without paying taxes. This is a superior advantage.

Recently some of these plans have been liberalized so that an individual may participate as a trustee-administrator in investment and reinvestment decisions. It is also possible in the case of some of these plans to invest in real estate as long as the plan has a clause permitting such investment. Furthermore, it is also possible to draft some of the plans to permit loans (e.g., insurance policy loans) to the individual from the plan without triggering income taxes. Thus, tax deferral to later years may be achieved, real estate investments may be made, and liquidity reserves and optional investment funds may be created with before-tax income under these relatively new laws.

In the past many taxpayers have avoided taking advantage of the tax set-aside privileges because in the earlier Keogh plan, for example, the money was frozen in the account until age 59, and the penalties for early withdrawal were severe. Such problems still exist, but they can be circumvented by choosing the appropriate plan and carefully drawing up the plan to achieve the flexibility that the law permits. In effect, loans from the funds and investments in real estate may even be managed by the individual investor.

Good sources of information on the opportunities for portfolio building by such devices are the magazine *Medical Economics* and, of course, tax planning counselors.

There are some disadvantages. For example, if one plan participant adopts borrowing privileges, all must have this right. Investment in illiquid assets like real estate could create liquidity problems when some plan participants become eligible for payout. Since depreciation write-offs may not be passed through, this tends to limit plan investments to those that maximize eventual capital gain.

Another disadvantage is that such individual plans require plan administrators, trustees, and so forth. Expert tax and legal advice is imperative to avoid prohibited transactions and conform to ERISA regulations.

Estate Planning

Building a portfolio with the objective of wealth accumulation creates problems of inheritance, gift, and death taxes. Generally, a personal portfolio-building plan that will create an estate of over $600,000 makes expert estate-planning advice mandatory to properly avoid some taxes. One should keep in mind that taxes can create particular problems for an estate that is concentrated in real estate because distress sales may be necessary. The Internal Revenue Service accepts only cash and U.S. government securities in payment of taxes. The law provides limited flexibility for extensions to permit orderly liquidation.

Those who are self-managing real estate projects should certainly consider the possibility of untimely death. The individual should designate some appropriate person who has the training to carry on management. Provisions must also be made for managing the real estate investment pending its disposal in an orderly manner.

Guidelines for Diversifying Real Estate Investments

Since real estate is particularly susceptible to rate-of-return and risk problems, the individual investor should develop a portfolio that consciously maximizes diversification possibilities. On the other hand, specialize—do *not* diversify—if you are self-managing, until you are handling all the assets you comfortably can, considering the sleep factor. Specialize in a particular *property type* (residential real estate is recommended for most beginners). Specialize in a *neighborhood* or neighborhoods within the metro area in which you are employed. Use leases with which you are thoroughly familiar. Concentrate on an age (remaining economic life) of building in which you are familiar with the types of maintenance problems you will encounter. Use an ownership form for which you know most of the legal ramifications. Finally, try to stay with projects in which you have control over property management problems. A goal should be to get into large enough projects so that economies of scale will permit the services of an independent property manager, allowing you to concentrate on venture (investment) management functions. Finally, stay with tax avoidance procedures with which you are familiar and for which you can predict likely outcomes. To these general rules we suggest the following *exceptions:*

Form of ownership. During the feeding stage some people prefer self-management. Such a person may build a substantial portfolio using proprietorship; joint tenancy; small, closely held corporations; or small general partnerships. As a self-manager reaches the latter part of the growth stage, however, an effort should be made to move out of such management-intensive ownership into more passive forms like the national partnership, blue-chip common stock, equity REITs, and the like. On the other hand, if primary career opportunities are superior, one should not divert energy to self-management, even during the feeding stage. One should seek interests in general or limited partnerships with competent, ethical managing partners, or consider the national partnerships or equity REITs.

Diversity in demand profiles. This is a worthwhile objective. We have recommended residential real estate for beginners because of the stability of demand and because the building cycles are less extreme than in other types of real estate. On the other hand, concentration in residential buildings bears the risk of rent control in many areas of the country. To get the advantage of lease terms that are quite different from the typical residential lease, we suggest diversifying into other types of property, such as warehouses or office buildings.

Diversity in financing terms. This hardly seems like typical real estate investment advice. All other things being equal, most counselors recommend maximizing leverage. We suggest that, once the growth stage has been reached or certainly by the benefit stage, one should consider real estate investments with 60 to 70 percent leverage in order to minimize the downside risks implicit in the business and residential construction cycles. Although this reduces the rate of return, it also minimizes the risk and the "hassle" factor. While we urge maximizing leveraging in the early stages, one should ease up on the lever as portfolio-building goals are achieved.

Diversity in disposition. Tax planning is a routine part of real estate investing. Some simple investment rules are suggested here:

• Exchange if you can; otherwise, seek an installment sale. If that is not possible, consider refinancing if the market permits, since that will give you more time to find an exchange or an installment sale.
• On the other hand, if your personal situation requires cash, seek a cash sale in spite of the capital gain tax.
• Finally, there are exceptions to every general decision rule. It may be better to make a gift to your children, create a trust, or choose some other unusual disposition device. This is especially true when you own a "cash cow" (see Chapter 17 for a general discussion on disposition techniques).

Assembling a Team of Advisers and Consultants

For most of us, it is profitable to concentrate on the primary career and bear the costs of employing professionals who have expertise in technical matters (e.g., tax-sheltered retirement plans). Generally, an individual portfolio builder might need attorneys, a CPA, an insurance agent, a stockbroker, a financial advisor, a real estate appraiser, and a real estate broker/counselor.

At no time in the portfolio life cycle are the frustrations of forming the team more intense than when one is formulating the initial personal financial plan. Recommendations made by one professional often prove unacceptable to another. A clearly defined written strategy will minimize the friction resulting from the diverse inputs of various professionals.

Some professionals have problems of ego-involvement, and working with them can produce much conflict. If you have little time for building a personal portfolio, consider a member of the International Association of Financial Planners as a personal adviser, or a recommended associate broker in a large stock brokerage firm who considers real estate an appropriate part of a personal portfolio. One must be careful to avoid "churners" and other "self-servers." Bank references and credit reports are recommended.

Implementing the Strategy

This is a difficult task psychologically for many investors. One feels that it is a step into an abyss of uncertainty. Actually, anyone who is engaged in some saving and intuitive investment is already operating the plan that we have labeled "no plan." Strategy simply imposes structure and system on saving and investment.

Monitoring and Evaluating Performance

An individual financial plan must be adapted to changes over time. If you are troubled by the subjective nature of adjustments to change, the highly structured nature of the management strategy in Chapter 16 should be helpful. If one adapts the criteria for managing a property to auditing and evaluating portfolio performance, the goal of above-average performance has a greater possibility of being achieved.

Adapting the Plan to Changing Circumstances

In a sense this is a reprise of Chapter 7. All portfolios are built in a milieu of dynamic change and future uncertainty. Most of us accept the risk of this uncertainty because the only way to achieve greater stability would be to sacrifice individual independence to a centrally planned economy.

The unpredictability of a market-oriented economy is a product of *an environment in which many of us have the power to influence decisions* that affect politics, the law, economics, and social affairs. The result is that the tools of investment simulation and portfolio management can provide only crude scenarios of the future. Furthermore, once we decide to commit funds to a particular investment we perceive it as an *opportunity*. Yet life in a market economy is such that others are free to find ways to improve on the way investments serve society. The resulting changes create *competitive threats* or *threats of obsolescence*. One must be ready to make a timely decision to move on to a more opportune investment.

Finally, *individual strengths and weaknesses* must be periodically reconsidered. Whether it is a new professional credential, a divorce, a birth, death, or marriage, life's changing events should and do enter the calculus of the individual investor. The strategy of portfolio management is a continuous process toward achievement of the benefit stage. Even in the benefit stage some effort must be given to investment management. With luck, all you need to do is supervise and control the managers to whom you have delegated powers and duties while you sail on your oceangoing yacht!

SUMMARY

Developing a personal portfolio with real estate forces one to diverge from the conventional wisdom that all the attributes of an investment can be compressed within two variables—return and risk. Most individuals do not define wealth accumulation as the transcendent life goal.

Adopting a strategy of personal portfolio building requires one to accept a systematic framework to handle the complexity, dynamism, and uncertainty of the future. We recommend that each person recognize the three stages of a portfolio life cycle: the feeding stage, the growth stage, and the benefit stage. Because the apparently precise and objective standards of measuring portfolio performance are based on the assumption that rational equity investors diversify sufficiently to eliminate unsystematic risk, we have to reject that premise for individuals building portfolios that contain real estate assets.

Real estate is chosen nonrandomly and is heterogeneous. Therefore, we recommend a strategic framework for personal financial management built around the development of a personal philosophy, a personal situation audit, and the development and implementation of a strategy for investing in cash equivalent reserves, liquidity reserves, an optional investment fund, investment real estate, possible collectibles, a home, life insurance, tax planning, estate and retirement planning, and liability management. We urge the investor to assemble a team of carefully selected professional advisers and consultants to succeed in this wealth-building strategy.

Finally, continuous monitoring is necessary because personal life situations change and one must adapt to changes in the environment, to new opportunities, to competitive threats, and to improved knowledge of one's own strengths and weaknesses.

27

The Real Estate Investment Outlook

In 1980 it was easier for a poverty-income teenager to pass a security guard in the suburbs than for a middle-income family to find a home in the inner city. Think of the hourglass as half full, you'll feel better about the future.

JRC

If one assumes that humans are rational, one must ponder our current state of confusion. Our social and economic structure at the beginning of this decade was in a muddle. There is uncertainty and instability not only in metro areas but in the world economy. The family is changing in ways that some people don't like or even comprehend; this increases anxiety and uncertainty. We suffer from high and rising crime rates, terrorism, kidnappings, and decreasing respect for social institutions like the church, the law, the press, and big business. Under these conditions, forecasting the future state of the U.S. economy is difficult.

We hear many conflicting proposals on the subject of what to do to end the confusion. A nation that thought it had eliminated the business cycle in the 1960s has come to realize that its ability to recommend sensible policies that will support a reasonable rate of economic growth, relatively stable prices, balance-of-payments equilibrium, and high levels of output and employment is woefully inadequate. It is unclear which proposals might gain the acceptance of an increasingly intransigent Congress and an undisciplined executive branch. However, we would be wise to keep in mind that many people in the United States are well fed, well housed, well clothed, and have enough disposable income to support investment. Half of humanity does not have any of these benefits.

Real estate investments are for the long term. In this book we have recommended a time horizon of five to fifteen years. We have related real estate investment projects to the life cycle of the individual investor and the portfolio management problems of the institutional investor. However, our primary focus has been on the analysis of specific projects and an ownership cycle that is usually shorter than the remaining economic life of the improvements to the project itself. We have emphasized that decision analysis should focus in part on a study of real estate market cycles, which operate independently of the business cycles. In Parts III and IV we developed a method for strategic planning and decision making in real estate investing and some tools for analyzing certain kinds of property.

We recognize that managers of large portfolios and developers and investors in satellite new towns and large industrial projects must be future planners in the true sense of the word. To that end, we recommend study of such periodicals as *Science News, The Technology Review, Futurist,* and the works of the Hudson Institute and the Rand Corporation, among others. However, the year 2000 and the twenty-first century are beyond the scope of this chapter.

Although real estate as an asset is highly illiquid, real estate decision making takes place in a very dynamic short-run environment. Therefore, we will limit our discussion of the outlook for real estate investing to the next five years.

First we will deal with the most important uncertainty—inflation.

Inflation—The Overriding Uncertainty

As this book was going to press, inflation was still a matter of crucial and immediate concern to everyone. Let's begin by eliminating all the silly excuses. Inflation has not been caused by OPEC. Other nations—Germany and Japan for example—have not suffered from as high a rate of inflation as the United States in recent years, even though they are more dependent on OPEC oil than the United States. Similarly, inflation has not been caused by farmers, labor unions, supermarket clerks, the neighborhood physician, or the people who sell real estate. They've all been around for years, with pretty much the same profit drive. Nor has inflation been caused by greedy oil companies or basic industries. Inflation has been caused by mismanagement of the dollar. The dollar has been depreciated by the excessive deficits of the federal government; the combination of easy money, interest ceilings, burgeoning credit demand, reduced savings, declining productivity, and irresponsible federal budget making.

In the winter of 1980 a rational interlude seemed to occur. The Federal Reserve Board tried to hold back on money creation and tighten the reins on credit. Congress and the White House joined hands in seeking to balance the budget, and inevitably a health-giving recession set in with all the unemployment and personal suffering that it entails. The people spoke through a landslide election in which they chose a man who promised to get them out of this economic mess. Your problem as a real estate investment decision maker is to predict the outcome of an economic decision-making system in the setting of a democratic society.

The following is our attempt to summarize the economic outlook for the period through the mid 1980s. We regret to say that we expect a continuation of the high rate of inflation. The forecast can probably best be described as a bimodal probability distribution: If the federal government is successful in bringing its spending budget under control and stimulating business expansion during the early 1980s, inflation should decline into the 7– 10 percent range; if not, inflation will most likely continue at the 10– 13 percent range experienced during the period 1979– 1981. Because controlling inflation is politically more hazardous than enduring it, we place a 40 percent probability on the lower range and a 60 percent probability on the higher range.

In recent years there has been a feeling that rapid inflation may be good for real estate. In fact, inflation has made millionaires out of many average and unknowledgeable equity investors and covered up many of their investment mistakes. However, much of that inflation phenomenon and investment thinking—as we have noted on several occasions—was a product of low annual mortgage constants that did not reflect or anticipate rising inflation rates and increasing rental income and property values that did respond favorably to inflation. For the equity investor the "good old days" of cheap mortgage money and high leverage ratios are gone. While money will continue to flow into real estate, it will bear a high cost and onerous terms, relative to historical standards. In the 1980s, developers and investors will need to adapt to mortgage rates and terms that closely parallel inflation rate volatility, and they will have to learn to hedge their financial positions by seeking creative financial structures that adapt more readily to changing inflation rates and capital market conditions.

The Overall Forecast

The year 1980 may have been the midpoint of the longest period of sustained real estate growth in American history. Therefore, the prospects immediately ahead are quite positive, although there is some haziness with respect to energy and inflation.

First, developers have become more experienced and more professional. They appear to be better capitalized, and investors and lenders are more aware of the need for market studies and marketability analysis. Thus, the traditional developer's entrepreneurial optimism is more likely to be tempered by rational decision making. Second, market demand for most land uses appears to be strong. The only generally weak sector appears to be recreational second homes. Finally, the U.S. system of real estate finance will become even more complex, thus providing various opportunities for participation by lenders in individual projects as an inflation hedge. However, one can expect substantial deviation from the traditional principal reduction, annual mortgage constant loan. The sources of funds will expand, and there will be more activity in the securities market and from the pension funds.

In summary, the short-term outlook for real estate should be good as long as the "greater fool" theory implicit in the psychology of overbuilding does not overwhelm sensible judgment.

THE MARKET OUTLOOK FOR DIFFERENT TYPES OF REAL ESTATE, 1982–1986

The outpouring of people from the Snow Belt states in the Northeast and upper Midwest to the Sun Belt in the South and the Southwest will continue. Northern California and the Pacific Coast states of Oregon and Washington will enjoy more modest growth rates than in the past. In terms of percentage increases, the greatest growth occurred in Nevada, Alaska, Arizona, Wyoming, and Florida through the early 1970s. Recently Vermont, New Hampshire, and Maine have shown sharp increases as a spillover from the southern New England states. (See Exhibit 27–1.) Population increases in absolute terms, a measure that is considered more relevant by many experts and investors, were presented in Chapter 4.

Generally, redistribution of population is attributed to climatic factors, the boom in retirement home construction, and people seeking a lower cost of living related to savings in energy costs. Statistically, however, the north-to-south moves are less important than the moves from central cities to suburbs. This is particularly true of the industrial sector of the economy; redevelopment of aging cities is largely dependent on new policies that will attract service and professional em-

---

EXHIBIT 27–1.   Percent Change in U.S. Population, by State, 1970–1979

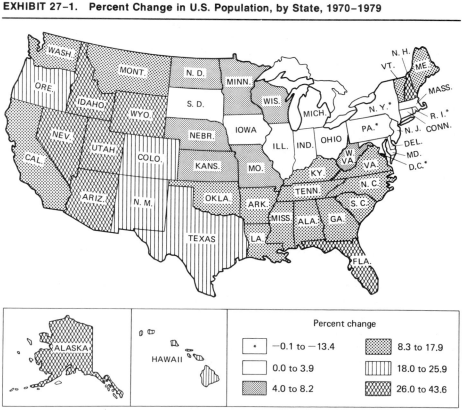

SOURCE: Bureau of the Census

ployment to replace the manufacturing sector employment that is going to the suburbs and to cities with populations under 100,000 in the West and Southeast.

While both political parties are working to "reindustrialize America," it is important to distinguish between their definitions of that slogan. On the one hand, *reindustrialization* may mean maintaining the ratio of blue-collar, semiskilled employment in mass production industries. But in the high-technology sectors of our economy there is a massive demographic shift out of manual work into "knowledge" work. In contrast to the situation in the 1950s, only half as many young people entering the labor force today expect to be employed in traditional blue-collar work. To many analysts, probably the only way for the United States to regain its international competitiveness as a producer and exporter is to encourage this shift. Indeed, it can be said that continuation of the policy of maintaining blue-collar employment in the coming years will diminish the competitive position of the United States. Promoting the shift to white-collar employment may be the only way to expand employment other than the artificial stimulus provided by a military boom. The problem for the real estate investor will be to determine the impact of these shifts on regional and metro areas.

The demographic and economic characteristics of the population that were discussed in Chapter 4 are expected to continue in the early 1980s. The median forecast of the Bureau of the Census projects that the U.S. population will grow by about 9.6 percent between 1980 and 1990, with the South and West accounting for a large part of the gain.

Projected Percentage Gains in U.S. Population, 1980–1990, by Region	
South	14.6
West	14.3
North–Central	5.0
Northeast	3.9

Within regions, higher growth areas are expected. The population of the eight mountain states of the West is expected to grow by 20.7 percent on a small base. This rate is nearly double that for the Pacific Coast states. In the South, the District of Columbia and the eight southeastern states will grow faster than the region as a whole. Florida is expected to lead the way with a 27.1 percent gain by 1990.[1]

As children born during the baby boom of 1947–1963 reach their peak potential child-bearing period during the 1980s, there is a possibility for substantial increases in the birthrate—for what has been called an "echo" baby boom. However, we do not expect the childbearing population to increase its fertility rate in the short term.

We see some significant social and economic changes having an impact on real estate use:

1. There will be more home-centered leisure pursuits, such as video tapes and games and microcomputers. Less discretionary disposable income will result in more at-home activity.

---

[1] The *Statistical Abstract of the United States,* published by the Census Bureau, is an inexpensive, compact source of 1980 census data and projections.

2. The workweek will continue to grow shorter. Vacation time will increase slightly, but only an energy shortage would increase the trend toward the four-day workweek.
3. The labor force will increase in size, and female participation will increase even more. More important, there will be a continuing shift from blue-collar to white-collar employment as automation, computer software, and other new technologies change the nature of the factory.
4. Crime rates will drop because a smaller proportion of the population will be in the "crime-prone ages" of 15 to 24. Further, there will be a broader adoption of victim indemnification programs. People in American cities will feel more secure.
5. Factory layout and size will change as a result of the impact of information systems on processing.
6. The service sector of the economy will increase sharply in both absolute and relative terms. More than 90 percent of new-job formations will be in the service sector. In addition, major evolutionary changes in the use of office space will occur more rapidly because of word processing, CRT terminals, and microcomputers. This will be translated into a continued increase in the demand for office space.

Industrial Buildings and Parks

It is more difficult to generalize about industrial space than about other real estate markets because each standard industrial classification has different locational requirements for manufacturing and distribution. We believe that decisions by national and international concerns to add new facilities will increasingly benefit southern and southwestern areas. This is especially true of high-technology operations with large proportions of white-collar workers. But expansion in the South and Southwest does not necessarily involve the closing of a northern plant. Distribution warehouse facilities for consumer products will follow the national population shift. Thus, there should be ample opportunity for industrial and warehouse development in all the growth areas of the nation.

Housing

The proportion of owner-occupied housing in the United States is now over 65 percent. Adult households are increasing as a proportion of the total. Condominiums may become the first step on the ownership housing path as well as the last step for empty-nesters. Thus, there is a large potential market for condominiums (especially townhouses) as the move toward more unit ownership in multiple-family buildings continues.

We will have yet another housing crisis as the public begins to perceive that the number of privately owned rental units is insufficient. The traditional rule of thumb of no more than one-fourth of pretax income for rent no longer holds. The production of subsidized housing units, especially for the elderly, will increase, but it will remain insufficient. Taking replacement housing into consideration, the demand for new housing units will be about 2.3 million annually through the mid

1980s. We can expect to see tension build as frustrated tenants argue for rent control and more limits on condominium conversions in order to prevent erosion of the relative supply. Indeed, rent regulation has spread to over 100 cities, and has discouraged building. In Los Angeles and San Francisco local governments have adopted various types of rent and building controls, with the result that construction of additional rental housing is at an all-time low. Thus, although the underlying demand for rental housing will remain high, serious political problems may affect production. If rents do not rise faster than costs because of the fear of rent control, it is probable that the supply will not begin to keep pace with demand. Because high financing costs will make much new construction unattractive to developers, there will be a significant shortfall in rental housing, and much social unrest as a result.

It appears that ownership units will remain the mainstay of housing starts. But because of high purchase prices in relation to family income, more new units will be townhouses, patio homes, planned-unit developments, and condominiums. The latter will represent an increasing proportion of housing starts nationwide by the mid-1980s. In part this is because they represent a form of ownership that can be afforded by a substantial portion of American households. Condominiums also provide a life style for singles, empty-nesters, and working couples who do not want to be responsible for exterior maintenance. Continuation of the homeowner's interest and real estate tax deductions is essential for this trend to ownership to continue. This tax policy, however, is under attack.

If home ownership remains the preferred choice of Americans, there will be an increasing need for government subsidies for middle-income households. The extent to which government housing programs respond will depend on creative new programs and the prevailing political and economic climate. We doubt that housing will receive any priority as long as the arms race continues.

Office Buildings

Rents in high-prestige new office space in Manhattan and Chicago are now well over $40 per square foot annually for the most sought-after locations (the average 1981 price was $24.50). The extent to which rent increases will reflect the balance between supply and demand in the next few years will depend largely on the capacity of the marketplace to pay higher and higher rents. That capacity is not infinite. Rent accounts for a small percentage of most firms' total operating costs, but efficient managers monitor square-foot occupancy costs closely. There are clouds on the horizon; isolated overbuilding has already emerged in some areas, such as the Chicago Loop (1980). With rents in New York and Chicago now double those in Atlanta and Dallas, corporate headquarters will be increasingly likely to move south.

More business corporations are expressing an interest in partial or even total ownership of the real estate they occupy by way of holding-company arrangements. Even smaller prime tenants are seeking equity positions. However, the prospects of office space markets are quite promising for the next several years because the shift from blue-collar to white-collar employment has intensified. In effect, fewer workers will be making and growing products and more will be doing the data processing, servicing, financing, and analyzing that goes on in offices. A substantial rise in service employment is projected, much of which will require additional office space. Concern must be expressed about the way office space is likely to be rationalized in the future. Simply reproducing past office layouts seems questionable in view of the evolutionary changes occurring as a result of the introduction of telecommunications and other electronic equipment.

On the other hand, the trend toward larger buildings and multiuse complexes will probably continue because of the possibility of economies of scale with respect to financing and developers' overhead costs, and increased involvement by large institutional investors. The increasing costs of new development will make it feasible to rehabilitate many larger, older office buildings in the central business districts. Tax incentives available under the 1981 tax act will promote this trend. Few significant exterior design innovations are expected in the early 1980s because efforts are being concentrated on energy conservation and efficient maintenance.

There will be more user ownership in office complexes. For example, by 1990 medical offices may be predominantly in condominium ownership. While this will be beneficial for the present equity owners of office buildings that have conversion potential and for developers of condominium office space, it will be detrimental to non-user equity investors seeking office building investments.

Shopping Centers

It will be helpful here and in the following section to classify the larger SMSAs by size. (See Exhibit 27–2.) A significant realignment in the use of retail space and the activities of shopping center developers is expected during the next five years.

There is some evidence that many of the strata 1 and 2 major metropolitan areas are now oversaturated with retail space, particularly regional shopping centers. It is expected that the national shopping center developers will increasingly penetrate downward to the second and third strata metropolitan areas, and it is doubtful that many new regional and superregional shopping centers will be built. Instead, marketing efforts will concentrate on promoting the many regional shopping centers with two or three anchor stores. The early 1980s will see more rehabilitation and renovation of well-located older retail centers, which will sharpen the competition for everyone.

Retailing in central business districts will increase in both relative and absolute terms in the largest centers (strata 1), in regional centers with good public transportation systems, and finally in smaller and emerging centers where there is a historically maintained, strong gravitational pull of retail customers toward the central business district in the SMSA.

The less viable central business districts, particularly those in the second and third strata metro areas, will continue to experience declines in retailing during the 1980s.

The drive toward energy efficiency, restrictions on development, and other planning regulations will work in favor of older retail districts and shopping centers

EXHIBIT 27–2.   Size Stratification of Large U.S. Metropolitan Areas (Population as of July 1976)

STRATA 1—NATIONAL CENTERS (OVER 3 MILLION)

Chicago	New York	San Francisco
Detroit	Philadelphia	Washington, D.C.
Los Angeles		

STRATA 2—REGIONAL CENTERS (1 TO 3 MILLION)

Anaheim/Santa Ana	Houston	Phoenix
Atlanta	Indianapolis	Pittsburgh
Baltimore	Kansas City	Portland
Boston	Miami	Riverside/San Bernardino
Buffalo	Milwaukee	St. Louis
Cincinnati	Minneapolis	San Diego
Cleveland	Nassau/Suffolk	San Jose
Columbus	Newark	Seattle
Dallas	New Orleans	Tampa
Denver		

STRATA 3—SMALLER REGIONAL OR EMERGING CENTERS (500,000 TO 1 MILLION)

Akron	Honolulu	Providence
Albany, N.Y.	Jacksonville	Richmond, Va.
Allentown	Jersey City	Rochester, N.Y.
Birmingham, Ala.	Louisville	Sacramento
Charlotte	Memphis	Salt Lake City
Dayton	Nashville	San Antonio
Flint	New Brunswick	Springfield, Mass.
Ft. Lauderdale	New Haven	Syracuse
Gary	Norfolk	Toledo
Grand Rapids	Oklahoma City	Tulsa
Greensboro	Omaha	Worcester
Greenville, S.C.	Orlando	Youngstown
Hartford		

STRATA 4—ALL OTHER SMSAs

SOURCE: Bureau of the Census, July 1976.

that are well organized and maintain an attractive appearance with sufficient parking. It is expected that community and neighborhood shopping centers will increase in number, but not in size, as the thrust of development shifts from new growth areas to meeting the need for retail service in areas that have been passed over.

It is expected that shopping centers will become more individualized as they seek to differentiate themselves and establish themselves in a niche of the market.

One may expect more boutiques, eating and drinking establishments, specialty shops, and possibly catalog retailers. Some centers will seek to develop themes like those of Salt Lake City's Trolley Square and the Galleria in Houston (see Chapter 20). It is expected that a number of centers will incorporate high-fashion elements into their tenant mix and promote neighborhood civic activities as they seek to maximize their share of the trading area's targeted shoppers.

Local developers and investors in the third and fourth strata metro areas will find increasingly stiff competition from more sophisticated major shopping center developers because oversaturation of first- and second-strata markets will increase interest in the smaller SMSAs, some of which are currently underserviced by the retail sector in relation to their size and aggregate income.

In summary, it appears that the retail outlook through 1985 is positive. However, the signposts read, "Proceed with Caution." New construction will continue, but on a more selective basis. Upgrading and revitalization of existing shopping centers will produce more intensive competition for new construction than in the past.

Hotels and Motels

The gas shortage in the summer of 1979 foreshadowed a condition of uncertainty for auto-oriented hotels and motels. In recent years with good gas supplies, including 1981, the hotel/motel industry has experienced very high levels of occupancy at escalating room rates. Although very little overbuilding had occurred through 1981, the rate of development that characterized recent years should not continue. Investing in hotels and motels, most of which are acutely sensitive to changes in vacation plans, driving patterns, and other use patterns, certainly remains risky.

The production of new hotels to cater to the traveling public will experience a sharp decline during the next five years. Investors in existing facilities may or may not experience high returns, depending on national energy policies.

The financial feasibility of new luxury motels and hotels is open to question. Construction costs for luxury downtown hotels in large cities range from $83,000 to $88,000 per room (1981). The room rates and occupancy levels necessary to amortize such construction costs and yield a business profit for the operators and investors appear somewhat discouraging in the short term.

Metro areas with active hotels in their central business districts that cater primarily to business and convention visitors have growth potential and should constitute profitable investment locations due to the restraint on financial feasibility for new construction. A large number of convention facilities have been built in recent years, encouraging the dispersion of small and medium-sized conventions in particular. Business and convention travel is highly sensitive to shifts in the national business cycle; both categories of travel tend to drop temporarily during an economic recession. In recent years HUD's UDAG program, which makes direct grants to developers by way of cities in order to stimulate private investment and job creation, has assisted in the development of a number of new central business district hotels that otherwise would not have been financially feasible.

The political sector may want to continue this public support in order to attract more visitors to inner-city areas.

In recent years there has been a dramatic growth in the number of foreign visitors to the United States, both business travelers and tourists, because of the decline in the value of the dollar. The greatest beneficiaries of foreign travel in recent years have been the central business districts of the first- and second-strata metro areas and resort areas like Miami. Some hotels are reporting that foreigners account for 25–35 percent of their overall business.

In the past few years (including 1980–1981), hotel/motel room rates have risen much faster than the consumer price index. Such a trend cannot be expected to continue. However, the hotel/motel industry should expect the trend to be good but probably not as strong as in 1975–1980. The factors of greatest concern are high construction costs per unit; the uncertainty of energy availability, both for new development and for users' travel; and the rate of inflation. Hotels are the most labor intensive of all income properties, except hospitals and nursing homes, and are vulnerable to sharp labor cost increases.

WHAT FINANCING WILL BE AVAILABLE?

Equity Financing   It appears that equity financing will be readily available in the first half of the 1980s. The attractions of real estate as an investment medium have led to increasing flows of funds from such relatively new investment entities as national, regional, and local syndications; pension funds; equity REITs; foreign investors; and the mortgage pools of portfolio managers. With inflation expected to continue at substantial rates during the next five years, real estate should continue to be attractive as an investment vehicle for both institutions and individuals.

This book has emphasized that real estate investing requires careful attention from the acquisition stage to the termination stage, and capable property management during the operation phase. Thus, the opportunities for passive investment on the part of individuals have historically been restricted. However, the increasing involvement of syndications, pension funds, and stock brokerage house pools will make it easier for smaller passive investors to invest in real estate.

Historically, it appears that few investments could compete with real estate, taking both risks and returns into account. Money was cheap because mortgage interest rates tended to lag inflation rates. Real estate appreciation outpaced the consumer price index, which itself far exceeded stock market performance. (See Exhibit 27–3.) However, we should not forget that the indiscriminate flows of funds into real estate investment trusts from 1971 to 1974 resulted in imprudent financing and a severe real estate depression as a result of overbuilding. Although it is unlikely that the performance of the early 1970s will be repeated, we should be forewarned that pressures—such as that created by foreign money invested in U.S. real estate and massive infusions of new capital by pension funds in the 1980s—may cause another round of euphoria and an undue increase in risk.

The liberal tax shelter provisions for real estate assets under the Economic

EXHIBIT 27-3.   Comparative Price Changes, 1970-1979 (1967 = 100)

Year	Average Selling Price, New Single- Family Homes	Average Value of Farm Land and Buildings	Consumer Price Index (All Items)	Standard & Poor's 500 Common Stock Index
1970	117.4	117	116.3	90.5
1979	262.6	308[a]	211.5	102.1
Percent change	+124%	+163%	+82%	+13%

[a] 1978 figure.

Recovery Tax Act of 1981 will provide increased stimuli for equity investment in all property types.

Debt Capital   With substantial rates of inflation, the availability of all types of permanent debt capital will remain restricted, both for housing and for commercial and industrial properties. Under our lower inflation rate scenario, medium- and long-term interest rates will fall significantly from current levels and more funds will become available. Historically, mortgage interest rates have averaged 2 to 4 percentage points above the inflation rate; thus, if inflation falls to the 7–10 percent range, and lenders are confident that such rates will continue, mortgage rates should fall to the 10–13 percent range. Under the higher inflation rate scenario, mortgage interest rates should remain in the 13–17 percent range.

In either case, investors will be forced to live with relatively conservative leverage strategies, and greater emphasis will be placed on creative debt financing techniques that simultaneously satisfy the cash flow needs of the equity investor and protect the lender against volatile inflation and interest rate risks. The equity investor should carefully assess the risks of short-term call or renegotiation provisions, widely varying interest rate adjustments, and equity participations by lenders. In many instances, the additional risk will not be compensated for in the expected IRR after tax.

High energy costs in addition to the high debt-capital costs will result in increased pressure for all users of real estate to economize on space. "Small is beautiful" will become the norm, and investors and developers will seek to reduce nearly all types of facilities in size—including single-family houses, apartments, retail stores, office space, hotel rooms, and industrial plants. The era of the sub-compact car will be followed by that of the subcompact dwelling unit (down as low as 500 square feet), and by subcompact motel and hotel rooms, office cubicles, and so on. Thus, while the average size of a real estate project will increase (increase in emphasis on large multiuse projects), the amount of space devoted to each real estate use or user will decrease.

Foreign Investors   To date, foreign investors have concentrated on high-quality existing properties—office buildings, industrial buildings, apartments, and shopping centers. As a group, they seem not to be very interested in residential buildings. However, there are major exceptions. Foreign investors are paying top dollar and have generally forced up the prices of high-quality projects and brought down capitalization rates in a number of metropolitan areas. It can be said that the involvement of foreign investors in those markets has been healthy to date. If the pace should accelerate, it is possible that they could act as a "wild card" in the marketplace.

Structural Changes in Financial Institutions The most striking development during the next five years will be the blurring of lines between financial institutions. The traditional separation of the thrift institutions and banks from life insurance companies and other lenders will lessen significantly. Banks and credit unions will expand their functions in real estate. Insurance companies and some large retail institutions (e.g., Sears) are expected to become important lenders in both construction and mortgage financing. Manufacturing concerns like General Electric Credit Corporation and Westinghouse Credit Corporation will become even more important. It is expected that mortgage-backed securities will be issued in smaller units and in forms that will become accessible to individual investors.

Strengthening Secondary Mortgage Markets The key to most of these changes is further development and rationalization of the secondary market for mortgages, mortgage-backed securities, and mortgage bonds, and even some fusion of the money and capital markets. It would not be surprising to see plastic money systems like VISA and MasterCard take on mortgage loan servicing functions for a fee. Such a development would certainly facilitate the entry of more intermediaries into the real estate financing market.

Although many people argue the need for commercial variable-rate mortgages (VRMs) or other techniques to index long-term debt in order to protect the lenders against inflation, it appears unlikely that such mortgages will become prevalent for income properties during the next five years. It is, however, more likely that renegotiable notes with three- to five-year balloon payment mortgages, lender demands for equity and/or cash flow participation, and fixed principal payments with varying interest rates and amortization durations will become a viable alternative to the traditional form of the variable-rate mortgage. Lack of understanding of the risk characteristics of these new debt instruments, coupled with a boom psychology, could result in investors' underestimating the risks of specific ventures and financing approaches, thereby increasing the uncertainty.

In summary, it appears likely that money will be available, but at interest rates that are historically high and on relatively onerous terms. Furthermore, there will be a much greater variety of debt instruments and, hence, a need for more sophisticated evaluations by both the equity investor and the lender.

THE SPRAWLING COSTS OF URBAN CONTAINMENT[2]

Conversion of prime agricultural land to urban uses in areas like Iowa, Illinois, and California is conversion of a national treasure to a dubious higher and better use. Converting cornbelt soil into middle-class subdivisions is a little like wrapping fish

[2] Wallace F. Smith, "The Sprawling Costs of Urban Containment," *California Management Review,* Spring 1976, pp. 40–45.

in the Dead Sea scrolls. However, the marketplace does not account for social costs. Because urban land uses are so highly interdependent, the price paid for an improvement does not reflect all of the costs incurred to produce it. This is a basic reason for urban land use planning, an exercise of police power that has stood up well in several decades of legal testing. We have become conscious of the finite nature of our space and the fact that air and water and the esthetic appeal of trees and scenery are not free.

The next five years will see increasing pressure for control of real estate investors and developers. It appears likely that proposals to develop land will increasingly be resisted by nearby owners because of anticipated environmental degradation, that users of newly developed land will be made to compensate the community for social costs, and that the pace of land development will be slowed.

More and more cities and counties are obligated to act as agents of the state in enforcing environmental-protection policies. Since private land development necessarily carries with it social costs to the surrounding community, while its benefits tend to accrue to the buyers and users, who are (often) not yet members of that community, the environmental-review process is loaded against the developer's pricing mechanism.

Recently, in the celebrated Mt. Laurel case, the New Jersey Supreme Court determined that a suburban community like Mt. Laurel could not regulate land use so as to carry out primarily local home rule objectives, but was required to accommodate a regional need for housing for low- or moderate-income families.[3]

The next five years will be difficult as we seek to rationalize the interests of various groups in land use planning and development. John Rahenkamp[4] has provided us with a schematic diagram of how developers see the development process of the future evolving. (See Exhibit 27–4.)

New Risks in Developing and Investing in Metro Areas

Development has always been a relatively risky business. In performing the entrepreneurial function, the developer commits substantial resources to some projects that do not come to fruition at all or, worse, take longer than expected to reach the rental phase. This phase of real estate investing has been stretched out and made more uncertain by the problems just discussed.

The very economic conditions that make new development financially unattractive make existing income-producing properties more attractive. There are reasons to expect that it will become more difficult to finance new projects to meet increasing demand in the various sectors of real estate investment. This should favor the existing stock in all the sectors of real estate.

However, operating costs continue to rise faster than rents. Furthermore, there seems to be a semipermanent upward shift in the cost of amortizing loans through annual debt service, with annual mortgage constants much higher than in

---

[3] Jerome G. Rose, "The Mt. Laurel Decision: Is It Based on Wishful Thinking," *Real Estate Law Journal*, Summer 1975, pp. 61–70.

[4] Robert W. Ditmer, John Rahenkamp, and Donald Ruggles, "Import Zoning, a Technique for Responsible Land Use Management," *Plan Canada*, March 1977, pp. 48–58.

EXHIBIT 27–4. Schematic Diagram of the Impact Zoning Development Process

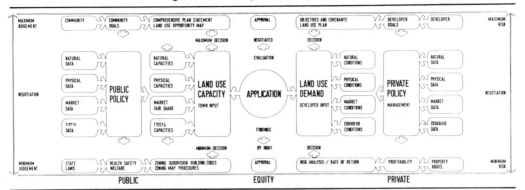

SOURCE: John Rahenkamp, Robert Ditmer, and Donald Ruggles, "Impact Zoning: A Technique for Responsible Land Use Management," *Plan Canada*, March 1977. Reproduced courtesy of John Rahenkamp and Associates, Inc.

the past. It is clear that property investment faces some serious uncertainty in the next five years as the market adjusts to the increasing burden on cash flow and to the market pressures on capitalization rates. Only if rents rise at a faster rate in the future than in the past can we expect the value of real estate properties to continue to rise as fast as they have in the recent past. Indeed, it is fair to say that some increases in property value in recent years have been in anticipation of rent increases yet to come—somewhat like the bidding up of glamour stocks in the late 1960s and early 1970s.

Following are some general observations about the new return/risk relationships:

1. Less favorable mortgage financing will be available. Higher equity contribution ratios—say, 25–50 percent—should be expected.
2. As a result of inflation and the influx of new money into equity investment, gross income multipliers have risen and equity capitalization rates (cash flow before tax/equity investment) have fallen. Consequently, the risk of negative cash flows during the early years of ownership has increased. Investors are "betting on the come."
3. Individuals are more knowledgeable and better able to discriminate among available investments. Tax shelter is no longer a justification in and of itself; investors want to see a meaningful cash flow from a real estate venture over the holding period. However, the 1981 tax act will increase investor emphasis on tax shelter as a primary source of return.
4. All of the foregoing point to less opportunity for financial and tax leveraging, and indicate that returns are more dependent on appreciation of property value and rising rental income and NOIs in future years.

In summary, equity investors will probably still be able to make higher-than-average returns in real estate relative to other investment media, but the increase in the level of knowledge and expertise in the marketplace will make it more difficult and competitive.

SCENARIOS IN REAL ESTATE INVESTMENT STRATEGY AND PLANNING

The level of uncertainty in real estate investment is increasing. Sudden changes in the social, political, technical, and economic environments are affecting operating profitability and asset appreciation. Interdependency and interactions between the private and public sectors and among political issues are increasing in both number and complexity. Unexpected and potentially disruptive events are becoming more commonplace.

The usefulness of the scenario technique for strategic planning in addressing this new environment in real estate investing was recognized in Chapter 8. One can expect increasingly sophisticated techniques to be added to real estate investing in an evolutionary way. Real estate investment analysis under conditions of uncertainty is barely in the idea stage, even though the ideas were first proposed in the late 1960s. Only a few models have appeared, but owing to a dearth of quality data the probability curves for the variables have not been correctly identified.

Pyhrr (1973)[5] used Monte Carlo simulation, but to date his model does not appear to be operational. It has some input–output flexibility, but there are problems of autocorrelation and multicolinearity. In effect, probabilities are not well understood or identified in the real estate investment field. Others have done little to follow Pyhrr's work, in spite of the severe need, except for Wofford, Gau and Kohlhepp, Findlay and Messner, et al.[6] In part, this is because modern quantitative concepts are not prevalent in real estate. Differences in the use of *typical* (implicit averages: mean, median, or mode?) or *most probable* are difficult to quantify. *Expected* and *most probable* value are not carefully differentiated in the literature. Real estate terminology has not yet incorporated *point estimate* or *distribution,* nor have the meanings of *naive* or *predictive* or *normative* been generally accepted. Sensitivity analysis has been misapplied or misinterpreted.

However, recent literature makes it clear that a new generation of professional practitioners and academics will quickly produce a substantial change in methodology and knowledge in this field. As scenario thinking takes over corporate planning and strategy, real estate investment analysis using scenario planning techniques (as illustrated in Exhibit 27– 5) will be used by the entrepreneur (generalist) who is in charge of the investment process.

We use the word *entrepreneur* to describe the manager in a real estate

---

[5] Stephen A. Pyhrr, "A Computer Simulation to Measure the Risk in Real Estate Investment," *Real Estate Appraiser,* May-June 1973, pp. 13– 31.

[6] Larry Wofford, *A Simulation Approach to the Appraisal of Income Producing Real Estate,* Ph.D. Dissertation (unpublished), University of Texas, 1977; George W. Gau and Daniel B. Kohlhepp, *OUPROB —A Discounted Cash Flow Model for Real Estate Investment Analysis* (Norman: University of Oklahoma, Center for Economic and Management Research, 1976); C. Chapman Findlay, III, Stephen D. Messner, and R. Tarantello, *FMRR Simulation Model and User Manual,* Real Estate Report No. 30, (Starrs: University of Connecticut, Center for Real Estate and Urban Economic Studies, March 1980).

EXHIBIT 27–5.   Real Estate Investment Scenarios

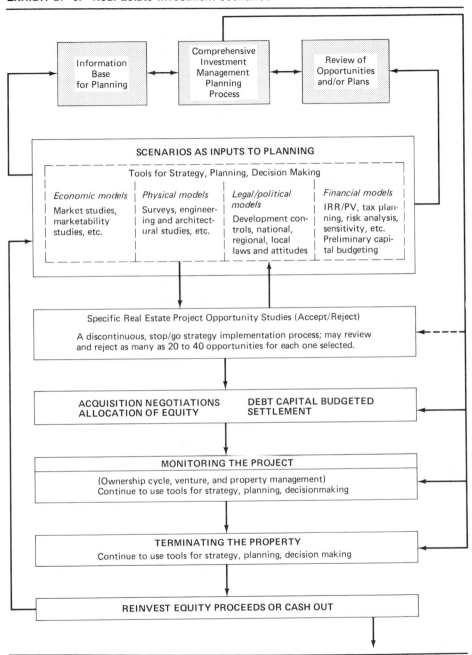

investment scenario planning process because it is important that such a person realize the utility of intuition and subjective judgment in return/risk analysis. Although we believe that in the near future we will see the development of more powerful models as inputs to the real estate investment process, the quality of the data still requires judgmental interpretation by people who are in touch with the dynamics of the marketplace.

The usefulness of case studies and scenarios to train managers in the environment of real estate investment has been recognized for some time, and the authors believe that the Pyhrr model for investment analysis and financial structuring (Exhibit 8–4) integrates the scenario concept into investment and financial analysis in a way that will serve as a forerunner for improved models.

Current Problems of Scenario Planning

As an aid to those who would do scenario modeling to improve the effectiveness of real estate investing, we have set forth some ideas concerning the difficulties we all face in intellectually modeling the real estate investment as a process.

The entrepreneur is currently necessary for success in real estate investing; at least it is necessary to have such a person as a top manager in an investing group. However, an entrepreneur has difficulty playing the role of employee or subordinate in an authoritarian environment. He or she tends not to want to be accountable to anyone else. In effect, then, the qualities that make people successful entrepreneurs make them marginally acceptable to conventional, established business and social networks.[7] But successful scenario planning requires the entrepreneur to cooperate with others and to accept short-term subordination of personal aims. The quality of real estate data and the highly politicized environment of real estate decision making require that such a person be characterized by breadth of education and training, high social awareness, and a sense of direct involvement. The entrepreneur must have a high degree of confidence in his or her own ability and an orientation toward solving problems for the uncertain future. It is apparent that if we are to integrate strategic planning into the real estate investment process, we must also find a way of making organizations feel comfortable working with entrepreneurial personalities and helping entrepreneurs feel at home in an organizational framework.

Framing the scenario is difficult today. Generally, the problems that must be solved in the future are the following:

1. Establishing parameters for scenarios of real estate investing—the first research would focus on defining the problem space.
2. Setting data base requirements within time and budget constraints so as to produce an appropriate information system for each scenario. Current data base requirements are a procrustean bed. It is hoped that structuring of appropriate scenarios will make data base needs more explicit.

---

[7] For greater insight into developing networks in our information based economy, see Marily Ferguson, *The Aquarian Conspiracy—Personal and Social Transformation in the 1980s* (Boston: Houghton-Mifflin, 1980).

3. More flexible and interactive computer software, readily accessible through microcomputers (stand alone and on-line), to facilitate the use of appropriate, well-developed scenarios. Such telecommunicating is necessary to maximize the use of an entrepreneur's thinking, as recent research has proven.[8]

4. From the early scenarios others must be developed. Early scenarios are often hierarchically at too high a level and tend to be insensitive to inputs from, say, the local environment and neighborhood events. The result is that they tend to be either too crude to be efficient or too detailed and therefore unwieldy. More effective scenarios will be developed that will be disaggregated but will be linked by a master scenario.

5. Many models are inadequately documented, so that only the author/user is capable of using the scenario.

6. Scenarios would be most useful if they enabled the user to forecast. Currently we tend to be limited to "most likely," "optimistic," and "pessimistic" analyses, which are often inadequate in a probabilistic environment.

7. There is a need to integrate various models—market, physical, political, and financial—into a single interactive program to enable academics and practitioners in the field to improve scenario planning.

Hopefully, with much dedicated research, study, experimentation, and hard work by academicians and practitioners alike, approaches and solutions to the problems enumerated above will be forthcoming in the 1980s. We encourage all of you to become involved and participate actively in this challenging process.

CONCLUSION

For the present, we hope this book has provided an information base for a comprehensive investment management plan, and the techniques and tools necessary to review opportunities in real estate investment. The short-term future should provide sophisticated, opportunistic real estate investors with a chance for above-average returns and accumulation of wealth. It is not easy to make money in real estate, but there is a higher probability of success for the educated and rational investor than in other investment mediums.

[8] Charles Hampden-Turner, *Maps of the Mind* (New York: Macmillan, 1981; London: Mitchell Beasley). Recommended.

Appendixes

APPENDIX A

The Time Value of Money: Problems for the Student

1. What is the value today of $10,000 paid in 7 years if the investor's desired rate of return is 7%?
2. What is the present value of $1 million to be received in 15 years if the investor's discount rate is 12%?
3. An investor has an opportunity to purchase an investment that will provide $10,000 at the end of the third year and $50,000 at the end of the fifth year. It is anticipated that the property may be sold at the end of the sixth year for $200,000. If the investor expects a 15% yield, what should he pay for the investment today?
4. To what amount will $1,000 accumulate in 10 years at 10% interest, with monthly payments?
5. Five thousand dollars is placed in a savings account today at 7% interest compounded monthly. An additional $10,000 will be placed in the account at the end of the sixth year. To what amount will the account have compounded at the end of the tenth year?
6. What is the monthly payment required for $100,000 to accumulate in a savings account at the end of the fifteenth year at 10% interest?
7. A lender makes a $100,000 mortgage at 9% interest, 25 years, with monthly payments.
   a. What is the monthly debt service required?
   b. What is the schedule for the principal and interest components of debt service for the first 3 months?
   c. What is the remaining mortgage balance at the end of the third year?
8. A borrower takes a loan for $250,000 for 30 years at 8% interest, with monthly payments. What are the monthly debt service payments?
9. An investor has a chance to purchase an apartment building that will provide estimated net operating income as shown in the following table. It will have an estimated resale value at the end of the third year of $38,000. If the investor wants a 12% return on the investment, what should be paid for the property?

End of Year	Payment
1	$12,000
2	10,500
3	25,500

10. Property under a step-up lease has the following payments due:

Year	Annual Rent, Paid at Beginning of Year
1–10	$50,000
11–15	55,000
16–20	75,000

When the lease terminates in 20 years, the market value is expected to be $600,000.

What is the justified investment price of the property if the investor expects an 18% rate of return?

11. An investor has an opportunity to purchase land for $50,000 and thinks it may be sold for $110,000 in 8 years. What is the internal rate of return, disregarding holding costs?

12. Land is expected to double in value in 10 years. What is the internal rate of return?

13. An investor has an opportunity to purchase a $10,000 annuity paid annually for 10 years for $60,000. What yield (IRR) will be received?

14. A property is available for $200,000 and is generating net operating income of $30,000. If the estimated resale value of the property in 7 years is $250,000,
    a. What yield will the investor receive?
    b. What portion of the $30,000 in periodic returns is return *of* investment and what part is return *on* investment?

15. A man purchased a commercial lot and is paying monthly interest only of $183.33. At an annual simple interest rate of 11%, what is the principal owed?

16. If you paid $30,000 for your house five years ago and its value has appreciated at an annual compound interest rate of 10%, what would it be worth today?
    What will the purchasing power of $1 be worth 50 years from now if inflation continues at an annual compound rate of 6%?

17. You have been offered a 30% interest in a partnership that plans to net $100,000 on the sale of a property at the end of 4 years. What would you pay for this interest if you wanted to earn 14% on your investment, compounded annually?

18. Some apartments that you own will need a complete renovation in 7 years. You estimate the total renovation cost to be $40,000. How much must you deposit monthly into an account earning 6%, compounded monthly, in order to have the money for renovation at the end of 7 years?

19. How much will you owe on a $55,000, 30-year mortgage at the end of 12 years, assuming a 12% interest rate compounded monthly?
    What percent of a mortgage will be unpaid at the end of 15 years on a 20-year mortgage? Assume a 10% annual interest rate with *annual* compounding.

20. A seller offers a small office building for the price of $100,000. The equity required from the buyer at closing is $30,000. Thus, the existing first-mortgage balance is $70,000. The existing mortgage is payable monthly for the 21 years remaining at an 8% interest rate. Negotiations occur. The seller agrees to take back a wraparound of $85,000, 10% interest rate for 21 years.
    a. Compute the true yield (IRR) on the wraparound mortgage to the seller. Assume that the full mortgage balances are repaid in accordance with their terms.
    b. Evaluate the transaction. Is it good from the seller's viewpoint? From the buyer's?

6.00% MONTHLY COMPOUND INTEREST TABLES 6.00%
EFFECTIVE RATE 0.500

	1 AMOUNT OF $1 AT COMPOUND INTEREST	2 ACCUMULATION OF $1 PER PERIOD	3 SINKING FUND FACTOR	4 PRESENT VALUE REVERSION OF $1	5 PRESENT VALUE ORD. ANNUITY $1 PER PERIOD	6 INSTALMENT TO AMORTIZE $1	
NTHS							
1	1.005000	1.000000	1.000000	0.995025	0.995025	1.005000	
2	1.010025	2.005000	0.498753	0.990075	1.985099	0.503753	
3	1.015075	3.015025	0.331672	0.985149	2.970248	0.336672	
4	1.020151	4.030100	0.248133	0.980248	3.950496	0.253133	
5	1.025251	5.050251	0.198010	0.975371	4.925866	0.203010	
6	1.030378	6.075502	0.164595	0.970518	5.896384	0.169595	
7	1.035529	7.105879	0.140729	0.965690	6.862074	0.145729	
8	1.040707	8.141409	0.122829	0.960885	7.822959	0.127829	
9	1.045911	9.182116	0.108907	0.956105	8.779064	0.113907	
0	1.051140	10.228026	0.097771	0.951348	9.730412	0.102771	
1	1.056396	11.279167	0.088659	0.946615	10.677027	0.093659	
2	1.061678	12.335562	0.081066	0.941905	11.618932	0.086066	

							MONTHS
ARS							
1	1.061678	12.335562	0.081066	0.941905'	11.618932	0.086066	12
2	1.127160	25.431955	0.039321	0.887186	22.562866	0.044321	24
3	1.196681	39.336105	0.025422	0.835645	32.871016	0.030422	36
4	1.270489	54.097832	0.018485	0.787098	42.580318	0.023485	48
5	1.348850	69.770031	0.014333	0.741372	51.725561	0.019333	60
6	1.432044	86.408856	0.011573	0.698302	60.339514	0.016573	72
7	1.520370	104.073927	0.009609	0.657735	68.453042	0.014609	84
8	1.614143	122.828542	0.008141	0.619524	76.095218	0.013141	96
9	1.713699	142.739900	0.007006	0.583533	83.293424	0.012006	108
0	1.819397	163.879347	0.006102	0.549633	90.073453	0.011102	120
1	1.931613	186.322629	0.005367	0.517702	96.459599	0.010367	132
2	2.050751	210.150163	0.004759	0.487626	102.474743	0.009759	144
3	2.177237	235.447328	0.004247	0.459298	108.140440	0.009247	156
4	2.311524	262.304766	0.003812	0.432615	113.476990	0.008812	168
5	2.454094	290.818712	0.003439	0.407482	118.503515	0.008439	180
6	2.605457	321.091337	0.003114	0.383810	123.238025	0.008114	192
7	2.766156	353.231110	0.002831	0.361513	127.697486	0.007831	204
8	2.936766	387.353194	0.002582	0.340511	131.897876	0.007582	216
9	3.117899	423.579854	0.002361	0.320729	135.854246	0.007361	228
0	3.310204	462.040895	0.002164	0.302096	139.580772	0.007164	240
1	3.514371	502.874129	0.001989	0.284546	143.090806	0.006989	252
2	3.731129	546.225867	0.001831	0.268015	146.396927	0.006831	264
3	3.961257	592.251446	0.001688	0.252445	149.510979	0.006688	276
4	4.205579	641.115782	0.001560	0.237779	152.444121	0.006560	288
5	4.464970	692.993962	0.001443	0.223966	155.206864	0.006443	300
6	4.740359	748.071876	0.001337	0.210954	157.809106	0.006337	312
7	5.032734	806.546875	0.001240	0.198699	160.260172	0.006240	324
8	5.343142	868.628484	0.001151	0.187156	162.568844	0.006151	336
9	5.672696	934.539150	0.001070	0.176283	164.743394	0.006070	348
0	6.022575	1004.515043	0.000996	0.166042	166.791614	0.005996	360
1	6.394034	1078.806895	0.000927	0.156396	168.720844	0.005927	372
2	6.788405	1157.680906	0.000864	0.147310	170.537996	0.005864	384
3	7.207098	1241.419693	0.000806	0.138752	172.249581	0.005806	396
4	7.651617	1330.323306	0.000752	0.130691	173.861732	0.005752	408
5	8.123551	1424.710299	0.000702	0.123099	175.380226	0.005702	420
6	8.624594	1524.918875	0.000656	0.115947	176.810504	0.005656	432
7	9.156540	1631.308097	0.000613	0.109212	178.157690	0.005613	444
8	9.721296	1744.259173	0.000573	0.102867	179.426611	0.005573	456
9	10.320884	1864.176825	0.000536	0.096891	180.621815	0.005536	468
0	10.957454	1991.490734	0.000502	0.091262	181.747584	0.005502	480

SOURCE: Paul Wendt and Alan R. Cerf, *Tables for Investment Analysis* (Center for Real Estate and Urban Economics, 1966; reprinted by the Institute of Business and Economic Research, 1977, 1979 and 1981, University of California, Berkeley).

6.00%   ANNUAL COMPOUND INTEREST TABLES   6.00%
                                     EFFECTIVE RATE   6.00

	1 AMOUNT OF $1 AT COMPOUND INTEREST	2 ACCUMULATION OF $1 PER PERIOD	3 SINKING FUND FACTOR	4 PRESENT VALUE REVERSION OF $1	5 PRESENT VALUE ORD. ANNUITY $1 PER PERIOD	6 INSTALMENT TO AMORTIZE $1
YEARS						
1	1.060000	1.000000	1.000000	0.943396	0.943396	1.060000
2	1.123600	2.060000	0.485437	0.889996	1.833393	0.545437
3	1.191016	3.183600	0.314110	0.839619	2.673012	0.374110
4	1.262477	4.374616	0.228591	0.792094	3.465106	0.288591
5	1.338226	5.637093	0.177396	0.747258	4.212364	0.237396
6	1.418519	6.975319	0.143363	0.704961	4.917324	0.203363
7	1.503630	8.393838	0.119135	0.665057	5.582381	0.179135
8	1.593848	9.897468	0.101036	0.627412	6.209794	0.161036
9	1.689479	11.491316	0.087022	0.591898	6.801692	0.147022
10	1.790848	13.180795	0.075868	0.558395	7.360087	0.135868
11	1.898299	14.971643	0.066793	0.526788	7.886875	0.126793
12	2.012196	16.869941	0.059277	0.496969	8.383844	0.119277
13	2.132928	18.882138	0.052960	0.468839	8.852683	0.112960
14	2.260904	21.015066	0.047585	0.442301	9.294984	0.107585
15	2.396558	23.275970	0.042963	0.417265	9.712249	0.102963
16	2.540352	25.672528	0.038952	0.393646	10.105895	0.098952
17	2.692773	28.212880	0.035445	0.371364	10.477260	0.095445
18	2.854339	30.905653	0.032357	0.350344	10.827603	0.092357
19	3.025600	33.759992	0.029621	0.330513	11.158116	0.089621
20	3.207135	36.785591	0.027185	0.311805	11.469921	0.087185
21	3.399564	39.992727	0.025005	0.294155	11.764077	0.085005
22	3.603537	43.392290	0.023046	0.277505	12.041582	0.083046
23	3.819750	46.995828	0.021278	0.261797	12.303379	0.081278
24	4.048935	50.815577	0.019679	0.246979	12.550358	0.079679
25	4.291871	54.864512	0.018227	0.232999	12.783356	0.078227
26	4.549383	59.156383	0.016904	0.219810	13.003166	0.076904
27	4.822346	63.705766	0.015697	0.207368	13.210534	0.075697
28	5.111687	68.528112	0.014593	0.195630	13.406164	0.074593
29	5.418388	73.639798	0.013580	0.184557	13.590721	0.073580
30	5.743491	79.058186	0.012649	0.174110	13.764831	0.072649
31	6.088101	84.801677	0.011792	0.164255	13.929086	0.071792
32	6.453387	90.889778	0.011002	0.154957	14.084043	0.071002
33	6.840590	97.343165	0.010273	0.146186	14.230230	0.070273
34	7.251025	104.183755	0.009598	0.137912	14.368141	0.069598
35	7.686087	111.434780	0.008974	0.130105	14.498246	0.068974
36	8.147252	119.120867	0.008395	0.122741	14.620987	0.068395
37	8.636087	127.268119	0.007857	0.115793	14.736780	0.067857
38	9.154252	135.904206	0.007358	0.109239	14.846019	0.067358
39	9.703507	145.058458	0.006894	0.103056	14.949075	0.066894
40	10.285718	154.761966	0.006462	0.097222	15.046297	0.066462
41	10.902861	165.047684	0.006059	0.091719	15.138016	0.066059
42	11.557033	175.950545	0.005683	0.086527	15.224543	0.065683
43	12.250455	187.507577	0.005333	0.081630	15.306173	0.065333
44	12.985482	199.758032	0.005006	0.077009	15.383182	0.065006
45	13.764611	212.743514	0.004700	0.072650	15.455832	0.064700
46	14.590487	226.508125	0.004415	0.068538	15.524370	0.064415
47	15.465917	241.098612	0.004148	0.064658	15.589028	0.064148
48	16.393872	256.564529	0.003898	0.060998	15.650027	0.063898
49	17.377504	272.958401	0.003664	0.057546	15.707572	0.063664
50	18.420154	290.335905	0.003444	0.054288	15.761861	0.063444

7.00%   MONTHLY COMPOUND INTEREST TABLES   7.00%
                               EFFECTIVE RATE 0.583

	1 AMOUNT OF $1 AT COMPOUND INTEREST	2 ACCUMULATION OF $1 PER PERIOD	3 SINKING FUND FACTOR	4 PRESENT VALUE REVERSION OF $1	5 PRESENT VALUE ORD. ANNUITY $1 PER PERIOD	6 INSTALMENT TO AMORTIZE $1	
MONTHS							
1	1.005833	1.000000	1.000000	0.994200	0.994200	1.005833	
2	1.011701	2.005833	0.498546	0.988435	1.982635	0.504379	
3	1.017602	3.017534	0.331396	0.982702	2.965337	0.337230	
4	1.023538	4.035136	0.247823	0.977003	3.942340	0.253656	
5	1.029500	5.058673	0.197680	0.971337	4.913677	0.203514	
6	1.035514	6.088184	0.164253	0.965704	5.879381	0.170086	
7	1.041555	7.123698	0.140377	0.960103	6.839484	0.146210	
8	1.047631	8.165253	0.122470	0.954535	7.794019	0.128304	
9	1.053742	9.212883	0.108544	0.948999	8.743018	0.114377	
10	1.059889	10.266625	0.097403	0.943495	9.686513	0.103236	
11	1.066071	11.326514	0.088288	0.938024	10.624537	0.094122	
12	1.072290	12.392585	0.080693	0.932583	11.557120	0.086527	
YEARS							**MONTHS**
1	1.072290	12.392585	0.080693	0.932583	11.557120	0.086527	12
2	1.149806	25.681032	0.038939	0.869712	22.335099	0.044773	24
3	1.232926	39.930101	0.025044	0.811079	32.386464	0.030877	36
4	1.322054	55.209236	0.018113	0.756399	41.760201	0.023946	48
5	1.417625	71.592902	0.013968	0.705405	50.501993	0.019801	60
6	1.520106	89.160944	0.011216	0.657849	58.654444	0.017049	72
7	1.629994	107.998981	0.009259	0.613499	66.257285	0.015093	84
8	1.747826	128.198821	0.007800	0.572139	73.347569	0.013634	96
9	1.874177	149.858909	0.006673	0.533568	79.959850	0.012506	108
10	2.009661	173.084807	0.005778	0.497596	86.126354	0.011611	120
11	2.154940	197.989707	0.005051	0.464050	91.877134	0.010884	132
12	2.310721	224.694985	0.004450	0.432765	97.240216	0.010284	144
13	2.477763	253.330789	0.003947	0.403590	102.241738	0.009781	156
14	2.656881	284.036677	0.003521	0.376381	106.906074	0.009354	168
15	2.848947	316.962297	0.003155	0.351007	111.255958	0.008988	180
16	3.054897	352.268112	0.002839	0.327343	115.312587	0.008672	192
17	3.275736	390.126188	0.002563	0.305275	119.095732	0.008397	204
18	3.512539	430.721027	0.002322	0.284694	122.623831	0.008155	216
19	3.766461	474.250470	0.002109	0.265501	125.914077	0.007942	228
20	4.038739	520.926660	0.001920	0.247602	128.982506	0.007753	240
21	4.330700	570.977075	0.001751	0.230910	131.844073	0.007585	252
22	4.643766	624.645640	0.001601	0.215342	134.512723	0.007434	264
23	4.979464	682.193909	0.001466	0.200825	137.001461	0.007299	276
24	5.339430	743.902347	0.001344	0.187286	139.322418	0.007178	288
25	5.725418	810.071693	0.001234	0.174660	141.486903	0.007068	300
26	6.139309	881.024426	0.001135	0.162885	143.505467	0.006968	312
27	6.583120	957.106339	0.001045	0.151904	145.387946	0.006878	324
28	7.059015	1038.688219	0.000963	0.141663	147.143515	0.006796	336
29	7.569311	1126.167659	0.000888	0.132112	148.780729	0.006721	348
30	8.116497	1219.970996	0.000820	0.123206	150.307568	0.006653	360
31	8.703240	1320.555383	0.000757	0.114900	151.731473	0.006591	372
32	9.332398	1428.411024	0.000700	0.107154	153.059383	0.006533	384
33	10.007037	1544.063557	0.000648	0.099930	154.297770	0.006481	396
34	10.730447	1668.076622	0.000599	0.093193	155.452669	0.006433	408
35	11.506152	1801.054601	0.000555	0.086910	156.529709	0.006389	420
36	12.337932	1943.645569	0.000514	0.081051	157.534139	0.006348	432
37	13.229843	2096.544450	0.000477	0.075587	158.470853	0.006310	444
38	14.186229	2260.496403	0.000442	0.070491	159.344418	0.006276	456
39	15.211753	2436.300456	0.000410	0.065739	160.159090	0.006244	468
40	16.311411	2624.813398	0.000381	0.061307	160.918839	0.006214	480

7.00%   ANNUAL COMPOUND INTEREST TABLES   7.00%
                      EFFECTIVE RATE 7.00

	1	2	3	4	5	6
	AMOUNT OF $1 AT COMPOUND INTEREST	ACCUMULATION OF $1 PER PERIOD	SINKING FUND FACTOR	PRESENT VALUE REVERSION OF $1	PRESENT VALUE ORD. ANNUITY $1 PER PERIOD	INSTALMENT TO AMORTIZE $1
YEARS						
1	1.070000	1.000000	1.000000	0.934579	0.934579	1.070000
2	1.144900	2.070000	0.483092	0.873439	1.808018	0.553092
3	1.225043	3.214900	0.311052	0.816298	2.624316	0.381052
4	1.310796	4.439943	0.225228	0.762895	3.387211	0.295228
5	1.402552	5.750739	0.173891	0.712986	4.100197	0.243891
6	1.500730	7.153291	0.139796	0.666342	4.766540	0.209796
7	1.605781	8.654021	0.115553	0.622750	5.389289	0.185553
8	1.718186	10.259803	0.097468	0.582009	5.971299	0.167468
9	1.838459	11.977989	0.083486	0.543934	6.515232	0.153486
10	1.967151	13.816448	0.072378	0.508349	7.023582	0.142378
11	2.104852	15.783599	0.063357	0.475093	7.498674	0.133357
12	2.252192	17.888451	0.055902	0.444012	7.942686	0.125902
13	2.409845	20.140643	0.049661	0.414964	8.357651	0.119651
14	2.578534	22.550488	0.044345	0.387817	8.745468	0.114345
15	2.759032	25.129022	0.039795	0.362446	9.107914	0.109795
16	2.952164	27.888054	0.035858	0.338735	9.446649	0.105858
17	3.158815	30.840217	0.032425	0.316574	9.763223	0.102425
18	3.379932	33.999033	0.029413	0.295864	10.059087	0.099413
19	3.616528	37.378965	0.026753	0.276508	10.335595	0.096753
20	3.869684	40.995492	0.024393	0.258419	10.594014	0.094393
21	4.140562	44.865177	0.022289	0.241513	10.835527	0.092289
22	4.430402	49.005739	0.020406	0.225713	11.061240	0.090406
23	4.740530	53.436141	0.018714	0.210947	11.272187	0.088714
24	5.072367	58.176671	0.017189	0.197147	11.469334	0.087189
25	5.427433	63.249038	0.015811	0.184249	11.653583	0.085811
26	5.807353	68.676470	0.014561	0.172195	11.825779	0.084561
27	6.213868	74.483823	0.013426	0.160930	11.986709	0.083426
28	6.648838	80.697691	0.012392	0.150402	12.137111	0.082392
29	7.114257	87.346529	0.011449	0.140563	12.277674	0.081449
30	7.612255	94.460786	0.010586	0.131367	12.409041	0.080586
31	8.145113	102.073041	0.009797	0.122773	12.531814	0.079797
32	8.715271	110.218154	0.009073	0.114741	12.646555	0.079073
33	9.325340	118.933425	0.008408	0.107235	12.753790	0.078408
34	9.978114	128.258765	0.007797	0.100219	12.854009	0.077797
35	10.676581	138.236878	0.007234	0.093663	12.947672	0.077234
36	11.423942	148.913460	0.006715	0.087535	13.035208	0.076715
37	12.223618	160.337402	0.006237	0.081809	13.117017	0.076237
38	13.079271	172.561020	0.005795	0.076457	13.193473	0.075795
39	13.994820	185.640292	0.005387	0.071455	13.264928	0.075387
40	14.974458	199.635112	0.005009	0.066780	13.331709	0.075009
41	16.022670	214.609570	0.004660	0.062412	13.394120	0.074660
42	17.144257	230.632240	0.004336	0.058329	13.452449	0.074336
43	18.344355	247.776496	0.004036	0.054513	13.506962	0.074036
44	19.628460	266.120851	0.003758	0.050946	13.557908	0.073758
45	21.002452	285.749311	0.003500	0.047613	13.605522	0.073500
46	22.472623	306.751763	0.003260	0.044499	13.650020	0.073260
47	24.045707	329.224386	0.003037	0.041587	13.691608	0.073037
48	25.728907	353.270093	0.002831	0.038867	13.730474	0.072831
49	27.529930	378.999000	0.002639	0.036324	13.766799	0.072639
50	29.457025	406.528929	0.002460	0.033948	13.800746	0.072460

8.00%   MONTHLY COMPOUND INTEREST TABLES   8.00%
EFFECTIVE RATE 0.667

	1	2	3	4	5	6	
	AMOUNT OF $1 AT COMPOUND INTEREST	ACCUMULATION OF $1 PER PERIOD	SINKING FUND FACTOR	PRESENT VALUE REVERSION OF $1	PRESENT VALUE ORD. ANNUITY $1 PER PERIOD	INSTALMENT TO AMORTIZE $1	
MONTHS							
1	1.006667	1.000000	1.000000	0.993377	0.993377	1.006667	
2	1.013378	2.006667	0.498339	0.986799	1.980176	0.505006	
3	1.020134	3.020044	0.331121	0.980264	2.960440	0.337788	
4	1.026935	4.040178	0.247514	0.973772	3.934212	0.254181	
5	1.033781	5.067113	0.197351	0.967323	4.901535	0.204018	
6	1.040673	6.100893	0.163910	0.960917	5.862452	0.170577	
7	1.047610	7.141566	0.140025	0.954553	6.817005	0.146692	
8	1.054595	8.189176	0.122112	0.948232	7.765237	0.128779	
9	1.061625	9.243771	0.108181	0.941952	8.707189	0.114848	
10	1.068703	10.305396	0.097037	0.935714	9.642903	0.103703	
11	1.075827	11.374099	0.087919	0.929517	10.572420	0.094586	
12	1.083000	12.449926	0.080322	0.923361	11.495782	0.086988	
YEARS							MONTHS
1	1.083000	12.449926	0.080322	0.923361	11.495782	0.086988	12
2	1.172888	25.933190	0.038561	0.852596	22.110544	0.045227	24
3	1.270237	40.535558	0.024670	0.787255	31.911806	0.031336	36
4	1.375666	56.349915	0.017746	0.726921	40.961913	0.024413	48
5	1.489846	73.476856	0.013610	0.671210	49.318433	0.020276	60
6	1.613502	92.025325	0.010867	0.619770	57.034522	0.017533	72
7	1.747422	112.113308	0.008920	0.572272	64.159261	0.015586	84
8	1.892457	133.868583	0.007470	0.528414	70.737970	0.014137	96
9	2.049530	157.429535	0.006352	0.487917	76.812497	0.013019	108
10	2.219640	182.946035	0.005466	0.450523	82.421481	0.012133	120
11	2.403869	210.580392	0.004749	0.415996	87.600600	0.011415	132
12	2.603389	240.508387	0.004158	0.384115	92.382800	0.010825	144
13	2.819464	272.920390	0.003664	0.354677	96.798498	0.010331	156
14	3.053484	308.022574	0.003247	0.327495	100.875784	0.009913	168
15	3.306921	346.038222	0.002890	0.302396	104.640592	0.009557	180
16	3.581394	387.209149	0.002583	0.279221	108.116871	0.009249	192
17	3.878648	431.797244	0.002316	0.257822	111.326733	0.008983	204
18	4.200254	480.086128	0.002083	0.238063	114.290596	0.008750	216
19	4.549220	532.382966	0.001878	0.219818	117.027313	0.008545	228
20	4.926803	589.020416	0.001698	0.202971	119.554292	0.008364	240
21	5.335725	650.358746	0.001538	0.187416	121.887606	0.008204	252
22	5.778588	716.788127	0.001395	0.173053	124.042099	0.008062	264
23	6.258207	788.731114	0.001268	0.159790	126.031475	0.007935	276
24	6.777636	866.645333	0.001154	0.147544	127.868388	0.007821	288
25	7.340176	951.026395	0.001051	0.136237	129.564523	0.007718	300
26	7.949407	1042.411042	0.000959	0.125796	131.130668	0.007626	312
27	8.609204	1141.380571	0.000876	0.116155	132.576786	0.007543	324
28	9.323763	1248.564521	0.000801	0.107253	133.912076	0.007468	336
29	10.097631	1364.644687	0.000733	0.099033	135.145031	0.007399	348
30	10.935730	1490.359449	0.000671	0.091443	136.283494	0.007338	360
31	11.843390	1626.508474	0.000615	0.084435	137.334707	0.007281	372
32	12.826385	1773.957801	0.000564	0.077964	138.305357	0.007230	384
33	13.890969	1933.645350	0.000517	0.071989	139.201617	0.007184	396
34	15.043913	2106.586886	0.000475	0.066472	140.029190	0.007141	408
35	16.292550	2293.882485	0.000436	0.061378	140.793338	0.007103	420
36	17.644824	2496.723526	0.000401	0.056674	141.498923	0.007067	432
37	19.109335	2716.400273	0.000368	0.052330	142.150433	0.007035	444
38	20.695401	2954.310082	0.000338	0.048320	142.752013	0.007005	456
39	22.413109	3211.966288	0.000311	0.044617	143.307488	0.006978	468
40	24.273386	3491.007831	0.000286	0.041197	143.820392	0.006953	480

8.00%   ANNUAL COMPOUND INTEREST TABLES   8.00%
                                  EFFECTIVE RATE 8.00

	1 AMOUNT OF $1 AT COMPOUND INTEREST	2 ACCUMULATION OF $1 PER PERIOD	3 SINKING FUND FACTOR	4 PRESENT VALUE REVERSION OF $1	5 PRESENT VALUE ORD. ANNUITY $1 PER PERIOD	6 INSTALMENT TO AMORTIZE $1
YEARS						
1	1.080000	1.000000	1.000000	0.925926	0.925926	1.080000
2	1.166400	2.080000	0.480769	0.857339	1.783265	0.560769
3	1.259712	3.246400	0.308034	0.793832	2.577097	0.388034
4	1.360489	4.506112	0.221921	0.735030	3.312127	0.301921
5	1.469328	5.866601	0.170456	0.680583	3.992710	0.250456
6	1.586874	7.335929	0.136315	0.630170	4.622880	0.216315
7	1.713824	8.922803	0.112072	0.583490	5.206370	0.192072
8	1.850930	10.636628	0.094015	0.540269	5.746639	0.174015
9	1.999005	12.487558	0.080080	0.500249	6.246888	0.160080
10	2.158925	14.486562	0.069029	0.463193	6.710081	0.149029
11	2.331639	16.645487	0.060076	0.428883	7.138964	0.140076
12	2.518170	18.977126	0.052695	0.397114	7.536078	0.132695
13	2.719624	21.495297	0.046522	0.367698	7.903776	0.126522
14	2.937194	24.214920	0.041297	0.340461	8.244237	0.121297
15	3.172169	27.152114	0.036830	0.315242	8.559479	0.116830
16	3.425943	30.324283	0.032977	0.291890	8.851369	0.112977
17	3.700018	33.750226	0.029629	0.270269	9.121638	0.109629
18	3.996019	37.450244	0.026702	0.250249	9.371887	0.106702
19	4.315701	41.446263	0.024128	0.231712	9.603599	0.104128
20	4.660957	45.761964	0.021852	0.214548	9.818147	0.101852
21	5.033834	50.422921	0.019832	0.198656	10.016803	0.099832
22	5.436540	55.456755	0.018032	0.183941	10.200744	0.098032
23	5.871464	60.893296	0.016422	0.170315	10.371059	0.096422
24	6.341181	66.764759	0.014978	0.157699	10.528758	0.094978
25	6.848475	73.105940	0.013679	0.146018	10.674776	0.093679
26	7.396353	79.954415	0.012507	0.135202	10.809978	0.092507
27	7.988061	87.350768	0.011448	0.125187	10.935165	0.091448
28	8.627106	95.338830	0.010489	0.115914	11.051078	0.090489
29	9.317275	103.965936	0.009619	0.107328	11.158406	0.089619
30	10.062657	113.283211	0.008827	0.099377	11.257783	0.088827
31	10.867669	123.345868	0.008107	0.092016	11.349799	0.088107
32	11.737083	134.213537	0.007451	0.085200	11.434999	0.087451
33	12.676050	145.950620	0.006852	0.078889	11.513888	0.086852
34	13.690134	158.626670	0.006304	0.073045	11.586934	0.086304
35	14.785344	172.316804	0.005803	0.067635	11.654568	0.085803
36	15.968172	187.102148	0.005345	0.062625	11.717193	0.085345
37	17.245626	203.070320	0.004924	0.057986	11.775179	0.084924
38	18.625276	220.315945	0.004539	0.053690	11.828869	0.084539
39	20.115298	238.941221	0.004185	0.049713	11.878582	0.084185
40	21.724521	259.056519	0.003860	0.046031	11.924613	0.083860
41	23.462483	280.781040	0.003561	0.042621	11.967235	0.083561
42	25.339482	304.243523	0.003287	0.039464	12.006699	0.083287
43	27.366640	329.583005	0.003034	0.036541	12.043240	0.083034
44	29.555972	356.949646	0.002802	0.033834	12.077074	0.082802
45	31.920449	386.505617	0.002587	0.031328	12.108402	0.082587
46	34.474085	418.426067	0.002390	0.029007	12.137409	0.082390
47	37.232012	452.900152	0.002208	0.026859	12.164267	0.082208
48	40.210573	490.132164	0.002040	0.024869	12.189136	0.082040
49	43.427419	530.342737	0.001886	0.023027	12.212163	0.081886
50	46.901613	573.770156	0.001743	0.021321	12.233485	0.081743

9.00% MONTHLY COMPOUND INTEREST TABLES 9.00%
EFFECTIVE RATE 0.750

	1 AMOUNT OF $1 AT COMPOUND INTEREST	2 ACCUMULATION OF $1 PER PERIOD	3 SINKING FUND FACTOR	4 PRESENT VALUE REVERSION OF $1	5 PRESENT VALUE ORD. ANNUITY $1 PER PERIOD	6 INSTALMENT TO AMORTIZE $1	
MONTHS							
1	1.007500	1.000000	1.000000	0.992556	0.992556	1.007500	
2	1.015056	2.007500	0.498132	0.985167	1.977723	0.505632	
3	1.022669	3.022556	0.330846	0.977833	2.955556	0.338346	
4	1.030339	4.045225	0.247205	0.970554	3.926110	0.254705	
5	1.038067	5.075565	0.197022	0.963329	4.889440	0.204522	
6	1.045852	6.113631	0.163569	0.956158	5.845598	0.171069	
7	1.053696	7.159484	0.139675	0.949040	6.794638	0.147175	
8	1.061599	8.213180	0.121756	0.941975	7.736613	0.129256	
9	1.069561	9.274779	0.107819	0.934963	8.671576	0.115319	
10	1.077583	10.344339	0.096671	0.928003	9.599580	0.104171	
11	1.085664	11.421922	0.087551	0.921095	10.520675	0.095051	
12	1.093807	12.507586	0.079951	0.914238	11.434913	0.087451	
YEARS							MONTHS
1	1.093807	12.507586	0.079951	0.914238	11.434913	0.087451	12
2	1.196414	26.188471	0.038185	0.835831	21.889146	0.045685	24
3	1.308645	41.152716	0.024300	0.764149	31.446805	0.031800	36
4	1.431405	57.520711	0.017385	0.698614	40.184782	0.024885	48
5	1.565681	75.424137	0.013258	0.638700	48.173374	0.020758	60
6	1.712553	95.007028	0.010526	0.583924	55.476849	0.018026	72
7	1.873202	116.426928	0.008589	0.533845	62.153965	0.016089	84
8	2.048921	139.856164	0.007150	0.488062	68.258439	0.014650	96
9	2.241124	165.483223	0.006043	0.446205	73.839382	0.013543	108
10	2.451357	193.514277	0.005168	0.407937	78.941693	0.012668	120
11	2.681311	224.174837	0.004461	0.372952	83.606420	0.011961	132
12	2.932837	257.711570	0.003880	0.340967	87.871092	0.011380	144
13	3.207957	294.394279	0.003397	0.311725	91.770018	0.010897	156
14	3.508886	334.518099	0.002989	0.284991	95.334564	0.010489	168
15	3.838043	378.405769	0.002643	0.260549	98.593409	0.010143	180
16	4.198078	426.410427	0.002345	0.238204	101.572769	0.009845	192
17	4.591887	478.918252	0.002088	0.217775	104.296613	0.009588	204
18	5.022638	536.351674	0.001864	0.199099	106.786856	0.009364	216
19	5.493796	599.172747	0.001669	0.182024	109.063531	0.009169	228
20	6.009152	667.886870	0.001497	0.166413	111.144954	0.008997	240
21	6.572851	743.046852	0.001346	0.152141	113.047870	0.008846	252
22	7.189430	825.257358	0.001212	0.139093	114.787589	0.008712	264
23	7.863848	915.179777	0.001093	0.127164	116.378106	0.008593	276
24	8.601532	1013.537539	0.000987	0.116258	117.832218	0.008487	288
25	9.408415	1121.121937	0.000892	0.106288	119.161622	0.008392	300
26	10.290989	1238.798494	0.000807	0.097172	120.377014	0.008307	312
27	11.256354	1367.513924	0.000731	0.088839	121.488172	0.008231	324
28	12.312278	1508.303750	0.000663	0.081220	122.504035	0.008163	336
29	13.467255	1662.300631	0.000602	0.074254	123.432776	0.008102	348
30	14.730576	1830.743483	0.000546	0.067886	124.281866	0.008046	360
31	16.112406	2014.987436	0.000496	0.062064	125.058136	0.007996	372
32	17.623861	2216.514743	0.000451	0.056741	125.767832	0.007951	384
33	19.277100	2436.946701	0.000410	0.051875	126.416664	0.007910	396
34	21.085425	2678.056697	0.000373	0.047426	127.009850	0.007873	408
35	23.063384	2941.784473	0.000340	0.043359	127.552164	0.007840	420
36	25.226888	3230.251735	0.000310	0.039640	128.047967	0.007810	432
37	27.593344	3545.779215	0.000282	0.036241	128.501250	0.007782	444
38	30.181790	3890.905350	0.000257	0.033133	128.915659	0.007757	456
39	33.013050	4268.406696	0.000234	0.030291	129.294526	0.007734	468
40	36.109902	4681.320272	0.000214	0.027693	129.640902	0.007714	480

9.00%   ANNUAL COMPOUND INTEREST TABLES   9.00%
                              EFFECTIVE RATE 9.00

	1 AMOUNT OF $1 AT COMPOUND INTEREST	2 ACCUMULATION OF $1 PER PERIOD	3 SINKING FUND FACTOR	4 PRESENT VALUE REVERSION OF $1	5 PRESENT VALUE ORD. ANNUITY $1 PER PERIOD	6 INSTALMENT TO AMORTIZE $1
YEARS						
1	1.090000	1.000000	1.000000	0.917431	0.917431	1.090000
2	1.188100	2.090000	0.478469	0.841680	1.759111	0.568469
3	1.295029	3.278100	0.305055	0.772183	2.531295	0.395055
4	1.411582	4.573129	0.218669	0.708425	3.239720	0.308669
5	1.538624	5.984711	0.167092	0.649931	3.889651	0.257092
6	1.677100	7.523335	0.132920	0.596267	4.485919	0.222920
7	1.828039	9.200435	0.108691	0.547034	5.032953	0.198691
8	1.992563	11.028474	0.090674	0.501866	5.534819	0.180674
9	2.171893	13.021036	0.076799	0.460428	5.995247	0.166799
10	2.367364	15.192930	0.065820	0.422411	6.417658	0.155820
11	2.580426	17.560293	0.056947	0.387533	6.805191	0.146947
12	2.812665	20.140720	0.049651	0.355535	7.160725	0.139651
13	3.065805	22.953385	0.043567	0.326179	7.486904	0.133567
14	3.341727	26.019189	0.038433	0.299246	7.786150	0.128433
15	3.642482	29.360916	0.034059	0.274538	8.060688	0.124059
16	3.970306	33.003399	0.030300	0.251870	8.312558	0.120300
17	4.327633	36.973705	0.027046	0.231073	8.543631	0.117046
18	4.717120	41.301338	0.024212	0.211994	8.755625	0.114212
19	5.141661	46.018458	0.021730	0.194490	8.950115	0.111730
20	5.604411	51.160120	0.019546	0.178431	9.128546	0.109546
21	6.108808	56.764530	0.017617	0.163698	9.292244	0.107617
22	6.658600	62.873338	0.015905	0.150182	9.442425	0.105905
23	7.257874	69.531939	0.014382	0.137781	9.580207	0.104382
24	7.911083	76.789813	0.013023	0.126405	9.706612	0.103023
25	8.623081	84.700896	0.011806	0.115968	9.822580	0.101806
26	9.399158	93.323977	0.010715	0.106393	9.928972	0.100715
27	10.245082	102.723135	0.009735	0.097608	10.026580	0.099735
28	11.167140	112.968217	0.008852	0.089548	10.116128	0.098852
29	12.172182	124.135356	0.008056	0.082155	10.198283	0.098056
30	13.267678	136.307539	0.007336	0.075371	10.273654	0.097336
31	14.461770	149.575217	0.006686	0.069148	10.342802	0.096686
32	15.763329	164.036987	0.006096	0.063438	10.406240	0.096096
33	17.182028	179.800315	0.005562	0.058200	10.464441	0.095562
34	18.728411	196.982344	0.005077	0.053395	10.517835	0.095077
35	20.413968	215.710755	0.004636	0.048986	10.566821	0.094636
36	22.251225	236.124723	0.004235	0.044941	10.611763	0.094235
37	24.253835	258.375948	0.003870	0.041231	10.652993	0.093870
38	26.436680	282.629783	0.003538	0.037826	10.690820	0.093538
39	28.815982	309.066463	0.003236	0.034703	10.725523	0.093236
40	31.409420	337.882445	0.002960	0.031838	10.757360	0.092960
41	34.236268	369.291865	0.002708	0.029209	10.786569	0.092708
42	37.317532	403.528133	0.002478	0.026797	10.813366	0.092478
43	40.676110	440.845665	0.002268	0.024584	10.837950	0.092268
44	44.336960	481.521775	0.002077	0.022555	10.860505	0.092077
45	48.327286	525.858734	0.001902	0.020692	10.881197	0.091902
46	52.676742	574.186021	0.001742	0.018984	10.900181	0.091742
47	57.417649	626.862762	0.001595	0.017416	10.917597	0.091595
48	62.585237	684.280411	0.001461	0.015978	10.933575	0.091461
49	68.217908	746.865648	0.001339	0.014659	10.948234	0.091339
50	74.357520	815.083556	0.001227	0.013449	10.961683	0.091227

10.00%   MONTHLY COMPOUND INTEREST TABLES   10.00%
                                EFFECTIVE RATE 0.833

	1 AMOUNT OF $1 AT COMPOUND INTEREST	2 ACCUMULATION OF $1 PER PERIOD	3 SINKING FUND FACTOR	4 PRESENT VALUE REVERSION OF $1	5 PRESENT VALUE ORD. ANNUITY $1 PER PERIOD	6 INSTALMENT TO AMORTIZE $1	
MONTHS							
1	1.008333	1.000000	1.000000	0.991736	0.991736	1.008333	
2	1.016736	2.008333	0.497925	0.983539	1.975275	0.506259	
3	1.025209	3.025069	0.330571	0.975411	2.950686	0.338904	
4	1.033752	4.050278	0.246897	0.967350	3.918036	0.255230	
5	1.042367	5.084031	0.196694	0.959355	4.877391	0.205020	
6	1.051053	6.126398	0.163228	0.951427	5.828817	0.171561	
7	1.059812	7.177451	0.139325	0.943563	6.772381	0.147659	
8	1.068644	8.237263	0.121400	0.935765	7.708146	0.129733	
9	1.077549	9.305907	0.107459	0.928032	8.636178	0.115792	
10	1.086529	10.383456	0.096307	0.920362	9.556540	0.104640	
11	1.095583	11.469985	0.087184	0.912756	10.469296	0.095517	
12	1.104713	12.565568	0.079583	0.905212	11.374508	0.087916	
YEARS							MONTHS
1	1.104713	12.565568	0.079583	0.905212	11.374508	0.087916	12
2	1.220391	26.446915	0.037812	0.819410	21.670855	0.046145	24
3	1.348182	41.781821	0.023934	0.741740	30.991236	0.032267	36
4	1.489354	58.722492	0.017029	0.671432	39.428160	0.025363	48
5	1.645309	77.437072	0.012914	0.607789	47.065369	0.021247	60
6	1.817594	98.111314	0.010193	0.550178	53.978665	0.018526	72
7	2.007920	120.950418	0.008268	0.498028	60.236667	0.016601	84
8	2.218176	146.181076	0.006841	0.450821	65.901488	0.015174	96
9	2.450448	174.053713	0.005745	0.408089	71.029355	0.014079	108
10	2.707041	204.844979	0.004882	0.369407	75.671163	0.013215	120
11	2.990504	238.860493	0.004187	0.334392	79.872986	0.012520	132
12	3.303649	276.437876	0.003617	0.302696	83.676528	0.011951	144
13	3.649584	317.950102	0.003145	0.274004	87.119542	0.011478	156
14	4.031743	363.809201	0.002749	0.248032	90.236201	0.011082	168
15	4.453920	414.470346	0.002413	0.224521	93.057439	0.010746	180
16	4.920303	470.436376	0.002126	0.203240	95.611259	0.010459	192
17	5.435523	532.262780	0.001879	0.183975	97.923008	0.010212	204
18	6.004693	600.563216	0.001665	0.166536	100.015633	0.009998	216
19	6.633463	676.015601	0.001479	0.150751	101.909902	0.009813	228
20	7.328074	759.368836	0.001317	0.136462	103.624619	0.009650	240
21	8.095419	851.450244	0.001174	0.123527	105.176801	0.009508	252
22	8.943115	953.173779	0.001049	0.111818	106.581856	0.009382	264
23	9.879576	1065.549097	0.000938	0.101219	107.853730	0.009272	276
24	10.914097	1189.691580	0.000841	0.091625	109.005045	0.009174	288
25	12.056945	1326.833403	0.000754	0.082940	110.047230	0.009087	300
26	13.319465	1478.335767	0.000676	0.075078	110.990629	0.009010	312
27	14.714187	1645.702407	0.000608	0.067962	111.844605	0.008941	324
28	16.254954	1830.594523	0.000546	0.061520	112.617635	0.008880	336
29	17.957060	2034.847259	0.000491	0.055688	113.317392	0.008825	348
30	19.837399	2260.487925	0.000442	0.050410	113.950820	0.008776	360
31	21.914634	2509.756117	0.000398	0.045632	114.524207	0.008732	372
32	24.209383	2785.125947	0.000359	0.041306	115.043244	0.008692	384
33	26.744422	3089.330596	0.000324	0.037391	115.513083	0.008657	396
34	29.544912	3425.389448	0.000292	0.033847	115.938387	0.008625	408
35	32.638650	3796.638052	0.000263	0.030639	116.323377	0.008597	420
36	36.056344	4206.761236	0.000238	0.027734	116.671876	0.008571	432
37	39.831914	4659.829677	0.000215	0.025105	116.987340	0.008548	444
38	44.002836	5160.340305	0.000194	0.022726	117.272903	0.008527	456
39	48.610508	5713.260935	0.000175	0.020572	117.531398	0.008508	468
40	53.700663	6324.079581	0.000158	0.018622	117.765391	0.008491	480

10.00%   ANNUAL COMPOUND INTEREST TABLES   10.00%
                                      EFFECTIVE RATE 10.00

	1	2	3	4	5	6
	AMOUNT OF $1 AT COMPOUND INTEREST	ACCUMULATION OF $1 PER PERIOD	SINKING FUND FACTOR	PRESENT VALUE REVERSION OF $1	PRESENT VALUE ORD. ANNUITY $1 PER PERIOD	INSTALMENT TO AMORTIZE $1
YEARS						
1	1.100000	1.000000	1.000000	0.909091	0.909091	1.100000
2	1.210000	2.100000	0.476190	0.826446	1.735537	0.576190
3	1.331000	3.310000	0.302115	0.751315	2.486852	0.402115
4	1.464100	4.641000	0.215471	0.683013	3.169865	0.315471
5	1.610510	6.105100	0.163797	0.620921	3.790787	0.263797
6	1.771561	7.715610	0.129607	0.564474	4.355261	0.229607
7	1.948717	9.487171	0.105405	0.513158	4.868419	0.205405
8	2.143589	11.435888	0.087444	0.466507	5.334926	0.187444
9	2.357948	13.579477	0.073641	0.424098	5.759024	0.173641
10	2.593742	15.937425	0.062745	0.385543	6.144567	0.162745
11	2.853117	18.531167	0.053963	0.350494	6.495061	0.153963
12	3.138428	21.384284	0.046763	0.318631	6.813692	0.146763
13	3.452271	24.522712	0.040779	0.289664	7.103356	0.140779
14	3.797498	27.974983	0.035746	0.263331	7.366687	0.135746
15	4.177248	31.772482	0.031474	0.239392	7.606080	0.131474
16	4.594973	35.949730	0.027817	0.217629	7.823709	0.127817
17	5.054470	40.544703	0.024664	0.197845	8.021553	0.124664
18	5.559917	45.599173	0.021930	0.179859	8.201412	0.121930
19	6.115909	51.159090	0.019547	0.163508	8.364920	0.119547
20	6.727500	57.274999	0.017460	0.148644	8.513564	0.117460
21	7.400250	64.002499	0.015624	0.135131	8.648694	0.115624
22	8.140275	71.402749	0.014005	0.122846	8.771540	0.114005
23	8.954302	79.543024	0.012572	0.111678	8.883218	0.112572
24	9.849733	88.497327	0.011300	0.101526	8.984744	0.111300
25	10.834706	98.347059	0.010168	0.092296	9.077040	0.110168
26	11.918177	109.181765	0.009159	0.083905	9.160945	0.109159
27	13.109994	121.099942	0.008258	0.076278	9.237223	0.108258
28	14.420994	134.209936	0.007451	0.069343	9.306567	0.107451
29	15.863093	148.630930	0.006728	0.063039	9.369606	0.106728
30	17.449402	164.494023	0.006079	0.057309	9.426914	0.106079
31	19.194342	181.943425	0.005496	0.052099	9.479013	0.105496
32	21.113777	201.137767	0.004972	0.047362	9.526376	0.104972
33	23.225154	222.251544	0.004499	0.043057	9.569432	0.104499
34	25.547670	245.476699	0.004074	0.039143	9.608575	0.104074
35	28.102437	271.024368	0.003690	0.035584	9.644159	0.103690
36	30.912681	299.126805	0.003343	0.032349	9.676508	0.103343
37	34.003949	330.039486	0.003030	0.029408	9.705917	0.103030
38	37.404343	364.043434	0.002747	0.026735	9.732651	0.102747
39	41.144778	401.447778	0.002491	0.024304	9.756956	0.102491
40	45.259256	442.592556	0.002259	0.022095	9.779051	0.102259
41	49.785181	487.851811	0.002050	0.020086	9.799137	0.102050
42	54.763699	537.636992	0.001860	0.018260	9.817397	0.101860
43	60.240069	592.400692	0.001688	0.016600	9.833998	0.101688
44	66.264076	652.640761	0.001532	0.015091	9.849089	0.101532
45	72.890484	718.904837	0.001391	0.013719	9.862808	0.101391
46	80.179532	791.795321	0.001263	0.012472	9.875280	0.101263
47	88.197485	871.974853	0.001147	0.011338	9.886618	0.101147
48	97.017234	960.172338	0.001041	0.010307	9.896926	0.101041
49	106.718957	1057.189572	0.000946	0.009370	9.906296	0.100946
50	117.390853	1163.908529	0.000859	0.008519	9.914814	0.100859

11.00%   MONTHLY COMPOUND INTEREST TABLES   11.00%
                              EFFECTIVE RATE 0.917

	1 AMOUNT OF $1 AT COMPOUND INTEREST	2 ACCUMULATION OF $1 PER PERIOD	3 SINKING FUND FACTOR	4 PRESENT VALUE REVERSION OF $1	5 PRESENT VALUE ORD. ANNUITY $1 PER PERIOD	6 INSTALMENT TO AMORTIZE $1	
MONTHS							
1	1.009167	1.000000	1.000000	0.990917	0.990917	1.009167	
2	1.018417	2.009167	0.497719	0.981916	1.972832	0.506885	
3	1.027753	3.027584	0.330296	0.972997	2.945829	0.339463	
4	1.037174	4.055337	0.246589	0.964158	3.909987	0.255755	
5	1.046681	5.092511	0.196367	0.955401	4.865388	0.205533	
6	1.056276	6.139192	0.162888	0.946722	5.812110	0.172055	
7	1.065958	7.195468	0.138976	0.938123	6.750233	0.148143	
8	1.075730	8.261427	0.121044	0.929602	7.679835	0.130211	
9	1.085591	9.337156	0.107099	0.921158	8.600992	0.116266	
10	1.095542	10.422747	0.095944	0.912790	9.513783	0.105111	
11	1.105584	11.518289	0.086818	0.904499	10.418282	0.095985	
12	1.115719	12.623873	0.079215	0.896283	11.314565	0.088382	
YEARS							**MONTHS**
1	1.115719	12.623873	0.079215	0.896283	11.314565	0.088382	12
2	1.244829	26.708566	0.037441	0.803323	21.455619	0.046608	24
3	1.388879	42.423123	0.023572	0.720005	30.544874	0.032739	36
4	1.549598	59.956151	0.016679	0.645329	38.691421	0.025846	48
5	1.728916	79.518080	0.012576	0.578397	45.993034	0.021742	60
6	1.928984	101.343692	0.009867	0.518408	52.537346	0.019034	72
7	2.152204	125.694940	0.007956	0.464640	58.402903	0.017122	84
8	2.401254	152.864085	0.006542	0.416449	63.660103	0.015708	96
9	2.679124	183.177212	0.005459	0.373256	68.372043	0.014626	108
10	2.989150	216.998139	0.004608	0.334543	72.595275	0.013775	120
11	3.335051	254.732784	0.003926	0.299846	76.380487	0.013092	132
12	3.720979	296.834038	0.003369	0.268747	79.773109	0.012536	144
13	4.151566	343.807200	0.002909	0.240873	82.813859	0.012075	156
14	4.631980	396.216042	0.002524	0.215890	85.539231	0.011691	168
15	5.167988	454.689575	0.002199	0.193499	87.981937	0.011366	180
16	5.766021	519.929596	0.001923	0.173430	90.171293	0.011090	192
17	6.433259	592.719117	0.001687	0.155442	92.133576	0.010854	204
18	7.177708	673.931757	0.001484	0.139320	93.892337	0.010650	216
19	8.008304	764.542228	0.001308	0.124870	95.468685	0.010475	228
20	8.935015	865.638038	0.001155	0.111919	96.881539	0.010322	240
21	9.968965	978.432537	0.001022	0.100311	98.147856	0.010189	252
22	11.122562	1104.279485	0.000906	0.089907	99.282835	0.010072	264
23	12.409652	1244.689295	0.000803	0.080582	100.300098	0.009970	276
24	13.845682	1401.347165	0.000714	0.072225	101.211853	0.009880	288
25	15.447889	1576.133301	0.000634	0.064734	102.029044	0.009801	300
26	17.235500	1771.145485	0.000565	0.058020	102.761478	0.009731	312
27	19.229972	1988.724252	0.000503	0.052002	103.417947	0.009670	324
28	21.455242	2231.480981	0.000448	0.046609	104.006328	0.009615	336
29	23.938018	2502.329236	0.000400	0.041775	104.533685	0.009566	348
30	26.708098	2804.519736	0.000357	0.037442	105.006346	0.009523	360
31	29.798728	3141.679369	0.000318	0.033558	105.429984	0.009485	372
32	33.247002	3517.854723	0.000284	0.030078	105.809684	0.009451	384
33	37.094306	3937.560650	0.000254	0.026958	106.150002	0.009421	396
34	41.386816	4405.834459	0.000227	0.024162	106.455024	0.009394	408
35	46.176050	4928.296368	0.000203	0.021656	106.728409	0.009370	420
36	51.519489	5511.216961	0.000181	0.019410	106.973440	0.009348	432
37	57.481264	6161.592447	0.000162	0.017397	107.193057	0.009329	444
38	64.132929	6887.228627	0.000145	0.015593	107.389897	0.009312	456
39	71.554317	7696.834582	0.000130	0.013975	107.566320	0.009297	468
40	79.834499	8600.127195	0.000116	0.012526	107.724446	0.009283	480

11.00%   ANNUAL COMPOUND INTEREST TABLES   11.00%
                                    EFFECTIVE RATE 11.00

	1 AMOUNT OF $1 AT COMPOUND INTEREST	2 ACCUMULATION OF $1 PER PERIOD	3 SINKING FUND FACTOR	4 PRESENT VALUE REVERSION OF $1	5 PRESENT VALUE ORD. ANNUITY $1 PER PERIOD	6 INSTALMENT TO AMORTIZE $1
YEARS						
1	1.110000	1.000000	1.000000	0.900901	0.900901	1.110000
2	1.232100	2.110000	0.473934	0.811622	1.712523	0.583934
3	1.367631	3.342100	0.299213	0.731191	2.443715	0.409213
4	1.518070	4.709731	0.212326	0.658731	3.102446	0.322326
5	1.685058	6.227801	0.160570	0.593451	3.695897	0.270570
6	1.870415	7.912860	0.126377	0.534641	4.230538	0.236377
7	2.076160	9.783274	0.102215	0.481658	4.712196	0.212215
8	2.304538	11.859434	0.084321	0.433926	5.146123	0.194321
9	2.558037	14.163972	0.070602	0.390925	5.537048	0.180602
10	2.839421	16.722009	0.059801	0.352184	5.889232	0.169801
11	3.151757	19.561430	0.051121	0.317283	6.206515	0.161121
12	3.498451	22.713187	0.044027	0.285841	6.492356	0.154027
13	3.883280	26.211638	0.038151	0.257514	6.749870	0.148151
14	4.310441	30.094918	0.033228	0.231995	6.981865	0.143228
15	4.784589	34.405359	0.029065	0.209004	7.190870	0.139065
16	5.310894	39.189948	0.025517	0.188292	7.379162	0.135517
17	5.895093	44.500843	0.022471	0.169633	7.548794	0.132471
18	6.543553	50.395936	0.019843	0.152822	7.701617	0.129843
19	7.263344	56.939488	0.017563	0.137678	7.839294	0.127563
20	8.062312	64.202832	0.015576	0.124034	7.963328	0.125576
21	8.949166	72.265144	0.013838	0.111742	8.075070	0.123838
22	9.933574	81.214309	0.012313	0.100669	8.175739	0.122313
23	11.026267	91.147884	0.010971	0.090693	8.266432	0.120971
24	12.239157	102.174151	0.009787	0.081705	8.348137	0.119787
25	13.585464	114.413307	0.008740	0.073608	8.421745	0.118740
26	15.079865	127.998771	0.007813	0.066314	8.488058	0.117813
27	16.738650	143.078636	0.006989	0.059742	8.547800	0.116989
28	18.579901	159.817286	0.006257	0.053822	8.601622	0.116257
29	20.623691	178.397187	0.005605	0.048488	8.650110	0.115605
30	22.892297	199.020878	0.005025	0.043683	8.693793	0.115025
31	25.410449	221.913174	0.004506	0.039354	8.733146	0.114506
32	28.205599	247.323624	0.004043	0.035454	8.768600	0.114043
33	31.308224	275.529222	0.003629	0.031940	8.800541	0.113629
34	34.752118	306.837437	0.003259	0.028775	8.829316	0.113259
35	38.574851	341.589555	0.002927	0.025924	8.855240	0.112927
36	42.818085	380.164406	0.002630	0.023355	8.878594	0.112630
37	47.528074	422.982490	0.002364	0.021040	8.899635	0.112364
38	52.756162	470.510564	0.002125	0.018955	8.918590	0.112125
39	58.559240	523.266726	0.001911	0.017077	8.935666	0.111911
40	65.000867	581.826066	0.001719	0.015384	8.951051	0.111719
41	72.150963	646.826934	0.001546	0.013860	8.964911	0.111546
42	80.087569	718.977896	0.001391	0.012486	8.977397	0.111391
43	88.897201	799.065465	0.001251	0.011249	8.988646	0.111251
44	98.675893	887.962666	0.001126	0.010134	8.998780	0.111126
45	109.530242	986.638559	0.001014	0.009130	9.007910	0.111014
46	121.578568	1096.168801	0.000912	0.008225	9.016135	0.110912
47	134.952211	1217.747369	0.000821	0.007410	9.023545	0.110821
48	149.796954	1352.699580	0.000739	0.006676	9.030221	0.110739
49	166.274619	1502.496534	0.000666	0.006014	9.036235	0.110666
50	184.564827	1668.771152	0.000599	0.005418	9.041653	0.110599

12.00%   MONTHLY COMPOUND INTEREST TABLES   12.00%
                                    EFFECTIVE RATE 1.000

	1 AMOUNT OF $1 AT COMPOUND INTEREST	2 ACCUMULATION OF $1 PER PERIOD	3 SINKING FUND FACTOR	4 PRESENT VALUE REVERSION OF $1	5 PRESENT VALUE ORD. ANNUITY $1 PER PERIOD	6 INSTALMENT TO AMORTIZE $1	
MONTHS							
1	1.010000	1.000000	1.000000	0.990099	0.990099	1.010000	
2	1.020100	2.010000	0.497512	0.980296	1.970395	0.507512	
3	1.030301	3.030100	0.330022	0.970590	2.940985	0.340022	
4	1.040604	4.060401	0.246281	0.960980	3.901966	0.256281	
5	1.051010	5.101005	0.196040	0.951466	4.853431	0.206040	
6	1.061520	6.152015	0.162548	0.942045	5.795476	0.172548	
7	1.072135	7.213535	0.138628	0.932718	6.728195	0.148628	
8	1.082857	8.285671	0.120690	0.923483	7.651678	0.130690	
9	1.093685	9.368527	0.106740	0.914340	8.566018	0.116740	
10	1.104622	10.462213	0.095582	0.905287	9.471305	0.105582	
11	1.115668	11.566835	0.086454	0.896324	10.367628	0.096454	
12	1.126825	12.682503	0.078849	0.887449	11.255077	0.088849	

							MONTHS
YEARS							
1	1.126825	12.682503	0.078849	0.887449	11.255077	0.088849	12
2	1.269735	26.973465	0.037073	0.787566	21.243387	0.047073	24
3	1.430769	43.076878	0.023214	0.698925	30.107505	0.033214	36
4	1.612226	61.222608	0.016334	0.620260	37.973959	0.026334	48
5	1.816697	81.669670	0.012244	0.550450	44.955038	0.022244	60
6	2.047099	104.709931	0.009550	0.488496	51.150391	0.019550	72
7	2.306723	130.672274	0.007653	0.433515	56.648453	0.017653	84
8	2.599273	159.927293	0.006253	0.384723	61.527703	0.016253	96
9	2.928926	192.892579	0.005184	0.341422	65.857790	0.015184	108
10	3.300387	230.038689	0.004347	0.302995	69.700522	0.014347	120
11	3.718959	271.895856	0.003678	0.268892	73.110752	0.013678	132
12	4.190616	319.061559	0.003134	0.238628	76.137157	0.013134	144
13	4.722091	372.209054	0.002687	0.211771	78.822939	0.012687	156
14	5.320970	432.096982	0.002314	0.187936	81.206434	0.012314	168
15	5.995802	499.580198	0.002002	0.166783	83.321664	0.012002	180
16	6.756220	575.621974	0.001737	0.148012	85.198824	0.011737	192
17	7.613078	661.307751	0.001512	0.131353	86.864707	0.011512	204
18	8.578606	757.860630	0.001320	0.116569	88.343095	0.011320	216
19	9.666588	866.658830	0.001154	0.103449	89.655089	0.011154	228
20	10.892554	989.255365	0.001011	0.091806	90.819416	0.011011	240
21	12.274002	1127.400210	0.000887	0.081473	91.852698	0.010887	252
22	13.830653	1283.065278	0.000779	0.072303	92.769683	0.010779	264
23	15.584726	1458.472574	0.000686	0.064165	93.583461	0.010686	276
24	17.561259	1656.125905	0.000604	0.056944	94.305647	0.010604	288
25	19.788466	1878.846626	0.000532	0.050534	94.946551	0.010532	300
26	22.298139	2129.813909	0.000470	0.044847	95.515321	0.010470	312
27	25.126101	2412.610125	0.000414	0.039799	96.020075	0.010414	324
28	28.312720	2731.271980	0.000366	0.035320	96.468019	0.010366	336
29	31.903481	3090.348134	0.000324	0.031345	96.865546	0.010324	348
30	35.949641	3494.964133	0.000286	0.027817	97.218331	0.010286	360
31	40.508956	3950.895567	0.000253	0.024686	97.531410	0.010253	372
32	45.646505	4464.650519	0.000224	0.021907	97.809252	0.010224	384
33	51.435625	5043.562459	0.000198	0.019442	98.055822	0.010198	396
34	57.958949	5695.894923	0.000176	0.017254	98.274641	0.010176	408
35	65.309595	6430.959471	0.000155	0.015312	98.468831	0.010155	420
36	73.592486	7259.248603	0.000138	0.013588	98.641166	0.010138	432
37	82.925855	8192.585529	0.000122	0.012059	98.794103	0.010122	444
38	93.442929	9244.292938	0.000108	0.010702	98.929828	0.010108	456
39	105.293832	10429.383172	0.000096	0.009497	99.050277	0.010096	468
40	118.647725	11764.772510	0.000085	0.008428	99.157169	0.010085	480

12.00%   ANNUAL COMPOUND INTEREST TABLES   12.00
                                   EFFECTIVE RATE 12.00

	1	2	3	4	5	6
	AMOUNT OF $1 AT COMPOUND INTEREST	ACCUMULATION OF $1 PER PERIOD	SINKING FUND FACTOR	PRESENT VALUE REVERSION OF $1	PRESENT VALUE ORD. ANNUITY $1 PER PERIOD	INSTALME TO AMORTIZE
YEARS						
1	1.120000	1.000000	1.000000	0.892857	0.892857	1.1200
2	1.254400	2.120000	0.471698	0.797194	1.690051	0.5916
3	1.404928	3.374400	0.296349	0.711780	2.401831	0.4163
4	1.573519	4.779328	0.209234	0.635518	3.037349	0.3292
5	1.762342	6.352847	0.157410	0.567427	3.604776	0.2774
6	1.973823	8.115189	0.123226	0.506631	4.111407	0.2432
7	2.210681	10.089012	0.099118	0.452349	4.563757	0.2191
8	2.475963	12.299693	0.081303	0.403883	4.967640	0.2013
9	2.773079	14.775656	0.067679	0.360610	5.328250	0.1876
10	3.105848	17.548735	0.056984	0.321973	5.650223	0.1769
11	3.478550	20.654583	0.048415	0.287476	5.937699	0.1684
12	3.895976	24.133133	0.041437	0.256675	6.194374	0.1614
13	4.363493	28.029109	0.035677	0.229174	6.423548	0.1556
14	4.887112	32.392602	0.030871	0.204620	6.628168	0.1508
15	5.473566	37.279715	0.026824	0.182696	6.810864	0.1468
16	6.130394	42.753280	0.023390	0.163122	6.973986	0.1433
17	6.866041	48.883674	0.020457	0.145644	7.119630	0.1404
18	7.689966	55.749715	0.017937	0.130040	7.249670	0.1379
19	8.612762	63.439681	0.015763	0.116107	7.365777	0.1357
20	9.646293	72.052442	0.013879	0.103667	7.469444	0.1338
21	10.803848	81.698736	0.012240	0.092560	7.562003	0.1322
22	12.100310	92.502584	0.010811	0.082643	7.644646	0.1308
23	13.552347	104.602894	0.009560	0.073788	7.718434	0.1295
24	15.178629	118.155241	0.008463	0.065882	7.784316	0.1284
25	17.000064	133.333870	0.007500	0.058823	7.843139	0.1275
26	19.040072	150.333934	0.006652	0.052521	7.895660	0.1266
27	21.324881	169.374007	0.005904	0.046894	7.942554	0.1259
28	23.883866	190.698887	0.005244	0.041869	7.984423	0.1252
29	26.749930	214.582754	0.004660	0.037383	8.021806	0.1246
30	29.959922	241.332684	0.004144	0.033378	8.055184	0.1241
31	33.555113	271.292606	0.003686	0.029802	8.084986	0.1236
32	37.581726	304.847719	0.003280	0.026609	8.111594	0.1232
33	42.091533	342.429446	0.002920	0.023758	8.135352	0.1229
34	47.142517	384.520979	0.002601	0.021212	8.156564	0.1226
35	52.799620	431.663496	0.002317	0.018940	8.175504	0.1223
36	59.135574	484.463116	0.002064	0.016910	8.192414	0.1220
37	66.231843	543.598690	0.001840	0.015098	8.207513	0.1218
38	74.179664	609.830533	0.001640	0.013481	8.220993	0.1216
39	83.081224	684.010197	0.001462	0.012036	8.233030	0.1214
40	93.050970	767.091420	0.001304	0.010747	8.243777	0.1213
41	104.217087	860.142391	0.001163	0.009595	8.253372	0.1211
42	116.723137	964.359478	0.001037	0.008567	8.261939	0.1210
43	130.729914	1081.082615	0.000925	0.007649	8.269589	0.1209
44	146.417503	1211.812529	0.000825	0.006830	8.276418	0.1208
45	163.987604	1358.230032	0.000736	0.006098	8.282516	0.1207
46	183.666116	1522.217636	0.000657	0.005445	8.287961	0.1206
47	205.706050	1705.883752	0.000586	0.004861	8.292822	0.1205
48	230.390776	1911.589803	0.000523	0.004340	8.297163	0.1205
49	258.037669	2141.980579	0.000467	0.003875	8.301038	0.1204
50	289.002190	2400.018249	0.000417	0.003460	8.304498	0.1204

13.00%   **MONTHLY COMPOUND INTEREST TABLES**   13.00%
                                  EFFECTIVE RATE 1.083

	1 AMOUNT OF $1 AT COMPOUND INTEREST	2 ACCUMULATION OF $1 PER PERIOD	3 SINKING FUND FACTOR	4 PRESENT VALUE REVERSION OF $1	5 PRESENT VALUE ORD. ANNUITY $1 PER PERIOD	6 INSTALMENT TO AMORTIZE $1	
MONTHS							
1	1.010833	1.000000	1.000000	0.989283	0.989283	1.010833	
2	1.021784	2.010833	0.497306	0.978680	1.967963	0.508140	
3	1.032853	3.032617	0.329748	0.968192	2.936155	0.340581	
4	1.044043	4.065471	0.245974	0.957815	3.893970	0.256807	
5	1.055353	5.109513	0.195713	0.947550	4.841520	0.206547	
6	1.066786	6.164866	0.162210	0.937395	5.778915	0.173043	
7	1.078343	7.231652	0.138281	0.927349	6.706264	0.149114	
8	1.090025	8.309995	0.120337	0.917410	7.623674	0.131170	
9	1.101834	9.400020	0.106383	0.907578	8.531253	0.117216	
10	1.113770	10.501854	0.095221	0.897851	9.429104	0.106055	
11	1.125836	11.615624	0.086091	0.888229	10.317333	0.096924	
12	1.138032	12.741460	0.078484	0.878710	11.196042	0.089317	
YEARS							**MONTHS**
1	1.138032	12.741460	0.078484	0.878710	11.196042	0.089317	12
2	1.295118	27.241655	0.036708	0.772130	21.034112	0.047542	24
3	1.473886	43.743348	0.022861	0.678478	29.678917	0.033694	36
4	1.677330	62.522811	0.015994	0.596185	37.275190	0.026827	48
5	1.908857	83.894449	0.011920	0.523874	43.950107	0.022753	60
6	2.172341	108.216068	0.009241	0.460333	49.815421	0.020074	72
7	2.472194	135.894861	0.007359	0.404499	54.969328	0.018192	84
8	2.813437	167.394225	0.005974	0.355437	59.498115	0.016807	96
9	3.201783	203.241525	0.004920	0.312326	63.477604	0.015754	108
10	3.643733	244.036917	0.004098	0.274444	66.974419	0.014931	120
11	4.146687	290.463399	0.003443	0.241156	70.047103	0.014276	132
12	4.719064	343.298242	0.002913	0.211906	72.747100	0.013746	144
13	5.370448	403.426010	0.002479	0.186204	75.119613	0.013312	156
14	6.111745	471.853363	0.002119	0.163619	77.204363	0.012953	168
15	6.955364	549.725914	0.001819	0.143774	79.036253	0.012652	180
16	7.915430	638.347406	0.001567	0.126336	80.645952	0.012400	192
17	9.008017	739.201542	0.001353	0.111012	82.060410	0.012186	204
18	10.251416	853.976825	0.001171	0.097548	83.303307	0.012004	216
19	11.666444	984.594826	0.001016	0.085716	84.395453	0.011849	228
20	13.276792	1133.242353	0.000882	0.075319	85.355132	0.011716	240
21	15.109421	1302.408067	0.000768	0.066184	86.198412	0.011601	252
22	17.195012	1494.924144	0.000669	0.058156	86.939409	0.011502	264
23	19.568482	1714.013694	0.000583	0.051103	87.590531	0.011417	276
24	22.269568	1963.344717	0.000509	0.044904	88.162677	0.011343	288
25	25.343491	2247.091520	0.000445	0.039458	88.665428	0.011278	300
26	28.841716	2570.004599	0.000389	0.034672	89.107200	0.011222	312
27	32.822810	2937.490172	0.000340	0.030467	89.495389	0.011174	324
28	37.353424	3355.700690	0.000298	0.026771	89.836495	0.011131	336
29	42.509410	3831.637843	0.000261	0.023524	90.136227	0.011094	348
30	48.377089	4373.269783	0.000229	0.020671	90.399605	0.011062	360
31	55.054699	4989.664524	0.000200	0.018164	90.631038	0.011034	372
32	62.654036	5691.141761	0.000176	0.015961	90.834400	0.011009	384
33	71.302328	6489.445641	0.000154	0.014025	91.013097	0.010987	396
34	81.144365	7397.941387	0.000135	0.012324	91.170119	0.010969	408
35	92.344923	8431.839055	0.000119	0.010829	91.308095	0.010952	420
36	105.091522	9608.448184	0.000104	0.009516	91.429337	0.010937	432
37	119.597566	10947.467591	0.000091	0.008361	91.535873	0.010925	444
38	136.105914	12471.315170	0.000080	0.007347	91.629487	0.010914	456
39	154.892951	14205.503212	0.000070	0.006456	91.711747	0.010904	468
40	176.273210	16179.065533	0.000062	0.005673	91.784030	0.010895	480

13.00%   ANNUAL COMPOUND INTEREST TABLES   13.00%
                              EFFECTIVE RATE 13.00

| | 1 | 2 | 3 | 4 | 5 | 6 |
	AMOUNT OF $1 AT COMPOUND INTEREST	ACCUMULATION OF $1 PER PERIOD	SINKING FUND FACTOR	PRESENT VALUE REVERSION OF $1	PRESENT VALUE ORD. ANNUITY $1 PER PERIOD	INSTALMENT TO AMORTIZE $1
YEARS						
1	1.130000	1.000000	1.000000	0.884956	0.884956	1.130000
2	1.276900	2.130000	0.469484	0.783147	1.668102	0.599484
3	1.442897	3.406900	0.293522	0.693050	2.361153	0.423522
4	1.630474	4.849797	0.206194	0.613319	2.974471	0.336194
5	1.842435	6.480271	0.154315	0.542760	3.517231	0.284315
6	2.081952	8.322706	0.120153	0.480319	3.997550	0.250153
7	2.352605	10.404658	0.096111	0.425061	4.422610	0.226111
8	2.658444	12.757263	0.078387	0.376160	4.798770	0.208387
9	3.004042	15.415707	0.064869	0.332885	5.131655	0.194869
10	3.394567	18.419749	0.054290	0.294588	5.426243	0.184290
11	3.835861	21.814317	0.045841	0.260698	5.686941	0.175841
12	4.334523	25.650178	0.038986	0.230706	5.917647	0.168986
13	4.898011·	29.984701	0.033350	0.204165	6.121812	0.163350
14	5.534753	34.882712	0.028667	0.180677	6.302488	0.158667
15	6.254270	40.417464	0.024742	0.159891	6.462379	0.154742
16	7.067326	46.671735	0.021426	0.141496	6.603875	0.151426
17	7.986078	53.739060	0.018608	0.125218	6.729093	0.148608
18	9.024268	61.725138	0.016201	0.110812	6.839905	0.146201
19	10.197423	70.749406	0.014134	0.098064	6.937969	0.144134
20	11.523088	80.946829	0.012354	0.086782	7.024752	0.142354
21	13.021089	92.469917	0.010814	0.076798	7.101550	0.140814
22	14.713831	105.491006	0.009479	0.067963	7.169513	0.139479
23	16.626629	120.204837	0.008319	0.060144	7.229658	0.138319
24	18.788091	136.831465	0.007308	0.053225	7.282883	0.137308
25	21.230542	155.619556	0.006426	0.047102	7.329985	0.136426
26	23.990513	176.850098	0.005655	0.041683	7.371668	0.135655
27	27.109279	200.840611	0.004979	0.036888	7.408556	0.134979
28	30.633486	227.949890	0.004387	0.032644	7.441200	0.134387
29	34.615839	258.583376	0.003867	0.028889	7.470088	0.133867
30	39.115898	293.199215	0.003411	0.025565	7.495653	0.133411
31	44.200965	332.315113	0.003009	0.022624	7.518277	0.133009
32	49.947090	376.516078	0.002656	0.020021	7.538299	0.132656
33	56.440212	426.463168	0.002345	0.017718	7.556016	0.132345
34	63.777439	482.903380	0.002071	0.015680	7.571696	0.132071
35	72.068506	546.680819	0.001829	0.013876	7.585572	0.131829
36	81.437412	618.749325	0.001616	0.012279	7.597851	0.131616
37	92.024276	700.186738	0.001428	0.010867	7.608718	0.131428
38	103.987432	792.211014	0.001262	0.009617	7.618334	0.131262
39	117.505798	896.198445	0.001116	0.008510	7.626844	0.131116
40	132.781552	1013.704243	0.000986	0.007531	7.634376	0.130986
41	150.043153	1146.485795	0.000872	0.006665	7.641040	0.130872
42	169.548763	1296.528948	0.000771	0.005898	7.646938	0.130771
43	191.590103	1466.077712	0.000682	0.005219	7.652158	0.130682
44	216.496816	1657.667814	0.000603	0.004619	7.656777	0.130603
45	244.641402	1874.164630	0.000534	0.004088	7.660864	0.130534
46	276.444784	2118.806032	0.000472	0.003617	7.664482	0.130472
47	312.382606	2395.250816	0.000417	0.003201	7.667683	0.130417
48	352.992345	2707.633422	0.000369	0.002833	7.670516	0.130369
49	398.881350	3060.625767	0.000327	0.002507	7.673023	0.130327
50	450.735925	3459.507117	0.000289	0.002219	7.675242	0.130289

14.00%   MONTHLY COMPOUND INTEREST TABLES   14.00%
                              EFFECTIVE RATE 1.167

	1 AMOUNT OF $1 AT COMPOUND INTEREST	2 ACCUMULATION OF $1 PER PERIOD	3 SINKING FUND FACTOR	4 PRESENT VALUE REVERSION OF $1	5 PRESENT VALUE ORD. ANNUITY $1 PER PERIOD	6 INSTALMENT TO AMORTIZE $1	
MONTHS							
1	1.011667	1.000000	1.000000	0.988468	0.988468	1.011667	
2	1.023469	2.011667	0.497100	0.977069	1.965537	0.508767	
3	1.035410	3.035136	0.329475	0.965801	2.931338	0.341141	
4	1.047490	4.070546	0.245667	0.954663	3.886001	0.257334	
5	1.059710	5.118036	0.195387	0.943654	4.829655	0.207054	
6	1.072074	6.177746	0.161871	0.932772	5.762427	0.173538	
7	1.084581	7.249820	0.137934	0.922015	6.684442	0.149601	
8	1.097235	8.334401	0.119985	0.911382	7.595824	0.131651	
9	1.110036	9.431636	0.106026	0.900872	8.496696	0.117693	
10	1.122986	10.541672	0.094862	0.890483	9.387178	0.106528	
11	1.136088	11.664658	0.085729	0.880214	10.267392	0.097396	
12	1.149342	12.800745	0.078120	0.870063	11.137455	0.089787	
YEARS							**MONTHS**
1	1.149342	12.800745	0.078120	0.870063	11.137455	0.089787	12
2	1.320987	27.513180	0.036346	0.757010	20.827743	0.048013	24
3	1.518266	44.422800	0.022511	0.658646	29.258904	0.034178	36
4	1.745007	63.857736	0.015660	0.573064	36.594546	0.027326	48
5	2.005610	86.195125	0.011602	0.498601	42.977016	0.023268	60
6	2.305132	111.868425	0.008939	0.433815	48.530168	0.020606	72
7	2.649385	141.375828	0.007073	0.377446	53.361760	0.018740	84
8	3.045049	175.289927	0.005705	0.328402	57.565549	0.017372	96
9	3.499803	214.268826	0.004667	0.285730	61.223111	0.016334	108
10	4.022471	259.068912	0.003860	0.248603	64.405420	0.015527	120
11	4.623195	310.559535	0.003220	0.216301	67.174230	0.014887	132
12	5.313632	369.739871	0.002705	0.188195	69.583269	0.014371	144
13	6.107180	437.758319	0.002284	0.163742	71.679284	0.013951	156
14	7.019239	515.934780	0.001938	0.142466	73.502950	0.013605	168
15	8.067507	605.786272	0.001651	0.123954	75.089654	0.013317	180
16	9.272324	709.056369	0.001410	0.107848	76.470187	0.013077	192
17	10.657072	827.749031	0.001208	0.093834	77.671337	0.012875	204
18	12.248621	964.167496	0.001037	0.081642	78.716413	0.012704	216
19	14.077855	1120.958972	0.000892	0.071034	79.625696	0.012559	228
20	16.180270	1301.166005	0.000769	0.061804	80.416829	0.012435	240
21	18.596664	1508.285522	0.000663	0.053773	81.105164	0.012330	252
22	21.373928	1746.336688	0.000573	0.046786	81.704060	0.012239	264
23	24.565954	2019.938898	0.000495	0.040707	82.225136	0.012162	276
24	28.234683	2334.401417	0.000428	0.035417	82.678506	0.012095	288
25	32.451308	2695.826407	0.000371	0.030815	83.072966	0.012038	300
26	37.297652	3111.227338	0.000321	0.026811	83.416171	0.011988	312
27	42.867759	3588.665088	0.000279	0.023328	83.714781	0.011945	324
28	49.269718	4137.404360	0.000242	0.020296	83.974591	0.011908	336
29	56.627757	4768.093468	0.000210	0.017659	84.200641	0.011876	348
30	65.084661	5492.970967	0.000182	0.015365	84.397320	0.011849	360
31	74.804537	6326.103143	0.000158	0.013368	84.568442	0.011825	372
32	85.975998	7283.656968	0.000137	0.011631	84.717330	0.011804	384
33	98.815828	8384.213826	0.000119	0.010120	84.846871	0.011786	396
34	113.573184	9649.130077	0.000104	0.008805	84.959580	0.011770	408
35	130.534434	11102.951488	0.000090	0.007661	85.057645	0.011757	420
36	150.028711	12773.889539	0.000078	0.006665	85.142966	0.011745	432
37	172.434303	14694.368869	0.000068	0.005799	85.217202	0.011735	444
38	198.185992	16901.656479	0.000059	0.005046	85.281792	0.011726	456
39	227.783490	19438.584900	0.000051	0.004390	85.337989	0.011718	468
40	261.801139	22354.383359	0.000045	0.003820	85.386883	0.011711	480

14.00%   ANNUAL COMPOUND INTEREST TABLES   14.00%
                              EFFECTIVE RATE 14.00

	1 AMOUNT OF $1 AT COMPOUND INTEREST	2 ACCUMULATION OF $1 PER PERIOD	3 SINKING FUND FACTOR	4 PRESENT VALUE REVERSION OF $1	5 PRESENT VALUE ORD. ANNUITY $1 PER PERIOD	6 INSTALMENT TO AMORTIZE $1
YEARS						
1	1.140000	1.000000	1.000000	0.877193	0.877193	1.140000
2	1.299600	2.140000	0.467290	0.769468	1.646661	0.607290
3	1.481544	3.439600	0.290731	0.674972	2.321632	0.430731
4	1.688960	4.921144	0.203205	0.592080	2.913712	0.343205
5	1.925415	6.610104	0.151284	0.519369	3.433081	0.291284
6	2.194973	8.535519	0.117157	0.455587	3.888668	0.257157
7	2.502269	10.730491	0.093192	0.399637	4.288305	0.233192
8	2.852586	13.232760	0.075570	0.350559	4.638864	0.215570
9	3.251949	16.085347	0.062168	0.307508	4.946372	0.202168
10	3.707221	19.337295	0.051714	0.269744	5.216116	0.191714
11	4.226232	23.044516	0.043394	0.236617	5.452733	0.183394
12	4.817905	27.270749	0.036669	0.207559	5.660292	0.176669
13	5.492411	32.088654	0.031164	0.182069	5.842362	0.171164
14	6.261349	37.581065	0.026609	0.159710	6.002072	0.166609
15	7.137938	43.842414	0.022809	0.140096	6.142168	0.162809
16	8.137249	50.980352	0.019615	0.122892	6.265060	0.159615
17	9.276464	59.117601	0.016915	0.107800	6.372859	0.156915
18	10.575169	68.394066	0.014621	0.094561	6.467420	0.154621
19	12.055693	78.969235	0.012663	0.082948	6.550369	0.152663
20	13.743490	91.024928	0.010986	0.072762	6.623131	0.150986
21	15.667578	104.768418	0.009545	0.063826	6.686957	0.149545
22	17.861039	120.435996	0.008303	0.055988	6.742944	0.148303
23	20.361585	138.297035	0.007231	0.049112	6.792056	0.147231
24	23.212207	158.658620	0.006303	0.043081	6.835137	0.146303
25	26.461916	181.870827	0.005498	0.037790	6.872927	0.145498
26	30.166584	208.332743	0.004800	0.033149	6.906077	0.144800
27	34.389906	238.499327	0.004193	0.029078	6.935155	0.144193
28	39.204493	272.889233	0.003664	0.025507	6.960662	0.143664
29	44.693122	312.093725	0.003204	0.022375	6.983037	0.143204
30	50.950159	356.786847	0.002803	0.019627	7.002664	0.142803
31	58.083181	407.737006	0.002453	0.017217	7.019881	0.142453
32	66.214826	465.820186	0.002147	0.015102	7.034983	0.142147
33	75.484902	532.035012	0.001880	0.013248	7.048231	0.141880
34	86.052788	607.519914	0.001646	0.011621	7.059852	0.141646
35	98.100178	693.572702	0.001442	0.010194	7.070045	0.141442
36	111.834203	791.672881	0.001263	0.008942	7.078987	0.141263
37	127.490992	903.507084	0.001107	0.007844	7.086831	0.141107
38	145.339731	1030.998076	0.000970	0.006880	7.093711	0.140970
39	165.687293	1176.337806	0.000850	0.006035	7.099747	0.140850
40	188.883514	1342.025099	0.000745	0.005294	7.105041	0.140745
41	215.327206	1530.908613	0.000653	0.004644	7.109685	0.140653
42	245.473015	1746.235819	0.000573	0.004074	7.113759	0.140573
43	279.839237	1991.708833	0.000502	0.003573	7.117332	0.140502
44	319.016730	2271.548070	0.000440	0.003135	7.120467	0.140440
45	363.679072	2590.564800	0.000386	0.002750	7.123217	0.140386
46	414.594142	2954.243872	0.000338	0.002412	7.125629	0.140338
47	472.637322	3368.838014	0.000297	0.002116	7.127744	0.140297
48	538.806547	3841.475336	0.000260	0.001856	7.129600	0.140260
49	614.239464	4380.281883	0.000228	0.001628	7.131228	0.140228
50	700.232988	4994.521346	0.000200	0.001428	7.132656	0.140200

15.00%   **MONTHLY COMPOUND INTEREST TABLES**   15.00%
                              EFFECTIVE RATE 1.250

	1 AMOUNT OF $1 AT COMPOUND INTEREST	2 ACCUMULATION OF $1 PER PERIOD	3 SINKING FUND FACTOR	4 PRESENT VALUE REVERSION OF $1	5 PRESENT VALUE ORD. ANNUITY $1 PER PERIOD	6 INSTALMENT TO AMORTIZE $1	
MONTHS							
1	1.012500	1.000000	1.000000	0.987654	0.987654	1.012500	
2	1.025156	2.012500	0.496894	0.975461	1.963115	0.509394	
3	1.037971	3.037656	0.329201	0.963418	2.926534	0.341701	
4	1.050945	4.075627	0.245361	0.951524	3.878058	0.257861	
5	1.064082	5.126572	0.195062	0.939777	4.817835	0.207562	
6	1.077383	6.190654	0.161534	0.928175	5.746010	0.174034	
7	1.090850	7.268038	0.137589	0.916716	6.662726	0.150089	
8	1.104486	8.358888	0.119633	0.905398	7.568124	0.132133	
9	1.118292	9.463374	0.105671	0.894221	8.462345	0.118171	
10	1.132271	10.581666	0.094503	0.883181	9.345526	0.107003	
11	1.146424	11.713937	0.085368	0.872277	10.217803	0.097868	
12	1.160755	12.860361	0.077758	0.861509	11.079312	0.090258	
YEARS							**MONTHS**
1	1.160755	12.860361	0.077758	0.861509	11.079312	0.090258	12
2	1.347351	27.788084	0.035987	0.742197	20.624235	0.048487	24
3	1.563944	45.115506	0.022165	0.639409	28.847267	0.034665	36
4	1.815355	65.228388	0.015331	0.550856	35.931481	0.027831	48
5	2.107181	88.574508	0.011290	0.474568	42.034592	0.023790	60
6	2.445920	115.673621	0.008645	0.408844	47.292474	0.021145	72
7	2.839113	147.129040	0.006797	0.352223	51.822185	0.019297	84
8	3.295513	183.641059	0.005445	0.303443	55.724570	0.017945	96
9	3.825282	226.022551	0.004424	0.261419	59.086509	0.016924	108
10	4.440213	275.217058	0.003633	0.225214	61.982847	0.016133	120
11	5.153998	332.319805	0.003009	0.194024	64.478068	0.015509	132
12	5.982526	398.602077	0.002509	0.167153	66.627722	0.015009	144
13	6.944244	475.539523	0.002103	0.144004	68.479668	0.014603	156
14	8.060563	564.845011	0.001770	0.124061	70.075134	0.014270	168
15	9.356334	668.506759	0.001496	0.106879	71.449643	0.013996	180
16	10.860408	788.832603	0.001268	0.092078	72.633794	0.013768	192
17	12.606267	928.501369	0.001077	0.079326	73.653950	0.013577	204
18	14.632781	1090.622520	0.000917	0.068340	74.532823	0.013417	216
19	16.985067	1278.805378	0.000782	0.058875	75.289980	0.013282	228
20	19.715494	1497.239481	0.000668	0.050722	75.942278	0.013168	240
21	22.884848	1750.787854	0.000571	0.043697	76.504237	0.013071	252
22	26.563691	2045.095272	0.000489	0.037645	76.988370	0.012989	264
23	30.833924	2386.713938	0.000419	0.032432	77.405455	0.012919	276
24	35.790617	2783.249347	0.000359	0.027940	77.764777	0.012859	288
25	41.544120	3243.529615	0.000308	0.024071	78.074336	0.012808	300
26	48.222525	3777.802015	0.000265	0.020737	78.341024	0.012765	312
27	55.974514	4397.961118	0.000227	0.017865	78.570778	0.012727	324
28	64.972670	5117.813598	0.000195	0.015391	78.768713	0.012695	336
29	75.417320	5953.385616	0.000168	0.013260	78.939236	0.012668	348
30	87.540995	6923.279611	0.000144	0.011423	79.086142	0.012644	360
31	101.613606	8049.088447	0.000124	0.009841	79.212704	0.012624	372
32	117.948452	9355.876140	0.000107	0.008478	79.321738	0.012607	384
33	136.909198	10872.735858	0.000092	0.007304	79.415671	0.012592	396
34	158.917970	12633.437629	0.000079	0.006293	79.496596	0.012579	408
35	184.464752	14677.180163	0.000068	0.005421	79.566313	0.012568	420
36	214.118294	17049.463544	0.000059	0.004670	79.626375	0.012559	432
37	248.538777	19803.102194	0.000050	0.004024	79.678119	0.012550	444
38	288.492509	22999.400698	0.000043	0.003466	79.722696	0.012543	456
39	334.868983	26709.518627	0.000037	0.002986	79.761101	0.012537	468
40	388.700685	31016.054774	0.000032	0.002573	79.794186	0.012532	480

15.00%   ANNUAL COMPOUND INTEREST TABLES   15.00%
                              EFFECTIVE RATE 15.00

	1 AMOUNT OF $1 AT COMPOUND INTEREST	2 ACCUMULATION OF $1 PER PERIOD	3 SINKING FUND FACTOR	4 PRESENT VALUE REVERSION OF $1	5 PRESENT VALUE ORD. ANNUITY $1 PER PERIOD	6 INSTALMENT TO AMORTIZE $1
YEARS						
1	1.150000	1.000000	1.000000	0.869565	0.869565	1.150000
2	1.322500	2.150000	0.465116	0.756144	1.625709	0.615116
3	1.520875	3.472500	0.287977	0.657516	2.283225	0.437977
4	1.749006	4.993375	0.200265	0.571753	2.854978	0.350265
5	2.011357	6.742381	0.148316	0.497177	3.352155	0.298316
6	2.313061	8.753738	0.114237	0.432328	3.784483	0.264237
7	2.660020	11.066799	0.090360	0.375937	4.160420	0.240360
8	3.059023	13.726819	0.072850	0.326902	4.487322	0.222850
9	3.517876	16.785842	0.059574	0.284262	4.771584	0.209574
10	4.045558	20.303718	0.049252	0.247185	5.018769	0.199252
11	4.652391	24.349276	0.041069	0.214943	5.233712	0.191069
12	5.350250	29.001667	0.034481	0.186907	5.420619	0.184481
13	6.152788	34.351917	0.029110	0.162528	5.583147	0.179110
14	7.075706	40.504705	0.024688	0.141329	5.724476	0.174688
15	8.137062	47.580411	0.021017	0.122894	5.847370	0.171017
16	9.357621	55.717472	0.017948	0.106865	5.954235	0.167948
17	10.761264	65.075093	0.015367	0.092926	6.047161	0.165367
18	12.375454	75.836357	0.013186	0.080805	6.127966	0.163186
19	14.231772	88.211811	0.011336	0.070265	6.198231	0.161336
20	16.366537	102.443583	0.009761	0.061100	6.259331	0.159761
21	18.821518	118.810120	0.008417	0.053131	6.312462	0.158417
22	21.644746	137.631638	0.007266	0.046201	6.358663	0.157266
23	24.891458	159.276384	0.006278	0.040174	6.398837	0.156278
24	28.625176	184.167841	0.005430	0.034934	6.433771	0.155430
25	32.918953	212.793017	0.004699	0.030378	6.464149	0.154699
26	37.856796	245.711970	0.004070	0.026415	6.490564	0.154070
27	43.535315	283.568766	0.003526	0.022970	6.513534	0.153526
28	50.065612	327.104080	0.003057	0.019974	6.533508	0.153057
29	57.575454	377.169693	0.002651	0.017369	6.550877	0.152651
30	66.211772	434.745146	0.002300	0.015103	6.565980	0.152300
31	76.143538	500.956918	0.001996	0.013133	6.579113	0.151996
32	87.565068	577.100456	0.001733	0.011420	6.590533	0.151733
33	100.699829	664.665525	0.001505	0.009931	6.600463	0.151505
34	115.804803	765.365353	0.001307	0.008635	6.609099	0.151307
35	133.175523	881.170156	0.001135	0.007509	6.616607	0.151135
36	153.151852	1014.345680	0.000986	0.006529	6.623137	0.150986
37	176.124630	1167.497532	0.000857	0.005678	6.628815	0.150857
38	202.543324	1343.622161	0.000744	0.004937	6.633752	0.150744
39	232.924823	1546.165485	0.000647	0.004293	6.638045	0.150647
40	267.863546	1779.090308	0.000562	0.003733	6.641778	0.150562
41	308.043078	2046.953854	0.000489	0.003246	6.645025	0.150489
42	354.249540	2354.996933	0.000425	0.002823	6.647848	0.150425
43	407.386971	2709.246473	0.000369	0.002455	6.650302	0.150369
44	468.495017	3116.633443	0.000321	0.002134	6.652437	0.150321
45	538.769269	3585.128460	0.000279	0.001856	6.654293	0.150279
46	619.584659	4123.897729	0.000242	0.001614	6.655907	0.150242
47	712.522358	4743.482388	0.000211	0.001403	6.657310	0.150211
48	819.400712	5456.004746	0.000183	0.001220	6.658531	0.150183
49	942.310819	6275.405458	0.000159	0.001061	6.659592	0.150159
50	1083.657442	7217.716277	0.000139	0.000923	6.660515	0.150139

16.00%   MONTHLY COMPOUND INTEREST TABLES   16.00%
                               EFFECTIVE RATE 1.333

	1	2	3	4	5	6
	AMOUNT OF $1 AT COMPOUND INTEREST	ACCUMULATION OF $1 PER PERIOD	SINKING FUND FACTOR	PRESENT VALUE REVERSION OF $1	PRESENT VALUE ORD. ANNUITY $1 PER PERIOD	INSTALMENT TO AMORTIZE $1
MONTHS						
1	1.013333	1.000000	1.000000	0.986842	0.986842	1.013333
2	1.026844	2.013333	0.496689	0.973857	1.960699	0.510022
3	1.040536	3.040178	0.328928	0.961043	2.921743	0.342261
4	1.054410	4.080713	0.245055	0.948398	3.870141	0.258389
5	1.068468	5.135123	0.194737	0.935919	4.806060	0.208071
6	1.082715	6.203591	0.161197	0.923604	5.729665	0.174530
7	1.097151	7.286306	0.137244	0.911452	6.641116	0.150577
8	1.111779	8.383457	0.119283	0.899459	7.540575	0.132616
9	1.126603	9.495236	0.105316	0.887624	8.428199	0.118649
10	1.141625	10.621839	0.094146	0.875945	9.304144	0.107479
11	1.156846	11.763464	0.085009	0.864419	10.168563	0.098342
12	1.172271	12.920310	0.077398	0.853045	11.021609	0.090731

YEARS							**MONTHS**
1	1.172271	12.920310	0.077398	0.853045	11.021609	0.090731	12
2	1.374259	28.066412	0.035630	0.727686	20.423539	0.048963	24
3	1.610957	45.821745	0.021824	0.620749	28.443811	0.035157	36
4	1.888477	66.635803	0.015007	0.529527	35.285465	0.028340	48
5	2.213807	91.035516	0.010985	0.451711	41.121706	0.024318	60
6	2.595181	119.638587	0.008359	0.385330	46.100283	0.021692	72
7	3.042255	153.169132	0.006529	0.328704	50.347235	0.019862	84
8	3.566347	192.476010	0.005195	0.280399	53.970077	0.018529	96
9	4.180724	238.554316	0.004192	0.239193	57.060524	0.017525	108
10	4.900941	292.570569	0.003418	0.204042	59.696816	0.016751	120
11	5.745230	355.892244	0.002810	0.174057	61.945692	0.016143	132
12	6.734965	430.122395	0.002325	0.148479	63.864085	0.015658	144
13	7.895203	517.140233	0.001934	0.126659	65.500561	0.015267	156
14	9.255316	619.148703	0.001615	0.108046	66.896549	0.014948	168
15	10.849737	738.730255	0.001354	0.092168	68.087390	0.014687	180
16	12.718830	878.912215	0.001138	0.078624	69.103231	0.014471	192
17	14.909912	1043.243434	0.000959	0.067069	69.969789	0.014292	204
18	17.478455	1235.884123	0.000809	0.057213	70.709003	0.014142	216
19	20.489482	1461.711177	0.000684	0.048806	71.339585	0.014017	228
20	24.019222	1726.441638	0.000579	0.041633	71.877501	0.013913	240
21	28.157032	2036.777427	0.000491	0.035515	72.336367	0.013824	252
22	33.007667	2400.575011	0.000417	0.030296	72.727801	0.013750	264
23	38.693924	2827.044294	0.000354	0.025844	73.061711	0.013687	276
24	45.359757	3326.981781	0.000301	0.022046	73.346552	0.013634	288
25	53.173919	3913.043898	0.000256	0.018806	73.589534	0.013589	300
26	62.334232	4600.067404	0.000217	0.016043	73.796809	0.013551	312
27	73.072600	5405.444997	0.000185	0.013685	73.973623	0.013518	324
28	85.660875	6349.565632	0.000157	0.011674	74.124454	0.013491	336
29	100.417742	7456.330682	0.000134	0.009958	74.253120	0.013467	348
30	117.716787	8753.759030	0.000114	0.008495	74.362878	0.013448	360
31	137.995952	10274.696396	0.000097	0.007247	74.456506	0.013431	372
32	161.768625	12057.646856	0.000083	0.006182	74.536375	0.013416	384
33	189.636635	14147.747615	0.000071	0.005273	74.604507	0.013404	396
34	222.305489	16597.911700	0.000060	0.004498	74.662626	0.013394	408
35	260.602233	19470.167508	0.000051	0.003837	74.712205	0.013385	420
36	305.496388	22837.229117	0.000044	0.003273	74.754498	0.013377	432
37	358.124495	26784.337116	0.000037	0.002792	74.790576	0.013371	444
38	419.818887	31411.416562	0.000032	0.002382	74.821352	0.013365	456
39	492.141422	36835.606678	0.000027	0.002032	74.847605	0.013360	468
40	576.923018	43194.226354	0.000023	0.001733	74.870000	0.013356	480

16.00%   ANNUAL COMPOUND INTEREST TABLES   16.00%
                              EFFECTIVE RATE 16.00

	1	2	3	4	5	6
	AMOUNT OF $1 AT COMPOUND INTEREST	ACCUMULATION OF $1 PER PERIOD	SINKING FUND FACTOR	PRESENT VALUE REVERSION OF $1	PRESENT VALUE ORD. ANNUITY $1 PER PERIOD	INSTALMENT TO AMORTIZE $1
YEARS						
1	1.160000	1.000000	1.000000	0.862069	0.862069	1.160000
2	1.345600	2.160000	0.462963	0.743163	1.605232	0.622963
3	1.560896	3.505600	0.285258	0.640658	2.245890	0.445258
4	1.810639	5.066496	0.197375	0.552291	2.798181	0.357375
5	2.100342	6.877135	0.145409	0.476113	3.274294	0.305409
6	2.436396	8.977477	0.111390	0.410442	3.684736	0.271390
7	2.826220	11.413873	0.087613	0.353830	4.038565	0.247613
8	3.278415	14.240093	0.070224	0.305025	4.343591	0.230224
9	3.802961	17.518508	0.057082	0.262953	4.606544	0.217082
10	4.411435	21.321469	0.046901	0.226684	4.833227	0.206901
11	5.117265	25.732904	0.038861	0.195417	5.028644	0.198861
12	5.936027	30.850169	0.032415	0.168463	5.197107	0.192415
13	6.885791	36.786196	0.027184	0.145227	5.342334	0.187184
14	7.987518	43.671987	0.022898	0.125195	5.467529	0.182898
15	9.265521	51.659505	0.019358	0.107927	5.575456	0.179358
16	10.748004	60.925026	0.016414	0.093041	5.668497	0.176414
17	12.467685	71.673030	0.013952	0.080207	5.748704	0.173952
18	14.462514	84.140715	0.011885	0.069144	5.817848	0.171885
19	16.776517	98.603230	0.010142	0.059607	5.877455	0.170142
20	19.460759	115.379747	0.008667	0.051385	5.928841	0.168667
21	22.574481	134.840506	0.007416	0.044298	5.973139	0.167416
22	26.186398	157.414987	0.006353	0.038188	6.011326	0.166353
23	30.376222	183.601385	0.005447	0.032920	6.044247	0.165447
24	35.236417	213.977607	0.004673	0.028380	6.072627	0.164673
25	40.874244	249.214024	0.004013	0.024465	6.097092	0.164013
26	47.414123	290.088267	0.003447	0.021091	6.118183	0.163447
27	55.000382	337.502390	0.002963	0.018182	6.136364	0.162963
28	63.800444	392.502773	0.002548	0.015674	6.152038	0.162548
29	74.008515	456.303216	0.002192	0.013512	6.165550	0.162192
30	85.849877	530.311731	0.001886	0.011648	6.177198	0.161886
31	99.585857	616.161608	0.001623	0.010042	6.187240	0.161623
32	115.519594	715.747465	0.001397	0.008657	6.195897	0.161397
33	134.002729	831.267059	0.001203	0.007463	6.203359	0.161203
34	155.443166	965.269789	0.001036	0.006433	6.209792	0.161036
35	180.314073	1120.712955	0.000892	0.005546	6.215338	0.160892
36	209.164324	1301.027028	0.000769	0.004781	6.220119	0.160769
37	242.630616	1510.191352	0.000662	0.004121	6.224241	0.160662
38	281.451515	1752.821968	0.000571	0.003553	6.227794	0.160571
39	326.483757	2034.273483	0.000492	0.003063	6.230857	0.160492
40	378.721158	2360.757241	0.000424	0.002640	6.233497	0.160424
41	439.316544	2739.478399	0.000365	0.002276	6.235773	0.160365
42	509.607191	3178.794943	0.000315	0.001962	6.237736	0.160315
43	591.144341	3688.402134	0.000271	0.001692	6.239427	0.160271
44	685.727436	4279.546475	0.000234	0.001458	6.240886	0.160234
45	795.443826	4965.273911	0.000201	0.001257	6.242143	0.160201
46	922.714838	5760.717737	0.000174	0.001084	6.243227	0.160174
47	1070.349212	6683.432575	0.000150	0.000934	6.244161	0.160150
48	1241.605086	7753.781787	0.000129	0.000805	6.244966	0.160129
49	1440.261900	8995.386873	0.000111	0.000694	6.245661	0.160111
50	1670.703804	10435.648773	0.000096	0.000599	6.246259	0.160096

18.00%   MONTHLY COMPOUND INTEREST TABLES   18.00%
                                  EFFECTIVE RATE 1.500

	1 AMOUNT OF $1 AT COMPOUND INTEREST	2 ACCUMULATION OF $1 PER PERIOD	3 SINKING FUND FACTOR	4 PRESENT VALUE REVERSION OF $1	5 PRESENT VALUE ORD. ANNUITY $1 PER PERIOD	6 INSTALMENT TO AMORTIZE $1	
MONTHS							
1	1.015000	1.000000	1.000000	0.985222	0.985222	1.015000	
2	1.030225	2.015000	0.496278	0.970662	1.955883	0.511278	
3	1.045678	3.045225	0.328383	0.956317	2.912200	0.343383	
4	1.061364	4.090903	0.244445	0.942184	3.854385	0.259445	
5	1.077284	5.152267	0.194089	0.928260	4.782645	0.209089	
6	1.093443	6.229551	0.160525	0.914542	5.697187	0.175525	
7	1.109845	7.322994	0.136556	0.901027	6.598214	0.151556	
8	1.126493	8.432839	0.118584	0.887711	7.485925	0.133584	
9	1.143390	9.559332	0.104610	0.874592	8.360517	0.119610	
10	1.160541	10.702722	0.093434	0.861667	9.222185	0.108434	
11	1.177949	11.863262	0.084294	0.848933	10.071118	0.099294	
12	1.195618	13.041211	0.076680	0.836387	10.907505	0.091680	
YEARS							**MONTHS**
1	1.195618	13.041211	0.076680	0.836387	10.907505	0.091680	12
2	1.429503	28.633521	0.034924	0.699544	20.030405	0.049924	24
3	1.709160	47.275969	0.021152	0.585090	27.660684	0.036152	36
4	2.043478	69.565219	0.014375	0.489362	34.042554	0.029375	48
5	2.443220	96.214652	0.010393	0.409296	39.380269	0.025393	60
6	2.921158	128.077197	0.007808	0.342330	43.844667	0.022808	72
7	3.492590	166.172636	0.006018	0.286321	47.578633	0.021018	84
8	4.175804	211.720235	0.004723	0.239475	50.701675	0.019723	96
9	4.992667	266.177771	0.003757	0.200294	53.313749	0.018757	108
10	5.969323	331.288191	0.003019	0.167523	55.498454	0.018019	120
11	7.137031	409.135393	0.002444	0.140114	57.325714	0.017444	132
12	8.533164	502.210922	0.001991	0.117190	58.854011	0.016991	144
13	10.202406	613.493716	0.001630	0.098016	60.132260	0.016630	156
14	12.198182	746.545446	0.001340	0.081979	61.201371	0.016340	168
15	14.584368	905.624513	0.001104	0.068567	62.095562	0.016104	180
16	17.437335	1095.822335	0.000913	0.057348	62.843452	0.015913	192
17	20.848395	1323.226308	0.000756	0.047965	63.468978	0.015756	204
18	24.926719	1595.114630	0.000627	0.040118	63.992160	0.015627	216
19	29.802839	1920.189249	0.000521	0.033554	64.429743	0.015521	228
20	35.632816	2308.854370	0.000433	0.028064	64.795732	0.015433	240
21	42.603242	2773.549452	0.000361	0.023472	65.101841	0.015361	252
22	50.937210	3329.147335	0.000300	0.019632	65.357866	0.015300	264
23	60.901454	3993.430261	0.000250	0.016420	65.572002	0.015250	276
24	72.814885	4787.658998	0.000209	0.013733	65.751103	0.015209	288
25	87.058800	5737.253308	0.000174	0.011486	65.900901	0.015174	300
26	104.089083	6872.605521	0.000146	0.009607	66.026190	0.015146	312
27	124.450799	8230.053258	0.000122	0.008035	66.130980	0.015122	324
28	148.795637	9853.042438	0.000101	0.006721	66.218625	0.015101	336
29	177.902767	11793.517795	0.000085	0.005621	66.291930	0.015085	348
30	212.703781	14113.585393	0.000071	0.004701	66.353242	0.015071	360
31	254.312506	16887.500371	0.000059	0.003932	66.404522	0.015059	372
32	304.060653	20204.043526	0.000049	0.003289	66.447412	0.015049	384
33	363.540442	24169.362788	0.000041	0.002751	66.483285	0.015041	396
34	434.655558	28910.370553	0.000035	0.002301	66.513289	0.015035	408
35	519.682084	34578.805588	0.000029	0.001924	66.538383	0.015029	420
36	621.341343	41356.089520	0.000024	0.001609	66.559372	0.015024	432
37	742.887000	49459.133342	0.000020	0.001346	66.576927	0.015020	444
38	888.209197	59147.279780	0.000017	0.001126	66.591609	0.015017	456
39	1061.959056	70730.603709	0.000014	0.000942	66.603890	0.015014	468
40	1269.697544	84579.836283	0.000012	0.000788	66.614161	0.015012	480

18.00%   ANNUAL COMPOUND INTEREST TABLES   18.00%
                              EFFECTIVE RATE 18.00

	1	2	3	4	5	6
	AMOUNT OF $1 AT COMPOUND INTEREST	ACCUMULATION OF $1 PER PERIOD	SINKING FUND FACTOR	PRESENT VALUE REVERSION OF $1	PRESENT VALUE ORD. ANNUITY $1 PER PERIOD	INSTALMENT TO AMORTIZE $1
YEARS						
1	1.180000	1.000000	1.000000	0.847458	0.847458	1.180000
2	1.392400	2.180000	0.458716	0.718184	1.565642	0.638716
3	1.643032	3.572400	0.279924	0.608631	2.174273	0.459924
4	1.938778	5.215432	0.191739	0.515789	2.690062	0.371739
5	2.287758	7.154210	0.139778	0.437109	3.127171	0.319778
6	2.699554	9.441968	0.105910	0.370432	3.497603	0.285910
7	3.185474	12.141522	0.082362	0.313925	3.811528	0.262362
8	3.758859	15.326996	0.065244	0.266038	4.077566	0.245244
9	4.435454	19.085855	0.052395	0.225456	4.303022	0.232395
10	5.233836	23.521309	0.042515	0.191064	4.494086	0.222515
11	6.175926	28.755144	0.034776	0.161919	4.656005	0.214776
12	7.287593	34.931070	0.028628	0.137220	4.793225	0.208628
13	8.599359	42.218663	0.023686	0.116288	4.909513	0.203686
14	10.147244	50.818022	0.019678	0.098549	5.008062	0.199678
15	11.973748	60.965266	0.016403	0.083516	5.091578	0.196403
16	14.129023	72.939014	0.013710	0.070776	5.162354	0.193710
17	16.672247	87.068036	0.011485	0.059980	5.222334	0.191485
18	19.673251	103.740283	0.009639	0.050830	5.273164	0.189639
19	23.214436	123.413534	0.008103	0.043077	5.316241	0.188103
20	27.393035	146.627970	0.006820	0.036506	5.352746	0.186820
21	32.323781	174.021005	0.005746	0.030937	5.383683	0.185746
22	38.142061	206.344785	0.004846	0.026218	5.409901	0.184846
23	45.007632	244.486847	0.004090	0.022218	5.432120	0.184090
24	53.109006	289.494479	0.003454	0.018829	5.450949	0.183454
25	62.668627	342.603486	0.002919	0.015957	5.466906	0.182919
26	73.948980	405.272113	0.002467	0.013523	5.480429	0.182467
27	87.259797	479.221093	0.002087	0.011460	5.491889	0.182087
28	102.966560	566.480890	0.001765	0.009712	5.501601	0.181765
29	121.500541	669.447450	0.001494	0.008230	5.509831	0.181494
30	143.370638	790.947991	0.001264	0.006975	5.516806	0.181264
31	169.177353	934.318630	0.001070	0.005911	5.522717	0.181070
32	199.629277	1103.495983	0.000906	0.005009	5.527726	0.180906
33	235.562547	1303.125260	0.000767	0.004245	5.531971	0.180767
34	277.963805	1538.687807	0.000650	0.003598	5.535569	0.180650
35	327.997290	1816.651612	0.000550	0.003049	5.538618	0.180550
36	387.036802	2144.648902	0.000466	0.002584	5.541201	0.180466
37	456.703427	2531.685705	0.000395	0.002190	5.543391	0.180395
38	538.910044	2988.389132	0.000335	0.001856	5.545247	0.180335
39	635.913852	3527.299175	0.000284	0.001573	5.546819	0.180284
40	750.378345	4163.213027	0.000240	0.001333	5.548152	0.180240
41	885.446447	4913.591372	0.000204	0.001129	5.549281	0.180204
42	1044.826807	5799.037819	0.000172	0.000957	5.550238	0.180172
43	1232.895633	6843.864626	0.000146	0.000811	5.551049	0.180146
44	1454.816847	8076.760259	0.000124	0.000687	5.551737	0.180124
45	1716.683879	9531.577105	0.000105	0.000583	5.552319	0.180105
46	2025.686977	11248.260984	0.000089	0.000494	5.552813	0.180089
47	2390.310633	13273.947961	0.000075	0.000418	5.553231	0.180075
48	2820.566547	15664.258594	0.000064	0.000355	5.553586	0.180064
49	3328.268525	18484.825141	0.000054	0.000300	5.553886	0.180054
50	3927.356860	21813.093667	0.000046	0.000255	5.554141	0.180046

APPENDIX C
Coefficients for Present Value of $1

$$\text{Coefficient} = \frac{1}{(1 + i)^n}$$

To be
received
at the
end of

Discount Rate

Period	1%	2%	3%	4%	5%	6%	7%	8%	9%	10%	12%	14%	15%
1	.990	.900	.971	.962	.952	.943	.935	.926	.917	.909	.893	.877	.870
2	.980	.961	.943	.925	.907	.890	.873	.857	.842	.026	.797	.769	.756
3	.971	.942	.915	.889	.864	.840	.816	.794	.772	.751	.712	.675	.658
4	.961	.924	.889	.855	.823	.792	.763	.735	.708	.683	.636	.592	.572
5	.951	.906	.863	.822	.784	.747	.713	.681	.650	.621	.567	.519	.497
6	.942	.888	.838	.790	.746	.705	.666	.630	.596	.564	.507	.456	.432
7	.933	.871	.813	.760	.711	.665	.623	.583	.547	.513	.452	.400	.376
8	.923	.853	.789	.731	.677	.627	.582	.540	.502	.467	.404	.351	.327
9	.914	.837	.766	.703	.645	.592	.544	.500	.460	.424	.361	.308	.284
10	.905	.820	.744	.676	.614	.558	.508	.463	.422	.386	.322	.270	.247
11	.896	.804	.722	.650	.585	.527	.475	.429	.388	.350	.287	.237	.215
12	.887	.788	.701	.625	.557	.497	.444	.397	.356	.319	.257	.208	.187
13	.879	.773	.681	.601	.530	.469	.445	.368	.326	.290	.229	.182	.163
14	.870	.758	.661	.577	.505	.442	.388	.340	.299	.263	.205	.160	.141
15	.861	.743	.642	.555	.481	.417	.362	.315	.275	.239	.183	.140	.123
16	.853	.728	.623	.534	.458	.394	.339	.292	.252	.218	.163	.123	.107
17	.844	.714	.605	.513	.436	.371	.317	.270	.231	.198	.146	.108	.093
18	.836	.700	.587	.494	.416	.350	.296	.250	.212	.180	.130	.095	.081
19	.828	.686	.570	.475	.396	.331	.276	.232	.194	.164	.116	.083	.070
20	.820	.673	.554	.456	.377	.312	.258	.215	.178	.149	.104	.073	.061
25	.780	.610	.478	.375	.295	.233	.184	.146	.116	.092	.059	.038	.030
30	.742	.552	.412	.308	.231	.174	.131	.099	.075	.057	.033	.020	.015

Period	16%	18%	20%	24%	28%	32%	36%	40%	50%	60%	70%	80%	90%
1	.862	.847	.833	.806	.781	.758	.735	.714	.667	.625	.588	.556	.526
2	.743	.718	.694	.650	.610	.574	.541	.510	.444	.391	.346	.309	.277
3	.641	.609	.579	.524	.477	.435	.398	.364	.296	.244	.204	.171	.146
4	.552	.516	.482	.423	.373	.329	.292	.260	.198	.153	.120	.095	.077
5	.476	.437	.402	.341	.291	.250	.215	.186	.132	.095	.070	.053	.040
6	.410	.370	.335	.275	.227	.189	.158	.133	.088	.060	.041	.029	.021
7	.354	.314	.279	.222	.178	.143	.116	.095	.059	.037	.024	.016	.011
8	.305	.266	.233	.179	.139	.108	.085	.068	.039	.023	.014	.009	.006
9	.263	.226	.194	.144	.108	.082	.063	.048	.026	.015	.008	.005	.003
10	.227	.191	.162	.116	.085	.062	.046	.035	.017	.009	.005	.003	.002
11	.195	.162	.135	.094	.066	.047	.034	.025	.012	.006	.003	.002	.001
12	.168	.137	.112	.076	.052	.036	.025	.018	.008	.004	.002	.001	.001
13	.145	.116	.093	.061	.040	.027	.018	.013	.005	.002	.001	.001	.000
14	.125	.099	.078	.049	.032	.021	.014	.009	.003	.001	.001	.000	.000
15	.108	.084	.065	.040	.025	.016	.010	.006	.002	.001	.000	.000	.000
16	.093	.071	.054	.032	.019	.012	.007	.005	.002	.001	.000	.000	
17	.080	.060	.045	.026	.015	.009	.005	.003	.001	.000	.000		
18	.069	.051	.038	.021	.012	.007	.004	.002	.001	.000	.000		
19	.060	.043	.031	.017	.009	.005	.003	.002	.000	.000			
20	.051	.037	.026	.014	.007	.004	.002	.001	.000	.000			
25	.024	.016	.010	.005	.002	.001	.000	.000					
30	.012	.007	.004	.002	.001	.000	.000						

Coefficients for Present Value of a $1 Annuity

$$\text{Coefficient} = \sum_{n=1}^{n} \frac{1}{(1+i)^n}$$

Received at the end of each period for:

Discount Rate

Period	1%	2%	3%	4%	5%	6%	7%	8%	9%	10%
1	0.990	0.980	0.971	0.962	0.952	0.943	0.935	0.926	0.917	0.909
2	1.970	1.942	1.913	1.886	1.859	1.833	1.808	1.783	1.759	1.736
3	2.941	2.884	2.829	2.775	2.723	2.673	2.624	2.577	2.531	2.487
4	3.902	3.808	3.717	3.630	3.546	3.465	3.387	3.312	3.240	3.170
5	4.853	4.713	4.580	4.452	4.329	4.212	4.100	3.993	3.890	3.791
6	5.795	5.601	5.417	5.242	5.076	4.917	4.766	4.623	4.486	4.355
7	6.728	6.472	6.230	6.002	5.786	5.582	5.389	5.206	5.033	4.868
8	7.652	7.325	7.020	6.733	6.463	6.210	5.971	5.747	5.535	5.335
9	8.566	8.162	7.786	7.435	7.108	6.802	6.515	6.247	5.995	5.759
10	9.471	8.983	8.530	8.111	7.722	7.360	7.024	6.710	6.418	6.145
11	10.368	9.787	9.253	8.760	8.306	7.887	7.499	7.139	6.805	6.495
12	11.255	10.575	9.954	9.385	8.863	8.384	7.943	7.536	7.161	6.814
13	12.134	11.348	10.635	9.986	9.394	8.853	8.358	7.904	7.487	7.103
14	13.004	12.106	11.296	10.563	9.899	9.295	8.745	8.244	7.786	7.367
15	13.865	12.849	11.938	11.118	10.380	9.712	9.108	8.559	8.060	7.606
16	14.718	13.578	12.561	11.652	10.838	10.106	9.447	8.851	8.312	7.824
17	15.562	14.292	13.166	12.166	11.274	10.477	9.763	9.122	8.544	8.022
18	16.398	14.992	13.754	12.659	11.690	10.828	10.059	9.372	8.756	8.201
19	17.226	15.678	14.324	13.134	12.085	11.158	10.336	9.604	8.950	8.365
20	18.046	16.351	14.877	13.590	12.462	11.470	10.594	9.818	9.128	8.514
25	22.023	19.523	17.413	15.622	14.094	12.783	11.654	10.675	9.823	9.077
30	25.808	22.397	19.600	17.292	15.373	13.765	12.409	11.258	10.274	9.427

Period	12%	14%	16%	18%	20%	24%	28%	32%	36%
1	0.893	0.877	0.862	0.847	0.833	0.806	0.781	0.758	0.735
2	1.690	1.647	1.605	1.566	1.528	1.457	1.392	1.332	1.276
3	2.402	2.322	2.246	2.174	2.106	1.981	1.868	1.766	1.674
4	3.037	2.914	2.798	2.690	2.589	2.404	2.241	2.096	1.966
5	3.605	3.433	3.274	3.127	2.991	2.745	2.532	2.345	2.181
6	4.111	3.889	3.685	3.498	3.326	3.020	2.759	2.534	2.339
7	4.564	4.288	4.039	3.812	3.605	3.242	2.937	2.678	2.455
8	4.968	4.639	4.344	4.078	3.837	3.421	3.076	2.786	2.540
9	5.328	4.946	4.607	4.303	4.031	3.566	3.184	2.868	2.603
10	5.650	5.216	4.833	4.494	4.193	3.682	3.269	2.930	2.650
11	5.938	5.435	5.029	4.656	4.327	3.776	3.335	2.978	2.683
12	6.194	5.660	5.197	4.793	4.439	3.851	3.387	3.013	2.708
13	6.424	5.842	5.342	4.910	4.533	3.912	3.427	3.040	2.727
14	6.628	6.002	5.468	5.008	4.611	3.962	3.459	3.061	2.740
15	6.811	6.142	5.575	5.092	4.675	4.001	3.483	3.076	2.750
16	6.974	6.265	5.669	5.162	4.730	4.033	3.503	3.088	2.758
17	7.120	5.373	5.749	5.222	4.775	4.059	3.518	3.097	2.763
18	7.250	6.467	5.818	5.273	4.812	4.080	3.529	3.104	2.767
19	7.366	6.550	5.877	5.316	4.844	4.097	3.539	3.109	2.770
20	7.469	6.623	5.929	5.353	4.870	4.110	3.546	3.113	2.772
25	7.843	6.873	6.097	5.467	4.948	4.147	3.564	3.122	2.776
30	8.055	7.003	6.177	5.517	4.979	4.160	3.569	3.124	2.778

APPENDIX D
Mortgage Constant: Monthly Payment in Arrears

Description: This table shows the percent of the principal amount of a loan needed each year to pay off the loan when the actual payments are monthly and are paid in arrears. Divide the percent by 12 to get the level monthly payment per $100 that includes both interest and principal.

Example: The Constant Annual Percent needed to pay off a 15%, 30 year loan if payments are made monthly and in arrears is 15.18%. Divide by 12 to get the actual monthly payment. The constant annual payment for a $50,000 loan is $7,590. The monthly payment is $632.50.

INTEREST RATE	5 yr	6 yr	7 yr	8 yr	9 yr	10 yr	11 yr	12 yr	13 yr	14 yr	15 yr	16 yr	17 yr	18 yr	19 yr	20 yr
4.00	22.10	18.78	16.41	14.63	13.25	12.15	11.26	10.51	9.88	9.35	8.88	8.48	8.12	7.81	7.53	7.28
4.25	22.24	18.92	16.55	14.77	13.39	12.30	11.40	10.66	10.03	9.49	9.03	8.63	8.28	7.96	7.68	7.44
4.50	22.38	19.05	16.69	14.91	13.54	12.44	11.55	10.81	10.18	9.65	9.18	9.78	8.43	8.12	7.84	7.60
4.75	22.51	19.19	16.83	15.05	13.68	12.59	11.69	10.95	10.33	9.80	9.34	8.94	8.59	8.28	8.01	7.70
5.00	22.65	19.33	16.97	15.20	13.83	12.73	11.84	11.10	10.48	9.95	9.49	9.10	8.75	8.44	8.17	7.92
5.25	22.79	19.47	17.11	15.34	13.97	12.88	11.99	11.25	10.63	10.11	9.65	9.26	8.91	8.60	8.33	8.09
5.50	22.93	19.61	17.25	15.48	14.12	13.03	12.14	11.41	10.79	10.26	9.81	9.42	9.07	8.77	8.50	8.26
5.75	23.07	19.75	17.39	15.63	14.26	13.18	12.29	11.56	10.94	10.42	9.97	9.58	9.24	8.94	8.67	8.43
6.00	23.20	19.89	17.54	15.77	14.41	13.33	12.45	11.72	11.10	10.58	10.13	9.74	9.40	9.10	8.84	8.60
6.25	23.34	20.03	17.68	15.92	14.56	13.48	12.60	11.87	11.26	10.74	10.29	9.91	9.57	9.27	9.01	8.78
6.50	23.48	20.18	17.82	16.07	14.71	13.63	12.75	12.03	11.42	10.90	10.46	10.07	9.74	9.44	9.18	8.95
6.75	23.63	20.32	17.97	16.22	14.86	13.78	12.91	12.19	11.58	11.07	10.62	10.24	9.91	9.62	9.36	9.13
7.00	23.77	20.46	18.12	16.37	15.01	13.94	13.07	12.35	11.74	11.23	10.79	10.41	10.08	9.79	9.54	9.31
7.25	23.91	20.61	18.26	16.52	15.16	14.09	13.22	12.51	11.91	11.40	10.96	10.58	10.25	9.97	9.71	9.49
7.50	24.05	20.75	18.41	16.67	15.32	14.25	13.38	12.67	12.07	11.56	11.13	10.75	10.43	10.14	9.89	9.67
7.75	24.19	20.90	18.56	16.82	15.47	14.41	13.54	12.83	12.24	11.73	11.30	10.93	10.61	10.32	10.08	9.86
8.00	24.34	21.04	18.71	16.97	15.63	14.56	13.70	12.99	12.40	11.90	11.47	11.10	10.78	10.50	10.26	10.04
8.25	24.48	21.19	18.86	17.12	15.78	14.72	13.87	13.16	12.57	12.07	11.65	11.28	10.96	10.69	10.44	10.23
8.50	24.62	21.34	19.01	17.28	15.94	14.88	14.03	13.33	12.74	12.24	11.82	11.46	11.14	10.87	10.63	10.42
8.75	24.77	21.49	19.16	17.43	16.10	15.04	14.19	13.49	12.91	12.42	12.00	11.64	11.33	11.06	10.82	10.61
9.00	24.92	21.64	19.31	17.59	16.26	15.21	14.36	13.66	13.08	12.59	12.18	11.82	11.51	11.24	11.01	10.80
9.25	25.06	21.78	19.46	17.74	16.42	15.37	14.53	13.83	13.25	12.77	12.36	12.00	11.70	11.43	11.20	11.00
9.50	25.21	21.93	19.62	17.90	16.58	15.53	14.69	14.00	13.43	12.95	12.54	12.18	11.88	11.62	11.39	11.19
9.75	25.35	22.09	19.77	18.06	16.74	15.70	14.86	14.17	13.60	13.12	12.72	12.37	12.07	11.81	11.58	11.39
10.00	25.50	22.24	19.93	18.21	16.90	15.86	15.03	14.35	13.78	13.30	12.90	12.56	12.26	12.00	11.78	11.59
10.25	25.65	22.39	20.08	18.37	17.06	16.03	15.20	14.52	13.96	13.48	13.08	12.74	12.45	12.20	11.98	11.78
10.50	25.80	22.54	20.24	18.53	17.23	16.20	15.37	14.69	14.14	13.67	13.27	12.93	12.64	12.39	12.17	11.99
10.75	25.95	22.69	20.39	18.69	17.39	16.37	15.54	14.87	14.31	13.85	13.46	13.12	12.84	12.59	12.37	12.19
11.00	26.10	22.85	20.55	18.86	17.56	16.54	15.72	15.05	14.50	14.03	13.64	13.31	13.03	12.79	12.57	12.39
11.25	26.25	23.00	20.71	19.02	17.72	16.71	15.89	15.23	14.68	14.22	13.83	13.51	13.23	12.98	12.78	12.60
11.50	26.40	23.15	20.87	19.18	17.89	16.88	16.07	15.40	14.86	14.41	14.02	13.70	13.42	13.18	12.98	12.80
11.75	26.55	23.31	21.03	19.34	18.06	17.05	16.24	15.58	15.04	14.59	14.21	13.89	13.62	13.39	13.18	13.01
12.00	26.70	23.47	21.19	19.51	18.23	17.22	16.42	15.77	15.23	14.78	14.41	14.09	13.82	13.59	13.39	13.22
12.25	26.85	23.62	21.35	19.67	18.40	17.40	16.60	15.95	15.42	14.97	14.60	14.29	14.02	13.79	13.60	13.43
12.50	27.00	23.78	21.51	19.84	18.57	17.57	16.78	16.13	15.60	15.16	14.80	14.49	14.22	14.00	13.80	13.64
12.75	27.16	23.94	21.67	20.01	18.74	17.75	16.96	16.32	15.79	15.36	14.99	14.68	14.42	14.20	14.01	13.85
13.00	27.31	24.09	21.84	20.17	18.91	17.92	17.14	16.50	15.98	15.55	15.19	14.88	14.63	14.41	14.22	14.06
13.25	27.46	24.25	22.00	20.34	19.08	18.10	17.32	16.69	16.17	15.74	15.39	15.09	14.83	14.62	14.44	14.28
13.50	27.62	24.41	22.16	20.51	19.26	18.28	17.50	16.87	16.36	15.94	15.58	15.29	15.04	14.83	14.65	14.49
13.75	27.77	24.57	22.33	20.68	19.43	18.46	17.68	17.06	16.55	16.13	15.78	15.49	15.25	15.04	14.86	14.71
14.00	27.93	24.73	22.49	20.85	19.61	18.64	17.87	17.25	16.75	16.33	15.99	15.70	15.45	15.25	15.08	14.93
14.25	28.08	24.89	22.66	21.02	19.78	18.82	18.05	17.44	16.94	16.53	16.19	15.90	15.66	15.46	15.29	15.15
14.50	28.24	25.05	22.83	21.19	19.96	19.00	18.24	17.63	17.14	16.73	16.39	16.11	15.87	15.68	15.51	15.36
14.75	28.40	25.22	22.99	21.37	20.14	19.18	18.43	17.82	17.33	16.93	16.60	16.32	16.09	15.89	15.72	15.59
15.00	28.55	25.38	23.16	21.54	20.31	19.37	18.62	18.02	17.53	17.13	16.80	16.53	16.30	16.11	15.94	15.81
15.25	28.71	25.54	23.33	21.71	20.49	19.55	18.80	18.21	17.73	17.33	17.01	16.74	16.51	16.32	16.16	16.03
15.50	28.87	25.71	23.50	21.89	20.67	19.73	18.99	18.40	17.93	17.53	17.21	16.95	16.72	16.54	16.38	16.25
15.75	29.03	25.87	23.67	22.06	20.85	19.92	19.19	18.60	18.12	17.74	17.42	17.16	16.94	16.76	16.60	16.48
16.00	29.19	26.04	23.84	22.24	21.04	20.11	19.38	18.79	18.33	17.94	17.63	17.37	17.16	16.98	16.83	16.70
16.25	29.35	26.20	24.01	22.42	21.22	20.29	19.57	18.99	18.53	18.15	17.84	17.58	17.37	17.20	17.05	16.93
16.50	29.51	26.37	24.18	22.59	21.40	20.48	19.76	19.19	18.73	18.36	18.05	17.80	17.59	17.42	17.27	17.15
16.75	29.67	26.53	24.35	22.77	21.58	20.67	19.96	19.39	18.93	18.56	18.26	18.01	17.81	17.64	17.50	17.38
17.00	29.83	26.70	24.53	22.95	21.77	20.86	20.15	19.59	19.14	18.77	18.47	18.23	18.03	17.86	17.72	17.61
17.25	29.99	26.87	24.70	23.13	21.95	21.05	20.35	19.79	19.34	18.98	18.69	18.45	18.25	18.08	17.95	17.84
17.50	30.15	27.04	24.88	23.31	22.14	21.24	20.54	19.99	19.55	19.19	18.90	18.66	18.47	18.31	18.17	18.06
17.75	30.31	27.21	25.05	23.49	22.33	21.43	20.74	20.19	19.75	19.40	19.11	18.88	18.69	18.53	18.40	18.29
18.00	30.48	27.37	25.23	23.67	22.51	21.63	20.94	20.39	19.96	19.61	19.33	19.10	18.91	18.76	18.63	18.52
18.25	30.64	27.54	25.40	23.86	22.70	21.82	21.14	20.60	20.17	19.82	19.55	19.32	19.13	18.98	18.86	18.76
18.50	30.80	27.71	25.58	24.04	22.89	22.01	21.34	20.80	20.38	20.04	19.76	19.54	19.36	19.21	19.09	18.99
18.75	30.97	27.89	25.76	24.22	23.08	22.21	21.54	21.01	20.59	20.25	19.98	19.76	19.58	19.44	19.32	19.22
19.00	31.13	28.06	25.93	24.41	23.27	22.41	21.74	21.21	20.80	20.47	20.20	19.98	19.81	19.67	19.55	19.45
19.25	31.30	28.23	26.11	24.59	23.46	22.60	21.94	21.42	21.01	20.68	20.42	20.21	20.03	19.89	19.78	19.69
19.50	31.46	28.40	26.29	24.78	23.65	22.80	22.14	21.63	21.22	20.90	20.64	20.43	20.26	20.12	20.01	19.92
19.75	31.63	28.57	26.47	24.96	23.84	23.00	22.34	21.84	21.43	21.11	20.86	20.65	20.49	20.35	20.24	20.16
20.00	31.80	28.75	26.65	25.15	24.04	23.20	22.55	22.04	21.65	21.33	21.08	20.88	20.72	20.58	20.48	20.39
20.25	31.96	28.92	26.83	25.34	24.23	23.39	22.75	22.25	21.86	21.55	21.30	21.10	20.94	20.82	20.71	20.63
20.50	32.13	29.10	27.01	25.52	24.42	23.59	22.96	22.46	22.08	21.77	21.53	21.33	21.17	21.05	20.95	20.86
20.75	32.30	29.27	27.20	25.71	24.62	23.80	23.16	22.68	22.29	21.99	21.75	21.56	21.40	21.28	21.18	21.10

SOURCE: *Thorndike Encyclopedia of Banking and Financial Tables,* Rev. Ed. (Boston: Warren, Gorham & Lamont, 1980), pp. 1–2 and 1–3.

Mortgage Constant: Monthly Payment in Arrears

INTEREST RATE	21 yr	22 yr	23 yr	24 yr	25 yr	26 yr	27 yr	28 yr	29 yr	30 yr	31 yr	32 yr	33 yr	34 yr	35 yr	40 yr
4.00	7.05	6.85	6.66	6.49	6.34	6.20	6.07	5.95	5.84	5.73	5.64	5.55	5.47	5.39	5.32	5.02
4.25	7.21	7.01	6.83	6.66	6.51	6.37	6.24	6.12	6.01	5.91	5.81	5.73	5.65	5.57	5.50	5.21
4.50	7.37	7.17	6.99	6.83	6.67	6.54	6.41	6.29	6.18	6.09	5.99	5.91	5.83	5.75	5.68	5.40
4.75	7.54	7.34	7.16	7.00	6.85	6.71	6.58	6.47	6.36	6.26	6.17	6.09	6.01	5.94	5.87	5.59
5.00	7.71	7.51	7.33	7.17	7.02	6.89	6.76	6.65	6.54	6.45	6.36	6.28	6.20	6.13	6.06	5.79
5.25	7.87	7.68	7.50	7.34	7.20	7.06	6.94	6.83	6.73	6.63	6.54	6.46	6.39	6.32	6.25	5.99
5.50	8.04	7.85	7.68	7.52	7.37	7.24	7.12	7.01	6.91	6.82	6.73	6.65	6.58	6.51	6.45	6.19
5.75	8.22	8.03	7.85	7.70	7.55	7.42	7.31	7.20	7.10	7.01	6.92	6.85	6.77	6.71	6.65	6.40
6.00	8.39	8.20	8.03	7.88	7.74	7.61	7.49	7.39	7.29	7.20	7.12	7.04	6.97	6.91	6.85	6.61
6.25	8.57	8.38	8.21	8.06	7.92	7.80	7.68	7.58	7.48	7.39	7.31	7.24	7.17	7.11	7.05	6.82
6.50	8.75	8.56	8.39	8.24	8.11	7.98	7.87	7.77	7.68	7.59	7.51	7.44	7.37	7.31	7.25	7.03
6.75	8.93	8.74	8.58	8.43	8.30	8.17	8.06	7.96	7.87	7.79	7.71	7.64	7.58	7.52	7.46	7.25
7.00	9.11	8.93	8.76	8.62	8.49	8.37	8.26	8.16	8.07	7.99	7.91	7.85	7.78	7.72	7.67	7.46
7.25	9.29	9.11	8.95	8.81	8.68	8.56	8.46	8.36	8.27	8.19	8.12	8.05	7.99	7.93	7.88	7.68
7.50	9.47	9.30	9.14	9.00	8.87	8.76	8.65	8.56	8.47	8.40	8.32	8.26	8.20	8.15	8.10	7.90
7.75	9.66	9.49	9.33	9.19	9.07	8.96	8.85	8.76	8.68	8.60	8.53	8.47	8.41	8.36	8.31	8.12
8.00	9.85	9.68	9.53	9.39	9.27	9.16	9.06	8.97	8.88	8.81	8.74	8.68	8.63	8.57	8.53	8.35
8.25	10.04	9.87	9.72	9.59	9.47	9.36	9.26	9.17	9.09	9.02	8.95	8.90	8.84	8.79	8.75	8.57
8.50	10.23	10.07	9.92	9.79	9.67	9.56	9.47	9.38	9.30	9.23	9.17	9.11	9.06	9.01	8.97	8.80
8.75	10.43	10.26	10.12	9.99	9.87	9.77	9.67	9.59	9.51	9.45	9.38	9.33	9.28	9.23	9.19	9.03
9.00	10.62	10.46	10.32	10.19	10.08	9.97	9.88	9.80	9.73	9.66	9.60	9.55	9.50	9.45	9.41	9.26
9.25	10.82	10.66	10.52	10.39	10.28	10.18	10.09	10.01	9.94	9.88	9.82	9.77	9.72	9.68	9.64	9.49
9.50	11.01	10.86	10.72	10.60	10.49	10.39	10.31	10.23	10.16	10.10	10.04	9.99	9.94	9.90	9.86	9.73
9.75	11.21	11.06	10.93	10.81	10.70	10.60	10.52	10.44	10.38	10.31	10.26	10.21	10.17	10.13	10.09	9.96
10.00	11.41	11.26	11.13	11.01	10.91	10.82	10.73	10.66	10.59	10.54	10.48	10.44	10.39	10.36	10.32	10.19
10.25	11.62	11.47	11.34	11.22	11.12	11.03	10.95	10.88	10.82	10.76	10.71	10.66	10.62	10.58	10.55	10.43
10.50	11.82	11.68	11.55	11.43	11.34	11.25	11.17	11.10	11.04	10.98	10.93	10.89	10.85	10.81	10.78	10.67
10.75	12.03	11.88	11.76	11.65	11.55	11.46	11.39	11.32	11.26	11.21	11.16	11.12	11.08	11.05	11.02	10.91
11.00	12.23	12.09	11.97	11.86	11.77	11.68	11.61	11.54	11.48	11.43	11.39	11.35	11.31	11.28	11.25	11.14
11.25	12.44	12.30	12.18	12.08	11.98	11.90	11.83	11.77	11.71	11.66	11.62	11.58	11.54	11.51	11.48	11.38
11.50	12.65	12.51	12.40	12.29	12.20	12.12	12.05	11.99	11.94	11.89	11.85	11.81	11.77	11.74	11.72	11.62
11.75	12.86	12.73	12.61	12.51	12.42	12.35	12.28	12.22	12.16	12.12	12.08	12.04	12.01	11.98	11.95	11.87
12.00	13.07	12.94	12.83	12.73	12.64	12.57	12.50	12.44	12.39	12.35	12.31	12.27	12.24	12.22	12.19	12.11
12.25	13.28	13.16	13.05	12.95	12.87	12.79	12.73	12.67	12.62	12.58	12.54	12.51	12.48	12.45	12.43	12.35
12.50	13.50	13.37	13.26	13.17	13.09	13.02	12.96	12.90	12.85	12.81	12.78	12.74	12.71	12.69	12.67	12.59
12.75	13.71	13.59	13.48	13.39	13.31	13.24	13.18	13.13	13.09	13.05	13.01	12.98	12.95	12.93	12.91	12.84
13.00	13.93	13.81	13.71	13.62	13.54	13.47	13.41	13.36	13.32	13.28	13.25	13.22	13.19	13.17	13.15	13.08
13.25	14.14	14.03	13.93	13.84	13.77	13.70	13.64	13.59	13.55	13.51	13.48	13.45	13.43	13.41	13.39	13.32
13.50	14.36	14.25	14.15	14.07	13.99	13.93	13.87	13.83	13.79	13.75	13.72	13.69	13.67	13.65	13.63	13.57
13.75	14.58	14.47	14.37	14.29	14.22	14.16	14.11	14.06	14.02	13.99	13.96	13.93	13.91	13.89	13.87	13.81
14.00	14.80	14.69	14.60	14.52	14.45	14.39	14.34	14.30	14.26	14.22	14.19	14.17	14.15	14.13	14.11	14.06
14.25	15.02	14.92	14.82	14.75	14.68	14.62	14.57	14.53	14.49	14.46	14.43	14.41	14.39	14.37	14.36	14.30
14.50	15.24	15.14	15.05	14.98	14.91	14.86	14.81	14.77	14.73	14.70	14.67	14.65	14.63	14.61	14.60	14.55
14.75	15.47	15.37	15.28	15.21	15.14	15.09	15.04	15.00	14.97	14.94	14.91	14.89	14.87	14.86	14.84	14.80
15.00	15.69	15.59	15.51	15.44	15.37	15.32	15.28	15.24	15.21	15.18	15.15	15.13	15.12	15.10	15.09	15.04
15.25	15.92	15.82	15.74	15.67	15.61	15.56	15.51	15.48	15.45	15.42	15.40	15.38	15.36	15.34	15.33	15.29
15.50	16.14	16.05	15.97	15.90	15.84	15.79	15.75	15.72	15.69	15.66	15.64	15.62	15.60	15.59	15.58	15.54
15.75	16.37	16.28	16.20	16.13	16.08	16.03	15.99	15.95	15.93	15.90	15.88	15.86	15.85	15.83	15.82	15.79
16.00	16.59	16.50	16.43	16.37	16.31	16.27	16.23	16.19	16.17	16.14	16.12	16.10	16.09	16.08	16.07	16.03
16.25	16.82	16.74	16.66	16.60	16.55	16.50	16.47	16.43	16.41	16.38	16.36	16.35	16.33	16.32	16.31	16.28
16.50	17.05	16.97	16.89	16.83	16.78	16.74	16.71	16.67	16.65	16.63	16.61	16.59	16.58	16.57	16.56	16.53
16.75	17.28	17.20	17.13	17.07	17.02	16.98	16.94	16.92	16.89	16.87	16.85	16.84	16.82	16.81	16.80	16.78
17.00	17.51	17.43	17.36	17.31	17.26	17.22	17.19	17.16	17.13	17.11	17.10	17.08	17.07	17.06	17.05	17.02
17.25	17.74	17.66	17.60	17.54	17.50	17.46	17.43	17.40	17.38	17.36	17.34	17.33	17.32	17.31	17.30	17.27
17.50	17.97	17.90	17.83	17.78	17.74	17.70	17.67	17.64	17.62	17.60	17.59	17.57	17.56	17.55	17.55	17.52
17.75	18.20	18.13	18.07	18.02	17.97	17.94	17.91	17.88	17.86	17.85	17.83	17.82	17.81	17.80	17.79	17.77
18.00	18.44	18.37	18.31	18.26	18.21	18.18	18.15	18.13	18.11	18.09	18.08	18.06	18.05	18.05	18.04	18.02
18.25	18.67	18.60	18.54	18.49	18.45	18.42	18.39	18.37	18.35	18.34	18.32	18.31	18.30	18.29	18.29	18.27
18.50	18.91	18.84	18.78	18.73	18.69	18.66	18.64	18.61	18.60	18.58	18.57	18.56	18.55	18.54	18.54	18.52
18.75	19.14	19.07	19.02	18.97	18.94	18.90	18.88	18.86	18.84	18.83	18.81	18.80	18.80	18.79	18.78	18.77
19.00	19.37	19.31	19.26	19.21	19.18	19.15	19.12	19.10	19.09	19.07	19.06	19.05	19.04	19.04	19.03	19.02
19.25	19.61	19.55	19.50	19.45	19.42	19.39	19.37	19.35	19.33	19.32	19.31	19.30	19.29	19.28	19.28	19.26
19.50	19.85	19.79	19.74	19.69	19.66	19.63	19.61	19.59	19.58	19.56	19.55	19.55	19.54	19.53	19.53	19.51
19.75	20.08	20.02	19.98	19.94	19.90	19.88	19.86	19.84	19.82	19.81	19.80	19.79	19.79	19.78	19.78	19.76
20.00	20.32	20.26	20.22	20.18	20.15	20.12	20.10	20.08	20.07	20.06	20.05	20.04	20.03	20.03	20.02	20.01
20.25	20.56	20.50	20.46	20.42	20.39	20.36	20.34	20.33	20.32	20.30	20.30	20.29	20.28	20.28	20.27	20.26
20.50	20.80	20.74	20.70	20.66	20.63	20.61	20.59	20.57	20.56	20.55	20.54	20.54	20.53	20.53	20.52	20.51
20.75	21.03	20.98	20.94	20.90	20.88	20.85	20.84	20.82	20.81	20.80	20.79	20.78	20.78	20.77	20.77	20.76

APPENDIX E
Accelerated Cost Recovery System Tables
for Real Estate Assets

TABLE 1. All Personal Property

If the Recovery Year Is	Purchased In 1981–1984		Purchased in 1985		Purchased after 1985	
	3-Year	5-Year	3-Year	5-Year	3-Year	5-Year
	THE APPLICABLE COST RECOVERY PERCENTAGE FOR PROPERTY IS					
1	25	15	29	18	33	20
2	38	22	47	33	45	32
3	37	21	24	25	22	24
4	—	21	—	16	—	16
5	—	21	—	8	—	8

TABLE 2. All Real Property (except Low-Income Housing)

If the Recovery Year Is	The Applicable Percentage Is (Use the Column for the Month in the First Year the Property Is Placed in Service)											
	1	2	3	4	5	6	7	8	9	10	11	12
1	12	11	10	9	8	7	6	5	4	3	2	1
2	10	10	11	11	11	11	11	11	11	11	11	12
3	9	9	9	9	10	10	10	10	10	10	10	10
4	8	8	8	8	8	8	9	9	9	9	9	9
5	7	7	7	7	7	7	8	8	8	8	8	8
6	6	6	6	6	7	7	7	7	7	7	7	7
7	6	6	6	6	6	6	6	6	6	6	6	6
8	6	6	6	6	6	6	5	6	6	6	6	6
9	6	6	6	6	5	6	5	5	5	6	6	6
10	5	6	5	6	5	5	5	5	5	5	6	5
11	5	5	5	5	5	5	5	5	5	5	5	5
12	5	5	5	5	5	5	5	5	5	5	5	5
13	5	5	5	5	5	5	5	5	5	5	5	5
14	5	5	5	5	5	5	5	5	5	5	5	5
15	5	5	5	5	5	5	5	5	5	5	5	5
16	—	—	1	1	2	2	3	3	4	4	4	5

Note: This table does not apply for short taxable years of less than 12 months.

TABLE 3. **Low-Income Housing**

If the Recovery Year Is	The Applicable Percentage Is (Use the Column for the Month in the First Year the Property Is Placed in Service)											
	1	2	3	4	5	6	7	8	9	10	11	12
1	13	12	11	10	9	8	7	6	4	3	2	1
2	12	12	12	12	12	12	12	13	13	13	13	13
3	10	10	10	10	11	11	11	11	11	11	11	11
4	9	9	9	9	9	9	9	9	10	10	10	10
5	8	8	8	8	8	8	8	8	8	8	8	9
6	7	7	7	7	7	7	7	7	7	7	7	7
7	6	6	6	6	6	6	6	6	6	6	6	6
8	5	5	5	5	5	5	5	5	5	5	6	6
9	5	5	5	5	5	5	5	5	5	5	5	5
10	5	5	5	5	5	5	5	5	5	5	5	5
11	4	5	5	5	5	5	5	5	5	5	5	5
12	4	4	4	5	4	5	5	5	5	5	5	5
13	4	4	4	4	4	4	5	4	5	5	5	5
14	4	4	4	4	4	4	4	4	4	5	4	4
15	4	4	4	4	4	4	4	4	4	4	4	4
16	—	—	1	1	2	2	2	3	3	3	4	4

Note: This table does not apply for short taxable years of less than 12 months.

Index

Abandonment, 496
Aberle case, 496n
Absorption rate, market, 114–115, 137
Accelerated basis, depreciation, 306
Accelerated cost recovery system (ACRS), 343
and depreciation, 354–360
Accelerated loan, 395
Acceleration clauses, 395
Accessibility, neighborhood, 123
Accommodation, and negotiations, 431–432
Accounting
cash vs. accrual, 364–366
controls and reporting system, in reducing risk, 331
and property management, 461–462
Accounting rate of return, 313
Accounts payable, current, 706–707
Accreditation, nursing homes, 638
Accredited Management Organizations (AMOs), 466
Accredited Resident Manager (ARM), 466
Accumulated earnings tax, corporation, 230
Acquisition, in ownership life cycle, 40
Acquisition period, tax shelter strategy, 374
Active investor, 13
Activity attributes, hotel/motel location, 629
Adams, John S., 79n, 84n
Adaptability, industrial building, 600
Add-on minimum tax, 360–361
Adjusted basis, in disposal of investment, 485
Adjusted gross income (AGI), and income tax formula, 344–345
Adjusted internal rate of return, 293–296
Ad valorem tax, on real property, 344
Advertising, in promoting projects, 454
Advisers, personal portfolio, 724–725
After-tax analysis, discounted cash flow, 297–309
After-tax cash flow, 484
Age, and migration, 89–91
Agglomerating tendency, industrial buildings, 591–592
Aging, of population, 88
Agricultural land, unimproved, and inflation, 155
Air rights, 493
Alderson case, 503, 504, 505
Aldrich, Peter C., 691
Allegheny Center, Pittsburgh, 544

Allen, Robert G., 616, 623
Allocations, general partnership, 221–222
Alternative minimum tax on capital gains, 360, 361
Alternative mortgage instruments (AMIs), 399
Alternatives, in investment analysis model, 193
Alternative uses, special-use properties, 624, 625
Amenities, neighborhood, 123
American Arbitration Association, 487
American Hotel and Motel Association, 631
American Institute of Real Estate Appraisers (AIREA), 33
American Trucking Association, 593
Amortization
and debt financing, 391–392
and tax shelter, 370
Amortization schedule, mortgage, 396–398
Amortization term, 390
Analysis
Aspen Wood Apartments sale, 512
balance sheet, 707–708
feasibility vs. investment, 25–35
industrial building, 600–601
internal rate of return, 306–309
investment, 23
land ownership expense, 653
macromarket, 100
present value, 306–309
See also Cash flow analysis; Demand analysis; Discounted cash flow analysis; Economic base analysis; Investment analysis; Marketability analysis; Market analysis; Operations analysis; Rate-of-return analysis; Ratio analysis; Risk analysis; Supply analysis
Anchor tenant, shopping center, 542
Anderson, Hershel M., 345n
Annual budget, adopting, 710–715
Annual debt service, in financial feasibility model, 258–259
Annualized net present value (ANPV), 323
Annual U.S. Economic Data, 164
Apartments
definitions, 524–527
discounted cash flow analysis, 537–538
financing and refinancing, 535–536
investing in, 528
investment decision, 538

investors and investor motivations, 528–529
market and marketability analysis, 529–532
operations analysis, 533–535
physical, legal, political, and environmental analysis, 532–533
returns and risks, 529
taxation and tax structure, 536–537
track records and trends, 527–528
See also Aspen Wood Apartments
Apgar, Mahlon, 331n
Appraisal, vs. investment and feasibility analysis, 33–35
Appreciation, small rental properties, 615
Appreciation leverage, in debt financing, 388
Archer, S., 702n
Architectural and engineering study, 32
Architecture
industrial building, 600
office building, 573
Area delineation, in market studies, 104
Arnold, Alvin L., 26n, 240n, 358n, 362n, 394n, 403n, 406n, 433n, 466n, 486n, 691n
Artificial accounting losses, 305
Artificial buffers, neighborhoods, 122
Aspen Wood Apartments, 187
balance sheet, 477
capital expenditures, 377–379
cash flow analysis, 380–381, 382
description, 206, 208–209
computer analysis, 298–309
depreciation schedules, 379
details, 277-278
discounted cash flow analysis, 297–309
feasibility research, 335, 339–340
financial package: decision, 423–424; input assumptions, 421–423
investment objectives and criteria, 210–211
investment philosophy, 207–211
joint venture, 244–245
loan schedules, 379–380
management organization, 470
negotiations with seller, 334–335
net cash position analysis, 381–383
operating assumptions, 380, 381
operating statements, 472–476
ownership decision matrix, 242–244
plans and policies, 211
property management, 469–477

Aspen Wood Apartments **(Continued)**
ratio analysis and final investment decision, 383–384
reports to investors, 471
sale, projection of net proceeds, 383, 384
sale contract, final, 444–447
sale structure proposals, 280–281
screening criteria, 211
seller's operating pro forma, 278–280
termination of investment, 511–514
valuation using financial feasibility model, 281–283
See also Apartments
Assessments, land, 653
Asset(s), 706
nature of, 707
priority of claim, lender vs. equity investor, 27
real vs. financial, and inflation, 161
Assets inventory, cost of producing, 704–705
Asset tests, REIT, 235
Association of American Geographers, 76
Assumed investment, at IRR, 294
Assumption base ratios, 314–315
Atlanta, Georgia, economic base analysis to forecast growth in, 108–111
Atlanta Regional Commission, 109, 118
Auction, 492
Audit, linked, 219
Authority, of property manager, 463–464
Avoidance, of risk, 330

Babcock, Guilford C., 296n
Bailey, C. W., 466n
Bailey, John B., 111n
Baird Publishing Co. case, 504
Baker, James A., 298, 377n
Balance sheet
analyzing, 707–708
Aspen Wood Apartments, 477
Balloon loan, 391, 395
Balloon payment, and amortization cost, 623
Balloon payment mortgages, industrial buildings, 604
Bandwagon cycle, 175
Bank deposits, 89
Bank of America Real Estate Fund, 695
Bank real estate funds, 691–692
Bargaining, cooperative, vs. confrontation, 429
Barlow, Raleigh, 77
Barr, Gary K., 413n, 414n
Basis
in disposal of investment, 484–486
in exchange of property, 508–509
BASS (Bay Area Simulation Study), 118
Beaton, William R., 60n
Beginning basis, depreciation, 301, 302

Bell, David E., 128n
Bell, Robert, 402
Beneficial owners, REIT, 235
Benefit stage, personal portfolio, 700
Bernard case, 504
Bernstein, Joel H., 411n
Best-fit approach, to real estate investment, 59–61
Biedenham Realty Co., Inc. v. US, 492n
Birthrate, and population, 87
Blazar, Sheldon M., 157n
Blind pool partnership, 717
Bloom, George, 54n
Blue-sky laws, 420
Bockl, George, 44n, 47–48
Body, Zvi, 161n
Boilerplate clauses, 394
Bonds, industrial real estate, 605–607
Bonus depreciation, 359
Boot, in exchange of property, 500, 505
Borelli, Donald, 483
Boundaries, neighborhood, and marketability, 122
Boyce, Byrl, 31n, 34n, 111n, 121n
Break-even leverage, 255
Break-even point, 64, 313
identifying, 452
Break-even ratio, 252–253
Brenner, Michael J., 401
Brigham, Eugene F., 254n, 290n, 293n, 294n
Britton, James A. Jr., 247n, 329n
Brock, Horace R., 345n
Brown, Lawrence E., 689
Budget, annual personal, 710–715
Budget motels, 626
Builder/developer, as investor, 13
Building analysis, industrial building, 600–601
Building maintenance, shopping center, 555
Building Owners and Managers Association International (BOMA), 571
Build-lease, industrial building, 603
Built to suit; industrial building, 603
Bureau of Economic Analysis, 104
Busch Gardens, 626
Business cycle, and real estate cycle, 170–171
Business insurance, 712
Business-related risk, portfolio, 701
vs. market-related risk, 670–672
Business risk, 319–320
and IRR, 321
Business Week, 164, 171
Buyer, predicaments in negotiations, 436
Buy-sell agreement, 487

CACI, Inc., 112, 128, 129, 130, 550
Called loan, 395
Campbell, Kenneth, 665n
Canadian rollover (CRO), 399
Capital
appreciation, 10
security of, 9
Capital additions policy, and property management, 453

Capital assets
in investment analysis, 25
and long-term capital gain, 348, 349
Capital budgeting approach
to inflation cycle strategy, 161–165
to real estate investment, 61–68
Capital expenditures
Aspen Wood Apartments, 377–379
vs. operating expense, 366
Capital gain
alternative minimum tax on, 360, 361
and depreciation recapture, 352–353
and ownership form, 215
Capital gain income, vs. ordinary income, 348–353
Capital improvements, deferred, and NOI, 272–273
Capitalization expenses, and NOI, 273
Capitalization rates, 436
small rental properties, 620–621
Capital outlay, and ownership form, 216
Cap rates, use in negotiations, 436
Capture rates, market, 138–139
Carlson, Don W., 449n
Carlton case, 503
Carlyle Real Estate Limited Partnership, 694
Carr, E. William, 494n
Cartography, urban, 76–77
Caruth case, 491n
Case, Fred E., 166, 167n, 173n, 196n, 570n, 648
Cash accounting, vs. accrual accounting, 364–366
Cash equivalent, 718
Cash equivalent reserves, 706
Cash flow, 26–27
computer analysis of data, 298–309
and inflation, 150
and IRR, 292–293
from operations, 27
and present value, 286–288
and refinancing, 408
small rental properties, 614–615
and taxable income, 369–370
Cash flow after taxes, 381
plus equity buildup plus appreciation to initial equity, ratio of, 312–313
plus equity buildup to initial equity, ratio of, 312
to initial equity, ratio of, 311–312
to total capital, 305
Cash flow analysis, 303–306
Aspen Wood Apartments, 380–381, 382
hotels and motels, 635
Cash flow before taxes, 27
in financial feasibility model, 259
to initial equity, ratio of, 311
Cash flow statement, 247–248
rental house, 621
Cash-on-cash return, 59, 253–254
Cash reserves, 712–713
Cash throwoff, 27

ash throw-off rate, 59
sh value, life insurance, 706
sualty losses, 498
iling height, industrial building,
    601
entralization of management, cor-
    poration, 228
ntrally located sites, industrial
    buildings, 594
ntral utility system, shopping cen-
    ter, 556
rt, Alan R., 63n, 142n, 197n, 676n
rtified Commercial Investment
    Member (CCIM), 451
rtified Property Managers (CPMs),
    451, 461–462, 466
ains, and investment in hotels and
    motels, 627
andler, Charles, 647n
apin, Stuart, 75n
aracteristic line, security, 671
aritable contribution, in disposing
    of property, 493
udleigh, Walter H. III, 689
ties, 72
    data, 145
    growth and decline, 82–85
    real estate cycles in, 172–173
ark, William Dennison Jr., 388n
asses of ownership interest, within
    same ownership vehicle, 412
assification, in market studies,
    104, 105
awson, Marion, 650n
ean Air Act amendment (1970), 6
ear span, industrial building, 586
fford trust, 237–238
osed-end offerings, in syndication,
    416–417
osed period, 393
osing
    and negotiations, 441–442
    timing of, 482–483
osing costs, proration, 445
osing date, Aspen Wood Apart-
    ments, 447
osing statement, Aspen Wood
    Apartments, 446
ustering tendency, industrial
    buildings, 591–592
astal Zone Management Act
    (1972), 6
ates, C. Robert, 188n
de controls, neighborhood, 123
hen, Jerome B., 40n
ldwell Banker Co., 196
llapsible corporations, 230–231
llateral, special-use properties,
    625
llateralized loan, 407
llectibles, 706, 715
lwell, Peter F., 57n
mmerce Department, 85–86
mmercial income property, and in-
    flation, 158
mmercial locations, 80–81
mmercial office buildings, 571
mmercial second mortgages, 402
mmitment, and track record, 520
mmitment fees and points, debt
    financing, 392

Common-area charges, shopping cen-
    ter, 555
Common-area maintenance, shopping
    center, 555
Comm'r v. Segall, 483n
Community development block
    grants, 401
Community shopping center, 541
Comparative locational advantage,
    principle of, 77–82
Comparative market analysis form,
    small rental properties, 616
Compatibility, of tenants, 456
Compatibility study, 32
Compensation, property manager,
    464
Compensation schemes, for investors,
    413–415
Competence, and track record, 519
Competition
    and changing property usage,
        269–270
    field survey, 131–135
    metropolitan areas, 84–85
    potential, analysis of, 97
Component depreciation, 354, 359
Composite basis, depreciation, 359
Compound interest, 145
Computer analysis, cash flow data,
    298–309
Computer mapping techniques, 76
Computer software, sources, 521–
    522
Condemnation, 497
Conditional sale, 487
Condominium, 611, 613–614
    defined, 526
    market outlook for, 733
Conduit tax treatment, REIT, 235
Conduit theory, 48
Conference, on property manager's
    goals and budget objectives,
    467–468
Confrontation, vs. cooperative bar-
    gaining, 429
Connecticut General Mortgage and
    Realty Investments, 695
Consolidated Capital Properties,
    717
Construction cycle, 171
Construction lender, as investment
    decision maker, 16–17
Construction loan costs, and infla-
    tion, 151
Construction work, supervising, 462
Constructive receipt, 365
Consultants, personal portfolio, 724–
    725
Consulting functions, property man-
    ager, 464
Consumer price index (CPI), 144
Consumer price inflation, 145
Contingencies, office building prepa-
    ration for, 573
Contingency fund, land ownership,
    654
Continuity
    corporation, 228
    limited partnership, 224
    and management form, 216
Contract, hotel management, 632
Contrary opinion, law of, 176–177

Control(s)
    government: as investment disad-
        vantage, 12; and ownership
        form, 211
    of large properties with minimum
        capital outlays, corporation, 229
    management, and ownership form,
        215–216
    personal, as investor motivation,
        8–9
    and real estate investment, 49
    and risk taking, 716–717
    See also Risk management and
        control
Control variables, 326
Convenience goods, shopping center,
    542
Conventional hotels, 626
Conversion, and property manage-
    ment, 451
Convertible mortgage, 411
Conveyors, industrial building, 601
Cooley, Phillip L., 255n
Cooper, James R., 6n, 75n, 142,
    197n, 326n, 421n, 450n, 481
Cooperative bargaining, vs. confron-
    tation, 429
Cooperative housing projects, 526–
    527
Corgel, John B., 358n
Corporate general partner, and lim-
    ited partnership, 225
Corporate surplus, and investment in
    industrial buildings, 591
Corporation
    capital gains taxation, 348
    and income tax formula, 347
    nominee, dummy, and straw, 233–
        234
    regular (Subchapter C), 228–231
    Subchapter S, 231–233
    tax year, 364
Cost
    of assets inventory, 704–705
    construction loan, and inflation,
        151
    equity, 309
    of holding land, 653–654
    office building refinancing, 580
    shopping center financing, 557–558
    of urban containment, 739–742
    vs. value, investment, 53
Cost equity, 309
Cost recovery. **See** Depreciation
Counseling of investor, and property
    management, 449
Counteroffers, estimating range in
    negotiations, 437–438
Coupe case, 504
Covariance, and portfolio, 668–670
Crane v. Cobb, 484n, 496n
Creative equity structures, 412–413
Creative financing, 406–407
Creative Solutions case, 497n
Credit, industrial building, 606
Credit report, tenants, 618
Creditworthiness, in selecting ten-
    ants, 455–456
Crow, Trammell, 16, 38, 519
Cultural traits, and negotiations, 433
Cumberland Mall, Atlanta, 544, 546–
    547

Cummings, Jack, 409n
Cumulative cash flow before and after tax, in cash flow analysis, 305
Curcio, Richard J., 676n, 683, 684
Current accounts payable, 706–707
Current equity position, 707
Current liabilities, 706–707
Current operating income and expenses
  apartments, 534–535
  hotels and motels, 632–634
  office building, 574–575
  shopping centers, 553–557
Cycles. **See** Inflation cycle; Life cycle; Real estate cycles

Dallas Transfer case, 499n
Dasso, Jerome, 466n
Davis, Joseph M., 359
Dealer, and long-term capital gain, 348, 349–351
Dealer activities, REIT, 235
Death, gift in contemplation of, 494
Death rate, and population, 88
Debatable deductions, 367
Debentures, industrial real estate, 605–606
Debt, in investment analysis, 25–26
Debt capital, outlook, 738
Debt coverage ratio (DCR), 64, 313
  in financial feasibility model, 258
  industrial building, 607
  and mortgage constant, 248–253
  office building, 580
  and risk, 252
  shopping center, 558
Debt financing
  creative, 406–407
  first-mortgage, 399–400
  government-sponsored loan programs, 400–401
  junior mortgage, 401–406
  leverage decision, 387–389
  mortgage amortization schedule, 396–398
  variables, 390–396
Debt service, 26
  and inflation, 150
Debt service costs, land ownership, 653
Debt-to-equity ratio, lender vs. equity investor, 27
Decision, investment, 23–24
Decision criteria, 200–201
Decision makers, in investment process, 15–19
Decision model, ownership, 213
Decision rule
  IRR, 293
  present value, 288–289
Declining-balance method, depreciation, 355, 357
Declining-credit option, 495
Default point, 252–253
Deferred-payment sales, 491
Deflation, as investment disadvantage, 12
Deglomerating forces, industrial buildings, 592
Demand, for real estate, 100
  and migration, 89–90

Demand analysis
  apartments, 529–531
  hotels and motels, 627
  industrial buildings, 591–592
  land investment, 652–653
  nursing homes, 639–640
  office buildings, 571–572
  shopping center, 549–550
  small rental housing, 616–617
  for specified use, 112–113
Demand indicators, urban space use, 102–103
Demand profiles, diversity, 724
Demand shifts, industrial buildings, 588
Depreciation
  and accelerated cost recovery system, 354–360
  claimed, 301
  deductions, and tax shelter strategy, 374–375
  hotels and motels, 634–635
  industrial building, 608
  recapture, and capital gain, 352–353
  and tax on sale of property, 306
  and tax shelter, 370
  of values, as investment disadvantage, 12
  write-offs, and tax shelter, 372
Depreciation information, cash flow data, 301–302
Depreciation schedules, Aspen Wood Apartments, 379
Descent, disposition of property by, 494–495
Desired rate of return on equity
  in financial feasibility model, 259
  industrial building, 608–609
  office building, 582–583
  shopping center, 561
Deterministic models, 675
  real estate investment, 63
Developer, as investment decision maker, 15–16
Development and design criteria matrix, hotels and motels, 629
Diegelman, David A., 354n
Differentiation, market, 627, 630
Direct utility approach, real estate investment, 64–65
Disability insurance, 712
Discounted cash flow
  most-likely output, and risk analysis, 322
  rate-of-return models, real estate investment, 62
Discounted cash flow (DCF) analysis, 194
  apartments, 537–538
  Aspen Wood Apartments, 297–309, 340, 383
  industrial building, 608–609
  land investments, 658–661
  office building, 582–583
  shopping center, 560–561
Discount rate, 285
Disposal of investment
  basis, 484–486
  defining gain or loss, 483–484
  in investment cycle, 478–480
  in ownership life cycle, 40

by sale, 486–491
  and tax planning, 482
  timing of closing, 482–483
Disposition of property
  by abandonment, 496
  by auction, 492
  by charitable contributions, 493
  diversity in, 724
  by exchange, 493
  financing purchaser to facilitate sale, 487–491
  by foreclosure, 498–500
  guidelines, 480–486
  involuntary conversions, 497–498
  options, 495–496
  partial, 492–493
  by sale, 486–491
  sale of personal residence, 493–494
  tax deeds, 496–497
  by will or descent, 494–495
Disqualification of participant, and exchange of property, 505
Distribution, 742
Ditmer, Robert, 656n, 740n, 741n
Diversification
  corporation, 229
  guidelines for, 723–724
  and ownership form, 216
  in reducing risk, 331
  and refinancing, 408
Dividend test, REIT, 235
Dollars and Cents of Shopping Centers, 458, 557
Downs, Anthony, 31n, 111n, 150n, 176n, 385n
Downs, James C. Jr., 142n, 449n, 451n
Downside risk, 319
Drucker, Peter F., 467n
Due-on-encumbrance clause, 394–395
Due-on-sale clause, 394
Dummy corporation, and ownership, 233–234
Duplex, 611
Dynamic business risk, 320

Earnings record, evaluating, 708
Earth science maps, 125
Eck, David Victor, 221n
Ecological concerns, industrial buildings, 589
Economic base analysis, 101–108
  abstract, 112
  to forecast growth in Atlanta, 108–111
Economic base ratio analysis, 102
Economic conditions, and portfolio, 667
Economic life, neighborhood properties, 123
Economic Recovery Tax Act (1981), 148, 238, 284, 343–344, 485, 494, 529, 581, 607, 635, 658
Economic standards, industrial building, 600–601
Economies of scale, and syndication offerings, 415–416
Edwards, Charles E., 255n
Effective marginal bracket, 347
Effective mortgage constant, 303

ficient diversification, portfolio, 667
ficient frontier, 672–673, 719
gbeer, William, 628n
dridge, Thomas, 566
ectrical installation, industrial building, 600
evators, industrial building, 601
mination, of risk, 330
lis, Robert M., 196n
wood valuation model of investment, 55–56, 57
npire State Building, sandwich lease, 406–407
MPIRIC model, regional planning, 118
nployees Retirement Income Security Act (ERISA) (1974), 665, 666–667
nployment
major shift, industrial building, 587
tenants, 618
nployment density, industrial building, 587
nployment rate, and new-job formation, 89
igineering expenditures, land ownership, 654
iglebrecht, T. D., 388n
trepreneur, 742, 744
trepreneurial leverage theory, 48
vironment, and industrial location, 80
vironmental factors
apartments, 533
hotels and motels, 631
industrial building, 601
nursing homes, 640
office building, 573–574
shopping center, 551–552
small rental properties, 618
vironmental impact statement, 125
vironmental quality, and land investment, 656
qual cash flow streams, and present value, 287–288
quipment trust certificates, industrial real estate, 606
quitable Life Assurance Society, Real Estate Account 8, 691
quity, 25
balancing, 506
conservation, 502
in investment analysis, 25
trading on, 479–480
quity buildup, small rental properties, 615
quity cash flow after tax, 303–305
quity cash flow before tax, 303
quity cash flow valuation model of investment, 54–55
quity cost, 309
quity dividend, 27
quity dividend rate, 59, 253–254
quity financing
compensation schemes for investors, 413–415
creative structures, 412–413
outlook, 737–738
and ownership form, 410–411
sources, 411–412

Equity investment, 25
lender requirements, special-use property, 624–625
maximum, in financial feasibility model, 259
Equity investor, 25
in industrial buildings, 590
and lender, 27–28
managing vs. passive, 17–19
strategy, 253
See also Investor
Equity kickers, 395–396
Equity position, current, 707
Equity real estate investment trusts (EREITS), 234, 666
and shopping ceners, 548
Equity value, 308–309
Erler, Raymond L., 388
Erosion, of leverage benefits, 389
Escalator clauses, lease, 458
in shifting risk, 330
Escrow accounts, required, 394
Estate building
corporation, 229
and exchange of property, 502
as investor motivation, 9
and ownership form, 216
Estate planning, 723
Estate tax, and ownership form, 215
Estey, Arthur S., 59n
Estoppel statements, 274
Etter, Wayne E., 389, 419n
Evaluation, 23
of property exchange, 506–509
of property manager's performance, 466–468
return/risk, 29
Evans, J., 702n
Ex ante model, 145
Excess depreciation, 302, 352
Excess investment interest, 362
Excess tax shelter, 371
Exchange, disposition of property by, 493
Exchange of property, 500–501
actual, 503–504
evaluating, 506–509
reasons for, 501–502
structuring considerations, 502–506
Exculpatory clause, 392
Executive Park, Atlanta, 566–567
Existing capture rate, 138
Existing properties, and inflation, 151–153
Expansion of portfolio, and refinancing, 408
Expected net appreciation, 322
Expected return, and variance, developing measures of, 673–676
Expected return on investment, and risk, 668
Expense(s)
analyzing variability in, 265–266
capitalization, and NOI, 273
forecasts, 139
hotels and motels, 628, 631
industrial building, 595, 598
office building, 579
operating vs. capital, 366
shopping centers, 553, 557
small rental properties, 615

Expense analysis, land ownership, 653
Experience Exchange Report of the Building Owners and Managers Association (BOMA) International, 575, 576–578
Expertise, management, and ownership form, 215–216
Exposure to risk, and disposal of investment, 479
External financial risk, 321
Extraordinary expenses, anticipating, 708, 710

Facilities nearby, effects on neighborhood, 123
Fair market value, 367
Fama, Eugene F., 10n, 141, 161n
Family partnership, 222–223
Farber, Sheldon, 625n
Farmers Home Administration (FmHA), Title V rural housing, 401
Feasibility, and feasibility analysis, 30–33
vs. appraisal, 33–35
vs. investment analysis, 25–35
See also Financial feasibility model
Feasibility research, 194
Aspen Wood Apartments, 335, 339–340
Federal Home Loan Bank Board, 613
Federal Reserve Board, 728
Feeding stage, personal portfolio, 699–700
Feldman, Sandor S., 430
Federal Home Loan Mortgage Corp. (FHLMC), residential appraisal form, 125, 126
Federal National Mortgage Association (FNMA), residential appraisal form, 125, 126
Federal Reserve Bank of St. Louis, 164
Federal Water Pollution Control Act (1972), 6
Feedback, investment, 25
Ferguson, Marily, 744n
Fertility rate, and population, 87
FHA Techniques of Housing Market Analysis, 531
Fiduciary relationship, investors, joint venture, 227–228
Field survey, competition, 131–135
Final sales contract, Aspen Wood Apartments, 444–447
Final settlement, and negotiations, 441–442
Financial decision approaches, to real estate investment, 53–59
Financial/economic study, 32–33
Financial feasibility model, 256–264
in analyzing property, 193
application, 264–271
developing detailed one-year pro forma, 271–275
formulas, 261
in negotiations, 431
in reducing risk, 331
revised, 260–264
and risk analysis, 322

Financial feasibility model **(Continued)**
  valuation of Aspen Wood Apartments using, 281–283
  See also Feasibility analysis; Financing
Financial institutions, outlook, 739
Financial levels, small rental properties, 615
Financially feasible site use, 127
Financial management rate of return (FMRR), 295–296
Financial objectives, vs. nonfinancial, 199
Financial package, Aspen Wood Apartments, 421–424
Financial planning, corporation, 229
Financial ratio analysis. **See** Ratio analysis
Financial risk, 320–321
  and IRR, 321
Financial structuring, and investment analysis, 191–195
Financial wealth, maximizing, 30
Financial worth, preparing statement of, 705–707
Financing
  apartments, 535–536
  decision model, 386–387
  hotels and motels, 634
  industrial building, 604–607
  land investments, 656–658
  neighborhood sources, 123
  office building, 579–581
  outlook, 737–739
  of purchaser to facilitate sale of property, 487–491
  shopping center, 557–559
  small rental properties, 622–623
  syndication offerings, 415–420
  See also Financial feasibility model
Financing costs
  apartments, 535–536
  small rental properties, 622–623
Financing terms, diversity, 724
Findlay, M. Chapman III, 67, 295, 296n, 668n, 676n, 683, 684, 742
Findlay-Messner rate of return, 295
Fireproof industrial building, 586
Fire protection, industrial building, 601
First-class industrial building, 598
First National Bank of Chicago, Fund F, 239
Fisher, Irving, 146
Fisher, Ted L., 388n
Five-year write-off, 360
Fixed option, 495
Flexibility, general partnership, 220
Flieller, James, 343
Floor area ratio, industrial building, 587
Floor loads, industrial building, 586
Floor space per floor, office building, 573
Footloose industries, location, 77–79
Forbes, 171, 173
Forecast, inflation, 162–164
Foreclosure, 395, 498–500
Foreign investors
  outlook, 738–739
  in shopping centers, 548

Forest land, unimproved, and inflation, 155
Form utility, 585
Forster, Pennell Kerr, 633n
Fortune, 593
Foundation work, office building, 573
Four-way benefit test, 48
Fox and Caskadon, 717
Fractional interests, 492
Fraud, discouragement, in syndication offerings, 418
Free and clear return, 253
Friedan, Bernard, 612
Friedman, Harris C., 10n, 67, 687, 717
Friedman, Jack, 481, 657n
Fringe benefits, corporation, 229
Full-credit option, 495
Full disclosure, syndication offerings, 418
Fully amortizing mortgage, 392
Functional obsolescence, overcoming, 451
Funds sources, industrial buildings, 604–605
Future population, and demand for urban space use, 102–103
Future value, 286

Gain
  allocation, and ownership form, 215
  defining, 483–484
  realized, 506
  recognized, 508
Gaines, James P., 676n, 683, 684
Galleria, Houston, 542, 544
Garden apartments, 524–525
Garrigan, Richard T., 262n
Gas installation, industrial building, 600
Gau, George W., 296n, 326n, 676n, 701, 702, 742
General and administrative expenses, shopping centers, 556
General business cycle, and real estate cycle, 170–171
General commercial office buildings, 571
General economic inflation, 143–145
General Electric Credit Corp., 739
Generalized model of investment value, 54
General ledger accounts, office building, 576–577
General partnership, 220–222
General-purpose industrial building, 586
Generative business, 81
Genetski, Robert J., 143, 147n
Geometric mean return, 668n
Ghiardelli Square, San Francisco, 542
Gibb, Jack R., 429
Gibbons, James E., 11
Gift, 494
  in contemplation of death, 494
  or trust, and tax shelter strategy, 375
Gift-trust/leaseback, 494–495
Gitman, Lawrence J., 322, 324n
GLITAMAD, property life cycle pyramid, 36–37

Glubetich, Dave, 623n
Goals, and personal portfolio, 703
Gobar, Al, 153n
Goebel, Paul R., 358n
Goggans, Travis P., 388
Government agency, and data on metropolitan areas, 85–86
Government controls
  as investment disadvantage, 12
  and ownership form, 216
Government-sponsored loan programs, 400–401
Graaskamp, James A., 3, 4, 5n, 31, 54n, 61n, 97, 320n, 329n, 676
Grace period, 395
Graduated payment mortgage (GPM), 399
Graduated rent, shopping center, 5?
Graham, Benjamin, 713
Grantor trust, 237
Grayson, C. Jackson Jr., 318n
Great American Growth Properties, Quad Cities, 548
Greenhut, Melvin L., 592n
Gross building area, 565
Gross income per leasable square foot, in financial feasibility model, 258
Gross lease, vs. net lease, 457
Gross national product price deflate 143
Gross possible income (GPI), in fina cial feasibility model, 258
Gross profit, 489–490
Gross profit percentage, 490
Gross rent multiplier (GRM), 314–3?
  real estate investment model, 61
  use in negotiations, 436
Ground lease, industrial building, 603
Growth potential, REIT, 236
Growth stage, personal portfolio, 7?
Guaranteed returns, equity investor, 414–415
Guntermann, Karl L., 6n, 75n

Half-year convention, 355, 357
Hall, Woodford L., 546
Hallmark Center, Kansas City, 652
Halper, Emanuel B., 392n
Halperin, Jerome Y., 230n, 351n, 401n
Halpern case, 503, 505
Halpin, Michael C., 142n, 174, 177
Hamel case, 499n
Hamilton, Carl W., 67, 676n,.683
Hammond, James H. Jr., 399
Hampden-Turner, Charles, 745n
Hanford, Lloyd D. Sr., 31, 60n
Haroldsen, Mark Oliver, 44n, 49
  approach, to real estate investment, 49–51
Harris, C. Jackson, 540n, 564n, 61(
Harris, Chauncy D., 75
Hawaiian technique, 412
Hayes, Perry, 408n
Hazard insurance, 712
Health, Education, and Welfare Department, Medicare certification form, 638
Health insurance, 710–711

ating, industrial building, 601
avy industries, location, 80
mmer, Edgar H., 676
nry Miller REIT, Dallas, 548
rd cycle, 175
rtz, David B., 326
cks, Tyler G., 44n
ggins, J. Warren, 301n, 350n, 363n
gh-credit-lease loan, 407
ghest and best use, in site analysis, 126–127
gh-rise apartments, 525–526
lton, Conrad, 50
lton, Hugh G., 157n
lton Head, South Carolina, 517, 651
nds, Dudley, 127n
nes, Mary Alice, 197n
te, Gailen L., 361n
ist, industrial building, 586
lding costs, land, 653–654
lding period return, 668n
lzman, Lee J., 213n, 221n, 231n, 233n
me
    as investment, 715
    market value, 706
    mortgage payable on, 707
    me furnishings, 706
    meowner, and inflation, 155–157
tel Astoria case, 499n
tels and motels, 625–626
    current operating income and expenses, 632–634
    financing, 634
    investing in, 626–627
    investment decision, 635–637
    investors and investor motivation, 627
    legal, political, and environmental factors, 631
    market and marketability analysis, 627–631
    market outlook for, 736–737
    physical analysis, 631
    property management, 631–632
    risk management, 634
    tax shelter, 634–635
tel management contract, 632
tine, Peter, 540n
ot market/overkill cycle, 174
useholds, composition, 88–90
ousing, market outlook for, 732–733
oward, Ronald A., 699n
ow-to approaches, to real estate investment, 45–53
oyt, Homer, 54n, 171n
ubbard, Elbert, 80n
udson Institute, 728
uff, David, 81n
uman nature, and negotiations, 433
unter, Jim, 523n, 564n
utton, E. F., 694
ybrid REITs, 234

Ikle, Fred C., 425
Illiquidity, as disadvantage, 10
Image, public, and ownership form, 216
Immigration, and population, 88
Impact model, regional planning, 118
Implicit price deflator, 143
Improvements, neighborhood, 123
Impulse goods, shopping center, 542
Imputed interest, 491
Incentives, property manager, 164
Income
    capital gain vs. ordinary, 348–353
    lender vs. equity investor, 27
    quality and variability, 707
    timing of, 364–366
    See also Net operating income (NOI); Rental income
Income analysis, land ownership, 653
Income averaging, and tax shelter strategy, 375
Income/expense analysis: apartments, 534
Income property
    commercial, and inflation, 158
    multifamily, and inflation, 157–158
Income tax
    deductions, and ownership form, 215
    formula, 344–347
Income-to-rent ratio, small rental properties, 620
Incorporated pocketbook, 230
Indexing
    and financing small rental properties, 622
    and portfolio selection, 686–687
Individual
    capital gain taxation, 348
    tax year, 364
Individual franchise owner, motivation, 627
Individual investors, need for property management, 450
Individual ownership, 218
Individual retirement account (IRA), 722
    and ownership, 239–240
Industrial buildings and parks, 585–587
    discounted cash flow analysis, 608–609
    financing and refinancing, 604–607
    investing in, 589–590
    investment decision, 609
    legal, political, and environmental analysis, 601
    market and marketability analysis, 591–598
    market outlook for, 732
    office, 571
    property management and leasing, 602–603
    risk management and control, 603–604

taxation and tax structure, 607–608
    trends, 587–589
Industrial land use competitive survey, 134–135
Industrial locations, 77–80
Industrial park, 588
    organized, 595
Industrial plant, 586
    layout, 598
Industrial real estate bonds, 605–607
Industrial sites, analyzing, 593
Industrial space, and demand for urban space use, 103
Inflation
    and commercial income property, 158
    and cycles, 141–147
    and existing properties, 151–153
    forecast, 162–164
    framework for forecasting, 162
    hedge, subordinated land leaseback, 405
    and homeowner, 155–157
    impact on investors and properties, 147–148
    as investment disadvantage, 12
    and leverage strategy, 150–151
    and mathematics of wealth transfer, 148–150
    measures of, 143–147
    and multifamily income property, 157–158
    and new properties, 151
    protection against, as investor motivation, 10
    and real estate investment, 728–729
    and time value of money, 285
    and unimproved land, 154–155
Inflation cycle, 159–161
    capital budgeting approach to strategy, 161–165
    and investment strategy, 158–165
    stages, 159
    See also Life cycle; Real estate cycles
Information
    lack, as investment disadvantage, 12
    on inflation, sources of, 164–165
Initial equity investment, 311
    and cash flow, 311–313
Initial no-prepayment period, 393
Installment sales, 488–491
    and tax shelter strategy, 375
Institute of Real Estate Management (IREM), 449, 451, 455, 462, 466
Institutional investor, 42
    in hotels and motels, 627
    in industrial buildings, 590–591
    need for property management, 450
    in shopping centers, 548
Institutional portfolio
    characteristics and performance, 690–695
    choice, 667–673

Institutional portfolio (**Continued**)
  problems and prospects, 695–696
  real estate vs. stock, 687–690
  See also Personal portfolio
Institutional second mortgages, 402
Insurance
  adequate, 710–712
  in shifting risk, 330
  shopping centers, 556
Insurance policy loans outstanding, 707
Integrity, and track record, 519
Interdependence, metropolitan areas, 84–85
Interest
  compound, 145
  deductions, and tax shelter strategy, 375
  imputed, 491
Interest-only loan, 391
Interest-only notes, 623
Interest, ownership form and transferability, 215, 224
Interest rate, and debt financing, 390–391
Interest rate method, of generating mortgage amortization schedule, 396–397
Internal financial risk, 321
Internal rate of return, 284, 290–293
  analysis, 306–309
  and business and financial risk, 321
  component analysis, 323
  model, real estate investment, 62–63
  modified, 293–296
  partitioning, and risk absorption analysis, 322
  See also Rate of return; Rate-of-return analysis
Internal Revenue Service
  audit, 367–368
  position on operating deductions, 366
International Association of Financial Planners, 725
Interval timesharing, 611
Intrastate offerings, 419
Inventory
  of assets, cost of producing, 704–705
  and property management, 460–461
  unsold, 113–114
Investment
  advantages and returns, 8–10
  in apartments, 528
  continuity, and exchange of property, 502
  disadvantages and risks, 10–13
  disposal as part of cycle, 478–480
  Ellwood valuation model, 55–56, 57
  equity cash flow valuation model, 54–55
  in hotel or motel, 626–627
  in income-producing property, 614

in industrial buildings, 589–590
  and investment analysis, 25–30
  in land, 651–652
  in nursing homes, 639
  in office buildings, 568
  participants in process, 13–19
  in shopping centers, 544–545
  vs. speculation, 19–20
  termination, Aspen Wood Apartments, 511–514
  transaction, 25
  See also Disposal of investment; Investment analysis; Land investments; Real estate investment
Investment analysis
  vs. appraisal, 33–35
  vs. feasibility analysis, 25–35
  and financial structuring, 191–195
  and investment, 25–30
  See also Investment; Real estate investment
Investment cost, vs. investment value, 53
Investment criteria, 190, 210–211
Investment decision
  apartments, 538
  Aspen Wood Apartments, 383–384
  hotels and motels, 635–637
  industrial building, 609
  nursing home, 641, 644
  office building, 583
  shopping center, 561
  small rental properties, 624
  time horizons for, 35–43
Investment environment, real estate, 4–5
Investment interest, limitations, 362–363
Investment objectives, 190, 197–200
  Aspen Wood Apartments, 210–211
Investment performance, and exchange of property, 501
Investment philosophy, 189, 195–196
  Aspen Wood Apartments, 207–211
Investment principles, 196–197
Investment real estate, 706, 714–715
Investment screening criteria, 86
Investment strategy, 189
  determination of, 193
  developing, 195–203
  framework, 189
  and inflation cycle, 158–165
  terminology, 189–191
Investment tax credits, and tax shelter strategy, 375
Investment time horizon, lender vs. equity investor, 27–28
Investment value
  decision rule, 53–54
  generalized model, 54
  real estate investment approach, 53–56
  using in negotiations, 436–437
Investors
  in apartments, 528–529

compensation schemes, 413–415
  counseling, and property management, 449
  fiduciary relationship, joint venture, 227–228
  hotels and motels, 627
  industrial building, 590–591
  land, 652
  life cycle, 40–42, 175
  market data sources, 179–183
  monthly reports, Aspen Wood Apartments, 471
  motivations, 8–13
  objectives, and exchange of property, 501
  office buildings, 569
  performing management duties, and NOI, 274
  shopping centers, 545, 548
  strategy on operating deductions, 366
  tax shelter game plan, 370
  See also Equity investor
Investor utility curve, 672–673
Involuntary conversions, 497–498
Involuntary disposition of investment, 480
Involvement, direct vs. indirect, 196
Irrevocable trust, 237
Isoquants, 672

Jaffe, Austin J., 290n, 450n, 464n, 481n
Jaffe, Jeffrey, 161n
Jean, William H., 293n
Jerrimad, B., 156n
JMB Properties, Ltd., 694, 695
Johnson, Irvin E., 55
Johnson, Robert, 285n
Joint Commission on Accreditation of Hospitals and Long-Term Care Facilities, 638
Joint tenancy, 218–219
Joint venture, 227–228, 268–269, 411
  Aspen Wood Apartments, 244–245
  land developers and investors, 652
Joint venture partner, as investment decision maker, 16
Jones, Charles, 668n
Judgment, and track record, 519–520
Junior mortgage, debt financing, 401–406

Kahn, Sanders A., 570n
Kamath, Ravindra, 400n
Kapplin, Steven D., 63n, 317n, 665n, 676n, 686
Kau, James B., 361n, 367n, 371
Keeney, Ralph L., 128n
Kelleher, Dennis G., 157n, 688–689
Kelley, Edward N., 462n, 534n
Kelting, Herman, 320n
Keogh plan, 722
  and ownership, 239–240
Kerwood, Lewis O., 247n, 329n
Key ratios, shopping center, 554
Killian Co. case, 499n
King, Donald A. Jr., 187n

nnard, William, 592
ntner regulations, 224
e Kiplinger Report, 171
ein, Roger, 19n, 143n, 147n, 149n, 160
emkosky, Robert, 702
1ab, Donald, 695
1ight, F. H., 318n
hlhepp, Daniel B., 296n, 326n, 676n, 701, 702, 742
sarowich, John T., 238n
atovil, Robert, 499n
aus, Egon H., 404
snet, Jack, 26n, 213n, 221n, 231n, 233n, 240n, 403n

bor market area, 104
den, Ben E., 154n
ke City, Florida, 626
nd
  holding costs, 653–654
  investors and investor motivation, 652
  subordinated leasebacks, 405–406
  See also Land investments
nd contracts, 488
  in shifting risk, 330
nd deal, anatomy of, 658–661
nd investments, 647–648, 651–652
  discounted cash flow analysis, 658–661
  financing, 656-658
  market and marketability analysis, 652–654
  physical, legal, political, and environmental analysis, 655–656
  risk management and control, 654–655
  taxation and tax structure, 658
  track record and trends, 648–651
nd use
  dominant factors, 77
  life cycle stages, 173
  in metropolitan areas, 74–77
  multiple-nuclei theory, 75
  patterns and controls, industrial buildings, 588–589
  and principle of comparative locational advantage, 77–82
  and urban cartography, 76–77
ngford, Janelle, 691, 692n
tane, Harry, 668n
w
  of contrary opinion, 176–177
  See also Tax law
wson, Fred R., 629n, 630n
yout and construction, industrial plant, 598–600
ase
  negotiations and terms, 456–459
  special concessions, and NOI, 274
aseback
  sale and, 487
  subordinated, 405–406
ase guarantee insurance, industrial building, 607
asehold approach, multiclass equity structures, 412–413

Lease-purchase contract, as debatable deduction, 367
Leasing
  apartments, 533
  industrial building, 602–603
  management, office building, 574
  shopping center, 552
Legal certainty, corporation, 229
Legal complexity, as investment disadvantage, 12
Legal expenditures, land ownership, 654
Legal factors
  apartments, 533
  hotels and motels, 631
  industrial building, 601
  land investment, 655
  nursing homes, 640
  office building, 573–574
  shopping center, 551–552
  small rental properties, 618
Legally permissible site use, 127
Legal/political barriers, neighborhood, 122
Legal study, 32
Leider, Arnold, 403
Lender, 25
  debt coverage ratio and mortgage constant desired by, 558, 580, 607
  equity investment requirements special-use properties, 624–625
  and equity investor, 27–28
  as investment decision maker, 16–17
  risk control and management, 536, 558–559, 580–581
Letter of intent, 335, 336–338
Leverage, 25
  criteria, 210
  and inflation, 150–151
  as investor motivation, 9
  in land investment financing, 657
  positive and negative, 254–256, 311
  and real estate investment, 50–51
  and tax shelter, 372–373, 375
Leverage decision, debt financing, 387–389
Leverage position, 300
Levi, Donald R., 419n
Levitt, William, 611
Liability, 25, 706–707
  limited, and ownership form, 215
Liberty Mirror Works case, 499n
Licensure, nursing homes, 638
Life cycle
  investor, 40–42
  ownership, 39–40
  personal portfolio, 699–701
  property, 35–39
  See also Inflation cycle; Real estate cycle
Life insurance, 710
  cash value, 706
Life Safety Code, nursing homes, 638
Like-kind properties, exchange of, 504–505
Limited liability
  corporations, 228
  and ownership form, 215

Limited partnership, 223–226
  real estate portfolios, 694–695
  in shifting risk, 330
Limited tax shelter, REIT, 236
Lindeman, J. Bruce, 154n
Linked audit, 219
Lintner, John, 161n
Liquidity
  and disposal of investment, 479
  and refinancing, 408
Liquidity reserves, 706, 713–714, 718
Listening, in negotiations, 430
Little, John D. C., 128n
Livingston, Richard J., 359n
Living trust, 237
Loan, 25
  amount and terms, in reducing risk, 330–331
  government-sponsored programs, 400–401
  multiple, 268–269
Loan amortization, 322
Loan approach, multiclass equity structures, 412–413
Loan balance
  as percent of original cost and property value, 313–314
  sales price, tax basis, and, 373
Loan information, cash flow data, 302–303
Loan-to-value ratio, industrial building, 607
Loan schedules, Aspen Wood Apartments, 379–380
Loan term, 390
Local markets, real estate, 100
Location
  criteria, 211
  hotel or motel, 626, 627, 628–629
  industrial buildings, 592
  and marketability, 121
  in market analysis, 97
  office building, 570
  real estate, 98–99
  in reducing risk, 331
  small rental properties, 616–617
Lock-in period, 393
Long, Clarence D., 171n
Long cycle, 165–166
Long-range goals, and personal portfolio, 703
Long-term capital gain, conditions for treatment as, 348–352
Long-term leases, with escalation clauses, in shifting risk, 330
Long-term liabilities, 707
Loss
  allocation, 215
  defining, 483–484
  casualty, 498
Lot sales, subdivision, 492
Lowenstern, Hugo H., 341n
Low-rise apartments, 525
Lowry, Albert J., 44n, 466n
Loye, David, 432n
Lucas v. **North Texas Lumber Co.,** 495n
Lusht, Kenneth M., 141–142, 157, 254n, 311n, 388n
Lyon, Victor L., 62n, 293n

Macromarket analysis, 100
Macro real estate cycles, 165–166
Mader, Chris, 142n
Maintenance
common areas, shopping center, 555
deferred, and NOI, 272
Maintenance plan, developing, 452–453
Maisel, Sherman J., 12n, 142n, 167n
Major institutions, office buildings for, 571
Major-shift employment, industrial building, 587
Major tenants, shopping center, 542
Malabre, Alfred L. Jr., 148n
Malat v. Riddell, 492n
Mall, shopping center, 542
Management
centralization, corporation, 228
control and expertise, and ownership form, 215–216
and control of risk, 329–331
defining scope of services, 462–465
duties performed by investor, and NOI, 274
office building, 574
organization, Aspen Wood Apartments, 470
style and functions, 196
See also Property management; Risk management and control
Management burden, as disadvantage, 10–11
Management fee, subordination, 414
Management plan, 136–137
IREM, 451
Managing equity investor, as decision maker, 17–18
Mandelker, Gershon, 161n
Mandell, Lewis, 80n
Mao, James C. T., 293n
Mapping, computer techniques, 76
Marginal tax rate, investor, and tax shelter strategy, 375
Market
analyzing ripeness, 482
characterization in negotiations, 436
geographic boundaries, 129
real estate, 98–100
standard reports, 132–133
Marketability
and ownership form, 215
and refinancing, 408
Marketability analysis
apartments, 529–532
defined, 120–121
field survey of competition, 131–135
hotels and motels, 627–631
industrial buildings, 591–598
land investment, 652–654
location, neighborhood, and site, 121
market absorption and capture rates, 137–139
marketing strategy and management plan, 135–137
and neighborhood analysis, 122–123

and neighborhood boundaries, 122
office buildings, 571–573
revenue and expense forecasts, 139
shopping center, 549–551
site analysis in, 124–130
small rental properties, 615–618
Market absorption rate, 114–115, 137
Market analysis, 32
apartments, 529–532
hotels and motels, 627–631
industrial buildings, 591–598
land investment, 652–654
office building, 571–573
real estate, 97
shopping center, 549–551
small rental properties, 615–618
Market area, delineation, 112
Market basket, 144
Market capture rates, 138–139
Market data, for real estate investors, 179–183
Market demand, indicators, 115
Market growth index, 130
Market-indexed loans, and risk, 330
Marketing and merchandising space, and property management, 453–455
Marketing strategy, 135–136
Market-oriented industries, location, 77
Market potential index, 130
Market promotion, and property management, 449
Market-related risk, vs. business-related risk, portfolio, 670–672
Market risk, and personal portfolio, 701
Market studies
current market conditions, 113–114
defined, 100–101
descriptive analysis, 111–116
economic base analysis, 101–108; abstract, 112
market area delineation, 112
projections of rent schedules, prices, and space needs, 114–116
supply and demand analysis for specified use, 112–113
Market trading area, shopping center, 542
Market value, 33–34
vs. investment value, 53
using in negotiations, 436–437
Markowitz, Harry M., 67, 667, 669–670
Marquardt, Raymond, 146n, 161n
Marshall, Richard D., 150n
Martin, Robert, 702n
Mason, oseph B., 81n
Master prospectus, syndication offering, 417
Master strategy, personal portfolio, 718–724
Materials-oriented industries, location, 77
Mathews case, 495n
Maturity, neighborhood, 123
Maximizing, vs. satisficing, in negotiations, 429

Maximum equity investment, in financial feasibility model, 259
Maximum loan, formula, 250–252
Maximum offering price, in financial feasibility model, 260
Mayer, Martin, 523
McLeister, Kathleen, 656n
McMahan, John, 131n, 142n, 452, 462n
McNeil, Robert, 519
McNeil Real Estate Fund, 717
Measurement
of inflation, 145–146
of return and risk, 23, 29
Medicaid, 637
Medical/dental office buildings, 571
Medical Economics, 722
Medicare, 637
certification form, 638
Member Appraisal Institute (MAI), 451
Merchandising
of industrial space, 602
vs. selling, 453
Merchandising study, 32
Merchants' association, shopping center, 543
Merit review, 420
Merrill Lynch, Pierce, Fenner & Smith Inc., 694
Messner, Stephen D., 31n, 62n, 6, 111n, 121n, 293n, 295, 296, 592n, 668n, 676n, 683, 742
Metro market economic base analysis, 106–108
Metropolitan area
and age of migration, 89–91
competition and interdependence, 84–85
defined, 72–73
growth and decline, 82–85
growth patterns, 73–82
land use, 74–77
risks in developing and investing in, 740–742
size stratification, 735
target, search for, 85–91
Middle-age investor, 41
Mid-rise apartments, 525
Migration, age of, 89–91
Migratory shift, 587
Miles, Mike E., 59n, 466n, 486n, 675n, 689, 691, 692n, 701
Mill construction, industrial building, 587
Miner, John B., 188n, 467n
Minimum cash-flow-through-leaseback arrangement, 414
Minimum tax, 360–361
Miscellaneous assets, 706
Miscellaneous liabilities, 707
MLH Properties, 694
Modernization
feasibility, office building, 573
and property management, 451
Modified internal rate of return (MIRR), 293–296
Monetary Trends, 164
Money, time value of, 285
Money, 171
Monte Carlo simulation, 65–67, 673
and risk analysis, 326–329

ontgomery, J. Thomas, 29n, 30n, 33n, 329n
oore, Charles T., 81n
oore, George, 128n
orris, Jackson L., 418n
orrison, Cathy A., 326n
ortgage
 amortization schedule, 396–398
 in disposal of investment, 485–486
 loan amount, in financal feasibility model, 259
 loan maturity, industrial building, 607
 terms, in negotiation with seller, 334
e Mortgage and Real Estate Executives Report, 164, 691
ortgage bonds, industrial real estate, 605
ortgage constant (K)
 and amortization schedule, 397–398
 and debt coverage ratio, 248–253
 in financial feasibility model, 259
 industrial building, 607
 and interest rate, 390–391
 office building, 580
 shopping center, 558
ortgaged out, 389
ortgage money cycle, 171–172
ortgage payable
 on home, 707
 on other real estate, 707
ortgage REITs, 234
oses, Edward A., 686
ost probable selling price, 33, 34
 vs. investment value, 53
 using in negotiations, 436–437
otels. See Hotels and motels
otivation of investor, 8–13
 in apartments, 528–529
 in hotels and motels, 627
 in industrial buildings, 590–591
 in land, 652
 in office buildings, 569
 in shopping centers, 545, 548
t. Laurel case, 740
ove-ins, tenants, 460
ove-outs, tenants, 460
ulticlass equity structures, 412–413
ultifamily income property, and inflation, 157–158
ultiple corporations, 230–231
ultiple loans, 268–269
ultiple-nuclei theory, land use, 75
ultiple-property offerings, syndication, 415–416
ultiple-rate-of-return problem, 293
ultiuse shopping center, 543

aive diversification, portfolio, 667
-asset calculus model, real estate, 681–685
ational Association of Home Builders, 612
ational Association of REALTORS®, 613
 Institute of Real Estate Management, 534

National Institute of Farm and Land Brokers, 657
National Environmental Policy Act (NEPA) (1969), 6, 125
National Fire Protection Association, 638
National/international markets, real estate, 99
National Real Estate Investor, 164
National Realtors Marketing Institute (NRMI), 451
Natural barriers, neighborhood, 122
Negative leverage, 254–256, 311
Negative tax shelter, 371–372
Negotiations
 achieving objectives, 435–441
 checklist, 442–443
 ending, 441–442
 estimating range of offers and counteroffers, 437–438
 for financial package, Aspen Wood Apartments, 421–424
 getting what you bargained for, 438–440
 lease, 456–459
 with property manager, 465–466
 psychology of, 432–435
 role of, 426–432
 with seller, 193, 194; Aspen Wood Apartments, 334–335
 site of, 434–435
Neighborhood
 boundaries, and marketability, 122
 economic and demographic profile, 127–130
 and marketability, 121–123
 real estate cycles, 173–174
 shopping center, 541
Nelson, Charles R., 161n
Net cash position analysis, Aspen Wood Apartments, 381–383
Net equity reversion, 484
Net income after debt service, 27
Net lease, vs. gross lease, 457
Net leased property, investment interest limitations, 363
Net monetary creditor, 149
Net monetary debtor, 140
Net operating income (NOI)
 detailed one-year pro forma, 271–275
 distortions in, 272–275
 division, lender vs. equity investor, 27
 in financial feasibility model, 258, 259
 in investment analysis, 26–27
 ratio of to property value, 314
 ratio of to total property cost, 311
 See also Income; Rental income
Net present value (NPV), 62, 289, 309
 annualized, 323
Net rentable area, office building, 565
Net sale proceeds, 484
 projection, Aspen Wood Apartments, 383, 384
Net selling price, 306
Net tax payable, and income tax formula, 347
Net worth, 25, 379, 707
 availability for investment, 710
 and limited partnership, 225

New concept/market overkill cycle, 174
New properties, and inflation, 151
Nickerson, William, 44n, 45–47, 52
Nierenberg, Gerard J., 425, 426, 428n
Nominal rate of return, 146–147
Nominee corporation, and ownership, 233–234
Noncorporate ownership, 217–228
Nonfinancial objectives, vs. financial, 199
Nonguaranteed returns, equity investor, 414–415
Non-owner-occupied property, financing, 622
Nonrecourse mortgages, in avoiding or eliminating risk, 330
Nonspecified property offerings, syndication, 416
North, Lincoln, W., 20n
Northridge Fashion Center, Northridge, Calif., 544
No tax shelter, 371
Notes receivable, 706
Nursing homes
 definitions, 637–639
 investing in, 639
 investment decision, 641, 644
 legal, political, and environmental factors, 640
 physical analysis, 640
 property management, 640–641
 supply and demand analysis, 639–640
 tax shelter, 641
Nursing hours, 638–639

OBERS projection, 106, 109
Obligations, of tenant, 459
Occupancy, and self-use, as investor motivation, 9
Occupancy rate, neighborhood, 123
Offer, estimating range in negotiations, 437–438
Offering price, maximum, in financial feasibility model, 260
Office area services, shopping centers, 555
Office buildings
 definitions, 565
 discounted cash flow analysis, 582–583
 financing and refining, 579–581
 investing in, 568
 investment decision, 583
 investors and investor motivations, 569
 market and marketability analysis, 571–573
 market outlook for, 733–734
 operations analysis, 574–579
 physical, legal, political, and environmental analysis, 573–574
 returns and risks, 569–570
 taxation and tax structure, 581–582
 track record and trends, 565, 568
Office competitive survey, 134
Office park, 565
Offshore trust, ownership, 238
Older investor, 41–42

Omni-Mega structure, Atlanta, 519
Onassis, Aristotle, 50
100 times formula, real estate investment, 51
150 percent declining-balance method, depreciation, 357
175 percent declining-balance method, depreciation, 357
Open-end offerings, syndication, 416–417
Open-end sales contract, 491
Operating assumptions, Aspen Wood Apartments, 380–381
Operating costs, and inflation, 150–151
Operating deductions, 366–367
Operating expense(s)
  vs. capital expenses, 366
  nursing home, 641, 642–643
  small rental property, 620–621
  and tax shelter strategy, 375
Operating expense ratios, 315
Operating income
  nursing home, 641, 642–643
  small rental property, 620–621
Operating management, special-use properties, 625
Operating period, tax shelter, 374–375
Operating revenue, and tax shelter strategy, 375
Operating statements, Aspen Wood Apartments, 472–476
Operating yield, as investor motivation, 9
Operations
  cash flow from, 27
  and management of property, 449, 459–462
  nursing home, 641, 642–643
  in ownership life cycle, 40
Operations analysis
  apartments, 533–535
  office building, 574–579
  shopping center, 552–557
Operations leverage, in debt financing, 388
Operations report, multitenant industrial building, 599
OPM (other people's money) formula, 50–51
Oppenheimer, 694
Opportunity cost, 285
Option, 495–496
Optional investment fund, 706
Ordinary annuity, 287
Ordinary income, vs. capital gain income, 348–353
Organized industrial parks, 594
Original basis, in disposal of investment, 484
Orrisch case, 500n
Other people's money, 25
  and OPM formula, 50–51
  pyramiding with, 46
Other tangible personal property, 706
Overage, 458
Overall capitalization rate, 314
Overall rate, 253
Owner, family partnership, 222–223
Owner-investor, industrial building, 606

Owner-occupant, industrial building, 606
Owner-occupied office building, 565
Owner-occupied property, financing, 622
Owner's cash investment, 25
Ownership, 707
  alternatives, 212–213
  corporations, 228–234
  decision model, 213
  and equity financing, 410–411
  general partnership, 220–222
  individual, 218
  joint tenancy, 218–219
  joint venture, 227–228
  limited partnership, 223–226
  noncorporate forms, 217–228
  real estate investment, 723–724
  real estate syndication, 240
  REIT, 234–236
  selection criteria, 214–217
  tenancy in common, 219
  trusts, 234–240
Ownership decision matrix, Aspen Wood Apartments, 242–244
Ownership life cycle, 39–40, 175
  optimizing, 480–482

Packager/syndicator, as investor, 13
Parisse, Alan, 240n, 417n
Parking, office building, 573
Part(s), and property management, 460–461
Partial disposition of property, 492–493
Partially amortizing mortgage, 391
Partial tax shelter, 371
Participants, in investment process, 13–19
Participations, 395–396
Partners
  joint venture, as investment decision maker, 16
  in negotiations, 435
Partnership
  family, 222–223
  general, 220–222
  tax year, 364
Passive equity investor, as decision maker, 18–19
Passive income tests, REIT, 235
Passive investor, 13
Payback, 305
Payback period model, real estate investment, 61
Pellatt, Peter G. K., 67, 674, 682, 684
Pension funds, real estate portfolios, 690–691
Pension rights, vested, 706
Pension trusts, 238–239
Percentage changes, in CPI, 144
Percentage lease, 458
Percentage rent
  shopping center, 552, 553
  subordinated land leaseback, 405
Perfectly negatively correlated assets, 669
Perfectly positively correlated assets, 668
Permanence potential, in selecting tenant, 456

Permanent lender, as investment decision maker, 16–17
Personal audit, and portfolio, 70, 718
Personal control, as investor motivation, 8–9
Personal financial plan, developing and implementing, 702–725
Personal holding company, 230
Personal liability, debt financing, 392–393
Personal loan, 407
Personal philosophy
  developing, 703
  reassessing, 718
Personal portfolio
  building strategy, 699–702
  identifying objectives, 717
  life cycle, 699–701
  managing risk in, 701–702
  naive vs. efficient, 719–722
  and personal financial plan, 70, 725
  See also Institutional portfolio
Personal property
  depreciation, 355, 357
  tangible, 706
  useful life, 358
Personal residence, sale of, 493–4
Personal situation audit, and person portfolio, 703–708
Peter Fuller Enterprises v. Manche ter Savings Bank, 393n
Peters, Clarence, 629n
Peterson, Robert A., 81n
Pfouts, Ralph, 102n
Phantom taxable gain, 485
Physical factors
  apartments, 532
  hotels and motels, 631
  land investments, 655
  nursing homes, 640
  office building, 573
  shopping center, 551
  small rental properties, 618
Physically possible site use, 127
Plan, 190
Planned industrial district, 588
Planned-unit developments (PUD), 5
Planning controls, neighborhood, 1
Planning phase, Haroldsen real esta investments, 49–50
Plans and policies, 201–203
  Aspen Wood Apartments, 211
Plant, layout and construction, 598 600
Plant area, industrial, 586
Plant site, industrial, 586
Point(s), debt financing, 392
Point estimate, 742
Police powers, to regulate private property, 5–6
Policy, 190
Political factors
  apartments, 533
  hotels and motels, 631
  industrial building, 601
  land investment, 656
  nursing homes, 640
  office buildings, 573–574
  shopping centers, 551–552
  small rental properties, 618

ole, John, 610n
or Richard's Almanac, 19
pularity cycle, real estate, 175
pulation
  aging, 88
  metropolitan areas, 86–87
  projections, 106
  redistribution, 730–731
rtfolio
  analysis, 67–68
  diversification, 408
  expansion, 408
rtfolio selection, 676–681
  adaptation, 686–687
  simplified approach, 685–686
rtfolio theory
  extended development, 681–687
  and large institutional investors, 687–696
  modern, 670–673
  and real estate investment, 673–681
rtman, John, 519
sitive leverage, 254–256, 311
ssible variability, of cash inflows, 141
tential capture rate, 138
wers, of property manager, 463–464
epayment penalty, 393–394
epayment provisions, debt financing, 393–394
esent value (PV), 284, 285–290
  analysis, 306–309
  and mortgage amortization schedule, 398
  real estate investment model, 61–62
esent value of 1 per period, 287, 288
ice, Donald, 146n, 161n
ice
  apartments, 535
  in excess of market value, as debatable deduction, 367
  projections, 114–116
  in reducing risk, 331
  and terms of sale, tax shelter strategy, 375
ice-level-adjusted mortgage (PLAM), 399
imary trading area, shopping center, 542, 549–550
ivacy, and ownership form, 216
ivate offerings, 418
obabilistic model, real estate investment, 63
obabilistic rate-of-return model, 327
ocess changes, and industrial buildings, 588
oducer price index (PPI), 144
ofessional insurance, 712
ofessional office building, 565
ofessional property management, 449–450
ofessionals
  in negotiations, 435
  property management, 449–450
ofitability index (PI), 54, 289–290, 309
ofitability ratios, 311–313

Profit à prendre, 493
Profit-sharing rights, vested, 706
Profit statement, office building, 578
Project, existing vs. development, 31–32
Projections, of rent schedules, prices, and space needs, 114–116
Property
  life cycle, 35–39, 175
  selection, 518–521
  types, 516
  See also Disposal of property; Exchange of property; Property management; Real estate; Real estate cycles; Real estate investment
Property information, cash flow data, 300
Property Investment Separate Account (PRISA), 198, 239, 691, 693
Property management, 17, 195
  apartments, 533
  Aspen Wood Apartments, 469–477
  capital additions policy, 453
  defined, 448–450
  hotels and motels, 631–632
  industrial building, 602–603
  lease negotiations and terms, 456–459
  maintenance plan, 452–453
  marketing and merchandising space, 453–455
  need for, 450
  nursing homes, 640–641
  and operation, 459–462
  planning use of space, 450–452
  process, 450–462
  professional, 449–450
  in reducing risk, 331
  selecting tenants, 455–456
  shopping center, 552
  small rental property, 618–620
  See also Management
Property manager
  evaluating performance of, 466–468
  as investor, 14
  negotiation with, 465–466
  scope of services, 462–465
  selecting, 462–466
Property-specific cycles, real estate, 174
Property usage, and competition, 269–270
Property value at end of year, in cash flow analysis, 306
Proration, of closing costs, Aspen Wood Apartments, 445
Prospectus, syndication offering, 417
Protection system, industrial building, 601
Prudential Life Insurance Co., 198, 407
  Property Investment Separate Account (PRISA), 198, 239, 691, 693
Psychology, of negotiations, 432–435
Public development agencies, as industrial building investors, 591
Public image
  corporation, 229
  and ownership form, 216

Public Law 89-97 (1966), 637
Purchase money junior mortgage, 402–403
Purchase money mortgage, 487–488
  in land investment financing, 657
Purchaser
  conditions required in negotiations, 438–441, 445
  financing to facilitate sale of property, 487–491
Purchasing policy, statement of, 204
Pyhrr, Stephen A., 28n, 63n, 142, 221n, 247n, 298n, 326n, 377n, 421n, 450n, 481, 675, 742
Pyramid, property life cycle, 36–39
Pyramiding with other people's money, 46
Pyramid properties, and refinancing, 408

Quadruplex, 611
Qualifying limitations, investment tax credits, 361–362
Qualifying properties, in exchange, 504
Quality, and marketability, 121
Quantity, and marketability, 121
Quasi-industrial office buildings, 571
Quirin, G. David, 318n

Rabinowitz, Alan, 165n, 166, 171n
Rahenkamp, John, 656, 740n, 741n
Rail installation, industrial building, 600
Raimer, Russell B., 400n
Rand Corp., 728
Range of sales and rentals, neighborhood, 123
Ranking, of objectives, 200
Ratcliff, Richard, 22, 34n, 53n, 64, 326n
Rate
  inflation, 144
  office building financing, 579–580
  shopping center financing, 557
Rate of return
  acceptable, 717–718
  of alternative investments, 481
  approach, to real estate investment, 48, 56–59
  calculation models, 58–59
  criteria, 210
  decision rule, 57–58
  and disposal of investment, 479
  real vs. nominal, 146–147
  See also Internal rate of return; Rate-of-return analysis
Rate-of-return analysis
  apartments, 537
  industrial building, 608
  office building, 582–583
  shopping center, 560
  small rental properties, 623
Rate of return on equity (ROE), 253–254
  achievable, 50
  after tax, 311
  cumulative probability distribution curve, 328
Rate of return on total capital (ROR), 253

Ratio analysis, 309–315
  apartments, 537-538
  Aspen Wood Apartments, 383–384
  assumption base ratios, 314–315
  economic base, 102
  hotels and motels, 635
  industrial building, 609
  office building, 583
  profitability ratios, 311–313
  risk, 64
  risk ratios, 313–314
  shopping center, 554, 561
  small rental properties, 623–624
Ratio of vacancy and operating expense to gross income, in financial feasibility model, 258
Reading Station, Philadelphia, 542
Real estate
  activities, and ownership form, 215
  defined, 3–6
  demand, and migration, 89–90
  financing outlook, 737–739
  forecast for, 729
  investment environment, 4–5
  investor motivations, 8–13
  market outlook, 730–737
  N-asset calculus model, 681–685
  opportunities, 6–8
  as space and money over time, 4
  as stewardship, 5–6
  See also Investment; Property; Real estate cycle; Real estate investment
The Real Estate Analyst, 165
Real estate cycle
  in avoiding and eliminating risk, 330
  causes and dynamics, 167–170
  construction, 171
  and general business cycle, 170–171
  and inflation, 141–147
  as investment disadvantage, 12
  macro, 165–166
  mortgage money, 171–172
  neighborhood, 173–174
  popularity, 175
  property-specific, 174
  seasonal, 175
  social change, 175–176
  strategies for dealing with, 176–177
  urban area and city, 172–173
  See also Inflation cycle; Life cycle; Real estate; Real estate investment
Real estate inflation, 144–145
Real Estate Investing Letter, 164
Real estate investment
  best-fit approach, 59–61
  capital budgeting approaches, 61–68
  diversification guidelines, 723–724
  financial decision approaches, 53–59
  framework for studies, 23–25
  how-to approaches, 45–53
  and inflation, 728–729
  internal-rate-of-return model, 62–63
  investment value approach, 53–56

and portfolio theory, 673–681
  present value model, 61–62
  rate-of-return approach, 56–59
  risk analysis models, 63–68
  scenarios in strategy and planning, 742–745
  and Subchapter S, 232–233
  See also Investment; Portfolio; Portfolio theory; Real estate
Real estate investment trust (REIT), 234–236, 665–666
  real estate portfolios, 691–694
Real estate investors. See investors
Real estate market analysis, 97
Real Estate Review, 688
Real internal rate of return, 146–147
Realized gain, in property exchange, 506
Real property
  depreciation, 355, 357
  useful life, 358
  tax, 344
Realtors National Marketing Institute (RNMI), 506
Reappraisal clauses, lease, 458–459
Reasonably probable site use, 126
Recapture
  in exchange of property, 509
  of original equity, 322
Recognized gain, in property exchange, 508
Record keeping, and property management, 461–462
Record maintenance, 708
Recovery deduction, 354
Recovery periods, 358
Redeveloped land, industrial, 595
Redford, K. J., 188n
Reduction, of risk, 330–331
Reed, John T., 410n
References, tenants, 618
Refinancing, 407–410
  apartments, 535–536
  industrial building, 604–607
  office building, 579–581
  shopping center, 557–559
  small rental properties, 622–623
Reforms, tax law, and tax shelter, 373
Refurbishing, and refinancing, 408
Regional data, 145
Regional markets, real estate, 99–100
Regional planning models, 117–119
Regional shopping center, 541
Registration, syndication offerings, 418
Regular (Subchapter C) corporations, 228–231
Regular return, and ownership form, 216
Regulation, of syndicates, 417–420
Regulation A, SEC, 419
Rehabilitation, and property management, 451
Rehabilitation expenditures, and investment tax credits, 362
Reiling, Williams S., 411n
Reilly, Frank K., 146n, 161n
Reilly's law of retail gravitation, 81
Reimbursement for taxes, subordinated land leaseback, 405

Reindustrialization, 731
Relationship of parties, and exchar of properties, 504
Remaining principal, 302–303
Renegotiated rate mortgage (RRM), 249, 399
Renovation, and refinancing, 408
Rent
  analyzing variability in, 265–268
  estimates, shopping center, 553
  and inflation, 150–151
  range, neighborhood, 123
  subordinated land leaseback, 405
Rental income
  apartments, 531–532
  hotel and motel projections, 6, 631
  industrial building projections, 595, 598
  nursing home projections, 640
  office building projections, 572
  shopping center projections, 550
  small rental property projectio 617–618
  See also Income; Net operating come (NOI)
Rental properties. See Small ren properties
Rent schedules, projections, 114–1
Rent-up guarantee, 414
Replacement period, 498
Replacement reserves, and NOI, 27
Reporting requirements, governme and ownership form, 216
Reports to investors, Aspen Wood Apartments, 471
Reputation, neighborhood, 123
Research
  feasibility, 194; Aspen Wood Apa ments, 335, 339–340
  financial feasibility, in reducing risk, 331
Reserves
  cash, 712–713
  liquidity, 713–714
Residential appraisal form, FHLM/ FNMA, 125, 126
Residential competitive survey, 131
Residential hotels, 626
Residential locations, 81–82
Residential rental property, deprec tion, 357
Residual net cash flow, nursing hom 644
Resort hotels, 626
Retail/commercial competitive survey, 134
Retail gravitation, Reilly's law of, 8
Retirement, and tax planning, 72 723
Retirement fund
  corporation, 229
  and ownership form, 217
Return(s)
  apartments, 529
  diversification, and syndication ferings, 415
  level of, 708
  office buildings, 569–570
  and refinancing, 409–410
  regular, and ownership form, 216
  and risk management, 30

shopping centers, 548–549
small rental properties, 614–615
See also Internal rate of return;
    Rate of return; Rate-of-return
    analysis
urn/risk evaluation, in DCF analy-
    sis, 340
enue forecasts, 139
erse annuity mortgage, 399–400
ersion cash flow, 306
iew, 164
ocable trust, 237
e, Michael, 689, 701
ks, Bruce, 156, 612n, 689
enbark, Richard, 714n
hts, of tenant, 459
g, Alfred A., 466
g, F. Lee, 698n
ger, Robert J., 433, 434
k(s)
apartments, 529
avoidance of, 330
criteria, 211
and debt coverage ratio, 252
in developing and investing in
    metro areas, 740–742
diversification, and syndication of-
    ferings, 415
and expected return on invest-
    ment, 668
management and control of, 329–
    331
nature and definition of, 318–319
office buildings, 569–570
in person portfolio, 701–702
in real estate investment, 50, 52
and refinnancing, 409–410
shopping centers, 548–549
small rental properties, 614–615
and time value of money, 285
types, 319–321
vs. uncertainty, 318
See also Risk analysis; Risk man-
    agement and control
k absorption analysis, and IRR par-
    titioning, 322
k absorption (RA) ratio, 322–324
k analysis, 318–329
apartments, 537–538
hotels and motels, 635
industrial building, 609
levels, 322–329
office building, 583
real estate investment models,
    63–68
shopping center, 561
small rental properties, 623–624
See also Risk(s); Risk management
    and control
k level, 708
k management and control, 329–
    331
apartments, 532, 535
hotels and motels, 634
industrial building, 603–604
land investment, 654–655
lenders, 536
office buildings, 573, 579
and return, 30
shopping centers, 550–551, 557
small rental properties, 618
See also Risk(s); Risk analysis

Risk profile, rate of return on equity,
    328
Risk ratios, 313–314
Risk/return framework, for analyzing
    inflation and cycles, 142–143
Risks of agency, protection from, 464
Risk taker, rating yourself as, 715–
    717
Robbins, Michael, 676
Roberts, Scott, 621
Robertson, Terry, 60n
Robichek, Alexander A., 318n
Robinson, C. D., 125n
Robinson, Gerald J., 220n
Roll, Richard, 671n, 696n
Rolling options, 495
Roosevelt, Theodore, 9
Rose, Jerome G., 740
Ross, Stephen A., 671n, 696n
Roulac, Stephen E., 12n, 28n, 40n,
    142, 167n, 187n, 193n, 199,
    239n, 412n, 413n, 417n, 658n,
    659n, 660n, 687n
Ruggles, Donald, 740n, 741n
Rule of 72, 648
Rule 146, SEC, 418
Rule 147, SEC, 419
Rushing, Philip J., 57n
Rushmore, Stephen, 11
Rutgers University, Urban Policy Re-
    search Center, 528
Rystrom, David, 157n

Sacks, Mason J., 232n, 351n, 355n
Safe Harbor rules, 225, 418
Safe Harbor for Intrastate Exemption,
    419
Salaries, of stockholder employees,
    231
Sale
    analysis, Aspen Wood Apartments,
        512
    calculation of proceeds from, 306
    contract, Aspen Wood Apartments,
        444–447
    disposition of property by, 486–491
    and leaseback, 487
    net proceeds projection, Aspen
        Wood Apartments, 383, 384
    of personal residence, 493–494
    price and terms, tax shelter strat-
        egy, 375
    range, neighborhood, 123
Sale-buyback, 406
Sale-leaseback
    industrial building, 603
    property or building, 406
Sales price
    allocation, and tax shelter strat-
        egy, 375
    loan balance, tax basis, and, 373
Sale structure proposals, Aspen Wood
    Apartments, 280–281
Salvage value, and depreciation, 354
Sanders, Anthony B., 316n
Sandwich lease, 406–407
S&B Realty Co. case, 497n
Satellites, shopping center, 543
Satisficing, vs. maximizing, in negoti-
    ations, 429
Scheduled net income, 273

Schneider, J. D., 81n
Schreiber, Irving, 62n, 293n
Schumpeter, J. A., 318n
Schwab, Bernard, 64, 326n
Schwartz, Sheldon, 359n
Schwert, G. William, 10n, 141, 161n
Science News, 728
Screening criteria, 203
    Aspen Wood Apartments, 211
Scribner, David Jr., 301n
Seasonal cycles, real estate, 175
Seasonal demand, and seller's note,
    623
Secondary data sources, in metropoli-
    tan areas, 85–86
Secondary mortgage markets, outlook,
    739
Secondary trading area, shopping
    center, 542, 550
Second mortgages, commercial vs. in-
    stitutional, 402
Section 8 housing program, 401
Section 179 deduction, 359
Section 202 housing program, 401
Section 1031 exchange, 500–501,
    502, 503–504
Section 1231 property, and long-term
    capital gain, 348, 349
Section 1237, tax code, 492
Securities Act (1933), 418–419
Securities and Exchange Commission,
    417
Securities Exchange Act (1934), 418–
    419
Security, of capital, as investor moti-
    vation, 9
Security deposit
    as debatable deduction, 367
    from tenants, 707
Security system, industrial building,
    601
Segmentation, market, 627, 630
Seldin, Maury, 36n, 142n, 203n,
    204n, 623n
Selection criteria, ownership form,
    214–217
Self-use and occupancy, as investor
    motivation, 9
Sellars, W. M. Jr., 599n
Seller
    conditions required in negotia-
        tions, 438, 440–441, 447
    financing, 402–403
    negotiation with, 193, 194; Aspen
        Wood Apartments, 334–335
    operating pro forma, Aspen Wood
        Apartments, 278–280
    predicaments in negotiations, 436
Seller's note, and seasonal demand,
    623
Selling, vs. merchandising, 453
Selling decision, evaluating, 480–
    482
Selling price
    computation of, 484
    most probable, 33, 34
    and refinancing, 408
Senior real estate analysts (SREAs),
    451
Sensitivity analysis, and risk, 64,
    323–326
Series, 143

Service contracts, and property management, 460–461
Set base rent, with additional charges, shopping center, 552
Sewage installation, industrial building, 600
Sewal, Murphy A., 128n
Shared appreciation mortgage (SAM), 400
Sharpe, William F., 670, 684, 685
Shenkel, William M., 466n
Shifting, or risk, 330
Shopping centers
definitions, 540–543
discounted cash flow analysis, 560–561
financing and refinancing, 557–559
investing in, 544–545
investment decision, 561
investors and investor motivations, 545, 548
market and marketability analysis, 549–551
market outlook for, 734–736
operations analysis, 552–557
physical, legal, political, and environmental analysis, 551–552
returns ad risks, 548–549
taxation and tax structure, 559–560
track record and trends, 543–544
Shopping goods, shopping center, 543
Short cycle, 166
Short-range goals, and personal portfolio, 703
Short run, vs. long run, 199
Short-term liabilities, 707
Shussheim, Morton J., 90n
Signs, in promoting projects, 454
Sills, Richard P., 352
Silverman, Jane A., 80n, 125n, 601n
Simon, Herbert, 429
Simple interest, 145
Simulation model, risk, 65–67
Single-family homes, 611
selling prices, 613
Single-property offerings, syndication, 415–416
Single-purpose industrial building, 586
Sirmans, C. F., 361n, 367n, 371, 689
Site
economic and demographic profile, 127–130
industrial building, 598–600
and marketability, 121
of negotiations, 434–435
Site analysis, in marketability analysis, 124–130
Site improvements, land, 653–654
Siteline™ system, 128
Site • Potential™ system, 128, 130
SITE II, 550
Situation audit, and personal portfolio, 703–708
60-month write-off, 360
Small Business Administration (SBA), 605
Small Business Investment Companies (SBICs), 604

Small rental properties
financing and refinancing, 622–623
investing in, 614
investment checklist, 619
investment decision, 624
legal, political, and environmental factors, 618
management, 618–620
market and marketability analysis, 615–618
operating income and expenses, 620–621
physical and structural analysis, 618
rate-of-return analysis, 623
ratio and risk analysis, 623–624
returns and risks, 614–615
tax problems and uncertainties, 623
trends and uncertainties, 612–614, 621–622
Smith, Halbert C., 387n
Smith, Owen, 433n
Smith, Wallace F., 739n
Smith case, 505
Social change cycles, real estate, 175–176
Social Security Act, 637
Social Security Administration, 640
Software, sources, 521–522
Soil conditions, office building, 573
Sources
office building financing and refinancing, 579
shopping center financing, 557
Space
projection of needs, 114–116
use planning, 450–452; and property management, 449
Space efficiency, office building, 573
Special allocations
and general partnership, 221–222
and limited partnership, 225–226
Special-purpose industrial building, 586
Specialty goods, shopping center, 543
Specialty shopping center, 541–542
Special-use properties, 624–625
hotels and motels, 625–637
nursing homes, 637–644
Specified property offerings, syndication, 416
Speculation, vs. investment, 19–20
Spellman, Lewis J., 142
Spetzler, Carl S., 326
Spieker, A. M., 125n
Spies, P. F., 111n
Spiro, Herbert T., 708n
Sprawl, neighborhood, 123
Sprinkel, Beryl W., 143, 147n
Sprinkler system, industrial building, 587, 601
Square-foot prices, use in negtiations, 436
Stability, metropolitan areas, 83–84
Staged equity investment, 415
Stagflation, and institutional portfolio, 667
Standard & Poor's Outlook, 713
Standard & Poor's Stock Guide, 713

Standard consolidated statistical areas (SCSAs), 72
growth derby, 91–95
Standard industrial classifications (SIC), 104, 105
Standard Manual of Accounting for Shopping Center Operations, 555
Standard metropolitan statistical areas (SMSAs), 72–73
growth derby, 91–95
Standing loan, 391
Stanley, Thomas J., 128n
Starchild, Adam, 238n
Starker II case, 504, 505
State laws, on syndication offerings 420
State variables, 326
Static business risk, 319–320
Statistical Abstract of the United States, 91
Steele, Robert W., 52n
Steiner, George A., 188n, 467n
Step-up options, 495
Stevenson, Howard W., 157n
Stockholder employees, salaries of, 231
Stolnitz, George J., 85n, 88n
Straight lease, industrial building, 603
Straight-line depreciation, 355, 357
and long-term capital gain, 348, 352
Straight-line basis, depreciation, 3 306
Straight sale, 486–487
Straight-term mortgage, 391
Strategy study, 32
Straw corporation, and ownership, 233–234
Strip shopping center, 543
Structural density, industrial building, 587
Structural factors
office building, 573
shopping center, 551
small rental properties, 618
Structure, criteria, 211
Subchapter C corporation, ownersh 228–231
Subchapter S corporation, ownersh 231–233
Subdivision lot sales, 492
Subordinated land leasebacks, 405–406
Subordination
of management fee, 414
in real estate financing, 622
Subsurface rights, 493
Suburban sites and acreage, industrial buildings, 594
Sumichrast, Michael, 142n
Summation estimating techniques, 138
Summerfeld, Raymond M., 345n
Sum-of-the-years'-digits (SOYD), depreciation, 355, 357
Superleverage, and real estate investment, 50–51
Superregional shopping center, 541
Supplies, and property management, 460–461

y, 112
real estate, 100
ly analysis
artments, 529–531
tels and motels, 627, 631
lustrial building, 593–595
d investment, 652–653
rsing homes, 639–640
ice buildings, 572
opping center, 550
all rental housing, 616–617
specified use, 112–113
ly/demand relationship, construction, 172
tener, 384
nik, Richard H., 36n, 142n,
203n, 204n, 623n
cate
nership, 240
gulation, 417–420
cation
d equity financing, 410
erings, 415–420
nership alternative, 213
al estate, 240
d shopping centers, 548
gle property, and REIT, 236
matic risk, 672
d personal portfolio, 701

s, and financial calculation, in
generating mortgage amortization schedule, 398
out letter, 392
, Janet, 676n
ran Co. case, 496n
ble personal property, 706
an, William J., 493n
tello, R., 742
t metropolitan area, search for,
85–91
s)
assessment due, 707
d general partnership, 220–221
ome, 215, 344–347
d ownership, 653
paid, 706
mbursement, subordinated land
easeback, 405
sale of property, 306, 307
selection of ownership form,
214–215
pping centers, 556
taxable income, 345–347
also Taxation and tax structure; Tax law; Tax planning;
ax shelter
le income
cash flow, 303, 369–370
taxes, 345–347
on and tax structure
rtments, 536–537
ustrial building, 607–608
d investments, 658
negotiations with seller, 334–
35
ce building, 581–582
estate asset transactions, 350
pping center, 559–560
ll rental properties, 618
al gain upon sale of property,
53

See also Tax(es); Tax law; Tax
planning; Tax shelter
Tax basis
and general partnership, 221
sales price, loan balance, and, 373
Tax benefits structure, 194
Tax deeds, 496–497
Tax depreciation, and tax shelter,
372
Tax-free exchange, and tax shelter
strategy, 375
Tax law, 341–343
capital gain vs. ordinary income,
348–353
depreciation and accelerated cost
recovery system, 354–360
income tax formula, 344–347
investment interest limitations,
362–363
investment tax credits, 361–362
minimum tax, 360–361
reforms, and tax shelter, 373
See also Economic Recovery Tax
Act; Tax(es); Taxation and tax
structure; Tax planning
Tax leverage, in debt financing, 388
Tax losses, pass-through, and ownership form, 214–215
Tax planning
corporation, 229
and disposal of investment, 482
and IRS audit, 367–368
operating deductions, 366–367
and retirement, 722–723
and tax shelter, 368–373; strategy checklist, 373–376
timing of income, 364–366
See also Tax(es); Taxation and tax
structure; Tax law
Tax preference, 360
Tax preference items, 360
Tax problems and uncertainties
industrial building, 608
office building, 582
shopping center, 560
small rental properties, 623
Tax rate schedules, for married individuals filing joint returns, 346
Tax Reform Acts (1976, 1978), 175
Tax shelter, 368–373
apartments, 536
complete, 371
hotels and motels, 634–635
industrial building, 607–608
as investor motivation, 10
nursing homes, 641
office building, 581–582
pitfalls, 372–373
and refinancing, 408
shopping center, 559–560
small rental properties, 615
stages, 371–372
strategy checklist, 373–376
See also Tax(es); Taxation and tax
structure; Tax law; Tax planning
Tax treatment
joint venture, 227–228
tenancy in common, 219–220
Tax year, 364–366
Technology Park, Atlanta, 595, 596–
597

The Technology Review, 728
Tenancy in common, 219–220
Tenant(s)
bona fide, and NOI, 274
compatibility, 456
move-ins and move-outs, 460
rights and obligations, 459
security deposits from, 707
selecting, 455–456
Tenant arrangements, and leases, industrial buildings, 602–603
Tenant-owner, industrial building,
606
10 percent rule, 50
Term(s), 390
apartments, 535
lease, 456–459
office building financing, 579–580
shopping center financing, 557
Terminal-value IRR, 294
Termination, 195
Aspen Wood Apartments, 511–514
in ownership life cycle, 40
Termination period, tax shelter strategy, 375–376
Terms of sale, and tax shelter strat-
egy, 375
Tertiary trading area, shopping cen-
ter, 542, 550
Thau, William A., 433n
Thematic image, in promoting proj-
ect, 453–454
Theme shopping center, 541–542
Theory of Interest (Fisher), 146
Third-class industrial building, 600
Thorndike, David, 248
Threat of condemnation, 497
Time horizons for investment deci-
sions, 35–43
lender vs. equity investor, 27–28
Timesharing, 611–612
Time value, of money, 285
Timing
of closing, 482–483
of income, 364–366
Title V Farmers Home Administration
(FmHA) rural housing, 401
Total cash proceeds, 322
Total employment, and demand for
urban space use, 102
Total gain, 352
Total income, and income tax for-
mula, 344
Total leasable square feet, in finan-
cial feasibility model, 258
Total operating receipts, shopping
areas, 555
Total present value of equity invest-
ment, 306
Total rent, shopping center, 554
Total terminal value, 295
Townhouse, 611
Townhouse complexes, 526
Track record and trends
apartments, 527–528
land investments, 648–651
office buildings, 565, 568
shopping centers, 543–544
Trade or business property, invest-
ment interest limitations, 363
Trading area, shopping center, 549–
550

Trading markets, real estate, 99–100
Trading on equity, in disposing of investment, 479–480
Traffic builders, in promoting project, 454–455
Train, John, 698
Transaction
  consideration for, Aspen Wood Apartments, 444–445
  investment, 25
Transaction costs, and disposal of equity, 479
Transfer, of risk, 330
Transferability of interest corporation, 228
  limited partnership, 224
  and ownership form, 215
Transportation, and industrial buildings, 587–588
Trends and uncertainties
  apartments, 535
  office buildings, 575, 579
  shopping centers, 556–557
  small rental properties, 621–622
Trends in the Hotel/Motel Business, 632, 634
Trimble, Harold G., 31n, 111n, 121n
Triplex, 611
Trolley Square, Salt Lake City, 542
True yield, 313
Trust
  ownership, 234–240
  and track record, 519–520
Tschappatt, Carl J., 387n
Turnover rate, 115
  neighborhood, 123
Tuttle, Donald, 668n
Twain, Mark, 40
200 percent declining-balance method depreciation, 357

Ullman, Edward L., 75
Uncertainty
  vs. risk, 318
  small rental properties, 621–622
Undepreciated balance, 301
Undeveloped land, investment interest limitations, 363
Unequal cash flow streams
  and IRR, 292–293
  and present value, 286–287
Uniform Limited Partnership Act (ULPA), 223, 224
Uniform Partnership Act, 220
Uniform System of Accounts and Expense Dictionary for Motels/Hotels, 631
Unimproved land, and inflation, 154–155
U.S. Financial Data, 164
USA Standards Institute, 586
Unrealistic objectives, 199
Unrelated business income, 239, 240
Unsold inventory, 113–114
Unsystematic risk, 672
  and personal portfolio, 701
Updegrave, Walter L., 411n
Upside, property life cycle, 36–38

Upton, King, 691
Urban cartography, 76–77
Urban containment, costs of, 739–742
Urban Development Action Grants (UDAG), 401, 589
Urban fringe, 72
Urbanized area, 72
Urban land, unimproved, and inflation, 154
Urban Land Institute, 458, 554, 555
  Project Reference Files, 544
Urban place, 72
Urban population, 72
Urban space use, demand indicators, 102–103
Use, neighborhood, 123
Useful life, 354
  determination, 358
Users, as investors in industrial buildings, 590
Usury, and straw corporation, 233
Utilities, neighborhood, 123
Utility system, shopping center, 556
Utilization Review Committee, nursing homes, 637

Vacancies
  hotel and motel projections, 628, 631
  industrial building projections, 595, 598
  and NOI, 273–274
  nursing home projections, 640
  office building projections, 572
  and rental income, apartments, 531–532
  shopping center projections, 550, 553
  small rental property projection, 617–618
Vacancy and operating expenses, in financial feasibility model, 258
Vacancy and operating expense to gross income, ratio of, 258
Vacancy rate, neighborhood, 123
Valachi, Donald, 262n, 293n, 322n, 410n, 493n
Valid purpose, and exchange of property, 505–506
Valuation, Aspen Wood Apartments, using financial feasibility model, 281–283
Value, depreciation, as investment disadvantage, 12
Value Line Investment Survey, 713
VanCaspel, Venita, 714
Variability, rent and expense, 265–268
Variable rate financing, and indexing, 622
Variable rate mortgage (VRM), 249, 399
Variance of returns, 668
Ventilation, industrial building, 601
Venture management, 17
  in reducing risk, 331
Vertical shopping center, 543

Vested pension and profit-sharing rights, 706
Vitt, Lois A., 411n
Volatility, real estate cycle, 170
Voluntary disposition of investme 480

Wall Street Journal, 171
Walk-up apartments, 525
Walters, David W., 449, 450, 463
Walters, William Jr., 466, 534n
Ward, Robert L., 31, 111n, 121n
Ward, William L., 402n
Wasson, H. Reed, 233n
Watching, in negotiations, 430
Water installation, industrial buil ing, 600
Water Tower Place, Chicago, 544
Wealth, maximization, in investme analysis, 28–30
Wealth transfer, mathematics of, 148–150
Wealth-pyramiding process, 46–4
Webb, James R., 689
Weimer, Arthur M., 54n
Weinstein, M. W., 493
Weisiger, William M., 448n
Weitzman, M. K., 111n
Welch, Russell, 258n, 285n
Wendt, Paul F, 63n, 118, 142n, 154n, 157n, 197n, 676, 688
Wenzlick, Roy 165
Werner, Raymond J., 499n
Westinghouse, Credit Corp., 739
Weston, J. Fred, 290n, 293n
White, John R., 33n
Wholesale price index (WPI), 144
Wiley, Robert J., 96n, 673n
Williams, John E., 523n, 540n, 5 610n
Williford, Jerry S., 358
Wofford, Larry E., 322, 324n, 326 686, 698n, 742
Wolf, Jack S., 76n
Wolman, William, 19n, 143n, 147 149n, 160
Wong, Sui N., 157n, 688
Woods, Donald H., 326
Wraparound mortgage, 261, 403
  Aspen Wood Apartments, 445
Wright, P. Bruce, 233n
Written objectives, 198
Wurtzebach, Charles H., 466, 486
Wyndelts, Robert W., 359

Yesavich, Peter, 630n
Yormark, Jonathan S., 67n, 676, Young, Michael S., 295n, 296n, 326n, 676n, 687
Young investor, 40–41

Zaloudek, Robert F., 81n
Zeckendorf, William, 188, 391, 4
Zeikel, Arthur, 40n
Zerbst, Robert H., 255n, 322, 32
Zinbarg, Edward D., 40n
Zoning, small rental properties,
Zoning controls, neighborhood, 1